V!VA
TRAVEL GUIDES

PERU

Lima - Cusco - Machu Picchu - Arequipa - Lake Titicaca - Huaraz - Coast

2nd Edition
February 2009

V!VA Travel Guides' Guarantee:
We guarantee our guidebook to be the most up-to-date printed guidebook available. Visit www.vivatravelguides.com/guarantee/ to learn more.

V!VA Travel Guide: Peru

ISBN-10: 0-9791264-3-6
ISBN-13: 978-0-9791264-3-7

Copyright © 2009, Viva Publishing Network.
Voice: (970) 744-4244
Fax: (612) 605-5720
Website: www.vivatravelguides.com
Information: info@vivatravelguides.com

www.vivatravelguides.com

Travel is inherently dangerous. While we use a superior process for updating guidebooks and have made every effort to ensure the accuracy of facts in this book, Viva Publishing Network, its owners, members, employees, contributors and the authors cannot be held liable for events outside of their control and we make no guarantee as to the accuracy of published information. Please travel safely, be alert, and let us know how your vacation went!

Contents

Introduction   21

Geography   21
Flora & Fauna   21
Climate   21
History   22
Politics   23
Economy   24
Population   25
Language   25
Religion   27
Culture   28
Social & Environmental Issues   33
Holidays And Fiestas   34
Visas   38
Embassies & Consulates   39
Quick Facts   41
Getting To and Away From Peru   42
Border Crossing   44
Departure Tax   44
Getting Around   44
Types of Tours   47
Adventure Travel   48
Sports & Recreation   48
Hiking   48
Sandboarding   49
Surfing   50
Horseback Riding   51
Mountain Climbing   52
Whitewater Rafting and Kayaking   53
Mountain Biking   54
Birdwatching   55
Sport Fishing   56
Studying Spanish   56
Studying Quechua   57
Living in Peru   57
Volunteering & Working   58
Teaching English   58
Lodging   59
Food and Drink   61
Shopping   64
The South American Explorers' Club   66

Peru Travel Tips   67

Health & Safety   67
Communications   69
Media   73
Money & Costs   74
Etiquette & Dress   74
Responsible Tourism   75
Photography   75
Women Travelers   76

GAY & LESBIAN TRAVELERS 76
SENIOR TRAVELERS 77
DISABLED TRAVELERS 77
TRAVELING WITH CHILDREN 77

LIMA 78

LIMA HISTORY 79
WHEN TO GO 80
GETTING TO AND AWAY 80
TRAVELING WITH KIDS IN LIMA 81
SERVICES 82
THINGS TO SEE AND DO 83
STUDYING SPANISH 85
VOLUNTEERING 87
TOUR OPERATORS 88
CENTRAL LIMA 90
SAN ISIDRO 104
MIRAFLORES 112
BARRANCO 129
PUEBLO LIBRE 137
CHORILLOS 139
SAN BORJA 140
MONTERRICO 141
AROUND LIMA 142

PACIFIC COAST SOUTH OF LIMA 145

THE PISCO EARTHQUAKE 146
WHEN TO GO 147
GETTING TO AND AWAY 147
THINGS TO SEE AND DO 147
PISCO 148
PARACAS 152
ISLAS BALLESTAS 156
ICA 159
HUACACHINA OASIS 168
NASCA 173
NASCA LINES 176
CAHUACHI 182

AREQUIPA AND THE COLCA CANYON 186

AREQUIPA 188
AREQUIPA HISTORY 189
WHEN TO GO 189
GETTING TO AND AWAY 191
THINGS TO SEE AND DO 192
STUDYING SPANISH 195
VOLUNTEERING 196
TOUR OPERATORS 196
COLCA CANYON 211
CHIVAY 215

Coporaque 218
Yanque 218
Maca 218
Cabanaconde 219
Huambo 220
Cotahuasi Canyon 220
Tacna 221

SOUTHERN PERUVIAN ANDES 232

When To Go 233
Huánuco 233
Junín 235
The mantaro Valley 235
Cochas Grande / Cochas Chico 236
San Jerónimo de Tunán 236
Hualhuas 236
Huancayo 207
Ayacucho 242

CUSCO, MACHU PICCHU AND THE SACRED VALLEY 249

When to Go 250
Cusco 251
Cusco History 252
Getting To and Away From Cusco 253
Things to See and Do 258
Studying Spanish 265
Volunteering 269
Cusco Tours 271
San Blas 287

Around Cusco 298
Chinchero 298
Andahuaylillas and San Pedro 298

The Sacred Valley 299
Sacred Valley History 299
When To Go 300
Things to See and Do 300
Sacred Valley Trekking 301
Sacred Valley Tours 305
Pisac 305
Urubamba 311
Yucay 313

Around Urubamba 314
Ollantaytambo 314
Aguas Calientes 323

Machu Picchu and the Inca Trail 330
Machu Picchu and the Inca Trail History 331
When To Go 331
Getting To and Away 331

ENVIRONMENTAL ISSUES	332
THE INCA TRAIL	332
MACHU PICCHU	336

LAKE TITICACA   341

LAKE TITICACA AND PUNO HISTORY	342
WHEN TO GO	344
THINGS TO SEE AND DO	346
LAKE TITICACA TOURS	346
JULIACA	347
LAMPA	350
LLACHÓN	350
PUNO	351
CHUCHITO	363
JULI	364
THE PERUVIAN ISLANDS OF LAKE TITICACA	364
ISLA UROS	364
ISLA AMANTANÍ	366
ISLA TAQUILE	366
ISLA SUASI	367
ISLA ANAPIA AND YUSPIQUE	367
THE BOLIVIAN SIDE OF LAKE TITICACA	368
THE BOLIVIAN ISLANDS	369
COPACABANA	369

CENTRAL PERUVIAN ANDES   373

WHEN TO GO	374
THINGS TO SEE AND DO	374
CORDILLERA BLANCA	375
CORDILLERA NEGRA	375
CORDILLERA HUAYHUASH	376
CENTRAL ANDES TOURS	377
HUARAZ	378
HUASCARÁN NATIONAL PARK	385
CHIQUIÁN	391
CARHUAZ	392
YUNGAY	393
CARAZ	395
MONTERREY	397

PACIFIC COAST NORTH OF LIMA   398

WHEN TO GO	399
THINGS TO SEE AND DO	400
PACIFIC COAST TOURS	400
TRUJILLO	400
TRUJILLO HISTORY	401
CHAN CHAN	412
HUANCHACO	413
CHICLAYO	420
PIURA	431
CATACAOS	437
CABO BLANCO	438

Paita and Around   439
Huancabamba   439
Zorritos   446
Máncora   450
Tumbes   455

NORTHERN ANDES   459

When To Go   460
Cajamarca   460
Chachapoyas   465
Kuélap   472
Jalca Grande   474
Yerbabuena   476
Leymebamba   478
Lámud   480

The Peruvian Amazon Basin   483

Environmental Issues   484
When to Go   485
Things to See and Do   486
Peruvian Amazon Tours   486
Puerto Maldonado   487
Tambopata   493
Manu   494
Manu Biosphere Reserve   494
Tarapoto   499
Abiseo River National Park   499
Iquitos   501
Around Iquitos   513
Santa Rosa   514

Index   516

Packing Lists   534
Useful Spanish Phrases   536
Tear-out Cheat Sheet   537

About V!VA Travel Guides

V!VA Travel Guides is a new approach to travel guides. We have taken the travel guide and redesigned it from the ground up using the internet, geographic databases, community participation and the latest in printing technology which allows us to print our guidebooks one at a time when they are ordered. Reversing the general progression, we have started with a website, gathered user ratings and reviews, and then compiled the community's favorites into a book. Every time you see the V!VA insignia you know that the location is a favorite of the V!VA Travel Community. For you, the reader, this means more accurate and up-to-date travel information and more ratings by travelers like yourself.

Community and Free Membership:
The accuracy and quality of the information in this book is largely thanks to our online community of travelers. If you would like to join them, go to www.vivatravelguides.com/ members/ to get more information and to sign up for free.

Your Opinions, Experiences and Travels:
Did you love a place? Will you never return to another? Every destination in this guidebook is listed on our website with space for user ratings and reviews. Share your experiences, help out other travelers and let the world know what you think.

Updates & Registering:
We update our books at least twice a year. By purchasing this book you are entitled to one year of free electronic updates. Go to www.vivatravelguides.com/updates/ to register for your free updates. Receive a free E-book by registering your views at www.vivatravelguides. com/register.

Corrections & Suggestions:
We are committed to bringing you the most accurate and up-to-date information. However, places change, prices rise, businesses close down and information, no matter how accurate it once was, inevitably changes. Thus we ask for your help: If you find an error in this book or something that has changed, go to www.vivatravelguides.com/corrections/ and report them (oh, and unlike the other guidebooks, we'll incorporate them into our information within a few days).

If you think we have missed something, or want to see something in our next book, go to www.vivatravelguides.com/suggestions/ and let us know. As a small token of our thanks for correcting an error or submitting a suggestion, we'll send you a coupon for 50 percent off any of our E-books or 20 percent off any of our printed books.

Coming soon on www.vivatravelguides.com
This is just the beginning. We're busy adding new features that our users have requested to our books and website. A few coming attractions are:
- Improved Community Functions: join groups, find travel partners, participate in forums.
- Write travel blogs and share travel photos from your trip
- And more!

How to Use This Book

This book is a best-of Peru taken straight from our website. You can check out the website to read user reviews, rate your favorite hotels and restaurants and add in information you think we are missing. The book also features highlighted sections on haciendas, eco-tourism and adventure travel in Peru. Use our helpful tear-out sheet, complete with emergency contact details and helpful numbers, while you are out and about in Peru.

ABOUT THE AUTHORS

Paula Newton is V!VA's operations expert. With an MBA and a background in New Media, Paula is the Editor-in-Chief and the organizing force behind the team. With an insatiable thirst for off-the-beaten-track travel, Paula has traveled extensively, especially in Europe and Asia, and has explored more than 25 countries. She currently lives in Quito.

Ricardo Segreda graduated with Departmental Honors from Manhattanville College in Purchase, New York, earning a B.A. in Religious Studies and Literature. Following a spell managing a hostel for Hostelling International in Washington State, and serving on its Board of Directors, Segreda relocated to Ecuador. In Quito, he divides his time between film critiquing for Ecuador's largest daily, La Hora and serving as a staff writer for V!VA. He pounded the streets of Peru to take a leading role in the production of this book.

Michelle Hopey has worked as a journalist for years, writing and editing for a number of magazines and newspapers across the United States. Upon earning an M.S. in Journalism from Boston University she set out to study Spanish in South America while she went through Machu Picchu and café hopped in Buenos Aires, finally landing in Quito, Ecuador. Michelle played a leading role in the editorial decision-making process and in gathering content for this book.

Upon re-declaring her independence at age 29, Lorraine Caputo packed her trusty Rocinante (so her knapsack's called) and began traipsing throughout the Americas, from Alaska to Patagonia. Her work has been published in almost 50 journals, 14 books, an anthology of women's travel writings and three recordings in the United States, Canada and Latin America. In addition to writing up the Northern Andes section of the book, Lorraine also played a key role in the editing process.

Dr. Christopher Minster, PhD, is a graduate of Penn State University, The University of Montana and Ohio State. He is the resident V!VA Travel Guides expert on ruins, history and culture, as well as spooky things like haunted museums. He worked for the U.S. Peace Corps in Guatemala as a volunteer from 1991 to 1994 and has traveled extensively in Latin America. He currently resides in Quito.

With an M.A. in journalism from University of North Carolina and a B.A. in English from Gonzaga University, Daniel Johnson knows two things: Something within him enjoys working with words, and he naturally gravitates toward exceptional basketball programs. A self-proclaimed international man of leisure, he has traveled to Latin America, Europe, Southeast Asia and the Middle East. When he's not traveling or thinking about traveling, Daniel works as a freelance journalist.

MANY THANKS TO:
All of our talented writing staff who contributed so many detailed and informative sections for this book, including: John Howison, Erin Helland, Caroline Bennett, Katie Tibbetts, Kristi Mohrbacher, Amanda Massello, Katie Hale, Jordan Barnes and Blessing Waung.

And special thanks to the V!VA editors who spent countless hours updating information to make this the most up-to-date Peru book on the market: Margaret Rode, Karen Nagy, Michelle Lillie, Laura Granfortuna, Alison Isaac, Tom Ravenscroft, Andrea Davoust, Rachael Hanley and Chris Hughes.

Also, thanks to all of our contributors, but in particular, thanks to Kris Dreessen, Rachael Daigle, Dave Britton, Jeff Yates, Sharon K. Couzens de Hinojosa, Luisa Michelsen, Carsten Korch of www.livinginperu.com and Kelley Coyner for their excellent coverage of various regions of Peru. Last, but not least, thank you to Miles Buesst for visiting Pisco and Ica after the earthquake to update our information.

A huge thank you to Tania Morales, the programming mastermind who keeps our parent website www.vivatravelguides.com running smoothly and always lends a hand to the not-always-computer-savvy staff. Also, Viviana Morales who helped with painstakingly creating all of our maps, and the whole Metamorf team for their ongoing support.

◇ Cover Design: Jason Halberstadt ◇ Cover Photo: Dave Stamboulis ◇
◇ Back Cover Photo (Llama): Dave Stamboulis ◇ Back Cover Photo (Girls): Alberto Romo
◇ Title Page Photo: Ricardo Segreda ◇

Get your writing published in our books, go to www.vivatravelguides.com

Peru Highlights

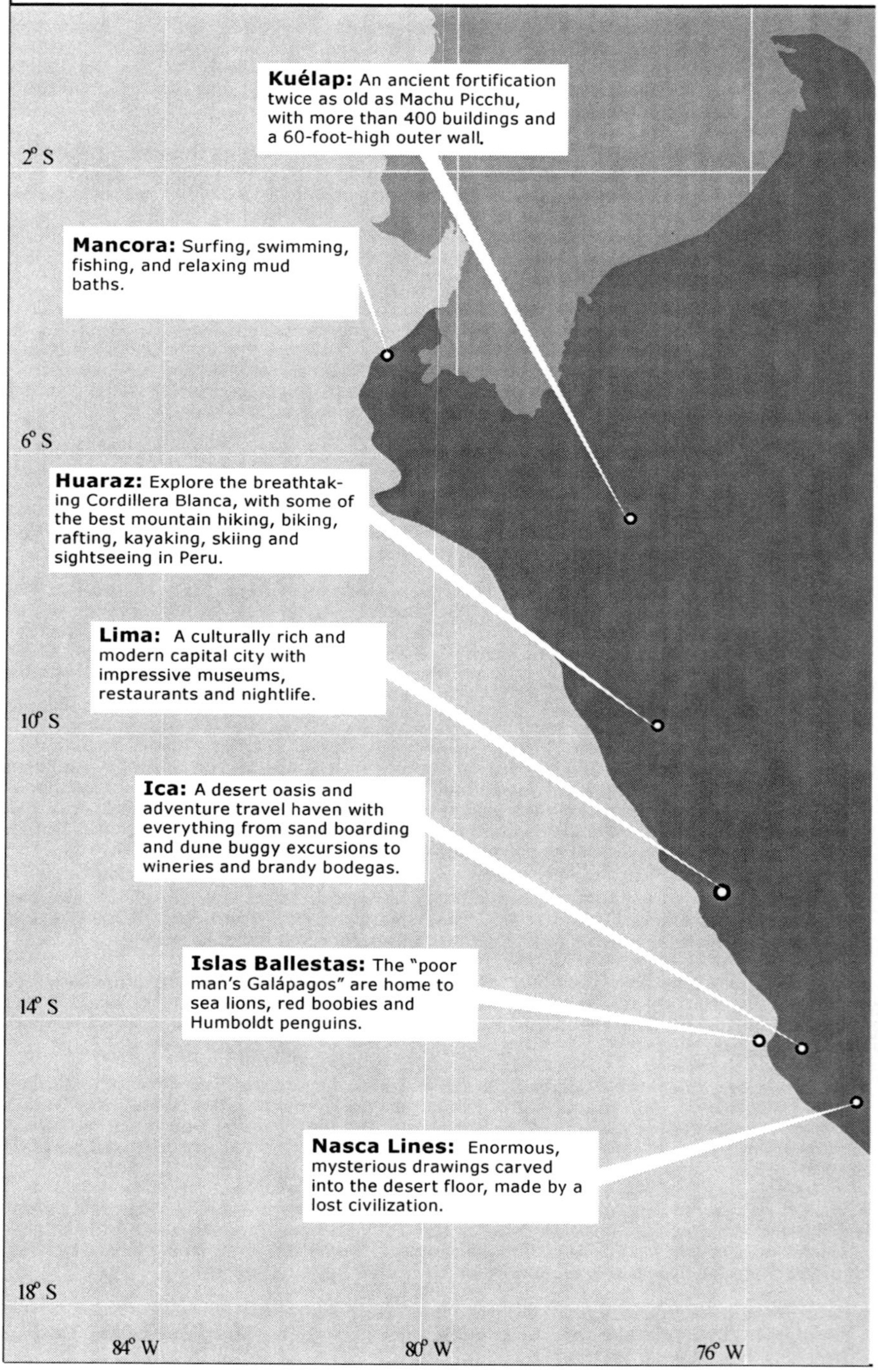

Kuélap: An ancient fortification twice as old as Machu Picchu, with more than 400 buildings and a 60-foot-high outer wall.

Mancora: Surfing, swimming, fishing, and relaxing mud baths.

Huaraz: Explore the breathtaking Cordillera Blanca, with some of the best mountain hiking, biking, rafting, kayaking, skiing and sightseeing in Peru.

Lima: A culturally rich and modern capital city with impressive museums, restaurants and nightlife.

Ica: A desert oasis and adventure travel haven with everything from sand boarding and dune buggy excursions to wineries and brandy bodegas.

Islas Ballestas: The "poor man's Galápagos" are home to sea lions, red boobies and Humboldt penguins.

Nasca Lines: Enormous, mysterious drawings carved into the desert floor, made by a lost civilization.

2° S

6° S

10° S

14° S

18° S

84° W

80° W

76° W

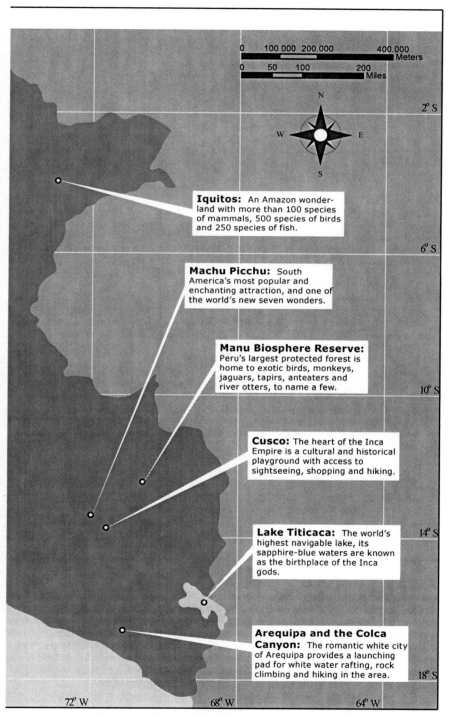

0   100.000 200.000   400.000
                                   Meters
0   50   100   200
                          Miles

N
W   E
S

2° S

6° S

10° S

14° S

18° S

72° W   68° W   64° W

Iquitos: An Amazon wonderland with more than 100 species of mammals, 500 species of birds and 250 species of fish.

Machu Picchu: South America's most popular and enchanting attraction, and one of the world's new seven wonders.

Manu Biosphere Reserve: Peru's largest protected forest is home to exotic birds, monkeys, jaguars, tapirs, anteaters and river otters, to name a few.

Cusco: The heart of the Inca Empire is a cultural and historical playground with access to sightseeing, shopping and hiking.

Lake Titicaca: The world's highest navigable lake, its sapphire-blue waters are known as the birthplace of the Inca gods.

Arequipa and the Colca Canyon: The romantic white city of Arequipa provides a launching pad for white water rafting, rock climbing and hiking in the area.

PERU HIGHLIGHTS

1. CUSCO, MACHU PICCHU AND THE SACRED VALLEY

Machu Picchu is South America's most popular tourist attraction and in 2007 was designated one of the world's new seven wonders. One's journey to Machu Picchu starts in the former seat of the Inca Empire, Cusco, with its historical buildings, before heading through the geographically and archaeologically rich Sacred Valley.

2. LAKE TITICACA

It's the world's highest navigable lake at 3,810 meters and one of the largest, covering an area of over 8,000 square kilometers. Its sapphire-blue waters are known as the birthplace of the Inca gods, and home to pre-Inca civilizations, such as the Aymara who continue to live on the man-made Uros Islets, that have changed little over the millennia.

3. NASCA LINES

It was lost to the world until it surprised pilots flying over this flat and desolate region of southern Peru in 1921. They looked down and saw lines and carvings extending as wide as 65 kilometers in the shape of a monkey, a spider, a pelican, hummingbirds, a whale, a dog and perhaps even an astronaut—or space alien. Archeologists are still debating the what, how and why of these remnants of a lost civilization.

4. AREQUIPA AND THE COLCA CANYON

Arequipa and the Colca Canyon represent urban and rural Southern Peru at its most intoxicating. Arequipa is the White City, named so because much of its exquisite architecture has been carved out of ashen volcanic rock. The pristine Colca Canyon provides opportunities for whitewater rafting, rock climbing, hiking, encounters with communities unchanged by colonization and even dinosaur tracks.

5. HUARAZ

Perched at 3,028 meters, Huaraz has always been a mecca and magnet for rogue adventurers ready to risk everything scaling a rock or a glacier. Forget about Huaraz as a city, still barely recovered from a devastating earthquake over 30 years ago. This area, made famous by the film *Touching the Void*, also offers some of the greatest opportunities for mountain biking, rafting, kayaking, bird-watching, paragliding, skiing and spectacular sightseeing.

6. IQUITOS

For many, Iquitos is a gateway to paradise with an array of exotic animals, from monkeys to macaws, herons to hawks, and turtles to toucans. Chartered boats provide the opportunity to see many of these creatures, as well as the eye-opening foliage which serves as their home. Nearby Pacaya-Samiria National Reserve shelters 100 species of mammals, 500 species of birds and 250 species of fish. There are also local museums and opportunities for shopping.

REGIONS OF PERU

The Andes form the spine of Peru, between the sterile beige desert of the coast and the verdant jungles of the Amazon lowlands. From surfing to mountain climbing; from ancient ruins to Spanish colonial architecture to modern skyscrapers; from world-class museums and restaurants to exotic birds and mammals; from lost civilizations to bloody battlefields of centuries of war; from oases nestled in sand dunes to alpine lakes sheltered by sky-scraping cordilleras—Peru has much to offer the visitor. If you sojourn on the Amazon River or through the back-roads of the highlands, you will discover a Peru very few have known. So pack your bags and strike out. Peru is so much more than just the former Inca Empire.

LIMA (P.78)

Lima, once the seat of a Spanish Empire Viceroyalty, is today a large metropolis. If arriving by air, your plane will slice through the infamous smog, especially during the *garúa* (Scotch mist) season when the cold and damp creep through the streets into your bones and spirit. But glimmering through the mist are the many jewels Lima has to offer you. Pre-Columbian ruins and numerous museums hide within the folds of modern neighborhoods like San Isidro and Miraflores. Step back into time before the Spaniards, before the Inca, at sites like Huaca Huallamarca and Huanca Pucllana. Admire the artistry displayed at the Museo de Arte, the Larco Museum or Italian Art Museum—or that by modern-day hands at the myriad markets and cooperatives. Learn about Peruvian culture at Museo Nacional de Arqueología. The Centro Histórico yet preserves much colonial architecture with numerous centuries-old churches and the imposing Plaza de Armas. Wander through the catacombs of Iglesia San Francisco or witness the horrific torture methods of the Spanish Inquisition at the interesting Museo de la Inquisición. Sample fresh seafood dishes and *ceviche* in Chorrillos, or sample the wines of Queirolo vineyards, considered by many to be the finest vintner in the country. There are beaches to comb or surf, night clubs to dance the night away, language schools to study Spanish or Quechua, supermalls in the suburbs and some of the country's finest restaurants. Don't let the city's reputation for crime and its pollution drive you away too soon—spend a few days here and admire the gems Lima hides.

PACIFIC COAST SOUTH OF LIMA (P.145)

South of Lima are the many beaches to which Limeños escape the grey, dank jungle of the city. Be warned, though—the water is icy due to the Humboldt Current. Stop in the vineyards near Ica, like Tacama Winery, Bodega El Catador or Vista Alegre, and sample some of the nation's best wines—and, of course, *pisco*. Ica's Museo Histórico Regional is worth a visit, for its excellent exhibits of mummies and *quipus*. You can watch amazing sunsets and gaze upon stars dazzling in a midnight-blue sky at Oasis Huacachina, hidden amongst the desert dunes, which go on for leagues to the Pacific Ocean. If you need a bit of a rush, sandboard or dunebuggy that desert expanse. Be sure to fly over the still little-understood Nasca Lines, and visit the fascinating museums, Casa-Museo María Reiche, Museo Antonini or the María Reiche Planetarium. Pre-Columbian civilizations left many other reminders of their existence in this region; be sure to spend an extra day or two exploring nearby Paredones, Cahuichi or Cementerios de Chauchilla, near Nasca, or Candelabra de los Andes, near Pisco. The coastline and off-shore islands are home to several nature preserves, often called the "Galápagos of Peru": Paracas National Reserve and Islas Ballestas, near Pisco, and San Juan de Marcona Marine Reserve, near Nasca.

On August 15, 2007 Southern Peru was rocked by an 8.0 earthquake, destroying a significant proportion of Pisco and Ica. One of our writers visited the region in late September / early October 2008, to update our content, but please visit us at www.vivatravelguides.com to let us know of any additional or updated information you may have.

PACIFIC COAST NORTH OF LIMA (P.398)

The Chimú dynasty that ruled the northern Peruvian coast worshipped the sea. The ruins of Chan Chan, their most important city—and perhaps the largest adobe city ever built in the Americas—lies near Trujillo. Molded into the walls are many intricate pictures, including fishnet designs, sea otters and pelicans.

Today the northern coast of Peru continues to attract worshippers of the sea. The ocean is cooled by the Humboldt Current for many kilometers north of Lima, until it finally veers westward, allowing the north coast of this country to enjoy warmer waters. You can surf one of the longest left-breaks in the world at Máncora, or hit the open sea in a totora raft in Huanchaco. Study Spanish or take surfing lessons in Huanchaco or Máncora. Beachcomb for fossils at Colán, near Piura.

The region is littered with dozens upon dozens of archaeological sites. Between Trujillo and Huanchaco, not only will you find Chan Chan, but also the Moche ruins Huaca del Sol y Huaca de la Luna with brilliant painted friezes. Near Chiclayo are Sipán, where a gold-adorned ruler and his entourage were uncovered in 1987, and Túcume, presently undergoing extensive excavation. Of course, with all this archaeological richness, northern Peru boasts some world-class museums: Chiclayo's Brüning Archaeological Museum, Sicán National Museum and Royal Tombs of Sipán Museum; Trujillo's Museo de Arqueología; and Piura's small but impressive Museo Municipal Vicas.

This region of Peru isn't just about ancient civilizations. It also boasts ports that were important throughout the Spanish colonial rule and the struggles for independence. You can visit a number of colonial mansions in Trujillo, including the Casa de la Emancipación. In Piura you can see the Casa Museo Gran Almirante Grau and about 12 kilometers from Piura is the port town of Paita, where Manuela Sáenz—Bolívar's *compañera*—lived in exile after the *Libertador's* death.

NORTHERN ANDES (P.459)

The northern Andes region presents you with a wide-ranging Peruvian world—from Cajamarca, where the last Inca emperor was murdered by the Spaniards, to unexplored ruins hidden in the Amazon jungles.

In Cajamarca, you can stand in the Cuarto de Rescate where Atahualpa, the last Inca ruler, was held for ransom by the Spaniards, and later stroll through the Plaza de Armas where he was executed. Dozens of colonial churches await your devotion and the Museo Arqueológico y Etnográfico is the perfect place for a history lesson. Outside of Cajamarca, soak in the Baños del Inca hot springs or explore the 3,500-year-old Cumbe Mayo aqueduct, Ventanillas de Otuzco funerary ruins or many quaint Andean villages nearby.

The mysterious realm of the Chachapoya awaits you in the cloud forests of the Río Utcubmaba River valley. Dotted with hundreds of unexcavated ruins connected with pre-Inca stone roads, it is said to be archaeologically richer than the Sacred Valley. Still seldom-visited by national or foreign tourists, you can explore the tremendous ruins of Kuélap, the stunning sarcophagi statues at Karajía and the colorful mausoleums at Revash. The traditional culture lives into this present day in the village Jalca Grande, the bartering market of Yerbabuena, and through the Yaraví music in Leymebamba and pottery workshops in Huancas. The region also shelters natural beauty: caverns, the emerald-green Huaylla Belén river valley, and Gojta, the third-highest waterfall in the world.

CENTRAL ANDES (P.373)

Often called the "Peruvian Alps," the Cordillera Blanca, Cordillera Negra and Cordillera Huayhuash mountain ranges boasts alpine lakes snuggled in high valleys and icy peaks. If you are a mountain climber or just enjoy hiking in spirit-moving scenery, you will have many opportunities here. Parque Nacional Huascarán, home of Huascarán, the highest peak in Peru, encompasses these Cordilleras.

Huaraz, the largest city, is a good base from which to arrange excursions into the national park or the Cordilleras. Caraz's focus is on adventure sports like rafting and kayaking as well as mountain climbing and hiking to Laguna Parón. From Chiquián you can reach Huayhuash, with over 165 kilometers of trails meandering through the mountains, or scale El Carnicero, Peru's second-highest peak. The entire central Andean region provides many weeks of adventure sports, like mountain climbing, long-range trekking, rafting, kayaking, mountain biking and paragliding. Such laid-back sports as birdwatching, fishing, day hikes and horseback riding, are also possibilities.

After wandering the Cordilleras, you can give your muscles a good, relaxing soak. Head for the hot springs at Monterrey, near Huaraz, or the Baños de la Merced, near Carhuaz.

If you are more culturally inclined, you will not be disappointed. Huaraz is home to the Museo Regional de Ancash, focused on archaeology, and the Sala de Cultura of Banco Wiese, an art museum. Within these sierras hide some of the oldest and most impressive archaeological sites of the Chavín people, a culture believed to be the ancestor of all other great pre-Columbian societies, including the Wari and the Inca. Explore the ruins of Chavín de Huántar, Tumshukaiko near Caraz, Huanoca Pampa, near Chiquián, or Willkawaína near Huaraz.

Ancient cities aren't the only ruins in this region. Yungay was the site of a devasting landslide that killed over 90% of the population in 1970. The site of the former town is now a cemetery. The town has been rebuilt up on higher ground and serves as a gateway to fine trekking in the Cordilleras.

SOUTHERN ANDES (P.232)

The southern Peruvian Andes are perhaps the least touristy place you will visit in Peru. For several decades, it was a zone abandoned due to the violence of the civil war, the Peruvian military and the *Sendero Luminoso* (Shining Path). Only in the past decade have tourists begun to return to know this region, discovering its *punas,* (high Andean plateaus) populated by small adobe villages, flamingos and tassel-earringed alpacas. There are craftspeople to chat with, ruins to wander and birds to scout.

The ancient Kotosh civilization was centered near Huánuco, a city teeming with colonial buildings, churches and vibrant markets. Five kilometers away is the 4,000-year-old Kotosh temple, Templo de las Manos Cruzadas.

Be sure to bring your binoculars to Reserva Nacional Junín, possessing the second largest lake in the country, Lago de Junín, as well as over 100 species of birds.

Railroad buffs are not left out of the action here. You can board the Highest Train in the World to Huancayo, or click-clack along on the last truly local train left in Peru, that from Huancayo to Huancavelica. Huancayo and the Mantaro valley are home to many crafts virtuosos. Call on artist-shaman Pedro Marticorena Oroña Laya at his Wali Wasi home in Huancayo. Drop in at the many artisan workshops in the valley's villages: Cochas Grande and Cochas Chico are renowned for carved gourds or *mates burilados*; Hualhuas, for weavings; and Jerónimo de Tunán for silver jewelry. Yes, of course, this region also has its museums and ruins to discover.

Ayacucho, the "Corner of Blood," has seen war throughout its history: from Inca to Spanish conquest, from Wars of Independence to the armed conflicts with the Sendero Luminoso. But it is also a university city with abundant culture: many poets and musicians who make their home here; there are 33 churches, the Museo de Arte Popular Joaquín López Antay and the Museo Arqueológico Hipólito Unánue, as well as the artisan neighborhood of Barrio Santa Ana. Outside of town are the ruins of Vilcashuamán, Baños Intihuatana and Wari. Join in the Semana Santa festivities, with flower-carpeted streets, solemn processions and bull effigies with firework horns.

AREQUIPA AND THE COLCA CANYON (P.186)

Under majestic volcano El Misti's shadow, the romantic city of Arequipa awaits you in Southern Peru. Pearly white, arcaded buildings made of white volcanic stone line the city's many plazas. Myriads of colonial churches, including the 400-year-old Monasterio de Santa Catalina (which you can visit), the Cathedral, La Compañía of the Jesuits and others, as well as colonial-era mansions scatter the city. You can learn more about the history and culture of Arequipa at the Museo Santuarios Andinos, home of the 13-year-old mummy Juanita, the Museo de Arte Contemporánea and the Museo Histórico Municipal.

If the mere altitude of Arequipa doesn't give you enough of a high, get your adrenaline pumping with a climb of one the neighboring volcanoes: El Misti (5,822 m / 19,101 ft), Chachani (over

6,000 m / 19,685 ft), or Ampato (6,288 m / 20, 630 ft). Beyond their *cordillera* lie two canyons much deeper than the U.S.' Grand Canyon. Delve into the depths of Colca Canyon (3,400 meters / 11,155 feet deep) or Cotahuasi Canyon (3,535 m / 12,000 ft — the deepest in the world), rafting through three- to five-grade white waters. Trek, mountain bike or ride horses through trails that wind along their lunarscape walls and visit the villages that preserve much of their ancient ways. Your thrill will only be heightened by the sound of a condor's wings swooping overhead. In the Colca Canyon, you can catch spectacular views of these high Andes and the Valley of the Volcanoes, and check out the Toro Muerto Petroglyphs. Be sure to drop by Reserva Nacional Salinas y Aguada Blanca, an area of stunningly beautiful salty lakes and grasslands teeming with wildlife, like flamingos, geese, black-faced Andean gulls, *vicuñas* and *vizcachas*. Take a relaxing bath in La Caldera hot springs near Chivay. Cotahuasi Canyon is home to Solimama volcano, the highest in Peru at 6,425 meters / 21,079 feet and Catarata Sipia, a 150-meter / 492-ft high waterfall.

In the southern-most reaches of Peru is Tacna, near the Chilean border. (Well, it was, at one time, part of Chile—from 1880 until 1929—until the people voted to once more be Peruvians.) If you get the chance, hop on the train to skip over the border—and before boarding, chug down memory lane at the Museo Ferroviario at the Tacna station. Also to entertain your hours, you can stroll around town, checking out the Catedral, designed by Gustave Eiffel (of Eiffel Tower fame), colonial houses and fountain-misted plazas. Further afield you can relax in the Caliente hot springs or investigate the San Francisco de Miculla petroglyphs.

CUSCO, MACHU PICCHU AND THE SACRED VALLEY (P.249)

Many dream of undertaking the four-day trek along the Inca Trail to that holy grail, Machu Picchu. If you are one, don't forget to make your reservation well ahead of time. Regulations instituted in 2002 limit the number of hikers that can be on the trail on any day. Don't forget that the Inca Trail is closed during the month of February for maintenance.

But many other Inca trails await your footfall here in the Sacred Valley, like those to Salcantay, Vilcabamba, and Ausangate in the Cordillera Vilcanota. And ruins? Well, there's way more than that new Seven Wonders of the Modern World. Drop by Sacsayhuamán, Q'enqo, Puca Pucara, Tambo Machay, Pisac and Ollantaytambo. Quaint *pueblos* also are to be checked out here, many producing good alpaca and llama wool products.

Cusco, the former capital of the Inca Empire was later razed and rebuilt by the Spaniards. While wandering the narrow streets you will encounter dozens of churches whose foundations are the massive-stone walls of Inca temples. You can spend hours or even weeks combing through the museums Cusco has to offer.

But two warnings before heading out for any exploration in this region: make sure you rest upon arriving to let yourself get acclimatized to the 3,500+ meter altitude — and don't forget to buy your Cusco Tourist Ticket, allowing you entrance into many sites.

LAKE TITICACA (P.341)

The teal-blue waters of Lago Titicaca shimmer at 3,821 meters (12,536 ft) above sea level. Sitting by golden-maroon fields of quinoa, women spin wool on hand-held spindles. Flamingoes wade through the marshes where *totora* reed boats bob. In the distance, on the Bolivian side, the snowy peaks of Cordillera Apolobamba scrape the crystalline sky.

According to legend, the glorious Inca dynasty rose from the depths of this, the highest lake in the world and South America's largest fresh-water body. Their ascent is marked by the Isla del Sol and Isla de Luna, most easily reached from the Bolivian town of Copacabana. Other great nations also developed in this region, most notably the Tiwanaku, on the Bolivian side. Here on the Peruvian shores you can visit such ruins as Sillustani, Pucará and Raqchi.

Not only ruins of those former civilizations dot the shores of Titicaca. Their Quechua & Aymara-speaking descendents continue to live here. The oldest and most enigmatic of these is the Uros peoples, whose agricultural expertise creates mat-based islands, which they continue to farm and live on to this day. You can visit their communities, as well as those on the other inhabited islands of the lake.

Puno is the transit point—whether you are traveling from Arequipa to Cusco or to the sister-nation Bolivia. From Puno you can catch the train to Cusco, and thus begin your exploration of the former Inca Empire heartland. The city affords brilliant views over the surrounding countryside, from Cerrito de Huajsapata and Mirador de Kuntur Wasi. There are also a number of charming *pueblos* to know, wandering through markets and entering simple colonial churches, like Llachón, Juli and Chucuito. Be sure to join in on one of the 300 festivals that happen in these villages throughout the year—especially the renowned *carnaval* of Puno, and the early-February Virgen de Candalaría celebrations in Copacabana, Bolivia. The region also offers fantastic trekking, biking and kayaking.

THE AMAZON (P.483)

The majority of Peru is a low, emerald blanket that stretches across the Amazon basin. Travel the rivers and get splashed by pink river dolphins, caiman or giant river otters. Wander virgin forests, where you can watch toucans, macaws and squirrel monkeys overhead. Rough it camping out, stay in indigenous communities, or in first-rate lodges.

You can visit the Napo and Amazon River basins at Iquitos. Gustave Eiffel's Casa de Fierro and the many fancy *azulejos* (decorative tiles) lend testimony to the city's fabulously wealthy past. Today, you can go to nearby nature areas, such as Laguna Quistococha or Reserva Nacional Pacaya-Samaria. While waiting for a boat to take you down the Amazon to Colombia or Brazil, you can shop at the lively markets.

The southern Amazon region is a warming experience after your stay in the heights of Machu Picchu, Cusco and Lake Titicaca. Take a swing down to Puerto Maldonado, from where you can jump off to Lago Sandoval, Parque Nacional Bahuaja-Sonene and Reserva Nacional Tambopata. Be sure to have your binoculars and bird guide at hand—and, of course, your camera to capture the macaws at the licks. If you want to hang out a bit longer, you can study Spanish here, or get involved in one of many environmental and animal-rescue projects in the area.

Also in the Madre de Dios region is the Manu Biosphere Reserve, home to thousands of species of plants and animals. Be ready to see screeching monkeys, elusive jaguars, cagey caimans, prismatic macaws and playful giant otters. If you are a birdwatcher, this is your paradise, with more than a thousand bird species.

SUGGESTED ITINERARIES

It is hard to get a good taste of Peru in little time. The country is large and overland travel can be long. If going into high altitude, allow for time to acclimatize yourself, especially if you are planning trekking, mountain climbing or other high-octane sports. Review the information on how to prevent *soroche* (altitude sickness). If your vacation is short, decide what is most attractive to you. Perhaps focus your stay on just one region, to really get the most out of your trip.

You can easily spend a week just in Huaraz, trekking through the Cordillera Blanca to little towns and Chavín ruins, or in the Chachapoyas realm, overflowing with mysterious archaeological sites like Kuélap, Revash and Karajía, as well as the Gocta waterfall. Flights to both these gateway cities can save you travel time. Many folks will choose to visit Machu Picchu. If you cannot get a reservation for the Inca Trail, or would like to make your holiday a bit different, consider doing one of the other less visited treks in the Sacred Valley, like Salcantay, Vilcabamba, or Ausangate in the Cordillera Vilcanota.

Get your writing published in our books, go to www.vivatravelguides.com

The following are just some suggested itineraries. For longer trips, mix and match them. Have fun creating your own. *¡Buen Viaje!*

ONE WEEK
CLASSIC TRIP
Day 1-3: Fly into Lima; continue on to Cusco by plane. Visit the many museums and churches Cusco city offers. Take in Ollantaytambo and other sites in the Sacred Valley. Day 4: Hop on the train to Machu Picchu (on your own, or arranged through a tour company). Return to Cusco, where you will stay overnight. Days 5-6: To Puno—Shop. Take an excursion on Lago Titicaca, visiting the Uros, Taquile and other islands. Visit Sillustani, Pucará and Raqchi ruins, and Llachón, Juli and Chucuito villages. Day 7: Travel to Juliaca to take your flight back to Lima.

MACHU PICCHU AND THE INCA TRAIL
Days 1-3: Fly into Lima; continue on to Cusco by plane. Take the next few days to acclimatize to the altitude, before embarking on your dream trek. Leisurely visit Cusco's many museums and churches, as well as the great Inca ruins at Sacsayhuamán, Q'enqo, Puca Pucara, Tambo Machay, Pisac and Ollantaytambo. Shop at the small-town markets. Relax. Days 4-6: The three-day Inca Trail to Machu Picchu. Day 7: Fly back to Lima.

NORTHERN COAST
Day 1: Fly into Lima; catch the afternoon flight to Trujillo. Overnight in Huanchaco, 20 minutes from Trujillo. Day 2: Visit the incredible Chan Chan, Huaca del Sol, Huaca de la Luna and Huaca Esmeraldas ruins. Ride the waves in a *totora* raft. Days 3-4: To Chiclayo. Check out the spectacular archaeological sites Sipán and Túcume, and Chiclayo's world-class Brüning Archaeological, Sicán National and Royal Tombs of Sipán Museums. Days 5-6: Travel to Máncora, by way of Piura. Enjoy the beach; surf (or take lessons). Dine on some fresh ceviche. Day 7: Bus down to Talara, where you can catch your flight to Lima.

SOUTHERN COAST
Day 1: Fly into Lima. Days 2-3: Travel to Pisco, only four hours away. Check out the mysterious Candelabra de los Andes. Take boat tour of the Paracas National Reserve and Islas Ballestres. Overnight in Pisco. Day 4: To Ica: Check out the impressive Museo Histórico Regional. Sample the pisco and other vintages at Tacama Winery, Bodega El Catador or Vista Alegre. Try your hand at sandboarding. Overnight at Oasis Huacachina. Days 5-6: To Nasca: Fly over the famous Nasca Lines and visit the museums: Casa-Museo Maria Reiche, Museo Antonini or the Maria Reiche Planetarium. Day trips to near-by ruins of Paredones, Cahuichi or Cementerios de Chauchilla, or to the San Juan de Marcona Marine Reserve. Overnight in Nasca. Day 7: Return to Lima by bus.

SOUTHERN PERU
Day 1: Arrive in Lima; if it is yet early enough, catch the flight for Arequipa. Days 2-3: Stroll around the *Ciudad Blanca* of pearly white colonial churches and mansions. Visit the 400-year-old Monasterio de Santa Catalina, the Cathedral, La Compañía church, Museo Santuarios Andinos, Museo de Arte Contemporánea and Museo Histórico Municipal. Days 4-5: To Colca Canyon where you can trek, bike or horseback ride to age-old villages and, with a bit of luck, spot condors. Day 6: Now that you are acclimatized to the altitude, climb El Misti—or just spend the day exploring Arequipa some more. Day 7: Catch a flight in Arequipa for your return to Lima.

TWO WEEKS
CLASSIC TRIP: THE INCA TRAIL AND THE JUNGLE
Days 1-4: Fly into Lima; continue on to Cusco by plane. Take the next few days to acclimatize to the altitude, before embarking on the Inca Trail. Leisurely visit Cusco's many museums and churches, and the Sacred Valley's great Inca ruins at Sacsayhuamán, Puca Pucara,

Ollantaytambo and elsewhere. Shop at the small-town markets. Relax. Days 5-8: The four-day Inca Trail to Machu Picchu. Day 8: Return to Cusco. Day 9-12: Fly to Puerto Maldonado for your stay at a jungle lodge. Day 13: Fly to Lima. Day 14: Take in some of the many cultural jewels Lima presents you, and do a bit of shopping for gifts and souvenirs.

NORTHERN JUNGLE JAUNT

Days 1-6: Arrive in Lima; catch a flight to Iquitos. Stay in a jungle lodge, or base yourself in Iquitos, cruising the Amazon and its tributaries to indigenous villages, Laguna Quistococha and Reserva Nacional Pacaya-Samiria. Shop in Iquitos' renowned floating river market, and witness the reminders of this city's glorious past, like the many azulejos and the Casa de Fierro. Days 7-11: Take a four-to-seven-day boat upstream to Pucallpa. (The trip is longest when the river is high.) Day 12: Check out this central jungle port, visit its zoo and drop by local artist Pablo César Amaringo Shuna's studio Usko-Ayar, before heading back to civilization. Day 13: Fly to Lima. Day 14: Take in some of the many cultural jewels Lima presents you, and do a bit of shopping for gifts and souvenirs.

Photo by Margaret Rode

Photo by Margaret Rode

INTRODUCTION

In Quechua, the language closest to that of the Inca, Peru means the 'land of abundance.' Peru is full of extremes: from lush, towering Andean peaks to rolling sand dunes on the coast to the largest, most diverse rainforest in the world, the Amazon jungle. Peru is also rich in pre-Columbian culture with millions of citizens in the Andes mountains who still live, speak and work the way their ancestors did thousands of years ago. On the Pacific coast of South America, between Ecuador and Bolivia and west of Brazil, Peru ranks among the world's top producers of silver, copper, lead and zinc. The Amazon makes up half of the Peru, the Andes mountains occupy a third and the rest is coastal desert.

GEOGRAPHY, CLIMATE, FLORA AND FAUNA

Peru features wildly diverse flora and fauna, thanks to its great natural and geological diversity. One of Peru's leading scientists, Dr. Javier Pulgar Vidal, completed extensive studies of the country in the 1930s, describing no less than eight climatological zones, divided into 96 sub-zones, each of which represents a different biological niche. The eight zones are Chala, or coastland; Yunga, lowland valleys; Quechua, a temperate, middle-altitude zone; Suni, highlands; Puna, inhospitable highlands; Janca, snowy mountain peaks; Omagua, high interior jungle; and Rupa-Rupa, lowland jungle.

The Chala, or coastal, zone features islands, mangroves, beaches, some marshes, and inland areas up to about 500 meters above sea level. The flora of this region is marked by palm trees, coconuts, olive trees, papayas, mangroves, *Chala* (maize plant in Quechua) and the variety of grape from which Peruvian *pisco* is made. The area is also home to certain reeds and rushes that are used commercially by the locals to make baskets, mats, etc. The fauna includes all sea animals and marine birds, such as fish, sea lions, frigates and boobies.

The lowland valleys and hills that make up the Yunga zone (500-2300 m/ 1600-7500 ft above sea level) are marked by fruit trees such as the avocado, plum, orange, grapefruit, and lime. Peru's extensive sugarcane fields are found in the Yunga ("warm valley"). The region is famous for orchids: more than 200 species are thought to exist here. It features many species of birds, including the rare white-winged guan. The Warm Valley is also home to some small species of wild cats as well as many reptiles, including boas and several types of lizard, and the Andean spectacled bear. The Yunga is currently considered a highly endangered ecosystem: a great deal of damage is being inflicted by agriculture and deforestation.

The temperate Quechua region (2300-3500 m/ 7500-11500 ft above sea level) is the most important agricultural zone for Peruvian grains, such as maize and wheat. Tomatoes, papayas and peaches also grow well in the Quechua area.

The Suni zone (3500-4,100 m/ 11500-13500 ft above sea level) is cold and dry, with some glacial lakes. *Suni* means "high" in Quechua. The flora of the region is tough—hardy plants and bushes, with very few trees. Little agriculture takes place here, but quinoa (a local grain) does well, as do some potatoes, barley, oats and the broad bean. The famous guinea pig, long a staple food of Andean cultures, is native to this region. The Lake Titicaca basin is considered to be a combination of Suni and Puna regions.

The Puna zone is the highest that supports human populations; *puna* means "altitude sickness" in Quechua. The region is home to iconic Andean creatures such as the llama, vicuña, guanaco and alpaca. Sheep, which were introduced into the area, also thrive here. The Puna has several highland lakes which are important stop-overs for migratory birds. Potatoes grow well, as do certain cacti.

The Janca ("white") region is the highest in Peru, and is characterized by glaciers and snow-capped peaks. Some grasses, moss and lichens thrive in the region, but little else. Some animals and birds, including the Andean condor, reside here as well. It is too inhospitable for people to stay there for long.

Get your writing published in our books, go to www.vivatravelguides.com

The Omagua region, or high jungle, gets its name from an indigenous word meaning "region of the fresh water fish." In Peru, there are vast stretches of virgin rainforest classified as Omagua. It is home to several species of mammals and reptiles, as well as many birds and insects. There are also, naturally, several species of fish that thrive in this climate zone, largest of which is the *paiche*. Several important species of plants, including the Brazil nut tree, mahogany and the hallucinogenic ayahuasca are found here.

Peru's steamy interior jungle lowlands are classified as Rupa-Rupa, from a Quechua word meaning "ardent." This thriving, vital ecosystem is home to countless species of plant and animal life. Many trees from this region are of commercial value, including the balsawood, rubber and oil palm trees.

HISTORY

The area now known as Peru was inhabited long before the arrival of the Spanish. Various smaller ethnic groups controlled regions and cities before the ascendance of the Inca from the Cusco region in about 1440 AD. The Inca conquered the region and established Cusco (p.251) as the center of their empire.

The Inca were talented mathematicians and stonemasons. They built formidable cities and fortifications, and they were skilled rulers. Interestingly, their civilization was not familiar with the wheel and axle (except in toys), and all of the heavy stones for their cities were transported by sled or rolled on logs. They did not have books and writing, but did have *quipus*, complex sets of colored cords knotted in certain patterns. At least in terms of mathematics, these cords were as accurate as writing. Although some quipus still exist in museums, the art of being able to decipher them has been lost.

When a Spanish expedition arrived in 1532 under Francisco Pizarro, it found an Inca Empire in chaos. A bloody civil war had torn the empire apart, with two brothers—Atahualpa in the north and Huáscar in the south—fighting for dominance. Not long after the arrival of the Spanish, Huáscar was captured by Atahualpa's forces. When Atahualpa was captured by the Spanish at Cajamarca, he ordered Huáscar executed so that he alone would be the ruler of the Inca. Unfortunately for Atahualpa, Huáscar was the elder brother, which under the European system of inheritance made him head of the Inca. The Spanish branded Atahualpa a traitor and usurper and murdered him after collection of a huge ransom of gold and silver. Subsequently, the Spanish would base their legal claim to Andean lands on the notion that since they had taken them from a "usurper," their continued occupation was just and legal.

In the 1540s, the Spanish conquistadores fell to warring among themselves in a series of civil wars that were every bit as brutal as the conquest had been. Francisco Pizarro himself was hacked down in the street. It wasn't until the arrival of a series of Viceroys in the latter half of the century that the situation calmed down. The most notable of the Viceroys was Francisco de Toledo, who ruled from 1569 to 1581. Toledo toured the vast lands of Peru, taking with him mapmakers, historians and bureaucrats. He often kept Inca policies and legal precedents in place when he could.

By the latter half of the 16th century, precious metals had been discovered in abundance in parts of Peru, and gold and silver from the region was shipped to Spain for more than two centuries. In the early 1800s, Peru was one of the last colonies to declare independence from Spain, largely because the capital city of Lima (p.78) was very loyal. Even so, Peru declared itself independent in 1821. What followed was a long period of instability: Peru had 59 presidents from 1821 to 1900. Although it fared a little better in the 20th century, there was still a great deal of chaos—Peru had five different presidents in 1931 alone. As late as 1980, Peru was ruled by the military, but in recent years a fragile democracy has seemingly taken root.

During the 1980s, Peru was plagued by the twin evils of cocaine production and revolts. The Maoist Shining Path controlled huge areas of the Peruvian countryside and operated with impunity in Lima at the height of its power. Atrocities were committed on both sides as the government sought to put down the rebellion. In the 1990s, the administration of Japanese-Peruvian mathematician Alberto Fujimori succeeded in bringing the economy under control and in eliminating the terrorism of the Shining Path. The group never recovered after its leader, Abimael Guzmán, was captured in Lima in 1992. Although he was re-elected in 2000, Fujimori was forced to flee to Japan in order to avoid indictment for corruption.

In the run-off election, the people of Peru elected Alejandro Toledo, one of 16 children and a former shoeshine boy who also happens to be native Andean. The Toledo administration was marked by several scandals, including everything from forging registration signatures to an illegitimate daughter. International observers, however, credit Toledo with sparking some limited growth in the economy. In June 2006, Alan García Pérez, who had served as president from 1985 to 1990, was re-elected president by popular vote to a five-year term.

Inca
The ancient and modern people of the Andes are often incorrectly referred to as the Inca. In fact, only the kings and ruling family were referred to as Inca. The closest translation for the word *Inca* is 'king,' at least in the way the people of the ancient Andes used it.

POLITICS
The Republic of Peru operates as a presidential representative democratic republic and is based on a multi-party system, whereby the president (Alan García as of writing, 2008) is elected for a five-year term and serves as both head of state and head of government. The legislative body is a 120-member elected unicameral Congress, and—though once a toothless body acting at the whim of the president—has seen a notable increase in powers in recent years and serves as an important counterbalance to the executive branch. The judiciary is independent of both the executive and legislative branches, and steps have been taken to reform its notoriously obsolete and corruption-ridden practices.

Peru's modern political history has been more a series of personality showdowns and power-politics struggles than an institution based on party platforms, though parties spring up and have maintained a prominent place in the face of Peruvian politics since the 1950s.

Peru is in an ongoing state of democratization. Largely due to corruption and poor leadership, it has struggled to achieve the development progress of neighboring countries, rendering the nation gravely impoverished and disposed to increased inequality. Peruvian politics have been continually compromised by corruption, with two of the last three presidents currently under investigation.

Remnants of the first major disappointment still linger after the erratic presidency of Alberto Fujimori, who was elected in 1990. Though the early years of his term looked hopeful and inspired a dramatic economic turnaround and significant progress in curtailing guerrilla activity, the president's increasing reliance on harsh authoritarian measures and economic decline in the late 1990s spawned rising dissatisfaction with his regime, contributing to its rapid fall. Fujimori resigned from office in 2000, fleeing to Japan (where he also holds citizenship) as charges of diverting vast government revenues closed in on him. He later returned to South America and based himself in Chile during the 2006 Peruvian elections in an attempt to clear his reputation, but was quickly held by authorities.

Alejandro Toledo, García's most recent predecessor and the first democratically elected Peruvian president of indigenous descent, later failed to make good on promises to both meet the needs of the poor and bring the country up to speed in light of globalization. Topping off his apparent inability to make any sort of progress, he is still under investigation for nasty scandals exposed during his term as president.

The presidential election of 2006 saw the return of García who, after serving a less than impressive term during the turbulent 1980s, returned to office with ideas for social reform and promises of major improvements of the economic situation. Thus far the government led by García seems far more interested in neo-liberal strategies such as free trade, than in adopting policies aimed at reducing poverty and advancing development goals.

Peru turned down the opportunity to address these issues when it elected García over the populist candidate Ollanta Humala, who showed greater interest in pro-poor policies and campaigned on the premise of bringing about a "revolution for the poor." But García cited Humala's open support of Venezuela's leftist president Hugo Chávez as dangerous for the independence of the nation and took the seat.

Poverty has been further exacerbated by the diversion of much-needed national resources to deal with internal conflict caused by rebel groups such as the Maoist Shining Path and the Tupac Amaru Revolutionary Movement (MRTA). Though much progress in curbing violence was seen during Fujimori's presidency, the campaign was expensive. Sporadic insurgencies have since plagued the nation. Drug trafficking and drug-related crime also remains a problem in Peru and involvement is often attributed to former members of these two groups.

The Shining Path

The Communist Party of Peru (El Partido Comunista del Perú, PCP)—more commonly known as the Shining Path or *Sendero Luminoso*—is a militant Maoist guerilla group founded in the late 1960s, in an attempt to restructure an impoverished Peruvian society perpetuated by a system deeply-rooted in race and class-based discrimination.

Established by former University professor Abimael Guzmán in response to a split in the Peruvian Communist Party, the Senderistas took up arms in 1980, launching their campaign in indigenous communities in the Andes and attracting sympathizers with ideas of replacing the traditional ruling elite with a peasant revolutionary authority. Using violence and intimidation, they quickly gained control over large regions of Peru throughout the 1980s, attacking any allusion to capitalist society and greatly disrupting the Peruvian economy.

By the time their influence began to wane with the capture of Guzmán in 1992, the Shining Path was responsible for an estimated 25,000 deaths in Peru. The group has been widely condemned for its brutality—victims were often hacked to death with machetes, and peasants, trade union organizers, popularly elected officials and civilians were regular targets. Though their new leader, Oscar Ramirez Durand, was sentenced to life imprisonment in 1999 under harsh anti-terror laws enacted by former president Alberto Fujimori, sporadic acts since have since served as reminders that the group still maintains a presence in society.

Throughout Fujimori's crackdown thousands of Peruvians were convicted of terrorism-related crimes and faced life sentences in prison, many of which may have been unjust, according to human rights activists. In 2003 the constitutional court struck down Fujimori's hard-handed laws, granting 1,900 Shining Path prisoners, including founder Guzmán, the right to request retrials in civilian court, . While the Shining Path is considered to be a terrorist group by major world authorities and maintains a place on the U.S. Department of State's "Designated Foreign Terrorist Organizations" list, both Peruvian and North American governments say that terrorism is not a prevailing problem in Peru today.

ECONOMY

When the Inca came to the region of Peru in the 15th century, they found several small tribes engaged in basic agriculture, notably corn and cotton. The Inca conquered the region and added limited mining and other agricultural practices. When the Spanish arrived in 1531, they established their own rule in the region. Using native labor, they greatly increased mining operations. The city of Lima was founded in 1535, in part, as a port city from which gold and silver could be shipped back to Spain.

During the colonial and republican eras, the economy of Peru remained based on mining, agriculture and fishing. In the 1840s, great deposits of saltpeter (also known as potassium nitrate) in the form of eons of accumulated bird guano were discovered on some Pacific islands off the coast of Peru. The guano made excellent fertilizer and saltpeter is an essential ingredient for explosives. Harvesting the guano brought in a great deal of revenue for Peru. The islands were so rich that Spain seized them in 1864, but the Peruvians eventually drove them off. By 1874 the accumulated guano had been mostly harvested.

In the 1980s, inflation was rampant in Peru and the economy was in dire shape. President Alberto Fujimori instituted several reforms and encouraged foreign investment, and in the 1990s the economy stabilized. From 1994 to 1997, the economy did particularly well, and GDP increased dramatically. After a few years of stagnation, the economy is again growing under the fiscally sound policies of successive administrations.

Today, Peru's economy is very diverse. Mining, fishing, metals, textiles, food, chemicals and tourism are all important sectors of a growing economy. Peru's main exports include coffee, minerals and fish. The U.S., China and Great Britain are Peru's largest trading partners.

Tourism is a steadily-growing and increasingly important part of Peru's economy. Machu Picchu (p.336), Cusco (p.251), Lima (p.78), the jungle (p.483) and mountaineering expeditions, among other tourism-related activities, have made Peru into one of Latin America's top tourism draws, especially now that the Shining Path has been all but eliminated.

POPULATION
Peru has a population of more than 29 million. The annual growth rate of the population is reported to be 1.26%. The population is fairly young — 30% of the people are estimated to be under the age of 14. Ethnicity is divided into four main groups: Amerindian (45%), *mestizo* or mixed (37%), white (15%) and other, including those of African, Japanese and Chinese descent (3%).

LANGUAGE
Spanish was brought to Peru in the 16th century by the *conquistadores* and today it is the most widely spoken language, used in most cities and towns. The majority of Peruvians speak at least some Spanish. English is not common, although most tourism professionals do speak it. Various dialects of Quechua are spoken across Peru, particularly in the Andean regions; some are very markedly different from one another. The use of Quechua has been declining over the past century, although there are initiatives underway in various areas to bring it back into the classroom, to maintain traditions. Aymara is spoken largely in the Lake Titicaca area, in and around Puno.

Spanish, Quechua and Aymara
In April 2006, two Peruvian congresswomen from Cusco proclaimed that they would communicate only in Quechua during plenary sessions in Congress. Thus another *salvo* had been fired in Peru's century-old struggle in the use of language to determine national identity and culture. Since 1975, Peru's constitution has recognized Quechua and Aymara along with Spanish as official languages of the Republic. However, since Spain's conquest of South America during the 16th century, Spanish has served as the dominant language of Peru, after the conquistadors excluded all indigenous languages from cultural and political discourse. In Peru, as in other Andean nations, the majority of the population speaks Spanish, but significant minorities (estimates range up to ten million) are also very proudly bilingual, speaking one form or another of Quechua or Aymara.

The word Quechua is used to denote both a people and a wide variety of spoken dialects that pre-date not only the Spanish empire, but also the Incan empire—by at least a millennium. Peru itself can lay claim to being the birthplace of Quechua, which then became the *lingua franca* of trade throughout the Andes. However, the language of Quechua itself has at

LORI BERENSON: AMERICAN BEHIND PERUVIAN BARS

A panel of hooded military judges sat speaking through microphones that distorted their voices. The verdict: guilty as charged. Twenty-six-year-old Lori Berenson's fate was sealed. She was sentenced to life in prison on January 11, 1996, for treason against the fatherland: Peru.

Lori Berenson grew up the daughter of university professors in New York, attending high school with Jennifer Aniston and Cher's daughter, Chastity Bono. However, Berenson dropped out of MIT and headed to Central America where she picked up a different kind of education, losing friends to the brutality of El Salvador's National Guard and working with the Committee in Solidarity with the People of El Salvador (CISPES) and the Salvadoran Popular Forces of Liberation.

Her curiosity about different cultures eventually led her to Peru in 1994. Her traveling companion was Pacífico Castrellón. He was deeply involved in the Tupac Amaru Revolutionary Movement (MRTA), one of the most wanted and watched terrorist groups in Peru. Berenson would later claim he was a Panamanian whom she met by chance in an art gallery in Panama City. Castrellón would claim their trip to Peru was arranged by the MRTA rebels and on their way to Peru they met with MRTA leader Néstor Cerpa.

In Peru, Berenson leased a large house in the suburbs of Lima with Castrellón. This house became the headquarters for the MRTA, storing seven automatic rifles with over 8,000 rounds of ammunition, 100 hand grenades and over 2,000 sticks of dynamite. Berenson claimed she knew nothing of this. She also claimed that she knew nothing of her housemates' involvement with the MRTA. In August 1995, she moved out of the house and rented her own apartment in Lima. Guards do not recall seeing any MRTA members enter her new residence—her activity seemed normal.

However, on November 30, 1995, Berenson was arrested along with Nancy Gilvonio, the wife of the MRTA leader Cerpa, while riding a bus in Lima after leaving Peru's Congress. The day after her arrest, Berenson's house was raided by security forces, a coded floor plan of Congress allegedly sketched by Berenson and a forged Peruvian election ID card bearing her photo were among the evidence seized. Thirteen months later, Cerpa led a takeover of the Japanese Ambassador's Lima residence. The MRTA rebels held 72 hostages for four months. They demanded freedom for hundreds of imprisoned comrades, with Berenson being number three on their list.

After Berenson's original trial in 1996, she was retried under lesser charges, due to international pressure. She was found guilty of collaboration. In prison, Berenson was subjected to horrific living conditions and became chronically ill. She was eventually moved to a lower elevation prison where her health problems seemed to improve.

In 2003, she married Aníbal Apari, a paroled MRTA member whom she met when both were serving time at Yanamayo prison. Berenson currently spends her days working in the prison bakery and speaking out against human rights. "I've been in jail many years now because of my beliefs, but I still have great hopes and I'm still convinced that there will be a future of justice for the people of Peru and all humanity."

Berenson's case went to the Inter-American Court of Human Rights, based in Costa Rica, in 2002. At that time, the court upheld the second ruling of the Peruvian Supreme Court. Former U.S. Ambassador to Peru, Dennis Jett, said the reason is simple: "She isn't innocent." Guilty or innocent, jail is where Berenson will stay until her release date in 2015.

least forty separate dialects that have evolved with wide variations according to geography. Indeed, within Peru, northern Quechua and southern Quechua cannot use their respective languages to communicate.

A commonly-held belief has evolved that the Cusco Quechua is the most authentic and complete Quechua, but some historians argue that was more due to Cusco being the seat of the Inca Empire which arose in the early 15th century and had mandated it as the official language of the realm, though they tolerated the use of other idioms. Ironically, it was the Spanish who actually spread the use of Cusco Quechua more so than Incan emperors, by utilizing it as a means of broadening their conquest of the New World even while curtailing its ability to serve the needs of its native speakers.

Quechua words that have become incorporated into the English language through Spanish include: coca, condor, gaucho, jerky, llama, potato, puma and quinoa. Huttese, language of the Huts in the Star Wars series, is largely taken from Quechua.

RELIGION

When the Spanish arrived in the region in the early 1530s and set about conquering the Inca empire, they brought their religion with them. Catholic churches and cathedrals sprang up in every new settlement. During the colonial period, the mendicant orders—the Dominicans, Franciscans and Augustinians—were prominent in society. The *conquistadores* were said to favor the mendicant orders, as the friars are not allowed to own personal property (and there would, therefore, be more loot for everyone else). Today, many important cities dating from the colonial period have cathedrals, monasteries and squares dedicated to San Francisco and San Agustín, reflecting this colonial legacy.

Before the arrival of the Spanish, the native Andeans worshipped a complex pantheon of deities. The greatest of the Inca deities was Viracocha, and some early Spanish missionaries saw in Vira Cocha an embodiment of their own Christian God (while other missionaries saw him as an incarnation of Satan). For a fascinating look at pre-Columbian Andean religion, check out The Huarochiri Manuscript, one of very few documents that deal with pre-Hispanic religious beliefs to have survived the colonial era.

In 1586, Isabel Flores de Oliva was born in Lima. She would later adopt the name Rosa. An extremely devout young woman, she refused to marry and eventually entered a Dominican convent. She was known for her acts of charity as well as extreme self-mortification, including constantly wearing a spiked crown, long fasts and sleeping on a bed full of stones, thorns and broken glass and pottery. Perhaps not surprisingly, she died at the young age of 31, and her funeral was attended by all of the city leaders of Lima. Many miracles have been attributed to her. She was canonized in 1671 as Saint Rose of Lima. She is the patroness of the Americas as well as of Lima, which remembers her with a holiday on August 30. St. Martin of Porras (1579-1639) was also born in Lima, and St. Turibius of Mongrovejo (1538-1606), although born in Spain, was Archbishop of Lima from 1579 until his death.

Over the centuries, Spanish priests managed to stamp out most of the traces of native religion, but some structures and beliefs remained. Cusco's temples were built over but not totally destroyed, and some of the foundations can still be seen. In a religious melding process known as syncretism, some churches combine elements of native religion with Christianity.

Today, Peru is still predominantly Roman Catholic (about 80%), but there are other religions as well. Mission-oriented groups, such as the Church of Latter-Day Saints (Mormons) and Jehovah's Witnesses, are growing, and there are communities of Muslims, Buddhists, Hindus and more. The reclusive Los Israelitas del Nuevo Pacto Universal (Israelites of the New Universal Pact) often put forth candidates for major elections from their compound in the hills near Huarochirí, but little is known about them and their mysterious founder, Ezequiel Ataucusi (The Illuminated One), although one of their candidates, Javier Noriega, was elected to congress.

Peru is often a destination for new age spiritual pilgrims. Shamans (both real and fake) in the Amazon offer experiences with ayahuasca, a hallucinogenic vine that is often credited with giving visions. Cusco is also considered a center for new age "energy."

CULTURE

More than any other Andean country, Peru embodies all the conflicts, cultures and contradictions of Latin American civilization. The city of Cusco was the seat of the Inca empire until the arrival of Spanish conquistador Francisco Pizarro in 1531, who executed the rival princes Huáscar and Atahualpa, and brought about the long and bloody reign of Spanish and Catholic domination, which was justified by defining the indigenous peoples of the Inca empire as "savages."

Up until then the Inca had demonstrated an impressive capacity for building and design, culminating in the archeological landmark, Machu Picchu. Music figured prominently in pre-Columbian Peruvian life, with songs and pan flutes integrated into the daily tasks of work. Many folk songs from that epoch are still sung today. Long-established traditions of dance often were used in religious rituals. High quality sculpture, pottery, textiles and jewelry were hallmarks of Inca culture.

However, with subjugation came integration. The Spanish introduced string instruments, such as harps and guitars, to native musical customs. In the ensuing 400 plus years, as races and cultures have mixed, so have traditions. The work of Peruvian composer Andrés Sas combines classical European rhythms with native Inca melodies. The arrival of African slaves in the 19th century, as well as Chinese and Japanese laborers for the construction of railways, added to the complexity of Peru's historical diversity.

Architecturally, cities such as Cusco still retain the imprint of their Inca past. Styles of European colonialism has itself left an impressive legacy in terms of churches and public buildings. Peru is also notable for a rich, and often very experimental, literary tradition that has attracted worldwide interest, most notably the works of Mario Vargas Llosa.

Art and Architecture

The arts have played a prominent role in Peruvian history and culture, coloring the nation with a wide variety of styles that can be seen across its regions in everything from literature and architecture to painting, crafts and dance.

While Spanish influence cannot be denied, the indigenous heritage of Peru is one of the richest in South America, with conspicuous traces of Inca tradition throughout Peruvian art and culture. Art forms from architecture to handicrafts are a unique fusion of Spanish and Native American forms. Descendents of the Quechua and Aymara peoples, who live in much of the Andean highlands, preserve and emulate the folklore and traditions of their ancestors, while other regions have incorporated these customs into modern designs, making for a vibrant melding of styles throughout Peru's artistic history and in contemporary works.

Painting and Sculpture

Spanish colonization brought European art into the new world, and influence spread rapidly throughout Peru as religious paintings were used to teach Christianity. By the 17th century, native artists began melding the imported art with local tradition and style, leading to the Peruvian-Euro influenced Cusco School of the 17th and 18th centuries. The Cusco School was the largest movement in Peru's art history, made up of *mestizo* painters and sculptors who produced countless depictions of religious figures adorned in gold. Artists of the era were largely influenced by Spanish and late Gothic works.

During the 20th century, artists began following the lead of the Mexican muralists, resulting in a Peruvian movement incorporating Andean accents and depicting the life and hardships of the nation's indigenous people. An indigenous movement led by painter José Sabogal (1888-1956) in the 20th century sought to integrate pre-Columbian influence and Peruvian style and tradition. Works largely depicted indigenous women and incorporated ancient motifs from weavings and pottery. By the mid-20th century, artists began experimenting with abstract art, though works today still maintain pre-Columbian and Peruvian patterns.

Architecture
While much of Peruvian architecture is of Creole style—blending Spanish and indigenous designs—there is also a prominent Moorish influence, brought in from North Africa to Spain, and then into the Americas. Of course Peru's proud array of ruins—from Machu Picchu to Moche—present a very real form of pre-conquest art, not to be ignored as part of the nation's architectural style.

Crafts
Peru is a haven for folk art and high-quality handcrafts, boasting one of the largest varieties of arts and crafts in the world, which can be found across the nation. Folk art is not only a fundamental activity for the cultural identity of Peru, but a way of life for many communities. A diverse array of brightly colored textiles—particularly from the highlands in Ayacucho and Huancayo—depict local Andean and coastal life, with large graphic pre-Hispanic shapes of animals and indigenous life, influenced by forms brought over by the Spanish. Pottery, woodwork, woven baskets, worked gold and silver jewelry, and hand-tooled leather goods are also prevalent across the nation. Passion comes through the imagery and threads of works made by a culture that communicates mainly through art. The Paracas region (p.152) is renowned for its long tradition of unique weavings.

Museums
Peru's ancient civilizations date back at least as far Egypt's and match it for sophistication and architectural achievements. The Museo de la Nación steers visitors through several millennia's worth of history, conquest, conflict and civilization. The 10,000-year-old legacy of Peru's oldest known people, the Chavín, comes to life in the displays of large perforated seashells used as horns and the Chavín pipes made of bone tubes carved with animals associated with ritual transformation. The Moche civilization, which followed, has permanently preserved its spirit in figurines, made of clay, copper, silver or gold, representing everything from sexual acts to anthropomorphized deities. Miniature scale models of some of Peru's key archaeological sites on three different floors help put the evolution of pre-colonial Peru in a comprehensible context. You are advised to spend at least three hours taking it all in.

Another museum of note to visit while you are in Peru is the Museo de Oro del Peru y Armas del Mundo, literally Peru's Gold Museum and Arms of the World. The latter half of the museum goes beyond Peruvian culture and bespeaks of Miguel Mujica Gallo's fascination with weapons. This Peruvian businessman collected armaments across the globe to create the single most impressive assembly of artillery housed under one roof.

Carbines and muskets compete for attention with the other half of the museum, dedicated to the mineral that moved Spain to conquer and control much of the western hemisphere for centuries, permanently Latinizing a continent and a culture. Textiles, silver, semi-precious minerals and ceramic idols from the Mochica, Chimu and Vicús epochs reverberate as tokens of civilizations that, like all civilizations, have mortal life spans. Also included is an educational metallurgy exhibit, highlighting the evolution of the craft.

For the ecologically-oriented, the Museum of Natural History Javier Prado, founded in 1918 and affiliated with Universidad Nacional de San Marcos, and the Universidad Ricardo Palma's Museum of Natural History, bring to light Peru's plentiful bio-diversity. Both past and present are highlighted, with artifacts ranging from sea dinosaur fossils to a vast collection of live amphibians, reptiles, fish, birds and foliage.

Religiously-themed museums point up the florid classicism of Catholic ecclesiasticism while an Inquisition museum evokes the darker side of religion. Other sites highlight in-

INTRO & INFO

digenous craftwork, and for the modern-minded, the Museo de Arte, designed by none other than Gustave Eiffel (of Eiffel Tower fame), serves as the gateway to Peru's contemporary art. Outside of Peru, notable archaeology and pre-Columbian museums can be found in Arequipa, Chiclayo, Cusco (also an art museum), Huamachuco, Lurín, Moquegua, Piura and Trujillo.

Music

Music in Peru presents an eclectic mix of sounds, beats and eras with roots in the Andes, Spain and elsewhere around the globe. Peru's pre-colonial history includes cultures that date back to before the Inca established dominance in the 1400s, and much of the nation's musical influence and instruments can be traced to those times, particularly the panpipes, flutes and drums of Andean music. Archaeological discoveries show that music has been played in Peru as long as 10,000 years ago.

Native music consists primarily of stringed instruments reminiscent of mandolins and Spanish guitars, including the *charanga*—Peru's national instrument. Though once considered music of the rural poor, the rise of the indigenous movement in the art world and the post- revolutionary environment after 1959 made native music and the charango popular among performers across classes. Music in the Andes has maintained much of its native tradition, incorporating Spanish touches with stringed instruments and vocals. The *huayno* is a soulful, chant-like style of music most popular in the southern Andean region. Huayno spread from the interior mountainous regions to the coast in the mid-20th century, taking off throughout Peru and other Andean nations.

In the Arequipa region (p.186), traditional Andean music is heavily accented with Spanish tones, particularly in the *yaraví* style, a sad and soulful sound of vocals accompanied by a Spanish guitar. Music in Puno (p.351), Cusco (p.251) and surrounding regions is similar, but even more melancholic and often incorporating violins and other stringed instruments into traditional Inca rhythms. Heading into the Central Andes, music becomes more lively and upbeat, particularly that of the *huaylas* heard around the Huanuco-Huaraz area (p.378).

Coastal music—*música criolla*—exhibits a myriad of rhythms with a generally livelier feel than those of the Andes, with beats rooted in traditional Spanish, African and Gypsy music. A significant slave population was brought to the coast, which made for a strong neo-African influence on the area. By the 1950s, Afro-Peruvian music had begun being recorded and had incorporated the Spanish guitar, the *quijada* (an instrument made from the jawbone of a mule), and the *cajón* drum. The *landó* and the *festejo* are two of the most popular forms of this *música*, often played to accompany equally lively dances.

Rock music from North America was introduced in the mid-1950s, paving the way for the first Peruvian rock bands. The 1960s saw new trends, blending in sounds of garage rock. Rock saw a lull in the late 1960s and 1970s during the reign of a military dictatorship that considered the music alienating and banned concerts. Though many bands lost momentum, several were able to endure underground into the 1980s. Rock became more diversified in the 1990s, and bands slowly became recognized in the mainstream later in the decade. Today rock music creates a thriving scene in Peru and has even had some commercial success on the international stage.

Dance

As with music in pre-Columbian Peru, dance was assimilated into the undertakings of farming, hunting and combat. There is the *llamerada*, for example, a still-performed dance that imitates the act of llama herding as a means of ensuring the successful realization of the task. As with the "sun dances" of Native North Americans, for the indigenous inhabitants of Peru, dance was considered a religious ritual with the supernatural ability to positively impact the quality of life for the tribe.

Among Peruvians, dances that can trace their origins to the pre-Columbian include the *huayno*, the most representative of Andean folkloric dances. Quite possibly it began as a ritual dance performed at funerals but now serves a purely celebratory function in the community. The dance is performed by couples in embroidered vests and colorful dresses—yellow, red and blue predominate—who circle the musicians while doing abrupt spins, hops and tap-like movements to keep time with the drums, harps, guitars and violins. Some variations include wind instruments such as trumpets and saxophones.

The *marinera* is Peru's most famous dance, a *pas de deux* in which both partners elegantly wave silk handkerchiefs and execute graceful and precise movements to the accompaniment of Spanish guitars, a Creole *cajón* (a percussive wooden box) and bugles. Frequently the woman, with her flowing, pleated and striped skirt, is barefoot, marking the rhythm and guiding her male partner, sharply attired and with a white-brimmed hat. The name refers to the coastal region where it originated, and the dance traditions of Spain, Africa and indigenous Peru all contributed to a dance that is associated with national pride.

Theater
There are several theatrical traditions in Peru; occasionally they have conflicted with each other, occasionally they have merged. In recent times the result has been a provocative work that has received worldwide acclaim. Before conquest and colonization, and as with ancient Greece, theater was a religious ceremony, celebrating such deities as the sun god Inti in the festival of Inti Raymi, or Feast of the Sun. The ceremony coincided with the winter solstice. Following the conquest, it was banned by the Catholic Church, which also incorporated many pagan elements into its own religious pageants.

The Inti Raymi celebration did not return until the 20th century, when a renewed appreciation of indigenous culture revived Inti Raymi as theater, proudly presented in Quechua. As performed in the city of Cusco, a local is chosen to represent an Inca ruler, adorned with helmet-like feathered crown and bearing a war hammer, and born aloft in his throne to the town center, where rituals and prophecies initiate nine days of celebrations. Other religious festivals integrate elements of both the Catholic veneration of saints and the Virgin Mary with Andean ceremonial traditions and archetypes. For its part, the Church instituted the theatrical-theological traditions of Old Spain to the New World, with the first play being performed in 1568 in Lima's Plaza de San Pedro. Over the centuries Peruvian theater secularized, obtaining wealthy patrons outside the Church, and by the 20th century playwrights such as Sebastián Salazar Bondy and Enrique Solari Swayne brought literary prestige and social conscience to the Peruvian stage.

However, Peru's most highly regarded contribution to the art of theater is the innovative company Yuyachkani. Formed in the early 1970s, Yuyachkani, being heavily influenced by the modernist, avant-garde philosophy of European directors such as Peter Brook and Jerzy Grotowski, brought about a renewed focus on the actor as the catalyst for stirring the political and spiritual conscience of the audience. The group itself survived Peru's volatile political and social history to serve as a virtual Greek chorus for the country.

The Yuyachkani's name is derived from the Quechua expression for "I am thinking and I am remembering," and has not been afraid to venture into some of the most socially ravaged sectors of Peru, addressing issues such as terrorism and social injustice, through a style that is abstract yet accessible to all Peruvians. A production of Sophocles' *Antigone,* done in Quechua and Spanish, serves a pointed commentary on the abuses of governmental power. The company has influenced a generation of theatre artists not only in Peru but also in neighboring Andean countries.

The active theater scene in Lima, Cusco and other Peruvian cities offers visitors a wide range of creativity, from classics to post-modernism. Notable theaters in Lima include the Teatro Municipal, the Centro Cultural de La Católica, and the Teatro Británico.

Get your writing published in our books, go to www.vivatravelguides.com

Comedy

Peruvian comedy, at least in the post-colonial era, began in the 19th century with Manuel Ascensio Segura, a journalist and playwright whose work, in the tradition of Aristophanes and Molière, tweaked and satirized the institutions and customs of the society he inhabited. Peruvian militarism was a frequent target of his work. He also poked fun at partisan politics, libelous journal-

YMA SUMAC—POP LIFE OF AN ANDEAN PRINCESS

The singer Yma Sumac stands alone as the most famous Peruvian in the world. Only novelist Mario Vargas Llosa approaches a comparable degree of international recognition. Appropriately, she is the only Peruvian with a star on the Hollywood Walk of Fame. She came into her own, globally, during the 1950s and could be described as a cross between the high art of María Callas and the high camp of Brazilian diva Carmen Miranda. "Exoticism" and novelty songs were an ongoing selling point in the United States in the pre-Elvis era of American music, and Yma Sumac, with her exotic Andean looks (she is reportedly a direct descendent of the last Inca king Atahualpa) and her four-and-a-half octave reach, found her niche with a wide audience.

Yma Sumac was born in 1922 in Ichocán, Peru, with the name Zoila Augusta Emperatriz Chávarri del Castillo. Biographical data states that she practiced singing by imitating the sounds of the many exotic birds of Peru. By the age of thirteen she was already singing before crowds of thousands, and her vocal range attracted the attention of the minister of education, who sent her and her family to Lima so she could attend a Catholic boarding school. By 1942 she adopted the stage name Imma Sumack, later modified to Yma Sumac, and was singing on the radio. Years later a rumor spread that "Yma Sumac" was an anagram for "Amy Camus" and that she hailed from Brooklyn, to which Yma jokingly responded, "Must all talent come from Brooklyn?"

During the Latin music boom of the 1940s she moved to New York and few years later was signed by Capitol records. Working with such pop music legends as Billy May and Les Baxter, she hit the charts, offering slick, Hollywoodized versions of Andean and South American folk tunes, as well as mambo songs in sync with the cha-cha-cha zeitgeist of the times. Her albums—now sought-after pop and camp items—also featured recordings of other people's novelty hits, such as Wimoweh, also known as The Lion Sleeps Tonight, but all arranged to showcase her famous bass-to-coloratura voice.

Her exotic allure, complete with elaborate "Inca Princess" costumes, attracted a lot of attention, and she appeared in major motion pictures, such as *Secret of the Inca*, which starred Charlton Heston and was filmed in her native Peru. She also recorded the song "I Wonder" for Walt Disney's Sleeping Beauty. Though her popularity peaked in the 1950s, she continued to perform in concert halls worldwide throughout the 1960s. She attempted to reach a new audience with a pop-rock album in 1971, and then returned to Peru in semi-retirement. She began to make a comeback in the 1980s, which included a turn in the Stephen Sondheim musical Follies in Long Beach, California, as well as recitals in New York and San Francisco.

But it was in the late 1990s and early 2000s which saw a renewal of interest in Yma Sumac's work, with songs (especially her standard Gopher Mambo) on the soundtracks to such movies as *Men with Guns*; *The Big Lebowski*; *Happy, Texas*; *Ordinary Decent Criminal*; *Confessions of a Dangerous Mind*; and *The In-Laws*. Now living in Los Angeles, in 2006 Yma Sumac was invited back to Lima to receive the Orden del Sol (Order of the Sun) award by then-President of Peru, Alejandro Toledo, as well as the Jorge Basadre Medal by the Universidad Nacional de San Marcos. Her return to her native Peru was one of the biggest media events in the country's history.

Photo by Peter Anderson

ism and Lima provincialism. Though classified technically as "comedy," today Segura's work, like Molière's, is more likely to evoke a knowing approval from a sophisticated audience for the acuity of his observations than belly laughs.

In terms of humor / ha-ha as opposed to humor / smart, a comedy troupe like Los Cómicos Ambulantes, or the Walking Comics, has been making several generations of Peruvians laugh since the 1970s. A rag-tag, loosely-assembled association of performers, some of the Cómicos Ambulantes had backgrounds as professional circus clowns; others were simply naturally funny men. They did street theatre, attracting crowds by parodying behavior and attitudes characteristic of cities like Lima and Cusco; in the latter they called themselves the Inca of Laughter. A turning point for them came when they were invited to perform on popular Peruvian talk shows such as Talking Straight and Between Us, where their perceptive pokes at Peruvians struck a chord with a popular audience. The result was their own programs, The Walking Comics Show and The Kings of Laughter. As with American comedy shows like Saturday Night Live, this served as a launching pad for individual careers, as in the case of comics such as Kike and Lonchera. Others did not fare as well and returned to their former poverty as street performers.

In the meantime, local street performers and comedy troupes, such as La Banda del Choclito, continue to amuse the local citizenry, who considering all that Peruvians have lived with and have to live with, could use all the humor they can get.

Social and Environmental Issues in Peru
Peru's Socio-Economic Climate

In Peru, as in all Latin American countries, social issues revolve around the economy. In Peru's case, it has meant sustaining economic growth after an extended bout of political unrest and economic turmoil following a 20-year civil war against radical insurgent movements.

The socio-political climate is complicated by race issues relating to Peru's colonial heritage. Eighty-two percent of the country is of either indigenous or mixed indigenous-Spanish descent, while 15 percent of the populace is Caucasian of purely Spanish heritage—yet that same 15 percent continues to make up the majority of Peru's upper-class with its attendant domination of industry and politics. This in turn has led to ongoing civil unrest resulting from large-scale poverty and resentment among the mostly disenfranchised non-white majority. This is further exacerbated by a lingering racism that originated in the arrival of the Spanish and still pervades popular culture, such as in television shows and advertising, which presents Caucasian rather than indigenous as closer to an ideal of physical desirability.

This came to a head with the emergence of two separate radical factions during the early 1980s: the Shining Path, which was Maoist, and Túpac Amaru, which was Marxist-Leninist. Both organizations recruited among the poorest in Peru's rural areas and used violence and

HOLIDAYS AND FIESTAS

The main holidays and *fiestas* of Peru are:

January 1: New Year's Day (*Año Nuevo*).

January 6: Epiphany.

February 2: Virgen de la Candelaría, Puno, Patron saint of Puno—The statue of the Virgin is paraded around the town accompanied by dancers of all ages.

Carnaval: Celebrated the weekend leading up to Ash Wednesday, Carnaval is the ultimate party in Latin America, and in Peru it is celebrated in most of the Andes. A popular custom is to throw water at people. As a foreigner you are likely to be a popular target! In Cajamarca, a *Carnaval* queen is elected and there are competitions of friendship and song.

Semana Santa: Semana Santa (Easter/Holy Week) is celebrated all over Peru, but Ayacucho is a special place to spend this period, hosting one of the most important Holy Week festivals in all of Peru. In the run-up to Easter Sunday, Ayacucho transforms into a city of flowered streets, processions, fireworks, dancing and more.

May 1: Labor Day.

June: Corpus Christi (Body of Christ) is celebrated fairly widely in the Andean regions.

June 24: Inti Raymi, Cusco—June sees Cusco turn into one big party in the period preceding this important Incan festival (see box next page).

June 29: Day of San Pedro and San Pablo—Peru-wide holiday.

July 16: Virgen del Carmen, Paucartambo, near Cusco—This celebration is in honor of the Virgen del Carmen, the patron saint of Paucartambo. Folk stories are acted out by local dance groups and there are processions through the steets to scare away demons.

July 28-29: Independence (Fiestas Patrias)—Independence day is an important public holiday for Peruvians, with many traveling during this period. Correspondingly, prices for accommodation rise. In Lima there are both military and civilian parades. Independence Day itself is July 28, while most of the celebrations take place on July 29.

August 30: Saint Rose of Lima.

October 8: Battle of Angamos, commemorating a decisive Chilean victory on this date in 1879, during the War of the Pacific.

October 18-28: Señor de los Milagros (Lord of the Miracles)—This is a very important Peruvian celebration for the patron saint of Lima, with huge processions through the streets, led by a select few who carry the statue.

November 1: Todos los Santos (All Saints Day).

November 2: Día de los Muertos (Day of the Dead)—Offerings of food, particularly of bread shaped like people and animals, are made to the dead.

December 8: Day of the Immaculate Conception—A festival celebrated throughout the whole of Peru, Chivay is an interesting place to observe this festival, where men dress in women's clothes and pretend to snatch the women!

December 24-25: Christmas—Festivities start on the 24th. Families gather to celebrate with a big meal on December 24. December 25 is a nationwide public holiday.

December 31: *Año Viejo*—New Year's Eve.

terror to achieve their aim of taking over the country—and for some time it seemed that the Shining Path movement might succeed; at one point 60 percent of the country, mostly the rural sectors, was under its control.

The presidency of leftist Alan García during this time was nothing less than an abject disaster. During his term inflation reached 2,200,200 per cent, resulting in three changes of currency as the Peruvian monetary notes kept losing its trade value. In addition, incomes dropped, foreign investment stopped and unemployment soared—all of which contributed to support for the two competing revolutionary movements, especially the Shining Path guerillas, who increased the degree and severity of violence against Peru's urban sector.

Peruvians then turned to the hard-line candidate, Alberto Fujimori, who intensified and broadened the military campaign against the rebels. He also reversed many of García's economic measures and introduced wide-sweeping free-market reforms, privatizing many industries and opening up greater sections of Peru's Amazon for oil-drilling. This measure, despite its positive effect on the economy, was widely criticized for the impact it had on Peru's ecology and the lives of Peru's indigenous tribes.

INTI RAYMI: THE FESTIVAL OF THE SUN

Every year in June, there is an opportunity to witness a beautiful exhibition of Peruvian culture and tradition: Inti Raymi, the Festival of the Sun.

The Inti Raymi festival originated as a celebration to honor the Sun God as insurance for plentiful crops in the harvest season. Each winter solstice, when the sun is farthest from the earth, the Inca would gather out of fear of the lack of sun, beseeching its return. In 1572, the colonial Spaniards banned the tradition because of its pagan rituals.

The festivities went underground, but today it is celebrated as one of the largest festivals in South America, second only to the carnival of Rio. Every year, hundreds of thousands of people gather in Cusco for the week-long festivities. From live music to street vendors to daytime fairs, the festival consists of different daily activities. Free concerts, put on by the best Peruvian musical troupes, are held nightly in the Plaza de Armas.

All activities lead up to June 24, the climax of the festival and the actual day of Inti Raymi. Scientifically speaking, the winter solstice begins June 21, but Peruvians follow the *pacha unachaq*, a sundial used by the Inca.

Over 500 actors are selected to enact the day-long ceremony. It is considered a great honor to be selected as Sapa Inca or his wife, as they are the two main characters for the day. Ceremonies commence in the Qorikancha square in front of the Santo Domingo church, which is built over the Temple of the Sun. Here, Sapa Inca calls on blessings from the sun. Afterwards, he is carried on a golden throne to Sacsayhuamán, a fortress in the hills above Cusco. Thousands of people await his arrival. He climbs the sacred altar. A white llama is sacrificed to ensure the fertility of the earth.

At sunset, haystacks are set afire and revelers dance around them to honor the Empire of the Four Wind Directions. The ceremony ends with the celebrants returning to Cusco, watching as Sapa Inca and Mama Occla are carried on their golden thrones. And so the sun's new year begins!

The Fujimori government was able to reverse Peru's economic tailspin as well as defeat both the Shining Path and the Túpac Amaru, but at the cost of curtailing democracy and permitting the country's security forces to commit human rights abuses. There was also evidence of extensive corruption occurring throughout the administration, including clandestine dealings with Colombian narcotraffickers.

After winning a questionable election in 2000, Fujimori abruptly resigned while on a visit to Japan, using his dual citizenship with that country to avoid prosecution for a variety of criminal charges that were being brought against him in Peru.

However, with Peru's economy on the rebound and the threat of a Maoist or Marxist takeover in recession, the work ahead for post-Fujimori Peru has been to keep moving forward. Unfortunately, the reconciliatory presidency of centrist Alejandro Toledo, while restoring some of the democracy that was restricted during the previous administration, was overwhelmed by corruption scandals and unpopular economic measures, which resulted in Toledo's approval dropping as low as eight percent.

Despite the failures of his first term in office, Alan García made a political comeback and was narrowly re-elected president against the Hugo Chávez-backed, leftist military candidate, Ollanta Humala. García now claims to have revised his political philosophy and hopes to approximate the success of Chile's free-market economy.

García announced a 13-point plan that includes increasing public and private investment, keeping inflation below two percent a year, building 250,000 new homes, teaching just as many Peruvians how to read and write, reducing poverty from 50 percent to 30 percent (poverty in rural areas is as high as 70 percent), reducing malnutrition from 25 percent to 16 percent, increasing access to electricity and running water to 90 percent, creating 1,500,000 new jobs, increasing federal reserves by $9 bn dollars, conferring property deeds to 800,000 landowners, and reducing Peru's national debt from 24 percent to 13 percent.

This is a daunting challenge. Currently the number of businesses that evade paying taxes is as high as 53 percent, though Carsten Korch, editor of www.livinginperu.com, claims that actual tax evasion is over 90 percent.

Curiously not on President García's agenda is the pervasive and profound issue of crime. The U.S. State Department has rated Peru as a Critical Threat post for crime, and Peru's National Police report in 2006 that in Lima a crime occurs every three minutes. Crime is virtually institutionalized in Peru, from petty theft to organized crime rings that traffic in drugs, sex slavery, illegal immigration and the unlawful sale of Peru's archaeological heritage. The problem is further exacerbated by Peru's often-corrupt law enforcement.

President García will be walking a careful tightrope in maintaining enough credibility for his centrist policies, but without the larger popular working class and indigenous support enjoyed by his more demagogic and leftist fellow Andean leaders in Venezuela, Bolivia and Ecuador, who represent the modern indigenous movement in Latin America. In the Hobbesian climate of Latin American politics, Ollanta Humala will be keeping a close watch on Alan García between now and the next election in 2011.

The Machu Picchu vs. Yale University Controversy

In this context, Alan Garcia has been fortunate to seize upon a nationalist and patriotic issue, one especially relevant to Peru's indigenous population: the relics removed by National Geographic explorer Hiram Bingham from Machu Picchu after his discovery of the historic city in 1912. They have resided at Yale University ever since. Yale claims that the government of Peru legally signed off on the artifacts, which comprise everything from crockery to clay deities, while Peru maintains that Yale's custody of them was only for the sake of research, with the understanding that they would eventually be returned.

In the nearly one-hundred years since Bingham's discovery, generations of Peruvians have lived and died without access to some of the most valuable tokens of their ancestral heritage. However, how much access they would have had if the items remained in Peru is an open question. In an investigative piece in The *New York Times*, Arthur Lubow noted that "Peru's record in safeguarding archaeological treasures...is spotted with the traces of disappearing objects." For example, in 1979, literally hundreds of pieces of Incan and pre-Incan pieces went missing from the National Museum of Archaeology. In 1993 almost the entire gold collection from Cusco's Museo Inka disappeared.

It is generally agreed that much of what is in Yale's Peabody Museum is less interesting and less impressive than what is on already on display on museums throughout Peru. Nonetheless, Alan Garcia scored a political and cultural victory on September 14th, 2007, when Yale agreed to return the artifacts, which would be made available to the general public in a traveling exhibition, and whose revenue would fund a new museum in Cusco. Yale and Peru will continue to work together in the study and preservation of the objects.

Environmental Issues

Peru has some of the richest and most abundant natural resources of any country in the world, but the economic crises and political turmoil of the last several decades has made safeguarding the country's environment secondary to exploiting it. As a result, Peru is experiencing many ecological problems that have raised the concerns of environmentalists around the world. These include air and water pollution, soil contamination and erosion, and deforestation.

Industrial and vehicle emissions in Peru create over 31 metric tons of carbon dioxide a year. In 2002, only 81 percent of the population had access to pure drinking water due to industrial, sewage and petroleum-drilling waste. Overgrazing in the *sierra* and the coast, meanwhile, has brought about soil erosion.

Half of Peru is forest, and the country experiences a deforestation rate of roughly 0.14 percent per year, largely as a consequence of subsistence farming resulting from migrant farmers exploiting a squatter's law that allows citizens to obtain public land if they can prove they have lived on it for at least five years. The greater degree of deforestation, however, is wrought by commercial logging, both legal and illegal, as well as mining, petroleum drilling and road development.

Most of the logging in Peru going on is illegal; estimates are that up to 95 percent of the country's mahogany is unlawfully cut and sold, much of it from national parks and federal reserves. However, with law enforcement underfunded and vulnerable to bribery and corruption, almost no commercial loggers are either charged or prosecuted.

Then there is the deforestation brought about by oil-drilling. In 2005 a contract was granted to the China National Petroleum Corporation in the Madre de Dios region of southern Peru, an area that is home to more than 10 percent of the world's bird species.

Coca production, both legal and illegal, has taken its toll as forests have been cleared in order to make way for coca plantations.

Gold mining also contributes substantially, since the process involves destroying river banks and clearing floodplain forests. Furthermore, this creates an incentive to bring independent miners who then cut trees for firewood and shacks. Mercury is a necessary component of the mining process, but the effect is to poison soil and water.

A very controversial project in Peru's Amazon basin is the construction of a transoceanic highway across the jungle connecting Peru to Brazil. There are concerns that the road will essentially urbanize everything along its path, endangering or possibly consuming all flora and fauna in the area, but there is hope that it may bring jobs and trade to rural areas.

Peru has up to 2,937 varieties of amphibians, birds, mammals and reptiles, and 17,144 species of plants. Currently, Peru's endangered species list includes 46 mammals, including the yellow-tailed woolly monkey and the black spider monkey; 64 types of birds, including the tundra peregrine falcon and the white-winged guan; and 653 plants, many of which are native only to Peru. A number of reptiles are at risk as well, including the hawksbill turtle, the leatherback turtle, the spectacled caiman and the Orinoco and American crocodiles.

VISAS

Passports are required of all countries regardless of visa status. If you are entering Peru for business, or to study at a Peruvian university, you must obtain a business or student visa regardless of the country you are from. Business and student visas are only good for 90 days, but renewals are allowed and are determined on an individual basis. Citizens of the following countries can travel to Peru for up to 90 days without a tourist visa:

South America:
Argentina, Bolivia, Brazil, Chile, Colombia, Ecuador, Guyana, Paraguay, Suriname, Uruguay, Venezuela.

North America:
Canada, U.S., Mexico.

Central America:
Antigua and Barbuda, Bahamas, Barbados, Belize, Costa Rica, Dominica, Dominican Republic, El Salvador, Grenada, Guatemala, Haiti, Honduras, Jamaica, Nicaragua, Panama, Saint Kitts and Nevis, Saint Lucia, Saint Vincent and the Grenadines, Trinidad and Tobago.

Europe:
Andorra, Austria, Belarus, Belgium, Bulgaria, Croatia, Cyprus, Czech Republic, Denmark, Estonia, Finland, France, Germany, Greece, Hungary, Iceland, Ireland, Italy, Latvia, Liechtenstein, Lithuania, Luxemburg, Macedonia, Malta, Moldava, Monaco, Iceland, Norway, Poland, Portugal, Russian Federation, San Marino, Serbia and Montenegro, Slovakia, Slovenia, Spain, Vatican City, Sweden, Switzerland, Ukraine, United Kingdom and Northern Ireland.

Asia:
Brunei Darussalam, Hong Kong, Indonesia, Israel, Japan, Malaysia, Philippines, Republic of Korea, Singapore, Taiwan, Thailand.
Oceania: Australia, Cook Islands, Fiji, Kiribati, Marshall Islands, Micronesia, Nauru, New Zealand, Niue, Palau, Papua New Guinea, Salomon Islands, Samoa, Tonga, Tuvalu, Vanuatu.

Africa:
South Africa.

All citizens of countries NOT listed are required to obtain a travel visa for entry into Peru, prior to arriving in Peru.

Visitors entering via plane or border crossings can stay in the country and will receive a tourist card valid for either 30, 60 or 90 days. It depends upon where you enter the country as to what that border crossing offers, but your best bet is to ask for the 90-day card, otherwise you may have to exit the country and re-enter again. You must also get a new tourist card upon each re-entry and always present it when you exit the country.

If your tourist card is stolen or lost, a new one needs to be obtained at the Oficina de Migraciones (Monday-Friday, 9 a.m.-1 p.m. Av. España 700 and Av. Huaraz, Breña, Lima, 51-1-433-0731 / 332-1268). If you do not have the card, you will be fined when you exit the country.

Embassies / Consulates

Argentina
Av. 28 de Julio 828, Lima
Tel: 51-1-433-3381 / 9966 / 4545
Fax: 51-1-433-0769
E-mail: embajada@terra.com.pe

Bolivia
Calle Los Castaños 235 San Isidro, Lima
Tel: 51-1-441-0738 / 51-1-440-2095
Fax: 51-1-440-2298
E-mail: postmast@emboli.org.pe

Brazil
Av. José Pardo, 850, Miraflores, Lima
Tel: 51-1-421-5660 / 421-5650
Fax: 51-1-445-2421
E-mail: embajada@embajadabrasil.org.pe
URL: www.embajadabrasil.org.pe

Canada
Bolognesi 228, Miraflores Lima
Tel: 51-1-319-3200
E-mail: lima@international.gc.ca
http://geo.international.gc.ca/latin-america/peru/

Chile
Javier Prado Oeste 790, San Isidro, Lima
Tel: 51-1-221-2221 / 51-1-221-2080
Fax: 51-1-221-1258
E-mail: emchile@terra.com.pe

Colombia
Av. Jorge Basadre 1580 San Isidro, Lima
Tel: 51-1-442-9648 / 51-1-441-0954
Fax: 51-1-441-9806

Costa Rica
Baltazar La Torre 828, San Isidro, Lima
Tel: 51-1-264-2999, 51-1-264-2711
Fax: 51-1-264-2799
E-mail: Costarica@terra.com.pe

Cuba
Coronel Portillo No. 110, San Isidro, Lima
Tel: 51-1-264-2053, Fax: 51-1-264-4525
E-mail: embcuba@chavin.rcp.net.pe

Dominican Republic
Tudela y Varela 360, San Isidro, Lima
Tel: 51-1-421-9765 / 51-1-421-9767
Fax: 51-1-222-0639
URL: http://www.embajadadominicanaperu.org

Ecuador
Las Palmeras 356, San Isidro, Lima
Tel: 51-1-212-4171 / 51-1-212-5481
Fax: 51-1-422-0711
E-mail: embajada@mecuadorperu.org.pe
URL: www.mecuadorperu.org.pe

Finland
Av. Victor Andrés Belaúnde 147
Edificio Real Tres, Oficina 502, San Isidro, Lima
Tel: 51-1-222-4466 / 222-4480
Fax: 51-1-222-4463
E-mail: sanomat.lim@formin.fi
URL: www.finlandia.org.pe

France
Av. Arequipa 3415, San Isidro, Lima
Tel: 51-1-215-8400, Fax: 51-1-215-8441
E-mail: france.embajada@ambafrance-pe.org
URL: www.ambafrance-pe.org/

Germany
Av. Arequipa 4210, Miraflores, Lima
Tel: 51-1-212-5016, Fax: 51-1-422-6475 / 51-1-440-4048
E-mail: kanzlei@embajada-alemana.org.pe
URL: www.embajada-alemana.org.pe

Greece
Av. Principal 190, Urbanización Sta. Catalina, La Victoria, Lima
E-mail: emgrecia@terra.com.pe
Tel: 51-1-476-1548 / 476-0798
Fax: 51-1-223-2486

Guatemala
Calle Inca Ripac 309, Jesús María, Lima
Tel: 51-1-460-2078 / 462-0920
Fax: 51-1-463-5885
E-mail: visa@embajadadeguatemalaenperu.org
URL: http://www.embajadadeguatemalaenperu.org

Honduras
Av. Las Camelias 491. Oficina 202, San Isidro, Lima
Tel: 51-1-422-8111 / 422-8112
Fax: 51-1-221-1677

India
Av. Salaverry 3006, Magdalena del Mar, Lima
Tel: 51-1-460-2289 / 51-1-261-6006
Fax: 51-1-461-0374
E-mail: hoc@indembassy.org.pe
URL: www.indembassy.org.pe

Israel
Natalio Sanchez 125, 6th floor, Santa Beatriz, Lima
Tel: 51-1-433-4431, Fax: 51-1-433-8925
E-mail: emisrael@electrodata.com.pe
URL: http://lima.mfa.gov.il

Italy
Venida Gregorio Escobedo 298, Jesus Maria, Lima
Tel: 51-1-463-2727, Fax: 51-1-463-5317
E-mail: italemb@chavin.rcp.net.pe

Japan
Av. San Felipe 356, Jesús María, Lima 11
Tel: 51-1-219-9550 / 219-9551
Fax: 51-1-219-9544
URL: http://www.pe.emb-japan.go.jp/
E-mail: consjapon@embajadajapon.org.pe

Mexico
Av. Jorge Basadre 710, San Isidro, Lima
Tel: 51-1-612-1600, Fax: 51-1-612-1627
E-mail: info@mexico.org.pe
URL: http://portal.sre.gob.mx/peru/index.php

Netherlands
Torre Parque Mar, Av. José Larco 1301, 13th floor, Miraflores, Lima
Tel: 51-1-213-9800 / 51-1-213-9800
Fax: 51-1-213-9805
E-mail: nlgovlim@terra.com.pe
URL: http://www.nlgovlim.com/

Panama
Av. Emilio Cavenecia 329 Office 2A, San Isidro, Lima
Tel/Fax: 51-1-421-4762 / 51-1-421-2836
URL: www.consuladopanamalima.com.pe

Portugal
Antequera 777, 3rd floor, San Isidro, Lima
Tel: 51-1-440-9905, Fax: 51-1-421-5979
E-mail: mail@sclim.dgaccp.pt

Russia
Av. Salavaerry, 3424, San Isidro, Lima
Tel: 51-1-264-0036 / 51-1-264-0038
Fax: 51-1-264-0130
E-mail: rosposol@amauta.rcp.net.pe
URL: http://www.lima.ruembassy.org/

South Korea
Av. Principal 190, 7th floor, Santa Catalina, La Victoria, Lima
Tel: 51-1-476-0815 / 476-0861 / 476-0874 / 51-1-225-0772,
Fax: 51-1-476-0950
E-mail: koremb-pu@mofat.go.kr
URL: www.mofat.go.kr/

Sweden
La Santa María 130, San Isidro, Lima
Tel: 51-1-442-8905
Fax: 51-1-421-3295
E-mail: konslima@speedy.com.pe

Switzerland
Av. Salaverry 3240, San Isidro, Lima
Tel: 51-1-264-0305
Fax: 51-1-264-1319
URL: www.eda.admin.ch/lima

Spain
Calle Los Pinos, 490, San Isidro, Lima
Tel: 51-1-513-7930, Fax: 51-1-422-0347
E-mail: cog.lima@mae.es
URL: www.consuladolima.com.pe/

Uruguay
José D. Anchorena 084, San Isidro, Lima
Tel: 51-1-264-0099 / 51-1-264-1286
Fax: 51-1-264-0112
E-mail: uruinca@embajada-uruguay.com

United Kingdom
Torre Parque Mar, 22nd floor, Av. Jose Larco 1301, Miraflores, Lima
Tel: 51-1-617-3000, Fax: 51-1-617-3100
Consular: consular.lima@fco.gov.uk
URL: http://ukinperu.fco.gov.uk/es

United States of America
Av. La Encalada, block 17, Surco, Lima
Tel: 51-1-434-3000, Fax: 51-1-618-2397
URL: http://lima.usembassy.gov/

PERU QUICK FACTS

Area: 1,285,220 sq km (496,414 mi)   Population: 29,180,900

Capital: Lima   Religion: Roman Catholic

Languages: Spanish, Quechua, Aymara   Literacy: 87.7%

Life Expectancy: 70   GDP Per Capita: U.S. $7,600

Currency: Peruvian Nuevo Sol (roughly 3 soles to $1, as of December 2008)

Industry: mining of metals, petroleum, fishing, textiles, clothing, food processing.

Agriculture: asparagus, coffee, cotton, sugarcane, rice, poultry, fish, plantains, grapes, oranges, coca, beef, dairy production, guinea pigs.

Exports: fish/fish products, gold, copper, zinc, crude petroleum and by-products.

Electricity: Peru uses a 220v system.

Tourist Visas

If you are from one of the countries NOT listed, you will need to obtain a tourist visa from the appropriate Peruvian consular representative before proceeding abroad. Allow a few weeks time for processing your visa application, especially if you are applying by mail. Most Peruvian consular representatives are located in capital cities. As soon as you receive your visa, check to make sure no mistakes were made. For more details see: www.consuladoperu.com.

Business Visas

Business travelers are issued three-month visas and they must be renewed quarterly at the Oficina de Migraciones in Lima (see contact information above). Your passport must have a remaining validity of at least the length of the trip. Application process:

- Fill out the visa form.
- Obtain a letter from your employer indicating the motive and the length of your stay.
- You must gather one passport picture, copy of the flight ticket, and a money order payable to Consulado General del Peru for US $ 30.
- Bring it to the nearest Peruvian consulate office, or if you are mailing your application, you must send a FedEx pre-paid envelope with your name and complete address to return the documents.

Student Visas

Students are issued visas for three-month stays through a Peruvian Consulate in their home country. Passports must have a remaining validity of at least the length of the trip.

Application process:

- Fill out the visa form.
- Obtain a letter from your university or educational institution in Peru, indicating the motive and the time of your stay.
- You'll need to gather one passport picture, copy of the flight ticket, and a money order payable to Consulado General del Peru for $30.

Get your writing published in our books, go to www.vivatravelguides.com

- Bring your application to the nearest Peruvian Consulate, or if this procedure is done by mail, you have to send a FedEx pre-paid envelope with your name and complete address to return the documents.
- Once you have been enrolled in a Peruvian school, student visas may be renewed at the Oficina de Migraciones.

Immigration

Duty Free: When leaving Peru, any one person is allowed to exit with 400 cigarettes, or 50 cigars or 250 grams of tobacco, 2.5 liters of alcohol, 2 kg of processed foods, and new articles for personal use or gifts up to value of $300.

Archeological items and art: The government of Peru prohibits the exportation of archaeological artifacts and colonial art. These restrictions include archaeological material from the pre-Hispanic cultures and certain ethnological materials from the colonial period of Peru. Many countries outside of Peru including the U.S.A. and U.K. have the authority to take action if you are found with any of these.

Extra passport photos: Bring an extra set of passport photos. If your passport is stolen, it could take several days to get a photo of the appropriate size taken. By already having additional passport-sized photos, you'll save yourself lot of time and frustration.

GETTING TO AND AWAY FROM PERU
FLYING TO PERU

The peak season for traveling via airplane to Peru runs from July to August, coinciding with summer vacations for teachers and students. Tickets in September sell out rather quickly, however, because air fares drop, and December is a busy time as well due to the high number of Peruvian immigrants returning home to visit their families for Christmas.

The main carriers offering flights from North America are Delta, Continental, American Airlines and three Latin American-based airlines: Lan Perú, Taca, and Copa.

The main carriers from the United Kingdom are Lufthansa, American Airlines, Continental Airlines, Delta Airlines (via the U.S.), United Airlines (via the U.S.), Iberia (via Madrid) and KLM (via Amsterdam).

From Australia and New Zealand one can take Air New Zealand, Aerolíneas (an Argentine airline), Lan Chile, Quantas and United Airlines.

ACCESSING PERU VIA LAND
From Ecuador

If you are accessing Peru by land from Ecuador, Transporte Cifa has buses leaving from such cities as Guayaquil, Loja, and Cuenca heading south to the border towns Huaquillas in Ecuador and Tumbes (p.455) in Peru. A little further inland is La Tina, the border crossing just south of Macará; Loja Internacional has direct buses from Loja through Macará to Piura (p.431), Peru. Your bus will stop at the migration office, where you will be expected to show your passport, tourist visa, and, perhaps, some proof of financial independence. Resist "help" from anybody who is not an official public servant. A third, more rustic, border crossing is at La Balsa; this route goes through the jungle mountains. For more information on these borders, see the respective sections.

From Colombia

The U.S. State Department warns that "the entire Peru/Colombia border" is highly dangerous due to narcotics trafficking and armed guerillas.

From Brazil
Land travel between Brazil and Peru has been very sparse due to the limited and poor-quality roads. There are, however, plans underway to construct major roads connecting São Paolo to Lima (p.78), and Iberia in Brazil to Puerto Maldonado (p.487) in Peru. In the latter region there already is a (muddy) road going to the Brazilian border, which you can access via a few minibuses and trucks, but most people prefer to be ferried by boat.

From Bolivia
The most common entry point into Peru from Bolivia is the road heading west from La Paz, which will take you to the border towns of Guaqui and Desaguadero. Some travelers will also depart via boat from the Bolivian coastal town of Puerta Costa on Lake Titicaca (p.341) to Copacabana (p.369), and from there enter Peru.

From Chile
There are buses, trains and taxis that will take you along the Pan-American Highway to the Peruvian border town of Tacna (p.221).

ACCESSING PERU VIA RIVER
Many travelers dream of sojourning up the Amazon and its tributaries by boat, from one country to another. Although not as common as it once was, you can still choose this adventure. It's a slow journey, stopping at villages along the way to drop off, pick up passengers and cargo. (Indeed, it can get quite crowded.) Here are a few things to keep in mind:

- Speak only with the captain of the boat; confirm departure date and time, and prices. Compare prices with different boats; inspect the vessel for cleanliness. Pay only the captain or another authorized person, and obtain a receipt.
- Larger boats have cabins (some even with air conditioning); however, these are more expensive than hammock space on the deck, and tend to be hot and stuffy. If you opt to travel swinging along in your hammock, be sure to choose a spot away from the fumes and noise of the engines, the insect-attracting lights and the bathrooms. Have rope not only to hang your *hamaca*, but also to hang cloth for privacy. Board early (often it is possible to do so the night before) to land a choice spot.
- Use a mosquito net and repellent, and don't forget to take your malaria medication.
- Secure your belongings extremely well; lock your berth or bags, and always keep the key with you.
- Food will be provided, as will drink (often made with river water). Bring along some fresh fruits, comfort foods and purified water. Have your own cup, as well and some diarrhea medication, just in case.
- It gets remarkably cool at night on the river; light, warm clothing and a blanket (or cloth hammock) will keep you warm.

From Ecuador
Twice a week, motorized canoes ply the Napo River from Coca to Nuevo Rocafuerte, Ecuador (full day, $30). Ecuadorian immigration is in Nuevo Rocafuerte, and Peruvian immigration in Pantoja. Another canoe takes you to Pantoja, Peru (two hours, $10 per person). Irregular boats go to Iquitos (four to five days, $20). Check in Coca for immigration and boat details before beginning this journey.

From Colombia
In the middle of the Amazon jungle is a triple border—Leticia, Colombia; Tabatinga, Brazil; and Santa Rosa, Peru—where the respective countries' immigration formalities are performed. Take a boat across the Amazon from Leticia to Santa Rosa ($1). Vessels leave the Peruvian port for Iquitos (speedboat, 11-12 hours, $50; slow launch, two days, $20 hammock, $30 cabin; buy your ticket the day before).

From Brazil

Many boats make the long journey up the golden Amazon River from Manaus to Benjamin Constant and Tabatinga. (It may be quicker to take the boat just to Benjamin Constant, then a fast local ferry to Tabatinga, 2 hours, $1.50.) This route takes seven to eight days upriver and costs $60 for a hammock and $120 for a double cabin. For immigration information and details, please see above.

From Bolivia

This sojourn is only for the most hardy (and patient) of souls. Three days or more can pass between boats. From Riberalta, Bolivia, you take a boat to Puerto Heath (three days, $15-20), and from there a canoe to Puerto Pardo, Peru (five hours, $5) and then to Puerto Maldonado. Check locally for the most accurate information, as it is quite scarce from the outside.

BORDER CROSSING IN PERU

For tourists from most non-Latin American countries, all you need to enter Peru from its official entry points with Ecuador, Colombia, Brazil, Bolivia and Chile is a current and valid passport. However, if you have been residing in any of these countries for more than 90 days, it is expected you will present an official "permission to leave" slip, usually obtained at your host country's immigration office. Due to Peru's limited public service budget, none of the terrestrial entry ports are open 24/7, so you need to bear this in mind.

A word of caution: the moment you get off your bus or step out your taxi, any number of locals will aggressively "offer" you help, and explain all sorts of "fees" and "taxes" you will need to pay, and how they will serve as your guide. They will also willing to change money for you. Use common sense and deal only with recognizable and verifiable border guards and immigration officials, and change your money only at banks or other legitimate businesses.

PERUVIAN DEPARTURE TAX

As of December 2008 the international departure tax for Peru is $30.25, which can be paid in dollars, soles, or both. The departure tax for flights inside Peru is $6.05, but both rates are subject to change. There is no departure tax for leaving the country by bus, car, bicycle or on foot.

GETTING AROUND PERU

Air

There are currently 68 main airports in Peru, and five major domestic airlines—Wayra, StarPeru, Aero Cóndor, Lan Perú and LC Busre, all of whom fly out of Peru's main airport, Jorge Chávez International in Lima, which is one of three international airports in Peru. As for the airports, approximately 16 receive commercial airlines; the rest serve private charter and military craft. All major tourist destinations in Peru, such as Cusco (p.251), Iquitos (p.501), Huaraz (p.378), Arequipa (p.188), Puno (p.351) and Puerto Maldonado (p.487), have airports and at least one major carrier to take you there. Some common sense rules when getting around Peru via airplane include confirming your flight at least 72 hours in advance, getting to the airport at least three hours early and having enough cash on hand—there are ATMs available—to pay departure and other taxes, only deal with official personal at airports (you will be hounded by so-called "helpers"), accept nothing from strangers and keep your money and passport safe at all times.

Bus

Due to the country's poor economy, Peruvians travel more by bus than any other form of transportation, and so do most tourists. Bus travel is inexpensive; however, the quality of buses varies, as do rates according to season. The higher-priced lines, such as Cruz del Sur and Ormeño, offer cleaner, safer and more comfortable seating, as well as faster service, but one should never be complacent regarding the potential of theft no matter what bus one is on. Buses traveling between large cities routinely sell out, so it is recommended that you purchase your ticket at least a day in advance. The larger buses do have toilets, but they are often out-of-order and rarely cleaned; if you talk to the driver, he will generally wait for you if you explain that you need to use a bathroom at a stop. Many buses between major tourist destinations only leave at night, so bringing a blanket is advised both for sleeping and keeping warm.

Trains
Due to their high-maintenance costs compared to buses, there are only a limited number of trains running in Peru. Most of those are tourist-oriented, getting you to where you want to go and providing beautiful vistas along the way. Among the more popular routes are from Cusco to Machu Picchu (p.336), Lima (p.78) to Huancayo (p.236), and Arequipa (p.188) to Lake Titicaca (p.341), which then goes through the Urubamba Valley to the edge of the Amazon. Tickets should be purchased at least a day in advance. The companies range from *Económico* (which the locals take) to Pullman (the most popular with tourists) to Inca, for the wealthy. A local train still runs several times a day between Huancayo and Huancavelica.

Taxi
Unlike Ecuador and other countries, taxis in Peru do not have meters to provide an objective price. With poverty and low wages being what they are in this country, even the most congenial taxi driver will not be above trying to pull a fast one on an inexperienced tourist, though the majority will be honest. Your best bet is to inquire, before you hail a cab, what the estimated price from point A to point B will be, and to let your driver know that. Peru's tourist police are very strict about curtailing unlicensed cabs, and they can tell you what sort of identifying sticker for legal cabs you should look out for. It is not uncommon for travelers, particularly in groups, to use a cab to get from one town to another, since the fare, when divided, is often not more expensive than a minibus, and the ride is considerably more comfortable.

Hitchhiking
As with most places in Latin America, some common-sense precautions should be used if you are going to try hitchhiking as a means of getting around. A woman traveling alone should never hitchhike, and even men are better off traveling with a partner, in terms of both safety and getting rides. The safety factor increases with the number of fellow travelers. Traveling during the day is preferred, and most drivers expect some compensation.

Car Rental
The ratio of cons to pros in assessing whether it is worth it to rent a car is at least a dozen to one: bad roads, high rental costs (including hidden costs), poor-quality vehicles, antagonistic drivers, high theft and vandalism risks, frequent and costly tolls, unreadable road signs, time-consuming drives between cities—and few gas stations along the way. By contrast, it is considerably cheaper and easier to get around via bus, taxi, plane or train. Still, some feel that it provides them a unique autonomy, so if you are going to rent a car, Hertz, Budget and Avis have franchises in Peru. A familiarity with driving standard transmission is recommended.

Cycling
With the increasing political stability that has developed in Peru over the last ten years, more and more adventure cycling enthusiasts attempt to see the width and breadth of this country on two wheels. For those wanting to do so, the following is recommended: A steel-frame bike will be the most durable. Bring a bike that has a 26-inch wheel, since such wheels are standard in Peru and thus finding replaceable parts for them will be easy. However, you should also bring your own tire replacements for long trips, since the quality of such is generally poor in Peru. You should also bring additional, high-quality spokes for long trips, as well as, of course, tubes. A mountain bike is best for traversing Peru's challenging geography.

To avoid accidents, always ride with a rear-view mirror, and avoid major highways, which have little to offer in terms of scenery or culture anyway. Since they share the road with horses, llamas or donkeys, drivers on smaller roads are more conscientious. Use sun block. Wearing long sleeves and riding pants will reduce your exposure to dirt, bugs and sun. Go slowly to

Get your writing published in our books, go to www.vivatravelguides.com

adjust to different climates and altitudes, and when arriving in a high-altitude city like Cusco (p.251), spend a few days acclimatizing before you move on. Connect with other cyclists and hostel and campground owners to keep current on what routes have higher-crime possibilities. Many cyclists stop at Casa Ciclista in Trujillo (p.400), where the owner Lucho Ramírez welcomes and registers all cyclists. The best times to go are from July through September. This trip can be made for as low as $20 a day. In terms of taking your bike to Peru, you can have it boxed before boarding and reassembled in Peru, all for less than $100.

Back Roads Cusco to Quito

Are you ready for an adventure few will ever take, through landscapes that sing to your soul, and villages and mining towns that prick your conscience? Then pack your bags for the rollercoaster journey from Cusco to Quito by back roads through the Andes, to heights of 4,330 meters (14,206 ft) and dips to 740 meters (2,428 ft), without descending to Lima and the coast. The trip takes many days, due to unpaved, hair-pinning roads, infrequent transportation and daytime-only travel. It is best during the dry months (May-September); frequent landslides during the rainy season cause delays and cancellations. Be warned in some areas, especially Huánuco-Cerro de Pasco, miner and *cocalero* strikes may disrupt transit. Keep your eyes on the news and ear to the ground.

Lodging and restaurants exist in all the transfer towns. All transportation is daily, except where noted.

Your journey begins in Cusco. The unpaved road to Abancay, Andahuaylas and Ayacucho wends across barren *puna* surrounded by glacier-blanketed mountains, scattered with flamingo-visited *lagunas* (399 km, 24 hours, $15).

From Ayacucho to Huancayo a poor road meanders through breathtaking scenery (319 km, 9-10 hours, $8-10). Several companies leave Huancayo for La Oroya and Cerro de Pasco (five hours, $5), a bleak town at 4,330 meters (14,206 ft), scarred by a gaping open mine. Frequent buses and *colectivos* depart Cerro de Pasco for Huánuco, a charming city at 1,894 meters (6,214 ft) (2-3 hours, $3-5).

From Huánaco, the coarse road soars to La Unión at 3,204 meters (10,512 ft) (colectivos and buses, 5-6 hours, $8-10). From La Unión's market, *combis* leave half-hourly for Huallanca (Huánuco) (1 hour, $1); a paved road continues to Huaraz (bus, three daily, 6 hours, $7).

The route from Huaraz rambles northward into the upper Marañón River valley and to the rarely visited Parque Nacional Río Abiseo. Travel to Sihuas (8:30 a.m. and 11 a.m., 8 hours, $9), from where buses depart for Tayabamba at 3,300 meters (10,826 ft) (Monday, Wednesday, Saturday, midnight-2 a.m., 7-8 hours, $8). The journey to the uninviting mining town Retamas (2,700 m/8,858 ft) lasts three hours (colectivos and combis, 7 a.m.-5:30 p.m., $6); quaint Llacuabamba (15 minutes, $1) offers a better night's sleep. Thrice-weekly buses travel from Retamas to pleasant Huamachuco (Monday, 8 a.m., Thursday, 8 p.m., Saturday, 4 a.m., 12 hours, $9; also daily combis, 10 hours, $12). The trip passes through Chahual (1,450 m/4,757 ft); from nearby Los Alisos you can make the ten-day trek to the Chachapoya ruins of Pajatén in Parque Nacional Río Abiseo (guide and permits needed). The road then climbs to a 3,900-meter (12,795-ft) pass before arriving at Chugay (3,400 m/11,155 ft), and descends to the Río Grande and Huamachuco. Frequent combis depart Huamachuco for Cajabamba (2½ hours, $2), from where you then catch one for Cajamarca (4 hours, $4).

The trip from Cajamarca into the mysterious Chachapoyas region is arduous. It first jolts along to Celendín (four buses daily, 112 kilometers, 4 hours, $4; also combis from Av. Atahualpa, 300-block). Microbuses leave Celendín for Leymebamba only three times per week ($6.60), and buses direct to Chachapoyas on Thursday and Sunday at 11 a.m. ($10). Combis leave early mornings from Leymebamba for Chachapoyas.

From Chachapoyas, you forge northward along the Andes' cloud-forested slopes, descending to 740 meters (2,428 ft) altitude at Jaén, to the La Balsa border crossing into Ecuador. (For specifics on this border crossing, see Getting To and Away From Chachapoyas.

Once entering Ecuador, you visit fascinating Andean towns like Vilcabamba, Loja, Cuenca and Riobamba, before reaching Quito, the second-highest capital in the Americas.

TYPES OF TOURS

Organized Peru tours are available to a wide range of attractions, landscapes, climates and cultures. A slew of reputable agencies offer a number of excursions, from scenic day trips to Lake Titicaca (p.341)—the world's highest navigable lake—to mystical multi-day hikes through Machu Picchu (p.336) and along the Inca Trail (p.332). Peruvian Amazon tours explore one of the most bio-diverse areas of the planet and highlight the unique flora and fauna in the rainforest, while Andes trips will take you high into the picturesque peaks. Choose an adventure trekking tour, or sit back and take in the sites by bus: there are trips for travelers of any spirit, with expeditions that can include hiking, mountain biking, rafting, culture tours and shopping. A wide range of itineraries means there is something to fit your interests, timeframe and budget. Tours can easily be booked internationally or in all of the major cities once in Peru.

Andes Tours

The snowcapped peaks and glacial lakes of the Peruvian Andes offer some of the most incredible scenery in the hemisphere, and a wide range of tours cater to both expert mountaineer and greenhorn trekker alike. It is not necessary to be "super fit" to hike in the Andes, but you do need to be of generally good fitness and a regular walker. Tours are rated by level of difficulty and often last a couple of weeks or more; many several-day trips are also available. The majority of Andes tours depart from Huaraz (p.378), though trips can be taken from several of the country's other mountain towns.

Amazon Tours

Amazon tours allow you to explore one of the most bio-diverse areas on the planet via boat trips down the Amazon tributary rivers, eco-lodge stays, or often a combination of the two. Typically, knowledgeable guides take you deep into the rainforest in search of the more than 1500 species of birds, 2500 species of fish, and more than 50,000 species of plants. Tours can last anywhere from two days to two weeks, and offer a wide range of accommodation.

Lake Titicaca Tours

Tours of the world's highest navigable lake offer a variety of single and multiple-day tours of the waters and the communities living on its shores and islands. Tours range from a few hours of island exploration to days of getting to know lakeside villages. Most travel agencies in Puno (p.351) handle the conventional tours of Lake Titicaca (p.341) and Sillustani, along with a handful of other ruins programs that can extend trips by a few days.

Inca Trail Tours

Hiking the Inca Trail (p.332) is by far one of the most popular activities in Peru, and there is a host of tour possibilities to guide you. Shorter jaunts of a few days touch on the sites, while trips of three days to more than a week will take you winding through an array of sceneries, altitudes, climates and ecosystems that range from high Andean plains to dense cloud forest. Many excursions end with a climactic arrival at breathtaking Machu Picchu (p.336). Most trips leave and return to Cusco (p.251), and if you haven't had time to acclimate to high altitudes it may be worth hanging out here for a few days before hitting the trail. Look around: trips vary greatly in levels of difficulty and price.

Organized Tours

There are a number of operators who can provide guided tours of Peru. Many of these are based in Peru and can be found in the tour operator listings sections for Peru and under the main travel areas. Alternatively, there are tour operators based in North America, Europe and Australia that offer a variety of tours taking in most of Peru's main highlights. Companies such as G.A.P. (www.gapadventures.com) based out of Canada, or U.K.-based Tucan Travel (www.tucantravel.com) offer a variety of trips from three days and upward, taking in just one or two destinations, or tours that explore the country pretty thoroughly, to tours that are multi-country, visiting Peru as part of a trip that may take up to six months and cover all of South America. These types of tours are often group trips where you will be traveling with a number of others from different countries and backgrounds from all over the world. They are more costly than going it alone, but for those who like to have everything organized upfront, they can be a good option.

Some tour operators and options are detailed below. Alternatively, check out the different sections of the book to find more information about tour operators in specific locations.

Andex Adventure
Tel / Fax: 51-1-251-6530.
URL: www.andex-adventure.com.

Sun God Expedition Tours
Tel: 51-8-423-2765.
E-mail: info@sungodperu.com, URL: www.sungodperu.com.

Santa Cruz Trek
Tel: 51-4-342-5661.
E-mail: info@santacruztrek.com, info@perubergsport.com, URL: www.santacruztrek.com.

Aventuras de Oro
Tel: 51-1-793-1352, Fax: 51-1-241-9172.
E-mail: info@aventuras-de-oro.com, URL: www.aventuras-de-oro.com.

ADVENTURE TRAVEL
Jagged mountains of the Andes, dense Amazonian jungle, endless desert sands and a rugged coastline make Peru a dreamscape for the outdoor enthusiast. From world-class mountain climbing and multi-day treks involving whitewater rafting, horseback riding, paragliding, surfing, and visits to ancient ruins — there's an adventure to suit every taste and season. Hike into Machu Picchu, or break off the tourist-trodden path on the high mountain Ausangate Circuit. Challenge the surf of the north coast, then dry your bones sandboarding in the monstrous dunes at Huacachina. Peru is an adventure playground.

SPORTS AND RECREATION
Like much of South America, football (*fútbol*) is something like religion in Peru. Kids play in the street, adults play in the parks, and when the national team is playing, the country shuts down. Be sure to take in a game if you can: it's an unforgettable experience. Many of Peru's best *futbolistas* play for teams in other nations, as they can get a great deal more money, but fans back home still like to follow their careers.

HIKING
Hiking in Peru affords travelers the opportunity to take in some of the best scenery the Andes have to offer. Often, hikes and treks will stop by Inca ruins too. Some of the best excursions in Peru are detailed below.

The most famous hike in Peru, perhaps in the world, is the Inca Trail (p.332). Thousands travel to Peru each year to trek this route and enjoy its final reward—Machu Picchu (p.336). However, with an Inca Trail bursting under the strain of the volumes of visitors, a number of alternative hikes are gaining in popularity. Don't limit yourself to the well-trodden path. Consider doing the Lares Trek which ends at Machu Picchu, passing through remote Quechua communities and glacial landscapes. Note: only 500 people per day area allowed to hike the Inca Trail (porters and guides included); to avoid disappointment, register at least three months ahead of the trek. Be aware that the Inca Trail is closed during the month of February. You will need to hike with a guide.

There is also great hiking in the Sacred Valley region (p.299). Ollantaytambo makes a good starting point. If you're a hiker who also appreciates history, you'll love the options in this area, many of which take in ancient Inca ruins or agricultural terracing. Varied and interesting treks include those of Pumamarca, Pinculluna, Salcantay, Ausangate, Vilcabamba and Choquequirao.

The Cordilleras Blanca (p.373), Negra and Huayhuash offer hikers of varying abilities an array of excursions through breathtaking landscapes of jagged peaks and sweeping valleys. If you want to hike in this region, Huaraz makes for an excellent base and starting point. It is better to hike in the dry season, between May to September, although often April, October and November can be fine, also. Some trekking highlights include the Santa Cruz to Llanganuco route, arriving at stunning blue lakes; the Olleros to Chavín trek, which terminates at the Chavín de Huantar fortress temple; Huayhuash; and Alpamayo.

Colca Canyon (p.211) is another part of Peru where hikers will be spoilt for choice with spectacular treks in one of the world's deepest canyons, with the possible bonus of spotting a majestic condor or two, more if you are lucky. Hikes in this area include steep forays into the canyon, to lush oases at the bottom. Close by, in the countryside surrounding Arequipa (p.188), hiking opportunities also abound. Great walks can be had on El Misti and Chachani, two of the mountains surrounding the city.

A lesser-known region that also affords great walking opportunities is the cloud forests of the Utcubamba River valley near Chachapoyas (p.465). Here you can visit pre-Inca *llactas* (villages) and burial ruins via ancient roads. The multi-day treks to Gran Vilaya and Laguna de los Cóndores are great adventures to partake.

When you are hiking in Peru, be aware of altitude sickness. Don't plan on doing long hikes within your first few days. It is important initially to rest for a few days and drink lots of bottled water. Once acclimatized and hiking, be on your guard for symptoms of altitude sickness, which include severe headaches, drowsiness, confusion, dry cough and/or breathlessness. If symptoms continue, it is important to get to a lower altitude and rest. Altitude sickness can come on suddenly if you experience a sudden change of altitude.

Also, make sure that you are appropriately equipped with a decent pair of hiking shoes, a wind/waterproof jacket, hat, scarf, gloves, quick-drying pants and plenty of warm gear. It get really cold at these high altitudes—don't head out unprepared, even if it looks nice and sunny. Don't forget your sunscreen; despite the cold, the sun can burn you quickly at these altitudes. Be sure to take lots of water and snacks too.

SANDBOARDING

Sandboarding is a specialty in Peru, particularly in the Ica Desert region. Many of the hotels and hostels at Huacachina Oasis (p.168) rent or provide sandboards, and most of the local tour companies offer trips as well.

Sandboarding is a lot like snowboarding, only on sand instead of snow. Typically, groups of tourists will select battered boards provided by the tour operator of their choice, and then pile into a questionable-looking dune buggy for a quick ride out into the desert. When a likely-looking dune is identified, the car will drop you off at the top. Helpful guides will show you how to "surf" down the dune without killing yourself. Before long, everyone will reach the bottom: the guide, who has effortlessly glided there on his board, and the tourists, who have either taken a sandy tumble or walked because there is no more wax on their boards.

Boards should be waxed between runs, and your guide will show you how as the buggy brings you to another dune. On a typical day, you may get in about a half-dozen different runs before heading back to Huacachina.

If you're near Nasca (p.173) and up for a challenge, you may want to check out Cerro Blanco, or White Mountain. At 2070 meters, it is one of the tallest sand dunes in the world (if not the tallest). It is certainly the most massive sandboard-able peak in Peru. Dune buggies can only get you close to the top of Cerro Blanco. You'll have to leave your hotel early, drive for a while, and then walk three hours to get to the top, carrying your board and gear. The descent usually takes about an hour. Cost depends on the tour agency you choose, but averages about $50-60.

What to bring: a lot of water: perhaps three liters or so. Sunscreen, hat, strong, comfortable shoes, sunglasses, camera.

Copa Sudamericana

Every year, the Dune Riders International World Tour of Sandboard sponsors the Copa Sudamericana in Peru, a sort of South American championship of sandboarding. Contestants come from around the world to compete in categories like Boarder Cross and Parallel Slalom. The competition is still in its initial years, so it often changes dates, venues and events. A good place to find information on this event is: www.sudamericansandboardcup.com

SURFING

Surfing has been a staple in Peru since the beginning of its civilization. Revered as a sport because of its spiritual ambience, wave riding was also a daily part of the fisherman's routine, when they surfed on their *totora*, or reed boats.

Since then, both the styles and methods of surfing in Peru have evolved, with synthetic surfboards replacing the wooden boats. However, Peruvian esteem has not diminished. The country has turned out legendary surfers, such as Sergio "Gordo" Barreda, a four-time Peruvian national champion and two-time international champion. Needless to say, many young locals take inspiration from him, beginning their surfing careers early. Peru is blessed with consistent surf along its 3,000-kilometer coast and constant sunny weather—unlike many of the countries in the world, where surfing is limited to a short period. The country also hosts one of the surf world's most sought-after waves: *chicama*.

Chicama, the world's longest wave, stretches over 2 kilometers, which means a good surfer can ride it for 3 minutes. On the downside, having reached the end of the swell, the surfer has to walk 20 minutes along te beach to get back to their starting point. The wave is definitely on every pro surfer's "to-do" list.

Reportedly, chicama was discovered by Hawaiian surfer Chuck Shipman from the window of a plane on his way home from the world surfing championships in Peru. Barreda's brother Sergio later returned to the wave with a few friends to film the phenomenon, but the film actually ran out before the ride was even completed.

There are dozens of other top surfing beaches, ranging from undiscovered stretches to always-happening hippie towns. Some beaches are specifically for experts, and dangerous for those who don't know what they are doing. Others are perfect beginning points for novices, though. The cold Humboldt Current and the warm Niño Current feed the waves year-round, thus creating huge temperature differences along the coast. It is best to check out surf reports online before heading out to a chosen destination.

Cabo Blanco, for those in the know, has the best waves in all of Peru. It was discovered, unsurprisingly, by Gordo Barreda in 1979. Advanced surfers that can handle the left reef break are rewarded with perfect tubes, when conditions are right—waves can get up to ten feet tall!

Máncora (p.452), known for its gorgeous coastline and good waves, is the most common surfing destination. Supposedly, this beach is sunny 365 days a year. During the early months of the year, a swell from the Pacific builds long waves. However, if the surf isn't to your liking, there are always the captivating white-sand beaches and lively bars to keep you busy.

The Peruvian surf scene motivated the Beach Boys to mention Cerro Azul in their 60s hit "Surfing Sufari" and Ernest Hemingway was reportedly inspired by Cabo Blanco to write his famous novel *The Old Man and the Sea.* You too can encounter some unforgettable breaks and undiscovered waves.

There are limitless choices to how you want to approach your surf journey through Peru. It is possible to book a surf tour through the numerous operators, many of which are based in Lima. There is also the opportunity to find a private guide to drive you along the coast to great spots; this is a good way to find the beaches that only locals know of. Or you can take a chance, and rough it on your own.

HORSEBACK RIDING

Peru is a country of spectacular vistas and incredible natural diversity, and one of the best ways to experience it is on horseback.

The Peruvian Paso horse is a specific breed, descended from the original horses brought by the *conquistadores* over 400 years ago. These horses feature a four-beat gait (called the *paso llano*) that makes them exceptionally smooth to ride. They are spirited, but well-trained, and easy to ride. Paso horses are a Peruvian breed and the people are very proud of them.

Peruvian horses are often trained differently than in other parts of the world. If you're an experienced rider, you may find that your horse does not respond to the commands you're used to. Simply take a little time to become accustomed to the proper commands and ask the guide if you have any problems.

Tips

Most horseback tour operators in Peru are reputable and take excellent care of their horses, particularly those that offer multi-day excursions. However, some of the smaller operators and those specializing in day trips don't take as good care of their horses as they should. If you think your operator is a little sketchy, ask to see the horses beforehand. If they look unhealthy or have saddle sores, you may want to find a different operator. Nothing can ruin a riding trip like thinking your mount has been abused. Please advise V!VA Travel Guides if you find inhumane situations at any stables.

Some of the horses are tamer than others, and some can be downright squirrelly. If you feel like you have no control over your horse, don't hesitate to ask for a change.
If the tack (saddle and bridle) looks old, cracked or too worn, ask to have it changed. A fall can lead to serious injury. Be sure the girth band is tight and make sure the stirrups are the right length: if they're too short or too long it will make your ride difficult.

Your guide will usually be the person who takes care of the horses. Chances are he will know more about horses than local culture, flora or fauna, and may not say much during the trip. If the horses are healthy, clean and well-behaved, be sure to tip at the end of the ride. A couple of dollars per rider should suffice.

Places to Ride

The north of Peru, the Cajamarca-Trujillo-Chiclayo area, is a popular one for multi-day horseback trips. Northern Peru receives significantly less visitors than the Cusco/Machu Picchu area, and the rides are therefore more rustic. There are still ruins to ride through, and many museums and hot springs to visit.

Get your writing published in our books, go to www.vivatravelguides.com

The Ayacucho area (p.242) is also celebrated, as it offers stunning Andean vistas along with good markets for shopping. Many multi-day horseback trips in the Ayacucho area go from the highlands to the coast, and take trips to Ica and the Nasca Lines.

The Sacred Valley (p.299), with its picturesque towns, Andean culture and ancient ruins, is a favorite horseback riding destination. There are also many nice hotels where you can spend the night. Longer tours may include side trips to Machu Picchu and Cusco. Expect to see fields of wildflowers, smiling children herding sheep and goats and spectacular mountain vistas. The Inca Trail (p.332) is generally considered a hiking trail, but it is possible to find outfitters and tour companies who can take you on horseback.

In the far south, Arequipa (p.188) is a popular destination for horseback riding, and it is easy to find trips into the nearby Colca Canyon. Several travel agencies in town can hook you up with a reputable horseback tour.

Operators
Hotel Las Dunas in Ica (www.lasdunashotel.com).
Hotel Ocucaje Sun and Wine Resort outside of Ica (www.hotelocucaje.com).
Hotel Incatambo Hacienda, outside of Cusco (www.peru-hotels.com/cuzhacie.htm).
Hotel Royal Inka Pisac in the Sacred Valley (www.royalinkahotel.com/hpisac.html).

Mountain Climbing
If summiting some of the world's grandest and most beautiful peaks is your thing, then Peru is the place for you. Peru boasts an incredible 32 mountains higher than 6,000 meters, the pinnacle of which is Huascarán at 6,768 meters, giving experienced climbers a plethora of options. However, many of the lower mountains can be tackled by relative amateurs and there are plenty of challenging peaks for aspiring climbers.

Some of Peru's mountains can be climbed year-round; but for the highest mountains, June to September is the only time a summit can be attempted. For Peru's grandest peaks be sure to plan your trip well in advance as guides are required and last-minute planning may significantly limit your climbing options.

The range with the highest concentration of peaks (and climbers) is the Cordillera Blanca, near Huaraz (p.378). With countless mountains for climbers of all ability levels. Further south are Arequipa (p.188) and Cusco (p.251) which are the country's second-best mountaineering areas, after the Cordillera Blanca.

For all three areas, acclimatization periods of four to seven days are recommended. Often this time can be filled with less-challenging day hike, giving climbers a chance to get used to the altitude as well getting their legs ready for the days ahead.
Every tour company has English and Spanish guides; you will pay a little more for the English speakers. They are in high demand and language education is expensive.

Cordillera Blanca
The Huaraz area in Peru attracts some of the world's best mountaineers each year to attempt the breathtaking peaks studding the Cordillera Blanca range and the other less heralded peaks nearby. It is unquestionably the climbing capital of Peru and has several world-class mountains. Climbers traveling to Peru solely to conquer 6,000-meter peaks often complete several in a couple of weeks. Many of the mountains are located within Huascarán National Park, meaning the climbs take place in protected and unspoiled nature. The Cordillera Blanca is also considered to be one of the most accessible climbing areas in the world, in addition to being one of the best places to climb.

The highest peak in the range is Huascarán (6,768 m), making it a favorite of climbers. Alpamayo (5,947 m) is the most-climbed mountain in the Cordillera Blanca and is considered by many to be the most beautiful one in the world due to its near-perfect pyramid shape.

The Ishinca Valley is another popular destination in the region because it offers climbs ranging from easy (by mountaineering standards) to difficult. The primary peaks in the Ishinca Valley are Urus (5,430 m), Ishinca (5,530 m) and Tocllaraju (6,034 m). Ishinca and Urus are considered easy and can be attempted year-round. Tocllaraju is rated moderate to difficult and can only be climbed from May through September.

Another favorite climb in the region is Chopicalqui (6,354 m). This mushroom-shaped peak is moderately difficult. The summit treats climbers to one of the best panoramic views of the Cordillera Blanca including a look straight across at Huascarán. The climbs listed above take from five to seven days each, depending on ability and fitness.

Huaraz and the surrounding area also host the Semana del Andinismo every June. This festival, celebrating all things mountain, attracts some of the best climbers, skiers and snowboarders from around the world. They descend *en masse* on Huaraz for a week of intense, friendly competition with Peruvian locals and others from around the world.

Arequipa

Although it doesn't have the number of peaks the Cordillera Blanca has, Arequipa offers beginners a few choices to try out mountain climbing. The three most popular climbs in Arequipa are El Misti (5,825 m), Chachani (6,057 m) and Ampato (6,318 m). El Misti looms as a backdrop within sight of Arequipa, while the others are further away. Reaching the summit of Misti is a straightforward two-day climb, and you will likely leave your hotel in the morning of the first day and return on the evening of the second.

Chachani is considered one of the easiest 6,000 meter peaks in the world; so if you simply want to notch one in your belt, this is the place to do it. Like the El Misti climb, this two-day tour departs Arequipa in the morning of the first day, whereupon you are driven up to the base of Chachani at over 5,300 meters. The following morning the summit trip begins early, and returns to Arequipa after a full day of travel up and down the mountain.

Reaching the summit of Ampato is the most challenging of the three primary mountain climbing expeditions operating out of Arequipa. This trip requires a commitment of four days and entails many more kilometers covered on foot than the other two. Three days of intense climbing and descending and multiple camps make this climb more strenuous and reflective of a real mountain expedition than the others. The peak of Ampato has added historical significance, Juanita, the superbly preserved Peruvian mummy, was discovered there in 1995.

The two most intimidating mountaineering expeditions from Cusco are the summits of Salcantay (6,271 m) and Ausangate (6,372 m). The only time for a summit of these peaks is between June and September. Salcantay takes eight to ten days to summit while Ausangate takes at least ten days. Neither of these climbs is appropriate for beginners and they should not be attempted without an experienced, certified guide.

WHITEWATER RAFTING AND KAYAKING

Whitewater rafting is soaring in popularity in Peru thanks to the abundance of world-class rivers in the country. Adding to the convenience, many of these rivers are located near two of the country's most-visited tourist destinations: Cusco (p.251) and Arequipa (p.188). Peru has whitewater options for every level of experience, from beginner Class II and III water to Class IV, V, and beyond. Although some rafting companies offer kayaking trips, these are not as common as rafting. Experienced kayakers should contact the tour operators in the whitewater areas for information. Some companies in Arequipa offer inflatable kayak trips down Class III water.

Cusco is Peru's rafting capital. The most popular excursions are day trips on the Río Urubamba. These leave the city at 9 a.m. and return at 3 p.m., giving visitors about three hours on the river. Many companies also offer three or four-day expeditions on the Río Apurímac, which is probably the best-known rafting destination in Peru. Despite operating out of Cusco, these trips require a four-hour drive to arrive at the river. The Apurímac is a special river because, as it is the largest contributor to the Amazon, some consider it the longest river in the world.

Another popular choice is a rafting trip which begin on Lake Titicaca and takes you down the Río Tambopata in southwestern Peru (p.341). These trips generally last over a week, meandering through the Tambopata Candamo Reserved Zone in the Peruvian Amazon (p.483). While an excellent adventure, be sure to ask how many days of your trip will include whitewater. Once you reach the Amazon, the water gets much tamer and involves more "floating."

Arequipa offers several rafting destinations. The most common are day trips to the Chili and Majes rivers. These trips include three to five hours on the river and return to Arequipa in the evening. Some companies also offer multi-day trips down the Colca Canyon, the deepest canyon in the world.

Expeditions down the Río Cotahuasi are also available in Arequipa. This trip takes rafters down what is considered to be one of the finest and toughest stretches of Class IV and V whitewater anywhere. The trip starts with a grueling high-altitude drive to the river, followed by a strenuous hike around Sipia Falls. Over the next 120 kilometers, paddlers will encounter not only huge whitewater but also spectacular campsites and Inca ruins. Doing research and booking in advance is a must, because these trips are offered infrequently. This tour is available with Mayuc Tours and Condor Journeys and Adventures, two local outfitters.

When choosing a rafting company, make sure all the necessary safety equipment (lifejackets, throw-bags and helmets) is provided. All guides should be certified. Most companies go beyond the requirements to ensure a safe, comfortable experience, but it's still important to take care that the safety standards meet your expectations.

Mountain Biking
Mountain biking is relatively new to Peru but due to nearly unlimited numbers of trails and routes it is quickly gaining ground. The two major mountain biking centers are Huaraz (p.378) in the Cordillera Blanca mountain range and Cusco (p.251) around the Sacred Valley (p.299), neither of which have a shortage of tour operators. Trips from one day to two weeks are available and most multi-day excursions include a support vehicle to transport your food, clothing, etc. Rentals are available in both locations but if you are planning a trip to Peru solely for biking it's best to bring your own. As with any rental, you get what you pay for. Cheaper bikes will cost about $15 per day; a decent bike with front suspension will cost closer to $25 per day. All rentals should come with a helmet, puncture repair kit, pump and a first-aid kit. Below are the brief descriptions of the main riding destinations.

Huaraz and the Cordillera Blanca
Huaraz is the primary location for mountain bikers in Peru. Experienced riders, especially those looking for a more physically challenging experience, tend to gravitate towards Huaraz. Huaraz has some of the more challenging riding in Peru, but most companies offer a range of options depending on ability and fitness level.

The most popular trip is the Huascarán Tour. Offered by most major tour companies, this trip lasts anywhere from five to 14 days and includes extensive touring of the Cordillera Blanca Range and Huascarán National Park. The vistas in the Cordillera Blanca are stunning and many consider it the most beautiful range in the world.

Given that many of the rides are in the Cordillera Blanca, there are loads of technical single tracks to be ridden. If you're looking to burn your quads, you can ride to the top before barreling down. But if you're only looking for the exhilaration of the downhill ride, many companies will drive you and your bike to the top.

Cusco and the Sacred Valley

Cusco is the best choice for mountain biking tours for less-experienced riders or those looking for an easier ride. Mountain biking tours from Cusco range from one day to over a week. There are numerous options for getting out and spending a day on a bike. Most of the day trips are straight forward, downhill cruises, taking riders past Inca ruins and through the striking surroundings of the Sacred Valley.

Arequipa

Many of the trekking and rafting companies based in Arequipa also offer mountain biking. Colca Canyon is reportedly the deepest canyon in the world at 3,400 m (11,333 ft) and is a popular destination for riders of all abilities. Another option is a downhill or cross-country ride on the sides of the snow-capped El Misti Volcano. Most companies drive you to the highest point of the trip and from there you get on your bike and begin to cruise downhill.

BIRDWATCHING

Peru ranks with Colombia as having the highest number of bird species in the Western Hemisphere—over 1,800, and second only to Brazil in its number of birds endemic to the country itself, nearly 300. The range of birds extends from tiny antbirds to magisterial condors, with macaws, parrots, owls, hummingbirds and nearly every other winged creature imaginable. There are more impressive statistics: 85 percent of Peru's birds are permanent residents; of the native species living within Peru, 120 cannot be found anywhere else. Peru is a record-holder for the highest number of species living in a single location — the Manu Biosphere Reserve (p.494). Peru in fact contains an impressive 20 percent of the world's bird population. The government of Peru, in recognition of this, has set aside roughly 15 percent of its territory for the protection and preservation of its environment, with 60 reserves and natural protected areas. While on your birding expedition, you are well advised to employ a local tour guide. Take your camera and binoculars along and get ready!

Manu Biosphere Reserve

The Manu Biosphere Reserve has the largest concentration and largest variety of bird life in the world: a staggering 1,000 species have been discovered so far. Manu holds one in every nine species of bird life found on the planet.

The Biosphere Reserve encompasses a great variety of altitudinal zones and habitat types. Altitudes vary from over 4,000 meters above sea level in the high Andes down to 350 meters in the lowland Amazonian rainforest. For every 1,000 meters gained or lost, the structure of the bird communities differs. This altitudinal variation, coupled with the variety of forest types, grasslands, lakes and micro-habitats such as bamboo stands, reed-beds and treefalls, has produced the highest bird count for any area in the world. The differences in altitudes, combined with the diversity in geography and plant life has contributed to what is the highest concentration of birds in the world.

Photo by Amanda Massello

On a two to three-week birding trip to Manu, from the highlands to the lowlands, birdwatchers regularly record a staggering

450 to 500 species. Among the birds one will see are the Grey-breasted Mountain-toucan, the Mountain Cacique, the Swallow-tailed Nightjar, the Barred Fruiteater, the Collared Jay, and most especially, the Andean Cock-of-the-Rock.

Tambopata and Madre de Dios

The Tambopata and Madre de Dios regions, the least developed and least populated in all of Peru, feature over 1,000 bird species as well as 200 mammals, 1,230 species of butterfly, and up to 3,000 plant species—a higher concentration in one area than anywhere else in the world. The bird species to be found here include the Russet-backed Oropendola, the Yellow-rumped Cacique, Sand-colored Nighthawks, Horned Screamers, Large-billed Terns, Sunbitterns and of course, macaws. Indeed, Tambopata offers the largest known collection of macaws in the world, and this area is also home to the Tambopata Research Center, dedicated to the study and preservation of the macaw.

Abra Málaga (Cusco)

This famous birdwatching spot near the Cusco-Quillamba road provides an opportunity to appreciate such critically endangered *rara avis* as the Ash-breasted Tit-Tyrant (*Anairetes alpinus*), *Leptasthenura xenothorax*, the Royal Cinclodes (*Cinclodes aricomae*) and the White-browed Tit-Spinetail, *Leptasthenura xenothorax*.

The Abra Málaga area itself, which comprises ten hectares of Polylepis woodland at 4,000 to 4,300 meters, is divided into three regions: the Peñas, the Pass, and the Canchayoc. The Peñas offers a spectacular variety of hummingbirds, including the Great Sapphirewing, Black-tailed and Green-tailed Trainbearers, Purple-backed Thornbill and Giant Hummingbird. The Pass, the most well-known section, offers the Tawny Tit-Spinetail, Puna Tapaculo, Stripe-headed Antpitta and Line-fronted Canastero. The Canchayoc features the Unstreaked Tit-Tyrants, the Pale-edged Flycatcher, the Puna Thistletail, the Chestnut-bellied Mountain-Tanager and the Scarlet-bellied Mountain-Tanager.

Ballestas Islands

The Ballestas Islands (p.156) features over 150 specie of marine birds, such as cormorants, boobies, flamingos, pelicans and penguins. Cold currents from Antarctica carry nutrients that feed fish, which in turn bring on the sea birds. During the months of February and March condors will also visit the islands to feast on carcasses of sea lions. The large bird population produces and, due to little rain, stores a high quantity of bird droppings known as guano, which sustained Peru's economy when it was exported to Europe in the 19th century. The birds on the Ballestas include the Humboldt Penguin, the Wilson's Storm-Petrel, the Peruvian Pelican, the Peruvian Booby, the Guanay Cormorant, the Red-legged Cormorant, the Blackish Oystercatcher, the Tawny-throated Dotterel, the Chilean Skua, the Gray Gull, the Kelp Gull, the Band-tailed Gull, the Gray-hooded Gull, the Inca Tern and even the land bird, the Seaside Cinclodes.

Iquitos

Deep in the heart of the Peruvian Amazon, Iquitos is home to the Pacaya-Samiria National Reserve, an iridescent array of hawks, herons and jacamas, among others. Read more about birdwatching in the Iquitos section.

SPORT FISHING

The world's largest black marlin, weighing a staggering 1,560 pounds (702 kg), was caught in Peruvian waters. Still need a reason to come try your luck? Peru offers first-class saltwater fishing on the coast and excellent freshwater fishing in the Amazon. Trout fishing is good in the highlands.

STUDYING SPANISH

Peru is home to a number of distinguished Spanish schools, most of which are located in cities with thriving tourist scenes, such as Lima (p.78), Cusco (p.251) and the Lake

Titicaca area (p.341). Arequipa (p.188), Huancayo (p.236) and Huaraz (p.378) are also growing in popularity as favorite spots to learn Spanish. Combined with a host of other things the area has to offer—mountains, jungle, rafting, history, etc.—Peru is an ideal locale to *aprender español.*

STUDYING QUECHUA

For those looking to live and work in certain Andean areas, or for those who simply want to try something different, you may want to take some classes in Quechua while visiting Peru. Quechua, the official language of the Inca Empire, is still spoken today by some 13 million people, most of whom are located in Peru, Bolivia and Ecuador. For English speakers, Quechua is fairly easy to learn, because the verbs are regular and there are few exceptions to the grammatical rules. The hardest part, according to those who have learned it, is the prefixes and suffixes that can be added to words to change or modify their meaning.

There are several schools in Peru where you can learn Quechua. Naturally, the best ones are in areas with a higher indigenous population. Cusco is a good place to learn the language. Some Spanish schools offer classes in introductory to intermediate Quechua in addition to their normal Spanish courses.

Quechua classes tend to focus on conversational language skills: there are relatively few books written or printed in Quechua, and therefore reading / writing skills are less important than speaking. The courses also tend to offer a great deal of culture as well, as tradition and history are important aspects of the indigenous Andean cultures. Some of the better schools offer organized excursions where students can practice Quechua in a real-life environment.

Is an introductory Quechua course for you? If you're very interested in Andean culture, have some time to spend, already speak some Spanish, and want to learn a language that has centuries of tradition, you may want to consider it!

LIVING IN PERU

With such attractions as Machu Picchu, Lake Titicaca, the Amazon and the Nasca Lines, Peru is the most visited country in all of South America. It is only natural that many travelers would take the extra step and move here. The strength of the dollar and the euro against the Peruvian sol is an additional incentive.

The majority of foreigners live in either Miraflores or San Isidro, two well-heeled neighborhoods outside of Lima, which have the highest property values. A one-bedroom apartment goes for $250 to $350 a month, while units in newer buildings start at $450. If you want real penthouse luxury with a view of the Pacific and access to a golf course, you are looking at a minimum of $1,000 monthly.

Weekly and daily apartment rentals are available, but pricey: between $40 and $250. You'd be better off in many cases renting a room in a clean hostel for $10 a night. However, if you try hard enough you might score a bargain. One lucky resident got an entire house in the Oxapampa district for $100 a month.

If you have capital to invest in property the Miraflores and San Isidro neighborhoods are the best bets both for their quality of living and for future market potential.

There are a variety of visa categories for those interested in migrating to Peru. The general requirements include a F-007 form, your passport, a roundtrip ticket to Peru, and proof of payment, via the Banco de la Nación, of the $25 fee for requesting a visa. Worker visas need to be approved by the Ministry of Labor, while resident visas require proof that you can bring in at least $1,000 a month into the country, or at least have $60,000 sent to Peru in a locked account, or invest $25,000 while guaranteeing the creation of five jobs for Peruvians in two years.

Get your writing published in our books, go to www.vivatravelguides.com

Student visas require a matriculation document from an official school stating that the student will be enrolled for up to a year. A document guaranteeing payment of the costs of education, room, and board, is also necessary, on top of the general requirements.

Volunteer visas can be arranged though an international migration NGO, and there are related categories such as missionary or religious worker.

The majority of foreigners, however, have tourist visas, which last for 90 days. There is a one dollar a day "penalty" for staying beyond that. As of June 2008, it is no longer possible to extend the initial tourist visa, but you can request 183 days under a tourist visa when you arrive at immigration. Or you can just leave the country for one night every three months to get another 90 days. People on tourist visas are technically not allowed to work, but such regulations are laxly enforced.

Volunteering and Working in Peru

If you would like to have a different experience in getting to know Peru, beyond the tourist glitter, consider volunteering. Projects with street children are common in Lima and the Cusco-Sacred Valley region, calling on you to just spend time with the children, teaching them basic living skills and English. A few projects provide room and board; however, many charge a fee. You can check with the South American Explorers Club in Lima or Cusco for opportunities, or with language schools.

If you are a medical or other professional, check with organizations like Médecins Sans Frontières or Maryknolls for long or short-term opportunities. Some have two and three-year stints, with expenses covered and a stipend provided.

You can also try the ol' stand-by: teaching English. Visit English language centers, résumé in hand, to find a job. Be wise, though, and research any prospective employer, as some schools have earned a reputation for not paying their teachers. Also, many high schools look for teachers; frequently they ask for no certification and will arrange for your work visa. You can also tutor privately, putting up signs around and relying on word-of-mouth.
Another option, requiring a good command of Spanish, is in tourism as a translator for tour groups, as a guide, or as restaurant, bar or hotel help. Ask around for these opportunities. Often you'll receive room and board; wages, if any, would be low.

Otherwise, there are entrepreneurial opportunities in business, exports and translating. If you are going to start a business, apart from the aforementioned price and conditions, one will be faced with much frustrating paperwork and bureaucracy, though knowing who to "tip," and for how much, can ease the process.

Whether for volunteer or work positions, check websites like:
www.goabroad.com
www.workingabroad.com
www.idealist.org
www.gapyear.com.

Teaching English as a Foreign Language

As more and more Peruvians are studying English, there is a greater need for English teachers. Although many people coming to Peru for a short time look for work in language institutes, if you are thinking of staying for a longer time, look for work in universities or schools. Not only is the pay better, (typical pay is $500–700 per month, plus benefits, compared to about $5 an hour at language institutes with no benefits), but it's more stable and the working environment is often more organized.

If you want to teach in a language institute, you should be a native speaker or have an appropriate English level. You will also be expected to commit a certain amount of time to the language institute (usually between three and six months), and be willing to work split-shifts and some Saturdays. Often these jobs will be under the table, so you will have to border-hop or get visa extensions in Lima. The majority of these jobs can be found in touristy cities, such as Lima (p.78), Cusco p.251), Arequipa (p.188) and Trujillo (p.400). Occasionally job openings will be advertised on TEFL websites, but you'll probably be better off looking at the Yellow Pages (www.paginasamarillas.com.pe) or going to the city center and presenting your CV or résumé at language institutes, which usually hire year-round and classes last between one and three months.

To get a job with a school or university, you may be required to have a TEFL Certificate, a degree in education, a valid license in education or teaching experience, in addition to being able to converse in the appropriate English level. You will also have to be available for the entire school year (March to December) and some schools have training in February. Places may arrange the appropriate working visa; others (usually universities, if you work part-time) will require you to have all your papers in order before they hire you. Job advertisements can be found in El Comercio, the national newspaper, or on the schools' websites. As many jobs are found word-of-mouth, try sending your CV or résumé out in November to school directors or directors of the Centro de Idiomas in universities. The following websites have school and university listings: www.universidadperu.com/colegios-peru.php, www.universia.edu.pe, www.peruhoo.com/Educacion/Colegios, www.internationaleducationmedia.com.

If you are a qualified teacher and can commit two years to living in Peru, try International Schools. Often you can arrange a job before you arrive and the pay is similar to rates that teachers receive in their home country. International School Job Fairs are held throughout the year; you can also look at: www.ibo.org, www.schools.ac, www.isbi.com, www.cobisec.org/bi_peru.htm. Remember that the school year starts in March, so plan to start sending out your résumé or CV (with a recent photo) in November.

LODGING
Hotels in Peru are as varied as the country's landscapes and people. Luxury five-star hotels are available in Lima. Stately boutique and historical hotels, monasteries and haciendas are a rewarding way to visit Cusco and the Machu Picchu area. Eco-lodges in the Peruvian Amazon provide a comfortable, up-close look into the wildlife of the world's largest rainforest. Small family-run hotels in Peru are perhaps the most intimate way to get to know the country, that is, except for an adventurous homestay where you'll come to understand the culture of Peru first hand with a Peruvian family.

Spas
Spa and relaxation tourism are growing internationally, and Peru is no exception. Many travelers come to Latin America from the United States and Europe, eager to spend a night or two at a nice spa, where a day of massages, Jacuzzis, mud baths and more costs a mere fraction of what it would at home. The best spas in Peru are currently found in the most important tourism centers, such as Lima, Cusco and Nasca. More remote locations such as Iquitos do not have as much to offer.

Most spas in Peru offer a variety of massages, steam rooms, aromatherapy and Jacuzzis. Some offer yoga, specialized treatments, sound therapy and more. Every spa has its own specialties, so check what services they feature before you go. Generally, massages and other services can be ordered individually,or as part of a package.

Some of Peru's better spas:
Cantayo Hotel Spa and Resort, Nasca
The Cantayo Hotel, one of the most elegant in dusty Nasca, is expanding its spa services. Currently, it offers yoga and hydromassages. URL: www.hotelcantayo.com.

Kallpa Wasi Spa, Yucay, Sacred Valley
About an hour from Cusco, those looking to relax after spending a few days hiking the Inca Trail or exploring Machu Picchu might want to head here. It's part of the Sonesta Posada del Inca Hotel and offers a full service spa with massage, sauna, and yoga. URL: www.sonesta.com/sacredvalley.

Stilos Spa, Cusco
This spa is not affiliated with any hotel—you can't spend the night. It does have a good reputation and a wide variety of massages and treatments. Tel: 0-84-22-1156.

Miraflores Park Hotel, Lima
This facility features massages at the Zest Spa, one of the best in Lima. It's expensive, but the hotel is run by the prestigious international Orient Express group, so you know you'll get top-notch service. URL: www.mira-park.com.

Haciendas
Like the rest of Latin America, Peru was once home to many *haciendas*, elegant country estate homes owned by wealthy citizens during the colonial and Republican periods. Some haciendas were administrative centers from which a single family could rule up to dozens of indigenous villages like medieval dukes. Although historically linked to oppression and exploitation of indigenous society, there is no denying that the stately buildings, often with balconies, gardens, stables and courtyards, are tranquil, beautiful and well worth a visit.

In some countries, such as Ecuador, many old colonial and Republican haciendas have been turned into first-rate guest homes, offering horseback riding, traditional food and elegant accommodations. Unfortunately for Peru, a number of the country's most attractive haciendas were taken over by the government between 1968 and 1972, during the agrarian reforms of President Juan Velasco. Many of the best haciendas were given to cooperatives, which allowed them to deteriorate into rubble, and some were looted and burned. In the best of cases, the marvelous old buildings were merely neglected.

A few haciendas have survived, however, and their owners are learning what Ecuador learned decades ago—restored haciendas make great hotels. Areas of high tourist traffic are seeing more and more of them, especially the Sacred Valley near Cusco. One of the best is Hacienda San José in Chincha, first established as a sugarcane plantation in 1688 (www.haciendasanjose.com.pe). Its owners managed to keep it during the Velasco administration, converting it into a hotel and restaurant soon thereafter.

A stay at a converted hacienda can be a highlight of any trip to Peru. There is something magical about staying at a place that has been around for centuries, especially if it has been nicely refurbished. Most of the haciendas in Peru are in the upper-middle price range: expect to pay roughly $70 per night for a double. Many offer a wide range of activities, from mountain biking to horseback riding, and all offer tranquil garden paths, beautiful rooms and scenery, terraces and gardens. If a stay at a colonial hacienda is within your budget, it is certainly worth checking one out.

Camping
As a hiking and trekking mecca, Peru boasts many camping opportunities. In general, travelers will not be responsible for their own equipment (tent, sleeping bag, camping stove, etc.) as most camping trips are organized through tour operators who provide (or rent) all types of gear. However, if you are planning on doing a lot of camping, it's not a bad idea to bring some of your favorite items. In the Huaraz and Cusco regions the number of options for trekking or climbing in combination with camping is almost unlimited. Camping is often combined with other multi-day activities, such as biking or whitewater rafting.

The majority of the camping is done in the Cusco region—where the combination of the jam-packed Inca Trail and the accompanying Sacred Valley provide visitors with a multitude of camping possibilities. Most treks in the region can be organized through guiding companies with offices based in Cusco.

Huaraz, Peru's climbing capital, predictably has lots of camping. However, the camping is merely a necessary element of summiting one of the several nearby peaks. For those not going up the mountains, there are also camping and trekking options in the Cordillera Blanca.

Peru's multi-day whitewater rafting trips also include camping. Most of them leave from Cusco (although you will put-in the river hours from the city). The outfitter will provide all necessary equipment.

Along the coast and in the mountains there are camping options as alternatives to hotels. If you plan on this style of camping you will want to make sure you place your tent in a safe place. Ideally the campground has a place to lock up valuables. People have been known to camp on the beach in Peru, but ask around before determing whether or not it's safe in that area.

Eco-Tourism

Eco-tourism in Peru has boomed in the last decade. There are many valid eco-lodges that have little-to-no negative effect on the environment and help you truly appreciate Peru's natural beauty. However, many hotels claim to be eco-lodges (many simply by adding the prefix "eco" to all goods and services) without taking basic steps to guarantee ecological protection. All good eco-lodges should follow these guidelines:

1. Minimal environmental impact should be the fundamental goal of every eco-operator. How a hotel or tour operator manages its impact will tell you immediately if it is truly ecologically minded. Ecologically responsible businesses recycle, conserve water and energy, manage waste properly (i.e. implement composting and gray water projects), and allow guests to choose whether or not to change linens or towels daily. These simple efforts make a huge difference in the long-term environmental impact of tourism.

2. Conservation may be practiced in many different ways. Habitat preservation is one of the principal forms of conservation. Habitats may be preserved by establishing private reserves, supporting established national parks and reserves, or funding native tree reforestation projects. Although protected areas may be visited by tourists, it is important to recognize that their primary purpose is preservation. Whenever visiting a protected area, your visit should have minimal impact.

3. Sustainability is vital to the long-term success of eco-tourism. The majority of products consumed at an eco-facility should be locally produced and local organic gardens should be the source of the majority of the food served. Furthermore, construction should be done using local materials and methods. Ultimately, sustainability means that a lifestyle that is in balance and that can be maintained indefinitely without depleting the earth's resources.

4. Community involvement is a crucial aspect of eco-tourism. Eco-tourism should generate revenue for the local economy without harming the environment. Ideally, the community should own the establishment. If this is not possible, the operation should at least employ local labor. Moreover, in addition to generating revenue and providing employment, eco-establishments should sponsor community development projects.

5. Environmental education teaches others to be ecologically responsible. Every guest should leave an eco-facility having learned something about environmental preservation and cultural sensitivity. This ensures the continued growth of environmental and cultural awareness.

FOOD AND DRINK

When the great culinary destinations of the world are discussed, Peru is not likely to be often mentioned. However, in recent years it has begun to be recognized as a place with an extremely diverse and delicious selection of cuisine. The country not only has an expansive variety of traditional fare, but also a unique selection of fusions. This is due to the land's unique geography, its openness to blend races and cultures, and its use of ancient cuisine techniques in modern dishes. Also, you tend to be able to get the most bang for your buck in Peru, with a fancy dinner running at around $20.

In fact, Peru's increasing recognition as a culinary destination has caused the number of culinary tours available to skyrocket. Most begin in Lima and travel through the country to Cusco, where Machu Picchu is located. They say they know the absolute best restaurants, some even claiming that the meals are free if they are not as wonderful as you expected. If you love food, these are a great way to explore Peru and experience fine Peruvian cuisine.

Because of Peru's geographical diversity and varying climates, there is a great variety of agriculture products that lend to the unique culinary dishes available in the country.

Peru has seen immigration from such countries as Spain, China, Africa, Japan and Italy. The cooking methods and cuisine types from these countries have been mixed with traditional Peruvian methods, thus creating very unique and flavorful dishes. The mixtures of cultures in cuisines are especially apparent in areas where people from a certain area settled. For example, on the coast, where Moorish, African and Chinese people settled, you will find dishes with these influences. One of the most popular mixed cuisine types in Peru is *chifa*, or Chinese food. You will find many Peruvian dishes, such as *lomo saltado*, which combine traditional Peruvian food with Chinese. Even the food that is considered to be 'true' Chinese food has definite Peruvian influences.

The most quintessential Peruvian coast food is *ceviche*, although you can find it pretty much anywhere in Peru. Ceviche varies from place to place, but in general it is seafood marinated in spices and citrus juice.

In the Andes, the diet of indigenous people remains nearly the same as it has been for hundreds of years. Staples include corn, potatoes, and meats from such animals as alpaca and guinea pig, or *cuy*. The idea of eating a furry little animal may seem repulsive to many foreigners, but cuy is a common food, even considered to be a delicacy. When in the area you are sure to walk down a street and see restaurant after restaurant roasting up guinea pig. If you are feeling brave, try one, it definitely will be an experience you will never forget.

A *pachamanca* is a special banquet that is meant to be a celebration. It is made from a cornucopia of meats, herb and vegetables slowly cooked underground on heated stones. It is a rather tedious process, requiring a very skillful cook.

Fruits and vegetables make up the basis of a jungle diet. If you make a trip to the jungle, you are sure to encounter many types that are foreign to you. A popular fruit is *camu camu*, a small reddish purple fruit that resembles a cherry and has high vitamin C content.

Those with a sweet tooth will not be disappointed during their visit to Peru. There are many delicious desserts to choose from. *Helados*, or ice creams, are one of the most popular. Besides traditional ice cream flavors, such as chocolate and vanilla, you can find exotic flavors made with local fruits. Another common desert choice is *alfajores*, which typically is a lemon -flavored pastry with a sweet, creamy filling. *Turrones*, similar to fudge, are also very popular. They are most commonly made from almonds, although some are made from honey.

The most popular drink in Peru is by far the pisco sour. It is made with *pisco*, which is a type of brandy distilled from grapes. The brandy is then mixed with egg white, lemon, sugar syrup and spirits. The wine industry in Peru has recently been gaining more attention. In particular good wines can be found in the Ica region, to the south of Lima. *Chicha* is a popular drink in the Andes. It is made with fermented *maize*, or corn, and other herbs.

As for non-alcoholic refreshments, soft drinks are very popular, in particular Inca Kola. Fresh juices are also very prevalent. Just be careful, because they are often prepared with tap water. Most restaurants in touristy areas know to make the juice with purified or boiled water, but a hole in the wall may not.

For many, food is a highlight of a trip. Peru is sure to not disappoint anyone looking for good culinary experiences during their holiday. Come with an open mind (and an empty stomach) and experience the unique flavors of this culturally rich country.

Wines of Peru

Few foreigners realize the tastiness and quality of wines produced in Peru, or the deep history of wine grape cultivation in the country. Though the grape growing region is quite small and doesn't boast the production scale or reputation of larger markets in neighboring Chile or Argentina, the quality of wines is comparable.

Wine grapes were first introduced in the 16th century when Spanish *conquistador* Marquis Francisco de Caravantes brought vines from the Canary Islands and initiated wine production in the region. As production expanded, Peru began exporting wine to other colonies, making Spanish wine producers nervous. They negotiated a ban on wine trade with the king, shifting focus away from wine trade to increased production of grape liquors using pre-Inca style earthenware containers, called piscos.

These early endeavors of Jesuit monk farmers established the foundation for the trading of pisco and new centers of production, particularly within the province of Ica (p.159), today's center for Peruvian wine culture. The Ica region enjoys fertile soils and the cool air of the Humboldt Current much like the Napa Valley, blessing the area with ideal conditions for the cultivation of wine grapes. Peru's best wineries—or *bodegas*—are located here, such as the larger Bodegas Tacama and Ocucaje. Grape harvest is annually celebrated with lively parades, marching bands and tastings in Ica every March during the National Vintage Festival.

INCA KOLA

During your time in Peru you are sure to encounter this sweet, yellow soft drink. Its flavor resembles bubble gum, and most in Peru enjoy it at room temperature from a glass bottle.

Launched in 1935, the cola has seen great success in Peru. It has consistently had higher sales then both Coca-Cola and Pepsi, declaring itself the drink of Peru. During the 70s and 80s the drink often used the slogan "Made of National Flavor!"

Both Pepsi and Coca-Cola strove to catch up with Inca Kola's sales during the 90s to no avail. A major hit for Coke during this time was when McDonalds forced them to allow Inca Kola to be sold in their restaurant. In 1997 Coca-Cola began to look into buying out Lindley Corporation, who produced Inca Kola.

By 1999 a deal had been worked out. Coca-Cola bought 59% of the Inca Kola Corporation and 30% of the Lindley Corporation for 300 million dollars. In return Lindley Corporation was given the rights to bottle all Coca-Cola products in Peru, and Coca-Cola was given permission to bottle and sell Inca Kola in other countries. However, Coca-Cola only bottles and sells Inca Kola in Ecuador and the Northeast part of the United States.

Today Inca Kola continues to dominate the soda market in Peru. Be sure to give it a try. Its flavor will make you understand why it has experienced such popularity in Peru.

Culinary Vocabulary

Ají—Ají is the Spanish word for chili pepper. It is a staple in Peruvian cuisine.

Arroz con leche—A rice and caramel pudding flavored with cinnamon and vanilla.

Arroz con pollo—A rice and chicken stew with *ají amarillo* and cilantro flavoring.

Arroz tapado—A sauté of meat, garlic, tomatoes, raisins, olives, egg and parsley, served in between two layers of rice.

Ceviche—One of the most popular Peruvian dishes, ceviche is the combination of raw fish or shellfish, lime juice, ají, onion, sweet potato and corn.

Charqui—Traditionally, dried llama meat used in Andean cooking, however today beef tends to be more commonly used.

Chifa—The name given in Peru to Peruvian Chinese cuisine and Chinese restaurants.

Cuy—Guinea pig, a Peruvian delicacy. They are usually roasted with garlic, or served with a peanut sauce.

Criollo or *al la criolla*—Types of spicy food, meaning "creole."

Lomo saltado—Sautéed beef and potatoes with ají and soy sauce, this is a good example of a combination of Peruvian and Chinese cuisine.

Pachamanca—A popular dish in the highlands that symbolizes the relationship between the Andean people and the Earth. It generally consists of several ingredients, usually including chicken, cuy, potatoes and corn. It is cooked inside a hole filled with stones covered in herbs.

Pisco—Pisco is a brandy distilled from fermented grape juice. It is considered to be Peru's national drink.

Pisco sour—The cocktail of Peru. It is a mix of pisco, lemon, egg whites, syrup and bitters.

Queso fresco—A typical Peruvian cheese, white and soft.

Salsa criolla—A sauce that is usually served with meals, consisting of onions, ají, lime juice and cilantro.

Tiradito—A dish similar to ceviche, but with a more subtle taste. Its main differing point from ceviche is its lack of onions.

Trucha—Trout

SHOPPING

Every country has its textile, pottery or art that it's famous for. But Peru is an exception. It has so many quality choices—almost too many. But if you're a shopper, you'll enjoy Lima and Cusco, and not only for cheap prices. From hand-woven tapestries, beautifully-crafted silver jewelry, knitted sweaters, scarves, gloves and clothing boutiques, it is a challenge to choose: traditional folk art or modern contemporary painting? Antique tapestries or newly-woven weavings? Ceramics or CDs?

Soft, cozy, finely-knit alpaca sweaters are one of the best buys in Peru. While they might be really expensive by Peruvian standards, the cost would still be much higher in Europe or the United States. Alpacas are descendants of camels and cousins to llamas. They evolved thousands of years ago, developing a fine hair with remarkable softness, fineness, length, warmth and strength. But finding the right Alpaca sweater involves some shopping around.

Alpaca creations, from sweaters and gloves to hats and ponchos, are abundant throughout Peru, especially in Cusco (p.251). There are 22 different natural colors of this wool. Baby alpaca makes the most luxurious and soft products. Alpaca became the fiber used to clothe the wealthy Inca. It is said that baby alpaca, the first shorn fiber produced by an alpaca, was reserved for royalty only; anyone not royalty found donning the cashmere-like product was penalized, on some occasions even sentenced to death.

A high number of stores and often stalls (especially in Cusco) advertise real baby alpaca or real, 100 percent pure alpaca products for 60 or 70 soles. In all likelihood, these are fakes, even if the store owner says it's real and gives you a long story about who made it. Don't get duped. Real alpaca products are beautifully made; the texture is super-soft and feels like cashmere. If it's too silky though, it's probably been spun with polyester. If the texture is too rough, it's been spun with sheep's wool, which still make fine products, but just aren't what you thought you were paying for. The label also makes

IS IT THE REAL THING?

You ignore the bustling hum of the market around you. You have found a beautiful sweater to keep you warm in the chilly Andes. "Oh, yes, it's wool," the vendor says with a friendly smile.

Ah, but the age-old question pops up in your mind: Is it the real thing—or synthetic?

You can still rely on touch to tell you—to some degree. Sheep wool is thick and "itchy." Alpaca wool is fine, soft—and rolls down compactly, yet springs back to its original density when unrolled. Synthetics—polyester, nylon and what-not—feels, well, synthetic, right? Uh, not any more. Increasingly these fibers have become almost equal in touch to their natural competitors.

But there is still one fool-proof way to know for sure whether that sweater you are yearning is the real, all-natural, 100% thing.

The secret is always to carry a pack of matches in your pocket when you head out to the market to shop for textiles. A lighter will work, also.

First, pick a bit of fuzz off the sweater, being careful not to pull the yarns of the garment. Twirl the fuzz to make a strand. Strike a match and burn your strand.

Plant fibers—cotton, linen, ramie and even silk (after all, it comes from mulberry leaves!)—will turn to a fine, light-colored ash.

Animal fibers—whether from lamb, sheep, alpaca, llama or even critters like qiviut and yak (yes, this test will work on any continent)—will singe and smell like burnt hair.

Synthetics will melt into a small black ball and smell like burnt plastic.

If that sweater is a mix of natural animal and synthetic fibers, it will both singe and melt; by how much it does of either, you can pretty much calculate the percentage of blend.

You might find yourself saying to that friendly vendor, "And from just what type of animal did this wool come from, a Polyester?"

a difference. A real alpaca sweater will have the label of the person who made it, or company. Most often, true alpaca items are found in mid-to high-end stores in Cusco and Lima (p.78). As always, don't wait for the airport; while well-advertised, they are also way overpriced.

Since you are in the land of the Inca, artists have designed some exquisite pre-Columbian art work that you can purchase nearly anywhere from street markets to museums. A range of Inca designs are painted in a variety of colors from bright oranges and reds to earthy browns and stone blues. Relatively cheap and beautiful, they make great wall hangings if you frame them later. Most artists and galleries have suitable packaging so that you can take them home without damaging them. And while we're on the art side of things, don't forget to pick yourself up a bottle of *pisco*, the delectable spirit used to make pisco sours. It is readily available more or less everywhere.

The closer you get south towards the silver mines of Bolivia, the more you will begin to see silver stores, or *platerías* as they are called in Spanish. Earrings, rings, necklaces, bracelets,

Get your writing published in our books, go to www.vivatravelguides.com

jacket pins, hair pins, silverware, serving plates, candle stick holders and frames can all be found in both Lima and Cusco. Many are one-of-a-kind and most are handmade.

Lima tends to be more expensive, but, at the same, there are a slew of exceptional silver stalls, especially at the market on Avenida La Paz in Miraflores. Here unique designs can be found, and many are created into Inca symbols, which are filled in with red, blue and green crushed stone to complete the arrangement.

Cusco, on the other hand — even though it is still a tourist town — tends to be cheaper for silver, probably because it is closer to Bolivia. But in Cusco there are many, many shops along Plaza de Armas, which although nice for variety, require more sifting through to make sure what you're buying is really silver. Since silver is a soft metal in its purest form, it is too soft to be used for jewelry and other items. It is, therefore, mixed with other metals to make it more durable. Only .925 is pure sterling silver, meaning that .075 is an additive. Usually copper is added to make a pure 1000 parts silver. So anything around .925 is a good bet that you're getting what you paid for. In Cusco you might also want to head up towards Calle San Blas, where you will come upon many small, funky independent jewelry boutiques that have some exciting finds.

Finally, follow the guidelines below for securing and buying some great quality Peruvian products regardless of which town you are in:

• September to May is considered low season and many shop owners are likely to cut you a deal.
• As in all of South America, it's tradition and culture to bargain. Don't feel bad or feel like you should give more because they are small indigenous shop owners. They expect you to bargain, and if you don't, many locals will actually be offended.
• If you can pay in cash, do. You are likely to get a better discount on the items you are purchasing. This includes even high-end stores where credit cards are readily accepted. The fees associated with credit-card payments tend to be higher than discounts, so it's worth the vendor's while.

Bargaining

Bargaining is the name of the game in Peru in the markets and often in the craft shops, too. In the markets there are no prices on display. You need to bargain prices with the stall holder. Wait until the seller suggests a price, and then offer to pay half to two-thirds of that price and take it from there. To find out the lowest price that a vendor will accept, ask *"el último?"*

It is worth checking out prices on a few different stands with similar products before entering into bargaining, to get a good idea of value. Also recommended is to buy a lot of things at the same stall. Sellers will often discount prices for those buying in bulk. Nooks away from the main arteries of markets will often have better bargains than those near strategic corners. Most importantly, don't pass up that unique sweater for the sake of a dollar. That dollar will mean more to the stall holder than to you, and you will surely regret it when you get home.

SOUTH AMERICAN EXPLORERS CLUB

The South American Explorers Club has a strong presence in Peru, with clubs in both Lima and Cusco. The clubhouses have a lot to offer to both travelers and ex-pats. They are usually a great place to meet other like-minded people. For travelers, the club is an excellent source for maps, guidebooks and general up-to-date safety and travel information. Sometimes excursions are organized, and there are regular weekly events as well. Club members get discounts on all of this, plus cheaper deals in many bars, restaurants and tour agencies in Peru.

Lima SAE Clubhouse: Calle Piura 135, Miraflores, Lima, Peru, Tel/Fax: 51-1-445-3306, E-mail: limaclub@saexplorers.org.

Cusco SAE Clubhouse: Choquechaka 188, Mailing Address: Apartado 500, Cusco, Peru, Tel: 51-8-424-5484, E-mail: cuscoclub@saexplorers.org.

PERU TRAVEL TIPS
HEALTH AND SAFETY

Pharmacies in Peru are fairly common and usually easy to find. Often you can save yourself a trip to the doctor's by getting advice from a pharmacist. Good chains are Boticas Fasa, Boticas Tassara and Superfarma. If you do get sick and urgently need to visit a doctor, in most instances your consulate can give you the contact details of an English-speaking doctor.

Bring prescription medicines with you, ideally with a copy of your prescription, so that you have the details to be able to pick up more if necessary. Keep your prescription medication in your hand baggage and be sure to carry an extra set of contact lenses or glasses.

MINOR HEALTH PROBLEMS
Altitude Sickness

When traveling in the Peruvian Andes, it is important to rest for a few days and drink lots of bottled water. Should you feel a severe headache, drowsiness, confusion, dry cough, and/or breathlessness, drink lots of water and rest. If the symptoms continue, you may want to move to a lower altitude. Anyone planning to hike at high altitudes is advised to relax in a high-altitude city for a few days before any physical exertion. Note that altitude sickness can come on rapidly if you experience a sudden change of altitude.

Sunburn/Heat Exhaustion

Peru is not far from the Equator; therefore, even at high altitudes where cool breezes constantly blow and snow can accumulate, the sun is incredibly strong. Apply sunscreen with at least an SPF of 30 every few hours you are outside. If you do get severe sunburn, treat it with a cream and stay out of the sun for a while. To avoid overheating, wear a hat and sunglasses and drink lots of water. Overweight people are more susceptible to sun stroke. The symptoms of heat exhaustion are profuse sweating, weakness, exhaustion, muscle cramps, rapid pulse and vomiting. If you experience heat stroke, go to a cool, shaded area until your body temperature normalizes and drink lots of water. If the symptoms continue, consult a doctor.

Motion Sickness

Even the hardiest of travelers can be hit by motion sickness on the buses in the Andes and on boats off the Peruvian coastline. Sit near the front of the bus or stay above deck on the boat and focus on the horizon. If you are prone to motion sickness, eat light, nongreasy food before traveling and avoid drinking too much, particularly alcohol. Over-the-counter medications such as Dramamine can prevent it: in Peru, go to a pharmacy and ask for Mareol, a liquid medicine similar to Dramamine. Ginger root, candy or tea, if taken a half-hour before the journey, can also help alleviate symptoms. If you suffer from severe motion sickness, you may want to get a prescription for something stronger, like a patch.

Traveler's Diarrhea

This is probably the most common problem for travelers. There is no vaccine to protect you from traveler's diarrhea; it is avoided by eating sensibly. Contrary to popular belief, it is usually transmitted by food, not contaminated water. Eat only steaming hot food that has been cooked all the way through in clean establishments. Avoid raw lettuce and fruit that cannot be peeled, like strawberries. Vegetables are usually safer than meat.

Make sure any milk you drink has been boiled. Avoid ice cream that could have melted and been refrozen, such as anything for sale in the street. If you do get diarrhea, the best way is to stay hydrated with clear soups, lemon tea, Gatorade and soda that has gone flat. Bananas are also a good source of potassium and help stop diarrhea. Pure coconut milk (not diluted with water) also helps stop loose stools. If you need to travel and can't afford to let the illness run its course, any pharmacy will give you something that will make you comfortable enough for a bus trip. If the diarrhea persists for more than five days, or is tinged with blood or mucus, see a doctor.

More Serious Health Problems

Hepatitis A and B

A vaccination against hepatitis A is recommended, since this strain of the disease can be caught from contaminated food or water. If you are planning to stay in Peru for more than six months or if you're going to work in a hospital, it may a good idea to get a vaccination against hepatitis B too. A hepatitis B vaccination is not considered necessary for short-term travelers. It is wise to stay away from any sort of questionable injection. It is not advisable to get a piercing or tattoo while traveling, especially at the popular outdoor markets.

Malaria

If you are only visiting Lima, Cusco, Machu Picchu, Lake Titicaca, Arequipa or Tacna, there is no known risk of malaria. In all other areas there is potentially a risk and you should take prevention pills. Malaria is caused by a parasite carried by mosquitoes. The disease produces flu-like symptoms: fatigue, lethargy, head and body aches, fever and chills. It can lead to death. If you are in a malarial area and start to have these symptoms, get to a medical facility quickly. Time is of the essence for successful treatment.

Dengue Fever

When travelling in Peru, be aware that the northern coast has one of the highest incidences of dengue fever in the country. Dengue fever is more common in populated areas than in rural zones. Dengue fever is caused by a virus. Its on-set is seven to ten days after exposure, and is also characterized by flu-like symptoms, high fever, body pains (and thus its nick-name, bone-break fever) and sometimes a red rash on the torso. The rarer hemorrhagic strain leads to internal bleeding. The only treatment is rest and plenty of liquids. Use a non-aspirin based pain killer (acetaminophen or paracetamol) to bring down the fever.

Rabies

There are stray dogs throughout Peru that are usually harmless. However, many home-owners train guard dogs to attack trespassers. On long hikes in rural areas, always carry a walking stick or rocks to defend yourself if a dog starts to attack.

Typhoid

An oral capsule or injection should be taken before travel, and the injection needs boosting every three years to be current.

Yellow Fever

This mosquito-borne disease is endemic to many parts of South America. Talk to your doctor before taking the vaccine, as it is not recommended for people with certain allergies, pregnant women and other special cases. The vaccine is good for ten years. You will be given a certificate after vaccination. Keep it with your person; after traveling in Peru, you may need it to enter other countries.

In addition to all of the above, be sure that you are up to date with polio and tetanus jabs.

Safety

Generally, travelers to Peru stand out, as is the case in most of the rest of South America. You are likely to be a head taller than the other passengers on buses, so people will notice that you're foreign. Unfortunately, this does make travelers easy targets for petty crime. In crowds, always hold your bag close to your body and in front of you where you can see it. Most thieves work in teams: one will distract you while the other slashes your bag or picks your pocket. If you are approached by a suspicious person asking for money or the time, or are splashed with mustard (or a similar substance), just walk away quickly. Don't let yourself get trapped. A bit of common sense goes a long way—it is better to keep expensive electronics and jewelry hidden away as much as possible.

Make photocopies of your documents and keep them separate from the originals. You can also scan your passport's information page and E-mail it to yourself. Additionally, it is sensible to distribute important documents into at least two stashes. Keep your passport, at least one credit card and most of your cash well protected under your clothes. This can either be in a money belt (worn under the beltline), sewn-in pocket or other contraption. Keep a wallet or coin purse within easy reach (but NOT in a hip pocket) with a small amount of money and perhaps a second credit card for daily food and shopping so that you don't have to reach into your main reserve when you aren't in a comfortable space.

Take particular care on public transportation, especially if it is crowded, as pickpockets tend to take advantage of these situations. Take care with your belongings on trains and buses. If space permits, keep your bag at your feet, with your leg through the straps. If you choose to take taxis instead, it is better to call a cab than to flag one on the streets.

In most cities in Peru the less-safe areas are usually easily identifiable. They are often around bus stations and major outdoor markets. Lodging is usually less costly in these areas, but it is better to spend a dollar or two more per night to get an upgrade for peace of mind. Researching the perfect spot beforehand is the best way to avoid being stuck in a neighborhood that makes you uncomfortable.

COMMUNICATIONS
Mail and Packages
Peru's postal service is reasonably efficient, especially now that it is managed by a private company (Serpost S.A.).

Sending Mail Locally
When addressing local mail, note that "Jr." doesn't mean "junior"; it is a designation meaning *Jirón*, or street. "S / n" is sometimes used in place of a number for a street address. This abbreviation simply means *sin número*, or no number. The house or building with such an address is unnumbered.

El Correo Central de Lima is located near the Plaza de Armas and is open Monday through Saturday from 8 a.m. to 8 p.m. and Sundays 9 a.m. to 2 p.m. Every larger city has a main post office that is usually located near the central plaza.

Sending Mail Abroad
Letters and postcards to North America take between ten days and two weeks, and cost around $1. To Europe, they cost $1.20. If you are purchasing large quantities of textiles and other handicrafts, you can send packages home from post offices, but it is expensive. You will pay more than $100 for ten kilograms (22 lbs.), similar to what it costs to use DHL, which will probably get your package to your destination faster. UPS is found in Arequipa and Lima, but its courier services cost nearly three times as much as those of DHL. Another option, if you have computer access, is L-Mail (www.l-mail.com). Through this ingenious website, you can write a letter, and the company will print it out and post it for you from a location close to your mailing destination.

Get your writing published in our books, go to www.vivatravelguides.com

INTRO & INFO

DON'T GET BITTEN!

Avoidance of mosquito bites is the key to preventing dengue and malaria. Unfortunately, the mosquitoes that carry these diseases are active at different times of the day: the *Aedes aegypti*, which transmits dengue, from dawn to dusk, and the *Anopheles*, which carries malaria, from dusk to dawn. This means mosquito bite prevention is a 24-hour job. Thoroughly apply insect repellent with at least 30% DEET (avoid contact with plastics) and wear long, loose garments. Avoid dark colors, shiny jewelry and scented soaps or perfumes, as these attract mosquitoes. Look for lodging that is away from standing pools of water, and that provides screens on doors and windows, or a mosquito net on the bed (or tote your own, preferably permethrin-treated). Burn mosquito coils in your room. Additionally, mosquitoes do not, as a rule, like moving air, so sleep with a fan blowing on you. Do not scratch bites; this can lead to infection in tropical climes. In malarial areas, use appropriate prophylactic medications; no such prevention for dengue exists. Upon returning home, have a check-up if you suspect that you have been exposed to malaria or dengue. That said, few travelers have any problems with either disease so long as they heed the above recommendations.

Select DHL Offices in Lima
(see www.dhl.com for complete listing)

Av. Gran Chimú 441-A Zarate, SJL, Lima 36
Hours: Monday-Friday, 9 a.m.-6 p.m., Saturday, 9 a.m.-1 p.m.

Av. Javier Prado Este 2875, San Borja, Lima 41
Hours: Monday-Friday, 9 a.m.-6 p.m., Saturday, 9 a.m.-1 p.m.
C.C. Larcomar Módulo MG-12, Miraflores, Lima 18
Hours: Monday-Saturday 10 a.m.-10 p.m.

Javier Prado Este 307, San Isidro, Lima 27
Hours: Monday-Saturday, 9:00 a.m.-9:00 p.m., Sunday 9 a.m.-5 p.m.

UPS Offices
Union Pak del Peru, S.A.
Av. del Ejército 2107, San Isidro-27, Lima
Tel: 51-1-264-0105, Fax: 51-1-264-6340

Union Pak del Peru S.A.
Av. del Ejército 506, Barrio Yanahuara, Arequipa
Tel.: 51-54-258-060
Fax: 51-54-258-128

Receiving Mail
You can have mail sent to you, care of any main post office (Correo Central). The post office will know to hold your mail until you pick it up, if you have letters addressed as following:

Your Full Name (last name in capitals)
Poste Restante
Lista de Correos
Correo Central
City / Town Name, Peru

The South American Explorer's Clubhouse in Lima and Cusco is also a place for members to receive mail and packages. Regular membership is $50 a year for individuals / $80 for couples, and is good in all four locations (Lima, Cusco, Quito and Buenos Aires). Groups, volunteers, nationals, and students with ID get discounts.

Mailing Address SAE Lima: Calle Piura 135, Miraflores, Lima, Peru.
Mailing Address SAE Cusco: Apartado 500, Cusco, Peru.

Telephones

In the mid-1990s Spain's Telefónica purchased the privatized national phone system, making it much more efficient. Many area codes in Peru were changed in 2003. Be wary of published telephone numbers, since many still contain old area codes.

Local

For local calls, you do not need to dial the area code (01 for Lima, three digits for all other cities); dial only the number. To make a long-distance call within Peru, dial the city code (including the zero) + telephone number.

To call information service, dial 103, for the operator 100, and international operator 108. In case of emergency, dial 105 for police, or in Lima, the tourist police at 01/225-8698.

Calling Abroad from Peru

For international calls, dial 00 + country code + city code + telephone number. The country code for Peru is +51, and the outgoing code is 00, followed by the relevant country code (e.g. 0044 for the UK). City/area codes are in use, e.g. (01) for Lima.

Calling to Peru from Abroad

If you have to call to Peru from abroad dial 51 (country code) + area code + phone number. If you want to save money and the person you are calling has access to a computer, look into an internet call via programs like Skype or iChat for very little cost or free.

Global Systems for Mobiles (GSM)

This is the wave of the future in the cell phone world. All Europeans, some Australians and a few Americans use this technology, which makes it possible to use a cell phone anywhere in the world. You need both a world-capable, multibandwidth phone using a GSM system. This allows you to communicate in Peru, Kenya, Nepal or anywhere. The possibilities are endless. Once you have acquired these two things (your phone provider will be able to assist you), call your provider before your trip and have "international roaming" activated. There is a downside to all of this technology—it isn't cheap. Roaming per minute can cost anywhere from $1 to $5 in some countries, so ask before you talk eight hours a day.

Another practical option, if you will be in Peru for an extended amount of time, is to buy a cheap cell phone. Local calls are relatively cheap, and incoming calls are free. You can choose a plan, or instead, simply load your phone with minutes from a prepaid calling card and when they run out enter more minutes. Text messaging is very cheap and popular because of this.

Prepaid Calling Cards

Phone cards, called Tarjeta 147, can be purchased at newspaper kiosks and street vendors. To use the card, first rub off the secret code number. Dial the numbers 1-4-7 and then dial the 12-digit number on the card. A voice recording will tell you (in Spanish only) the value remaining on the card and instruct you to dial the desired telephone number. It will then tell you how many minutes you can expect to talk with the amount remaining. These cards can be made to make-long distance, including international, calls.

Cell Phones

Peru, even though a third world country, has not escaped being stricken with cell phone mania. Upon arrival to the airport you may find vendors renting cell phones for the duration of your stay in Peru. Many travelers have had a positive experience with the Peru Rent a Cell company. In general, all incoming calls are free, long distance rates are lower, no international/roaming charges are applied, there is a free concierge service and rates are lower than prepaid rates. There are a couple of plans to choose from.

Plan A has an activation fee of $9.99 and the rate is $1.49 per minute, but there is no charge for incoming calls. Plan B has no activation fee, and is available for a daily charge of $9.99 and a rate of $0.99 per minute.

E-mail: informes@proturismo.com.pe
URL: www.proturismo.com.pe

You can also look into getting a Peruvian SIM card to use with your cell phone from home.

As of April 2008, Movistar and Claro cell phone numbers changed, and it is now necessary to add a 9 in front of old cell phone numbers, if there wasn't one there before, for example in Lima and Callao. The local area code then needs to be inserted after the first 9 (For instance, if an old Cusco number was 51-952-3475, it would now be 51-9-**84**-52-3475). All cell phone numbers should now read 51-9-(Area code)-XXXXXX.

Local Area Codes in Peru:
1 - Lima
54 - Arequipa
74 - Chiclayo
44 - Chimbote, Trujillo
84 - Cusco
64 - Huancayo
65 - Iquitos
73 - Piura

Accessing Your Home Computer from Afar
If you need to access files on your office computer while abroad, look into a service called GoToMyPC (www.gotomypc.com). It will allow you to get into all your files and programs on your desktop computer or laptop left behind at the office or at home. This allows you the comfort of working from abroad, without worrying about losing a laptop or having to make too many phone calls to the office.

Using Your Own Laptop
If you have WiFi or Blue Tooth in your laptop, you may be lucky enough to pick up a signal from local networks if you are in a big city, or you can use your computer at an array of internet cafés or hotels that provide login codes for WiFi surfing.

If you're traveling outside the reach of your ISP, the iPass network has dial-up numbers in most of the world's countries. You'll have to sign up with an iPass provider, who then tells you how to set up your computer for your destination. For a list of iPass providers, go to www.ipass.com and click on "Individual Purchase."

Although obvious, don't forget to back up all your work on your laptop. Thieves love to steal these electronics and if you take your eye off of your laptop for one moment in a public location, it is bound to be gone for good.

Internet Cafés
Peru is well connected to the internet with an abundance of inexpensive internet kiosks, called *cabinas pública*, available on just about every other street corner in most towns and every big city. Internet cafés, too, are popular and easy to locate. Connection speeds are usually fast

and reliable. Fees per hour usually run between 50 cents and $1. Youth hostels, hotels, bars and restaurants commonly have internet for tourists and travelers to use for a fee.

MEDIA

The government of Peru officially recognizes free mass media. Unfortunately, from 1968 until the rule of Alberto Fujimori during the 1990s, the country saw little media independence. Ironically, it was the media that brought the Fujimori scandal to light. The government continues to exert power over media outlets by purchasing advertising that promotes pro-government views, but there is much more freedom of expression attained by many journalists in the press today.

Privately-owned and operated broadcasting and newspaper companies control the media scene in Peru. State-run stations have a home on the radio and TV waves, but are not popular. The leading Lima daily newspapers are El Comercio, Ojo, and Expreso, distributed throughout the nation. Official government decrees are published in the official government newspaper, El Peruano, which was founded by Simón Bolívar in 1825.

Prominent Press in Peru
Daily Newspapers:
- El Comercio
- El Peruano
- Ojo
- Ajá
- La República
- Perú 21
- El Bocón
- El Popular
- Correo
- Libero

TV Channels:
- Frecuencia Latina
- America Televisión
- Panamericana Televisión S.A
- Canal 9
- ATV, Andina de Televisión
- Vision Peru

Magazines:
- Caretas
- Gente
- Cosas
- Business
- Comercio y Producción
- Medio Empresarial
- Caucus
- Rumbos de Sol and Piedra
- América Economía
- Expectativa

Radio Stations:
- Radioprogramas del Peru (RPP)
- Radio Nacional del Peru
- Radio Libertad Mundo
- Radio LD Stereo

Get your writing published in our books, go to www.vivatravelguides.com

- Oxígeno
- Ovacion
- CPN
- Radio San Borja
- Studio Bacán
- Studio 92
- Doble 9

MONEY AND COSTS

For the last several years Peruvian currency has stood at roughly three soles to the dollar, making the cost of travel in this country especially economical for budget-minded tourists.

With this three-to-one ratio in mind, you can calculate costs accordingly. Frequently housing, food and transportation costs are relatively cheap; you can buy a decent lunch for $3 in cities such as Lima or Cusco.

Indeed, if your intention is to see as much of Peru on as low a budget as possible, your daily costs can go for no more than $15 a day. But that means hostels with shared bathrooms and taking some of the cheaper (and riskier) buses between cities. If you are willing to spend at least twice that you can upgrade your comfort level and avail yourself to such activities as museums and guided tours.

Travelers with few budget restrictions will be able to glide through Peru. There are many top-quality hotels, restaurants and tour operators that are relatively inexpensive by first-world standards. Some actually charge first-world prices as well for millionaire-level comfort. But sometimes such a price is little more than a reassurance for people equate high cost with quality.

ETIQUETTE AND DRESS

South Americans are polite, and Peruvians are no exception to this rule. When entering restaurants, a store, or even browsing goods at an outdoor market, it's expected to greet the staff with a *buenos días, buenas tardes* or *buenas noches*, depending on the time of day and to say *gracias* or *hasta luego* when you leave. Greetings involving women are a kiss on the right cheek and between two men, a handshake.

How to Dress

Peruvians are generally better dressed than most North Americans and Europeans. So if you are wearing old, tattered travel clothes and flip flops, you will invariably get some stares. That said, Peruvians are patient with the ways of the traveler and will treat you respectfully regardless of how raggedy your outfit—as long as you aren't trying to get into a nice restaurant, bar or club dressed like a bum.

In the Andes, people tend to cover up a lot more than on the coast, partially because it is much colder and partially because the culture tends to be a bit more conservative. You will rarely see an Andino wearing shorts off the *fútbol* field, and flip flops are an oddity. Men should never plan to travel bare-chested in the Andes. Likewise, women should never wear just a sports bra or swimsuit around town. If blending in is important to you, wear pants more often than shorts, don't fly in a t-shirt and shorts, don't wear flip flops, and when going out at night, men should wear collared shirts and women should wear clean, stylish clothes—pants are fine. On the coast and outside of the main cities, these rules are much more relaxed.

Food Manners

Like all countries, there is a certain way to eat all typical meals. Table manners are more relaxed, though, so don't worry too much about them. Don't be surprised that tables at casual, crowded restaurants are often shared. When you get up to leave or join someone's table, it is appropriate to say *buen provecho*—bon appétit.

Etiquette When Visiting Someone's Home

If visiting someone's home for a party or meal, it is polite to bring a small gift, like a cake for dessert or a bottle of wine. Bigger gifts can be overwhelming and the host may feel like he or she needs to give you something in return, so stick with something small. Peruvians are generous by nature and will want to feel one ahead in gift exchanges, so try not to confound your host with expensive presents.

If you are staying with your host for an extended period of time, offer to help out with groceries and bring fresh flowers. A memento from your hometown like a photo, postcard or small book will be appreciated. Also remember that, unless you are staying with one of Peru's handful of insanely rich families, your visit will probably be something of a financial strain. You can make it less so by taking short showers—hot water is expensive—and minimizing electricity use—also expensive. Phone calls to cell phones should never be made from land lines—they are very costly. Phone and internet service in general tends to be very pricey, so try not to run up your host's bill.

RESPONSIBLE TOURISM

Tourism is an extremely important source of income to Peru. Support this nation by encouraging local industries. Eat at local restaurants and stay at locally-owned hotels as opposed to international chains. There is a wide selection of comfortable, clean and reasonably priced hotels all over the country, owned and operated by Peruvians. V!VA Travel Guides usually mentions if the owners are foreign, so choose wisely.

Use water and electricity carefully. When city officials cut down on the community's supply, travelers are usually given preference, so don't abuse the privilege.

Beggars

Don't give money or candy to children begging. You are just encouraging this destructive cycle by financing parents willing to send their little ones out onto the streets to work. Many disabled adults and senior citizens also beg; you can decide if you want to help them out or not; many Peruvians do.

Photography

ALWAYS ask before taking photographs or videos of people. Just because people look and dress differently doesn't mean you're in a zoo. Show your respect by talking to people before making them a souvenir of your vacation.

Environmental Awareness

An eco-tourism movement is slowly but surely making its way through Peru. Unfortunately, the habits of throwing trash out bus windows and littering in general are deeply engrained in Peruvian collective consciousness. Be responsible by not participating in these bad habits and make a point of leaving camping sites, nature walks, picnic grounds and such areas cleaner than you left them. Peruvian cities have started putting up "Do Not Litter" signs, but there is a long way to go. Consider staying at an eco-lodge or volunteering for an organization working to educate the community and preserve the environment.

PHOTOGRAPHY

Peru provides amazing photographic opportunities, from the sweeping vistas at Machu Picchu (p.336) to the still waters of Lake Titicaca (p.341).

High-quality film can be found in most tourist locations and in all large cities. Fuji, Kodak, Konica, Polaroid and Forte film brands from 50 ASA to 400 ASA are commonly sold, but the higher speeds, especially 1600, are scarce. Color, black and white, and slide film are widely available. The most common formats are 35 mm, 120 mm and Advantix (from Kodak). Professional formats like 6 x 6 are rare, but can be acquired at specialty stores. These stores also sell camera accessories such as batteries, cleaning kits, lenses, bags, tripods, flashes and filters and will perform technical services.

Get your writing published in our books, go to www.vivatravelguides.com

Pack an extra camera battery or camera charger (make sure you also pack and adapter for any electrical equipment: Peru uses 220 V, 60 Hz), as these accessories will be harder to come by. You will not want your camera to run out of battery life when you are in the middle of Colca Canyon or the Amazon jungle.

Camera equipment should be packed in airtight plastic bags when traveling to the rainforest to protect against the humid climate; a dehumidifying sachet is also wise. When going through airport X-ray machines, ask to have your camera and film excluded from the screening process, as it can cause damage. If you are taking photographs of local people, always ask their permission beforehand. Do not take photographs of military installations or airports. There may be a charge to take pictures at museums or national tourist sites.

Film Development and Camera Repair
Laboratorio Color Profesional
Av. Benavides 1171, Miraflores, Lima
Tel: 51-1-214-8430 / 242 7575
Hours: Monday-Friday, 9 a.m.-7 p.m., Saturday, 9:30 a.m.–1 p.m.
Professional quality developing. One-day service available, highly recommended. Advantix, Color, B/W.

Foto Cristina
Kodak Pro Center
Calle Víctor Maurtua 110, San Isidro, Lima
Tel: 440-4898, E-mail: fotoscristina@infonegocio.net.pe
Hours: Monday-Friday, 9 a.m.-8:30 p.m., Saturday, 9 a.m.-6 p.m.

Kodak Express
Jr. de la Unión 790, Lima
Tel: 428-6025

also:
Av. Larco 1005, Miraflores
Las Begonias 670, San Isidro, Tel: 441-2800
Hours: Most stores open Monday-Saturday, 9 a.m.-9 p.m.

Taller de Fotografia Profesional
Av. Benavides 1171, Miraflores
Tel: 51-1-241-1015 / 446-7421
Hours: Monday-Friday, 9 a.m.-7 p.m., Saturday, 9:30 a.m.-1 p.m.
Recommended for repairs.

WOMEN TRAVELERS
Female travelers should expect local men to call out to them and/or whistle. However, realize that this is as big a part of Latin and Peruvian culture as the food or the art. Usually ignoring the comments or actions is sufficient, but occasionally words will need to be said. Either way, keep walking. A good way to avoid this type of harassment is to cover up and avoid flirting. If the attention is really bothersome, wearing a wedding band on your left hand may help. Traveling in groups and especially with males will also cut down on the unwanted attention. Use discretion when traveling alone: take cabs after dark, avoid deserted areas and always go with your gut instinct when it comes to safety. Tampons and other female care products are difficult to find outside of the big cities so it is recommended that women stock up before heading out of an urban environment.

GAY AND LESBIAN TRAVELERS
As throughout most of Latin America, notions of gender have been experiencing significant upheaval over the years. For example, despite traditional *machista* notions that men are de-

fined as being providers and physically strong, and women as obedient mothers and wives, women who can afford it are now routinely obtaining education and pursuing careers. Similarly, despite traditional homophobia, homosexuality was officially decriminalized in 1999, and in the years since, gay businesses along with a gay subculture have grown in Lima, Arequipa and other cities with both a large population and a notable urban culture.

However, while urban culture might be moderately gay-tolerant, it is still not gay-friendly and many gay men and women lead closeted, double lives. Within certain areas, such as theatre or the arts, it is easier to be "out" than in business or politics. Many gays and lesbians chose not to come out to their families.

Be prepared, as harassment of homosexual males still takes place. A common slang term for a male acting at all effeminate is *maricón*. It's best to avoid public affection of any kind, hetero- or homosexual, and keep a low profile while outside of a gay-friendly area.

Still, the anonymity of the internet has facilitated the promotion of a gay culture. Ambiente.com and Gayperu.com are good Spanish resources for gay and lesbian travelers, and http://lima.queercity.info/index.html is a good English-language source with gay or gay-friendly bars, restaurants, hotels and hostels in Lima.

SENIOR TRAVELERS

Energetic, enthusiastic seniors will find Peru extremely satisfying. Many travel agencies offer group tours of everything from the big cities to the ruins to hiking up mountains. Most health care providers do not cover travel, so seniors should check with their provider before traveling and buy special travel insurance if necessary. Generally, senior citizens are treated with respect and consideration by the locals. Retirement homes and senior care facilities—typical among gringos—are almost unheard of among South Americans. In Peru, it is customary for older patrons to live with their children or other younger family members when they can no longer care for themselves.

DISABLED TRAVELERS

As in most Latin American countries, travel can be difficult for disabled persons in Peru. Uneven sidewalks, roads and a lack of wheelchair accessible hotels and restaurants can be frustrating. However, Peru is making strides to be more inclusive through nation-wide laws to prevent discrimination against disabilities, to broaden social coverage to persons with disabilities, and to improve wheel-chair accessibility. New hotels and restaurants often have wheelchair ramps, though few hotels will have specially-designed rooms. The best bet for travelers in wheelchairs is to maintain an upbeat attitude and to travel with companions willing and able to lend a hand if need be. Call hotels and restaurants beforehand to ensure their accessibility. We suggest staying at more-expensive international chain hotels as they tend to be more accommodating.

TRAVELING WITH CHILDREN

Take special care when traveling with children. It's necessary to pay the full amount if they take up a seat, but sit them on your lap and they often ride for free on domestic buses. Generally traveling families have few problems as locals tend to treat children with a lot of respect. Teach your child to say *gracias* and *por favor* and the locals will get a real kick out of it. Bargaining is appropriate, if not encouraged, for family rates at hotels. Sharing food between children at a restaurant is fine. Discounts are often given for children on airplanes. Make sure to ask your travel agent about special packages and itineraries for families.

LIMA

A culturally rich yet modern city on the rise, Lima has an edge worth exploring. Its raw vibe mixed with its new sense of pride is sure to bring this once-Spanish capital back into the spotlight. Lima is home to Peru's best museums, most notably the Museo de Oro del Peru (Peruvian Gold Museum) and the Museo de la Nación (The National Museum), one of the largest museums in South America. Other highlights include colonial architecture at Iglesia de San Francisco, pre-Inca pyramids at Pachacámac and catacombs in Central Lima (p.90).

The recently renovated Plaza de Armas (or Plaza Mayor) has been Peru's governmental center since 1535, with the Palacio de Gobierno (Presidential Palace) and the Archbishop's Palace at its center. Recently, up-scale restaurants and cafés have sprung up in the area right around the plaza. The coastal suburbs of Miraflores (p.112), San Isidro (p.104) and Barranco (p.129) are popular places to stay to avoid Central Lima's smog and chaos. Barranco is especially popular for its nightlife and performing arts center.

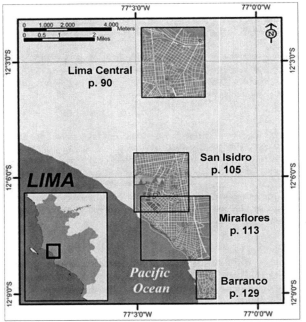

While high unemployment rates in the 1980s and 90s contributed to the deterioration of the city and rise in crime, Lima also suffered from intense pollution, mostly emitted by the large number of cars and emerging industry. The smog, combined with a heavy fog, called *garua*, blankets the city from June to December, making Lima seem dark, gloomy and scary. But under it all, Lima is a colorful city, and in recent years the government has cracked down on crime and made many tourist areas safer. As a result, the city as a whole, with its reputable gastronomic scene, including signature fish dishes, musical talents, lively historic and contemporary art scene, terrific performing arts and cosmopolitan shopping venues, has become a great place to explore.

In 2003, under the mayor's orders, the old city got clean. For years, the historic center, El Centro, has been considered an unsafe area not worthy of any attention. But like in so many South American cities that hold exquisite architecture and rich history, all that was needed was a bit of money and a whole lot of loving. Today, the Plaza de Armas, located in the historic center, shows off its beauty. Lima declared its independence from Spain here in 1821. The renovation of this area has also made it easier and safer to visit some of the center's most unique treasures, such as the Iglesia de San Francisco, which houses catacombs whose tunnels reportedly hold bones from 75,000 people, or the Museo de Arte de Lima, a Peruvian art museum.

If you are just using Lima as a portal to Cusco, your flight will most likely arrive late at night and leave for Cusco early in the morning. You can either tough out the layover in the airport or go to a hotel for a few hours until your flight leaves. The Miraflores district is your best bet for a reasonable rate on a room and you won't have to travel too far. Central Lima is about 30-45 minutes from the airport. Be sure to get to the airport early, as the flights to Cusco are usually packed and often delayed due to cloudy weather in this mountainous city.

HIGHLIGHTS OF LIMA

' The Parque de la Exposición— Also known as "Cultura",their is a tribute to Lima's urban planners from the 19th century. It was conceived and built in 1868 as the Parque de la Exposición, and is still referred to this way by many locals. Its mix of fountains, Victorian houses and modern art make this a popular favorite. Avenida Wilson and 28 de Julio, Central Lima.

' El Museo de la Nación—The largest museum in Peru features four floors of history and exhibits in a large, sprawling building in the San Borja neighborhood. The museum provides a fairly complete overview of Peruvian history and culture. Of particular interest are the sections on pre-Spanish life in the area and the reproductions of Peru's major archaeological sites. Av. Javier Prado Este 2465, Tel:51-1-476-9875.

' Parque de la Muralla—This new park, complete with a pedestrian walkway, sits on the banks of the Rio Rimac. During its construction diggers unearthed the remains of 500-year-old city walls that were once meant to repel both the rising river and Dutch pirates. A small museum on the site explains some of the history of wall. Avenida Abancay and Jiron Amazonas.

' Iglesia de San Francisco—This Franciscan church and monastery is one of the most haunting (almost literally) and memorable sites in all of Lima. Originally constructed in 1546, it is the oldest church in South America. It also served as the first official Catholic cemetery in Lima, at a time when the dead were laid to rest in catacombs beneath the church. You get to visit the catacombs and view the hundreds of centuries old bones and scores of skulls as part of the guided tour. The church also has one of the oldest and most historically significant libraries in the Americas as well as dramatic collections of religious and secular art, including Renaissance-era tiles imported from Spain. Plaza San Francisco, Jiron Ancash and Lampa, Tel: 51-1-426-7377 / 427-1381, ext 111, URL: www.museocatacumbas.com.

' The Gold Museum—Exotic is probably the best word to encapsulate what the Gold Museum has on display. The permanent collection includes not only headdresses, masks and gold figures, but also knives and other artifacts dating from pre-Inca to colonial times. Ancient mummies are also featured. Experts have questioned the legitimacy of the museum's pieces; in 2001 the museum was wracked by scandal when many artifacts were proven to be fakes. Unfortunately, all the pieces are real today, so there's no fool's gold to be found here anymore. Alonso de Molina 1100, Tel: 51-1-345-1271.

' Plaza de Armas—Throughout its history, the Plaza de Armas has been a focal point of Lima. Created in 1650 and flanked by cathedrals, ornate buildings and the government palace, the Plaza de Armas spans four large blocks and surrounds a park in the center. A bronze fountain with an angel perched on top is its centerpiece. There is a ceremonial changing of the guard six days a week, as well as regular marching band performances.

LIMA HISTORY

Lima's central colonial district is the most historic in the whole city and one of the most historic in all of Latin America. Established by Francisco Pizarro on January 18, 1535 as the City of Kings on January 18, 1535, it was home to 40 viceroys (no kings!) during the colonial era. The central square (Plaza de Armas) was laid out by Pizarro himself, with the cathedral on one side, the Cabildo (town hall) on another side and Pizarro's own house on another. Pizarro lived in what is now known as the Presidential Palace until his death in 1541; he was murdered in the street by rival conquistadores. His remains are in the cathedral.

After Pizarro, Lima continued to be very important historically. It became the seat of one of only two Spanish viceroyalties in the New World; the other was in Mexico City. A third was

Photo by Freyja Ellis

added later, in Buenos Aires. As such, it was the political and spiritual hub of Spanish South America for centuries. Spanish civil and religious authorities set up shop in Lima, ruling the part of the Spanish Empire that stretched from Quito to Chile. The discovery of rich mineral deposits in parts of Bolivia and Peru meant that a great deal of wealth flowed into Lima, and some of the old colonial homes still reflect this.

The Holy Office of the Inquisition was established in Lima, and began looking for heretics to prosecute. Under the Inquisition, there was a great deal of paranoia and witch-hunting. The Inquisition was charged with extirpating idolatry, but was forbidden to persecute indigenous Andeans. The idea was that the natives, recently pacified and brought to Catholicism, needed time to adapt to Christianity. Therefore, they were given a "free pass" of sorts; hey were punished when they were found to be continuing to practice their traditional rituals, but not executed or burned at the stake (not always, anyway).

Since the natives were off limits, the Inquisition went after crypto-Jews (Jews who had "converted" but who continued to practice Judaism in secret) and Protestants with a vengeance. Lima's central square was often the site of Auto de Fé's, which were public penances for those tried and convicted. Some, but not all, of those convicted were later executed, some by burning at the stake.

In 1746, a devastating earthquake hit the city, killing thousands and toppling many buildings. The city was rebuilt, although a great deal of historic architecture was lost. In 1988, Lima's Historic Center was named a UNESCO World Heritage site; one of its acclaimed architectural features are the city's colonial balconies. By some estimates, there are still more than 1,600 balconies that have survived since Lima's earliest days. In the late 1990s, local efforts were made in Lima to significantly clean up downtown Lima. Street vendors were kicked out, more police were sent in on patrol and street crime diminished significantly.

When to Go
Winter in Lima is from April to December, when a coastal fog, or *garúa*, blankets the city's skyline. From January to March (the summer months), the sun comes out and the beaches are packed with people.

Getting To and Away From Lima
Lima's airport, Aeropuerto Internacional Jorge Chávez, is located 16 km northwest of Lima, about 30 minutes away from the Miraflores area. It is recommended that for do-

mestic flights you arrive at least two hours in advance, and for international flights at least three hours in advance.

At the time of press, the airport fee, or TUUA, was $6.05 for domestic flights and $30.25 for international flights. It tends to change often, so you may have to pay a bit more. You pay the fee at the airport payment teller windows, which are located across from the Mini Market on the second floor.

Taxis
Although taxis are a bit more expensive than other modes of transportation from the airport, they are by far the easiest. This way, there is no lugging your luggage to the bus station, plus you will get dropped off at exactly where you need to be. The taxi ride from the Lima Airport to the center of Lima will take anywhere between 30 minutes and an hour, depending on traffic.

Upon arrival in Lima it is best to book a taxi in the reception area, rather than catching one of the taxis waiting outside, which will surely overcharge you. Ask for information at the Customer Care counters, which are located in the international and domestic arrivals area before the terminal exits. Expect to pay between $10 and $20 for the taxi ride.

Lockers
If you are going to be in the airport for a long period of time and would rather not deal with you luggage, the airport does have lockers available for rent. The suitcase storage service is located in the domestic arrivals area.

Parking
There is both hourly and long-term parking available at the airport. The hourly rate is 3.50 nuevos soles. The payment teller windows can be found in front of the terminal. Long-term parking costs 17.50 nuevos soles per day. The long-term parking lot is the parking lot located on the right, directly following police control.

Internet and Telephone Services
Recently the Lima airport became Wi-Fi compatible. However, there is a charge to use this service. You can buy Wi-Fi cards at the coffee shops located in Peru Plaza, in the domestic and international terminals and in the public call center of the Telefónica, which is on the second level. Telephone booths are located throughout the airport, with the highest concentration being in the Telefónica.

Buses
There are no actual bus stations on the airport premises, so if you have a lot of stuff it is probably best not to go looking for a bus.

TRAVELING WITH KIDS IN LIMA
As with most travel, there seldom is anything more helpful than tips from an on-site parent about where to take kids. Here are a few suggestions for the little ones:

Cieneguilla
At 30-40 minutes from Lima, Cieneguilla is a short drive by local standards. Typically the weather is much nicer than downtown. There are a variety of restaurants that have good food, large kid-friendly play areas and reasonably good service. These play areas have playgrounds complete with trampolines and sometimes even horse rides. Avoid more crime-prone parks downtown and be selective, there are some parks in Miraflores that are ok. Ask desk clerks or locals for their assessments of local green spaces before hanging out with your tot. URL: www.cieneguilla.com.

The Museo de la Nacion
The museum is home to a children's theatre. It also features a variety of exhibits of native Peruvian artwork and hosts different art-related events, including an evening of art called Noche de Arte. URL: www.nochedearte.com.

LIMA

Restaurant Rosa Náutica

Enjoy the sweeping view of Miraflores from your table. You will feel as if you are right over the surf as it comes to shore at sunset. If you or your small companion insist on sand between your toes, park near the restaurant and walk the beach looking for shells, rocks or observing the local surfers catching a wave. Tips on ordering in a restaurant: Stick with the appetizers and skip the main courses. The appetizers are simply more varied. The variety makes for a great shared dining experience. URL: www.larosanautica.com/rn_homeing.html.

San Francisco Church and Catacombs

The church and its design are grandiose and magnificent especially from the perspective of a seven-year-old. The catacombs are chilling and fascinating for parent and child. You can go to the underside of the church building and look at all of the bones of the people interred there.

LIMA SERVICES

Banks in Lima

ATMs are readily available in Lima, with many offering 24-hour service. Just approach them with caution, in particular at night, since many thieves target them. In general *casas de cambio*, or foreign-exchange bureaus, tend to give better rates than a bank for cash. They can be found throughout the city, with the highest concentrations being in touristy areas, such as Miraflores.

American Express

Lost or stolen travelers checks can be replaced here; however, they do not cash checks. They are open from 9:00 a.m. to 5:30 p.m. on Mondays through Fridays, and 9:00 a.m. to 1:00 p.m. on Saturdays. Santa Cruz 621, Miraflores, Tel: 51-1-221-8204, E-mail: amex-card@travex.com.pe.

Banco Continental

This bank chain in Lima is open from 9:00 a.m. to 6:00 p.m. on Monday through Friday, and 9:30 a.m. to 12:30 p.m. on Saturdays.

BCP

One of the more prevalent bank chains in Lima. All branches have 24-hour ATMs that give cash advances on Visa. Their bank also will change Amex, Citicorp and Visa travelers checks. They are open from 9:00 a.m. to 6:00 p.m. on Mondays through Fridays, and 9:30 a.m. to 12:30 p.m. on Saturdays.

Moneygram

If you need money wired to you, this is a good option. They are open from 10:00 a.m. to 6:30 p.m. Monday through Saturday. Alfredo Benavides 735, Miraflores, Tel: 51-1-241-2222, E-mail: moneyecpress@terra.com.pe.

Western Union

Another strong choice if you need money wired to you in Peru. There are various locations in all of the country, so you are sure to find one that is convenient for you. The best way to find the one that will work best for you is to visit their website where you can find addresses, phone numbers and hours for the different agencies. URL: www.westernunion.com.

Emergency Medical Care in Lima

The U.S. Embassy maintains a list of medical providers in Lima; although they do not officially recommend any, the list is of places used by embassy staff. Generally, the places listed will have someone on duty who speaks English. A couple of clinics they list:

Clínica San Borga:
Av. Guardia Civil 333, San Borja, Tel: 51-1-475-3141.

Clínica el Golf:
Av. Aureliano Miro Quesada, San Isidro, Tel: 51-1-264-3300.

The complete list includes specialists, including cardiologists, dentists and more. You can find the complete, up-to-date ducument here: http://lima.usembassy.gov/medical.html.

Gold's Gym Peru

With 11 locations in and around the city, Gold's Gym Peru is far more than a weight training center and suits most workout needs. Catering to all ability and exercise levels, the facilities are fully equipped, clean and modern. Equipment is in excellent and new condition, and feature Stair masters, Elliptical machines, treadmills and stationary bikes. There are also large studios for aerobic, dance and strength training classes. A sample of classes include Pilates, yoga, step aerobics, spinning, strength training, cardio kickboxing, among others. Gold's Gym Peru also has extensive weight-training equipment for both males and females. Most locations also have nutritionists, personal trainers, daycare, small cafeteria, massage services and on-site sauna. It also provides a running club and outdoor athletic excursions. Prices vary amongst clubs and member sign-up discounts are frequent. Miraflores, San Miguel, Camacho, San Isidro, Lima Norte, Las Begonias, Ovalo Higuereta, Minka-Callao, San Borja, Jesús María, Chorrillos. E-mail: miraflores@goldsgymperu.com.pe, URL: www.goldsgymperu.com.

Ibero Librerías

With some of the most helpful staff around, Ibero Librerías is a great bookstore to hunt down that hard-to-find souvenir or to simply browse around. While most titles are in Spanish, they do carry some English-language books. Stocked with a variety of literature, the store also offers exceptional travel, art, history and reference selections. If you are on the hunt for a Peruvian cookbook, you won't want to miss the collection of traditional and modern cuisine. Cookbooks always make great souvenirs, and many of these are translated in Spanish and in English within the same book. There are several locations around Lima proper, three within Miraflores. Av. Oscar Benavides 500, Tel: 51-1-242-2798.

THINGS TO SEE AND DO IN LIMA

There are enough activities in Lima to entertain the most determined sightseer. A tentative itinerary may begin with a morning stroll to one of Lima's many plazas or parks. These quiet refuges in a bustling city will ease you into a busy day, rich with Peruvian history. Surrounding these areas are landmark buildings and beautiful testaments to colonial architecture. Next, wander into a church or monastery that highlights the dominating role of religion throughout Peru's history. If religious anecdotes inspire your appetite, you will want to step into a Peruvian café to sample authentic foods from the country. Next, be sure to make time to visit one or two of the country's most extensive and fascinating museums followed by a traipse through various Inca ruins that are set against Lima's modern backdrop. Exhausted, take a quick nap and refresh yourself for an exciting evening. Enjoy a dinner of the freshest seafood available overlooking the ocean and dance the night away to the lively rhythms that define South America.

Spend a day or a week in Lima, and you will undoubtedly find yourself awed, inspired, enlightened and thoroughly entertained at every moment. Try not to miss a single activity in Lima, with its rich history, bold culture and warm people.

Lima Museums

Perhaps due to its unpleasant climate, Lima is home to numerous excellent museums. Although some of them are clustered in the old town near the Cathedral, many of the other good ones are spread out over the city, making them sometimes difficult to find. If you're stuck in Lima for a few days, chances are that you'll find a museum that will interest you. Some museums—such as the Archaeology Museum or the Larco Museum—are worth spending time in Lima for.

National Archaeology Museum (Entrance: $0.30 - $3)

This museum, whose full name is El Museo Nacional de Arqueología, Antropología, e Historia, is a must-see for history buffs visiting Lima. Like the National Museum, it provides an overview of the history of the region, mostly before the arrival of the Spanish. It is easier to navigate than the National Museum, however, and most visitors prefer it to its larger cousin. The museum oversees one of the largest collections of pre-hispanic art and relics in the world. Some of the highlights include exceptionally well-preserved mummies from the Nasca region and the Estela Raimondi, an enormous carved stone that once resided at Chavín de Huántar, a major pre-Columbian site. It is carved with snakes, animals and gods. The building that houses the museum is also beautiful and historic and is included on the tour. As not all of the exhibits are labeled in English, a guide is suggested if your Spanish is not very good. Tuesday-Saturday, 9:15 a.m. - 5 p.m., Sunday, 10 a.m.-5 p.m., Closed Mondays. Plaza Bolívar, Tel: 51-1-463-5070.

Larco Museum / Museo Larco (Entrance: $6.60)

The Museo Arqueológico Rafael Larco Herrera, commonly known as the Museo Larco or Larco Museum, is one of the most popular in Lima. Set in a gorgeous old hacienda, the museum is the private collection of Rafael Larco Herrera. It is considered by many to be the largest and most complete collection of pre-Columbian artifacts and relics in the world. It is comprised of more than 40,000 pieces of pottery and 5,000 pieces of gold and textiles.

Of particular interest is the section on erotic art and ceramics, politely set off from the rest of the exhibits by a garden. The pieces show that the early inhabitants of South America were quite uninhibited. The artifacts on display are quite interesting and occasionally humorous.

The museum is located in the neighborhood of Pueblo Libre, to the south of central Lima. As Lima museums go it is slightly expensive, but well worth a visit. Monday-Saturday, 9 a.m. - 6 p.m., Sunday, 9 a.m. - 1 p.m. Av. Bolívar 1515, Tel: 51-1-461-1835, URL: www.museolarco.org.

Museo de la Nación (Entrance: $0.30-$2)

The largest museum in Peru, the National Museum features four floors of history and exhibits in a large, sprawling building in the San Borja neighborhood of Lima. Of particular interest are the sections on pre-Spanish life in the area and the reproductions of Peru's major archaeological sites. The galleries often feature temporary exhibits as well. The museum provides a fairly complete overview of Peruvian history and culture. Tuesday - Sunday, 9 a.m. - 5 p.m., Av. Javier Prado Este 2465, Tel: 51-1-476-9875.

Museo de Oro (Entrance: $10)

The Gold Museum is considered one of Lima's premier attractions. It houses the private collection of Miguel Mujica Gallo, who spent years amassing it, often by purchasing relics from grave robbers. It features gold figures, jewelry, masks, knives and artifacts from the Inca and colonial periods. It also contains mummies, headdresses and other ancient relics.

In 2001, a huge scandal broke out. It was proven that many of the pieces in the museum were fakes. Experts had been suspicious of many of the pieces for years. The Mujica Gallo family claimed that the fakes had been purchased by mistake and that the museum now only houses genuine pieces. However there is still a cloud of skepticism that hangs over the exhibits.

Upstairs from the Gold Museum is the equally fascinating Arms museum, which houses weapons and armor from many cultures. Artifacts from Peru's history, such as items owned by the Pizarro brothers and Simón Bolívar, are also on display. You may want to do both museums as part of a tour, since the displays are not always clearly marked. Daily, 11:30 a.m. - 7 p.m. Alonso de Molina 1100, Tel: 51-1-345-1271.

Bullfighting Museum / Museo Taurino
The Museo Taurino, or Bullfighting Museum, has information on everything you could ever want to know about the art of bullfighting, comprising displays, photos, weapons, relics and more. Monday-Saturday, 9 a.m. - 4 p.m. Hualgayoc 332, Rímac, Tel: 51-1-481-1467.

Museo de los Descalzos (Entrance: $1.60)
El Museo de los Descalzos, (literally, "The Museum of the Shoeless Ones") is housed in a convent that formerly was a spiritual sanctuary for the Franciscan order. Today it contains a great deal of religious and colonial art, as well as a restored chapel with gold-covered altars, an old wine-making area and a pharmacy. The museum is quite interesting, particularly for those who wish to know more about the colonial era or the art of Peru's early history. English-speaking guides are often available. Mass is still celebrated, generally in the hours before the museum opens in the morning and after it closes at night. Tuesday-Sunday, 10 a.m. - 1 p.m. and 3 p.m. - 6 p.m. Northern end of the Alameda de los Descalzos, Tel: 51-1-481 0441.

Museo de Arte de Lima (Entrance: $2)
The Lima Art Museum has the best collection of Peruvian art in the country. The paintings cover the colonial era to the present, and there is also a selection of woodcarvings, furniture, etc. There is also a coffee shop, gift shop and movie theater. Check with the museum before you visit, as they often arrange interesting temporary exhibits. Daily, 10 a.m. - 3 p.m., closed Wednesdays. Paseo Colón 125, Tel: 51-1-423-4732, URL: museoarte.perucultural.org.pe.

Museo del Banco Central (Entrance: Free)
The Central Bank Museum has three sections: archaeology, numismatic (coins and money) and art. The archaeology section is located in the basement and has an interesting pottery collection. The currency exhibit is on the first floor and features colonial-era coins. The art exhibit on the top floor features paintings from the 19th and 20th centuries, many by Peruvian artists. Tuesday to Friday, 10 a.m. - 4 p.m., Saturday and Sunday, 10 a.m. - 1 p.m. Lampa and Ucayali, Tel: 51-1-427-6250, Fax: 51-1-427-5880, E-mail: cbakula@bcrp.gob.pe, museo@bcrp.gob.pe, URL: museobcr.perucultural.org.pe.

Museo de la Inquisición (Entrance: Free)
Located on the Plaza Bolívar, which is also home to the Peruvian Congress building, the Inquisition Museum is one of Lima's most popular and often visited museums. Housed in the building that was home to the Inquisition from 1570 to 1820, the museum has exhibits which explain the impact and importance of the Inquisition in Peru's history.

Imported from Spain in the late 16th century, the Inquisition was responsible for eliminating heresy and blasphemy in the New World. Some of their targets included Spanish Jews and their descendents, who were often accused of maintaining their practices in secret. In this museum, you can visit the lightless dungeon cells where those accused awaited judgement or punishment. It was also from this location that the public burning of heretics was ordered. Daily, 9 a.m. - 5 p.m. Plaza Bolívar.

STUDYING SPANISH IN LIMA

Academia Castellana ($220 / week, individual course)
Academia Castellana offers Spanish classes in Lima, including a variety of levels and business Spanish. Classes begin whenever the students want, and time and hours per day are flexible. Lodging is with host families or in student residences, and the academy offers organized trips and activities, such as cooking courses, volunteer opportunities, guided visits to the city center, etc. Ernesto Diez Canseco 497, Tel: 51-1-247-7054 / 51-1-444-2579, E-mail: acspanishclasses@gmail.com, URL: www.acspanishclasses.com.

EEC Spanish School ($189 / week, intensive course)
The EEC Spanish School is a professional school with tailor-made courses for different needs. They offer professional spanish courses that will train students to effectively interact and conduct busi-

ness with Latin Americans and standard Spanish courses that will help students to learn about the local culture, habits and traditions. With a minimum age of 20 and no more than six students per class, EEC provides a fun atmosphere with a focus on personal attention for each student. Immersion activities such as Spanish films, presentations, speakers, discussions and outings are also offered. Classes help to prepare students to take the DELE. There is a $30 mandatory registration fee and prices range from $18/hr for private classes to $249 for 26-hr programs. Mariano de los Santos 120, San Isidro, Tel: 51-1-442-1509, E-mail: administration@ eec-spanishschool.com, URL: http://eec-spanishschool.com/index.php.

El Sol Spanish School ($235 / week, intensive course)
A quaint, friendly Spanish language school in the heart to Miraflores, El Sol Spanish School offers a range of courses, from beginner and advanced Spanish grammar to Peruvian cooking. Salsa classes are also offered in the late afternoon, along with a variety of weekly social activities. It has a great international mix of students from Europe, Canada, Australia, New Zealand and the United States. Homestays are available, as are apartment accommodations. Grimaldo del Solar 469, Tel: 51-1-242-7763 / 241-3806; from US or Canada: 1-800-381-1806, E-mail: elsol@idiomasperu.com, URL: elsol.idiomasperu.com.

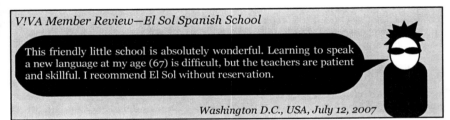

V!VA Member Review—El Sol Spanish School

This friendly little school is absolutely wonderful. Learning to speak a new language at my age (67) is difficult, but the teachers are patient and skillful. I recommend El Sol without reservation.

Washington D.C., USA, July 12, 2007

Caminante School ($200 / week, individual course)
The Caminante School has branches in several areas of Peru, including Arequipa, Ica, Cusco, Lima, Lambayeque, Puno and Trujillo. It intends to open another branch in Iquitos in the near future. They have a great variety of options for Spanish instruction and lodging; see their web site for details. The programs in Lima are more expensive than in the other cities. If you're on a budget, you may want to look into some of the different programs. Tel: 51-1-915-63835 / 51-8-425-2233 / 51-8-425-4927, URL: info@caminanteschool.org.

Conexus Language Institute ($190 / week, intensive course)
Conexus is a small school in Lima offering courses in Spanish and English. Class size varies, but never more than five students, and individual classes are available. They accept walk-ins, and are very flexible with their scheduling. Conexus is best for travelers who just want to learn Spanish, but who don't want to be tied down to a rigid schedule and don't need college credit or a diploma. Students can be housed with Peruvian families and are encouraged to go on Conexus' regularly planned excursions. Av. Paseo de la República 3195, Oficina 1002, San Isidro, Tel: 51-1-421-5642, Fax: 51-1-442-2828, E-mail: info@conexusinstitute.com, URL: http://www.conexusinstitute.com/home.htm.

Hispana Spanish Language School
Excellent school to study Spanish and speak it from the very beginning. There are extra-curricular activities such as excursions in Lima, salsa dancing and Peruvian cooking lessons and a great library with excellent bilingual books. Centrally located in the heart of Miraflores district. Calle San Martin 377 Miraflores, Tel: 51-14-463-045, E-mail: spanish.school@hispanaidiomas.com, URL: hispanaidiomas.com.

Universidad del Pacífico Centro de Idiomas
The Spanish program at the Universidad del Pacífico is a serious, rigorous course of study designed for those who really need to learn the language, such as businessmen, diplomats, etc. Courses start regularly, but run on the university schedule, not that of students. Classes

usually meet in the evening. The center also offers classes in French, Portuguese, Italian, and Mandarin Chinese. Av. Prescott 333, San Isidro, Tel: 51-1-421-1628 / 421 3483 /421 2969, E-mail: idiomas@up.edu.pe, URL: www.up.edu.pe/idiomas.

Pontífica Universidad Católica del Peru Instituto de Idiomas
The Pontífica Universidad Católica del Peru, recently celebrating its 90th birthday, is a fully accredited and prestigious Peruvian university. They offer Spanish classes to foreigners, but without the flexibility of smaller walk-in places. If you're planning on being in Lima for a while, or if you need a diploma or college credit, you may want to consider this option for learning Spanish. Camino Real 1037, San Isidro, Tel: 51-1-626-6500 / 51-1-626-6430, Fax: 51-1-442-6719, E-mail: idiomas@pucp.edu.pe, URL: http://www.idiomas.pucp.edu.pe.

S.I.I.E School
S.I.I.E School offers a wide variety of Spanish programs and courses designed for each student's individual needs, from absolute beginners to advanced (DELE Certificate and credits awarded), Spanish for careers; professionals, one to one, academic rrograms for scholars, school group cultural tours, voluntary work/ experience and homestays with and without lessons. S.I.I.E will also coordinate housing with local bed and breakfasts or hotels with some meals provided. Programs cost approximately $100 (20 hrs) with lodging and meals additional. Tel: 556-2-555-2909, E-mail: siieinfo@netline.cl, URL: http://www.studenttravel-siie-chile-peru.cl.

ICPNA Spanish School
ICPNA is much more than a simple, garden-variety walk-in Spanish school for foreigners, the sort of which are found from Cuernavaca to Santiago. This large institution offers English classes for Peruvians, cultural programs, testing prep (SATs, etc.) and more. The Spanish program can be taken monthly, with classes meeting Monday through Friday in the morning from 8:45 a.m. until 10:15 a.m. A complete Spanish course can be taken in a year. A very serious school, ICPNA has been recognized by several international organizations, and has five branches throughout Lima. Avenida Angamos Oeste 160, Miraflores, Tel: 51-1-706-7000, E-mail: postmaster@icpna.edu.pe, URL: http://www.icpna.edu.pe/ingles.

VOLUNTEERING IN LIMA
Volunteers for Peace
This Burlington, VT-based organization sends volunteers to various work-camps in Lima as well as Ayacucho, Peru. Trips average a length of three weeks. 1034 Tiffany Road, Burlington, VT, 05730, Tel: 1-802-259-2759 / 1-802-259-2922, E-mail: vfp@vfp.org, URL: www.vfp.org.

Global Volunteers
Global Volunteers provides volunteers with short-term placements working in orphanages in Lima. 375 East Little Canada Road, St. Paul, MN, 55117, USA, Tel: 1-800-487-1074 / 651-482-0915, E-mail: E-mail@globalvolunteers.org, URL: www.globalvolunteers.com.

I-to-I
I-to-I (based in the UK) offers-short term volunteer opportunities from one to twelve weeks. They also offer help in finding short-term teaching jobs abroad. Volunteer placements in Peru have included positions on archaeological digs in the past. Programs run between $1000 and $1500 average for three weeks. Woodside House, 261 Low Lane, Leeds, Yorkshire, LS18 5NY, Tel: 44-800-011-1156, E-mail: info@i-to-i.com, URL: www.i-to-i.com.

VolunTourism
VolunTourism specializes in organizing short trips to volunteer in numerous countries. Their website lists about twelve different NGO's and organizations that operate internationally, connecting volunteers with opportunities to serve in local communities. 717 Third Avenue, Chula Vista, California, USA 91910, Tel: 1-619-434-6230 / 1-619-426-6664, E-mail: vt@voluntourism.org, URL: http://voluntourism.org.

Cross Cultural Solutions

Cross Cultural Solutions offers listings of volunteer positions in education and social justice. The organization charges fees but provides in-country assistance to volunteers in exchange. 2 Clinton Place New Rochelle, New York, USA, 10801, Tel: 1-800-380-4777 / 1-914-632-0022 / 1-914-632-8494, E-mail: info@crossculturalsolutions.org, URL: www.crossculturalsolutions.org.

Earthwatch Institute

Earthwatch Institute is an environmental organization that lets volunteers and students join archaeological and conservation projects for a fee. One to three-week programs run around $1700. 3 Clock Tower Place, Suite 100, Box 75, Maynard, MA, USA, 01754, Tel: 1-800-776-0188 / 978-461-0081 / 978-461-2332, E-mail: info@earthwatch.org, URL: www.earthwatch.org.

LIMA TOURS

As a huge, thriving metropolis, Lima can be overwhelming when it comes to planning the day. There are enough museums, churches and colonial buildings to exhaust even the most ambitious tourist in town. There are many parks and plazas to explore and most are within walking distance of each other. For the history buffs, there are a handful of Inca ruins scattered around the city that oddly contrast with the more modern additions. Athletic travelers can combine their love for exercise with their love of exploration and experience any of the biking, swimming, surfing or paragliding tours in town. For the traveler who would like to sample a little of everything, careful planning will make the best of their time.

There are quite a few companies that offer tours in Lima as well as trips around Peru and it's well worth doing a little research to compare operators and individual tours. Tours outside of Lima tend to be cheaper if organized in cities closest to tour destinations. Additionally, there are travel agencies in Lima that can assist with your plans and offer advice.

Andex Adventure

Andex Adventure are not just about visiting an area; the company prefers to help travelers discover people, countrysides, wildlife, cultures, adventures and beaches. It offers tours throughout Peru, from the snowy heights around Huaraz to the jungles of Manu, of Kuélap, from the ancient ruins of Kuélap to (of course) Machu Picchu and Cusco. Avenida Paseo República 1730, Tel: 51-1-251-6530, Fax: 51-1-251-6530, E-mail: info@andex-adventure.com, URL: andex-adventure.com.

Lima Visión

Lima Visión has a decent tour offering, taking three hours to look around all of Lima, both modern and old. The tour includes the Plaza Mayor, the City Hall, the Government Palace, the Cathedral and the San Francisco church. Following the old town stint, the tour heads over to the new town, to San Isidro, visiting the Huaca Huallamarca, which is of an adobe pre-Inca style. The tour finishes up in Miraflores, in the Parque del Amor. As with many of the other tour companies, Lima Visión offers tours all over Peru. Jr. Chiclayo 444, Miraflores, Tel: 51-1-447-7710, Fax: 51-1-446-9969, E-mail: peruvisi@peruvision.com, URL: www.peruvision.com.

Enjoy Peru

Enjoy Peru offers Lima tours; in fact, they can provide a two-day "Archaeological Tour of Lima," which takes in the historical central part of the city, most of the historically important churches and religious buildings and a few museums, including the Government Palace and City Hall, the Church of Santa Domingo and the tomb of Santa Rosa, the Convent and Church of San Francisco and the Larco Herrera Museum. It also takes a trip around the areas of Miraflores and San Isidro. On the second day, the tour goes to Pachacámac, the important ancient pre-Columbian archaeological site. Tel: USA: 1-888-317-3383, URL: www.enjoyperu.com.

Contacto Lima

This tour agency specializes in tours of the city of Lima, offering both half and full-day tours of the city. It also provides tours to sites around Lima, such as Nasca and Paracas. Tel: 51-1-224-3854, E-mail: contactolima@tsi.com.pe.

The Mirabus ($12)

The only one of its kind so far in Lima, the Mirabus tour bus is highly recommended for newcomers to Lima, especially upon arriving. They offer a variety of urban tours on their open air double-decker bus, some for one hour around the historical district and some for a more inclusive three hours, going as far as the beach towns of Miraflores and Chorillos. The guide explains the history and background of many Lima landmarks, letting you know which monument, for example, was built by Gustave Eiffel, of Eiffel tower fame, or that the Palace of Justice is almost an exact duplicate of the one in Brussels. Private excursions are also available. However, they only offer tours in Spanish. Plaza San Martín and Jr. Quilca, Tel: 51-1-476-4213 / 51-1-242-6699 / 51-1-243-7629, E-mail: reservas@mirabusperu.com.

Info Peru

Officially a travel agency, capable of booking travel via bus or plane, as well as stays in any variety of hotels, hostels, lodges and cabins, Info Peru also serves, completely free of charge, as an information outlet for anyone who comes by to seek out virtually any information having to do with travel in Peru: where to go, what to do, and whom to contact. They boast 15 years experience in the business and fluency in both English and French. Jr. de la Unión 1066 (and Belén), Office 102, URL: www.infoperu.com.

Fertur Peru Travel

Fertur Peru has a well-established reputation as one of the best travel agencies and tour operators in the country. A four-day excursion to Machu Picchu can be easily arranged through them for as low as $230. A three-day trip from Iquitos to the Amazon rainforest can go as low as $185, and two nights in Lake Titicaca from Puno, in a room with a private bath, as low as $94. Siduith Ferrer, owner and founder, is devoted to eco-friendly and sustainable travel in Latin America. Open Monday to Saturday: 9 a.m. - 7 p.m. Jr. Junín 211, Tel: 51-1-427-2626; 427-1958, TeleFax: 51-1-428-3247, USA and Canada: 1-877-247-0055, UK: 020-3002-3811.

Kolibri Expeditions ($99 - 400 / day)

Based in Lima, Kolibri Expeditions provides birding trips to all corners of Peru and South America. Owned and operated by ex-pat, veteran bird lover guide and biologist from University of Stockholm, Sweden, Gunnar Engblom, Kolibri offers a variety of birding tours for both amateurs and serious field birders. If you want to see rare and exotic birds, or just a vibrant variety of birds, Engblom and his knowledgeable staff can make it happen. The company works with local communities so the tours will help conserve the habitat and lead to sustainable development. With a range of comfort levels--some tours sleep in hostels and others are more safari-style with tents--there are trips for every kind of bird and wildlife connoisseur. Groups can organize to have customized trips. Urban birding in Lima and whale watching are also available. Calle Luis Arias Schreiber 192, oficina 300, Urb. La Aurora, Miraflores, E-mail: admin@kolibriexpeditions.com, URL: www. kolibriexpeditions.com.

LIMA LODGING

With approximately 50 distinct districts, each neighborhood in Lima offers varying accommodations to suit individual travelers. Depending on the atmosphere and price range you are looking for, there are multiple hotels in Lima that will suit your tastes.

For history-loving travelers who want to devote their time to exploring colonial buildings and historic plazas, the Lima Centro neighborhood has everything from cheap, clean hostels to high-end hotels overlooking the city.

For business travelers interested in a quiet, luxurious stay, consider San Isidro, Lima's business and residential area. The area has many restaurants and bars to enjoy late into the evening and accommodations tend to cater to the middle and upper class.

For cultured travelers interested in delicious restaurants, happening clubs and excellent shopping, consider staying at one of Lima's hotels in the Miraflores neighborhood. This area sits atop the cliffs overlooking the beach, is residential and is packed with great restaurants, clubs and shops. For artistic, fun-loving night owls, head straight to the more popular neighborhood of Barranco. The architecture and sights in this area appeal to the world's traveling artists. Inspiring by day and wild by night, Barranco is up-and-coming with some of the most friendly and colorful chic hostels and budget accommodations in Lima.

Scattered amongst the more well-known districts are the smaller neighborhoods of Chorrillos and Pueblo Libre. These neighborhoods tend to be a little less touristy. Both have lodging options that range from inexpensive to high end.

CENTRAL LIMA

The heart of Lima is found in its historic center. Once an Inca city of some importance, Lima became a major city under the Spanish, who decided to establish a port here. Although their first efforts at building a city on the site were destroyed in a 1746 earthquake, the city was rebuilt and today is home to some of the most impressive architecture in the Americas.

Any visitor to Lima will probably visit the historical center at some point. All of the important churches, monasteries, and plazas are located there, as well as many of the most interesting museums. There are also a number of hotels and hostals, the most interesting of which are stately colonial homes that have been converted to hotels. The backpacker set in particular will find Central Lima's hotels affordable and unique.

CENTRAL LIMA HISTORY

Lima's central colonial district is the most historic in the whole city and one of the most historic in all of Latin America. Since Lima was established in 1535 by Francisco Pizarro, the center has been a site of great importance.

Pizarro founded Lima as the City of Kings on January 18, 1535, and although no kings ever visited during its early history, it was home to 40 viceroys during the colonial era. The central square (Plaza de Armas) was laid out by Pizarro himself, with the cathedral on one side, the Cabildo (town hall) on another side and Pizarro's own house on another. Pizarro lived in what is now known as the Presidential Palace until his death in 1541; he was hacked down in the street by rival conquistadores. His remains are in the cathedral.

After Pizarro, Lima continued to be very important historically. Lima became the seat of one of only two Spanish viceroyalties in the New World; the other was in Mexico City. (A third was added in Buenos Aires later.) As such, it was the political and spiritual hub of Spanish South America for centuries.

Spanish civil and religious authorities set up shop in Lima, ruling the part of the Spanish Empire that stretched from Quito to Chile. The discovery of rich mineral deposits in parts of Bolivia and Peru meant that a great deal of wealth flowed into Lima, and some of the old colonial homes still reflect this.

CENTRAL LIMA SERVICES
Teleperu Telephone

The Teleperu telephone cabinas provide an inexpensive and expedient manner to call outside the country: the USA and Canada are only 25 céntimos a minute, or 9 cents US, while Spain, Italy, and Japan are at 12 cents, and the rest of the world at 20 cents. Calling within South American and within Peru is also available. These cabinas can be found throughout most tourist-trafficked areas of Peru, and usually operate from 8:00 a.m. to 10:00 p.m.

Correo Central de Lima (Free)

Not just a post office, this very big and ornate edifice behind the Palace of the Governor in the historical center is worth visiting simply for appreciating its architecture. The building also serves as a historical museum, complete with displays of notable stamps. They detail the importance of the Peruvian postal service as a hub of communications technology from its founding in the 19th century, when it provided the first telegraph and later radio services to the country. The interior is divided by a walkway under elegant metal arches. Be prepared for merchants who will very aggressively try to get you to purchase the postcards that they have for sale. Open 8 a.m. - 8:45 p.m. (4:00 p.m. on Sunday). Pasaje Piura, next to the Palacio de Gobierno. Tel: 51-1-533-2005 / 533-5152.

Belmundo en Línea

This particular Internet station is clean, cool and well-ventilated, with modern computers, large monitors, webcams and headsets with microphones, making calls via Skype and other software programs possible. It also offers scanning and other copying services, as well as printing. The cost is about 45 cents an hour, and there is a minor offering of juice, snacks and stationary supplies. The only drawback is that their well-used keyboards wear out frequently, so you might find yourself having to type with extra-tactical tenacity. Av. Petit Tours 3006 and Javier Prado.

Photo by Freyja Ellis

Diana Net and Tattoo Parlour

Diana Net could be considered an attractive option for travelers considering two different purchases: an hour's worth of surfing the 'net and a tattoo. That is, this Internet cabina on the mercantile Jirón de la Reunión offers both, though the owner, Augusta, said she would prefer not to work on you while you are instant messaging. All the computers come with webcams and microphones. International long-distance calling services are also available. The cost of time on the computer is only a sol an hour. Jr. de la Union 518, Suites 203 and 204, Tel: 51-1-428-2793, E-mail: Blackline_tatto@hotmail.com.

DJ Tattoo Machines

Leave Peru as a new you--literally. With the exchange rate favoring the dollar over the sol, one to three, go ahead and put that Chinese dragon on your thigh or the Sun God Viracocha on your chest, or simply your mom's name on your arm, at an exceptionally low cost but very skillfully and professionally done by owner and tattoo pro David Manuel Fernández. The process is sterile and hygienic, and David is committed to a solid rapport with his all clients, ensuring a harmony between what you want and the artist can provide. The staff will work on literally any requested area. Cuadra 5 Jr. de la Unión, Galería Espadero, Sótano 103, Tel: 51-1-972-93-218, E-mail: dmfc8@hotmail.com.

Lima Municipal Tourism Information Office (Free)

Most visitors to the historical center of Lima will be pleased to take advantage of Lima's Tourism Municipal Information Office, located on the Plaza de Armas and in between some of the best restaurants in the area. With a concierge who can communicate in English as well as Spanish, this is one of the best first places to go before you start taking advantage of Lima's urban and coastal niceties. The office provides any number of brochures, maps and refer-

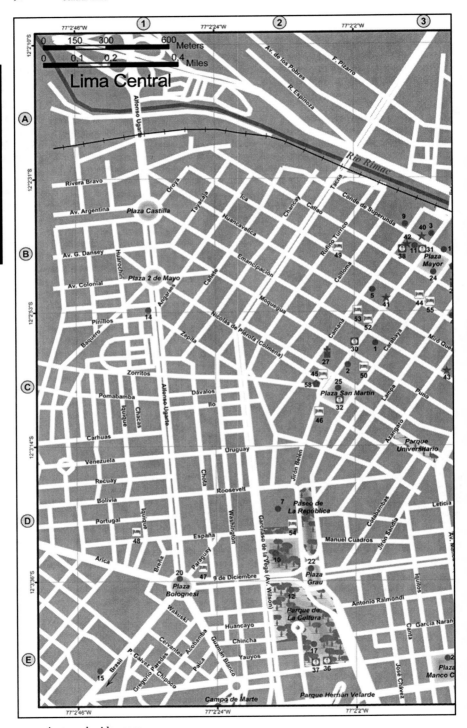

Activities ●
1 Almacén Metro C3
2 Arte en Cuero Sánchez C2
3 Casa de Aliaga B3
4 Casa Goyeneche C3
5 Casa Riva-Agüero B3
6 Casa Torre Tagle C3
7 Centro Cívico D2
8 Cerro de San Cristóbal A3
9 Convento de Santo Domingo B3
10 Italian Art Museum D2
11 Librería El Virrey B3
12 Museo de Arte de Lima E2
13 Museo de la Inquisición B4
14 Museo de la Nación B1
15 Museo Larco A1
16 Palacio de Gobierno B3
17 Parque de la Exposición E2
18 Parque de la Muralla B4
19 Plaza Bolívar B4
20 Plaza Bolognesi D1
21 Plaza de Acho A4
22 Plaza Grau D2
23 Plaza Manco Cápac E3
24 Plaza Mayor B3
25 Plaza San Martín C2

Church ⛪
26 Catedral de Lima B3
27 Iglesia de Jesús C2
28 Iglesia de San Pedro C3
29 Iglesia San Francisco B4

Eating 🍽
30 Aero Club del Peru C2
31 Consentino Gourmet B3
32 El Estadio Fútbol Club C2
33 Jimmy's Baguetería C4
34 La Catedral Restaurant and Bar B3
35 La Muralla B4
36 Laguna Dorada E2
37 Palacio de Sancochado E2
38 Pardo's Chicken B3

Services ★
39 Belmundo en Línea C4
40 Correa Central de Lima B3
41 Diana Net and Tattoo Parlour B3
42 Lima Municipal Tourism Information Office B3
43 Teleperu Telephone C3

Sleeping 🛏
44 El Balcón Dorado B3
45 Gran Hotel Bolívar C2
46 Hostal Belén C2
47 Hostal de las Artes D1
48 Hostal Iquique D1
49 Hostal Roma B2
50 Hotel Continental C3
51 Hotel España B4
52 Hotel Inka Path C3
53 Hotel Kamana B3
54 Hotel Lima Sheraton and Casino D2
55 Hotel Maury B3
56 The Wiracocha Hotel B3

Tour Operator ♠
57 Fertur Peru Travel B3
58 Mirabus C2

LIMA

ences about where to go and what to see--not only in Lima, but throughout Peru. Open from 10 a.m. - 6 p.m. daily. Jr. de la Union 300 / Jr. Conde de Superunda 177, Tel: 51-1-315-1300, E-mail: turismo@munlima.gob.pe, URL: www.munlima.gob.pe.

THINGS TO SEE AND DO IN CENTRAL LIMA

The colonial center is the heart of Lima, and a can't-miss for any visitor. It is where you'll find the best museums, restored homes and city parks, as well as numerous good hotels and restaurants. There are many churches and other religious buildings, plus good shopping.

Plaza de Armas

Inca temples once stood here. Spanish conquistador Francisco Pizarro was assassinated here. Accused sorcerers were brutally punished around the square in the 17th century. Throughout history, the Plaza de Armas, or Plaza Mayor, has been a focal point of Lima, with its cathedrals, ornate buildings and government palace. Now, it is a UNESCO World Heritage Site. Plaza de Armas spans four large blocks, with a park in the center. A bronze fountain with an angel perched on top blowing a trumpet is its centerpiece. It's also the oldest remaining structure, created in 1650.

On the north end of Plaza de Armas is the Palacio de Gobierno (governor's palace), which is now home to Peru's president and is open for tours. Visitors can see a traditional changing of the guard (Monday through Saturday, at 11:30 a.m.), but guards are always on duty here if you just want a dose of presidential (and military) ambiance. Catedral de Lima is home to a religious museum and what are believed to be Pizarro's remains, which are encased in a casket. The Iglesia de Merced dominates another block and the main post office is right off the plaza. Several other historic buildings and churches are within a few blocks, including the San Francisco monastery and church. Catacombs are its claim to fame and open for tours.
At night, hundreds of people stroll the park and sit on the church steps to experience the culture. There's also an information office here to get tips on the next sightseeing stop. Located about two blocks south of the Río Rímac.

Lima Cathedral / Catedral de Lima (Entrance: $1 - 1.40)

The Lima Cathedral, known simply as La Catedral in the city, is a highlight of any visit. The first stone of the cathedral was laid by Francisco Pizarro, the Spanish conquistador who defeated the Inca. Ironically, Pizarro would be laid to rest in the same cathedral less than ten years later, when he was murdered in the streets during the brutal warring among Spanish factions that followed the fall of the Inca. There are 15 smaller chapels within the larger cathedral structure, each of which is dedicated to a different saint or religious figure. The cathedral is famous for the ornately carved choir stalls and several impressive paintings. There is a museum which contains sacred items and relics as well as a collection of religious paintings, mostly from the colonial era. The museum is open 9 a.m.-4:30 p.m. daily except Sunday, and Saturday from 10 a.m. to 4:30 p.m. Entrance to the museum costs 5 soles / $1.60. Catedral de Lima is open Monday through Friday 9 a.m. to 4:30 p.m. and Saturday 10 a.m. to 4:30 p.m. Admission is $1.40 (4.50 nuevo sols) for adults and $1 for kids (3 nuevo sols). Call 51-1-427-9647.

Palacio de Gobierno (Free)

On the northeast side of the Plaza de Armas, the Government Palace is one of the city's architectural delights. The home of the president was built in the 1920s and 30s in several phases by several architects, and was once the home of Marquis Francisco Pizarro, founder of the city of Lima. The mostly baroque style is reminiscent of Peruvian colonial art. There is a ceremonial changing of the guard every day at noon worth seeing, and a free guided tour of the palace that must be arranged 48 hours in advance at the Office of Public Relations around the corner. Plaza de Armas. Monday - Friday, 9 a.m. - 4.30 p.m. (closed for lunch from 1 -2 p.m). A tour of the presidential palace is free but reservations are required through the Office of Public Relations, Jr. de la Unión, Plaza Pizarro. Call 51-1-311-3908.

San Francisco (Entrance: $1.60)

San Francisco is a sixteenth-century church and convent located in central Lima. Visitors can stroll around the gorgeous courtyards and marvel at the woodwork, tiles and paintings that adorn the inside of the convent. One highlight is the catacombs, a public cemetery where bodies were stacked like wood and allowed to decompose before being stored elsewhere. Also, look for the painting of the last supper in which the disciples are eating cuy, or guinea pig, a traditional Andean dish. Part of the San Francisco convent has been set aside as a museum (admission: 5 soles / $1.60, open 10 a.m.- 5:45 p.m. daily). It houses an impressive collection of colonial and republican era paintings and religious art, such as carved crosses, urns, etc. The museum prides itself on its collection of paintings by Francisco Zurbarán, a well known artist. Aficionados of colonial or religous art will enjoy the museum. San Francisco is located in central Lima, only about two blocks away from the Plaza Mayor and the Cathedral.

The San Francisco Catacombs

This Franciscan church and monastery is one of the most haunting (almost literally) and memorable sites in all of Lima. Originally constructed in 1546, it is one of the oldest churches in South America. It also served as the first official Catholic cemetery in Lima, at a time when the dead were laid to rest in catacombs beneath the church, itself an echo of an old Roman custom. You will get to visit the catacombs and view the hundreds of centuries-old bones and scores of skulls as part of the guided tour. The church also has one of the oldest and most historically significant libraries in the Americas and dramatic collections of religious and secular art, including renaissance-era tiles imported from Spain. Plaza San Francisco, Jirón Ancash and Lampa, Tel: 51-1-426-7377 / 427-1381, ext. 111, Fax: 01-427-4831, E-mail: informes@museocatacumbas.com, URL: www.museocatacumbas.com.

Plaza de Acho

The Plaza de Acho was founded in 1766 by the Viceroy Amat and stands proudly as the primary bullring of Lima. It is also considered the oldest in South America. Various celebrations are held here, such as the Señor de los Milagros Fair. The Museo Taurino is nearby. The bullring is made of adobe and wood and has survived earthquakes for centuries. Tuesday - Sunday, 10 a.m. - 6 p.m. Jr. Hualgayoc 332, Tel: 51-1-481-1467.

Cerro de San Cristóbal

A large cross at the summit of a 409-meter (1,342 feet) high hill, this attraction provides visitors a great view of Lima extending out to the sea. The cross itself, erected in 1928, supplanted various predecessors, beginning with a wooden cross planted by Francisco Pizarro in 1535 to honor the "miraculous" victory of his 500 troops against an army of 25,000 Incan resistors to Spanish domination. An interpretive museum offers more detail of San Cristóbal's history. It is now also the site an annual religious pilgrimage. Any number of touring vans in front of the municipal building will take you there for five soles, which comes to about $1.70. There are any number of vans leaving the Plaza del Gobierno in downtown Lima that will take you there.

Parque de la Cultura / Parque de la Exposición (Free)

Featuring some of the most exquisite architecture in Lima, the Parque de la Cultura downtown is a tribute to Lima's urban planners in the 19th century, when it was conceived and built in 1868 as the Parque de la Exposición, as it is still referred to by many locals. Its mix of fountains, Victorian houses and modern art make this a popular favorite for Lima families and lovers. It is also home to two theatre companies that showcase cutting-edge work for both children and adults. Currently, and perhaps as a way of reducing crime and litter, only one or two of its high-iron gates are open at any time. Avenida Wilson and 28 de Julio.

Italian Art Museum / Museo de Arte Italiano

Only a short distance from the Parque de la Exposición, the Museo de Arte Italiano (Italian Art Museum) is a pleasant detour into Renaissance culture, complete with a neo-classical building and well-manicured front yard that evokes 16th-century Rome. Designed by Milanese architect Gaetano Moretti and donated by Peru's Italian community to commemorate the centennial of Peru's independence, it features a combination of contemporary and classical art, sculptures, paintings and furniture, as well as works by local artists. Open daily, 9 a.m. - 2:30 p.m. Paseo de la República 250.

Casa Torre Tagle (Free)

One of the oldest and most accomplished expressions of Spanish colonialism, the Casa Torre Tagle merits a visit. It is named after the Marquis Torre Tagle, a former treasurer of the Spanish Armada. Built in 1735, this is one of the last examples of Baroque design found in the Americas, with imperial staircases, ballrooms and tiling that alludes to the influence of the earlier Moroccan conquest of Spain. A gilded, 16th-century carriage is also on display. The coat of arms itself was designed by the Marquis. Its very ornate balconies and stone carvings on the outside evoke all the grandiose presumption of the Spanish empire. As headquarters for the Ministry of Foreign Affairs, public access is limited to the courtyards. From the Plaza de Armas, head west on Jirón Wiese, then left on Jirón Ucayali. Jirón Ucayali 363, between Jirón Azangara and Jirón Lampa, Tel: 51-1-311-2400.

Casa de Aliaga

Casa de Aliaga, or the Aliaga Home, is a fascinating home and museum. Jerónimo de Aliaga was one of Francisco Pizarro's most trusted lieutenants during the exploration and conquest of Peru, and he was rewarded in 1535 with a huaca, or Indian temple, which he converted into a home. In places, the original stonework is still visible. The home has since remained in the Aliaga family for an astonishing 17 generations. Today it is a restored colonial home, and features a series of rooms that represent life in Lima in the 16th, 17th, and 18th centuries. Casa de Aliaga is not open to the public: all visits must be arranged beforehand through Lima tours. Tel: 51-1-424-9066 / 7560.

Casa Goyeneche (Free)

Across the street from the Casa Torre Tagle, is the Casa Goyeneche, also known as the Casa Rada, constructed 40 years later. These side-by-side buildings provide a striking opportunity to observe the shift from early 18th-century Baroque to the late-18th century, somewhat sparer, style of Rococo. By any standard, however, its carefully carved balconies are models of elegance. The building is now under the auspices of Peru's Banco de Crédito. From the Plaza de Armas go west from Jirón Wiese to Jirón Ucayali. Turn left and walk two blocks. Jr. Ucayali 358, Tel: 51-1-349-0606 / 2349.

Parque de la Muralla

This new park, complete with a track for children to cycle and a pedestrian walkway, sits on the banks of the Río Rímac. During its construction diggers unearthed the remains of 500-year-old city walls that were once meant to repel both the rising river and Dutch pirates. A small museum on the site explains some of the history of the wall and the city of Lima. There are also modern restaurants and tourist shops. It is clearly designed for families with children, but even on your own, it is a surprisingly pleasant experience, and worth visiting if you are already in the Historical Center. Avenida Abancay and Jirón Amazonas, URL: www.serpar.munlima.gob.pe.

Casa Riva-Agüero (Entrance: $0.70)

Twenty-seven-rooms big, the Casa Riva-Agüero is yet another echo of a distant past in which the rich and powerful built large homes as tributes to their own hubris. The last owner, Don José de la Riva-Agüero, at least had the good sense to donate the building to Peru's Pontifica Catholic University. It is now home to both a folk-themed Museum of Popular Art and a historical library, and at any given moment features some interesting scientific or cultural exhibit. Its colonial balconies and courtyard are worth looking at themselves. The house is open Tuesday through Saturday from 10 a.m. to 1 p.m. and 2 to 7:30 p.m.; admission costs 2 soles ($0.70). Camaná 459, Tel: 51-1-626-2000, E-mail: matp@pucp.edu.pe, URL: www.pucp.edu.pe/ira.

Plaza San Martín

Plaza de San Martín is one of the largest and most impressive city squares in Lima. Built in 1921 and named for José de San Martín, a hero of South American independence, the plaza is paved with stones and decorated with antique-looking lights and benches. There is an impressive stature of San Martín in the center of the park. On one side of the plaza is the seen-better-days Gran Hotel Bolívar. The Teatro Colón and El Club Nacional are also located on the plaza at the end of Jiron Bolognesi, near La Punta in the Callao neighborhood.

Iglesia de La Merced

One of the oldest churches in all of South America, founded in 1535 by Fray Miguel de Orenes, who was reputed to be 110 years old at the time, the Iglesia de la Merced features a very elaborate, impressive façade. Inside, the neoclassic altar is home to a Virgin of Mercy, which was adopted in 1823 as patroness of the Peruvian Army. Parts have been added or reconstructed after earthquakes, resulting in an interesting hodgepodge of styles. Open daily from 8 a.m. - noon and again from 5 p.m. - 8 p.m. It is located not far from the central square. Jirón de la Unión 621.

Iglesia de San Pedro (Free)

A stunning church built by the Jesuits starting in the 16th century, St. Peter's Church is one of Lima's best-known landmarks. It is now a major visitor destination, as it features an impressive collection of fascinating colonial art. This church was built over the course of 200 years and as such contains a mish-mash of techniques and styles making it of particular interest to architecture students. Jr. Ucayali at Jr. Azángaro, Lima.

Iglesia de Jesús, Maria y José (Free)

Although this smallish church doesn't look like much from the outside, inside the Baroque interior is considered one of the best in Lima. It's worth a look if you're nearby. Jr. Camaná and Jr. Moquegua.

Convento de Santo Domingo (Entrance: $1)

Two saints for the price of one! The remains of Lima's two saints, Santa Rosa de Lima and San Martín de Porres, rest forever at the Convento de Santo Domingo. Like other religious buildings in Lima, the convent was built over a long period of time and reflects varying architectural styles and movements. A very popular place to visit for Limeños and travelers alike, it is well worth checking out. Monday - Saturday, 9 - 11 a.m. and 3 - 6 p.m., Sunday, 9 a.m. - 1 p.m. Conde de Superunda and Camaná.

Shopping
Palacio de la Esmeralda

According to legend, the Egyptian goddess Isis wore the emerald. It was later valued by the Romans for its calming, peaceful qualities. The green gem is also associated with good luck and cosmic energy. Along with gold, it helped build the Spanish empire. At Palacio de la Esmeralda you can pick out an exquisitely polished and mounted sample of this valued rock, presented on rings, amulets, bracelets, necklaces and earrings, and shaped in a variety of forms: heart, tear, oval, square or simply round. The creative designs include incorporations of Incan motifs. Palacio de la Esmeralda also sells other high quality folk art. Plaza de Armas. Pasaje Santa Rosa 119, Tel: 51-1-426-7432, URL: www.emeraldsandgems.com.

Arte en Cuero Sánchez

Another great bargain for tourists, here is your chance to get custom-made, personally designed leather goods at prices that would be cheap even for vinyl. A top-notch leather jacket can be tailored for less than $60. Owner Lourdes Sánchez and her expert staff can also fashion such suede and/or leather items as hats, pants, skirts, belts, wallets, handbags, ties and even undergarments, in a variety of tones, shades, cuts and zippers – in three days or less. Jirón de la Unión 835, Tel: 51-1-427-3951 / 520-8352.

Feria Manos Artesanas

Just outside the north entrance to the Parque de la Exposición is your opportunity to sample a tradition that pre-dates Peru itself: the folk bazaar. Under a bright yellow and red tent, this event sponsored by a variety of indigenous retail and cultural associations is a colorful, sometimes gaudy spectacle of folk art and services. Which is to say, beyond the crafts, you can also have your future divined or your back massaged. There are also a number of food vendors selling shish kabobs and ice cream, and even one restaurant, the Plazuela de los Artesanos, with indoor and outdoor seating, the latter being recommended due to the warm weather. Daily, 9 a.m. - 11 p.m. Plaza de los Artesanos, Avenida 28 de Julio, Tel: 51-1-424-1937.

Librería El Virrey

This handsome bookshop in the historical center has a larger and more cosmopolitan selection than most in Lima. It is one of the few that stocks both foreign language books and magazines. El Virrey also offers a variety of useful maps and guides. It is open every day, early to late, and takes all credit cards. Pasaje los Escribanos 107-115, Tel: 51-1-427-5080, E-mail: libreria@elvirrey.com, URL: www.elvirrey.com.

Palacio de las Maletas

With a name that translates literally into the Palace of Suitcases, it offers exactly what it promises: total luggage lunacy. Leather, canvas, plastic? Briefcases, suitcases? With wheels, without? Portfolio, travel bag? Backpack, rucksack, knapsack? Duffel bag, satchel, wallet, handbag, purse? They also promise to reconstruct and repair all suitcases in accordance with the highest standards of quality. They are the exclusive representatives in Peru of the Airliner, Pagani and Arena Milano brands. Daily, 9 a.m. - 9 p.m. Jr. Junín 405, Tel: 51-1-427-9671 / 427-3278.

Almacén Metro

There are any numbers of stores along Jirón de la Reunión selling clothes, food and office supplies, but you might prefer to cut to the chase and simply stop at the massive Metro, occupying an entire block of Avenida Cusco between Calles Carabaya and Lampa. Part of the Almacenes Metro chain, one of the most extensive in Latin America, this superstore is your Wal-Mart south of the equator. There is a large supermarket downstairs, a food court upstairs, and everywhere else all you need for just about everything. Av. Cusco, between Lampa and Carabaya.

CENTRAL LIMA LODGING

There are many advantages and disadvantages to staying in Central Lima. The disadvantages include much more noise than other parts of the city, smog and pollution, lack of parking and the general chaos that characterizes the downtown centers of many of Latin America's largest cities. On the plus side, you'll be staying in the historical center of one of the New World's oldest and most important cities. You'll be close to important historical structures and places as well as some of Lima's best museums and an assortment of restaurants. There are a variety of hotels to choose from, the most interesting of which are the converted colonial mansions. These vary greatly in quality, cleanliness, comfort and cost, so if you're interested in staying at one, shop around. They tend to have a lot of character: crooked, creaky floorboards, maze-like floor plans, and no two rooms exactly alike. The only general rule in the area is that you'll pay more for a room with a private bathroom.

BUDGET
Hotel España (Rooms: $3.50 - 17)

Located on the same block as the San Francisco church and only a couple of blocks from the main city plaza, Hotel España is a boisterous, fun hostel favored by many international backpackers. Check out the rooftop garden and café: they keep interesting birds and other animals there. The dorm-style rooms are among the cheapest in Lima. Bring your own lock to use one of their small lockers to store your things. Jr. Azángaro 105, Tel: 51-1-428-5546, URL: www. hotelespanaperu.com.

Hotel Inka Path (Rooms: $6 - 39)

Very conveniently located on the Jr. de la Reunión, the long and very mercantile walkway linking the Plaza San Martín with the Plaza de Gobierno, Hotel Inka Path offers fresh newness—it is less than a year old—and high quality but low-cost rooms. The rooms themselves, inside a refurbished old building, have ample space (and very high ceilings). They all come equipped with cable TV and hot running water. Continental breakfast and free internet access come as part of the package. Jr. de la Unión 654, Tel: 51-1-426-1919 / 426-9302, E-mail: gerencia@inkapath.com, URL: www.inkapath.com.

The Wiracocha Hotel (Rooms: $9)

For very undiscriminating travelers, the Wiracocha Hotel has one advantage: its proximity to the Plaza de Armas and all the other attractions in the Historical Center. Apart from that, Wiracocha is about as minimalist as a low-cost lodge in Peru can offer: rooms with or without bathrooms, lacking shower curtains. There is no electric fan and no television (though few people would miss the latter), and the rooms, while not filthy, could be described charitably as "institutional." Jr. Junín 284, Tel: 51-1-427-1178.

Hostal de las Artes (Rooms: $9 - 24, Dorm: $5)

The Hostal de las Artes is located in Lima's historical center, not far from Paseo Colón and Plaza Bolognesi. The hostel itself is in a nicely restored 19th-century home, most of which is relatively original (their website points out that their plumbing and hot water system have been modernized). They offer an array of lodging options in different rooms, such as single with bath, single without bath, double with bath, double without, etc. Whatever option you need, their rates are among the lowest in Lima. Rates are tax-free for foreigners. Jr. Chota 1460, Tel: 51-1-433-0031, E-mail: artes@terra.com.pe, URL: arteswelcome.tripod.com.

El Lava (Rooms: $15)

Near the historic Plaza San Martin, of which the rooms provide a view, this is one of the best deals in Lima. It offers nearly first class-hotel rooms at hostel rates. This was in fact, once upon a time, one of Lima's premier hotels. It is still well-maintained and, for the price, you not only get your own room, but a private bath, electric fan, cable TV and a continental breakfast included. The rooms themselves are clean and fresh. The El Lava hotel also comes with its own bar and restaurant. Av. Nicolás de Piérola 850, Tel: 51-1-242-5860 / 339-0545, E-mail: hplazareservas@terra.com.pe.

Hostal Belén (Rooms: $15 - 20)

If you can book a room in this former military officers' club turned hostel and restaurant, consider yourself lucky: it has only ten rooms. Rooms come with private bathrooms, hot running water and cable TV, and all in an elegant, classy environment. The hotel has its own cafeteria, and is located in one of Peru's most attractive areas (in front of Plaza San Martín on Av. Nicolás Piérola) Guests have access to theatres, taverns and a generally exciting nightlife. Laundry, banking and internet services are ubiquitous throughout the neighborhood. Av. Nicolás de Piérola 953, Tel: 51-1-427-7391, E-mail: ryexport2000@yahoo.es.

Hostal Roma (Rooms: $10 - 40)

The well-regarded Hostal Roma is something of a Lima institution and has been in business for 35 years. Travelers can say they slept in a converted mansion that dates from 1892, located mere blocks away from the central square, cathedral and other points of interest. Hostal Roma has 36 rooms, all of which are singles, doubles or triples. During high season rates may go up, and they suggest you make reservations ahead of time through their website. Jr. Ica 326, Tel: 51-1-427-7572, URL: www.hostalroma.8m.com.

Mami Panchita (Rooms: $10 - 40)

Hostal Mami Panchita, located in the San Miguel district, is highly rated by past visitors. With only about 15 rooms, Mami Panchita is small, neat and comfortable. The owners speak Spanish, English and Dutch. Airport transfers available for an additional cost. Av. Federico

Gallesi 198, San Miguel, Tel: 51-1-263-7203, Fax: 51-1-263-0749, E-mail: raymi_travels@perusat.net.pe, URL: www.bed42.com/mamipanchita.

MID-RANGE
Hotel Kamana (Rooms: $28 - 60)
Hotel Kamana is located one block from the pedestrian street Jr. de la Unión, which is packed with restaurants, cafes, internet, shops and more. Important tourist sites can be visited by a short walking tour and the airport is just 30 minutes from the hotel. The hotel offers pleasant simple, double, triple and matrimonial rooms that come with cable TV, security box, telephone with national and international long distance access, a private bathroom and 24-hour hot water. Other services include the Mr. Koala Restaurant (serving traditional Creole cuisine and international dishes), the Koala Bar, WiFi internet service, foreign currency exchange, tourist information, laundry service, taxi service and free luggage storage. English and French are spoken. Jr. Camaná 547, Tel: 51-1-426-7204, E-mail: reservas@hotelkamana.com, URL: www.hotelkamana.com.

El Balcón Dorado (Rooms: $30 - 60)
This bright little hotel offers a range of accommodations for backpackers, students and budget travelers. Rooms are furnished with cable TV, private bathrooms and hot water 24 hours a day. The hotel also has a travel desk, telephone/fax facilities, smoking rooms, restaurant, laundry, internet access, 24-hour reception and luggage storage. Breakfast and linens are included. Credit cards are accepted and airport pickup is available. You can check in any time of the day. Jr. Ucayali 199, Tel: 51-1-427-6028, E-mail: balcondorado@hotmail.com.

HIGH-END
Gran Hotel Bolívar (Rooms: $50 - 150)
Conveniently located on the Plaza de San Martín, the Gran Hotel Bolívar is a stately, elegant white building that was first built in 1924. It was specifically constructed to accommodate visiting heads of state and dignitaries who were coming to Lima to celebrate the 100-year anniversary of the pivotal battle of Ayacucho, and it shows. Arched doorways, crystal chandeliers and tasteful rooms and corridors abound. There are several large salons for special events such as meetings and weddings. Their list of previous guests includes many presidents and leaders of Latin American countries, as well as Ernest Hemingway, Orson Welles and even the Rolling Stones. Although expensive by old town standards, the room rates are surprisingly reasonable for such a historic and well-located building. Mid-range travelers may want to consider upgrading for a night. Breakfast is included in the rates. Jr. de la Unión 958, Tel: 51-1-619-7171, Fax: 51-1-619-7170, E-mail: reservas@granhotelbolivarperu.com, URL: http://www.granhotelbolivarperu.com.

Hotel Maury (Rooms: $70 - 130)
Hotel Maury was one of the best-known hotels in Peru for most of the second half of the 20th century. They closed their doors during the 90s, but reopened in 2000 with a completely redone interior. The hotel offers all the services of an upscale hotel such as internet, air conditioning, room service and private parking. Jr. Ucayali 201, corner of Jr. Carabaya, Tel: 51-1-428-8188.

Hotel Lima Sheraton and Casino (Rooms: $72 - 275)
The Sheraton Lima is one of the finest hotels in the city and almost certainly the best luxury hotel in the historic district. It is in a modern, stately building with 431 rooms and features all of the amenities you would expect from a five-star hotel: comfortable rooms, good service, fine dining, a spa and more. The price is competitive with other hotels in the city in the same class. A good option for those who want to be close to the old town without sacrificing any comfort or luxury. As the name implies, there is also a casino on the premises. Av. Paseo de la República 170, Tel: 51-1-315-5000, Fax: 51-1-315-5015, E-mail: reservas@sheraton.com.pe, URL: www.sheraton.com.pe.

CENTRAL LIMA RESTAURANTS

As in the rest of Lima, there are plenty of diverse and great tasting options for every budget in Central Lima. The streets that are most populated with restaurants happen to be Pasaje Olaya, on the Plaza de Armas, and between Jr. de la Unión and Jr. Carabaya. Jr. Carabaya is a small pedestrian walkway that sees a lot of businessmen during lunch hour. Prices are a little higher in this area.

Cocolat Café

This chic and attractive spot on the Plaza de Armas, near the official tourist information office, charges more (a cappuccino goes for $4), but you get your money's worth. Expert preparations of such continental favorites include chicken cordon bleu, smoked salmon with olives, fettuccine alfredo, spaghetti putanesca and filet mignon. The menu, offered in both English and Spanish versions, starts with a coffee list that includes coffee cioccolata. The dessert includes items such as ice cream with brandy and pecans. Credit cards are accepted. Open Monday - Saturday, 7 a.m. - 6 p.m., breakfast and lunch only. Pasaje Nicolás de Rivera El Viejo 121, Tel: 51-1-427-4471.

La Posada del Márquez

Facing the Palacio de Gobierno, La Posada del Márquez offers well-cooked versions of such local favorites as beef cooked with beer and grilled chicken breasts that come with a side order of cheese-filled potatoes. The red and green interior also comes with both an upper and lower floor and seats 100. They accept all credit cards and are open every day for breakfast, lunch and dinner. Jr. Huallaga 140, Tel: 51-1-427-4830.

Restaurante La Rana Verde

La Rana Verde (The Green Frog) has made a name for itself over the last 30 years and should be on your agenda, as it serves some of the best seafood in town. The restaurant is built on stilts over the water, and although it is a little on the expensive side, the cuisine is superb and is served in generous quantities. Of course, being on the ocean and all, the specialty is fish: flounder, sea bass and scallops, which are all caught daily. You can even watch your lunch being delivered, freshly caught, to the restaurant's pier by fishing boats. Served a variety of ways, it is up to you to decide how you would like your fish cooked. Since the restaurant is built of wood, it is kind of creaky and damp, and you may get splashed when the sea is high, but with open windows all around, you can watch the coming and going of the boats and ships of one of the largest ports in South America. Plan carefully, it is only open for lunch. Parque Gálvez, La Punta, Callao.

Hotel Continental Restaurant

The Hotel Continental Restaurant provides a more professional and cosmopolitan ambience than most in the area, though the menu items are rather provincial. This is not to say that they aren't tasty. That includes items such as the *pescado a la chorrillana*, a Mexican-style plate with tomatoes, fish and vegetables, with variations that include sliced beef. In Peru's winter season they are open for breakfast, lunch and dinner; during their summer only lunch and dinner. All credit cards are accepted. Jr. Puno 196, Tel: 51-1-427-5890, 426-1633, E-mail: hotelcontinental_04@yahoo. es, URL: www.hotelcontinental.com.pe.

San Remo los Escribanos

Now in its seventh year, this fashionable restaurant, well-located near the Palacio de Gobierno has a graceful and creative design (the internal harp of a piano is incorporated into a stairwell), along with high-quality preparations of Italian and Peruvian cuisine, sandwiches, vegetarian selections and European coffees. The prices here are a little bit higher than average for Lima, though falling into midrange for people accustomed to dollars and euros. It is open every day and accepts all credit cards. Nicolás de Ribera El Viejo 137, Tel: 51-1-427-9102, E-mail: miraf@free.com.pe.

Cosentino Gourmet

Inside the Palacio de la Unión and facing the Palacio del Gobierno, Cosentino Gourmet has a look that could be described as "classy" and a specialized, limited item menu, but you still pay no more than at any other restaurant in the area. The menu changes every day, but a typical offering is a choice between grilled chicken with oriental sauce or spaghetti with marinara. All items come with salad, bread and dessert. The facility is large and can seat upwards of 120, ideal for groups. Jr. de la Union 364, Tel: 51-1-426-2279 / 426-2418, E-mail: cosentinogourmet@hotmail.com, URL: www.cosentinogourmet.com.

España Restaurant

Nothing like some fettuccine, a salad, steak with chips or even a vegetarian soyburger for lunch while a pair of large turtles walk between the restaurant's tables. All in a day's work for the Restaurant España, on the top floor of the popular and idiosyncratic Hotel España. You don't have to be a guest to enjoy this place and its laid-back bohemian vibe. Just be open to the unexpected. Jr. de Azángaro 105, Tel: 51-1-427-9196, E-mail: cmundo@hotmail.com.

El Estadio Fútbol Club

"Our motto is good food, good times and soccer" is what El Estadio Fútbol Club claims, and with a large stained-glass soccer ball in the window and life-size models of some of Latin America's most famous soccer players sitting at tables, what else could you expect? This sports-pub-to-end-all-sports-pubs is a Latino Bubba's dream, with a native menu that includes *milanesa de pollo a la pobre* (fried chicken, French fries, fried banana, fried egg, white rice and salad). With three stories, El Estadio Fútbol Club can accommodate 300, making it an ideal location for groups. Nicolás de Piérola 926, (Plaza San Martín), Tel: 51-1-428-8866.

De César Restaurant

The style of this small restaurant points to an affection for Amerian pop culture, decorated as it is with posters of Elvis and Marilyn (as well as Chaplin and Laurel and Hardy), race cars, and other iconic evocations of the United States of America. Here is where you will also find 18 selections of coffee and 13 alcohol-spiked options, such as espresso with vodka, gin, amaretto, and that Peruvian favorite, Pisco. There are also approximately 200 main course selections on the menu. Jr. de Ancash N 300, Tel: 51-1-428-8740.

Rincón Chileno

Now in its 42nd year, Rincón Chileno qualifies as an institution around the Plaza de Armas, serving as a goodwill ambassador of Chilean cuisine and culture since 1965. Here, if nowhere else in Lima, you will be introduced to popular Chilean favorites such as *loco mayo*, a seafood platter with mayonnaise; *empanadas caldúas*, a juicier version of the traditional meat pastry; *pastel choclo*, a fondue in a clay pot with chicken and beef; and *poroto granado*, a stew with squash and white corn. The restaurant, with its multiple rooms, is a lively tribute to Chilean culture, especially its music. Rincón Chileno is open from Monday - Saturday, 10 a.m. - 7 p.m., and Sundays and holidays until 4 p.m. Jr. Camaná N 228, Tel: 51-1-428-8640, E-mail: rinconchileno@yahoo.com.

Chifa Fuc Seng

One of the brighter Chinese restaurants, or as they call them here, "chifas," that you will find near the Historical Center, Chifa Fuc Seng's offerings include chicken chijaukay, tempura-fried chicken breast served with soy dipping sauce, lobsters with mushrooms, pork with peach, and of course, Beijing duck. Hungry already? It is open every day from 11:30 a.m. onwards. Sorry, no credit cards accepted. Also, the staff speak very limited Spanish and absolutely no English. Jr. de Carabaya 612, Tel: 51-1-427-3223.

R.H. Atlantic

R.H. Atlantic is the closest you will get to an American diner in Lima. Indeed, one of their offerings is an "American-style steak," complete with, yes, an order of fries and a coke. The checkered red and black tablecloths help contribute to a 1950s pop ambience. However, the local cuisine is not forgotten, so you can sample fried yucca with cheese sauce, as well as a few pasta dishes. They also have many sandwich items and an extensive coffee list. Jr. Huallaga 146, Tel: 51-1-426-9627.

Aero Club del Peru

You walk into the courtyard, where there is an authentic early model single-passenger airplane, and then into the restaurant, the formal and elegant environment of the Aero Club of Peru. The grounds are home to an aviator's association, but its restaurant is open to the general public. They offer plates such as as anticuchos de carne, beef heart marinated in cumin, garlic, chili and vinegar, or alcachofa rellena de marisco, a roasted artichoke heart stuffed with seafood. The prices are within budget range. With multiple rooms and a capacity for 300, it is an ideal location for large assemblies. Jr. de la Unión 722, Tel: 51-1-427-0092 / 8749, E-mail: queenperuviangourmet@hotmail.com.

Villa Natura

Villa Natura is such a popular vegetarian restaurant that, if you come alone, you might have to share a table. They offer varieties of meatless cuisine, with or without eggs and dairy, fruit juices, carrot and other vegetable extracts, and such specialties as maca punch and quinoa drink. The service is somewhat sloppy, but the food is good. This restaurant also serves as a natural health store, with many organic herbs and remedies for sale. Villa Natura is open every day from 7 a.m. - 10 p.m. Jr. Ucayali N 320, Tel: 51-1-426-3944.

San Paolo

One of the few restaurants with a distinctly European atmosphere in the historical center, San Paolo features 13 selections of tea and 14 of coffee, including "banana café," made with actual bananas. This could be described as an Italian restaurant—many lasagna and ravioli items, and pizza—with a large selection of traditional Peruvian offerings as well. The wall display across the entire facility, a glass panel exhibiting vintage wine bottles, is original and appealing. No credit cards accepted. Jr. de Ancash 454, Tel: 51-1-427-5981.

T'anta

They promise dishes that range from "light to forceful." Another fashionable and pricey restaurant at the Plaza de Armas, the T'anta menu features exotic dishes like chicharroncito, sliced pork with creamed sweet potato, orange sauce and Peruvian criolla, and cheeses of the world, which as it promises is just that, with as many varied cheeses you can put on a plate. They serve up to 100 persons, and are open Monday through Saturday from 9 a.m. to 9 p.m., and on Sundays until 6 p.m. They accept all credit cards. Pasaje Nicolás de Rivera El Viejo 142, Tel: 51-1-428-3115, E-mail: lima@tanta.com.pe.

Rincón Cervecero

With life-size models of jolly guys in lederhosen and buxom barmaids, the spirit of an eternal Oktoberfest reigns supreme at Rincón Cervecero (literally, "beer corner"), a veritable Disneyland of drinking holes. They do serve food, and proudly boast quality meals "guaranteed by a graduate of Le Cordon Bleu," Peru's most prestigious culinary school. They also serve beer fresh out of a barrel, and honor not only Oktoberfest (in September), but the Peruvian Beer Festival in January. Rincón Cervecero has an ample dance floor, too, making this one a lively place to spend an evening drinking, dancing and cheering on the favored soccer teams. Av. Nicolás de Piérola 926, Tel: 51-1-428-8866, E-mail: eliasumber@estadio.com.pe.

Rusti Bar

You walk up a flight of stairs that features logs as banisters. Then you step inside and you see a pile of logs bound together to form a bar, logs and sticks forming chairs, and a general jungle atmosphere worthy of the backlot of an old Tarzan movie. You are in the Rusti Bar, near the main square of the Plaza de Armas. Open every day from 11 a.m. - 3 a.m., though generally filling up later in the day, the Rusti Bar offers live music in addition to beer and pizza. They have an on-site wood stove where the chef tosses and bakes the pizza right before you. Jr. Callao 177, Tel: 51-1-439-9620.

Jimmy's Baguetería and Pastelería

Local bakeries are a mainstay of the Latin American economy, as much in Peru as anywhere else. Jimmy's Baguetería and Pastelería, specializing in breads and pastries, is no exception. Featuring

LIMA

a large assortment of chicken, beef and pizza empanadas, along with fresh-baked bread and stylish wedding cakes, you'll have a hard time saying no to anything once you step inside. Av. Abanca 296, and Huallaga, Tel: 51-1-428-8942.

La Muralla

The newly constructed riverside Parque la Muralla, along the Jr. de Amazonas in Lima, includes a slick, modern-style restaurant, La Muralla, complete with glass walls. Seafood, sandwiches and salads, as well as a variety of pies, custards and other desserts are typical menu items. The prices are about average for Lima, inexpensive for most tourists. They can seat up to 150; a group wanting to enjoy the park and other nearby attractions could book space at La Muralla. Jr. de Amazonas, Parque la Muralla, E-mail: restaurantelamuralla@hotmail.com.

Pardo's Chicken

One of a great many competing restaurant chains in Peru, Pardo's Chicken boasts a more professional but less manufactured environment than most. Their location on the Plaza de Armas is a bonus for those who want to eat a traditional but well-made dinner in a pleasantly stylish setting without having to pay the higher charges of other restaurants in the vicinity. Chicken is their specialty and they feature a variety of different preparations to suit most tastes. Monday through Sunday their happy hour includes two-for-one Pisco Sours, Cuba Libres and Piña Coladas. All credit cards are accepted. Pasaje Santa Rosa 153, Tel: 51-1-427-2301, URL: www.pardoschicken.com.pe.

Raulito's (Entrees: $1.25 - 4)

From its corrugated tin ceiling and artificial foliage decorating its spare white walls to its simple name, "Raulito's," named after its owner Raúl, is pure working-class Peruvian. The place is clean, the staff treats you like you're a member of the family, the food is decent and the price is cheap. Hamburgers with frijoles, ceviche, steak and potatoes, and fresh fruit juices are some of the menu items, handwritten by the staff on a whiteboard. Jr. Lampa 148.

Miski Wasi (Entrees: $2 and up)

The other vegetarian restaurant on Jr. de Ucayali has a very funky design, with East Indian, Cambodian and Tibetan folk art on display. The food is a competent offering of tempeh, soy and other vegetarian favorites, along with meatless South American offerings, such as *choclo*. The service is so-so, but the prices are very reasonable.. It also has its own gift shop, selling many of the same folk crafts as in the restaurant, as well as some Peruvian work. Jr. de Ucayali 212, Tel: 51-1-247-0877.

Laguna Dorada (Entrees: $3 and up)

While visiting the Parque de la Cultura, the Food Rotunda is a fast, pleasant and convenient stop for your group. This food court is located beneath the stands of the outdoor Teatro de Exposición, and its climate, no matter how hot and humid the park may be on a given day, is always cool and dry. The food itself is inexpensive by foreign standards, and very filling. They offer what Peruvians like most: ceviche, arroz con pollo, batter-fried seafood and other native plates. Av. 28 de Julio, inside the Parque de la Exposición, Tel: 51-1-424-6015 / 9671-6380, E-mail: francon@yahoo.com.

Belén Restaurant (Entrees: $4 and up)

If you are hosting a special group event, or simply want to impress your friends while staying within your budget, look no further than the Belén restaurant. Once a former military officers' club, it still retains an imperial ambience, complete with high ceilings, ornate trim, columns, marble floors and, most importantly, a bust of former military president Marshall Óscar Raymundo Benavides Larrea, whose imposing presence accompanies your dining. The focus is on native cuisine, with such exotic-sounding plates as *sancochado* (soup with chicken, beef, rice, potatoes and herbs). Av. Nicolás de Piérola 953, Tel: 51-1-427-7391, E-mail: ryexport2000@yahoo.es.

Palacio de Sancochado (Entrees: $6)

A uniquely Limeña legend for 25 years, the Palacio de Sancochado relies on word of mouth and little else. Owner Juan Ruggiero offers up more than just lunch (served from noon to 5 p.m.), which comprises just one plate, and all without coffee or desert. He has converted his elegant 70-year-old childhood home into a virtual temple of time past. His home features everything from first–model jukeboxes to tintypes and just about anything uniquely obsolete. The total effect is intoxicating. Juan's local clientele, stone-soup like, has made its own donations. The food? The one-entrée-only special is a proudly Peruvian platter of potatoes, yams, yucca, carrots, cabbage, garbanzos, rice, creole sauce and a half–kilo of beef—all for $6. You can forget about eating anything else the day you dine there. Av. 28 de Julio 990, in front of the Parque de la Exposición, Tel: 51-1-331-0789.

Los Vitrales de Gemma (Entrees: $7 - 10)

A former colonial mansion converted into a slick, modern restaurant with a classy edge, the Vitrales de Gemma is a great place for groups: it can seat up to 210. This restaurant is definitely more upscale; its appetizers start at around $5 and main courses go for $7 to $10. The menu offers variations of traditional Peruvian favorites, such as ceviche, steak, and shrimp-filled crepes. It accepts all credit cards and is open for breakfast, lunch and dinner. Jr. Ucayali 332, Tel: 51-1-427-5799 / 428-2474, E-mail: losvitralesdegemma@hotmail.com.

La Catedral Restaurant and Bar (Entrees: $10 and up)

If you are walking around the Plaza de Gobierno and in the mood for a more professional and modern environment in which to dine, La Catedral should satisfy you, from its checkered maroon and beige marble tiles to its carefully designed wooden chairs meant to echo the twin spirals of the Catedral de Lima. This restaurant offers appetizers that start at $4 and main courses, such as a Hawaiian steak, priced at $12. There are eight varieties of the perennial Peruvian favorite, ceviche, as well as a bar and a large selection of drinks. Jr. Junín 288, Tel: 51-1-856-4465, E-mail: Lacatedral_carowa@viabcp.com.

NIGHTLIFE

Concert Disco

The past and present meet at Concert Disco, a dance club in an antique building with imperially high ceilings, columns and rococo trim for what was most likely an old-money dynasty. Located on the Calle de Baquijano, near Cusco and Jirón de la Reunión, it is now where Limeños take their sweethearts and even children to dance to a mixture of salsa, merengue, reggaeton, electronic rock and much more. Sunday through Thursday admission is free, on Fridays and Saturdays the DJ has a special mix of 80s and 90s hits. The bar serves beer and sangria and everything in between. Baquijano and Cusco.

Palace Concert

Fast, loud and new, the Palace Concert dance club and bar will keep you on your feet from when it opens at 6 p.m. to when it closes the next morning at 9 a.m. You will find it right on the corner of Calle de Baquijano and the Jirón de la Reunión; admission is free, but the only requirement to get in, besides being over 18, is that you are a party of at least two. The DJ plays a mix of Latin genre favorites such as reggaeton, meringue and salsa, along with international pop hits and 80s and 90s favorites. Jr. de la Reunión 700.

SAN ISIDRO

The San Isidro district of Lima is one of the city's most affluent zones, known for green areas, nice residential neighborhoods, fine hotels and dining, and decent nightlife. Visitors favor San Isidro for its hotels and good food.

SAN ISIDRO HISTORY

Originally the site of an extensive olive grove outside of Lima, San Isidro wasn't founded until 1931, so it does not possess as much history as other neighborhoods. San Isidro is a mon-

LIMA

eyed zone, home to upscale shopping, a financial district and many of Lima's finest hotels. Most of the foreign embassies also take up residence in San Isidro, adding to its debonair atmosphere. Switzerland, France, Morocco, and Mexico are just a few of the countries whose embassies are located here. San Isidro is intellectual, too—the San Isidro Municipal Library is considered the most complete and extensive in Lima. Visitors and inhabitants come to San Isidro for its green areas. The swank Lima Golf Club is located right in the heart of the district. For those with no clubs in tow, more green patches can be found in the famous El Olivar park, named for its groves of olive trees, some of which were planted centuries ago. The park was established as a national monument in 1959.

SAN ISIDRO SERVICES
DHL
DHL is easily accessible for all of your mailing and shipping needs. Ausejo Salas 153, floor 3, Tel: 51-12-321-976, Monday – Friday last drop at 5 p.m., Saturday / Sunday closed.

Dr. Victor Aste
Should you need to see a doctor while visiting San Isidro, Dr. Victor Aste speaks English and will be able to assist with most non-emergency needs. In the event of an emergency, please visit an area hospital. Antero Aspillaga 415, Oficina 101, Tel: 51-14-417-502.

iPeru
iPeru features a tourist information and assistance service where visitors can ask about information on Peru, as well as assistance if the tourist feels the service paid for was not provided as advertised. Please note that iPeru does not give recommendations for travel agencies, lodgings or transport services, nor does it make reservations or file applications for customs or immigration. Monday - Friday 8:30 a.m.- 6 p.m. Jorge Basadre 610, Tel: 51-14-211-627, E-mail: iperulima@promperu.gob.pe.

THINGS TO SEE AND DO IN SAN ISIDRO
As one of Lima's residential districts, San Isidro has fewer activities than surrounding areas, but is no less interesting. There are a handful of museums with private collections of pottery, jewelry, textiles and ceramics, fascinating archaeological and anthropological artifacts and interesting tidbits of Peruvian history.

Sights
Museo de Historia Natural UNMSM (Entrance: $1.65 Adults, Concessions $0.85)
The Museum of Natural History, founded on February 28, 1918, consists of four main divisions: botany, zoology, ecology and geoscience. Browse Peruvian landscapes and a modest taxidermy collection that highlights the region's mammals, primates, invertebrates, birds, botany, fossils, dinosaurs, fish and minerals. Open from Monday–Friday, 9 a.m. - 3 p.m., Saturday 9 a.m. - 5 p.m. and Sunday 9 a.m. - 1 p.m. Av. Arenales 1256, Jesús Maria. Tel: 51-1-471-0117, E-mail: museohn@unmsm.edu.pe.

Huaca Huallamarca (Entrance: $1.75)
This ancient Maranga monument seems out of place, sandwiched between neighboring hotels and apartment buildings. Constructed with adobe bricks dating from 200 to 500 AD, this landmark has been lovingly restored and now offers interesting views of San Isidro. Tuesday – Sunday, 9 a.m. - 5 p.m. Nicolás de Rivera 201, Tel: 51-1-222-4124.

El Olivar (Entrance: Free)
Surrounding the El Olivar Historical Monument is a lush park made up of a plantation of olive trees that dates back more than 450 years. This park serves as a great reminder of Lima's history and offers visitors a pleasant stroll under the olive trees. Jr. Choquehuanca s/n.

Activities ●

1 Huaca Huallamarca B2
2 Museo de Historia Natural UNMSM B3
3 Parque El Olivar B3

Eating 🍴

4 Alfresco A3
5 Antica Pizzaría A3
6 Como Agua Para Chocolate B3
7 El Cartujo B3
8 Matseui A3
9 News Café A3
10 Punta Sal C3
11 Punto Italiano A3
12 Tai Lounge B3
13 Trattoria San Ceferino A3

Services ★

14 Camino Real Shopping B3
15 DHL B1
16 Dr. Astor Aste B3
17 Ilaria A2
18 Segunda Vuelta D3

Sleeping 🛏

19 Casa Bella B2
20 Country Club Lima Hotel B1
21 Hotel Libertador San Isidro Golf B1
22 Hotel Los Delfines B2
23 Sonesta Lima Hotel El Olivar B3
24 Suites Antique A2
25 Suites del Bosque B3
26 Swisshotel B3
27 Youth Hostel Malka A4

Parque Combate de Altao (Entrance: Free)

San Isidro is Peru's premier business district: Men in black suits with silk ties, cell phones in the left and briefcases in the right, scurry by in droves. Movement and chaos abound. Skyscrapers tower above, surveying the bustle below. But calmly sleeping amidst all the energy, the endless commotion, is the Parque Combate de Altao. The park is large and square, perhaps a former plaza. The lush vegetation, the broad overhanging trees and the healthy moist fragrance of the grass, welcomes you into the park. The fresh air, the roaming dogs, the feasting pigeons and the desolate jungle gym all contribute to a feeling of peace, a deep exhalation of relief. If you're in the area and need to relax, check it out. Corner of Av. Las Orquídeas and Andréas Reyes, only a few blocks away from Av. Arequipa and Javier Prado.

Shopping
Camino Real

This is a large mall with a collection of smaller, less pretentious shops than in shopping areas in Miraflores. Belaunde 147.

Ilaria

Browse this stylish jewelry and silverware shop for unique and beautiful creations by master jewelers. Silver and gold are intricately combined with precious materials such as amethyst, pearl, sapphire, and ruby to create stunning necklaces, bracelets, rings, and more. Additionally, contemporary and traditional silverware sets including wood and silver home accessories are available. Prices tend to be high in this shop. Av. 2 de Mayo 308, Tel: 51-14-417-703.

El Virrey

Following their recent move to a much bigger and nicer store, El Virrey now offers three times their original selection of books. Founded 30 years ago by the Sanseviero family, this store offers a large selection of local and imported books on nearly every subject you could possibly be interested in. With the additional space, you'll find plenty of room to sit down and enjoy a good book in one of their comfortable reading rooms. Plan on browsing for awhile. Miguel Dasso 147, Tel: 51-14-400-607.

Segunda Vuelta

For the fashionable traveler with a weakness for unique designs, this tiny shop features clothes by young Peruvian designers. If you don't find anything to suit your taste from this selection, don't miss the excellent assortment of second-hand and vintage garments. The shop is small and partly hidden from view, so be careful not to miss it. There is no sign out front, just a big number 330. Av. Conquistadores 330, Tel: 51-14-217-163.

SAN ISIDRO LODGING

The affluent San Isidro district is known for some of the best upscale hotels in Lima. This residential and quiet area caters to the mid to high-end visitor, and you will find many business travelers in the area. There are a few exceptions, however, and the tourist with a lower budget can find places to stay as well. The area is safe and recommended for travelers who plan to stay for an extended period of time.

BUDGET
Youth Hostel Malka ($8 - 20)

One of the only low-budget options in San Isidro, Youth Hostel Malka is clean and pleasant, with a garden, climbing wall and ping-pong tables. It is very popular among budget travelers and backpackers, and word-of-mouth in South America has it as one of the best low-cost options in all of Peru. They are particularly proud of their comfortable mattresses. Prices include tax, breakfast is $2 extra. Los Lirios 165, Tel: 51-14-420-162, Fax: 51-12-225-589, URL: www.youthhostelperu.com.

Hostal Collacocha (Rooms: $26 - 49)

Located on a tranquil tree-laden street, Collacocha is pleasantly small and unassuming. Easily one of the best deals in San Isidro. The atmosphere inside is even better and it will be hard to find a lobby that rivals Collacocha's in character and taste: The décor is rustic, eclectic and even eccentric. One finds delft tiles and gold-framed orthodox reliefs on the walls, stained-glass lamps, a fireplace and a pool table. The rooms though basic, are cozy and nice with beds, carpet, cable TV, private bathrooms, hot water and linens. One room is newly remodeled for handicap accessibility with a private bathroom. Although simple, all rooms have a really cozy feel to them. It's definitely a place you should check out (and into). Price includes tax for foreign tourists. Andrés Reyes 100, Tel: 51-14-423-900, Fax: 51-14-424-160, E-mail: collacocha@viabcp.com, URL: www.hostalcollacocha.com.

Casa Bella (Rooms: $35 and up)

Casa Bella is a pleasant, quiet spot in San Isidro. It's not too far from the action, however: Miraflores is only 10 minutes away. A converted private home, Casa Bella does not have a lot of rooms, so best to book ahead. Free internet access, breakfast and airport pick-up for those staying three or more nights. Ask for one of the rooms that has a garden view. Taxes are included. Las Flores 459, Tel: 51-14-217-354, URL: www.casabellaperu.net.

MID-RANGE
El Marqués Hotel (Rooms: $70 - 150)

An excellent option if you want to treat yourself, but not spend a fortune. The hotel is beautiful--inside and out. The red brick building, with its surrounding foliage and broad shutters, resembles something of a chalet in the Swiss Alps. The interior—the lobby, bar and restaurant-—is very quaint and provides for a relaxing stay. The rooms are clean, comfortable and individually decorated. A good, solid economic choice. Av. Chinchon 461, Tel: 51-14-420-046, Fax: 51-14-420-043, E-mail: reservas@hotelelmarques.com, URL: www.hotelmarques.com.

Suites Antique (Rooms: $85 - 100)

Suite Antique hotel is located in central San Isidro, so nearby restaurants, embassies, banks, parks, supermarkets, shopping malls, museums, markets and evening entertainment centers are just close enough to be convenient but far enough away to provide a quiet, restful stay. Rooms are comfortable and spacious with warm décor. Biarritz, the on-site restaurant-café, serves Peruvian and international dishes. The staff is friendly and the service is good. The property also features a business center, free parking, 24-hr front desk service and garden or city views. Av. 2 de Mayo 954, Tel: 51-12-221-094, URL: www.suitesantique.com.

HIGH-END
Hotel Libertador San Isidro Golf, Lima (Rooms: $105 - 210)

The Hotel Libertador faces the Golf Club. The 53 rooms have been decorated to provide the highest levels of comfort and quality. The Ostrich House Restaurant will dazzle you with the diversity of dishes and the Bar El Balcón will delight you with his special Pisco Sour. Wireless internet access, fitness center, sauna and jacuzzi are offered. Rates do not include taxes but do include buffet breakfast. Los Eucaliptos 550, Tel: 51-14-216-666, Fax: 51-14-423-011, E-mail: reservaslima@libertador.com.pe, URL: www.libertador.com.pe.

Basadre Suites Hotel (Rooms: $130 - 177)

Located in the San Isidro district of Lima, the Hotel Basadre Suites offers quick access to the best tourist spots and shopping centers. A great hotel for business as well as vacationing travelers, the hotel is 15 minutes from the international airport. Four room types are available: Single Room, Double Room, Junior Suite or Senior Suite. The inviting restaurant with garden and swimming pool view is a special place to start or your day with a hearty breakfast, or to enjoy a delicious lunch or dinner with a select variety of dishes of traditional Peruvian cuisine or international specialities. There is a shuttle from the airport to the hotel for $22-$80. Taxes are included, as is breakfast. Av. Jorge Basadre 1310, Tel: 51-14-422-423, Fax: 51-12-225-581, E-mail: reservas@hotelbasadre.com, URL: www.hotelbasadre.com.

Sonesta Lima Hotel El Olivar (Rooms: $135 - 209)

Smack in the middle of Lima's San Isidro business district, Sonesta Lima Hotel El Olivar is perfect for business folks, along with families and travelers looking to stay in a safe nice area away from Miraflores. The large rooms have comfortable beds, cable TV, phones, carpet, air conditioning, minibar and a safe. The décor is bright and cheery, with colorful Incan fabrics. If you choose your hotel on the basis of bathrooms, look no further; the large, beautiful, marble bathrooms are perhaps this hotel's best feature. Well, that and the fact that the seven-story hotel overlooks Parque El Olivar and the fact that its one of the best bangs for your bucks in all of Lima. Prices include taxes and breakfast. Childen under 8 stay free. Pancho Fierro 194, Tel: 1-800-Sonesta (US and Canada) / 51-12-224-273 (locally), E-mail: reservations@sonesta.com, URL: www.sonesta.com.

Suites del Bosque (Rooms: $140-200)

These upscale suites boast a cozy and pleasant atmosphere designed for the most aristocratic of travelers. With 54 contemporary suites that include all the latest in gadgets and luxuries including among others internet, kitchenette, and air conditioning, the Suites del Bosque will accommodate almost any need. Dine on-site at the Crystals Restaurant that serves a variety of pastas and salads in addition to their buffet. There is also a business center with fax, phones, photocopier and computer access and laundry service available. Paz Soldan 165, Tel: 51-12-211-108, URL: www.suitesdelbosque.com.

Country Club Lima Hotel ($209 - 549)

The Country Club Lima Hotel was built in 1927 and refurbished in 1998. Today it stands as one of Lima's finer hotels. Popular with business and pleasure travelers, the hotel has everything you would expect from a five-star hotel: good service, comfortable rooms, amenities (a good restaurant and travel desk, etc) and decadently huge and well-decorated rooms. Included are luxuries such as internet, cable TV, safe box, air conditioning, and more. No-smoking and handicap accessible rooms are available. Los Eucaliptos 590, Tel: 51-16-119-000, Fax: 51-16-119-002, E-mail: country@hotelcountry.com, URL: www.hotelcountry.com.

Swissôtel (Rooms: $240-1400)

Swissôtel's mission is to make your stay a memorable one, and with their luxury offerings--including sophisticately royal rooms, some of the most comfortable beds ever, top-of-the-line staff, and let's not forget to mention every amenity you'd ever want, it doesn't get much better than this. From their state-of-the-art spa services, fitness facilities (even a tennis court), spotlessly clean quality, the hotel is a great place to indulge. Well-equipped for business people wanting space for work (all rooms have desks and internet), it's also great if you have lots of people in your party. The 18-floor hotel with 244 rooms has ample space, but of course, it will cost you a few hundred a night. But even the most ragged traveler who wants serious luxury won't be disappointed. Three fabulous restaurants serving Swiss, Italian and Peruvian fare are also on the premises. Prices include tax. Vía Central 150, Centro Empresarial Real. Tel: 51-16-114-400, Fax: 51-16-114-401, E-mail: reservations.lima@swissotel,com, URL: www.swissotel.com/lima.

Hotel los Delfines (Rooms: $220 - $1000)

Another luxury hotel in the swank San Isidro district, Los Delfines is in an attractive, modern building. It sets itself apart by actually having two dolphins in residence there,

Yaku and Wayra, who are quite popular with the guests. The rooms are pleasant and spacious, and there are a variety of suites and special rooms to choose from. The hotel features a cafe, bar and restaurant. The restaurant specializes in international cuisine. According to the web site, it has "an extraordinary view of the Dolphinarium," which is presumably a fancy name for the dolphin tank. The hotel also features a gym, spa and bakery that offers delivery. Los Eucaliptos 555, Tel: 51-12-157-000, Fax: 51-12-157-073 / 157-071, E-mail: reservas@losdelfineshotel.com.pe, URL: www.losdelfineshotel.com.pe/ingles/default.asp.

San Isidro Restaurants

Like Miraflores, the upscale San Isidro district of Lima is home to many excellent restaurants. Some of the best of them can be found in the international hotels that dot San Isidro, but many of the best restaurants are independent. If you're hungry for some local flavor, try lunch at a cevichería.

Como Agua Para Chocolate

This colorful little cantina offers deliciously traditional Mexican entrées in a vibrant atmosphere. Enjoy specials like barbacoa de cordero (lamb steamed in avocado leaves) or albóndigas al chipotle (spicy meatballs and yellow rice). A creative lunch menu boasts many choices and the dessert menu includes tasty sweets doused in chocolate. Pancho Fierro 108, Tel: 51-12-220-297.

News Café

This delightful coffeehouse/café, serves up excellent, real strong coffee and a light menu of sandwiches and tasteful gourmet salads. Anyone looking for international newspapers will be in heaven here with an array of daily and weekly papers from around the world to choose from. Intellectual sorts tend to hang out here and so if you're looking for conversation, you're likely to find it at News Café. Av Conquistadores and Santa Luisa, Tel: 51-14-216-278.

Antica Pizzería

Antica Pizzería is one of Lima's most popular Italian restaurants, specializing in wood-burning oven-style pizzas and standard but well-done Italian meals. The long, wooden tables can be awkward, but the pizza is first-rate. Av. 2 de Mayo 728-744, Tel: 51-14-227-939 / 229-404.

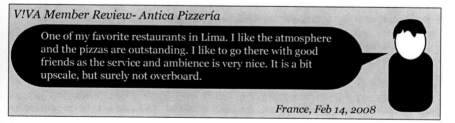

V!VA Member Review- Antica Pizzería

One of my favorite restaurants in Lima. I like the atmosphere and the pizzas are outstanding. I like to go there with good friends as the service and ambience is very nice. It is a bit upscale, but surely not overboard.

France, Feb 14, 2008

La Carreta

La Carreta is a steak house favored by Lima locals. It is located in the San Isidro financial district and attracts an interesting power-lunch crowd of bankers, lawyers and politicians. The décor is colonial hacienda and quite pleasant. A carnivore's delight, La Carreta offers various cuts of meat prepared in different ways. It is expensive by Lima standards, but still one of the best steak houses in town. Rivera Navarrete 740, Tel: 51-14-422-690.

LIMA

Tai Lounge

This exclusive restaurant and bar tends to attract the swankiest of Limeños who don't mind paying the elevated prices for drinks. Enjoy the lavish surroundings and lush lounging areas, watch the sophisticated patrons. and even if you're just stopping in for a drink, don't rule out sampling the tasty Thai food. Conquistadores 325, Tel: 51-14-227-351.

Los Delfines

Join the posh clientele for pricey (and refreshing!) cocktails at this upper class hotel and casino. The Oceanus Lounge is the perfect place to relax and enjoy good company in a marvelous setting. Should there be a lull in the conversation, let the resident dolphins entertain you with their antics in the surrounding tanks. Los Eucaliptos 555, Tel: 51-12-157-000.

Fuente de Soda "Amy's" ($1 - 1.75)

This small family-owned restaurant, run by the same three señoras day-in, day-out, offers a great alternative to the more expensive, tourist-hungry establishments in Miraflores. Located in the Lince district, only a ten-minute taxi or bus ride from Miraflores, the restaurant offers an excellent meal at unbeatable prices. The restaurant's decorum is austere and simple, with only a capacity to seat twelve; but the workers' calm and friendly personalities, along with the tranquil pace at which locals dine, makes you feel right at home. Amy's joint offers a fine *menú del día*, where one can delve into classic Peruvian dishes. For only $1.50 you can have a two-course meal, consisting of a hearty, vegetable and pasta-filled soup or a portion of the fresh and zesty ceviche, along with a chicken, meat or fish main platter. Monday - Saturday, 8:30 a.m – 5:30 p.m. Bartolomé Herrera 149, Lince.

La Casa Verde (Entrees: $2 - 4.50)

Located on Avenida Arequipa, merely a block away from the intersecting Javier Prado, La Casa Verde is in a central, convenient location. On the surface, it seems that it would be an excellent choice for the price, between $2-4.50 a plate. The exterior is quite impressive, almost café-like, with its broad green and white-striped awning. The seating area is spacious and you can enjoy an abundance of natural light pouring through the many windows. Unfortunately, the inattentive service can be a turn-off, and the food is nothing to write home about, but it does fill you up and keeps the budget low. Monday - Sunday, 7 a.m. - 11 p.m. Av. Arequipa 2795, Tel: 51-12-221-672.

El Buen Sabor (Entrees: $2 - 5)

If you're looking to sample cheap, classic Peruvian dishes as well as to try Peru's most renowned dish, ceviche, this is it. Well-lit, clean and spacious, the service is professional and efficient. Only a block away form to Avenida Arequipa, you shouldn't have too much trouble finding it. Open Monday-Sunday 9 a.m.-6 p.m. Open Monday - Sunday 9 a.m. - 6 p.m. Av. Petit Thouars 3320, Tel: 51-14-229-737.

Lalo's (Entrees: $3 - 5)

Lalo's is in Lima's modern San Isidro financial district, on the corner of Augusto Tamayo. They serve traditional Peruvian food like ceviche, mixto, lomo saltado, papa a la huancaína, aguadito de pollo, chupe de camarones and escabeche de pescado. Daily specials also feature international dishes from other South American cuisines. The food is fresh. Eduardo Garland Barón, the executive chef and owner, was born in Peru and has operated restaurants in Cancun, Costa Rica and Houston. The restaurant modern decor is brightly colored. It is a great setting to enjoy a wonderful meal. Drop by for a frozen margarita or pisco sour. Augusto Tamayo 196, Tel: 51-14-214-471.

T'anta (Entrees: $5 - 9)

For quick eats in the café or for takeout, T'anta makes tasty salads, paninis, Peruvian sandwiches, homemade pastas and excellent desserts. This chic café is comfortably stylish and there is bound to be something on the menu that will hit the spot. Stop in for a coffee and to sample the exceptional passion-fruit tart. Pancho Fierro 117, Tel: 51-14-219-708.

El Cartujo (Entrees: $6 - 8)

Enjoy your meal in the tranquil atmosphere of El Cartujo. Removed from the activity of the city, this restaurant boasts a quiet location near a park. Stop in for a drink at the long wooden bar, a light salad, or order a delicious lunch from a menu that features anything from pasta, to sole-stuffed lobster to Argentine beef. The food is complimented by an excellent wine list. Reservations are recommended. Los Libertadores 108, Tel: 51-12-214-962.

Punta Sal (Entrees: $9 - 15)

Serving the freshest in seafood, Punta Sal offers top-notch ceviche, scallops and other gourmet nationally and internationally famous dishes at reasonable prices. With excellent service and a well-rounded South American wine list, Punta Sal delivers a satisfying dining experience. Conquistadores 958, Tel: 51-14-417-431.

Punto Italiano (Entrees: $10 - 16)

This traditional trattoria-style restaurant features Italian dishes that are sure to satisfy the hungriest of travelers. Dine on handmade ravioli stuffed with tasty ingredients. Don't miss the pizza unless, of course, it is to try one of the rich pasta dishes with the meat of your choice. Av. 2 de Mayo 647, Tel: 51-12-213-167.

Alfresco (Entrees: $10 - 18)

This popular oceanfront seafood shack is part of a well-known chain and offers diners a delightful meal overlooking the water. With excellent seafood selections such as reasonably priced ceviche, a delicious charcoal fillet of sea bream, a tasty pulpo a la brasa (grilled octopus) or fetuccini negro con camarones (squid ink pasta with shrimp), you'll experience a dish you've never tasted before. Complement your meal with a South American wine from the extensive list and you'll leave with a full tummy. Santa Luisa 295, Tel: 51-14-228-915.

Trattoria San Ceferino (Entrees: $11 - 19)

Centrally located in the heart of San Isidro's comercial centre, this Italian restaurant serves traditional Italian dishes, such as pasta, pizza, lasagna, ravioli and spaghetti. Frequent diners of the Trattoria San Ceferino often request the famous shrimp dish timbal de camarones, the bife de chorizo (a large strip steak) or the unique potted duck and green risotto dish. Av. 2 de Mayo 793, Tel: 51-14-228-242.

Matseui (Entrees: $12 - 17)

Often described as the best sushi bar in Lima, this popular and classy establishment was co-founded by Nobuyuki Matsuhisa (founder of world-renowned Nobu Restaurants). Even the most critical sushi lovers will approve of the sashimi and maki rolls, and delight in the tempura and yakitori dishes. Manuel Bañon 260, Tel: 51-14-224-323.

MIRAFLORES

Miraflores is one of Lima's most upscale districts, full of fancy hotels, good shopping, elegant restaurants, bookstores, banks and more. Better nightlife is to be found in the Barranco neighborhood, but that's not to say there's none to be found in Miraflores. There is an archaeological site in Miraflores, Huaca Pucllana which is open daily and has a small but interesting attached museum.

MIRAFLORES HISTORY

This attractive area, with its ocean views and cliffs, was one of the first areas to be settled by the Spanish after Lima was founded. It was named San Miguel de Miraflores in 1535. From 1879 to 1884, Peru and Bolivia united to fight Chile in South America' s bloodiest war, the

War of the Pacific. One of the most famous battles was the Battle of Miraflores, in January 1881, in which 2,000 dedicated Peruvians fought the invading Chileans in Miraflores. They were Lima's last line of defense. The Peruvians, short on munitions and outnumbered, were defeated and Lima was sacked. Nevertheless, the bravery of the Miraflores defenders is remembered today: Miraflores' official nickname is "the heroic city." One famous resident of the Miraflores district was Ricardo Palma (1833-1919), one of Peru's most celebrated writers.

In the 19th century, the area became known as a beach resort of sorts and its popularity grew. By the 1950s, it was one of Lima's most important districts. In 1992, the infamous Sendero Luminoso ("the Shining Path") detonated a car bomb in Miraflores; weeks later, terrorist leader Abimael Guzmán was captured in nearby Surcillo, only blocks away from Miraflores.

Today, Miraflores is one of the most affluent and attractive sectors of Lima. The streets are lined with trees, the buildings are well-kept and street crime is closely controlled (although not nonexistent). An effort has been made to preserve green space in Miraflores, and the dedication of the famous "Lover's Park" is a step in the right direction. The central square, Parque Kennedy, is great for strolling and hosts occasional art shows and flea markets.

MIRAFLORES SERVICES
Dragón Internet ($0.50 / Hour)
This little internet café is located along a tiny boulevard adjoining the busy Av. José Larco. It's a quiet, friendly place offering both internet access and international calling stations, but the internet cabins lack partitions. It's a good choice if you want to avoid the crowds and congestion of central Miraflores. Open constantly. Tarata 230, Tel: 51-1-446-6814.

Jedi Travel Service—Internet Cafe ($0.60 / Hour)
Located in the dead-center of Miraflores, across from Parque Kennedy, this café is a convenient option to check your E-mail and make international phone calls. The environment is clean and orderly, and the cabins are spacious and private. Open 8 a.m. - 2 a.m. Av. Diagonal 218 (second floor), Tel: 51-14-454-227.

MacPlanet Internet Café ($1 / Hour)
This cozy little internet café is comfortable, with 11 private terminals, multimedia equipment, and services including E-mail, FTP, international calls, chat, printing capabilities, document scanning and webhosting. Monday – Saturday 9 a.m. – 11 p.m., Sunday 10 a.m. - 3 p.m. Av. Aviacion 3380.

RadioShack
It's not uncommon to leave home without bringing all the necessary gadgets and adapters. Without these essentials, say goodbye to your cell phone, MP3 player and hairdryer. But in foreign countries like Peru, RadioShack with a large offering of electronics and products of the sort can be a godsend. Av. Salaverry 3310. Tel: 51-1-264-2600, URL: www.radioshack.com.

THINGS TO SEE AND DO IN MIRAFLORES
With interesting daytime sites to complement the exciting nightime antics, activities in Miraflores abound. Visit one of a number of museums, Inca ruins other landmarks. Relax in the shade of a local park and peruse the markets selling handicrafts, jewelry, artwork and food. Try your hand at surfing or wade through one of the more sandy beaches in Lima. Take a Spanish class to brush up on the language or hit a local club to taste the dance scene.

Huaca Pucllana (Entrance: 7 soles / $2.35)
Machu Picchu may get all the glory, but ruins even older than the Cusco giant can be explored without ever leaving downtown Lima. Indigenous peoples started building Huaca Pucllana in 400 A.D.—nine centuries before the Incas started setting stones at mighty Machu Picchu. Those earliest residents gathered, traded, made community decisions, worshiped and sacrificed

women and children at Huaca Pucllana for 300 years. They abandoned the site when the Wari empire conquered the area in 700 A.D., and built a cemetery for its elite on top of the pyramid. The Incas moved in some three centuries later.

Although Huaca Pucllana is ancient, it's a relatively new attraction. Grounds opened for tours in 1984 and excavation is ongoing. On the top, take in a panoramic view of downtown Lima and a bird's eye view of just how intricate the ruins are. Huaca Pucllana once stretched nearly eight square miles. Development whittled it to less than two and a half. There's a small flora and fauna park on the grounds, and a gift shop with a small selection of native crafts. Staff has built animal pens for animals that were used (or eaten) through the centuries, including guinea pigs. Even though the tour is guided, don't expect to be hurried. Guides are committed to Huaca Pucllana's preservation and welcome questions. If you want to grab a coffee or snack and savor the sight after the tour, the mid-range Restaurant Huaca Pucllana is right beside the ruins. The ruins are lit at night and nearly every table has a view. The archeological site is at the end of Calle General Borgoño block 8, between block 4 of Avenida Angamos Oeste and block 45 of Avenida Arequipa.

Parque Kennedy
Smack dab in the middle of Lima's upscale Miraflores neighborhood is Parque Kennedy, flanked by two major thoroughfares—Avenida José Larco and Diagonal. The park is a small oasis among tall buildings and the congested traffic for which Lima is famous. A paved walkway runs through the center of Parque Kennedy, which draws a good number of people from all walks of life, at all times of day. Young couples snuggle on benches, men in business suits sit on a small field of concrete stools and read the paper while they get their shoes shined, and vendors sell salty popcorn from red and white carts. The southern end of the park is home to a children's playground. There's a good view of the very ornate Iglesia de la Virgen Milagrosa on the north end. Parque Kennedy is across the street from Restaurant Row, famous for its dozens of restaurants and bars that range from Italian and wood-oven pizzerias to Brazilian barbecue and Cuban dance floors. Get ready to make a run for it—crossing Diagonal is like dodging speeding bullets. Restaurant Row is pedestrian only and hopping at night, even during the work week. Competition is fierce: Nearly every eatery or bar has a tout outside, shouting out drink specials and personally beckoning you in. It's difficult to decide if a place is packed because it's got great food or because they offer the cheapest pisco sour. In the evening, Parque Kennedy takes on the atmosphere of a little fiesta. Diners on their way to restaurants and clubs that ring Parque Kennedy stroll through. Some nights, the elevated cement circle in the park center plays host to artists selling woodwork, jewelry and other handiwork or vendors selling antiques. Outside cafés are usually full and decorated with white outdoor lights and table canopies. A meal at the parkside cafés will run you about $7 (22 nuevo sols) and up.

Parque del Amor
Finish your cup of coffee or glass of wine at Larcomar and head north along Malecón de la Reserva. Walk along the scenic path for ten minutes and you'll see a little yellow bridge; behind the bridge is an imposing red sandstone sculpture, sitting atop a black marble pedestal, which will immediately steal your attention. This is Parque del Amor and the sculpture depicts a man embracing his love. The park's charm and character compensate for its small size. Beds of crimson roses, daffodils and violets, carved in various shapes, stud the green grass. A white concrete bench, decorated with colorful mosaic tiles, presses against the cliffs' edges. Various couples, young and old, cuddle in the little enclaves and savor the sunset. The park truly embodies its name and is as safe as a hug. Av. Malecón Cisneros and Av. Diagonal

El Faro de la Marina
El Faro de la Marina is a blue and white candy cane-striped lighthouse that faces the ocean. El Faro de la Marina doesn't have the cutting originality of Parque del Amor but it affords beautiful, expansive views of the ocean and the softly eroded cliffs. On the broad patches of grass, families picnic, dogs sprint back and forth, and couples lay teasing one another. Like Parque del Amor, it has a distinct magnetism and is best accented by the pastel strokes of peach and purple at sunset. Av. Malecón Cisneros and Av. Diagonal.

Find more reviews from travelers at www.vivatravelguides.com

LIMA

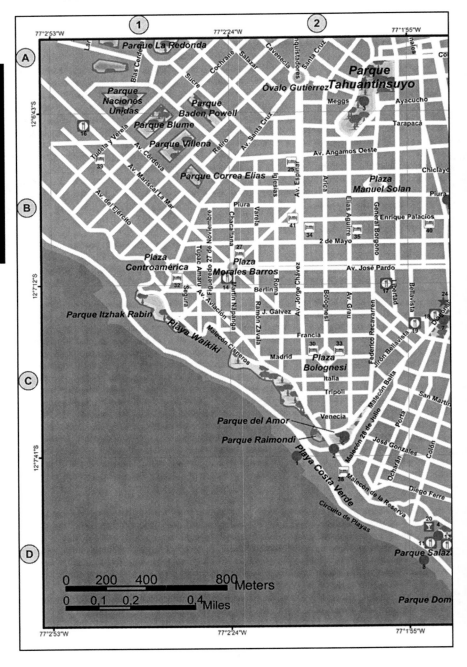

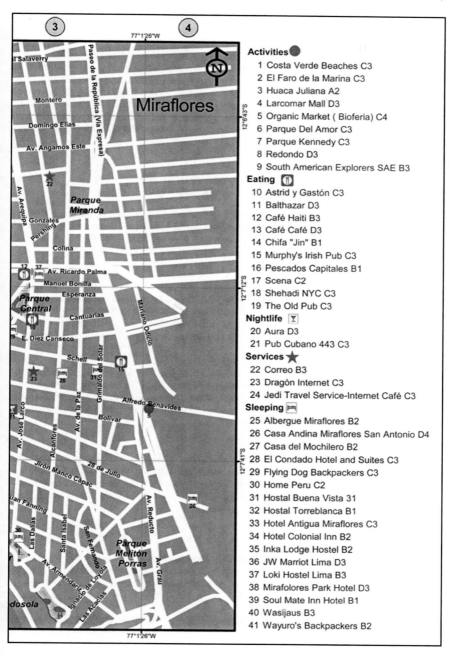

Miraflores

Activities ●
1 Costa Verde Beaches C3
2 El Faro de la Marina C3
3 Huaca Juliana A2
4 Larcomar Mall D3
5 Organic Market (Bioferia) C4
6 Parque Del Amor C3
7 Parque Kennedy C3
8 Redondo D3
9 South American Explorers SAE B3

Eating 🍴
10 Astrid y Gastón C3
11 Balthazar D3
12 Café Haiti B3
13 Café Café D3
14 Chifa "Jin" B1
15 Murphy's Irish Pub C3
16 Pescados Capitales B1
17 Scena C2
18 Shehadi NYC C3
19 The Old Pub C3

Nightlife 🍸
20 Aura D3
21 Pub Cubano 443 C3

Services ★
22 Correo B3
23 Dragón Internet C3
24 Jedi Travel Service-Internet Café C3

Sleeping 🛏
25 Albergue Miraflores B2
26 Casa Andina Miraflores San Antonio D4
27 Casa del Mochilero B2
28 El Condado Hotel and Suites C3
29 Flying Dog Backpackers C3
30 Home Peru C2
31 Hostal Buena Vista 31
32 Hostal Torreblanca B1
33 Hotel Antigua Miraflores C3
34 Hotel Colonial Inn B2
35 Inka Lodge Hostel B2
36 JW Marriot Lima D3
37 Loki Hostel Lima B3
38 Mirafolores Park Hotel D3
39 Soul Mate Inn Hotel B1
40 Wasijaus B3
41 Wayuro's Backpackers B2

LIMA

Costa Verde Beaches

There are four main surfable beaches along the Costa Verde beach road in Miraflores, Lima, and all are within a 15-minute walk of each other. South of the pier at Rosa Náutica Restaurant's is Redondo, and from there head north of the pier to find the breaks of Makaha, Waikiki and La Pampilla. All breaks are fairly consistent year round but best with a swell from the southwest. The shore and beach area of all four beaches consists primarily of large and small pebbles, making walking and entering/exiting the water difficult. The water can be very polluted. When you think you've just paddled through a jellyfish, it's more likely a just plastic bag or other plastic product. All breaks handle up to a maybe a little overhead wave, but consistently see waist-high to head-high surf. At Waikiki parking is tight, but the other three beaches have plenty of parking.

Waikiki

Not to be confused with Hawaii's famous Waikiki, Lima's Waikiki, may not have crystal clear, warm waters, but when the surfs breaks, it's a Lima favorite.

With consistently good waves, Waikiki is made of an exposed reef break and has a more northerly swell than the other Costa Verde Beaches. It's not typically crowded, but when the waters get moving, the people come running. Along the Costa Verde Beach Road in Miraflores, go north of the pier at Rosa Náutica Restaurant and you'll hit Waikiki, near La Pampilla Beach.

La Pampilla

Of all the Costa Verde beaches, La Pampilla is by far the most popular break for intermediate and advanced surfers—and it should only be surfed by those who are skilled and know what they are doing; novices need not apply. All breaks can see very good outer break wave formation, especially as the swell passes head-high. To get to La Pampilla head along the beach road in Miraflores then go north of the pier at Rosa Náutica Restaurant. It's near Makaha and Waikiki.

Makaha

Makaha is the most popular for beginner surfers, with both good inside and outside left and right breaks from an exposed reef. Schools and newbies occupy the inner break, and be warned, it can get fairly crowded on weekends. This beach, north of Rosa Náutica Restaurant's pier, has several kiosks along the sidewalk which rent boards and wetsuits for 20 soles / $6.60 per hour or less, and offer lessons for about 40 soles / $ 13.30 per hour.

Redondo

Picturesque Redondo is the only Costa Verde beach located south of the pier at Rosa Náutica Restaurant. The waves here break closer to the beach, providing an easier paddle. It is also less damning on the feet, as Redondo has less rock and more sand than the other Costa Verde beaches. The breaks here tend to be better with a more southerly swell. Costa Verde Beach Road—head south of the pier at Rosa Náutica Restaurant in Miraflores.

Shopping
Organic Market (Bioferia)

Every Saturday morning locals flock to Parque Reducto in Miraflores to buy fresh organic produce and to taste an assortment of organic breads, jams and coffee as part of the weekly Bioferia, or organic market. With a wide selection of fruits and vegetables, the Bioferia is cheap, delicious, unique and definitely is worth a visit.

Nearly a block long, the market is largely made up of a local organic farmers and environmental, education and natural health organizations, along with NGOs. It is a child-friendly zone, as there are many hands-on education activities for the young ones and many presentations on ecology and organic food production. Aside from fresh organic fruits and vegetables, you can pick up items such as chicken, eggs and a number of cow and goat milk products, including cheese. Perhaps the best, though, are the organic baked-goods and jams--and of course, don't forget to wash it down with a fresh organic guanábana juice or a sip of organic coffee. Open only on Saturdays. Parque Reducto, Avenida Benavides and the Vía Expresa.

Larcomar

From the street, Larcomar looks like a nice cliffside park with fountains, a few palm trees and a crowd of people hanging along the railing looking out to sea. Walk a few steps closer and discover a three-story mall packed with restaurants, fast-food joints, shops, discos, a 12-screen movie theater and a 24-lane underground bowling alley. Visitors gather topside for nightly sunset shows or to take take a breather from the fanfare below. On clear, calm days, a paraglider may drift by on their way to the beaches below. On the first level, which is open-air, shoppers can browse under the sun and watch daredevils get strapped to bungee cords and bounce around in a metal frame near the edge of the cliff. No one's going over on this ride, but it looks like it from the rumble seat. Stores vary from mainstream jean and T-shirt shops to bookstores and boutiques that specialize in Peruvian handicrafts. American staples like RadioShack, KFC and Burger King make an appearance here. People who forgot to pack guidebooks and film can find it at Larcomar, as well as sleeping bags and other outdoor gear at Tatoo Outdoors. There's also a Western Union. People looking for more obscure things, like Che Guevara shirts, should head to the small trendy stores on Av. José Larco. If you're looking for crafts sold by the artists themselves or a bargain on crafts, Mercado de los Indios (Petit Thouars 5245) has a massive collection of artists and sellers under one roof. Larcomar's draw is its dramatic location with views of the Pacific. Av. Malecón de la Reserva 610, URL: www.larcomar.com.

RadioShack

It's not uncommon to leave home without bringing all the necessary gadgets and adapters. Without these essentials, say goodbye to your cell phone, MP3 player and hairdryer. But in foreign countries like Peru, RadioShack can be a godsend, supplying most common needs. Monday - Friday 9 a.m. - 6 p.m., Saturday and Sunday, 10 a.m. - 3 p.m., Av. Salaverry 3310. Tel: 51-1-264-2600. URL: www.radioshack.com.

MIRAFLORES TOURS

KTM Peru Motorcycles (Tours: $200+ / day)

KTM Peru Adventure Tours has been around officially since 1997, though their guides have been riding motorcycles and dirt bikes since the 1970s. Do the math: that is more than 30 years of experience. KTM caters to the most adventurous traveler and guarantees an exciting tour. There are one, two and three-day tours through the dunes of Ica. Prices are roughly $200 per day. They have every kind of bike for whichever adventure you would like: sport, racing, off-roading, adventure or sport minicycles. Safety is a primary concern of theirs, and their expert guides are very careful to supply all the knowledge and advice a rider may need. Av. Benavides 2854, Tel: 51-1-260-8854, E-mail: informes@ktmperu.com, URL: www.ktmperu.com.

Bike Tours of Lima

Biking in Lima is an unforgettable experience. The tours cover the best neighborhoods and spots of this big city, mainly using bicycle lanes and less-traffic roads and streets. The bikes are also comfortable and safe. It's a great way to see the city with a very cool and friendly staff. Bolivar 150, behind Atlantic City Casino, Miraflores. Tel: 51-1-4453172, E-mail: info@bike-toursoflima.com, URL: www.biketoursoflima.com

MIRAFLORES LODGING

Miraflores is one of Lima's swankier neighborhoods with fancy hotels and chic hostels. Accommodations for the traveler interested in low-budget travel include many clean, cheap hostels. The atmosphere tends to be laid back and sociable with youthful staff excited to offer advice about the city. There is also a variety of mid-range to high-end hostels and hotels offering many luxuries and great views overlooking the ocean. The area is generally safe; however, like all cities, it is recommended that you be aware of your surroundings, as things do happen. The neighborhood attracts many young travelers and weekends can get pretty noisy.

BUDGET

Casa del Mochilero (Dorm: $4)

Casa del Mochilero ("House of the Backpacker") is a clean, efficient hostel just a few blocks from Kennedy Park in Miraflores. It has bunk rooms and visitors must share a bathroom, but at about $4 per night, the price is right. Chacaltana 130-A, Tel: 51-1-444-9089.

Flying Dog Backpackers (Dorm: $8, Rooms: $22)

Flying Dog Backpackers is a clean, airy hostel located very close to Kennedy Park, which puts it near most of the sites of interest in the Miraflores district. It has a variety of options ranging from dorm-style rooms with shared bath to more private double rooms. The staff is very knowledgable about the surrounding areas: where to eat, good bars, etc. They speak English and Spanish and understand Portuguese and Italian. There are discounts for longer stays. Diez Canseco 117, Tel: 51-1-445-6745 / 445-0940, Fax: 51-1-445-2376, E-mail: flyingdog@mixmail.com, URL: www.flyingdog.esmartweb.com.

Wasijaus (Rooms: $8 - 25)

Wasijaus is a clean, comfortable and secure bed and breakfast. Conveniently located in the Miraflores district, it is close to restaurants, travel agencies, supermarkets, banks and other services. Coronel Inclan 494, Tel: 51-1-445-8025, Fax: 51-1-445-8025, E-mail: reservas@wasijaus.com, URL: www.wasijaus.com.

Home Peru ($8 - 28)

Home Peru, located in the swank Miraflores district, is a restored colonial mansion popular with the backpacker crowd. Although it's a little bit more expensive than your typical dorm-style hostel, the comfortable rooms and new bathrooms make up for it. Av. Arequipa 4501, Tel: 51-1-241-9898, E-mail: reservations@homeperu.com, URL: www. homeperu.com.

Wayruro's Backpackers (Dorm: $9)

Wayruro's Backpackers is a small, clean backpacker's hostel in Miraflores. Rooms are dormitory style. There is a game room with ping-pong, a pool table and *sapo* (a local game in which the object is to throw coins into the mouth of a brass frog). Enrique Palacios 900, Tel: 51-1-444-1564, E-mail: wayruros@wayruros.com, URL: www.wayruros.com.

Stop and Drop Lima Backpacker Hotel and Guest House (Dorms: $9 / per person, Rooms: $30)

Part surf haven, part hotel, Stop and Drop might feel a bit more like crashing at a friend's house. Rooms and common areas are basic, but the service is friendly and knowledgeable. Stop and Drop offers a number of services, including Spanish and/or surf lessons, personal lockers in each room, cable TV, movies, music, internet and kitchen. The reception is open 24 hours per day. Prices include tax. Berlin St. 168, Tel: 51-1-243-3101, Cell: 51-99-823-1953, E-mail: info@stopandrop.com, URL: www.stopandrop.com.

Loki Hostel Lima (Dorm: $9 - 12.50, Rooms: $32)

Formerly called Incahaus, this hostel is the new little brother of the stunning Loki Hostel in Cusco. Built in the 1920s, this house was used until 2000 as an office building. In 2005, it was beautifully transformed into the place to stop and party in Lima slam-bang in the heart of Miraflores. The friendly, outgoing staff will point you in the right direction to all the best bars, clubs, restaurants and markets. The hostel also has all the services that a backpacker could possibly want: free internet, free continental breakfast, comfy beds, excellent showers, a movie room with a DVD collection and Loki's famous barbecue nights. The in-house bar offers great views of Miraflores Park and surrounding areas. Av. Larco 189, Tel: 51-1-242-4350, Fax: 51-1-241-3701, E-mail: info@lokihostel.com, URL: www.lokihostel.com.

Inka Lodge Hostel ($10 - 25)
The Inka Lodge is a modern, friendly hostel. All of the facilities are new and well-maintained. There is a pleasant patio and space to relax on the roof. The decor is an interesting mix of modern with ancient Inca themes. The hostal has space for 30 in a variety of dorm rooms and doubles. Breakfast included in price. Elias Aguirre 278, Tel: 51-1-242-6989, URL: www.inkalodge.com/home.htm.

Albergue Miraflores House (Dorms: $11 / Person, Rooms: $13 - 32)
If you're looking for a clean, secure and comfortable place to stay after an exhausting trip, the friendly staff at Miraflores House will welcome you. They offer travel advice on local sights, planning trips and assistance with purchasing tickets for your next destination. Enjoy the lounge room, watching DVDs or cable TV, using the free internet, playing board games, or jamming on the musical instruments provided. Airport pickups can be arranged. Albergue Miraflores House has a late check in/out, offers free lockers for your valuables, free luggage storage, free kitchen and laundry service. Taxes and are breakfast included, as is internet, water and tea. Av. Comandante Espinar 611, Tel: 51-1-447-7748, Cell: 51-1-998-231-953, E-mail: fchauvel@terra.com.pe, URL: www.alberguemirafloreshouse.com.

Inka Frog Hostel ($13 - 46)
The hostel has brand new equipment and pleasant decorations. Rooms are equipped with cable TV, safe deposit box, radio-alarm clock and walk-in closets. Inka Frog also has a deluxe floor with double rooms (ensuites), triples and group rooms, all with private bathrooms and TVs. There is also the backpacker floor with shared rooms, but separate dressing rooms and bathrooms for each gender. The hostel is located one block away from two main avenues (Pardo and Comandante Espinar) where there are restaurants, coffee shops, travel agencies and movie theaters, among other services. Calle General Iglesias 271, Tel: 51-1-445-8979, E-mail: info@inkafrog.com, URL: www.inkafrog.com.

MID-RANGE
Lima Lodging (Rooms: $20 - 40)
A traveler's lodge run by an ex-backpacker turned travel agent, this is an ideal place if you don't want to spend much money yet want a pleasurable stay in a private and homey inn. Rooms are comfortable and pleasantly outfitted. Prices include tax, discounts available if you stay more than a week. Av. Roca and Boloña, Tel: 51-14-461-621, Cell: 51-19-911-78801, E-mail: info@limalodging.org, URL: www.limalodging.org.

Hostal Eiffel (Rooms: $30 - 80)
Only 15 minutes from downtown Lima and 30 minutes from Jorge Chávez International Airport, Hostal Eiffel, in the middle of Miraflores, enjoys a central location near banks, shopping centers and entertainment. The hostel is comfortable, secure and quiet. Each room is equipped with cable TV, private bathroom and hot water. Prices include breakfast and taxes. Juan Fanning 550, Tel: 51-1-99-61-1737, Fax: 51-1-565-0016, E-mail: hotelsperu@yahoo.es.

Residencial el Farro (Rooms: $30 - 80)
More along the lines of a U.S. beach motel than hostel, the rooms at the Faro Inn Hostel are loaded with simple features and have a bland decor. All 20 of the hostel's rooms come with a TV and queen-sized bed, and features such as a small refrigerator and larger closets come as you move from standard to suite and executive-level rooms. The senior suite, at the top end, comes with a Jacuzzi tub in the bathroom. There is a sea view from the building's terrace. Prices include breakfast and tax. Calle Francia 857, Tel: 51-1-242-0339, Fax: 51-1-243-2651, E-mail: residencialelfaro@hotmail.com, URL: www.elfaroinn.com.

Hostal El Patio (Rooms: $35 - 65)
Hostal El Patio is a small, cozy mid-range hotel in Miraflores. A bit chic by design, it looks more like a B&B than a hostel, with wonderfully decorated common areas and a relaxing patio. If

you need a break from the more raucous hostels, this place is worth checking first. The hostel is very charming but has limited space, so reservations are suggested. Cash payments may receive a discount. Diez Canseco 341a, Tel: 51-1-444-2107, Fax: 51-1-444-1663, E-mail: hostalelpatio@qnet.com.pe, URL: www.hostalelpatio.net.

Hostal Buena Vista (Rooms: $35 - 65)

Hostal Buena Vista is well-located in the Miraflores district: It is close to old town as well as the hip Miraflores nightlife. The streets immediately surrounding the Buena Vista are, however, relatively quiet and tranquil. The common areas have a bit more pizzazz. Av. Grimaldo del Solar 202, Tel: 51-1-447-3178, E-mail: hostalbuenav@bonus.com.pe, URL: www.hostalbuenavista.com/index3.htm.

V!VA Member Review- Hostal Buena Vista

I loved this place! The front courtyard is beautiful, gated and you feel very safe here. The people are warm and friendly. The morning breakfast is out of this world. Don't miss out. This place is packed with Old World charm.

Washington, USA, May 13, 2007

APU Peru, International student house (Rooms: $50 - $70 / week)

APU Peru helps foreign students and volunteers by providing furnished international student housing. Homey and economical, APU has two houses and an apartment located in Miraflores. While not a hostel, foreign visitors, including students, internship recipients, workers and volunteers, can rent a room for one week to 12 months. Both cozy houses have WiFi internet access, laundry, fully furnished rooms, common rooms and a large kitchen. The houses are also a great place to meet other longer-term international residents. Salsa classes are available, as are Spanish classes, and a there is also a discount at a gym nearby. Prices can't be beat and the staff is super friendly. APU 1: 355 Diego Ferre, APU2: 815 Coronel Inclan, APU Apartment: 354 Libertad apartment 118, Tel: 51-1-446-8909 / 99-780-5153 E-mail: apuperu@student-houses-peru.com, apuperu@hotmail.com, apuperu@yahoo.com, URL: www.student-houses-peru.com.

Hotel Colonial Inn (Rooms: $50 - 80)

Hotel Colonial Inn is an attractive mid-range hotel, with elegant and comfortable rooms; two have a jacuzzi. There is a pleasant lobby and a bar for relaxing, and a restaurant and terrace. The Colonial Inn welcomes all visitors but particularly caters to business travelers, providing a business center and conference room. The hotel also boasts a restored vintage automobile; city tours in the car are available. Av. Comandante Espinar 310, Tel: 51-1-241-7471, Fax: 51-1-445-7587, E-mail: hotel@hotelcolonialinn.com, URL: www.hotelcolonialinn.com.

Soul Mate Inn Hotel (Rooms: $50 - $90)

The Soul Mate Inn Hotel offers comfortable rooms, a cafeteria, a select bar, facilities for social activities and special events (for up to 50 people) and room service 24 hours per day. Additionally, suites have free internet. The hotel's Sky Bar, on a wide terrace with a view to the sea, serves up barbecue. The hotel is located just 20 minutes from the airport. Toribio Pacheco 350, Tel: 51-1-221-5046 / 421-4167, Fax: 51-1-421-5134, E-mail: reservas@soulmate-inn.com, URL: www.soulmate-inn.com.

Hostal Torreblanca (Rooms: $53 - 77)

Hostal Torreblanca is a pleasant mid-range hotel which offers a wide variety of services, including cable TV in every room, taxis, business services (copies, internet, etc.) and more. They also arrange tours and excursions, such as visits to the Nasca Lines and Lima city tours.

The attached restaurant specializes in steaks and pasta. Breakfast is included in the price. Av. José Pardo 1453, Tel: 51-1-447-3363, Fax: 51-1-447-3363, E-mail: hostal@torreblancaperu.com, URL: www.torreblancaperu.com/ing/index.htm.

Best Western Embajadores (Rooms: $65 - 80)

Unlike the U.S. chain, Best Western South America is not just a motel on the side of the highway. While not over-the-top luxury, Best Westerns in Latin America tend to be more upscale than their northern counterparts. Best Western Embajadores is no exception. The hotel is a good, safe choice without too many frills. Comfortable beds, cable TV, a mini-bar, telephones and clean bathrooms are what you get for a reasonable price, and the swimming pool and mini gym don't hurt either. Tax and breakfast included. Juan Fanning 320, Tel: From the US or Canada: 1-800-780-7234; Locally: 51-1-242-9127, Fax: 51-1-242-9131, E-mail: hotelembajadores@mixmail.com, URL: www.bestwestern.com.

HIGH-END
Casa Andina Miraflores San Antonio (Rooms: $74.50 - 117.70)

Although not in the heart of Miraflores like its sister hotel, Casa Andina Miraflores, Casa Andina Miraflores San Antonio is perfect for the traveler who wants to be out of the hustle of Miraflores, but within walking distance of the major attractions and amenities. Unlike the Miraflores-proper hotel, San Antonio includes an on-site restaurant, Waykuna Andean. The hotel has cable TV, phones, clean rooms, modern bathrooms and firm beds; local and international companies often hold conferences and meetings at this location, which also has a 25-person conference room, free wireless internet, parking and, of course, food. As with all Casa Andina hotels, if you're traveling the tourist circuit you're likely to see many of the same foreigners at one Casa Andina and then at another, as the company makes it super easy to book all hotels (which are scattered throughout tourist areas of Peru) from just one location. Prices include breakfast and taxes. Av. 28 de Julio 1088, Tel: 51-1-241-4050, Fax: 51-1-241-4051, URL: www.casa-andina.com.

Hotel Antigua Miraflores (Rooms: $79 - 154)

A charming turn-of-the-century mansion that has since been converted to a hotel, Hotel Antigua Miraflores has the homey feel of a bed and breakfast with fully modern facilities. The staff provides excellent service. The hotel is expensive, but good value for the money. Prices include service and breakfast. Av. Grau 350, Tel: 51-1-241-6116, Fax: 51-1-241-6115, E-mail: info@peru-hotels-inns.com, URL: www.peru-hotels-inns.com.

Casa Andina Miraflores Hotel (Rooms: $85.30 - 117.70)

Upscale but not over the top is the best way to describe Casa Andina's Miraflores location. A small hotel chain in Peru, Casa Andina is decorated in colorfully bright Incan décor with super comfortable beds and clean, carpeted rooms. The Miraflores location has all the standard American and European amenities, including: cable TVs, air conditioning, phones and modern, marble baths with 24-hour hot water. The hotel is expanding from 42 rooms to 58, which are scheduled to include new deep bathtubs. The super friendly staff and a suburb location--smack in the middle of bustling Miraflores-make this a great hotel to call home. Tax and buffet breakfast included in the price of stay. Av. Petit Thouars 5444, Tel: 51-1-447-0263 / 241-3160, Fax: 51-1-447-0336, URL: www.casa-andina.com.

El Condado Hotel and Suites (Rooms: $110 - 170)

A tranquil boulevard, lined with various quaint bars and restaurants, separates El Condado from the chaotic, casino-lined Avenida Larco. The hotel is close to the action, but the narrow one-way street contributes to a detached, relaxed vibe. The whole hotel--the individual rooms and the common areas-are decorated with class and subtlety. All rooms are equipped with a standard mini-bar and wireless connection, not to mention private baths, hot water, comfy beds, cable and phones. With a gym, hot-tub, classy bar and restaurant, El Condado is

LIMA

a definite contender for those willing to spend the cash. Tax included. Alcanfores 465, Tel: 51-1-444-0306, E-mail: ventas@condado.com.pe, URL: www.condado.com.pe.

Miraflores Park Hotel (Rooms: $350 - 1650)
The Miraflores Park Hotel is one of Lima's finest. Owned by the prestigious international Orient Express group, the hotel offers everything you would expect from a $350 per night hotel: impeccable service and facilities, comfortable rooms, swimming pool, squash court, etc. The Miraflores Park Hotel caters to well-heeled tourists and international business travelers. It features business facilities, a five-star restaurant and even an English pub. Miraflores Park is a great place to stay if you can afford it. Prices may not include taxes and service fees. Contact the hotel for information on specials and packages. Av. Malecón de la Reserva 1035, Tel: 51-1-242-3000, Fax: 51-1-242-3393, E-mail: mirapark@peruorientexpress.com.pe, URL: www.mira-park.com.

JW Marriott Lima
The Marriott hotel chain is well-known for luxury lodgings, and their Lima branch is no different. JW Marriot offers everything you would expect from a five-star hotel. Malecón de la Reserva 615, Tel: 51-1-217-7000, Fax: 51-1 217-7100, URL: marriott.com/property/propertypage/LIMDT.

MIRAFLORES RESTAURANTS
The Miraflores district of Lima is home to some of the best food in the city. There is a variety of options, from five-star restaurants to street vendors. If you love fish and other dishes from the sea, you'll want to splurge for a fine meal at one of Miraflores' many seafood restaurants.

BUDGET
Chifa "Jin" (Entrées: $2 - 4)
While in Lima you have to try the Chifa "Jin." The Chinese food here, however, is distinct from western countries: it's more flavorful and fresh, and the ingredients, especially the spices, are far more eclectic. Chifa "Jin" in Miraflores is an excellent place to sample this unique Asian food; the atmosphere is relaxed and the food is high quality. Try the *sopa wantan, wantan frito* or *pollo chi jau kay*, some of the local favorites. Head away from Parque Kennedy on Av. José Pardo and get off at the first circle you see, about a mile away. Right on Ca. Moore, only a few shop fronts from the circle. Moore 152, Tel: 51-1-445-0122.

Restaurant Aries ($2 - 6)
If you want to save some money and taste some excellent, typical Peruvian cuisine, be adventurous and head to Restaurant Aries. Across from Ripley's Department store, only four storefronts from the corner of Ca. Lima and Ca. Schell, family-run, Aries forms part of the pulse of Miraflores downtown. The frank simplicity—the faded mustard-yellow walls, the worn tile floors—nicely complements the authenticity of the food. Two dollars will get you the two-course menú del día. Try ceviche or *papa rellena* (a fried potato stuffed with ground beef, onions and olives) for the entrada, and for the main dish, you can't go wrong with *cabrito* (goat meat) or *picante de mariscos* (shrimp, octopus and squid covered in a creamy garlic sauce). Lima 110, Tel: 51-1-446-5708.

Super Rueda ($3 - 4)
Super Rueda is a nice joint with tasty, greasy fast food. A popular spot on the weekends, it's a pit stop for revelers after a night of partying at local bars. With an outdoor patio, it creates a pleasant atmosphere for chatting and drinking some more beers. The food selection is varied—Peruvian-style tacos, empanadas (beef- and chicken-filled pastries) and hamburgers are typical fare. If you want to indulge yourself a bit and chill out in a relaxed ambience, you've got to check out Super Rueda. Open Monday - Sunday, 8 a.m. -2 a.m. Av. José Pardo 1224, Tel: 51-1-445-6919.

Café Haití (Entrées: $7 - 12)
The bamboo chairs and plastic cream-colored tables exude a pungent air of 1960s Havana. Along the sidewalk, you see a broad, maroon awning with golden rails and dozens of full tables that emit a hum of excited, amicable conversation. Discussions are on all sides: politi-

cal corruption, literature, fútbol. Whether you're sipping on a coffee or sampling one of their three most popular dishes-ceviche, lomo saltado (marinated strips of steak over rice and potatoes) or sopa criolla (Creole soup)-you'll appreciate the ambiance of this 45-year-old Miraflores relic. Diagonal 150, Tel: 51-1-445-0539, E-mail: fafg@infonegocio.net.pe.

El Parquetito Café ($7 - 12)

Hip Parque Kennedy attracts bar-goers, sightseers and park strollers to central Miraflores, and diners at El Parquetito Café have a ringside seat to the daily parade. Candles light individual tables, which stretch from the restaurant front to the park. The tiny white lights illuminate the eating area in a soft glow. The menu offers traditional Peruvian dishes such as cebiche, which is raw shrimp or fish marinated in lemon juice and served chilled, as well as beef dishes such as grilled steak served with an egg, rice and fried plantains. Fresh juices, Pilsener and other beers, and mixed drinks are served, as well as a fairly extensive list of desserts, including cakes and flan. Patrons who order breakfast can relax with a cup of coffee and juice, eat toast and eggs and watch other people hurry off to work. Ambiance is the draw here. Hours: Open for breakfast at 8 a.m. Dinner until late. Jirón Diez Canseco 117, Tel: 51-1-444-0490.

Coco de Mer (Entrees: $7 - 12)

This is an excellent home-away-from-home when you're feeling lost in Lima's hectic core. The place has a lovely atmosphere and the British owners have given it a classy yet casual feel. One of the interesting aspects is that they have local art on the walls and it isn't the usual artesany, poncho-style stuff! The other great thing is that the restaurant serves food and drinks all day long, unlike most places, and the prices are very reasonable. Coco de Mer is highly recommended if you are passing through Lima. Av. Grau 400, Tel: 51-1-243-0278, E-mail: cocodemerlima@gmail.com.

Shehadi NYC (Entrées: $7 - 14)

Directly across the street from Parque Kennedy, in the center of the tourist mecca of Miraflores, you will find this excellent café/restaurant. Decked out with soft orange lighting, a chic bar, tasteful wooden décor and a nice sidewalk vista, you would expect the place to be more expensive. For a reasonable price you can enjoy classic Peruvian cuisine, pizza or a broad array of salads. One of the best bets in central Miraflores. Diagonal 220, Tel: 51-1-444-0630.

> *V!VA Member Review—Shehadi NYC*
>
> Shehadi's is THE place to go in Lima. Anyone used to the upscale lounges of LA, NY or Playa Del Carmen will feel at home at Shehadi's. I was amazed out how great the food is compared to the local alternatives. I practically ate there for a week!
>
> *San Francisco, U.S.A., July 27, 2007*

MID-RANGE

Murphy's Irish Pub

Open 6pm till late Monday to Friday. Live music Thursday, Friday and Saturday. Free pool table and darts. Ca. Schell 627, Tel: 51-1-242-1212, E-mail: irishpublima@yahoo.es, URL: www.irishpublima.com.

Balthazar

This modern café/restaurant is a tasty, affordable option if you want to eat in the popular Larcomar shopping complex. With comfortable, stylish sofas, a beautiful ocean view and a comprehensive menu of gourmet sandwiches, salads and desserts, Balthazar is not a bad place for a pit stop. Larcomar shopping complex, Tel: 51-1-242-0140.

Find more reviews from travelers at www.vivatravelguides.com

Arúgula

Arúgula is a quiet after-theatre or -cinema restaurant a few blocks from Larcomar and the centre of Miraflores. The décor is quiet and unassuming with a played-down elegance. Arúgula is one of the favorite hangouts for Peru's best writers and artists, who usually are found conversing in the corner tables over the excellent wines. Dishes of the day are written on a blackboard and include such delicacies as tuna tartare, rabbit ravioli and osobucco with saffron, among other wonders. The three-mushroom pizza is wonderful. Salads are delicious and include items such as squash flowers filled with prosciutto, fresh dates with blue cheese or grilled chicken breast rolled in sesame, all served over a bed of arugula. Ca. San Fernando 320, Tel: 51-14-440-132.

Patagonia Art-Bar

Owned by a couple of Argentine artists, this art bar's ambience feels like Buenos Aires and its cultural life. The bar is divided into three main areas: a comfy bar lounge at the entrance, a European-style dining area and an open-air terrace. They also have a room for alternative events like theatre, poetry or dance. Photos and paintings adorn the walls. Not surprisingly, the kitchen serves a variety of Argentinean cuisine, like *matambre* and their famous steaks. Tango workshops are held twice a week. Open Monday - Saturday, 6 p.m. until everyone leaves. Ca. Bolívar 164, Tel: 51-14-451-165.

Café Café

As the name suggests, this is the place for coffee, twice-over-good coffee. However, you can also enjoy large breakfasts, lunches and dinners with generous servings of well-cooked, down-to-earth food at reasonable prices, plus a well-stocked bar. The dessert trolley is frighteningly sumptuous. But really the main reason for making this a must, is the suspended-over-the-ocean view that you have. Being 200 meters vertically over sea level, you can sit outside on the balcony and be nicely blown away as you watch airplane wings swoop past at eye level, and watch the tiny cars below you, with the ocean stretching away to the horizon. At night, it is equally impressive, as you can see the lights of the neighboring coastal districts strung like a diamond necklace around the bay. They do have a large cozy indoor area for those who prefer creature comforts. They have branches in Avenida Diagonal, close to the Central Park of Miraflores and another in downtown Lima. Inside Larcomar Mall. Tel: 51-1-445-1165.

La Dalmacia

This is a place where people from Miraflores go for coffee, for a drink or to eat, and, of course, to look and be seen. The daily special is chalked on a board and the food is displayed around their horseshoe-styled bar. Tapas are popular, and great for a light lunch or supper. La Dalmacia is candlelit. It is full by about 10 p.m., so if you want a table, get there early. Slices of home-baked bread served with seasoned olive oil for dipping greets you as you decide what to order. La Dalmacia has a good selection of wines and a bar. Quiches are very popular as well as soufflés of spinach and artichoke. If you are a vegetarian, try the outstanding veggie lasagna. When La Dalmacia is full, the noise level is high. It is within walking distance from Larcomar and the center of Miraflores. Open Monday-Saturday, 8 a.m.-2 a.m., Sunday, 8 a.m.-11 p.m. San Fernando 401, Tel: 51-1-445-7917.

La Isla del Mono

La Isla del Mono offers Lima's seafood at its best. Offerings include their mouth-watering Ceviche de Lenguado, or sole ceviche-raw sole, served dripping in a delicious lemony-chili sauce. You also can partake in a variety of other fishy treats. If you're lucky, they may offer you a free pisco sour or two. New as of October 2007, the restaurant's decor is modern and chic but minimal, located in one of the few remaining older buildings in Miraflores. San Martín 835. Tel: 51-1-243-3080, URL: www.laisladelmono.com.pe.

Fluid

For great Thai food right in the heart of the Miraflores district, head to Fluid. This new, British-run venue serves Asian cuisine amid a chilled ambience and funky decor. It is popular with the backpacker set and trendy Limeños alike. The food is carefully prepared, tastefully presented and exquisite. Try the red chicken curry, for an authentic Thai experience, or go at lunchtime (12 noon to 4 p.m.) for the generous set "Thai Combo" menu for 15 soles. Owners Kia and Richard Haylett go out of their way to ensure that your experience is a good one. Oh, and in case you're not sold already, this place has a happy hour ever day from 6 til 9 p.m., WiFi internet, a book exchange and a pool table to boot. The restaurant is open from midday every day except Sunday, and from 6 pm to midnight it is happy hour. Berlín 333. Tel: 51-1-242-9885, URL: www.fluidperu.com.

HIGH-END

Las Brujas de Cachiche

You'll find this impressive restaurant tucked away in the tranquil backstreets of Miraflores. A fusion of international techniques with classic Peruvian recipes, you can't find Peruvian food much better than Brujas. The menu is broad and features an excellent three-course buffet as well as a long list of individual entrees. Located in a large, wooden chalet-like mansion—high wooden ceilings with basic, yet tasteful interior design—Brujas has a very relaxed, unpretentious ambience. If you're going to spend the bucks, Brujas is something you shouldn't miss. Open Monday - Sunday, 10 a.m. - 10 p.m. Bolognesi 460, Tel: 51-1-444-5310 / 447-1883, E-mail: alcorta@brujasdecachiche.com.pe.

El Kapallaq

El Kapallaq is an upscale cevichería, considered one of Lima's best by locals. Try a ceviche or one of the traditional stews, made in clay pots. Open only for lunch. Av. Petit Thouars 4844, Tel: 51-1-444-4149.

Pescados Capitales

Pescados Capitales is an excellent seafood restaurant hidden away in a corner of the Miraflores district, it serves good desserts, too. La Mar 1337, Tel: 51-1-421-8808 / 222-5731.

Astrid y Gastón

Consistently rated as one of Lima's best restaurants, Astrid y Gastón is located on a little side street not far from Parque Miraflores. The food is outstanding. Don't forget to save room for dessert. Be sure to call ahead for reservations. Cantuarias 175, Tel: 51-1-444-1496.

Scena

If you don't feel like you're in a swanky New York City bar when you walk into Scena, it might be for the lack of New Yorkers. And like a Big Apple bar, Scena is a place to see and be seen. A more upscale restaurant and bar with bright colors and bright lights, Scena takes its name literally from "The Scene," as in theatre. Don't be surprised to see champagne on multiple tables here. As for the food, the menu is influenced by the Middle East and combined superbly with fresh Peruvian ingredients. More fun arrives at 10 o'clock when a surpise 20-minute performance begins. The lights lower and the entertainment begins—a trapeze show, a tight rope walker or perhaps a harlequin flirting with the audience. The decoration is nicely bizarre. A surprising touch is a man's voice dictating yoga lessons in the ladies' restroom, which can be quite a shock for the unprepared. Open for lunch, Monday - Friday, 12:30 - 4 p.m. and for dinner, Monday - Saturday, 7:30 p.m. - 12:30 a.m. Francisco de Paula Camino 280, Tel: 51-1-445-9688 /241-8184, URL: www.scena.com.pe.

La Rosa Náutica (Entrées: $9 - 49)

La Rosa Náutica is not only a top-of-the-line, first-class restaurant with elegant décor, but its cuisine includes some of the freshest, most creative gourmet dishes in all of Lima. Perched out on Pier 4 along Lima's beachfront in Miraflores, the restaurant is literally on the water, allowing patrons to overlook the waves and out into the horizon. La Rosa serves everything from unique seafood combos like the *ceviche norteño* (a mix of sole, scallops and flounder in a large sea scallop with corn, chili pepper and fried yucca) to grilled meats, poultry, pastas and outstanding salads like the warm goat cheese salad (tossed with mixed greens, sun-dried tomatoes and caramelized figs). Although La Rosa Náutica serves up a serious selection of seafood, the restaurant is sure to please even the vegetarian in your party, as they also have many vegetarian options, including the mushroom ceviche: a savory mix of mushrooms, peppers, garlic, ginger and hot chilis. If you can't afford the prices, go for just for a drink at the restaurant's bar, El Espigón Bar. You can watch the sunset while drinking a Pisco sour overlooking the ocean—it's a surreal, romantic experience that is difficult to be had anywhere else in town. Espigón 4 (Pier 4) Circuito de Playas, Tel: 51-1-445-0149 / 447-0057 / 447-5450, E-mail: ventas@larosanautica.com, URL: www.larosanautica.com.

MIRAFLORES NIGHTLIFE

Pub Cubano 443

Always packed on the weekends, this club is the hotspot for Cuban salsa. Though the club isn't too big, it packs in a lot of energy and movement. Hidden down an inconspicuous side street, it attracts a more local, less touristy crowd, but the drinks can be steep. It's a good option if you feel like dancing and absorbing the local vibe. Monday - Thursday, 10 p.m. - 2 a.m., Friday - Sunday, 10 p.m. - sunrise. San Martin 443, Tel: 51-1-242-2038 / 9-921-8684 E-mail: pubcubano@443pubcubano.com, URL: www.443pubcubano.com.

Jazz Zone (Cover: $3.30 - $6.80)

Located in the heart of Miraflores in a garden walk-through passageway, this cozy jazz bar also hosts art exhibitions from local artists. Their musical variations range from Latin jazz fusions to contemporary jazz live performances. International bands play throughout the year. Jazz Zone is fond of supporting young and innovative artists, and offers musical instrument workshops for anyone who wants to feel the jazz. La Paz 656, Tel: 51-1-241-8139.

Tumbao VIP (Cover: $5 - 7)

Near Parque Kennedy, at the end of the touristy Calle de los Pizzas ("Pizza Street"), this salsa club is a good option for those who want to get down, get dancing and get to know the locals. Of the many clubs on Calle de las Pizzas, Tumbao VIP is one of the largest and most impressive. It also features renowned salsa artists monthly. Open Monday - Sunday, 10 p.m. until the party slows. Ca. Bellavista 237, Tel: 51-1-446-5530.

The Old Pub

Oddly enough, the most authentic English pub in Lima, The Old Pub, is centrally located in Lima's "Little Italy," or as some call it, "Pizza Street," Ca. San Ramón, a short road near Parque Miraflores. But don't let a whiff of Italy deter you; after all, it's an English pub, owned by a proper Brit—and it's in Peru—so you've probably come searching for that refreshing taste of home and comfort. Quickly upon entering, you know you've got the real deal with the large display of beers on tap, the colorful mosaic of old drink coasters pinned to the wall, and of course, the dart board, one of only a few in town. The super friendly crowd (not surprisingly many ex-pats and travelers) and the nostalgic environs of the The Old Pub will fill you with a sense of place and some jolly good cheer. Sadly, you won't be able to satisfy those hunger pangs with a plate of old fashioned English fish and chips—the pub doesn't serve food. But let it be known that seafood in Lima is plentiful and delicious, and you can always find a place for some fresh fish after a few good beers and merrymaking. Open till 2-3am. San Ramon 295.

Tasca Bar

Under the same ownership as the Flying Dog, and located conveniently underneath the Diez Canseco branch of the hostel, Tasca Bar is a popular hangout. It is all too easy to drop in from the hostel above, joining the trendy Limeños. Bar stools are arranged around a long, narrow bar, from which patrons can (and do) purchase all manner of alcoholic drinks and cocktails. They have the local brew, Cusqueña on tap, for about 5 soles ($1.5) a glass. 117 Diez Canseco.

El Latino

Head to El Latino, if you feel like dancing but aren't in the mood for a club that is too overwhelming. One of the many dance clubs on Calle de las Pizzas, El Latino is a small club, with a medium-sized dance floor, dark lighting and a big screen TV. If you're looking to chill out and relax to some music, you probably won't find that here: salsa, samba and reggaetone always hold sway. So, if you want the fast upbeat music and have your dancing shoes on, this is where it's at. Monday - Thursday, midnight - 2 a.m., Friday and Saturday, midnight - 4 a.m. Closed Sunday. Pasaje San Ramón 234, better known as Calle de Las Pizzas or "Little Italy," Tel: 51-1-242-7176.

Aura (Cover: $12.50)

Located in Larcomar, Aura is the premier upscale dance club in Miraflores, and for that matter, in all of Lima. A huge dance floor, several bars and lots of lounge areas turn it up with a mix of pop (Latin, US and Brit), electrónica, and techno. It's is the place for posh, youthful 20-something Limeños to be seen. Sophisticated, classy dress is typically the attire, men should plan to wear collared shirts; oddly enough, jeans are okay. Reminiscent of the Buenos Aires nightlife scene with a little LA and Manhattan spice thrown in, neon lights and modern decor keep it fresh. Aura is open until sunrise on the weekends and doesn't really pick up speed until 2 a.m., giving party-goers three to four hours of non-stop dancing. Any traveler who wants to keep the party going past the typical 3 a.m. closing hour, won't be sad, even to pay the pricey 40 soles (or $12.50) to get in. As long as you dress nicely and pay the cover, you can get in. The drinks are cheap and the club is very safe. Larcomar local 236, Tel: 51-1-242-5516, E-mail: informes@aura.com.pe, URL: www.aura.com.pe.

BARRANCO

Like San Isidro and Miraflores, Barranco is an upscale district of Lima. Barranco is located south of the city center; San Isidro and Miraflores, on the waterfront. It is home to several hotels and restaurants. Formerly a beach resort of sorts in Lima, today the district is known for a thriving arts and music scene, but there are also good bars and nightclubs.

BARRANCO HISTORY

The village of Barranco was founded by early Spanish settlers and soon became known as a popular seaside resort. By the time Peru became independent, it was a thriving retreat for Lima's wealthiest families. It was also a favorite for international families. Now it is an upscale district of Lima.

Barranco has a great deal of history. According to local legend, one night, a group of fishermen were lost at sea, enshrouded in Lima's famous dense fog. They prayed for salvation, and a luminous cross appeared, guiding them back to shore. The Ermita church was constructed on the site where the cross allegedly appeared, and since has become the preferred church for fishermen. Although the church was sacked by invading Chilean troops in 1881, is has been rebuilt and is an interesting site to visit.

Barranco was once known as "the city of windmills," as early settlers often used windmills to draw water from their wells. In 1870, the famous "Bajada a los Baños," a series of stairways that leads to the ocean, was constructed, and has since become an important Barranco landmark. Nearby, lovers meet on the Puente de Los Suspiros, "the Bridge of Sighs."

Find more reviews from travelers at www.vivatravelguides.com

In 1940, a strong earthquake hit the region and did a great deal of damage to Barranco. The town recovered, however, and rebuilt. There are many architectural wonders in Barranco, most of which date from the Republican era. Check out the Casa Nash or the Casa Checa Eguren, both of which are fantastic examples of older architecture. Today, Barranco is a romantic, bohemian, artistic district, known for lively nightlife.

According to local legend, one night, a group of fishermen were lost at sea, enshrouded in Lima's famous dense fog. They prayed for salvation, and a luminous cross appeared, guiding them back to shore. The Ermita church was constructed on the site where the cross allegedly appeared, and since has become the preferred church for fishermen. Although the church was sacked by invading Chilean troops in 1881, is has been rebuilt and is an interesting site to visit. Barranco was once known as "the city of windmills," as early settlers often used windmills to draw water from their wells. In 1870, the famous "Bajada a los Baños," a series of stairways that leads to the ocean, was constructed, and has since become an important Barranco landmark. Nearby, lovers meet on the Puente de los Suspiros, "the Bridge of Sighs."

In 1940, a strong earthquake hit the region and did a great deal of damage to Barranco. The town recovered, however, and rebuilt. There are many architectural wonders in Barranco, most of which date from the Republican era. Check out the Casa Nash or the Casa Checa Eguren, both of which are fantastic examples of older architecture. Today, Barranco is a romantic, bohemian, artistic district, known for lively nightlife.

THINGS TO SEE AND DO IN BARRANCO

Barranco's activities are not of the tree-swinging, white-water variety. Instead they highlight the art and culture of one of Lima's nicest neighborhoods. If you find yourself in Barranco, make sure you check out the galleries and art shops, because even if you're not buying, looking is worth the effort. This cliff-top town also showcases beautiful colonial architecture and a bridge that has inspired thousands of artists and poets the world over.

Museo Galería Arte Popular de Ayacucho

The Museo Galería Arte Popular de Ayacucho in Barranco, Lima, flaunts an excellent permanentcollection of art from the Ayacucho region, known for its painted religious panels. The anonymous murals found in the churches and basilicas of Ayacucho since the colonial period, afford great insight into the social customs of bygone areas. Pieces range from pre-hispanic to contemporary. Check out artifacts from the conquista such as El Cajón de San Marcos and several examples of Cruces de Camino. For a lesson in recent history, check out the Retablo Cayara, a representation of the 1998 standoff between the military and the Sendero Luminoso in which around 30 people were assassinated and another 45 "disappeared". Monday - Saturday, 9 a.m - 5 p.m. Closed Sundays. Av. Pedro de Osma 116, Tel: 51-1-247-0599, E-mail: info@mugapa. com, URL: http://www.mugapa.com/.

Puente de los Suspiros

The Puente de los Suspiros (Bridge of Sighs) was built in the late 1800s, and to this day remains a romantic landmark for couples and families to enjoy the company of loved ones. Overlooking the waters that gently run down to the beach, the Puente de los Suspiros has inspired musicians and artists with its antique planks and quaint cobblestone road that lead to a great ocean view atop a cliff. The old bridge connects the streets of Ayacucho and La Ermita and is surrounded by little eateries and sidewalk vendors selling local foods at good prices. Calle Ayacucho and Bajada a Los Baños.

Galería Lucía de la Puente

This famous commercial gallery is known as "the" art center in Lima. It is located in an old, fully refurbished Barranco mansion. Huge rooms with tall walls that reflect natural light onto the walls offer a great opportunity to appreciate works of art. Paseo Sáenz Peña 206, Tel: 51-1-477-9740, Fax: 51-1-247-4940, E-mail: ldelapuente@gluciadelapuente.com, URL: www.gluciadelapuente.com.

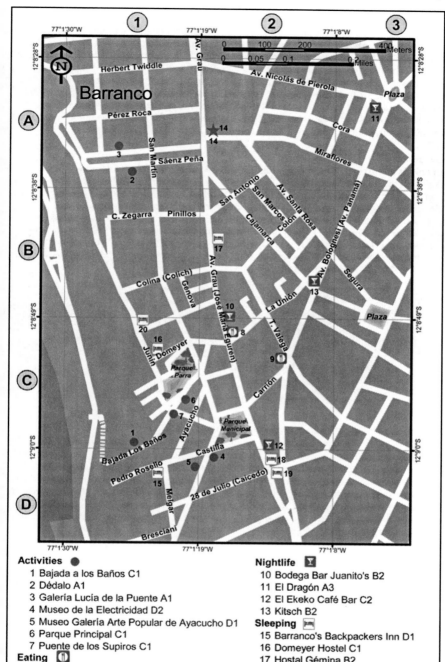

Activities ●
1 Bajada a los Baños C1
2 Dédalo A1
3 Galería Lucía de la Puente A1
4 Museo de la Electricidad D2
5 Museo Galería Arte Popular de Ayacucho D1
6 Parque Principal C1
7 Puente de los Supiros C1

Eating 🍽
8 El Mortal C2
9 La Noche C2

Services ★
14 Lavandería Neptuno

Nightlife 🍸
10 Bodega Bar Juanito's B2
11 El Dragón A3
12 El Ekeko Café Bar C2
13 Kitsch B2

Sleeping 🛏
15 Barranco's Backpackers Inn D1
16 Domeyer Hostel C1
17 Hostal Gémina B2
18 Mochilero's Backpackers D2
19 Quinto de Allison D2
20 The Point C1

Parque Principal

This is one of Lima's most beautiful and unique parks, planted in one of Lima's most charming and rustic areas. This little park serves as a plaza—and surrounded on four sides by beautiful Spanish architecture, tasteful restaurants and bars, an imposing crimson catholic church. The originality of the ambience is refreshing and invigorating. You can simply sit on the bench and consume all the energy and color. In the distance a green marble stage, reminiscent of a Greek amphitheatre, rests below the prominent, white marble neoclassical columns. Statues of Cupid, figures of Roman Goddesses, spring from the vibrant, decorative patches of flowers. And above, the large trees spread outwards, serving as umbrellas against Lima's piercing summer sun. Av. Grau (José María Eguren) and Av. Carrión.

Dédalo

Dédalo is a must see. Even if you don't plan to spend any money, it is well worth the visit. Staged in an old refurbished house in Barranco, a block away from the sea, it offers Peruvian non-traditional workmanship at its best. You will find beautiful handmade ceramics, blown glass, design-winning woodwork, stone carvings and the latest in textile design, among other works of art on a world-class level. They have a nice coffee shop on the inside patio, a children's toy area, handmade jewelry and a permanent exhibition of unique objects made out of recycled materials. There is no pressure to buy, so you can just wander at your leisure through the treasure-filled rooms. Monday-Saturday, 10 a.m.-9 p.m. Closed Sundays. Paseo Sáenz Peña 295, Tel: 51-1-477-0562, Fax: 51-1-477-5131.

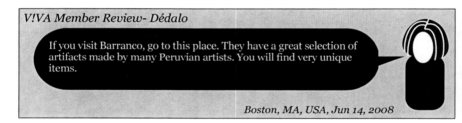

V!VA Member Review- Dédalo

If you visit Barranco, go to this place. They have a great selection of artifacts made by many Peruvian artists. You will find very unique items.

Boston, MA, USA, Jun 14, 2008

Museo de la Electricidad (Entrance: $0.60)

Directly adjacent to Parque Principal, this miniature museum-better said, exhibit-may be a 15-minute visit, but worth it. Posted to the walls are some charming old photos of Peru, and there's a room dedicated to antique, outdated electrical devices: telephones, record players, jukeboxes. Spanish speakers interested in Peru's history of electrical technology will also get something out of this simple, unassuming museum. This museum also has resources in Braille for the visually impaired and guides are available upon request. Daily, 9 a.m. - 5 p.m., Av. Pedro d'Osma 105, Tel: 51-1-477-6577, E-mail: museoelectri@speedy.com.pe, URL: museoelectri.perucultural.org.pe.

BARRANCO LODGING

Barranco's demographic has changed over the years and is now known as one of Lima's most lively districts. Beautiful colonial architecture combined with a vivacious nightlife tends to draw the younger, more transient crowds, and this is exactly who accommodation is geared toward. There are several top-notch hostels that will meet any backpacker's needs. There are also plenty of good mid- to high-end accommodations for the wealthier traveler wanting a piece of the nightlife.

La Casa Barranco ($7 per person)

La Casa Barranco is a small (ten beds), home-style hostel in Lima's Barranco district. Friendly, neat and clean, it's popular among the backpacker crowd. There is a kitchen and cable TV for the use of the guests. If you contact them, they'll pick you up at the airport for $14 (the airport is out of town a ways). Av. Grau 982, Tel: 51-1-477-0984 / 967-27449.

The Point (Rooms: $7 - $9)

The Point Backpacker's Hostel considers itself Lima's "original party hostel," a joint immensely popular among the international backpacker set. It is relatively new but becoming well known due to its lively, welcoming atmosphere. There are a number of entertaining extras here, such as a bar, ping-pong table, Nintendo, and more, that you don't find at every youth hostel. The nightly organized events and convenient location near some of Lima's best nightlife guarantee an enjoyable stay. Malecón Junín 300, Tel: 51-1-247-7997.

Safe in Lima (Dorm: $7, Rooms: $10 - 18)

Travelers will indeed feel safe in this wonderfully cozy hostel with a warm family atmosphere, located in a quiet, green area and just 20 meters from ocean view. the main square in Barranco is a ten minute stroll away and surrounding neighborhoods can be easily accessed. All rooms have a private bathroom and double rooms have a queen-sized bed. Rooms are clean, comfortable and spacious and guests can use the kitchen for free. Safe in Lima also offers a pick up service from the airport or bus terminal, offers free information and maps about Lima and will help organize tours of the city. Alfredo Silva 150, Tel: 51-1-252-7330, E-mail: info@ safeinlima.com.

Barranco's Backpackers Inn (Dorm: $8 - 9, Rooms: $12)

Located in a quiet and scenic area, Backpacker's Inn is a short walk from surfing, a plaza, bars, live music, restaurants and shows just down the street. Ocean views from this renovated mansion are stunning, and rooms for two, four or six people are clean and comfortable. There is 24-hour hot water and showers, complimentary cable TV and internet access, laundry service, housekeeping and airport pick-up at below average rates. Tours, trips and surfing can be organized by the hostel. The staff also speaks both Spanish and English. Mariscal Castilla 260, Tel: 51-1-247-1326, URL: www.barrancobackpackers.com.

Mochilero's Backpackers (Rooms: $8 - $25)

Mochilero's Backpackers is one of Lima's best backpacker options. A converted old mansion, it is located close to the Parque Municipal, which is a bus hub for the city. It is very popular with students, and for good reason: present your student ID and you get a discount. There is a bar and pub right next door. Av Pedro de Osma 135, Tel: 51-1-477-4506, Fax: 51-1-477-0302, E-mail: backpacker@amauta.rcp.net.pe.

La Quinta de Allison (Rooms: $10 - 20)

The La Quinta de Allison resides on a quiet side street in Barranco. Inconspicuous and modest, this is one of the cheaper hotels in the area. Rooms tend to be smaller but are very comfortable. The bathrooms are decent, and some of the more expensive rooms have whirlpool tubs. Interior rooms tend to be a little darker and rooms with windows onto the street can be noisy at times. There is also an on-site restaurant, room service and bar. Jr. 28 de Julio 281, Tel: 51-1-247-1515.

Hostal Gemina (Rooms: $30 - $50)

This modern hotel, located above a shopping center, houses 31 small but comfortable rooms that have cable TV, decent bathrooms (with endless hot water!) and friendly service. Rates are negotiable, there is an on-site cafeteria and room service is 24-hours. Av. Grau 620, Tel: 51-1-477-0712, E-mail: gemina@tsi.com.pe.

Domeyer Hostel (Rooms: $40 - $80)

Stroll down this placid side street in Barranco and, as you approach the Domeyer Hostel, you'll be greeted by a friendly Labrador retriever who calls the funky, colonial Domeyer Hostel home. With boldly painted walls, bright bedspreads, vivid Peruvian tiles, local artwork decorating the walls and bronze statues setting about, this sophisticated hostel boasts comfortable rooms with high ceilings, tall windows and shutters that open to a fresh ocean breeze. Domeyer Hostel also has a guest kitchen with barbecue area, a small bar and lounge

LIMA

and the rates include free internet access and continental breakfast. Airport pickups can be arranged. Jr. Domeyer 296, Tel: 51-1-247-1413.

Second Home Peru (Rooms: $75 - $95)

Second Home Peru embodies the spirit of the Peruvian culture combined with the tranquility of the Pacific. This majestic B&B with five private rooms is conveniently anchored in central Barranco. To enter the once the home of Peruvian sculptor Victor Delfín, is to enter an artist's imaginative world replete with its creative works. You do not need to search far to find seedlings of inspiration; they abound in the gardens, terrace and Pacific view of this historic Tudor mansion. Taxes are included in their rates. Domeyer 366, Tel: 51-1-477-5021, Fax: 51-1-247-1042, E-mail: Secondh@aol.com, URL: www.secondhomeperu.com.

BARRANCO RESTAURANTS

Barranco's gastronomic scene reflects Lima's diverse and colorful food culture and has many options for a satisfying dining experience. If you aren't quite hungry enough for a big meal, meander through the passageway under El Puente de los Suspiros and pick up a quick treat from one of the various vendors along the way. If you're hungry enough for a large meal or want to make dinner a memorable experience, you'll find options for every pocketbook. For a special treat, you may want to consider a big bowl of ceviche on the beachfront.

La Posada del Ángel

If you like angels you'll find them here, hanging from the roof, peeking at you around corners, staring from the walls. This dark, cozy, rustic setting is blessed. Another enchanting, old "Barranco-style" house with many small rooms leading through a maze of antiques, found objects and cuckoo clocks that make you forget time. Tables and chairs are scattered around in a storybook atmosphere. Mainly beer and wine are served, but spirits abound. Pizza is a good choice, freshly made and not very expensive, among other starters. Music is performed live every night, mainly Latin American "nueva trova," with songs from well-known Cuban socialist Silvio Rodríguez, often described as the Latin American Bob Dylan. Av. Prolongación San Martín, Tel: 51-1-247-5544.

Restaurante Vida

Vida is a fantastic bar and restaurante located under the Puente de los Suspiros, arguably the most romantic place in Lima. This restaurant features haute Peruvian cuisine, but not haut prices, a zen garden, top-notch chef and sommelier. Bajada de Baños 340, Tel: 51-1-252-8034/ 252-8035, E-mail: info@restaurantevida.com, URL: www.restaurantevida.com.

Las Hamacas

Las Hamacas is a typical beach restaurant, but uniquely charming. You can sit in the open dining area or have your food and drink taken to your beach umbrella and lounge chairs. The food is very tasty, and it should be; owner Carlos looks after every detail, buying everything himself and also supervising the kitchen. You may want to try a *jalea*, an assortment of deep fried seafood on top of a delicious piece of fish, served with crispy golden yams and a salad. One plate is enough to feed about four people, but of course you've got to have a ceviche, either before or after the jalea, to complete the meal. There is private parking and this spot might be a good lunch choice if you want to explore the ruins at Pachacámac in the morning. Km 42 Panamerican Highway, Playa Punta Rocas.

El Mortal

Stumble out from the bars, walk a few steps and you're there. An excellent place to indulge that drunken appetite of yours-grease, grease and more grease. We're talking cheeseburgers, eggs, bacon, ham and french fries, fried chicken and heavy-duty sandwiches. But you can't deny the tastiness and the price. It's an easy sell for food and alcohol-lovers. It's got a cool atmosphere, too, in a rustic-dive-charming sort of way. So go eat and forget the consequences. Open 9 a.m.-3 a.m. Av. Grau 230, Tel: 51-1-255-9730.

El Delfín (Entrées: $4 - $8)

A soft ocean breeze filtered through the ravine below, softly brushes against the plants that hang from the wooden rafters. You stand up, approach the deck's railing and gaze in both directions-to the left, a calm moonlit ocean; to the right, a quaint lamp-lit path ascending towards Puente de Los Suspiros. You return to your seat, pick up your fork and delve into your papa a la huancaína (sliced potatoes topped with a creamy, slightly spicy sauce) and anticucho (fried cow hearts), which taste better than you ever thought possible. Scattered about the restaurant sit whispering couples and boisterous groups of friends. With everything from ceviche to burgers, El Delfín if perfect if you're looking for a relaxed restaurant with tasty food. Open from 11 a.m.-3 a.m., Monday-Sunday. Bajada de Baños 403, Puente de Los Suspiros, Tel: 51-1-477-6465.

El Suizo (Entrees: $7)

When asked if they know "El Suizo," most Limeños will respond, "Is that still there?" And yes, after 50 years it is still churning out the same wonderful dishes—mussels a la suisse, fresh sea bass and their most famous recipe (which isn't even on the menu), Corvina al Pardo, a delicious sea bass wrapped in a spinach sauce. Cooked however you'd like, the fish can also be steamed and served with burnt butter and capers over a perfectly boiled potato; this delicacy has a savory, delicate flavor. For dessert, try the apple pancakes with caramel. Hint: Eat them warm with a scoop of vanilla ice cream or else you will have to use a chisel. While catering to Lima's intelligentsia and academic crowds, the restaurant is situated on a small bay surrounded by impressive cliffs. You can easily watch surfers from here, and when the sea is high it has some of the best waves in all of the Pacific, fit only for professional surfers. Prices are average and the wine list limited, but you can bring your own bottle. The pisco sours are classic and the strawberry cocktails are unique. Taxes included in prices. Arrange for a taxi to pick you up. Located on Playa La Herradura, Tel: 51-1-467-0163.

Chala (Entrées: $15 - 20)

One of the newest upscale restaurants to hit Barranco is Chala, located in an old colonial-style house converted into a very hip, minimalistic restaurant and bar. Photographs taken of Lima at the beginning of the last century are shown, from which you can get an idea of the changes that have taken place. The veranda where lunch and dinner are also served is the same as it was 100 years ago, overlooking a tree-lined, cobbled pathway going down to the sea. From there you can see the two main features of Barranco, the Bridge of the Sighs (El Puente de Los Suspiros) and the old La Ermita church. The food at Chala is spectacular and inventive. Many of Peru's exotic fruits are used in its preparation. As a starter try the shrimp, which includes three extra-large shrimp stuffed with seasoned yam, and served with a thick sauce of passion fruit. For an entrée, taste the fresh tuna fish steak with a Peruvian berry topping. The complimentary, homemade nut-herb bread is delicious. The wine list is extensive and the service is excellent. Reservations are a must. Prices include tax. Bajada de Baños 343, Tel: 51-1-252-8515.

Punto Blanco (Set Lunch: $15.50)

You'll find Punto Blanco along a new promenade by the sea. A circular white building with glass windows overlooking Lima's bay, it offers an extensive and creative buffet, a large selection of ceviches, sushi and traditional creole Peruvian dishes. The staff is helpful and service is excellent. You can choose to sit on the terrace overlooking the beach or have a slightly more formal meal inside the main building. Prices are set for the lunch buffet at 49 soles, including desserts and an optional drink. Circuito de Playas Costa Verde, Tel: 51-1-252-8454 / 8423.

BARRANCO NIGHTLIFE

Bar Mochileros

Near the main square park of Barranco, Bar Mochileros is a former backpacker hostel now transformed into a series of bars and a cultural center where you can enjoy live circus-like performances, dance, music and emerging local DJ concerts. A young hip crowd gathers around the porch and the different terraces of this museum-like house. Concerts mainly take

LIMA

place in the basement bar which has a Liverpool "Cavern" feeling. All kinds of drinks are served at a moderate to inexpensive rate. Av. Pedro de Osma 135, Tel: 51-1-477-0302.

La Noche

One of the most famous venues in this bohemian district, over the years it has become a widely known cultural stage for music, film, photography and performing arts. It is located in a traditional wooden building with two milieus and two floors, each one with its own bar; one has daily live performances and the other, an art gallery. They have jazz every Monday night from 11 p.m., with no cover. Definitely a place that's alive any night of the week. Beer is mostly served in pitchers at a good price, as well as traditional Peruvian cocktails made out of pisco. Their food is well served and could be described as Spanish tapas. Av. Bolognesi 307 (El Boulevard), Tel: 51-1-477-5829.

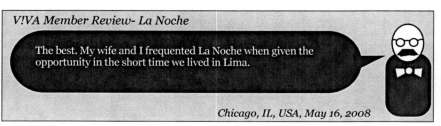

V!VA Member Review- La Noche

The best. My wife and I frequented La Noche when given the opportunity in the short time we lived in Lima.

Chicago, IL, USA, May 16, 2008

Bodega Bar Juanito's

Popular and well-established, this bar has been a landmark of Barranco for more than 60 years. Founded by Juan Casual Villacorta and still run by Juan and his family, Juanito's is loved by locals and its not out of the ordinary to see writers scribbling thoughts and lyrics on napkins. Cozy and friendly, Juanito's is a great place to share a pitcher of beers with friends. Does not accept credit cards. Open Monday – Saturday 11 a.m.-3 a.m. and Sunday 11 a.m.-1 a.m. Monday – Saturday 11 a.m. - 3 a.m. Av. Grau 274, Tel: 51-1-994-96176.

Kitsch (No Cover)

For travelers who packed their dancing shoes, the main dancing drag in Barranco is Av. Grau with a variety of discos and raucous clubs. One of Lima's hottest bars is Kitsch, boasting flamboyant décor and tunes that range from 70s and 80s pop to Latin and techno. This bar is gay-and-straight friendly, and you'll most likely see a variety of people from all backgrounds. Open 19:00 to late. Bolognesi 743.

El Ekeko Café Bar (Cover: $2.85 - 5.70)

Not quite as wild as other popular joints in Barranco, this artsy locale boasts two levels with live music Wednesday through Saturday. Most acts tend to be Latin, including Cuban, tango, musica folklorica and cha-cha-chas. There are free poetry readings on Monday evenings and El Ekeko also offers a range of hors d'oeuvres. Open Monday – Wednesday 10 a.m.– midnight and Thursday – Saturday 10 a.m.-3 a.m. Av. Grau 266, Tel: 51-1-247-3148.

El Dragón (Cover: $3.15)

A typical barranquino-styled house is the home of this well-established cultural bar, one of the first to promote bands with a special kick on fusing funk and Latin rhythms with local jazz elements. Inside El Dragón you can see a collection of wall paintings done by young local artists. The week starts on Tuesdays with blends of Afro jazz, funk and reggae; Wednesdays they turn electronic; Thursdays is a mix of local, well-known bands; and Fridays and Saturdays DJs perform to a lively, buzzing, fun crowd. All events are performed live so you may have to pay an entrance fee of generally 10 soles, depending on which band is playing; this usually includes a free drink. They have a large dragon-tailed bar fully stocked to satisfy your thirst for exotic or classic drinks. Av. Nicolás de Piérola 168.

PUEBLO LIBRE

Pueblo Libre is a quiet residential district located not far from the historic center of Lima. Originally founded in 1557 as Magdalena Vieja, this section of town was given a new name in 1821 by none other than José de San Martín, one of the Great Liberators of South America. The town was renamed for the great patriotism and desire for freedom that San Martín saw in the inhabitants. In 1881, during the disastrous War of the Pacific, the government of Peru briefly used Pueblo Libre as the seat of government. Pueblo Libre is also sometimes called "Villa de los Libertadores" because different leaders of the independence movement, such as Bolívar, Sucre, Córdova and others, maintained official residences there. Well known for its museums, including two of Lima's best, the Rafael Larco Herrera Archaeological Museum and the National Anthropology Museum, this part of town is also good for shopping.

THINGS TO SEE AND DO IN PUEBLO LIBRE

Plaza Bolívar

Away from the bustle of Lima's downtown lies the green park of Plaza Bolívar, flanked by three of Lima's more interesting museums. Travel back 8,000 years as you peruse the Pre-Columbian artifacts at the yellow painted monolith, the Museo Nacional de Antropología, Arqueología e Historia del Perú, home to two 2,500-year-old mummies recovered near the Nasca Lines and other national gems not to be missed. The private Museo Arqueológico Rafael Larco Herrera, just across the plaza, equally warrants a visit. Larco's museum has one of the largest collections of Peruvian cultural artifacts as well as an exhibit of ancient erotic art that never ceases to amaze visitors. Don't forget the Museum of National History, which displays art and artifacts from the colonial and republican eras. Getting to Pueblo Libre on public transportation is a little tricky but can still be done. Hop on the bus marked Todo Brasil and ask the driver to drop you on Av General Vivanco, a short walk away. A taxi from Miraflores will set you back about $2. Av. Abancay and Jr. Ayacucho

Sidrik's Peruvian Handicraft

Sidrik's is one of the leading alpaca wool retail outlets in Peru, and it is worth going out to Pueblo Libre in order to take advantage of dazzling array of native clothing items, includingbut not limited to the world famous chullo, the somewhat pointed wool cap designed to keep ears warm in high and cold attitudes--perfect for your hike to Machu Picchu. There is also the accompanying floor-length scarf, as well as alpaca trousers, skirts, vests and ties--with many colorful varieties of indigenous designs and patterns. With the current exchange rate favoring the dollar over the sol, the prices are a fraction of what you would pay for these clothes as exported items. Avenida la Marina 612 (and Sucre), Tel: 51-1-461-6095 E-mail: sidriks@hotmail.com, URL: www.sidriks.com.pe.

Bodega Santiago Queirolo

There are two huge wooden wine barrels on the right, and antique model car on the right, which is how you will know you are in the Santiago Queirolo Winery, one of the largest manufacturers of Peruvian wine in the area. Their selection includes dry, semi-dry, sangria, champagne and, of course, the popular Peruvian favorite, pisco. A bottle of wine goes from $5 to $7, a great bargain for an exceptionally high-quality product. Av San Martín 1062, Tel: 51-1-463-1008 / 463-6503, E-mail: vtas_sq@millicom.com.pe, URL: www.santiagoqueirolo.com.

PUEBLO LIBRE LODGING

A quiet and less popular area for tourists, Pueblo Libre does not have as many colorful or varied accommodations options as nearby Miraflores or other sections of Lima. However, there are still options available with all the basic amenities and the area is conveniently located to surrounding landmarks, tourist spots, restaurants and activities.

LIMA

Casa Marfil (Rooms: $6 - 7)
Casa Marfil is an interesting option for travelers who are looking for a quiet, more personal experience in a large city. This eco-friendly guest house provides a comfortable stay with a local family in their home. Enjoy cable TV, laundry facilities, kitchen, internet, free luggage storage, hot water all day and travel information. English is spoken. Parque Ayacucho 126, Tel: 51-1-463-3161, E-mail: casamarfil@yahoo.com.

Hospedaje Residencial Santa Fé (Rooms: $10 - 15)
This is a family-run guest house/hostel located in the residential area of Pueblo Libre, 15 minutes from the Jorge Chávez International Airport. All rooms have private toilets and bathrooms, hot water and cable TV. The hostel is near popular museums, churches, markets, restaurants and services such as banks, exchange money offices, travel agencies and supermarkets. Private airport pickup or transport into the city can be easily arranged. Jr. Santa Fé 328, Tel: 51-1-461-8263, URL: www.santafehostel.com/bienvenido.htm.

Hotel Mamatila
Hotel Mamatila is a simple, comfortable option with 20 single, double and triple rooms. All rooms have hot and cold water 24-hours a day, television with cable, telephone and 24-hour room service. The hotel also provides internet, continental breakfast, an on-site restaurant, safe-deposit box, fax, laundry and open areas to relax. Additionally, tourist information and airport pick up can be arranged. Antonio Arrieta 110 Esq. Cdra 16 Av. Brasil, Tel: 51-1-463-1573, URL: www.hotelmamatila.com.

Bait Sababa Lodge
The Bait Sababa Lodge prides itself on making you feel at home. Unlike most other hotels in the area, they speak Hebrew. Their rooms have hot water and breakfast is included. Bait Sababa is centrally located, and close to internet, laundry, banks, museums, hospitals, restaurants and the bus terminal. No credit cards are accepted. Av. San Martin 743, Tel: 51-1-261-4990, URL: www.geocities.com/sababalodgelimaperu.

PUEBLO LIBRE RESTAURANTS
Though not as large as nearby neighborhoods, Pueblo Libre offers some nice, quiet places to dine on authentic, Peruvian fare and other popular favorites. Prices are decent, and the experience will be memorable.

Antigua Taberna Queirolo
This large, attractive and stylish restaurant, with its swinging wood doors, is modeled on what a 16th-century European tavern would have looked like. There are also displays of nostalgic photos of old Peru on its walls. The taberna's 14-item menu includes such choice offerings as *chorolitos a la chalaca* (mussels on the shell) with generous helpings of corn, tomato and spices. As an extension of the Santiago Queirolo Winery next door, it offers a naturally great selection of beverages. No credit cards are accepted. Av San Martín 1062, Tel: 51-1-460-0441, E-mail: tabernaqueirolo@yahoo.com, URL: www.antiguatabernaqueirolo.com.

El Bolivariano
Step into one of the many rooms at El Bolivariano and enjoy a unique dining experience. Choose between a more formal meal in the Comedor Manuelita or enjoy a cocktail in the Boli-Bar and catch up with friends. If you are looking for an intimate, romantic experience, dine in La Pergola. If you happen to come in on a Sunday afternoon, be sure to try a little bit of everything on the Creole Buffet. El Bolivariano serves a wide variety of seafood, Creole food, salads, desserts and creative drinks. Pasaje Santa Rosa 291, Tel: 51-1-261-9565, E-mail: reservas@elbolivariano.com, URL: www.elbolivariano.com.

CHORRILLOS

Chorrillos, which means a "constant trickle of water," is a lesser-known neighborhood in Lima. Once a beach resort town, it was the scene of heavy fighting during the war between Peru and Chile in 1880-1881, and much of it was destroyed. Today, Chorrillos is tucked up against the Pacific Ocean and offers stunning panoramic views of the bay of Lima and the island of San Lorenzo in El Callao. With an atmosphere that resembles a fish market and décor to match, the mood is very relaxed in Chorrillos. Famous for its beach resorts at La Herradura and restaurants specializing in spicy dishes, this neighborhood is not without its attractions. The astronomical observatory El Planetario is located here and built on the historical Morro Solar. El Malecón is the area's boardwalk and a great place to spend a lazy afternoon.

CHORRILLOS SERVICES
Claro Cell Phone Service
Claro is one of the largest providers of cellular phone service in Peru, and travelers considering an extensive or even short-term stay in Peru might look into what Claro offers. For an investment of 89 soles ($25) you can purchase a cellular along with 210 minutes, with additional minutes available through inexpensive phone cards. Claro's office in Chorrillos is located in the Centro Comercial Plaza Lima Sur shopping mall, at the Paseo de le República. Av Paseo de la República and Matellini, URL: www.claro.com.pe.

Centro Comercial Plaza Lima Sur
This massive and modern shopping complex in Chorrillos is a consumer heaven. Featuring Peru's largest retailer, Metro, and a glossy array of local and North American corporate franchises, including Ace Hardware and the Canadian Scotiabank, Lima Sur has outlets for every need or want, including health facilities and electronics. Bring your credit card. Av Paseo de la República and Matellini.

Supermarkets
Plaza Vea is located on Av. República de Panama and Metro.

THINGS TO SEE AND DO IN CHORRILLOS
El Malecón
Once considered the soul of Chorrillos this boardwalk, used to be where local spend lazy afternoons and moonlit evenings. Since then, El Malecón has undergone two transformations, the first after the war with Chile, and the second at the beginning of the 20th century. Now, the once wooden planks have been replaced with bright tiled mosaics and the lighting system is electric instead of gas. With panoramic views of the bay of Lima, El Malecón proudly remains on the map and indestructible.

Pantanos de Villa
The only protected area in metropolitan Lima, the Villa Swamps is an Ecological park just 30 minutes from downtown Lima. The swamps, or *humedales* (humid lands), cover more than 2,000 hectares and are home to many migrating birds.

El Planetario
This astronomical observatory was erected on the historical Morro Solar, a landmark location of important events during the war with Chile (1879-1883). From this spot, spectacular views of the Lima coast and San Lorenzo Island can be enjoyed.

CHORRILLOS LODGING
As a less touristy area of Lima, Chorrillos enjoys a quieter and less raucous environment. After a crazy night out in Miraflores or Barranco, plan on coming back to Chorrillos for a deep, peaceful sleep.

LIMA

Hotel Olaya (Rooms: $18 - $30)

Hotel Olaya is located in a quiet, residential area just 20 minutes from Lima's Historical Center and 45 minutes from the airport. Other easily accessible sights and attractions include Barranco and Miraflores, both distinguished cultural, commercial and entertainment centers. The hotel has 38 basic but comfortable rooms with hot and cold water, telephone, cable TV and 24-hour room service. Hotel services include airport pickups, travel agency, cafeteria-bar and E-mail access. Av. Huaylas 710, Tel: 51-1-467-3047, E-mail: holayareservas@infonegocio.net.pe, URL: www.hotelo-laya.com.pe.

CHORRILLOS RESTAURANTS

The dining scene in Chorrillos, formerly a bustling fishing village, is reminiscent of its seaside history. There are many good *cevicherías* and small restaurants along the fish market that offer excellent samples of fresh fish. Also popular here is the *chorrillana* style of cooking that uses tomatoes and chilis. Careful, it's very spicy.

El Hornero

If you want meat, if you really, really want meat, we're talking a nice, big, juicy steak served with golden, crisp fries, a freshly tossed salad topped with an impeccable dressing, and all served with warm rolls and a fine red wine, head to El Hornero, a family-owned and-managed restaurant in Chorrillos. The beauty is of it is that you can indulge in all this while under an open window terrace, letting in a soft sea breeze and a view that stretches to the horizon. Of course, instead of a single meal, you could order an individual BBQ to be brought to your table, which easily feeds three or four hungry people. The BBQ comes with sausages, chicken, pork, steak. The meal sounds is perfected when you throw in the great Pisco Sours, sublime desserts, damask napkins, large goblets, friendly service and reasonable prices—yes, you've got it all at El Hornero. Open for lunch and dinner, but more popular at lunchtime. Try to get a table on the second floor. Malecón Almirante Miguel Grau 983, Tel: 51-1-251-8109.

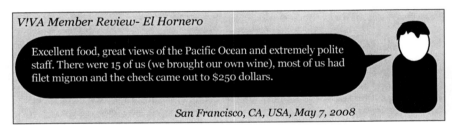

V!VA Member Review- El Hornero

Excellent food, great views of the Pacific Ocean and extremely polite staff. There were 15 of us (we brought our own wine), most of us had filet mignon and the check came out to $250 dollars.

San Francisco, CA, USA, May 7, 2008

Puntarenas Restaurant (Entrees: $9 - 12)

Staying true to Chorrillos's fishing roots, this restaurant serves up fresh seafood at a reasonable price. Jr. Santa Teresa 455, Tel: 51-1-467-0053.

SAN BORJA

San Borja is primarily a residential neighborhood of Lima, though it is also home to one of the city's most important museums, the Museo de La Nación. Upon entering the Banco de la Nación building, one will find a plethora of cultural offerings. The Museo Peruano de Ciencias de la Salud is also located here, with an extensive collection of mummies and models of all the Inca ruins to be found in the country accompanied by both Spanish and English explanations. Towards the basement you'll find the Instituto Nacional de Cultura's bookshop. There's also a café next door where you can sit down, mull over your purchases and relax after a full day of museum-hopping.

THINGS TO SEE AND DO IN SAN BORJA

Huaca San Borja

This archaeological zone, constructed by the Ichma culture, resembles pyramid foundations made of mud. Inside there are enclosures, passages and uneven floors to explore. A guided visit will explain the origins of these strange ruins. Corner of Av. Canada y Av. de la Arqueologia.

LIMA

The National Library
Originally located in Central Lima, this expansive library was established in 1821. Despite having most of the library's works stolen during the war with Chile, the library was able to build up its collection and moved to a new building in 2006. The new building houses a theater, cafeteria, exhibition halls, 12 reading rooms, storage areas and administrative offices. The library also contains the largest selection of newspapers and magazines in the country. Av. de la Poesia 160, Tel: 51-1-513-6900, URL: www.bnp.gob.pe/portalbnp.

SAN BORJA LODGING
Hotel Britania (Rooms: $40 - 80)
Located in a quiet area and just minutes from important places of business, the Hotel Britania tends to target business travelers. There are single, double and triple executive suites all outfitted with a modern environment including air conditioning, Jacuzzi and sauna and a comfortable living room. There is also an on-site restaurant featuring national and international cuisine and a bar that hosts happy hour. A basic gym with cardio machines and weights is available as well. Staff is helpful and room service is prompt. Av. San Borja Sur 653, Tel: 51-1-224-2006, E-mail: reservas@hbritania.com, URL: www.hbritania.com.

Prince Hotel Suites Spa (Rooms: $99 - 172)
This higher end property offers a choice of either the Prince Suite or the Executive Suite. Both have a king-size bed, sauna and Jacuzzi. WiFi internet and airport pickup is also included. The Executive Suite come with an adjacent living room with guest bathroom. This property is somewhat removed from restaurants, shopping, and the business district but is only a short cab ride away. Av. Guardia Civil 727, Tel: 51-1-225-3025, E-mail: reservas@princehotel.com. pe, URL: www.princehotel.com.pe.

SAN BORJA RESTAURANTS
Edo Sushi Bar
This Japanese restaurant offers amazing flavors, the freshest in seafood ingredients and is reasonably priced. Although it has only been around for less than a year, Edo Sushi Bar has already won over a devoted following. San Borja Sur 663, Tel: 51-1-225-0881.

MONTERRICO
Most famous for its horse racing, Monterrico is one of Lima's less touristy neighborhoods. Monterrico's Hippodrome gets packed four days a week, hosting both national and international races, Tuesday and Thursday at 7 p.m. and Saturdays and Sundays at 1 p.m. There's also a Gold Museum, Textile Museum, and Arms Museum all housed within one building. Here clothing samples over a thousand years old can be found, as well as feather capes hailing from Western Peru. Gun enthusiasts won't want to miss the Spanish colonial firearms that are on display here.

MONTERRICO LODGING
Golf Los Incas Apart Hotel (Rooms: $200 - $700)
Los Incas is a 5-star, all-suite hotel with large, luxurious rooms. The hotel is located just a short drive from the entertainment and business districts of Lima, the U.S. Embassy, museums and the horse track. Lima's main streets are easily accessible from here. Most of the rooms include a Jacuzzi bath, nice views, internet, microwave and mini-bar, cable TV and air conditioning. A full American breakfast is included in the rate. There is an on-site restaurant and 24-hour room service. Av Cerros de Camacho 500, Tel: 51-1-437-7701, E-mail: reservas@golfincahotel.com, URL: www.golfincahotel.com.

El Polo Apart Hotel (Rooms: $425 - $495)
El Polo is mostly frequented by business travelers who like to be comfortable, if not spoiled. Opened in 1997, this seven-story luxury building is close to one of the most modern shopping centers in Lima. The Centro Comercial El Polo has cinemas, cafés, bars, restaurants and any other kind of shop you might need. There are 38 rooms in total and each has a living room, dining room and fully furnished kitchen. The hotel also has laundry service, an on-site res-

taurant, 24-hour room service, business facilities and a fitness club. Av. La Encalada 1515, Tel: 51-1-434-2050, E-mail: reservas@.hotelelpolo.com, URL: www.hotelelpolo.com.

MONTERRICO RESTAURANTS
Sushi Ito
Do not let the small size of this restaurant deter you from enjoying the delicious sushi creations that Sushi Ito is reputed to serve. Start with light appetizers and move on to the sushi and sashimi. Share a traditional spicy tuna roll with your dining companion or enjoy a Ninja roll all to yourself. For customers who prefer their fish cooked, there is an extensive menu of yummy entrees to choose from. Finish the meal with a brulée or fruit sorbet. Av. El Polo 740, Tel: 51-1-435-5817, URL: www.sushi-ito.com.

THINGS TO DO AROUND LIMA
Day Trips to Callao and La Punta
If you are looking to escape the city scene for a day, head to Callao, the port of Lima, and to La Punta, a residential area of Callao. Here you'll find the Maritime Museum where you can explore the inside of a submarine, visit the Fort of San Felipe, and if you can fit it in, a boat trip around the bay of Callao. Tickets can be bought from the museum, and all are within easy walking distance.

La Punta is a narrow peninsula which separates the bays of Miraflores and Callao. It was once joined to the islands San Lorenzo and El Frontón, which you can see close by, until a tidal wave drowned half of the town many years ago. The Naval Officers' School is based here, as well as the Peruvian Yacht Club. It is an older area with a markedly Italian flavor due to the immigrants who arrived after the last war. Many of the houses have now been catalogued as National Historical Treasures by the government, which means that they can not be altered in any way or sold. You can walk all around the peninsula following the promenades on both sides. Many migratory birds can be found on the south side as well. At the tip of the peninsula there are a few economical restaurants, the best being Brisas Marinas.

SURFING LIMA'S WAVES
Surfers come from around the world to board the waves of Peru, and Lima's coast is no different. For the beaches near Lima you will need a 3-mm full wetsuit pretty much year round, but come Peru's summer months, January and February, you can just trunk it. Most folks ride their short boards year round, so much so, that they vastly outnumber the long boards, even when the waves are small.

Punta Hermosa Beaches
The area around the coastal town of Punta Hermosa is lined with numerous world-class breaks. It is no coincidence that Peruvian champ Sofía Milanovich owns a prime location beach house here. Heading south from Lima to around the 40 km. mark, it is best to take the side road beach access highway from the Pan-American Highway. In addition to numerous decent and cheap restaurants along the road, well-marked signs mark off each major beach from there, starting with Caballeros. A few of the many other notable breaks within a few kilometers south include Señoritas, La Isla and Punta Rocas.

Caballeros
Caballeros is a right point break and one of the few tubing options in Peru, as the wave becomes perfectly hollow at about a head-high swell. It can hold up to about a meter overhead. This place is good for the skilled surfer. It is 40 kilometers south of Lima. Near Punta Hermosa, take the beach access road from the Pan-American Highway towards the ocean.

Señoritas
Just south of Caballeros, Señoritas beach is just around the headland south. It's is a nice left point break. The reef here can be fairly well-exposed in low tides, and can handle a swell of up to about a meter overhead.Forty kilometers south of Lima, near Punta Hermosa. Take the Pan-American Highway and then the beach access road towards Punta Hermosa. Follow the beach road south of Punta Hermosa and you'll find Señoritas Beach.

Punta Hermosa—Playa Norte and La Isla

At the town of Punta Hermosa, not only will you find larger resorts and good restaurants along the beach, but you'll have two great surf beaches to choose between. The board-breaking shore-break of Playa Norte is north of the headland, and the large rollers of La Isla, is to the south. La Isla breaks from the left and right and can get a big hold-up to double overhead. A beach paddle can take 20 minutes or more if a good swell exists, but you also make similar time if you enter the water over the rocks near the headland. It is located 40 kilometers south of Lima, along a beach access road easily reached off the Pan-American Highway.

Cerro Azul

Famously listed, just after "Laguna" in the Beach Boy's song "Surfin' Safari," Cerro Azul is a consistent left point break located about 130 kilometers south of Lima. It sees the best waves with a swell from the southwest that will wrap nicely around the headland, and can take you 150 meters or more all the way to the pier. Another left and right closer to the pier starts breaking at about chest high. The typical surf is chest-high, and can tube up. It occasionally sees waves up to a meter overhead. The outer breaks stay fairly light with surfers on the weekends, but the take-off zone can be jam-packed when the waves are really good. The inner breaks are often crowded with kids and body boarders. The beach is very family-friendly and attracts most of the town on the nicer weekends.

The town of Cerro Azul, 130 km south of Lima, has numerous hostels, all with easy beach access and a big plate of fresh ceviche can be had for 20 soles / $6.60 at the numerous restaurants.

Punta Negra and Punta Rocas

Three kilometers south of Punta Hermosa you'll find Punta Negra, home of the world-famous Punta Rocas break. Located in the northern part beach, this area is usually full of families and is lined with umbrellas and restaurants.

Punta Rocas is one of the most consistent waves in Peru. It has good shape from all directions of a swell. Waves here are typically a half-meter larger or more than other breaks, and it can hold up well, with up to a double overhead swell. It has good left and right breaks over a reef, but Punta Rocas can quickly get blown out if there is wind of any kind. This beach is 3 km south of Punta Hermosa Route, located 43 kilometers south of Lima, along the beach access road off the Pan-American Highway.

RUINS

Pachacámac (Entrance: $0.35 - 1.85)

Roughly 40 kilometers south of Lima you will find the ancient city of Pachacámac. The city was originally constructed by a pre-Incan culture, but has been occupied by other civilizations. This causes the site to have a very interesting mix of architecture styles. There is a gift shop, if you want to take something home to remember it by, and café located in the ancient city, if you need a snack after admiring the ruins. Antigua Panamericana Sur Km. 31.5 / Distrito de Lurín, Tel: 51-1-430-0168, E-mail: museopachacamac@perucultural.org.pe

PARAGLIDING

Aeroxtreme

Paragliding instructor Michael Fernández has more than 15 years of experience. He offers tandem flights year-round that fly over the beautiful Costa Verde in Miraflores. Flights are 10 to 15 minutes long and no experience is necessary. Be sure to bring your camera.

Mike also offers one-day courses allowing you to fly solo close to the ground with proper instruction. This includes five solo glides on a small dune in Lurín, one tandem flight over Costa Verde or Pachacámac and transportation to the flying sites from Miraflores.

A beginner pilot course is offered during which you will learn the basic techniques of flight in eight classes and includes the use of paragliding equipment, flight manual and transportation to the fly-

LIMA

ing sites. Contact Mike for more information. Trípoli 345 Apt. 503 - Miraflores, Tel: 51-1-242-5125 / 51-1-999480954 / 981064128, E-mail: mike@aeroxtreme.com, URL: www.aeroxtreme.com.

HORSEBACK RIDING
Cabalgatas Horseback Riding

Visitors to Lima who want to explore ancient ruins, sandy beaches and the Peruvian countryside can do so in a traditional way riding a Peruvian paso horse. Pasos are pure descendants of the steeds Spanish conquistadors brought to the Americas 400 years ago and are a great source of national pride today. Known for their unique gait, pasos seem to kick their feet to the side instead of to the front. It's an uncommon sight in the horse world, and purely Peruvian. Cabalgatas, in the Mamacona stable complex outside Lima, will suit everyone up, from novices to experienced riders, for a trail ride through the Pachacámac ruins.

Begun in 200 A.D., Pachacámac was expanded by the Wari tribe and then incorporated into the Inca empire. It's the closest major archeological site to Lima. Riders tour the Templo del Sol (Temple of the Sun) and Palacio de Mamacuña (House of the Chosen Women) and other sun-drenched remains before heading along tree-lined dirt roads. Riders pass several small ranches where foals and horses graze. A long stretch of deserted beach is the final destination. Seagulls soar overhead as the horses wade through the surf, ankle-to knee-deep.

Beginners may want to hang on because more frisky horses may break into gallop. Before the bump becomes too breathtaking, the guides will easily rein the horses back to a walk. Except for the occasional rumble of a truck passing on the highway behind, riders are alone. The entire trail ride is about three hours long, but the time on the beach seems endless because the sand goes on and on. Trail riding at Cabalgatas is an authentic paso experience. Watching the Cabalgatas guides prepare the horses and cool them down after the tour is a glimpse into the real cowboy life. Cabalgatas riders compete in the National Paso Horse tournament, which is conveniently held right on Mamacona grounds every April.

Go at the right time and you've got a front-row seat to the country's most heralded paso competition. Breeders from all over Peru strut their stuff, decked out in traditional white pants and shirts, hats and serapes. You can hang out right where the competitors warm up, watch the action in the tournament ring and hobnob with owners and spectators alike. The easiest way to reach Cabalgatas stable is by taxi, to Mamacona, 15 miles (24 kilometers) south of Lima. The Mamacona entrance is before the entrance to Pachacámac ruins. Look for the shield that says Asociación del Caballo Peruano de Paso. Cell: 51-1-9837-5813 / 9507-8444, Fax: 51-1-221-4591, E-mail: informes@cabalgatas.com.pe, URL:www.cabalgatas.com.pe.

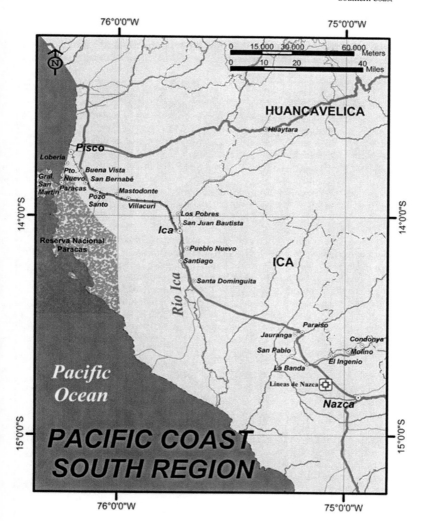

PACIFIC COAST SOUTH OF LIMA

If you're looking to bum on the beach, stick to Peru's northern coast as the Pacific coast south of Lima is mostly desert. There's plenty here however, and in your quest for coastal archaeological travel, sandboarding down dunes and close access to some of the highlights in the Andes, your best bet is south.

Highlights of the Southern Coast

• See diverse species of aquatic birds and marine life such as sea lions, red boobies, and Humboldt penguins while on a boat tour of the Islas Ballestas (near Pisco), nicknamed the poor man's Galápagos. Ubiquitous white droppings left by the colony of red bobbies have also earned the islands the name of Islas Guaneras. If the fauna is not enough muse over a giant sandstone carving on the face of one of the islands, the Candelabro de Los Andes, whose mysterious image and creation has caused just as much controversy as the Nasca lines.

• Ponder centuries-old carvings in the desert sand near Nasca. The Nasca Lines are not just images and figures cut into the rock. Archaeologists believe they may be representations of a lost culture. The very shapes one finds there support the idea that their authors were traders, nomads, or even men from outer space, as the whale and the monkey are not spe-

SOUTHERN COAST

THE PISCO EARTHQUAKE: A YEAR AFTER

On August 15, 2007, a magnitude-8 earthquake struck Peru's Southern Pacific Coast. The epicenter was located 48 kilometers (30 miles) west-northwest of Chincha, about 144 kilometers (90 miles) south of Lima. The tremor destroyed 80% of Pisco and caused a tsunami that swiped Pisco Playa, and Playa Chaco and Lagunillas at Paracas. Over 500 persons were killed. About 360 are still listed as missing.

Reconstruction in the areas has been slow, dependent on the personal abilities of its denizens and amid allegations of corruption. With the one-year anniversary of the earthquake approching, Pisco residents declared massive demonstrations. Their frustrations were many-fold. After the pull-out of the military, crime soared. Houses donated by Turkey, Venezuela, Chile and other countries still hadn't been fully distributed. The mayor would not allow a Cuban medical brigade to set up within the city, despite the hospital being barely functional. A citizens group was demanding a recall election of the mayor, but, it claims, signed petitions were stolen at gunpoint. Rubble yet piled high in lots and streets. The cemetery's deadline for burying the dead in private graves was running out. But many did not have the money for burials or for rebuilding. Just a few weeks before the one-year mark, the government sent in 100 national police reinforcements. Finally ruins were cleared away. But, Pisqueños say, the debris hadn't been checked for bodies of the missing. Nor do they know where the bodies they couldn't rebury were dumped.

Pisco's rebuilding has been slow. The donated provisional houses are now being erected, so families may protect their claims to lots. New constructions of earthquake-resistant buildings are going up, like the Compañía church and the planned Minimercado Santa Rosa. Those hotels and restaurants that were not damaged by the quake or whose owners had money to rebuild have reopened. Many of the budget hostels, though, were totally destroyed. Electricity still is subject to brownouts. Some travelers are now choosing to stay in Pisco, and their money is helping the base economy of the city. After the quake many tourists opted to stay in Paracas and Playa Chaco, which were less affected, and are using that as their base for visiting Islas Ballestas and the National Reserve.

Though swept by the tidal wave, Paracas Peninsula protected Chaco from being more heavily damaged. Reconstruction is apace in the village. Its mayor has taken the opportunity to build new kiosks for the small eateries along the seafront. Ica was also shattered by the 2007 tremor. Almost every church was damaged and still are closed. Santuario del Señor del Lurén has a temporary home built by the community itself. Repair of the old church is projected to take up to five years. The majority of hotels and restaurants, however, survived the tremor's brunt. The tourism information office, which had been in the damaged city hall, is yet to reopen. Most businesses have found new locales and again are providing services. Rubble from destroyed homes still mound in lots.

Universally, people in the affected towns complain about access materials for rebuilding their businesses and homes. Those that had money can rebuild. But for many, the hope remains distant, as prices for cement and other materials have tripled in price. The government, they state, has not implemented any policies to prevent such gouging. But with time and our tourism money, families will have the funds for rebuilding.

cies indigenous to this region of Peru. Dating the Nasca lines has proved a difficult science, adding to the enigma of their creation.

• Pair mystery with adventure—the Nasca lines are only 8 km away from the chance to sandboard alongside the nearby desert oasis Huacachina. Surf down sand dunes in Ica from a height of 2, 000 meters (the highest on the continent).

• Find out what makes the sweet in the Pisco sour by taking a tour of a brandy bodega in Ica. Assume Peruvian nationality for a day by paying tribute to the drink on February 8th, the National Pisco Sour Day.

When to Go to the Southern Coast
During the summer months, from December to March the weather conditions are wonderful on the southern coast of Peru. The air is hot and humid and the sky is blue. During the winter months of May to November, however, the weather can be rather unpleasant. In the mornings it gets quite chilly. Also, the moisture in the air tends to condense and form a drizzle called *garúa*.

Another thing to keep in mind when planning your trip is that prices tend to vary depending on the season you visit. High season is considered the months of December to March, and July to August as well as various national holidays. During these times prices undoubtedly will be higher. Also during some holiday seasons, such as Easter, things may be more costly at some places.

Getting To and Away from the Southern Coast
Most people visiting the Pisco area begin their trip in Lima. There is no airport in Pisco, so you will either have to drive, take a bus or hire a taxi out of the city. Pisco is about 242 km south of Lima by way of the Pan-American Highway. You can expect the ride to take three and a half hours and cost between $4-8 per person.

The following bus companies that have daily regular service to Pisco: Ormeño, Royal Class service; Cruz del Sur, Crucero service and Soyuz / Peru Bus.
These two bus services tend to be good and dependable.
Ormeño: Av. Calle Carlos Zavala 177, Lima centre, Tel: 427-5679. They also have an office at Avenida Javier Prado Este 1059, Tel: 472-1710, URL: www.grupo-ormeno.com.
Cruz del Sur: URL: www.cruzdelsur.com.pe.

Buses to Pisco depart from their bus station located at Jr Quilca 531, Lima center, Tel: 51-1-424-6158.

You can also find organized tours in Lima that will take you to Pisco that also include tours of attractions within and around Pisco.

Safety Along the Southern Coast
As with any foreign travel, it is best to use good judgment in everything that you do. Foreign travelers tend to be the target of petty crimes such as pick-pocketing. Be aware of your surroundings, and don't carry around unnecessary credit cards or cash. At night, it is best to take taxis rather than walking, even if the distance is short. Also beaches are to be avoided at night, since there tends to be a high danger of robberies after dark.

THINGS TO SEE AND DO ALONG THE SOUTHERN COAST
The area on the Pacific Coast south of Lima may be mostly desert, but there are plenty of attractions that bring in thousands of tourists every year. In Nasca, one can find the famed Nasca Lines, a collection of lines and figures that were etched into the landscape. No one is quite sure what their purpose is, which is part of their allure.

The Islas Ballestas, located in the Paracas National Reserve, are another popular site in the area. They are host to a vast wildlife population, for this reason they are often called the Poor Man's Galapagos. They offer visitors an opportunity to see exotic animals, without a steep price tag.

If you are looking to try something a little out of the ordinary-sandboarding might be just the thing for you. There are many places for people to sandboard in the area, particularly in the areas outside of Ica and Nasca.

Surfing sand might not be for everyone, and more museum-oriented people will not be dissapointed with this area. All of the major cities, Nasca, Ica and Pisco deliver their share of interesting museums. Most are dedicated to indigenous cultures and study of nearby ruins.

PISCO

This small fishing village is the largest port between Callao and Matarani, and is perhaps best known for its intoxicating white grape brandy of the same name. The town's two sections, Pisco Pueblo and Pisco Puerto have expanded into one another over time, creating an eclectic mix of colonial-style homes and fisheries.

The town was once home to one of the greatest civilizations in Peru, the Paracas, who left a number of intriguing archaeological artifacts that are now on display at museums throughout Peru.

Although the town has a few interesting churches, it primarily serves as a jumping off point for travelers headed to the nearby Islas Ballestas. These remarkable islands off the coast of the Paracas Peninsula are part of the Paracas National Reserve and are home to an abundance of marine animals and birds. Miscellany-mongers will also be interested to know that February 8 is the annual National Day of the Pisco Sour.

Note: Since the devastating earthquake on August 15, 2007, Pisco is struggling and has undergone some major changes. See the Pisco Earthquake page for a full report on the disaster and it's aftermath.

When to Go
Pisco has a dry climate. The best weather comes with summer, mid-December to March. Skies are clear and temperatures warm both day and night. August is windy, whipping up the sandy soil into dust devils. The first week of September in Pisco marks the Expedición Libertadora del General José de San Martín, which commemorates the launch of the Liberator's fight.

Getting To and Away from Pisco
Finding your way to Pisco will probably include a quick bus change on Latin America's most famous highway, the Pan-American, as most buses don't go to Pisco directly. From Lima, expect to pay $5-10 for a four hour bus. Buses from Ica, $3-5, up to two hours, twice daily, and Nasca, $6-12, four hours.

To Arequipa, $12-18, 12-15 hours. Ask the driver to let you off at San Clemente, where minibuses ($0.50) and colectivos ($1, ten minutes) are sure to be awaiting to take you the 6 km into Pisco's center. Three companies do, however, have service into Pisco center: San Martín (on Avenida San Martín), Costeño (Conde Monclova 637) and Ormeño (Calle San Francisco and Pedemonte).

To Lima: Costeño (3 morning departures plus 3 p.m.) and San Martín (6 a.m., 2 p.m., $5). Ormeño (1:30 p.m., 4:30 p.m., $10). To Nasca: Ormeño (11:30 a.m., 1 p.m., $6.70-13.35) Some of Ormeño's buses leave from San Clemente, though tickets can be purchased in Pisco: Arequipa (11:30 a.m., $33.35, 12.5 hours), Tacna (4:30 p.m., $20, 17.5 hours; also 1:30 p.m., via Moquegua, $27, 19.5 hours), Ayacucho (8:30 p.m., $10, 8.5 hours). Ormeño also has a depot in Paracas, as does Cruz del Sur (see Paracas for more information).

To San Clemente: Combis (minibuses) depart from Pedemonte and 4 de Julio (when full, 6 a.m.-6 p.m., $0.50, 10 minutes). Colectivo taxis leave from the same place, as well as from the Plaza de Armas ($1).

To Paracas: Combis from the market district at Beatita de Humay and Fermín Tangüis (when full, 6 a.m.-6 p.m., $0.50, 15 minutes). Colectivo taxis leave from the market and the Plaza de Armas ($0.70).

Getting Around
The only way to presently zip around town is in one of the enclosed motorcycle taxis that look like beetles ($0.35-0.50).

Safety in Pisco
Immediately after the 2007 earthquake security actually improved in Pisco, thanks to the presence of military troops. Once they pulled out however, the crime rate soared. With the one-year anniversary of the quake, national police reinforcements were sent in. The city has become a bit safer, though locals continue to take care on the streets away from the Plaza de Armas where, they say, thieves hide out in abandoned lots. Some advise that for a time it is best to stay in Paracas. It is advisable to take a taxi after dark in Pisco.

PISCO SERVICES
Pisco has no public tourism office. But, the numerous tour companies at the corner of San Francisco and Progreso are eager to help. Banks are located around the Plaza de Armas. All exchange American Express traveler's checks (US dollars only), cash dollars and Euros. Their ATMs handle Visa, Plaus, Cirrus and Mastercard.
• BCP (Monday-Thursday 9 a.m.-6:30 p.m., Friday 9 a.m.-7:30 p.m., Saturday 9 a.m.-1 p.m. Calle Pérez Figuerola and Independencia)—ATM also American Express.
• Scotiabank (Monday-Friday 9:15 a.m.-6 p.m., Saturday 9:15 a.m.-12:30 p.m. Calle Comercio, between Calle Callao and Avenida San Martín)—also is Western Union agent.
• Interbank (Monday-Friday 9 a.m.-6:15 p.m., Saturday 9:15 a.m.-12:30 p.m. Corner of San Martín and Calle Comercio)—its GlobalNet ATM also accepts American Express and Diners Club cards.

Banco de la Nación is the MoneyGram agent; its ATM takes only Visa and Plus cards, and the bank exchanges only US cash dollars (Monday-Saturday 8 a.m.-5:30 p.m. Calle San Francisco and San Juan de Dios).

Telecommunications is still affected by kinks in the electrical grid, even a year after the earthquake. Internet cafés are mostly on the streets off the Plaza de Armas and charge $0.35-0.50 per hour. Phone providers are scarce and charge a bit more than in other parts of the country. Of course, old-fashioned mail, provided by Serpost, continues to function, rain, shine or blackout (Monday-Friday 8:30 a.m.-5:30 p.m. Calle Callao, between Comercio and Pedemonte).

The Hospital San Juan de Dios is functioning, though not at full capacity (Calle San Juan de Dios, between Calle San Francisco and Calle Pueblo Nuevo). Several pharmacies are across from the market at Beatita de Humay and 4 de Julio.

The police station is (finally) being rebuilt where it had been before the earthquake, but presently is on the opposite corner, on the Plaza de Armas.

PISCO LODGING
It should be noted that, during reconstruction, most of the occupants of Pisco's hotels are NGO workers. That doesn't mean rooms aren't available. Despite having fewer lodging options than other tourist destinations in Peru, it does have options that will appeal to every type of vacationer. Truly rugged backpackers will enjoy camping for free on the beaches in the Paracas

SOUTHERN COAST

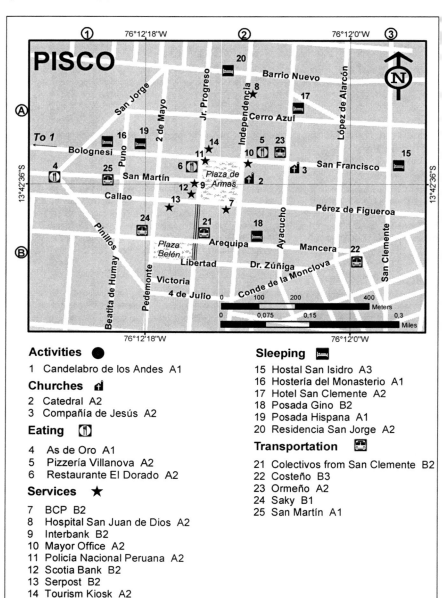

Activities ●
1 Candelabro de los Andes A1

Churches ⌂
2 Catedral A2
3 Compañía de Jesús A2

Eating ⌘
4 As de Oro A1
5 Pizzería Villanova A2
6 Restaurante El Dorado A2

Services ★
7 BCP B2
8 Hospital San Juan de Dios A2
9 Interbank B2
10 Mayor Office A2
11 Policía Nacional Peruana A2
12 Scotia Bank B2
13 Serpost B2
14 Tourism Kiosk A2

Sleeping 🛏
15 Hostal San Isidro A3
16 Hostería del Monasterio A1
17 Hotel San Clemente A2
18 Posada Gino B2
19 Posada Hispana A1
20 Residencia San Jorge A2

Transportation 🚌
21 Colectivos from San Clemente B2
22 Costeño B3
23 Ormeño A2
24 Saky B1
25 San Martín A1

Reserve. Less adventuresome travelers will find hostels that are nothing fancy, but well worth their low costs. Whats more, tourists seeking a bit more luxury will be pleased to find a couple of hotels with a more resort-like atmosphere.

Posada Hospedaje Gino (Rooms: $5 - 10)
A small hostel with a family atmosphere, Posada Hospedaje Gino is one of the few true budget options that survived the 2007 Pisco earthquake. Owner Gino provides six rooms that are a bit small and sparsely furnished, but clean and with cable TV (a recent upgrade) and private hot-water bath-

rooms. It is also conveniently located, just two blocks from the Plaza de Armas and two from the Ormeño bus depot. Márquez de Mancera 241, Tel: 53-1428, E-mail: posada_gino@hotmail.com.

Hostal San Isidro (Rooms: $17 - 27, Dorm: $10)

Reopened August 20, Hostal San Isidro is a favorite among Pisco visitors. It is located in a quiet area of town, which tends to be safer than other areas. However, still be careful, especially at night. The owners, the Alejandros, and workers at the hostel are very friendly and helpful; they can help you arrange tours to places such as Islas Ballestas and Paracas, but it might be slightly more costly booking with the hotel. Unfortunately, the pool is not filled with water, as it is in short supply. Progreso 171, Plaza de Armas.

V!VA Member Review- Hostal San Isidro

The hostel has very friendly owners who will help you in all situations. Located in a safe area of the city, the rooms are spacious and very clean. Everything is very well maintained. Absolutely recommended budget hostel in the Pisco area.

Holland, Jun 29, 2007

San Jorge Residencial (Rooms: $17 - 27)

Scheduled to reopen in November, Residencial San Jorge is a nice, 13-room hotel with over 10 years of experience in the tourism industry. Its located in the heart of Pisco, just two blocks from the main square, near banks, restaurants, travel agencies and local attractions. Jr. Barrio Nuevo 133, Tel: 53-2885, E-mail: hotel_san_jorge_residencial@hotmail.com, URL: www.hotelsanjorgeresidencial.com.

La Hosteria del Monasterio (Rooms: $27 - 37)

The sister hotel of the Posada Hispana, this 11-room hotel suffered very little damage from the earthquake. Rooms come with hot water, cable TV, and breakfast. Av. Bolognesi 326, Tel: 51-5-6-53-1383, E-mail: reservaspisco@hotmail.com, URL: www.hosteriadelmonasterio.com.

Hostal Posada Hispana (Rooms: $27 - 39)

The hostel is conveniently located just one block from the main square, Plaza de Armas. The rooms are clean but sparsely decorated. The hotel also operates a café which serves both Spanish and Peruvian dishes. Bolognesi 236, Tel: 51-56-536363, E-mail: posadahispana@terra.com.pe.

PISCO RESTAURANTS

Places to eat in Pisco tend to be no-nonsense, and generally well-priced. Seafood is the specialty of the area, in particular a Peruvian delicacy called ceviche, which is raw fish marinated in lemon juice. The highest number of restaurants are located in the Plaza de Armas. Also, most of the hotels in Pisco hold their own restaurant and bar areas-convenient if you don't feel up to venturing out to find a place to eat or hang out for the night. A lunch special is $1.50-3, the cheaper options are found in the bustling market district, on Beatita de Humay and 4 de Julio.

As de Oro (Entrees: $3 - 11)

As de Oro is a clean and modern restaurant that serves mostly traditional Peruvian food. After 9 p.m. on the weekends, it transforms into a discoteca, so come early if you want to eat dinner without interruption. Open Tuesday through Saturday from noon until 11:30 p.m., and Sunday from noon from 11 p.m. San Martin 472.

El Dorado (Entrees: $4 - 18)

Like a Phoenix rising out of the rubble of the devastating 2007 earthquake, El Dorado has reopened its doors with larger facilities. The bistro is a bit fancier than in its pre-earthquake incarnation. Now inside seating is at cloth-covered tables beneath chandeliers. On the back patio is a slightly more informal arrangement, beneath broad umbrellas. El Dorado still serves the delicious Peruvian food it has always been known for and moderate prices. Lunch special costs $2.70-3; à la carte entrées $2.70-10.70. Open daily 7 a.m.-11 p.m. San Martin 472.

Pizzaría Villanova (Entrees: $6 - 10)

For a break from seafood and the usual Peruvian cuisine, Pizzaría Villanova is the place to go. Ten types of pizza appear on the menu (including some with seafood), as well as old-time Italian favorites like fettuccini a lo alfredo and al pesto, lasagna, ravioli and canelones. Lots of good options for vegetarians. It's a glass-walled restaurant attached to Hostal Villa Manuelita and a half-block from the Plaza de Armas. Open daily 7-11 p.m. Calle San Francisco 225, Tel: 53-5218.

PARACAS

Paracas refers to a peninsula, bay, pre-Inca culture and the National Reserve (Reserva Nacional de Paracas). It is located roughly 150 miles from Lima, 50 miles from Ica and 130 miles from Nasca.

PISCO SOUR

Want to see the gloves come off? Gather a Peruvian and a Chilean, then ask them where the best Pisco comes from. Make sure you stand far back, because the fight could get dirty; a huge controversy surrounds this grape brandy.

The history of Pisco production dates back to the beginning of the colonial era and the early wine-producers in what would become southern Peru. In order to supplement their income, these viticulturists produced a stronger, cheaper drink, which they sold at the port of Pisco. Today, Peruvian Pisco production is highly sophisticated and heavily regulated. The spirit comes in several varieties, including Pisco puro, made from a single grape (usually Quebranta or Italia), and Pisco acholado, made from a blend of several grapes. Pisco can be found throughout the Andean region in the form of Pisco Sour, a cocktail made with Pisco, lime juice, sugar, egg whites, and angostura bitters. This delicious drink, an excellent accompaniment to ceviche, is deceptively mild and famous for sneaking up on the unwary.

A veritable war is now being fought between Peru and Chile over the rights to claim Pisco as their respective national drink. While Peru claims its historic origin, Chile was the first to expand its production and create a massive export market. Chileans argue that foreign taste buds recognize their product as the "authentic" version. Peruvians counter that the Chilean version, which allows additives and is yellow in color as opposed to clear, is not "authentic" because it deviates from the traditional method of production. The Pisco battle is not likely to be settled anytime soon. In the meantime perhaps each side could try to kick back, and have a strong Pisco Sour—made with Pisco from their origin of choice.

Ingredients: 2 oz. Pisco; ¾ oz. lime juice; ½ oz. simple syrup (granulated sugar melted in water); 1 egg white; 3 oz. ice or enough to fill a cocktail shaker; a few dashes of Angostura bitters.

First make the simple syrup then blend together Pisco, lime juice, simple syrup, and egg white with ice. Take an old-fashioned or highball glass, dip the rim in egg white and then sugar. Strain the drink into the glass and sprinkle with a few drops of Angostura bitters. Salud.

PARACAS HISTORY

Between 750 BC and 100 AD, the Paracas culture thrived on the Paracas Peninsula. Information from excavations tells us that they had a detailed knowledge of irrigation and water management. The large excavation known as Wari Kayan uncovered intricate subterranean burial chambers in which dead ancestors were placed. The mummies were wrapped with layers of incredibly ornate and finely-woven textiles. The Paracans are best known for these woven textiles. The bay also holds historical significance, as it was the spot where Jose de San Martin disembarked with liberation forces and began the campaign for independence to end the Spanish viceroyalty.

The beautiful Reserva Nacional de Paracas is a coveted destination for birdwatchers and hikers. Its geographical and biological features make the sea of Paracas one of the richest marine ecosystems in the world as well as one of the most peaceful and serene. Aside from the National Reserve, there are also sites such as the petroglyph, Candelabro and various museums featuring information on the Paracas.

From Pisco, the road for Reserva Nacional de Paracas heads for Playa Pisco, which was wiped virtually clean from the tidal wave. The route then follows the ocean. Beaches all along the way are mounded with rubble from the 2007 earthquake. After San Andrés, fish meal factories become the common feature of the landscape. Then you arrive at Playa Chaco, a village on the edge of the Reserva.

Since the devastating 2007 quake that destroyed Pisco, Chaco has become the center for tourism to the national reserve and Islas Ballestas. Even though a tidal wave washed over Chaco, taking out businesses along the waterfront, reconstruction here has been rapid. At the entrance of Playa Chaco, on a hill to the east is El Mirador, a lookout point over the bay with a monument commemorating Liberator San Martin's expedition launched from here during the Wars of Independence. At this point, the road branches, the left fork heading for Reserva Nacional de Paracas and the right, called Avenida Paracas, heading to Playa Chaco. Along the *avenida* are hotels, restaurants and tour operators. Plazuela Quiñónez is the focal point for tourism.

Two blocks away is the Bahía de Paracas, along which runs Boulevard Playa Chaco, the seaside promenade. Along the nice stretch of beach are rows of souvenir kiosks and restaurants. Past the hotels on the main drag, the road divides at the Bolognesi roundabout. From this point, the road forms a broken loop. The classic Hotel Paracas and other fine hotels are located on Avenida Paracas, where the old section runs along the shore. It later becomes Avenida Independencia, then Avenida Santo Domingo. Since the tidal wave, this leg no longer arrives at the control post, or garita of the national reserve. The newer road on to the left of the Bolognesi statue goes inland, shadowed on one side by worn hills, arriving at the garita.

When to Go to Paracas

The best months to visit Paracas are from mid-December through March. The days are hot, the skies clear and the sea warm enough for modest bathing. This is also a popular time for vacationing Peruvians to come and see the local wildlife. Prices rise accordingly. Another high season is during the Fiestas Patrias from the end of July to the beginning of August. Some hotel and tour operators also claim there is an additional European high season during August, September and other months , which results in raised prices. From April to December, days are cloudy with clear, cold nights and misty dawns.

Getting To and Away from Paracas

Two of Peru's best bus companies now have depots in Paracas: Cruz del Sur (Hotel Zarcillo Paradise, Avenida Independencia A20, Tel: 53-6636) and Ormeño (Paracas Explorer, Avenida Paracas, Manzana D, Lote 9, Tel: 53-1487 / 54-5089, E-mail: paracasexplorer@hotmail.com / operaciones@pparacasexplorer.com, URL: www.pparacasexplorer.com).

Get your writing published in our books, go to www.vivatravelguides.com

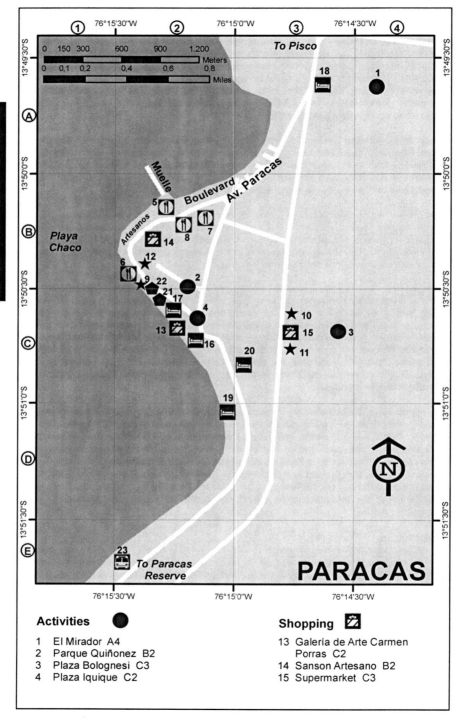

PARACAS

Activities ●

1 El Mirador A4
2 Parque Quiñonez B2
3 Plaza Bolognesi C3
4 Plaza Iquique C2

Shopping

13 Galería de Arte Carmen
    Porras C2
14 Sanson Artesano B2
15 Supermarket C3

Eating

5	Cheap Eateries B2
6	Cheap Eateries B2
7	El Chorito B2
8	Johnny & Jennifer B2

Services ★

9	Botica Niño Jesús B2
10	Centro de Salud C3
11	Community Phone Center C3
12	Internet B2

Sleeping

16	Hospedaje Shalom C2
17	Hostal Frailes C2
18	Hotel Mirador A3
19	Hotel Paracas D2
20	Posada del Emancipador C3

Tour Operator ⬠

21	Carol Travel Adventure C2
22	Paracas Explorer C2

Transportation

23	Cruz del Sur E2

To Lima: Cruz del Sur (11:30 a.m., 2:30 p.m., 5:30 p.m., $29-33, 3.5 hours), Ormeño (1:30 p.m., 4:30 p.m., $10, 4 hours).

To Ica: Cruz del Sur (7:45 a.m., 10:30 a.m., 5 p.m., $7-10, 1 hour).

To Nasca: Cruz del Sur (7:45 a.m., 10:30 a.m., 5 p.m., $12-15), Ormeño (11:30 a.m., 1 p.m., $6.70-13.35) For other destinations, go to San Clemente, by way of Pisco (see Getting To and Away From Pisco.

Getting Around Paracas

A taxi to or from the Cruz del Sur terminal costs $0.70. The Pisco-Chaco-Paracas combi goes as far as the Hilton, about 300 meters from the Reserva Nacional de Paracas entry. The minibus passes by the Cruz del Sur depot and Hotel Paracas. The combis operate from 6 a.m. to 6 p.m. (Pisco-Chaco $0.50, Pisco-Paracas $0.80, Chaco-Paracas $0.25). Collective taxis (*colectivos*) from Paracas to Pisco cost $0.80-1.

Safety in Paracas

The 2007 tsunami that swept over Paracas is a reminder that this earthquake-prone continent is subject to tidal waves as well. In the case of a tremor, head for as high of ground as possible as fast as possible and follow instructions from public officials. In the realm of personal safety, things are pretty calm in Paracas, although common sense should be exercised against petty theft. Camping anywhere is not recommended.

PARACAS SERVICES

In Paracas there is no municipal tourism office. Private tour operators are willing to dispense information, and eager to sell tours. Inrena, the institute responsible for the management of the national reserve, has offices at the entry to the park, about three kilometers (1.8 miles) south of the village.

There are no formal money facilities in Paracas. The nearest banks and ATMs are in Pisco. Some tour operators may change US dollars.

The only internet provider is an unnamed place on Plazuela Quiñónez with a large sign on the roof that says "Internet Llamadas Internacionales." It has Skype and charges $0.70 per hour (daily 10 a.m.-11 p.m., but may close early if electricity to the village is low). A community phone center with coin-operated phones is down from the church next to the supermarket (daily 10 a.m.-8 p.m.). Several independent locutorios on the street parallel to the highway and beach also have call services.

Serpost has no post office here.

Get your writing published in our books, go to www.vivatravelguides.com

SOUTHERN COAST

Shopping

The Centro de Salud is next to the church, left from the Plaza Bolognesi roundabout. On the corner of Plazuela Quiñónez is Botica Divino Niño Jesús (24-hour service, Tel: 77-2003). Galería de Arte Carmen Porras has original artwork, ceramics, handmade journals and other fine crafts (irregular hours. Avenida Paracas, Manzana D, Lote 4, next to Hostal Los Frayles). Along Paracas' main beach, Playa Chaco, are a multitude of stands selling everything including t-shirts and other souvenirs, geared for the Islas Ballestas tourists. Most close by mid-afternoon. At the far right end of the row of restaurants is an artisan shop where Sansón and his family from Iquitos forge sterling silver jewelry, woodcarvings, sand paintings and other creations. They also sell postcards, regionally produced liquors and other items (daily 7 a.m.-9 p.m., E-mail: samvideo9@hotmail.com).

Things to See and Do in Paracas

Paracas National Reserve (Entrance: $2)

The Paracas National Reserve comprises most of the Paracas peninsula and surrounding waters. It is a land and marine reserve, and also an archaeological zone, containing more than 100 small sites from the Paracas people, who flourished in the area from 700 to 100 BC.

The main attraction of Paracas is the animals. Crabs, sea lions, orcas, whales, sea turtles and sea otters can be seen. There are also over two hundred species of birds who visit the area, such as the Humboldt penguin, boobies, flamingos and petrels. It is a beautiful park, full of beaches, cliffs and rock formations.

Within the park is the Julio C. Tello Museum, renowned for its impressive collection of pre-Columbian textiles. There is also a collection of mummies and ceramics and a good deal of information about the Paracas people. It also features an interesting re-creation of a typical Paracas dwelling. (Admission: $2, open daily 7 a.m. - 4 p.m. daily).

Islas Ballestas

Just north of the Paracas Peninsula sits the popular wildlife retreat of Islas Ballestas. As visitors are not allowed on the islands, the focus of any trip to this area is a four-hour boat tour of the islands, although boats are not allowed to enter the cave. Some tour operators will take their boats inside as a bit of added rush. If they do go in, it is safe only when the tide is low and the sea calm. The tour supplies visitors with ample views of resident wildlife, including endangered turtles, Humboldt penguins, red boobies, pelicans, turkey vultures and red-footed cormorants, to name a few.

Some have gone as far as calling the Islas Ballestas the "Peruvian Galápagos," though in reality this is probably a bit of a misnomer. About 110 species of migratory and resident sea birds have been documented on the islands, and the area is a rest stop along the Alaska-Patagonia migration route. The high level of bird traffic on the islands is what prompted locals to give the islands another nickname: *las islas guaneras*. The hundreds of thousands of birds that come to roost on the islands leave behind their own unique mark: massive amounts of guano. Containing 20 times more nitrogen than cow manure, these bird droppings make excellent fertilizer and during the mid-19th century massive amounts were harvested from the islands.

Today the Peruvian government operates a program to ensure sustainable guano removal. Besides nitrogen-rich aves-excrement, the islands are also home to penguins, seals and sea lions. In the summer months, from January to March, baby sea lions are born and the islands swell with new life. Lucky travelers may catch a glimpse of dolphins, humpbacked whales, or even more rarely, Andean condors.

The route to the islands passes the famous Candelabro, a large drawing carved into the cliff jutting out of the bay. The *malecón* at the dock has several seafood restaurants, street performers and good handicrafts with unusual natural gems, fossils and even sea lion fangs for sale. From Paracas tours cost $10-11.70, plus $0.35 dock charge, departing from the municipal pier and the yacht club. They are more than twice as expensive from Pisco. Trips to Ballestas leave at 8 a.m., returning in time to hook up with tours to Reserva Nacional de Paracas. There are one or two extra tours during the high season depending on demand. Tours include transportation and Spanish-English speaking guide. They usually leave from the reserve Paracas at 11 a.m.

Candelabro de los Andes

An image carved into the sandstone cliffs along the Pisco Bay is said to be one of the most mysterious archeological sights in South America. It is often called the Candelabro de los Andes, which translates to Candlestick of the Andes, because of its resemblance to a candlestick. It can be seen from sea from as far as 12 miles.

It is often attributed to the Paracas Culture of the first millennium BC, but in reality no one is sure exactly when or why it was made. Because of this, there are many conspiracy theories regarding the carving. One of the stranger and more farfetched theories was begun by a man named Frank Joseph. He suggested that it resembles jimson, which is a plant sometimes used as a hallucinogenic drug. He thought that those who made the carving journeyed to Northern California, the nearest location jimson can be found, and used the carving as a way to help them navigate their way home.

It is doubtful we will ever know the real origin of this carving. However, we can be sure that the mystery surrounding this carving will always be part of what draws so many tourists to the site.

PARACAS LODGING

Lodging options in Paracas range from the mid to high end. A year after the tsunami budget hostels are almost non-existent as some inns continue to be booked by aid organizations. The less expensive hotels are located in the Playa Chaco district, near Plazuela Quiñónez. It is always worth asking if a cheaper price might be without breakfast. Prices are higher mid-December through March and for the Fiestas Patrias holidays. Some establishments further have a "European vacation" high season, lasting into September. For those travelers properly equipped, camping in the Reserva is the cheapest alternative. Soon on the market will be a Hilton Hotel, near the entrance to Reserva Nacional de Paracas. (Unfortunately the construction of this lodge has displaced a flamingo colony.

Hospedaje Shalom (Rooms: $6.70 - 13.35)

Doña Edna's Hospedaje Shalom has been occupied by aid relief workers since the earthquake and tidal wave, but that hasn't kept her still. On the backside, just a block from the beach, she has been building new rooms to accommodate the growing number of tourists. The rooms are spacious and simply furnished with large picture windows. The beds are excellent. Private baths are nicely finished, with hot water on request. Doña Edna and her family are very friendly and helpful. Av. Paracas, Manzana D, Lote 2, Tel: 53-1588.

Hostal Los Frayles (Rooms: $12 - 24)

Hostal Los Frayles' 11 rooms are medium-sized, clean and nicely decorated. All have private bath with hot and cold water showers. Windows are screened. A few sport TVs, for those visitors who think the natural environment and plethora of seabirds on the beach are not enough entertainment. The two rooms with an ocean view are considerably more expensive. The rooftop terrace is a great place to rest and look out over the bay. The family that owns this also operates Hotel Ballestas Island and Paracas Explorer tour agency. Price includes breakfast and taxes though it is cheaper without breakfast. Prices double in the high season. Av. Paracas, Manzana D, Lote 5, E-mail: hostallosfrayles@hotmail.com, URL: www.hostal-losfrayles.com.

El Mirador (Rooms: $28 - 54)
Located on Paracas Bay, El Mirador allows you to appreciate the views and wildlife of the bay. The hotel also has a pool and gameroom on-site so you can make the most of your stay. The hotel offers tours to all the major attractions in the area. An American breakfast is included in the price of a room. High Season: December 15 to March, and from July 5 to August 31. C. Paracas KM. 20, Tel: 51-967-2163 (cellular), E-mail: info@elmiradorhotel.com, URL: www.elmiradorhotel.com.

Posada del Emancipador (Rooms: $35 - 120)
Currently home to the Canadian Red Cross (for earthquake volunteer work), this collection of five modern bungalow-style condominiums is near Hotel Paracas. Services include cable TV, private bath with hot water, laundry service and a private guard. Prices include breakfast and tax. Accepts US dollars, Euros or soles, and only Visa traveler's checks. Tel: 51-56-54-5086, Fax: 54-5085, E-mail: hotel@elemperadorhotel.com, URL: www.posadadelemancipador.com.

Hotel Paracas (Rooms: $145 - 389)
Open since 1944, Hotel Paracas is located near the Paracas National Reserve. Its proximity to the reserve offers for wonderful views of the water and a good chance to see wildlife from the window of your hotel room. The hotel has a Mediterranean feel, with good sized rooms offering either a view of the bay or of the gardens. The cost of staying at this hotel varies dramatically according to the high and low seasons. High season rates are applied from December 16 to March 31 and from July 16 to August 3. Av. Paracas 173, Tel: 51-1-445-9376 / 446-5079, E-mail: ventas@hotelparacas.com, URL: www.hotelparacas.com.

Camping in Reserva Nacional de Paracas
Experience the nighttime's billions of stars, the sound of the waves and the morning's flocks of birds while camping at Reserva Nacional de Paracas. Campsite are at the Interpretive Center (six kilometers / 3.5 miles from the garita), Lagunillas (six kilometers / 3.5 miles from the control post) and at Playa Yumaque (10 kilometers / 6 miles). There is no camping gear available to rent, including food, drink and stove, since open fires are not allowed. Camping is free, though you will have to pay for each day in the park ($1.70 adults, $0.50 children 6-12 years old, 5 and under free; ticket valid from midnight to midnight). If you are not in your own vehicle, you can still get to the Centro de Interpretación and Lagunillas on your own by hiking along the road. Take a Chaco-Paracas combi as far as the new Hilton Hotel (tell the driver to let you off there; $1 from Pisco, $0.50 from Playa Chaco), then walk the destroyed road up to the garita, from there continue walking up the road until the campsites.

PARACAS RESTAURANTS
Food in Paracas is expensive compared to many other places in Peru. Even the produce vendors and shops tend to be a bit pricey. A supermarket, Autoservicio Municipal, is just down from the Centro de Salud, near the Plaza Bolognesi (daily 10 .am.-8 p.m.). As can be expected, many varieties of fish and seafood (especially scallops) make their way onto local menus. Note: a *lomo* is a thin-cut steak; a *churrasco* is thicker. In the center of the promenade are more expensive dining options popular with tourists. À la carte is the norm, though some have special plates at about half the cost. These eateries are open well into the evening.

Restaurant Row (Entrees: $1.70 - 10)
Along the malecón Boulevard Playa Chaco are a number of restaurants. The ones flanking either end of the beach are cheaper, with daily specials (soup, plus main course of fish or chicken) and à la carte dishes. They now have homes in the newly built kiosks, which replaced the post-tsunami shacks. Many close at sunset. Cevichería Edith is a good choice; the señora is willing to do special orders. Lunch specials $1.70-6.70; à la carte $3.35-6.70.

Johnny y Jennifer (Entrees: $3.70 - 10)
Out of the more up-scale restaurants along the malecón, Johnny y Jennifer consistently dishes up well-prepared food. Meals are generous: a regular order is sufficient for two. Be sure

to ask about the specials for one, since they are not on the menu. The service is attentive, without the hustling of customers other restaurants practice. Open 6 a.m.-8 p.m. (or later, if there are customers). Boulevard Playa Chaco, third from left, Tel: 54-5006.

El Chorito (Entrees: $7.35 - 10)

Hostal Santa María's restaurant, El Chorito, is one of Paracas finest dining establishments. Crystal and white linen is the theme, with draped tables and glass walls. Patio seating under white cloth umbrellas and a bougainvillea arbor provides a backdrop for a menu that focuses on seafood. Some beef and chicken entrées are also prepared. Only Peruvian wines from Ica are served. Open daily noon-9 p.m. Av. Paracas s/n, Tel: 54-5045, E-mail: restaurant_elchorito@hotmail.com.

ICA

Ica, population 152,000, is a pleasant, palm-tree filled oasis of a city adjacent to the Ica Desert. The desert is known for adventure travel: popular activities are sandboarding, dune buggy trips and fossil hunting. It is also possible to get flights from Ica to see the famous Nasca Lines, although flights from the town of Nasca are cheaper.

This wonderful city stands out, thanks to its warm climate, gorgeous white sand dunes and to a mysterious lagoon, known by the locals as Huacachina, just a few kilometers outside of town. Huacachina Lake is a popular visitor spot with a variety of hotels and restaurants.

The nearby Paracas National Reserve has excellent birdwatching; it is a shorebird sanctuary and home to Andean condors. This city also has one of the best museums of the country, "The Regional Museum," which displays stunning relics and mummies collected from the various cultures that flourished in the south of Peru, including the Paracas, Nasca, Wari and Inca Culture. In addition, visitors may spend a great time at one of the traditional vineyards located in the countryside and learning to prepare Peruvian Pisco, which is a sort of grape brandy slightly reminiscent of tequila. It is used to make the Pisco sour, Peru's national drink. The grape-harvest season runs from February to April. Early Spanish settlers planted grapes, which thrived in the arid conditions. Today, the Ica region is known as Peru's premier winemaking region, and there are more than 80 wineries in the area, many of which accept visitors.

When to Go

Ica has a desert climate with sunny days and temperatures reaching to 32°C (89°F). Nights tend to be cool, falling to 9°C (49°F). The warmest months are December to March. Ica has several festivals to salute the noble grape and its spirits:

March—Festival de la Vendimia—The grape harvest festival with fairs, contests, parades, concerts and a Harvest Queen, who stomps the first grapes of the season.

End of August—Festival Regional de Pisco—to judge the region's best pisco brandy.

September—Semana Turística de Ica—bodega tours, wine competitions and pisco tastings are part of Ica's Tourism Week, as are Peruvian Paso horses, cockfights and an international sandboarding competition.

Ica also has its share of religious observations:
March / April—Semana Santa (Easter Week)—Begins on Palm Sunday with the procession of Señor del Triunfo and Easter Sunday with the marking of Christ's resurrection and the Procesión del Borrachito. Streets are decorated with carpets and triumphal arches, throughout the celebrations.

Second and third weeks of October—Fiesta del Señor de Lurén—Legend says the patron saint of Ica came from Lima in 1570, but got lost in the desert, where he was found by the Lurén couple. The biggest day of the festivity is the third Monday of October, when his statue traverses the streets of the city from dusk to dawn.

Get your writing published in our books, go to www.vivatravelguides.com

Getting To and Away from Ica

Most of the major bus companies are just a few blocks west of the Plaza de Armas: Soyuz / Peru Bus and Flores in the Terminal de Ica (Avenida Matías Manzanilla 164), Cruz del Sur (Fray Ramón Rojas s/n) and Ormeño (Lambayeque 180). Cial is quite far from the center, at the roundabout on Manzanilla.

To Lima: Flores (every 15 minutes 5 a.m.-8 a.m., $6.70), Soyuz / Peru Bus (every 15 minutes, 24 hours per day, $8.35-9.35), Cruz del Sur (1:30 p.m., 4:30 p.m., 7:30 p.m., $18.70-22), Ormeño (1 p.m., $5-13.35), 4.5-5 hours.

To Pisco (San Clemente): Soyuz / Peru Bus (every 15 minutes, 24 hours per day, $1.35, 1 hour) or any Lima-bound bus to the San Clemente crossroads. See Getting To and Away From Pisco for more information.

To Paracas: Ormeño (3:30 p.m., $7), Cruz del Sur (1:30 p.m., 4:30 p.m., $7-10), 1 hour.

To Nasca: Flores (half-hourly 5 a.m.-6:30 p.m., $2.35), Soyuz / Peru Bus (half-hourly, $3-3.35), Ormeño (1 p.m., 6 p.m., 8:30 p.m., $2.70-8:35), 2-3 hours.

To Tacna: Cruz del Sur (6 p.m., 9:30 p.m., $40.35-46.70), Ormeño (3 p.m., 6 p.m., $20-23.35), 15 hours.

To Arequipa: Cruz del Sur (6 departures 5 p.m.-10:30 p.m., $17-45), Ormeño (1 a.m., 3 buses 7-10 p.m., $20-30), 10.5-11 hours.

To Cusco: Cruz del Sur (6 p.m., 9:30 p.m., $47-60, 15.5 hours). All of Ormeño's international bus routes pass through Ica.

To La Paz: 1 p.m., $90.

To Huacachina: Hail a cab on the street ($1-1.70) or take "official" ones from inside the bus depots ($1.35-1.70). Prices are per cab. There are no *combis*. The airport is Aeródromo de Ica (Carretera Panamericana Sur, Km 299, Tel.: 25-6230). At present, there is no passenger service.

Getting Around

Mototaxis cost $0.70 within the city. Taxis are $1-1.35. City minibuses charge $0.50.

Safety in Ica

Beware of thieves and bag slashers at the bus terminals and stops (especially for Nasca), even during broad daylight. Also be careful with motorcycle taxis. Locals warn to take care after dark on streets away from the city center, especially north of Salaverry.

ICA SERVICES

Since the earthquake damaged city hall, Ica no longer has a tourism office. Get information at www.regioica.gob.pe and www.peru.info/ica. The Soyuz / Peru Bus station has a tourism information desk with good maps of the city, but some of the information given by staff about attractions can be wrong. Tour agencies are another place to get the rundown about, and buy excursions to, local sites. Other useful addresses are:
• Policía Nacional (Avenida J.J. Elías, cuadra 5 s/n, Tel: 23-5421 / 22-4553)
• Touring y Automóvil Club del Perú (Camino a la Huacachina s/n, Tel / Fax: 23-5061, E-mail: ica@touringperu.com.pe).

Most banks in Ica are near the Plaza de Armas or on Calle Grau. The main ones, exchange American Express travelers checks and US dollars. ATMs that accept Plus, Visa, MasterCard and Cirrus cards are:

• BCP (Monday-Thursday 9 a.m.-6:30 p.m., Friday 9 a.m.-7:30 p.m., Saturday 9 a.m.-1 p.m. Corner of Grau and Lima, AtMs on Grau)—ATM also accepts American Express cards.
• Scotiabank (Monday-Friday 9:15 a.m.-6 p.m., Saturday 9:15 a.m.-12:30 p.m Bolívar 160, Plaza de Armas)—Western Union agent.
• Interbanks (Monday-Friday 9 a.m.-6:15 p.m., Saturday 9:15 a.m.-12:30 p.m. Calle Grau and Ayacucho)—ATM also takes American Express and Diners Club.
• Banco de la Nación is a MoneyGram agent and exchanges US dollars. Its ATM takes only Visa and Plus cards (Monday-Friday 8 a.m.-5:30 p.m., Saturday 9 a.m.-1 p.m. Calle Grau 161).

Street money changers in fluorescent green and blue vests hang out on Bolívar near Scotiabank. Take the usual precautions on safety and be aware that fake bills are in circulation. It's not hard to find an internet café ($0.35) or *locutorio*. Many internet providers are open until 10 p.m. on weeknights and closed Sundays. For those travelers still into snail mail, Serpost is at San Martín 521 (Monday-Friday 8 a.m.-8 p.m., Saturday 8 a.m.-7 p.m.).

Hospital Félix Torrealva Gutiérrez provides 24-hour attention (Avenida Cuitervo, between Lima and Piura, Tel: 23-4798 / 23-4450). Pharmacies are most common on Calle Municipalidad, between the Plaza de Armas and Avenida Juan José Elías.

Getting laundry done in Ica is quite an expensive affair. One of the cheapest is on the main plaza, identified only by a sign that reads "Lavandería." It has next day service for $2.70 per kilo (Monday-Saturday 9 a.m.-1 p.m., 4-8 p.m., Libertad 169).

If you're not making a trip up to Cusco and Lake Titicaca, get good quality sweaters, scarves, bags and other woolens at Artesanía de Puno, a mini-mall of four shops. Bargain hard, as prices come with the "gringo tax" (Monday-Saturday 9 a.m.-10 p.m., Sunday 9 a.m.-9 p.m., Callao 203).

THINGS TO SEE AND DO IN ICA

For being a town that is in a large desert, there is a surprising amount of things to do in Ica. Within the city there are a few interesting museums, such as Museo Regional de Ica, which displays mummy artifacts.

Right outside of Ica, Huacachina Lake is a big attraction. It offers visitors an oasis from the dusty hot desert surrounding it. In that area dune buggy trips and sandboarding are very popular activities.

The Paracas National Reserve, which is located near Ica, is probably the most popular tourist attraction in the area. It is comprised of the Paracas penisnsula and the surrounding area. One can see many animals there, including crabs, sea lions, orcas, whales and sea turtles. Within this reserve is the Ballestas Islands, which are often referred to as the poor man's Galapagos, and host a great array of wildlife. See Things to See and Do in Paracas.

Marquis of Torre Hermosa House

Home to a bank, there is no signage to set this building apart from others around it. Still, having survived devastating earthquakes and urban development, this is one of the only examples of viceregal architecture still standing. The Rococo façade worked in stone is beautiful. Having accommodated the Liberator, it is also known as the Casa Bolívar. Ca. Libertad, Block 1, Plaza de Armas.

Museo de Piedras Grabadas de Ica

In 1961 the Río Ica flooded and exposed a strange phenomenon in the Ocucaje desert, 40 kilometers (24 miles) south of Ica. Locals found engraved stones and began selling them to tourists. Dr. Javier Cabrera Darquea received one as a birthday gift in 1966, his obsession, collecting more than 11,000 of the rocks that depict ceremonies, flora, fauna and mysterious scenes of

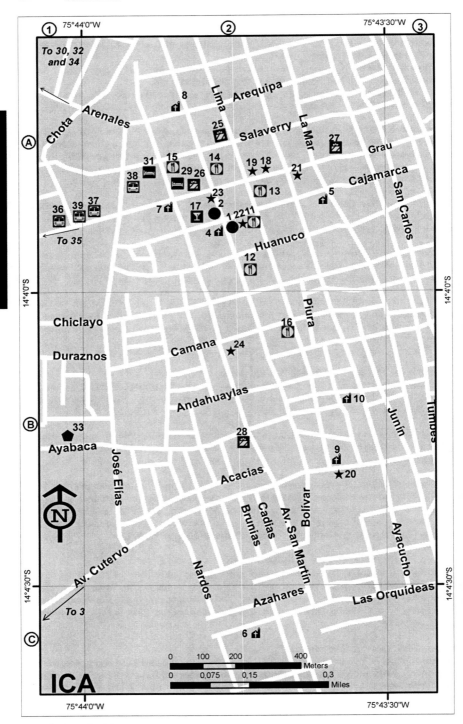

Activities ●

1 Marquis of Torre Hermosa House A2
2 Museo de Piedras Grabadas A2
3 Touring and Automovil Club del Perú C1

Churches ⛪

4 Catedral A2
5 Iglesia de Jesús María A2
6 Iglesia Sagrada Familia C2
7 Iglesia San Francisco A2
8 Iglesia San Juan de Dios A2
9 New Señor de Luren Shrine B2
10 Santuario del Señor de Luren B2

Eating 🍴

11 Anita A2
12 El Otro Peñoncito A2
13 Plaza 125 A2
14 Restaurant Riollo A2
15 Restaurante Vegetariano El Paraíso A2
16 Restaurante Venezia B2

Nightlife 🍸

17 Lovera A2

Services ★

18 Banco de la Nación A2
19 BCP A2
20 Hospital B2
21 Interbank A2
22 Lavandería A2
23 ScotiaBank A2
24 Serpost B2

Shopping

25 Artesanía de Puno A2
26 Ica Market A2
27 Mercado Central A2
28 Mercado La Palma B2

Sleeping 🛏

29 Hospedaje Loreto A2
30 Hotel Las Dunas A1
31 Posada del Sol A2
32 Residencial Angostura A1

Tour Operator ⬠

33 Huancachina Tours B1

Transportation 🚌

34 Airport A1
35 Cial A1
36 Cruz del Sur A1
37 Flores A2
38 Ormeño A2
39 Soyuz/Perú Bus A1

SOUTHERN COAST

humans hunting dinosaurs. Some detractors claim these stone carvings are recent works by the locals. Others argue that they are pre-historic creations. Dr. Cabrera wrote a thesis on his theory of the rocks' origins and Dennis Swift did microscopic analyses. To add fuel to the controversy, two Spaniards in 2002 found six such stones in the Occucaje Desert. The Universidad Autónoma de Madrid has tested two and found them to be 61,000 and 99,000 years old. The two Spaniards, María del Carmen Olázar Benguría and Félix Arenas Mariscal, penned a book about their 2002 find, which contains the lab report of the dating of the stones: *La verdad sobre las piedras de Ica* (Madrid: Editorial Sirio, 2008). Bolívar 170, Plaza de Armas, Tel: 23-1933 / 21-3026 / (Lima) 01-9965-24106, E-mail: eugeniacabrerac@gmail.com / bibliotecadepiedra@viabcp.com.

Adolfo Bermúdez Jenkins Regional Museum / Museo Regional de Ica

The building suffered some minor damage during the earthquake, but fortunately none of the artifacts inside were affected, which means you can still get up close and personal with shrunken heads and other mummy remains in this museum located in the southwest corner of Ica. This museum has a collection of pieces from Paracas, Nasca, Huari, Ica and Inca cultures, as well as Colonial canvases and Republican objects. To get there take a taxi or *colectivo* (bus 17) from Plaza de Armas. Adults: $3, Kids: $0.30, Students: $0.70. Visiting hours are Monday - Friday, 8 a.m. - 7 p.m., Saturday and holidays 9 a.m. - 6 p.m. and Sunday 9 a.m. - 1:30 p.m. Av. Ayabaca, block 8, Tel: 51-5-623-4383.

Lord of Luren Sanctuary

The Lord of Luren is considered the patron saint of Ica and is celebrated during the Holy Week and the third week of October. The neoclassical sanctuary was built in his honor and during these celebrations, thousands of believers follow his statue in a procession. Unfortunately the sanctuary was damaged in an earthquake, and will be under repair for an estimated five years. A provisional shrine is being built a block west at Avenida Cutervo and Lima. Calle Ayacucho, block 10.

Ica Cathedral

The Ica Cathedral was originally constructed back in the 18th century, but was remodeled in 1814. The Baroque style interior is evident in the pulpit and altars and the exterior of the church tends to be neoclassical. It was originally part of a Jesuit monumental complex. The Cathedral unfortunately suffered quite extensive damage: the bell towers and apse walls were partly destroyed and the apse roof partially collapsed. The Ica Cathedral is on the corner of Calle Bolívar and Calle La Libertad, Main Square.

Ica Desert

The Ica desert was once a shallow ocean basin before tectonic movements millions of years ago thrust it upward. Today, it is a dry, arid, starkly beautiful desert known for adventure travel. Popular Ica Desert sports include sandboarding and dune buggy trips.

The area is known to scientists as a hot spot for finding marine fossils. Many fascinating marine animals lived in the area that would become the Ica desert, including *Carcharocles megalodon*, an enormous shark that may have measured fifty feet in length. At approximately 25 tons, it was one of the largest predators ever. It ate whales.

Fortunately for today's visitor, there are no more Carcharocles megalodons in the Ica desert, but if you're lucky, you may see some fossils.

Tours to the Ica desert are available in the town of Ica. They range from day trip for dune buggy riding and sandboarding to weeklong outback adventure camping.

Sandboarding and Dune Buggying in Ica ($14)

You've most definitely heard of surfing and skiing, and probably snowboarding, but sandboarding? Believe it or not, one of the most popular activities in the deserts stretching across southern Peru is surfing the sands. At nearly 2,000 meters (6,560 feet), the sand dunes located just 8 kilometers from Nasca are the largest in South America, and have become popular destinations for adventure-seekers keen to try their luck tearing it up on a sand board. Other gnarly dunes can be found around Huacachina Oasis near Ica.

A wild morph between skiing and snowboarding, sandboarding is quickly becoming one of the most popular ways to enjoy the deserts unfolding around the Nasca region. Unlike its icier cousin, this sport involves hot desert sun and frequent sand spills, so it pays to bring plenty of sunscreen and get some instruction before you give it a go. A number of agencies and hotels around Ica rent boards.

The best time to go is early morning or late afternoon before heat and desert winds make for a sandy, scorching adventure. If sandboarding doesn't sound like your style, you can also enjoy the dune-covered landscapes of southern Peru from the seat of a dune buggy. Another popular desert pastime, dune buggy riding is a great way to see the sand if you're not inclined to surf it. Local agencies offer a number of dune buggy trips around Huacachina Oasis, which are sure to get the adrenaline pumping.

Huacachina Lake

Only six kilometers from Ica, Huacachina Lake is a popular attraction. A true oasis, it is a green spot in a sea of sand. The area around the lake is known for dune buggy trips and sandboarding. It is possible to swim and boat in the lake as well. Huacachina Lake is home to several nice hotels and restaurants, if you find downtown Ica too noisy.

Ica Wineries

If heaping plates of home-cooked food and glasses teeming with wine spark your interest, then you should definitely head to one of the 85 traditional wineries spread throughout the Ica countryside. These welcoming retreats woo visitors with sensational food, a charming, down-home atmosphere and, more importantly, the opportunity to taste locally produced wines. The region is also well-known for producing pisco, a kind of grape brandy distilled from sweet grapes that grow in abundance in the desert near Ica. Bodega tours are a great way to experience another facet of Peruvian culture as they don't usually draw big crowds and consequently offer a more intimate and authentic experience. Depending on your preference you can choose to visit either a small or large bodega, both of which will probably charm you into a food (or more likely alcohol) induced stupor.

Perhaps the best time to visit is between January and March during harvest season, or *vendimia*. Visits outside of harvest season tend to be quieter, and you might have trouble finding a wine guide. You may, however, have the opportunity to share a glass or two with the bodega's owner. Most winery tours are in Spanish only, though Tacama Winery offers tours in English, and others can probably arrange English-speaking guides with a little advanced notice. The best way to get to these countryside wine retreats is to check in with one of the travel agencies in Ica about organized tours.

Two nearby wineries Bodega, El Catador and Vista Alegre provide the chance to sample Peruvian spirits of the earthly kind. Pisco, the national drink, are in abundance, but the local wines are tasty as well. A tour of each winery is also part of the deal.

Bodega El Catador: Fondo Tres Esquinas 102, Subtanjalla Tel.: 40-3295 / 40-3427. From Ica, take Bus no. 6 from Moquegua, block 2 (half-hourly, $0.50).

SOUTHERN COAST

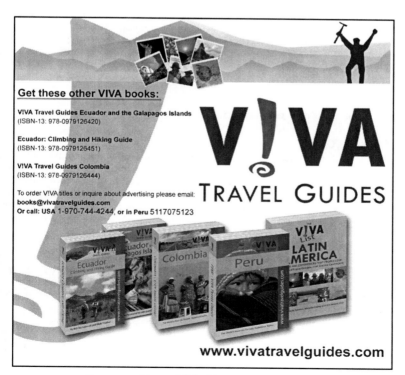

Get your writing published in our books, go to www.vivatravelguides.com

Vista Alegre: Bodega El Catador is some 10km north of Ica. Small vans leave for that direction from the street Moquegua before noon, and from Loreto after. Vista Alegre is a mere 3km northeast of town. It's best to take a taxi there. Camino a Tingüina, Km 25, Tel: 23-2919.

Tacama Winery
About ten kilometers away from Ica, the Tacama Winery is open for tours 9 a.m. to 4:30 p.m. (except December 25-January 1). It produces Peru's best dry wines. Tacama employs French wine experts to help with grape selection and other wine-related consultations, and the result is several outstanding wines. The winery itself is an interesting mix of a century-old hacienda with modern winery technology and methods. Tacama produces about 1.5 million liters of wine and pisco annually. The website is quite useful, with everything from a virtual tour of the winery to a pisco recipe book. Tel: 054-22-8395, E-mail: vinatacama@tacama.com, URL: http://www.tacama.com/english/index.html.

ICA TOURS
Ica is a large playground with tons to do and see. From exploring the desert, to wandering through ruins, seeing the Nasca lines, archaeological tours, paleontological tours, city walks and visiting Ballestas Islands, any tour company in the area will be more than happy to share the region's beauty with you.

Huacachina Tours
Huacachina Tours offers trips to Ballestas Islands, the Tambo Colorado Ruins, and the Nasca Lines (over flight), as well as archaeloical and palentoloical excursions. Contact Huacachina Tours for more information. Av. Angostura 355 L-47, Urb. Residencial La Angostura (front of the Hotel Las Dunas), Tel: 51-5-625-6582, E-mail: gerencia@huacachinatours.com.

Desert Adventures
Explore the desert like you never have before! Cruise over the sandy dunes in a dune buggy or by toboggan. Or learn how to sandboard from licensed professionals with over 20 years of experience in sand sports. Try the paleontology tour and visit the great fossil deposit to see prehistoric marine animals from over 8 million years ago. The Virgin Beach tour will take you through the desert to the cliffs and beaches of the coast where you will enjoy lunch overlooking the water. Finally, for the ultimate in exploration, spend two days in the desert, at the fossil deposit, on the beach, swimming in natural pools and fishing. Prices range from $17-$170, depending on the tour and number of participants. Huacachina s/n, Tel: 51-5-622-8458, E-mail: info@desertadventure.net, URL: www.desertadventure.net.

ICA LODGING
Hotels in Ica are relatively plentiful and you will usually be able to find a decent room for an equally decent price. Ica also has some great high-end accommodation options, including up-market resorts with swimming pools and bike rentals as well as out-of-town haciendas. Wherever you stay in Ica you're sure to find something to suit your budget and tastes. It is recommended you reserve rooms in advance for stays in Ica, particularly during summer months when tourism to the area soars.

Hospedaje Loreto (Rooms: $9 - 12)
Inexpensive lodging is a bit hard to find in Ica. Hospedaje Loreto is one of the cheapest. The staff is friendly, though they don't quite seem to know what to do with foreigners. Most of this hostel's clientele are one-nighters in transit to further destinations. The rooms are clean, sparsely furnished and have private bathrooms with hot water on request. Rooms vary in quality, so look at several before choosing. Calle Loreto 124, Tel: 50-5008.

Hotel Posada del Sol (Rooms: $10 - 20)
Hotel Posada del Sol is a tall monument a few blocks from the Plaza de Armas and bus depots. The rooms are very large, bright and shiny clean. They all come with private, hot water baths

and TV. Accommodations on the fifth floor roof terrace have an added feature—spectacular views of the mountains and sand dunes surrounding Ica. The only disadvantage is Posada del Sol has no elevator—just a broad sweeping staircase to the upper floors. The street-side sign announces cheaper prices, but these are only for guests staying a month or more. Salaverry 193, Tel: 23-8446.

La Florida Inn (Rooms: $15 - 30)
La Florida is a small, neat hotel not far from the middle of Ica and only a couple of blocks from the regional museum. It has TV, hot water and a variety of budget options. The hotel can also arrange tours to nearby sites of interest, such as the Nasca Lines. Tel: 23-7313, E-mail: lemco3@aol.com, URL: http://hometown.aol.com/lemco3/laFloridahtml.

Hacienda San José (Rooms: $25 - 120)
Before the earthquake, the Hacienda San José was a well-preserved colonial hacienda located between Lima and Ica. Unfortunately, the earthquake caused massive damage to the structure, leaving this lodging option in doubt. Word is that the owners are currently seeking public funds to repair/rebuild. It's worth calling or checking the hacienda's website (contact information below) to see if any progress has been made. Juan Fanning 328, Of. 202, Miraflores, Lima, Tel: 51-444-5242, Fax: 51 444 5524, URL: www.haciendasanjose.com.pe/.

Hotel Hacienda Ocucaje (Rooms: $64 - 102)
Located between the towns of Ica and Nasca (it is closer to Ica), Hotel Hacienda Ocucaje was for years been a popular tourist destination for Peruvians and foreigners alike. A winery and pisco manufacturer with a history spanning back to the 16th century, hard luck has fallen on the entire operation since the Pisco Earthquake. According to travelers, the hacienda is not currently offering tours, and, with half the building demolished by the earthquake, lodging is out of the equation for the time being as well. Av. 28 de Julio 810 (Lima office), Tel: 51-1-444-4059, Fax: 51-1-445-2133, E-mail: reservas@hotelocucaje.com, URL: www.hotelocucaje.com/index.htm.

Hotel Las Dunas (Rooms: $103 - 480)
A complete resort-hotel, Las Dunas offers a bit of everything: three pools with slides, tours to the desert, tennis, golf, dance lessons, you name it. The rooms are comfortable and cool. The food is excellent and the restaurant features a variety of theme meals. Other offered activities include horse riding, massage and a presentation on the Nasca Lines (all available in either English or Spanish). Prices include taxes and services. Prices for single and double rooms are higher on weekends. Av. La Angostura 400, Tel: (51-1) 25-6224 (Ica), Fax: (51-1) 446-6280 (Lima), E-mail: reservas@invertur.com.pe, URL: http://www.lasdunashotel.com.

ICA RESTAURANTS
Ica offers a decent array of restaurants to satisfy most palates and budgets. As well as the usual Peruvian offerings that are fairly ubiquitous, you can find decent Italian eateries and good places for breakfast or sandwiches. There are also a couple of more upscale restaurants, if your budget can stretch to it. Chifas are a fixture in Ica, though few have vegetarian dishes. Pizza places selling by the slice or pie surround the Plaza de Armas. Small cafés in town of regional bodegas are the place to go to sample Ica's wines and piscos without going out of the city. Several are on Calle Lima, two blocks from the main square. Other local treats to try are all types of dishes prepared with *pallares* (butter beans), and the *chocotejas*, a delicious mouthful of chocolate filled with soft caramel and pecans, lemon rind, *güinda* (sour cherry), *castañas* (cashews), fig, coconut or *pasas borrachas* (raisins soaked in pisco). Daily specials run from $1.35-4.70. Ica Market is a centrally located supermarket (Avenida Municipalidad 260). Mercado La Palma (San Martín and Ayabaca) and the mercado central (Calle Grau, between Amazonas and Tumbes) are open daily 6 a.m.-6 p.m., with eateries serving only until 2 p.m.

Restaurant Vegetariano El Paraíso (Entrees: $1 - 4)

Slip into the sunny-colored retreat of the Restaurant Vegetariano El Paraíso. This two-room eatery provides a respite from the bustling city. Quickly, Doña Marta and her staff will be at your table to take your order. Traditional Peruvian favorites like *bistec a lo pobre* (steak with egg), *milanesa* (breaded steak) and *lomo saltado* are all prepared with soy "meat." Pastas and omelettes are also on the menu. The breakfast and the three-course lunch specials are especially easy on the wallet. Open Monday-Thursday 8 a.m.-8:30 p.m., Friday and Sunday 8 a.m.-5 p.m., closed Saturday. Loreto 178, Tel: 22-8308.

Restaurant Riollo (Entrees: $2 - 9)

Restaurant Riollo is one of several inexpensive family eateries on this block. The main feature during lunch is the daily special with the choice of appetizer, entrée and drink (made with boiled water). Also on the board are à la carte beef and chicken dishes. At night, Riollo rolls out the rotisserie to offer clients roasted chicken. Open daily 8 a.m.-12 p.m., rotisserie at 6 p.m. until midnight. Tacna, between Grau and Salaverry.

Cevicheria 'El Portal' (Entrees: $3 - 5)

Still open after the earthquake, this cheap and cheerful restaurant offers local fare, with an emphasis on, you guessed it, ceviche. Opposite the Restaurant Venezia.

Lovera (Drinks: $3 - 6)

If your schedule doesn't allow for you to make a special trip out to a bodega near Ica, sit down and try the fruits of the vine in this local vineyard. Lovera has been distilling wines and other spirits since 1866. Its Pisco Quebranta has won a number of national and international awards since 1976. Lovera also makes Pisco Acholada and Pisco Torontel, as well as wines. Half-pitcher of wine or pisco for $2.70, full pitcher $5.35. Open Monday-Saturday 10 a.m.-9 p.m., Sunday 10 a.m.-3 p.m. Libertad 204, Tel: 22-9006.

El Otro Peñoncito (Entrees: $3 - 9)

If in the mood for a refined dining experience, the linen table cloths and respectable wine glasses lend this restaurant a distinguished air. The prices match, of course. Seafood, pastas, Peruvian dishes can all be had here to be topped off with a nice wine or pisco from the area. Open daily from 7 a.m. to midnight. Bolívar 255, Tel: 23-3921, Fax: 23-1804.

Plaza 125 (Entrees: $3 - 17)

Plaza 125 is similar to Anita in menu, prices and location. It's caddy corner to the other restaurant on the Plaza de Armas. You can go the ordinary route with a typical breakfast, sandwich or pasta or choose the Peruvian counterparts. The staff are friendly and hardworking. Open daily from 7 a.m to 2 a.m. Lima 126, Tel: 056-21-1818.

Anita (Entrees: $4 - 16)

Entering the Plaza de Armas, this restaurant café takes the center spot on Libertad. It offers your general fare of sandwiches, Peruvian dishes, chicken, meat and seafood with a set meal for lunch. Piscos are on tap, but the bakery is nothing to salivate over. Open daily from 9 a.m. to 11:30 p.m. Libertad 133-137, Tel: 056-21-8582.

HUACACHINA OASIS

Located just 5 kilometers outside of Ica, this small desert oasis consists of a quiet lagoon surrounded by sand dunes, palm trees and *huarangos* (carob trees). A local legend completes Huacachina's enchanting atmosphere: when the moon is full you can hear the mournful cry of a woman who drowned herself in the lagoon after discovering her fiancé was killed at war. Beautiful houses line the lagoon's shores and while the water can be a bit murky at times, it makes a great place to escape from the desert heat after a day of sandboarding or cruising around in a dune buggy. A boardwalk encircles the lagoon, and a variety of enticing

ANCIENT MONSTER OF THE SEA

Carcharodon Megalodon ate whales. A member of the shark family, this monster of the sea had a bad attitude and teeth the size of frisbees. One of the largest predators ever, it probably measured as many as 20 meters (65 feet) and weighed as much as 25 tons. With a maw that measured 1.8 meters (6 feet) wide by 2.1 meters (7 feet) this beast of beasts could swallow a buffalo ... whole!

The bones of the mighty Carcharodon Megalodon, as well as many other marine animals, can be found in the parched stretch of land known as the Ica desert. Located near Ica, Peru, this desert was once a shallow ocean basin before a tectonic upheaval pushed it above sea level. Local guides know all of the best places to find fossils in this parched wasteland, and the lucky visitor may even find a Carcharodon Megalodon tooth. Some of its teeth have survived, deeply embedded in whale bones.

The sands of the Ica desert hide more than the bones of dead fish, however. Before the arrival of the Spanish, local cultures used the desert as a sacred burial ground. Unfortunately, grave-robbing is still something of a local industry. Those relics that have survived the rampant scavenging can be viewed in the regional museum in Ica.

The desert surface is also conducive to a number of active adventures, equally as interesting. Among these sand-sports, sandboarding is one of the most popular. As the name implies, it involves sliding down a sandy dune on a sort of surfboard. You can also tear through the desert on dune buggies, mountain bikes or four-wheelers: you can rent them (and guides) in the nearby town of Ica. Most travelers stay at the Huacachina Oasis, a speck of green in the gray desert. There is a small lake there, surrounded by numerous hotels and tour operators.

Beyond its bones, burial grounds, and sandboards, the Ica desert still holds at least one mystery: the Ica stones. According to local legend, a farmer discovered a cave full of more than 15,000 stones with designs etched into them after a heavy rain. He was busted for selling them to tourists, and then sold his collection to Dr. Javier Cabrera, who maintains a private museum of the stones in Ica. The designs show many different scenes, such as medical procedures including heart and brain surgery, as well as humans hunting dinosaurs. Most scientists believe the Ica stones to be a total hoax, but the curious may find the museum to be well be worth a visit. Either they're a legitimate historical find, or they're evidence of how much work people will put into creating and propagating a profitable scam. Questionable authenticity aside, the stones are intriguing and make for an interesting excursion.

Fortunately for swimmers and surfers, the last Carcharodon Megalodon went to shark heaven about 1.2 million years ago (although there are those who say there could still be some lurking in secret corners of the world's deepest seas). If you want to see one, you'll have to go to Ica, and don't forget your sandboard!

Excerpt by Crit Minster Ph.D., taken from V!VA List Latin America, April 2007

> ### V!VA Member Review- Huacachina Oasis
>
> *Huacacina is a small two street town crammed with possibility and adventure. Centered around a green oasis fringed by palm trees, visitors can expect to enjoy blood red desert sunsets and heart-stopping buggy rides across the dunes. The sandboarding is not to be missed, and if you have the time, pop in to meet the affable owner of the only bar in town.*
>
> Malta, January 2009

restaurants and hotels line the town. According to locals, the lagoon's sulfur-rich waters contain curative properties. Whether or not this theory has merit, you're bound to leave the Huacachina Oasis feeling a little more relaxed than when you arrived. The only way to get to this desert dream is by taxi.

When to Go

Huacachina's climate is much like that of the city of Ica. Expect clear skies day and night with plenty of sun and star shine. Daytime temperatures can reach to 32°C (89°F) and nighttime to 9°C (49°F). The hottest months are during summer, December through March. Many Peruvians vacation here in those months, as well as Fiestas Patrias (at the end of July). The last weekend of March, the oasis celebrates the Festival Internacional de la Sirena de Huacachina, held in conjunction with Ica's Festival de la Vendimia.

Getting To and Away Huacachina Oasis

Buses for other Peru destinations depart from Ica. See Getting To and Away from Ica for details. In the oasis, taxis congregate between the entrance road and the Boulevard Alta. Per cab, the price to Ica is $1.35-1.70. There are no *combis* or buses.

Getting Around

Huacachina is a small enough hamlet to get anywhere on foot. If you need assistance in getting around or you are feeling particularly lazy, you could wave down one of the motorcycle rickshaw taxis that sometimes come in from Ica ($0.50).

Safety in Huacachina Oasis

Sandboarding on large dunes can be a tricky proposition, if not down-right dangerous for the novice. Do not go out on the dunes in the dark, lest you get lost in the desert or worse assaulted. The village itself is fairly laid back; though take common-sense precautions against petty theft.

HUACACHINA OASIS SERVICES

Huacachina has no tourism office, though hotels and tour operators gladly step up to the plate. The police station is located across from the village church, next to Hotel Mossone. There are no banks or ATMs in this hamlet. Among all the trades it practices, Da Silva House exchanges US dollars, Euros and soles (Angela de Perotti, Lote 3). The number of internet providers can be counted on one hand. All charge $1 per hour.
- Oasis Net at Hostal Salvatierra (Monday-Saturday 9 a.m.-10 p.m.)
- Desert Nights (daily 8 a.m.-10 p.m.)
- Hotel Mossone—only for guests
- Restaurant La Sirena (daily 8 a.m.-10 p.m.), with Skype.

Forget mailing anything from this postcard-pretty oasis—there is no post office here.

The nearest doctor and pharmacy are in Ica. Some shops may have the most basic of medications.

Along the south side of the lagoon and the passageway next to Hotel Mossone are artisan stands with the usual hand-made jewelry, postcards and other memorabilia of your stay at this magical spot. Da Silva's small general store has a book exchange.

HUACACHINA OASIS HOTELS

Huacachina Oasis is just as it sounds, a thriving lagoon teeming with life and surrounded by scenic sand dunes. Enjoy all the dunes have to offer by day and by night, rest peacefully within this verdant paradise at a pleasant hotel with staff who are waiting to spoil you. Or consider packing a tent and stay at one of the campsites at Da Silva House, where there are fire pits, tipis to shelter tents and common baths for $2.70 per person (Angela de Perotti, Lote 3.

Hostal Desert Nights (Rooms: $2.70 - 3.35)

At last Huacachina has a true backpackers place to hang the hat. The brainchild of a young Vermonter and her Peruvian mate, Desert Nights is a classic hostel, in true International Hostelling style. On the shores of the lagoon, it has two roomy dorms with bunk beds galore. Thick blankets keep the chill away. Common baths are huge, clean and designated by gender. The whole lodge is decorated with relics of those by-gone days when Huacachina was a first-class resort. Common rooms are cozy places to read, share travel tales over a beer or write. Boulevard Principal s/n, next to the ramp down from Boulevard Alta, Tel: 22-8458.

Hostal Rocha (Rooms: $5 - 15)

Located outside of Ica on Lake Huacachina, Hostal Rocha is a good option for the budget traveler or backpacker who wantes to spend some time at the lake. The hostal's 15 rooms vary in size, ammenities and price, with some having private bathrooms or balconies. A volleyball court, a pool, and a camping area are also located behind the hostel itself. It rents bikes and sandboards, and you can arrange desert tours from there. Breakfast not included and note that the hostal does not accept credit cards. Tel: 51-5-622-2256.

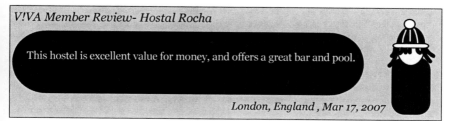

V!VA Member Review- Hostal Rocha

This hostel is excellent value for money, and offers a great bar and pool.

London, England , Mar 17, 2007

Casa de Arena (Rooms: $7 - 17)

The Casa de Arena lodge offers rooms with private bath rooms, a swimming pool, laundry service, luggage storage, safety boxes, public telephones, lockers, comfortable beds, and hot water. They can also provide tourist information about sandboarding and other activities in the area.Balneario Huacachina, Tel: 054215274, E-mail: casa_de_arena@hotmail.com.

Hostería Suiza (Rooms: $13 - 52)

Hostería Suiza is located in the Huacachina Oasis and is surrounded by scenic sand dunes. The hosteria sits on the quietest spot on the lagoon and is owned and managed by Heidi Baumgartner, daughter of Swiss hoteliers. The hosteria has a cozy atmosphere and a total of 22 beds including 3 matrimonials, 3 doubles, 2 triples and 1 quad. The hosteria also has a living room with TV, dining room, bar, porch over the lagoon, swimming pool and private parking. All prices include tax. Tel: 23-8762, E-mail: hostesuiza@terra.com.pe, URL: www.hostesuiza.5u.com.

Hotel Mossone (Rooms: $68 - 129)

On the shores of Huacachina Lake, the venerable Hotel Mossone was a plush resort back in the 1920s. Time and desert winds took their toll, however, and the Mossone has seen better days, although a recent restoration project has made a lot of difference. It is still a charming place and probably the fanciest hotel in the Ica region (it is certainly the most famous as the Peruvian elite used to regularly visit). There is an outdoor pool and modern facilities. Sandboards and mountain bikes are available for the adventure crowd. Tel: (011-51-56) 213-630, Fax: 056/236-137, E-mail: reservas@derramajae.org.pe.

Huacachina Oasis Restaurants

Food is, to put it mildly, quite expensive in Huacachina. But then, is that a surprise at a resort like this? Daily specials cost $3.35-11.70, with most establishments charging $5. The cheaper eateries are on the south side of the lake. The Da Silva general store is just about the only place you can pick up on food supplies.

Da Silva House (Entrees: $3 - 5)

By day the front space is a beverage store, but peer beyond the open shelves stocked with multi-colored bottles. Behind here is Huacachina's hottest nightclub. Its walls vibrate with the multi-lingual greetings and drawings of the travelers from Korea, Mexico, Euskara and other lands. There are just few tables and comfy floor pillows in one corner, all to make room for what is the most important activity here: dancing the night away. Da Silva guarantees to make the most of your outing, with Happy Hour 10 p.m.-midnight, salsa lessons and fire shows. Open daily 10 p.m.-dawn (even on Sunday). Angela de Perotti, Lote 3, Tel: 956-86-7777, E-mail: arturos1986@hotmail.com.

Restaurant-Bar Desert Nights (Entrees: $3.35 - 7.50)

Journeyers staying at Huacachina are raving about the food at Restaurant-Bar Desert Nights. Tastily prepared Peruvian and international dishes are quickly served up. Vegetarians have their own menu. And Desert Nights has something few places in Peru can boast: real milkshakes. Enjoy the evening out on the front porch with a view of the *laguna* or in one of the intimate interior rooms with art exhibits. The fully stocked bar provides a safe atmosphere for women travelers looking for a bit of nightlife. Open daily 8 a.m.-midnight. Boulevard Principal s/n, next to the ramp down from Boulevard Alta Tel: 22-8458

Restaurant Moroni (Entrees: $3.35 - 8.35)

On the very shores of the lake is Restaurant Moroni, the only bistro in Huacachina that affords you an up-close setting of these enchanting waters. In an open-air pavilion, the bilingual waiters quickly attend to the diners seated at clothed tables. The menu covers the whole range, from fish to chicken to beef prepared à la Peruvian and International. Of course, *ceviche*, rice dishes and pastas also grace the plates. Lunch specials are generous portions of appetizer, main plate and drink. Open daily 8:30 a.m.-9 p.m. Boulevard Principal, left side of lagoon, Tel: 23-8471.

The Mossone (Entrees: $3.35 - 12)

The Mossone has been around since those olden days when people came to this oasis to bathe in the medicinal waters. The restaurant continues to serve the finest of foods with a touch of class. The daily special are quite expensive, but the à la carte dishes, surprisingly, are about the same price as other restaurants in the village. So go ahead, have a romantic night out. Afterwards, retire to the English bar to have a coffee or nightcap. Open for breakfast 6-10 a.m., lunch 1-4 p.m., dinner 7-11 p.m. Tel: 21-3630, Fax: 23-6137, E-mail: reservas@derramajae.org.pe.

Restaurant La Sirena (Entrees: $4 - 10)

On the large front porch of La Sirena, a group of travelers share stories as they await the quick arrival of the waiter with scrumptious pasta and pizza, savory garlic bread and good drinks. Inside, others are having drinks or Skyping home. This is the place to be, for good food and good times. La Sirena has several specials to choose from, most notably the personal pizza (a dozen varieties) with choice of appetizer. Salads are an incredible toss of the usual fixings with brocoli, cauliflower, asparagus and a delicious, Green Goddess-styled dressing. Open daily 8:30 a.m.-10 or 11 p.m. Balneario de Huacachina 100 (right side of malecón), Tel: 21-3239, E-mail: restaurant_lasirena_huacachina@hotmail.com.

NASCA

The town of Nasca is a dusty outpost in the San José desert. The town and area would be unremarkable if it were not for the Nasca Lines, a series of 70 or so large designs etched into the dry desert outside of town. Nasca itself is a ramshackle town that has learned how to live off the tourist trade. Visitors to the town who arrive by bus will be greeted by a small swarm of pushy locals wishing to sell tours to the lines or try to get them to stay in certain hotels. The best way to see the lines is to go through reputable agencies, of which there are several available in town. The best hotels are located outside of the town itself, though with blooming tourism there are several hotels with a range of prices and services to chose from.

The town is also a taking-off point for adventure travel: visitors can go sandboarding on Cerro Blanco, a nearby enormous dune, or go mountain biking or horseback riding. There is good hiking as well, and four-wheel safaris to several points of interest can be arranged at the Hotel Cantayo. The town boasts two museums: the Museo Antonini highlights the ancient cultures from the region and has an excellent pottery collection, and Casa-Museo Maria Reiche is dedicated to preserving the life work of Maria Reiche, a German mathematician who spent decades studying and documenting the Nasca lines. For shoppers, the town is known for pottery.

Four kilometers outside of town is the Cantayo Aqueduct and the Inca ruins of Paredones. Both sites can be reached by taxi, or go with a guide from the city. Travel agencies can also take you to the Chauchilla cemetery, about a half-hour from town. Some of the ancient tombs have been restored, but mostly the area, littered with skulls and bones, is interesting as a testament to the destructiveness of grave robbers, who have plundered the area for years, occasionally with the use of modern tools such as bulldozers. Cahuachi is another archaeological site nearby: it is a complex that consists of about 40 pyramids.

When To Go to Nasca

In the summer months (mid-December through March) it is just plain old hot in Nasca. The rest of the year, days usually dawn with *garúa* (and may delay flights over the Lines) that quickly burns off. Also expect windy afternoons and chill nights. No-one seems to quite agree on when the tourism high season is. Some tour operators and hotels charge the higher prices only December-March and June-July, others into September. In the off season, prices drop up to 50%. Throughout the year though Nasca has quite a calendar of events:

• **January 23**—Aniversario Provincial de Nasca—Celebration of the province's founding
• **April 6**—Day of the Declaration of the 7 Wonders of Peru (the Nasca Lines came in first place)
• **Second / third week of May**—Semana Turística—All sorts of tourism promotions events, plus the celebration of Maria Reiche's birthday on May 15
• **May 27**—Cruz de Socos—religious processions and masses
• **August 30**—Santa Rosa de Lima—Patron saint of Peru and the Policia Nacional
• **September 8**—Fiestas Patronales de Nasca—With novenas to the Virgen de Guadalupe, beginning on August 29 and processions
• **September 9-10**—Virgen del Carmen de Nasca—The town's patron saint, with an all-night procession on the 10th
• **December 15**—UNESCO's Declaration of Nasca as a Patrimonio Cultural de la Humanidad site. The surrounding villages also have their special days: http://fiestasdenasca.blogspot.com/.

Getting To and Away from Nasca

Most fruits and vegetables are banned from entering Tacna and Moquegua Departments. Bags and vehicles are checked upon entering these districts. Most buses depart Tacna from Terminal Terrestre Manuel A. Odría (Calle Hiólito Unanue s/n, Tel.: 42-7007, Fax: 42-3009). To the left of the roadside is the national terminal, with police post, restaurant, bag keep ($0.50-0.70 per hour), shops, bathrooms, tourist information office, internet, phones and GlobalNet ATM (Visa, Plus, MasterCard, Cirrus, American Express, Diners Club).

- To Lima: Buses leave mostly noon-7:30 p.m., 18-20 hours—Cial ($24-37), Flores ($20 económico, $27-34 first class), Ormeño ($33), Civa ($17-25 economical, $40-47 first class), Cruz del Sur ($36-54 cruzero).
- To Arequipa: 6-7 hours—Flores (hourly 5:30 a.m.-10 p.m., $9-12), Cruz del Sur (2 p.m., 6 p.m., $12), Ormeño (2:30 p.m., 9:15 p.m., $6), Civa (9 p.m., $7). Also Moquegua, Angelitos Negros, Pacífico and other companies.
- To Ica: Take any Lima-bound bus (expect to pay full fare to Lima).
- To Puno: Pacífico, or go by way of Arequipa.
- To Cusco: Cruz del Sur (12:30 p.m., $42, 14 hours).

Other buses for Puno, Cusco and Desaguadero depart from Terminal Terretsre El Kollasuyo (Emancipación s/n and Avenida Haití, Distrito Alto de la Alianza, Tel.: 31-2538). Ormeño has internacional buses South to Chile and Argentina, and North to Ecuador, Colombia and Venezuela. Various companies also have service to Moquegua and Ilo. Colectivos (shared taxis) and busetas (minibuses) leave from the international section of Terminal Terrestre Manuel A. Odría, opposite the national terminal (daily 4 a.m.-11 p.m.). This terminal has an iPeru office, shops, restaurant, phones, internet, bathrooms, exchange houses, travel agents and other facilities. See Peru-Chile Border Crossing for details on transportation to that country.

For combis and other transport to towns within the Tacna region, including the coast, go to Terminal Terrestre Francisco Bolognesi, commonly called Terminal Pesquero (4 a.m.-9 p.m. Avenida Circunlación s/n, Tel.: 41-1786). Agencia de Viajes Caminos al Sur downtown sells Civa and Cruz del Sur tickets, and fares for Chilean buses (daily 9 a.m.-9 p.m. Downtown: Calle Ayacucho 96, Tel.: 24-6149, E-mail: haza71@hotmail.com; also Terminal Internacional D-1, 2nd floor, Tel.: 24-2872, E-mail: pullmanbus_tacna@hotmail.com). Arica-Santiago (6 departures daily, $76, 30 hours), Arica-Antofagasta (10 a.m., 8:30 p.m., 11 p.m., $24-32, 10 hours), Arica-Calama-Salta, Argentina (Monday, Friday, Saturday 9 p.m., $76, 18 hours), Arica-La Paz, Bolivia (daily 10 a.m., $16, 8 hours). Payment for tickets only in Chilean pesos (change at any exchange house). All buses leave from Arica's bus terminal. Twice daily Monday-Saturday a train departs for Arica, Chile. See Peru-Chile Border Crossing for details (Avenida Gregorio Albarracín 412, Tel.: 24-7126).

Aeropuerto Carlos Ciriani Santa Rosa is five kilometers (3 miles) south of the city (Carretera Panamericana Sur s/n, km 5, Tel.: 31-4672). Lan Perú has two daily flights to Lima (7:20 p.m., 8:50 p.m., $137-180, 1 hour 50 minutes) and thrice-weekly to Cusco (Wednesday, Friday, Sunday 11:30 a.m., $144-200, 1 hour). Lan takes major credit cards (Monday-Friday 8:30 a.m.-7 p.m., Saturday 8:30 a.m.-4 p.m. Apurímac 101, Tel.: 42-8346, Fax: 24-6102, URL: www.lan.com).

Getting Around Nasca

Most of the services and facilities that will be of interest to tourists are within walking distance of each other, including the major bus terminals. This makes getting around Nasca a cinch for newcomers. It also means you don't have to rely heavily on local transportation to get around. Upon arrival in Nasca you will likely be hounded by various agents promoting hotels, tours and restaurants, some of which may offer you a free ride downtown. The walk into town is less than one km, so there is no need to take any of them up on their offer. Plenty of *taxistas* will undoubtedly hound you but walking is easy and cheaper (not to mention it will save you the hassle of a taxi driver pushing a certain hotel). Most of the tour operators are located within the downtown area and tours of the Nasca Lines the other attractions all leave within walking distance of the hotels. Jirón Bolognesi is also known as the "Boulevard." In Nasca, people use Jirón and Calle interchangeably for street names; Callao would be called Calle Callao or Jirón Callao.

Safety in Nasca

Hotel and tour solicitors hang out at the bus terminals. They have a bad reputation. Do not speak with them, tell anything about yourself, or in which hotel you plan to stay. You may be setting yourself up to be ripped off. When buying a tour, always obtain a receipt with the company's name, address and phone number printed on it. Go to archaeological sites only with registered guides that have an official identification card.

NASCA SERVICES

The public tourism office is in the back of the municipalidad, or city hall (Monday-Friday 7:45 a.m.-1 p.m., 1:30-3:30 p.m. Tel.: 52-3150, URL: www.muninasca.com). SERENAZGO, a tourism police kiosk on the point of Plaza Bolognesi, also provides information, as well as 24-hour emergency assistance to tourists (Tel.: 52-4401). Another kiosk is in front of the Policia Nacional commissary on Avenida Los Incas, across from the Flores bus station.

To pick up on more soles, these facilities are available in Nasca:
• GlobalNet ATM (next to Casa Andina hotel, Bolognesi 367)—Accepts Visa, Plus, MasterCard, Cirrus, American Express and Diners Club cards.
• BCP (Monday-Friday 9 a.m.-6:30 p.m., Saturday 9 a.m.-1 p.m. Lima 495)—Exchanges American Express travelers checks; ATM: Visa, Plus, MasterCard, Cirrus, American Express. • Banco de la Nación (Monday-Friday 8 a.m.-5:30 p.m., Saturday 9 a.m.-1 p.m. Lima, between Grau and Fermín de Castillo)—Exchanges US dollars; MoneyGram agent; ATM: Visa, Plus.
• Banco Azteca (daily 9 a.m.-9 p.m. Lima 429)—Quick service on changing US dollars.

Money changers hang out around the banks. Many souvenir and other shops also change money. Most tour operators accept US cash in payment.

You won't have much problem finding internet in Nasca. Check along Bolognesi and around the Plaza de Armas. Most are open 9 a.m.-10 p.m. and charge $0.35. *Locutorios* are also common. A handy one is Nazcatel with local and national service, along with international calls from $0.15 per minute (daily 8 a.m.-10 p.m. Bolognesi 472).

Serpost's main office is two blocks from the Plaza (Monday-Friday 9 a.m-5:30 p.m., Saturday 8 a.m.-3:30 p.m. Fermín de Castillo 379). Sending postcards from the enigmatic lines must be popular, as many shops also have Serpost mailboxes.

Hospital de Apoyo de Nasca provides 24-hour attention (Callao s/n, and Morsesky, Tel.: 52-2010). Pharmacies are along Bolognesi and Lima, between Plaza Bolognesi and the Plaza de Armas.

Lavandería-Piñatería Alegría does same and next-day laundry service, charging $0.35 per piece. On your way out, you can also pick up a piñata and other party favors (daily 8 a.m.-8 p.m. Lima 760, Tel.: 52-2959).

At Taller de Cerámica Emilia, Felicita Calle Benavides (daughter of the great master Andrés Calle) and her family continue with the tradition of making excellent replicas of Wari, Nasca and Tiahuanaco pottery (Parque Artesanal Turístico de Vista Alegre, main entrance to the airport, Tel.: 52-1269 / 956-80-64444, E-mail: ceramica_emilia@hotmail.com). The women of Casa de Mujer Artesana Nasca work primarily in leather, and do ecological, rural and gastronomic tours (Jirón Italia 122, Tel.: 52-1386, E-mail: casamujerartesana@hotmail.com.

Get your writing published in our books, go to www.vivatravelguides.com

SOUTHERN COAST

THINGS TO SEE AND DO IN NASCA

Although Nasca is probably best known for the Nasca Lines, there are other activities that will interest visitors in the area. Sand boarding is a popular activity, in particular on the dune Cerro Blanco. Mountain biking and horseback riding are other popular activities in the area.

The town of Nasca has two museums: The Museo Antonini, which highlights pottery of the area, and the Casa-Museo Maria Reiche, which has artifacts and information about historical sites in the area.

A little bit outside of the city is the Cantayo Aqueduct and the Inca ruins of Paredones. Also outside of the city is the Chauchilla cemetery, which has ancient tombs for visitors to see.

The Nasca Lines

Ages ago, a mysterious culture etched more than 300 figures and shapes into the barren desert rock outside of the present-day town of Nasca, Peru. No one knows for certain why they did it. The culture that created them vanished into the dusty desert winds, and for centuries the drawings waited alone in the ageless wasteland. They weren't discovered until the 1920s when they were spotted by pilots of the first commercial flights in the region. Those who went to investigate dubbed them "The Nasca Lines."

From ground level, the intricate designs appear to be nothing more than a confused jumble of shallow ruts in the sand and rock of the parched desert. When viewed from the air or an observation tower, however, the shape of these drawings — called "geoglyphs" by scientists — becomes apparent. Some of them are massive: one of the hummingbirds measures 123 meters (400 feet) in length. Another line is 65 kilometers (40 miles) long. Some of the figures are geometric, such as trapezoids and triangles, and others represent animals such as a spider, birds and a lizard. The "astronaut" is a bulb-headed humanoid with round eyes. Some say the figure represents an alien; others say he's a man in a space suit. Interestingly, two of the designs, the whale and the monkey, represent animals that are not found anywhere near the lines. They're considered evidence that the makers of the lines were traders or pilgrims... or space aliens.

The age of the lines is unknown. The Nasca culture did live in the region for several centuries (roughly from the 1st to the 9th century), but there is no concrete way to date the lines. The recently discovered city of Cahuachi, located nearby, may yet reveal some answers. The Nasca Lines remain a mystery today.

Maria Reiche, a German mathematician who devoted her life to unlocking the secrets of the lines, believed that the designs represent an astrological calendar, and that each of the designs may correspond to a constellation. This theory is disputed by a number of reliable sources, and a National Geographic study completed in 1968 seems to disprove it. Her work is preserved in her old home, which is now The Maria Reiche Planetarium and museum, dedicated to her memory.

Erich Von Däniken, a Swiss writer, suggested in his 1968 book *Chariots of the Gods,* that the lines were intended as a sort of landing strip for extraterrestrial beings. Others believe that the lines were made as walking or running paths: priests or participants would follow the trails during elaborate ceremonies meant to please the Gods. Still others argue that the lines show underground rivers of water.

Preserving the Nasca Lines is one of the challenges facing Peru today. The elements in the desert are harsh, and the lines are naturally eroding. Human intervention, however, is proving much more destructive: sadly advertisers and political campaigns have carved messages in the rock between the designs. New copper and gold mines threaten some of the lines as well and grave robbers threaten to loot the recently discovered tombs at the nearby Cahuachi archaeological site. The area has recently been designated a UNESCO World Heritage Site, which should help in preservation efforts. If these efforts fail, perhaps the aliens will come back and fix their landing pad.

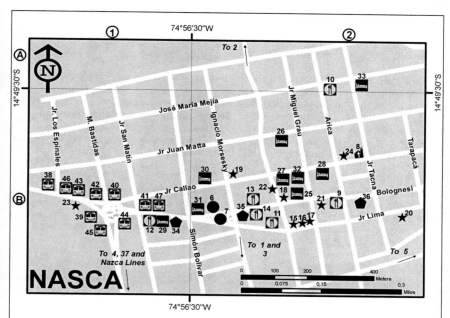

NASCA

To 2
To 4, 37 and Nazca Lines
To 1 and 3
To 5

Activities ●

1   Cahuachi B2
2   Casa Museo María Reiche A2
3   Chauchilla B2
4   Mirador B1
5   Museo Antonini B2
6   Planetario María Reiche B2
7   Plaza Bolognesi B2

Churches 🛕

8   Iglesia Matriz de Nasca B2

Eating 🍴

9   Chifa Namkug B2
10 El Huarang A2
11 La Taberna B2
12 Restaurant La Kañada B1
13 Restaurante Las Cañas B2
14 Vía la Encantada B2

Services ★

15 Banco Azteca B2
16 Banco de la Nación B2
17 BCP B2
18 GlobalNet ATM B2
19 Hospital B2
20 Lavandería Alegría B2
21 Nascatel B2
22 Serpost B2
23 Tourism Info Kiosk/Police Commisary B1
24 Tourism Office B2

Sleeping 🛏

25 Casa Andina B2
26 Friend´s House B2
27 Hospedaje Latino B2
28 Hospedaje Nasca Sur B2
29 Hostal Alegría B1
30 Hotel Oro Viejo B2
31 Nasca Lines Hotel B2
32 Sol de Nasca B2
33 Walk-On Inn A2

Tour Operator ⬟

34 Alegría Tours B1
35 Mystery Perú B2
36 Nasca Trails B2

Transportation 🚌

37 Airport B1
38 Cachipa B1
39 Civa B1
40 Collective Taxis for Ica B1
41 Cruz del Sur B1
42 Cueva B1
43 Flores B1
44 Minibus for Marcona B1
45 Minibus for Marcona B1
46 Ormeño B1
47 Terminal(Soyuz, Cial, Tepsa, Wari, Palomino) B1

The best way to see the lines is from a small plane. These depart from nearby Nasca, and also from the town of Ica, which is slightly farther away. Costs of a fly-over vary, but are not too expensive: from Nasca, the over flight costs about $50. A two-day, one-night tour from Lima to the area, including the flight, runs about $200-$250.

A cheaper but less satisfying option is to take the highway into the desert (by bus or taxi) and visit the three-story observation tower, which affords decent views of three of the lines. There are a variety of hotels in Ica and Nasca, including some nice ones at the Huacachina Oasis. If you plan to view the Nasca Lines from the air, beware that the chartered planes fly in a zig-zag in order to obtain the best possible views; as a result, they can be airsick-inducing, so take the proper precautions. The flight is worth it, though, as the views are far superior to the viewing tower and the trip by road is long and poorly maintained.

Nasca Lines Flights with Helicopters

This is a different way to observe the wonderful Nasca Lines. This smooth flight takes you over the enigmatic Nasca and Palpa Lines, stopping over each figure to take amazing pictures. This unique flight lasts about 35 minutes and allows visitors to see the most popular Nasca drawings, such as the monkey, the hummingbird, the whale, the condor, the astronaut and many other impressive geometric designs.

Museo Didactico Antonini

Museo Antonini's stunning collection is worth escaping to one afternoon. The museum heads up excavations at Pueblo Viejo and Cahuachi archaeological sites, and houses finds from them, including some extremely impressive recently uncovered ceramics. But, it isn't just about pottery shards. Metal work, beads, jewelry and plant remains are displayed as well. Excellent exhibits reveal the natural environments, customs and ethno-botany of the ancient peoples that once inhabited this desert. The grounds include part of the Cantalloc aqueduct system. Walk down Bolognesi or Lima past the Plaza de Armas. These two streets merge to form Avenida La Cultural. It is about one kilometer walk from town. Ring the bell for entrance. The display explanations are in Spanish. Ask at the desk to borrow a guide to the museum (available in English, French, German, Japanese, Italian). The museum has a giftshop with books on not only archaeology of the regions, also plants and birds as well.

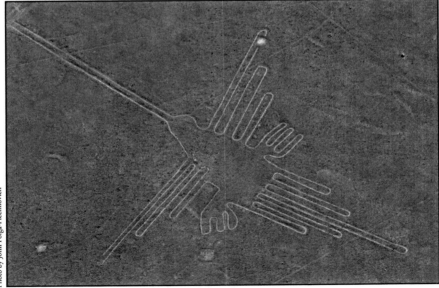

Photo by John Polga-Hecimovich

SOUTHERN COAST

Museo Antonini also offers tours to the Cahuachi site ($23 one person, $3 each additional person plus $17-24 transportation for all). Avenida La Cultura 600.

Mirador and Cerro

The Nasca Lines, located approximately 25 kilometers (15 miles) North of Nasca, can be viewed from a plane weaving the sky above them, or from other, more down-to-earth vantage points. The cerro is a solitary hill in the midst of this vast desert. Climbing to the top, you can see lines criss-crossing the desert. One series of lines to the northeast join to form a giant triangle pointing to a source of water in the mountains. Another line further west is over seven kilometers (4.2 miles) long and perfectly designates the winter solstice day. A kilometer up the highway is the *mirador*, a 12-meter (39-foot) high metal lookout tower. From the top you can view the Tree and the Hands. As well, the remnants of the Lizard, which construction of the Pan-American Highway cut in two. (Look for the tail on the west side of the road, and a paw on the east side).

Tours, which include the Cerro, Mirador and the Casa-Museo Maria Reiche, cost on average $15 per person (check if entries are included). To get there on your own, take a bus heading for Ica or other northern destination and hop off at the Cerro (there is no roadside sign, so inform the driver; $0.70). The look-out tower is one kilometer up the road, on the same side of the highway. It is best to do this outing in the early morning or late afternoon, to avoid the mid-day heat and strong sun. This outing can be combined with a trip to Casa-Museo Maria Reiche, three kilometers north. However, the highway is quite dangerous as it goes through a narrow cut. It's best to await another bus to go up there ($0.70).

Cemetery of Chauchilla

This graveyard from the Chincha period (1000-1460) makes an interesting day trip from Nasca. Located about 8 kilometers off the Panamerican Highway, approximately 30 minutes south of Nasca, this somber collection of human remains is a stark reminder of the presence of looting in the area. Thousands of sun-bleached human bones, accompanied by scraps of textiles and snatches of human hair, are haphazardly strewn about the desolate landscape. Both time and looters have robbed the site of much of its archaeological integrity, leaving behind a jumble of bones and mess of human artifacts. Local archaeologists scramble to identify and piece together remnants of this desert graveyard, in a desperate attempt to salvage any historical information they can from the site. It is the only archaeological site in Peru, in which ancient mummies are seen in their original graves, along wth ancient artifacts, dating back to 1000 AD. Like the Cahuachi complex, there is no formal public transport to the site, but tours can be arranged through local agencies. Open dawn to dusk.

María Reiche Planetarium

Located in the Hotel Nasca Lines in town, the Planetarium offers nightly shows (7 p.m.) concerning the Nasca lines and the various theories about their purpose and origins. You do not need to be staying at the hotel to attend. The planetarium was named for Maria Reiche was a German mathematician and scientist who studied the lines for decades. Open daily 7 p.m. and 9 p.m. (English), 8 p.m. (Spanish); also 6 p.m., by previous arrangement (French, Italian or Japanese. Bolognesi 300 (Hotel Nasca Lines), Tel: 056/52-2293, E-mail: edgarstar5@hotmail.com, URL: www.concytec.gob.pe/ipa.

Casa-Museo Maria Reiche

For decades Maria Reiche lived in a simple, dirt-floored house just to the north of the Nasca Lines where she spent most of her life studying the patterns in the lines. Her bedroom is left just as it was when she studied and lived here. The grounds now include a museum with the tools she used and the charts she meticulously drew of the lines, as well as old aerial photographs of them and some archaeological finds. In a new building are ceramics and a mummy. Maria and her sister are buried in the xero-scaped garden. The museum is located approximately 30 kilometers (18 miles) north of Nasca. Tours, which include the Cerro, Mirador and the Casa-Museo Maria Reiche, cost on average $15 per person (check if entries are included). To get there on your own, take a bus heaing for Ica or other northern destination and hop off at the Cerro (there is no roadside sign, so inform the driver; $1). The look-out tower is one kilometer up the road, on the same side of the highway. It is best to do this outing in the early morning or late afternoon, to avoid he mid-day heat and strong sun.

NASCA TOURS
Mystery Peru
Travel with Mystery Peru aboard a dune buggy across the desert and explore the ceremonial center of Cahuachi, these ancient burial sites feature mummified corpses from the Nasca Culture, a fertile oasis and amazing dune formations. The Usaka desert features gorgeous sand to practice one of the ultimate sports in Peru, sandboarding. Ignacio Morsesky, 126 Arica 576, Tel: 51-56-52-2379 E-mail: info@mysteryperu.com, URL: www.mysteryperu.com.

Nasca Trails
This tour company, run by Juan Tohanilo Vera, offers guided tours to cemeteries outside of Nasca as well as to the local museums. They can arrange for a flight over the Nasca Lines as well. Juan Tohanilo Vera speaks English, Spanish, Italian, French and German, and is an inspiration for language students traveling Peru. At approximately $50 (depending on the season) his flights over the Nasca Lines are slightly more expensive than other operators in town. He comes highly recommended and is very knowledgeable about the history of Nasca. Bolognesi 550, Tel: 51-56-52-2858, Fax: 52-3582, E-mail: nascatrails@terra.com.pe, URL: www.nascatrails.com.

Alegría Tours
Alegría Tours offers a variety of tours operating out of Nasca. Their list of options includes simple archeological tours of Nasca, sandboarding, guided museum tours, trips to a nearby goldmine and hotspring, and of course, Nasca's calling-card, flights over the Nasca Lines. For every tour except the flight over the Nasca Lines there are discounts for bigger groups, so if you're traveling alone it's worth it to try and find a few friends to join you with this reputable tour agency. Additionally, they offer first class bus service to Lima, Ica and Arequipa. Private car transportation by English speaking guides to Ica and Lima is also available. This option is faster, more personal and quite a bit more expensive. Calle Lima 168, Tel: 51-34-52-2444, E-mail: info@alegriatoursperu.com.

Peru Adventure Tours
Peru Adventure Tours offers half-day bicycling trips around Nasca, which take visitors to see the aqueducts created by the Nasca culture, the Nasca lines from atop a small hill. the Paredones archeological site, the Nasca ceramics museums and an old gold mine. The tour return is by bike back to your hotel. In order to qualify for a discount you must have a valid ISIC card and South American Explorers membership. Half-day biking tours $35 per person, Cerro Blanco 1 day tours $85-135 per person. Jerusalén Street 410, Tel: 0051 (0)54 221658, Fax: 0051 054 221658, E-mail: info@peruadventurestours.com, URL: www.peruadventurestours.com.

NASCA LODGING
Although there is lodging located within the actual town of Nasca, it is probably not the best option when staying in the area. Nasca village tends to be a bit run down, and the hotels within it are no exception. Outside of the town, you will find much higher quality accommodations in a more tranquil setting. The hotels have varying rates and amenity types, and most will be happy to help you arrange tours of the surrounding attractions.

Hospedaje Latino (Rooms: $5 per person)
An up-and-coming hostel on the Nasca scene, Hospedaje Latino offers rooms for two or more guests. A narrow staircase leads up to the hotel's reception and tour agency. Rooms are like a mini-maze here, all of differing sizes. The private baths are clean and the attention good, making this another nice option for the shoe-stringer having to count the cents. Ignacio Morsesky 272, Tel: 52-2738 / 965-9281, E-mail: tavera70@hotmail.com.

Walk On Inn (Rooms: $5 - 8)

Under new management and a new name, the former Hostal Vía Morburg is located two blocks from the main square, behind the church. The Inn has a pretty exterior and its guests enjoy the use of the swimming pool and roof terrace. For those with their laptops, the hotel features WiFi. There is also a cozy restaurant and bar. The hotel is popular and reliable. SAE members get a 20 percent discount. José María Mejía 108, Tel: skype:walkoninn.

Hostal Sol de Nasca (Rooms: $5 - 10)

Hostal Sol de Nasca is a budget traveler's choice in the crowded Nasca lodging market. Located midway between the bus stations and The Plaza de Armas, this inn is convenient for walking around the city. The rooms are large with windows to let the light and fresh air in. They are no-nonsense, without cable TV, but comfortable. Two rooms on the uppermost floor share a common bath. The top floor dining room has a stunning view of Cerro Blanco. Callao 586A, Tel: 52-2730, E-mail: hostal_soldenasca@hotmail.com.

Friend's House Hostel (Rooms: $8 per person)

A relative newcomer in town, Friend's House is not a bad place to lay your head. Clean and comfortable with 24 hour hot water, this Nasca hotel is centrally located. It boasts a pleasant roof terrace furnished with sofas and plants which is a great place to kick back for a while. There is also a kitchen and TV room. This is a good place for those who want to spend quality time and meet people. There have however, been reports that the hostel can be a noisy place due to local discos, so this one is perhaps just for heavy sleepers. Free transport is provided to and from the bus terminals. Friends House along with Mochilero's Explorer arrange flights over the Nasca lines and sand boarding at Cerro Blanco, the highest sand dune in the world (2078 meters). Price includes breakfast and free transport from bus terminals. 712 Calle Juan Matta, Tel: 52-4191 / 52-2684, E-mail: elmochilero_1000@hotmail.com, friends_house_nasca@hotmail.com.

V!VA Member Review- Friend's House Hostel

This is probably the best place we found: nice, comfortable hostel. The staff is very friendly. We really liked them.

UK, Aug 19, 2008

Hospedaje Nasca Sur (Rooms: $10 - 17)

Hospedaje Nasca Sur is another well-placed hotel in the city, between downtown and the bus depots. Rooms vary in size but they and the adjoining private baths are immaculately clean. All come with cable TV. Be forewarned, though: this place is an echo chamber. Whether it is an upstairs neighbor watching a soccer match or other guests returning late from clubbing, you might find your sleep disturbed. Even though Hospedaje Nasca Sur's ads claim 24-hour hot water, the heater is turned on only 5 p.m.-11 a.m. Callao 568, Tel: 31-1236 / 994-4575, E-mail: nascasur@hotmail.com.

Hostal Alegría I (Rooms: $10 - 50)

Hostal Alegría is located in downtown Nasca. It is owned by Alegría Tours, who keep an office at the hotel. It is a good value for a mid-range hotel, featuring neat, airy rooms and a pool. Some of the rooms even have air conditioning. The on-site travel agency is reputable and convenient. Good value for a mid-range hotel. Lima 166, Tel: 056-52-2444, URL: www.nazcaperu.com.

Casa Andina Nasca (Rooms: $25 - 39)

Done out in coastal architecture, Casa Andina's Nasca offering comes with 60 rooms, all tastefully furnished. The hotel has the benefit of cable TV in all rooms, breakfast buffet and an outdoor

CAHUACHI

Excavations in the low-lying hills located just 28 kilometers (17 miles) northwest of Nasca have uncovered a 24 kilometer (15 mile) network of walls, staircases, and plazas that once comprised a city larger than Trujillo's Chan Chan. The site includes nearly 40 pyramids, including the 25-meter (82 ft) high and 100 meter (330 ft) long Great Pyramid. The complex faces the Nasca Lines and occupies a sacred spot where the Río Nasca flows out of the desert floor. In charge of excavations at Cahuachi since 1985, Giuseppe Orefici contends that the pyramids were used almost exclusively for ceremonial rituals in order to thank the gods for water.

Construction of the Cahuachi complex spanned from 400 BC to 400 AD, when the site was abandoned due to flooding. The sheer size of the pyramids parallels the scale of those pyramids built by the Moche and Sicán in Northern Peru. Much of the site and its structures have been defaced by looters, but in spite of this, Orefici and his team have uncovered a number of tombs and ancient Nasca artifacts. Although there is no official public transport to the site, a number of agencies are starting to include the site in their tour packages.

swimming pool. It has a range of services, including restaurant, safe deposit box, car parking and laundry service. Just one block from the main square, this hotel is a convenient five-minute ride from the airfield from which you can take your Nasca Lines flight. SAE members get a 10 percent discount. Prices do not include tax, which foreigners do not pay (only Peruvian nationals and residents pay it.) Jr. Bolognesi 367, Tel: 51-56-52-3563, Fax: 51-56-52-1067, E-mail: cac-nasca@casa-andina.com, URL: www.casa-andina.com.

Oro Viejo Hotel (Rooms: $33 - 110)

Oro Viejo is a popular but small, nine-room hotel. Located in central Nasca, it is close enough to offer access to travel agencies, cafés, etc., but far enough away to be peaceful and quiet. From the street, it looks like a regular house; inside it is roomy, cool and shaded, and features a pleasant garden and patio with a bar and lounge. The patio and garden are full of chairs for guests to relax. Callao 483, Tel: 056-52-2284, E-mail: oro_viejo@terra.com.pe, URL: www.hoteloroviejo.net.

Nasca Lines Hotel (Rooms: $91 - 176)

One of the best hotels in Nasca city, Nasca Lines is a converted hacienda with a courtyard, tennis courts, fountains and swimming pool. The rooms are tastefully decorated and comfortable. There are 34 rooms. The German mathematician and expert on the Nasca lines, Maria Reiche, lived here for several years and the on-site planetarium features informational shows based on her life work. The restaurant is excellent. Prices include buffet breakfast, taxes and tips. Bolognesi s/n, Tel: 56-52-2293, Fax: 52-2112, E-mail: hnasca@dematourshoteles.com, URL: www.dematourshoteles.com.

Hotel Cantayo Spa and Resort (Rooms: $185 - 320)

Perhaps the most luxurious place to stay in the Nasca area, the Hotel Cantayo Spa and Resort was built on the ruins of a spacious old hacienda, and still maintains some of the arches, floors, and hallways. Today it is a deluxe hotel and spa. A very relaxing place, it offers spacious rooms, flowered gardens, swimming pools and fine dining. It has become more of a spa and relaxation resort in recent years, and now features a gym, Jacuzzi, sauna, hydro-massages, steam room and a yoga area among all else. Cantayo also offers adventure tours including horse rides, sandboarding, swimming lessons and 4x4 trips to some of the more remote points of local interest, such as the coast, where you can see penguins, condors and sea lions. You can also visit Pampa Galenas Nature Reserve, an hour and a half from the hotel. Prices do not include taxes, but breakfast is included. Reservations made via internet may get a discount. Tel: 51 56 522345, Fax: 51 56 522283, E-mail: info@hotelcantayo.com, URL: http://www.hotelcantayo.com/eng/el_hotel.html.

NASCA RESTAURANTS

The actual city of Nasca gets a lot of hit-and-runs. Tourists stop by on their way to peek at the ancient lines, stay a night in town and pick up their trail the next morning. Although the town has adjusted to the high influx of tourism, there isn't an abundance of restaurants. That said, the available eateries do have character. For an Italian or seafood dinner, go to one of the restaurants linked to the hotels. Plates are more expensive but come with the works. If you're in the mood to sample traditional food in a relaxed environment, wander a little farther from your hotel to hit up one of the unique restaurants around town. At one locale, backpackers have left their signatures on the graffiti-filled walls. Another restaurant offers outdoor seating on a second-floor terrace. Well-priced vegetarian, Peruvian and seafood dishes are on the menu at most places. Plus, on the weekends live music and happenin' vibes throng in a few of the restaurant-bars.

The daily lunch special runs from $1 to $10, with most diners charging $2-2.70. A slew of cheap eateries are on General Varela, north of Avenida Augusto B. Leguía. Tacna's two markets are other places to eat inexpensively, as well as to pick up supplies: Mercado 2 de Mayo on Av. 2 de Mayo, between Pasaje Calderón de la Barca and Meléndez) and the Mercado Central (Avenida Bolognesi and Pallardelli). Both are open daily 6 a.m.-4 p.m. Empanadas are sold all over and make for a good snack or light meal for budget travelers ($0.35-0.70). They come in a variety of fillings, from cheese to *ají de gallina*. Many restaurants close early on Sundays or don't open at all. The main market throbs with activity along Lima, between Grau and Arica (daily 7 a.m.-7 p.m.) Nearby is Supermarket Raulito (Monday-Saturday 8 a.m.-10 p.m., Sunday 8 a.m.-9 p.m. Grau, between Bolognesi and Lima). Another market, much larger and more rustic, is one block from the Plaza de Armas, on Callao. The cheapest diners in Nasca line the east and west sides of the main plaza. Nasca has no vegetarian-only restaurant, but many eateries do offer meatless dishes.

Chifa Nam Kug

Chifa Nam Kug allows a break from Nasca's usual Peruvian and Italian offerings. Following in the great tradition of chifas throughout Peru, the Chinese owners stir-fry Sino favorites like Kanlu Wantan, Taypa and Chuakay. Specials, which include wantan soup or fried wantans with a main dish, are a delicious way to stay on budget. À la carte entrées come in all sauces and preparations, including vegetarian options. For the Peruvian touch, accompany your meal with Inca Kola. For an even more authentic Chinese experience, ask for the chop sticks. Open daily noon-4 p.m., 6-11 p.m. Bolognesi 448, Tel: 52-2151.

Hotel Cantayo Restaurant

The restaurant at the Hotel Cantayo is considered to be the best in the Nasca area. Much of the food is organic. There is a full menu specializing in gourmet Italian food. Hotel Cantayo, outside of Nasca, Tel: 51 56 522345, Fax: 51 56 522283, E-mail: info@hotelcantayo.com, URL: http://www.hotelcantayo.com/eng/servicios.html.

Las Cañas (Entrees: $2 - 7)

Built purely of bamboo cane, roofed with petate mats, Las Cañas is a pleasant place to enjoy a leisurely breakfast, lunch or dinner. Special meals at lunch and dinner come with choice of soup or appetizer, plus one of a dozen entrées. In the evenings they offer several options for vegetarians. For the ultimate romantic corner, there's a loft with only a table for two. Open daily 8 a.m.-11 p.m. Bolognesi 279, Tel: 985-1199, E-mail: megaparedes@hotmail.com.

El Huarango (Entrees: $2 - 7)

One of Nasca's better restaurants, El Huarango is popular with the local set and travelers alike. This restaurant serves up good sized portions of tasty food, across two floors. One of the nicest places to sit is on the roof terrace that has a great view. The food is reasonably priced too. Open daily from 11:30 a.m.-10 p.m. Calle Arica 602, Terraza (third floor), Tel: 52-2141, E-mail: restaurantehuarangonasca@hotmail.com.

SOUTHERN COAST

Restaurant La Kañada (Entrees: $2 - 8)

This place is a reliable choice with travelers to Nasca. The restaurant has a good variety of delicious Peruvian regional dishes, delivered in a tranquil setting. For a treat, try any of the shellfish options. Open daily from 8 a.m.-11 p.m. Lima 160, Tel: 52-2531.

La Taberna (Entrees: $3 - 8)

La Taberna's trademark is a series of grafitti on the wall, scribbled by other travelers over the years. This is one of the best restaurants in town and serves up a veritable feast of international meals, including vegetarian options. The restaurant frequently has live music to enjoy as you eat. Open daily from 9 a.m.-4 p.m., 6-11 p.m. Lima 321, Tel: 52-3803.

Restaurant Vía La Encantada (Entrees: $3 - 13)

Restaurant Vía La Encantada does lead you to an enchanted land of international dishes with French and Thai flairs to Peruvian creativity and real "American" breakfasts (complete with eggs scrambled with ham or bacon). The wicker-bamboo and brass furnishings, tables draped with Nasca-Line-weave cloths and a balcony add to the bewitchment of this pricey bistro—as does the torturously translated menu. Aside from some salads and pastas, vegetarians have few options here. Vía La Encantada serves authentic coffee and capuccinos. Open daily 7 a.m.-midnight. Bolognesi 282, Tel: 52-4216 / 964-3426, E-mail: laencantada_nasca@yahoo.com / laencantada_nasca@hotmail.com, URL: www. vialaencantada.com.

THINGS TO SEE AND DO AROUND NASCA

Cantayo Aqueduct and the Inca Ruins of Paredones

Two-thousand years ago, in pre-Inca times, the inhabitants of Nasca developed a system of underground aqueducts to irrigate dry lands that lacked of surface water. Thus, they were able to combat the ever-growing desert. The system is unique in Peru and perhaps in the whole world. In spite of the harshness of the desert, in the Nasca region still exist over 30 underground channels, which are used by local farmers, to grow mainly cotton, corn, beans and potatoes, as well as a variety of fruits. In addition to the channels, nearby visitors may also see various lines etched on the desert floor representing geometric forms, as well as the Inca ruins of Paredones. For further information, contact www. mysteryperu.com.

Mummies on the Nasca Desert

Located some 40 km west of Nasca, is one of the strangest cemeteries on Earth. The place is called the Death Valley, and it is inhabited by a group of farmers who make a living plundering the ancient tombs of their ancestors. The Death Valley has been totally destroyed by this people, who are also known as *huaqueros*, or graver robbers. On the desert surface, one can see hundreds of bones, skulls, complete human bodies, and old tombs. The bodies are found naked due to the robberies, but their state of preservation is amazing.

San Juan de Marcona Marine Reserve

Located on the Pacific coast to the west of Nasca, the San Juan de Marcona Marine Reserve is relatively small — only 54 hectacres — but has an interesting variety of wildlife. The area is known for large populations of Humboldt Penguins and sea lions, as well as a number of sea birds. Ask about trips to the reserve at any of the reputable travel agencies in Nasca or Ica.

Vicuña Reserve of Pampas Galeras

The Vicuña National Park of Pampas Galeras is located about 90 kilometers from the city of Nasca (598 meters, 1962 ft, above sea level), following a steep, winding road that leads high into the Andes to an elevation of 4200 meters, 13,780 ft, above sea level. This area is home to two south american camels, the vicuñas and guanacos, which can be seen running freely through the Andean plateau. Unlike their cousins, the llamas and alpacas, the vicuñas and guanacos are wild animals, as they have not been domesticated and have adapted to high altitudes where drought and freezing nights are the natural rules. The Vicuña Reserve of Pampas Galeras houses roughly 70% of vicuñas in the world, therefore a tour to Pampas Galeras guarantees any visitor a good experience with these wonderful Andean animals. In addition to these camels, one also can see the famous Andean rodent known by the locals as *viscacha,* as well as eagles, ducks and condors.

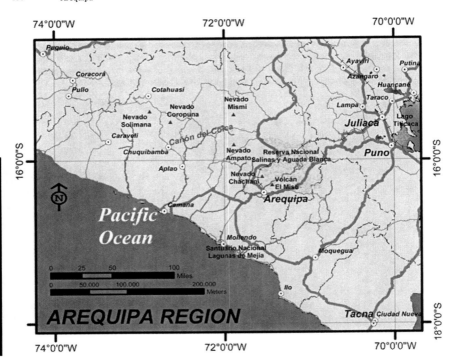

AREQUIPA AND THE COLCA CANYON

In Southern Peru, Arequipa and the Colca Canyon offer plenty to keep travelers occupied for several days, with spectacular scenery, fascinating history and a large number of outdoor activities to boot.

Arequipa itself is held in high regard for both its colonial charm and rich cultural heritage, and is a designated UNESCO World Cultural Heritage site. Beautiful churches, convents and colonial mansions, perfectly framed by majestic snow-capped mountains, set Arequipa aside from its neighbors. The town and its mountains draw culture buffs and adventure junkies from around the world.

The Colca Canyon is famous for its natural beauty, cultural history, and adventure trekking. The canyon was largely forgotten until the late 1970s when engineers visited the canyon to build the area's first road. Due to their relative isolation from the modern world, the people and villages in this region have maintained their ancient traditions and ways of life. A great way to explore the region is on foot, via the numerous ancient trails that wind their way between villages. Along with Cusco and Huaraz, Colca has become known as a magnet for adventure sport, drawing hikers, bikers, trekkers, and rafters from around the world.

If you're heading into the Canyon and you're not coming from Cusco, stay in Arequipa a few days to acclimatize. The most popular point to view the canyon is the Cruz del Condór.

Highlights of Arequipa and the Colca Canyon

The Arequipa and Colca Canyon region is packed with things to see and do for travelers with all tastes. Arequipa has a number of decent Spanish schools. There are a couple of very interesting museums and lots of colonial buildings drenched in history, such as La Compañia or La Catedral. For the outdoorsy traveler, Arequipa's activities include horseback riding, whitewater rafting, mountain biking, hiking and climbing. For those heading out of town, activities in the Colca Canyon include all of the hiking, rafting and climbing opportunities that are also available in close proximity to Arequipa, but there is the hopeful chance to see the mighty condor. Colca Canyon has its own historical draws too—take a trip to Coporaque to see one of the oldest churches in the region.

• Catch a glimpse of the condors in Colca Canyon – Single or multi-day trips can be made to the Colca Canyon. If time permits the multi-day option is worthwhile as it allows visitors to see and explore the bottom depths of the canyon—twice as deep as Arizona's Grand Canyon! The Colca Valley is also a prime location to see the massive Andean Condors soaring in their natural habitat.

• Pay a visit to Momia Juanita – See one of the best preserved mummies in the world at the Museo Santuarios Andinos in downtown Arequipa. Discovered in 1995 by an American-Peruvian climbing team, Momia Juanita had been frozen for over 500 years after being sacrificed atop 6288 m Mt. Ampato.

• Raft Peru's white waters – Experienced rafters can tackle the Río Colga while those new to rafting can splash down the Río Majes. The Río Colga offers visitors much bigger, faster water but both rivers offer stunning views of the surrounding Andean scenery.

• "Swiftly" summit a 6000 meter peak – The Andes surrounding Arequipa have numerous 6000 m peaks including one of the easiest in the world in Chachani. With a base camp above 5000 m the Chachini's peak can be summited in 8 hours, giving those with relatively little mountaineering experience an opportunity to feel what it's like above 6,000 meters.

• Promenade around the Plaza de Armas – The Plaza de Armas in Arequipa is one of the largest and most striking in South America. Featuring many of the white sillar buildings that Arequipa is known for, no visit is complete without time spent exploring the plaza and its rich colonial legacy.

Getting To and Away from Arequipa and the Colca Canyon

Most navigation of the Colca Canyon valley will require a layover in the beautiful white-washed city of Arequipa. Arequipa may be accessed by air from Cusco or Lima and by bus from Cusco, Juliaca or Puno. While train services may be reintroduced in the future, at the time of writing there are none in or out of Arequipa (check www.perurail.com). Overnight buses to and from Arequipa are not advisable due to many reported robberies in addition to weather related incidents during the wet season. Lying at the base of the canyon, Chivay serves as the most popular starting point for treks to the Colca Canyon. Two hours further along the road lies Cabanaconde, Chivay's peaceful sister to the south of the canyon. Cruz del Cóndor is best reached from here.

Safety in Arequipa and the Colca Canyon

Petty theft is common in Arequipa, so be sure to leave anything of value back at the hostel. Also, beware of unregistered ticket vendors who may try to sell you fake entrance passes and especially all-in-one package deals to points of interest around the canyon. Always check weather conditions before trekking, especially during the wet season as trails become more difficult. Travelers should also think twice about taking an overnight bus into or out of the area during the wet season, as road conditions worsen and accident rates increase.

AREQUIPA AND THE COLCA CANYON TOURS

In Arequipa and the Colca Canyon, there is an abundance of tours that the traveler can take, with both locations offering distinct options. Arequipa offers city tours, including a chance to visit some of the fascinating old colonial buildings. There are also adventure excursions near the city for hiking, climbing, mountain-biking, whitewater rafting or horseback riding.

In the Colca Canyon, organized tours are also available for all of these same activities, particularly for hiking. A couple of good trekking tours can be taken from the village of Cabanaconde. Tours for trips to the Cruz del Cóndor can also be purchased in Arequipa or in the Colca Canyon.

AREQUIPA AND THE COLCA CANYON LODGING

Arequipa and the Colca Canyon region has just about as wide an array of hotels as one might expect for an area so diverse. Arequipa has something for every taste and budget. Many Arequipa hotels are based very close to the historical part of town, in the streets surrounding the Plaza de Armas and close to main landmarks. Some hotels in Arequipa offer lovely views of the spectacular scenery surrounding the city. If you're looking for help getting around and seeing the city, many hotels offer their own city tour service.

In the Colca Canyon, hotels are mainly clustered around Chivay and Cabanaconde. More remote options are also available. In this area, many of the hotels come with an adjoining restaurant. There are some stunning places to stay in the countryside surrounding Colca Canyon, often with nearby hotsprings.

AREQUIPA

When he arrived in the present-day Arequipa with his army, Inca Mayta Cápac declared *arique-pay*, meaning "Yes, stay here," and they formed the beginnings of the city at the base of El Misti mountain. Nearly six centuries later, this oasis of pearly white buildings rising out of the valley retains its captivating beauty.

Highlights of Arequipa

Nicknamed *la ciudad blanca*, or "the white city," for its unique buildings made entirely of sillar, a white volcanic stone, Arequipa offers an easy and romantic atmosphere. The striking Plaza de Armas, lined with palm trees and dominated by the sprawling neoclassical La Catedral, is one of the most beautiful main squares in all of Peru. From here you can take a stroll to the 400 year old Monasterio de Santa Catalina, La Compañia, the church of San Francisco, Chapel of the Third Order, or Santo Domingo. Similarily charming are the colonial mansions in the city center and the revived colonial neighborhoods such as Los Tombos and Barrio San Lázaro.

Arequipa's history provides ample options for lovers of the past. There are a number of interesting museums, including the new Museo Santuarios Andinos, home to the famous mummy of 13-year-old Juanita, Museo Histórico Municipal, and Museo de Arte Contemporáneo. Arequipa also has several colonial mansions which are worth visiting. Some of these *casonas* are located outside the city in the picturesque countryside. To see the houses and enjoy the fresh air, take a three-hour tour *campiña*, which can be arranged by one of Arequipa's tour agencies.

If you prefer spectacular views that don't require physical labor, Yanahuara, 2 km northwest of the city, offers excellent views of El Misti. For active adventurers looking for more than a languorous countryside tour, head to one of the three volcanoes towering over the city. Chachani is the most achievable 6,000 meter summit, while El Misti and Ampato promise more challenging treks. Beyond these peaks, in the extraordinary Valley of the Volcanoes, are two of the world's deepest canyons—the Cotahuasi and the Colca. Trips to either of these places provide vivid images of some of the country's most spectacular scenery, and if you're lucky, glimpses of the noble condor.

The celebrated Colca Canyon wasn't connected to the modern world until the late 1970s, and as such, its villagers continue to practice ancient traditions and ways of life. In comparison with other areas, this is also one of the safest places for trekking, mountain biking, and rafting. For tourist information, head to i-Peru (Portal de la Municipalidad 110, Tel: 51-54-221-

228). Travelers should also be warned that theft can be a problem in the market areas, particularly after dark. You should also be careful when taking taxis at night, as car-jacking has been reported. Because Arequipa is a commercial center for southern Peru, it has a number of hotels and restaurants, which cater to a broad spectrum of tastes and budgets.

AREQUIPA HISTORY
Arequipa Today
Arequipa of yesterday is a tale of two stories: one of the Aymara indigenous people who had been settled in the area for centuries and another of the Spanish colonialists, who "founded" the city in 1540. Archaeological findings in the valleys around Arequipa suggest that the Aymara had been settled in the area for thousands of years before being conquered by the Inca Empire in the 1400s. The Aymara had developed advanced irrigation and agriculture techniques, the remains of which can still be seen in the valleys surrounding Arequipa. Upon takeover by the Incas, the Aymara and their land were relied on heavily by the Inca Empire to produce food and other agricultural products. The Inca rule over the Aymara, however, was brief as the Spanish arrived and conquered soon after.

Modern Arequipa was "founded" on August 15, 1540 by Garcí Manuel de Carbajal. Under Spanish colonial rule, agriculture continued to serve as Arequipa's principal economic engine, as European crops such as wine, liquor and olive oil were established and cultivated in the region. In July of 1821, José de San Martín declared Peru a nation independent from Spain. During the 19th century, Arequipa was a hotbed for Peruvian nationalism. It was in this period that Arequipa became known throughout the continent as a "land of leaders" because of the often brave and daring rebellions of the Arequipeños.

Arequipa had a relatively isolated history until 1870 when it became connected to the Pacific Ocean by rail. It joined the intercontinental trading loop in the 1930s when road expansion gave Arequipa a direct link to the Pan-American Highway.

Arequipa Today
While once an important agricultural center for the Churajon culture, the main contemporary driver of the Arequipan economy is tourism. Often considered to be the second most beautiful city in Peru after Cusco, Arequipa is bustling with attractions for all stripes of tourists. Visitors come to Arequipa to hike the volcanoes, visit the nearby Colca Canyon or walk around the downtown area to admire the colonial architecture. It was this stunning engineering that led to the city's designation as a UNESCO World Heritage Site in 2000 for the unique combination of European and native characteristics. Walking around the city will allow a visitor to appreciate the beauty of Arequipa's white sillar buildings, whose façades shine in the high afternoon sun.

The city's Plaza de Armas is one of the grandest on the whole continent and features many of the city's most remarkable buildings—some of which have been completely rebuilt as a result of earthquakes in the area. When the Spanish initially descended upon Arequipa in 1540 it created the largest Spanish population in all of Peru. The second half of the 20th century saw large migrations from the highlands, greatly changing the demographic and cultural makeup of the city. Today, Arequipa's population is a mixture of Spanish, indigenous and *mestizo* (mixed) inhabitants. Many of Arequipa's colonial buildings have been converted into hotels and restaurants serving the city's thriving tourism industry.

When to Go
The best time to visit Arequipa is during the dry months of June through September. That said, Arequipa averages over 300 days of sunshine every year, so visiting during the so-called rainy season probably won't spoil your trip.

Each year on August 15th there is a city-wide party celebrating the day Garcí Manuel de Carbajal settled the city in 1540. On this day and those surrounding it, the city is

AREQUIPA

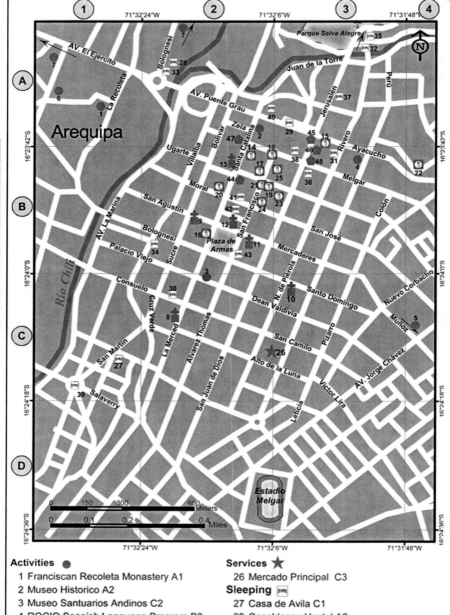

Activities ●

1 Franciscan Recoleta Monastery A1
2 Museo Historico A2
3 Museo Santuarios Andinos C2
4 ROCIO Spanish Language Program B3
5 Sabandía Mill C4
6 Toro Muerto Petroglyphs A1
7 Yanahuara A1

Church ▟

8 Iglesia de La Merced C2

Services ★

26 Mercado Principal C3

Sleeping 🛏

27 Casa de Avila C1
28 Casablanca Hostal A2
29 Colonial Palace A3
30 Hostal Casona Solar C2
31 Hostal Solar B3
32 Hotel La Gruta A3
33 Hotel la Posada del Puente A2

9 Iglesia de San Agustín B2	34 Hotel Lari House B2
10 Iglesia de Santo Domingo C3	35 Hotel Libertador A3
11 Iglesia La Compañía B2	36 La Casa de Melgar Hostal B3
12 La Catedral B2	37 La Casa de mi Abuela A3
13 Monasterio de Santa Catalina B2	38 La Casona de Jerusalén Hospedaje B3
Eating	39 La Plazuela C1
14 Deja Vu B2	40 La Posada del Cacique A2
15 D'La Casa A3	41 Los Balcones de Moral y Santa Catalina B2
16 El Cerrojo B2	42 Posada de Sancho B2
17 El Turko II B2	43 Sonesta Posada del Inca B2
18 El Viñedo B2	**Tour Operator**
19 Gianni's B2	44 Al Travel Tours B2
20 La Boveda Social Club B2	45 Colca Trek A3
21 La Italiana B2	46 Cusipata Viajes y Turismo B3
22 Lakshmivan B4	47 Naturaleza Activa A2
23 Mandala Vegeterian Restaurant B3	48 Peru Adventures Tours B3
24 Ras el hanout y los 40 sabores B2	
25 Sonccollay B3	

packed and last-minute accommodations are hard to come by. It is a great time to see Arequipa if you want to mix with locals and see how they kick-back. However, if you are planning on being in Arequipa in mid-August, be sure to arrange accommodations well in advance.

Getting To and Away from Arequipa

Daily flights are available to and from Lima, on LAN or TANS, as well as to and from Cusco on LAN. The Rodríguez Ballón airport is located about 8km away from the city center (for info call 51-54-443-464). Terminal Terrestre (Av Andrés Avelino Cáceres) houses all the long distance bus companies, however some buses also depart from the smaller Terrapuerto next door. Both are located 10-15 minutes by bus or taxi ($1) headed south from downtown. Fares from Cusco run from $7.50-$21, 17 hours on average. Headed towards Puno, buses cost $4.50 and take six hours. It is best to avoid overnight buses to and from Arequipa as many accidents and hijackings have been reported in the surrounding area. Perúrail (Arica 200 y Av Tacna, www.perurail.com or call 51-54-215-350) also runs rail service to Arequipa from Cusco via Juliaca as well as from Puno. However, at the time of writing these had been suspended except for chartered groups.

AREQUIPA SERVICES

For tourist information, head to i-Peru (Portal de la Municipalidad 110, Tel: 51-54-221-228).

Shopping

As the center of Peru's thriving wool industry, Arequipa offers a number of wool and fine clothing shops. One of the best places to start any shopping adventure is Pasaje Catedral, an inviting street behind the cathedral. Offering a wide selection of men's and women's sweaters, coats, and scarves, Millma's Baby Alpaca is one of the nicer shops in town. For baby alpaca sweaters, scarves, and pashminas, head to Links Fashions. Michell is a large outlet store that, in addition to selling sweaters, scarves, and coats, also demonstrates to visitors the process of hand-sorting alpaca fiber and loom weaving. Of course, if you're really anxious to learn the trade of wool-sorting you can arrange a visit to one of the factories or highland ranches specializing in alpaca and vicuña. El Centro Turistico Comercial de Arequipa is the premier shopping center of Arequipa. Located at Mercaderes 141 (half a block from the Main Square) they sell handicrafts, alpaca garments, jewelry, silverware, souvenirs, decorations, chocolates and handbags. Services include internet, money exchange, call center, video room and more.

Help other travelers. Publish your favorite places at www.vivatravelguides.com

Patio Del Ekeko

If you are going to shop for souvenirs in just one place in Arequipa, it should be the Patio del Ekeko mall, just off the Plaza de Armas. A wide variety of shops offer a dizzying array of high-quality handicrafts: alpaca knitwear, jewelry, house decorations, hats, liquors, chocolates and coffees. There is also a restaurant, internet café, money change and shipping service. Mercaderes 141, Arequipa. Tel: 51-54-215-861. E-mail: info@cecotur.com, URL: www.cecotur.com.

Police Station

The Police station is located at Jerusalen 315.

THINGS TO SEE AND DO IN AREQUIPA

Arequipa has silently become one of Peru's most popular visitor draws: a gorgeous colonial city constructed of white volcanic stone with pleasant parks and friendly people. There is no one thing to do or see that defines Arequipa (like the enigmatic Nasca Lines in Nasca, for example). Instead, there are many lower-key activities that can easily fill a week or more in this lovely city and region.

There are several good Spanish schools in Arequipa, almost as many as you'll find in Lima or Cusco. The city features some interesting museums, including the Contemporary Art Museum, the Municipal History Museum, and the Andean Sanctuary Museum. There are also some well-preserved colonial mansions that are open to the public. La Compañia is a beautifully restored Jesuit church from the colonial era. La Catedral, which has been destroyed twice by natural disasters and subsequently rebuilt, is an impressive sight. When you're done with the museums, there is also decent shopping to be done in Arequipa, especially if you're interested in wool. If you're craving something a little more active, there are horseback riding tours and some beautiful mountains nearby, such as El Misti and Ampato. There are also a lot of hiking trails, whitewater trips and mountain biking opportunities, enough to delight any active adventure traveler. If you want to explore the region and get out of town for a while, head for the famous Cruz del Cóndor to see some of these magnificent birds in flight, or to the Mirador de Los Andes to get a great view.

Photo by Cate Batchelder

GAY AREQUIPA

Arequipa is notable as one of the few cities in Peru outside of Lima to have openly gay businesses—two dance clubs and a video store—along with a few gay-owned and gay-friendly hotels. The city population of one million does guarantee the existence of a sizable gay community. The exceptional level of culture, such as theatre groups and art associations signify at least a minimal level of tolerance. Gary Lee and his Peruvian partner manage the Casa Arequipa, an upscale bed and breakfast, and he notes that the more openly gay businesses provide an opportunity for individuals to get into what is still considered a low-profile community. Lee adds that while there is still a lot of anti-gay prejudice, and that while the lesbian community is much more closeted than the gay male community, Peru is nonetheless an evolving, changing culture. The two gay dance clubs are SKP at 205 Villalba, and Open Night, on the corner of Salaverry and Jorge Chavez. Both clubs open late and stay open late.

Franciscan Recoleta Monastery (Entrance: $1.60)

One of the most impressive historical monuments in Peru, the Franciscan Recoleta Monastery dates back to 1648. This museum offers a microcosmic illustration of the two dominant cultures that shaped Peru. One of these is pre-Columbian, featuring Nasca, Chavín and Chancay pottery, stones and mummies. The other is the legacy of the Catholic Church, with an extensive display of religious art and their monastery's library, which houses no less than 20,000 books. In the three and a half centuries since its creation, the Recoleta Monastery has been rebuilt and renovated following various earthquakes that impacted the region. Open daily, 9 a.m.-5 p.m. Recoleta 117, Tel: 51-54-270-966.

La Compañía (Entrance: $2)

Founded by Jesuits in 1573, La Compañía is a large church composed of three naves and a cupola. This Arequipa attraction is best known for its elaborately carved stone entrance and the Chapel of San Ignacio de Loyola. Inside is a delicately carved cedar main altar, whose details are accentuated by a gold leaf covering. Adorning the chapel's walls are works from the Mannerist master Bernardo Bitti. In the sacristy located nearby, the gigantic murals of jungle plants and animals recall an earlier period when missionaries were sent into the depths of the Amazon to seek out native converts. Craft markets now inhabit the Jesuits' less significant cloisters, which are located further down on General Moran Street. Open Monday - Friday, 9 a.m. - 12:30 p.m., 3 p.m. - 6 p.m., Saturday, 11:30 a.m. - 12:30 p.m., 3 p.m. - 6 p.m., and Sunday 9 a.m. - 12:30 p.m., 5 p.m. - 6 p.m. Thomas Álvarez and General Morán, Tel: 51-54-212-141.

La Catedral (Entrance: Free)

Framed by the majestic snow-capped peaks of El Misti and Chachani, La Catedral is truly one of the most spectacular sites in Arequipa. While construction of the church began in 1544, much of its edifice was destroyed during an earthquake in the 17th century. Then, in 1844 it was completely destroyed by fire. The present-day façade that dominates the Plaza de Armas bears a neoclassical style. Inside you'll find one of the largest organs in South America, and an elaborately carved wooden pulpit adorned with a menacing serpent-tailed devil. Open Monday - Saturday, 7 a.m. - 11:30am, 4:30 p.m. - 7:30pm and Sunday, 6:30 a.m. - 1:30 p.m., 4:30 p.m. - 7:30 p.m. La Plaza de Armas Tel: 51-54-232-635.

Monasterio de Santa Catalina (Entrance: $9)

Like a city within a city, the astounding Monasterio de Santa Catalina is probably one of the best architectural sites in Arequipa. With architecture reminiscent of Andalusian Spain, the convent contains a hundred houses, 60 streets, a main square, church, and cemetery. The painting gallery houses more than 400 paintings from the Cusqueña School. Until 1970, when it was opened to the public, this place was shrouded in mystery. During the 17th and 18th centuries, hundreds of nuns lived here, in addition to the daughters of wealthy families. The nuns who currently call this place home have the pleasure of living in modern quarters, complete with fully equipped kitchens. Some of the convent's highlights include the Orange Tree Cloister, with painted arches; Calle Toledo, an expansive boulevard that ends in a communal *lavandería*, where the nuns wash their clothes; and the rooms of Sor Ana, a 17th century nun who the Vatican is eager to canonize. Mass is held daily at 7:30 a.m. Santa Catalina 301, Tel: 51-54-229-798, URL: www.santacatalina.org.pe.

Colonial Mansions

Arequipa boasts some of the best preserved and finest colonial architecture in all of Peru. Because most *casonas* were built as single story structures, they have withstood the various earthquakes that leveled other buildings in the city. One of the best houses is the Casa del Moral (Moral 318, Tel: 51-54-214-907, Monday - Saturday, 9 a.m. - 5:30 p.m., $1.50, students $1), which dates back to around 1700. The house gets its name from the beautiful *mora* (mulberry tree) which graces the courtyard, paved with river stones and surrounded by gorgeous ochre walls. Perched on the front doors of the house are elaborately carved pumas and serpents, and the interior of the house is decorated with art and furniture from the period.

Down the street from Casa del Moral is the beautiful Casona Iriberry (San Agustin on the Plaza de Armas, Tel: 51-54-204-482, Open daily 9 a.m. - 1 p.m., 4 p.m. - 8 p.m., Free). The house was built in 1793 and was recently converted into the Centro Cultural Chávez de la Rosa. The house's spacious rooms open onto a series of elegant stone patios, and the doorways don carved messages in Spanish.

Other houses of interest include the Casa Tristán del Pozo, recently converted into a cultural center and offices for the Banco Continental, and Casa Goyeneche, which features an ecclesiastical coat-of-arms of José Sebastián Goyeneche (1784-1872), the former bishop of Arequipa. Arequipa's three-hour *campiña* (country) tour also gives travelers a chance to see some other fine examples of colonial houses.

Museo de Arte Contemporáneo (Entrance: $1)

Art lovers and photography buffs should find this museum interesting. Dedicated to painting and photography from 1900 onwards, the museum houses an intriguing collection of 20th century art, and photography exhibits of Miguel and Carlos Vargas. The famous Cusco photographer, Martín Chambi, was mentored by these two brothers, who themselves were famous for documenting the daily life and customs of 20th century Arequipa. A more contemporary section, which exhibits work by a range of young local artists, will surely suit those with more modern tastes. Paintings of some of Peru's most famous artists, such as Fernando de Szyszlo and Enrique Polanco are also featured in the museum. A restored dining car-turned-café and gardens out back are also worth a peek. Open Tuesday - Friday, 10 a.m. - 5 p.m., Saturday - Sunday, 10 a.m. - 2p.m. Tacna and Arica 201, Tel: 51-54-221-068, E-mail: mac_arequipa@yahoo.es.

Museo Histórico Municipal (Entrance: $0.75)

Located near San Francisco Church, the Museo Histórico Municipal features a naval museum and historical photographs of Arequipa. One of the museum's highlights is a series of caricatures and paintings by local artist Jorge Vinatea Reynoso (1900-31). Plaza San Francisco 407.

Museo Santuarios Andinos (Entrance: General, $6, Students, $3)

This museum, dedicated to high-altitude archaeology and its pioneer Johan Reinhard, is most famous for housing the mummified remains of 13-year-old Juanita. Shortly after arriving in the area, the Incas implemented the practice of sacrificing children on the peaks of the area's highest volcanoes. Archaeologists believe that the children were sacrificed as part of a Capac Cocha ceremony aimed at appeasing the *apus*, or mountain gods. While the idea of human sacrifices may seem a bit gruesome by modern day standards, such a death was considered an honor during the Inca period. In addition to Juanita, the museum is home to 18 other mummies discovered atop volcanoes in Peru, Argentina, and Chile. The mummies are displayed with the textiles, gold, ceramics, and woodcarvings that were found in their tombs. The entrance fee includes a mandatory one-hour tour that features a National Geographic documentary. Open Monday - Saturday, 9 a.m. - 6 p.m., and Sunday, 9 a.m. - 3 p.m. La Merced 110, Tel: 51-54-215-013, URL: www.ucsm.edu.pe/santury.

STUDYING SPANISH IN AREQUIPA

With its Spanish colonial charm and picturesque surroundings, Arequipa offers a wonderful alternative venue for learning Spanish. There are few places in the Andes where the language is spoken as clearly and correctly, but a host of language schools in Arequipa offer solid programs.

CEICA Centro Estudios e Interacción Cultural Arequipa

This small school was founded by a group of Spanish teachers in 1996 and is owned by locals. Classes from basic to advanced are small (1-4 students) and held outside in a pleasant open-air courtyard. CEICA is 25-minute walk from the city center. Urbanización Universitaria G-9 Cercado, Tel: 51-54-221-165 / 51-54-231-759, E-mail: Info@ceica-peru.com.

Casa de Avila Spanish School

Opened in 2004 and located in the center of the city, this school specializes in one-to-one programs and small groups. Classes are tailored to your abilities, with all levels available. Classes take place in a wide open courtyard, and accommodation is offered in the famous Casa de Avila Hostel or in family houses. The program includes immersion activities to reinforce your learning. Several schedules are available, including a special "Spanish for volunteering" program. Online registration offered. Av. San Martin 116, Vallecito, Tel: 51-54-213-177, URL: www.spanishschoolarequipa.com.

EDEAQ Escuela de Español Ari Quipay Arequipa ($120 for 20 hours)

EDEAQ has recently been reopened in the 18th century home of famous Arequipa writer, jurist, and former Peruvian president José Luis Bustamante y Rivero near the colonial heart of town. The school takes pride in its small size and family-like atmosphere; don't expect hoards of fellow students blabbering in their native languages in the hallways. The program is personal and the prices straightforward, with a good chunk of the fees actually making it to teachers' and host families' pockets. Casilla 11, Tel: 51-54-257-358 / 51-54-226-784, Cell: 51-54-95-999-2995, Fax: 51-54-257-358, E-mail: contact@edeaq.com, URL: www.edeaq.com.

ROCIO Spanish Language Program (From $6 / hour)

Classes in Quechua, Aymara, and standard Spanish are available at ROCIO, along with a host of slightly different extracurriculars like Peruvian dance and cooking, as well as bird watching in Chiwata. ROCIO also offers a "Learn and Teach" program where you can take Spanish in exchange for teaching lessons in your own tongue. Calle Melgar No. 209 - Of. 22, Tel: 51-54-224-568 / 51-54-969-4582, Fax: 51-54-286-929, E-mail: info@spanish-peru.com, URL: www.spanish-peru.com.

Llama Education (From $120 for 20 hours)

Housed in a new central location downtown, Llama Education is another decent option for a normal Spanish school program. Casabella lote A6 Cerro Colorado, Tel: 51-54-274-069, E-mail: info@llamaeducation.com

Spanish Café Arequipa

Laid-back and a little different from the rest, the Spanish Language Café is a good choice for those looking to escape the usual Spanish school bubble and spend the days practicing grammar and conversing in a chill café bar. By day the place hums with Spanish murmurings, while a small bar and live music keep the place going into the night. When things get rowdy, classes are held in a more private section of the building. Andean Integration, Tel: 51-54-222-052, E-mail: info@spanishcafeperu.com

VOLUNTEERING IN AREQUIPA

Arequipa's urban and natural beauty and rich culture do not shelter it from many of the same social problems that affect the rest of Peru, especially the children. The underfunded and understaffed educational system is in particularly high need of assistance, and for this Arequipa provides many volunteer prospects, as well as opportunities to learn Spanish.

I-to-I Volunteers

The I-to-I volunteer program in Arequipa needs helpers to work with disadvantaged children, doing work such as feeding, washing, helping with physical therapy, organizing games and activities, and maintaining the facility. Work is between five to six hours a day, serving the poorest children in Arequipa. Apart from meal preparation, volunteers are needed in areas such as arts, crafts, and teaching English. You will also have an opportunity to play *fútbol* and other sports with the children. The cost is US$ 1795.00 for 4 weeks, and includes accommodations and meals. URL: www.i-to-i.com.

The Point Hostel

The Point Hostel in Arequipa needs volunteers to receive guests, tend bar, organize events and do other work as needed. Compensation includes free lodging, dinner, and discounts on drinks. Volunteer positions are open throughout the year. This is an excellent opportunity for travelers on a tight budget to enjoy the extraordinary city of Arequipa and its surrounding environment. E-mail: btblow@yahoo.co.uk.

San Vincente de Paul

The San Vincente de Paul program is run by three nuns who provide care and education to a group of 30 children whose parents work all day as street vendors, often earning no more than $50 a month. Volunteers are needed to assist the teachers, set-up games and physical exercises. An intermediate grasp of Spanish, at the very least, is essential, as well as a minimal four-week time commitment. Work is scheduled from 8 a.m. to 4:30 p.m. Tel: 51-84-262-345, Fax: 51-84-241-422, URL: www.volunteerprograms.org.

Global Vision International

Global Vision International's program in Arequipa needs foreign volunteers to assist teachers in Arequipa's underfunded and understaffed educational system, from early morning to the afternoon, particularly in the area of literacy, math, and English. Help is also needed in setting up auxiliary schools in the region and sending adults back to school (or in some cases, going to school for the first time). Part of your fee goes towards the cost of the program itself, buying books and other teaching material for the children, and even food. Volunteers will stay in their own rooms within the homes of local families. Tel: 1-888-653-6028 (toll free), E-mail: info@gviusa.com.

INABIF Children's Home

The INABIF Children's Home serves male orphans and also those from severely dysfunctional homes, some rescued from lives of petty crime and drug use. The goal of INABIF is to teach basic life skills, from personal hygiene to housekeeping and cooking, to learning interpersonal cooperation, and above all, self-discipline. Since few of the boys in the facility can leave the home, volunteers are needed to help prepare these children for the outside world, conversing with them, sharing experiences and demonstrating an interest in the boys' lives. Volunteers also help prepare games and activities, as well as tutor English. Tel: 51-84-262-345, Fax: 51-84-241-422, URL: www.volunteerprograms.org.

AREQUIPA TOURS

Located in the heart of canyon country, Arequipa is a great place to scout around for hiking and trekking tours. Most tour companies located on Jerusalén, Santa Catalina and near Plaza de Armas offer tours of Colca, Cotahuasi, Toro Muerto, and the city tours in Arequipa itself. You can also buy air, train, and bus tickets, and inquire about longer trekking excursions.

Prices fluctuate significantly so your best bet is to shop around. In general you get what you pay for, so make sure you know what's included in cheaper tours. Always make sure your company and its guides are official. The Asociación de Operadores y Promotores de Turismo de Aventura y Ecoturismo is group of nature lovers that have set a standard for the quality of service and environmental impact that Arequipa tour operators are responsible for. Only the businesses that meet their standards receive their seal of approval. To inquire about a tour operator you can send an E-mail to aptare@gmail.com.

GSA Arequipa

GSA Arequipa has more than ten years of experience as a tour operator based out of Arequipa, running tours in both Peru and Bolivia. Tour packages offered in Arequipa run for either three days ($149) or four days ($199) and include guides, hotel, and some meals. The four-day package includes a city tour, a visit to Santa Catalina Convent and the Sabandía Mill, and stopovers at popular sites outside of Arequipa: the Colca Canyon, the Reserva Nacional de Aquada Blanca y Salinas, the Cruz del Cóndor, some hot springs, and the towns of Chivay, Yura, Yanque, Puente Cervantes, Achoma and Lari. Three-day tours visit Arequipa and a few major sights, and include outings in the towns of Tingo and Cayma. Prices are not fixed and depend on which type of accommodation you choose. Visit GSA's website for more information on available tours. Portal de San Agustín, Tel: 51-54-202-427, E-mail: gsa_aqp@hotmail.com, URL: www.gsaperutravel.com.

Eco Tours

Eco Tours is a travel agency and tour operator that specializes in conventional ecotourism and adventure trips in the Colca and Cotahuasi Canyons, Inca Trail, Amazon Rainforest, Nasca Lines over flight and more. They can also organize climbing, trekking, rafting, horseback riding, paragliding, bicycling, birdwatching or city tours. Eco Tours can also assist with plane, bus and train tickets, accomodations or book exchange. Jerusalén 409, Tel: 51-54-202-562, E-mail: ecotours@terra.com.pe.

Peru Explorer

For $60, Peru Explorer will offer a comprehensive three-day tour of Arequipa and its surrounding countryside. The morning of the first day is a guide through the stunning religious architecture of the area, including the 450 year-old Holy Catalina Monastery, the Founder's Mansion, even a visit to a *discoteca*! The second day includes tours of alpaca farms and opportunities to check out the volcanoes and white-capped sierras surrounding the city, finally ending at a natural thermal spring. Rounding out the trip, day three allows for condor-watching and pre-Inca ruins. The range of Peru Explorer's options extend beyond Arequipa, though, and they also offer multi-day package tours that include the Cotahuasi Canyon, Cusco, Puno, Pisco, and Nasca. Portal San Agustín 131, Tel: 51-54-225-684, E-mail: arequipaexplorerperu@hotmail.com.

Peru Incas Explorer (PIE) Peru

Owned by the same family as the popular Home Sweet Home hostels, PIE now has offices and hostels in Arequipa, Cusco and Ollantaytambo in the Sacred Valley, and offers a range of tours all over the country. In Arequipa it operates trekking trips to the Colca Canyon, always trying to combine culture and history with adventure. The tours include stays in small villages, school visits, as well as hiking, climbing and biking in the area. Calle Rivero (Home Sweet Home Hostel), E-mail: info@pie-peru.com, URL: www.pie-peru.com.

Land Adventures

A relatively new tour operator, Land Adventures is geared towards backpackers, offering affordable trips packed with adrenalin inducing options. It offers the standard Colca Canyon tour, as well as trekking options in the Cotahuasi Canyon, and mountain biking and climbing trips in the area. Land Adventures follows a responsible tourism policy and can also set you up with volunteer work in isolated communities in the Colca Canyon. Santa Catalina 118-B, 2nd Floor, Tel: 51-54-204872, E-mail: informes@landadventures.net, URL: www.landadventures.net.

AREQUIPA

Cusipata Viajes y Turismo

Cusipata Viajes y Turismo presents an array of adventure services including whitewater rafting, hiking, trekking, horseback riding, paragliding, mountain biking, kayaking (in fact they have their very own kayaking school, teaching everything from paddling to rolling); their prices range from $30 for a one-day introduction to rafting to $2,000 for a 5-day excursion hitting the rapids in one of the deepest canyons in the world, the Cotahuasi. This is a family operation, managed by the Vellutinos who are all experienced and certified guides. Jerusalén 408–A, Tel: 51-54-203-966, E-mail: gvellutino@terra.com.pe, URL: www.cusipata.com

Arequipa Bustour

This guide to Arequipa will, for four hours and $10, gives you one heck of a ride on a double-decker open air bus, starting at the Plaza de Armas where English (and French) speaking guides will explain the history and architecture of the White City, before touring the sparkling valleys and historic monuments surrounding Arequipa. The stops include visits to farms where exotic fruits are harvested, viewing towers that give breathtaking views of the region, an 18th century mill still in use, the colonial mansion, which was home of the city's founder, and a stop at a local alpaca, vicuña, and llama wool outlet, where you can pet said animals. An ideal introduction to the region. Portal de San Agustin 111, Tel: 51-54-203-434, E-mail: bustour@terra.com.pe

PeruMotors

PeruMotors is a small and flexible travel-organization under Dutch management, specializing in guided motor tours in South America. They organize moto and 4x4 tours for reasonable prices. They have "Desert to Jungle" tours, which all visit Machu Picchu (Cusco), Nasca (Lines) and Lake Titicaca. Tour durations range from 13 to 21 days. Calle Álvarez Thomas 102, Urb. Selva Alegre, Tel: 51-54-223-984, Fax: 51-54-289-899, E-mail: geert@perumotors.com, URL: www.perumotors.com.

Caframi Tours (Tours: $30 - 270)

Caframi Tours offers a full lot of guided trips ranging from a few hours around downtown Arequipa (walking tours as well) to 6-day trips into the Peruvian Amazon (the longer ones are based out of Iquitos and transportation to and from Iquitos is not included or arranged). They also offer single and multi-day rafting trips down both the Majel and Chili Rivers. For those looking to get a little altitude, Caframi Tours can take you up the snowless Misti Volcano or to the summit of snow-capped Ampato or Chachini. The tours range in price from $30 for short city tours to $270 for a 5-day trek to Machu Picchu during low season. Caframi offers student discounts, so if this applies to you, be sure to ask. Prices rise during Semana Santa so plan accordingly. Jerusalén 402-B Cercado, Tel: 51-54-220-447, E-mail: caframitours@hotmail.com or carframitours@yahoo.es, URL: www.caframitours.com.

Peru Adventures Tours

Peru Adventure Tours offers the full gamut of hiking and walking tours around Arequipa as well as sandboarding to nearby Ica. Unlike many operators in the area, they do not have rafting trips but instead, ATV tours and horseback riding trips.

A four hour tour of Arequipa costs $35 for an English speaking guide, including transportation and entrance to all attractions. During high season a 5-day trek to Machu Picchu costs $345. Their tours are more expensive than other operators but they claim to pay Peruvian taxes that many companies cleverly evade due to Peru's loose tax structure. Additionally, their employees are paid higher guaranteed wages than other operators in the area. They also have a "responsible tourism" policy that all guides and staff have been trained in. Make the decision for yourself, but understand this is one of the reasons for the higher prices. 410-A, Jerusalén Street, Tel: 51-54-221-658, E-mail: info@peruadventures-tours.com, URL: www.peruadventurestours.com.

Pablo Tour

The Pablo Tour agency is regionally certified in ecotourism and by the Peruvian Association of Adventure and Ecological Tourism of the Colca and Cotahuasi Canyon. It offers nearly every tour in Arequipa you could conceive of: rafting, paddling inflatable kayaks through Class II and III rapids, mixed rafting-hiking-mountain biking tours, multi-day ascents of the volcanoes around Arequipa, and single or multi-day hikes in and around the Colca Canyon. A 4-day trek costs $145. Jerusalén 400 AB-1, Tel: 51-54-203-737, Fax: 51-54-203-737, E-mail: pablotour@hotmail.com, URL: www.pablotour.com.

Ideal Travels SAC

Friendly, reliable guides lead trips to the Colca and Cotahuasi Canyons, Toro Muerto, and nearby Valley of the Volcanoes. Jeep and microbus rentals are also available. International ticket reservations can be made, and credit cards are accepted. Urb San Isidro F-2, Vallecito Tel: 51-54-244-439, E-mail: idealperu@terra.com.pe.

Zárate Expeditions

This is one of the most professional and experienced agencies in Arequipa. Specializing in climbing and trekking, they can organize expeditions to most of the nearby mountains and volcanoes, including El Misti, Nevado Chachani, Nevado Ampato, Volcano Ubinas, and the Colca Canyon. Treks to the source of the Amazon, and mountain biking and 4x4 trips can also be arranged. The company is run by professional mountain guide Carlos Zárate, who gladly provides information and advice about climbing around Arequipa.Santa Catalina 204, Office 3, Tel: 51-54-202-461 / 51-54-263-107, URL: www.zarateadventures.com.

Naturaleza Activa

This is a relatively new adventure company that specializes in adventure tours. Climbing and mountain biking excursions can be arranged. Guides are experienced and extremely knowledgeable. Santa Catalina 211, Tel: 51-54-695-793.

Colca Trek

Colca Trek is one of the best options for Colca Canyon tours. Vlado, the owner, is very knowledgeable and helpful, and can provide tours to the Colca and Cotahuasi Canyons for hiking and trekking. Just be sure to ask for Vlado Soto specifically. Tours of the Colca Canyon run from two to five days, where Cotahuasi tours run for four, five, six, seven or ten days. Ask also about rafting tours (on the Colca River and the Cotahuasi River) and mountain biking trips. Jerusalén 401-B Tel: 51-54-206-217 E-mail: colcatrek@gmail.com URL: www.colcatrek.com.pe.

Inka Fest

Inka Fest is a travel agency specializing in adventure, mystical, cultural, and ecological tours. With Inka Fest, you can discover the Andes, the jungle, or North or South Peru. They offer good prices and the workers are very helpful and patient in helping you organize a tour according to your needs. Calle El Carmen 509 - Miraflores, Zip: 0 54, Tel: 005154487755, Fax: 005154487755, E-mail: info@inkafestravelperu.com, URL: www.inkafestravelperu.com.

AREQUIPA LODGING

Arequipa is an important tourism travel hub, as well as one of Peru's more important cities for business and commerce. That means that there is a wider variety of hotels and lodging than you might normally expect for a city of this size. Look around and you'll be able to discover something for every taste and budget. You can find hotels in colonial buildings set around courtyards or newer, more modern options. Many Arequipa hotels are based very close to the colonial center, sprawling out from the Plaza de Armas and close to main historical landmarks. This is convenient for strolling around and sightseeing. If you prefer a quieter area, shop around because there are hotels in residential areas of Arequipa too. Some accommodation options offer pretty views of El Misti or the other spectacular scenery surrounding the city. If you're looking for help getting around and seeing the city, many hotels in Arequipa offer their own city tour service. It is worth booking in advance because Arequipa is popular and hotels fill up quickly.

BUDGET

La Posada del Cacique (Rooms: $4.50 - 9 per person)

A laid-back hostel in a colonial-style building with a large patio, La Posada del Cacique offers a lounge, kitchen and internet. Rooms come with a private or shared bath. Prices include tax. To get there from the Plaza de Armas, walk four blocks up Av. Santa Catalina past the Monastery. Once at the intersection with Calle Puente Grau, the hostel is 40 m up the street to your right on the opposite side of the road. Calle Jerusalén 404, Tel: 51-54-202-170, E-mail: laposadadelcacique@gmail.com, URL: www.laposadadelcacique.com.

Los Andes Bed & Breakfast ($5 – 8 per person)

Los Andes is comfortable, tranquil and secure, half a block from the Plaza de Armas. Popular with volunteers and long-stay travelers, there is a well-equipped kitchen for guests to use, a dining room and two large TV rooms with comfy couches. Internet is available for guests, although at the time of writing it was a little temperamental. Rooms are clean, well-decorated and reasonably priced. The only drawback is that it is often necessary to book a room in advance. Calle La Merced 123, Tel: 51-54-247-473, E-mail: information@set.peru.com, URL: www.losandesbb.com.

Posada del Parque (Dorm: $5 per person / Room: $9 per person)

Just 3 blocks from the Plaza de Armas, Posada del Parque is a backpackers' gem, with lots of great perks such as internet access for guests, a TV room with cable and a large selection of DVDs, table football, a variety of board games. Let's not forget the huge rooftop terrace where breakfast is served every morning. Both dorm and private rooms are available, with either private and shared baths. There is also a travel agency on the top floor that can offer information and help with booking onward bus tickets. Dean Valdivia 238, Tel: 51-54-212-275, E-mail: posadadelparque@hotmail.com, URL: www.posadadelparque.com.

Hotel Lari House (Rooms: $5 - 15)

Lari House is located two blocks away from the main square of Arequipa. It has hot and cold water all day long and there is a kitchen available for all the guests. In Lari House, the slogan is "Our house is your house and the customer is the first." Calle Cruz Verde 119 - Cercado, Tel: 51-54-220-680, E-mail: larihousearequipa@hotmail.com, URL: www.hotelsarequipa.com.

Colonial Palace (Rooms: $5 - 15)

The Colonial Palace lives up to its name, one of many enterprises in Arequipa that have taken advantage of the city's surplus of 17th and 18th century constructions to provide visitors with an elegantly ambient experience. In the Colonial Palace you get to sleep in rooms with

curved stone ceilings and large wooden doors. It is within walking distance of the Plaza de Armas, but its rooms are free of any street noise. Amenities include a continental breakfast, hair dryers, Internet access, and cable television. The Colonial Palace also offers its own tour operator and travel agent service. Pte. Grau 108, Tel: 51-54-913-5101, E-mail: colonialpalace_aqp@hotmail.com, URL: www.colonialpalace.com.

Home Sweet Home (Rooms: $5 - 22)

This friendly hostel is loved by backpackers and known for its big breakfasts, family atmosphere and cute rooms. There is a community television and kitchen as well. Rates include American breakfasts and taxes. Home Sweet Home, Calle Rivero 509 -A, Zip: 054, Tel: 51-54-405-982, Fax: 51-54-220-323, E-mail: reservas@homesweethome-peru.com, URL: www.homesweethome-peru.com.

Colonial House Inn (Rooms: $7 per person and up)

A large, creaky old backpackers pad, Colonial House Inn offers cheap rooms and a friendly atmosphere. Rooms, although threadbare in some cases, are clean and comfortable, and many boast the high-domed sillar ceilings of colonial Arequipa. There are two indoor patios, a small garden, and a rooftop terrace. Breakfast costs $2 extra. The staff is helpful and happy to give free tourist information. Puente Grau 114, Tel: 51-54-223-533, E-mail: colonialhouseinn@hotmail.com, URL: www.colonialhouseinn-arequipa.com

Bothy Hostel (Rooms: $7 - 10 per person)

Run by the same enthusiastic adrenaline seekers as Land Adventures, Bothy Hostel provides basic accommodations and a party atmosphere for backpackers, with regular nighttime barbeques on the roof-top terrace. Other facilities include a guests' kitchen, TV room with DVDs, luggage storage, free internet and shared common areas great for having a beer and meeting other guests. All rooms have shared bathrooms, and the cramped dorms sleep up to 5 people. Puente Grau 109, Tel: 51-54-282-438, E-mail: info@bothyhostel.com, URL: www.bothyhostel.com

The Point Arequipa (Rooms: $8 - 16)

The Point Arequipa was established in the middle of 2005, overlooking the impressive snow-capped Andean volcanoes. The hostel offers a travel center and a big, comfy hot tub outside in the garden. Prices include continental breakfast, internet, storage, cable TV and taxes. You can take a taxi from the bus terminal, but be sure to emphasize that you want to go to the "Vallecito" neighborhood, as there's more than one Avenida Lima. Av. Lima 515, Vallecito, Tel: (054) 286 920, E-mail: arequipa@thepointhostels.com, URL: www.thepointhostels.com.

La Compañía (Rooms: $8 - 25)

Hostal La Compañia is located in an old republican building in the heart of Arequipa. After undergoing a complete renovation in 2005, the original charm and character of the building remain complimented by modern amenities. Spacious rooms open up to a sunny patio, dining area and lounge. Baltic pine floors and high ceilings are a unique touch at this classic hostal. Rooms are clean, comfortable and bright. Additional services include laundry, safety deposit boxes, airport transport, internet, 24-hour room service, hot water, and breakfast included with the price. Spanish classes at competitive rates can also be arranged upon request. General Moran 109, Tel: 51-54-201-807, E-mail: info@lacompaniahostal.com, URL: www.lacompaniehostal.com.

El Caminante Class (Rooms: $9 per person and up)

One of the oldest and the best backpackers hotels in Arequipa, Caminante Class opened a second location in 2008 to keep up with demand. Rooms are comfortable and clean, if a little cramped, and many lead en-suite style into communal bathrooms (make sure all the doors are closed!). Some rooms also have balconies, and there is an indoor terrace where you can sit back and enjoy the sunny Arequipa afternoons. El Caminante offers breakfast and laundry services at low prices, and you will find staff members friendly and willing to help. Santa Catalina 207-A, 2nd floor, and Santa Catalina 223, Tel: 51-54-203-444, E-mail: caminanteaqp@hotmail.com.

La Casona de Jerusalén Hospedaje (Rooms: $10 - 15)

The Casona de Jerusalén Hospedaje has a charming open-air deck with an awning, tables, and a coffee bar. Many guests might feel extra secure knowing that the hostel is right in front of the National Tourism Police office. The rooms themselves are pleasant, complete with hot running water and cable television, with prices that start at $10 for a private room, going only as high as $15 for a "matrimonial" suite. A short walk from the Plaza de Armas, they also have their own travel agency and offer free transportation from Arequipa's bus terminals. Jerusalén 306 Altos, Tel: 51-54-205-453, E-mail: hjerusalén@terra.com.pe.

Hostel Casona Solar (Rooms: $12.50 - 17.50)

Hostal Casona Solar offers the best of both worlds: the beauty of Arequipa's white-stone, colonial architecture *and* modern bathrooms. Constructed in 1702, the building has high-arched roofs and large doors. As you would expect of any mansion, there are several garden courtyards and a fireplace. The hostel calls itself "a beautifully restored colonial gentleman's house." To make it more of an inn, the owners have added a bar/lunchroom. In the morning, you can sit down to a home-made breakfast of fresh juice, fruit salad and bread inside, or if it's nice weather, you can eat your meal in the patio while basking in the sun. Group and extended-stay discounts are available. Prices include tax and a homemade breakfast. From the Plaza de Armas you walk to the Compania church, 2 blocks down on Alveres Thomas. When you reach Calle Consuelo, turn left and you will see Casona Solar on your right handside. Calle Consuelo 116 Zip: Cercado Tel: 51-54-228-991 Fax: 51-54-228-991 E-mail: info@casonasolar.com URL: www.casonasolar.com URL: www.casonasolar.com.

V!VA Member Review- Hostel Casona Solar

Casona Solar is one of the best hotels I have ever stayed at in traveling through Latin America. It is a restored 18th century mansion and has both modern conveniences (hot water, modern shower) and historic ambiance.

San Francisco, CA, USA, Feb 13, 2008

Buena Vista Hostal (Rooms: $13 - 45)

Get one of the best paranomic views of the volcanoes or the city and a relaxed, comfortable stay at this hotel. It is close to downtown, in a quiet and secure area. Just five minutes by taxi or bus and four blocks away from the Mirador de Yanahuara. Relax in Buena Vista's Mirador with astonishing views of the surroundings. They provide a free transfer from the airport or bus station to the hostel when you book a room for a minimum stay of two nights. Price includes continental breakfast, access to internet and all taxes. Calle Ugarte 623, Yanahuara (after Calle Quesada), Tel: (51-1) 997-205646, Fax: (51-54) 27-1686, E-mail: buenavistahostal@yahoo.com, URL: www.buenavistahostal.com.

Casa de Ávila (Rooms: $15 - 30)

Casa De Avila was built in 1930 as a hotel in the middle of town. Reconditioned and re-opened in 2004, the hotel now offers 18 nice, clean rooms surrounding a pleasant garden dotted with chairs and umbrellas. Single, double, twin, and triple rooms are available. All rooms have comfortable beds, basic furniture and a private bathroom with hot water and WiFi Internet (some have cable TV). Linens are included and towels are changed daily. Other services include a cafeteria, internet room, guest's kitchen, lobby, and restroom. Information on area tours, flights, buses and activities is available. Av. San Martin 116 - Vallecito, Tel: 51-54-213-177, E-mail: info@casadeavila.com, URL: www.casadeavila.com.

Helena de Santa María (Rooms: $18 and up)
The Helena de Santa María is at a bit of a remove from the center of Arequipa, rather being situated in a quiet residential (and very middle-class) neighborhood, a short distance from the Parque Libertad de Expresión. This is a new facility, with an attractive modern design, and clean, spacious rooms, also offering free Internet access and a continental breakfast. The Helena de Santa María also offers discounts for groups. Owners Alfredo and Fiorella Sanchez generously provide any tourist information you might need. Calle José Santos Chocano 28 y Umacollo, Tel: 51-54-273-165, E-mail: hotelhelenaaqp@yahoo.com.

La Casa de Sillar (Rooms: $18 - $35)
Previously known as Colonial House II, La Casa de Sillar, is made entirely of the white "sillar" volcanic rock, for which Arequipa is famous. Services include phone and internet for guests, cable TV in every room, tourist information, and free pick-up from the bus station. All rooms have private baths with 24-hour hot water. Calle Rivero 504, Tel: 51-54-284-249, E-mail: reservas@lacasadesillar.com, URL: www.lacasadesillar.com

MID-RANGE
La Compania Jerusalen (Rooms $25 - 48)
Hostel Jerusalen is just one block away from the Plaza de Armas, in a charming white brick colonial building. Although the modern building in the back patio is slightly less charming, all rooms are cozy and come with private bathrooms. Breakfast is included in the price and beverages are available on request. There also is internet access and a laundry service. If you are staying longer than a week, you can get a discount on the room or else rent an apartment. The hostel can also arrange Spanish classes. Jerusalen 530, Tel: 51-54-201-807, E-mail: info@lacompaniahostal.com, URL: www.lacompaniahostal.com/jerusalen.

Los Balcones de Moral y Santa Catalina (Rooms: $25 - 55)
This beautiful big house dates back from colonial times and is located in the city center of Arequipa. The first floor was recently declared a national historical monument in Peru and houses reception with a telephone, tax station and luggage lockers. The second floor has a republican façade and contains remodeled interiors, rooms, a cafeteria, an internet hall and service area for storage and laundry. There are 16 rooms available. Each bathroom has hot water while all rooms have cable TV, telephone service, a desk and closet. The rooms each have individual balconies with nice views. Moral 217, Tel: 51-54-201-291, E-mail: losbalconeshotel@hotmail.com, URL: www.balconeshotel.com.

Casablanca Hostal (Rooms: $25 and up)
Casablanca is a little more expensive than other hostels in the area, with single rooms starting at $25 a night. But you are more than compensated by the superb use of an authentic, exciting colonial facility made of lava pumice that evokes an aura of Spanish Gothic; they even have a wine cellar. In addition, there is a large and pleasant common area that includes a cafeteria. Internet access includes wireless service, and they also offer breakfast and laundry services. At the moment, however, they do not accept credit cards. Puente Bolognesi 104, Tel: 54-221-327, E-mail: casablancaaqp@hotmail.com, URL: www.casablancahostal.com.

Hostal Solar (Rooms: $28 - 32)
The Hostal Solar has eight traditional rooms decorated in colonial art with modern touches. Many of the rooms have high ceilings and are all built with the volcanic stone sillar. All rooms are equipped with private bathroom (hot water 24-hours a day), cable TV, telephone and thermal quilts. Breakfast is included (taxes not included in price). Other services include cafeteria, laundry, internet, parking, tourist information, ticket/tour reservations, activities and BBQs can be arranged for groups. Complimentary airport pickup also provided. Calle Ayacucho 108, Tel: 51-54-241-793, E-mail: reservas@hostalsolar.com, URL: www.hostalsolar.com.

La Casa de Melgar Hostal (Rooms: $35)

Walking through the gates of this charming hotel you travel back into time. Decorated with antiques and colonial art, La Casa de Melgar, once the home of bishops and poets, is an excellent example of 18th century Arequipana architecture. The thick, richly-painted walls, arches and pleasant, airy garden give the whole place a romantic, if a tad musty, air. The rooms come with private bathroom, hot water and cable TV. There also is a cafeteria. Melgar 108, Arequipa, Tel: 51-54-222-459, E-mail: lacasademelgar@terra.com.pe, URL: www.lacasademelgar.com.

La Hosteria (Rooms: $45 - 55)

Located behind the Santa Catalina Monastery, La Hosteria is a welcoming colonial-style hotel, with plenty of flowers and a fountain in the middle of the patio. The rooms are spacious and airy, with minibars and views of the monastery from some. For a colonial-era hotel, it is exceptionally sunny and you can take in the views of the snow-capped volcanoes from the decks on the second floor. Calle Bolivar 405 Cercado, Tel: 51-54- 289-269, E-mail: lahosteria@terra.com.pe.

La Plazuela (Rooms: $45 - 65)

La Plazuela is a quaint garden house located within the residential district of Vallecito in Arequipa, just five minutes from the main square. Each room includes a private bathroom and shower with hot water all day. The rooms come with TV, minibar and a direct dialing phone. Services include free internet, fax, safety box, laundry and a taxi service. There is also a restaurant that offers Peruvian and international food. Ovalo de Vallecito 105, Tel: 51-54-222-624, URL: www.hostal-laplazuela.com.

La Gruta Hotel (Rooms: $45 - 65)

This hotel with beautiful gardens is located in an elegant residential area, yet just a few minutes away from the colonial city and commercial area. La Gruta has a helpful and friendly atmosphere, with large, clean and very comfortable carpeted rooms. Price includes tax. Calle La Gruta 304, Tel: 51-54-224-631, Fax: 51-54-289-899, E-mail: lagruta@lagrutahotel.com, URL: www.lagrutahotel.com, URL: www.lagrutahotel.com.

La Casa de mi Abuela (Rooms: $47 - 74)

Pretty fittingly for a place named "My grandmother's house," this three-decade-old hotel is a converted family house, with comfortable modern rooms and a rustic restaurant built in the spacious, pleasant gardens. Service is friendly and consistent. Though as the hotel is a favorite of tour operators, you occasionally may get swamped by a large group. Ask for a garden suite, though, as the rooms in the older house tend to be a bit musty. Amenities include cable TV, private parking, WiFi, a library, a games room, a pool and even a playground for kids. Jerusalen 606, Cercado, Arequipa, Tel: 51-54-241-206, E-mail: lacasa@tierra.com.pe, URL: www.lacasademiabuela.com.

Mirador Del Monasterio (Rooms: $50 - 70)

This simple hotel is just across the street from the Santa Catalina monastery and its main attraction is the beautiful terrace, where you can lounge in deck chairs, admiring the view over the Monasterio and the volcanoes surrounding Arequipa. The 18 rooms are somewhat bland, but service is friendly and amenities include a taxi service, laundry service and cafeteria, as well as safes for your valuables. Zela 301, Cercado, Tel: 51-54-224-923/ 225-122, E-mail: miradordelmonasterio@terra.com.pe, URL: www.miradordemonasterio.com.

HIGH-END
El Balcón (Rooms: $75 -165)
A very large colonial house, the formerly budget Los Balcones was refurbished in 2008 and turned into an upscale hotel with vast, modern, clean rooms and sprawling balconies. While the location is convenient, just a block away from the Plaza de Armas, you may expect early morning street noise. The service is excellent and includes laundry, free transfer to the hotel and medical assistance if necessary. Negotiate a discount if staying more than one night. Calle Moral 217, Cercado, Tel: 51-54-201-291, URL: www.balconeshotel.com, E-mail: losbalconeshotel@hotmail.com.

Sonesta Posada del Inca (Rooms: $83 - 118)
The Sonesta Posada del Inca hotels always seem to find the best locations in the cities they serve, and their Arequipa branch is no exception. The hotel is right next to the cathedral in the center of town. It is a classy place with an elegant interior, clean, neat rooms and all of the amenities you expect from a hotel in the upper-mid range. There is a fine restaurant on the premises specializing in local and international cuisine. Prices do not include applicable taxes and service fees. Check their website for discounts and specials -- they often have them. Portal de Flores 116, Tel: 51-54-215-530, Fax: 51-54-234-374, E-mail: salesarequipa@sonestaperu.com, URL: http://www.sonesta.com/peru_arequipa.

Hotel la Posada del Puente (Rooms: $85 - 200)
Hotel la Posada del Puente is an elegant, well-maintained inn near the Grau Bridge. Popular with business travelers, the hotel features a view of the Misti Volcano and well-landscaped grounds. The rooms are simple, neat and comfortable. Rates include fees and taxes. Esquina Puente Grau y Avenida Bolognesi 101, Tel: 51-54-253-132, Fax: 51-54-253-576, E-mail: hotel@posadadelpuente.com, URL: http://www.posadadelpuente.com.

Hotel Libertador Arequipa (Rooms: $220 - 345)
The hotel has the privilege of being in a peaceful though central place, five minutes away from the main square. Their 88 rooms are spacious, comfortable and have been elegantly decorated in a colonial style. In the Los Robles restaurant you will enjoy exquisite typical and international cuisine, followed by cocktails at the Bar Los Montoneros. During your day you have the opportunity to relax using the sauna, Jacuzzi, fitness room. Rates include buffet breakfast, but not taxes. Plaza Bolívar S/N Urb. Selva Alegre, Tel: 51-54-215-110, Fax: 51-54-241-933, E-mail: arequipa@libertador.com.pe, URL: www.libertador.com.pe.

AREQUIPA RESTAURANTS
Make sure to bring your appetite if you make the trip to Arequipa. Arequipeños are famous throughout Peru for their sumptuous cooking, and many restaurants in the area specialize in traditional regional specialties. The historic center is chock-full of great-value casual restaurants, and even the best eateries are affordable. Whether you're in the mood for Peruvian, Turkish, French, Italian, or Mexican, Arequipa is ready to accommodate your taste buds (and your wallet). If you get a chance, try the most famous local dish: *ocopa a la arequipeña*. This traditional appetizer consists of boiled potatoes drenched in a cheese and peanut sauce. At some places you can dive into the mouth-watering dishes while your eyes feast on spectacular views of the surrounding volcanoes.

La Ibérica Chocolates
The chocolates sold in La Ibérica shops are absolutely exquisite. Favorites are the *pastillas*, bite-sized bits of heaven. You can also try the dozens of varieties of dark chocolate, toffees, *mazapanes* (marzipan) and *turrones* (nougat). You can find these world-class chocolates and

treats in several La Ibérica shops in Arequipa as well as in Lima and Cusco. Jerusalén 136, Cercado, Centro Comercial Cayma, Tienda 22-A, Tel: 51-54-215-670, E-mail: chocolates@laiberica.com.pe. La Ibérica also has locations at: Mall Saga Falabella, Tienda 11; Casona Santa Catalina 210, Tienda 103B-C; Aeropuerto Rodríguez Ballón, Tienda 3.

V!VA Member Review- La Iberíca Chocolates

This is the Sees Candies of Peru. The shop is based in Arequipa and is always busy. You can also buy the candies (toffees are the best!) at the airport in Lima.

California, U.S.A., July 13, 2007

Deja Vu
Deja Vu is a restaurant and pub offering lunch and dinner. At night, the place comes to life with a happy hour and from Tuesday to Friday patrons can enjoy live music. Saturday is Latin night, with live DJ's and pumping music. San Francisco street 319-b, Tel: 51-54-422-1904, E-mail: broccetta@hotmail.com URL: dejavu.com.pe.

El Cerrojo (Entrees: $1.70 - 50)
El Cerrojo is one of the restaurants fortunate enough to be located in Arequipa's Plaza de Armas, with seating in a second-floor terrace offering a scenic view of the square. They start with low-price items, such as sandwiches, going for 5 solés, or $1.70, with their costliest platter, "shrimp of seven flavors," at 150 solés, or $50. In between, their standard price averages at $6.00 for a lunch or dinner platter. They have one section called the *plato tipico*, or typical dish. The rest a standard selection of common international favorites, including pizzas. They accept all credit cards. Portal San Agustin 111-A, Plaza de Armas, Tel: 51-54-213-786.

D'la Casa (Entrees: $1.50 and up)
This quaint little corner diner, inside a typically Arequipeño building complete with a curved ceiling, will sell you a decent hamburger or "coq au vin" for little more than a dollar. Modesty is its own virtue here, and this place is recommended for its low-cost but high-quality preparations of simple beef, pork, and chicken plates. And, they don't skimp on the portions. D'la Casa is a short walk from the Plaza de Armas. Calle San Francisco 218-A, Tel: 51-54-282-791.

Café Casa Verde (Entrees: $2)
This little cafe is on the main drag of Jerusalen but is easy to miss from the outside. It is well worth seeking out, not only for its delicious German breads, pastries, cakes and fresh coffee, but also because of its humanitarian mission. With money raised in the café, the organization provides a home for 30 abandoned children. The café can also set you up with volunteer work if you are staying in Arequipa for a while. Jerusalen 406, Tel: 51-54-226-379.

Lakshmivan (Entrees: $2 - 5)
Vegetarians and their budgets will be delighted by Lakshmivan's well-priced and delicious dishes. Choose from a menu that includes seven different soy meat dishes, spinach lasagna, tofu and soy hamburgers, vegetarian paella, 16 different salads (all under $2), and pumpkin soup. You can also fuel up in the morning with a wholesome breakfast of muesli, yogurt, and homemade bread. Daily 7 a.m. to 10 p.m. Jerusalén 402, Tel: 51-54-228-768.

La Salchichería Alemana (Entrees: $3)
Literally translating as "The German Sausage Shop," this diner-style restaurant lives up to its name, with various types of sausage and cured meats on the menu. A very popular lunchtime stop for locals, it is often packed out. But not to worry—you can also buy the sausages to cook back at your hostel, particularly good if you have a barbeque. San Francisco 137, Tel: 51-54-255-512.

La Italiana (Entrees: $3 - 15)

They call themselves "La Italiana," and this Italian joint features more than just the usual cheese pizza and spaghetti. Their "special pizzas" push new limits of creativity, with tasty combinations like *prosciutto con palmito*. There is also a separate, exclusively seafood menu and a nouveau Arequipa selection, with many variations of guinea pig. The design itself evokes the proud elegance of old Italy, with linen napkins folded into glasses. They take all credit cards. San Francisco 303-B, Tel: 51-54-202-080, E-mail: informes@consorciobongourmet.com, URL: www.consorciobongourmet.com.

Mandala Vegetarian Restaurant (Entrees: $4)

They call themselves "your vegetarian house" and offer everything from soy sausages, soy pizza, curried soy, soy rolls, as well as tofu options galore. There are also a number of items featuring gluten, such as stir-fried gluten with broccoli. For those whose vegetarian palette includes milk and eggs, there are some tasty, home-made ice cream deserts. Prices run at about $4, and the restaurant is open for breakfast, lunch, and dinner. Calle Jerusalen #207, Tel: 51-54-229-974, E-mail: mandalaqp@hotmail.com.

Gianni's (Entrees: $5 - 6)

A popular place among the locals, Gianni's is characterized by red-and-white-checked tablecloths and some of the best pizza in town. The ingredients are fresh and meals are served with copious amounts of wine. Besides pizza, the menu also offers traditional Italian dishes like handmade fettuccini, gnocchi, ravioli, lasagna, and cannelloni. Meat lovers can try the steaks, or for something lighter, sample the fish dishes. This is a great place to grab a bite and a beer before hitting the nearby bars and dance clubs. Monday - Saturday, 6 p.m. - 1 a.m. San Francisco 304, Tel: 51-54-287-138.

Ary Quepay (Entrees: $5 - 10)

This laidback, rustic restaurant specializes in traditional Peruvian cooking, as prepared by the friendly husband-wife team Marcos and Gloria Verapinto. Diners can enjoy traditional Arequipeño plates, such as grilled guinea pig and peppers stuffed with veggies. Enjoy your meal in the relaxing garden-like dining room beneath the bamboo roof and skylights. The family recipe starters of *pastels de papas* and *soltero de queso* are highly recommended. The menu also offers a number of good

AREQUIPA

vegetarian dishes. Every night at 6:30 p.m. the restaurant comes to life with live folkloric music. In the mornings, the restaurant serves an excellent breakfast and a variety of fresh juices. Open 11 a.m. to 11 p.m. Jerusalén 502, Tel: 51-54-204-583, E-mail: restaurant@aryquepay.com, URL: www.aryquepay.com/restaurant.htm.

Tradición Arequipeña (Entrees: $5 - 10)

Among the restaurants in Arequipa, Tradición Arequipeña is one of the most highly recommended by locals. Located a few kilometers outside of town in the district of Paucarpata, this restaurant has an elegant atmosphere with gardens and spectacular views of the snow-capped peak of El Misti. The menu includes such traditional Peruvian dishes as cuy, adobo, ceviche, and a variety of *chupes*, or seafood soups. In addition to the stunning views, the restaurant serves its heaping plates of Peruvian food with a side of live music, and on Saturdays at 5 p.m. an orchestra will accompany your meal. Open Sunday - Thursday, noon to 8:30 p.m., Friday, noon - midnight. Dolores 111, Tel: 51-54-426-467.

El Turko II (Entrees: $5 - 10)

If you're in the mood for Middle Eastern food, then El Turko II is definitely the place to go. The immaculate wood floors, high sillar ceilings, and intriguing modern art provide a great atmosphere to savor the Middle Eastern flavors so rarely found in Peru. Choose from a menu of mouth-watering hummus, falafel, lamb kebab, and eggplant dishes. A slightly smaller, more affordable version of this restaurant is located down the street. El Turko I (San Francisco 216-A, Tel: 51-54-203-862) serves delectable Turkish pita sandwiches and other Middle Eastern treats. The kabobs are highly recommended. Open 8 a.m. to 12 a.m. daily. San Francisco 311, Tel: 51-54-215-729.

Las Quenas (Entrees: $5.50)

Popular with locals as well as tourists, Las Quenas serves all the typical dishes from Arequipa and the region. There is live music and a traditional dance show every evening except Sunday, starting at 8 p.m. A good place to try cuy *chactado* (guinea pig flattened and cooked between hot stones), if you have gotten away without eating any guinea pig so far. There are also drinks offers in the afternoons. Book a table for dinner in advance to avoid disappointment, as it gets busy in th evenings. Santa Catalina 302 (opposite the Monastery), Tel: 51-54-281-115 / 206-440.

La Bóveda Social Club (Entrees: $6)

La Bóveda Social Club is more than just a restaurant and tavern; located on the Plaza de Armas, owner Jose Manuel Delgado has cultivated his establishment as a favorite of Arequipa's literary, musical, and artistic community. An indoor theatre is used both for staging new works by young playwrights and for lively political discussions. The menu offers a combination of standard Peruvian and continental favorites, at prices averaging $6. They offer breakfast, lunch, and dinner, with the doors opening at 7:00 a.m. Portal San Agustin 127, Arequipa, Tel: 51-54-243-596, E-mail: bovedesa@viabcp.com.pe.

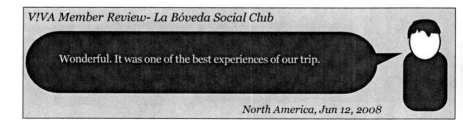

V!VA Member Review- La Bóveda Social Club

Wonderful. It was one of the best experiences of our trip.

North America, Jun 12, 2008

Retro (Entrees: $6)

Retro opens at 6:00 p.m., an index of its nocturnal orientation and spirit, with its funky American rock posters and ear-shattering sound system. But if you canhandle the deafening music, there's pizza, barbecued chicken salad (average about $6 a plate) and all the beer and drinks you can imagine. Retro is but one part of the larger Casona Forum, a collection of clubs and bars on Calle San Francisco in Arequipa. Calle San Francisco 317, Tel: (054) 204294, E-mail: retro@forumrockcafe.com, URL: http://www.forumrockcafe.com/retro.html.

El Viñedo (Entrees: $11)

This classy restaurant on the Calle San Francisco serves standard continental favorites, with some original items, such as Minestroni Argentino—with meat, chicken, sausage, cheese, and vegetables—along with some uniquely Arequipeña favorites such as shrimp omelette or fried guinea pig with salad. They also have a few ostrich plates. Additionally they have a tavern and charming little lounge. Prices are higher than average, about $11, but they take all credit cards. San Francisco 319, Tel: 51-54-205-053, E-mail: hosteliayturismoelrestaurador@hotmail.com, URL: www.hosturesgastronomia.com.

Paquita Siu Gourmet

Paquita Siu Gourmet whips up fusions of Japanese, Thai and Chinese cuisine with a Peruvian twist. The food is excellent; the restaurant prides itself on always using high-quality ingredients. The dining room is small: 12-14 tables in a very quiet and clean environment. Here you can sample everything from sushi to Thai curry. Try the deep-fried snapper in sweet chili sauce. And Paquita Siu Gourmet delivers! Calle Granada 102, Cayma, Tel: 51-54-251-915,URL: www.paquitasiugourmet.com.

Ras el Hanout y los 40 Sabores

With its Moroccan theme, the café and tavern Ras El Hanout (subtitle: "and the 40 flavors") is a perfect complement to the Spanish colonial architecture of Arequipa. Owner Egmond Gamero offers an elegant Moorish ambience, from the old-world incense in the air to classic North African dishes, such as *Haira* soup (with beef, cilantro, chick peas, lentils, and lemon), or spicy *tagine kefta* meatballs, or artichoke heart with egg filling, mozzarella, tuna, lemon, and falafel. Exotic teas served from long-necked tea kettles and *narguilas*, Middle Eastern hookahs for smoking tobacco, only add to the fun. San Francisco 227, Tel: 51-54-227-779, E-mail: goethe3m@hotmail.com.

V!VA Member Review- Ras el Hanout y los 40 Sabores

Unbelievable, great, great, great! We went back!

Belgium, Nov 07, 2008

Sonccollay

Sonccollay is a Quecha word which means "my little heart" or "from the heart." This warm, welcoming restaurant serves Inca and pre-Inca cuisine that has survived over 9,000 years. Alpaca, guinea pig, and shrimp are served over hot stones and roasted on a wood fire and complimented by chili peppers stuffed with sweet and spicy ingredients. Sonccollay also offers tasty soups and stews, old style coffee and desserts, sweet juices, native beer and area wines. All dishes are based on original recipes with the finest meats and vegetables. Enjoy beautiful views of surrounding Arequipa while you dine. Open from 8am to 10pm. Portal San Agustin 149, Main Square Terrase, Tel: 54-969-568-184 / 959-673-517, E-mail: sonccollay@gmail.com / reservas@sonccollay.com, URL: www.colcaperu.com.

Things to See and Do Around Arequipa

Yanahuara

Sporting stone archways and magnificent views of El Misti, the lovely neighborhood of Yanahuara is a great place for a relaxing afternoon stroll. The 18th century Iglesia San Juan Bautista (Monday - Friday, 9 a.m. - noon, 4 p.m. - 8 p.m., Saturday - Sunday, 7 a.m. - 1 p.m., 3 p.m. - 8 p.m.) is also worth a look. With walls that are nearly two meters thick and an exquisitely carved façade, the church is one of the best examples of mestizo art in Peru. Be sure to check out the carved *cherubim*, a pre-hispanic symbol of power that was outlawed in Peru during colonial times. When you've seen enough of the church, hop in a taxi (or walk if you prefer) and head towards the Mirador de Carmen Alto, which has spectacular views of all the nearby volcanoes, Arequipa, and an abandoned Spanish *sillar* quarry.

Toro Muerto Petroglyphs

Stretching 200 meters wide for about 2 kilometers 165 km west of Arequipa, the impressive Toro Muerto petroglyphs are one of the largest collections of petroglyph drawings in the world. Figures of animals, birds and people– some of them are even mysteriously flying "ancient astronauts" carved into volcanic rock which appear as if they came out of nowhere in the vast valley. Though the roots of the drawings have not been confirmed, most historians agree that they were likely created by the Huari culture between 500 and 1200 AD. The site is often visited in conjunction with a trip to the Valley of the Volcanoes 100 km away. Guided tours leave from Arequipa, or you can make the trip yourself, but leave plenty of time when taking public transportation. Buses to Corire depart from Arequipa (3 hours), from where you can either walk to the site (about 1 ½ hours), or ask to be let off 2 km outside the town at the start of a dirt road with a sign that leads to the petroglyphs.

Sabandía Mill (Entrance: $2)

Built in 1621, only less than thirty years after Columbus set foot in the Americas, this stone mill powered by a nearby waterfall is still in operation, grinding grains and flours, after being restored in 1973. This historical landmark is worth visiting both for its historical architecture, as well as the natural beauty surrounding it, from the alpacas and vicuñas that freely wander outside to the spectacular views of the Misti and Chachani volcanoes. The Sabandía Mill is about five miles from Arequipa's downtown, in the Sabandia Valley, and can best be accessed by taxis or tour buses. Daily, 9 a.m.-5 p.m., Huasacache, via Paisajista.

La Mansión del Fundador (Entrance: $3)

Its name in Spanish translates into "The Mansion of the Founder," the "founder" being Don Garcí Manuel de Carbajal, who was among many knights order by Francisco Pizarro to establish cities across Peru as a means of consolidating the territory under Spanish rule. Don Carbajal accomplished a relatively peaceful settlement in this high and dry region. His mansion here was later appropriated by the Jesuits and then by a captain in the Spanish army. It fell into disuse and neglect before being restored by landmark preservationists in 1978, who hoped to revive 500 years worth of Peruvian history, exquisite architecture, artwork, and furnishings. It is about 12 miles (20 km) from the Plaza de Armas, in the peaceful pueblo of Huasacache, and can be accessed by municipal buses, tour buses, and taxis. Daily, 10 a.m.-5 p.m., Huasacache, via Paisajista, Tel: 51-54-442-460.

Rent a Horse with Colca Tours ($59 / day)

This stable of horses for rent and instruction is located next to the famous and historic Sabandía Mill. Experienced instructors and guides Roberto del Carpio and Natalio Cutipa offer lessons in equestrianism as well as guided tours around the sparkling Chilina Valley and the terraced slopes of Parcuapata. Rates start at 10 solés, or $3 an hour, for lessons. Molino de Sabandia, Tel: 51-54-991-0174 / 51-54-991-5157, E-mail: info@colcatours.com.

Chachani

Less experienced trekkers and climbers seeking to summit a high altitude peak should head to Chachani (6,095 m). Just a three hour drive from Arequipa, this gorgeous snow-capped volcano is perhaps also one of the easiest 6,000 meter peaks in all of Latin America. The road from Arequipa ascends to 5,100 meters, from where climbers make the two or more hour climb to base camp. From camp, the summit is another five to six hours, a climb that is usually made the following morning. In spite of its reputation for being an easy peak to summit, it is still a high altitude climb and should be treated with caution. An ice ax and crampons are the equipment of choice, and it is recommended that a guide accompany you, which is easy to arrange with one of the many Arequipa tour companies. The truly fit can climb Chachani in one day from Arequipa, but two days is recommended for the un-acclimatized, or anyone who wants to actually enjoy the views. Though Chachani is less popular than its neighbor, El Misti, it is still a well-trodden trek. You may be lucky enough to have the mountain to yourself, but be prepared to share it.

El Misti

El Misti, the closest volcano to Arequipa, offers a fairly straightforward opportunity to summit a high peak. Trekkers should start their journey from the hydroelectric plant, after first registering with the police there. Due to reports of assaults in 2001, climbers should avoid the route that starts near the outskirts of town. From the entrance give yourself a day to reach the Monte Blanco shelter, at 4,800 meters. Prepare for an early morning, preferably dawn, to make the 4-to-6-hour climb to Misti's summit by 11 a.m., before mists blanket the mountain and obscure the view. If you start your descent by noon it is possible to reach the hydroelectric plant by 6 p.m. If you're not feeling quite up for a six hour trek, then take a jeep from 3,300 meters to the end of the rough road, and make the 45-minute hike to the campground at 4,600 meters. Be aware that there's only space here for three tents, and that you should bring plenty of food, water, and inclement weather gear. Further information can be obtained from Arequipa tour companies.

Ampato

This peak is popular both for its grace and beauty, and its proximity to other accessible mountains nearby. You can drive to 4,900 meters, and from there it is a two-hour climb to base camp at 5,200 meters. The summit is another six hours to climb. Another route starts from Cabanaconde, in the Colca Canyon. This trek begins at an Incan ceremonial center, sitting at 5,000 meters on the northeast side of the volcano. From there, the summit is about seven hours away. If you've got happy feet and are keen for more climbs, the nearby volcanoes of Sabancaya (5,995m) and Hualca Hualca (6,095m) can also be climbed from this camp.

Majes River Lodge ($20 - 31 per person)

This family farm is located in one of the deepest canyons on earth and runs thrilling rafting adventures. The Majes Valley offers a mild climate, spectacular scenery, archaeological treasures, dinosaur prints and an enchanting castle. Rooms here are comfortable with hot water. Other ammenities include a dining room, bar, barbecue, campfire, *pachamama* (mother earth) ceremony with a shaman. Raft with professional guides, who supply life jackets and inflatable self-bailing river rafts. Rafting is open from April through December with trips beginning everyday at 9 a.m. The river is run in the morning only. La Central Ongoro, Aplao Castilla, Tel: 51-54-979-7731, E-mail: jzuniga74@hotmail.com, URL: www.majesriver.com.

COLCA CANYON

Set amidst 6,000 meter peaks that plunge into a lunar-like landscape decorated with rocks, ichu grass and the bizarre-looking *yareta* plant, the Colca Canyon is famous for its natural beauty, cultural history, and adventure treks. The Collagua and Cabana people lived here for nearly 2,000 years, carving a network of remarkable terraces into the canyon walls.

In the 15th century Inca Mayta Cápac arrived with his army and, according to historians married Mama Tancaray Yacchi, daughter of a local Collagua chief, to secure the conquest. According to legend he built Mama Tancaray, a house of copper that was eventually melted to make the gigantic bells that hang in Coporaque's towers today. When the Spanish arrived, they forced local peoples into *reducciones*, and put them to work on plantations or in the nearby Caylloma silver mine.

Help other travelers. Publish your favorite places at www.vivatravelguides.com

COLCA FESTIVALS

Like Huancayo, Puno, and the shores of Lake Titicaca, Colca has a reputation for vibrant festivals. If you can, plan your trip around any of the following festivals:

La Virgen de Candelaria: celebrated in Chivay, Acoma, and Maca on February 2-3

Carnival: celebrated in late February in Colca

Easter Week: celebrated in April in Colca

La Fiesta de San Juan: celebrated in Yanque and several other Colca towns on June 13

Virgen del Carmen: celebrated in Cabanaconde and Chivay on July 16

Santiago Apóstol: celebrated in Coporaque and Madrigal on July 25

La Virgen de la Asunción: an eight day festival celebrated in Chivay starting on August 15

Spring Festival: celebrated in Yanque on Sept 23

La Fiesta de la Virgen del Rosario: celebrated in Chivay, Achoma, Ichupampa, Maca, and Yanque on October 7

Todos Los Santos (All Saints' Day): celebrated throughout Colca Canyon on November 1-2

Los Fieles Difuntos (All Souls' Day): celebrated throughout Colca Canyon on November 1-2

La Virgen Imaculada: celebrated in Chivay and Yanque on December 8; celebrations include performances of the five-day Wititi dance.

For further information regarding Peruvian festivals, check out www.peru.org.pe, the government's tourist agency page. (Note: you can change the language to English by clicking on the drop down list located in the upper right-hand corner of the screen).

In spite of this forced labor, the Collaguas assimilated much of the Spanish culture into their own traditions. In particular, Catholic imagery was absorbed into many of their festivals, and women adopted the Spanish-style petticoat as a form of dress. Without roads or communications, Colca Canyon was largely forgotten until the late 1970's when engineers visited the canyon to build the area's first road. Due to their relative isolation from the modern world, the people and villages in this region have maintained their ancient traditions and ways of life.

A great way to explore the region is on foot, via the numerous ancient trails that wind their way between villages. In 1981, a crew of six Polish adventurers and local rafter Antonio Vellutino discovered another facet of the Colca Canyon: extreme adventure. Today, in addition to its rich cultural heritage, the canyon offers tremendous outdoor adventure opportunities. Along with Cusco and Huaraz, Colca has become known as a magnet for adventure sport, drawing hikers, bikers, trekkers, and rafters from around the world. At 3,400 meters, Colca Canyon is more than twice as deep as Arizona's Grand Canyon.

Travelers usually start off in Arequipa, and make the bumpy four-hour journey across the spectacular Andean landscape. Most of this region is part of the Reserva Nacional Salinas y Aguada Blanca, an area of stunning beauty, rich in wildlife. Flamingos, geese, and black-faced Andean gulls lounge in salty lakes, while vicuñas graze in nearby grasslands and vizcachas, (despite appearances it's a rodent not a rabbit) scurry across the rocky landscape. Towering over this natural playground is El Misti, the 5,830 meter peak that draws altitude-hungry trekkers and climbers.

The traditional route from Arequipa climbs as high as 4,700 meters, passing the petroglyphs at Sumbay cave, and crossing the desolate Patapampa plain dotted with mysterious stone piles built by the Collagua. From here, the road drops into Chivay, the gateway to Colca Canyon. From Chivay there are a number of roads that lead into the canyon. Villages on the right (north) side of the canyon are less frequented by tourists, and boast a number of interesting colonial churches.

Soloists should bear in mind that the canyon is extremely large, with a lot to offer in terms of sites and activities, so if you want to do a lot, or are limited by time, you may want to consider going with an agency. In most cases, agency deals are cheaper than do-it-yourself travel. If you do decide to travel Lone Ranger-style, it's easy to catch a bus to Chivay or Cabanaconde, and explore the canyon on foot or by colectivo. Whether traveling with a tour, or independently make sure you bring a wide-brimmed hat, sunscreen, and plenty of water. Besides sun exposure, the other threat in this region is *soroche*, or mountain sickness.

If you're not coming from Cusco, stay in Arequipa a few days to acclimatize. The most popular point to view the canyon is the Cruz del Condór. Look down and you'll see spectacular scenery. Look up, and if you're lucky, you'll see the massive Andean condor sky-surfing thermal waves high above the canyon walls. The best time to spot this elusive bird is early in the morning, preferably between 7 a.m. and 10 a.m. The nearby Tapay lookout is less frequented by tourists, but also seems to be less popular among condors. There is a $2 entrance fee to the canyon, which is usually not included in agency prices.

The Communities of the Colca Canyon

The Colca Canyon, whose inhabitants have ancestral roots in the region going back 7000 years, is home to a number of small pueblos, including Chivay, Cabanaconde, Maca, Coporaque and Huambo. They all feature historical churches and plazas that date at least to the 19th century.

COLCA CANYON HISTORY

The Colca Canyon has been the traditional home of the Collagua and Cabana peoples for ages: they are thought to be descended from the Aymara culture. The canyon has always been remote: although it was part of the Inca Empire, it maintained a high level of autonomy from Inca rule, mostly because the geography made it difficult to govern. The world Colca comes from the holes in the valley walls, which were dug by natives as places to store food and bury their dead. When the Spanish came, they established several towns in the area, but they did not last and have been lost to time. It wasn't until the 1980's, when the river was harnessed for hydroelectric power, that usable roads were built in the region. Even so, the drive from Arequipa to Chivay—about 50 miles as the condor flies—is a four-hour trip, minimum. The Colca Canyon remains a very traditional area: you'll surely see modern-day Collagua and Cabana men and women, who still speak their traditional language and wear the same sort of clothes that their ancestors have worn for centuries.

When to Go

January to April is the rainy season, when the canyon springs to life with flowers and greenery. The warmest and driest weather is from May through November, with condor-watching at its best from June through September.

Getting To and Away From the Colca Canyon

Most people who visit the Colca Canyon from Arequipa hire a professional tour guide, which is fairly inexpensive: costs run an average of $15 a day for two days. However, some may want to head out on their own, in which case they are advised to start by taking any one of a number of minibuses (about 20 solés/ $6.50) that leave from Arequipa. The six hour trip north, traversing 165 km (103 miles) will take one to the village of Cabanaconde, which is the starting point for those who want to explore the Colca Canyon.

THINGS TO SEE AND DO IN COLCA CANYON

Most people travel here to the Colca Canyon looking to spot the majestic condor at the aptly named La Cruz del Cóndor. However this canyon has much more to offer: in addition to the spectacular scenery at the Valley of the Volcanoes, there are countless adventure opportunities including trekking, horseback riding, kayaking and whitewater rafting. Stay at any of the little towns surrounding the canyon and you will find interesting local activities, including the hot springs at Chivay, one of the oldest churches in Peru in Coporaque and the Toro Muerto Petroglyphs.

Reserva Nacional Salinas y Aguada Blanca (Entrance: Free)

With a surface area of 366, 936 hectacres, the Reserva Nacional Salinas y Aguada Blanca is a nature preserve of diverse vegetation and wildlife that encompases almost the entire of the Canyon region. Named for the Laguna Salinas and the pampa Aguada Blanca, a plethora of marine and land life abounds on this large swath of protected land. Lazy flamingos, black-beaked Andean gulls and slender wooly vicuñas dot the landscape, adding to its natural beauty. To get there, take any road heading out of Arequipa towards the Colca Canyon. Altough entrance is free, you do have to record your name and passport number at the checkpoint.

Mirador de Los Andes

The Mirador de Los Andes ("Andes Lookout"), also known as the Patapampa Pass, is a breathtaking lookout point between Arequipa and Chivay. Most tours will stop here for a little while to allow visitors to stretch their legs and take some photos of the mountains. At 4,850 meters (about 16,000 feet), it is one of the highest passes in the world. On a clear day, you can see four volcanoes: El Misti, Chachani, Ampato and Sabancaya. Look for the *apachetas*, small mounds of stones made by superstitious travelers hoping for divine blessings; in the distant past, locals believed this region was home to the gods.

La Cruz del Condor (Entrance: $13)

La Cruz del Cóndor ("the condor's cross") is one of the Arequipa region's major visitor draws. It is a lofty lookout over the beautiful Colca Canyon, home to a relatively large population of Andean condors. Every morning, as the sun rises, it creates warm thermals which rise from the canyon floor. Without these, the heavy and ungainly condors cannot fly. So every morning they wait, and at about 8 a.m., there are enough thermals for them to leave their nests in the canyon walls and soar gracefully above the river in search of food. The condors attract the tourists; the tourists attract the region's other notorious scavengers: trinket and souvenir sellers that crowd the lookout, hawking postcards, t-shirts and piles of assorted junk. If it gets too much for you, head over to the Tapay lookout, which although is in the flight path of fewer condors, also has fewer vendors. The best way to get to Cruz del Cóndor is to catch any bus running between Cabanaconde and Chivay and ask to be let off there. The overlook is about an hour and a half from Chivay.

Valley of the Volcanoes

Characterized by an unearthly, ostensibly endless lava field dominated by the majestic snow-capped peaks of Coropuna and Escribano, the Valley of the Volcanoes is a spectacular museum of natural wonder. This small valley, nestled between the geological giants of Colca and Cotahuasi, is home to more than 80 volcanic cones, some only 24 meters high. The 65 kilometer stretch of utterly amazing scenery also has a lake and the Río Andagua, which runs underground through most of the valley. The village of Andagua sits at the head of the valley, and makes a good point from which to start any journey into the valley. Few people make it to this region, and those interested in trekking it must be sure to bring plenty of water. A few days trek from Andagua is Lago Mamacocha near the village of Ayo. Adventure seekers can make the five day trek through Chacas to Cabanaconde in Colca Canyon. This arduous journey traces the original route that U.S. pilots Robert Shippee and George Johnson traversed in 1929 during an aerial geographic expedition.

Colca Canyon Trekking

Colca Canyon has a good range of trekking opportunities, from easy day hikes to longer, more intense treks in and around the canyon. A popular trek begins in Cabanaconde and plunges 1,200 meters to Sangalle, a riverside oasis where you can choose to stay in one of three campgrounds: Paradise, Oasis, and Eden. In contrast to chilly Chivay, the climate here is subtropical and lends itself to lounging with a good book or playing in the nearby pools. You can camp here for a few dollars a night or rent huts with makeshift beds. The huts sell food, but you're probably better off packing a stove and cooking your own outdoor feast. You can leave your organic trash with the campsite manager, but take all cans, glass, and plastic with you. The abundance of trash strewn throughout the area should remind you of the importance of being environmentally conscious.

From the campsite you can continue another two or three hours, where you'll find another good camping spot further upstream on Río Colca. The path leading away from the camp heads uphill about 1,200 meters to the Cruz del Condór, where you can view the famous birds. The whole trip takes about two or three days. Other treks follow the canyon rim, along a number of ancient Collagua and Inca paths that connect most of the villages in the canyon area. The best trekking can be found on the canyon's northern side, which is relatively devoid of tourists. Provided that you have plenty of water, can speak a little Spanish, and bring plenty of sun protection, Colca Canyon is a great place to meander in a choose-your-own-trek sort of style. A longer, more adventurous trek leads from Cabanaconde to the Valley of the Volcanoes, which boasts legendary scenery.

COLCA CANYON TOURS

The majority of tours in the Colca Canyon will take in the highlights such as the Cruz del Condor, however for the more adventurous travelers, hiking, trekking, climbing, mountain biking and rafting tours are all available. The Canyon has trekking opportunities to suit all levels of fitness and Cabanaconde acts as the base camp for a great range of hikes of varying difficulty levels and lengths, from two to ten days. It is strongly recommended to go with a knowledgeable guide from an established tour operator; this requires planning ahead as most of the best operators are based in Arequipa. See Arequipa Tours to plan your adventures into Colca Canyon.

COLCA CANYON LODGING

The tiny canyon towns of Chivay and Cabanaconde contain hostels and hotels of varying price and quality. Grander, out-of-town options are also available. In general, you get what you pay for. Some really delightful choices are available that have hot springs nearby and superb vistas of the surrounding scenery. Most hotels have restaurants attached as there aren't many other eateries in the towns.

CHIVAY

At 3,652 meters, Chivay is the most popular entry point for the Colca Canyon. Chiva is the first village on the edge of the canyon and the major connection between the two sides and as such is a tourist haven, containing a variety of good hotels, restaurants, and bus services. Due to its popularity, however, the town is a bit touristy and shows the wear of world traveler traffic. Those in search of a slightly more laidback atmosphere should head to nearby Cabanaconde, which is also closer to the Cruz del Cóndor.

To its credit, Chivay has the only Internet in Colca, the best-equipped clinic, and is the headquarters for police and mountain rescue. The area also boasts excellent hiking and trekking opportunities. Chivay is host to various points of historical interest including ancient Inca stone grain stores, a bridge constructed with visible Inca foundations, and the 18th century Nuestra Señora Asunción church. The area's most popular attraction, however, are the thermal hot springs just 2 kilometers outside of Chivay.

Getting To and Away from Chivay

Finding your feet in Chivay is fairly straightforward, as buses arrive in the centrally located Plaza de Armas. From Arequipa, the trip takes four to five hours and costs around four dollars. The bus trip to Cabanaconde is between two to three hours. Tourist information is available at the Plaza.

Help other travelers. Publish your favorite places at www.vivatravelguides.com

THINGS TO SEE AND DO IN CHIVAY
La Calera Hotsprings (Entrance: $3 for foreigners)
After a day spent condor spotting in the canyon, what better way to relax than to visit the hot springs, taking in the beautiful mountain scenery. Grab a drink and unwind in the five different pools of varying temperatures, or check out the steam room. Heat varies from warm to downright hot and the temperature within the pools also differs depending on where you sit. Note that the pools do not have lockers to secure your belongings, so it is better not to take too much cash with you. The springs are found on the opposite side of the canyon from Chivay. (Open daily 4:30 a.m.-7 p.m.)

Colca Lodge Hotsprings
Less accessible but worth the visit, the upscale Colca Lodge has natural volcanic thermal springs, purposely designed to not interfer with the surrounding habitat. Some say these are the best hotsprings in the area, and possibly all of Peru. To get to Colca Lodge from the town of Chivay it is possible to rent a private car through the hotel, however a taxi will cost around $16. Full use of the hotsprings is free for paying guests. They also offer a package for non-guests, including enterance to the thermals and lunch for $22. Closed February and March. Tel: 51-54-531-191, Fax: 51-54-531-056, E-mail: info@colca-lodge.com, URL: www.colca-lodge.com.

CHIVAY LODGING
Condor Wasi (Rooms: $25 - 35)
Condor Wasi is a rustic, peaceful lodge located on the banks of the Colca River between the town of Chivay and the La Calera hotsprings. All rooms have private bathrooms and some have views of the Colca River. There is a small outside dining area where traditional food is served. Condor Wasi may appeal to those looking for a more authentic stay in the Colca Canyon. Rooms are clean and well-kept, and service is friendly and personal. Chivay – La Calera Road, Tel: 51-54-95-944-9656, E-mail: condorwasi@hotmail.com, URL: www.colcacondorwasi.com.

Hostal Colca Wasi Kopling (Rooms: $26 - 45)
Hostal Colca Wasi Kopling is a relatively small hotel, offering only one single room, nine double rooms and two triples, all with private bathrooms and hot water. While the hostel is centrally located, just 300 meters from the city center and close to all local amenities, it also has green areas for wandering. The hotel is adapted so that it is suitable for senior citizens, physically challenged people and families. In the cafeteria/restaurant, lunch or dinner can be provided for $4, and room rates include breakfast and taxes. The hotel also has a laundry service and a garage, as well as a telephone-fax service. Cheaper rates are available for groups and during the low season. Siglo XX s/n, Casilla Postal 1817, Tel, Fax: 51-54-531-076, E-mail: colcawasikolping@hotmail.com, URL: www.hotelskolping.net/colcawasi/colcawasi_eng.html.

Colca Inn Hotel (Rooms: $30 and up)
Not much to look at from the outside, the Colca Inn Hotel is a reasonable choice for budgeters, and is fairly central to the main square—just two blocks away. The hostel offers a bar, cafeteria and a restaurant which serves good hearty food, or if you're too tired, the hostel also has 24 hour room service. Rooms have private bathrooms and hot water. An American-style breakfast is included in the price of the room. The hotel has a games room, a safe and both a telephone and a laundry service. No credit cards are accepted. Salaverry 307, Tel: 51-54-531-088, URL: www.hotelcolcainn.com.

Pozo del Cielo Hotel (Rooms: $45 - 109)
The Pozo del Cielo Hotel is tastefully constructed from local stone and consists of twenty large rustic rooms decorated with local handicrafts. Singles, doubles and triples are available. The hotel boasts hot water, heating and carpeting, which in this part of Peru is necessary as the temperature can get down to 0ºC. In the restaurant, traditional foods are served, along with freshly baked homemade bread and herbal teas. For something stronger, head to the bar, which promises, "Classic and exotic drinks." Guests of Pozo enjoy panoramic views and the option of a Mystical Tour which includes a visit to community spiritual doctors and local crafts manufacturers. In addition to all of this the hotel offers money

exchange, tourist information, a laundry service, taxi service and board games. Calle Huascar and Sol de Sacsayhuaman, Tel: 51-54-531-041, E-mail: reservas@pozodelcielo. com.pe, URL: www.pozodelcielo.com.pe.

V!VA Member Review- Pozo del Cielo Hotel

A lovely rustic property with great views over the town of Chivay... warm and cozy. We had a very large room, with a massive double bed. Excellent breakfast.

U.K., July 5, 2007

Colca Lodge (Rooms: $60 - 70)

Affiliated with the Hotel Libertador chain, the Colca Lodge is located approximately six miles from Chivay's town center. Constructed from stone and mud with thatched roofs, the rooms are solar heated. On the outdoor terrace, you can take in the spectactular scenery. Rooms have a private bathroom with heating and hot water. The hotel restaurant offers fairly pricey but tasty meals, and a buffet breakfast is included in the room price. To relax, there is a pleasant living room, a bar and a games room; however, the highlight of this place is the hot springs where water from local volcanic sources is channeled into pretty pools. For a fee, non-guests can visit these hotsprings as well. Tel: 51-54-531-191, Fax: 51-54-531-056, E-mail: info@colca-lodge.com, URL: www.colca-lodge.com.

Casa Andina-Colca (Rooms: $69 - 92)

Four blocks from the central square in Chivay, this hotel is Casa Andina's Chivay offering. The hotel's 52 rooms are comfortable and well-appointed and ten of the rooms are non-smoking rooms. The hotel boasts an Andean-style restaurant and a bar. For communication, internet access is available and there is a telephone service at the front desk. The hotel also offers currency exchange and a laundry service. Calle Huayna Cápac, Tel: 51-54-531-020, Fax: 51-54-531-098, URL: www.casa-andina.com/peru_hotels/colca_hotel-1-4-4.htm.

Hotel Collahua (Rooms: $80 and up)

The relatively new development of Collahua consists of 40 bungalows offering single, double, triple and quad accommodations, all with private bath and solar-powered hot water. The bungalows are situated around a central garden in the town of Yanque, seven kilometers from Chivay. There is also a restaurant with a capacity of 150 people where buffet meals are served. Usually, there is traditional music and dancing at dinner time. Reservations through Arequipa office: Mercaderes 212, Galerias Gamesa, Of. 502, Tel: 51-54-507-078, E-mail: hotelcollahua@star.com.pe, URL: www.hotelcollahua.com.

Las Casitas del Colca (Rooms: $500 - 845)

Las Casitas del Colca is an all-inclusive lodge hotel nestled on the banks of the Colca River, offering twenty individual luxury casitas. Las Casitas features supreme privacy and exclusivity in a fascinating destination. Transfers with a private guide can be arranged from Arequipa airport via the hotel. Las Casitas del Colca, Parque Curina s/n Yanque, Tel: +5 11 610 8300, E-mail: colca@peruorient-express.com.pe, URL: www.lascasitasdelcolca.com.

CHIVAY RESTAURANTS

Chivay has only a small number of restaurant options to choose from, several of which are adjoined to the accommodations detailed above. As a general rule, food is fairly cheap. Chivay is a popular lunch stop for tourists who come to view the condors in the canyon.

Casablanca

Conveniently located on the main square, Casablanca offers a variety of options at reasonable prices. The food is tasty and the service is good, too. If you have the stomach for it, try the alpaca steak, a regional delicacy. It is very rich, but delicious. For those who prefer their greens, the restaurant also serves a fair selection of vegetarian options. Plaza de Armas 705.

McElroy's Irish Pub

Easy to find on the Plaza de Armas, McElroy's is a decent Irish bar in Chivay. The bar is fairly small, but sports a free pool table and a TV. Sometimes the pub has a happy hour. This is a place where you are sure to come across other travelers heading to the canyon for condor spotting. There isn't too much that is recognizably Irish about the bar, but it is a great place to kick back for an evening. Plaza de Armas.

COPORAQUE

Coporaque is a small village located across the river from Chivay, about eight kilometers to the west. There are no services here; the only phone in the area is a payphone in the plaza, so don't plan on calling home from here. The town's claim to fame is the oldest church in the Colca Canyon, El Templo de Santiago Apóstol de Coporaque. Another less famous church, La Capilla de San Sebastián, has an interesting façade, and is also worth a visit.

THINGS TO SEE AND DO IN COPORAQUE

El Templo de Santiago Apóstol de Coporaque

Built in 1569, Templo de Coporaque is the oldest church in the Colca Canyon area and is still in use today. While many of the other churches in the area fell victim to the numerous earthquakes over the years, the church here has survived relatively unscathed. The church's white brick exterior is typical of the region. Its square *campaniles* contain the bells that were purportedly forged from the melted copper of Mama Yacchi's house. Inside the church, a variety of 16th century images adorn the altar.

YANQUE

Just 10 kilometers west of Chivay, Yanque is a small town characterized by dirt streets and a quiet, laidback atmosphere. The baroque church, Inmaculada Concepción, has an interesting carved mestizo face, adorned with various saints, including Santa Rosa de Lima. East of the Plaza de Armas, a path winds its way about 1 kilometer into the country side to an ancient stone bridge spanning the Río Colca. From the bridge, you can view the adobe walls of ancient Inca hanging tombs in the cliff face. If you've got the energy and about four hours worth of daylight, head across the Colca and make the climb up to the ruins at Uyu Uyu, which rise above Coporaque. This is where the Collagua lived before the Spanish forced them to relocate to present day Coporaque. You can return by crossing the bridge located downstream of Yanque. To sooth those sore muscles, seek out the public hot springs (4 a.m. - 7 p.m., $.50), or head to nearby Colca Lodge.

MACA

This little village, situated 23 kilometers west of Chivay, was very nearly destroyed by repeated eruptions of Sabancaya in the late 1980's, and then an earthquake in 2001. The village church, Santa Ana, was severely damaged, but continues to stand proudly today. The façade is decorated with miniature false pillars, carved flowers and a balcony once used by missionaries to preach to the indigenous peoples. A curious site awaits visitors just outside of town: the Choquetico Stone. Similar to Saywite Rock near Abancay, this stone is a carved scale model of nearly 10,000 hectares of Collagua terracing in Colca Canyon. Archaeologists believe it may have been used in ancient rainmaking rituals. The surrounding hills are adorned with *colcas*, adobe stone granaries, from which the canyon gets its name.

CABANACONDE

A popular alternative to the tourist hangout of Chivay, Cabanaconde is the last of five villages stretching across the southern edge of Colca Canyon. Although the road doesn't end here, it does become a bit rougher as it heads into more remote landscapes. The town's quiet atmosphere and inexpensive hostels make it a good place to rest and relax before making the 15-minute bus trip (or three-hour walk) to the nearby Cruz del Condór. For a less touristy view of the birds, head to the hill just west of the village, a 15-minute walk from the plaza. (We can't guarantee that you'll see the birds, but it's worth a shot). There is also a path that leads from town down into the canyon and up to the village of Tapay. While you're in town, check out San Pedro Alcán, which was rebuilt after an earthquake in 1784 and has a sun, moon, and stars carved onto its foreboding façade. Electricity is scare in town, so be sure to bring your torch or flashlight.

Getting To and Away From Cabanaconde

Cabanaconde is a five to six-hour bus journey from Arequipa (two hours on from Chivay). Bus companies servicing this route include Reyna and Andalucia; they arrive and leave from the main plaza in Cabanaconde. While it is possible to take an overnight or early morning bus and begin hiking on the same day, those planning to hike from Cabanaconde are advised to stay overnight in Cabanaconde prior to their hike, as the journey from Arequipa can be fairly gruelling. Buses leave Arequipa at 12 p.m., 2 p.m., 2 a.m. and 6 a.m.

THINGS TO SEE AND DO IN CABANACONDE

Aside from Condor viewing at the Cruz del Cóndor, Cabanaconde is a kick off point for many interesting and scenic hikes into the Colca Canyon. Two favorites treks are: to the Sangalle Oasis, which can be done in one day or over a more leisurely two days, including camping at the oasis; and a four-to-six-day hike, starting in Cabanaconde and ending in Andagua.

Sangalle Oasis Trek

The trek to the Sangalle Oasis at the bottom of the Canyon can be made in one day, or at a slower pace, in two. Most people who hike down camp overnight at the pleasant oasis, enjoying the more moderate climate and relaxing in the swimming pool to be found there. The trail can be treacherous in places and the way down can take two to three hours with the steeper return route taking up to four hours. Snacks, simple food and water can be purchased at the bottom. It is also possible to hire tents or hut-style accommodation there. Beware of locals posing as officials, trying to take money from you. At the time of writing you do not have to pay to hike here. Make sure to take lots of water, sunscreen and snacks with you on the hike.

Andagua Trek

The Cabanaconde-Andagua Trek into the Colca Canyon is challenging but worth the effort. The route passes through unspoiled scenery with craggy volcanic peaks, isolated villages, terraces, lava flows and people in traditional costume. Along the way it is sometimes possible to spot condors, eagles, deer and vizcacha. The trail heads out from Cabanaconde, through the villages of Choco, Miña and Chachas, finally arriving in Andagua anywhere from four to six days later. While the hike is only approximately 60 km, it is recommended to do this hike over five days as the terrain makes for difficult hiking in places with steep ascents and drops. The hike is best enjoyed in the dry season, between May and September. Accommodation along the way varies between camping and simple homestays in the little villages. The hikes usually include the cost of mules to carry the luggage, the guide, accommodation and food. Take care on the trek. There are risks of altitude sickness due to the steep rises and descents, sunburn and dehydration. Make sure you take a sleeping bag, warm clothes (it can get chilly at altitude at night), rain wear, decent footwear, a flashlight, a hat, sunblock, toiletries and insect repellent. Also, don't forget snacks and water—distances between villages can be lengthy.

CABANACONDE LODGING
Hostal Valle del Fuego

Hostal Valle del Fuego is in an adobe house with a distinctly rustic feel, conveniently located in the town center of Cabanaconde. The welcoming owners have a lot of knowledge about the locale. Don't expect perks like heating, hot water or blankets; however the breakfasts are outstanding. The hotel has a restaurant and a bar where you can relax over a beer and an alpaca steak after a day of condor-viewing or hiking. Corner of Grau / Bolívar, Tel: 51-54-203-737 / 51-54-830-032, E-mail: hvalledelfuego@hotmail.com.

La Posada del Conde (Rooms: $25 - 42)

This hotel is a good choice with a pleasant atmosphere and comfortable and clean rooms which have private bathrooms and 24-hour hot water. La Posada del Conde has 24 rooms spread over four floors, a bar and a restaurant with a varied menu, including regional and international options. Service is friendly and helpful. Other amenities are continental breakfast, room service, laundry service, money exchange, luggage storage, a garage and tourist information. They accept Visa, Mastercard and American Express. Prices do not include taxes. Calle San Pedro, Tel: 51-54-440-197, Cell: 51--54-95-983-0166, E-mail: pdelconde@yahoo.com, URL: espanol.geocities.com/pdelconde/Hotel.html.

Kuntur Wassi (Rooms: $45 - 70)

This hotel is arguably the best spot in town, in an attractive building surrounded by a pretty garden. Close to the Plaza de Armas in Cabanaconde, the hotel has 24 rooms split across six terraces or levels. From the upper levels there is a great view over the town. If you fancy a splurge, stay in a suite where you will have amenities such as a Jacuzzi and mini-bar. The hotel offers room heating and 24-hour hot water—a blessing at this altitude. The restaurant serves Peruvian and international food, and an American-style breakfast is offered. The hotel provides a plethora of services, including room service, bar, parking, auditorium, library, video library, telephone, internet, safe, luggage store and laundry. Taxes are included in the prices, and the hotel takes all major credit cards. Cruz Blanca 195-197, Tel: 51-54-812-166 / 51-54-830-034 / 51-54-958797217, E-mail: reservas@kunturwassi-colca.com / info@arequipacolca.com, URL:www.arequipacolca.com.

HUAMBO

Huambo is located in the lower part of Colca Canyon, in the Caylloma province. During its very sunny days the men wear reed hats, and the clear nights have made this a favorite of astronomers. The region is home to much exotic flora, including the *Queñua* tree, the *lloque* tree, cactuses, and rare fruits such as the *membrillo* (quince) and the *vicchun* (the Andean papaya). The range of native animals includes the *tarucas* (a type of reindeer), *vicuñas*, the *vizcacha* (the Andean rabbit), the *huallata* (the Andean duck), many exotic reptiles and amphibians, and even shrimp.

COTAHUASI CANYON

The deepest canyon in the Americas at 3,535 meters (12,000 ft), the Cotahuasi Canyon is on the rise as a tourist magnet, attracting adventurers form all over the world. The abysses and ravines provide passage for the Cotahuasi River, which begins at the 5,474 meter (17,960 ft) peak of Cerro Supramarca and flows over the spectacular Sipia, a 150 meter (492 feet) high waterfall. This river offers some of the world's best Class 5 whitewater rafting and kayaking and the same area also offers excellent mountain biking and climbing opportunities.

The Canyon became a National Tourist Reserve in 1988 and is home to both the Solimama and Coropuna volcanoes; the latter, at 6,425 meters (21,000 ft), is the highest in Peru. Within the reserve, one will also discover hanging bridges and historical ruins (including Aymaran mummies), the remains of such previous civilizations as the Waris and the Incas, and glaciers, lakes, medicinal hot springs, and rare flora and fauna. If you're lucky you may also encounter the locals, whose culture and language has changed little over the years due to their limited contact with the outside world.

The town of Cotahuasi is the usual starting point for trips to the canyon, waterfall and reserve, although tours can also be arranged from Arequipa. Make sure you get a window seat for the twelve-hour bus ride north from Arequipa, as on the way you will pass Umahuarco, the legendary "place of execution." This is one of the places where the Incas bound their prisoners, Prometheus-like, to precipices and made them available as living prey for hungry condors. Amazingly enough, one can still see the sun-bleached skeletons of their victims.

TACNA

Located 36 km from the Chilean boarder and 56 km from the port of Arica, Tacna is an important commercial center frequented by Chileans in search of cheap medical and dental treatment. As Peru's southernmost city, Tacna is also a popular point for travelers to hop across the boarder to Chile. From 1880 to 1929 Tacna was officially governed by Chile, until its people unanimously voted to return to Peru. This notorious vote gave Tacna its nickname, Heroic Tacna. Just 8 km away from the city, off the Panamericana Norte, is Campo de la Alianza, the site of a 1880 battle between Peru and Chile. The main points of interest in town are located in the Plaza de Armas. Facing the plaza is the cathedral, which was designed by the famous Gustave Eiffel. The bronze fountain located in the plaza was also designed by Eiffel, who designed similar ones for Buenos Aires, Lisbon, Paris and nearby Moquegua. Standing menacingly on either side of the Arco de los Héroes, a triumphal arch that serves as the city's symbol, are gigantic bronze statues of Admiral Grau and Colonel Bolognesi, two heroes of the War of the Pacific.

When to Go

The summer months (December-March) are warm day and night, with temperatures 25-28°C (77-83°F). The rest of the year, days dawn cloudy, usually clearing by mid-day. Evenings and nights are chilly, necessitating a sweater or jacket. In winter (June-August), temperatures reach 6-13°C (43-55°F). Many of the special days celebrated in Tacna have to do with the War of the Pacific and subsequent liberation from Chile:

• **May 26**—Homenaje a los Defensores del Campo de la Alianza—Parades and various civic acts pay homage to those who defended the region from the Chilean invasion.
• **August 24-30**—Exposur—A commercial fair exhibiting the agricultural and artisan production of the Tacna region.
• **August 28**—Reincorporación de Tacna al Perú—The biggest celebration in Tacna, marking its reincorporation into the country of Peru.
• **November 1-2**—Día de los Todos Santos—Observances of departed family members, of particular interest in Tacna because of the diverse Peruvian and international population of the city. Traditions include cleaning the tombs, *curanderos* rituals honoring the dead with food, drink, and serenades.

Getting To and Away From Tacna

Tacna is a bit of a transportation hub, serving as the crossing point into Arica, Chile. Buses can be picked up here to head across the border. The bus terminal, called Terminal Terrestre, is located north of the Plaza de Armas and is a twenty minute walk away. The terminal is located on Hipólito Unanue. Buses to Lima take between 18 to 20 hours. Ormeño offer a service to Arequipa, a journey of about six hours. Buses also head to Puno (12 hours), Cusco (18 hours) and to various coastal towns. Aero Condor offers flights to Lima, sometimes stopping off via Arequipa.

For those interested in crossing the border, one of the best ways is to catch one of the huge sedans that leave from either the international bus terminal in Arica or the Tacna bus terminal (leaves when full, 6 a.m. - 11 p.m.). Be sure to bring your passport, tourist card, a terminal departure tax ticket, and $30 to prove you have the means to travel. If the driver takes your passport during the ride, no worries, it's standard procedure for him to present all the passports at customs. If you need a Chilean visa, get it in Tacna. The border gets crazy on the weekends, when the traffic is heaviest. Peruvian time is one hour earlier than Chilean time from March to October and 2 hours earlier from February to March.

Getting Around

Combis, or microbuses, run throughout the city ($0.25). From Terminal Terrestre Manuel A. Odría to downtown, take the "A"; from the centro to the terminal, catch the number 4 at 2 de Mayo and Arias Aragüez. To go to Terminal Bolognesi, hop on any along 2 de Mayo that says "Terminal Pesquero." Taxis usually charge $1 for destinations anywhere in town, including from the national / international bus depot. From the city to the airport the costs is $2.70-3.35.

Help other travelers. Publish your favorite places at www.vivatravelguides.com

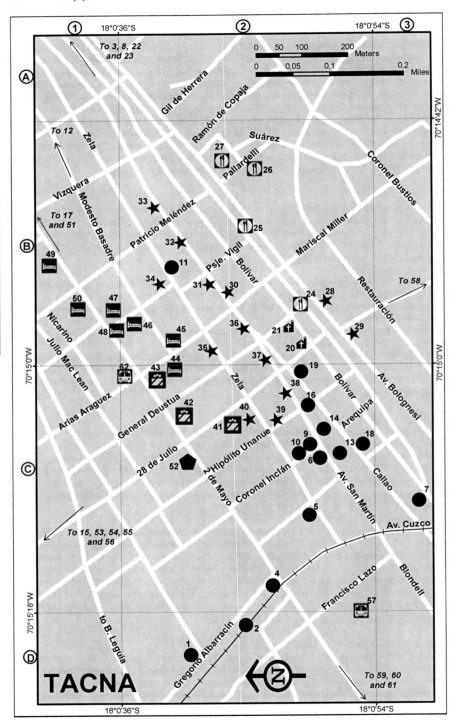

AREQUIPA

Activities ●

1 Alameda Bolognesi D2
2 Arco Parabólico D2
3 Calientes A1
4 Casa Basadre C2
5 Casa Jurídica C2
6 Casa Museo Basadre C2
7 Casa Zela C3
8 Cementery A1
9 Galería de Arte C2
10 Mesquita Bab-Ui-Islam C2
11 Museo Casa de la Comisión Jurídica B2
12 Museo de Sitio Las Peñas B1
13 Museo Ferroviario C2
14 Museo Histórico C2
15 Museo Sitio Campo de la Alianza C1
16 Pila Ornamental C2
17 San Francisco de Miculla B1
18 Teatro Municipal C2
19 Teatro Orfeón C2

Churches ⛪

20 Catedral B2
21 Iglesia Espíritu Santo B2

Eating 🍴

22 Benvenuti A1
23 Boccatto da Cardenale A1
24 Cevichería a Todo Vapor B2
25 Fu Lin Restaurante Vegetariano B2
26 Rancho San Antonio B2
27 Restaurant Comida Pakistaní B2

Services ★

28 Banco Azteca B2
29 Banco de la Nación B2
30 BCP B2
31 Bolivian Consulate B2
32 Chilean Consulate B2
33 Hospital Regional Hipólito Unanue B2
34 Interbank B2
35 Lavandería Tacna B2
36 Museo Postal/Serpost B2
37 Oficina de Migraciones B2
38 Policía Nacional C2
39 ScotiaBank C2
40 Tourism Police C2

Shopping 🛍

41 Mercado 2 de Mayo C2
42 Mercado Central C2
43 Mercado de Artesanías C2

Sleeping 🛏

44 Hospedaje Bon Ami C2
45 Hostal Inclán B2
46 Hotel Casa Kopling B2
47 Hotel Copacabana B1
48 Hotel Mesón B1
49 Maximo´s Hotel B1
50 Tacna Grand Hotel B1
51 Takana Inn Hotel B1

Tour Operator ⬠

52 Dircetur C2
53 LAN C1
54 Soma Tours C1

Train Station 🚂

55 Train Station C1

Transportation 🚌

56 Airport Carlos Ciriani C1
57 Buseta to Bus Terminal C2
58 Caminos al Sur B3
59 National and International Bus Terminals D2
60 Tacna Centro D2
61 Terminal Terrestre Bolognesi D2
62 Zesal C2

AREQUIPA

Safety in Tacna

Tacna is generally a safe city—but a city nonetheless. Take care in the market areas and the bus terminals. It is best to take a taxi to your destination late at night and before dawn; use only authorized services. Be aware of changing money on the street (official changers wear a colored vest and ID) or using ATMs. At the bus terminals, buy your tickets only from agencies and ticket offices. Do not consume food, drink or other products offered to you or from strolling vendors. And—as testimony to the growing role of Tacna in the drug trade—do not carry packages for other people.

Help other travelers. Publish your favorite places at www.vivatravelguides.com

TACNA SERVICES

The main office of iPeru is in the old red and white municipalidad building (Monday-Saturday 8:30 a.m.-7 p.m., Sunday 8:30 a.m.-2 p.m. San Martín 491, Tel.: 42-5514, E-mail: iperutacna@ promperu.gob.pe, URL: www.peru.info.com.pe). Branch offices are at the international bus terminal (Monday-Saturday 8:30 a.m.-3 p.m.) and the airport. Dircetur, the regional tourism office, is also very helpful (Monday-Friday 8 a.m.-3 p.m. Blondell 50, oficina 109, Tel.: 74-6944, Fax: 72-2784, E-mail: tacna@mincetur.gob.pe, URL: www.mincetur.gob.pe/regiones/tacna).

Other useful offices are:
• Police station (24-hour hour attention. Pasaje Calderón de la Barca 354, Tel.: 41-4141). Tourism police (Calle Callao, across from the Catedral).
• Oficina de Migracions (Peruvian immigration) (Monday-Friday 8 a.m.-1 p.m. Avenida Circunvalación s/n, Urbanización El Triángulo, Tel.: 74-3231).
• Chilean Consulate (Monday-Friday 8 a.m.-1 p.m. Présbitero Andía and Gregorio Albarracín, just past the train station, Tel.: 42-3063, URL: www.minrel.cl).
• Bolivian Consulate (Monday-Friday 9 a.m.-3 p.m. Bolognesi 1721).
• Touring y Automóvil Club del Perú (Miraflores 365, Urbanización Los Granados, Tel. / Fax: 24-4237, E-mail: tacna@touringperu.com.pe, URL: www.touring peru.com.pe).
The following banks change American Express travelers checks (no commission) and have ATMs that accept Visa, Plus, MasterCard and Cirrus cards:
• BCP (Monday-Thursday 9 a.m.-6:30 p.m., Friday 9 a.m.-7:30 p.m., Saturday 9 a.m.-1 p.m. San Martín 574)—ATM also American Express, Diners Club.
• Interbank (Monday-Friday 9 a.m.-6:15 p.m., Saturday 9:15 a.m.-12:30 p.m. San Martín 646). GlobalNet ATM also accepts American Express, Diners Club; travelers checks, also MasterCard, Thomas Cook.
• Scotiabank (Monday-Friday 9:15 a.m.-6 p.m., Saturday 9:15 a.m.-12:30 p.m. San Martín 476). Also Western Union agent.
• Banco de la Nación is a MoneyGram agent; it also exchanges US cash dollars; ATM Visa and Plus only (Monday-Friday 8 a.m.-5:30 p.m., Saturday 9 a.m.-1 p.m. San Martín, between Unanue and 28 de Julio).
• Banco Azteca exchanges US cash dollars every day and is a MoneyGram agent (daily 9 a.m.-9 p.m. San Martín 760).

Exchange houses are very common all along San Martín and Avenida Bolognesi. Most close at 7 p.m. and on Sundays. They change US dollars, soles, Chilean pesos and Euros—and some even Argentine pesos, bolivianos and yens. Official money changers hang out near the iPeru office. It is best to get rid of soles in Tacna before heading into Chile.

Internet exists on almost every block of the city. Average hours are 8 a.m. (10 a.m. on Sunday) to 10 p.m., and costs $0.35 per hour. Some have half-price specials on weekends. Skype is common. Locutorios, likewise, are found everywhere and charge standard prices.

The post office is Serpost (Monday-Saturday 8 a.m.-8 p.m. Bolognesi 361). Hospital Regional Hipólite Unanue is just west of the Cathedral (24-hour attention, Blondell s/n, Tel.: 24-2121).

Many pharmacies are along San Martín in the heart of Tacna. Boticas Arángel delivers (Tel.: 24-4074).

To make a good impression on Chilean official before crossing the border, make a stop at Lavandería Tacna. It has next day service (same day, if you get it in early enough) and charges $2 per kilo (Monday-Saturday 8 a.m.-1 p.m., 3-8 p.m. Zela 374A).

The entire length of Pallardelli, near the Mercado Central, is known as the mercado artesanía. Here are many small shops selling sweaters, ponchos, bags and souvenirs at good prices. Behind the Instituto Nacional de Cultura (INC) are workshop-galleries of regional Tacna artists and craftspersons (daily 10 a.m.-7 p.m. Ayacucho, between San Martín and Bolívar).

THINGS TO SEE AND DO AROUND TACNA

Most people arriving in Tacna just cross the street from one bus terminal to the other, rushing to get over the border and on to another hot tourist destination. Tacna, though, is worth a day or two stay. To explore the many museums, stroll down the Paseo Bolognesi and take a jaunt to local. The public cemetery is a curious mix of tombs reflecting the ethnic diversity of the city. Bird watchers will find many prime sites here, like the virtually deserted beaches near Tacna and the Humedales de Ite. To top the adventure off, ride the train into Chile.

Plaza de Armas

A wander around the Plaza de Armas is one of the highlights of a visit to Tacna. Opposite the civic center, the Catedral de Tacna is a simple but stunning cathedral, designed by Gustave Eiffel and completed in 1854. The structure is built form quarry stone and the inside is less ornate than other churches. The beautiful Ornamental Fountain, completed during the 19th century, can be found in the middle of the civic center. Also, the Arch of the Heroes can be found in this plaza, commemorating the figureheads of the War of the Pacific: Gua and Bolognesi, after which streets are also named.

Centro Cultural Teatro Orfeón

Teatro Orfeón, constructed in 1848, is Tacna's oldest theater. Unlike most playhouses we know today, with rows of seating facing the stage in front, the Orfeón was designed along traditional Spanish and Mediterranean lines. The original performance space was the outside patio surrounded by a portico from under which the audience watched; later, the theater was moved inside. The large room with an elevated stage at one end is where the performance occurs and on both sides are raised platforms for the audience. Since 1998 this has been the center for Deciertopicante and Artilandia, groups working in educational and therapeutic dance, theater and other arts. Café Thespis upstairs hosts *tertulias*, or literary readings every Thursday night and is a wonderful place to have a local wine, coffee or mate and chat. Functions usually are at 7:30 p.m. weekend evenings. The café is open Tuesday-Saturday 5-11 p.m. and after events. Pasaje Calderón de la Barca 310, Tel: 962-2292 / 997-3605, E-mail: deciertopicante@gmail.com.

Casa Del Zela

History fiends should head to Casa de Zela, one of the oldest colonial houses in Tacna, and home to Francisco Antonio de Zela y Arizaga, who shouted Peru's first cry for independence in 1811. Zela 542.

Train across the Northern Atacama Desert

Few ordinary, working-class trains run anymore in Peru. An even rarer ride is the international railroad, crossing from one country to another. But from Tacna to Arica, Chile, departs what is called the world's shortest train line, measuring only 60 kilometers (36 miles). Its schedule fits the needs of the people on either side of the border.

In the pre-dawn hours, Peruvians queue up with overstuffed bags to labor on the other side of the border. Shortly after arriving in Arica, the *autovagón* (railbus) departs, bringing Chileans to Tacna for shopping or dental appointments. In the afternoon, Chileans go home, sacks overflowing with new clothes and bright smiles. The train then returns to Peru, taking its riders home after another workday.

From Tacna, the train clacks and sways across the desert, low hills off to the east. The land changes with each passing kilometer. Occasionally a small settlement or a garden plot, an orchard floats in the beige sea of sand. In the midst of this mostly barren scape rises a low white obelisk signifying the Peru-Chile border, past which this sole car continues on its way, engine humming. The marker is not merely a division of countries, but also of development. Blacktop roads crisscross the desert, yards are parceled by thin-limbed trees, and a soccer field anticipates Saturday's game.

Help other travelers. Publish your favorite places at www.vivatravelguides.com

AREQUIPA

Getting there: Trains depart Tacna Monday-Saturday 8 a.m. and 6 p.m. (adults $2.35 Monday-Friday, $3 Saturday, children under 8 years old free, 1 hour 15 minutes). Avenida Gregorio Albarracín 412 Tel: 24-7126. From Arica, the autovagón leaves at 9 a.m. and 7 p.m. See Peru-Chile Border Crossing for more information. An autovagón (called a *ferrobus* in other Latin American countries), is a railbus, or a one-car train with the locomotive built in. Immigration procedures are taken care of at both stations. It is probably not possible to do this as a day jaunt, due to immigration (you would have to have your passport stamped at both stations, which may affect your ability to return to the station of origin. Check with immigration and consulate officials).

Humedales de Ite

Humedales de Ite, 90 kilometers (54 miles) north of Tacna, is Peru's largest wetlands. In part a man-made swamp (from mining activities in the early 1960s), these humedales now cover 1360 hectares and are 11.7 kilometers (7 miles) long and at points up to 2000 meters (1.5 miles) wide.

The four types of ecosystems—reed swamp, grass plains, sandy beach and delta—are a birdwatcher's paradise. Humededales de Ite has 85 species of resident birds, among them *pato colorado* (cinnamon teal duck, Anas cyanoptera cyanoptera), *pollo de agua* (Common Moorhen, Gallinula chloropus) and *choca* (American coot, Fulica Americana). This is also a resting spot for almost 60 types of migratory birds coming from Canada, the US, as well as the Andean altiplano. Visitors include the *rayador* (Black Skimmer, Rynchops niger), Franklin's gull (Leucophaeus pipixcan), *yanavico* (Puna Ibis, Plegadis ridgwayi), *jerga grande* (Yellow-billed of brown pintail duck, Anas georgica) and *pariguana chilena* (Chilean flamingo, Phoenicopterus chilensis). From Terminal Bolognesi in Tacna, take a bus heading for Ilo and debark at Ite (frequent 7 a.m.-9 p.m., $2.70, 1.5 hours). From Ite village, the humedales are a 10-15 minute walk. September is the best month to pull out the binoculars, especially for observing the flamingos.

Museo Regional Histórico

The Museo Regional Histórico (also known as La Casa de Cultura) serves as both public library and museum, and houses local pre-Inca artefacts and massive oil paintings depicting the War of the Pacific (open Monday - Saturday, 9 a.m. - 1 p.m., 1:30 p.m. - 3:30 p.m. Apurimac 202, at Bolívar.

Museo Ferroviario

The Museo Ferroviario has two exhibit rooms with displays of old newspaper clippings, route maps, and collections of train stamps from all over the world. Antique locomotives are on display across the tracks towards the end of the station (Open Monday - Saturday, 7 a.m. - 5 p.m.) 2 de Mayo 412, Tel: 24-6572.

Museo Postal y Filtélico

Stop into the small museum with the first hundred stamps of Peru, stamps from around the world and postal implements from the past century. Best yet its free! (Monday-Saturday 8 a.m.-8 p.m. Bolognesi 361).

Casa Museo Basadre

This Republican-era house was the childhood home of Jorge Basadre Grohmann (the man on the 50 soles note), renowned historian and key figure in Tacna's independence from Chile. The museum, no entry fee, has his personal effects and writings, plus a gallery of Tacneño artists (Monday-Friday 8 a.m.-5p.m. San Martín 212).

Museo Casa de la Comisión Jurídica

Here is where the ceremony to reincorporate Tacna into Peru took place in 1929. Several rooms display the history of this momentous act and period furnishings. It is also the Regional Archives, with records from the 17th to mid-20th centuries. (Monday-Friday 7:30 a.m.-3:30 p.m. Zela 716, Tel.: 41-5225. Entry: free).

Museo Sitio Campo de la Alianza

Located at kilometer 8 of the Pan-American Highway Norte, this museum and monument are on the site of a major battle of the Guerra del Pacífico, May 26, 1880. The monument is composed of white stone spires with fallen soldiers atop. It is free to enter the complex and the museum just costs $0.35 (daily 8 a.m.-5 p.m.). Only on August 28 is there public transport to this museum; the rest of the year, go on tour ($9) or take a taxi ($3.35 round trip).

Museo de Sitio Las Peañas (Entry: $1)

Displays of archaeological finds (mostly ceramics) from the 8000 BC to Inca times (Monday-Friday 10 a.m.-1 p.m.) Prolongación Jorge Basachre, Pocollay District. From 2 de Mayo, catch a "B" minibus and tell the driver you want to get off at the museum, as some "B" combis go direct to Calana (7 a.m.-2 p.m., $0.20); or take a taxi there ($1.35 one way), and a minibus back. From Peañas you can also make a circuit of the wineries at Pocollay, peach-rich Calana, Calientes hot springs and Miculla.

Calientes Hot Springs

For those wanting to get out of the city for a bit and relax, the baths of Calientes are a good option. The waters of the baths are said to have medicinal qualities and are supposed to be good for the skin. The hot springs typically fill up on Sundays. The town Calientes is located approximately 22 kilometers (13.5 miles) outside of Tacna and the journey takes around 30 minutes. Catch a minibus from Tacna Centro on 2 de Mayo ($1, 40 minutes) or go by taxi $3.35-5 one way, 30 minutes) and take a *combi* back into town. Another option is staying at the lodge on site. Calientes can be combined with a trip to Miculla (about 30 minutes away walking).

San Francisco De Miculla Petroglyphs

Close to Tacna (22 kilometers/ 13.5 miles) are the San Francisco de Miculla Petroglyphs. The drawings are of dancing, fighting and people hunting animals. The age of the petroglyphs is a point of debate with age estimates varying between 500 and 1445 BC. The carvings are of all different sizes and are on the surface of red silica rocks. It takes about a few hours to truly see the site, as the pertoglyphs are quite dispersed. It's a good idea to bring snacks, as there is no place to buy food or water. Miculla can be combined with a trip to Calientes hot springs (about 30 minutes away walking). Catch a minibus from Tacna Centro on 2 de Mayo ($0.70, 30 minutes). It will let you off at the roadside, from where it is still about a 10-minute hike to the site. Or, go by taxi ($3.35-5 one way, 30 minutes) and take a *combi* back into town.

Paseo Bolognesi

The commercial artery of Tacna is Av. Bolognesi. In the center of the broad boulevard is a several-kilometer-long park, the Paseo Bolognesi. To stroll down the palm-lined Paseo is to walk through Tacna's history. At the east end of the avenue is the Universidad Nacional. Just west, towards Calle Amazonas, are several Republican-era mansions built after the August 1868 earthquake.

At Amazonas, make a detour one block north to Iglesia Espíritu Santo. Designed by Juan Batenero, this unusual church has a trefoil-shaped ceiling and floor plan. Returning to Bolognesi, about midways, at Pallardelli, is the market district, with the *mercado central* and *mercado artesanía*. The median park begins to widen in front of the Hotel Gran Tacna, one of the city's premier hotels.

At Av. Grau is an old steam locomotive. Continuing past the railroad tracks is a park with statues to the various heroes of Tacna's independence movements. At the very end of the Paseo, at the roundabout, is one of the newest architectural features of Tacna, reflecting a new member to its ethnic diversity: Mesquita Bab-Ul-Islam, the Pakastani community's mosque. Iglesia Espíritu Santo is open during the day. Mesquita Bab-Ul-Islam is open to visitors, usually around 4 p.m. (or ring the bell). Also, city tours include this stop on their itinerary. An unsual feature of the Paseo are the irrigation gates one occasionally sees. This controls the flow of the Río Caplina, which runs right under the boulevard.

Boca del Río and Other Beaches

Tacna has its own beaches to which its denizens escape the sweltering summer months. The air may be hot, but the water of the Pacific along this coast is cold. A dip into the surf is refreshing. During the rest of the year, almost no-one comes, providing a peaceful get-away for travelers needing a big chill. A paved road connects Tacna with Boca del Río, Los Palos and other beaches.

Boca del Río, 52 kilometers (31 miles) away at the mouth of Río Sama, is the most popular of the resorts. Along the broad band of sand, heaps of boulders form shallow pools in which to soak. Drop a line in, as fishing is said to be good. Boca del Río has the most developed services for the tourist, with simple hotels and restaurants, as well as grocery shops, a medical post and gas station.

Los Palos is closer to the city, 41 kilometers (25 miles) to the south. Both the Panamericana Sur and the coastal road go there. Olive groves and fruit orchards embroider the edge of this blanket of fine sand washed by gentle waves. Services are limited to a few restaurants and bungalows to rent.

Quebrada de Burros, 75 kilometers (45 miles) from Tacna, is of ecological importance, with a number of endemic and endangered species. Archaeological digs here also show the area was inhabited by fishing hamlets 6000-9800 years ago.

Other more isolated beaches along the coast are Santa Rosa (the southernmost in Peru), La Yarada, Llostay, Puerto Colorada Vila Vila, Caleta Sama ad Caleta Meca. From Terminal Bolognesi catch a bus to any of the major beaches (6 a.m.-1 p.m., last back to Tacna 4 p.m., $1.70, 30-45 minutes or more, depending on distance). Some, like Quebrada de Burros, are only accessible in private vehicle. Several tour agencies in Tacna offer all-day excursions to discover these beaches ($30). In the off-season (April-December) services are limited, but room prices are much lower.

TACNA TOURS

Most agencies in Tacna deal with selling bus and plane tickets. Very few offer tours to the many attractions in and near the city. One is Samatours (San Martín 824, piso 2, oficina 2, Tel.: 42-6325, E-mail: samatoursperu@hotmail.com). Another is Zesal (Monday-Friday 8 a.m.-7 p.m., Saturday 8 a.m.-5 p.m., Av. 28 de Julio 102, Tel: 24-4842, E-mail: info@zesal. net / zesaltacna1@hotmail.com, URL: www.zesal.net; also, on the second floor of the international bus terminal, Tel.: 24-2851). Both have tours of the city, to Campo de Alianza, Calientes, vineyards and archaeological sites like Miculla. Zesal also runs trips to Boca del Río and other beaches, as well as prime Peruvian destinations like Cusco and Machu Picchu, and sells bus tickets for Chile, Argentina, Peru and other points.

TACNA LODGING

Tacna is a popular shopping destination for Chileans who spend the weekend looking for bargains. Hotels usually fill up at these times, as well as during Chilean holidays. Tacna has many hostels of all classes, though, that you should be able to find something available at these times. In a pinch, try the row of *hospedajes* across from the national/international bus terminals.

Hostal Inclán (Rooms: $4 - 12.50)

Hostal Inclán is popular with Chilean bargain hunters. It's a perfect place for budget travelers, too, looking to spend a day or two in Tacna. A half-block from the Plaza de Armas and four from the train station, the hotel is close to many of the city's main attractions. Single bathless rooms are on the small side with shared common baths that are as large as the sleeping room. Those accommodations with private bath also have cable TV and are considerably more spacious. All may be a bit worn in this five-story hostel, but it is clean. Inclán 171, Tel: 24-4848.

Hospedaje Bon Ami (Rooms: $5 - 8.50)

Otherwise known as Buen Amigo, Hospedaje Bon Amigo proves to be a good friend in Tacna. These accommodations have built-in closets (to stow the backpack out of the way) and decent beds, making it a good place to rest for a day or two. The rooms on the top floor of this three-story hostel are sunnier than those on the lower floors, but all are decently clean. Both common and private baths have solar-heated hot water. Bon Ami is located equidistant from the 2 de Mayo market, downtown and the train station. Buses from the terminal pass right in front. Av. 2 de mayo 445, Tel: 74-4847.

Hotel Casa Kolping (Rooms: $16 - 36)

Casa Kolping has 26 rooms, all equiped with private bathroom and hot water. For an extra charge, TV sets are available. They can offer excursions in the surrounding area and even have a chapel and facilities for conferences. Lunch or dinner is offered for a bargain $3, while they can provide snacks for $1.50. A buffet is available and hotel prices include continental breakfast and tax. Discounts are offered for booking in advance during January through April and it is worth trying to negotiate better rates for groups. Parking available. Av. Rufino Albarracín 1002, Para Chico, Tel / Fax: 51-5-231-4141, E-mail: casakoplingtacna@hotmail.com, URL: www.hoteleskolping.net/tacna/tacna_eng.html.

Takana Inn Hotel (Rooms: $17 - 32)

A family business, Takana Inn Hotel is conveniently located close to the commercial center, in the heart of the French zone of Tacna. The hotel offers comfortable rooms with cable TV and private bathrooms with hot water. The rooms are decorated in colors thought to be relaxing to the clientele. Additional services include breakfast, parking, a safety deposit box, broadband internet, shoe-shine service, laundry, room service and they can even arrange massages in the room. When you are tired of checking all this out, head to the bar where the barman can pour you a cocktail, alcoholic or otherwise. Credit cards accepted. Av. Coronel Mendoza 1337, Tel: 51-24-6555, Fax: 51-52-24-7682, E-mail: reservas@takanainnhotel.com, URL: www.takanainnhotel.com.

Hotel Copacabana (Rooms: $22 - 29)

Hotel Copacabana is close to the main square in Tacna, making it central for sightseeing opportunities. They boast rooms with private bathroom and hot water 24 hours per day. All rooms have cable TV and the hotel offers room service as well as a restaurant with a decent set menu, or alternatively a café for sandwiches and juice. Other services the hotel offers, include fax, e-mail and internet as well as a laundry service and a garage. Prices include tax and continental breakfast. All major credit cards are accepted. Arias Aragüez 370, Tel: 51-5-242-1721 / 242-158 / 242-603, E-mail: hotelcopacabana@speedy.com.pe, URL: http://www.copahotel.com.

Maximo's Hotel (Rooms: $27 - 55)

In business since 1997, Maximo's is l centrally placed in the city. The hotel has plenty of eateries too, including a restaurant and a snack-bar/bakery/café. For families, Maximo's offers the service of looking after your children. They are geared up for travelers and can arrange tours of the city, currency exchange and they even have a souvenir shop. When you're done with exploring the city, kick back in the hotel's sauna. Arias Aragüez 281, Tel: 51-5-224-2605, E-mail: maximoshotel@hotmail.com, URL: www.grupomaximos.com.

Hotel Meson (Rooms: $27 - 60)

Hotel Meson provides comfortable rooms in sizes ranging from single to quadruple. Rooms have cable TV and minibars. There is a restaurant, "José Antonio", which serves a mixture of tasty treats from a national and international menu, or you can relax in the café bar, "El Mirador". The hotel can offer city tours to those who are interested. They also have a conference room, room service, rent-a-car and internet provision. Hipólito Unanue 175 (on the corner with Zela), Tel: 51-52-41-4070 / 42-5841, Fax: 51-5-242-1832, E-mail: mesonhotel@terra.com.pe, URL:www.mesonhotel.com.

Tacna Gran Hotel (Rooms: $55 - 85)

Centrally located, on Bolognesi, the Tacna Gran Hotel is positioned conveniently for business visitors. The hotel is fairly large, boasting 75 rooms, with private bath, direct dial telephones and TV. Eating options abound—the hotel offers a restaurant and a cafeteria or room service if you prefer. Definitely a luxury option, the hotel provides all manner of other amenities, including bar, *discotheca*, conference room, swimming pool, parking and a safe. All rates include an American-style breakfast and the 10% service charge. The hotel accepts all major credit cards. Av. Francisco Bolognesi 300. E-mail: reservas@granhoteltacna.com, URL: www.granhoteltacna.com.

TACNA RESTAURANTS

Due to its proximity to the Chilean border, Tacna restaurants serve up an interesting mixture of dishes from both the Peruvian Andes and Chile. Typical local treats include *choclo con queso* (corn with cheese), *cuy frito* (fried guinea pig) and *pastel de choclo* which is a kind of corn cake often filled with pork, but sometimes with raisins. Other popular regional specialties include tripe soup, or *patasca*, fried pork with corn or stew-style dishes served with potatoes which can be washed down with a Pisco Sour.

Fu-Lin Restaurant Vegetariano (Entrees: $1.50 - 2.50)

It's a small corner affair, but a great refuge for vegetarians (and vegans, for that matter). The Chinese owners of Fu-Lin Restaurant Vegetariano whip up the most delicious menu (lunch special: appetizer, soup, main plate and drink). Each dish, touched with subtle flavors, are a delight for the taste buds. Fu Lin also sells soy milk, yogurt and tofu. If you can't make up your mind which main dish to have, ask for the combinado. There are also a few à la carte choices. Open Monday-Friday 10 a.m.-4 p.m. Calle Arias Aragüez 396.

Boccatto da Cardenale ($2 - 3.50)

During the day, folks come to Boccato da Cardenale to relax on the front patio, enjoy a leisurely coffee and perhaps a snack, people watch and soak up warm rays. Once the sun goes down, this club comes alive with people sitting down to Happy Hour (Monday-Thursday 7:30 p.m.-10 p.m.). After 10 p.m. on Tuesday and Thursday, 11 p.m. Friday and Saturday, the inside pulsates with romantic, *criollo* (Afro-Peruvian) and other music live from the large stage. Open 8:30 a.m.-12:30 a.m. (or until the last person goes home, even at 3 a.m.). San Martín 631, Tel: 42-6570, E-mail: boccattodcl@hotmail.com.

Benvenuti Trattoria (Entrees: $2 - 10)

A newcomer to Tacna's dining scene, Bevenuti Trattoria has already been welcomed by a loyal following of customers. Its luncheon specials are quite a treat, coming with a choice of starter, main course (including pasta and a vegetarian option), dessert and drink. After lunch, the beehive oven is fired up to bake any of the 39 pies on the menu or special requests. Some imaginative creations make the grade, like ratatouille with artichokes and cheese. Two words sum up the food at Benvenuti Trattoria: *muloa bene*. Open Monday-Saturday 8:30 a.m.-7 p.m. Avenida 2 de mayo 380, Tel: 57-4288, E-mail: Benvenuti_eirl@hotmail.com.

Rancho San Antonio Restaurant (Entrees: $4 - 19)

Rancho San Antonio is a popular joint serving up both international and national cuisine in a relaxing and laidback setting. There is a mixture of delicious seafood and meaty offerings, including *parrilladas*, shrimp and some of the best steak in town. It is also possible to try the local specialty of choclo con queso. They also make great Pisco Sour. Open Monday through Saturday noon to 11 p.m., and Sunday noon to 5 p.m. Col. Bustíos 298.

Cevichería A Todo Vapor (Entrees: $5 - 12)

As the name suggests, for fans of seafood, Cevichería A Todo Vapor has a fine selection of delicious Peruvian ceviche and shellfish options available for very reasonable prices. One of the most respected seafood restaurants in Tacna. Don't be surprised to see Chilean tour buses parked out front. Open daily from 9 a.m. to 4:30 p.m. Alfonso Ugarte 419.

Cafe Genova

Café Genova is a long established favorite with travelers and locals alike, popular for its simple but tasty options, from healthy salads to hearty pasta dishes, through to sandwiches and desserts for those just looking for a snack. Open for lunch and dinner with tables both inside and outside for those who prefer to people watch while they eat. It's also a great place to stop off for a coffee after a morning sightseeing in the city. Av. San Martín 649.

Restaurant Comida Pakistaní

Primarily serving the resident Pakistani community in Tacna, Restaurant Comida Pakistaní also opens its doors to the public at large. In a faded-green building trimmed with dark-green wrought iron, right across from the steam locomotive park, the best of that Asian country's delights can fill the stomachs of meat eaters and vegetarians alike. The traditional Muslim family prepares halal food and closes on important holidays like Ramadan. Tacneños recommend this diner highly to those who want to take a gastronomic journey to a far-away land. Avenida Grau 342, Tel: 24-1931.

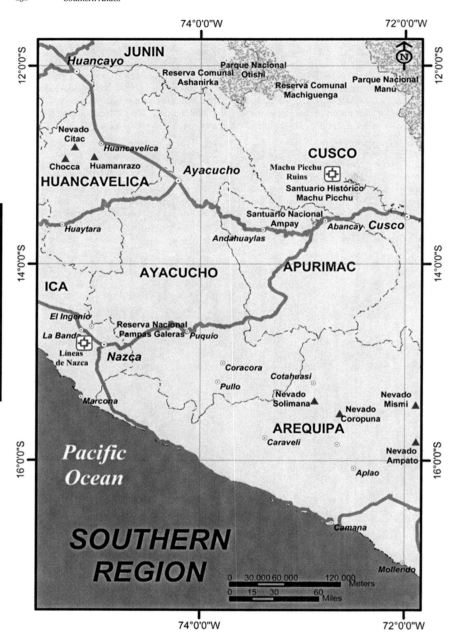

SOUTHERN PERUVIAN ANDES

The Southern Peruvian Andes is a picturesque region known mostly to the outside world as the birthplace and center of operations of the Sendero Luminoso, or "Shining Path," a communist guerilla organization that terrorized Peru in the 1980's and 1990's. Today the Shining Path is barely visible, making it possible once again to visit the region and its beautiful colonial city, Ayacucho (p.242).

Arguably the best feature of the Southern Peruvian Highlands is that the area has not decided to focus exclusively on tourism. Sure, there is reliable tourism infrastructure but the towns and villages are not overrun with options. The Southern Peruvian Highlands has gorgeous mountains dotted with enough lakes, views, and bumpy roads to last a lifetime. The villages scattered throughout the countryside are not often visited by tourists, and still exist and operate largely the same as they have for centuries.

Since locals often lead simple lives, visitors are afforded amenities that locals rarely enjoy. Despite this the residents are still likely to invite tourists to participate in the various celebrations and festivals that continue to flourish. This is the best part of the Southern Peruvian Highlands—you can wind your way through the towns without feeling intrusive, but that the same time not feel like you're just another tourist.

Highlights of The Southern Peruvian Andes

• Lago do Junín—The second largest lake in Peru is a must-see, not just for the water but for surrounding wildlife refuges.

• Markets of Huancayo—Loaded with clothes and crafts from the nearby villages—stop here for souvenirs.

•Huancavelica—Get off the beaten track and experience Peruvian life without many (if any) other *extranjeros* around.

• Ayacucho—Learn about the interesting history of the Shining Path in and around this area.

When to Go

The Southern Peruvian Andes do not see a lot of weather and climate variation, so visitors are able to come any time of year. In June and July, the daily lows drop to about 4°C. The rest of the year the highs hover between 23°C and 27°C and the lows are about 10°C. The high season coincides with the coolest weather, so come during the low season to experience warmer weather and fewer crowds.

Safety in the Southern Peruvian Andes

The towns are all relatively small, and since there seems to be a correlation between big cities and crime, the towns and villages in the Southern Peruvian Andes are all pretty safe. When traveling on the buses, make sure to always keep an eye on your personal belongings. Your things under or on top of the bus will be fine, but keep your daypack close. Crowded buses present the most problems, as pickpockets have an easier time when everyone is squished together. In general, simply take common-sense precautions and there should not be safety issues.

SOUTHERN PERUVIAN ANDES LODGING

Accommodations here tend to be budget or mid-range options. There are very few high-end choices, but you can still expect to find hot showers (ask first!) and numerous mid-range options have a television. Some accommodations appear run down to the naked eye but still offer a good night's sleep.

HUÁNUCO

Situated on the Upper Huallaga, northwest on the road from Junín, the city of Huánuco serves as the capital of the Huánuco Department. The bustling city is a crowd of fast-food joints, hotels, and bars, which often overshadow Huánuco's vibrant local markets and more charming colonial buildings. Despite the modern and slightly drab trappings, the city's origins can be traced back to 2,000 BC when the Kotosh people ruled the surrounding lands. In fact, Huánuco's pride and joy (and not surprisingly most popular site) are the Kotosh Temples, located five kilometers from town. Dating back approximately 4,000 years, these structures are some of the oldest in Peru.

SOUTHERN ANDES

Getting To and Away from Huánuco

Huánuco has its own airport if you want to make the Temple of Kotosh one of your destinations but are pressed for time. The airport David Figueroa Fernandini (Tel: 062-51-3066) has no regular scheduled flights, though many charter and private flights. To get to town, it's five kilometers by taxi on the Carretera Huánuco.

THINGS TO SEE AND DO IN HUÁNUCO

Temple of Kotosh

Tread foot on ancient ground at the Temple of Kotosh—the oldest evidence of human civilization in Perú, dating between 4, 000 and 5, 000 years old. Built during the Mito Period, (2000–1800 BC) the area around the temple is suspected to have been sacred land, due to the limited amount of houses uncovered near the site.

The temple takes its name from the pile of rocks uncovered there, as kotosh cleverly translates to mean "pile". Multiple sculptures resembling a set of crossed hands are carved into the temple walls, which gives it the second name of El Templo de las Manos Cruzadas. Archaeologists believe the hands to represent the concept of duality in Huanca cosmology, as each hand rests on the other, though they are crossed. There are many different interpretations, though, including: the image of a sacrificial offering to the gods, a symbol of protection against enemies, a symbol for male and female, and even a simple representation of a common ritual.

Museo de las Ciencias Naturales

After spending a few hours pondering the pre-Columbian marvel of the Temple of Kotosh, it is worth it to stop at the Museo de Ciencias to investigate its collection of archaeological artifacts uncovered near the temple, which include a few mummies from Huánuco. A broad range of stuffed birds and animal life from the jungle are also on display.

Huánuco Churches

The city of Huánuco, founded in 1539, was part of an important cultural movement during the colonial era. One can see this evidenced in the intricate architecture of the city's many churches—La Catedral, la Iglesia San Francisco, la Iglesia de Cristo Rey, la Iglesia de la Merced and la Iglesia San Cristóbal—all displaying neoclassical, baroque and romantic styles.

Iglesia San Francisco
Jr. Dámaso Beraún y Huallayco
Monday-Thursday, 9 a.m. - 1 p.m., 4 - 6 p.m., Friday - Saturday, 9 a.m. - noon.

Iglesia de San Cristóbal
Jr. San Cristóbal y Jr. Dámaso Beraún, Plazuela San Cristóbal
Open only during mass hours.

HUÁNUCO LODGING

Gran Hostal Miraflores

The Gran Hostal Miraflores is clean, simple, and convenient, located just two blocks off the central plaza on Hermilio Valdizán. They offer laundry, breakfast and lunch upon request, private bathrooms, hot showers and cable TV. Single, double, triple and quad rooms available as well as a safe deposit box. Hermilio Valdizán 564, Tel: 06-251-2848, E-mail: hostalmiraflores@yahoo.com, URL: www.granhostalmiraflores.com.

El Grand Hotel Huánuco

For a luxurious stay in Huánuco, look no further than El Grand Hotel Huánuco—a pool, jacuzzi and billiards room, all on the premises! Laundry, internet, cable TV, purified water, conference room and money exchange also available. Offers single, double, triple, or queen rooms. On-site Majestic Restaurant offers national and international dishes. Jr. Dámaso Beraun 775, Tel: 51-62-512-410 / 51-62-514-222, E-mail: reservas@inkacomforthoteles.com, URL: www.grandhotelhuanuco.com.

Villa Jennifer Eco-Lodge (Rooms: $12.50 - 30)

The Villa Jennifer Eco-Lodge is located outside of Huánuco right near Tingo Maria. Each room here is unique as is the experience of staying here, where you can bird watch from the lodge's doorstep. Chill in the restaurant-bar, by the swimming pool, on the playing fields, or saunter through Villa Jennifer's mini-zoo. *Desayuno*'s are included. Laundry service is available and there's cable TV in every room. Tingo Maria, Provincia de Leoncio Prado, Tel: 51-62-794-714, E-mail: villajennifer53@hotmail.com. URL: www.villajennifer.com.

JUNÍN

With a population of about 5,000 people, the tiny town of Junín is surprisingly the jumping off point for the second largest lake in Peru: Lago del Junín. Although most tourists breeze past the lake and its surrounding beauty, it is definitely worth a look if you have the time, and are keen for an off-the-beaten-trail adventure.

Bird-lovers bring your binoculars, because abutting the lake's shores is the Lago Junín National Reserve, home to one of the largest bird-watching sites in the central Andes (bird-lovers bring your binoculars). Trips to the area offer visitors the opportunity to spot giant coot, flamingos, and many a number of other colorful feathered friends. The best time of year to visit is during the spring and fall when the greatest variety of birds can be spotted.

The scenery unfolds along the road as it winds toward the lake's shores and Lago Junín National Reserve is spectacular. Visitors can enjoy observing the traditional stone houses and quiet countryside dotted with alpacas. Whether or not you remember your binoculars (or even cared to bring them in the first place) the area boasts enchanting views, of Andean landscape—and of course, the majestic Lago Junín.

Junín National Reserve (Entrance: $5)

More than 100 species of aquatic and land birds can be found in Lago Junín, Peru's second largest lake, making it a very popular destination for birders. Twenty different rivers and 12 streams feed the lake and various kinds of wetlands, creating an ecosystem of amazing biodiversity. The Reserva Nacional Junín surrounding the lake covers a total of 53,000 hectares of land. Among the many species to be scouted are two of Junín's own rare bird breeds—the black-nosed Junín Grebe and the Junín Coot—which are both in danger of extinction. Chilean flamingos and Andean gulls may also be spotted in the silvery waters of the lake, while pampas cats, mountain guinea pigs, vicuna and wooly alpaca graze the shores. Fishermen are usually quite willing to take birdwatchers out on a cruise, so don't be afraid to ask one.

THE MANTARO VALLEY

The scenic Mantaro Valley is located not too far to the east of Lima, and is easily reached from Huancayo. This fertile valley is known for its potatoes, corn, quinoa, artichokes, barley and a variety of vegetables. Besides being rich in agricultural, Mantaro Valley also produces an abundance of Andean artesanía. The charming adobe villages that line the valley are famous for their handicrafts, and some of the artisans have even received national awards for their work.

In particular, the twin towns of Cochas Grande and Cochas Chico specialize in the ancient art of gourd carving; Hualhuas is known for finely woven tapestries, and San Jerónimo de Tunán produces a lot of fine silver jewelry. In short, visitors are bound to encounter some of the finest crafts in Peru.

Perhaps more valuable than the goods themselves is the opportunity to sit and chat with the artisans as they deftly work on their latest creation. And unlike the more touristy dives around Peru, the people in Mantaro Valley seem innocently oblivious to foreign visitors. Having maintained their traditional ways of life, the inhabitants of this region provide a refreshing, remarkably un-touristy glimpse of life in the valley.

SOUTHERN ANDES

There are a number of interesting sites sprawled across Mantaro, including ruins from the Xauxa and Huanca cultures. Adventurers and active travelers can explore the area on foot or with mountain bikes. For trail information make your way to Incas del Peru (Giráldez 652, Tel: 51-64-223-303, URL: www.incasdelpuru.org, Open Monday - Saturday 9 a.m. - 1 p.m. and 4 - 7 p.m., Sunday, 10 a.m. - 1 p.m.). Owner Lucho Hurtado is a fountain of knowledge about the area and can organize a number of different activities and itineraries, including excursions to nearby Cordillera Huaytapallana, archaeological tours, and visits to crafts shops. For a good night's sleep and bite to eat before heading out into the valley, Huancayo is your best bet. Although not particularly attractive, the town is a bustling commercial and cultural hub where you can surely spend a few days exploring.

COCHAS GRANDE / COCHAS CHICO
Mates burilados-or carved gourds-are the attraction in the small towns of Cochas Grande and Cochas Chico. If you've been traveling around Peru for a while, you've probably already seen these gourds, which are sold in hotel gift shops and other gringo places from Huancabamba to Arequipa. These intricately etched gourds generally tell a story about some aspect of Peruvian life: if you purchase one, be sure to ask about it. You can't miss the various shops in town.

Cochas Grande is not big enough to have places to stay or much to offer in the way of food: most people day trip from Huancayo, which is only a half hour away by bus.

SAN JERÓNIMO DE TUNÁN
A quaint village only a few miles to the north of Huancayo, San Jerónimo de Tunán is known for artisans who specialize in making silver jewelry. There are a few shops, or get to the morning market on Wednesdays. Stop in and check out the Baroque church once you've finished shopping.

HUALHUAS
Hualhuas is a small town a few miles to the north of Huancayo known for fine weaving. The style and materials used here are very traditional. The visitor will find a wide array of colorful tapestries, rugs, and more. The quality also varies greatly, with some of the more artistic and intricate pieces going for up to several hundred dollars (but don't worry if that's out of your budget: you'll find something affordable). Hualhuas is not big enough to have hotels or much in the way of restaurants: most visitors day trip from Huancayo (about 20 minutes away by bus).

HUANCAYO
Characterized by clusters of non-descript concrete buildings and streets crowded with buses, Huancayo is a visually unspectacular town. What it lacks in optical allure, however, it more than makes up for in cultural draw. Located in the heart of the Mantaro Valley, the city has garnered a reputation as the center of Andean *artesanía*. Although tourism to the area dwindled from late 1980 to early 1990, when the region was at the stage of a bloody conflict between the Shining Path and Peruvian army, the town and its vibrant inhabitants seem to have recovered. Huancayo has re-emerged as a bustling commercial hub and cultural center that draws people from around the world for its food, crafts, dancing and music.

The town's Sunday Market on Huancavelica Street is worth a wander, though it is probably better to head toward one of the local villages for handicrafts. If you do not make it into town for the market, there is also a daily market located behind the railway station, and a handicrafts market between Ancash and Real, which are both worth a look.

Besides shopping, the town has a couple of interesting sites, which can be reached by taxi or on foot. Some of the highlights include the sandstone towers of Torre Torre and the Parque de la Identidad Huanca, which boasts interesting surrealistic sculptures dispersed

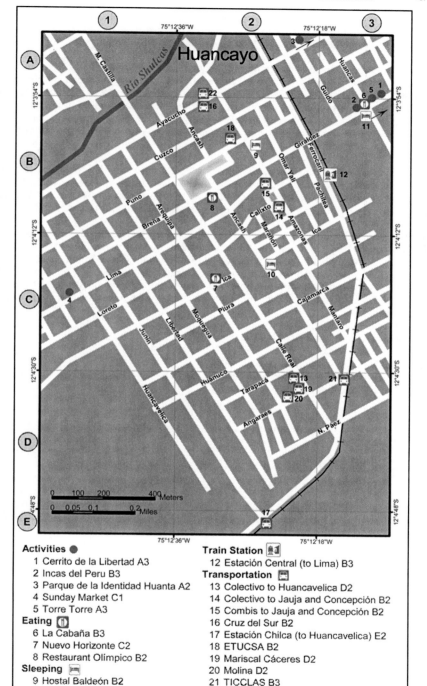

Huancayo

SOUTHERN ANDES

Activities ●
1 Cerrito de la Libertad A3
2 Incas del Peru B3
3 Parque de la Identidad Huanta A2
4 Sunday Market C1
5 Torre Torre A3
Eating
6 La Cabaña B3
7 Nuevo Horizonte C2
8 Restaurant Olímpico B2
Sleeping
9 Hostal Baldeón B2
10 Hotel Turismo Huancayo C2
11 La Casa de la Abuela B3

Train Station
12 Estación Central (to Lima) B3
Transportation
13 Colectivo to Huancavelica D2
14 Colectivo to Jauja and Concepción B2
15 Combis to Jauja and Concepción B2
16 Cruz del Sur B2
17 Estación Chilca (to Huancavelica) E2
18 ETUCSA B2
19 Mariscal Cáceres D2
20 Molina D2
21 TICCLAS B3
22 Turismo Central A2

among a variety of indigenous plants and markers highlighting the history of the Mantaro Valley. There are also a variety of good value Peruvian restaurants located in this area. The Cerrito de la Libertad offers a good view of the city and a small park.

The city makes a great base for exploring the surrounding Mantaro Valley, which is lined with vibrant villages and attractive artesian communities. The craftspeople of this region produce an amazing variety of high-quality handicrafts and artwork. If you've been to Lima, Cusco, or any hotel with a gift shop, you'll recognize these Andean treasures. Visiting the towns around Huancayo is easy—they're surprisingly close—and fun. You'll get a better price than in the big cities, plus the awareness that your money is going directly to the artist and not some middleman.

In addition to its fine crafts, Huancayo and the Mantaro Valley are also famous for their local festivals. In particular the Festival de Apóstal Santiago is a can't-miss occasion if you're around for it. Kicking off on July 25, the festival presents an eclectic mix of Christian and pre-Hispanic traditions, featuring spectacular dances and ritualistic cattle branding.

Plan on staying a couple of days in Huancayo—see our Huancayo Hotels section for lodging advice—and day trip out to see the small artisan towns in the region. Try to arrange your trip so that you can see the Sunday market (on Huancavelica Street). It is worth a wander, though you may be better off heading to one of the local villages for handicrafts. If you don't make it into town for Sunday's market, there is also a daily market located behind the railway station, and a handicrafts market between Ancash and Real, which are both worth a look.

Telephone: Country code: 51, City code: 64.

Getting To and Away From Huancayo

Getting buses to and from Lima from Huancayo is fairly easy. Buses run regularly and the trip normally takes about six to seven hours.

Huancayo to Lima:
Cruz del Sur: (Jr, Ayacucho 281, 51-6-423-2650) has four departures daily (8 a.m., 1:30 p.m., 11 p.m. and 11:30 p.m.).

Ormeño (Av. Mariscal Castilla N⁰ 1379, 251-199) offers three departures to Lima daily.
E.T.U.C.S.A. (Puno 220, 226-524) offers several departures daily, including three overnighters.

Mariscal Cáceres (Calle Real 1245, 216-635) Leaves twice a day (9:30 a.m., 10:30 p.m.) but the buses stop along the way and may not have a bathroom (don't forget: seven-hour trip).

Pullman (Avenida Ferrocarril 601, 266-120) has one overnight bus that leaves daily at 11:30 p.m.

Rogger (Jirón Lima 561, 212-687) offers one daily overnight bus (no bathroom).

Bus Peru (Paseo la Breña 235, 808-053) has three departures daily (8:30 a.m., 9 p.m., 10:45 p.m.). The last of these three is an overnight bus with sleeper facilities.

Judith (Ayacucho 282, 219-276) has one overnight bus to Lima (11:30 p.m.).

Lima to Huancayo:
Cruz del Sur has four departures daily (7:45 a.m., 1:30 p.m., 10:45 and 11:30 p.m., be sure to get there early). You can book online at: http://www.go2peru.com/ecs3_ing_b.htm.

Huancayo to Jauja/Concepción:
Little buses leave regularly from the corner of Jr. Amazonas and Av. Giraldez, or you can catch a colectivo at Calle Calixta 531. The trip to Concepción takes about 20-30 minutes, and about 50 minutes to Jauja.

Huancayo to Huancavelica:
The train is the best way to reach the city. The station is at Av. Ferrocarril 461 in Chilca (51-6-421-7294). There are two trains daily, at 6:30 a.m. and 1 p.m. (2 p.m. and 6 p.m. on Sundays), taking four to five hours. Prices vary depending on class. If you do not want to take the scenic train, and would rather streamline your trip, there are other transportation options. Bus TICLSAS Chilca (corner of Ancash and Angaraes) has several departures leaving daily. Traveling time is about five hours.

By car: Autos depart for Huancavelica whenever they fill up with four passengers from Real 1241, Chilca. (365-417). At three hours, this is the quickest way to go.

Huancayo to Ayacucho:
This grueling but scenic 12-hour trip is serviced by two companies:
Exp Lobato (Jr. Omar Yali 148-158, 51-6-231-892) has one daily overnight departure (8:30 p.m.).

Molina (Angaraes 334 Chilca, 224501) has four departures (6:30 a.m., 8:00 a.m., 8 p.m. and 9 p.m.). Some buses have bathrooms, others do not so check ahead to reserve a seat on one that does for a more comfortable trip.

Huancayo to Satipo:
A scenic trip down into the jungle. Via La Merced, the trip takes about nine hours.

Exp Lobato (Jr. Omar Yali 148-158, 51-6-231-892) has four daily departures: 7 a.m., 11 a.m., 9:30 p.m. and 10 p.m.

Huancayo to Huánuco:
Turismo Central (Ayacucho 274, 51-6-422-3128) departs daily at 10:15 p.m. (seven hours).

Huancayo Travel Tips
•Huancayo has one of the highest crime rates in Peru: locals attribute it to gang activity. Take extra caution.
•The Sunday Market is fantastic: Be sure to explore it if you pass through town.
•Rainy season in Huancayo lasts from October to March. From April to September it is usually quite pleasant.
•In Huancayo, "Panchamanca" is a feast saved for special occasions. Meaning fruits of the earth, it is created by placing meats and vegetables underground with hot rocks. You may be able to find it at some restaurants.

THINGS TO SEE AND DO IN HUANCAYO
El Tren Macho
El Tren Macho, clacks alongside the Ríos Mantaro and Ichu toward Huancavelica. It is the only real local train left in all of Peru. Tourists journey together, unsegregated, with inhabitants of the pueblos scattered along its route. This is a heck of a ride, with a breathtaking landscape and vendors vying each other for your business. The train traverses 128 kilometers punctuated by 38 tunnels and 15 bridges. So hop aboard. Eat, chat with your seatmates—and experience the Peru behind the tourism façade.

Departs from and arrives at Huancayo's Chilca Railroad Station on Av. Ferrocarril and Jr. Junin. For complete information on schedules, fares and other information visit www.fahrplancenter.com, www.ferrocarrilcentral.com.pe.

Find more reviews from travelers at www.vivatravelguides.com

The High Train (Lima-Huancayo Train)

The Lima-Huancayo line was built from 1870 to 1908 by Henry Meiggs. Based on a design used in the Himalayan, in its time it was an engineering marvel. Although the passenger service was suspended due to terrorist activity between 1992 to 1995 it is currently running and has been featured on the BBC's Great Rail Journeys of the World.

The journey on "The Highest Train in the World" departs from the capital city at 100 meters (328 feet) above sea level and heads along the Río Rímac, continually rising into the Andes. As the locomotive zigzags higher into the sierra it crosses over the Infiernillo Bridge, the world's highest at 3,300 meters (10,827 feet), across barren puna and through the 1,176 meter (3861–feet) long Ticlio Tunnel. The train arrives at Galera, the highest passenger train station in the world at 4,781 meters (15,881 feet), before descending to the desolate mining town of La Oroya. It then continues across a broad fertile valley to its final destination, Huancayo (3,261 meters / 10,699 feet). By the end of this 336 kilometer (209 mile) journey, you will have traversed through six climatic zones, 69 tunnels, up six zigzags and across 58 bridges.

Prices range from $20-60 for children and $32-84 for adults depending ticket class. In the cheaper *clásico* class, 1950s British and 1980s Romanian carriage seating is provided on slightly uncomfortable straight-back benches. However, the brand new *turístico*'s 48-passenger cars are complete with reclining seats, air conditioning, heating and panoramic windows, make the journey significantly more enjoyable. In the bar car, turístico class passengers receive a complimentary pisco sour. Oxygen and coca tea are also available if you begin to develop soroche (high-altitude sickness).

In Lima, the train departs from Estación de Desamparados (behind the Palacio de Gobierno). In Huancayo, the train departs from Estación Central on Av. Ferrocarril between Pichis and Calixto. So, a-a-all abo-o-oard!

Torre Torre

Torre Torre features several sandstone pillars that have been naturally eroded over the years by wind and rain. It's also a good place from which to see the Montaro Valley. Look for the formation known as the "Priest's face", just 1 km from Cerrito de la Libertad.

Cerrito de la Libertad

El Cerrito de la Libertad is a small hill from which the entire city of Huancayo can be seen. It is an easy walk from downtown. The hill also features a small recreation area with a children's playground and a small, somewhat battered zoo (animal lovers might want to skip it).

HUANCAYO TOURS

Incas del Peru

Aside from booking train tickets, Incas Del Peru offers Montaro valley day trips, mountain exploration and jungle adventures. Language and cooking classes are also available. Av. Giraldez 652, Tel: 064-223303, Fax: 64-222-395, E-mail: incasdelperu@gmail.com, URL: www.incasdelperu.org/trip-list.

HUANCAYO LODGING

Lodging choices in Huancayo are a mixed bag. Budget travelers and backpackers will find a variety of attractive options, but high-end, luxury visitors have fewer choices, most of which are fancy ranches outside of town.

Hostal Baldeón (Rooms: $3.30 per person)

Conveniently located between the Catedral and the station for the Lima-bound trains, Hostal Baldeón provides you with a safe place to rest. The rooms, set around a nice courtyard, may be a bit small, but the beds are good. The family is friendly, and will stoke up the hot water heater upon request. There's a kitchen where you can whip up some of that comfort-food-from-home you've been craving, and an area to wash your clothes. An excellent deal. Jirón Amazonas 543, Tel: 51-64-231-634.

La Casa de la Abuela (Rooms: $6 - 10)
La Casa De La Abuela is located near bus and train stations, local markets, and is opposite a travel information center and restaurants La Cabaña and El Otro Lado. Clean, safe and friendly, the establishment also has a game room, bar area, library, cable television with DVD and VCR, dining room and travelers' kitchen. Av. Giraldez 691, Tel: 51-64-233-303, Fax: 51-64-222-395, URL:www.incasdelperu.org/CasaReservation.htm.

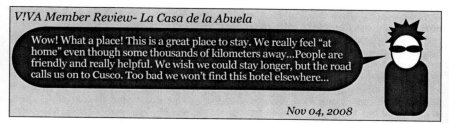

V!VA Member Review- La Casa de la Abuela

Wow! What a place! This is a great place to stay. We really feel "at home" even though some thousands of kilometers away...People are friendly and really helpful. We wish we could stay longer, but the road calls us on to Cusco. Too bad we won't find this hotel elsewhere...

Nov 04, 2008

Posadas "Casa Real" (Rooms: $12 - 35)
Located in central downtown and open 365 days a year, Posadas "Casa Real" offers both private and shared rooms. Safe, clean and comfortable, this hostel is located near the Sunday market, as well as local shops and restaurants. There is also an on-site pick up for Adventure's Tours. Calle Real 555, Tel: 51-64-234-140, E-mail: posadascr@yahoo.com, URL: http://www.posadacasareal.blogspot.com.

Hotel Turismo Huancayo (Rooms: $50 - 95)
Located in the heart of Huancayo, on Plaza Huamanmarca, Hotel Turismo Huancayo offers first-class accommodations for traveler and businessperson alike. The rooms are tastefully appointed, with heating, private hot-water bath, telephone and cable TV. Also there is room service, WiFi access throughout the hotel, parking, executive transportation and elegant restaurant. If you are on business, the conference rooms come equipped with a mini-bar. Group reservations are accepted. Probably the best of the hotels in Huancayo, at a price comfortable for those on a higher budget. Prices are higher during Easter and on Independence Day. Jirón Ancash 729, Tel: 51-64-231-072, Fax: 51-64-235-611, URL: www.hoteles-del-centro.com/t_en_reservaciones.html.

HUANCAYO RESTAURANTS
Restaurant Nuevo Horizonte (Entrees: $1 - 2)
Located a block down from the Centro Cívico in a colonial house, Restaurant Nuevo Horizonte dishes up traditional Peruvian meals like *lomo saltado* and *cau cau*, with a twist: instead of using meat, it uses soy. Nuevo Horizonte also prepares other creative vegetarian fare. Dishes range are priced low, easy on any vegetarian's wallet. If you are in need of teas, vitamins or other health food products, you can stock up here. Jirón Ica 578.

Restaurant Olímpico
An olympian in the Huancayo restaurant market, Restaurant Olímpico has been serving a menu full of classic Peruvian dishes to the community for six decades. The economical, daily blue-plate special is popular amongst both locals and travelers. You can also order à la carte specialties (do not miss out on the *cuy*, or the home-town creation, *papas a la huancaína*). Jirón Giráldez 199, Tel: 51-64-234-181.

SOUTHERN ANDES

Huancahuasi Restaurant
Huancahuasi restaurant, featuring two locations (one in Lima, the other in Huancayo) offers an intriguing mixture or traditional Andean food such as the *piqueo huancahuasi* (guinea pig, fried pork and potatoes) and newer creations such as the *coctel de trucha* (trout cocktail). They unabashedly cater to tourists, but locals do eat there as well. One of their specialties is a traditional breakfast, every day from 8 a.m. to 11 p.m. Early risers looking for a huge breakfast before a packed day might want to check them out. For lunch on Saturdays and Sundays, they offer a traditional *pachamanka*, which is a sort of feast prepared by filling a hole in the ground with burning charcoal before adding meat and vegetables and letting the whole mixture steam and cook for a while.

Open daily (except Tuesdays) from 8 a.m. to 7:00 p.m. On Fridays and Saturdays, they are open until midnight and feature *noches andinas*, with traditional music. Av. Mariscal Castilla 2222 and Progreso, across from Mariscal Castilla Stadium, Tel: 51-64-223-303, E-mail: informes@huancahuasi.com, URL: www.huancahuasi.com/index.asp.

La Cabaña
La Cabaña is a swinging dinner spot that fills nightly with travelers and Peruvians. Décor ranges from folkloric to the pop-cultural, and a great atmosphere is easily created every night. Av. Giraldez 652, Zip: 510, Tel: 51-64-223-303, Fax: 51-64-222-395, E-mail: luchoh@yahoo.com, URL: http://www.incasdelperu.org.

AYACUCHO
A lost jewel of a colonial city, Ayacucho is a flourishing cultural community located in the remote Peruvian Andes. Although it is a favorite of Peruvians, it is often overlooked by tourists, who are put off by the difficult roads that lead there. Those who do make the journey, however, are amply rewarded: the city is packed with colonial churches and cathedrals, is conveniently located near Inca ruins, and boasts some of the best markets and most interesting local cuisine in Peru.

The peaceful, relaxed atmosphere that pervades the city's streets and squares is a far cry from the tumultuous Ayacucho of days gone by. During the 1980s and 1990s the city was the site of bloody fighting between the government and the Shining Path, Maoist revolutionaries led by local philosophy professor Abimael Guzmán. Recently, however, the city seems to have shaken off its violent past and, thanks to municipal investment in colonial preservation, emerged a stronger, more brilliant city.

Surrounded by artisan villages and home to one of the oldest universities in the Americas, the city has rapidly developed into a popular cultural center. Among its local traditions, Ayacucho is famous for hosting one of the most important Holy Week festivals in all of Peru. In the 10 days leading up to Easter Sunday, Ayacucho transforms into a city of flowered streets, processions, fireworks, dancing, and more. Peruvians and foreigners alike flood the city and all of the hotels are sold out: if you plan to attend, be sure to make arrangements (including transportation) in advance.

The city is also a great place to explore on foot. With an abundance of Renaissance and Baroque churches, colonial homes and interesting museums, the city is sure to keep you busy. To see everything Ayacucho has to offer, it is best to rise early, eat a hearty breakfast, and be sure to put on your walking shoes. Highlights of any city walk include: Santo Domingo, Santa teresa, San Cristóbal, La Universidad San Cristobal de Huamanga, Museo de Arte Popular, and Museo Arqueológico Hipólito Unánue. The lookout at Cerro Acuchimay also offers excellent views of the city. Even if you cannot cover all the sites above, you should definitely head to Barrio Santa Ana, a bustling artisan community graced with cobblestone streets and plenty of craft workshops. See Things to See and Do in Ayacucho for more suggestions.

When you've had your fill of Ayacucho's seemingly infinite sites, you can head to the Inca ruins of Vilcashuamán, once an important provincial capital. Tours of Vilcashuamán, and nearby

Inca baths at Intihuatana, can be arranged with agencies in Ayacucho. The ruins at Huari also make for an interesting day trip, and can be combined with a visit to La Quinua, a small village 37 kilometers northeast of Ayacucho, which boasts some excellent handicrafts.

There is a small selection of hotels in Ayacucho, although there are options in every budget category. Many of the rates are quite reasonable, even at the fancier places. Be ware that rates will go up by as much as three times during Holy Week.

Getting To and Away from Ayacucho
Bus
Be forewarned: trips are long, often overnight, and into the high Andes. Bring along water, food, warm clothing and sleeping bag or blanket.

To Pisco and Lima:
The new, paved road goes via Ica, making the trip only nine to 10 hours long. For Pisco, alight at San Clemente, then catch a combi. These companies go: Cruz del Sur ($21-29); Expreso Wari (9 a.m., 10 p.m., $20); Ormeño (7:30 a.m., $9 and 8:30 p.m., semi-cama, $15); and ReyBus ($6).

To Andahuaylas, Abancay and Cusco:
In the dry season the unpaved road is good; in the rainy season, expect delays and landslides. Only Los Chankas provides direct service, changing busses in Andahuaylas (daily, 7 p.m., 24 hours, $12). Otherwise, bus to Andahuaylas (10-11 hours) with Expreso Wari (daily, 4 p.m.), ReyBus (Monday-Saturday, 6:30 p.m.) or Los Chankas (daily, 6:30 a.m. and 7 p.m.). In Andahuaylas, catch another bus to Abancay (138 kilometers, five hours) or Cusco (333 kilometers, 10 hours).

To Huancavelica:
No direct road exists between the two cities. The shorter route is to arrive to Rumichaca in time to take the10:30 a.m. combi to Huancavelica, four hours further away. Or take a Huancayo-bound bus as far as Izcuchaca, then another to Huancavelica.

To Huancayo:
The road is paved as far as Huanta, after which it is rough.
Los Chankas—Pasaje Cáceres Nº 150, Tel: 51-66-312-391
Cruz del Sur—Avenida Mariscal Cáceres Nº 1264, Tel: 51-6-311-5050 (main)
Expreso Wari—Av. Manco Capac 177, Tel: 51-66-316-906
Ormeño—Libertad Nº 257, Tel.: 51-66-312-495
ReyBus—Pasaje Cáceres 166, Tel.: 51-66-319-413

Air
Two companies service Ayacucho from Lima. Aero Cóndor flies via Andahuaylas Tuesday, Thursday and Sunday (to Ayacucho, 6 a.m.; to Lima, 8:15 a.m.; flight time, 1 hour 45 minutes; $90 + 19% I.G.V. taxes). LC Busre has two daily flights (from Lima, 5:25 a.m., 5:15 p.m.; from Ayacucho, 6:45 a.m., 6:55 p.m.; flight time, one hour; , $92 each way + 19% I.G.V. tax). Presently there is no service to Cusco.

The Ayacucho airport is 3 kilometers east of the city, on Avenida Castilla. Taxis to the town center charge two dollars. Bus and colectivo to the Plaza de Armas leave half-block from airport.

Aero Cóndor—in Ayacucho: Calle 9 de Diciembre Nº123, Tel.: 51-66-313-060, aypreservas@ aerocondor.com.pe, baseayacucho@aerocondor.com.pe, www.aerocondor.com.pe); in Lima: Aeropuerto Internacional Jorge Chávez, Tel.: 51-1-575-1536; also in Miraflores, San Isidro and San Borja.

LC Busre—in Ayacucho: Jirón 9 de Diciembre 160, Tel.: 51-66-316-012, ayacucho@lcbusre.com. pe; in Lima: Calle Los Tulipanes 218, Urbanización San Eugenio, Tel.: 51-1-611-300, lcbusre@ lcbusre.com.pe, www.lcbusre.com.pe.

Find more reviews from travelers at www.vivatravelguides.com

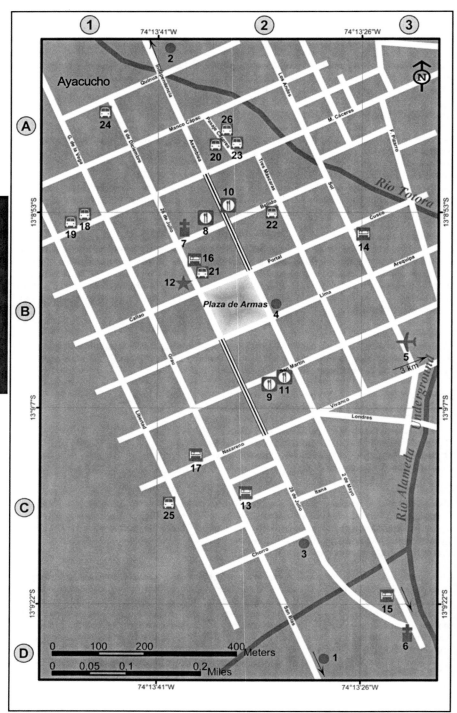

Activities ●
1 Barrio Santa Ana D2
2 Museo Arqueológico Hipólito Unanue A2
3 Museo de Artes Populares Joaquín López Antay C2
4 Universidad San Cristóbal de Huamanga B2
Airport ✈
5 Airport B3
Church
6 Iglesia Santa Teresa D2
7 Iglesia Santo Domingo B2
Eating 🍴
8 La Casona B2
9 Mía Pizza B2
10 Nueva Era A2
11 Restaurant Cámara Comercio B2
Services ★
12 Aero Cóndor B2

Sleeping 🛏
13 Hostal Grau C2
14 Hostal La Florida B3
15 Hotel Marquez de Valdelirios C3
16 Hotel Plaza B2
17 La Crillonesa C2
Transportation 🚌
18 Civa B1
19 Cruz del Sur B1
20 Expreso Wari A2
21 LC Busre B2
22 Libertadores B2
23 Los Chankas A2
24 Molina A1
25 Ormeño C2
26 Rey Bus A2

THINGS TO SEE AND DO IN AYACUCHO

Complejo Arqueológico Wari

Complejo Arqueológico Wari sprawls along the highway from Ayacucho to Quinua. Five signed entrances lead to the ruins of this once-great Wari capital. You can yet see the thick walls towering 12 meters (39 feet), tunnels, underground burial chambers, ceremonial plazas and homes of its estimated 50,000 residents.

Built around 600 A.D., archaeologists believe this was the first walled urban center in the Andes. The Wari (Huari) were one of the most important pre-Incan societies in Peru, with an empire stretching from Cajamarca to Cusco. Their urban, military and administrative organizations probably influenced the Inca.

The Complejo Arqueológico Wari is part of a 300-hectare site that also includes the fields of the Battle of Ayacucho, marked by an imposing 40-foot white obelisk, and the village of Quinua, renowned for craftworks, where there is a museum of the Battle ($1; open 10:30 a.m.-4 p.m.). Guided tour from Ayacucho costs $8-20. Or you can go on your own: Catch a Quinua-bound bus from Ayacucho's Barrio Magdalena and alight at the ruins.

Ruinas Vilcashuamán and Baños Intihuatana

A four-hour (110-kilometer) bus journey south of Ayacucho brings you to Vilcashuamán (meaning Sacred Falcon), the Incan provincial capital at the crossroads of their Cusco-Pacific and north-south highways. Notable ruins are a double-seated stone throne upon a five-tiered *usnu* (platform pyramid) and a Spanish church constructed atop the former Pyramid of the Sun. Walking an hour from these ruins, you arrive at Baños Intihuatana. Beside the lagoon here, a palace, tower, baths, altar and sun temple are among the Incan ruins awaiting your exploration. Be sure to keep an eye out for the 17-sided boulder in one of the structures. A tour with a travel agent will cost about $30. Travel tips: Alternatively, you could catch a combi on Tuesday, Thursday or Saturday from Avenida Castilla; however, you will need to stay overnight in Vischongo (45 minutes by car, two hours on foot from Vilcashuamán), as combis return to Ayacucho only every other day.

Museo de Arte Popular Joaquín López Antay

Named for Joaquín López Antay, one of Ayacucho's great retablo artists, the Museo de Arte Popular features folk art from Ayacucho and surrounding villages. On display are textiles, filigreed silver, ceramics and, of course, retablos—multi-tiered sculptures of religious and every-day-life scenes. The photo exhibits allow you to step into the history of the region and into the talleres of craftspersons at work. Portal Unión 28, across from the Plaza de Armas.

Find more reviews from travelers at www.vivatravelguides.com

Museo Arqueológico Hipólito Unánue (Entrance: $0.65)

The small Museo Arqueológico Hipólito Unánue, set in the botanical garden of the Universidad, exhibits artifacts of the Wari, who were the rulers of these lands before the Inca conquest in the 15th century. Also featured are local finds of Chimú, Moche, Chavín, Ica, Nasca and other pre-Columbian cultures. The museum additionally has an anthropological section, exhibiting the clothing, artwork, customs and ceremonies of the Ayacucho (Huamanga) region. In the near-by library is a collection of funerary remains, including mummies. Avenida Independencia 502, Complejo Cultural Simón Bolívar (at the north end of town, across from the University Residences).

Semana Santa in Ayacucho

Semana Santa, or Holy Week, Latin America's most important religious holiday, begins on Palm Sunday and culminates on Easter Sunday. Ayacucho's celebrations are amongst the most traditional. Spectacular processions are accentuated by flower-carpeted streets and *ninatoros* (bull effigies with firework horns). Scents of incense, gunpowder and bonfires mingle with aromas from street vendors' stall offering *chorrizo ayacuchano* (a savory pork sausage served with potatoes and salad), pisco punch and *mazamorra de llipta* (a milk and corn drink). Canticle songs in Spanish and Quechua weave through cerulean daytime skies and starry nights.

For 10 days, beginning the Friday before Palm Sunday, fervent Catholics faithfully crowd Ayacucho's streets. They share the joys and sorrows of the last days of Christ's life: His Palm Sunday arrival on a white donkey, accompanied by 12 devotee "apostles" and 300 llamas and donkeys. Good Friday night, beneath the light of a thousand candles upon statues' palanquins, they mourn his death. His resurrection on Sábado de Gloria is celebrated with horse parades and bull runs through Ayacucho's streets and a huge fair on Acuchimay hill. Dancing and drinking until dawn follow while awaiting the appearance of the resurrected Christ statue.

As Semana Santa often draws tens of thousands of visitors to Ayacucho, it is important to make hotel reservations months in advance. The tourism office also keeps names of families renting rooms.

Barrio Santa Ana

Sprawled along the steep streets leading uphill from Ayacucho's Plaza Mayor is the funky artisan community of Barrio Santa Ana. Quechua culture and crafts flourish here among the cobblestone streets lined with galleries and workshops. On any given day the streets are teeming with local craftspeople selling their wares, which include textiles, paintings, rugs and a variety of other handmade crafts. At several family-run galleries around Plazuela de Santa Ana you can observe locals in the creative moment.

Keep an eye out for the rugs here: some are very valuable and have received international recognition. Among the galleries and artisan workshops located in Barrio Santa, Ana Galería Latina is an excellent place to visit. Owners Alejandro and Alexander Gallardo represent the third and fourth generation of Gallardo weavers; their crafts reflect a tradition of quality and craftsmanship. Plazuela de Santa Ana 105, Tel: 51-6-652-8315, E-mail: wari39@hotmail.com.

Local craftsman Gregorio Sulca also has a studio full of spectacular pieces. A renowned textile and plastic artist, his work is deeply influenced by the local Quechua culture; many of his rugs and paintings have been displayed in Germany and the U.S. Anyone who happens to catch him in his studio (and can speak some Spanish) should engage this local prodigy in conversation; it's a great opportunity to learn more about the historical and philosophical origins of the Quechua culture and its art. Other worthwhile galleries include Alfonso Sulca Chávez (Plazuela de Santa Ana 83, Tel. 51-6-681-2990) and Galería Arte Popular de Fortunato Fernández (Plazuela de Santa Ana 105, Tel. 51-6-681-3192).

Quinua

Not far from Barrio Santa Ana is another great spot to search for local art and crafts. Located 37 kilometers from Ayacucho, the small Quechuan village of Quinua is one of the best places to buy ceramics. The area is known for its Iglesias de Quinua, miniature clay churches that locals place on rooftops for good luck. You can also browse a number of other hand-made ceramic pieces. Most of the pieces depict religious images or humorous caricatures of local public figures, and almost all are shaped from the rich red clay found in the region and then decorated with colorful mineral paint. There are a few good restaurants and you can stay at Hotel Qenwa, which is owned by the Quinua's mayor who organized a local militia against the Shining Path.

AYACUCHO LODGING

There are fewer hotels in Ayacucho than in other cities in Peru, but nonetheless, a decent variety and selection, and any budget level can be found. Hotels in Ayacucho tend to have very little internet presence: you will not find much information about them on-line and few of them have web sites, which makes making reservations challenging. If visiting Ayacucho, try to arrive early in the day to look around at the different lodging options.

Hostal Grau (Rooms: $4 - 7)

Hostal Grau is located a few blocks from the mercado. Climb the staircase to the reception, and you will be led to a sparse, gray-painted room--comfortable enough to lay your head during your stay to explore the city. There is hot water in the evening. Rooms with common bath are cheaper than those with private. You can wash your clothes in laundry area up on the roof--and enjoy the commanding view of the valleys and mountains surrounding Ayacucho. The Hostal Grau is a good value, and safe (though perhaps a little noisy). Jirón San Juan de Dios 192, Tel: 51-66-812-695.

La Crillonesa (Rooms: $5 - 18)

The Residencial La Crillonesa, across from the main market three blocks from the Plaza de Armas, is a popular choice among budget travelers. It offers small rooms, a rooftop terrace with incredible vistas of the city, laundry facilities and a restaurant. The private and shared bathrooms have hot water 24 hours per day, a nicety in the chill climate of Ayacucho. The staff is helpful with tourist information. Jirón Nazareno 165, Tel: 51-66-312-350, Fax: 51-66-818-350, E-mail: hotelcrillonesa@latinmail.com, URL: www.hotelcrillonesa.cib.net.

Hostal La Florida (Rooms: $10 - 14)

Located just three blocks from the main square, Hostal La Florida is among the better places to stay. With clean, quiet rooms that include cable TV and electric showers (hot water in the mornings), this hostal is popular among budget travelers. The hostel also has a small cafeteria and a garden where you can eat and relax. Jr. Cusco 310, Tel: 51-66-812-565.

Hostal El Marquez de Valdelirios (Rooms: $14 - 18)

Across from Plaza Mayor and set in a colonial-style mansion, this hotel offers a great place to stay for the price. Rooms are clean and nicely decorated, each with a hot shower, a telephone and cable TV. The hotel also has a bar and a garden. Breakfast is included in the price. Alameda Bolognesi 720-724.

Ciudadela Warpa Picchu (Rooms: $40 - 60)

Located five kilometers outside town, Ciudadela Warpa Picchu provides a bit more in terms of amenities for the price, including a gym, a restaurant, an outdoor pool and a spa. Price includes taxes and airport transfer if necessary. Km. 5 Carretera al Cusco, Tel: 51-66-819-462.

AYACUCHO RESTAURANTS

La Casona (Entrees: $2 - 6)

If looking for food typical to the region, head to La Casona. This Peruvian restaurant serves up local specialties at very decent prices set in pleasant surroundings. Jr. Belido 463, Tel: 51-6-681-2733.

Urpicha (Entrees: $2.30 - 6.60)

If you want to try such Peruvian specialties as roast *cuy, ají de gallina* or *puca picante con chicharrón* (potatoes swathed in a spicy peanut sauce, served with rice and pork), then you have come to the right place. The au fresco setting on a garden patio whets your appetite for the great down-home cooking at Urpicha. Or, opt for a table inside this cozy colonial home decorated with artesanía. Weekends feature local folk bands; you may want to make a reservation for then, as it is a popular place with locals. Jirón Londres 272, Tel: 51-66-813-905.

Restaurant Cámara Comercio

Restaurant Cámara Comercio is popular amongst locals and budget travelers for one good reason: great, filling food at a cheap price. It serves the usual Peruvian lunch menú, consisting of soup, the main dish (meat and, of course, rice, with a bit of salad) and drink for about $1. Come and get it while it's hot! Jr. San Martín 400.

Mía Pizza

You'll be greeted with smiles, a "Buenas noches" and, most importantly, the aroma of good, down-home Italian cooking. Pull up one of the wooden tables, warmed by the leña-fueled oven. The cheese of the pizza will soon be draping over your fingers as you eat slice after delicious slice. Or try the pastas, like spaghetti, canneloni and other goodies. Buon appetito! Jirón San Martín 420, Tel: 51-66-315-407.

Nueva Era

For vegetarians, one of the best bets in town is Nueva Era. The menu includes fixed-price options. The restaurant offers good value for money and the food is very tasty. Asamblea 204.

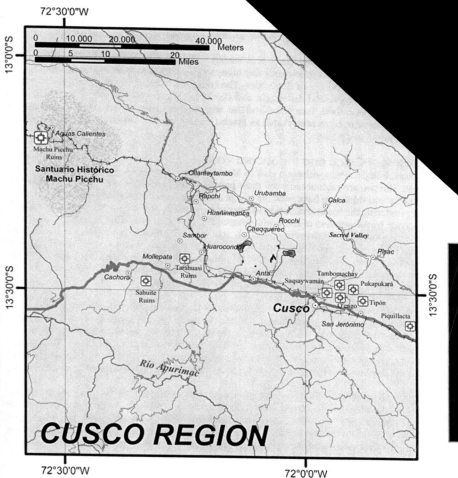

CUSCO, MACHU PICCHU AND THE SACRED VALLEY

Nestled among spectacular snow-capped mountains and decorated with contrasting quaint Andean villages and commanding Inca Ruins, the Sacred Valley and Cusco area tempt visitors with their cultural charm and natural wonders. Because it offers such an array of activities and attractions, this area is great for the rugged adventurer and world traveler alike. Even the briefest of excursions around the Sacred Valley area is sure to yield unforgettable images of rugged mountains, lush green terraces and ancient Inca ruins. Once you've acclimatized, and with average altitudes of 3500 meters altitude sickness is a serious matter in this area, there are a number of enticing destinations in the Sacred Valley. Besides acclimating to the altitude, perhaps the most difficult aspect of any trip to this area is figuring out how to see and do everything it has to offer.

The two biggest attractions which draw travelers from all over the world to this section of Peru, are the Inca Trail and Machu Picchu. While both promise an unforgettable travel experience, neither attraction embodies the full scope and scale of natural beauty and cultural richness that you're sure to encounter just beyond their reach. For those in search of ruins, the Inca's capital city of Cusco is worth a visit. Among the must-see Cusco activities are the nearby ruins of

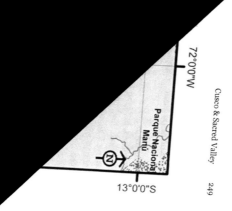

lachay. Also be sure to schedule a stop at the
. Here you can check out the Ollantaytambo
:xamples of Inca stonemasonry.

Valley area also offer a number of trekking
) grueling week-long excursions into the re-
ails wind their way up the rugged slopes of
illera Vilcanota and boast some of the most
dean landscape. The ruins of Choquequirao,
Picchu, are also worth the challenging climb.

ley
u Picchu and the Inca Trail qualifies as social
ular attractions of South America. Despite the
nd legend of Machu Picchu, an hour (or days)
reveal all the mysteries of this, one of the seven
ided high above the Río Urubamba, the clouds
which often sweep in to cover the ruins only add to its enigma. At least a visit will let you bear
witness to the accomplishments of the Incan Empire in Cusco. At an altitude of 11, 500 feet,
set amidst a valley of mysterious cities in the clouds, Cusco provides a good initiation into the
Incan way of life. On site check out the mixed Spanish-Incan architecture, some great museums
dedicated to Incan culture, as well as the Sacsayhuamán ruins.

Machu Picchu is the only fully preserved, not to mention still inhabited, Incan town in Perú. Ollantaytambo's sixteen stepped terraces remain a testament to the Inca's mastery of stonework
and agricultural planning. The Baño de la Ñusta (Bath of the Princess), and Temple of the Sun
are spectacular examples of Incan architecture. The rose-colored granite walls of Ollantaytambo are a source of wonder in itself. Some guides will tell you that the stone was mined in another
valley, while others say it is a blanket of tangerine lichen which gives them their unusual color.

It's just a thirty minute walk up hill along Pumacurco from the Plaza de las Nazarenas to the ruins of Cusco's temple to the Sun, the Sacsayhuamán Ruins, laid waste by Pizarro and his troops
in 1536 after three years of unsuccessful attempts to invade Cusco. All that remains today are
the outer walls of the religious complex. Llama sightings are common both on the ruins itself
at the base of the steep stone stair leading back down to Cusco from the far end of the ruins, so
keep your eyes peeled.

Both bigger and less frequented than Machu Picchu, the ruins of Choquequirao are veiled in the
same mystique that Machu Picchu had before Hiram Bingham rediscovered the site some 90
years ago and National Geographic turned Machu Picchu into a household name. Perched atop
a canyon ridge that conjoins three valleys, at 1, 600 meters, the newly discovered Choquequirao
is accessible only by foot. Treks to the top start in the small village of Cachora, and include a
journey through dense cloud forest.

You can load up on souvenirs such as weavings and ceramics at the famous Pisac market, held
three times a week. Drop in on a Sunday, and you will be rewarded with more than just foods
and wares, as costumed Pisqueños march across the main plaza following the 11am Quechua
church service at Iglesia San Pedro Apóstolo. Most organized tours only allow for a very brief
visit to the market, which is a shame as Pisac has a lot to offer.

When to Go

The best time to visit Cusco is April through October, when the days are hot and dry. However,
temperatures drop drastically in the evening, and can approach freezing even in the dry season. November to April sees some rainfall and lower temperatures during the wet season.
From September to May, during the rainy season. tourist numbers drop, as do prices. Cusco

becomes packed with Peruvians and foreigners alike during all the major holidays, so book ahead. Travelers should also be forewarned that the Inca Trail closes for maintenance for the entire month of February. Cusco is the center of much festival activity, so check the festival calendar before planning your route.

Safety in Cusco, Machu Picchu, and the Sacred Valley

The best season to hit Cusco is April through October, when the region is hot and dry during the day. However, temperatures drop drastically in the evening, and can approach freezing even in the dry season. November to April sees some rainfall and lower temperatures during the wet season; however, the advantage is that from September to May tourist numbers drop and as do prices. Cusco becomes packed with Peruvians and foreigners alike during all the major holidays, so book ahead. Travelers should also be forewarned that the Inca Trail closes for necessary maintenance for the entire month of February. Cusco is the center of much festival activity, so check the festival calendar before planning your route.

CUSCO

In addition to serving as a gateway to nearby attractions like Machu Picchu and the Inca Trail, Cusco offers travelers a host of culturally enticing museums, cathedrals and markets. This city an excellent addition to any itinerary. For outdoor enthusiasts, the Cusco area presents a number of spectacular trekking opportunities. And for those who want to stretch their legs a bit but aren't up for a week-long adventure over mountainous terrain, the nearby Inca ruins of Sacsayhuamán, Q'enqo, Puca Pucara, Tambo Machay, Tipón, and Pikillacta and Rumicolca make excellent day trips.

In Quechua Cusco translates as "belly button of the world," and at its height Cusco truly was the center of the great Inca Empire, which stretched across parts of South America from Northern Chile to Colombia. In terms of architectural prowess and political importance, Cusco paralleled the well-known Aztec capital of Tenochtitlán as one of the great imperial capitals of America. Today, Cusco is known for its inviting and intriguing blend of Spanish and Inca culture, most evident where Spanish churches and convents have been built squarely on top of perfectly laid Inca walls. While the Spanish did their best to pillage and plunder the city, they failed to completely destroy the massive network of Inca stonework, which continues to withstand both time and the elements. The Spanish buildings in contrast have begun to crack and crumble.

The Quechua people, the present-day ancestors of the Incas, have also been a city building block, they bring the charm, humility and beauty that keep tourism booming in Cusco. Because the city is a popular destination along the Gringo Trail, it has a variety of hotels and restaurants to accommodate any traveler's tastes, from world-class hotels to hostels the most miserly of backpackers will find affordable. Cusco is an extremely visitor-friendly city, with

Enter photo competitions at www.vivatravelguides.com

tour agencies on every block and very helpful locals. Most of the major Cusco activities are within walking distance of one another and can be covered in about half a day, though you may want to devote a little more time to browse the various shops and markets you encounter along the way. Some Cusco highlights include the Cusco Cathedral, Iglesia San Blas, San Blas, Qoricancha Templo del Sol and Santo Domingo, Museo Histórico Regional, Museo de Arte y Monasterio de Santa Catalina.

CUSCO HISTORY

Cusco is best known for its Incan and colonial periods; however, those two epochs represent only about one-third of Cusco's settled history. The city's first settlements, located in the eastern part of the current city, date as far back as 3,000 years. As a result, some consider Cusco to be the longest continually settled city in the Americas. In the years those first residents, various settlers have come and gone, including the Wari invaders around 750 AD—a period which preceded the construction of the buildings which today are called Pikillacta.

The Inca Civilization began around 1200 AD, and with it came the development of Cusco into a major political and religious center, one that could serve a relatively large population. A large expansion phase began around 1400 AD, when the Incas laid out the city in the shape of a Puma, their sacred animal. The expansion was short-lived as the Spanish would arrive next century, on November 15, 1533. Thus began violent and ruthless attempts to conquer the city. In 1536 the Incas rebelled against the Spanish in an attempt to regain control of the city. The ensuing war lasted 36 years, finally ending when the head of Túpac Amaru, the Inca dynasty's last emperor, was lopped off in Cusco's Main Square.

Cusco experienced a large earthquake in 1650, after which nearly every colonial building needed to be rebuilt (further emphasizing the quality of the Inca architecture, much of which remains standing today). A valiant attempt at emancipation was attempted in 1780 by José Gabriel Thupa Amaro Inga. When he was betrayed by his followers, and he and his whole family were executed in Cusco's Main Square. Independence was finally achieved in 1821, following a long, bloody process that served as the template for Latin America.

Once a stunning Inca capital, Cusco today offers one of the finest mixes of pre-Columbian, colonial and modern mestizo culture of any South American city. Cusco is often referred to as the archeological capital of South America. The colonial history of the city is not completely untouched, but the central historical area has not undergone an overwhelming number of alternations despite the high concentration of stores, hotels, restaurants, tour operators and other tourist-driven enterprises. A quick walk through the city allows visitors to see the influence of different periods of history with the naked eye. Inca ruins such as the Temple of the Sun contrast with Spanish churches and mansions, underscoring Cusco's various phases of development.

Cusco's unique mix of Amerindian and mestizo culture has persevered despite a massive influx of tourism. The best example is Inti Raymi, an Inca tradition that celebrates the winter solstice, according to the ancient Inca sundial. Locals and tourists alike are welcome to participate in the day-long event, in a show of how Cusco has reconciled its indigenous history with its recent tourism boom.

Lake Titicaca and the Founding of Cusco

Legend has it that when the ancient sun god made his two children, Manco Capac and Mama Ocllo, they emerged out of Lake Titicaca and on an island in the lake, he gave them a great golden staff to be used for a specific task. The task? Founding the Peruvian Incans and finding the most appropriate location by sticking the staff into the ground. Manco and his sister, Mama, searched Peru high and low for the right spot, but the staff would not stick into the ground. Finally, they came upon the most beautiful place they had seen yet. They stuck the staff in the ground and it stuck. They founded the city of Cusco, conquering

CUSCO

the tribes already living there and ruling them under the Incan Empire. Manco married his sister and they ruled side-by-side.

Some legends say that in the spot where they stuck the golden staff, Manco and Mama also built a Temple of the Sun dedicated to their father. If the legends are correct Manco would have been ruling the Incans in about the 12th century. During the 17th century, the Santo Domingo Church and Qoricancha were built on the site of the Temple of the Sun; the spot remains one of the biggest and most impressive tourist attractions in Cusco.

Getting To and Away From Cusco

For convenience sake, most people get to Cusco via airplane; a bus from Lima can cost $35 but takes 26 hours. You can break up the trip by stopping over in Nasca, but you would still have to leave at night to resume your trip. By contrast, a plane trip costs $70 and only takes an hour. Except for chartered planes, there are no international flights to Aeropuerto Internacional Velasco Astete in Cusco. The train stations, Estación de Huanchaq and Estación de San Pedro, connect to Aguas Calientes (Machu Picchu), Arequipa, Puno, and the Oriente (the Amazon jungle). There is also bus service between Cusco and those four regions.

Alejandro Velasco Astete International Airport

For those travelling to Cusco from Lima who do not want to take the over 24-hour, non-stop bus ride needed to access--or depart from--the region, there is the Alejandro Velasco Astete International Airport. The airtime between the two cities is one hour. Freshly remodeled, this is one of the most modern of all Latin American airports; the only one featuring boarding bridges between the terminal and the planes. It is named after a Peruvian pilot who in 1925 was the first man to fly over the Andes. The airport has mostly domestic flights, though it does receive some international charter flights. Due to its high altitude (10,860 feet / 3310 meters above sea level), all flights to Cusco from Lima leave in the morning. The airport is about three miles (5 kilometers) east-southeast of the city; a cab will take you there for 6 soles ($2), or you can take a bus for one sol. There are no hotels at the airport, so an early departure may end up choosing to sleep on the floors. It is safe and well-patrolled by guards. An ATM dispenses cash with most cards. A special feature of this airport is the domesticated and people-friendly alpacas that will greet you, and are open to both petting and pictures.

Getting Around Cusco

Most of what you will want to see in Cusco is within walking distance of the central Plaza de Armas, but if it is late, if you are in a hurry, or going to or from the outlying residential areas, there are plenty of cabs available. The tourist police recommend that tourists only use cabs that have the diamond-shaped sticker of official approval in their windshields. Apart from that, there are many combis or mini-vans, which can take you to the airport and other points around town.

Holidays and Festivals

Cusco plays host to several yearly festivals, some driven by Amerindian influences, others by post-Columbian traditions and some that blend both. The most well attended and most popular festival in Cusco is Inti Raymi, the yearly Inca festival celebrating the winter solstice on June 24, according to the Inca Sundial (modern science has since pinned the date to June 21).

Qoyllur Rit'i usually takes place on the Sunday before Corpus Christi. People make the pilgrimage from all over to pray to the Lord of Qoyllur Rit'i who they believe has powers to bring them success in love, school, etc.

The festival is capped off by a procession on the final night when hundreds of people climb the surrounding glaciers and lug down huge icicles. The icicles are melted to produce holy water which is thought to help the sick community members. As in pretty much all Latin American cities, Cusco lets loose for Carnival. The celebration peaks the Monday and Tuesday before Ash Wednesday and is a great time to visit Cusco if you want to party.

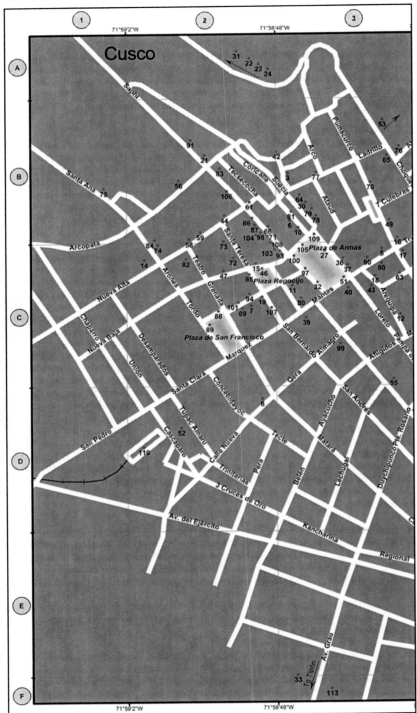

Cusco

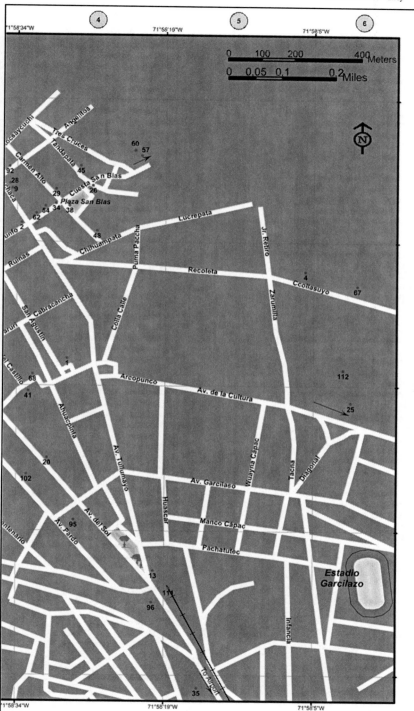

CUSCO

Activities
1 Acupari Language School
2 Aldea Yancay Project
3 Amauta Spanish School
4 Amigos Spanish School
5 Artesanías Pachúcatec
6 Body Show Spa Cusco
7 Cusco Spanish School
8 Excel Spanish Language Center
9 FairPlay Language School
10 Gringo Alley
11 La Cholita
12 Macchu Picchu Spanish School
13 Mercado Artesanal
14 Mundo Verde Spanish School
15 Museo de Arte Contemporáneo
16 Museo de Arte Religioso
17 Museo de Arte Religioso
18 Museo de Arte y Monasterio Santa Catalina
19 Museo de Historia Regional
20 Museo de Sitio Qoricancha
21 Proyecto Peru Language Center
22 Puca Pucará
23 Q'engo
24 Sacsayguamán
25 Salapunco
26 San Blas Spanish School
27 Seminario Ceramics
28 South American Explorers
29 South American Spanish School
30 Spanish in Peru
31 Tambo Machay
32 Tesoros del Ande
33 Tipón
34 Wiracocha Spanish School
Airport
35 Aeropuerto Velasco Astete
Church
36 Cusco Cathedral
37 El Triunfo
38 Iglesia San Blas
39 Iglesia y Convento de la Merced
40 La Compañía de Jesús
41 Qoricancha Templo del Sol and Santo Domingo
42 San Cristóbal
43 Santa Catalina
44 Santa Teresa
Eating
45 Vuelto
46 Govinda's
47 Kachivache
48 Macondo
Nightlife
49 Mandela's Bar
50 Paddy Flaherty's
51 Up Town
Services
52 Mercado Central
53 Mercado Mollina
Transportation
112 Bus to Pisac
113 Bus to Urubamba

Sleeping
54 Amaru Hostal
55 Cristina Hostal
56 El Balcón Hostal
57 Hospedaje El Artesano de San Blas
58 Hospedaje Emanuel
59 Hospedaje Granada
60 Hospedaje Inka
61 Hospedaje Qáni Wasi
62 Hospedaje Turístico San Blas
63 Hostal Casa Grande
64 Hostal Corihuasi
65 Hostal Rumi Punku
66 Hotel Cáceres
67 Hotel Emperador Plaza
68 Hotel Libertador Palacio del Inka
69 Hotel Marqueses
70 Hotel Monasterio
71 Hotel Oblitas
72 Hotel Royal Inka I
73 Hotel Royal Inka II
74 Intiq Samana
75 Loki Hostel Cusco
76 Los Apus Hotel and Mirador
77 Munay Wasi
78 Pirwa Lodging Hostel
79 Sol Innka Plaza
80 Sonesta Posada del Inca
81 Sumac Wasi
82 Teatro Inka Bed and Breakfast
83 Teqsiqocha Hostal
84 The Niños Hotel
Tour Operator
85 Action Valley
86 All Trek Cusco Tours
87 Andean Life Adventure
88 Andes Nature Tours
89 Apumayo
90 Big Foot
91 Cóndor
92 Eco Trek Peru
93 Eric Adventures
94 Explorandes
95 Manu Expeditions
96 Manu Nature Tours
97 Mayuc
98 Mountain Biking and Trekking
99 Peru Inkas Adventures- Mountain Biking
100 Peru Travel Sustainable Tourism
101 Peru Treks and Adventure
102 Peruvian Andean Treks
103 Quad Bike Tours
104 Sacred Land Adventures
105 SAS Travel
106 Sun Gate Tours
107 Turismo Inkaiko
108 United Mice
109 Vilcabamba Expediciones
Train Station
110 Estación San Pedro
111 Estación Wanchac

Likewise, Semana Santa, held during Easter, is celebrated all over Latin America. Cusco celebrates by holding numerous processions through the streets, including an Easter Monday procession led by El Señor de los Temblores (Lord of the Earthquakes). For the Santuranticuy festival, on December 24, hundreds of artisans head to Cusco's Plaza de Armas to spread their wares out on blankets. It is one of the largest craft fairs in Peru.

CUSCO SERVICES

Tourist Information Office
Monday - Friday, 8 a.m.-6:30 p.m., and Saturday, 8 a.m.-2 p.m. Portal Mantas 117-A (next to the La Merced Church), Tel: 51-84-222-032.

I-PERU / PROMPERU
Monday - Saturday, 8.30am-7.30pm. Av. El Sol 103, Office 102, Tel: 51-84-234-498. Also at Velasco Astete Airport Arrivals hall, Tel: 51-84-247-364. For tourist information and assistance.

Tourist Police
The following services may be helpful for tourists while in Cusco: Tourist Information Office Portal Mantas 188 (next to the La Merced Church) Telephone: 51-84263-176 Hours: Monday-Friday, 8 a.m.-6:30 p.m., and Saturday, 8 a.m.-2 p.m. Tourist Police Saphi 510 Telephone: 51-84-249-654 The Tourist Police will provide information and will also investigate crimes that are committed against tourists, such as theft of property. More serious crimes are handled by other law enforcement organizations. Immigration Av. el Sol 620 (1/2 block uphill from the post office) Telephone: 51-84-224-741 Hours: Monday-Friday, 8 a.m.-1 p.m. and 2 p.m.-4:30 p.m.

Immigration
Visas can be renewed for 30 days without leaving the country for $20. Monday - Friday, 8 a.m.-4:15 p.m. Av. el Sol 620 (1/2 block uphill from the post office), Tel: 51-84-222-741

CIMA Hyperbaric Center
Cusco is often breathtaking...in more ways than one. Even the most athletic are not immune to high altitude sickness if they are not accustomed to high up climates. Altitude sickness a condition which can affect people at over 2,400 meters (8,000 feet) over sea level. Cusco is 3,536 meters (11,600 feet), and such symptoms as dizziness and fatigue can develop into high altitude pulmonary edema (HAPE) or high altitude cerebral edema (HACE). The CIMA Hyperbaric Center, with its hyperbaric chamber, has become one of the most respected clinics in Cusco for treating high altitude sickness. They also provide any and all needed vaccinations and medical assistance relating to outdoor sports. 978 Avenida Pardo, Tel: 51-84-255-550, E-mail: info@cimaperu.com ,URL: www.cimaperu.com.

Shopping
San Pedro Market / Mercado Central (Entrance: free)
Located across from the San Pedro train station; a few blocks southwest of the Plaza de Armas, the central market offers one-stop shopping for the traveler with a grocery list and limited needs in the souvenir department. Though the Mercado Central is largely dedicated to sales of fruits, vegetables, meats and bread, there are a few vendors hawking souvenirs to those tourists who wander in. For practical goods, like socks or batteries, the Mercado Central gets the job done, although the range of goods is infinitesimal compared to Mercado Mollina. most markets in Peru, the Mercado Central has plenty of cheap local eats for the traveler with a sense of adventure and an iron stomach. Open Daily.

Cusco Tourist Ticket / Boleto Turístico Cusco
What is it? Even if you plan to visit only a few places in and around Cusco, it is wise to purchase the Cusco Tourist Ticket (Boleto Turístico Cusco, or BTC). It's the only way to get into some of Cusco's main attractions, and includes useful maps of the regions and the city. Although,

CUSCO

recently the tourist ticket has changed and you have to buy tickets for the different sites individually. How much is them? $10 adults $5 students under age 26 with ISIC card Note: The ticket only lasts ten days but can be renewed at any one of the two offices below. Where can I get them? Although it's theoretically available from all the sites on the ticket, your best bet is to buy it from one of the following two tour offices in Cusco: OFEC Avenida El Sol 103, #106 Telephone: 51-84-227-037 Monday-Friday, 8 a.m.-5 p.m. Casa Garcilaso corner of Garcilaso and Heladeros Telephone: 51-84-226-919 Monday-Friday, 7:45 a.m.-6 p.m., Saturday, 8 a.m.-4 p.m., Sunday 8 a.m.-noon. They cover Cusco Cathedral, Museo de Arte Religioso, Iglesia San Blas, Museo Histórico Regional Museo de Arte y Monasterio de Santa Catalina, Museo Palacio Municipal, Museo de Sitio Qoricancha Sacsayhuamán, Q'enqo, Puca, Pucara, Tambo, Machay, Pikillacta, Tipón and the Pisac, Ollantaytambo and Chinchero ruins.

THINGS TO SEE AND DO IN CUSCO

Plaza de Armas

With a commanding spot at the center of the city, the Plaza de Armas is perhaps the best point from which to start exploring the city. From here you can access all of the Cusco's major attractions, which spread out across the city along all four points of the compass. Within the Plaza de Armas you will find the Portal de Panes, Cusco Cathedral, Chapel of the Immaculate Conception, Chapel of El Señor de los Temblores, Museo Inka, and Iglesia de la Compañía de Jesús.

Following Callejón Loreto to the west of the Plaza de Armas will bring you to the spectacular stone walls of ancient Acclahuasi, or Temple of the Sun Virgins, where the Spanish built the Convent of Santa Catalina in 1610. Today about thirty sisters continue to live and worship here; inside is the Museo de Arte y Monasterio de Santa Catalina. Southeast from the convent, at the intersection of Avenida El Sol and Calle Santa Domingo, is the complex of Qoricancha Templo del Sol and Santo Domingo, a wonderful example of the city's characteristic mix of Spanish and Inca cultures. Within three minute's walk of this architectural amalgamation is the Museo de Sitio Qoricancha, which offers an interesting display of various archeological artifacts.

To the southwest of the Plaza de Armas are the Iglesia y Convento de la Merced and the Plaza de San Francisco, where you will find the Museo y Convento de San Francisco. Further to the south is the Central Market, which is known for its quality alpaca goods and antique textiles. Another area of interest lies near the Plaza Regocijo, just a block southwest of the Plaza de Armas. In the southwest corner of the plaza stands the Museo Histórico Regional, the residence of a prolific half-Inca, half-Spanish poet and author, and now the home to pre-Inca ceramics, Inca artifacts and numerous examples of Cusco's historic art. If you're in need of a drink but don't want to stray too far, then follow Calle Santa Teresa from Plaza Regocijo to the House of the Pumas, a small café whose entrance sports six pumas carved by the Spanish during the rebuilding of Cusco. Not far from the café is the Iglesia de Santa Teresa, which features beautiful paintings of St. Teresa, usually illuminated by candlelight.

Wander northeast of the Plaza de Armas, along Calle Córdoba del Tucmán, and you'll stumble across Plaza Nazarenas, a small and quiet section of town that boasts the Chapel of San Antonio Abad, Museo de Cerámica, and Museo Taller Hilario Mendivil. This area also has four other important attractions: the Museo de Arte Religioso, Hathun Rumiyoq, the most famous Inca passageway in the city; and Iglesia San Blas and San Blas, a bustling artisan neighborhood whose steep cobblestone streets offer fantastic views of the city. NOTE: Whether or not you plan to visit all the attractions in Cusco, it is worth purchasing the Cusco Tourist Ticket (Boleto Turístico General, BTG), which covers many of the historic museums, cathedrals, and ruins in the Cusco area.

Cusco Cathedral

Located in the center of Cusco on the Plaza de Armas, Cusco's massive stone cathedral is well worth a visit. construction began in 1560; much of the stone used to build the cathedral was brought from Sachsayhuamán and other Inca sites. Time and earthquakes took their toll on the cathedral; an ambitious resotration project took place between 1997 and 2002. Much of

GAY LIFE IN CUSCO

The official flag of the city of Cusco is almost identical to the Rainbow Flag, universally adopted by the gay community as its banner. And as globalization, via the information superhighway, has brought the rest of the world to Peru, including a nascent gay-rights movement, cusqueños themselves have become uneasy; some locals have proposed adopting a new flag without actually announcing why. Cusco has a gay bar/discothèque by the name of "Queen," (at the intersection of the Lorena and Cementerio Streets). This is a small venue located in a poor and dangerous section of the city that would not appeal to most international visitors. However, it is at least a sign of an emerging, if fragile, tolerance for the community. Some gay cusqueños will let you know that at least in the tourist-heavy sections of Cusco, hand-holding and light-kissing is tolerated. Gay-owned cafés and restaurants, such as Macondo and Fallen Angel, have a stylishly camp sensibility. A gay visitor who is planning on an extended stay in Cusco might patronize these establishments and might even find fellow gay men to socialize with. Options for lesbian travelers are more circumscribed, since women have to fight against machismo as well as homophobia.

the stonework has been shored up and the magnificent paintings have been delicately wiped clean of centuries of grime. Be sure to check out the Matia Angola bell in the bell tower, made with more than fifty pounds of gold. The entrance is no longer included as part of the Cusco Tourist Ticket. You now have to buy a ticket separately for 25 soles. Plaza de Armas.

Iglesia y Convento de la Merced

The Church and Convent of Mercy was originally built in 1535, making it one of the oldest religious institutions in South America. It was rebuilt after an earthquake destroyed it in 1654, and is still host to the white-robed Order of Mercy priesthood. The impressively designed courtyard and select rooms, all filled with centuries-old religious art (including a 16th century menorah), are open to general public. The wall murals were originally reproductions of Catholic iconography from the order's home in Seville, Spain, and they include what may be considered a very controversial depiction of the Virgin Mary. This is essential touring for those who want to understand Cusco's colonial past. Manta 121 ,Tel: 51-84-231-821.

Iglesia San Blas (Entrance: $5.50 or with BTC)

Iglesia San Blas is just one of the Cusco attractions located in the bustling artisan neighborhood of San Blas. Built in 1563, Iglesia San Blas is thought to be one of the oldest parishes in Cusco. Although unremarkable from the outside, this small, white-washed adobe church houses, one of the most exquisite examples of woodcarving in the world. Carved in a churrigueresque style from a single tree trunk, the famous cedar pulpit features intricately carved images of the Virgin Mary, apostles, cherubs, a sun-disc and bunches of grapes. Perhaps as interesting as the pulpit is the story that accompanies it. According to legend (you'll have to decide for yourself if it's true), the carpenter who created the pulpit's skull was placed inside the masterpiece, at the top beneath St. Paul's feet. While you're looking for the skull (let us know if you find it!) be sure to check out the baroque gold-leaf main altar. Plaza San Blas.

Palacio Arzobispal / Museo de Arte Religioso

For art aficionados and architecture fiends alike, the Museo de Arte Religioso is one of the most interesting spots in the city. Like many other attractions in Cusco, the museum sports a rich cultural history that appears in both the architecture outside and artwork inside.

The museum itself is located inside the Palacio Arzobispal, which sits adjacent to Hatunrumiyoc, a magnificent pedestrian alleyway lined with Inca stone masonry. The name Hatun Rumiyoc means "Street with the Big Stone," which is a reference to the massive 12-sided stone situated perfectly in the center of the wall. Originally the site of Inca Roca palace, the building has also served as the residence of the former Spanish marquis and the Archbishop of Cusco.

Enter photo competitions at www.vivatravelguides.com

CUSCO

Today, this building houses a collection of colonial religious paintings. One room in particular is filled with paintings by Marcos Zapata, an 18th century mestizo artist whose work often mixed indigenous elements with religious themes. In addition to the artwork, you're sure to admire the Moorish-style doors, ornately carved cedar ceilings and spectacular stained-glass windows. For a breath of fresh air, step out into the courtyard, adorned with blue and white tiles from Seville. Monday-Saturday, 8-11:30 a.m., 3-5:30 p.m., Corner of Hatun Rumiyoc and Palacio, Tel: 51-8-422-5211.

Casa Garcilaso / Museo Histórico Regional
Formerly the residence of one of Peru's most famous writers and Inca historians, Garcilaso de la Vega, the Museo Histórico Regional now offers an excellent review of Peruvian history, from pre-Inca civilizations to the Inca and colonial periods. Though the museum is not particularly well labeled, it does have interesting displays of Inca agricultural tools, colonial furniture and paintings, including a mummy with braids 1.5m long and photos of the damage incurred after the 1951 earthquake. In terms of Cusco attractions, this is an excellent place to start, as it provides a thorough archeological overview of the Chavín, Moche, Chimú, and Chancay cultures, in addition to exhibits that trace the evolution of the Cusqueña School of painting. Whether you're an avid historian, or just want to learn more about Peruvian culture, plan to spend a couple of hours exploring the exhibits. Plaza Regocijo (corner of Garcilaso and Heladeros), Tel: 51-84-223-245, Monday-Saturday, 8 a.m.-5 p.m.

Museo de Sitio Qoricancha
Located under the garden below Santo Domingo, the Museo de Sitio Qoricancha consists of three small rooms, which contain a pre-Columbian collection, Spanish paintings from the 18th century and photos of the excavation of Qoricancha. Although it is one of the smaller attractions in Cusco, this museum also has a decent collection of ceramics, metalwork and textile weavings dating back to Inca and pre-Inca civilizations. Avenida El Sol (across from Qoricancha).

Sacsayhuamán (Entrance: $15 or with BTC)
Perched forebodingly in the hillsides rising above Cusco, the fortress of Sacsayhuamán make up some of the most impressive and closest ruins in the area. Few structures now remain inside, but the massive 20-meter-high outer walls that zigzag together like razor-sharp teeth have stood stalwartly against past battles, earthquakes and time.

Emperor Pachacútec began building the hillside citadel in the 1440s, but the massive complex wasn't completed for almost another 100 years. Every Inca citizen was required to spend at least a few months a year building it, which involved dragging the massive stone blocks (one block is estimated to weigh an astounding 300 tons) via a system of log sleds and levers from as far as 32 kilometers away. Legend has it that 3,000 people died while dragging a single stone into place. During Manco Inca's great rebellion, the fortress was the scene of a massacre of an estimated 1,500 Inca soldiers who became trapped inside the three stone towers. Rather than face death at the Spaniards hands, many Incas leapt to their deaths from the high towers. The next morning condors feasted on the pile of corpses; the image was captured forever on Cusco's coat-of-arms.

Even today engineers marvel at the scope and scale of the ruin's stonework, which fits together perfectly without mortar. Like other ruins in the Cusco area, Sacsayhuamán exemplifies the Inca's extraordinary architectural prowess. A huge trapezoidal door leads into the ruins from the walkway. From here you can explore inside the ruins, which once consisted of an intricate network of small streets and buildings overshadowed by three main towers. Today, adjacent to the grassy esplanade in front of the main defensive walls, is Rodadero (Sliding Place), an intricately carved volcanic outcrop where the Inca throne once stood. In ancient times, this area was probably used for ceremonial gatherings. Even today you may be lucky enough to catch one of the many sun ceremonies still held throughout the year. If you can, plan to visit the ruins around the Inti Raymi festival held in June, during the summer solstice. From Sacsayhuamán you can also reach the Inca ruins of Q'enqo, Puca Pucara, and Tambo Machay. 2

kilometers from Cusco, getting there: From the Plaza de Armas, it's a 45-minute steep climb 2 kilometers uphill. Follow Calle Suecia to Calle Huaynapata, to Calle Pumacuro, which winds its way uphill past a small café. From the café it's about a 10-minute walk via signposts. Travel tips: Night tours available 8-10 p.m., but bring a flashlight and some friends.

Q'enqo (Entrance: $10 or with BTC)

The temple and amphitheater ruins of Q'enqo are located east of the giant white statue of Christ, perched on the hill next to Sacsayhuamán, and are only about a 20-minute walk from the famous fortress ruins. The Q'engo ruins derive their name from the Quechua word meaning "zig-zag," a reference to the series of perfectly carved channels adorning the upper western edge of the temple's stone. In ancient times these channels probably flowed with chichi, sacrificial llama blood used by priests during annual fertility festivals and solstice and equinox celebrations. In addition to the channels, Q'enqo sports a series of intricately carved designs, including steps, seats, geometric reliefs, pumas and condors. The hollowed-out limestone outcropping which comprises the main altar emphasizes the importance of the Rock Cult in Inca cosmological beliefs, and similar rock carvings can be found throughout the surrounding foothills. The complex also offers visitors the opportunity to explore a series of caves and tunnels beneath the rock. If you're up for a walk, you can also access the ruins of Puca Pucara and Tambo Machay from here. Near Sacsayhuamán ruins, to get there follow the signs posted on the main road from Sacsayhuamán.

Puca Pucara (Entrance: $7 or with BTC)

Though perhaps the least impressive of the ruins around Cusco, Puca Pucara offers stunning views of the Cusco Valley and glaciers to the south. Located about 11 kilometers outside the city, right beside the main Cusco-Pisac road, the ruins can also be reached via a one to two hour cross-country walk uphill from Sacsayhuamán and Q'enqo. In Quechua its name means Red Fort, and the complex was probably used by Emperor Pachacútec as a *tambo*, or out-of-town lodge. It's likely that the Emperor's court was stationed here when the Emperor came to visit the nearby baths of Tambo Machay. Beneath the complex there are several chambers to explore; the platform on top offers spectacular views. To get there go 11 kilometers from Cusco down the Cusco-Pisac road.

Tambo Machay (Entrance: $10 or with BTC)

Located just a 15-meter walk along a sign-posted path from the main road past Puca Pucara, Tambo Machay ruins are one of the more impressive examples of Inca baths, which can be found at nearly every important Inca temple, including Pisac, Ollantaytambo, and Machu Picchu. Water was worshipped by the Incas as a vital life element, and the painstakingly carved network of aqueducts and canals that comprise these baths are a reminder of their fascination with water. The complex consists of three tiered platforms which ingeniously channel spring water into three impressive waterfalls. All of the waterworks still function today. The quality of stonework indicates that the site was probably restricted to higher nobility, who might have used the baths only on ceremonial occasions. The site also has an impressive Inca wall that rises above the ceremonial niches. Near Puca Pucara.

Pikillacta and Rumicolca (Entrance: $7 or with BTC)

Much of the ancient Inca's organizational expertise and city planning abilities originated from the pre-Inca Huari Empire, which dominated the lands of Peru from 500 to 1000 A.D. An interesting example of Huari engineering is Rumicolca, an ancient aqueduct poised on a valley along the side of the highway, about 32 kilometers (22 miles) from Cusco. After their rise to power, the Incas converted this ancient water channel into a massive gateway to Cusco. Not far from Rumicolca is Pikillacta, the largest provincial outpost ever built by the Ayacucho-based Huari and one of the only pre-Inca sites of importance near Cusco. Were it not included on the Cusco Tourist Ticket, this 47-hectare, adobe-walled compound might go unnoticed; and, it affords visitors a great opportunity to check out pre-Inca architecture. Though little is known about the site's history, we can tell you that the little turquoise figurines displayed in Cusco's Museo Inka, were discovered here.

Gringo Alley

Taxis won't drive up it, and you'll have a hard time finding your hotel if it's on it, but for some reason the tight, narrow cobblestoned street, Calle Procuradores, just off the west side of Plaza de Armas is known among locals as "Gringo Alley." Unless your hostel is down the alley, you're likely to pass by the unassuming entrance, which looks like a barren road. But take a stroll down and you will find a handful of charming hostels, a slew of authentic artisanal shops, several internet cafes and a few great, mouth-watering, mid-range restaurants and bars you won't want to miss. Its tall colonial buildings and narrow streets capture the air of old Europe. Calle Procuradores leads to a maze of small, seemingly endless alleys where you'll find even more shops and hotels. The nickname, Gringo Alley may be a bit deceiving since it's not really all gringos; in fact, it's less gringo than the tourist glitz of Plaza de Armas. So, what makes this quaint sector a gringo zone exactly? Well, it is where gringos have been going in recent years to get away from the hustle of the Plaza de Armas and, of course, it has a steady flow of tourists. Whoever started this trend was on to something--it's close to everything a tourist needs, but feels more like a piece of San Blas.

San Blas

Characterized by steep cobblestone alleys with spectacular views of the city, San Blas is one of the oldest and most picturesque neighborhoods in Cusco. A thriving artistic community lives here—some families have been operating in San Blas for decades—and it is known for producing fine traditional and contemporary artwork. As many streets are pedestrian-only, San Blas is an excellent place to explore on foot. A relaxed stroll through streets lined with studios and workshops is a great way to soak in the artistic atmosphere and do some window-shopping. While you're in the neighborhood, you may want to head over to Iglesia San Blas, home to one of the New World's most famous woodcarvings. As you wander, be sure to look out for your belongings, as tourists aren't the only people scoping out the area; thieves operate here too.

The Stone Puma

North of Cusco's Plaza de Armas towards Cuesta San Blas, you will come upon one of the most haunting tokens of a civilization: the foundation for the one-time palace of 14th century Incan ruler Inca Roca. Throughout Cusco, the Spanish attempted to establish their hegemony by demolishing a century's worth of physically impressive architecture from the Incan and pre-Incan civilization. But there couldn't quite destroy it all. The stone blocks were too large, too heavy and, above all, too tightly fit. The wall on Calle Hatun Rumiyoc is particularly fascinating; locals will approach you and point out how the Incas were able to so tightly fit irregular blocks of stone, is a mystery yet to be solved by archaeologists and architects. The stones have the distinct outline of a puma, an animal considered sacred in Inca religion. The original city of Cusco itself is also supposed to resemble this animal. At the wall, the animal is seen in a crouching position. The smaller stones at the base of the wall serve as a reminder of Incan ingenuity, in that they functioned as shock absorbers for the wall itself, which accounts for how it endured though all the earthquakes in the region's history.

Tipón (Entrance: $7 or with BTC)

Located 23 kilometers southeast of Cusco, these ruins are not particularly popular among travelers who want to visit some of the bigger-name ruins around the Sacred Valley area. Despite its position off the beaten tourist trail, this extensive temple complex is one of the best examples of Inca stonemasonry, and some might say it is equal to the more celebrated ruins of Pisac, Ollantaytambo, and Chinchero. The temple includes well-preserved agricultural terraces, baths, irrigation canals and aqueducts that emphasize the Inca's skillful building technique. The ruins can be reached via a steep one-hour climb up a lovely path, or up a dirt road by car. If you're feeling especially agile, you can check out the ruins located about a 2-hour climb above Tipón. Note: It's virtually impossible to visit the ruins during the rainy season. 23 kilometers (14 miles) southeast of Cusco.

Qoricancha Templo del Sol and Santo Domingo

Of the numerous attractions in Cusco, this should be on the top of your list. Once home to nearly 4,000 of the Empire's highest ranking priests and their attendants, Qoricancha was an extraordinary display of Inca masonry and wealth. Dedicated to the worship of the sun, the Temple of the Sun was the main astronomical observatory for the Incas. The complex also included smaller temples and shrines dedicated to the worship of less important deities of the moon, Venus, thunder, lightning and rainbows. In Quechua its name means Golden Courtyard, which is an appropriate title for a temple once adorned with gold panels, life-size gold figures, solid gold altars and a gigantic golden sun disc all intended to reflect sunlight and drench the entire temple in golden light. During the summer, light enters a strategically placed niche, where only the Inca Chieftan was allowed to sit.

When the Spanish ransacked the city during their conquests, this glorious shrine to the sun was stripped of its golden accoutrements and most of its aesthetic glory. The Temple of the Sun was awarded to Juan Pizarro, younger brother of Francisco, who willed it to the Dominicans after he was wounded during the siege of Sacsayhuamán. Eventually the temple's carefully constructed stones were used as the foundation for the Convent of Santo Domingo, a baroque church built in the 17th century.

Today the site of Qoricancha and Santo Domingo is a magnificent testament to the cultural collision that occurred when the Spanish descended on the Inca Empire. Recent excavations have uncovered five chambers once belonging to the temple, in addition to some of the best stonework visible in Cusco. The 6-meter curved wall beneath the west end of the church, which has withstood repeated earthquakes, is perhaps the best example of Inca masonry this site offers. Excavations below this wall have uncovered a garden of gold and silver animals, as well as maize and other plants. Another remarkable stretch of Inca masonry extends from Calle Ahuacpinta, located outside the temple to the east of the entrance. Though not as spectacular as either Qoricancha or Santo Domingo, the nearby Museo de Sitio Qoricancha offers visitors a chance to further investigate and explore the development of Inca and Spanish cultures in the area. Plazoleta Santo Domingo, Tel: 51-84-222-071.

Museo de Arte y Monasterio de Santa Catalina (Entrance: $3, no longer included on BTC & closed for renovation at time of writing)

Built by the Spanish between 1601 and 1610 on top of Acllahuasi, where the Inca emperor once housed his chosen Virgins of the Sun, this convent and museum houses an interesting collection of colonial and religious art. Like other attractions in Cusco, the museum has a number of pieces from the Cusqueña School, an art movement emphasizing the union of both Inca and Spanish culture. In addition to baroque frescoes depicting Inca vegetation, the chapel also houses macabre statues of Jesus, beautifully painted arches and 17th century tapestries. Perhaps the highlight of this site is a series of 3-D figurines which recount the life of Christ. Objects such as this were popular devices used by the Catholic Church's "traveling salesmen," who were responsible for converting many of the indigenous people throughout Peru. Santa Catalina Angosta, Tel: 51-84-226-032.

Museo Inka

For spectacular views of Inca artifacts head over to Museo Inka. This recently renovated colonial home, run by the Universidad San Antonio de Abad, is located down an alley to the left of the Cusco Cathedral. Focused on the development of pre-Inca and Inca culture, the museum contains an intriguing collection of jewelry, ceramics, textiles, mummies, trepanned skulls, and a number of metal and gold pieces. Explanations are in English. Be sure to check out the stunning collection of miniature turquoise figures, among other examples of offerings to the gods. You may also have a chance to partake in the weaving demonstrations that take place in the courtyard. Among the attractions in Cusco, this museum is famous for housing the world's largest collection of wooden *queros*, which the Incas once used for drinking. Allow 1 ½ to 2 hours to see the whole collection. Cuesta del Almirante 103, Tel: 51-84-237-380.

Activities
Salapunco (Entrance: free)
Salapunco is a group of small caves that housed the mummies of Inca priests and other Inca elite. Inside the caves, the walls and altars are decorated with pumas, snakes and other important cultural symbols. This hauca is dedicated to worshipping the moon, and the position of the entrance allows the interior to be lit up once a month by the light of the moon. Km. 5, Highway to Pisac.

Body Shop Spa Cusco
Body Shop Spa Cusco is a modern relaxation center where you can relieve your fatigue and reenergize after visiting the tourist attractions. It offers massages, sauna, Jacuzzi, skin cleansing and foot therapy by reflexology. Calle Procuradores # 50, Tel: 51-84-236-647, URL: http://www.perucuzco.com/hotel_alquiler/sauna_real_state.htm.

Yin Yang Massage
Yin Yang Massage offers deep tissue massage, reiki, shiatsu or reflexology to help reduce stress, altitude sickness, sore muscles, twisted neck or backache. Music and Aromatherapy is included in the massages. Yin Yang has a staff of ten professional massage therapists on hand to take care of you. Portal Comercio 121 (upstairs), Tel: 51-84-258-201, E-mail: info@ yinyangtherapeuticmassage.com, URL: www.yinyangtherapeuticmassage.com.

Shopping
Artesanías Pachacútec (Sweaters: $25 - 75)
With the large number of vendors all claiming to sell 100 percent alpaca, it's often difficult to determine which sweaters are real and which are synthetic. But Artesanías Pachacútec sells the real deal and, better yet, the merchandise is affordable too. The super-soft alpaca sweaters come in a rainbow of colors, so you have your choice. With three locations spread about in Cusco, the sales staff are accustomed to working with tourists and are very accommodating and will want to help you find the right color and fit. Other items sold here include ponchos, hats, bags, ceramics and silver jewelry; but by far, sweaters are their thing. Triunfo N 388; Portal Nuevo N 270; Taller: Avenida Libertad F-B-3 Zarzuela, Santiago, Tel: 51-84-243-093 (Triunfo); 244-152 (Triunfo) / 237-708 (Taller), E-mail: pacha51@mixmail.com.

Mercado El Molino
Mercado Mollina is a shopper's dream. Forget Machu Picchu logo t-shirts, watercolor paintings and llama postcards. You won't find a single souvenir or craftsy trinket in any of the mercado's several hundred stalls. Instead, you'll find nearly anything you may ever want to use. Underwear, socks, jeans, shoes, sandals, belts, electronics, shirts, winter coats, plates, appliances, make up, toiletries...and of course, heaps and heaps of obscenely underpriced DVDs and CDs. Sprawled over the space of several city blocks and including temptations for all consumers, Mollina is the kind of shopping experience that dares to suggest that if you can't buy it at Mollina, then it can't be bought. Collectivos run from Choquechaca ($0.25) and taxis from the city center cost less than $1.

Tesoros del Ande
One of the more chic-looking shops in the Portal Comercio facing the Plaza de Armas, Tesoros del Ande offers high-quality, hand-made silver jewelry. They also sell fancy alpaca scarves, wool caps, shirts and skirts, not to mention hand-made leather handcrafts. There is a choice selection of ceramic and clay pottery and sculpture with many Incan and pre-Incan motifs. They take credit cards. Use one of yours here, because one would be wise not to carry the cash needed to pay for such items. They also sell maps, books, and other tour guide information. Portal Comercio 125, Tel: 51-84-234-231.

Seminario Ceramics
The artist Pablo Seminario is a local legend amongst cusqueños. He virtually invented a new form of ceramic artwork that integrates abstract modern styles with traditional Incan and

pre-Incan motifs. The story most commonly told was that years ago Pablo Seminario toiled at his craft with such dedication that he was near the point of utter destitution, as he had a family to care for. Then a visiting journalist took notice of his work. The rest is history, including the frequent imitation of his style by Cusco copycats. Why buy imitations? Seminario Ceramics on the Plaza de Armas sells original pottery and art overseen by the artist himself. Portal de Carnes N 224, Tel: 51-84-246-093, E-mail: kupa@terra.com.pe, URL: www.ceramicaseminario.com.

La Cholita

Why this little chocolate manufacturer, after 50 years, has not attained the global clout commensurate with such continental competitors as Toblerone may be one of the biggest mysteries of Cusco yet. Indeed, you can only get La Cholita chocolate in Cusco, so make the most of it while you are in this area. Handmade from the purest cocoa grown in the Sacred Valley, all-organic ingredients...well, just sample the coca-cocoa combination, or any other creative variations mixing chocolate with a variety of indigenous roots, herbs, fruits and spices. Yes, chocolate does go with everything. And this is not even to speak of their incredible diversity of shapes and sizes. Real chocolate addiction begins here. Portal Espinar 142-B, Tel: 51-84-225-181, E-mail: gbarbarberis@yahoo.com.mx.

STUDYING SPANISH IN CUSCO

If you want to take part of your vacation to learn Spanish, or if, upon arriving in Cusco, you realize your Spanish skills are less sharp then you thought, there are a great number of language schools within Cusco to choose from. Classes vary in level and length, with both group settings and private instruction widely available. Many schools offer social and volunteer opportunities, if you want them, and most can set up homestays as well. There are a lot of options, but with a little research you are sure to find a program that's right for you.

Mundo Verde Spanish School

This non-profit school is located four blocks from the Plaza de Armas in Cusco. The school assists a conservation project in the rainforest and the Health Fund for the Needy and runs a school in Urubamba. The Standard Spanish Course includes 20 hours of lessons, 4 hours per day. Groups rates are $110: for individuals, $150. The Intensive Spanish Course includes 30 hours of lessons, 6 hours per day. Groups cost $150 and individuals, $225. The Total Immersion Spanish Course includes 40 hours of lessons, 8 hours per day, lunch with the teacher, daily visits to local spots and transportation expenses. For groups, the cost is $300 and for individuals, the cost is $400. Family stays can be arranged for $100 per week, and additional activities such as cooking classes, tai chi, salsa classes, workshops and city tours are offered. Calle Nueva Alta 432-A, Tel: 51-84-221-287, E-mail: pabmirj@hotmail.com, URL: www.mundoverdespanish.com.

Excel Spanish Language Center (Lessons: $5 - 7)

All programs at the Excel Spanish Language Center include optional activities, in addition to the curriculum that are included in the tuition. The frequency and availability of activities depends on the time of year (and the season). Examples include day hikes, tours of historical ruins and religious sites, cultural and historical lectures and dance lessons. Prices are based on 20 hours per week: individual lessons are $7 per hour; group lessons are $5 per hour (2-5 people); the homestay option is $120 for 7 days/nights and includes 3 meals a day. Calle Cruz Verde 336, Tel: 51-84-235-298, E-mail: info@excelinspanish.com, URL: www.excel-spanishlanguageprograms-peru.org.

Cervantes Spanish School

The Spanish language study program at the Cervantes Spanish School includes salsa classes, cooking classes and walking city tours. Volunteer work can also be arranged. Individual lessons are $120 per week; group lessons, with a maximum of 4 people, are $90 per week. Both options include 20 hours of classes. Urb. Fideranda, Calle Camino Real 10, Wanchaq, Tel: 51-84-507-051, E-mail: cervantesschool@yahoo.es.

CUSCO

South American Spanish School

South American Spanish School in Cusco has some uniquely blended programs. One is Spanish mixed with Inca culture and the other is Spanish mixed with modern Peruvian culture. Half of the day is spent learning Spanish and the other half is spent learning about the other topic. They can also set up students with volunteer activities. Carmen Alto Street 112, San Blas, Tel: 51-84-223-012, E-mail: info@sasschool.org, URL: www.sasschool.org, URL: www.sassschool.org.

Cusco Spanish School

Cusco Spanish School is a small, personal, and flexible Spanish language school with more than 8 years of experience. It is made up of professional Peruvians with a broad knowledge of the teaching of Spanish as a foreign language and certain expertises, such as history, literature, economics, and sociology. The professionals of Cusco Spanish School teach Spanish, in an easygoing entertaining manner, without the stress typical of a conventional school, which allows students to develop their abilities and improve at their own pace. It also offers several volunteer opportunities that give students a chance to practice Spanish while helping out in the Cusco community. They also offer lessons in Urubamba, the heart of the Sacred Valley of the Incas, surrounded by beautiful country side, mountains and tiny villages. Cusco Spanish School teaches Spanish and Quechua. Urbanización Constancia A-11-2 Apartment 103, Fourth Floor, Tel: 51-84-226-928, E-mail: info@cuscospanishschool.com, URL: www.cuscospanishschool.com.

Spanish in Peru

Learn Spanish in three of the Inca empire's most enigmatic strongholds: the archeological capital Cusco, Urubamba in the Sacred Valley of the Incas, and the rainforest of Manu. The Cusco branch of the Spanish in Peru language school is located near the Plaza de Armas. You can choose to stay with a host family, or to volunteer with local projects. Suecia 480, Tel: 51-84-262-345, Fax: 51-84-241-422, E-mail: informatica4@spanishin-peru.com, URL: www.spanishinperu.com.

Amigos Spanish School

Amigos Spanish School is a non-profit language school. With every four hours of classes you pay for one child's education and food at The Amigos Foundation, to help child workers have a more promising future. Individual lessons are offered at $8 per hour. Group lessons (4-person maximum) are $108 for 20 hours per week, and can be combined with a homestay for $215. The homestay includes private bedroom, laundry, all meals and airport pick-up. Additional activities include salsa, meringue, traditional Andean dancing classes, cooking classes and city tour. Zaguan del Cielo B-23, Tel: 51-84-242-292, E-mail: amigo@spanishcusco.com, URL: www.spanishcusco.com.

Academia Latinoamericana de Español

The key to learning and understanding a language lies in your experience and the degree to which you are able to delve into the culture. At Academia Latinoamericana de Español, you will find yourself swiftly learning Spanish amidst the warm Peruvians and rich history that defines Peru. Regardless of your level of proficiency, students will find a program that suits their needs, goals and learning styles. Classes are 60 minutes in length for four hours per day. The maximum number of students per class is four. Students learn using the four language skills: listening, grammar, oral and written comprehension. Students homestay with native, middle-class families who live no further than a ten-minute bus ride from the school. The homestay is a great opportunity to learn about Peruvian customs and way of life. Programs range from $275-$470 per week, depending on the course that is chosen. Additionally, there are volunteer programs, activities and other arrangements that can be made to enhance the students' stay. Plaza Limacpampa 565, Tel: 51-84-243-364, E-mail: info@latinoschools.com, URL: www.latinoschools.com.

Acupari Language School

Acupari Language School offers lessons in not only Spanish, but also Quechua. Lesson packages include conversational practice, salsa lessons, cooking lessons and excursions. Individual Spanish lessons for one week are $140, and small group lessons (two to five persons) for one week is $100. Both options include 20 hours of lessons. Additional Spanish lessons can be arranged for $6 per hour. Quechua lessons for those with existing Spanish skills can also be arranged for an additional cost of $7.50 per hour. Homestays can be arranged for $12 per day, and include breakfast and either lunch or dinner. San Augustín 307, Tel: 51-84-242-970, E-mail: acupari@terra.com.pe, URL: www.acupari.com.

FairPlay Spanish School

FairPlay is an NGO based out of Cusco that employs single Peruvian mothers to train and empower them to support themselves as capable Spanish teachers. You pay your teachers directly so they earn a fair income. All teachers have successfully finished an intense seven-month training course. The school also uses a unique learning method that combines grammar and real-world practice. Only private lessons are offered: 20 hours per week costs $120 and 30 hours per week costs $190. The price includes the grammer and practice books, as well as a set of flashcards for beginners. FairPlay also offers homestays with Peruvian middle class families. One week costs $72 for a private room with a shared bathroom and three meals a day. $82 will get you a room with a private bathroom and three meals a day. Individuals pay $15 a week to FairPlay and the rest to the family. Choquechaca 188, Tel: 51-84-978-9252, E-mail: support.fairplay@gmail.com, URL: www.fairplay-peru.org.

Machu Picchu Spanish School

Machu Picchu Spanish School has several activities to get students involved in the community and within the school. Each Monday there is a welcome dinner for that week's new stu-

CUSCO

dents. Additionally, there are dancing and cooking classes available for interested students. Most of the activities are included in the course fees, but other more elaborate activities can be planned with extra costs. All of the teachers at Machu Picchu Spanish School are native speakers and are university graduates in either languages or literature. Calle Arequipa 251, Pasaje Q'aphchik'ijllu, Tel: 51-84-257-635, E-mail: www.machupicchuschool.org/contactus, URL: www.machupicchuschool.org.

Cusco Mania Spanish School
Cusco Mania Spanish has several long-term packages ranging from a few weeks to six months. All teachers are fully qualified. The school also has several other extensive programs such as cooking, dancing and volunteering in and around Cusco. Cusco Mania is not a school focused on intensive language programs like many of the others. But if you want to settle down in Cusco and do a variety of things besides Spanish school, it's a great option. Urb los Portales B-7, Tel: 51 984 966 694, E-mail: info@cuscomania.com, URL: www.cuscomania.com.

Proyecto Peru Language Centre
Proyecto Peru Language Centre offers a wide-range of free activities, such as Peruvian cooking classes, a quiz night, Spanish movie night, dance classes and free internet. It also has several different language school options. Traditional, 20-hour-a-week programs are the most popular, but there are also half-courses, and special purpose courses to teach people vocabulary for health care, business or technical fields. Proyecto Peru Language Centre also has a special program for children between the ages of 5 and 12. Calle Tecsecocha 429, Tel: 51-84-984 683016 / 984 954184, E-mail: info@proyectoperucentre.org, URL: www.proyectoperucentre.org.

Lingua Cusco
Lingua Cusco Spanish School is also part of the Asociacíon Pukllasunchis which works with the Cusco community to provide aid to under-privileged children. The project is well-regarded throughout Peru, and students can participate in the program. One-on-one lessons cost $9 per hour; two or three-person groups are $5 per hour, per person; and four or five-person groups are $4 per hour, per person. The homestay options are more flexible than those at many schools, as students can choose the number of meals they want each day. Siete Diablitos 222, San Blas, Fax: 51-84-237-918.

Inticahuarina Spanish School
Inticahuarina Spanish School is a school that offers a full range of language school options. More importantly, Inticahuarina can arrange volunteer opportunities in and around Cusco. This gives students a chance to give a little back to the community they are studying in while also getting out and practicing their Spanish. Inticahuarina Spanish School also arranges (and recommends) homestays for students. Zarumilla Bloque 5-A 103-105, Tel: 51-84-251481 /978-1844, E-mail: info@inticahuarinaspanishschool.com, URL: www.inticahuarinaspanishschool.com.

San Blas Spanish School
If brushing up on your Spanish skills is a priority in Cusco, San Blas Spanish School is one of the most visible tutoring outfits in town. It's located in the center of a cluster of popular cafés just above Plazoleta San Blas, and if the school's conspicuous sign doesn't catch your attention, the ever-present crowd of students lingering outside will. Full-immersion classes are offered in one-week blocks to students of all abilities, in four-hour morning or afternoon sessions. Placement exams are given to students with Spanish experience, and group, as well as individual lessons, are offered. At the conclusion of each week's sessions, classes close with a field trip and a Friday night social gathering (usually salsa dancing or pisco sour making lessons) which offers students from all classes a chance to socialize together. Family stay opportunities are also available, as are sessions at a second campus in the small village of Cai Cay about an hour from Cusco. Tandapata 688, Plazoleta San Blas, Tel: 51-84-247-898, E-mail: info@spanishschoolperu.com, URL: www.spanishschoolperu.com.

Amauta Spanish School

Amauta Spanish School offers the unique opportunity to study Spanish while immersed in Peruvian culture. Other activities make Amauta Spanish School a distinct educational destination in Cusco, former capital of the legendary Inca Empire, including Quechua language courses, workshops on Latin American and Peruvian Culture, and free daily student activities, such as lectures, Latin American cinema and salsa dance classes. Amauta Spanish School offers different accommodation options and, for every one interested, great volunteer work opportunities. It also has schools in the Sacred Valley and the Peruvian rainforest. Placement tests are given to all students, and university credit is available. Lessons start from $106 per week. Suecia 480, Tel: 51-84-241-422, E-mail: info@amautaspanish.com, URL: www.amautaspanish.com.

Wiracocha Spanish School

If you're interested in brushing up your Spanish skills while in Peru, then you should check out Wiracocha Spanish School. Offering a fun, friendly and professional environment, the school has a variety of beginner, intermediate and advanced programs. With so many options to choose from, the programs are almost as diverse as the Peruvian culture itself. Depending on your needs and how much time you have, you can choose from part-time, intensive, super intensive, immersion and individual courses. A number of special courses combine learning Spanish with another facet of Peruvian culture. You can study Spanish while volunteering or learning about Latin American Culture. Preparation courses for the DELE exams and other advanced Spanish certifications are also available. Besides Spanish classes, you can enjoy free salsa and Latin American dance classes, archaeological visits to town with your teacher, cooking classes and walks around town. For a truly enriching experience, you can choose to live with a local family. All teachers have university degrees and a genuine passion for teaching Spanish. Lessons range from $50 to $350 per week or $6 per hour. Calle Inka Roca 110, Tel: 51-84-967-0918, URL: www.wiracochaschool.org.

VOLUNTEERING IN CUSCO

South American Explorers

Internships in PR, travel research/writing, member services and volunteering resources are available year round at SAE Cusco. Positions run for a minimum of 12 weeks and are unpaid, though volunteers are provided with lunch as well as Spanish and yoga classes. Subsidized housing is also occasionally available. Choquechaca 188, Apt. 4 (2 Blocks from the Plaza de Armas); PO Box Apartado 500 Tel: 00-51-84-245484, E-mail: cuscoclub@saexplorers.org, URL: http://www.saexplorers.org.

Amauta Spanish School Volunteer Program

Amauta Spanish School runs a combined program to learn Spanish and volunteer in Cusco. Eight weeks is the minimum commitment. Volunteers are placed on social service projects in: hospitals, orphanages, schools, centers for street children among others. The standard price of the program, including language instruction, a small volunteer fee, and accommodation, is $1,379 (up to $2,200 if you choose a different option). Suecia 480, Tel: 00-51-8-426-2345, Fax: 00-51-8-424-1422, E-mail: info@amautaspanish.com, URL: http://www.amautaspanishschool.org/amautaspanish/english/volunteer.asp.

Global Crossroad

Global Crossroad offers social service volunteer projects and internships in health and education at local hospitals, schools, and orphanages. Opportunities to work on conservation projects in re-forestation and on indigenous rights campaigns in local communities are also available. Programs run from around $1,400-$1,600 for four weeks ($2,074-$2,174 for eight) and include food, accommodation, insurance and project placement. 11822 Justice Avenue Suite A-5 Baton Rouge, LA, USA Zip: 70816, Tel: 001-800-413-2008 (USA);0-800-310-1821 (UK), E-mail: info@globalcrossroad.com, ukinfo@globalcrossroad.com.

Volunteer Visions

Volunteer Visions places volunteers on health projects in understaffed medical clinics on the outskirts of Cusco. Projects run from two to 12 weeks. Food and accommodation is included. Volunteers in Cusco are expected to work 8:30 am. to 1 pm., Monday to Friday. Basic Spanish skills are recommended. The Program costs: $650/2 weeks, $1050/6 weeks, $1,340/8 weeks, $1,800/12 weeks. Tel: 001-330-871-4511, E-mail: info@volunteervisions.org, URL: http://volunteervisions.org.

United Planet

United Planet runs unique programs working in orphanages, state hospitals, mental institutions and in rural villages. All volunteers live with host families. The program fee includes insurance, accommodation, food, a trip to Machu Picchu for 2 days with a guide, as well as 4 hours of Spanish instruction per week. There is a minimum of one week at $1,395 and the cost is $200 per week thereafter for up to twelve weeks. There areDiscounts for families of three or more. 11 Arlington Street, Boston, MA, USA Zip: 02116 Tel: 001-800-292-2316 or 001-617-267-7763, Fax: 001-617-267-7764, E-mail: quest@unitedplanet.org, URL: www.unitedplanet.org.

Institute for Field Research Expeditions (IFRE)

Work as a volunteer in education (teaching English as a volunteer), health, conservation and development projects part-time, 20 hours a week, in Cusco, Peru. There is an application fee of $349. Placements can run for as little as 4 days or as long as twelve weeks. Program fee includes a donation to the project, insurance, room and board plus two hours of Spanish instruction per week. 8500 N Stemmons Frwy #4015 F, Dallas, Texas, USA Zip: 75247, Tel: 001-800-675-2504, (USA); 0-800-310-1437 (UK), Fax: 001-214-295-8585, E-mail: info@ifrevolunteers.org, URL: http://www.ifrevolunteers.org.

Q'ewar Project

Among the volunteer opportunities in Cusco is the Q'ewar Project, a non-profit that employs indigenous women to make high-quality, hand-made dolls for export to markets in Europe and North America. Attempting to redress issues of ethnocentrism, sexism and ignorance, the project pays a fair wage to women. Their dolls, made from alpaca and sheep wool, use ancient techniques for dying, incorporating indigenous foliage and even insects. Volunteers are needed for their social development and day care programs and knowledge of Spanish is a must. At the local chapter of the South American Explorers Club, former volunteers have written very favorably of their time with the Q'ewar Project. E-mail: juhebu@hotmail.com, URL: www.qewar.com.

Aldea Yanapay Project

The Aldea Yanapay website states "another way of living." For many of the children cared for by Aldea Yanapay, that means undoing the effects of abuse promulgated at home and even in schools, where a very casually applied corporal punishment has taught violence more than it has

reading or math. Aldea Yanapay, an alternative school for children from the age of six to 14, is founded on the principles of love and acceptance. Aldea Yanapay is open to volunteers who want to help children with educational and development needs, as well as teaching English, or anything else related to the well-being of children. Volunteers are compensated with lodging and food, and of course, the smiles of children regaining their self-confidence. Avenida Alta 466, Tel: 51-84-245-779, E-mail: subeli@hotmail.com, URL: www.aldeayanapay.org.

Fundación Selva Inka

A relatively new project based in Pilcopata in the cultural zone of Manu National Park, Fundación Selva Inka was set up by a local family from the area to promote sustainable tourism and provide employment for local people. Volunteer projects in the local school run year-round and include accommodation and meals in the no-frills but comfortable lodge. Special projects run from December to March during the school holidays in which volunteers help run workshops and activities for the children. Urb. Marcavalle C-25, Huanchaq, Tel: 084-231-625, 084-984-756-207, E-mail: info@selvainka.com, URL: http://www.selvainka.com.

Inca Educa

A well-established educational center in Cusco, Inca Educa offers low-priced vocational courses to underprivileged young people, giving them the opportunity to support themselves and to contribute to society in a positive way. They also sell many of the hand-made products from their workshops in Cusco and online. Volunteers are always needed to teach English and sometimes to help out with the administration and promotion of the organization. Av. Cusco 563, San Sebastian, Cusco, Tel: 51-84-275994E-mail: inca-educa@speedy.com.pe, URL: http://www.inca-educa.org.

CUSCO TOURS

Tours in Cusco vary from trips to local archaeological ruins to multi-day visits at sites outside the city. It is very possible to plan your trip from your home country; that can be a smart choice if you have limited time in Peru and want to see and do specific things. You can find also find a plethora of Peruvian tour operators just by taking a brief walk through the streets of Cusco. Chances are, upon landing in the small airport in Cusco, you'll be bombarded by solicitous tour operators. Most of them offer similar services, but here's one bit of advice: when planning a visit to the Inca Trail tour, pick carefully, as some provide better tours than others.

Turismo Inkaiko

Turismo Inkaiko is a well-established tour operator that offers trips to Cusco, Puno, Nasca, Paracas, Iquitos and Puerto Maldonado. The agency has a friendly and helpful staff who can offer an array of advice on expeditions as well as cultural and conventional trips throughout Peru. The agency is also partnered with hotels in a number of cities. Av. Jose Pardo 610, Of. 4 - Miraflores - Lima 18-Peru, Tel: 511 446-7500 / 446-4247 / 495-1283, Fax: 511 445-2532, E-mail: postmaster@turismoinkaiko.net, URL: www.turismoinkaiko.net.

Peru Treks and Adventure Tour Operator

Based in Cusco, Peru Treks and Adventure is a licensed tour operator offering a variety of packages for different budgets. The company can not only take you on the classic, four-day Inca Trail trek to Machu Picchu, but also on one-day tours of Cusco or the Sacred Valley; or white rafting and mountain biking excursions. All packages are offered on a group or private basis. Peru Treks and Adventures prides itself on being an agency that practices socially and environmentally responsible tourism. It pays particular attention to the wages and work conditions of its cooks, porters and other staff, yet provides competitive prices and quality service. This company also supports a number of education projects in small villages. In 2006 Peru Treks and Adventures was awarded Best Cusco Travel Agency by the Ministry of Tourism. Calle Garcilaso 265, Office 11, 2nd Floor, Tel: 51-84-505-863, Fax: 51-84-221-032, E-mail: info@perutreks.com, URL: www.perutreks.com.

SAS Travel

SAS Travel is owned and operated by an Australian-Peruvian couple, and provides professional tours of Machu Picchu, Manu National Park and Puerto Maldonado. The company also offers many adventure daytrips in the Sacred Valley, including river rafting, horseback riding, mountain biking and rock climbing. SAS can arrange trips to the Floating Islands in Puno, to the Nasca Lines and to Colca Canyon in Arequipa. A reputable agency, SAS is very busy and can occasionally overbook; however, sometimes they add on extra tours if need be. Portal De Panes 167, Plaza de Armas, Tel: 51-84-237-292, E-mail: info@sastravelperu.com.pe, URL: www.sastravelperu.com.

United Mice

A company specializing in guided tours of the Inca Trail, United Mice offers reasonable prices, good food, quality camping equipment and English-speaking guides. Due to their popularity, however, their tours during the high season are often large. Calle Plateros 351, Tel: 51-84-221-139 E-mail: reservations@unitedmice.com, URL: http://www.unitedmice.com.

Trekperu

Trekperu has been one of Peru's leading tour agencies since 1986. Their mission is to create the perfect trip that doesn't negatively impact the environment or adversely affect local communities. They offer custom trips featuring horseback riding, city tours, visits to archaeological ruins, climbing, cultural tours, and adventure trips. Tours are available in Spanish, English, German, and French. Av. Republica de Chile B-15 , Tel: 51-84-261501, Fax: 51-84-238591, E-mail: info@trekperu.com, URL: www.trekperu.com.

ATV-Adventures/ Quad Bike Tours

ATV Adventures is fairly new to the tourist circuit in Cusco. While the rookie company started in 2002, the company has no shortage of offerings. ATV arranges hiking, trekking mountain biking, rafting, ATV tours and trips to the jungle. There are 11 and 15 day multi-city tours which are also available. Plateros 324, Tel: 51-8-425-2762, E-mail: resevas@atv-adventureperu.com, URL: www.atv-adventureperu.com.

Andean Enjoy Perú

Andean Enjoy Peru travel agency is based in Cusco, and specializes in ecotourism, trekking, jungle and traditional tours and adventure sports. The company offers tours to places such as the Inca Trail, Choquequirao, Salkantay, Reserve Manu and Reserve Tambopata. Calle Tandapata 1028, Tel: 051 084 237214, Fax: 051 084 237214, E-mail: andeanenjoyperu@gmail.com, URL: http://www.andeanenjoyperu.com.

Trek in the Chicón Valley

Haku Trek is a new development in the Chicón valley and is a collaborative project between NGO ProPeru and the local community. The traditional village of Chicón is situated deep in the Chaquihuayjo valley, just outside Urubamba in the Sacred Valley of the Incas. All hikes are led by Chicón natives, ensuring that tourists have the opportunity to learn about nativeculture and language as we are learning about the regional wildlife. The Chicón eco-tourism project aims to educate tourists about the natural environment while providing an alternative form of employment and income for the inhabitants of Chicón. The funds generated from the project are used toward the reforestation of the Chicón Valley and queuñal forest. As such, every trek contributes to the conservation of endangered plant and animal species in the area. Tel: 51-84-961-3001, E-mail: hakutrek@hotmail.com, URL: www.hakutrek.com.

Mayuc

Mayuc is a reliable company with plenty of experience organizing a variety of custom tours. Trips range from an extended Inca Trail trek to visiting areas in and around Cusco and Peru. The company specializes in white-water rafting, offering a standard four-day/three-night package which includes 2, 3, 4, and 5-grade rapids. Portal Confiturias 211, Tel: 51-84-242-

824 / 1-866-777-9213 (US and Canada), Fax: 51-84-232-666, E-mail: info@mayuc.com, chando@mayuc.com, URL: www.mayuc.com.

Manu Nature Tours

Manu Nature Tours provides nature-based adventure tours, with a focus on the jungle. Longer tours, including mountain biking, birdwatching and rafting, are also available. Avenida Sol 582, E-mail: postmaster@mnt.com.pe

APU Expediciones

APU Expediciones offers cultural, adventure, educational/academic programs, nature tours and jungle packages to Manu and Tambopata. Guides are bilingual and extremely knowledgeable. Tel: 51-84-271-215 / 995-7483, E-mail: apuexped@yahoo.co.uk, watay71@yahoo.com, becimar@ yahoo.com, URL: www.geocities.com/apuexpeditions.

Explorandes

At the Cusco office of Explorandes you can only book Inca Trail tours, but on the company's website you can arrange a variety of trekking, rafting and cultural tours in Cusco and throughout Peru. Trips include visits to Ausangate, Salcantay, Colca Canyon, Cordillera Blanca and Huayhuash. The company can also arrange special tours if you are interested in orchids, ceramics or textiles. Avenida Garcilaso 316-A, Tel: 51-84-244-308, Fax: 51-84-233-784, E-mail: postmaster@explorandes.com, URL: www.explorandes.com.

Cóndor

Condor Travel can plug guests into a pre-arranged tour or create a custom-made tour from scratch, depending on your needs. The company has a great deal of experience with archeological tours, particularly if you want to learn more about the Inca Empire or any other of Peru's pre-Columbian civilizations. Condor Tours also plan a wide range of hiking and trekking excursions. Calle Saphi 848-A, E-mail: info@condortravel.com, URL: www.condortravel.com.pe

Inka Express

If you're bored of just taking the regular bus, one option is to upgrade to the Inka Express, which provides both transportation between Cusco and Puno as well as touring opportunities. The buses are very comfortable and free tea, coffee and mineral water for the entire trip is included in the price. The trip makes five stops, all-in-all, a 10-hour-journey, a whopping 4 hours longer than the normal bus. Note that costs are also much higher, and often your ticket does not include entrance fees to the sites, however this is a great option if you have the money and you have kids on board. While younger kids may not be too thrilled about the historical sites, they will appreciate getting off the bus and having a change of scenery every hour or so. Cusco office: Urb. El Ovalo Av. La Paz C-32, Puno office: Jiron Tacna 346, Lima office: Av. Cantuarias 140 Oficina 2 1 5, Miraflores E-mail: reservas@inkaexpress.com.pe, URL: www.inkaexpress.com.

CUSCO

A-31 Kennedy "A" Wanchaq CUSCO - PERU
Telefax: (51-84) 247489 | Mobile: 9696169 /E-Mail: info@amazonandesperu.com

Enter photo competitions at www.vivatravelguides.com

Apus Peru Adventure Travel Specialists
Apus Peru Adventure Travel Specialists is a small, Australian-Peruvian company that focuses on alternative and sustainable tourism. The company has 15 years of tourism experience, and offers private or group tours to a range of spectacular destinations around Cusco and Peru, with affordable prices and focus on understanding Peruvian culture. 366 Cuichipunco, Tel: 51 84 938 3049 E-mail: apusperu@westnet.com.au, URL: www.apus-peru.com.

Inka Legacy Tours
Inka Legacy Tours, based in Cusco, offers guided treks to Machu Picchu, Choquequirao, Ausangate and Lares. The company provides quality, small-group, classic and adventure excursions. Urbanización San Isidro F-7, Tel: 51-084-227-958, Fax: 51-084-227-958, E-mail: info@inkalegacytours.com, URL: www.inkalegacytours.com.

Peru Adventure Tours
Peru Adventure Tours features a variety of private excursions: cycling, trekking, climbing, horseback riding, leisurely jungle tours, 4x4 tours, trips along the Inca Trail to Machu Picchu and many more. Cusco: Triunfo Street s/n Down Town, Zip: 054, Tel: 005-105-422-1658,Fax: 005-105-422-1658, E-mail: info@peruadventurestours.com, URL: www.peruadventurestours.com.

Andes Landmark
Andes Landmark provides a wide variety of travel programs in adventure, conventional, specialized, fixed-departure and private trips organized according to your personal requirements. The company like most other tour operators in the area offer Lima city tours, as well as multi-day excursions to Huaraz and the Cordillera Blanca, the Amazon and the ancient trails of Cusco, Andes landmark also takes groups up the Inca Trail to Machu Picchu. Avenida La Paz 434, Oficina 501, Tel: 51-1-444-0931, Fax: 51-1-444-2462, E-mail: info@andes landmark, URL: www.andeslandmark.com.

Sacred Land Adventures Tour Operators
Sacred Land Adventures Tour Operators is a travel agency located in Cusco. the company specializes in adventure travel, offering guided Inca Trail treks to Machu Picchu; the Lares Trek; the Inca Jungle Trail; the Salkantay Trek; as well as tours of Lake Titicaca and Colca Canyon. Plateros 364, Zip: 084 Tel: 051-08-423-1610, Fax: 051-08-423-1610, E-mail: sacredland_adventures@hotmail.com, URL: www.sacredlandcusco.com.

Sun God Expeditions Tours
Sun God Expeditions Tours offers luxury expeditions along the length and breadth of Peru, with a particular focus on those with limited schedules. The guides speak English and Spanish, and tour escorts are multi-lingual. Personalized tours can be arranged. Sun God Expeditions Tours is an excellent choice for couples or families. Villa El Periodista A-3 Huanchaq, Tel: 51-84-9754759, Fax: 51-84-232765, E-mail: afl12@yahoo.es, URL: www.sungodperu.com.

The Inka Adventure
If you are looking for the ultimate bungee jumping experience over the verdant jungle, or want to see the Sacred Valley from a different viewpoint, The Inka Adventure can help you. The company offers what is considered to be the highest bungee jump leaping point in the Americas. On its website, the company explains the security measures it uses to insure a safe adventure for its clients. The actual jump takes about 10 to 15 minutes: three minutes to go up the 122 meters to the take-off point, and the rest spent on having the time of your life. Pasaje Sinchiroca 110, Tel: 51-84-233-742 / (Cell) 967-0918, E-mail: info@theinkaadventure.com, URL: www.theinkaadventure.com.

Peru Inkas Adventures
Peru Inkas Adventures offers great mountain biking, trekking, rafting and historic activities. The company is owned by passionate mountain bikers with many years of experience

leading groups through the best trails in Peru. Wayo, one of the guides, is not only a nice guy to ride with, but also the winner of multiple National Champion titles. Diego de Almagro 535 Jesus Maria, Zip: L11 Tel: (511) 95117026 ,E-mail: wayo@inkasadventures. com, URL: www.inkasadventures.com.

Globos de los Andes

Globos de los Andes offers hot air balloon excursions around Cusco and the surrounding Andes. You can fly over the Nasca Lines or experience Huaca de la Luna and Salkantay. Globos can also organize excursions for photographic or journalistic special events, promotional hot air balloon tether flights and Cusco Land Rover 4x4 transportation. Contact the company for prices. Av. de la Cultura 220, Suite 36, Tel: 51-84-232-352, E-mail: info@globosperu.com, URL: www.globosperu.com.

Action Valley

Action Valley is located just outside of Cusco and it is open from Monday through Saturday 9 a.m. to 8 p.m. The company will provide transportation to and from Action Valley for $2 roundtrip. Videography and photo services are also available. Activities include bungee jumping ($64), slingshot ($59), swing ($20), free rappel ($20), flying fox ($10), climbing wall ($10) and the acrobatic bungee ($10). Calle Santa Teresa 325, Plaza Regocijo, Tel: 51-84-240-835, E-mail: info@actionvalley.com, URL: www.actionvalleycusco. com.

Apumayo

Apumayo offers a wide variety of tours for every traveler's needs. The company's one to multi-day adventure tours include river rafting, Inca Trail trekking, mountain biking, multi-sport adventures and sea kayaking. There are also cultural tours like the Classical Tour, the Archaeological Tour or the Inti Raymi Classic. Expeditions include visits to the Apurimac, Tambopata River, Cotahuasi River, Colca River and Pongo Mainique. One-day cultural trips around the city and surrounding ruins or one-day adventure tours are also available. Travelers with disabilities are welcome; contact Apumayo for prices of custom itineraries. Avenida Garcilazo 316-A, Tel: 51-84-246-018, E-mail: contact@apumayo. com, URL: www.apumayo.com.

Amazonas Explorer

Amazonas Explorer caters to groups of 4 to 16, departing on fixed dates from Peru and Bolivia. Whether it is trekking, rafting, canoeing, mountain biking, cultural tours, multi-activity, family adventures, exploratory expeditions or customized adventures, this tour company has something for everyone. Trips are one to 16 day long, depending on the activities chosen. Prices include ground transportation, internal flights, airport transfers, lodging, rafting, canoeing and camping equipment, professional multi-lingual guides and meals while camping. Avenida Collasuyo 910, Tel: 51-84-252-846, E-mail: sales@amazonas-explorer.com, URL: www.amazonas-explorer.com.

Big Foot

Big Foot offers three main tours: hiking and trekking in Machu Picchu; hiking and trekking outside of Machu Picchu; and cultural tours. The company has are four treks in Machu Picchu, they include a four-day Inca Trail trek, a two-day Inca Trail trek, a seven-day Salkantay trek and a six-day Santa Teresa trek. Tours outside of Machu Picchu include a seven-day trek to Ausangate, famous for the traditional pilgrimage of Q'oyoriti each year and for being the highest mountain in southern Peru at 6,384 meters. There is also a ten-day trek to Vilcabamba, the place where Manco Inca retreated after being defeated by the Spaniards, and where he was tracked down and murdered. Cultural tours include a historical tour of Cusco, a tour to the Sacred Valley of the Inca and a one day tour of Machu Picchu (no hiking). All trips can be customized. Calle Triunfo 392, Centro Comercial, 2nd floor, Tel: 51-84-238-568, E-mail: info@bigfootcusco.com, URL: www.bigfootcusco.com

CUSCO

Eco Trek Peru

Eco Trek Peru is dedicated to making unforgettable, customized trips. It offers a variety of excursions: four to five-day jungle trips into the Pongo De Mainique gorge, 100 miles from Cusco; one to ten-day mountain biking trips on numerous trails that connect some of the most beautiful and challenging areas in Peru and the Andes; half-day to seven-day cultural tours visiting legendary archaeological and historical sites in and around Cusco, with bilingual guides; and custom-designed walking and treks off the beaten paths to Salkantay, Inka, Choquequirao, Apu Auzangate, Lares Trek and Espíritu Pampa. Canchipata 560, Tel: 51-84-247-286, E-mail: info@ecotrekperu.com, URL: www.ecotrekperu.com.

Manu Expeditions

Manu Expeditions is one of the longest running operators in the Manu Biosphere Reserve and has been guiding tours since 1983. Owned and run by a husband and wife team this company relies on a trustworthy team of boat-crews for rainforest trips, wranglers for the mountains and trained camp cooks for remote areas. Leaders are fluent in English and Spanish, as well as experts in their fields. Manu Expeditions offers more than just trips to the Manu Biosphere Reserve; it also provides a variety of activities, including horseback riding and birdwatching. Custom itineraries can be arranged. Calle Humberto Vidal Unda G-5, Segunda Etapa, Tel: 51-84-226-671, E-mail: manuexpeditions@terra.com.pe, URL: www.manuexpeditions.com.

Perol Chico

Perol Chico specializes in exclusive, multi-day equestrian tours that are off the beaten track. Founded in 1996, the riding center is located in the Sacred Valley of the Incas, between Cusco and Machu Picchu. It is surrounded by dramatic scenery; snowcapped mountains, deep blue lakes and lush flora and fauna make this a gorgeous base for your tour. The rides include stunning vistas, exciting trails and fascinating ruins. Perol Chico is dedicated to promoting ecological awareness while sustaining the local cultures and traditions. All horses are Peruvian Pasos trained through traditional Peruvian horsemanship and are kept in immaculate condition. Prices range from $720 for a three day ride to over $3,000 for a 12 day ride. Custom itineraries are available. Tel: 51-84-213-386, E-mail: info@perolchico.com, URL: www.perolchico.com.

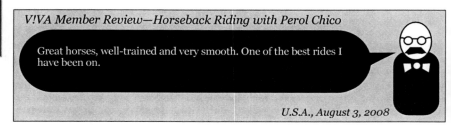

V!VA Member Review—Horseback Riding with Perol Chico

Great horses, well-trained and very smooth. One of the best rides I have been on.

U.S.A., August 3, 2008

Alma Mestiza

Alma Mestiza is a Hispanic-Peruvian travel agency and tour operator dedicated to designing itineraries based around mysticism and therapy. The focus of the trips are not solely the landscape or archaeological wonders, but are based on the excitement and learning that occurs on a personal and spiritual level while traveling. Mingling with the local people and culture, and to interacting with the living part of the country are all elements of an Alma Mestiza tour. The company offers five categories of tours: nature, mystical, traditional, adventure and therapeutic. Itineraries can be completely customized for each individual. Comunidad Campesina de Ticapata, Tel: 51 84 273 682 / 984 856 776, E-mail: info@almamestiza.com, URL: www.almamestiza.com.

Andean Life Adventure Tour Operator

Now in its tenth year, Andean Life Adventure Tour Operator has established itself as one of the most trust-worthy and high quality outfits in Cusco. Owner William Amaru is a native of Peru and has an intimate knowledge of everything--the Inca Trail, the Sacred Valley,

Machu Picchu--that makes Peru the single most visited nation in South America. Andean Life Adventure is an official tour operator according to Cusco's Municipal Council, an honor many other tour companies lack. The Andean Life's staff is educated in all areas of travel and trekking, ranging from biology to history and culture. Calle Plateros 372, Tel: 51-84-255-537, E-mail: andeanlife01@terra.com.pe, URL: www.andeanlife.com.

Eric Adventures

Eric aAdventures offers experiences in rock climbing, canyoning, rappeling, kayaking, white water rafting, horseback riding, mountain biking and paragliding. Whatever suits your adrenaline-rush needs, it's likely that Eric Adventures will help you find that rush. Owner Eric Arenas, an international kayaking and rafting champ, has been operating tours in Cusco since 1993. The company has an array of half as well as full-day activities to three or four day trekking trips. City and cultural tours and, of course, tours to Machu Picchu are also available. Eric Adventures can also arrange for private group tours. Plateros 324, Tel: 51-84-228-475 / 234-764, E-mail: cusco@ericadventures.com, URL: www.ericadventures.com.

Sun Gate Tours

Sun Gate Tours offers nearly every hike imaginable in the Sacred Valley region. The company can also arrange trips outside the region, in Arequipa or other major tourist destinations throughout Peru. Some of Sun Gate's most unique excursions are those which head to the jungle for up to eight days. Saphy Street 476, Tel: 51-84-232-046, E-mail: davidlx@hotmail.com, URL: www.sungatetours.com

Inca Land Adventures

Inca Land Adventures offers tours of all types, from the "Gringo Trail" to high-altitude adventure tours. Inca Land Adventures has several seasoned, bilingual Peruvian guides who can explain the natural and cultural history of Peru. Inca Land Adventures can also arrange multiday adventure tours. Urbanización Flor de la Cantuta, B-2, Tel: 051-84-275-973, Fax: 051-84-275-973, E-mail: info-cusco@incalandadventures.com, URL: www.incalandadventures.com.

Misterios Peru Travel

Misterios Peru Travel offers rafting, hiking, cultural and ecological tours among others. The company can arrange for guests to be picked up from either their hotel or the airport and, likewise, dropped off where necessary. Misterios offers all the usual tours in Peru, but for those wanting a more plush trip, Misterios Peru can organize excursions that bring guests to some of the finest restaurants and hotels in the country. Recoleta Street 501, Tel: 51-84-237-522, Fax: 51-84-237-522, E-mail: reservas@cuscohotelguide.com, URL: www.cuscohotelguide.com.

Peru Travel Sustainable Tourism

Also known as Llankay Peru Travel, Peru Travel Sustainable Tourism specializes in adventure and cultural tours throughout Peru, with an eye to protecting the country's the environmental and cultural heritage. Calle Espaderos 288, Tel: 51-84-235-645, Fax: 51-84-252-535, E-mail: theperutravel@terra.com, URL: www.theperutravel.com.

Andes Nature Tours

Andes Nature Tours has over 25 years of experience, and specializes in natural history and trekking, botany and birdwatching tours. The company can also tailor treks to almost any destination. Owner Aurelio speaks superb English. Garcilaso 210, Casa del Abuelo, oficina 217 Tel: 51-84-245-961, E-mail: ant@terra.com.pe.

Tierras Inkas

Cusco-based Tierras Inkas offers high-quality trips to the Sacred Valley, Maras, Moray, Tipón, Pikillacta, Andahuaylillas, Machu Picchu, Salkantay, Ausangate, Choquequirao, Vilcabamba, Manu and Puerto Maldonado. You can choose any of these destinations, or a simple tour of Cusco, or the classic Inca Trail. Horseback riding, rafting and birdwatching excursions are also a specialty of Tierras Inkas.La Florida ll-3 Los Pinos, Tel: 051-84-253-736, E-mail: Tierrasinkas@hotmail.com.

All Trek Cusco Tours
This outfit can create a complete Peru experience, whether hiking, trekking, having a cultural adventure or meeting Andean people. One of the most unique tours it offers takes visitors into the small villages throughout the Sacred Valley—a great way to get out of Cusco for a taste of rural Peruvian life. Calle Plateros 399, San Judas Chico 3 B-8, Tel: 54-81-262-605, Fax: 54-81-233-766, E-mail: alltrekcusco@yahoo.com, URL: www.alltrekcusco.com.

Llama Path
With only 4 years under its belt, Llama Path has quickly become one of the principal Inca Trail and alternative trekking operators. With a real interest in porter welfare, fair working conditions and social and ecological responsibility, Llama Path offers a strong, responsible tourism option for treks in the Cusco area. Treks are reasonably- priced, with good, bilingual guides and high-quality service. The company can also book mountain biking, rafting and adventure sports trips, although trekking is their speciality. San Juan de Dios 250, Tel: 51-84-240-822, E-mail: reservations@llamapath.com, URL: www.llamapath.com.

Wayki Trek
Run by a guide from a mountain community, Wayki trek has become one of the most popular operators for the Inca Trail and alternative treks. It offers the exclusive "Wayki option" on Inca Trail treks, in which participants have the chance to spend the night in the local community of the porters who will be accompanying them. The company is also an advocate of responsible tourism initiatives and often seeks volunteers for community projects. Procuradores 351 and Av. Pardo (right by the arch), Tel: 51-84-224-092, E-mail: info@waykitrek.net, URL: www.waykitrek.net.

Expediciones Vilca
Expediciones Vilca has years of experience operating affordable tours to Manu National Park. Most trips incorporate a combination of tented-camps and the Machiguenga lodge, which is run by local people. All trips offer the choice of taking a private bus or flights in and out of Manu. The best trip is the 8-day / 7-night program with land transportation in and out of Manu, because it gives you an adequate amount of time to get to know the park and an increased chance of spotting wildlife. Calle Plateros 359, Tel: 51-84-244-751, E-mail: manuvilca@terra.com.pe, URL: www. manuvilcaperu.com.

Enigma
Pioneers in the concept of "luxury trekking," Enigma offers the option of going on guided treks of a different standard, as well as the usual adventure treks offered by many Cusco-based tour operators. The company provides specialized programs designed for family travel or special interest programs such as photography or weaving tours. Their regular treks boast a high level of service; all their guides are well-trained professionals who are always bilingual and sometimes trilingual. Clorinda Matto de Turner 100, Magisetrio 1st etapa, Tel: 51-84-222-155, E-mail: info@enigmaperu.com, URL: www.enigmaperu.com.

Cusco Lodging
The variety of hotels in Cusco is amazing. The range of places to stay in the city runs from $4 youth hostels to internationally renowned hotels that charge several hundred dollars per night. In general, the quality of the hotels in Cusco is very good. Youth hostels tend to be clean and friendly, the mid-range hotels are charming and comfortable, and the luxury hotels offer some of the best facilities and services in the world. Higher-end hotels, are often located in a beautiful old colonial building. If you stay in a lower-budget place, beware that it can get pretty chilly at nights in Cusco, so check that there are sufficient blankets for your needs. Whatever your budget, you'll find the right place in Cusco. Reservations are always recommended, as the best Cusco hotels tend to fill up fast, especially in high tourist seasons,

such as May to November. Out of season, prices tend to be a bit lower. If you're in Cusco and looking around for a quiet spot, try a place off one of the main roads, as parts of the city can get very noisy.

BUDGET

La Casa de Kishkashta

A small, peaceful house with 12 beds, La Casa de Kishkashta provides guests with free WiFi internet access, a fully-equipped kitchen and a small TV room with a DVD player and PS2. The water is always hot and the breakfasts are always tasty. La Casa de Kishkashta is located in the center of Cusco, a block and a half from the main plaza. The owners can also help you arrange everything that Cusco has to offer-- rafting, bungy, trekking, trips to Machu Picchu and more. Marquez 259, Tel: 51-84-224465, E-mail: avi-tili@hotmail.com.

Hostal Suecia I

Suecia I is a small, cozy, and familiar bed and breakfast hostel in a carefully restored and conditioned 16th century house. It is located just off the Main Square, at the very heart of Cusco. Suecia provides simple, affordable, and quality service as well as friendly staff and is all-around good value. Suecia 332 Cusco Peru, Tel: 51-84-233-282, E-mail: hsuecia1@hotmail.com, URL: www.hostalsuecia1.com.

Hostal Procurador (Rooms: $5 - 9)

Hostal Procurador one of several inexpensive hostels along the narrow and cobblestone Coricalle. The rooms have a spare and even stale quality while also they are clean and secure. Hostal Procurador also features a small common area kitchen and a roof terrace, complete with outdoor furniture, which provides an opportunity to relax and enjoy a nice view of the Cusco skyline and a wide sea of red-tiled roofs. We talked to some young visitors, and they reported being pleased with the price and the quality. The staff is warm and considerate of the guest's needs, and the location is convenient. Corricalle 425, Tel: 51-84-243-559.

Hospedaje Tumi (Rooms: $5 - 10)

This inexpensive but likeable lodge makes good use of its old colonial structure and offers attractive, clean, freshly painted rooms, and--most notably for its low price--electric heaters for coping with Cusco's notoriously brisk nights. There is a common area kitchen and television, the latter set up on a patio, along with sofas for lounging and relaxing. Breakfast is available; even though Hospedaje Tumi is within walking distance of the Plaza de Armas, it is also sufficiently distant by several blocks from nighttime noise. Internet, phone and money exchange services are also available.The hotel also serves as a travel agency, and sells bus tickets to as far away as Puno and La Paz. Calle 7 Cuartones 245, Tel: 51-84-253-937, E-mail: hosphatuntumi@hotmail.com.

Hospedaje Félix (Rooms: $5 - 10)

The old building, with two-foot-thick walls, that houses the Hospedaje Félix looks like it was built at least 110 years ago and served as lodging for wandering gauchos and wayward vaqueros. It also does not look like it has been very aggressively looked after since the 19th century. For many the rough appearance of the building, along with the cheap price might be part of its appeal. It does have its own Internet cabinas, with what looks like fairly new computers. The location, near to the Plaza de Armas and the San Blas neighborhood, is another plus. Tecsecocha 171, Tel: 51-84-241-949.

Munay Wasi (Rooms: $7 - 12)

If your main priorities for a hotel are cheap and secure rooms, you might want to go to for the Munay Wasi. Apart from its proximity to the best of Cusco, the cost and security are its main assets. It boasts of being in an "old colonial building," but some might be put off by the flies inside the entrance way. This is a family-run business; the staff treat you with courtesy and kindness. The rooms are clean, but if you are over 5'10" (1.78 meters) you would do well to remember to duck when entering. Munay Wasi is a few blocks further than the other hostels

CUSCO

from downtown, and thus the rooms are quieter with less nighttime noise. Calle Waynapata 253, Tel: 51-84-223-661.

Hospedaje Q'ani Wasi (Rooms: $7 - 12)
On the very short Calle Tigre, in the Plaza de Armas neighborhood, is the Hospedaje Q'ani Wasi. You walk past the entrance into a corridor with rooms on both sides. The place is a bit run down but the rooms are clean, and most importantly, to budget travelers, very cheap, complete with hot running water. The proximity to all the attractions of the Plaza de Armas and the surrounding neighborhood is also an advantage. The management also points out that the rooms all come with color televisions --but who manufactures black and white sets these days? Calle Tigre 124,Tel: 5184-240-273/242-659, E-mail: eliseoadventures3@hotmail.com.

Loki Hostel Cusco (Rooms: $7-25)
In a newly restored, 450-year-old house, four seasoned backpackers have created a backpackers' oasis. The owners have made Loki Hostel a combination of all the things they liked in a good backpackers' hostel. A fun, comfortable and safe place with good-quality services, where you also can meet other like-minded travelers. During the building's history, it has been a traveler's inn and a home to a few of the mayors of Cusco and a Peruvian president wannabe. It is also where one of the biggest revolutions against the Spanish took place. Cuesta Santa Ana 601, Centro Histórico, Tel: 51-84-243-705, E-mail: info@lokihostel.com, URL: www.lokihostel.com.

Mirador Hanan Qosco (Rooms: $7 - 18)
This simple and inexpensive but well-maintained hostel along the cobblestone Coricalle has the same attraction as its competitors: cheap rooms within walking distance to both the Plaza de Armas and San Blas. The rooms and beds are slightly more stylish than what you would expect at this price, though you may not get used to the old and uneven wooden floors. If you are taller than the average Peruvian, you should also watch for the Mirador's low-entrances. A newly renovated and modern common-area kitchen is currently under construction. Coricalle 445, Tel: 51-84-437-618.

Hotel Cáceres (Rooms: $8.50 - 21)
The fancy-lettered sign for this place is sure to catch your gaze, but the entrance might be the most promising feature of this low-cost facility. Hotel Cáceres promises "comfortable rooms," with or without private bathrooms, and many of the same amenities that you will find in competing hotels, but this hotel is recommended only if 1) you are short on cash, 2) better but similarly priced facilities are rented out and 3) you want to stay near the Plaza de Armas. The rooms are stale and small, and at the high end of the price scale. There are better options during most of the year. Plateros Street 368, Tel: 51-84-232-616, E-mail: hotelcaceres@hotmail.com.

Hospedaje Emanuel (Rooms: $10 - 12)
This lodge south of the Plaza de Armas has only ten rooms and four bathrooms. Hospedaje Emanuel has a bar/cafeteria, hot water, luggage security, fax, mail and laundry service. For the ten to twelve dollars that you pay for a single room (depending on the season), the amenities might be enough to compensate for its being in an ugly location, within a dirty building complex. When we paid a visit there was a low-key smell of cat urine in the lobby. Siete Cuartones 284, Building 02, Tel: 51-84-261-507.

Hospedaje Posada del Viajero (Rooms: $10 - 14)
A new facility, the Hospedaje Posada del Viajero has an edge over its competitors in the eight-dollar-a-room market due to the freshness of its rooms and the newly constructed lounge and dining areas. Located within a building complex the Santa Catalina Ancha neighborhood, this inn also benefits from being at a quiet, distant and safe remove from the street. Both breakfast and cable TV are available for an additional $1.50 each. All the other expected amenities, such

CUSCO

as laundry service, safety boxes and access to medical services, come as part of the regular room rate. There are also clean, common-use kitchen, dining and lounge spaces. Santa Catalina Ancha 366-J, Tel: 51-84-261-643, E-mail: laposadadelviajerocusco@hotmail.com.

Teqsiqocha Hostal (Rooms: $10 - 25)

As that old song goes, "you gotta have a gimmick," and for Tecsecocha it is that each room is out-fitted with Castilian-Rococo furniture, which may or may not be authentic. There are fancy bed-spreads, too, which might lead you to overlook the threadbare quality of the rooms themselves. The manager admits that the hostel is still very much a work-in-progress. This hostel might appeal to travelers wanting to save a few dollars, and it is within walking distance of the Plaza de Armas, San Blas, and many restaurants and shops. The hostel also offers an on-site medical service, breakfast, a safety deposit box, and free movies in the coffee lounge, every day, from 5 to 7 p.m. Calle Tecsecocha 474, Tel: 51-84-248-720, E-mail: teqhostal@yahoo.com.

Gloria Pareja Guest House (Rooms: $11 - 15)

Gloria Pareja Guest House is a clean and safe inn located in downtown Cusco, and boasts of per-sonalized attention. The Hotel is intimate, with double rooms (with private or shared bathrooms) and a triple with private bath. Calle 250 Matará, 3rd floor, E-mail: vilcanotatour@yahoo.es.

Hostal Santa María (Rooms: $12 - 22)

The hostel's most attractive selling point: being right next door to the historic Compañía Catholic Church on the Plaza de Armas. Particularly pleasant is Hostal Santa María's second floor, where you can sit on the terrace and marvel at the church from a closer and more elevated angle than from the street. Continental breakfast is included. The hostel also has its own on-site massage clinic. For the sake of culture and/or art, each room has a wooden cross displayed. Hostal Santa María has been in business for 18 years, and has a good reputation.Santa Catalina Angosta, 158 Tel: 51-84-252-746, E-mail: hostalsantamaria@hotmail.com.

Pirwa Hostel Bed and Breakfast (Rooms: $12.50 and up)

Falling within the mid-range price for Cusco (though very cheap by euro and dollar standards), the Pirwa Bed and Breakfast is one of the best hostels in the Plaza de Armas area, and one of four hostels owned by Pirwa throughout Cusco. Owner Fernando Pilares deserves credit for both the creativity and care he has invested in the B & B in terms of the high-quality of its rooms and common areas. Guests are treated to a welcome drink and breakfast, served in a pleasant com-mon area, included in the price. Some rooms are more quiet than others in terms of distance from street noise, so you may want to ask about a room that fits your needs your needs. In room facilities include free internet access, WiFi and TVs. Check their website for more information on other Cusco Pirwa hostels. Calle Suecia 300, Tel: 51-84-244-315 / 970-6148, E-mail: reservas2-fpc@hotmail.com, URL: pirwahostelscusco.com.

Intiq Samana (Rooms: $15 - 25)

Intiq Samana is one of the best buys in Cusco, with its attractive, clean, stylish and comfort-able rooms belying its mid-range (though cheap by first-world standards) price of $15 for a single room and $25 for a double. Besides the expected storage space, hot water, private bath-rooms, safety boxes, breakfast, a clean and spacious common-area kitchen, laundry service and cable TV, this hostel also features free Internet access for its guests. The owner, Richard Flores, has done a great job in not just relying on the natural charm of an old building, but remodeling it so it looks both fresh and traditional. Calle Meloc 422-2, Tel: 51-84-232-101.

Imperial Palace (Rooms: $15 - 25)

This high-quality, but affordable, hostel has clean, carpeted rooms, hot running water, safe-deposit boxes, laundry service and a restaurant that serves a variety of breakfasts, which are included in the price. Single rooms start at $15, double rooms at $25. The location is a short walking distance from the Plaza de Armas, and within the same neighborhood in which you will find many colorful shops, taverns and restaurants. The owner proudly boasts of 30

CUSCO

years in the travel industry, and is one of the more informed sources of travel and touring in Cusco, the Sacred Valley and Machu Picchu. Calle Tecsecocha 490-B, Tel: 51-84-223-324, E-mail: imperialpalacehostal@hotmail.com.

MID-RANGE
Hostal Rojas (Rooms: $18 - 28)
The Hostal Rojas has been in business for 15 years, and you can tell the Rojas family takes its work seriously: the rooms are not only clean and comfortable, but belie their low-cost with high-quality furniture and bedspreads. The bathrooms are currently undergoing renovation, one at a time, so if you choose to stay here yours may, or may not, be outfitted with fresh tiles and modern plumbing. By next year the facility itself should look totally brand new. The hostel has a cafeteria, laundry, safety box and medical service are also included in the price. Calle Tigre 129, Tel: 51-84-228-184, E-mail: hostalrojas@hotmail.com.

The Chaksi Inn Hostal (Rooms: $18 - 36)
An affiliate of Hostelling International (HI), this hostel a little more expensive than the norm, although HI members do get a five dollar discount. A breakfast is included in the cost, and all credit cards are accepted, but with a 10 percent add on. For those who want comfort right in the heart of everything in Cusco, the Chaksi Inn Hostal is an attractive option. The hostel claims to be both clean and quiet, though considering some rooms overlook the Plaza de Armas, the latter might be disputed. Portal Confiturias 257, Tel: 51-84-245-230, E-mail: perutravel@hotmail.com ,URL: www.vientosdelperu.com.

Hostal Casa Grande (Rooms: $20 - 25)
Many hostels use "family-managed" as a selling point, but Hostal Casa Grande is one of the few in which it has some real meaning In a 19th century building constructed over what once was the Palace of Inca Yupanqui and featuring actual Inca-era blocks in its courtyard, the Casa Grande is managed by owner Sonia Mercado and her family. In terms of low-cost hostels, the rooms here are cleaner and have a more personal touch, though a few could use a fresh coat of paint. Additionally, there is a charming on-site museum, showcasing family lore, religious art, and Peruvian and cusqueño history, such as a display on the history of the sol, with actual bills and coins from the 19th century onward. Santa Catalina Ancha 353 Tel: 51-84-264-156 Fax: 51-84-802-582.

Plateros Hostal (Rooms: $20 - 40)
The Plateros Hostal is located on the street of the same name. The hostel offers a few extras such as a salon with a wide-screen television, free Internet access for guests and a cafeteria. Here's the rub: the rooms are of uneven quality, some are excellent, some are mediocre, and you might resent afterwards paying the same as another guest for a room that was much smaller and of a lower quality. To avoid problems simply request to see the room beforehand. The large, second-floor salon is pleasant if you can tolerate a low-key smell of mildew, which is due to a leaking roof. Calle Plateros 348, Tel: 51-84-236-878 / 252-878, Fax: 51-84-233-986, E-mail: plateroshostal@hotmail.com, URL: plateroshostal.pe.tripod.com.

Hostal Posada del Corrigedor (Rooms: $21 - 35)
If the price is within your budget you will not be disappointed. The management of Hostal Posada del Corrigedor has invested more creativity and care in this hostel than at most of the other hostels you will find in this level. The rooms are clean, comfortable and attractive. The hostel also has its own restaurant, the Plus Café, with a balcony view of the Plaza de Armas. Portal de Panes 151, Tel: 51-84-502-362, E-mail: 2fcp@hotmail.com.

Sumac Wasi (Rooms: $25 - 30)
Sumac Wasi (Beautiful House) is in a large, 400-year-old colonial house located 50 meters from the main square, in the heart of the Cusco city. It has comfortable and pleasant rooms with private bathrooms, 24-hour hot water, heaters and televisions. Continental breakfast

is part of the price for a night's stay here. Procuradores 366 Zip: Cusco, Tel: 51-84-240-664, Fax: 51-84-206-64, E-mail: informes@sumacwasi.com, URL: www.sumacwasi.com.

Sol Innka Plaza (Rooms: $25 - 35)
With higher-end price of things, with private rooms starting at $25, the Sol Innka should appeal to older travelers or those looking for an alternative to the standard backpacker lodging. The quality of the facility is first-rate in terms of comfort, cleanliness, security and design. There are additional niceties (beyond the cable TV, private bathrooms and continental breakfasts) such as a fax machine and WiFi. Calle Suecia 420-B, Tel: 51-84-431-350, E-mail: solinnkaplazahotel@hotmail.com, URL: www.solinnkaplazahotel.com.

Villa Mayor (Rooms: $30 and up)
It is hard not to like this very attractive and upscale hotel which faces the peaceful Plaza Regocijo. If you are planning to spend a little more money during your stay in Cusco, then this is one of the more appealing options. In addition to everything you expect from a Hotel at this price, which includes heated rooms, the Villa Mayor has its own restaurant and spa, with the latter offering services that range from waxing to pedicures. It is still close enough to the rest of old Cusco, but at an enough of a distance to be fairly tranquil.Portal Nuevo 246, Plaza del Regocijo, Tel: 51-84-263932, Fax: 51-84-252-688, E-mail: villamayorcusco@terra.com.pe, URL: www.villamayorhostal.com.

Rey Antares Mystic Hotel (Rooms: $35 - 55)
The more expensive room prices at the Rey Antares Mystic Hotel means a little bit extra, spiritually speaking. For interested guests, manager Yarly la Torre offers access to local shamans who will facilitate Earth ceremonies, and on its top floor the hotel has a salon for meditation and yoga. The Rey Antares' lobbies and rooms are painted in a calming light blue and green congruent with the stated tranquil and spiritual intentions of the facility. The Hotel also has great rooftop views of Cusco and the valley, as well as a café and restaurant. Even though all single rooms are priced the same, they are not all the same size, so one might want to take this into consideration. The location, in a non-tourist area, is more distant than other similar-range hotels from the Plaza de Armas, but taxis in Cusco are very inexpensive. Calle Cascaparo 172, Tel: 51-84-225-420, E-mail: info@reyantareshotel.com, URL: www.reyantareshotel.com.

Sol Plaza Inn (Previously Hotel Oblitas) (Rooms: $38 - 59)
One of several hotels on Calle Plateros at the south end of the Plaza de Armas, Hotel Oblitas offers money exchange services, tourist information, airline ticket reservations and purchases, faxing and free Internet access. The rooms start at $15 during the low-season and go as high as $42 during the high season. The rooms, complete with private bathrooms, are clean, fresh and pleasantly designed. Safety boxes, a cafeteria and on-site security guard are part of the package. Proximity to everything that the neighborhood has to offer is, of course, an advantage. Calle Plateros 358, Fax: 51-84-223-871 and 51-84-249-031, E-mail: info@solplazainn.com/solplazainn@hotmail.com, URL: www.solplazainn.com.

Hostal Corihuasi (Rooms: $38 - 66)
Hostal Corihuasi is a charming mid-range hotel in a good location. The building is in a converted 17th century home. The view of the city from some of the rooms and terraces is great. Each room is unique, though some are better than others so ask to see yours beforehand. The hotel also has an elegant lounge with fireplace. If you pay in cash, Hostal Corihuasi offers a $10 discount. Breakfast, taxes, and transport to and from the airport are included in the cost. Calle Suecia 561, Tel: 51-84-232-233 / 51-84-260-502, E-mail: hostal@corihuasi.com, URL: www.corihuasi.com.

The Niños Hotel (Rooms: $40 and up)
The Niños Hotel has large, comfortable rooms, inside an old and neatly refurbished colonial property, attractively stylish and heated. The hostel accepts payment in cash only,

though exceptions can be made for groups booking through travel agencies. The rooms are not numbered, but named after children, accompanied by childhood photos provided by owner Jolanda van den Berg. There is a reason for this. The Niños Hotel (and its restaurant), donates all its profits to help a foundation, which provides daily hot meals and assistance to 500 of Cusco's poorest. The overall quality of the facility justifies the price, and the knowledge that you are contributing to the humanitarian work should enhance the quality of your visit to Cusco. Calle Meloc 442, Tel: 51-84-231-424, E-mail: ninoshostel@terra.com.pe, URL: www.ninoshotel.com.

Teatro Inka Bed and Breakfast (Rooms: $40 - 62)
Located in the neighborhood just south of the Plaza de Armas, the Teatro Inka--named after Teatro Street, rather than an actual theatre--offers the luxury and quality you'd expect for a place whose rooms start at $40. Amenities include heat, cable TV, breakfast, medical assistance (in case of high altitude sickness), airport pick-up and drop-off and Internet access. For a little bit extra, you also get laundry service and a massage. Both the common areas and the rooms themselves are old west-style with a modern deco twist, and have won prizes for their design. Calle Teatro 391, Cusco Tel: 51-84-255-077 / 228-104, E-mail: info@teatroinka.com, URL: www.teatroinka.com.

Cristina Hostal (Rooms: $40 - 65, Apartments: $50 - 110)
Rustic, indigenous décor creates a true Peruvian ambiance at Cristina Hostal. While the rooms are basic, they have such amenities as comfortable beds with private baths, 24-hour hot water, telephones, carpeting, cable TV and comes with continental breakfast. For a bit more money, the hostel also rents apartment-styled rooms with a kitchenette, refrigerator, dining table, ample closet space and a sofa. Avenida El Sol 341, Cusco, two blocks from Plaza de Armas, Tel: 51-84-227-233, Fax: 51-84-227-251, E-mail: info@hcristina.com, URL: www.hcristina.com.

Hotel Carlos V (Rooms: $40 - 70)
Rooms are fresher, cleaner and simply better than what you get at most cheaper hotels and hostels in the area, and they come with all the expected niceties, such as hot running water, cable TV, a continental breakfast, security boxes, and most importantly for Cusco's chilly evenings, heated rooms. Hotel Carlos V also has its own restaurant, La Gruta. Strangely enough, it does not accept credit cards, only cash. Calle Tecsecocha 490, Tel: 51-84-223-091, Fax: 51-84-228-447, E-mail: reservas@carlosvcusco.com, URL: www.carlosvcusco.com.

El Balcón Hostal (Rooms: $40 - 90)
Located in the colonial center of Cusco, only three blocks from the Plaza de Armas, El Balcón overlooks the city and the surrounding mountains. This hostel was originally constructed in 1630 atop Inca agricultural terraces, and was meticulously restored in 1998 to the beautiful condition it is in today. El Balcón has 16 rooms, each with a private bathroom. Bathrooms are spacious, with showers and hot water 24 hours a day. The beds are custom made (extra long!), with 100% cotton linen sheets, 100% alpaca and wool blankets and feather pillows. The hostel also features space heaters, cable TV, local, national and international phone service, free WiFi internet access and room service. It has suites, matrimonial, single, double and triple rooms. In addition, El Balcón also offers airport pickup service, storage room, terraced garden, restaurant, laundry service and tourism information. Tambo de Montero, Tel: 51-84-236-738, E-mail: info@balconcusco.com, URL: www.balconcusco.com.

La Casona Real (Rooms: $50 - 80)
La Casona Real is perhaps one of the best hotels in Cusco. Located only a stone's throw from the Plaza de Armas, La Casona Real is on Calle Procuradores ("Gringo Alley") and is probably the best bang for your buck. Tastefully decorated with a modern Peruvian motif, the rooms are spacious, elegant and impeccably clean which may make you feel like you are truly at a home away from home. All rooms have comfy beds, private modern baths, 24 hour hot water, heat, phones, cable TV and room service. Also included in the price is continental breakfast

in the courtyard and free airport pick-up. The breezeway opens into a large airy and bright indoor courtyard with a fantastic bar for sipping wine or an ice cold *cerveza*. La Casona Real is exceptionally safe (the large outside double doors close early and you have to ring the bell to get in); the staff at La Casona Real are attentive, friendly and efficient, and will help you arrange anything you may need, including medical assistance.Calle Procuradores 354, Tel: 51-84-224-670, E-mail: reservations@casonarealcusco.com, URL: www.casonarealcusco.com.

HIGH-END

Hotel Marqueses (Rooms: $50 - 150)

Hotel Marqueses is only a block and a half from the Plaza de Armas, the perfect distance from many day and evening activities. A charming, safe and spotlessly clean place to stay, the hotel is adorned with a colonial motif suits the building's 400-year-old history. The open-air courtyard is a real gem. The hotel offers two types of rooms: standard and deluxe. The deluxe rooms have more sunlight and are more spacious because of their positioning near the courtyard. All rooms include hot water, heat, cable TV and a private bath. The friendly staff will accommodate most needs, including airport pick-up and drop-off service. Internet is available, free of charge, and so is a full breakfast buffet. Hotel Marqueses is one of the only hotels in Cusco that has suites, for a more spacious stay. Calle Garcilaso 256, Tel: 51-84-264-249, Fax: 51-84-257-819, E-mail: info@hotelmarqueses.com, URL: www.hotelmarqueses.com.

Hotel Rumi Punku (Rooms: $70 - 140)

Hotel Rumi Punku is an attractive hotel in old Cusco. Rumi Punku means "stone door" in Quechua: the entrance to the hotel leads through an ancient stone door, obviously of Inca design. The doorway is all that has survived of an Inca palace; today the door is considered a historic relic by the city of Cusco. The hotel itself is quite charming and the rooms are airy and neat. The restaurant is friendly; there is a small courtyard and chapel on the premises. Breakfast is included, as is airport pick-up if you call ahead. Calle Choquechaca 339, Tel: 51-84-221-102, E-mail: info@rumipunku.com, URL: www.rumipunku.com.

Sonesta Posada del Inca (Rooms: $70 - 200 + tax & services)

Owned and operated by the international Sonesta chain, Posada del Inca is strategically located right in the center of old Cusco. The rooms are bright and airy, there is a relaxing lounge with a fireplace, and the service is very good. The hotel has a tour desk which can help with trips and arrangements in Cusco (there is even an on-line "virtual concierge" so that you can book tours before you arrive). The Posada del Inca is fairly expensive; it falls somewhere around the upper mid-range or lower upper range in terms of costs, but the location is perfect and the value is good for the money. Portal Espinar 108, Tel: 51-84-227-061, Fax: 51-84-248-484, E-mail: salescusco@sonestaperu.com, URL: www.sonesta.com/peru_cusco.

Hotel Royal Inka I (Rooms: $72 - 120)

Hotel Royal Inka I is in a Cusco landmark; the building was originally built by Inca Pachacútec and later became the home of Francisca Zubiaga de Gamarra, a heroine of Peruvian independence struggle and wife of Peru's first president. There are a variety of comfortable rooms and suites to choose from. The hotel bar and restaurant are full of colonial character. The rates are competitive for a hotel of this class: check it out if you're ready for a little splurge. Plaza Regocijo 299, Tel: 51-84-222-284 / 231-067, Fax: 51-84-234-221, E-mail: royalinka@aol.com, URL: www.royalinkahotel.com/hotels.htm.

Hotel Royal Inka II (Rooms: $72 - 120)

Like its sister, the Royal Inka I, Hotel Royal Inka II occupies a converted colonial home. This hotel is a little more formal and expensive, and the rooms are more uniform. The entire establishment is more modern, which will appeal to some. The hotel is very conveniently located to all of Cusco's main attractions. The restaurant and bar on the top floor are pleasant and worth a visit even for those who do not stay there. 335 Santa Teresa, Tel: 51-84-222-284, Fax: 51-84-234-221, E-mail: royalinka@aol.com, URL: www.royalinkahotel.com/hotels.htm.

CUSCO

The Garden House, Cusco (Rooms: $89 - 219)

The Garden House is a country haven located only ten minutes from the center of Cusco. The balconies and garden terraces have commanding views over the former Inca capital and the mountainsides. The rooms are large and well furnished, all with private, hot-water bathroom and extra-long beds. Inter-connecting suites are available, for families. There's a beautiful cloistered patio, garden and orchards. The Garden House also has a library, spa facilities, dining room with extensive wine list and two sitting rooms with fireplaces. Other amenities include babysitting, internet, WiFi, cable TV, luggage storage, secure parking and airport pick-up. Larapa Grande B-6, Tel: 51-84-271-117, E-mail: info@cuscohouse.com, URL: www.cuscohouse.com.

V!VA Member Review—The Garden House

This place is great if you want to be able to take it easy in the altitude of Cusco. Luxurious, wonderful attention, spacious, and ten minutes from the centre of town in what must be the most beautiful (and enormous) garden in Cusco. We had a great time.

London, U.K., March 30, 2007

Hotel Arqueólogo Exclusive Selection (Rooms: $97 - 160)

Arqueólogo Exclusive Selection Hotel is in a restored colonial house located in the historical heart of Cusco. The hotel's original Inca walls, exceptional vistas of Cusco and wood-beam ceilings make it very cozy. The rooms have private bathrooms with 24-hour hot water, telephone, cable TV, heating, WiFi, balconies and private security boxes. Rates include buffet breakfast, served in its cafeteria with a lovely panoramic view of Cusco. Pumacurco 408 Zip: 5184, Tel: 51-84-232-522, Fax: 51-84-235-126, E-mail: reservation@hotelarqeuologo.com, URL: www.hotelarqueologo.com.

Hotel Libertador Palacio del Inka (Rooms: $270 - 340 + tax)

Hotel Libertador Palacio del Inka is located within the ancient city of Cusco, facing the impressive Qoricancha, or Temple of the Sun. Its 254 rooms have been especially designed to make your stay unique. You can enjoy excellent modern Andean and international cuisine in the Inti Raymi restaurant, have a light meal in the Kero Café or try special cocktails in the Rumi Bar. The hotel also has WiFi internet service, a fitness room, a spa, 24-hour room service, conference rooms and different stores where you will find all sorts of souvenirs you can imagine. Plazoleta Santo Domingo 259, Tel: 51-84-231-961, Fax: 51-84-233-152, E-mail: reservascusco@libertador.com.pe, URL: www.libertador.com.pe.

Hotel Monasterio (Rooms: $495 - 1,590 + tax & services)

Owned and operated by the prestigious Orient Express Hotels group, the Monasterio is one of the most luxurious hotels in Cusco. The hotel complex was formerly the San Antonio Abad seminary, which was built over 300 years ago and served as an actual monastery and seminary until recently. The seminary foundations themselves were constructed on Inca stonework. The monk's cells have been converted to elegant, comfortable rooms, the courtyards still have ancient trees, and much of the colonial art and paintings still adorn the walls and hallways. You can live like the monks did--only much, much better. The Hotel Monasterio has even installed a system to pump more oxygen into the rooms, to counteract the effects of altitude sickness on their guests. The hotel is huge: it has over 100 rooms plus several suites. There are two restaurants and a bar on the premises, as well as an original chapel which is still considered to be consecrated ground. There is an on-site travel agency which can arrange all sorts of tours. Calle Palacios 136, Plazoleta Nazarenas, Tel: 51-84-241-777, Fax: 51-84-246-983, E-mail:info@peruorientexpress.com.pe,URL:www.monasterio.orient-express.com/web/ocus/ocus_a2a_home.jsp

Machu Picchu Sanctuary Lodge (Rooms: $815 - 1,085)

For the jet-setting traveler who has no interest in staying in dusty, rabble-filled Aguas Calientes, there is the Machu Picchu Sanctuary Lodge. The Sanctuary is the only hotel right up on the top of the hill next to the ruins; the entrance is a short walk away (as in about fifty feet). The hotel has two suites and 29 rooms, some of which have an incredible mountain view (be prepared to pay more if you want a scenic room). The hotel is Run by the internationally renowned Orient Express hotel group where you'll get luxurious comfort and great service. The Sanctuary Lodge offers all of the expected amenities for a hotel in its class: internet, room service, etc. For those who really want to keep their exposure to riff-raff to a minimum, the hotel can help you book a helicopter flight from Cusco. If you cough up several hundred dollars to spend the night, be sure to be first in line to visit the ruins in the morning before the train arrives, bringing hordes of tourists with it. There is an excellent restaurant on the premises as well. Check their web site for special rates and promotions. Tel: +51 1 610 8303, Reservations +51 16 10 830, Fax: + 51 84 21 1053, E-mail: info@peruorientexpress.com. pe, URL: http://machupicchu.orient-express.com/web/omac/omac_a2a_home.jsp.

SAN BLAS LODGING
This charming neighborhood, full of art and *artesanía*, is a fun place to stay within Cusco. With options for all types of travelers, it's worth staying a night or two to explore San Blas' zigzagging streets and artist's workshops.

BUDGET
Hospedaje Granada (Rooms: $3)
There is little to recommend the Hospedaje Granada beyond its extremely low price: $3. There are 27 rooms and four bathrooms, but each room is outfitted with a *basinilla*, a small pot to urinate in. The hospedaje has spare wooden floors, a common-area kitchen, and within its limited plumbing facilities, hot water. The Hospedaje Granada is by-and-large a bracing reminder of the limited options for many of the poor of Peru and Latin America. The rooms at least look clean, and it is within a few blocks of the Plaza de Armas neighborhood. Siete Cuartones 290, Tel: 51-84-223-281.

Hospedaje El Artesano de San Blas (Rooms: $3 - 5)
If you stroll up Cuesta San Blas and keep heading north, the name changes to Suytucato, and on your left you will see the sign for the Hospedaje El Artesano de San Blas, one of the best little secrets for those really wanting a bargain without giving up a decent night's comfort. This is a first-rate backpacker's hostel; located in a clean and well-maintained Spanish colonial facility, with hot water, spacious rooms and a well-kept common kitchen area, all for a mere ten soles, or $5 for a private room, $3 for a shared room. Suytucato 790, Tel: 51-84-263-968, E-mail: manosandinas@yahoo.com.

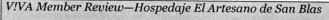

V!VA Member Review—Hospedaje El Artesano de San Blas

This place was wonderful- clean rooms, hot water, beautiful courtyard, very tranquilo atmosphere, and CHEAP. It is perfect for those who want a more authentic Cusco experience, off the gringo trail, and aren't interested in the international hostel vibe.

U.S.A., August 7, 2008

Hospedaje Sambleño (Rooms: $6 - 18)
Around the corner from the Plazoleta San Blas, Hospedaje Sambleño offers a cheap price- -single rooms at $6--in a great location. You can buy breakfast for a little extra at its own in-house Niña Niña restaurant. The rooms are spare and even a bit stale, with bare wooden floors. When we visited it, the receptionist was smoking a cigarette behind his desk in the lobby, an indication of what you can expect here. If none of this is an issue for you, and you are on a tight budget, you might not mind. Otherwise, as the Romans used to say, caveat emptor. Carmen Alto 114, Tel: 51-84-262-979, E-mail: sambleno@hotmail.com.

Hospedaje Inka (Rooms: $6 - 20)

This inn is located at the very summit of Suytucato on the path leading north from San Blas. Owner Américo Pacheco will welcome you into his rustic Hospedaje Inka, a former ranch home now serving as a backpacker palace, complete with an outdoor grill and, spare wooden floors (as well as private bathrooms). Américo is proud of what he calls his "orthopedic" beds and his breakfast featuring real cusqueño chocolate and barley bread. Take a deep breath of the fresh, mountain air and enjoy the spectacular views of Cusco and the mountain ranges surrounding it. This is one of the few hostels that offers parking and is a good way to sample both Cusco's urban and rural charms. Suytuccato 848, Tel: 51-84-231-995, E-mail: americo-pacheco@hotmail.com.

Arrieros (Rooms: $8.50 - 12)

Blink and you might miss this charming little hostel a little to the right, off the Cuesta San Blas, on a street called Kurkurpata. The owner himself does not go out of his way to advertise his facility too well, using a paper sign to announce rooms over a more conventional sign calling attention to his café and gift shop. Perhaps with reason, since he only has five rooms; but consider yourself lucky if you can rent one. Rooms have private bath rooms, hot water, and great views of the Cusco valley and city. As advertised Arrieros has its own in-house restaurant and gift shop. Calle Kurkurpata 122, Tel: 51-84-237-386.

The Blue House (Rooms: $8)

This cute, rabbit-warren of a place started off as a family renting out an extra room or two and has become one of the most popular hostels for long-stay travelers. With a shared kitchen and dining room for guests, a friendly family vibe, two outside terraces with stunning views, a TV room, and reasonable rates – it's easy to see why. Located high up in San Blas, the Blue House is only accessible on foot, so it's only a good option if you don't plan to stagger back alone from one of the many discotecas in the plaza late at night. A monthly rate of $150 is also available. Kiskapata 291, San Blas, Tel: 51-84-242-407, E-mail: info@thebluehouse.info, URL: www.thebluehouse.info.

Mirador de la Ñusta (Rooms: $10 - 20)

This hostel is blessed with one of the best spots in Cusco: at the head of the fountain of Plazoleta de San Blas. There is a nice garden patio inside, and the rooms are clean, comfortable and attractive. The very colorful owner, Daríos Segovia, provides local tours, starting at $100, to the Sacred Valley and other noteworthy archaeological sites, with himself as the guide. Breakfast is offered by request, and laundry as well as taxi service--at any hour, says Darios--is also include in the price. Calle Tandapata 682, Tel: 51-84-248-039.

Hostal Hatun Wasi (Rooms: $15 - 20)

This hostel is managed by the Mendivil family, whose religious and indigenous-themed folk art has gained recognition beyond Peru. This hotel has a great location and offer rooms designed with an artistic flair commensurate with the talent that made them famous. If you are fortunate to reserve a room on the terrace, there will be a great view of Cusco. Heating is available for an extra $3. There is also an attractive bar and cafeteria on the first floor. The owner, Francisco Mendivil, is often willing to personally show his art to you. Cuesta San Blas 619-B, Tel: 51-84-242-626 /233-247, E-mail: hostalhatunwas@hotmail.com.

MID-RANGE

Casa de la Gringa (Rooms: $20)

Just around the corner from the San Blas plaza is the Casa de la Gringa, which is owned by Lesley from South Africa. All the rooms have been individually decorated, and each has its own spiritual vibe, so ask which rooms are available when making a booking. There is also a mixed dorm for those who are content to soak up the energy of the house as a whole. There is a pleasant common area and a variety of board games to keep you busy on cold Cusco nights. The agency Another Planet is run by the same people and can organize spiritual tours for you, such as San Pedro trips in which you take the hallucinogenic cactus with a shaman. Tandapata 148 (corner of P'asnapaqana), San Blas, Tel: 51-84-241-168, URL: www.casadelagringa.com.

Hospedaje Turístico San Blas (Rooms: $20 - 25)

Located in the trendy, bohemian San Blas neighborhood north of the Plaza de Armas, Hospedaje Turístico San Blas is slightly more than mid-range in its price (a single room starts at $20 during the low-season and goes to $25 during the high season), but its high quality rooms in an area full of stylish shops and restaurants should appeal to many tourists. The interiors are a model of moderated elegance. Free internet access comes with the usual amenities, such as heated rooms and a continental breakfast, and their terrace offers pleasant views of the beautiful city of Cusco. Cuesta San Blas 526, Tel: 51-84-225-781 / 244-481, E-mail: sanblascusco@yahoo.com, URL: www.sanblashostal.com.

Amaru Hostal (Rooms: $20 - 25)

Many hostels just north of the Plaza de Armas in the "artist community" of San Blas are a little bit more expensive, but the Amaru Hostel is the only one that includes "American breakfast," featuring eggs and fruit salad, rather than the standard continental breakfast, that is included in the price. The hotel is a very pleasant place to stay, with large-windows in its rooms and a garden in the back. For colder nights, heating is available for an additional $3, negotiable for groups. There is a book exchange, and an overall friendly atmosphere. Cuesta San Blas 541 Tel: 51-84-225-933.

Hostal Marani (Rooms: $28 – 72)

Set around a colonial courtyard in San Blas, Hostal Marani offers good-quality accommodation at relatively low prices. All rooms are spacious and have private bathrooms. Breakfast in the sunny courtyard or small cafeteria is included. The Hostal Marani supports socially responsible tourism and has close ties to the Dutch Hope Foundation. Carmen Alto 194, San Blas, Tel: 51-84-249-462, E-mail: info@hostalmarani.com, URL: www.hostalmarani.com.

HIGH-END

Los Apus Hotel and Mirador (Rooms: $89 - 109)

The independent Swiss Los Apus Hotel and Mirador opened in December 1999. It is nestled in the foothills of the unspoiled historical site of San Blas, three blocks from the Plaza de Armas. The hotel is just 10 minutes from the Velasco Astete International Airport and the San Pedro rail station to Machu Picchu. Los Apus' 20 rooms, some with balconies, have wooden floors, double-paned windows, extra long beds, cable TV, smoke detectors, telephones, private baths and central system. Non-smoking and rooms for the disabled are available. Other services include: free airport pickup, WiFi and an internet cabin down at the patio, mail service, fax, money exchange, laundry and flight and train reservations. Hair dryers and safes are available upon request, as are oxygen and a doctor. The El Mirador Restaurant and Bar is on the roof terrace and has magnificent panoramic views. El Patio Restaurant is surrounded by stone columns and features international and regional cuisine. Atocsaycuchi 515, and Choquechaca, Tel: 51-84-264-243, Fax: 51-84-264-211, E-mail: info@losapushotel.com, URL: www.losapushotel.com.

Casa San Blas Boutique Hotel (Rooms: $95 - 160)

Casa San Blas Boutique Hotel offers superior service and hospitality. A warm atmosphere and clean, comfortable rooms are not even the hotel's main bent: this meticulously restored 18th century colonial-style house is also located in the historic artisan's quarter of San Blas. Spend the day browsing local wares, from woodcarvings and jewelry to weavings and paintings, and pass the night sampling gourmet dishes at the hotel's Cava de San Blas restaurant. Service, style and a spectacular location make Casa San Blas a traveler's gem. Tocuyeros 566, Tel: 51-84-251-563/ 1-888-569-1769 (US) / 1-303-539-9300 (US), Fax: 51-84-237-900 E-mail: info@casasanblas.com, URL: www.casasanblas.com.

CUSCO

Cusco Restaurants

Cusco is a good place to eat. A city steeped in tradition, with fine Peruvian restaurants on almost every corner. But the growth of tourism as an industry has created a market for everything from international fine cuisine to fast food.

Peruvian / Traditional

Cava de San Rafael

Cava de San Rafael serves up a modern Andean menu that includes local trout and grilled alpaca (for the daring). But it offers more than just fine cuisine to its clientele; it has a panoramic view of Cusco's Plaza de Armas, and has an ancestral and folk dance show. The restaurant on the itinerary of most first-class tours. Santa Catalina Ancha 370, Tel: 51-84-261-691, E-mail: cavadesanrafael@infonegocio.net.pe.

Fallen Angel

A funky, artsy restaurant featuring tables made out of bathtubs (full of live fish!) and barbed wire on the toilets (it's tasteful), Fallen Angel is popular among visitors. They have a varied menu—rumor has it that their steaks are excellent. Fallen Angel occasionally has parties and other special events—check in if you're in town. Plazoleta Nazarenas 221, Tel: 51-84-258-184, URL: www.fallenangelincusco.com.

Inka...Fe

Set in the artsy San Blas neighborhood, Inka...Fe Café is a find. Step off the cobblestone streets into this welcoming little restaurant and for between 15 to 25 soles ($5-$8) you can have your choice of a wide variety of international and Peruvian cuisine. From pasta and sandwiches to chicken, beef, pork and vegetarian options, this menu is sure to keep even the pickiest eater happy. Dishes are of a very generous size. The restaurant is small, intimate and homey, and the service impeccable. Calle Choquechaca 131-A, Tel: 51-84-254-073, E-mail: reservas@inkafe.com.pe.

Tampu Restaurant Bar

Tampu Restaurant Bar is an à la carte restaurant a short stroll away from Machu Picchu's entrance, within the Machu Picchu Sanctuary Lodge. The restaurant serves international and Peruvian food for breakfast, lunch and dinner, along with high tea in the afternoon. Prices are high but with Tampu's prime location, well-known reputation and lack of competition, the restaurant can get away with charging more. Machu Picchu Sanctuary Lodge has two dining choices — Tampu and Tinkuy Buffet Restaurant, a fixed-price buffet only open for lunch. Of the two, Tampu is the better choice. The restaurant is less crowded, entrée prices are generally cheaper than the buffet and you get a great view of the Andes. Machu Picchu, Tel: 511 610 8300, E-mail: reservas@peruorientexpress.com.pe, URL:http://www.orient-express.com/web/omac/omac_dining_tampu.jsp.

Tinkuy Buffet Restaurant

Tinkuy Buffet Restaurant is a part of Machu Picchu Sanctuary Lodge, the only hotel within walking distance of Machu Picchu. The buffet is pricey if you're only looking for a light meal, though the price does include salad, main course, dessert and nonalcoholic beverages. Tinkuy fills quickly with day trippers, and the noisy, crowded room can make it easy to forget this restaurant is part of a high-end hotel. Machu Picchu, Tel: 511 610 8300, E-mail: reservas@peruorientexpress.com.pe, URL:http://www.orient-express.com

Pacha-Papa

Located in the bustling artesian neighborhood of San Blas, Pacha-Papa offers an intimate setting filled with modern art and candlelit tables. For more informal dining, there is also a fireplace area with comfy sofas. Like the restaurant's art and music selection, the dishes are funky and flavorful with a distinct Peruvian and international flair. In fact, owner Tanya Miller previously worked in several London restaurants. On the menu you'll find roasted guinea pig and alpaca *anticucho*, in addition to other Peruvian specialties like tamales and quinoa soup. Also recommended are the beef tenderloin in red-wine-and-onion sauce, and the tropical chicken curry with bananas, peaches and strawberries. The hip, laidback atmosphere and reasonable prices appeal to a young crowd who come for the food and popular happy hour (daily 6:30 p.m.-7:30 p.m.). The Sunday roast (by reservation only) has become famous among locals and features a roast chicken, potatoes, veggies and homemade apple pie. Plaza San Blas 120, Tel: 51-84-241-318, E-mail: pachapapa@cuscorestaurants.com.

Khipus Restaurant

One of the main reasons people may want to visit Khipus is that it is the restaurant of choice of Edilberto Mérida, one of Peru's most famous painters and sculptors. Merida first created the now-common image of the poor Latin American with outstretched and massive hands. A new and very large Mérida sculpture of an Andean folk musician greets visitors to Khipus, along with other displays of his work. This is also an excellent restaurant with three stories and multiple rooms, each with its own theme. Expert preparations of traditional and continental cooking are also offered at reasonable prices. Carmen Alto133, Tel: 51-84-241-283, E-mail: khipusfood@hotmail.com, URL: www.khipusfood.com.

Moloko

A very chill café with free Internet downstairs and a movie room with comfy couches upstairs, Moloko is an easy place to socialize or to hunker down and enjoy a movie. Films show twice daily (pick up a monthly schedule at the café or have a look at the day's movies posted outside the front door), and admission is free, although movie watchers are expected to buy food or drink. The dinner menu is an unimpressive collection of sandwich and pizza selections; at lunch, the set menu is a basic but very economical and has tasty choices. The staff is young and friendly (and prone to periodically throwing great parties in lieu of a weekend film), and if the crowd is thin and the scheduled movie isn't a popular choice, it's possible to persuade the movie manager to change the selection. Choquechaca 216, Tel: 51-84-240-109 /967-8241, E-mail: molokoperu@hotmail.com.

Sky Restaurant (Entrees: $2.50 - 5)

This new restaurant offers a great deal: purchase any menu item over eight soles ($2.50) and you get a free Pisco Sour. Purchase any menu item over 15 soles ($5) and you get a free glass of locally made wine. And if that is not enough, if you come in as a group of six, you can invite a seventh for free. In terms of food, the restaurant has several alternative of different menus, such as Peruvian, Mexican and Italian. Its desert entrées include a *banana granita*, fried banana with marmalade and cheese. It is conveniently located over a discothèque, if you feel like dancing afterwards. Tecsecocha 415 A, E-mail: rosseus_sky@hotmail.com.

Pachacútec (Entrees: $3 and up)

Pachacútec, on the Plaza de Armasis a first-class restaurant with an appealing ambience that could be described as "Inca deco." A large portrait of legendary warrior Pachacútec hangs on the wall along with other samples of local art that incorporates indigenous motifs. Its menu, offered not only in Spanish and English, but French as well, is a mix of continental and native dishes, including asparagus rolls with ham, marinated mackerel ceviche and a "warm salad" that includes grilled peaches and roasted onions served over a cool bed of greens. Surprisingly, this high-quality eatery is quite inexpensive, with a three-course meal going for as little as $3. Portal de Pones 115, Fax: 51-84-245-041, E-mail: reservas@pachacutecrestaurant.com, URL: www.cuscoperu.com/pachacutec.

Drews (Entrees: $9)

Drews serves fantastic authentic Peruvian cuisine prepared by a chef trained in France. The restaurant is very reasonably priced, its location one block off of the Plaza means prices are lower than elsewhere. Drews has an intimate, comfortable atmosphere. Plateros 327, Tel: 51-84-22-4203.

CUSCO

Inka Grill (Entrees: $15 - 20)
According to some, this is the best restaurant in town. With a relaxing rustic charm, complimented by live Andean music, views of the colonial churches and a menu that will please any palate, it is hard to disagree. Specializing in modern Andean cuisine, Inka Grill serves a variety of tantalizing dishes, from fried calamari and stuffed Amarillo chili peppers to chicken satay, fresh trout and gourmet pastas. If you're not in the mood for gourmet, you can try one of Inka Grill's tempting pizzas. And what better way to compliment outstanding food than an extensive selection of fine international wines? As you can imagine, a restaurant this good doesn't stay empty very long, so reservations are recommended. Portal de Panes 115, Plaza de Armas, Tel: 51-84-262-992, E-mail: info@inkagrillcusco.com.

ASIAN
Kintaro Japanese Restaurant
Kintaro is the only Japanese restaurant in Cusco, and one of the few that can be found in Peru overall. Moriya Daisuke, a native of Japan, offers his customers as authentic an experience as possible, complete with a second floor where you sit barefoot in order to enjoy such specialties as anjonjoli and tofu, vegetable noodle soup, tempura, trout sashimi and white fish cake. Open every day from 2 to 10 p.m., it takes cash only and can seat up to forty. This restaurant also sells authentic, traditional, hand-dyed Japanese fabrics. Heladeros 149, Tel: 51-84-226-181, URL: www.kintaro-cusco.com.

Tika Bistro Gourmet
Tika Bistro Gourmet is a unique restaurant in Cusco. The cuisine you'll find at Tika is unlike anything you've ever tasted, combining Thai and Vietnamese flavors and techniques with traditional Peruvian ingredients. Tocuyeros 5663, Tel: 51-84-251-563 Fax: 51-84-237-900, E-mail: ayb@pebhl.com, URL: www.casasanblas.com/tikabistro/index.php.

Govinda's (Entrees: $2 - 5)
Govinda's has what is most likely the healthiest food in all of Cusco. Managed by local affiliates of Hare Krishna, and with a slant towards Indian-style cooking, the all-vegetarian, heavy on soy, menu offers such items as *apana de cusqueño*, that is, soy steak with fried bananas, cheese, and rice, or *palta rellena*, avocado stuffed with vegetables and yogurt sauce. Portraits of traditional Hindu religious figures, most notably Krishna, are prominently featured. Religious music plays on the sound system and a low-key smell of incense all contribute to a unique dining experience. Calle Espaderos 128, Tel: 51-84-504-864, E-mail: raghuraram@hotmail.com.

Bar Restaurant Indigo (Entrees: $5.50)
Serving up what is without a doubt the most authentic Thai food in Cusco, Indigo is a hidden treasure, just around the corner from the Plaza de Armas. Chose from all the Thai favorites, including pad-thai, green, red and yellow curries, and pick a spice-level from one to five. For those who enjoy a challenge (and pain) it is worth noting that a "five" has yet to be consumed at the restaurant. Other interesting features are comfy alcoves, a fireplace and swinging chairs, as well as an all-day happy hour with cheap cocktails. Tecsecocha 2, Tel: 51-84-260-271, E-mail: indigocusco@hotmail.com.

Maikhana Namaskar Indian Restaurant (Entrees: $10)
Maikhana Namaskar is a well-kept secret in Cusco. So well kept, in fact, that even locals who profess a love of Indian food don't know that a purveyor of samosas and hot chai tea even exists in San Blas. Coyly hidden in the Galería de Arte Señor Mérida, it's easy to pass right on by the restaurant, even if you know exactly what you're looking for. However, a well-honed sense of direction and a little persistence will be handsomely rewarded with spicy curries and homemade chutneys, hot rice, soft naan and a menu thick with options for vegetarians. The service requires some patience, and tandoori fans may be disappointed at the semi-permanent absence of tandoori-cooked options on the menu, but the food (prepared by Indian

chefs) is some of Cusco's best ethnic fare. Av. El Sol 106, Int. 201, 207 & 307, Galeria La Merced, Tel: 51-84-252-044, E-mail: maikhana@gmail.com, URL: www.maikhana.net.

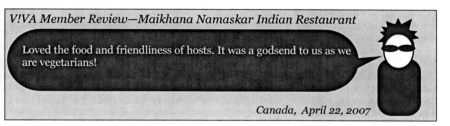

V!VA Member Review—Maikhana Namaskar Indian Restaurant

Loved the food and friendliness of hosts. It was a godsend to us as we are vegetarians!

Canada, April 22, 2007

Blueberry Lounge(Entrees: $10 - 12)
Great music, comfy couches and unbeatable food make Blueberry Lounge a popular place for travelers. The menu is Thai/Asian-influenced, but boasts a variety of internationally inspired dishes. Try the Vietnamese summer rolls or Teriyaki Alpaca, or any one of the soups, salads, or sandwiches. Vegetarian options are also available. And make sure you save room for dessert. On Friday and Saturday nights the walls vibrate with music from live DJs, making this place a great spot for kicking back and relaxing with a drink. Blueberry Lounge is open daily, 8:30 a.m.-midnight. Portal de Carnes 236, Tel: 51-84-249-458, E-mail: blueberry@cuscorestaurants.com, URL: www.cuscorestaurants.com/blueberry.

INTERNATIONAL
Restaurant Aldea Yanapay
As you walk up the flight of stairs to the Restaurant Aldea Yanapay, you are greeted by the colorful crayon impressions of children's artwork. The Restaurant Aldea Yanapay itself could be mistaken for a kindergarten, with cushions tossed on the floor as an indicator of its relaxed atmosphere. This is indeed a real restaurant, open from morning until night, offering up everything from *huevos rancheros* and Greek bread with tzatziki sauce, to pasta with bacon, mushrooms and tomatoes, Irish coffee and sangria. The Restaurant Aldea Yanapay raises funds for the non-profit Aldea Yanapay Project, an alternative school for disadvantaged children. Local musicians, clowns, and, not infrequently, tourists inspired to show off their guitar-picking aptitude also tend to perform there. Ruinas 415, Tel: 51-84-245-779, E-mail: mariellaaldave@hotmail.com, URL: www.aldeayanapay.org.

Witches' Garden
Owned and run by a hospitable French Canadian expat who gladly chats up her clientele and doles out loads of free traveling advice, Witches' Garden is arguably one of Cusco's best all-around culinary experiences. The candlelit dining room is very mod and yet cozy and relaxing. The menu is almost too big and too tempting. And the cocktail list—like the bar stocked with imports not found in any other Cusco watering hole—has one of the best selections of concoctions in town. The menu is heavy on favorites borrowed from all over the world (for example, the starter menu offers stuffed baked potatoes, Greek spanikopita, and oriental spring rolls), but also offers an alpaca option on most entrées, lending the restaurant a decidedly Peruvian flare. Lamb and vegetarian options make a humble appearance for diners less enthusiastic about the Andean meat. Be sure to save room for dessert (or be daring and start your meal with it) because the Black Hole Cake (Oreo cookie, vanilla ice cream, hot fudge and hot whiskey butterscotch) deserves its rumored "world-famous" reputation. Loreto 125, Tel: 84-244-077 / 984-741569 / 984-733068, E-mail: witchesgardencusco@post.com, URL: www.witchesgarden.net.

Granja Heidi Restaurant
Owner Karl Heinz-Horner grew up in Germany but proudly considers himself Peruvian, having settled here and started his own dairy farm, where he sells his own milk, yogurt and

CUSCO

cheese. He is also the proprietor of Granja Heidi, one of the best restaurants in Cusco, midway between the Plaza de Armas and Cuesta San Blas. Karl's level of consideration for his customers extends to providing menus in up to six languages, including Japanese, with an expertly prepared variety of Peruvian and Central European dishes, along with a good wine list. And of course, don't forget to try the deserts, made with fresh milk and cheese from Karl's dairy. Cuesta San Blas 525, Tel: 51-84-238-383.

Victor Victoria

Thirteen years old and going strong, Victor Victoria has made itself into a Cusco institution, winning the hearts and stomachs of young travelers with its cheap, tasty and filling breakfasts, including pancakes, French toast and special-order omelets. The restuarant is also open for lunch and dinner; the menu features native cuisine as well as old standards like hamburgers and fried chicken. There is also offers a salad and pasta bar. Owner Rosa Victoria graciously welcomes all customers with maternal kindness. And, no, the name of the restaurant has nothing to do with the 1983 movie. Calle Teqsaqocha 466, Tel: 51-84-252-284, E-mail: cleocardenas@yahoo.com.

Jack's Café Bar (Entrees: $2 - 6)

Manager Jane Berthelsen said she wanted "the sort of food from back home that you miss" when she came up with the idea of Jack's. Her vision included hearty pea and ham soup, and a big, juicy cheeseburger," not to mention Jack's antipasto which she calls, "a mixed plate of yummy things." And, Tex-Mex nachos. Located in the Plaza de Armas neighborhood, Jack's offers large, well-made platefuls of North American favorites, and that includes hummus with crispy ciabatta and a roasted pumpkin soup with fresh herbs. The restaurant is open every day from 6:30 a.m. to 11:00 p.m. and also has a bar. Corner of Choquechaka and Cuesta, San Blas, Tel: 51-84-254-606 / 506-960, E-mail: janeb34@hotmail.com.

Macondo (Entrees: $4 - 10)

This bar and restaurant in the San Blas district provides a chic, art-gallery ambience, with contemporary artwork displayed on its walls and candles on each table providing a mellow glow. The menu items include chicken with mango and orange sauce, trout salmon with curry sauce, or a local specialty, *papas locas*, which consist of potatoes in a creamy mint sauce and pickles. There is also a selection of fancy coffees to complement your dinner, and an extensive wine and spirits list. Macondo is open for breakfast, lunch and dinner, with prices ranging from $4 to $10. Cuesta San Blas 571, Tel: 51-84-229-415, E-mail: macondo@telsar.com, URL: www.macondoincusco.com.

Tupana Wasi (Entrees: $6 - 8)

Restaurants that claim to offer meals as varied as Italian, Mexican, Peruvian often arouse suspicion that none of those options will really be very good. This is not true in the case of Tupana Wasi Grill Bar. This intimate little restaurant, with capacity for 25 diners, offers an excellent variety of entrees and provides great service too. The restaurant is close to the heart of the San Blas district and is colorfully, but tastefully, decorated in a Peruvian / Mexican style. Cuesta de San Blas 575, Tel: 9358920 (cell).

El Truco Restaurant (Entrees: $8 - 15)

You will definitely not soon forget dining at the Truco Restaurant on the south end of the charming Plaza Regocijo, the latter a smaller and more tranquil compliment to the Plaza de Armas. El Truco is in a capacious and elegant building whose origin goes back to the 18th century, when it served as home to the Viceroy La Serna. It was later a coin plant, manufacturing gold and silver currency, then a gambling house. El Truco's limited, but choice, menu offers expert versions of continental favorites such as fillet mignon, trout menier and Napolitan spaghetti. Live music is common. The facility can easily accommodate over a 150 people, and is recommended for large groups. Plaza Regocio 261, Tel: 5184-235-295, Fax: 5184-262-441, E-mail: eltruco95@hotmail.com, URL: www.cuscuperu.com/eltruco.

ITALIAN/PIZZERÍA
Chez Maggy (Entrees: $3)
The original family-run pizzeria in Cusco, Chez Maggy now has several restaurants around the main plaza. The restaurant offers a delicious selection of fresh, thin-crust pizzas with a large choice of toppings, as well as several pasta dishes, including lasagna and ravioli. All restaurants are small, intimate, and kept warm by the clay pizza ovens inside. Since they are popular with tourists, you may have to wait for a table. You may also be treated to live music by local musicians who will expect a tip. Procuradores 344, 356 and 374, and Plateros 348, Tel: 51-84-234-861/ 246-316. URL: www.pizzeriachezmaggy.com.

Babieca Tratoria (Entrees: $3.50)
One of the most popular pizzerias in town, the Babieca boasts the table-sized *pizza kilometrica*, which can feed up to eight people. A good selection of toppings is available, as well as homemade pasta. Although the ground floor dining room is quite large, it can feel cramped as tables and chairs have been squashed in to make room for all the hungry pizza eaters fresh off the various trails in the area. Babieca also offers set lunch menus, but they do not usually include pizza. Tecsecocha 418, Tel: 51-84-221-122.

Bohème (Entrees: $5 - 10)
Just a few blocks from the Plaza de Armas, the Bohème Bar, Restaurant and Pizzeria is both an informal pizzeria and a slightly more formal but still convivial dining area. There is also a bar you can sit at and order drinks. The pizzeria includes pizza with alpaca, white corn or frijoles toppings. The Bohème itself, having opened in 2006, still conveys a fresh, clean, upbeat air. It is large enough to accommodate parties of up to 60 diners. Calle Saphy 476, Tel: 51-84-247-381.

FRENCH
Le Nomade
Le Nomade offers a relaxed Bohemian ambience of couches and narguile pipes, the latter with a variety of tobaccos. The menu has more of an emphasis on French cuisine, with such plates as *bistec con roquefort* and *boeuf bourguignon*, but there are a number of sandwiches as well. There are no standard chairs, except for two that face windows with mini-balconies. The restaurant is open from 8 a.m. to 2 p.m., with happy hour from 3:30 to 7 p.m. Choquechaka 207 and Cuesta San Blas, Tel: 51-84-438-369, URL: lenomade.net.

ISRAELI
Restaurant Narguila
Head to Narguila if you want to try *shakshuka*, a spiced egg and tomato specialty; served with *jahnun*, the pride of Yemen's bakeries. Or perhaps with a *malawach* puffed pastry. The eatery also serves *meorav*, a mixed grill serving of chicken giblets with onions. After eating you can relax by smoking cured tobacco in a long-stemmed narguile pipe, a time-honored Israeli tradition. Narguila offers a taste of the land of milk and honey in the South American Andes. *L'chaim!* Tecsecocha 405, Tel: 51-84-931-3107 (cell), E-mail: wilfred783@hotmail.com.

CAFÉ/BARS
Pepe Zeta Bistro Lounge
Take a bit of pub atmosphere, mix it with a touch of lounge and you might get an idea of Pepe Zeta's flavor. Its menu is varied and unpretentious, offering many appetizers and a wide selection of cocktails. Cozy sofa areas, a beautiful fireplace to keep you warm, a huge screen by the bar area to watch sports or movies, and soft house or bossa nova music makes it a relaxing option. Every weekend the bar has live music until the wee hours of the night. Tecsecocha 415, 2nd floor, Tel: 51-84-223-082, Fax: 51-84-223-082, E-mail: pepezeta@gmail.com, URL: www.pepezeta.com.

CUSCO

Velluto Crepes

Among party-loving travelers, Cusco has a reputation for hosting daily fiestas, for the traveler with a mean sweet tooth, Velluto is the best place to be during happy hour, with two-for-one crepes from 3 to 6 p.m. The happy hour selection has slightly slimmer pickings than the proper menu's long list of the sweet and the savory crepes, fresh salads and a variety of sandwiches; but the prices are a bargain for such rich food. Satisfy your sweet side with toppings like Nutella, fruit, ice cream or caramel, or make the nutritionally responsible decision with Velluto's oh-so-simple yet oh-so-delicious tomato, basil and mozzarella on ciabatta. Fine espresso and a nice selection of wine round out the café's European flavor. Plazoleta San Blas Tandapata.

Cappuccino Café

Cappuccino Café is a made-for-tourists specialty, with 22 varieties of coffee and a simple menu specializing in hamburgers, sandwiches and omelets. Located on the upper floor of the Portal Comercio, this eatery benefits from a spectacular view of the Plaza de Armas and the Catedral, particularly at sunset. Its apple pie is notable for a soft and fluffy pancake-like crust with a light filling. Cappuccino Café also has computers: with Internet access, costing around 0.50 cents per hour. This is a popular place with tourists and expatriates who come to hang out, commiserate and/or to write home. Portal Comercio 141.

Kachivache

While the owners call it a coffee shop, Kachivache is much more. This restaurant has a clean, artistically rustic atmosphere—with local art on the walls— and is perfect for a break from the city. Chefs at Kachivache use fresh seasoning and spices to create bold, rich, flavorful entrées. Mediterranean overtones dominate the eclectic menu which includes a variety of international dishes. Especially tasty are the kabobs plates with a choice of marinated chicken, beef or seafood and fresh grilled vegetables. The Spanish omelet is another excellent option, as are the assortment of gourmet sandwiches, which are a deal at only $1.25 each. If you are in search of a good cup of joe, there is a reason Kachivache is called a coffee shop, it has some of the strongest, boldest beans in town and will satisfy almost any craving. It is open Monday-Saturday, 9 a.m. - 11 p.m. but sometimes they do close randomly. San Juan de Dios 260, Tel: 51-84-974-6638 / 256143, E-mail: Kachivache_peru@yahoo.es.

The Film Lounge and Danish Café

Part movie salon, part cafeteria and part crash pad, the Film Lounge and Danish Café at the far end of Gringo Alley (a.k.a. Calle Procuradores) is an opportunity to relax and hang with travelers as well as locals. Owner Dorthe Sandbeck cooks up favorites from her native Denmark, such as meatball sandwiches, baguettes and home-made soups; she also offers screenings from her selection of more than 450 film titles in the movie salon, complete with surround sound. Or you can just hang out in the lounge area and share travel stories with friends, old and new. Procadores 389, 2nd floor, Tel: 51-84-123-236, E-mail: dorthesandbeck@hotmail.com.

Café Trotamundos

The name translates into "world trekker" and this eatery has its own trekker icon, a stick figure with a backpack. As much a tavern as a café, Trotamundos has a great view of the Catedral on the Plaza de Armas, along with a large fireplace to keep the place warm. It has a large selection of sandwiches, rolls and juices, along with drinks and coffee, and also makes and sells its own leather handbags and polo shirts featuring the Trotamundo mascot. A fine selection of wine can be purchased by the bottle. Portal de Comercio 177, Tel: 51-84-239-590.

Sweet Temptations

For those seeking a cozier and quieter corner of Cusco to relax and reflect, Sweet Temptations is a peaceful place in which to enjoy a light bite, like a salad or sandwich. The specialty, as the name suggests, are pastries, such as *alfor de ponca*, layers of thin cake with a caramel-like filling in between, courtesy of Argentine-trained chef Jimmy Flores. Jimmy also makes cheesecake, chocolate and carrot cake. Sweet Temptations has select gift items, all at very affordable prices. Herrajes 138-A, Tel: 51-84-244-129/ 227-510, E-mail: swetemptationcafe@yahoo.com.

Panadería El Buen Pastor

Truly, the best way to find El Buen Pastor is to follow your nose. Each morning, Monday through Saturday, the aroma of freshly baked bread and pastries wafts from the walk-in oven at El Buen Pastor through the streets of San Blas and drives tastebuds to distraction in anticipation of *pan con crema* and buttery *empanadas*. Personal pizzas, cream-filled cakes, caramel *churros*, fluffy empanadas, dozens of varieties of bread and goodies of all shapes and sizes can be promptly wrapped up to go or quickly served with a cup of coffee in the upstairs dining area. Because it's a non-profit organization benefiting a home for orphan girls, pastry lovers can feel slightly less guilty about making multiple trips in a single day. Cuesta San Blas 575.

CUSCO NIGHTLIFE

Mandela's Bar (Entrees: $3 and up)

Mandela's Bar is a fantastic bar/restaurant hidden behind the Cathedral, serving a mixture of Peruvian, contemporary and traditional South African food (spicy chicken, etc.) and a full bar (juices and cocktails). This bar has the best views in Cusco at night, by far, over the main Plaza and beyond. Mandela's also has regular live music on weekends and weeknights (local tribal groups, jazz, rock and blues) from 10 p.m. The atmosphere is homey, with candles in the main area, sofas in the lounge area and a chill-out section with cushions. Average costs: $3+ for a main course. Calle Palacio 121, 3rd Floor.

Los Perros Wine and Couch Bar (Entrees: $2 - $4)

This is a very popular and extremely trendy hangout where you'll find travelers lounging about with snacks and drinks. In addition to fabulous food, the restaurant also has a variety of board games, books and magazines. The artsy décor and funky music add to the laid-back atmosphere. On the weekends there is usually jazz music. Tecsecocha 426, Tel: 51-84-241-447.

PUBS

Paddy Flaherty's

Paddy Flaherty's calls itself "the highest Irish pub in the world." And at Cusco's altitude, who wouldn't want to treat themselves to the only place in town where you down a Guinness or English draft beer? At Paddy Flaherty's you can also sample authentic shepherd's pie, not to mention bread and butter pudding and other Celtic cuisine. Open every day from 11:00 a.m. to 2:00 a.m., including lunch, which features salads and roast chicken specialties. The main fun is hanging with the crowd every night for rousing revelry. Calle Triunfo 124 Tel: 51-84-247-719 / 225-361.

The Real McCoy (Entrees: $3)

Although not officially a pub, The Real McCoy an English restaurant, hosts regular pub quizzes and offers traditional pub fare – pie and mashed potato with gravy, big greasy breakfasts, baguettes and baked potatoes with a choice of fillings. With lots of genuine ingredients imported from the UK (including PG tips tea-bags), they have a devoted following among resident ex-pats in Cusco, and English food is always authentic. The Real McCoy also has a four-hour happy hour every night with cheap cocktails, live sports on their giant TV, magazines and board games. Calle Plateros 326, 2nd Floor (upstairs from a traditional goods store, sandwiched between two travel agencies), Tel: 51-84-261-111.

The Cross Keys Pub (Entrees: $3)

A Cusco nightlife institution, the Cross Keys recently moved from its old location in the Plaza de Armas to Calle Triunfo around the corner. Still the most authentic English Pub in Cusco, it is packed with memorabilia and has pool tables and darts. Cross Keys offers bar snacks and a small selection of pub classics, including giant juicy burgers, home-made lasagne and a huge choice of drinks. Look out for happy hour specials on cocktails and wine. Calle Triunfo 350, 2nd Floor, URL: www.cross-keys-pub-cusco-peru.com.

CUSCO

CLUBS

Mythology

Gringos living here could just as well name Mythology "cool central." It has a movie salon, a restaurant and an all-night dance floor. The cool location in the northwest corner of the Plaza de Armas is also where they offer regular salsa lessons. There are movies that play every day at 2:00 p.m., 4:00 p.m., 6:10 p.m., and 8:10 p.m., with rows of comfortable sofas facing a wall-sized screen. Neo-psychedelic art takes up the rest of the walls and the ceilings, and a $25,000 sound system keeps the best of old, new, international and local pop music pulsating until the roosters crow and the vicuñas come home. Portal de Carnes 298, 2nd Floor, Tel: 51-84-255-770.

Up Town

One part movie house, one part dance club, Up Town is one of the most popular stops on the Plaza de Armas. Its second-story location is a bit hidden from street traffic, but thanks to a persistent and insistent street team who dutifully hand out coupons (and enjoy a fairly high rate of success in dragging merrymakers up to the lounge), it's a well populated hangout. Twice a day, a crowd gathers in the corner of the bar that has been converted into a modest movie theatre and democratically chooses a film from Up Town's selection. The never-ending happy hour seems to only get happier as the night continues, especially once patrons have watched a film, a bite to eat and have found their dancing shoes; the staff gives free salsa lessons. Portal de Belén 115.

Mama Africa

A well-established bar and dance club, Mama Africa is like stepping onto a Caribbean island, with its world-class reggae-funk music and sweet, smooth cocktails. The club is located on the second story along the Plaza de Armas; the restaurant-turn-nightclub turns out some of the best dance music in town, playing everything from reggae, funk and electrónica to Latin pop, salsa and samba. The DJs here know how to spin it up and, if you like to dance, you won't be disappointed. While traditional Peruvian and international cuisine is served up during the day, most people come to Mama Africa in the daylight hours to watch one of the 3:30 p.m. movies (daily), nibble food and sip happy hour specialties - the perfect way to rest before the dancing begins. The club hosts special African and Brazilian dance performances throughout the year. Portal Harinas 191, 2nd Floor, Plaza de Armas, Tel: 51-84-246-544, E-mail: mama-frica@mamaafrica.com, URL: www.mamafricaclub.com.

AROUND CUSCO

CHINCHERO

Located 28 kilometers northwest of Cusco, the sleepy Andean town of Chinchero is one of the best places in the valley for Andean textiles and basic goods like hats, gloves, and shawls. Commanding sweeping views of the Salcantay and Vilcabamba mountain ranges, this traditional Andean village will captivate visitors with its natural beauty and cultural integrity. In the main square, which is dominated by a formidable Inca wall composed of huge stones and 10 trapezoidal niches, you'll find the famous Chinchero markets. Here you'll be greeted by bustling artisan sellers, dressed in traditional clothing, and eager to win your attention (and secure a purchase). The market is divided into two sections, one focusing on handicrafts and the other on produce. Even on Sunday, the busiest day, the Chinchero's markets seem more authentic than the Pisac markets. For the best bargaining chances, visit the markets on Tuesday or Thursday, when there are fewer crowds. If you're looking for a lively atmosphere, you may want to check out Pisac market, which is bigger and more flamboyant.

ANDAHUAYLILLAS AND SAN PEDRO

This small colonial village, located 37 kilometers south of Cusco, is home to one of Peru's most beautiful churches. Whether or not San Pedro is the "Sistine Chapel of the

Americas," as some have claimed, is a hotly debated subject (and one which we'll let you make up your own mind about). Built in 1631 in accordance with Spanish tradition, on top of ancient Inca foundations, the church charms visitors with an explosion of Baroque art and religious imagery.

In contrast to its rather dull looking exterior, the church's interior is lavishly decorated with wall-to-wall colonial paintings from the Cusqueña School, frescos and painted ceilings. To maintain the decadent theme, the altars and wood carvings are accented in gold leaf. Also worth a look is the mural by Luis de Riaño, which flamboyantly depicts the road to heaven and the road to hell, each paved with its own respective set of alarming images. The town itself is also visually appealing, with a charming plaza draped in blossoming red-flowered pisonay trees. Most excursions to Andahuaylillas can be combined with trips to the ruins of Rumicolca and Pikillacta. If your visit to San Pedro wasn't spiritual enough, you can always head to the Centro de Medicina Integral (Garcilaso 514, tel. 51-84-251-999, 9 a.m.-7 p.m., medintegral@hotmail.com) where you can relax in the aesthetically pleasing stone courtyard or spend the night in one of the center's plain rooms. Travelers from around the world come here for massages, meditation, harmonizing energy therapy (if you try it, let us know what this is) and other treatments.

THE SACRED VALLEY

The Sacred Valley is west of the sloping edges of the mountain town of Cusco. This area is rich, not only in fields, farms and views, but also in ancient Inca ruins. The famous ruins at Machu Picchu neighbor other Inca ruins at Pisac, Ollantaytambo, Vilcabamba and Choquequirao. Compared to the chilly city of Cusco, the Sacred Valley is a sunny paradise where travelers can explore the remains of numerous Inca palaces, fortresses and temples, and wander through charming Andean villages that continue to produce some of the country's finest handicrafts. Carefully sculpted by the Incas, the valley and its major attractions constantly echo the importance of lunar and solar movements in Inca culture. The temple fortresses of Pisac and Ollantaytambo both exemplify the Incas ability to integrate nature with magnificent feats of human engineering.

Due to its lower elevation, the Sacred Valley area is also an ideal place for travelers to acclimatize to altitude, before tackling any of the major mountains around Cusco. *Soroche*, or mountain sickness is a real threat in the area, and should be taken seriously by anyone arriving by plane from sea level. Adventure travelers will especially love this section of Peru. Some of the most spectacular hikes in the world are found here. The Inca Trail, leading to Machu Picchu, is the most popular, but there are many other, lesser known trekking opportunities in the Sacred Valley that are equally breathtaking. With spectacular Inca ruins and countless colonial churches and modern markets, this area has plenty to see and do while you prepare to surmount the area's higher-altitude attractions. The best time to visit is from April to May or October to November, when you can avoid the flocks of tourist that arrive during the high season from June to September. Even if you don't plan to see all the attractions in the Sacred Valley area, it is recommended that you purchase the Cusco Tourist Ticket, which covers many of the main ruins' entrance fees. If you make your arrangements through a tour operator, the entrance fees are usually included.

HISTORY OF THE SACRED VALLEY

In Quechua it is known as Vilcamayo, and in Spanish El Valle Sagrado de los Incas. This fertile valley, irrigated by the Urubamba River that stretches from Pisac to Ollantaytambo, has a settlement history going at least as far back as 800 B.C. to the Chanapata civilization. The valley provided some of the best agrarian opportunities in the region, and as the early tribes of Peru shifted from nomadic hunters to a settled society of farmers it became a popular place to live. The Sacred Valley was central to pre-Columbian Peru's development. Other pre-Incan civilizations that lived in the valley included the Qotacalla, who were there lived from 500 to 900 A.D., and the Killke, who continued to reside in the valley until Incan domination of the region in 1420. The Incas, regarded in turn lasted until the arrival of the Spaniards one hundred years later. The valley itself was regarded as sacred by the Incas as the territorial correlation to the Milky Way. Their mythology had the founding fathers of the region, the Ayar Brothers, emerging from the Ollantaytambo pyramid.

Ollantaytambo also served as the battleground for one of the last successful defeats of the Spanish army, when the Manco Inca withdrew from Cusco and his forces redirected the Río Patacancha to keep Pizarro's soldiers at bay, while at the same time enlisting the support of jungle tribes. Pizarro retreated, but eventually returned with reinforcements. Ironically, despite the subsequent attempt to remake the region and its people under Spain, much of the culture has remained unchanged throughout the centuries. People still speak Quechua, and farming methods are still very basic.

When to Go
The best time to visit the Sacred Valley is during the dry season, which lasts from mid-April until November. The Sacred Valley is no different from the rest of Peru, and the dry season coincides with high tourist season. June through September is especially busy; if you plan on hiking the Inca Trail, be sure to book well in advance as last-minute spots are very hard, if not impossible, to come by. During the wet season, from November to April, there are significantly less tourists but, hiking can be tougher. The Inca Trail is closed during February for maintenance, but other treks in the region remain open.

Sacred Valley Safety
The main safety consideration for most trekkers in the Sacred Valley is proper acclimatization and physical fitness. Pushing yourself into a trek without being fit enough or giving you enough time to get used to the altitude can be dangerous. Many of the guides speak several languages, and it is important to get a guide that can speak the language your most comfortable with in case there is an emergency. With regard to safety, the guides have the final say on all treks if they feel that something is unsafe or if the group should take a break. Respect your guide's decision and understand that they have superior experience and knowledge of the area, and considering the safety of the group as a whole.

Acclimatization
While neighboring Cusco sits at approximately 3,300 meters above sea level, the Sacred Valley's elevation is approximately 2,500 meters, making acclimatization easier. If you are arriving by air from sea level it is generally recommended to give yourself at least two days to get used to the altitude.

The best advice to beat potential altitude sickness, or soroche, is to drink lots of water and lay off the alcohol. Your appetite may be affected, and eating smaller meals may also help your body adjust. If you plan on doing any trekking or climbing while you are in the area, you will want to give your body at least a few days to adjust. Strenuous physical activity may exacerbate symptoms of altitude sickness.

THINGS TO SEE AND DO IN THE SACRED VALLEY
The Sacred Valley offers much to see and do, and a few days spent checking out the sights is recommended. Base yourself in one of the little towns, such as Pisac, Urubamba or Ollantaytambo, and explore the surrounding area from there. Pisac, in particular, makes a great kick-off point. The town features the famous and not-to-be missed Pisac Market. Aside from the market, the ruins of the Pisac fortress should be visited. The Sacred Valley also boasts a few interesting museums, such as El Museo Catcco in Ollantaytambo, which provides information about the fascinating local history. But the main reason for visiting this region is the seemingly limitless number of scenic hikes and treks through Sacred Valley. Many of the hikes combine walking through beautiful countryside on your way to or via various ruins sites.

Sacred Valley Trekking

The Sacred Valley and Cusco area is prime territory for anyone keen to get out and stretch their legs in spectacular mountain scenery. In addition to the famous Inca Trail, the area offers a variety of other treks and trails that cater to a range of fitness abilities. Whether you're a natural mountain goat or someone who prefers leisurely afternoon strolls, you're sure to find something to suit your tastes. Ollantaytambo and Yucay, in particular, make excellent bases for exploring the hills of the Urubamba Valley. The Cusco office of the South American Explorers is an excellent source for trip and trail reports. For most of the longer treks, permission from the Instituto Nacional de Cultura (Calle San Bernardo s/n, tel. 246-074 / 232-971) is required, and it is strongly suggested that guides accompany you on longer, more arduous trips.

The best time of year to hike is from May to November, and possibly December, when the trails are dry. Also, before embarking on any trip it is imperative that you acclimatize to the higher altitudes, as mountain sickness is a serious threat in this region. A few of the highly recommended hiking opportunities in the Sacred Valley are listed below:

- Pumamarca Ruins--Enjoy spectacular views of Andean mountains and remote Andean villages on your way to the Pumamarca Ruins.

- Pinculluna--Spend a great day hike through ancient Inca agricultural terracing.

- Huayoccari--Check out ancient Inca rock hangings and magnificent mountain views on this remote trek winding its way towards Huayoccari village.

- Salcantay--Summit the challenging slopes of Nevado Salkantay and descend towards the ruins of Patallacta, near the entrance to Machu Picchu.

- Ausangate and Cordillera Vilcanota--Visit one of the more remote and pristine areas in Peru. This tourist-free trek meanders past Andean llama herders and up to Nevado Ausangate.

- Vilcabamba--Challenge yourself with a trek that takes you to Espíritu Pampa and the famous Vitcos ruins.

- Choquequirao--Avoid the tourist trails and make the climb up to the Machu Picchu sibling ruins of Choquequirao.

What to Bring Trekking

Most of the treks in the Sacred Valley are done with a guide and an outfitting company that provide all the necessary camping gear (tents, sleeping bags, stoves and cooking equipment).

You will be responsible for your own clothing, and the most important items are broken-in hiking boots, comfortable pants (many people use quick-dry pants although they are by no means a necessity), a mixture of short and long-sleeve shirts suitable for layering, an insulating layer (preferably fleece or wool as both keep you warm even when wet), and an outer shell to block the wind and gain protection from precipitation. A warm hat to wear at night is a good idea, as well as one to protect your face from the sun during the day. A second pair of shoes to wear around camp at night will be appreciated after a long day in hiking boots. Two common items that are prohibited on the Inca Trail are plastic water bottles and trekking poles with exposed metal tips. To avoid the water bottle issue, bring along refillable containers or hydration systems. If you are bringing trekking poles, plastic tips are preferable but metal tips with duct tape on them are allowed.

Other Items To Bring Along:
• Camera
• Film
• Flashlight (and spare batteries)
• Bug spray
• Sunscreen
• Pocket knife
• Roll of toilet paper
• Personal toiletries
• Some large garbage bags to keep your things dry in the rain.

Trekking Fees

The cost of trekking in the Sacred Valley has risen sharply in recent years (especially on the Inca Trail), mostly due to the enforcement of minimum pay standards for guides and porters. However, there is still quite a bit of variation for the prices of similar tours. The higher-priced options generally offer better tents, sleeping bags and meals.

By far the most popular trek in the Sacred Valley (and in all of Peru) is the Inca Trail. The 2007 fee for four days on the Trail is $73, over four times what it was in 2000. For the shorter, two-day version, the fees are $25 for adults and $15 for students. Porters also now have to pay to enter as well, but this fee will be included in your overall tour price. More information is available in our Inca Trail section.

The fee to enter Machu Picchu is $40 for foreign adults and $20 for foreign students with a valid International Student Identification Card (ISIC) card. The ISIC card is the only accepted form of student identification.

The Lares Valley Trek is a popular alternative to the Inca Trail because it also finishes at Machu Picchu. Depending on your group size, the four-day trek costs between $260 and $420. There is no trail fee for the Lares Valley Trek, but your entrance to Machu Picchu at the end is included.

There is also a six-day Salcantay trek leading into the Inca Trail that costs about $450-650 depending on group size. Included in this are the fees for both the Inca Trail and Machu Picchu.

In order to save money, book a tour with a local operator. Although booking through an agency in your home country may seem easier, many of the local operators have extensive websites and booking through an agency in Cusco can sometimes cost half the price of foreign agencies.

Nearly all tours include the train ride back to Cusco from Aguas Calientes. There are two prices: one is about $46 while the cheaper option costs $15. Most companies include the train ride back and if your company has you booked for the $46 ticket you can save a few bucks by asking them to remove it from your package. The catch is that the cheaper ticket can only be bought in person, in Aguas Calientes, one day in advance. The train will take you to Ollantaytambo where you can catch a bus (about $3) to Cusco. Be warned, however, that this option is a bit risky in the high season, as tickets are sold on a first-come, first-serve basis.

The 'fees' associated with Sacred Valley treks are mostly in relation to the Inca Trail. Aside from outfitter costs, there are no trail fees for the other Sacred Valley treks. Guided hikes of the other major trails in the Sacred Valley cost approximately the same per day as the Inca Trail. The majority of tours offer discounts to those carrying valid ISIC cards and some give discounts to members of South American Explorers, so ask around.

The following are approximate prices for some of the more popular hikes in the Sacred Valley. The price variations are due to changes in price between low and high season:

Vilcabamba--$700 for 7 days
Choquequirao--$545 for 3 days, 4 nights
Salkantay--$450-650 for 6 days
Lares Valley--$260-450 for 4 days.

Salkantay

In terms of trekking opportunities in the Sacred Valley, this one requires a bit more physical and logistical preparation. The crowning jewel of the Salkantay trek is Nevado Salkantay (6,271 meters), the massive mountain that looms above the Inca Trail and plunges into the magnificent mountain city of Machu Picchu. Most Cusco tours offer a four-day trek from Mollepata, located in the Limatambo Valley about three and a half hours from Cusco. You can reach Mollepata by hopping on a bus heading from Cusco to Abancay. From Mollepata it's a three-kilometer walk to Parobambo, where you can hire mules and guides. The route itself stretches across Cordillera Vilcabamba and includes a steep ascent up to the Incachillasca Pass (5,000 meters a.s.l.) followed by a sharp descent along the glaciers of Salkantay. Though physically demanding, the trail offers rewarding views of snow-covered peaks and glacial valleys. On the last day you'll depart your campsite at Acobamba and head towards the Inca ruins of Patallacta, near the popular tourist gateway to the Inca Trail, Km. 88. From here you can catch a train to Machu Picchu or Cusco. Alternatives to the Salkantay Trek are also possible for those who would like something more off-the-beaten-path.

Lares Valley Trek

If you're looking to get off the beaten path but don't want to miss out on stellar scenery, then the Lares Valley Trek is an excellent option. In contrast to the popular Inca Trail Trek, the Lares Valley Trek has yet to fully appear on the tourist radar. Trekkers traverse high mountain passes, plunge into sub-tropical valleys rich in intriguing flora and fauna, and weave past tranquil lagoons, natural hot springs and Inca remains.

This less-traveled trek passes through the remarkable pastoral regions of the Cordillera Urubamba, and presents travelers with a unique opportunity to experience the enchanting Andean landscape and its Quechua culture. Due to the area's relative remoteness, its inhabitants have maintained their traditional ways of life, holding steadfastly to age-old practices of llama and alpaca herding, potato cultivation and colorful weaving. The area has changed very little over the last 500 years, and provides travelers remarkable insight into the lives of Andean farmers. Trekking through the Lares Valley, past thatched stone houses, herds of llamas and farmers dressed in their traditional brightly colored ponchos, is like traveling back in time.

On this trek, tradition and scenic splendor collide, leaving those lucky enough to experience the combination wondering why the Lares Valley is still just a whisper among the traveling community. Or perhaps those who do complete the Lares Valley Trek leave with pursed lips, in an attempt to preserve the pristine culture and landscape that make this area so inspiring. Although the trek is rated as moderate, it does include high passes over 4,000 meters so pre-trail acclimatization is essential. If arriving from sea level, it is recommended that you spend at least 3 days in Cusco before attempting the trek.

Peru Treks and Adventure has put together a series of special non-profit trek packages aimed at spreading the financial benefits of tourism to the local people. Trekkers on these tours have the opportunity to distribute warm clothes and school equipment to the mountain communities located along the trail—a great way to meet and interact with the people of this remarkably beautiful region.

SACRED VALLEY

Have a great travel story? Tell it at www.vivatravelguides.com

Vilcabamba

For a true adventure, make the knee-buckling climb up to Espíritu Pampa, believed by some to be the true "Lost City of the Incas." Here you'll discover the captivating ruins of Vitcos, where the Incas launched their 35-year rebellion against the Spanish. The trail offers some of the most diverse and intriguing scenery you'll encounter while trekking in the Sacred Valley. The journey through time and up mountains begins in Huancacalle, which can be reached by taking a bus or truck from Cusco over the Abra Málaga to Quillabamba and getting off at the Huancacalle turnoff. From Huancacalle a path will bring you to where the Inca emperor was originally exiled to the resting place of the sacred rock of Chuquipalta. From here the trail heads to New Vilcabamba, a colonial-era mining town, and ascends towards a 3,800-meter pass before dropping into the jungle below. The ascent to the ruins involves a steep climb up ancient Inca staircases and offers magnificent views of the valley below. Instead of walking back to Huancacalle, you can trek another one to two days along the river to a small town called Kiteni and take a bus back to Quillabamba. The whole trip takes between seven to 10 days, depending on your fitness level.

Ausangate and Cordillera Vilcanota

The trail that winds its way through the Cordillera Vilcanota and up to the sacred Nevado Ausangate (6,384 meters) goes through one of the more pristine, untouched-by-tourists areas in Peru. For those seeking to avoid the tourist trails this is a good choice among trekking opportunities in the Sacred Valley. You can choose from a number of trekking routes through this range, but the classic seven-day trek offered by most Cusco tour agencies begins in Tinki, a small town situated high in the puna grasslands, and gradually loops around Ausangate. The trail traverses up and across four very high mountain passes (two over 5000 meters), and offers magnificent views of the glacial faces of all the mountains in the range, including Colquecruz and Jampa. Passing through some of the more remote areas in Peru, the trail also affords trekkers glimpses of Andean llama herders and weavers.

Choquequirao

Among trekking opportunities in the Sacred Valley this trail entices trekkers with the chance to view magnificent, albeit less well-known, Inca ruins. This huge complex of Choquequirao sits precariously on a ridge-top in the Vilcabamba area and consists of magnificent Inca walls and double recessed doorways. Most likely, it was built as a winter palace for Inca Túpac Yupanqui, in the same fashion that his father, Pachacútec, built Machu Picchu. Since Hiram Bingham discovered the ruin in 1911 it has remained the relatively less-traveled sibling of Machu Picchu. The trek to Choquequirao starts at Cachora, which you can reach by taking a bus to Abancay and getting off at a dirt road past Saywite Stone. If you're keen, you can hitch-hike the final stretch to Cachora, where you can rent guides and mules. The first day involves a hike down to Río Apurímac, and on the second day you'll embark on an arduous six-hour climb straight up the other side to the cloud forest ridge where the city sits. Some Cusco tour agencies offer a combined ten-day trek from Choquequirao to Machu Picchu. Another approach to Choquequirao is to start at Huancacalle and make the eight-day trek across the Cordillera Vilcabamba via the Vitcos ruins.

Huayoccari

For the adventurous solitude-seeker, this hike is a sure win. In contrast to other trekking opportunities in the Sacred Valley, this one offers slightly less tourist-trodden trails. Along this two-day hike one way from Yucay to the small Andean village of Huayoccari, you'll encounter some of the most enchanting mountain scenery, from Inca terraces overlooking the San Juan River ravine to Sakrachayac and ancient rock paintings. After one night of camping you'll make the arduous ascent to Tuqsana Pass (4,000 meters) and then descend to Yanacocha Lake. From here you'll follow the trail to Huayoccari.

Pinculluna

If you're not up for a full-day's journey, Mt. Pinculluna, rising up behind Ollantaytambo, is an excellent choice among short trekking opportunities in the Sacred Valley. The trail offers a pretty couple-hour walk up past agricultural terracing. Because the trail isn't well marked in some spots, you may be better off hiring a guide in town to avoid getting lost.

Pumamarca Ruins

Among trekking opportunities in the Sacred Valley, this one rewards trekkers with spectacular views of Andean mountains and remote villages. The trail follows the banks of the Río Patacancha, where you will eventually encounter the small but well-preserved Inca ruins of Pumamarca. To complete the loop from Ollantaytambo requires about five hours. To begin, take the road north of Ollanta along the Patacancha. When the road crosses the river it becomes a footpath and you'll follow this past Munaypata village. Take a left and follow the path towards the valley and terracing and then make a sharp left towards the agricultural terraces in front of you.

SACRED VALLEY TOURS

Making arrangements to see the Sacred Valley through a tour operator, either in Peru or your home country, can be an excellent way to get to know this spectacular valley rich in Inca ruins, agriculture and magnificent views. In particular, there are several tour agencies in Cusco that will gladly help you plan an itinerary. Hiking tours are especially popular in this area. The Sacred Valley offers literally some of South America's most beautiful and historic hikes. Another extremely popular option are archaeological tours in the Sacred Valley. These are best for travelers who want to see as many of the incredibly preserved Inca ruins throughout the valley as possible. Aside from purchasing Sacred Valley tours in Cusco, for those who are a little more adventurous and perhaps have a decent smattering of Spanish, it is possible to base yourself in any of the smaller towns, such as Pisac, Urubamba or Ollantaytambo and get local advice and information about the best trips on offer. Biking tours can also be arranged. This mountainous region offers some excellent rides and gives travelers a chance to experience the exhilaration of cliff-side roads up close.

SACRED VALLEY LODGING

Hotels in the Sacred Valley are by and large good value, with friendly hospitable staff and low ceilings. Take care if you're tall! It is worth checking what the hotel rates include, as most don't include breakfast, but you can usually get it for a reasonable fee. Many hotels in the Sacred Valley can arrange local tours, often at a good rate. There are a range of hotels in Pisac to suit all budgets. Some have a great view of either the surrounding spectacular countryside or of the ruins. There are places conveniently close to the Pisac Market and local transportation. Just a bit further up the valley, accommodation in Urubamba is limited to just a few lodgings. This is a great place for budget travelers to pick up cheap accommodation. Ollantaytambo hotels are, on the whole, a good bet with cheap bed and breakfast options, through to more expensive places set around pretty courtyards or in well-kept gardens. Several places here offer a scenic vista over the ruins or a backdrop of the mountains. Shop around for a good deal.

PISAC

Pisac (32 km northeast of Cusco) is popular because of both ancient and modern attractions. The ancient ruins at the top of the mountainside featuring a small Inca village with temples, palaces, solstice markers, baths and water channels draw archaeologists from around the world. Its modern attraction is the weekly market on Sundays, which attracts travelers from around the world looking for bargains on indigenous weavings, souvenirs and knit clothing.

Getting To and Away From Pisac

In terms of making it to Pisac from Cusco, most travelers take either *combis* or *colectivos*, vans or mini-buses that depart from the corners of Puputi and La Cultura in Cusco, or Tullumayo and Garcelazo, when they have enough passengers, which is usually every fifteen minutes. The cost is about two soles, or $0.70. The trip itself takes about 45 minutes. To return to Cusco or head on to Urubamba and other cities, the colectivos and combis arrive and depart continuously from near the town market. Cabs can take you back and forth for about $5. There are also chartered bus tours which can be arranged through any travel agency.

Have a great travel story? Tell it at www.vivatravelguides.com

Things To See and Do in Pisac

Pisac Market

The Pisac market is a must-see for those visiting the Cusco region. Every Tuesday, Thursday and Sunday, the streets fill to overflowing with artisans selling their goods and tourists of every stripe buying them. Even if you must go to Pisac on another, non-market day, you'll find a lot of the same stuff for sale in little shops around town. Sunday is the best day to visit by far, as there is also a smaller market for locals. Villagers from miles around pack up their llamas and donkeys in the wee hours of the morning in order to arrive and set up stalls where they sell vegetables and other produce. Often, the preferred method of commerce is to barter, as opposed to buying and selling, a tradition that goes back to before the Inca. Even if you're not a shopper, the market is worth a visit. It's a great place to take photos and people-watch. Many of the cafés around the market have second-story balconies with good views of visitors from around the world haggling and bargaining with locals. The quality of the goods is a little sketchy. If you're looking to spend a lot of money on any one item, you're better off in a fine gallery in Cusco or Lima. But prices are low and the market is a great place to buy memorable souvenirs for friends back home.

Most of the goods sold at the Pisac market are textiles, jewelry, carved gourds, ceramics, felt hats, antiques (buyer beware) and sweaters, to name a few. Bargaining is standard practice in the Pisac market. There are no price tags; pay the price agreed to with the seller. Some tips: Never make the first offer. Wait until the seller starts with a price. Don't be afraid to walk away from a price you don't like; chances are you'll see the same thing from another seller. Another good tip is to buy a lot of things at the same stall, even if they're not of the same type (for example, gourds, sweaters, tapestries, etc.). Vendors will often discount prices for those buying in bulk. Be aware of your location; stalls tucked into back regions of the market far away from where the tour buses from Cusco disgorge their passengers will often have better prices than stalls nearer the bus stops and on strategic corners.

The Pisac market ends around five o'clock when the last of the tour buses goes back to Cusco. If you're staying in town, the end of the day is also a good time to look for bargains, since some of the sellers may be a little more willing to make a deal rather than pack their goods for next time. Shopping at markets like the one in Pisac can be a lot of fun if you lighten up and allow yourself to wheel and deal in a friendly way.

Awana Kancha

Opened in 2003, Awana Kancha is an interesting project to visit just a 10-minute drive outside Pisac at Km 23 of the Cusco-Pisac road. There is an exhibition of different types of Camelids, including llamas, alpacas and vicuñas, all of which are very happy to be fed a continual supply of long grass, which you will be handed upon arrival. The project works with different communities in the area who employ traditional techniques for spinning and dying wool, using all natural materials and weaving traditional designs. There is a large shop selling these high-quality weavings, as well as exhibits on the natural substances used to dye the thread. Afternoons are the best time to visit, as in the mornings the community is often busy with tour groups. Contact them in advance to organize a guided tour. There is no fee for the guided tour of the project, however donations are welcome. Km 23 Cusco-Pisac road, Tel: 51-84-203-289, E-mail: info@awanakancha.com, URL: www.awanakancha.com.

Pisac Ruins (Entrance: $15)

The ruins of the fortress at Pisac are among the most interesting in Peru. Today, historians and archaeologists believe that Pisac was a compound that mainly served as a line of defense against the Anti Indians, who held lands to the east of Cusco and were the implacable enemies of the Inca. The Pisac complex is made up of several different areas. Outside of the walled complex is Qanchisracay, a small compound of rough stone buildings. This area probably served as a military garrison and may have housed local villagers in case of attack. There are also some ruins of aqueducts. The area might have been home to farmers who worked the lower terraces. From Qanchisracay, the Inca Trail heads up the hill to a crossroads of sorts, known as Antachaka. There are four baths at the crossroads, with water brought in by duct. To the west, you'll see the cemetery known as Tankanamarka, an important pre-conquest site that has been largely looted by grave robbers. According to Inca belief, the dead could carry their possessions with them into the next life. For that reason, there were often treasures left in grave sites, a fact that the conquering Spanish soon realized and exploited. By some estimates, there may have been as many as 10,000 graves at the site at one time. The looters took everything and left only holes.

Continuing the hike, you'll pass through the wall through Amarupunku, the Door of the Serpent, and into Upper Pisac. The Incas' amazing skills with stonework are on display here: note how they cut this path through the rock and remember that they did not have iron tools or explosives to help them tunnel. Upper Pisac is the most important and impressive section of the ruins, because most of the ceremonial and religious structures in the complex are located there, and the stonework is incredible. There are several temples in Upper Pisac. Unfortunately, it is not known today which temples corresponded to which deity. One exception is the impressive Temple of the Sun, an oval building built directly into the rock. From the top of the building, Inca astronomers could track the movements of the sun, moon and stars. There is also an altar that may have been used to sacrifice animals for purposes of divination. Sadly, some of the decorative stonework on the temple of the Sun was recently chipped off by thieves. There are also a series of restored baths in Upper Pisac. The last area of the Pisac ruins is the residential area known as P'isaca, from which the ruin complex gets its name. It is a series of terraces and stone buildings. Some archaeologists believe that these were homes for the elite. From here, there is a trail you can take back to the town of Pisac.

PISAC LODGING

If you're planning on visiting either the Pisac ruins or markets you may want to spend the night in town. Pisac has a variety of accommodation types, which range from backpacker havens to modern luxury hotels. The only time you may have trouble finding a place to stay is in September, when pilgrims heading towards nearby Huanca descend on the town.

Hospedaje Kinsa Cocha (Rooms: $5 - 9)

Run by the friendly Chalco family, the inviting Hospedaje Kinsa Cocha offers simple, clean dorm-style rooms. The shared bathrooms have wood-heated hot water, so be sure to throw some logs on before showering! Calle Arequipa 307, Tel: 51-84-203-101.

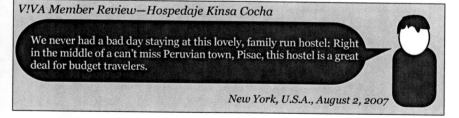

V!VA Member Review—Hospedaje Kinsa Cocha

We never had a bad day staying at this lovely, family run hostel: Right in the middle of a can't miss Peruvian town, Pisac, this hostel is a great deal for budget travelers.

New York, U.S.A., August 2, 2007

Hospedaje El Artesano (Rooms: $6 - 12)

Hospedaje El Artesano is probably the most minimal of hostels in Pisac. You have to walk through a soiled corridor with exposed wiring coming out the walls to access the reception. It has only five rooms, none of them with private bathrooms. They all go for about $6. The rooms themselves are fresh and clean, and the bathrooms do have hot water. Apart from that there are no other amenities, though laundry and such is easily available elsewhere. The hostel has neither a phone nor an e-mail address. If you are thinking of your stay strictly in terms of just crashing for a night, and nothing better at a similar price is available, this is at least serviceable, and the staff is friendly. Calle Vigil 244.

Have a great travel story? Tell it at www.vivatravelguides.com

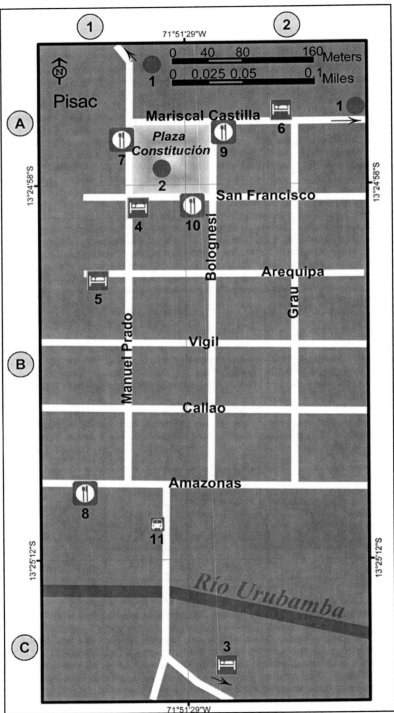

```
Activities ●                    Eating ⬤
 1 Pisac Ruins A1 A2              7 Ulrike's Café A1
 2 Pisac Market A1                8 Restaurant Valle Sagrado B1
Sleeping 🛏                      9 Restaurant Samana Wasi A2
 3 Hotel Royal Inka Pisac C2     10 Mullu B2
 4 Hotel Pisaq B1               Transportation 🚌
 5 Hospedaje Kinsa Cocha B1      11 Bus Station B1
 6 Hostal Varayoq A2
```

Hospedaje Linda Flor (Rooms: $6 - 12)

Hospedaje Linda Flor offers good clean and inexpensive rooms, some without bathrooms, some with, and little else. Single rooms without bathrooms are priced at $6, while private, double, matrimonial (with queen-sized beds) rooms go for $12. The rooms themselves have spare wooden floors and are freshly painted, and the bathrooms are newly remodeled. You register through the convenience store that owns it, and walk up a dirty stairway to access the rooms. Some of the ceilings are low, so if you are tall, be mindful. It is only a few blocks walk to the center of Pisac and its markets, buses and restaurants. Pardo Esquinal and Vigil, Tel: 51-84-203-035.

Hostal Samana Wasi (Rooms: $8 - 12)

On the corner of the Plaza de Armas, Samana Wasi offers friendly, family-run accommodation around a small central courtyard filled with flowers and chirping birds. Rooms are basic but clean, mostly with shared bathrooms. For a small extra fee you can have breakfast at the Samana Wasi restaurant, which includes some courtyard tables, a dining room and tables outside on the sidewalk where you can watch market sellers setting up their stalls. Plaza Constitución 509, Pisac, Tel: 51-84-203-018.

Hotel Pisaq (Rooms: $10 - 16)

Hotel Pisaq is a bright, friendly bed and breakfast located on the plaza in Pisac. The owners, a Peruvian-American couple, go out of their way to make their guests feel at home. There are a number of features that lower mid-range hotels don't usually offer, such as a sauna, well water and a café. The interior of the hotel is painted in a Native American theme, "which reflects the spirit of the indigenous nations of the Americas," according to their web site. They are very knowledgeable about the surrounding areas, and can arrange tours and visits to sites of interest. On the Plaza Constitución, Tel: 51-84-203-062, Fax: 51-84-203-062, E-mail: hotelpisaq@terra.com.pe, URL: www.aart.com/aart/HOTELPISAQ.html.

Hostal Varayoq (Rooms: $14 - 28)

Hostal Varayoq has the look and feel of higher-end hotel, yet is still available for hostel prices: single rooms start at $14, doubles and matrimoniales go for $28, with an American breakfast (with eggs, milk and fruit) included. This is probably the best bargain in this beautiful village that many stop at for a day, usually during the famous market fairs, on their way to Machu Picchu. Hostal Varayoq also has its own in-house restaurant, El Helecho, with $5-7 prices for well-made local and continental cuisine. Mariscal Castilla 380, Tel: 51-84-203-263, E-mail: manudiaz@hotmail.com.

Paz y Luz Bed and Breakfast (Rooms: $20 - 35)

For a rustic retreat, this gorgeous bed and breakfast next to the sacred Urubamba River is an excellent choice. With spectacular views of the enchanting Andean mountains and the nearby Pisac ruins, Paz y Luz offers visitors a relaxing atmosphere to contemplate the surrounding beauty. For active travelers, there are a number of trails nearby to explore the countryside. Rooms are comfortable, tastefully decorated and include brand new bathrooms. In the central area you'll find a dining table, woodstove and an immaculately polished wood staircase.

SACRED VALLEY

In a separate building in the rear is a one-bedroom apartment with its own kitchen. One kilometer from Pisac Bridge (to the right), Tel: 51-84-203-204, E-mail: dianedunn@terra.com.pe, URL: www.maxart.com/window/gateway.html.

Hotel Royal Inka Pisac (Rooms: $54 - 115, Monthly, $850 - 1200)

Hotel Royal Inka Pisac is a converted hacienda and chapel on the road out of Pisac on the way to the ruins. The hotel is attractive and offers a view of the ruins, and the rooms are large if a little bit dull. It is definitely the place to stay in Pisac if you're looking for a little bit of luxury: it features an indoor swimming pool, Jacuzzi and spa. They also offer classes taught by local artisans, such as woodworking. Carretera Pisac Ruinas s/n, Tel: 51-84-203-064, Fax: 51-84-203-064, E-mail: royalinka@aol.com, URL: www.royalinkahotel.com/hpisac.html.

PISAC RESTAURANTS

Pisac offers an array of restaurants that are sure to suit any traveler's taste or budget. Even vegetarians can find some good eats in this small city. A number of restaurants serve up tasty Peruvian fare, and a particular treat in this region is fresh trout. For those on a quest for something quick to eat, take a short stroll to the bakery on Mariscal Castilla 372, just across from the plaza. Here you can grab vegetarian empanadas and hot breads straight from adobe ovens. The bakery treats are particularly popular on market days.

Mullu

This little slice of bohemia is a hang-out lounge and art gallery/craft shop downstairs and a café/restaurant upstairs. The lounge part of the place has rows of black bean bag cushions along the wall facing a large-screen television. On the second floor, you can order yourself an alpaca cheeseburger, trout tartare or a plate of Andino-Thai sushi. Another Thai-influenced item, *tomka*, is a chicken dish cooked with coconut milk and lemon grass. Carrot juice and various mixes with other extracts are also available, like a banana-honey-nutmeg smoothie and *té piseño*, made from the local muña herb, for starters. Plaza de Armas 352, Tel: 51-84-203-073, URL: www.mullu.com.pe.

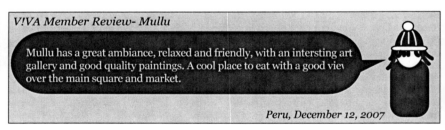

V!VA Member Review- Mullu

Mullu has a great ambiance, relaxed and friendly, with an intersting art gallery and good quality paintings. A cool place to eat with a good view over the main square and market.

Peru, December 12, 2007

Miski Mijuna Wasi

Facing Pisac's famous pisonay tree in the central plaza and, three days a week, the colorful market fair that takes over the town, Miski Mijuna Wasi restaurant offers traditional Peruvian and more standard cooking in a pleasant Andean setting, complete with native folk music complimenting the tranquil environment. Treat yourself to the indigenous *tarwi* soup made of broth, local vegetables and legumes, cheese, and local herbs and spices. Or how about diced kidney cooked in wine sauce? Miski Mijuna Wasi can accommodate up to 96, one of the larger options for groups in this small village, and its in-house pastry chef will whip up any number of flavorful desserts. Plaza de Armas 345, Tel: 51-84-203-266, E-mail: michell776@hotmail.com.

Restaurant Samana Wasi (Entrees: $2 and up)

For tasty and inexpensive dishes, check out Restaurant Samana Wasi. Among the restaurants in Pisac, this is one of the best. Enjoy the popular trout, salad and fried potatoes plate while relaxing in the cozy little courtyard situated towards the back. With great service and a pleasant atmosphere, complete with majestic mountains looming in the background, this restaurant is an excellent option for almost any hungry traveler. It is priced very reasonably, with appetizers starting at $1 and entrees at \$2. The restaurant also has a couple of basic rooms for rent. Calle Mariscal Castilla and Plaza Constitución 509, Tel: 51-84-203-018.

Restaurant Doña Clorinda

To try some excellent traditional Peruvian food make your way to Restaurant Doña Clorinda. Despite its rather humble looking façade, the restaurant serves up some delicious dishes, such as *lomo saltado* and *rocoto relleno*. If you ask for a table upstairs, owner doña Clorinda will take you on a semi-tour of her house to a spacious dining room that overlooks the plaza. Try the basic lunch menu for \$2, or splurge and get the slightly more extravagant version for \$5. Plaza de Armas 350, Tel: 51-84-203-051.

Restaurant Valle Sagrado

If you're in the mood to try some of the best trout in the Cusco area, then head over to Restaurant Valle Sagrado. At lunch this place is packed with locals, who flock to the restaurant for owner Carmen Luz's tasty soups and sandwiches, and trout, chicken and lamb rib dishes. The building's faux-Inca walls distinguish it from the numerous other restaurants situated nearby. Avenida Amazonas 116, Tel: 51-84-203-009.

Ulrike's Café

This classy new café promises some of the most creative menus in town. Even vegetarians can find something delectable to eat here. If you're in the mood for something sweet, try one of the delicious homemade cheesecakes. With art-adorned walls and a relaxed music-filled atmosphere, the café is a great place to take a break and grab a bite to eat. Plaza Constitución, Tel: 51-84-203-195, E-mail: ulrikescafe@terra.com.pe.

URUBAMBA

Located smack-bang in the middle of the Sacred Valley, Urubamba is an attractive little town, making it a good base for traveling around the area, exploring the countryside and visiting the Inca ruins. Urubamba tends to be passed over more than other towns in the region, making it a quieter place to kick back for a few days. The pleasant palm-fringed Plaza de Armas has a small fountain at the center. The town boasts a decent array of services, hotels and restaurants and is close to Cusco, within about an hour's drive. There are excellent hiking opportunities surrounding the town, especially in the area of Moray, a town close-by with Inca terraces that have been sculpted into the hillsides. Alternatively, nearby Salinas makes for an interesting stop with its Inca salt pans, still in production, following an ancient tradition.

Getting To and Away from Urubamba

The same busses that depart from Cusco to Pisac will also take you to Urubamba, as well as to the next town heading north, Ollantaytambo. The point of departure is at Avenida Ferrocarril, several blocks away from the Urubamba Plaza de Armas. There are plenty of inexpensive mototaxis that can take you to your hotel or hostel. Departures and arrivals are continuous from morning until night. Cabs, of course, are also an option, and if you have enough fellow riders the split cost is roughly equal to what you would pay on a bus.

URUBAMBA SERVICES

Pl@net.Com (\$0.32 / hour)

Whatever your communication needs while visiting Urubamba--writing or talking to your loved ones, catching up on news from home or anywhere else, or downloading and sending photos from your Peru journey--Pl@net.Com at 449 Jirón Grau, facing the Plaza de Armas, is by far the best Internet station in town. Not just by default, in that most of the others here have older-model computers with barely functioning keyboards in cramped spaces. Pl@net.Com features twelve fresh-model computers with high-speed access. Each is in a large, spacious, private cubicle, complete with headphones and a microphone. It is open every day from 9 a.m. to 10 p.m., and costs only one sol an hour. It also has telephone cabins that allow you to make inexpensive international and local calls. 449 Jirón Grau, Tel: 51-84-201-420, E-mail: rvvlap@hotmail.com.

URUBAMBA TOURS

Viento-Sur

Adventure Club Viento-Sur offers a unique combination of eco-tourism, adventure, sport and culture through a variety of outdoor activities: horseback riding, mountain biking, paragliding, walking, treks and cultural trips. It also provides exclusive, customized, multi-adventure travel programs. Pricing ranges from $100 to $500 depending on the activity. Tel: 51-84-201-620, E-mail: info@aventurasvientosur.com, URL: www.aventurasvientosur.com.

Sacred Valley Mountain Bike Tours ($40 - 180)

It is one thing to visit the Sacred Valley, but how about mountain biking across it, pushing up and across its slopes for the tour of a lifetime? The Sacred Valley Mountain Bike tour guides rent bicycles and gear for half-day, one-day and two-day trips through some of the world's best scenery, stopping now and then to appreciate sites such as the Inca Fortress of Ollantaytambo, or better yet, riding along some of the very same downhill trails used by the Incans in the competitive events in order to train young warriors for battle. The tour guides are as knowledgeable about local geography as they are about bicycles, and all bikes are thoroughly inspected before usage. Jirón Convención Nº 459, Tel: 51-84-201-331 / 201-884, E-mail: tourjardin@hotmail.com, URL: www.machawasi.com.

URUBAMBA LODGING

Hotel Urubamba (Rooms: $3 - 10)

When visiting a country where the majority of the population lives in poverty, it may not be fair or kind to criticize the efforts of its citizens who are trying to do the best they can with limited resources. The Hotel Urubamba is only recommended for those traveling on the cheap with a general indifference to where they are crashing for the night. It offers not only shared bathrooms, but shared rooms, as in more traditional hostels, at $3 a night, with private rooms going for $10. The rooms featured ragged, old, green carpet. The owners will fix a breakfast for $2, and they are at least considerate and friendly. The hotel also has its own convenience store. Bolognesi 605, Tel: 51-84-201-400 / 201-062.

Hospedaje los Jardines (Rooms: $12 - 27)

A little bit away from the Plaza de Armas in Urubamba, but closer to the foothills of the looming mountains of the Sacred Valley, the Hospedaje los Jardines has increasingly become the hostel of choice in this city for travelers from all over the world. As regards its name, it has a great, big, beautiful garden and a manicured lawn you can unwind on and contemplate the view of the aforementioned valley--if you are not distracted by the in-house jungle monkey, Juanito. A private room with a bathroom goes for $14, and a room for two is priced at $20. Breakfast is available for an additional $2. Hospedaje los Jardines rents bicycles and offers tours. Jirón de Convención 459, Tel: 51-84-201331 / 201-884, E-mail: info@machawasi.com, URL: www.machawasi.com.

Hospedaje Mach'a Wasi

In the town of Urubamba, Mach'a Wasi is a convenient and comfortable place for visitors to stay while exploring the natural, historic and cultural wonders of the Sacred Valley of the Incas. The owner places a strong emphasis on running the business in harmony with Mother Nature as much as possible and encouraging the guests to do likewise. Mach'a Wasi is a totally non-smoking environment. Drunken behavior is not tolerated either. The accommodation can house 13 people in five rooms featuring comfortable mattresses. Three of the rooms have their own shower, with another shower and a bath available for the remaining rooms. Hot showers are available at any time. Three rooms have a double bed; one of those rooms also contain two single beds, making it suitable for a small family. The other two rooms have three and two single beds respectively. Besides accommodation, the services of the hostel also include mountain rental bike tours, using quality Trek and GT mountain bikes, to suit small to large people, with front suspension, disc brakes, 24 gears, bell helmets, trek gloves and tire repair kits. Jirón Padre-Barre, Tel: 51-84-201-612, URL: www.machawasi.com.

URUBAMBA RESTAURANTS

The Muse

It opens at either 10 or 10:30 a.m., depending on the season, but still serves breakfast, probably because it rightly assumes that it's mostly young and mostly fun-loving foreign customers were up late the night before. You can order your eggs or pancakes any time throughout its work day. The Muse is made-to-order with its throw pillows and lounging chairs, its bohemian art, and variety of vegetarian and non-vegetarian options. An example of the latter is its Thai-style vegetables with chicken...or you can order it without. Live music, pub quizzes and movies are all part of the experience. Calle Comercio and Jirón Grau, Tel: 51-84-246-332, E-mail: claritadean@hotmail.com.

Cusco Café and Bar (Entrees: $3 - 8)

Located in one corner of the city of Urubamba's Plaza de Armas, the Cusco Café and Bar shows off a flashy sense of design and décor, from its ornately carved banister (you walk up a flight of stairs to access the place) to gallery displays of modern art on its walls. It features continental and Peruvian cooking, the latter with a more creative edge than you will find in local restaurants, such as a wheat risotto with Andean curry and banana chips. The prices range from $3-8, though they rise slightly during peak tourist season. It is one of the few restaurants you will find here that accepts credit cards. Calle Comercio 515, Tel: 51-84-201-681.

Café Plaza

This charming little restaurant on the Plaza de Armas in Urubamba offers a variety of filling but inexpensive Peruvian and continental favorites. It also has a large selection of coffees, including a variety of liquor-spiced cafés, not to mention liquor-spiced hot chocolates. Chocolate pancakes are also on the menu as a dessert. Café Plaza also features a large selection of fruit smoothies, cocktails and sandwiches. There is a magazine rack with a diverse selection of foreign and local publications, and an attractive selection of framed black-and-white photo portraits of locals adorning the walls. 440 Jirón Bolívar, Tel: 51-84-201-118.

YUCAY

Located a few kilometers east of Urubamba, Yucay is a peaceful town with a few interesting colonial homes and the restored colonial church of Santiago Apóstol. Inside the church, you'll find exquisite oil paintings and fine altars. The main square is divided by a large, grassy plaza where *futból*/soccer games are held. Facing the Plaza Manco II is the adobe palace of Sayri Túpac, who settled here after arriving from Vilcabamba in 1588. In the hillsides near the town there are extensive Inca terraces, perfect for an afternoon excursion. Aside from the hotels clustered around the main square, there are few services in Yucay.

One of Cusco's best kept secrets is also located near Yucay. Huayoccari Hacienda Restaurant is an elegant, converted country manor perched on a ridge overlooking the Sacred Valley, about two kilometers outside of Yucay. In addition to walls decorated with colonial paintings and ceramics, and a rustic courtyard, the hacienda has some of the best cuisine in all of Cusco.

Huayoccari Hacienda Restaurant ($35 per person)

Nestled high above the Sacred Valley, about two kilometers outside of Yucay, Huayoccari Hacienda Restaurant is one of the best places to grab a bite to eat and relax. The cooking is completely organic and based on the hacienda's original recipes. The menu includes homemade soups, fresh cheeses, steamed river trout and mouthwatering chicken. Save room for dessert, as the sweets are as delectable as the main meals. Though a bit out of the way, this place is definitely worth the trek. Who can say no to spectacular food and a to-die-for atmosphere? Be sure to make reservations in advance, as there are only a few tables. Kilometer 64 off the Pisac-Ollantaytambo highway. Call for directions beforehand. Tel: 51-84-962-2224 / 226-241, E-mail: hsilabrador@latinmail.com.

SACRED VALLEY

AROUND URUBAMBA
Moray (Entrance: $7)

Located about 38 kilometers from Cusco, Moray is a very interesting archaeological site. Discovered in 1932, Moray is a series of three circular terraced depressions which at first glance appear to be some sort of amphitheatre or coliseum. The terraces are finely made and have stood up very well over time. It is believed that the terraces are a sort of agricultural laboratory, as each terrace represents a different microclimate suitable for different sorts of crops and plants. The locals have started calling it the "Inca Laboratory." The site is very serene and located amidst much natural beauty. That, and the otherworldly appearance of the terraces and circles, have caused Moray to gain a bit of a reputation as a mystical hotspot. In any event, the site is well worth a visit for ruins buffs, history fanatics and anyone interested in a low-key yet beautiful visit to a part of the Sacred Valley that not every tourist gets to see. The nearest town is tiny Maras, which is easily reachable by bus from Urubamba. Moray is about 9 kilometers away from Maras. There is a small entry fee to see Moray. It is close to Salinas and the two can easily be combined into a good day trip.

Salinas

For centuries, native Andeans living in the highlands made their own salt by diverting a salt water hot springs into thousands of small pools and pans, which are then dried out. Today, there are more than 5,000 such *salineras* still in use, creating a patchwork of white rectangles on the hillside. The pools are topped off every three days or so, and after a month a few inches of solid salt will have accumulated. It is then broken up and carted off in sacks. Each salinera can produce about 150 kilos of salt per month. Nearby, a small mill processes the salt. Iodine is added and the salt is graded and sold. The sight of many terraces of salt pools cascading down the side of the steep mountain is guaranteed to leave an impression. The only drawback to visiting Salinas is that modern-day tourism has definitely discovered this timeless, traditional practice, and sometimes there are many buses of tour groups at the site. Nevertheless, it is well worth a visit. If you're up for a hike, you can get there in about 45 minutes from Urubamba or sign on for a tour. Be sure to bring some water—it can get quite warm in the area around Salinas. The closest town to Salinas is tiny Pichingoto, a scenic little spot carved right into the mountain. It is close enough to Moray that the two can be combined into one day.

OLLANTAYTAMBO

Poised in the northeastern end of the Sacred Valley, about 97 km from Cusco, this little town is a cultural haven well worth the visit. Surrounded by snow-capped peaks on both sides, Ollantaytambo boasts spectacular views of both Andean scenery and ancient Inca ruins. The town itself offers a number of hotels and restaurants, and it is recommended that you spend the night in town to ensure that you get to the ruins early, before the crowds. For a truly unique experience, rise early and watch the sun rise over the mountains. Because the scenery around Ollantaytambo is some of the most remarkable in the region, it's a great place to wander while you explore nearby ruins and other landmarks of the Inca Empire. Of the marks left by the Incas, some of the most intriguing are the Inca *andenes*, or agricultural terraces, that adorn either side of the massive gorge surrounding the town.

The town itself, with its adobe brick walls draped in blooming bougainvillea and perfectly carved canals that continue to carry water down from the mountains, is testament to the Incas' engineering and architectural genius. Take a stroll through the characteristic grid of streets and you'll be astounded by the site of locals lingering in the doorways of ancient Inca residential *cachas*, once inhabited by several families during the 15th century.

As you meander through town you may want to stop by El Museo Catcco, which has displays of textiles and archeological objects recovered from the local ruins, in addition to a plethora of ethnographic and archaeological information. If you get lost just follow the Ollantaytambo Heritage Trail, denoted by blue plaques, which highlights the most important historical sites around town.

Onwards from the main plaza, towards the outskirts of town, are a number of enchanting Inca ruins. Perhaps the biggest attraction is the massive fortress, perched among steep stone terraces carved into the hillside. Representing one of the Inca Empire's most impressive architectural examples, the fortress successfully held the Spanish at bay during an attack in 1537. Despite its forbidding façade, however, the edifice was probably originally intended as temple for worship and astronomical observation rather than military purposes.

Between the temple fortress and town, adjacent to the Patacancha River, you will encounter another interesting site: Baño de la Ñusta (Bath of the Princess). This ancient ruin composed of grey granite was once used for ceremonial bathing, and offers excellent views of ancient granaries built by the Incas. If you've got a keen eye you may also make out the face of an Inca carved into the cliffs rising high above the valley. Ollantaytambo can be reached from Cusco by train. You can also leave from here for Machu Picchu: the train has seven daily departures.

OLLANTAYTAMBO HISTORY

As the only standing fully preserved Inca Town in all of Perú, the town of Ollantaytambo is an important national heritage site. The word Ollantay has its roots in the Aymara (*ulla nta wi*) for "place that looks downwards," while tambo comes from the Quechua *tampu*, meaning "lodging and rest-stop for weary travelers." In one popular myth, Ollantaytambo is held to be the birthplace of the Incan people. However, most hold that Ollantaytambo was named after Ollantay, the Inca General whose military prowess helped to extend the borders of the Incan empire northwards and southwards. He is famous for having asked Inca Pachacútec for his daughter's hand in marriage. Being summarily denied the honor of marrying his love, Cusi Coyllor, due to his lower social origins, the indignant Ollantay rebelled against his ruler and was thrown in prison. A play written in the 16th century dramatized their tragic tale of love.

Militarily, Ollantaytambo is celebrated as the outpost of the most victorious defeat of the Spanish *conquista*. Manco Inca retreated with his troops here from Sascsayhuamán in 1537. The fortress of Ollantaytambo was important to the Inca defense against the *conquistadores*.

It was originally constructed as a fortification against the Amazonian Antis (generic term used for the indigenous Peruvians of the jungle). However, the discovery of remains of ritual baths and a Sun temple, archaeologists are questioning the defense theory. Historians also believe that Ollantaytambo may have held even more significance than Machu Picchu to the Incan Empire. Today, Ollantaytambo serves as a popular transportation hub for getting to and from Aguas Calientes (at the base of Machu Picchu) by train.

Getting To and Away from Ollantaytambo
The most popular way to visit Ollantaytambo is with a tour agency on a day trip from Cusco. Usually tour operators combine a stop in Ollantaytambo with several other surrounding villages like Chinchero or Piscac, and prices start at what is a called "bargain" $10. The most economic, and arguably the most enjoyable, way to explore Ollantaytambo is at your own leisure and on your own time by going it alone without a guided tour.

Bus
Though rumors abound of buses running directly between Cusco and Ollantaytambo, the easiest thing to do is to catch a bus from Cusco to Urubamba from one of two Cusco stations that service Urubamba, and then to change buses. The terminal on Grau runs via Chinchero (1.5 hours) while the terminal on Avenida Tullumayo takes the Pisac route (2 hours). Fares to Urubamba are $1-$1.50. Once at the Urubamba bus terminal, there's no shortage of collectivos running to Ollantaytambo or any question about where to find them. Collectivo operators bound for Ollantaytambo greet passengers from Cusco the moment they step off the bus and usher them into a waiting mini-van. From Urubamba, the ride into Ollantaytambo takes about 30 minutes in a collectivo ($0.30) or, for those with deep pockets, taxis make the trip slightly quicker for about $3.

Train
Ollantaytambo is the mid-point for trains running between Cusco and Aguas Calientes (the point of disembarkation for Machu Picchu and the last stop on the train). Though it's tempting to stop in Ollantaytambo en route or returning from Aguas Calientes, it can be an expensive endeavor if done solely by train, as fares to and from Ollantaytambo to Aguas Calientes are the same as from Cusco. Keep in mind that while it's possible to get to Ollantaytambo by road, Aguas Calientes can only be reached by train, and therefore travel between Aguas Calientes and Ollantaytambo requires train travel. The rail station in Ollantaytambo is about 1200 meters from the town proper, and the road is currently under serious construction, so be prepared to walk most of the distance.

Nine trains, offering a variety of classes and rates, stop in Ollantaytambo from Cusco every morning before continuing on to Aguas Calientes. It's possible to disembark in Ollantaytambo from a morning train, as well as embark on any of the trains en route to Aguas Calientes. Though a number of trains return to Cusco from Aguas Calientes every day, only three trains returning to Cusco stop in Ollantaytambo, so be sure to correctly book your ticket if you plan to alight at Ollantaytambo from Aguas Calientes. Trains leave Ollantaytambo bound for Cusco everyday between 5 p.m. and 6:45 p.m. Schedules and exact times are subject to change, so check with the train station directly or visit www.perurail.com for information.

THINGS TO SEE AND DO IN OLLANTAYTAMBO
The Sacred Valley abounds with opportunities to get your adrenaline fix en route to ruins. Leave the tour bus behind, and mountain bike to the Moray Ruins or take a ride down the 14,400-foot Abra Málaga Pass. Trek to the Choquequirao ruins (a journey also known as "the other Inca Trail") or whitewater raft the Apurímac Canyon. Ollantaytambo is an ideal jump-off point for outdoor adventures throughout the valley, whether you're interested in half-day, full-day or multi-day trips. All organized trips require a minimum of two people; however, with a group of three or more, prices are lower per person. Full-day mountain bike trips start about $35 (for do-it-yourself types, it's also possible to rent bikes, helmets and gear for about half the price), rafting starts at $20 and myriad multi-day combo trekking/biking

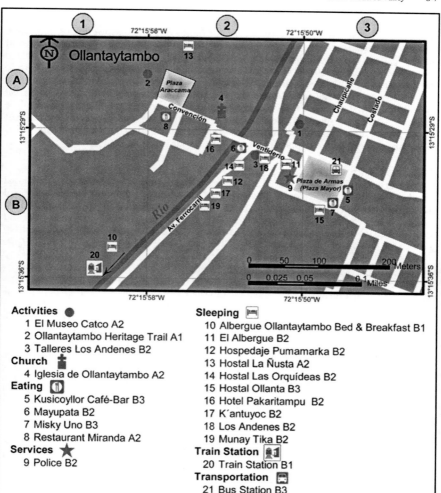

Activities ●
 1 El Museo Catco A2
 2 Ollantaytambo Heritage Trail A1
 3 Talleres Los Andenes B2
Church ♁
 4 Iglesia de Ollantaytambo A2
Eating 🍴
 5 Kusicoyllor Café-Bar B3
 6 Mayupata B2
 7 Misky Uno B3
 8 Restaurant Miranda A2
Services ★
 9 Police B2

Sleeping 🛏
 10 Albergue Ollantaytambo Bed & Breakfast B1
 11 El Albergue B2
 12 Hospedaje Pumamarka B2
 13 Hostal La Ñusta A2
 14 Hostal Las Orquídeas B2
 15 Hostal Ollanta B3
 16 Hotel Pakaritampu B2
 17 K'antuyoc B2
 18 Los Andenes B2
 19 Munay Tika B2
Train Station 🚉
 20 Train Station B1
Transportation 🚌
 21 Bus Station B3

SACRED VALLEY

trips start as low as $150 per person, but do cost as much as $250 per person for longer, more involved excursions. For an outdoor adventure on a smaller scale, it's possible to book city walking tours and short horse riding trips at various locations around Ollantaytambo, including restaurants and tour agencies in the Plaza Mayor.

Ollantaytambo Heritage Trail

The Ollantaytambo Heritage Trail is a collection of about a dozen sites of importance throughout town. If you're visiting on a day trip, most guided tour groups from Cusco, as well as city walking tours booked in Ollantaytambo, stroll through the small town, pointing out various stops along the trail, including Manay Raqay, the CATCCO Museum and the Temple of Santiago Apóstol. If you're self-guiding, blue plaques mark some of the sites, but the most complete list of trails stops, as well as a map, can be found just inside the entrance to the fortress on the wall outside the INC (Instituto Nacional de Cultura) office building. It's a giant mural map of the town and surrounding area, marked with the Rutas Ancestrales, the Heritage Trail and main parts of the fortress.

Have a great travel story? Tell it at www.vivatravelguides.com

Shopping at Manay Raqay (Square of the Request)

Nearly all visitors to Ollantaytambo pass through Manay Raqay as it's the only entrance to the fortress and in addition, it's a designated stop on the Heritage Trail. The Incan square's most unique feature (aside from the looming fortress obviously) is the water element, a forceful channel of water flowing openly through the square from the ruins just up the valley. With so many tourists taking the walk through Manay Raqay to enter the fortress, tourism officials have, of course, taken full advantage of the wide open space to erect several rows of market stalls. From afar, it looks like there's more shopping to be had than you'll actually find, as the stalls are sparsely occupied and those that are open for business hawk the same collection of books, jewelry, bags and walking sticks. However, the square is the most shopping you'll find in one place, and it is a great place to buy a book on your way in to the fortress.

El Museo Catcco

Despite its relatively small size, El Museo Catcco (Centro Andino de Tecnología Tradicional y Cultural de las Comunidades de Ollantaytambo) is an excellent source for historical and cultural information on Ollantaytambo. The museum has interesting displays of textiles from local ruins, and ethnographic and archaeological information. All exhibits are in English and Spanish. The museum also has a ceramic workshop where you can buy some quality pottery pieces. One block from plaza in Casa Horno, Tel: 51-84-204-034.

The Fair Trade Association in Ollantaytambo

For cultural and conscientious collectors, the Fair Trade Association outlet in Ollantaytambo on the Jirón de la Convención is a must-visit in their Peru journey. It is the retail outlet for the Patacancha Women's Cooperative, created with the intention of preserving and reviving the art of weaving done with traditional methods and natural dyes, a practice going back centuries. *Lliqllas* (a sort of very wide and long scarf), *chullos* (caps), handbags, ponchos, blankets and other hand-woven products are all produced with an authenticity that is priceless. As regards the Fair Trade Association's practice, the women employed earn a living wage for their work. In cooperation with the Casa Ecológica, this store also sells organic honey, soy, and sesame oil, among other products, not to mention pottery and ceramics. Please note that at the time of writing The Fair Trade Association in Ollantaytambo was looking to change their name and website. The E-mail and address will stay the same. Jirón de la Convención, E-mail: ollantaytextiles@gmail.com.

Talleres Los Andenes

A veteran weaver Félix Calla, proprietor of Hospedaje Los Andenes, also sells a creative assortment of alpaca wool, hand-made ponchos, handbags, shawls, vests, belts, wallets and hats, all at reasonable prices. In terms of stone and clay, his gift shop features goods, animals, deities, Incan symbols and other features central to Andean culture, which are also represented in Felix's colorful collection of expressive wooden masks. Old-fashioned irons--actually made from iron--should appeal to antique collectors. Calle Ventiderio, Tel: 51-84-204-095.

OLLANTAYTAMBO TOURS

Ollantaytambo Adventure Center (OAC)

Tour agencies in Cusco would have you believe that trekking or riding the train between Cusco and Aguas Calientes are your only two options to get to the lost city. Do something a little different with Ollantaytambo Adventure Center. OAC offers a two-day trip starting in Ollantaytambo, that's heavy on the trekking with a stint in a car. It's $240 for two people, and $230 with three or more. For a map, more information or to hire a guide, visit the INC office located in the fortress monument.

KB Tours

What to do in Ollantaytambo--apart from ascending the monumental Incan Pueblo steps? How about rafting, horseback riding, mountain-biking, and even simple hiking? KB Tours will organize any of the above, with excursions offered at beginning, intermediate and advanced levels, both for individuals and groups. KB Tours can take you for a ride through the Class II and Class III rapids of the Urubamba River, or on bicycle to the famous Incan quarries above the Sacred Valley or the salt mines of Marcas. Tours range from a half-day price of $25 to a four-day price of $189. Plaza de Armas, Tel: 51-84-204-133 / 994-7608, E-mail: kbtours_2@hotmail.com.

OLLANTAYTAMBO LODGING

Despite its relatively small size, Ollantaytambo boasts a variety of accommodation options. In particular, the city has plenty of good budget options for backpackers taking the train to Machu Picchu. If you're really penny-pinching, then head towards the San Isidro neighborhood, where many families have turned their homes into hostel rooms ($3-5 per person). You can reach this hostel haven by following the main road through town and heading left towards the ruins.

Andean Moon

Set back from the main square, up one of Ollantaytambo's pretty cobblestone streets, the Andean Moon is a pleasant place to crash for a day or two. The owner is friendly and accommodating, and you can barter with her in low season for a reduced rate. Rooms are a generous size and have beamed ceilings, bare wooden floors and are tastefully adorned with the works of local artists. Head up the spiral staircase to the roof, from where you have a first class view of the fortress. Later, take a dip in the Jacuzzi - although it will set you back a bit at $25 for a group of four people. This place has 24 hr hot water and the prices include a simple continental breakfast. Calle del Medio S/N, Tel: 51-84-246-398 (Cell: 9605360), E-mail: info@andeanmoonhostal.com, URL: www.andeanmoonhostel.com.

Hostal El Bosque

This hostel is about a two-minute walk from the train station. It has small and comfortable rooms with private bathrooms and hot water. The inviting courtyard and gardens are a great place to relax. Breakfast is included. Av. Ferrocarril s/n, Tel: 51-84-204-148, Fax: 51-84-204-148, E-mail: reservas@elbosqueollantaytambo.com.

Hospedaje Pumamarka (Rooms: $3 - 5)

With only four rooms in an old rustic building, the Hospedaje Pumamarka evokes the pioneer spirit of a romantic past. In terms of budget accommodation, if you are looking for cheap but quality, this is one of the better deals in Ollantaytambo. Prices for a single room vary from $3-5 depending on the season, and the rooms are top-notch: spacious, comfortable and artfully fashioned, with great window views of the looming green Sacred Valley mountains. One caution: this really is an old building, and the second floor hallway and entrances have low-ceilings. The owners also rent horses, arrange tours and offer money exchange services. Patecalle and Plaza de Armas, Tel: 51-84-204-128, E-mail: pumamarka40@hotmail.com.

Las Portadas (Rooms: $3.50 - 14)

Don't panic when you step through the gate at Las Portadas and find yourself in an ultra cozy courtyard surrounded by only a handful of rooms. The path winds through the flowered courtyard and opens up into a second, much more spacious communal outdoor area and another two-story building with plenty of rooms. The rooms differ in character, some with squeaky wooden floors and others with smooth tile, so check out a few to find one that suits your needs. Electric showers provide hot water. There is also a garage and camping facilities on the premises. Ca. Principal s/n, Tel: 51-84-204-008.

Hostal Ollanta (Rooms: $4.50 - 9)

Offering simple, clean rooms with wood floors, Hostel Ollanta is great for anyone on a budget. The shared bathrooms are brand new, and have hot water. Plaza de Armas, Tel: 51-84-204-116.

Hostal La Ñusta (Rooms: $4.50 - 9)

At Hostal La Ñusta dark, basic rooms give way to spectacular views of nearby mountains and ruins. Among the hotels in Ollantaytambo, this is one of the friendliest. Always ready to extend a hospitable hand to guests, owner Rubén Ponce is also a fountain of knowledge about the town's ruins. For those prepared to explore the area on horseback, you can also rent horses here for $10 per day. Carretera Ocobamba, Tel: 51-84-204-035.

K'antuyoc (Rooms: $7 - 20)

Perched on a very slender piece of land between the road and the river, K'antuyoc may be as close to sleeping in a grove of eucalyptus as it gets without actually swinging from a hammock. From the café downstairs (which boasts a menu with seven different flavors of pancakes, typical plates like *saltado de lomo*, chicken and trout, and a healthy list of soups, salads and pastas), you can nearly reach out and touch the river as it slides narrowly between tree trunks. The rooms are few, but well kept by the friendly proprietor, and all have hot water. Avenida Ferrocarril s/n, Tel: 51-84-204-147 / 994-7005.

Hotel Munay Tika (Rooms: $9.25 - 38)

From the front courtyard of Hotel Munay Tika you can hear the hum of the river as it tumbles down from Incan ruins and makes its way into the Río Urubamba. If the lull of babbling brook doesn't suit your fancy, weave around the bright yellow and red buildings and cozy up with your book among the flowers and silence in the back courtyard. It is run by a family who has taken great care to manicure the inside of the accommodation as well as the outside. The rooms are tidy, colorful and each has a private bath with hot water. The hotel also offers Internet service, national and international calling, and room service. And because it's located on the road connecting the rail station and town, the only noise you're likely to contend with is that of the river. Avenida Ferrocarril 118, Tel: 51-84-204-111, E-mail: reserves@munaytika.com, URL: www.munaytika.com.

Hospedaje Los Andenes (Rooms: $10 - 20)

This minor hostel offers inexpensive but pleasant rooms that start at $10 for an individual, $20 for two. All rooms come with bathrooms and hot running water. The rooms themselves are spacious, clean, comfortable and attractive for this price range, with colorful, heavy wool blankets for warmth once night falls. The owners, Félix Calla and María Palomino, will also fix you breakfast for an additional $2.50-3. They are also proprietors of a folk art and wool product shop. As with so many old frontier buildings now serving as hostels, even though ceilings in individual rooms are high, hallways and entrances are low, so the vertically advantaged should be careful. Calle Ventiderio, Tel: 51-84-204-095.

Hostal Las Orquídeas (Rooms: $15 - 45)

Small, but comfortable rooms with a private bath and hot water ensure that any visit to Hostal Las Orquídeas will be a restful one. Of the hotels in Ollantaytambo, this is definitely one of the coziest. The inviting courtyard and gardens are a great place to relax, and if you're hungry individual meals can be ordered. Estación s/n, Tel: 51-84-204-032.

Home Sweet Home Ollantaytambo (Rooms: $17 - 40)

A unique house offering every traveler's dream: a cozy, comfortable place with services of the highest level that does not overcharge. The breathtaking views of the Ollantaytambo Fortress, seen from many points in the hotel, make Home Sweet Home a unique quality B&B accommodation. Prices are per room per night with breakfast included, and reduced rates are available for visitors staying more than two nights. Ca. Principal A2, Tel: 084-9203637, Fax: 054-220323, E-mail: ollantaytambo@homesweethome-peru.com, URL: www.homesweethome-peru.com/ollantaytambo/pages/location.html.

El Albergue (Rooms: $58 - 94)

This peaceful establishment is perfect for travelers seeking a place to kick back and relax. Owned by Wendy Weeks, a painter from Seattle, the hotel has spacious whitewashed rooms tastefully adorned with wooden tables and beds. The inviting rooms are accented by a tranquil atmosphere and graceful decorations that include local weavings, Wendy's paintings and vases blossoming with flowers. Grab a seat on the wood balcony overlooking the lively garden and thumb through your favorite book, or try a wood-fired, eucalyptus steam sauna. In the morning, enjoy homemade French toast and coffee, and afterwards head to the hotel's shop where you can browse through an interesting collection of books, weavings, Ekeko dolls and Waq'ullu dance masks. For the more adventurous individuals, private transport to the salt mines, Moray or Abra Málaga for bird-watching can be arranged. Located near Ollantaytambo train station, Tel: 51-84-204-014 / 204-049, E-mail: albergue@rumbosperu.com, reservations@elalbergue.com, URL: www.elalbergue.com.

Hostal Sauce (Rooms: $88 - 145)

An upscale establishment offering cozy, sun-filled rooms overlooking the Ollantaytambo ruins, Hostal Sauce invites visitors to relax in its tranquil atmosphere. Of the places to stay in Ollantaytambo, this one offers some of the most spectacular views of Inca ruins. On cold nights, snuggle into the comfy couches and warm yourself in front of the central fireplace. When your tummy starts to grumble, head over to the hotel's restaurant and choose from a menu of delicious salads, meats and pastas. Calle Ventiderio 248, Tel: 51-84-204-044, E-mail: hostalsauce@viabcp.com, URL: www.hostalsauce.com.pe.

Hotel Pakaritampu (Rooms: $127 - 276)

Life in Ollantaytambo doesn't get much swankier or much more relaxing than Hotel Pakaritampu. Located on Av. Ferrocarril, which links the railroad station with the city center, the country grounds at Hotel Pakaritampu quickly whisk away any residual city stress after a stint in Cusco. The hotel campus itself is a rambling ranch-style hotel that captures scenic views of the valley below and ruins above. In addition to plenty of green space to wander, Hotel Pakaritampu has indoor and outdoor dining areas, a TV room, a library and reading room, and alpacas on site. All rooms include private baths with hot water, and the hotel provides telephones for international calls, safety deposit boxes, laundry services and internet access. Prices include tax and breakfast buffet; however, for non-Peruvian residents, the 19 percent tax will be deducted from the price upon proof of country of residency. Av. Ferrocarril s/n, Tel: 51-84-204-020 / 204-104, URL: www.pakaritampu.com.

OLLANTAYTAMBO RESTAURANTS

Ollantaytambo has a number of great eateries, each catering to a variety of budgets, palates and styles. From sophisticated modern cafés to popular gringo dives and Peruvian-style restaurants, Ollantaytambo has it all. The majority of cafés are centered near the main plaza, which is also a great place to scout for vegetarian options. For the truly adventurous, drop by any one of the private houses displaying a red plastic bag on a pole outside the door. Here you can try the local chicha maize beer, and mingle with the lively and ever-hospitable local hosts.

Sonccollay Restaurante Café Bar Pizzeria (Entrees: $2.75 - 10)

Despite its faraway corner location in the Plaza Mayor, Sonccollay attracts a fair amount of attention from visitors (thanks, partly, to its giant heart-shaped sign). A smattering of outdoor tables creates a modest patio, which unfortunately sits in the street proper and forces diners to contend with the noise and pollution of large tour buses as they pass within inches. Inside service may not allow for the same fantastic views of the surrounding ruins, as the atmosphere is severely no-frills, but the family who runs the café is eager to chat up the clientele. The menu is well-priced and offers the standard fare from Peruvian typical dishes to gringo favorites like pizza, pasta, burgers and sandwiches in addition to breakfast choices like omelets and pancakes. (Breakfast is cheaper, and ranges from $1.25 to $3.25.) If you have your backpack in tow, Sonccollay offers free backpack storage while you gallivant on a day's excursion, which you can book through the restaurant as well. Plaza de Armas.

Cactus Bar (Entrees: $3)

Tucked around the corner from the Main Plaza, Cactus Bar is one of the only places in Ollantaytambo that is open late. With modern, funky décor and a relaxed atmosphere, it serves up generous portions of bar snack type food as well as a selection of drinks. The owners, local guide Arturo and wife Louise from the UK, can offer lots of insider information about things to see and do in the area. Calle Principal s/n, Ollantaytambo, Tel: 51-84-797-162, E-mail: louise@leaplocal.org.

Hearts Café (Lunch: $5)

Hearts Café is becoming something of a backpacker favorite. Set right on the Plaza de Armas, Hearts offers "mainly wholefoods," in well-sized portions to its patrons. Try the delicious chicken casserole, complete with mashed potatoes and veggies, or stop by to pick up a take-out breakfast before heading to the ruins. What's great about this place is that the donate profits to children's projects in the region - while you wait for your food, check out the walls that are adorned with the pictures of the help that the owner has provided to the local region. You can eat well here, knowing that your cash is going to a good cause. Open from 7 am to 9 pm daily. Plaza de Armas, Tel: 51-84-204-078, E-mail: hearts.cafe@hotmail.com, URL: www.heartscafe.org.

Misky Uno (Entrees: $5 - 11)

Misky Uno's owner stands in the restaurant's doorway dressed in a tuxedo, grinning from ear to ear and beckoning the hungry for a fine meal. The cozy dining room feels more like an enlarged nook. The tables are elegantly set with linen napkins and wine glasses just waiting for visitors, and the sound of big band music drowns out any noise from the kitchen, nearby diners and, almost, your dining companion. To wine and dine in Peruvian style, Misky Uno focuses on typical dishes of ceviche, alpaca and trout, as well as a few comestibles that are high brow in any country, like filet mignon. Calle Convención s/n.

Tayta Pizzeria-Trattoria

Tayta Pizzeria-Trattoria has a stunning view of the Ollantaytambo fortress. This artsy dive specializes in homemade wood-oven pizzas and Italian pasta. Cheap and good, the menu also includes an array of appetizers and a wide wine selection, including a tasty pisco sour among many other cocktails, and of course beers are on hand as well. The right place for a perfect cup of Italian espresso. Av. Ferrocarril s/n Ollantaytambo, Tel: 204114, E-mail: reservas-tayta@hotmail.com.

Quechua Blues Bar Cafe

More of a bar than a restaurant (although you can get international food here), the Blues Bar Cafe is great for sinking a beer early evening after most of the tourists have left town. Their marketing materials boast, "the best view in Ollantaytambo," and they're probably right--the bar looks out over the fortress and has a pleasant, chilled out atmosphere. It is quiet early on, but livens up later with a mixed crowd. Food offered includes burgers and standard international fare. It's a bit on the pricey side, but with the best view in town, it is to be expected. From the fort, first right, Tel: 204130, E-mail: ketsaleoat@hotmail.com.

Mayupata

For a taste of home, make your way to restaurant Mayupata, which specializes in international treats like thin-crust pizzas and massive burgers smothered in cheese. On cold nights the inviting central fireplace is a popular spot to gather for drinks, and on any night you can chill out and enjoy the relaxing atmosphere paired with spectacular river views and great food. Meals cost between $3-8. Jirón Convención s/n (across from bridge, on the way towards the ruins), Tel: 51-84-204-009.

Alcázar

A popular joint for breakfast and lunch, Alcázar is praised for its simple, cheap breakfasts and mouth-watering vegetarian lunch options. Try the French toast or honey-and-banana-pancakes, which can be washed down with one of their delicious fresh juices. This is a great place to grab a snack or midday meal if you're in a rush to head off and explore the city. Or, if you've got some time to sit and relax, savor a glass of wine while you contemplate a menu of vegetarian dishes, spaghetti, steak fillet, chicken, ham, sausages and dessert. Calle del Medio (one block from main square), Tel: 51-84-204-034.

Restaurant Miranda

Compared to the number of touristy restaurants in Ollantaytambo, Restaurant Miranda has a refreshingly local feel. Early risers can enjoy a $2 breakfast of fresh juice, eggs, tamal and coffee, and those who prefer to sleep late can head here for a cheap but filling $3 lunch. Even vegetarians can find something to munch on here, and owner Alicia Miranda is always eager to please. Near Patacancha bridge, between the plazas, Tel: 51-84-204-097.

Il Capuccino

For a little more sophistication, Il Capuccino is the ideal place to relax, sip on a drink and sink into a pleasant conversation. In addition to excellent coffee, the café also has a selection of fine wines, tempting desserts and a book exchange. Stop by in the morning and prepare for a day of Andean adventure by fueling up with a good American-style breakfast. Ventiderio s/n.

Kusicoyllor Café-Bar

International treats and Peruvian delicacies collide at Kusicoyllor Café-Bar, where you can choose from a diverse menu of novo-Andean dishes, homemade croissants, real espresso and homemade ice cream (the only Ollantaytambo). The restaurant also has a fairly extensive selection of fine wines. With great food, friendly service and a full bar, this place has all the ingredients for a fantastic night out. A meal here will run you between$5-8. Plaza Araccama s/n, Tel: 51-84-204-114.

Inka Traveler

The Inka Traveler bar has a narrow winding staircase, decked out in stained wood bark, which you carefully walk up in order to access the restaurant itself, an efficient provider of well-made and inexpensive items from spaghetti and pancakes, to fried chicken and alpaca cutlets. Owner John Walter Serrano opens his restaurant at 6:00 a.m., one of the few to do so in Ollantaytambo, making pancakes and other carb-rich items for visiting early risers eager to get a head start on their climb up Machu Picchu. You can enjoy your meals with a view of the world-famous Ollantaytambo Fortress. Calle Ventidiero 2nd floor, Tel: 51-84-967-5995.

Ollantay Bar and Restaurant

It calls itself a "pizzeria, café, and restaurant," and what it claims is pretty much what you get. The menu includes pasta, soup, salad, steak, chicken, wines, lots of trout dishes, sandwiches, fruit juices, coffees and wines. Meals are generally in the $3-6 price range, and the locals of Ollantaytambo prove they can prepare such items as well as anyone else. It deserves kudos for the Old Spanish West atmosphere, especially in the brighter second floor. The restaurant itself is open from 7 a.m. to 10 p.m. every day. With a capacity for 70, groups are welcome. Discounts are available for members of the South American Explorers club. Plaza de Armas (east side), Tel: 51-84-204-001, E-mail: ollantay@ollantaytambo.org, URL: www.ollantaytambo.org.

AGUAS CALIENTES

The town below Machu Picchu, Aguas Calientes is the final train stop from Cusco. From here, just a few blocks from the train station, you can catch a 20-minute bus up a winding mountain road to the park entrance. To avoid crowds at Machu Picchu, we recommend staying one night at Aguas Calientes and taking the bus up to Machu Picchu before the first train arrives in the morning. Aguas Calientes is an unremarkable town, and you won't want to spend more than one night there, but there are a number of international restaurants and tourist-friendly hotels that live off the Machu Picchu crowds. There are some nice hikes in the area with decent bird and butterfly watching.

Getting To and Away from Aguas Calientes

There are no buses or roads that go to Aguas Calientes, the stopping-off point to access Machu Picchu – at least not all the way. The closest you can get via bus or taxi is Ollantaytambo, and from there, like everyone else you have to board a train. For those wanting to board a train

SACRED VALLEY

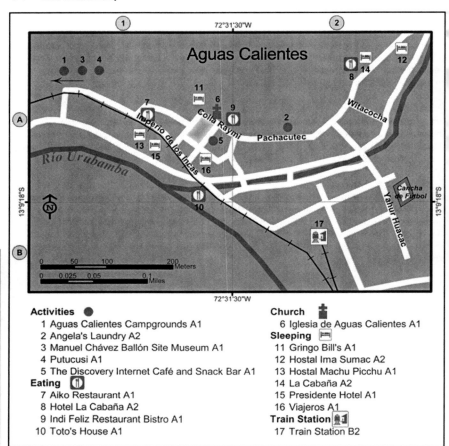

Activities ●
1 Aguas Calientes Campgrounds A1
2 Angela's Laundry A2
3 Manuel Chávez Ballón Site Museum A1
4 Putucusi A1
5 The Discovery Internet Café and Snack Bar A1
Eating 🍴
7 Aiko Restaurant A1
8 Hotel La Cabaña A2
9 Indi Feliz Restaurant Bistro A1
10 Toto's House A1

Church ✝
6 Iglesia de Aguas Calientes A1
Sleeping 🛏
11 Gringo Bill's A1
12 Hostal Ima Sumac A2
13 Hostal Machu Picchu A1
14 La Cabaña A2
15 Presidente Hotel A1
16 Viajeros A1
Train Station 🚉
17 Train Station B2

directly from Cusco, there are two options.

At the San Pedro Station in Cusco, at the intersection of Cascapara and Santa Clara, PeruRail has two daily departures, a "Vistadome" which leaves at 6:00 am and arrives at Aguas Calientes three-and-a-half hours later, and a "Backpacker" which leaves at 6:15 am and arrives in four hours. The Vistadome at $110 is the luxury trip, includes snacks, beverages, and a sky dome (ergo the name). The Backpacker, at $75 is the budget trip, but still comfortable. The return trips leave at 3:30 pm and 3:55 pm respectively. There are also morning departures from Aguas Calientes, beginning at 5:45 am. Schedules are subject to change, however, so one is best advised to purchase ahead. And be prepared to bring cash – credits cards of any sort are not accepted.

Those who can afford it and want luxury and convenience can take the new Hiram Bingham Deluxe Train, which departs from the city of Poroy, about 20 minutes north of Cusco. This train leaves at 9:00 am and gets to Aguas Calientes at 12:30 pm. The train, complete with a bar car, is modeled on the classic Orient Express train of its eponymous owner. The $470 price includes exclusive buses to the ruins of Machu Picchu and guided tours. The trip back includes cocktails and a four-course supper.

Once you are in Aguas Calientes you must head over to the Tourist Information office at their Plaza de Armas, and purchase two things: 1) a three-day access pass to the ruins, priced at $43, and 2) a round-trip bus pass for $12. The bus itself leaves from the Plaza.

Santa Maria-Santa Teresa Road Route / Inca Jungle Trail

Since 2005 when the strict regulations on the Inca Trail were imposed and Peru Rail began steadily increasing its prices, industrious backpackers have been taking a new route to Machu Picchu from Cusco. Taking an average of two days, as opposed to four hours on the train, but costing around a fourth of the price, it is a route for those with more time than money.

From Cusco, you can take either a bus or colectivo to Santa Maria. Buses leave from Paso Santiago and take around six hours to Santa Maria ($5), while colectivos leave from outside Almudena Cemetary and take around four hours ($12). From Santa Maria, it is an eight-hour trek along a dirt track, or a one-hour bus ride to Santa Teresa. From Santa Teresa you can take a colectivo or taxi to the Hydroelectric Plant from where there are four daily trains to Aguas Calientes (one hour, $8). There are basic hotels and restaurants in Santa Maria and Santa Teresa, and the hot springs just outside Santa Teresa make a welcome break from all the bone-shaking bus rides.

Some agencies in Cusco are running a version of this route dubbed the Inca Jungle Trail. Often, this means mountain biking down from Abra Málaga to Santa Maria, and then trekking to Santa Teresa. Be aware that many of the agencies running this trail are less professional than those who operate the Inka trail and will try to cut costs as much as possible, sometimes compromising safety standards. For the most up-to-date information about which are the most trustworthy agencies or how to make this trip alone, pop in to the South American Explorers Clubhouse in Cusco.

AGUAS CALIENTES LODGING

The closest stopover to Machu Picchu, staying overnight at Aguas Calientes allows you to catch the first bus to Machu Picchu and the last one to return home, thus avoiding the crowds from Cusco. The close proximity has encouraged a slew of hotels to pop up and there are many options for every budget. Prices are higher in the high season, but can be negotiated down in the low season. Camping is also an option. The cheapest hotels in Aguas Calientes are to be found along the railroad tracks, though they are little more than a place to lay your head. If you're prepared to spend a bit more, there are a number of places along the river, some with balcony views.

BUDGET

Camping ($5)

Aguas Calientes is one of the few pueblos you will find in Peru that offers its own campgrounds. It is a walk of about 2 kilometers north of Aguas Calientes, on the road leading to the winding trail towards Machu Picchu. The entrance fee is $5 per night and per tent. It features the roaring river, lots of lush green grass, a bathroom and---when the shop is staffed--snacks and drinks for sale.

Cusi Q'oyllor Hostal (Rooms: $5 - 30)

This simple, efficient hostel offers breakfast, hot water, telephone and fax service, a safety box, luggage storage, a row of computers in the lobby with Internet access, an in-house massage therapist, free tourist information and even pool. Not the swimming variety, but billiards. The rooms start at the low-rate of only $5 for a single unit without bathroom during the low-season, and go only as high as $30 for a double-bed unit with a private bathroom during the high season, and when you consider that breakfast comes with the package, it makes this one of the best deals in town. Las Orquídeas Mz 23 Lote 10, Tel: 51-84–211-113, E-mail: rjarc@hotmail.com.

Hostal Mandor (Rooms: $6 - 15)

This is another small, efficient, clean hostel on the popular and touristy Avenida Pachacútec for travelers just wanting to be close to everything before and/or after their Machu Picchu ascent. The rooms and bathrooms are small; indeed, it seems that the shower stalls are right over the toilet for those who want an all-in-one experience, but the prices range from a mere $6 to $15 depending on season. Towels are an additional $2. Each room features an empty beer bottle amusingly outfitted in miniature folk dress garb. Avenida Pachacútec, Tel: 51-84-435-804, E-mail: hostalmandor_2005@hotmail.com.

Yakumama (Rooms: $12 - 15)

A new addition to the plethora of cheap hostels in Aguas Calientes, this one is built well, clean and modern with neatly tiled bathrooms and relatively tasteful décor. Hot water is unreliable as in all the budget options in Aguas Calientes, but when it's hot, it's very hot. Staff do not speak much English, so a basic knowledge of Spanish will be useful when staying here. Tucked just off the main drag of Pachacutec, rooms on the top floors have views of the river. Av. Inka Roca (just off the 3rd block of Pachacutec), Tel: 51-84-211-185, E-mail: alfreyaku@hotmail.com.

Hostal Ima Sumac (Rooms: $20 - 30)

This is one of the more mid-range hostels you will find along the tavern-and-tourist filled Avenida Pachacútec, with prices fluctuating between $20 and $30 for single rooms with bathrooms, depending on the season. There are only 14 rooms, all of them spacious, clean and nice to look at, and they are the main *raison d'etre* for the higher price. If you are looking for a more comfortable stay but don't want to pay high-end hotel rates, this could be considered an attractive option. However, they don't take credit cards, so a stop at the local ATM is recommended. Breakfast, of course, is included. Avenida Pachacútec, Tel: 51-84-211-021, E-mail: reservas@hostalintiwasi.com, URL: www.hostalintiwasi.com.

Viajeros (Rooms: $25 - 45)

Cozy, comfortable and safe, Viajeros (which calls itself a "bed and breakfast" hostel) is run with the same efficiency as its sister agency, SAS Travel in Cusco. While it provides twin and doubled-sized beds, it's a great place to meet other hikers without feeling like you are at a youth hostel. Perhaps the best part is the helpful staff, who can offer advice and tips about the area. How water is available 24 hours a day, and some great, hearty meals are available at their on-site café and restaurant. A full breakfast is also included in an overnight stay. Ca. Inka Roca N 13, Tel: 51-84-211-237, E-mail: david@sastravel.com.

MID-RANGE

Hostal Machu Picchu (Rooms: $30 - 45)

Located right next door to the Presidente Hotel, the Hostal Machu Picchu is managed by the same company (except that it defines itself as a "hostel" rather than "hotel"), and virtually functions as the no-frills version of its more expensive next-door neighbor, Presidente Hotel. The prices are fixed, regardless of season, and there is no cable television and no bathtubs with Jacuzzi jets (there are rather standard shower stalls, however). Otherwise you are treated to the same breakfast buffet in the same in-house restaurant as guests at the more upscale Presidente Hotel. Imperio de los Incas 135, Tel: 51-84-211-212, E-mail: reservas@siahotels.com.

Presidente Hotel (Rooms: $50 - 65)

The Presidente Hotel justifies its higher price by amenities such as Jacuzzi bathtubs in the rooms. Located between railroad tracks and the roaring Urubamba River, it offers great views of the steep, moss-covered mountains surrounding Aguas Calientes. Other services such as cable television and a buffet breakfast are included in the price. This is a popular stay for international tourists who want the reassurance of quality that paying more money entails. Imperio de los Incas 135, Tel: 51-84-211-212, E-mail: reservas@siahotels.com.

Wiracocha Inn (Rooms $55 - 85)

A well-established favorite in Aguas Calientes, the Wiracocha Inn is in a convenient location close to the action. Its spacious and well-lit rooms offer spectacular views of the rushing

Urubamba River that slices through the town. With separate gas tanks for hot water for each room, you can be assured of a hot shower at any time of day. Friendly owner Gregorio is always around and trying to make your stay as pleasant as possible. Advance booking is recommended. Calle Wiracocha s/n, Tel: 51-84-211-088, E-mail: wiracochainn@hotmail.com, URL: www.wiracochainn.com.

Rupa Wasi Eco-Lodge (Rooms: $67 - 96)
Heading up a hill away from the bustling center of Aguas Calientes, the Rupa Wasi Eco-lodge offers a peaceful getaway. Rooms are plush, the food at the onsite restaurant is delicious and staff is friendly. And Eco-lodge is not just a name, the owners are dedicated to environmental projects and come up with new and innovative ways to recycle – check out the "bricks" in their garden, made from non-biodegradable rubbish. Other services such as cooking lessons, cultural tours and local walking tours can be arranged. Book in advance. Calle Huanacaure 180, Tel: 51-84-211-101, E-mail: info@rupawasi.net, URL: www.rupawasi.net.

Hotel Apu Majestic (Rooms: $70)
Hotel Apu Majestic is within a short walking distance from the Peru Rail Station in Aguas Calientes, though so is pretty much everything else. Its other listed amenities include heating, cable TV, room service, laundry (at an extra price), and ecological tours (ditto). And a hairdryer in every bathroom. You can hear the roaring Urubamba River outside your room, which is good or bad depending on your taste, and there is a pervasive smell of mildew throughout the whole facility. Both a modest buffet breakfast and lunch come with the price, which is $70 per person per night. Alameda Hermanos Ayar, Tel: 51-84-211-127, E-mail: reservas@go2machupicchu.com, URL: www.go2machupicchu.com.

HIGH-END
Hotel Restaurant La Cabaña (Rooms: $75 - 96)
Hotel Restaurant La Cabaña is a friendly hotel and restaurant not far from the center of town. It offers a variety of services not always found in a mid-range hotel, including a travel desk, internet, guides for the ruins and a TV with DVD library. They will also pick you up at the train station if you let them know in advance. The rooms are cozy and tastefully decorated, and the restaurant is quite pleasant and neat. Av. Pachacútec M-20 - L3, Tel: 51-84-211-048, E-mail: lacabana_mapi@latinmail.com

Gringo Bill's (Rooms: $75 - $150)
Something of an Aguas Calientes institution, Gringo Bill's has been around for at least 20 years. Although it calls itself a hostel, it is actually a bit more upscale and expensive than your typical hostel: the rooms are bright and airy, and some of them feature balconies. The restaurant is spacious. They offer trip packages and bag lunches for those visiting the ruins. Colla Raymi 104, Tel: 51-84-211-046, Fax: 51-84-211-046, E-mail: info@gringobills.com, URL: www.gringobills.com.

Hatuchay Tower (Rooms: $235 - 335)
Hatuchay Tower has 42 spacious rooms, all equipped with modern amenities such as satellite TV, telephone, in-room safe, 24-hour room service, and hot and cold water 24-hours. Smoking rooms are available. The on-site restaurant serves specialty Peruvian dishes and international cuisine. The restuarant is open 5 a.m. - 10 p.m. You can enjoy a relaxing cocktail with friends in the Hatuchay Tower Bar, open 2-10 p.m. Av Hermanos Ayar M-24, Tel: 51-84-211-201, E-mail: reservas@hatuchaytower.com, URL: www.hatuchaytower.com.

Machu Picchu Pueblo Hotel (Rooms: $435 - 930)
Probably the best luxury option in Aguas Calientes, the expensive but beautiful Machu Picchu Pueblo Hotel is located just on the outskirts of town, about a five-minute walk from the station. The hotel is a complex of guest bungalow cabins and finely tended gardens. A nature lover's paradise, the gardens boast several hundred species of orchids, ferns and other cloud forest foliage, and more than 150 species of birds and hummingbirds have been identified

SACRED VALLEY

on the hotel grounds. The hotel has won numerous awards, including being named one of Travel and Leisure Magazine's top 25 hotels in Latin America. If you can afford it, you won't be disappointed with this place. Machu Picchu Km. 110, Tel: 51-84-211-122 (USA: 1-800-442-5042), E-mail: central@inkaterra.com, URL: www.inkaterra.com/en/machu-picchu.

AGUAS CALIENTES SERVICES
The Discovery Internet Café and Snack Bar
There are plenty of Internet cafés throughout Aguas Calientes, and this one is slightly more expensive by charging you four solés rather than three an hour, but you more which get your extra 33 cents back. This is the only cybercafe in the area with genuine high-speed access, and that never falters at that. The computers are all latest models, connected to large flat screen monitors. Furthermore, this is located in a terrific spot, in a corner of the Manco Capac plaza, and the cybercafe's wide, spacious windows offer a great view of such. And they actually do serve coffee and snacks besides. International phone call service is also available. Manco Capac Plaza, Aguas Calientes, Tel: 51-84-211-355 / 211-040.

Angela's Laundry
The little things you don't take into account when you set off to conquer the Inca Trail...such as your dirty laundry. Dubious tourist rates apply here in a popular destination spot like Aguas Calientes as anywhere else, so here is the scoop: Angela's is the cheapest and the best, washing your smelly clothes for $2 a kilo. Feathered coats washed for $3, sleeping bags and sneakers for $4, all guaranteed washed, dried, and returned in four hours or less. Avenida Pachaqutec 150, Aguas Calientes, Tel: 51-84-211-105.

THINGS TO SEE AND DO IN AGUAS CALIENTES
Putucusi
This is an excellent walk up the mountain opposite of Machu Picchu that offers breathtaking views of Machu Picchu and the surrounding area. It can be steep and part of it requires going up wooden ladder rungs that get slippery in the wet season and tends to deter many hikers. The scenery is worth the hike though. 250 meters west of Aguas Calientes.

Manuel Chávez Ballón Site Museum
Anyone interested in a more thorough appreciation of Machu Picchu should pay a visit to this museum outside Aguas Calientes and named after Peruvian archeologist Manuel Chávez Ballón. Due to the fact that most of Machu Picchu's artifacts were removed by American explorer Hiram Bingham and kept thereafter at Yale University, the focus of the museum is on the discovery of Machu Picchu and the findings therein. There some remaining artifacts, as well as maps and video presentations. The botanical garden across the way showcases some of Peru's most impressive orchids and other flora.

The Thermal Baths of Aguas Calientes
The town of Aguas Calientes derives its name—Hot Waters--from the natural, geothermally-heated sulfuric waters here, near the base of the world's most famous lost city. They have long been considered to have medicinal properties, and in consideration of their popularity, the local government has set up changing rooms and even a cafeteria so you can enjoy as much leisure time as you need to unwind and relax, especially if you have just completed the Inca Trail as well as explored Machu Picchu. Swimwear, towels and sandals are mandatory (the latter can be rented). The cost is three dollars for foreigners.

The Mandor Gardens and Waterfalls
Machu Picchu is the main attraction in the area, but many visitors, while they are here, stop over and visit the Mandor gardens and waterfalls. Your options for accessing it are: 1) take a cab; 2) walk for two-hours; or 3) take the train that leaves at 12:30 p.m. Entrance to the gardens comes to $1.20, and there are places to eat while you are there. In addition to the waterfall, there is much exotic flora and fauna, including rare birds). The cost is $3 for foreigners.

Aguas Calientes Restaurants

Just as hotels sprung up to cater to the tourists, so have restaurants. Little cafés serving cheap Peruvian fare dot the railroad tracks, and vegetarian options, meat dishes, buffets and pizza joints line Pachacútec on the way to the hot springs. Again, prices tend to be a little higher due to the town's popularity with tourists traveling to Machu Picchu, so be prepared to pay a little more in some restaurants.

Restaurant El Manu (Entrees: $3 and up)

Situated on the main drag of Pachacútec, El Manu is not hard to spot, with its jungle-themed dining room fully visible from the entrance and a large pizza oven at the back. Offering standard fare at reasonable prices, and some tasty hot chocolate, El Manu is mostly notable for its warm, friendly atmosphere as well as its funky jungle theme. Popular with travelers, El Manu is a good place to hang out and meet other people. Av. Pachacútec 139.

Govindas (Entrees: $3 and up)

Run by the Hare-Krishna, the Govindas restaurant in Aguas Calientes is notable for serving up large portions of wholesome vegetarian food – a big contrast to the pizzas and steaks favored in most other eating establishments. Offering a set lunch and dinner menu every day at reasonable prices, as well as other à la carte options, Govindas is definitely the best place for vegetarian fare in Aguas Calientes. Av. Pachacútec 20.

Chez Maggy – Clave del Sol (Entrees: $5 and up)

Part of the family-run chain of Chez Maggy pizzerias expanding across Peru, this branch was one of the first. It offers good quality pizzas with a variety of toppings (including the "tropical" with pineapple, peaches and condensed milk for those with a sweet tooth). There is a warm and lively atmosphere inside as pizza chefs try to keep up with demand. Chez Maggy will also deliver to your hotel if your really can't move those legs any more after the trail! Av. Pachacútec 156, Tel: 51-84-211-006, URL: www.pizzeria-chezmaggy.com.

El Charro (Entrees: $5 -15)

This restaurant has style to spare, from the stained and varnished logs holding up its roof to the combination of dyed cotton and black leather tablecloths on its tables to the sheepskins on it its benches, El Charro is fun simply to look at. They offer Peruvian, Mexican and Italian dishes, with fixed-item menús. A three-course meal goes for $5. Their à la carte items, such as roast chicken, are a bit more expensive at $8, and their house specialty, roast guinea pig, goes for $15. They also have three computers set up with high-speed Internet access. They open at 9 a.m. and serve breakfast as well as lunch and dinner. Imperio de los Incas, Tel: 51-84-211-286, E-mail: elcharrosrestaurantmapi@hotmail.com.

Yakumama II Restaurant (Entrees: $8)

This standard but very decent restaurant on Manco Capac Plaza offers standard Peruvian food along with, of course, the universal favorite, pizza. There is an amusing touch in terms of its look: sitting on every table there are folk-art dolls representing classical stereotypes of rural Peruvians, playing harmonica, resting, etcetera. They are open from 8 a.m. until the last customer goes home, for breakfast, lunch and dinner, and they do accept credit cards. Lunch and dinner items go for about $8, which is about average for Aguas Calientes. Calderón Quispe Saturnino, Tel: 51-84-211-185.

Indi Feliz Restaurant Bistro (Entrees: $12)

As a restaurant, Indi Feliz has acquired a reputation--not just in Aguas Calientes, but in all of Peru--that is nothing less than legendary. In ten years they have won eight prizes, including, in two consecutive years, top honors in a national contest as Peruvian Business of the Year. It is the restaurant of choice for dignitaries and celebrities on their way to Machu Picchu. What

Machu Picchu and the Inca Trail - Environmental Issues

The principle environmental issue facing the Inca Trail and Machu Picchu is the increasingly demanding presence of tourism on the fragile natural environment. Prior to implementation of restrictions on tourism by the Peruvian government in 2001, the Inca Trail and Machu Picchu were getting run-down to a point many feared would soon be beyond repair. The trampling of the shallow dirt, the trail-side deforestation for firewood, human waste and other garbage left on the side of the Inca Trail were major environmental threats facing the famous 'lost city.' It was deteriorating to such a degree that UNESCO repeatedly threatened to add Machu Picchu to the World Heritage in Danger sites.

In 2001 Peru responded by creating a series of restrictions to protect the Inca Trail and began seriously enforcing them in 2003. There is now a limit of about 500 people per day on the trail, including all tourists, guides and porters. This works out to approximately 200 tourists per day. Additionally, all trekkers must be accompanied by a certified guide. The idea is that having guides present with all visitors not only provides employment for many local residents, but also that environmental standards and regulations will be enforced. All reputable tour agencies promote a 'pack-in, pack-out' policy, meaning that anything taken on the trek will be taken out. Open-fires are prohibited on the trail (deforestation for firewood was out of control), so make sure your company uses gas stoves. Permanent toilets have also been installed to combat the human waste problem.

Before the implementation of the regulations visitors could find bargain-basement tour prices, most often through operators that were skimping on protecting the natural environment that was paying their bills. Prices have increased significantly, but the porters now have a guaranteed daily wage and other standards (maximum carrying weight, sleeping pads, acceptable meals, accident insurance). As the prices have gone up, companies are cutting fewer corners and are able to invest in the preservation and protection of the Inca Trail and Machu Picchu. Many of the critical environmental issues the Trail and Machu Picchu were facing--litter, human waste, literal pounding of the trail--have been curbed or eliminated. So don't sigh and lament about the good ole days when hiking the Inca Trail could be done for under $200. Instead, relish the fact you are contributing to environmentally responsible, sustainable tourism in Peru and helping provide a decent, living wage for those who guide you on your trek.

The Inca Trail

Characterized by rugged ascents boasting magnificent views of Andean scenery and trails that wind their way through the cloud forest and past ancient archaeological sites, the Inca Trail is perhaps the most eminent of South American experiences. While other trails in the Sacred Valley area and around Cusco offer the same spectacular scenery, is the only Inca Trail that leads to the awesome gates of Machu Picchu, the ultimate climax to any trekking experience. This world-famous trail is part of the Sanctuario Histórico de Machu Picchu, an area of over 32,000 hectares set aside by the Peruvian state to protect the host of flora and fauna that flourish here. In 2001, in an attempt to restrict the number of hikers and damage to the trail, the Peruvian government established new regulations requiring all Inca Trail hikers to be accompanied by a licensed guide. Currently, a maximum of 500 hikers are allowed on the trail per day. Recently, regulations involved in obtaining an Inca Trail trekking permit have changed.

Please note: In order to secure your permit you must now provide your passport information no later than 90 days before your departure. So plan ahead, book early and avoid added stress.

Tours can be arranged through a number of tour companies in Cusco, and most cost between $200 and $300, which includes the entrance fee ($50 for adults, $25 for students and free for children under 11), transportation to and from the trail, an English-speaking guide, tents, mattress, three daily meals and porters who carry group gear. For about $50 extra/trip a personal porter can be hired to carry your gear. If you are inclined (and it's recommended)

SACRED VALLEY

you can tip your porters and guides. Independent travelers will generally be placed with a mixed group of travelers, and groups tend to be between 12 and 16 people. For premium-class service, groups are generally smaller and an upgrade on the return train is included. Prices for these treks range from $275 to $650 per person. Be cautious if the price is under $180, as the company may be cutting corners, or not adhering to the strict environmental regulations recently imposed. Only purchase your ticket from officially licensed agencies, and be sure to make your payments at the physical tour agency office. Direct any questions you may have regarding a tour company to the main tourism office in Cusco. You can save a little money by arranging your own transport back to Ollantaytambo, either for the last day of your tour, or by staying an extra night in Aguas Calientes and taking the early morning train, then catching a bus back to Cusco.

If you do take the train back to Cusco after your tour, make sure your return ticket has your name on it for the tourist train, or you will have to pay for any changes. Be sure to inquire if the guide for the Inca Trail and Machu Picchu will be the same, as some companies save money by sending a less experienced guide on the trail and hiring a new, certified guide at Machu Picchu. Also, if you have any concerns regarding the working conditions of the porters, contact Porteadores Inka Ñan, Dept. 4 Choquechaca 188, Cusco, Telephone: 246829.

When to Go

The single most important factor in planning your Inca Trail experience is making sure you give yourself plenty of time to acclimatize to the high altitude before attempting the physically demanding trail. The best way to avoid *soroche*, or altitude sickness, is to spend a few days in the Sacred Valley area, which is slightly lower in elevation. The first two days of the climb involve arduous ascents, so do not attempt them if you're feeling unwell. In most cases, four days will ensure a comfortable journey, and you should allow an extra day to see Machu Picchu after recovering from the hike. Usually the best month for trekking the Inca Trail is May, when the weather is fine and skies are clear. From June to September, the trail is a busy stretch of mountainside, with people from all over the world flocking to its rugged peaks and lush valleys. During the rainy season, from October to April, it is less busy but for obvious reasons: it's slightly wetter. Note: the trail is closed every February for cleaning and repair.

For a truly unique experience on the Inca Trail, try to depart two to three days before a full moon. According to the locals, the weather is best at this time and at night the Andean skyline is fully illuminated by the moonlight.

What to Bring

The trail involves rugged ascents and unpredictable weather, so it is imperative that you be prepared with the proper equipment. Be sure to pack strong footwear, rain gear and warm clothing, in addition to food, water (no plastic water bottles are allowed, canteens only), water purification, insect repellent, plastic bags, a torch, durable sleeping bag, items such as tents and cooking equipment will be provided by your tour operator.

What to Expect

The popular 4-day trek will take you along the ancient stone Inca highway, past dozens of archaeological sights, rushing rivers and uncountable views of the cloud forest and eye-captivating mountain scenery. Along this 43-kilometer trek you will tackle three formidable mountain passes and cruise to a maximum altitude of 4,200 meters. The trek begins at Qorihuayrachina near Ollantaytambo, often referred to as Km. 88 of the Cusco railway.

Another, slightly less intense version of the classic four-day trek is also growing in popularity. The two-day version, referred to as the Camino Sagrado del Inca, or "Sacred Trail," is a good alternative for time-pressed or fitness-deficient individuals. Along this journey you'll reach a maximum altitude of only 2,750 meters, which involve less arduous ascents, yet still leads to the wondrous mountain-mecca, Machu Picchu. This mini-trek begins at Km. 104, just 14 kilometers away from the ruins, and groups spend the night near the ruins of Wiñay Wayna

SACRED VALLEY

before departing at sunrise for the gates of Machu Picchu. There are also a limited number of permits for this trail, costing $50 per person, so like the 4 day Inca Trail, it is necessary to book in advance. However, if you're looking for divine mountain scenery, then the four-day trek is your best bet, as most of the best views and ruins are not included in the two-day tour.

4 Day Inca Trail Trek

To give you a better sense of what the four-day trek involves, we've put together a brief day-by-day summary of the trip.

Day 1 Total Distance: 10 to 11 kilometers

Arrive by train from Cusco, getting off at Km. 88, or by bus at Km. 82. From the station, cross the footbridge spanning the Río Urubamba and begin the gentle ascent up to the Inca ruins of Llactapata, where Bingham and his team first camped on their way to Machu Picchu. The trail then slopes upwards, following the Río Cusichaca, until it reaches Huayllabamba. To reach this small village, the only one along the trail that is still inhabited, it's about a three-hour climb. This is a good place to hire horses or mules, if you're so inclined. Most groups spend the night here, in preparation for the arduous journey up to the aptly named Dead Woman's Pass.

Day 2 Total Distance: 11 kilometers

Although equal to the first day in terms of distance, Day 2 is perhaps the most difficult day of the trip. From Huayllabamba, you're in for a steep, one-hour climb to the ruins of Llulucharoc (3,800 meters). Catch your breath and prepare for another 90-minute to 2-hour steep climb through the cloud forest to Llulluchapampa, an isolated village situated in a flat mountain meadow. Spectacular views of the valley below will keep your mind off the steep ascent. From Llulluchapampa make your way up the quad-killing climb towards Abra de Huarmihuañusca (Dead Woman's Pass), the first pass and highest point of the trek (4,200 meters). The 2 ½ hour climb is a mental and physical challenge, subjecting trekkers to a killer sun on the way up, and thin air and bitterly cold winds at the summit. Don't be surprised if snow or freezing rain greets you at the summit. Inevitably, however, the mind-blowing views will distract you from the body-numbing cold and physically demanding ascent. Do make sure that you shelter yourself from the wind while you check out the valley below.

Between Huayllamba and Huarmihuañusca there are three places to camp, if you're in need of a rest. The most popular among these is Three White Stones. From the summit the trail descends sharply via stone steps into Pacamayo Valley (3,600 meters). This area also offers excellent camping, and if you're lucky, you can catch a glimpse of the ever-playful spectacled bears.

Day 3 Total Distance: 15 kilometers

About an hour's trek towards the next pass, Abra de Runkuracay, you'll come across the intriguing ruins of Runcuracay. The name means "basket shaped" and is an appropriate title for the circular ruins unique among those on the trail. From the ruins it's about a 45-minute to one-hour steep climb to the second pass (3,900 meters). Just over the summit is another camp site, where you'll encounter magnificent views of the Vilcabamba mountain range. Follow the trail through a naturally formed tunnel and up a spectacular stone staircase to the ruins of Sayacmarca (3,500 meters). These beautiful ruins include ritual baths and terrace viewpoints overlooking the Aobamba Valley. It is believed that this tranquil area was once a resting spot for ancient travelers traversing the Inca Trail. You can camp near the remains of an aqueduct that once supplied water to the ancient settlement.

From Sayacmarca the trail descends via a remarkably well-preserved Inca footpath into thick cloud forest where you'll be astounded by exotic flora like orchids and bromeliads, and unique bird species. The trail winds its way towards Conchamarca, another rest stop for the weary. Pass through another Inca tunnel and follow the path up a gentle two-hour climb towards the third pass and the ruins of Phuyupatamarca (3,800 meters). This section of trail, whose name translates to "Town Above the Clouds," offers spectacular views of the Urubamba valley in one direction and in the other a grand view of the snow-covered peaks of Salcantay (Wild

Mountain). The ruins include six small baths that, during the wet season, are teeming with constantly running fresh water.

There is an excellent place to camp here, where you may even catch a glimpse of wild deer feeding. Also, keep an eye out for the massive backside of Machu Picchu peak. From the ruins the trail forks and you have two options. Follow the knee-buckling 2,250 step stone staircase to the terraces of Intipata, or head towards the stunning ruins of Wiñay Wayna. Only discovered in 1941, the ruins of this ancient citadel, named "Forever Young," for the perpetually blossoming orchids that flourish here, include spectacular stone agricultural terraces and ritual baths. A nearby hostel offers weary wanderers hot showers, food and the well-deserved beer. Be aware, however, that during peak season this hostel area can appear more like a tourist circus than peaceful mountain retreat.

Day 4 Total Distance: 7 kilometers
The final leg of this journey is all about getting to Intipunku (Sun Gate) and Machu Picchu. Be prepared for an early rise, as most groups depart camp at 4 a.m. to arrive at the ruins by 6:30 a.m. This climatic journey involves a 60 to 90-minute trek along narrow Inca stone paths, and a final push up a 50-step, nearly vertical climb to the ruins of Intipunku. The descent to Machu Picchu takes about 45 minutes. Upon reaching the ruins, trekkers must deposit their packs at the entrance gate and get their entrance passes stamped. From here you can bask in the glory of having completed the rugged journey to one of the world's greatest attractions.

Inca Trail Porters
You've waited so long to trek these rugged 43 kilometers to that Incan Holy Grail, Machu Picchu. But after two days, your feel muscles you never knew existed, another blister is welling up. As you momentarily rest on a rock, gasping for breath in this rarefied air, you see one of the porters striding smoothly by you, on his way to set up this night's camp for you and the others. Almost like *The Motorcycle Diaries*.

The lot of the porter changed with new regulations instituted in 2002. Before, it was not uncommon for one to carry 45 kilos, sleep under mere plastic and a blanket, receive the trekkers' leftovers or cook for himself, be paid only four dollars per day. Frequently porters would have to cut firewood to keep warm and eat, thus augmenting deforestation. Now the load limit is 25 kilograms (20 of trekkers' equipment, five for the porter's personal effects). The minimum wage is 35 soles per day. Unfortunately, some tour companies are getting around the new regulations by paying 15 soles per day (to be able to offer you a bargain price), and making trekkers carry their own packs across the weigh-in spot, then shifting the weight to the porters or denying porters their personal allowance.
Porters are the work horses of the trek—but they should not be treated that way. As consumers, we have responsibilities to ensure porters' fair treatment. How can you help to make sure the regulations are followed:

• Familiarize yourself with the regulations of the Inka Trail; see http://www.andeantravel-web.com/peru/treks/incatrail_regulations.html.
• Ask the tour company how much porters are paid, and if they are provided with food and proper camping equipment. Make clear your concern for the porters' welfare.
• If you don't like the answers, look for a different company or hire your own porter. You'll be supporting the local economy by providing employment.
• Ask the company precisely what equipment you are expected to take (sleeping bag, etc.—and, of course, warm clothing, canteen, etc.). Leave all unnecessary items stowed at your hostel. Don't unnecessarily weigh down the porter.
• During the trip, remember common courtesies. Learn a little Quechua. Thank them. Share your coca leaves.
• Talk with them about their lives and culture. Ask them to sing. Share photos of your family or homeland with them.
• Pool tips for the porters with other travelers; 20-25 soles total per porter is fair. If you feel like

SACRED VALLEY

SACRED VALLEY

Photo by Peter Anderson

giving a higher tip, donate money to projects supporting porters rights or their communities.

Mistreatment of porters should not be shrugged off with "Well, that is the way things are in these countries."

• File complaints with MINCETUR (Ministerio de Comercio Exterior y Turismo), Avenida de la Cultura 734, 3rd floor; Telephone: 51-84-241-508, FAX: 51-84-223-761, webmaster@mincetur.gob.pe, www.dirceturcusco.gob.pe; 7:30 a.m.- 12:45 p.m., 2:15-4:30 p.m.
• If you are a member, inform the South American Explorers Club.
• Drop line to us here at Viva Travel Guides, or make a posting on our site to share your experience with others.

To learn more about the porters' life, read the BBC's Inca Trail Porter Photo Journal. The Inka Porter Project (http://www.peruweb.org/porters) has information about porters' rights.

MACHU PICCHU
Despite the peace and tranquility conjured up by its astounding natural beauty, Machu Picchu is a fervently protected place, inhabited by numerous whistle-blowing guards who noisily herd unsuspecting travelers who have strayed from the main path. To explore the ruins in peace, the best option is to hire a guide or buy a map and stick to the specified routes. Guides are available on the site and often prove to be extremely knowledgeable. For a spectacular experience, obtain permission from the Instituto Nacional de Cultura in Cusco to enter the ruins before 6 a.m. and watch the sunrise over the Andes. From the ticket booth, you'll enter the south side of Machu Picchu through the Guard's Quarters, now the modern-day entrance. From here, there are a number of ways to explore the ruins, all of which offer striking views of intricate Inca architecture, Andean mountains and terraced staircases. A few of the can't-miss Machu Picchu attractions include the Temple of the Sun, Royal Tomb, Three-Windowed Temple, Chamber of the Princess, Principal Temple, Intihuatana, Huayna Picchu, Temple of the Moon and Intipunku.

Temple of the Sun
Upon entering the main ruins you'll cross over a dry moat and come across the first site of major interest, the Temple of the Sun. Once used as a solar observatory, this unique complex is the only round building at Machu Picchu. At sunrise during the summer solstice, the sun's rays flood through the window and illuminate the tower with a precision only the Incas could have executed. Also known as the Torreón, the temple presents a spectacular, semicircular wall and carved steps that fit seamlessly into the existing surface of a natural boulder, forming some sort of altar. Although access inside the temple is not permitted, the outside architecture is spectacular in and of itself. The temple displays some of Machu Picchu's most

superb stonework, and has a window from which the June solstice sunrise and the constellation of Pleiades can be observed. In Andean culture the Pleiades continues to be an important astronomical symbol, and the locals use the constellation to calculate the arrival of the rains and to determine the best time of year to plant crops. Next to the Temple of the Sun is the Chamber of the Princess, and below the temple is The Royal Tomb.

Chamber of the Princess
The two-story structure adjacent to the Temple of the Sun is the Chamber of the Princess. The building was most likely used for Inca nobility, which may explain why Yale archaeologist Hiram Bingham chose its name. A three-walled house standing next to the chamber has been restored with a thatched roof and provides a good illustration of how Inca buildings might have once looked. From here you can follow a staircase that leads upwards past the Royal Area (denoted by characteristic imperial Inca architecture) and to the two most impressive buildings in the city: the Three-Windowed Temple and the Principal Temple.

Three-Windowed Temple
Not far from the Chamber of the Princess is the spectacular Three-Windowed Temple. It is part of a complex situated around the Sacred Plaza, a ceremonial center that some argue is the most captivating section of the city. The temple's unusually large, trapezoidal windows perfectly frame the mountains unfolding beyond the Urubamba River valley. To your left as you face the Three-Windowed Temple is another popular Machu Picchu attraction, the Principal Temple.

Principal Temple
Situated next to the Three-Windowed Temple, this magnificent three-walled building derives its name from the immense foundation stones and fine stonework that comprise its three high main walls. The wall facing farthest east looks onto the Sacred Plaza. In contrast to most ancient temples in the Americas, whose entrances face east, the Principal Temple's entrance faces south. White sand found on the temple floor suggests that the temple may have been tied symbolically to the Río Urubamba, a theory that is not too farfetched considering the importance of water in the ancient Inca culture. The kite-shaped sacred stone sitting in the small square around the temple is thought to represent the Southern Cross constellation. A short stroll uphill from here brings you to one of the most spectacular sites of Machu Picchu, the Intihuatana, or Hitching Post of the Sun.

Intihuatana
A brief walk uphill from the Principal Temple will bring you to one of the most important shrines at Machu Picchu. Intihuatana, or Hitching Post of the Sun, is an intriguing carved rock whose shape mimics that of Huayna Picchu, the sacred peak rising beyond the ruins. Though the Incas created rocks like this for all their important ritual centers, Intihuatana is one of the few not destroyed by the Spanish conquistadores. Overlooking the Sacred Plaza, this sundial-like rock served as an astronomical device used to track constellation movements and to calculate the passing of seasons. Given its shape and strategic alignment with four important mountains, many scholars have conjectured that Intihuatana is symbolically linked to the spirit of the mountains on which Machu Picchu was built. If you follow the steps down from here, past the Sacred Plaza and towards the northern terraces you'll arrive at the Sacred Rock, gateway to Huayna Picchu.

Huayna Picchu
Just down the steps from Intihuatana and across the Sacred Plaza is the Sacred Rock, a massive piece of granite curiously shaped like the Inca's sacred mountain of Putucusi, which looms on the eastern horizon. Little is known about this rock, except that it serves as the gateway to Huayna Picchu. Access to the sacred summit is controlled by a guardian from a kiosk behind the Sacred Rock. The trail is open daily 7 a.m.-1 p.m., with the last exit by 3 p.m. The steep walk up to the summit takes about one to two hours and includes a 20-meter climb up a steep rock slab using a ladder and rope. (Those afraid of heights may want to pass on this

climb.) Your physical labors will be rewarded, however, with a spectacular panoramic view of the entire Machu Picchu complex and the Andean mountains and forests which cradle it. About two-thirds of the way down the trail behind the summit, another trail leads to the right and down to the exquisitely situated Temple of the Moon.

Temple of the Moon

Situated about 400 meters beneath the pinnacle of Huayna Picchu (about a 45-minute walk each way from the summit) is The Temple of the Moon, another spectacular example of Inca stonemasonry. The temple consists of a large natural cave with five niches carved into a massive white granite stone wall. Towards the cave's center is a rock carved like a throne, next to which are five carved steps that lead towards darker recesses where even more carved rocks and stone walls are visible. The temple's name originates from the way it radiates with moonlight at night, but many archaeologists believe that it was also symbolically aligned with the surrounding mountains. Steps on either side of the small plaza in front of the temple lead to more buildings and some interesting stone sanctuaries below. For equally incredible views of Machu Picchu and Huayna Picchu you can take the other trail leading down from the guardian's kiosk behind Sacred Rock. The thirty minute climb to Intipunku, the main entrance to Machu Picchu from the Inca Trail, is slightly less demanding and a good option for anyone lacking time or energy.

Royal Tomb

The Royal Tomb is a bit of a misnomer due to the fact that neither graves nor human remains have ever been encountered here. Though it may lack the macabre history that some travelers may expect, this cave-like structure is an excellent example of the Inca's stonemasonry genius. Located inside is a magnificent stepped altar and a series of tall niches, once used to present offerings, which capture the sun's rays to produce brilliant patterns of morning shadows. Just down the stairs leading from the Royal Tomb is a series of interconnected fountains and a still-functioning water canal.

Intipunku

If you don't have the time or energy to make the climb up to Huayna Picchu and Temple of the Moon, then you may prefer to take the trail leading from the guardian's kiosk behind the Sacred Stone to Intipunku, the main entrance to Machu Picchu from the Inca Trail. Intipunku, also known as the Sun Gate, consists of two large stones that correspond to the winter and summer solstices, and on these dates the gates are illuminated by laser-like beams of light. In addition to their symbolic importance, the gates also provide remarkable views of Machu Picchu and Huayna Picchu.

Wiñay Wayna

A rough two or three-hour descent from the ruins of Puyupatamarca, located on the Inca Trail, will bring you to the spectacular ruins of Wiñay Wayna. Here you will find a hotel and restaurant where you can grab a cold drink and hot shower. Originally a companion site for Machu Picchu, these ruins nestled high above the Río Urubamba probably served as a ceremonial and agricultural center. Like today, they may also have served as a rest stop for weary travelers on their way to the grand gates of Machu Picchu. The complex is divided into two architectural sections, with temples at the top and more rustic structures below. As many as 19 different springs carry water to various stone baths located at different levels throughout the characteristic Inca terracing. If you're up for a bit more walking (about 2 hours), you can take the well-marked trail from the ruins to Intipunku, the gateway to Machu Picchu.

MACHU PICCHU TOURS

Some people wait years to be able to get a chance to see the majestic Inca ruins at Machu Picchu, so if you get a chance to reach the spectacular cloud-enshrouded green peaks that are home to the ancient and incredibly well-preserved UNESCO World Heritage site, you want to be sure to do the trip right.

It is entirely possible to travel to Machu Picchu independently. However, because of its popularity and the limited number of visitors allowed on the site each day, it pays to plan ahead; tour operators can be an invaluable help. If you book with a tour operator in your home country, you will have the advantage of planning well in advance; however, you may pay more than if you plan the trip when you are in Peru. Peruvian tour operators based out of Lima, Cusco or any other major Peruvian city can also help you book your tour--usually at a slightly lower price than international operators. During the day, there are always guides available at the entrance to Machu Picchu. More expensive guides can be hired at the nearby Sanctuary Lodge. Most local operators offer a one-day excursion from Cusco to Machu Picchu, which includes all transport and a professional guide. (It's usually a good idea to make sure the guide speaks English.) From Cusco, you'll have to take a train to Aguas Calientes, the nearest town to Machu Picchu. From Aguas Calientes it's a 20-minute bus ride up to the ruins.

If you're visiting Machu Picchu as part of a day tour, you'll usually spend about four hours at the ruins. Two of these hours are spent as part of the guided tour. If you want to stay longer, or see the ruins at sunrise (highly recommended), spend the night in nearby Aguas Calientes or in the expensive Machu Picchu Sanctuary Lodge--the only hotel adjacent to Machu Picchu. Some tour companies offer tours spread over two days, but you may have to pay for the additional costs of accommodation. In addition to Machu Picchu tours, treks of the Inca Trail can also be arranged at one of the many Cusco tour agencies.

MACHU PICCHU LODGING

There are very limited accommodation options at Machu Picchu itself--most who don't head back to Cusco look in the town of Aguas Calientes for hotels close to Machu Picchu. This town offers an array of different lodging options, ranging from extremely cheap and basic to considerable luxury. The cheapest hotels in Aguas Calientes are to be found along the railroad tracks. These don't consist of much more than a place to lay your head. If you're prepared to spend a bit more, there are a number of places along the river, some with balcony views of the river. A number of the better hotels have adjoining restaurants. There are also a couple of decent lodges, one extremely close to the ruins, but be prepared to pay a premium.

Machu Picchu Sanctuary Lodge (Rooms: $715 — $1165)
For the jet-setting traveler who has no interest in staying at the bottom of the hill in dusty, rabble-filled Aguas Calientes, there is the Machu Picchu Sanctuary Lodge. The Sanctuary is the only hotel right up on the top of the hill next to the ruins: the entrance is a short walk away (as in about fifty feet). The hotel has two suites and 29 rooms, some of which have an incredible mountain view (be prepared to pay more if you want the scenic room). Run by the internationally renowned Orient Express hotel group, you'll get high-end comfort and service. The hotel offers all of the expected amenities for a hotel in its class: internet, room service, etc. For those who really want to keep their exposure to riff-raff to a minimum, the hotel can help you book a helicopter flight from Cusco. If you cough up several hundred dollars to spend the night, be sure to be first in line to visit the ruins in the morning before the train arrives, bringing hordes of tourists with it. There is an excellent restaurant on the premises as well. Check their web site for special rates and promotions. Phone (cell) 51-84-984-816-953; Reservation (Lima) 51-16-108-300, E-mail: res-mapi@peruorientexpress.com.pe homepage: http://machupicchu.orient-express.com/web/omac/omac_a2a_home.jsp.

Sumaq Machu Picchu Hotel
Sumaq Machu Picchu Hotel is an exclusive luxury hotel at the base of Machu Picchu. This four-star hotel blends in well with its location: everything from the architecture to the cuisine borrow from Andean influences. The exterior design aims to blend with the landscape, while interior decorations reflect Inca culture and Peruvian craftsmanship. The resort has 60 ample and luxurious rooms, equipped with alarms, WiFi, mini-bar, mp3 radios, and cable TV. The Qunuq Restaurant and Suquy Café-Bar, serves exquisite and varied samples of gourmet, novo-Andean, regional and international gastronomy. Menus are elaborated by well-recognized Peruvian Chef Rafael Piqueras. After trekking to Machu Picchu guests can relax in the

"Natural Spa Aqlla" which employs ancient Inca therapeutic techniques, including saunas, thermal baths, reflexology and massages that use essential oils and local herbs to heal your weary soles. Hermanos Ayar mz 1 lote 3, Tel: 51-14-470-579 / 51-16-281-082, Fax: 51-14-457-828, E-mail: reservas@sumaqhotelperu.com, URL: www.sumaqhotelperu.com.

V!VA Member Review- Machu Picchu Hotel

Lovely hotel with luxurious atmosphere. Excellent food with beautiful presentation. What a wonderful place to return to after a day at Macchu Picchu Sanctuary.

Florida, U.S.A., July 20, 2008

Hostal Varayoc

Just a stone's throw from the train station and buses to Machu Picchu, the Varayoc has a prime location. Blink and you'll miss it - it can be found right above the internet cafe. This place is simple and lacks any real character, but is good nonetheless. There is 24-hr hot water, much appreciated after a long hike. It is a bit noisy early evening, but soon quiets down as everyone gets to bed early, ready to hit Machu Picchu before the crowds. Imperio de los Incas Av. 114, Tel: 51-84-211-334, Fax: 51-84-211-334, E-mail: hostal.varayoc@hotmail.com.

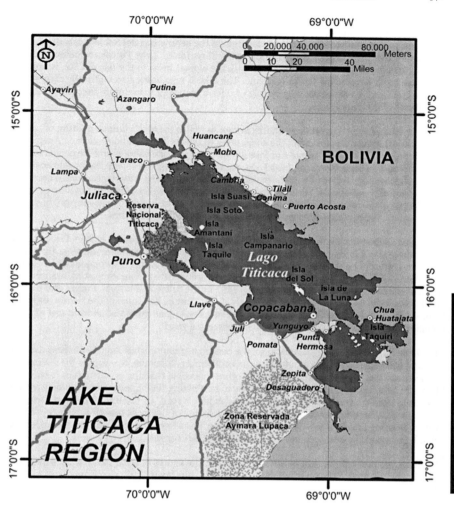

LAKE TITICACA

Sitting at an astounding 3,821 m above sea level, Lake Titicaca is the highest commercially navigable lake in the world. With a surface area of approximately 8,300 square km, it is also the largest freshwater lake in South America. About 25 rivers empty into the lake's ocean-like waters, which are dotted with 41 islands, both inhabited and uninhabited.

Forming a natural border between Bolivia and Peru, the lake can be characterized by the diversity of its cultural and natural attractions. Even the briefest exploration around these emerald-blue waters yields memorable encounters with the local people and their way of life. That the Spaniards bequeathed this majestic lake and its people to a king, rather than a *conquistador* (as was the custom), suggests the impression its grandiosity left on the explorers.

Before the Spaniards, the shores of Lake Titicaca were a center of wealth and a focal point for ancient civilizations. So powerful was the image of her sun-baked shores and brilliant blue waters that the Incas formulated a creation myth centered on the lake. According to ancient

The Inca civilization began to assert itself in the Puno region during the 15th century. Inca mythology asserts that Inca Manco Capac and his sister Mama Occla rose out of Lake Titicaca's waters with the divine purpose of creating and uniting a kingdom of peace and civilization. Puno and Lake Titicaca gained increased importance to the Incas because of the plethora of silver and gold in the area. Additionally, the Incas raised alpacas and llamas for wool and meat and cultivated high-altitude crops such as potatoes and coffee.

The Spanish arrived in Puno in 1534, led by Francisco Pizarro. Initially, colonization went relatively smoothly for the conquistadors. Within the century, the presence of precious metals caused an increase in fighting, especially over the silver and gold rich Laykakota Mines west of Puno. In the 1660s the fighting reached such a level that the Spanish viceroy at the time, Viceroy Conde de Lemos, arrived to quell the situation with drastic measures. He closed the mine, executed the one of the owners (probably the richest man in Latin America at the time), burned down the town that had grown up around it and founded Puno eight kilometers down the road. The exact location of the mines still remains a mystery today.

Fighting again erupted in Puno in the 1780s when indigenous communities began fighting for independence. They continued until 1821 when Peru was granted independence.

At this point Bolivia filled the void left by the Spanish and Puno became one site of the territory war between Peru and Bolivia. The warring between the two countries continued until 1847 when the countries agreed on boundaries and the fighting stopped.

Puno and Lake Titicaca Today

While Puno has a rich and interesting history, the city today is a relatively non-descript municipality of approximately 90,000 people. The city's major drawing card is its proximity to the shores of Lake Titicaca. Puno's tourism industry is well-developed and can accommodate the needs of all types of travelers. The problem is, that aside from the lake, the city has little to offer.

At 3,800 meters, Lake Titicaca is the highest navigable body of water in the world and is home to the famous Uros Floating Islands. Indian communities sometimes as small as just a couple of dozen people building floating islands out of totora reeds.

Contemporary Puno and Lake Titicaca have maintained their significance to Peru's indigenous populations. Those living around the Lake are mainly of Aymara descent and for many, Spanish is their second language. Many Peruvians think Lake Titicaca is the magical place birthplace of their people. According to Inca mythology the first Inca chief, Manco Cápac, rose out of Lake Titicaca. Hence, Puno's festivals and celebrations are among the most vibrant in Peru. A chance to see the dances, listen to the music or attend the fiestas of Puno's indigenous population should not be missed.

One interesting Lake Titicaca tidbit is that according to legend, when the Spanish invaded Peru, the Incas took Inca Huascar's massive gold chain that weighed 2200 kilos and dumped in into Lake Titicaca. The legend was taken seriously enough that legendary underwater explorer Jacques Cousteau mounted an expedition searching for it. Unfortunately, however, he found nothing more than a 60 cm, tri-colored frog that never surfaces. Not 2200 kilos of gold, but not far off.

When To Go

Given its elevation (3,860 m) and inland location far away from the Peruvian coast, Puno has dry, cool weather for most of the year. The average temperature throughout the year is about 8ºC, but the daily lows in July and August make this a less ideal time to visit (unless you brought some warm clothes). The best time to visit is between November and February when the weather is warmest, although it may be wet. Puno also hosts the Virgen de la Candelaria fiesta in February which brings the city to its full celebratory capacity.

LAKE TITICACA HOMESTAY EXPERIENCE

My first stop after arriving in Puno for the trip to Lake Titicaca was the Uros Floating Reed Islands. The area consists of 45 artificial Totora Reed islands anchored by poles in the ground, although only a few are accessible to tourists. On the island, I was treated to a tour and introduction to the Uros who still live a traditional lifestyle of hunting and raising cattle, although signs of the 21st century are evident in solar power panels and TV.

While on the island I was offered the chance to ride in one of the traditional reed boats, something that is not only relaxing, but also a good insight into how the Uros travel.

After an hour, I boarded the boat again and headed a few hours across Lake Titicaca, the highest navigable lake in the world at 3,800 m (12,467 ft), to Amantaní Island. Here, we disembarked and the guide assigned us our families, trying to closely match them to our preferences. I was assigned, with two others, to a family with four children. The lady of the house met us at the pier. The host families live in simple houses and the accommodation offered is basic. My family had no electricity and only an outside toilet with a single room for guests. Conversation can be difficult, as Quechua is the primary language, despite the basic phrase sheet our guide gave us prior to our arrival. Luckily the children spoke Spanish, so with the help of phrase books and sign language, we managed some basic conversation.

After a quick settling-in period, we were offered a lunch of potato soup, followed by potatoes and boiled eggs. Afterwards the locals and boat passengers enjoyed a game of football before a tour around the island, with our guide explaining the history of the island and islanders. The island itself is barren but beautiful, with a handful of villages and ruins situated between the two peaks of the island, Pachatata (Father Earth) and Pachamama (Mother Earth). A walk three times around the ruined temple at the top of the island is said to grant wishes.

After watching the sunset, we headed back to our respective families for dinner and the evening's entertainment. We were dressed in traditional clothing. Men wore ponchos and hats; the women wore petticoats, bulky skirts, white embroidered blouses and black embroidered scarves. A dance was put on in the local school to the music of local bands. The dancing was traditional, but easy to follow. The cold beer and the resplendent night sky rounded out a fun night.

The following day, after a coffee and pancake breakfast, we were taken down to the pier, where we said goodbye to our host families and sailed the short distance to neighboring Taquile Island, where roles are reversed and the men are renowned for their knitting. Yet protective of its local customs, the islanders have adapted to tourists and supply several small restaurants and a co-operative store.

The island itself is rugged with many Inca and pre-Inca ruins dotting the terraced hillside and paths shared by an assortment of cows, sheep and locals. Traditional dress is also worn on Taquile Island, and the men wear embroidered, woven red waistbands (*fajas*) and embroidered wool stocking caps that indicate marital status: red for married men, and red and white for those who are single. After a time exploring the island we headed back to the boat and I relaxed on the deck as we sailed back to Puno, arriving late afternoon.

Excerpt by Freyja Ellis, from V!VA List Latin America, April 2007.

Things To See and Do in Lake Titicaca

Lake Titicaca is the highest navigable lake in the world. With this status comes plenty of activities that can't be experienced anywhere else. Visit the remaining funerary towers of the ancient Colla people who once dominated Lake Titicaca. The towers once contained the remains of tribal families and their belongings. Island hop from floating island to floating island on a reed boat. Spend the night with local families who are warm and will welcome you to experience their traditions. Buy unique handicrafts, clothes and jewelry from markets throughout the lake. Photograph the deep hues of the lake against the bright white snowcapped peaks. Visit old churches and even older ruins scattered around the islands and shores of Lake Titicaca. Taste local foods or learn native dances. This is just the beginning of what the shores and depths of Lake Titicaca have to offer!

Sillustani (Entrance: $3)

Perched on a peninsular bluff overlooking Laguna Umayu, a salt lake situated in the midst of the altiplano, Sillustani harbors some of the most intriguing and best preserved ruins on the Peruvian end of Lake Titicaca. The gravity-defying towers, which have an uncanny resemblance to upturned inkwells, showcase the Colla's masterful stonemasonry skills. These stone tombs, or *chullpas*, served as the final resting places for entire families and their riches. Whether the Collas developed this unique architecture to show off their engineering prowess or to prevent looting is not clear.

Today, this ancient burial site is still used by Sillustani's chamani, or spiritual guide, who performs an annual agricultural fertility ceremony in the temple adjacent to the tombs. Not for the faint of heart, the ceremony includes the sacrifice of a pregnant llama. The fetus is extracted and presented as a symbol of future agricultural prosperity. Be sure to check out the ingeniously constructed *waru waru*, an agricultural device developed during the Tiwanaku Empire to protect crops from frosts.

One of the best ways to see Sillustani is through a Puno tour agency, which will pick you up at your hotel and provide a guided tour of the ruins (in English and Spanish). Most trips also included a brief stop at a local family's house. Sillustani is open 6 a.m. - dark.

Lake Titicaca Tours

A variety of single and multiple-day tours of the world's highest navigable lake are offered, ranging from a few hours of island exploration to days of getting to know lakeside villages. Most travel agencies in Puno handle the conventional tours of Lake Titicaca and Sillustani, along with a handful of other ruins programs and homestays that can extend trips by a few days.

Lake Titicaca Hotels

Lake Titicaca is a beautiful area with lodging options as varied as the views. Beginning in Juliaca, which is not a destination as much as a stopping point for travelers wanting to set up visits to surrounding villages, there are cheap hostels and even cheaper guesthouses. There are also some decent, mid-range hotels. The area around Juliaca includes the charming town of Lampa with its cheap, friendly *hospedajes* or the sleepy village of Pucara with very small, basic places to stay. The market towns of Ayaviri and Abra la Raya offer little in the way of accommodation.

The small port town of Puno is an excellent jumping-off point to visit Lake Titicaca's various islands. Accommodations here range from the most basic of hostels with icy cold showers to mid-range hostels and inns offering a little more luxury for a higher price. The high-end options in Puno include gorgeous views and the best comforts available to fight the sometimes chilly conditions. Choose to camp where allowed, or stay in a more comfortable hostel in the towns of Juli and Pomata.

The many islands each offer very simple accommodations and some islands offer fairly expensive hotels. Chose familial guesthouses that sleep up to ten people or lake-side hotels with stunning alpine views.

Choose a homestay that will allow you to truly experience Lake Titicaca and the generations of people who have lived there. You will be greeted by a family member who will welcome you into your new home. Meals are included and the homestays often include various family activities around the island. Homestays are unique, once-in-a-lifetime opportunities!

Lake Titicaca Homestays

The best way to experience Lake Titicaca and its rich culture is to organize a homestay with a local family. As homestays are fast becoming a signature part of the lake experience, this is not hard to do. Most Puno tour companies can organize a family homestay for you, along with transportation to the island. You can also catch a boat from the Puno public peer and attempt to arrange your own homestay once you arrive on the island. (Of course, being able to speak Spanish or Quechua would be pretty helpful). Usually, a member of your family will greet you, and guide you to your new island home. Homestays can vary greatly, but often include afternoon hikes with your family, football matches in the village square, and neighborhood fiestas. Meals are included in the cost, and also vary. The socially conscious company All Ways Travel also runs a homestay program on Islas Anapia and Yuspique. Homestays through this company are highly recommended for their quality and because proceeds help support sustainable tourism and community development. Regardless of how you arrange your homestay, it is an enriching experience and an opportunity that shouldn't be passed up.

JULIACA

Lacking the glorious lake views and cultural fanfare of Puno, Juliaca has assumed the role of a commercial travel conduit. What it lacks in cultural attractions, however, it makes up for in convenience. Despite its unattractive appearance, Juliaca has the closest airport to Lake Titicaca, and rail and highway connections to Puno, Arequipa and Cusco. The roads originating from Juliaca are also conducive to making the trek to Bolivia along the serpentine backroads winding their way along the northern shores of Lake Titicaca. If you decide to spend the night here, the best hotels and services are located near Plaza Bolognesi, where you can also find the city's train station.

THINGS TO SEE AND DO IN JULIACA

Culture buffs, have no fear: the town does offer a few attractions that will tide you over until you can reach your next destination. In the Plaza Bolognesi you will find the Iglesia La Merced, and a few blocks northwest is another colonial church, the Iglesia Santa Catalina. If you happen to be in town on a Sunday, make your way to Plaza Melgar, which has a huge market where you can browse and buy cheap alpaca wool sweaters. A more touristy market is held daily in the plaza outside the railway station, but keep an eye on your valuables as pickpockets regularly frequent this area.

Getting To and Away from Juliaca

The airport in Juliaca, known as the Inca Manco Cápac International Airport, is a short distance from the city itself, northwest of it by more than 5 kilometers (or 3 miles). It is managed by a government agency and features the longest runway in all of Latin America. It is a domestic, rather than international airport, and is used only by the three Peruvian airlines – Wayra, StarPeru and Aero Condor – as well as the Chilean airline, LAN. There are approximately 28 domestic flights that leave Juliaca airport every week. If you are in a hurry and are willing to spend extra, you can fly directly from Juliaca airport to Puno and Lake Titicaca, rather than take a bus. There are buses and taxis that will take you directly from this airport to the village of Llachón.

If you prefer to take a bus, there is a service from Cusco to Juliaca and Puno. The bus from Cusco to Juliaca can take anything from five to six hours and the road is relatively new and decent. The cost is around $10. Buses run onward to Puno, approximately another 45 km away. There is also a train service that runs from Cusco through Juliaca and Puno on Mon-

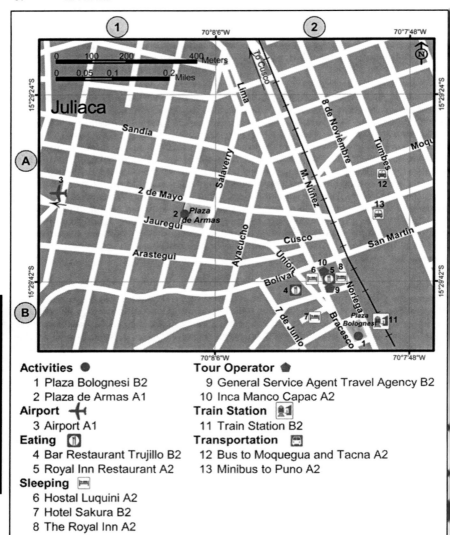

Activities ●
1 Plaza Bolognesi B2
2 Plaza de Armas A1
Airport ✈
3 Airport A1
Eating 🍴
4 Bar Restaurant Trujillo B2
5 Royal Inn Restaurant A2
Sleeping 🛏
6 Hostal Luquini A2
7 Hotel Sakura B2
8 The Royal Inn A2

Tour Operator ♠
9 General Service Agent Travel Agency B2
10 Inca Manco Capac A2
Train Station 🚉
11 Train Station B2
Transportation 🚌
12 Bus to Moquegua and Tacna A2
13 Minibus to Puno A2

days, Wednesdays and Saturdays. The train makes a scenic stop at La Raya, the highest point of the journey (literally). Tickets cost $130 first class and $19 "backpacker class". If you buy the cheap tickets you can't pre-reserve seats. The train leaves Cusco at 8 a.m. and arrives in Juliaca at 4.30 p.m. and Puno at 5.30 p.m. The return journey leaves Puno at 8 a.m. and Juliaca at 9.15 am, arriving in Cusco at 5.30 p.m. Tel: 51-51-321-391.

JULIACA TOURS
General Service Agent Travel Agency
A short walk from the Plaza Bolognesi, General Service Agent can book tours to some of the more interesting destinations on the Collao Plateau, such as the Sillustani pre-Inca burial ground, Lake Titicaca and the city of Arequipa, not to mention numerous other destinations throughout Peru and beyond that can be accessed via the Juliaca International Airport. Jiron San Román #114, Tel: 51-51-324-891.

JULIACA LODGING

Juliaca is not necessarily a destination for most tourists, but merely a stopping point on their way to visit the outlying islands or to organize tours. That said, should you need to stay over in Juliaca, many decent options appeal to your budget and needs. There are cheap hostels with warm water and comfortable beds and higher-end hotels with luxuries such as cable TV.

Hostal Luquini (Rooms: $5 - 15)

Here you can opt for a single room for only $5, with no private bathroom, or for $10 with. A double with a private bathroom goes for $15. The rooms are serviceable and clean, and come with cable TV. There is a nice patio inside the hostel. Rooms are well insulated from most street noise. Apart from that, this hostel, located in front of the Plaza Bolognesi, is recommended only if the superior Hotel Sakura and the Royal Inn are full. Jr. Bracesco 407, Tel: (054) 32-1510.

The Royal Inn (Rooms: $10 - 14)

The Royal Inn is Juliaca's most upscale accommodation. Rooms come with room service, heating, cable TV, hot water, internet access and telephone. The hotel has a conference room capable of hosting up to 40, as well as fax, laundry and cab service. Naturally a continental breakfast is also included. Jr. San Román #158, Tel: 51-321-561 / 51-328-626, E-mail: gerencia@royalinnhoteles.com, URL: www.royalinnhoteles.com.

V!VA Member Review—The Royal Inn

My wife and I loved this hotel. Clean, friendly, excellent service. Enjoyable!

U.S.A., December 30, 2007

Hotel Sakura (Rooms: $11 - 16)

This facility offers good rooms, private bathrooms, hot water, cable TV, fax services, and breakfast. The place is clean, the look and design a bit threadbare, but recommended as an alternative if the Royal Inn across the street is full. San Ramon 133, Tel: 51-322-072, E-mail: hotelsakura@hotmail.com.

JULIACA RESTAURANTS

Sitting down to a meal in Juliaca, you will most likely find yourself looking at a plate overflowing with Peruvian specialties. The food is decent and the prices can be even better. There are good spots for coffee and fresh bread or cake, as well as decent options for drinks. If you find your food tastes better with a little live music, there is a handful of bars or clubs with live folkloric music for your eating and listening pleasure.

Confitería Meli Melo

If in Juliaca you feel your diet is challenged by a massive carbohydrate craving, you can resist it or visit Meli Melo, where for a few *soles* you can avail yourself of a large helping of freshly prepared chocolate mousse or cheesecake, not to mention a panoply of pies, puddings and cakes with multiple layers with multiple fillings. Incidentally, it also serves breakfast and lunch, the latter mostly hamburgers and sandwiches. Jiron San Ramon #167.

Bar Restaurant Trujillo (Entrees: $2 - 4)

A favorite among locals in Juliaca, this moderately large restaurant, capable of seating 70, features 200 menu items. As owner Ricardo Onores proudly likes to point out, the Trujillo specializes in Northern Peruvian cuisine, such as lamb with frijoles, duck with rice, and Tacu-

LAKE TITICACA

Tacu, a fried rice pastry filled with black beans. The restaurant is open from 7:00 a.m. to 10:00 p.m. Jiron San Ramón #163, Juliaca Tel: 51-321-945.

Royal Inn Restaurant (Entrees: $4 - 6)

Part of the high-end Royal Inn, the restaurant matches the rest of the hotel; its clean, classy interior constitutes a mini-vacation of sorts from Juliaca's unpleasant downtown. The menu items are a standard mix of Peruvian and continental favorites. Lunch and dinner will cost you from $4-6. They open early at 6:30 a.m. and remain open until 10:00 p.m. A section of the restaurant can be used for private occasions. They take Visa and Diner's, but as with so much of Peru, not MasterCard. Jr. San Román 158, Tel: 51-321-561 / 51-328-626 E-mail: gerencia@royalinnhoteles.com, URL: www.royalinnhoteles.com.

LAMPA

Due to its remote location beyond the shores of Lake Titicaca and busy streets of Puno, Lampa has managed to maintain a quiet grace and colonial charm. Characterized by clean, open streets and 17th century *casonas* tinted ochre, maroon, and salmon (hence its nickname La Ciudad Rosada), Lampa is conducive to quiet mornings and languid afternoon strolls. Indeed, time seems to have bypassed this quaint colonial town, preferring instead to inhabit the rushing tourist-trodden cities of Puno and Juliaca.

Don't let Lampa's tranquil atmosphere fool you, however, as it has plenty to offer travelers in search of things to see and do. You can, for example, make your way to *Iglesia Santiago Apóstol*, the massive colonial church gracing Lampa's main square. Construction on the Latin-cross shaped church began in 1675 using a combination of lime mortar with river stones. In the 1950s Enrigue Torres Belón, a mining engineer, began restoration of the church. Belón even made the trip to the Vatican to obtain a rare copy of Michelangelo's Pietá. The interior of the church is adorned with huge colonial paintings and an exquisite pulpit whose awe-inspiring grace echoes the one in San Blás in Cusco.

In another section of the church is the Torres Belón mausoleum, in which the remains of Torres Belón and his wife are located. This eerie crypt is decorated with the bones of hundreds of priests, hacienda owners, and Spanish miners, which were removed from their original resting place beneath the church when Belón ordered the church's catacombs to be cemented shut. A number of ancient Inca tunnels left over from an earlier temple wind their way beneath the church.

A number of colonial homes in town are worth the visit, if you're keen to stretch your legs. During the independence wars, Simón Bolívar addressed the town from the beautiful Casona Chukiwanka located in Plaza Guru. Some of the houses even have old colonial games, in the form of white and black stones laid out in courtyards to form huge game boards.

The dirt roads stretching beyond Lampa towards Cusco make for an excellent bike ride or drive. On the way you can stop at the forest of *queña*, the Colla *chullpas*, well preserved remains of two colonial mines, a forest of *puya raimondi*, or the intriguing geological formations at Tinajani Canyon. If you take the other road leading westward from Lampa you'll come across a cave dawning animal carvings and burial towers similar to those at Sillustani.

If you can, plan to visit between July 29-31 when the town comes alive with colonial-style bullfights and traditional dances for the Fiesta de Santiago Apóstol. Another good time to visit is from December 6-8 when you can watch the religious processions of *La Virgin de la Immaculada*.

LLACHÓN

This inviting little village located between Puno and Juliaca promises a less touristy experience than the nearby Isla Taquile. While it does not harbor the same rustic restaurants as the more popular tourist spots, it does have Valentín Quispe, the gregarious local who runs a bucolic lodge on the outskirts of town. The lodge consists of small, whitewashed cabins with thatched roofs on a hillside promising spectacular views of Lago Titicaca. The lodge also serves as the departure point for kayaking around the lake. Always ready to help, Valentín can also arrange homestays with other families on Llachón. Or you can rough it for the night and enjoy the spectacular star-studded sky from the convenience of your own tent. There is a nice beach with a free campsite on one end, and on the opposite end a French-owned campground that rents tents and provides meals. For a change of scenery, find one of the local fishermen, who will gladly take you (of course there's fee!) to nearby Isla Taquile or Isla Amantaní. A sailboat usually costs around six dollars and a private motor boat $36.

PUNO

Characterized by sprawling, traffic-infested streets lined with barking men and women selling their brightly-colored crafts, the city of Puno lacks the grace and charm of its vastly more attractive neighbor, Lake Titicaca. Were it not for the dozens of tour agencies lining Puno's dusty streets, the placid shores of this natural gem may be all but swallowed up by the sites and sounds of a bustling city. Indeed, it's slightly ironic that the Quechua named for this hectic city translates to "place of rest."

Honking buses and pedestrian-packed streets aside, Puno has a number of redeeming qualities, which make it a great place to start any trip to Lake Titicaca and the surrounding area. As the central hub for lake excursions and trips to more attractive destinations, Puno has a number of hotels, restaurants and tour agencies to accommodate almost any traveler's tastes and needs. A recently built bus station now serves as a connection point for all major bus companies and is conveniently located within walking distance of the port, from where you can catch a boat to Isla Amantaní and Isla Taquile.

Dominated by the Aymara to the south and Quechua to the north, Puno was shaped by the confluence of two notably different cultural currents. Referred to by some as the folklore capital of the world, Puno boasts some of the most fascinating and vibrant folklore festivals. Three major festivals are unique to the city: Fiesta de la Virgen de la Candelaria, Puno Week and Adoración del Sol. Perhaps the most interesting attraction in Puno lies just outside the city limits. The Yavari is one of the world's great antique ships, and the story of how it came to rest in Puno is almost as interesting as the ship itself.

Within the city there are a number of interesting attractions, all within walking distance of one another. If you're feeling particularly energetic, spend the day exploring the city on foot. Gracing the Plaza de Armas is the city's 17th century cathedral, whose elaborately-carved façade gives way to a rather spartan interior accented by a brilliant silver-plated altar. Next to the cathedral is another 17th century relic, the Casa del Corregidor. There is an inviting courtyard on the grounds, where javaholics can savor a coffee from one of Puno's most delightful cafés.

From the Plaza de Armas you can head towards Parque Huajsapata where you'll find a massive mirador with a huge sculpture of Manco Cápac, the first Inca. Be aware, however, that a number of robbery assaults on single tourists have been reported here. Up the street from the plaza, on the corner of Conde de Lemos and Deústua, is the Balcony of the Conde de Lemos, former residence of Peru's viceroy and the current home of the Cultural Institute of Peru. Across the street you'll find the Museo Dreyer Municipal, which has a collection of pre-Inca and Inca artifacts and documents citing the history of the Spanish foundation of Peru.

From the museum, head downhill two blocks to Puno's pedestrian street, Lima, which connects the Plaza de Armas to Parque Pino. Here you can refuel at some of the city's best restaurants and cafés. Parque Pino boasts an 18th century church dedicated to San Juan Bautista, and home of the Virgen de Candelaria, Puno's most important patron saint. From the park, you can head towards the Arco Deústua, a huge stone arch built in honor of those killed in battles for independence in Junín and Ayacucho.

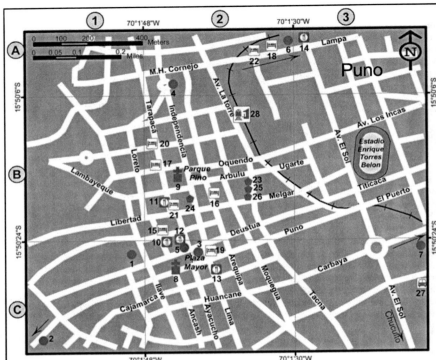

Activities ●
1 Cerrito de Huajsapata C1
2 Mirador de Kuntur Wasi C1
3 Plaza Mayor C2
4 Raqchi A2
5 The Casa del Corregidor C2
6 The Yavari A2
7 Vendors on the Puno docks C3

Church ✝
8 Catedral de Puno C2
9 San Juan Bautista B2

Eating 🍴
10 CECOVASA Café C2
11 IncaBar B2
12 La Casa del Corregidor B2
13 Mojsa Restaurant C2
14 The Yavari A3

Sleeping 🛏
15 Casa Andina Puno Plaza B2
16 Colón Inn B2
17 Hostal Los Pinos B2
18 Hotel Libertador Puno A2
19 Plaza Mayor C2
20 Posada Wary Nayra B2
21 Qelqatani Hotel B2
22 Sonesta Posada del Inca A2

Tour Operator ●
23 All Ways Travel B2
24 Edgar Adventures B2
25 Titicaca Expedition B2
26 Zarate Expeditions B2

Transportation 🚌
27 Bus Station C3

Train Station 🚊
28 Train Station B2

If city-sightseeing isn't your cup of tea, you can always meander through Puno's huge central market, or catch a boat to one of Lake Titicaca's islands. Active travelers may want to inquire about kayaking on Lake Titicaca, or horseback riding in the valley just north of Puno. A number of companies in Puno offer island tours to Isla Uros, Islas Taquile and Amantaní, Islas

Anapia and Yuspique, and Isla Suasi. You can also arrange a visit to nearby attractions like Sillustani and Chucuito. For free tourist information and maps head to i Peru (Deústua with Lima, Tel :51-365-088, 8:30 a.m. - 7:30 p.m. daily). Or, for more detailed information pay a visit to the Regional Tourism Office (Ayacucho 682, Tel: 51-364-976, Monday - Friday, 7:30 a.m. - 5:15 p.m.

Getting To and Away from Puno

The most scenic option for getting to Puno is from Cusco by rail service. If pressed for time, you can also fly to the airport in Juliaca (p.347), which is 45 minutes from Puno. Buses will get you there in less time and for cheaper, but of course will not be as plush, although Ormeño offers a first class bus service for $17, departing daily at 9 a.m. from the terminal terrestre. Imexso and Civa run buses for around $5-6 at 7:30 a.m. and 7:30 p.m. from the same station. Cruz del Sur also has a 1 p.m. bus. Another option is the Inka Express bus which stops along the way. The Puno bus station is located southeast of the centre, so you'll have to take a taxi into town. For those heading into Bolivia, there are regular direct buses for Copacabana and La Paz leaving from the main terminal. Alternatively, you can take a combi to Yunguyo (for Copacabana) for about $1, for the hour and a half ride, leaving from the corner of Av. El Puerto and Av. El Sol. Buses and combis only leave up to around 3 pm daily, so that they get to the immigration offices of Peru and Bolivia before they close for the day.

The Train from Cusco to Puno ($16 - 143)

The train ride from Cusco to Puno is one of the highest in the world, 3,500m (11,500 ft), and one of the most picturesque, apart from the train ride to Machu Picchu. The first half of this ten-hour journey provides some breathtaking views of Peru's Andean mountains that loom over deep valleys and the Huatanay River. The second half offers pleasant views of the Andean plains. The first-class coaches are oxygenated to mitigate the possibility of altitude sickness.

Travel options vary from first to economy class. First class includes an open-air observation deck. As in all your travels through Latin America, a certain degree of common-sense caution is advised in safeguarding your valuables.

The train for Puno departs from Estación Huanchaq (tel. 084-238-722) at the end of Avenida Sol, leaving every Monday, Wednesday and Saturday at 8:00 am. The trip from Cusco from Puno has the same schedule, with the Puno train station at Avenida La Torre 224 (tel. 051-351-041). Reservations for the latter must be made at least one day in advance. For more information, go to www.perurail.com.

Inka Express

If you don't want to spend the $143 to take the first-class train to Puno, but don't want to settle for a regular bus, Inka Express is a good option. Leaving from Cusco at 8 a.m. daily, they offer a "day-trip" with a difference: you will visit the site of Raqchi and the picturesque village of Andahuaylillas, home to the "Sistine Chapel of the Americas," enjoy lunch in a country restaurant, and end your day arriving in Puno at around 6 p.m. Urb. El Ovalo Pachatutec C-32, Cusco, Tel: 51-84-247-887, and Jr. Tacna 346, Puno, Tel: 51-51-365-654, URL: www.inkaexpress.com.

PUNO SERVICES

For free tourist information and maps head to i Peru (daily, 8:30 a.m.-7:30 p.m. Deústua with Lima, Tel :51-51-365-088). Or, for more detailed information, pay a visit to the Regional Tourism Office (Monday-Friday, 7:30 a.m.-5:15 p.m. Ayacucho 682, Tel: 51-51-364-976).

There are three main banks close to the main square in Puno, including the Canadian Scotia-bank, all of which have functioning ATMs that allow you to withdraw solés at any hour. Some common sense is advised, however, and you should be cautious about withdrawing cash after dark, particularly when there are no police or guards in the vicinity. ScotiaBank, on Deústua

LAKE TITICACA

and Jiron Lima, is right across the street from Puno's official tourist information office. Just a short walk away , on Jiron Lima and Grau, you will find the Banco Credito de Peru (BCP), as well as InterBank.

Shopping
Vendors on the Puno Docks
One advantage of walking as you head east towards Lake Titicaca and the main port of departure in Puno, Puerta Lacustre, is that you can to check out the scores of local vendors selling folk art, hand-made clothing, food, and many other items. Combined with the view of Lake Titicaca looming to the east, hanging out on the docks provides a pleasant immersion into local culture and geography.

Central Market
At Puno's Mercado Central, shoppers can enthusiastically dig among colorful alpaca sweaters, small stone carvings, hand-crafted jewelry, hats and artwork to find the ideal souvenir to take home. Street vendors sell local foods and tasty treats (not always the easiest on a foreigner's tummy, so be wary) and little children play at your feet while you shop. As in all markets, stay aware of your belongings and keep your valuables tucked deep in your bag. 8 a.m.-6 p.m., approximately. Near the train station, two blocks east of Parque Pino.

THINGS TO SEE AND DO IN PUNO
Though Puno is generally used as a starting off point to visit the surrounding islands, there are still a few activities to enjoy here. Visit Puno's baroque cathedral built in 1757, and afterwards, explore the oldest house in the area (now a cultural center). There are a handful of museums in the area showcasing the lake's history and ancient archaeological artifacts. There is a charming little park, old ruins and of course, many activities that can be organized outside of Puno.

Puno Cathedral (Entry: Free)
The Puno Cathedral was built in 1757, and as such has a distinctly baroque design. However, its religious art expresses both European and indigenous influences. The native *panti* plants that grow in the front were originally smuggled into town as contraband, and are reportedly capable of relieving physical pain. A skirmish between factions of miners in the 18th century resulted in a bullet being lodged in one of the paintings, which was thereafter referred to as the Lord of the Bullet, and petitions are made to this work by local farmers when they need rain. A fire in 1930, alas, destroyed much of the historical artwork in the cathedral. Bring a camera. Jiron Ayacucho and Jiron Puno, in front of Plaza de Armas.

Parque Pino
Parque Pino (Pino Park) is connected to the the larger Plaza de Armas of Puno by a walkway. It was built in 1901 seven years after Peru's decisive victory over Chile in honor of the local "puneño," Dr. Manuel Pino, who emerged as the hero of the war. A statue of the doctor stands atop a column in the center of the park, and busts of other notable Puno "puneños" who partook in this campaign can be found below. One side of the park is taken up by the "Glorious National College of San Carlos," founded by the "liberator" of South America, Simón Bolívar. Walk four blocks north on Jiron de Independencia from the Plaza de Arma. Jiron de Independencia y Jiron Alfonso Ugarte.

Jirón Lima
The pedestrian walkway Jirón Lima begins at the Plaza de Armas and continues until the Arco Deústua. This is the heart of town, where you will find most of the hostels, hotels, taverns, tour operators, street vendors and restaurants. It is not much in and of itself, but it does provide you an opportunity for a pleasant night out and a chance to meet other travelers.

Casa del Corregidor
This exquisite little structure near the heart of Puno is worth a visit both for itself as one of the few architectural and historical places of interest in Puno, and for the productive use of

its space. Casa del Corregidor's history dates to the 17th century. The name *corregidor* refers to a "corrector," a title traditionally associated to a sovereign who served as magistrate, governor and tax-collector. The Casa was later appropriated by the Catholic Church, and then by a private family, who eventually sold it to the city who declared it a historical landmark.

Casa del Corregidor is now home to a handful of progressive enterprises: the Café Cecovasa, the Fair Trade Folk Art shop, and the All Ways Travel Agency, which sponsors cultural tourism and works with NGOs to bring in much-needed volunteers to help poor children in the area. The Casa also sponsors a number of culturally edifying experiences, such as art expositions, talks, workshops and shows. Open 8 a.m-11 p.m. Jr. Deústua 576, Tel: 51-51-365-603, URL: www.casadelcorregidor.ciap.org.

San Juan Bautista Church
San Juan Bautista Church is the focus of the main festival in Puno, in honor of the Virgin of Candlemas, which takes place in the first week of February. The Virgin was adopted as the city's spiritual guardian following the victory of Spanish troops over local tribes in the 16th century, though some others claim it due was to the Mother of God's appearance to some miners during the 19th century. The church itself has a history going back 200 years, when it began as a chapel. In 1876 it was rebuilt as a formal church, with a distinctly French-style façade on the outside and three gothic-styled altars on the inside.

Arco Deústua Memorial
Head north on Calle Lima from the main Plaza and you will arrive at the Arco Deústua Memorial, built in 1847 to commemorate Peru's fallen soldiers in the battles of Junin and Ayacucho during the Independence War with Spain. Just a few blocks uphill, in the Parque San Juan, the arch serves as a good lookout point over Puno.

The Yavarí
The Yavari is a medium-sized, iron-hulled ship, one of the first two commissioned by the Peruvian government in 1861. They were forged in England and then shipped to Peru. What happened next was a fascinating chapter in Peruvian history: the two ships had to be packaged in small enough bundles that they could be carried by mules over stretches of Peru's barren highlands. Parts were lost, the government ran out of money, and a series of calamities threatened to derail the project, but in the end the ships were built and the Yavari was christened in 1870, beginning more than a century of service. In the early years, fuel was so scarce that the ship was modified so that it could run on dried llama dung! There has been a recent effort to preserve the Yavari, which has met with some success. Today, it is a tourist site and restaurant/café popular with visitors. Don't miss it on your trip to Puno. Located on a pier near Puno. Tel: 051/36-9329.

Mirador de Kuntur Wasi
With its metal wingspan 11 meters (36 feet) long, and perched on a hill 3,990 meters (13, 091 feet) high overlooking Puno, the Kuntur Wasi condor is the most dramatic expression of this community's pride in its Andean heritage. The lookout provides a breathtaking view of the city and Lake Titicaca. You can access it via cab for approximately $2, or you can walk east from the Plaza de Armas towards the base of the monument and begin a careful ascent of the 620 steps, which rise from sea level to the condor's talons.

Cerrito de Huajsapata
This imperial tribute to the founder, Manco Capac, of the Incan Empire is 45-meters (148 feet) high and can be found west of the city. As with the Kuntur Wasi lookout, the Cerrito of Huajsapata provides a spectacular view of the city and Lake Titicaca. Manco Capac stands before a wide concrete lot, popular with young amateur football players. There are rumors that inside the monument are subterranean portals that connect Puno to the Qoricancha Temple in Cusco. Of course, if there really were such a thing, local Peruvians would long since have capitalized it for maximum profit.

Find more reviews from travelers at www.vivatravelguides.com

Raqchi

Perhaps the most impressive aspect of the Raqchi ruins is the line of nearly 200 round stone houses that parallels the gigantic adobe Inca wall. At one time each one of the houses was filled to the brim with quinoa, freeze-dried potatoes and corn. The wall, nearly 15 meters high and 90 meters long, was part of a ceremonial center built by Inca Pachacútec. The now-crumbling walls once supported a huge hall with a roof—another testament to the Inca's architectural ambition and engineering skills. One of the supporting columns has been restored, and on one side of the wall there are six stone buildings, which probably once served as soldiers' barracks. Though the great hall of Raqchi has long since succumbed to time and the elements, the remaining five-story high wall is one of the best preserved examples of Inca adobe architecture, and definitely a site worth checking out.

Volunteering in Puno

Puno, being smaller than such large cities as Cusco and Lima, has fewer opportunities for volunteering, but no less great a need. Fortunately All Ways Travel and Nueva Acrópolis are available to address the needs of people living on Lake Titicaca and in Puno.

All Ways Travel World Challenge Volunteer Program

To address the unique needs of the children of indigenous communities, of Puno and various islets of Lake Titicaca, All Ways Travel and the non-profit World Challenge Organization work together to organize groups of high-school-age volunteers. The students raise funds to help purchase books and other educational materials, medicine and even toys. Volunteers also teach literacy to children while staying with their families on Anapia, Taquile, Sausi and Uros Islands. The program won a national award for their work as Best Participative Community-Based Project. Jr. Deústua 576, Tel: 51-51-353-979, E-mail: allwaystravel@titicacaperu.com, URL: www.titicacaperu.com.

Nueva Acrópolis

Nueva Acrópolis, or "New Acropolis," is an international organization dedicated to preserving and fostering culture, learning, science and philosophy. It has forty chapters around the world, including one right in Puno. Acropolis means High City, which considering Puno's 11,000 ft (3,300 m) altitude makes a chapter here very fitting. The organization has a volunteer program during the months of July and December, where help is needed on any number of quality-of-life projects, such as teaching painting, offering workshops on disease prevention, medicinal plants, hygiene, and providing healthcare services, as well as restoring monuments, and cleaning rivers, parks, and shorefronts. Jr. Moguegua 181, Tel: 51-51-368-876, E-mail: puno@acropolisperu.org, URL: www.acropolisperu.org.

Puno Tours

You'll have no problem finding tour companies in Puno; however, you should be wary of unofficial tour sellers, *jalagringos*, who target tourists. A good policy is to compare prices, only use official agencies, and only pay at the main office, not in the street. Most agencies organize trips to the islands of Taquile and Amantaní, as well as other places. Kayaking trips around the lake can also be arranged at a number of companies. For a unique experience inquire about island homestays, which offer unforgettable encounters with local communities.

Edgar Adventures

Run by Peruvian husband and wife team Edgar Apaza and Norka Florez, Edgar Adventures is one of the busiest tour agencies in Puno, and is highly recommended. This daring-duo runs tours departing daily to a number of Lake Titicaca Islands. Transport to and from Cusco, Arequipa and Bolivia can also be arranged through the company. Jr. Lima 328, Tel: 51-51-353-444, E-mail: manager@edgaradventures.com, URL: www.edgaradventures.com

All Ways Travel

This socially-conscious company managed by Victor Pauca and his daughter, Eliana, offers trips to various islands around Lake Titicaca and Sillustani, including Uros, Amantaní,

Anapia, Yuspique, and Taquile. The independent company works in collaboration with British company World Challenge Expeditions to place volunteers in local communities. All Ways Travel is a bit more expensive than other tour agencies, but it is worth it for the quality of service, and the benefits received by the local community. The company also runs a homestay program on Islas Anapia and Yuspique, so if you're keen to get to know the locals, this is a great option. Tacna 234, Tel: 51-5-135-5552, URL: www.titicacaperu.com.

Mystery Peru

Mystery Peru has been operating tours in Puno and Lake Titicaca since 2004. The guides speak English and are very knowledgeable about Lake Titicaca, area traditions, customs and local culture in general. Ignacio Morsesky 126, Arica 576, Tel: 51-56-522-379, Fax: 51-56-522-379, E-mail: info@mysteryperu.com, URL: www.mysteryperu.com.

Pirámide Tours

This company offers both classic tours and more unique trips to remote areas around Lake Titicaca. Service is flexible and friendly, and launches are fast. Transport to and from Cusco, Arequipa, and Bolivia can be arranged. Jr. Deza 129, Tel: 51-51-367-302, URL: www.titikakalake.com.

Solmartour

With over 30 years of tourism experience, customer service and tailor-made itineraries are deeply ingrained within Solmartour's philosophy. Their menu of tours is diverse with options for adventure tourism, esoteric tourism and experiential tourism. From floating down the Amazon River, to visiting the Manu Nature Reserve, to experiencing the Lord of Sipán or Machu Picchu, you'll find your perfect adventure here. Solmartour stands behind their statement that they want to "ensure that the travelers who come to Peru as tourists will return to their countries as our friends." As itineraries are customized, contact Solmartour for pricing information. Jr. Libertad 229 - 231, Tel: 51-54-352-901, E-mail: solmartour@ventanavirtual.com.pe.

Titicaca Expedition

Titicaca Expedition claims to offer the best team and best service for making the most of your visit to Titicaca. It does charge double what the other boat operators will charge to take you to the Uros islets or to Taquile Island, $6 rather than $3, but owner Sesbastian Grundy asserts that unlike the other operators, he will pick you up right at your hotel, and his boats come with actual, informative guides. All things considered, the rates to such landmark geographical and cultural points such as Sillustani and Amantaní are inexpensive, and the range of Titicaca Expedition's services include two and three-day excursions, including camping trips. Tel: 54-367-929, E-mail: titicaca-expedition@speedy.com.pe, URL: www.titicaca-expedition.com.

LAKE TITICACA

Titikayak

Partially owned by the reputable ExplorAndes agency, Titikayak is a fairly new company offering a range of safe, well-planned kayak trips that leave from Llachón. The equipment is excellent and everything you'll need for the trip is provided. The agency offers half-day trips around the peninsula, a full-day trip that goes to Isla Taquile and back, and a three-day trip that explores the island in detail. For those with arms-of-steel, longer 10-day trips to more remote places can also be arranged. Bolognesi 334, Tel: 51-51-367-747, E-mail: postmast@titikayak.com, URL: www.titikayak.com

Zárate Expeditions

From rappelling off of the mountain cliffs around Puno to visiting the Totorani waterfalls, Zarate really will take you out there in the wild surrounding Lake Titicaca. Apart from rock-climbing, they also do trekking, motorcycling, mountain biking (on Lake Titicaca's Capichica peninsula no less), camping (in the Chilligua canyon), and kayaking, of course, in the world's highest lake. Their day adventures are no more than forty dollars per person, and this is an ideal way to really experience this part of the world, not just look at it. Jiron Tacna 246, Tel: 51-36-9551, E-mail: zarateexpeditionpuno@hotmail.com, URL: www.viajeros.com/empresa-zarate.

PUNO LODGING

In terms of accommodation, Puno caters more tobudget-backpackers than those seeking first-class service. The best options are located on the banks of Lake Titicaca, and are worth the taxi ride if you can afford to splurge. Most hotels and hostels are more than willing to bargain outside the high season (June-Sept), and you should always check out the place first (in particular it pays to ask if they have hot water). Despite its reputation for less-than-sparkling dives, Puno does have some luxury accommodations that are worth a look if your wallet can manage.

BUDGET

El Manzano (Rooms: $8 - $16)

This small but charming hotel is a little way from the bustling center of Puno, towards the port. Rooms are basic but comfortable enough, and there is a sheltered, sunny dining room where you can sit and relax. Most rooms have shared baths; the 24 hour hot water is powered partly by gas, and partly by solar power. The staff is friendly, helpful and very knowledgeable about the area, so ask their advice if you are planning any independent trips. Av El Puerto 449, Tel: 51-51-364-697, E-mail: elmanzanopunoperu@hotmail.com, URL: www.elmanzanolodge.com.

Hostal Los Uros (Rooms: $10 - 15)

Clean, cozy rooms and 24-hour hot water make Hostal Los Uros a popular place among backpackers—so popular, in fact, that it's often full. The oak beds come furnished with plenty of comforters, important for those chilly Puno nights. Breakfast is served in the cafeteria, and laundry service and luggage store is available for a small charge. Other conveniences include internet, tourist information and a baby alpaca handicraft shop. Teodoro Valcárcel 135, Tel: 51-51-352-141, E-mail: huros@speedy.com.pe.

Hostal Los Pinos (Rooms: $14 - 32)

Of the places to stay in Puno, Hostal Los Pinos is one of the best budget options. This family-run hostel has spacious, light-filled rooms with new private baths and electric hot water showers. Those seeking to save a few pennies can request rooms with a shared bathroom. Other amenities include breakfast, luggage storage and laundry facilities. The staff is extremely helpful. Cheap tours can be arranged. Tarapacá 182, Tel: 51-51-367-398, E-mail: hostalpinos@hotmail.com.

Helena Inn Hostal (Rooms: $18 - 30)

Helena Inn Hostal is one of the few higher-end facilities in Puno. For those wanting to spend a little bit more for a quality stay while anticipating a trip to Lake Titicaca, the Helena Inn is not a disappointment. The design and décor is a slightly more updated version of 1930s style art deco, the rooms are carpeted, and there is free Internet access on every floor. The best part is the cafeteria, situated on the top floor, where you can enjoy a continental breakfast with a wide, winning view of Lake Titicaca. Cable TV, safety boxes, room service and even private parking all come as part of the package. Located just two blocks north of Puno's main square. Jiron Ayacucho 609, Tel: 51-51-352-108.

Hostal Taquile (Rooms: $20 - 35)
This basic hotel has a good location and friendly staff. The rooms are adequate, even with the worn furniture and bed covers. Although the brochure states 24-hour hot water, agua caliente is not always available. Beds come with multiple blankets, a nice addition since the heat is often on low. A simple breakfast of bread, coffee and juice is included with the price of your room, in addition to a pick-up from the Puno bus station. A computer with a slow internet connection is available for use in the lobby. Jr. Ayacucho 515-517, Tel: 051-351927/9733095, E-mail: hostaltaquilepuno@hotmail.com, www.taquilehostal.com.

MID-RANGE
Don Julio Youth Hostel (Rooms: $22 - 44)
Associated with Hostelling International, Don Julio is a well-run hostel with lots of extra services including internet for guests, TV room, an on-site café-bar and storage lockers. Rooms are pleasant and most are bright and airy. Breakfast is included in the price. Major credit cards are accepted. Jr. Tacna 336, Tel: 51-51-363-358, E-mail: hostaldonjulio@hotmail.com, URL: www. http://www.hihostels.com/dba/hostels-Puno---HI-Don-Julio-044039.en.htm.

El Buho Hotel (Rooms: $30 - 55)
A delightful, spacious hotel with well-decorated rooms and all-important gas heaters for those cold Puno nights. The hotel feels luxurious, yet homey at the same time. Services include carpeted rooms with private bath and 24 hour hot water, Cable TV, telephones in each room, an on-site bar and internet for guests. Staff are friendly and attentive. Jr. Lambayeque 142-144, Tel: 51-51-366-122, E-mail: reservas@hotelbuho.com, URL: www.hotelbuho.com.

Hotel Italia (Rooms: $33 - 55)
The Hotel Italia is located in the center of Puno and offers reasonably priced (if a little small) rooms. If you are in a group of three, the triple rooms are a good value. They also offer several vegetarian options in the in-house restaurant—a rarity in Peru and something to be sought out by vegetarians. All rooms have 24-hour hot water, private bathrooms and cable TV, with optional room service. They also offer valet service, which might be of interest to travelers arriving with their own transportation. Prices include taxes and breakfast. The low price is for a single room and the high price is for a triple. Theodoro Valcarcel Nº 122, Tel: 51-51-363-639, Fax: 51-51-367-706, E-mail: mail@hotelitaliaperu.com, URL: www.hotelitaliaperu.com

Hotel Ferrocarril (Rooms: $33 - 55)
Hotel Ferrocarril is a mid-priced inn conveniently located in downtown Puno. The rooms are clean, spacious, reasonably priced and feature twin reading lights above the beds. Each room has a private bath, 24-hour hot water and cable TV. There is also an on-site restaurant and cafeteria, and a garage for visitors with private cars. For those without their own wheels, Hotel Ferrocarril is within walking distance of both the bus and train stations. Guests can also rent out the conference center that accommodates up to 600 people. Price includes tax. The low price is for a single room and the high price is for a triple room. Av. la Torre 185, 51-51-351-752 / 35-2011, Fax: 51-51-351-752, E-mail: mail@hotelferrocarril.com, URL: www.hotelferrocarril.com.

Posada Spa Wary Nayra (Rooms: $34 - 56)
Puno's luxurious Posada Spa Wary Nayra, one block west of busy Jr. Lima, is a modern, comfortable hotel that is perfect to call home while traveling around Lake Titicaca. All rooms have comfortable beds, clean modern bathrooms, hot water with great pressure, new carpet,

LAKE TITICACA

"Estacion de Bus Hacia Chucuito" ($0.50, 12 minutes). The bus will leave you at the main square. From there, ask for the football field and walk one block beyond. Pasaje La Glorieta s/n, Chucuito, Puno, Tel: 51-54-220-323, Fax: 51-54-220-323, E-mail: reservas@laglorietahotel.com, URL: www.laglorietahotel.com.

Albergue Las Cabañas (Rooms: $22 - 34)

For the best accommodation in town, check into the charming Albergue Las Cabañas. Inside you'll be welcomed by the sight of high adobe walls looming over a beautiful garden of yellow *retama* and *queña* flowers. The bungalows consist of immaculately polished wood floors, stone hearths, and new bathrooms. Members of Hostelling International only pay $7 per person. Near Plaza de Armas at Tarapaca 538, Tel: 51-351-276, E-mail: lodgecabanas@chucuito.com.

JULI

The 84-kilometer stretch of road winding southwards from Puno to Juli is dotted with small towns set back from Lake Titicaca. The unfolding scenery includes towns like Platería, once known for its silver works, Acora, and Llave, a commercial crossroads clearly lacking in the colonial architecture found in so many other small towns in the region. Shortly after Llave, the road winds its way back towards the lake where it meets up with Juli. At one time, this was a resting point for silver caravans traveling between the coast and the Potosí mine. The Jesuits and Dominicans also once used Juli as a place to train missionaries. Today, Juli's attractions include four churches dating from the 16th and 17th centuries.

Located on the main plaza, San Pedro Mártir presents a fascinating Renaissance façade, which opens towards an intricate Baroque altar and paintings by the Italian master Bernardo Bitti. A short jaunt from San Pedro Mártir is San Juan Bautista. In addition to a magnificently carved altar and sacristy door, and walls adorned with 80 paintings from the Cusqueña School, the church has gorgeous windows composed of a unique translucent stone known as *Piedra de Huamanga*.

Santa Cruz de Jerusalén presents an enchanting mix of sacred wonder and natural beauty, with magnificent doors and spectacular views of Lake Titicaca. The skeletal remains of Nuestra Señora de la Ausunción have an undeniably sepulchral atmosphere, accented by a large door and intact tower rising above the crumbling remains. In July, the church ruins spring to life with a colorful fair held every Thursday.

THE PERUVIAN ISLANDS OF LAKE TITICACA

No trip to Lake Titicaca is complete without a visit to the charming islands anchored in its deep blue waters. A one-day boat tour will take you to the floating reed islands of the Uros people. However, an overnight homestay on one of the islands comes highly recommended, if only for the chance to watch a majestic Lake Titicaca sunset from one of the islands' shores. Each island has its own impressive and unique traditions stemming from Quechua culture. On the beautiful Islas Amantaní and Taquile one can hike to ruins; on an All Ways Travel tour of Isla Anapia or Isla Yuspique one can rest easy knowing that the tour company contributes to sustainable development.

ISLA UROS

Bullied by the Collas, then the Incas, and later the Spanish, the Uros people did the unthinkable in the name of cultural preservation: they isolated themselves by constructing floating islands out of the tótora reeds that grow abundantly around the lake. Today 32 islands still bob on the water's surface in a cluster about a 30 minute motorboat ride from Puno. The largest island manages to support a clinic, school, and Seventh Day Adventist church! To keep the islands afloat, the Uros must frequently rebuild the top layers, as the bottom layers rot and return to the lake's bottom. The pungent odor unique to the islands stems from the decomposition of the lower layer of reeds.

Like their ancestors, the Uros people continue to uphold their unique traditions and way of life. Family units are governed by a grandfather and marriages are often prearranged—sometimes from birth. The massive Viking-esque tótora rafts, adorned with carved dragonheads, are the same vessels as used centuries ago. Most inhabitants subsist by hunting and fishing, though the advent of tourism has significantly altered the economic structure of the islands. Twenty of the islands have managed to secure deals with tourist agencies in Puno and now garner much of their daily income from trafficking tourists.

The flourishing tourism industry, which first sprouted on the islands in the late 1960s, has created a dynamic tug-of-war between the positive and negative effects on the local culture. To a great extent, tourism has rescued the Uros from the threat of poverty and helped sustain their current population of several hundred. However, it has also created an undercurrent of aggressive adults and suppliant children who pressure tourists to buy their trinkets, or pay for posed pictures. A good rule of thumb for any visit to Islas Uros is not to give begging children money. Instead, give them fruit or buy one of their goods.

Tours to Islas Uros can be arranged through most Puno tour agencies or you can catch a boat to the islands from the Puno public pier.

Isla Uros Lodging
Kamisaraki Inn / Lodge Los Uros (Rooms: $15 - 20)
It is one thing to have visited the world-famous floating islands, but how about telling your friends you actually slept on them, in a reed hut no less? This is what the Kamisaraki Inn/ Lodge Los Uros offers, your opportunity to know what it is like to live among the inhabitants. Unlike the Uros homes, the reeds here are stacked, tee-pee like, with two beds, pillows, and several wool blankets each. The owner, Silverio, also manages a restaurant, in case you are extending your trip for more than an evening, and once there you can negotiate for visits, via traditional reed boat, to the other islands. The nights do get cold, however, so be prepared. The cost is about $15/person and it includes breakfast, lunch and dinner. For $20/person you get the three meals, a tour of the islands, cultural exchange, and a cultural night with bonfire. Ask for Silverio Lujano Jilapa.

Photo by Cate Batchelder
Find more reviews from travelers at www.vivatravelguides.com

There are many tourist boats leaving from the main dock in Puno, charging anywhere from $3 to $6 a ride, depending on the number of passengers available. There is also the Brisas del Titikaka to help you arrange your trip around the floating islands. Located at Av. Titicaca 579, Los Uros, Tel: 51–835-016 / 951-049-493 / 951-059-299, E-mail: kamisarakilodge@hotmail.com/reservas-kamisarakilodge@hotmail.com, URL: www.kamisarakilodge.tk.

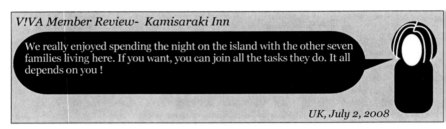

V!VA Member Review- Kamisaraki Inn

We really enjoyed spending the night on the island with the other seven families living here. If you want, you can join all the tasks they do. It all depends on you !

UK, July 2, 2008

ISLA AMANTANÍ

This picturesque little island receives less tourism than nearby Isla Taquile and is perfect for anyone seeking an authentic experience. While the islanders speak Quechua like their neighbors, their culture and customs are more strongly influenced by their Aymara ancestry. The community is divided into subsections of adobe houses, each divided by stone walls. Two hills tower over the island, and each crest is graced with a temple. The taller hill is dedicated to Pachatata (Father Earth), while the shorter hill is dedicated to Pachamama (Mother Earth). Because they are sacred sites, no one is permitted to enter either temple, except on the annual feast day, January 20. On this special day, the island's population divides in two, and each half gathers at its own respective temple.

A race is held from the summit of each hill to a specified point between the two, and a representative from each temple is chosen to partake in the event. According to tradition, a victory by Mother Earth means a bountiful harvest. Is it merely a coincidence, then, that Pachamama always seems to win? The Inca paths, which wind their way under graceful stone archways and over ancient agricultural terraces, are conducive to day hikes and island exploration. Be aware, however, that night's curtain falls quickly over the island, and the paths should not be attempted in the dark. Homestays can also be arranged on Amantaní, and it's polite to present your hosts with a small gift of some sort.

ISLA TAQUILE

In spite of the tourism wave that has swept across many of the Lake Titicaca islands, Isla Taquile has managed to maintain a significant degree of authenticity. Located about a 35-km boat ride from Puno, the island harbors a unique and rich local culture. The locals still speak Quechua and continue to don the traditional dress. Women wear brightly colored *polleras* (skirts) and drape themselves with black headscarves, a practice implemented by the conquistadores. For the men, it's the hat, not the ringfinger, that reveals their marital status. Single males wear caps with white tops, red bottoms and tips folded to the sides, while married men wear solid red caps with tips folded to the back.

In addition to transporting tourists, the islanders on Taquile sustain themselves with the production and sale of finely crafted textiles. Interestingly, while the women spin the wool, the men are contracted to do all of the knitting. Don't be surprised if you spot a group of men, armed with needles, fervently knitting on the streets of Taquile. In the high season, which extends from June to August, Taquileños set up stands in the Plazas de Armas, where they sell exquisite scarves, hats, belts and gloves. Having adopted the communal ayllu system, a method to ensure that wealth is distributed evenly, all earnings are shared.

Homestays can be arranged through a Puno tour company, but always make sure that you go with a socially responsible agency, and ensure that they pay islanders the going rate

LAKE TITICACA

for lodging and food. You should also confirm that no more than two people stay with each family. For a more authentic experience, ask to stay away from the touristy area near the town square. You can also arrange your own homestay by catching a boat from Puno's public pier (daily, 7:30 a.m.-8 a.m.). Upon arrival you will be assigned to a family, after paying a one dollar arrival fee.

As Taquile is only six km long and one kilometer wide, it is very accessible and can be traversed in about two hours. The islands' various beaches are great for relaxing or diving into the frigid waters of Lake Titicaca. Perched on the hilltop are pre-Inca ruins and a beautiful stone arch.

In 2004, the island gave birth to its first lodge, Tika Wasi, which offers visitors comfortable foam beds, clean white-washed walls, a terrace with lake views, running water and solar-heated showers. If you're hungry head to the main square where you'll find a dozen restaurants offering the same basic menu of quinoa soup, steamed or fried pejerrey, and tortilla mixed with potatoes and vegetables. Families also serve meals, though the quality and type of food offered varies.

In addition to a sense of adventure, travelers are advised to bring their own snacks and beverages, a sleeping bag to keep warm, a water bottle, soap and toilet paper.

ISLA SUASI

For a bit of luxury, head to Isla Suasi where you can relax at the Albergue Suasi—one of the lake's most chic lodges. The owners of the lodge have converted all 43-hectares of the island into an environmental preserve, which includes a trout farm where you can try your luck at catching dinner. A variety of nearly-extinct native flowers, herbs, trees and plants are being cultivated in the greenhouse. If you catch the rapid boat service offered by All Ways Travel, you can reach this island paradise in about two hours.

ISLAS ANAPIA AND YUSPIQUE

Floating in the southernmost waters of Lake Titicaca, Islas Anapia and Yuspique have become part of a package tour organized by the socially conscious tour company All Ways Travel. Implementing a new economic strategy of higher prices and better quality, this father-daughter team based in Puno has created a form of sustainable tourism that benefits local communities. Recently, the company was honored by the Ford Foundation as the "Best Community-Based Project in Peru."

The prepaid tour to these islands includes a two-hour scenic drive along the southern coast of Lake Titicaca, with stops at the charming towns of Juli, Pomata, Yunguyo, and finally the port of Punta Hermosa. From here, travelers board a sailboat and make the two hour journey to Isla Anapia. Upon arrival, visitors are welcomed by the father of their host family, and then brought to their island home. Typically, the afternoon involves a hike on nearby Isla Yuspique, accompanied by your host family. This afternoon adventure usually culminates with a beach picnic, and the chance to try some of the local food. Other activities include evening meetings with neighbors, herding animals, fishing, or lending a hand at building a house. Since its inception in 1997, All Ways Tours and its participants have built a library and a puppet theater and painted the local school.

This unique opportunity lends itself to cultural immersion and community development, and typically costs $65 per person for one night or $75 per person for two nights. If you're planning on crossing the border either to or from Bolivia, this trip is an excellent option. You can also combine this trip with a visit to Tiwanaku or Isla del Sol and Isla de la Luna.

LAKE TITICACA

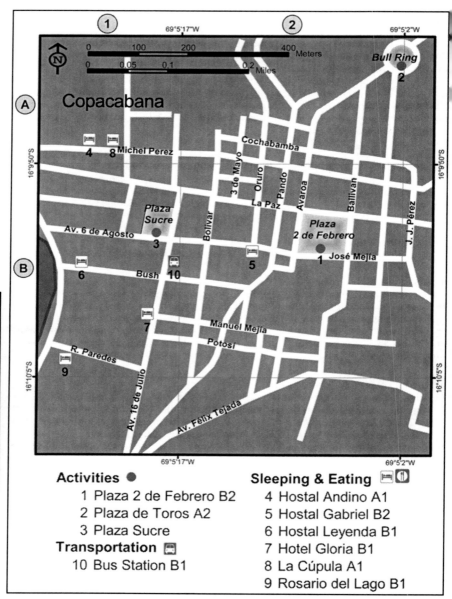

Activities ●
1 Plaza 2 de Febrero B2
2 Plaza de Toros A2
3 Plaza Sucre
Transportation 🚌
10 Bus Station B1

Sleeping & Eating 🛏️🍴
4 Hostal Andino A1
5 Hostal Gabriel B2
6 Hostal Leyenda B1
7 Hotel Gloria B1
8 La Cúpula A1
9 Rosario del Lago B1

THE BOLIVIAN SIDE OF LAKE TITICACA

Any trip to the Bolivian side of Lake Titicaca will include at least a brief stop in the hip Copacabana, which overshadows Puno as the Lake's cooler port city. Nestled between two imposing Andean peaks, Copacabana affords resplendent views of the Bolivian side's major attractions—the frequented Isla del Sol and more remote Isla de la Luna. Jump on a dinghy to the Isla del Sol, spend the night, and you will feel as if Pachamama (Mother Earth) has blessed you as you watch the sun sink into the horizon of the altiplano, on the island where the sun was born, according to local mythology.

THE BOLIVIAN ISLANDS
The Sun and Moon Islands

Lake Titicaca, which spans both the Peruvian and Bolivian sides of the Altiplano at a height of 3,810 meters is not only famed as the cradle of Andean civilization, but also lays claim to being the birthplace of both the sun and moon, and man and woman. Many travelers journey to the Bolivian Islands of the Sun and Moon to explore desolate Inca ruins and to witness one of the most visually spectacular sunsets on earth, on an adventure some might qualify as spiritual.

COPACABANA

Many tourists to the Lake Titicaca region base themselves in Copacabana, a sleepy little town on the southern shores, not far from La Paz. Perched between two peaks with views of the lake, the setting is stunning, and makes the town an excellent base from which to visit nearby attractions such as the Isla del Sol. Copacabana has a good range of tourist services including internet access and a bank (but no ATM). It is well known for its festivals; if you can arrange to be present for one of them, so much the better. While staying here, don't miss the Moorish-style Basilica of Copacabana.

COPACABANA HISTORY

This area was highly valued by the Inca civilization long before the Spanish discovered its allure. The Isla Del Sol, an island near Copacabana in Lake Titicaca, was a very important holy site for the Inca people. They believed that the god Viracocha, who created the universe, came from the waters of Lake Titicaca and created the sun at this island.

When the Spanish came to the area in the 16th century, they built the Basilica of Our Lady of Copacabana, a Moorish styled church that houses the statue of La Virgen de la Candelaria, which is said to have healing powers.

Getting To and Away from Copacabana

The journey from La Paz to Copacabana takes three to three and a half hours. In general, bus travel in Bolivia costs $1 per hour, so expect to pay $3 to $4, or more if you prefer a more luxurious bus. Buses leave from La Paz's cemetery bus terminal. The majority leave at 8:00 am. During the bus ride there is a stop where you will need to take a ferry across Tiquina Strait to meet the bus, which will also be ferried, on the other side. The bus will arrive in Copacabana at Plaza 2 de Febrero. Buses leave from the city at Plaza Sucre.

Also note that it may be best to take larger tourist buses on this journey, since they tend to be safer. In rare instances there have been reports of kidnapping and robbery on smaller minibuses. This is by all means not always the case, but just be aware of the possibility, and choose your bus company carefully.

Border Crossing from Peru to Bolivia: Hydrofoil Boat Ride

For country-hoppers and travelers bent on exploring the whole of Lake Titicaca, Tambo Tours offers a hydrofoil boat ride to the Bolivian Isla del Sol, departing from both Puno and Juli. Tickets are pricey however, at around $259, so most people choose to cross the border by land, reinitiating their aquatic tour in Copacabana, where a boat to the Islands of the Sun and Moon can easily be caught. See www.tambotours.com.

Safety in Copacabana

Outside of the bustle of Copacabana's backpacker-filled downtown, the night-time streets lack adequate light, so visitors should ensure they return to the city before nightfall. Copacabana, is also heavily frequented by pickpockets not afraid to slash into your bag, pack, etc., so be careful in crowded areas like markets and bus stations.

LAKE TITICACA

COPACABANA SERVICES

If you chose to visit Copacabana, cash up before you arrive; accessing ready money is a tricky matter in this city, despite tourism being the main business. Bolivia being one of the poorest countries in Latin America, the city does not have the resources to safeguard ATMs, so consequently there aren't any. There is only one bank in town, PRODEM, on the 6 of Agosto (between Bolívar and Pando), and the tellers will arrange withdrawals for you, but only during bank hours. If you arrive with no cash on a bank holiday, you have no choice but to return to Puno in Peru or continue south to La Paz. Also, many businesses will exchange *bolivianos* for the Peruvian *sol* or the US dollar (the current exchange rate is eight bolivianos per dollar) at usurious fees, but most Copacabana business owners will accept Peruvian or US currency. Few, however, will take credit cards.

COPACABANA TOURS

Today for You Tours

This Copacabana operator sells tours to a wide variety of locations, going north to Peru or heading south through Bolivia. That includes the Uyuni Salt Flats, the Isla del Pescado, the towns of Llica, La Paz and Los Yuncas. Its package tours—ranging anywhere from two to five days—come with bilingual guides, lodging and food. 16 de Julio, Tel: 591-2-280-9498, E-mail: todayforyou_@hotmail.com.

Titicaca Tours

Titicaca tours offers an all-day tour from Copacabana to the world-famous Islas del Sol and Islas la Luna, the former featuring such attractions as the Gold Museum, the Footprints of the Sun, the Sacred Rock, the Northern Ruins, the Inca Fountain, the Puma Museum and the Pilcocaina Temple. On the Moon Island you can visit the Temple of the Virgins of the Sun. Both islands offer lots of scenic walking trails as well, all for under $10. Av. 6 de agosto Final Caseta #2, Tel: 591-2-862-2060, E-mail: titicaca@yahoo.com.ar.

COPACABANA LODGING

This sleepy, lakeside *pueblo* offers an excellent selection of accommodations with unparalleled views of Lake Titicaca and the far-off islands. A handful of hostels cluster along the shore while others line the streets behind quaint stalls full of Bolivian handicrafts. On the west end of town you will find the most luxurious places to stay that guarantee stunning views, comfortable beds, delicious food (including the famous Lake Titicaca trout) and the friendliest staff around. Towards the center of town you will find budget deals that provide all the basics for a comfortable stay.

Hostal Gabriel (Rooms: $2.50)

This simple hostel, centrally located on 6 de Agosto, within walking distance of all the restaurants, taverns, nightclubs, docks and the bus terminal, offers clean and decent rooms. Private accommodations start at around 20 Bolivianos—little more than $2. A few extra dollars brings you television and breakfast. Laundry service is also available. For most backpackers looking to save money, this will do. Nights are cold, however, so if you are sleeping alone you might consider asking for an extra blanket. 6 de Agosto, Tel: 591-2-762-22357.

Hostal Andino (Rooms: $2.50 - 5)

The Hostal Andino offers rooms ranging from 20 to 40 *bolivianos*, and when you consider that comes to between $2.50 and $5.00, the modest virtues of this well-run hostel are a pleasant surprise. The rooms are not only clean, nice-looking and comfortable, but come with hot water and television too, a laundry service is also available. 1156 de Agosto, Tel: 591-2-862-2158.

Hostal Leyenda (Rooms: $10 - 20)

This charming hostel is on the shores of Lake Titicaca, of which all of its windows offer a great view, and you can hear the surf and seagulls late at night. The inn itself has a unique beach-gothic design, with cobblestone paths cutting through an elegant garden in the front. The rooms are clean, spacious and decorated with creative care. Breakfast is included, and the hostel also has its own restaurant. And also offers inexpensive tours of the famous Isla del Sol. Av. Constanera and Busch.

Hostal La Cúpula (Rooms: $10 - 40)

The hostel sits on a hilltop overlooking the town of Copacabana and Lake Titicaca. In the distance, guests have an excellent view the Cordillera Real of the Andes. The Cúpula architecture is eccentrically arabesque with rooms of every dimension and geometric shape. Getting your luggage up the hill is a bit of a challenge. Fortunately, a taxi driver can be convinced for a few *bolivianos* to serve as porter. An alternative is to rent a three-wheeled flatbed cycle from the main plaza. Be attentive about room selection. Size, shape, vistas and price are unique to each accommodation. The hotel staff will give you a *tarifario*, or list of room prices. Rooms range from the spectacular to somewhat odd. Be polite but assertive in selecting a room that matches your *gusto*. Private baths are clean and served by solar-powered water heaters. Breakfast is not included in the room price. The hostel's attractive international restaurant serves delicious continental and national dishes. An American breakfast costs about $2.50 and a full lunch or dinner entrée will run approximately $5. The Cúpula is surrounded by well-kept gardens including several multi-level patios. Prices include tax. Final Calle Michel Pérez 1-3, Tel: 591-2-862-2029, E-mail: bolivia@hotelcupula.com, URL: www.hotelcupula.com.

Hotel Gloria (Rooms: $28 - 42)

The Hotel Gloria is a basic, mid-size hotel managed by the Gloria Hotel chain of La Paz. The company bought up the rural Hoteles Prefecturales from the departmental government and runs similar establishments in Coroico, Nor Yungas and at the Urmiri Hot Springs. Rooms and suites are very clean, spacious, and most have excellent views of Lake Titicaca. The adjoining private bathrooms have abundant hot water. An American-style breakfast is included. Staff begin setting up a buffet with breads, pastries, cereals, coffee and juices as early as 7:00 a.m. If you want complimentary ham and eggs, just ask the waiter. This three-story hotel has a number of public areas including a comfortable lobby, large game room and a cozy television theater. There is no elevator. Parking is available in a secured lot. Calle 16 de Julio s/n, Tel: 591-2-240-7070 (La Paz), E-mail: gloriatr@ceibo.entlenet.bo.

Hotel Rosario del Lago (Rooms: $34 - 82)

Hotel Rosario del Lago is a luxurious lodge on the shores of Lake Titicaca with a prime location to catch every breathtaking sunset that spills over the lake. This colonial resort is decorated with local indigenous blankets, artwork and relics, perfectly tied in with modern amenities such as the internet. There are 24 rooms, a mix of singles, doubles, suites and *cabañas*, all with hot water, cable TV, large windows overlooking Lake Titicaca and lots of space. The restaurant is open for breakfast (buffet included in the rate), lunch and dinner. The cooks whip up delicious local fare. The famous trout that thrives in Lake Titicaca is cooked in a variety of ways, all of which are tasty. Prices are great too. Tours can be organized through Turisbus, the in-house travel agency, and the guides are extremely knowledgeable and friendly. Av. Costanera and Rigoberto Paredes, Tel: 591-2-862-2141, URL: www.hotelrosario.com/lago.

COPACABANA RESTAURANTS

Regardless of where you decide to eat, chances are good that *trucha* (trout) will be on the menu, and you are not going to want to miss it. "Homegrown" in the chilly waters of Lago Titicaca, the trout is pulled directly from the lake and cooked in any number of ways (all delicious) and served fresh as can be. Even the pickiest diner will agree that the trout is excellent! There are plenty of other options, from street vendors selling snacks along the main market streets to dives selling chicken, beef and vegetable options.

Puerta Del Sol (Entrees: $2.50 - 7)

For a typical Bolivian meal and traditional atmosphere, the Restaurant Puerta del Sol is a decent choice. Located near the center of Copacabana, the cooks here serve up a variety of national seasonal dishes of trout, pork, chicken and beef. The *milanesa* (breaded cutlets) and *churrasco argentino*, a marinated round steak served with Bolivian-style fries, are favorites. In addition to national cuisine, this 25-year-old restaurant also offers a few Continental/European selections, such as spaghetti and other pastas. Also on the menu are several vegetarian choices. Uniquely, the Puerta del Sol can prepare a box lunch upon request for those planning an all-day outing. Open noon to 10:00 p.m. on weekdays and noon to 11:00 p.m. or later on weekends. Closed Mondays during the low season (November through January). Av. 6 de Agosto s/n, near the corner of Bolívar, Tel: 591-2-862-2232.

Pacha (Entrees: $3.50 - 9)

Ask any hotel clerk in Copacabana for a restaurant recommendation and the Pacha is sure to be at the top of the list. The full name of the establishment is Café Restaurant Pizzería Pacha, quite a mouthful in itself. House specials include vegetarian dishes, a set course luncheon (a bargain at only $3.50), both national and international cuisine, and a variety of hot drinks coffees, espressos, cappuccinos and teas. The restaurant offers seating in a garden *terraza,* as well as in a warm and inviting indoor salon. On weekend evenings a small *conjunto* offers popular Latin music. South American wines and Bolivian beer are available, along with other liquors. The most popular dishes are pastas, pizza and Lake Titicaca trout. Opening hours are noon to 3:00 p.m. and 7:00 p.m. to approximately 10:00 p.m. on weeknights and until after midnight on Fridays and Saturdays. Av. 6 de agosto, between Bolívar and Pando, Tel: 591-2-862-2206.

Nimbo Café Restaurant and Bar

Welcome to the unique world of owner Miguel Gómez' ornate jungle-goth Nimbo Café Restaurant and Bar, complete with baubles, bangles and beads, not to mention sheepskins laid out on every chair. (There is a slightly stale smell.) The menu, a little on the exotic side, features quinoa burgers, trout stroganoff and coca-cola sautéed pork. Drinks? Besides the extensive wine list, Miguel can prepare you a coconut tequila. He also does his own music mixes for an evening of eating, drinking and partying that continues until the last customer leaves. Doors open at 3:00 p.m. Av. 6 de Agosto and Cabo Zapana, Tel: 862-36276.

Wayky's

Wayky's Restaurant-Pub-Bar is worth visiting simply for the fact that it has an honest-to-goodness monkey on the premises, one that you can play with—though be careful, since it does nip on occasion. Wayky's is a two-part business: on one side of the street is a restaurant, which opens at 6:00 a.m., serving continental and American breakfasts, as well as a lunch featuring standard spicy Bolivian items. When the restaurant closes at 7 p.m., the owners open the bar and club across the street, with drinks, music, movies, pool, games and darts. And perhaps the monkey. Av. 6 de Agosto y 16 de Julio.

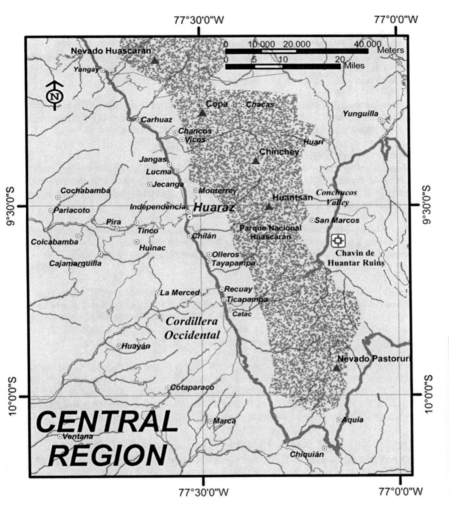

CENTRAL PERUVIAN ANDES

The Central Peruvian Andes are home to the famous Cordillera Blanca, or White Mountain Range. The region is known for excellent hiking, trekking and mountain climbing. It is also where you will find Huascarán National Park, the location of Peru's tallest peak (also named Huascarán).

The Central Peruvian Andes are best known for the variety of world-class mountaineering options they offer. They are not, however, a playground restricted to elite mountain climbers. Anyone with an appreciation for the massive ridges of the Cordillera Blanca can find things to enjoy in the area.

There are plenty of alpine lakes, ruins and deserted trails begging to be explored. Therefore, even if your goal isn't to summit a bunch of sky-scraping peaks you'll find more than enough to keep you busy in the Central Peruvian Andes.

Several ruins left behind by the various pre-Inca cultures are found in the region. The Chavín culture left the largest legacy, including Chavín de Huántar. Here you can see the work of this nation, one of the first pan-Andean cultures that influenced the development of many succeeding civilizations, such as the Wari and Inca cultures.

The largest city in the region is Huaraz (pop. 100,000) and it is definitely the most cosmopolitan of all Peruvian cities in the Central Andes. Many tour operators are based in Huaraz and can take visitors on single-day or multi-day trips.

Caraz also has many climbing and trekking operators, however, the city is much smaller and more focused on adventure tourism than Huaraz. If you are not looking to climb or trek great distances then it may be best to stick around Huaraz.

Highlights of the Central Peruvian Andes
• Huascarán–Huascarán, at 6768 m, is the highest peak in the Peruvian Andes. If you're a climber, this is a summit not to be missed. If you're not into mountain climbing, many tour companies offer tours to the base or treks and walks through the valley with good views of the mountain itself.

• Chavín de Huántar—30 km south of Huari, the Chavín de Huántar temple complex should be on the to-do list of anyone with an interest in Peruvian archaeology. It features the largest stone carved buildings in Peru and was declared a World Heritage Site in 1985.

When to Go
The best time to visit the Central Peruvian Andes is between May and September. During this period, there is consistently dry weather and storms are less frequent than in other comparably sized ranges in other parts of the world. There is less rain and all the peaks in the Cordillera Blanca can be attempted during this time. Naturally, this is also the high tourism season for the entire country so you will encounter much traffic.

Many of the lower peaks in the region can be climbed during the rest of the year, but the weather is both less predictable and less desirable. In June, Huaraz hosts the Semana del Andinismo, a world-renowned festival to celebrate all things to do with the surrounding mountains. You can see the town in full-swing, celebrating the life force of the Andes. It will also be the busiest time so make sure to book ahead.

THINGS TO SEE AND DO IN THE CENTRAL ANDES
This stunning region offers thrills for the most experienced adrenaline junkies and most demanding outdoor enthusiasts. There is no shortage of trails to backpack on, and no single trek fully encompasses the area. Towering glaciers and deep valleys balance each other perfectly.

Spend the day ice climbing. Or if speed is more appealing, excite your heart with a challenging day of mountain biking. Take a break with an introspective tour of area ruins. Finally, end the day recounting your adventures with a relaxing drink in front of a fire.

The glacier-topped Cordillera Blanca is the main climbing and hiking center of Peru. Mountain biking, horseback riding, rafting and canoeing are also popular activities in this area. Most tours are multi-day and all should include gear, food, transportation and guides.

If you plan to book a tour locally, head to Llanganuco where you can acclimatize as you hunt for the best deal. International operators also offer tours of this magnificent peak.

WARNING: Be alert to the threat of avalanches and mudslides before setting out to the mountains or taking trips in the area. Check locally to find out which areas should be avoided.

Cordillera Blanca

Running 180 kilometers from north to south across the Ancash region, the spectacular snowclad peaks of the Cordillera Blanca form a natural barrier between the desert coast and the Amazon basin. Rugged peaks descend toward massive glaciers, dropping into U-shaped valleys where cattle graze among the rich puna grasslands. Besides the range of Andes situated along the Chile-Argentina border, the Cordillera Blanca boasts the highest mountains in South America.

These hulking alpine beauties are visible throughout the region, and provide a number of challenging trails for intrepid hikers and travelers to explore. From the trekking hub of Huaraz alone, over 23 peaks exceeding 5,000 m are visible, most notably Huascarán (6,768 m). Every year this region receives thousands of trekking junkies eager to get out and test their skills on the nearby paths. Almost the entire chain is protected by the Huascarán National Park, home to 663 glaciers, 269 lakes, 41 rivers and 33 archaeological sites.

The largest concentration of glaciers found in the world's tropical zone is found here, as is one of Peru's most important pre-Inca sites: Chavín de Huántar. Because the range is quite narrow, it is easy to access trekking areas from roads. Many of these trails were created centuries before the dawn of recreational hiking, serving as natural highways for Andean inhabitants.

Rural villages line the region and provide trekkers with the unique opportunity to mingle with locals who continue to maintain many aspects of traditional Andean culture. Agencies in Huaraz can arrange a variety of itineraries, ranging in degree of difficulty and number of days. Most trails are easy to navigate, but include high passes between 4,000 and 5,000 meters. Proper equipment and acclimatization are essential.

Cordillera Negra

Noticeably devoid of snow, the brown mountains of the Cordillera Negra create a sharp contrast to the snow-covered peaks of the neighboring Cordillera Blanca. This mountain range offers some great hiking and biking opportunities, in addition to inspiring views of the surrounding scenery. Many of the tracks for exploring this area have been used for centuries, and wind their way past remote Andean villages and agricultural fields. Mountain bikers can test their skills on a range of trails, from easy, broad treks to hold-onto-your-helmet, narrow downhill slopes.

CENTRAL PERUVIAN ANDES: DOS AND DON'TS

Do
- Allow yourself adequate time to acclimatize before attempting any high altitude climbs or treks.
- Get in proper physical shape before arriving if you intend to do difficult climbs or treks.
- Be familiar with safe alpine practices, as many excursions take you days away from medical care.
- Take the same precautions with baggage, cameras and passports as you would in the rest of Peru.

Don't
- Push yourself too far beyond your comfort zone—the Peruvian Andes can be unforgiving and mistakes at high altitude are magnified.
- Think yourself more knowledgeable or a better judge than your guide—they are there for your safety and their decisions are final.

Regardless of how you choose to tackle this mountain range, the views are sure to please even the most discerning adventurers. You can access the Cordillera Negra via a number of dirt roads leading from Huaraz and other towns throughout the Río Santa Valley, such as Yungay, Caraz, Huallanca and Carhuaz.

Cordillera Huayhuash

Characterized by rugged snowcapped peaks, and wide alpine pastures dotted with tranquil blue lakes, the Cordillera Huayhuash is one of the most beautiful and least-known mountain ranges in South America. Although it is only 30 kilometers long, this cordillera packs a strong panoramic punch. Composed of one jagged ridge that gives way to rippling snow faces and massive glaciers, the Huayhuash is a physically challenging and visually rewarding trek.

With seven peaks exceeding 6,000 meters and another seven just over 5,500 meters, including the highest peak, Yerupajá (6,634 m), the 12-day loop around the entire range is sure to keep the heart pumping and legs pounding. Unlike the Cordillera Blanca, which is characterized by broad U-shaped valleys, the Cordillera Huayhuash is composed of rocky ridges that force trekkers to climb up and over a succession of passes between 4,500 and 5,000 meters. To navigate these high-altitude obstacle courses, most trekkers use *arrieros* (muleteers) and *burros* (donkeys), both of which can be hired at the start of the excursion.

Another factor setting Huayhuash apart from its more well-known siblings of Cordillera Blanca and Cordillera Negra is its remoteness. Compared to the highly-traveled ranges in the Cordillera Blanca, the trails blazing up, over and around Cordillera Huayhuash are remarkably quiet. Despite a network of new roads, getting into the region still takes one or two days. Consequently, the area remains an isolated, wild place—the perfect playground for solitude-seekers.

Hikes in this area usually begin in the city of Chiquián (3,400 m), about 111 kilometers south of Huaraz. Guides and trekking routes can be arranged at agencies in Huaraz. In 2002 the Peruvian government declared the range a protected area, a decided attempt to protect the zone from such deleterious enterprises as the Mitsui Mining and Smelting Company, which deposited industrial wastes in the wetlands on the range's west edge.

Lagunas de Llanganuco

Like turquoise teardrops poised at the base of the Cordillera Blanca's highest peaks, these two alpine lakes offer a delicate contrast to the massive glacial faces of the nearby Chopicalqui (6,354 m), Huandoy (6,395 m) and Huascarán (6, 768 m) mountains. Glacial silt deposits give this pair of alpine beauties their characteristic bright blue color, and at 4,000 meters above sea level they seem to glow and sparkle in the midday sun. Row boats can be rented on the first lake, Chinacocha; the second lake, Orconcocha, offers some of the best views of the surrounding mountains.

Both lagunas are situated within the Huascarán National Park. They are a popular starting point for the four-to-five-day Llanganuco-Santa Cruz trek, which some regard as one of the most beautiful hikes the continent has to offer. Agencies in Huaraz can organize day tours of Llanganuco, and those keen to get out and hit the trails can organize day treks to the lagunas. Independent travel to the lakes is possible via Yungay, about 26 kilometers away. From Yungay catch a *combi* or truck up to the lakes from the Plaza de Armas. Regardless of how you get to the lakes you are sure to be astounded by their unearthly beauty. An entrance fee of $1.50 is charged for day trips to the lakes.

Chavín de Huántar

Located about four hours east of Huaraz, the massive temple fortress of Chavín de Huántar is one of the last remaining large scale reminders of the Chavín culture, which stretched across the northern highlands of Peru from Cajamarca and Chiclayo in the north to Ayacucho and Ica in the south, from 900-200 BC. As one of the first pan-Andean cultures, the Chavín established a rich set of traditions that would infuse succeeding cultures like the Tiahuanaco, Wari and even the Inca. The fortress itself was built around 800 BC and was declared a World Heritage Trust Site by UNESCO in December 1985.

The main attractions include intricate stone carvings of symbolic figures and a network of tunnels that snake their way beneath the fortress floor. Three of these passages converge underground at the famous Lanzón stone monolith, which dates to 800 BC. The northern part of the pillar points upward towards a gallery where priests may have once performed rituals. Some areas are closed to the public in order to preserve the site, but public areas are illuminated by electric lights. A small museum at the entrance houses interesting carvings and Chavín pottery. Camping nearby is also possible, with permission from the guards.

Agencies in Huaraz offer a day trip to the site, which leaves around 8 a.m. If you decide to take the do-it-yourself tour you may want to hire one of the Spanish-speaking guides at the entrance. For active travelers there is a great trek that winds its way across the southern end of Cordillera Blanca from Olleros to Chavín. Relatively free of tourist traffic, the trail follows an ancient trade route that ascends to the Yanashallash Pass (4, 700 m).

Monumento Nacional Wilcahuaín

Just eight kilometers northeast of Huaraz is the Wilkawaín archaeological site. The ruins date to the Wari Empire, which dominated the region from 700 to 1000 AD. Gravity-defying vertical stone slabs and several smaller structures lead into finely constructed sepulchral stone chambers. The temple is done in Tiahuanaco style and means "grandson's house" in Quechua. Mummified bodies of prominent leaders were once laid to rest in the chambers of these three-story structures and kept dry using a complicated ventilation system.

Compared to other ruins in Peru, the Wilkawaín ruins require very little imagination as they are remarkably well preserved. For an additional fee you can enjoy a tour of the ruins, organized by charming and very articulate eight-year-olds.

To get there, take a combi from Huaraz (13 de Diciembre and Comercio) for about 30 cents direct to Wilkawaín; a taxi will cost a few dollars. On foot, walk past Hotel Huascarán, and cross the small bridge over the Río Quilcay, about a half-hour journey. Take the second right, which is marked by a blue sign, and continue uphill for about two hours. You may have to ask for directions as it's easy to lose your way along the myriad of trails used regularly by locals. About 500 meters beyond Wilkawaín is Ichiwilkawaín, which contains several other smaller structures. Take a torch if it's late. There is also an alternative road from the ruins to Monterrey, where you can relax with a hot soak in the thermal baths.

NOTE: There have been armed robberies on this small trail.

CENTRAL ANDES TOURS

Tours in the Central Peruvian Andes are aimed at the adventure seeker and fearless mountaineer. Whichever guide or operator you choose to lead you to the ultimate vista, be sure to research his or her experience and certifications. Many agencies will organize tours that include guides, equipment, food, transportation and porters. If you are more confident in your trekking skills and would prefer an individual guide (not necessarily all of the "luxuries" that come with an organized tour), it can be arranged. Be advised that it pays off to research the different itineraries that tour companies offer, follow up on reviews of different treks and of course, heed the advice of other travelers who have been there.

CENTRAL ANDES LODGING

Due to the area's status as a premier destination for outdoor activities, lodging in the Central Peruvian Andes caters to the backpacker market. However, there are still options available in the mid-range and high-end. In Huaraz, there are many great hostels and it's not rare for locals to offer rooms in their home to travelers. Be careful with this option as there is no way to know exactly what you are getting until you've committed. There are some beautiful mid-range B&Bs, hostels and hotels. Further into the mountains, you'll find charming lodges and inns as well.

Multiple tours and treks in the surrounding Cordilleras include accommodations (camping, etc.) at base camp. Monterrey offers lodging within a short walk of each other and the hot springs. Charming and a tad more expensive than the average hostel, these are decent places to stay. In Carhuaz, Yungay and Caraz are basic hostels with clean rooms and hot water as well as nicer options for the pickier traveler.

HUARAZ

This little town perched at 3,028 meters is a trekking and climbing center, drawing a crowd of international outdoor enthusiasts every year. The town itself, with its jumble of concrete buildings and muddy rivers, is a bit rough around the edges, but peek behind its ragged façade and you're bound to discover a number of charming hotels, restaurants and coffee houses.

The main focus of the area is the Callejón de Huaylas, the section of the Río Santa valley separating the Cordillera Negra to the west from the Cordillera Blanca to the east. A paved road cuts through the length of the valley, linking villages and providing access to the area's three famed cordilleras: Cordillera Blanca, Cordillera Negra, and Cordillera Huayhuash. With a bit of gusto and common sense it's entirely possible to show up without equipment and immediately head off on a trek or climb. Be watchful, however, for con artists and phony guides eager to swindle unsuspecting tourists.

Despite its rather drab appearance Huaraz has friendly, outgoing locals and an undeniably festive atmosphere. The Plaza de Armas is often blocked off for children's parades, *marinera* dance contests and military formations. Luzuriaga, the town's main street, has the greatest concentration of restaurants, gear shops and agencies. More establishments can be found farther north on either side of Río Quilcay. During Peruvian holidays, when the town overflows with *limeños*, prices rise along with the town's population; beware of overcharging.

While you acclimatize (and even the most Herculean of individuals should take at least two days before embarking on any mountain excursion) you can explore the streets or duck into one of the town's museums. The Museo Regional de Ancash houses artifacts from the Recuay, Wari, Chimu and Inca cultures. Art fanatics should head to the Sala de Cultura in Banco Wiese (Sucre 766), which has interesting art and photography exhibitions by local artists (free!). Uphill from the plaza is the Iglesia Soledad, which survived the 1970 earthquake that nearly leveled the entire city. A few good hotels are located up here, where you get some of the best views of the Cordillera Blanca and sunsets over the Cordillera Negra.

For more spectacular views of the surrounding peaks and valleys, head to the Rataquena, which is marked by a giant cross. This is a popular acclimatization hike, taking about an hour from town. To get there, walk up Villón or Confraternidad Este to the cemetery and turn right, following the switchbacks that crisscross through the forest. If you're keen for a bit more walking, continue uphill to Pukaventana, where you'll find even more spectacular views of the valley. There have been reports of armed hold-ups at Mirador, so always travel in a group.

The nearby ruins of Wilkawaín also make for an excellent day trip. From Huaraz you can organize a number of adventure sport activities, including mountain biking, rafting and kayaking, birdwatching, fishing, horseback riding, paragliding, skiing, rock and ice climbing, hiking and trekking, and sightseeing tours—you name it, Huaraz probably has it. The town is also a base for excursions to cordilleras Blanca, Negra and Huayhuash, Parque Nacional Huascarán, Lagunas de Llanganuco and the ancient Chavín capital of Chavín de Huántar. If you're keen to touch ice, but aren't quite up to the physical demands of a full-blown climb, then check out the Pastoruri glacier. Note: As of early 2008 this glacier has been closed to the public due to conflicts between the local communities and the National Park. It is unknown when it will reopen.

Basic tourist information can be found at Policía de Turismo, located in a small alley between the post office and the Municipalidad (Tel. 51-43-721-341, ext. 315, Monday - Friday 9 a.m. - 1 p.m. and 4 p.m. - 7 p.m., Saturday 9 a.m. - 1 p.m.). Always keep an eye on your backpack and be careful where you eat: Huaraz is unfortunately known for its food poisoning as well as its adventure sports.

Getting To and Away From Huaraz

In terms of getting to Huaraz from Lima, go to either Avenida Raymondi or Avenida Fitzcarrald, where you will find the following bus companies: CIVA, Cruz del Sur and Móvil Tours. A variety of buses depart throughout the day and into the evening; the trip generally takes eight hours and costs $10. There is no airport.

Most people leaving Huaraz will either head north to Trujillo or south to Lima. Heading south, most of the above companies will offer departures during the day. Heading north, however, they offer only overnight buses, and you are advised to book at least a day in advance. If you prefer to head to Trujillo in the morning from Huaraz, Empresa de Transportes (located on Av. Manco Cápac) offers a bus leaving at 8 a.m. for about $6 for the coastal town of Casma, and from there you take another bus company, América Express, which has buses heading north along the coast for little more than $2. Brace yourself, however; the trip down the mountain ranges heading towards the coast is both scenic and scary, with many zigzag turns on narrow, unpaved roads. The same buses can also take you from Trujillo to Huaraz— and with the same risks.

Leaving near the bridge in Huaraz, there are vans—combis—that depart routinely from Huaraz every half-hour or so, depending on how full they are, and head towards the towns of Carhuaz, Yungay and Caraz. The price ranges from $0.50 - $1.

CIVA 51-1-332-5236
Móvil Tours 51-43-342-255 (Huaraz)
Cruz del Sur 51-1-424-615
Empresa de Transportes 51-14-286-621
América Express 51-1-353-473

Safety in Huaraz

In addition to hikers' concerns in and around Huaraz, the city itself poses a few dangers. Even if you're not going hiking (for which you should allow two days to acclimatize), you'll still feel the effects of Huaraz's high altitude. Be sure to drink lots of water and avoid caffeine, alcohol and excessive exertion, as not to become dehydrated. Coca tea tends be a great help and is generally served everywhere. In 2002 and 2003 a few armed robberies of tourists trekking outside of Huaraz were reported. You may want to check with tourist information for the best advice on traveling outside of the city center.

THINGS TO SEE AND DO IN HUARAZ

Huaraz is an adventurers' paradise and there is no shortage of outdoor activities to try out. Hiking is one of the main things to do here, with numerous options available. The best time for this is between June and September. It is better not to head off on hikes around Huaraz without a knowledgeable guide. Climbers will not be disappointed with the volume of climbing activities in the Huaraz area. Talk to a reputable agency to find the best (and safest) deals. To rest your weary bones after some energetic hiking or climbing, there are hot springs five kilometers away from Huaraz in Monterrey. As to be expected, whitewater rafting and horseback riding options are also available. Or check out some of the local historical sites, such as

CENTRAL ANDES

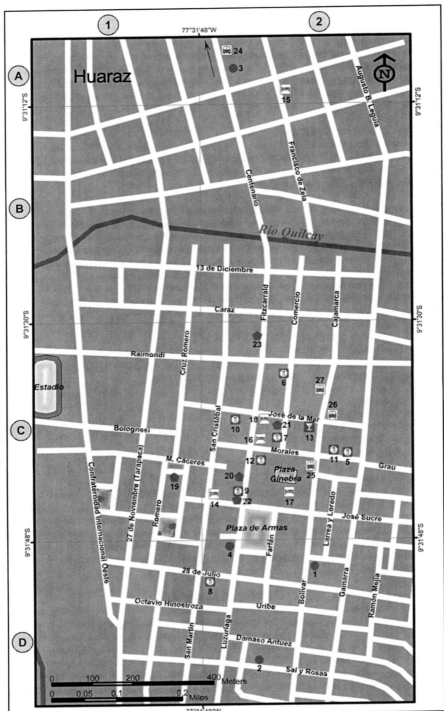

Activities ●
1 Diablo Club Huaraz D2
2 Huascarán National Park D2
3 Monumento Nacional Wilcahuain A2
4 Museo Arqueológico de Ancash D2

Eating 🍴
5 Bistro de los Andes C2
6 Café Creperie C2
7 Café Andino C2
8 California Café D2
9 Chilli Heaven C2
10 Fuente de Salud C2
11 La Luna Café C2
12 Piccolo Restaurant C2

Nightlife 🍸
13 Tambo Bar and Dance Club C2

Sleeping 🛏
14 Andino Club Hotel C2
15 Hotel Colombia A2
16 Hotel Huaraz C2
17 Hotel Pirámide C2
18 Oscar's Hostal C2

Tour Operator ♠
19 Galaxia Expeditions C1
20 Monttrek C2
21 Mountain Bike Adventure C2
22 Peru Andes Travel C2
23 Pyramid Adventures C2

Transportation 🚍
24 Bus Station A2
25 Civa C2
26 Cruz del Sur C2
27 Móvil Tours C2

Chavín de Huántar, the remnants of an early civilization from this area. There is plenty in and around Huaraz to keep you occupied for a number of days.

Museo Arqueológico de Ancash (Entrance: $1.50)
In terms of museums in Huaraz, Museo Arqueológico de Ancash is one of the most extensive. Inside you can browse a well-organized collection of stone monoliths and *huacos* from the Recuay culture (200-700 AD) and Chavín culture (800-200 BC). Upstairs are displays of pottery, textiles and metal objects from later Wari, Chimu and Inca nations. Open Monday-Saturday, 9 a.m.-1 p.m and 2:30-5 p.m. Luzuriaga 762, Plaza de Armas, Tel: 51-43-721-551.

El Señor de la Soledad
The festival for Huaraz's patron father, el Señor de la Soledad, is the city's large festival starting May 3 and ending May 10. It's a week-long party in the streets. Parades display traditional colorful costumes, music and dancing. The night brings fireworks and a *fiesta* atmosphere, filled with drinking and celebration. The festival also includes ski races and tons of live music along with traditional Peruvian dances. People come from all over Peru to celebrate what is referred to as both the Festival de Mayo or the Festival del Señor de la Soledad.

HIKING AND TREKKING AROUND HUARAZ
Planning Your Trek
Most people venture to Huaraz with one thing in mind: getting out into the countryside and up into the mountains. Due to its reputation as the "trekking capital," Huaraz is full of agencies offering a variety of trekking itineraries. Signing up for a trip through one of these agencies is an easy way to hit the trails.

Most companies will take care of the nitty-gritty details like transport, food, lodging, porters, horsemen, cooks and local guides, leaving you time to contemplate the area's sublime beauty (and perhaps concentrate on making it up to the next pass). Larger groups can custom-design a trip and contract an agency to take care of the trip's logistical details. When choosing an agency it is important to focus on reputable, rather than cheap companies. A private trekking or climbing guide can sometimes be hired from the Casa de Guías in Huaraz for between $35-40 per day. If you book a trek after arriving in Huaraz, you can usually get a better price, but before you pay make sure that both the agency and your guide adhere to the Leave No Trace principles, which have slowly been adopted in order to protect the natural beauty and ecological integrity of the region.

Get your writing published in our books, go to www.vivatravelguides.com

Photo by Cate Batchelder

For detailed topographic and general maps of the area, head to the South American Explorers Club in Lima. Most guide agencies in Huaraz sell maps and guidebooks. Café Andino and Casa de Guías in Huaraz are also excellent places to find climbing and trekking information.

Huaraz Hiking: When to Go

The main trekking and climbing season around Huaraz is from May to September, with the best weather and snow conditions falling between June and July. During the high season most of the best hotels in Huaraz are completely booked. Accommodation is particularly hard to find during the Fiestas Patrias weekend around July 28. Keep in mind that weather in the months leading into and out of the high season are often just as good for trekking. Trail conditions and the degree of technical skill required can change depending on the amount of annual snowfall. It's a good idea to check in with a local guide agency regardless of what season you go. Of course, given the fact that this region is literally riddled with treks, you can quite easily alter your alpine itinerary at the last minute.

Huaraz Hiking: Tailor-made Treks

If you're keen for some solo time, or want to organize a trip for just you and your buddies, you can plan your own trek. However, there are a few important things you should remember before you strap on the high altitude gear. Due to the extreme altitude (treks through the Cordilleras Blanca, Negra and Huayhuash region involve a series of calf-burning, 4,000- to 5,000-meter peaks) even experienced mountaineers may have difficulty carrying a pack. Many trekkers choose to hire donkeys and *arrieros* (muleteers). In addition to keeping your donkey in line these guys make your trip safer and are a great way to get to know the local culture. You can also feel warm and fuzzy about contributing to the local economy.

Most arrieros can be hired on the spot, so you can head to an area and then hire one; however, you should make sure the deal is clear from the beginning. For a list of recommended cooks and handlers, head to the Casa de Guías. Be a responsible traveler and pay the people you hire fairly. Also be aware that it is your duty to provide your arrieros, porters or cooks with food and a tent during the trip.

CENTRAL ANDES

Huaraz Hiking: Acclimatization

Before hefting the knapsack to head out, even very experienced adventurers should follow a few common sense steps to ensure a safe journey. The most important is to acclimatize gradually. The first camps along many of the treks are high enough to trigger altitude sickness. It's advisable to spend your first couple days in Huaraz taking it easy and exploring some of the lower-altitude sites in the area. An easy walk up to the Mirador Rataquena above Huaraz is a great way to spend the afternoon. Or you can catch a combi going east from Huaraz to the Callán Pass (4,225 m). A network of trails and dirt roads head from here back to Huaraz, and are perfect for a less strenuous day of exploration. On the second day, make your way to Laguna Churup (4,485 m) or to nearby Quebrada Quilcayhuanca. For further information on how to spend your first few days acclimatizing, head to either Café Andino or Casa de Guías.

Huaraz Hiking: Fees

By Peruvian standards the entrance fees to Parque Nacional Huascarán are high; however, the park is in dire need of financial support to help with trail maintenance, trash removal, endangered species protection, community-based programs and funding for search and rescue teams. Entry for the day is $1.50, and anyone planning to stay in the park for two or more days must purchase a $20 pass, which is valid for one month. Entrance fees can be paid at the park's headquarters in Huaraz (Sal and Rosas 555, Tel: 51-84-722-086, Monday-Friday, 8:30 a.m.-1 p.m., 2:30-6 p.m.) You can also find ticket booths at Lagunas de Llanganuco, Quebrada Ishinca, Pastoruri Glacier and Musho village en route to Huascarán.

Huaraz Hiking: Gear

Most people arriving in Huaraz have their own gear, but top-notch equipment can be rented from a number of places in Huaraz. E-mail agencies ahead of time to request certain gear, inquire about prices or make reservations. You can also buy equipment in Huaraz, but be warned that the prices can be inflated. Gear can also be sold in Huaraz, so if you're in a spot and find you have to purchase equipment, you may be able to re-sell it once you return. Due to the strong tropical sun, sun protection (sunscreen, sun hat, sunglasses and long-sleeved shirt) is essential. Be aware that the region's extreme altitude and tropical location mean that weather conditions can vary. Better to be safe than sorry; prepare for all weather conditions, especially wind and rain. A sturdy tent, warm sleeping bag and stove are also must-haves.

Huaraz Hiking: Safety

Every year climbers of all skill levels perish after failing to take weather conditions seriously in this region. The intense sun makes mountain snow more porous and causes glaciers to move more rapidly, which means even the most experienced climbers should take the proper precautions. In particular, Huascarán's ice fall has become increasingly more unstable in recent years.

Although both Huascarán and Alpamayo are among the most popular peaks in the Cordillera Blanca, a number of other equally challenging options exist, which do not pose the same inherent danger. You should always report to Casa de Guías before departing, leaving a date at which a search should begin. It's also a good idea to leave your embassy's phone number with the Casa.

A 35-member rescue team known as Unidad de Salvamento de Alta Montaña was established in 1999 by the Policía Nacional de Peru. This organization has 24-hour phone service and VHF/UHF radio dispatch, in addition to two rescue helicopters and trained search and rescue dogs. In the event of an emergency, contact either the Unidad de Salvamento de Alta Montaña (Monday-Friday, 24 hours a day. Tel: 51-43-793-333 / 327 / 291, E-mail: usam@pnp.gob.pe, URL: www.huaraz.info/usam, www.pnp.gob.pe/direcciones/altamontana.asp), or the Casa de Guías (Monday-Friday, 9 a.m.-1 p.m., 4-8 p.m., Saturday, 9 a.m.-1 p.m. Parque Ginebra 28-G, Tel: 51-43-721-811, E-mail: agmp@terra.com.pe).

Though the majority of visitors to the region leave without encountering problems worse than sore legs and the occasional blister, the influx of travelers from around the world has also triggered a rise in local crime. Reports of robberies, sometimes at gun- or knife-point, have been reported in the Huaraz area; be especially vigilant around popular base camps in the Cordillera Blanca. To reduce your chances of being robbed, hire a guard to watch over your base camp while you're away (usually around $15 per day).

Assaults on trails have also been reported. Trekking and climbing in groups of four or more is highly recommended. An even better option is to hire a local arriero who knows the area and can steer you clear of trouble. A number of more remote areas, especially the valleys above Huaraz, offer safer alternatives to the major routes, and provide ample opportunities to get out and explore.

If you're traveling through the Cordillera Huayhuash, be sure to bring supplies. Although basic items can be bought in larger villages located in the range, such as Llamac, Pocpa and Huayllapa, there are few other places on the trail, and evacuations can take several days.

Some final words of wisdom: Always respect the locals' property, and don't leave garbage behind. Giving out money and sweets to children on the street may attract unwanted attention.

Huaraz Hiking: Routes
The mountains surrounding Huaraz boast a seemingly infinite number of trekking and mountaineering routes to suit adventurers of all levels and abilities. Perhaps the most difficult aspect of planning an excursion in this area is choosing where to start. Among the host of trekking circuits, some of the highlights include Santa Cruz-Llanganuco, Olleros-Chavin, Huayhuash and Alpamayo.

Santa Cruz-Llanganuco Trek
The four-to-five-day, 45-kilometer Santa Cruz trek is a very popular hike near Huaraz. Weaving its way past massive Huascarán and the azure lakes at Llanganuco, the trail encompasses some of the most spectacular scenery you'll encounter in the Huaraz region, with views of all the principal snow-clad peaks. Although the route can be trekked in either direction—starting from Vaquerí and finishing at Cashapampa, or vice versa—most independent travelers choose to begin at Vaquerí. From Huaraz there is a daily bus to Vaquerí, which enables trekkers to make it to the camp site on the first day and then head up the first high pass the following day. The high point of the pass is Punta Unión (4,760 m); from here trekkers follow the Quebrada Santa Cruz downhill, all the while enjoying great views of peaks like Artesonraju, Quitaraju, Alpamayo and Taulliraju. For a longer hike (about two days longer) start at Lagunas Llanganuco and make your way over the Portachuelo Llanganuco pass (4,767 m).

Olleros-Chavín Trek
This visually astounding and physically accessible trek starts from Olleros, a small village located a few kilometers south of Huaraz. The three-day hike to the spectacular fortress temple of Chavín de Huántar (800 BC) follows a pre-Columbian trade route that cuts through the mountains on its way up and over Punta Yanashallash at 4,700 meters. Depending on your level of fitness (or your desire to carry your own pack) you can choose to hire a donkey to carry your equipment. The trek can usually be completed in three to four days.

Huayhuash Trek
With some of the most pristine mountain scenery, this 160-kilometer trek weaves past turquoise, trout-filled lakes, through wide open grasslands and up knee-jarring ridgelines. The 12-day circuit starts in the village of Chiquián and makes a loop around the entire range. Remarkable views accompany eight high passes between 4,600 and 5,000 meters; if the scenery doesn't take your breath away, the ascents certainly will. Because the trail is quite demanding, it is only recommended for acclimatized individuals in good physical condition. Recently-built roads from Chiquián to Llamac and Hualanca offer shortened versions of the original hike. Trekkers can now start in Huallanca to the north (between Huaraz and Huánuco), or catch a combi to Matacancha. From here most people head up the Cacanpunta Pass

(4,700 m) to the first campsite at Lago Mitacocha. This route encompasses about half the Huayhuash circuit, and is a good option if you're pressed for time. If you've got time to kill, then definitely consider doing the whole loop; beauty of this magnitude deserves more than a passing glance. Both the Chiquián and Huallanca starting points are equipped with hotel and restaurant services for travelers.

Alpamayo Trek

In addition to the challenge of tackling the rugged slopes of Alpamayo, this 150-kilometer trek promises captivating views of remote mountain scenery. Adventurers have several trekking options in this area, ranging from fairly easy, one-way treks to full-on 14-to-16-day expeditions. The ice-clad Alpamayo Peak (5,947 m) is famous for its nearly perfect conical shape, and should only be scaled by experienced mountaineers with proper equipment. A common starting point for this area is Cashapampa, located at the base of Quebrada Santa Cruz.

Huascarán National Park

Established in July 1975, the spectacular Parque Nacional Huascarán is a UNESCO World Biosphere Reserve and part of the World Heritage Trust. This area of intense natural beauty is located in the Ancash region near Huaraz, 404 kilometers northeast of Lima.

The park—also referred to as the Huaraz Area, Cordillera Blanca or Callejón de Huaylas—boasts stunning mountain scenery comparable to the beauty of the Himalayas around Annapurna in Nepal. The Huaraz region is unique, however, because it is home to Huascarán, Peru's highest peak and the world's highest tropical mountain. This 340,000-hectare garden of natural wonders encompasses all of the Cordillera Blanca above 4,000 meters (except for Nevado Champará), with more than 50 peaks exceeding 5,700 meters and more than 300 lakes. Hulking mountains and massive glaciers dominate the terrain, which drops into a low valley where a variety of microclimates thrive.

Inside the park, nearly 770 species of flora flourish, including the *Puya raimondii*, the largest bromeliad in the world. Meander through forests of endangered *Polylepis*—the world's highest altitude trees—where you may encounter such endangered mammals as the pampas cat, Andean cat, spectacled bear, and hippocamelus. Birdwatchers can keep an eye out for more than 100 species of birds, among them the torrent duck and kula. The lucky few may spot Andean condors soaring high above herds of *vicuña* and white-tailed deer.

The park is also home to the 3,000-year-old Chavín culture. The road to the enigmatic ruins of Chavín de Huántar tunnel through the lowest pass at 4,450 meters, exposing travelers to spectacular mountain views. In the Callejón de Conchucos, a valley on the far side of the range, is a string of isolated villages whose inhabitants continue to follow traditional ways of life. These bastions of culture are linked by dirt roads only. Most of the inhabitants in this region live below the poverty line, subsisting on maize, quinoa and *kiwicha* grains, and a variety of potatoes and other tubers. The latest source of income in this region is providing donkeys to foreigners passing through.

One of the park's aims is to raise the quality of life in the region by promoting sustainable tourism practices. Another corollary to the park's foundation is preservation of its flora, fauna, geology and archaeological sites. The park charges a fee of $1.25 for a day visit (a small price to pay for a lifetime of natural beauty). For visits up to seven days, a permit costing $20 is required. Permits can be purchased at the park office, located in the Ministry of Agriculture at the east end of Avenida Raymondi in Huaraz (open mornings only, Tel: 51-43-722-086). The roads winding through the Cordillera Blanca provide great access for day hikes. You can stay in any of the villages along Callejón de Huaylas, such as Huaraz, Carhuaz and Caraz. From any of these hamlets you can catch a taxi, horse or combi to your next destination, but be sure to plan for afternoon transportation. Agencies in Huaraz offer cheap day excursions to nearby sites, such as the Pastoruri Glacier and Lagunas de Llanganuco, and in most cases can pick you up at any one of the nearby towns.

CENTRAL ANDES

Get your writing published in our books, go to www.vivatravelguides.com

Huaraz Tours

Huaraz is a dream for those looking to climb the countless peaks in the Cordillera Blanca and the Cordillera Huayhuash. There is a plethora of tour operators with reputable records, experience and guides. The prices are usually similar, but of course it won't hurt to shop around a little. If you are planning on being in Huaraz during the peak season for climbing, June to September, make sure to book your trips ahead of time. All options can be discussed with the tour operators before you get to Huaraz.

Alpamayo Climbing and Santa Cruz Trek ($800 / person)

Santa Cruz Trek, adventure tour operators specializing in the Cordillera Blanca and Huayhuash, is part of Peru Bergsport. It combines four days trekking with a visit to Alpamayo mountain. Monday-Saturday, 9 a.m.-7 p.m. Tel: 51-43-425-661, E-mail: santacruztrekking@yahoo.es, URL: www.santacruztrek.com.

Explorandes

Explorandes operates a number of guided, five-day trekking tours out of Huaraz through the stunning Cordillera Blanca. Passing several peaks (but never climbing them), the expedition showcases Huascarán, Alpamayo and other jewels of the region. This company does not offer any mountain climbing trips. Unlike many Huaraz operators, Explorandes also has single day trips that are not physically demanding, to suit a variety of abilities. It also offers a 17-day extended tour of the Cordillera Blanca and Huayhuash; however, this package tour originates in Lima. Av. Centenario 489, Tel: 51-43-721-960, Fax: 51-43-728-071, E-mail: postmaster@explorandes.com, URL: www.explorandes.com/peru.

Galaxia Expeditions

Galaxia Expeditions is one of the most reputable and professional outdoor adventure outfits in Huaraz. It offers possibly the most comprehensive service for taking advantage of all that a geographical landmark like the Cordillera Blanca has to offer: from mountaineering to mountain biking, from rock climbing to ice climbing, with rafting, trekking and exploring canyons, among other activities. Galaxia's guides are all licensed and certified. It also rents everything you need for your escapade, at reasonable rates. In addition, its Huaraz office has its own climbing wall where lessons are offered, and café-bar, a great place to meet and socialize with like-minded risk-takers. A one-day bike tour, food included, goes for $35.

V!VA Member Review- Galaxia Expeditions

I found the guides quite competent and the service was very good. I met a lot of mountain lovers and I found a very good atmosphere. The people working there are very good and I always felt safe during the climbing.

Brussels, Belgium, March 16, 2008

Motorbike Tours ($165 / Day)

Motorcycling can be done in Huascarán National Park. Bring strong boots. Daily, 9 a.m.-10.30 p.m. Chilli Heaven, Parque Ginebra, Tel: 51-43-396-085, E-mail: simon1359@hotmail.com.

Mountain Bike Adventures

Mountain Bike Adventures is run by Julio Olaza, a Huaraz native and mountain biking enthusiast. Having biked the Cordillera Blanca his entire life, and spent stints in the United States mountain biking, Julio has turned his passion into his livelihood. He knows the landscape inside and out, and can lead or point bikers in the right direction for their ability and desired excursion. He is focused on safety and comes highly recommended everywhere. Rates average approximately $20 per day for equipment rentals and $30 for one-day tours. Multiday excursions can also be arranged. Lucar y Torre 530, 2nd Floor, Tel: 51-43-424-259, E-mail: julio.olaza@terra.com.pe, URL: www.chakinaniperu.com.

Monttrek

With more than 20 years' experience in activities surrounding Huaraz, Monttrek organizes ascents to many nearby peaks, ice and rock climbing, mountain biking excursions, horseback riding, rafting and more. Equipment can be rented through it, and it is a great source of information for serious adventurists. Av. Luzuriaga 646, 2nd Floor, Tel: 51-43-721-124.

Peruvian Andes Adventures / Pyramid Adventures

Peruvian Andes Adventures offers trekking, hiking, tours and mountain climbing around Huaraz, providing a wide range of adventure activities to individuals and groups. The company is operated by Hisao and Eli Morales. Jr. José Olaya 532, Tel/Fax: 51-43-421-864, E-mail: hisao@peruvianandes,com, URL: www.peruvianandes.com.

Peru Andes Travel

This all-purpose tour operator and travel agency offers experienced and certified guides that will facilitate access to all the best of the Cordillera Blanca, including the turquoise-blue Llanganuco Lagoon, shimmering, multicolored Puman Shimin, and the majestic ancient Chavín temples. Day trips cost as little as $8. They also provide mountain biking, bridge jumping, scaling canyons, rafting, rock climbing, ice climbing and trekking tours. As well, it sells, rents and repairs equipment, from sleeping bags to mountain bikes. Flights and bus trips across Peru can also be arranged. Av. Luzuriaga 627, Tel: 51-439-941-617, E-mail: pbrb7@hotmail.com.

Santa Cruz Expeditions

Santa Cruz Expeditions, with offices in Edinburgh, Scotland, and Huaraz, provides guides for climbs and treks throughout the Cordillera Blanca and Cordillera Huayhuash. It can create an itinerary to suit the needs of any level of climber. Santa Cruz Expeditions also leads treks in the region. It has a complete gear rental shop, and sometimes sells off its used gear— if you're looking to invest in some equipment, don't hesitate to ask. An English-speaking guide for two people to summit Huascarán costs $130/day, plus all other expenses (food, porters, cooks etc). Tel: 44-131-467-7086 / 100, E-mail: info@santacruzexpeditions.com, URL: www.santacruzexpeditions.com.

HUARAZ LODGING

Hotels in Huaraz are on the whole, decent and reasonably priced, but prices can rise during holiday periods. With the quantity of budget hotels, it is worth shopping around, as some hotels in Huaraz have good views of the Cordillera Blanca. For a relatively small town, there is plenty of choice, reflecting the importance of Huaraz as an outdoor adventure center.

BUDGET

Oscar's Hostal (Rooms: $6 - 13)

This competent facility close to downtown offers decent rooms. The most expensive is a triple. All rooms have private baths, with hot water 24/7, and cable television. No breakfast is included in the price, but there are plenty of restaurants nearby. Jr. la Mar 624, Tel: 51-43-422-720, E-mail: cvmonical@hotmail.com.

Hotel Huaraz (Rooms: $7 - 25)

Prices fluctuate depending on the season, and they are more than adequate; clean, comfortable and congenial. Rooms come with cable TV, and the hotel itself has a common-area kitchen, conference room, garage and laundry service. If you are willing to spend a little more, you can score a room with a Jacuzzi. Av Luzuriaga 529, Tel: 51-43-421-314.

CENTRAL ANDES

MID-RANGE

Morales Guest House (Rooms: $19 - 35)
Located five blocks from the Plaza de Armas in a quiet and safe area, the Morales Guest House has rooms with private bathrooms for two, three or four persons. The owners, the Morales Family, pioneers in climbing and trekking in the Cordillera Blanca and Huayhuash, are particularly friendly and willing to share their knowledge of the area, as well as help you to plan your activities while in Huaraz. Excellent, inexpensive family-style breakfast is available in the morning. You get great views of the mountain from guest rooms, as well as from the roof. Lounge chairs are also available for lying out in the sun. English is spoken. Prices do not include taxes. Jr. José Olaya 532, Tel/Fax: 51-43-421-864, E-mail: info@peruvianandes.com, URL: www.peruvianandes.com.

Colonia Hotel (Rooms: $20 - 60)
This hotel is located in the heart of Huaraz, just six blocks from the Plaza de Armas. The Colonia is an ecological hotel that attracts primarily adventurous travelers. The big garden is the perfect place to unwind after a day of excitement. The 13 rooms are spacious with hot water 24-hours a day and have balconies with views of the Cordillera Blanca. Hotel amenities include bar, restaurant, private parking, travel agency and internet. English is spoken. Tours can also be organized for climbing and trekking in Peru. Credit cards are not accepted unless booking is done online. Huandoy Street 103, URL: www.peru-hotels.com/huarcolo.htm

Hostal Alfredo (Rooms: $25 - 70)
Hostal Alfredo is in a quiet district nine blocks from the main plaza. Each of the 12 rooms in this historic building has phone, cable TV, private bath, intercom, Jacuzzi and hydromassage. The amenities of Hostal Alfredo are numerous: continental breakfast, room service, internet access, bar, restaurant, gardens, laundry, private parking, transfers and a handicrafts store. English and German are spoken. The hostel requires prepaid reservations; Mastercard, AMEX, Visa, Diner's Club and travelers' checks accepted. Av. Centenario 184, Tel: 51-43-421-632, E-mail: info@hostalalfredo.com, URL: www.hostalalfredo.com.

Hotel Pirámide (Rooms: $35 - 80)
This relatively new hotel is surprisingly expensive for a city that isn't: rooms start at $35, going as high as $80. They are a bit small, but clean and pleasant to look at. The Hotel Pirámide also offers a nice view of the Huascarán, Peru's highest mountain, and the Cordillera Blanca. Breakfast, served in its café, is included in the price, as is internet service. Top-floor suites feature Jacuzzis. Parque Ginebra, Tel: 51-43-425-801, E-mail: hotelpiramide@yahoo.es.

Hotel Colomba (Rooms: $38 - 45)
The first ecological lodge in Huaraz, Hotel Colomba is a beautiful old hacienda with accommodations in bungalows set in large, secure gardens full of plants. It's located in a quiet residential area of Huaraz, with modern hotel services, making it a great place to stay. The family who runs the hotel can help you organize tours and trekking. Includes taxes and service. Jr. Francisco de Zela 278, Tel: 51-43-421-241 / 421-501 / 427-106, Fax: 51-43-422-273, E-mail: colomba@terra.com.pe, URL: www.huarazhotel.com.

The Lazy Dog Inn (Rooms: $40 - 80)
The Lazy Dog Inn is an ecological adobe B&B. The lodge has small cabins with fireplaces, home-cooked meals, horses, outdoor firepit and community volunteer projects. It borders on the national park and is 1.2 hours from the town on foot, or about 10 minutes in a car. To get there, you can either take a 3.1 km road from Marian/Cachipampa, but beware, this road is rutted and occasionally impassable. Another alternative is to take the 12 km road, called Via Wilcahuaín Ruins, from Huaraz. The second route is better maintained and more easily passable by car. Prices are based on two persons and include meals. Some rooms are cabins, while others are in the main house. Apdo 94, Serpost, Tel: 51-43-943-789-330, E-mail: dbmorris@andeanalliance.com, URL: www.thelazydoginn.com.

Pastoruri Hotel (Rooms: $43 - 86)

The Pastoruri Hotel opened its doors to guests in 2005. Panoramic views and an array of amenities are complemented by quality service. The 27 comfortable rooms (singles, doubles and suites) have 24-hour hot water, private bath, cable TV, internet access (in some rooms), telephone and safe deposit box. Upper-level rooms also have a view of the mountains. Hotel facilities include a fully-equipped gym, restaurant, room service, laundry service and car parking. Rates include taxes, American breakfast, access to the gym and use of the lobby PC with internet. Mastercard, AMEX, Visa, Diner's and travelers' checks are accepted. Jr. Corongo 145, Independencia, Tel: 51-43-429-878, E-mail: ventas@pastorurihotel.com, URL: www.pastorurihotel.com.

HIGH-END

El Patio de Monterrey (Rooms: $59 - 112)

El Patio de Monterrey offers "modern comfort in a traditionally rustic atmosphere." The architecture is reminiscent of an *hacienda*, with chimneys, patios and beautiful gardens which create a romantic ambiance. Each of the 25 rooms are cozy and have TV, telephone and a private bathroom. The onsite restaurant serves breakfast and dinner. A bar, room service and internet are also available. Continental breakfast is included in the rate. The hotel accepts Mastercard, AMEX, Visa, Diner's and travelers checks. Carretera Huaraz-Caraz, km 206, Tel: 51-43-724-965, E-mail: elpatio@terra.com.pe, URL: www.elpatio.com.

Andino Club Hotel (Rooms: $85 - 632)

Just a 15-minute walk from the main plaza, Andino Club Hotel is often considered to be one of the best accommodations in town. The friendly owners are Swiss and some of the rooms have stunning views of the beautiful Huascaran Mountain. All rooms have private bathrooms with 24-hour hot water, cable TV, safety box, heaters and phone. The restaurant, Chalet Suisse, serves international cuisine in a beautiful setting and there is a business center with mail service, internet, fax and a conference room. There is a laundry service and transfers in/out can be arranged. Additionally, there is a travel agency that specializes in trekking, climbing, biking and horseback riding. Credit cards accepted: VISA, MasterCard, Diners, American Express. Travelers' checks are not accepted. Pedro Cochachín 357, Tel: 51-43-421-662, E-mail: informes@hotelandino.com, URL: www.hotelandino.com.

HUARAZ RESTAURANTS

Huaraz has a little bit of everything to satisfy the wide variety of appetites that traipse through the city. Start the day with an early morning continental breakfast of freshly-baked breads and jams. As your tummy starts grumbling in the afternoon, try one of the local dishes prepared with guinea pig, poultry, pork or lamb. No meal is complete without a popular bowl of soup (if you find you really like the guinea pig, try the *picante de cuy* soup, a spicy treat served with boiled potatoes). Later in the evening, you may crave something more familiar; you can find this at local Chinese or Italian restaurants. Enjoy!

Café Creperie (Entrees: $3 - 4)

This place features no less than 18 varieties of crepes. For your main course, try an Italian crepe with spinach, mushrooms, chicken, mozzarella and pesto sauce, or curry chicken with glazed apples and other unusual treats. Apples also feature in the desert crepes, as do sweet crepes sautéed in wine with vanilla ice cream. Sandwiches, salads and pizzas are also on the menu, and there is a full bar. Jr. Lucar y Torre 490, Tel: 51-43-424-541.

Piccolo Restaurant (Entrees: $5 - 7)

A self-described Italian restaurant, Piccolo Restaurant serves standard international favorites as well as Italian. Among the more original items on its menu are *conejo a la mostaza*, or rabbit à la mustard. Wine-sautéed alpaca, and a combined curried chicken-shrimp platter are also offered. Apart from that, there is lots of pasta and lots of pizza. Daily 7 a.m.-midnight.. Jr. Julián de Morales 632, Tel: 51-43-509-210, E-mail: piccoloservicios@hotmail.com.

Bistro de los Andes

Bistro de Los Andes comes highly recommended and the trout has been praised more than once. It specializes in French and Peruvian cuisine and also offers vegetarian dishes, like a yummy vegetable stir-fry. The owner speaks English, French and German. Open daily, 5 a.m.-1 p.m., 5-11 p.m. Morales 823, Tel: 51-44-726-249.

Café Andino

Stop in for a snack at Café Andino and leave with much more. This scrumptious little café is American-run, and is also home to La Cima, an adventure travel company and the Sierra Verde Spanish school. As you sit down to your steaming cup of coffee, enjoy the spectacular views of the Andes. This is a great place to relax, peruse the book exchange, chat with friends or explore your options for discovering the surrounding mountains. Jr. Lucar y Torre 530, Tel: 51-43-721-203, URL: www.cafeandino.com.

California Café

Ten years old, California Café has long been a Huaraz institution for foreign travelers and adventurers. Come in, put down your knapsack, grab a paperback, and relax in one of its wicker chairs or comfy sofas. Manager Tim Norris has recreated the look and feel of a bohemian Berkeley hang-out, complete with a wide selection of coffee and tea (including chai). He and his wife, Louisa, prepare an awesome breakfast and lunch menu, including large and fluffy pancakes to fuel you up for your next trek or bike tour around the Cordillera Blanca. Open every day until 6 p.m., this is one of the best places to meet other travelers and share stories and information. Jr. 28 de Julio, URL: huaylas.com/californiacafe/california.htm.

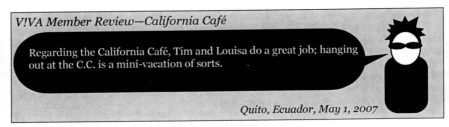

V!VA Member Review—California Café

Regarding the California Café, Tim and Louisa do a great job; hanging out at the C.C. is a mini-vacation of sorts.

Quito, Ecuador, May 1, 2007

Chilli Heaven

Chilli Heaven is a cozy, small restaurant serving authentic Indian and Mexican food. This place is well recommended for those who want to splurge. Parque Ginebra, next to Casa de Guías, Tel: 51-43-396-085.

Fuente de Salud

Called the Fountain of Health, this intimate vegetarian restaurant is a great place to give your body a break from the stresses of traveling. A good selection of meals are available at a decent price, from good soups and breakfasts to meat (yes, a vegetarian restaurant that serves meat) and pasta dishes. José de la Mar 562.

La Luna Café

With a pleasant and friendly atmosphere, the restaurant also houses a book exchange and games. It serves a good breakfast buffet until noon, followed by excellent Mexican food for lunch and dinner. Jr. Julián de Morales 820, E-mail: lalunacafe@peru.com.

HUARAZ NIGHTLIFE

Tambo Bar and Dance Club

This popular bar and dance club is made to accommodate up to 250—which means it is pretty dang big. Opening no earlier than 8 p.m. and remaining open until the last customer leaves, Tambo is for people who seriously intend to party. The usual creative mixes of popular North

American, European and Latin American music is what you'd expect, of course, but it also provides live music and even special performances by locals showcasing indigenous dance. There is not much food beyond some munchies to accompany your drink orders, but there is no cover charge. Jr. José de la Mar 776, Tel: 51-43-423-417.

Diablo Club Huaraz

Diablo Club is one of the most happening hot spots in Huaraz, and one of the largest clubs. Located close to the Plaza de Armas. Guests are served by a multinational staff. Open from 8 p.m. Jr. Simón Bolívar 715, E-mail: diabloclub@gmail.com URL: www.diablohuaraz.com

CHIQUIÁN

Tucked away in the Cordillera Huayhuash—111 kilometers from Huaraz—Chiquián is a hidden gem, forgotten by the tourist circuit which has been rerouted onto a new highway. Chiquián is a perfect base for trekking the mountains nearby, exploring the Jahuacoa Lagoon and visiting the Huanoca Pampa ruins. The inhabitants of this traditional cheese-making village bemoan the loss of tourists coming to Chiquián. For the odd traveler however, Chiquián's new-found tranquility is an attraction unto itself. Ask anyone in town and they will tell you why it's best to live here; in Chiquián you are *3,500 metros más cerca de las estrellas*—3,500 meters closer to the stars.

Most come to Chiquián to stray off the beaten path and trek the 165-kilometer network of paths around Huayhuash, taking in its natural riches. For day-trippers, there are waterfalls close to the pueblo, as well as trails affording views of the imposing Yerupajá, or El Carnicero (the Butcher), summit, which looms at 6,634 meters (21,766 feet), making it the second-highest mountain peak in Peru.

CHIQUIÁN HISTORY

Located at the base of the Cordillera Huayhuash, the small Andean mountain village of Chiquián is home to 6,500 inhabitants. This charming sierra town gets its name from the Quechua word for *amanecer—achikyay*—or sunrise in English.

Chiquián was formerly dominated by traditional haciendas, but the *patrones* (plantation masters) let loose their tight grip on the valley in the 1970s. Shortly after, Chiquián became a popular tourist destination, creating a new economy. Hotels, restaurants, shops and professional tour guides sprang up to meet the needs of travelers. Cheese production expanded in the 1990s, securing this community of dairy farmers' traditional way of life. The Asociación San Marcelo de Chiquián also runs a community-owned business in natural textiles and wools, harvested from the coats of the valley's abundant herds of sheep and alpaca.

CHIQUIÁN TOURS

Andes Top

Andes Top Peru offers five trekking routes in the Cordillera Huayhuash, ranging from four to 15 days. Most treks will summit the Yerupajá, the second-largest mountain peak in Peru. A four-day journey includes a stopover at the Jahuacoa Lagoon, whilst longer treks afford the possibility of also visiting the Laguna Viconga (11 days) as well as the Huanoca Pampa (12 days), an astrology complex built in the late 15th century. Two days of acclimatization to the altitude in Huaraz, before climbing the Huayhuash Mountains, is highly recommended; be sure to include this when calculating your dates. Jr. Comercio 1301, Tel: 51-43-447-121, E-mail: info@andestop-peru.com, URL: www.andestop-peru.com/site/homees.htm.

CHIQUIÁN LODGING

Gran Hotel Huayhuash (Rooms: $15 - 50)

Climbers wishing for a comfortable night's stay to prepare them for roughing it in the mountains for the next two weeks, need look no further than Gran Hotel Huayhuash, the plushest accommodation to be found in Chiquián. Jr. 28 de Julio 400, Tel: 51-43-425-661 Fax: 51-43-447-049, E-mail: info@hotelhuayhuash.com / perubergsport@yahoo.es.

Yungay had previously been the setting of a political and historical debacle in 1836—a decisive battle that defeated an attempt by Bolivia and Chile to co-opt Peru into a confederacy, and thus led to the permanent establishment of Peru as an independent nation.

On Sundays the people who now populate Yungay still pay tribute to their past and culture in an open-air market in which they don colorful, traditional garb. They also speak more Quechua here than in other parts of the Ancash region. For most travelers, Yungay matters most as its role as the gateway to some of the most spectacular geography in the central Andes, such as the Llanganuco lagoon, itself containing the biosphere reserve Huascarán.

THINGS TO SEE AND DO IN YUNGAY

Yungay is best known for its proximity to the dirt road that leads to Lagunas Llanganuco, two stunning lakes approximately 30 kilometers outside of Yungay. Otherwise, tiny Yungay doesn't have a lot of activities for travelers. That said, there are some little sights around to check out on the way to Lagunas Llanganuco.

Campo Santo

Old Yungay is presided over by a tall white statue of Christ to the north, overlooking the devastating path of destruction left by the 1970 *aluvión*, a deadly mix of avalanche, waterfall and landslide caused by an earthquake. The aluvión is responsible for destroying Old Yungay and killing its 18,000 inhabitants. Today, this quiet area allows for silent reflection on such a disaster among gardens and gravestones towards the northern end of town.

YUNGAY LODGING

Yungay is a small, serene little town that doesn't receive a lot of tourists, thus leaving it with little need for such services. There are just a couple of options for lodging and they are very basic. Accommodations are cheap and clean, and have the minimum for what travelers will need—a good night's rest.

Huascarán Hostal (Rooms: $3)

This hostel, just on the edge of the city of Yungay, charges $3 a night for a private room that also has its own bathroom. And for this price range the rooms are above average, especially when you consider that they also come with cable TV, laundry service, and even a parking garage. The facility itself is not high on design, but rather simply utilitarian. Jr. Leoncido Prado, Tel: 51-43-393-023, E-mail: ct_huascaran@hotmail.com.

Hostal Yungay (Rooms: $5 and up)

Rooms start at $5, and the owners are proud to let you know that the price includes a private bath, hot water, color TV, 24-hour service and security. For an extra cost, they also offer laundry service. Overall, these are decent quality rooms, clean, with fairly new beds. It also has the convenience of being close to downtown and within walking distance of stores and eateries. Hostal Yungay also has a terrace with clotheslines for hanging your wet garments. Jr. Santo Domingo 01, Tel: 51-43-393-053.

YUNGAY RESTAURANTS

Yungay has little to offer in the way of food. The good news is the food is cheap and will fill you up. There are several places to eat in Yungay's market, next to the plaza. Otherwise there are a couple of rustic restaurants in the area that could fulfill your needs.

Chicken Progreso (Entrees: $2 - 4)

Chicken Progreso is the cleanest and most modern restaurant in Yungay. It offers both a *menú ejecutivo*, featuring standard Peruvian and continental cuisine, and a *chifa* menu, that is, Chinese. The plates average $3, and many people passing through Yungay may not want to eat anywhere else. Av. Arias Grazzian, Tel: 51-43-504-818.

CARAZ

Located at in the foothills of the San Juan range in Ancash, at an altitude of 2,250 meters (7,382 ft), the city of Caraz is also known as *Caraz Dulzura*, or Sweet Caraz, perhaps because sugar cane was once a popular crop, which in turn might have led to the community's love of ice cream and pastries (most notably the milk-and-sugar confection, *manjar blanco* in its many pastry shops).

Unlike the other cities in the Ancash region, Caraz suffered little structural damage during the 8.0-magnitude earthquake that devastated so much of Peru in 1970. Thus it offers more neocolonial and 19th century architecture than Carhuaz, and is free of the prevalent eyesore of the exposed skeletal construction of buildings abandoned in mid-repair found in Huaraz. Historically, Caraz served as the last outpost for Simón Bolívar and his regimen in the decisive battles at Ayacucho and Junín that saw the end of Spanish rule in South America.

With its year-round temperate climate, Caraz is a rich source of agricultural produce. Besides the aforementioned sugar, the area also produces rice, cotton, potatoes and corn. Additionally, Caraz raises cattle, llamas, alpaca, vicuñas and sheep; the latter three providing the wool used in the many colorful and folkloric ponchos, scarves and caps sold in the area.

Caraz's main festival is in January, the celebration of the Virgin of Chiquinquirá, featuring processions, costumes, dancing, even bull fights, and of course, a lot of drinking. Apart from the modest cultural charms of the city itself, the main attraction is the access it provides to breathtaking scenery and adventure.

From Caraz, tour guides will take you to snow-capped Alpamayo at an altitude of nearly 6,000 meters (19,685 ft). In 1966, UNESCO declared it to be the "most beautiful mountain in the world." Other natural wonders include the sparkling Parón Lake, and *Pato* (Duck) Canyon, popular with mountain bikers (though you will not find many ducks within). The nearby Río Santa attracts many eager kayakers, canoeing and rafting enthusiasts.

THINGS TO SEE AND DO IN CARAZ

Outdoor activities and stunning vistas are the highlight of Caraz. Adventurists will find no shortage of hiking and trekking trails that give way to spectacular scenery and snow-covered peaks. Like other Peruvian towns, Caraz is not without ruins, so be sure to work a visit into your daily itinerary.

Laguna Parón

The turquoise waters of Laguna Parón sparkle and reflect the surrounding snow-capped peaks in the depths of the lagoon, making them appear even taller and more magnificent. At the end of the lake, the Pirámide de Garcilaso sits proudly. There is also a challenging rock climbing wall called the Torre de Parón, or the Sphinx. The drive to the Laguna is spectacular; ambitious and fit hikers can trek to it. Public transport is available. 32 km east of Caraz.

Tumshukaiko

Approximately two kilometers north of Caraz you'll find the Chavín ruins of Tumshukaiko. There is no fee or sign, and the ruins are only partially excavated. It takes the shape of a pyramid with seven tiers (very little is visible). There is also an underground tunnel that leads to a stone chair. Be sure to take a flashlight, and know that you will get dirty in the spots where it's a tight fit.

CARAZ TOURS

Apu Aventura

Apu Aventura boasts 15 years experience as a tour operator. For those looking to make the most of their visit to the Cordillera Blanca, this company offers well-organized adventures ranging from rock climbing, mountain biking, horseback riding to whitewater rafting. A four-day trek through Santa Cruz, complete with guiding and gear, goes for $450. There is also a cross-country exploration, via a Land Rover, that goes from Huaraz all the way to Machu Picchu. Parque San Martín 103, Tel: 51-43-392-159, E-mail: reserves@apuaventura.com, URL: www.apuaventura.com.

CARAZ LODGING
A little town growing in popularity, Caraz has not quite experienced the onslaught of tourism development that is inevitable. Thus, lodging options are very simple and provide an atmosphere to appreciate the surrounding panoramas and to relax. The budget prices stay relatively stable all year.

Los Pinos Lodge (Rooms: $8 - 40)
The Los Pinos Lodge is one of the most attractive accommodations in Caraz, largely due to the creative enthusiasm that its owner, Luís Rojas Lara, brings to the facility. The common area features an extensive library of books and maps, as well as DVDs and internet service. The cafeteria has a full-service bar, and this is one of the few hostels you will find that actually has a garage. Prices start at $8 for a private room with a shared bath and go to $40 for a family room. Breakfast is included in the price. Parque San Martín 103, Tel: 51-43-391-130, E-mail: lospinos@apuaventura.com, URL: www.apuaventaura.com.

Hostal Perla de los Andes (Rooms: $11 and up)
With its three-story, neo-classical design and location facing the Plaza de Armas, this hotel should be a perennial favorite for travelers for some time to come. Among its amenities are a restaurant, room service, cable TV, hot water both day and night, and international call service. Jr. Daniel Villar 179, Tel: 51-43-392-007, E-mail: hostalperladelosandes@hotmail.com.

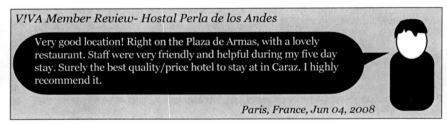

V!VA Member Review- Hostal Perla de los Andes

Very good location! Right on the Plaza de Armas, with a lovely restaurant. Staff were very friendly and helpful during my five day stay. Surely the best quality/price hotel to stay at in Caraz. I highly recommend it.

Paris, France, Jun 04, 2008

Caraz Dulzura Hostal (Rooms: $12 and up)
This hostel is a little further away from the center of town, but mototaxis will take you there for only a *sol*, or $0.33. The prices start at $12 for a private room that is clean and comfortable. The hostel features its own restaurant and bar, and a pleasant interior patio. The Caraz Dulzura Hostal also offers storage and laundry service. Jr. Sáenz Peña 212, Tel: 51-43-391-523, E-mail: hostalcarazdulzura@hotmail.com, URL: www.huaraz.com/carazdulzura.

CARAZ RESTAURANTS
In the town affectionately known to some as *Caraz Dulzura* (Sweet Caraz), visitors will notice its many displays of sweet cakes and other pastries in window after window, while ice cream shops proudly serve homemade treats to customers. If you are in the mood for something more substantial (and not quite as sweet) there is no shortage of cafés and restaurants serving local Peruvian dishes, hearty meat entrées, cuy (guinea pig) and veggie dishes too! Ask around for local recommendations.

Café la Terraza (Entrees: $1 - 5)
This nice, medium-size eatery's most notable feature is its internal terrace, complete with hanging plants, that add a touch of kitsch to your quiche. Open all days except Sunday, they sell sandwiches and hamburgers that go from $1 to $3, not to mention a standard offering

of beef, chicken, trout, pasta and pizza. It also has a better-than-average selection of coffees, cocktails and ice cream. Jr. Sucre 1106, Tel: 51-43-301-226.

Chifa Restaurant (Entrees: $2)

One thing you can't get away from, virtually anywhere in Peru, is Chinese food, and Caraz is no different. Young entrepreneur Juan Fidel Tolentino showcases his own flair for this decidedly non-indigenous cuisine with such dishes as Chicken Kontausi, Chicken Konmensi and Won Ton soup. The prices in this small, somewhat average-looking venue are no higher than $2. A big-screen television in the corner helps jolly along your eating experience. Daily 8 a.m.-11 p.m. Carretera Central 51, E-mail: conteplfrilaf@hotmail.com.

La Punta Grande

La Punta Grande makes an immediate impression due to its sheer size, seemingly incongruous in a town with such a small population: its seating capacity is close to 250, and offers as many tables outdoors as it does indoors. By contrast its menu offerings are small in number, offering standard variations of beef-chicken-pork-trout-venison...venison? Yes, that's right. Not only that, La Punta Grande raises its own deer, who wander freely around the restaurant. And being used to human contact, they are responsive to petting and stroking, and will gladly lick your hands...before they wind up on your plate. Daniel Villar 505, Tel: 51-43-391-320, E-mail: restlapuntagrande@hotmail.com.

MONTERREY

Six kilometers north of Huaraz along the road to Caraz is the laidback village of Monterrey. There are a few hotels and restaurants here, but the main attraction is the thermal baths (7 a.m.-6 p.m., $1). The baths consist of two large pools, each varying in temperature, and a range of private bathing rooms for one or two people. The upper pool is nicer, but is teeming with people on weekends and Peruvian holidays. The pools are closed on Monday for cleaning. Despite its brownish color—the result of mineral deposits—the water and the pools are among the cleanest and most hygienic in the area. If you can, get up for an early morning soak, as the pools are quietest and cleanest at this time. From Huaraz catch a city bus along Av. Luzuriaga ($0.22, until 7 p.m.). You can also catch a taxi ($2-3).

PACIFIC COAST NORTH OF LIMA

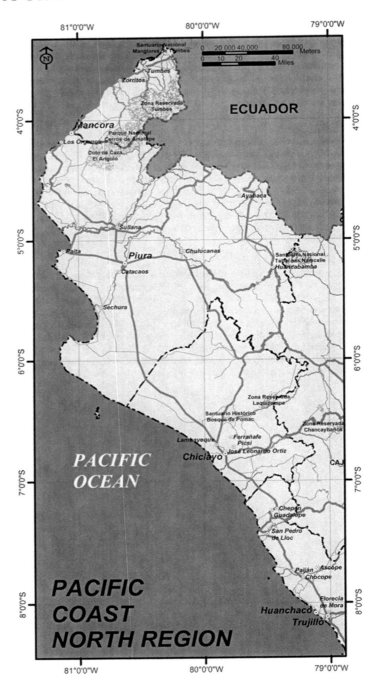

Because of its location, the Pacific Coast north of Lima does not get as many visitors as the rest of the country—it is simply too far away from Cusco, Machu Picchu and the Sacred Valley. This is unfortunate as the northern coast has much to offer visitors.

Trujillo (p.400) is one of Peru's largest cities with a population of 650,000, and is a great as a launching point to visit Chan Chan (p.412).

A few of the more noteworthy places to visit in the north coast region are:

• Tombs of Sipán—Considered to be South America's King Tut; upon discovery in 1987, the tombs were still largely intact and full of riches, unlike most tombs which had already been plundered by grave robbers.

• The Museo Sicán in Ferreñafe—This intriguing museum features an elaborately- reconstructed tomb of a Sicán royal personage containing, amongst other things, 20 sacrificed women and two massive golden arms.

• The Citadel of Chan Chan—The ruins of the largest pre-Columbian city in South America are a must-see for those on the Northern Pacific Coast. It was the capital of the Chimú kingdom around 1300 AD. Some archaeologists believe it was the largest adobe city ever. They are located a mere five kilometers (3 mi) west of Trujillo.

• Máncora—Sporting the largest left-hand point breaks in the world, Máncora is a prime vacation destination for Peruvians. It is busy but not overrun with tourists, giving visitors a more authentic Peruvian beach experience.

When to Go

Ironically, the northern coast of Peru is sunniest during December through April, when the rest of the country is in the rainy season. The overall climate of Peru's northern coast is very dry, making it attractive to visitors any time of the year.

In cities such as Piura and Máncora clouds are rare and rain is almost non-existent. The busiest time is June through August, during the rest of the country's dry season. The dry season coincides with the North American and European summers, and is the time when the majority of foreigners visit Peru. The North, however, has significantly less tourism than the South, so even a visit during high tourist season will afford tourists with plenty of available accommodation and activity options.

Safety on the Pacific Coast North of Lima

Visitors to Peru should take the necessary precautions against insect bites. The northern coast region has one of the highest incidences of dengue fever transmission in Peru and malaria is also passed along through mosquito bites. Unfortunately the mosquitoes that carry these diseases are active at different times of the day: the *Aedes aegypti* from dusk to dawn, and the *anopheles* from dusk to dawn. That means that mosquito bite prevention is a 24-hour job. Use DEET-based mosquito repellent and wear long garments. In malaria areas, use preventative medication; there is no prevention for dengue. See the More Serious Health Problems section for more advice.

Also, take sun protection especially seriously on the north coast of Peru. The sun is strong, and if you are not careful, it can burn you quickly. Your skin is most vulnerable in the middle of the day, so stay out of the sun between 11 a.m. and 4 p.m.

The northern coast does not require any safety precautions above those normally taken while traveling in Peru. Nonetheless, you should never wear expensive jewelry or flash around large sums of money. If you need to carry cash and important documents, carry them in a money belt underneath your clothes.

NORTHERN COAST

Help other travelers. Publish your favorite places at www.vivatravelguides.com

NORTHERN COAST

PACIFIC COAST NORTH OF LIMA THINGS TO DO
Although the area on the Northern Coast in Peru is less visited than other areas, there are a plethora of activities available, perhaps more so than any other region. This area is especially rich in archaeological sites. Some of the most noteworthy are the Tombs of Sipán, which were discovered in 1987 and showcase a large collection of extravagant artifacts. The adobe ruins of Chan Chan, thought to be the largest pre-Columbian city in South America, are the premier archaeological attraction of the Pacific coast.

Within Trujillo, Chiclayo and Piura, the major cities in this area, visitors can find a variety of museums and city sights to keep them entertained. The towns also have various markets, which are worth a visit to experience the local culture and find some goodies to take home. If you are more into a beach scene, Máncora is the perfect place for you. This Peruvian beach town has prime surfing. Máncora is very popular amongst the locals, giving visitors a less touristy beach experience.

PACIFIC COAST NORTH OF LIMA TOURS
When looking for tours in the northern Pacific coast region, keep in mind a few things: what you want to see, how long you want to see it and how much you are willing to spend. Most of the attractions located in this area are archaeological sites. A tour allows visitors to see more of the area and its sights, and learn more about what they are seeing.

PACIFIC COAST NORTH OF LIMA LODGING
Hotels in the Pacific coast north of Lima have it all, so much in fact, that you need to be sure to do ample research before settling on a place. There have been reports that some low-end accommodations have rooms that are visited by critters in the night. Also some of the cheaper places often do not have amenities such as hot water, so be sure to ask about that as well. For those looking for a more, shall we say, comfortable stay during their time in the area, many options are available. All of the main cities in the area—Trujillo, Piura, Máncora, Chiclayo and Huanchaco—have places to stay sans bugs and with hot water. There are even some high-end options affording guests a more luxurious stay in this region of Peru.

TRUJILLO
The north of Peru has often been described as the Egypt of South America, due to the abundance of pre-Inca treasures found in this area. Settled on the Pacific coast, Trujillo is one of Peru's largest cities, with a population of 690,000, and is the perfect starting point for anyone interested in exploring these ancient treasures. Founded in 1534 by Diego de Almagro and named after the birthplace of Francisco Pizarro, this colonial city was inhabited long before the arrival of the Spanish. From Trujillo one can travel to the historical landmarks of both the ancient Moche and Chimú cultures. Of particular interest are the archeological sites of Huaca del Sol y Huaca de la Luna, El Brujo and the mud-brick city of Chan Chan.

The city of Trujillo offers all the sights and sounds of a bustling metropolis, while maintaining an undeniable small-town feel. The greenness of the city contrasts nicely with the Andean mountains draped in brown, and a variety of restaurants, bars, hotels, churches and museums invite visitors to explore and enjoy Trujillo's modern and historical landscapes. The city is best explored on foot, and most of the popular plazas, hotels, restaurants and colonial *casas antiguas* are located in Old Town. Allow at least half a day to wander around Trujillo's colonial core, where you'll find a score of well-preserved homes and churches located to the north of the Plaza de Armas.

Art enthusiasts and history buffs should definitely plan a visit to Iglesia y Monasterio El Carmen, which offer Trujillo's best collection of colonial art. Located nearby is the Museo Arqueológico, which specializes in Peruvian history from 12,000 BC to the arrival of the Spanish. Be aware that in Trujillo *siestas* are taken seriously and most sites are closed from 1-4 p.m.

If you desire an escape from the honking *taxistas* and bustle of city life, check out nearby Huancha-co, a small fishing and surfing village teeming with hotels, guest houses and restaurants, famous for its narrow-pointed fishing rafts. Another point of departure from Trujillo is Puerto Malabrigo (Chicama), known to surfers as the best surf beach in Peru, and located just 70 kilometers (43 milles) north of the city.

TRUJILLO HISTORY

The city, 563 kilometers (350 miles) north of Lima and now known as Trujillo has been a thriv-ing metropolis as long as people have lived there—and that is a long time, going back millennia. The fertile earth of the Río Moche valley, a linear oasis running north-south through northern Peru's arid regions, served as the cradle of many early civilizations, most notably the Moche (pro-nounced Moh-Chey), whose strong agriculture and fishing-based economy led to the rise of one of the largest pre-Columbian empires, from 200 BC to 700 AD—before the rise of Chimús, and the later Incas.

The Moche became expert craftsmen, excelling in ceramics (offering detailed depictions of all fac-ets of daily life for the Moche, including some of the most sexually explicit figures in the western hemisphere), textiles and metallurgy. The large pyramids in the centers of their towns were trib-utes to their gods, but today serve as tributes to the Moche aptitude in building and design. Now their legacy is historical ruins, some of the biggest and most detailed in all of Latin America.

The Spanish arrived in 1534, and Diego de Almagro named it Villa Trujillo, after Trujillo in Ex-tremadura, Spain, birthplace of Francisco Pizarro. Three years later, Charles I of Spain officially designated Trujillo a city. Its coat of arms claims Trujillo as *la Ciudad de la Eterna Primavera*, The City of Eternal Spring. Trujillo soon became a major trading and commercial port. Indeed, its success was such that in 1685, a wall was constructed along the city perimeter to curb pirate raids on Trujillo. The enclosed sections of Trujillo are now a historic colonial center, featuring elegant classic houses, churches and public squares.

Trujillo is now the second largest city in Peru, home of the famous *marinera* dance, which com-bines European and indigenous styles, and is the taking off point for Peru's largest crop export, asparagus. Trujillo has a reputation of being a cleaner city than Lima, and the charm of its colonial heritage is enhanced by its proximity to archaeological wonders such as the ancient city of Chan Chan, and the Huaca del Sol pyramid.

Getting To and Away from Trujillo

Three areas serve as the central points for bus offices. On Avenida del Ejército, just past Avenida España, are the offices for Ormeño, Cial, Civa, Oltursa, Flores and Vía. The office for Cruz del Sur is around the corner on Amazonas and Emtrafesa, two blocks from Túpac Amaru 185 and across from the cemetery.

The second grouping of bus agency offices is on Avenida Mansiche, between Avenida Juan Pablo II and Ovalo Cassines. There are Ittsa (two stations: one for buses to Lima, another for north-bound buses), Chinchay Suyo, El Sol and Ethmopesa.

The third major area for interdepartmental buses is on Avenida América. Móvil Tours is near Ovalo Larco and Línea is midways between Ovalos Larco and Grau. Línea has in-town ticket offices at Carrión 140, a half-block from Avenida Mansiche, and at Orbegoso 300. Open Monday-Saturday 8 a.m.-9 p.m., and Sunday 8 a.m.-noon, 4-8 p.m.

To Lima: Most buses leave between 11 a.m. and 1 p.m. and from 10 p.m. to midnight, the ride takes eight to nine hours. Many companies have different levels of service that are sold for dif-ferent prices: Cial, $14-24; Cruz del Sur in addition leaves at 8:30 a.m. ($12-32); Ittsa, $19-37; Línea additionally has five buses running from 8 a.m.-noon ($12-40); and Móvil has special tick-ets for $27. Other companies that also take the route to Lima are: Oltursa, Flores, Vía, Civa and Emtrafesa.

NORTHERN COAST

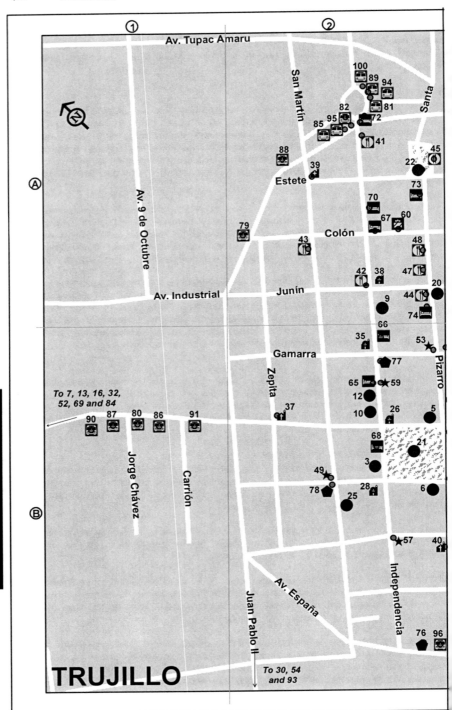

TRUJILLO

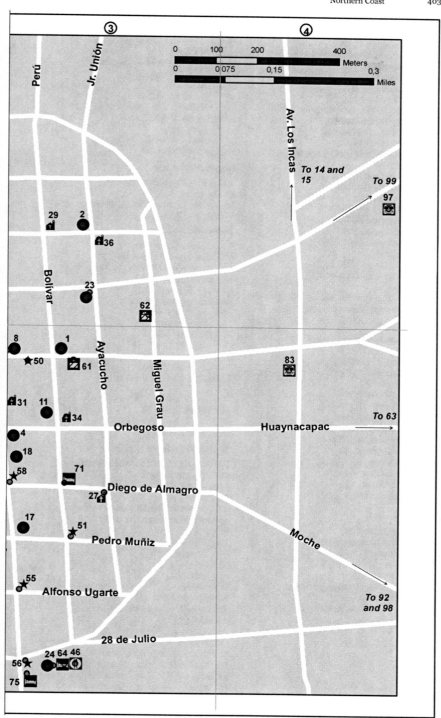

Activities

1 Aranda B3
2 Arqueológico de la UNT A3
3 Bracamonte B2
4 Calonge o Urquiaga B3
5 Catedralicio B2
6 Cavero y Muñoz B2
7 Colección Privada Cassinelli B1
8 De la Emancipación B3
9 Ganoza Chopitea A2
10 Garci Holguín B2
11 Gran Mariscal de Orbegoso B3
12 Hoyle B2
13 Huaca Arco Iris
14 Huaca de la Luna A4
15 Huaca del Sol A4
16 Huaca Esmeralda B1
17 Mayorazgo de Facalá B3
18 Municipalidad B3
19 Museo de Sitio Chan Chan
20 Palacio Iturregui A2
21 Plaza Mayor B2
22 Plazuela El Recreo A2
23 Risco A3
24 Touring y Automóvil Club del Perú B3
25 Museo de Zoología Juan Ormea B2

Churches

26 Basílica Menor Catedral B2
27 Belén B3
28 De la Compañía de Jesús B2
29 El Carmen A3
30 Huamán B2
31 La Merced B3
32 Mansiche B1
33 María del Socorro
34 San Agustín B3
35 San Francisco B2
36 San Lorenzo A3
37 Santa Ana B2
38 Santa Clara A2
39 Santa Rosa A2
40 Santo Domingo B2

Eating

41 Ajos y Maní A2
42 Café y Museo del Juguete A2
43 Canana A2
44 El Sol A2
45 El Tambo A2
46 Restaurant Romano Rincón
    Criollo B3
47 Restaurant de Marco A2
48 Restaurante Romano A2

Services ★

49 Banco de la Nación B2
50 BCP B3
51 Hospital Belén de Trujillo B3
52 Hospital Regional B1
53 Interbank B2
54 Migraciones B2
55 ScotiaBank B3
56 ScotiaBank B3
57 Serpost B2
58 Tourism Office B3
59 Tourism Police B2

Shopping

60 Liga de Artesanos A2
61 Mercado B3
62 Red de Empresarios Artesanales del
    Circuito Turístico A3

Sleeping

63 Casa de Clara B4
64 El Escudero Lodge B3
65 Hospedaje El Conde de Arce B2
66 Hostal Colonial B2
67 Hotel Ensueño A2
68 Hotel Libertador B2
69 Hotel Primavera B1
70 Korianka Hotel A2
71 Mochica B&B B3
72 Peregrino Hotel A2
73 Pullman Hotel A2
74 Real Hotel Pizarro A2
75 Residencial Vanini B3

Tour Operator

76 Chicón Tours B2
77 Guía Tours B2
78 Trujillo Tours B2

Transportation

79 Arco Iris-Chan Chan-Huanchaco A2
80 Chinchaysuyo B1
81 Cial A2
82 Civa A2
83 Combis to Huanchaco B4
84 Combis to Huanchaco B1
85 Cruz del Sur A2
86 El Sol B1
87 Elimapesa B1
88 Emtrafesa A2
89 Flores A2
90 Ittsa B1
91 Ittsa Lima Bus B1
92 Línea Bus Terminal B4
93 Móvil B2
94 Oltursa A2
95 Ormeño A2
96 Paradero Arco Iris-Chan Chan-Huanchaco B2
97 Stop for Huacas Luna y Sol A4
98 Terminal Terrestre Interprovincial B4
99 Terminal Terrestre Interurbano A4
100 Vía A2

NORTHERN COAST

To Huaraz-Línea: 9 p.m., 9:15 p.m., 9 hours ($14-24), Móvil: 9 p.m., 8:30 p.m., also to Caraz, 8-9 hours ($14).

To Cajamarca-Emtrafesa: 9:45 p.m., 6 hours, Línea: 10:30 a.m., 1:30 p.m., every 15 minutes from 10-11:30 p.m., 8 hours ($7-14)

To Jaén-Línea: 1:30 p.m., 11 p.m., 7 hours, transfer in Chiclayo ($6-8)

To Chachapoyas-Móvil: 4 p.m., 16 hours ($22)

To Tarapoto-Móvil: 3 p.m., 18 hours ($29-35)

To Chiclayo-Emtrafesa: half-hourly, 4:30 a.m.-8:30 p.m., 3 hours ($5), Línea: hourly, 3.5 hours ($4)

To Piura-Emtrafesa: 10:30 a.m., 1:30 p.m., 11:30 p.m. for 6 hours ($3), Ittsa: 1:30 p.m., 11:30 p.m., 11:45 p.m., 6 hours ($9-15), Línea: hourly 6 a.m.-4 p.m. with transfer in Chiclayo, 2:15 and 11 p.m. direct, 6-7 hours ($10-12). There are also buses to Piura with Chinchay Suyo (on to Sullana) and Ethmopesa.

To Paita-Ittsa: 11:40 p.m., 7 hours ($9)

To Máncora / Tumbes-Emtrafesa: 7 p.m., 8-10 hours ($7-9), El Sol: (8:30 p.m., 7 hours ($8)

Ormeño's north-bound international buses pass through Trujillo on their way to Guayaquil, Ecuador daily at 11:45 p.m. ($75), to Quito, Ecuador ($80), to Cali, Colombia ($145) and to Bogotá, Colombia on Monday and Fridays at 10:30 p.m.($170). More buses pass through Trujillo headed north to Cúcuta, Colombia ($180) and Caracas, Venezuela on Mondays at 10:30 p.m. ($180). For southern destinations (La Paz, Bolivia; Santiago de Chile; Mendoza and Buenos Aires, Argentina), buses leave from Lima.

Aeropuerto Carlos Martínez de Pinillos is off the highway toward Huanchaco (Tel: 51-44-464-013). A taxi to the airport costs $3.35-5. Huanchaco combis drop you off about one kilometer (0.6 miles) from the airport. LanPeru has three daily flights to Lima (starting at $129, 1 hour) (Monday-Friday 9 a.m.-7 p.m., Saturday 9 a.m.-12:30 p.m., Amaru 490, Tel: 20-1859).

Getting Around

Taxis around town typically cost $1, and more for longer distances. A combi ride within the city limits costs $0.25-0.40.

Safety in Trujillo

Visitors are warned frequently about walking beyond the Avenida España ring that circles the city, as well as walking in the vicinity of the bus stations. Other problematic areas, even in daylight, are the Buenos Aires Beach and the roads near Chan Chan, Huaca Arco Iris, Huaca Esmeraldas (especially) and Huaca El Brujo. It is better to take tours through agencies to these places or hire a taxi. Take exceptional care at the bus stop to Huacas Luna and Sol and at the Terminal Terrestre Interurbano, where many drug addicts and drunks hang out on the street, waiting to rob pedestrians. Best to take a taxi.

TRUJILLO SERVICES

Trujillo's iPeru office has good maps and information about the city and surrounding region Open Monday-Saturday 8 a.m.-6:30 p.m. and Sunday 8 a.m.-2 p.m. Jirón Pizarro 402, Mezzanine, Tel. / Fax: 51-44-294-561, E-mail: perutrujillo@promperu.gob.pe, URL: www.peru.info/eng/lalibertad.

Other useful addresses are:
· Tourism police (daily 8 a.m.-8 p.m. Jirón Independencia 630, tel.: 51-44-291-705)
· Touring y Automóvil Club del Perú (Argentina 258, Urb. El Recreo, via Huanchaco, Tel.: 51-44-603-131, Fax: 51-44-290-736, E-mail: trujillo@touringperu.com.pe)
· Consulates: Chile (Avenida Juan Pablo II 893, Dpto. 303, Tel.: 51-44-285-869), Finland (Avenida Perú s/n, Las Delicias, Tel.: 51-44-465-265), Italy (Túpac Yupanqui 990, Urb. Santa María, Tel.: 51-44-235-026), Spain (Guillermo Charum 238, Urb. San Andrés, Tel.: 51-44-465-265), United Kingdom (Flor de Canela 885, Urb. Las Palmeras del Golf, Tel.: 51-44-245-935).

Shopping

Like all major cities in Latin America, Trujillo has its share of chain shopping malls and supermarkets selling typical global corporate products. For tourists with more specialized tastes, the Gamarra neighborhood has a number of clothing shops. The Museo de Arqueología and the Museo Cassinelli sell Chimú and Moche ceramics, and Avenida España offers a craft market. Neighboring Huanchaco has more options, including a folk art market along its beach that sells jewelry and other crafts.

THINGS TO SEE AND DO IN TRUJILLO

As one of Peru's largest cities, Trujillo has a wide variety of activities within and surrounding the city to keep even the most stir crazy tourists entertained. In Trujillo's Plaza de Armas, you can watch the locals stroll about this quaint park. Trujillo has a couple of museums, including Museo del Juguete and Museo de Arqueología. The colonial mansions are also worth a visit, many have been maintained and give you a sense of what things were like here hundreds of years ago. Outside of Trujillo many archaeological sites are worth your exploration.

Plaza de Armas

All of the downtown city streets lead to the plaza where a baroque-style center monument that salutes liberty, created by Edmundo Müller can be seen. Or, as is always allowed, you can pass the day in this open and grandiose plaza.

Visiting Colonial Mansions

As a historically commercial center, Trujillo is home to a number of colonial mansions. The following are visiting hours for the most popular: Casa del Mayorazgo, 9:15 to 12:30, Mon. to Fri. Casa Bracamonte, visits restricted. Casa Ganoza Chopitea and Casa de la Emancipación, 9:15 a.m. to 12:30 p.m. and 4:00 to 6:30 p.m., Monday to Friday.

Museo de Arqueología (Entrance: $1.70 Adults, $0.35 Students)

Highly recommended by the guides of the archaeological sites outside of town, the museum highlights the distinct pre-Hispanic cultures of the region. On display here are reproductions of murals found in Huaca de la Luna, which is presently under excavation. Open Monday, 9:30 a.m.-2 p.m., Tuesday-Friday, 9:15 a.m.-1 p.m., Saturday-Sunday, 9:30 a.m.-4 p.m. Junín 682. Tel: 51-44-249-322

Museo del Juguete

If you make it to Café y Museo del Juguete, definitely take the trip upstairs to the Museo del Juguete, where you will encounter a modest but interesting display of rattlers, whistles, figurines, and other Chancay, Moche and Chimú toys dating as far back as 1000 BC. Art aficionados should walk over to the gallery next door where there are paintings by Gerado Chavez and his lesser-known brother. Open Monday-Saturday from 10 a.m.to 6 p.m., and Sunday from 10 a.m. to 1 p.m. Independencia 705. Tel: 51-44-297-200.

More Trujillo Museums

Museo de Historia Natural de la UPAO has a collection of flora, fauna and fossils of the region (Monday-Friday 8 a.m.-noon, 3-5 p.m., Saturday 8 a.m.-noon., Avenida América Sur 3145. Entry: free).

Museo de Zoología Juan Ormea Rodríguez has exhibits of taxidermy animals and birds from the coastal and Andean regions (Monday-Friday 7 a.m.-7 p.m., Jirón San Martín 368. Entry: foreigners $0.70, national adults $0.20, students $0.10).

Museo de Arte Moderno exhibits local artist Gerardo Chávez's personal collection of works by Guzmán, Wifredo Lam and others, as well as his own work (Monday-Saturday 9:30 a.m.-5:30 p.m., Sunday 9:30 a.m.-2 p.m., Prolongación Avenida Francisco Villareal y Carretera Industial Km 3.5, Tel: 51-44-215-668. Entry: adults $3.35, children $1.70).

Museo Catedrálico has religious art and a mural-decorated crypt (Monday-Friday 9 a.m.-1 p.m., 4-7 p.m., Jirón Orbegoso 419, Plaza de Armas, adjoining the cathedral. Entry: adults $1.35, university students $0.70, children $0.35).

Museo Cassinelli houses more than 6,000 pieces of pre-Columbian pottery, jewelry, textiles and musical instruments (daily 9:30 a.m.-1 p.m., 3-7 p.m., Avenida Nicolás de Piérola 607. Entry: free).

NOTE: Most museums are centrally located. For the Museo de Arte Moderno: on Avenida Los Incas, catch a north-bound "A-Huanchaco" combi. Tell the driver to let you off at La Villa Real, which is a half block from the museum ($0.50). A taxi costs about $3 one way.

TRUJILLO TOURS
Chacón Tours
Recommended by many, Chacón Tours offer a number of tours in and around Trujillo. It prides itself on the ability to provide tours in five languages. Chacón Tours is open daily, although get there early on Sundays—it closes at 2 p.m.The office can also assist in booking flights with most of the major airlines. Don't bother with its website—it is a disappointing array of unhelpful links. Instead, drop by and chat with its staff about what you want. España 106-112, Tel: 51-44-246-245 / 51-44-255-722, E-mail: chacontours@terra.com.pe, URL: www.chacontours.com.

Guía Tours
In operation since 1975, Guía Tours is a reliable choice for your Trujillo tour. It provides two to four-day excursions in Trujillo, as well as in Chiclayo and Cajamarca. The four-day Trujillo tour takes in the unforgettable Chan Chan, the Pirámides Sol y Luna, El Brujo and a Trujillo city tour, interspersed with trips to museums. The two-day Trujillo option is limited to Chan Chan and the Trujillo city tour, with stops at the museums. Jr. Independencia 580, Tel: 51-44-245-170, E-mail: guiattru@guiatours.com.pe, URL: www.guiatours.com.pe.

Trujillo Tours
A good bet, Trujillo Tours offer a number of half-day options including city tours and outings to Pirámides Sol y Luna, Chan Chan and Huanchaco. Tours by knowledgeable guides are available in several languages. Daily, 9 a.m.-1 p.m., 4-8 p.m. Diego de Almagro 301, Tel: 51-44-233-091, E-mail: ttours@terra.com.pe.

TRUJILLO LODGING
Because Trujillo is a popular stop along the South American tourist trail, the city offers an abundance of hotel types and locations. From budget hostels ($3 and above) to upscale luxury hotels ($100-150), Trujillo can accommodate almost any traveler's needs. For those interested in exploring the city and its numerous architectural attractions, it is wise to look for lodging in the downtown district, which has a pleasant colonial feel, but can also be noisy and overcrowded. Those in search of a more relaxed atmosphere may want to look for a place to stay in nearby Huanchaco (p.413), only 12 kilometers (7.5 mi) from Trujillo. This laid-back beach town is also an excellent choice for those heading towards Chan Chan. Whether you choose a hotel in Trujillo or nearby Huanchaco, it is a good idea to make reservations beforehand, especially if traveling in September when the Festival Internacional de la Primavera y la Marinera is held and the city swells with visitors.

BUDGET
Hospedaje El Conde de Arce (Rooms: $5 - 7)
This quaint little hospedaje provides an inviting and tranquil atmosphere away from the bustle of Trujillo's city center and the other hotels in Trujillo. In addition to offering hot water and rates that are a fraction of what you pay at neighboring establishments, Hospedaje El

NORTHERN COAST

Conde de Arce also comes with Carmilla, the extremely friendly owner who is sure to mother anyone who walks through the door. Independencia 577, Tel: 51-44-291-607.

Hospedaje Huascar (Rooms: $5 - 9)

On a cul-de-sac off Avenida Los Incas, five blocks from the Plaza de Armas, is a budget traveler's find. The neighborhood edges on a bit sketchy, but Hospedaje Huascar is reported to be a safe retreat. Rooms come with private or common bath and vary in size and quality, so check several before accepting one. In general, the two-person rooms are sufficiently large. Also, all areas of this second-floor hotel are kept clean. Huáscar 453, Tel: 51-44-243-869.

Casa de Clara (Rooms: $7 - 17)

For newcomers seeking a bit more information on activities in Trujillo, Casa de Clara is an excellent choice among Trujillo's hotels. The establishment is run by Clara Bravo and Michael White, both helpful and experienced tour guides who collectively speak German, French, Italian and English. Groups can be accommodated, and tours can be organized for any day of the week. Facilities include hot showers/baths, games, barbecue, sun patio, garden, library, music area, two cable TV lounges, videos and more. Meals can also be arranged per request. Cahuide 495, Tel: 51-44-299-997, E-mail: microbewhite@yahoo.com.

V!VA Member Review- Casa de Clara

In a quiet park away from the traffic congestion, fumes & honking. Everything you need in one place. Good, cheap, typical meals. Loads of info on tours. Cable TV, fast free internet with wireless for my laptop. Many languages spoken. International library & book swap.

Australia, Apr 12, 2008

Residencial Vanini (Rooms: $7 - 24)

In terms of the hotels in Trujillo, Residencial Vanini is probably the best budget option. Run by the charismatic Señora Marcela Vanini, who converted her family home into a hotel after her seven children grew up, Residencial Vanini offers half a dozen wood cabins on the roof, with shared showers. The terrace is an ideal spot to relax and enjoy a few drinks, or perhaps take in a sunset. Slightly more expensive rooms inside the house come with private bathrooms, and are conveniently located near the only phone and TV. Av. Larco 237, Tel: 51-44-200-878, E-mail: enriqueva@hotmail.com.

MID-RANGE

El Escudero Lodge (Rooms: $13 - 30)

El Escudero Lodge provides you with comfortable, super clean, hot/cold water, private baths, cable TV, internet service, telephone, laundry service and a helpful and accommodating staff. Puerto Rico 361,Urb. El Recreo (In a taxi: Close to Ave 29 de Diciembre y Santo Domingo, El Recreo Urbanization), Tel: 51-44-294665, E-mail: elescuderolodge@hotmail.com, URL: www.elescuderolodge.com.

Hotel Primavera (Rooms: $15 - 27)

The Hotel Primavera is far from the center of Trujillo, in a relatively safe neighborhood and within walking distance of a local bus terminal for travelers wanting to head north to Ecuador or south to Lima. The building and its rooms seem fairly new, making the starting price of $15 for a single room not unreasonable. Av. Nicolás de Piérola 872, Tel: 51-44-231-915

Mochica's Bed and Breakfast (Rooms: $18 - 29)

Mochica's Bed and Breakfast provides a familiar atmosphere where you'll feel like you're at home during your visit. The comfortable rooms are nicely decorated and come with private bath and closets. Warm and personal attention and low rates make it a good choice. Prices include breakfast. Located 15 minutes from Huanchaco Beach, 5 minutes from commercial centers, banks, bars, restaurants, discotheques and close to the bus station. Mz. E, Lt. 19, La Arboleda, Tel / Fax: 51-44-422-006, E-mail: ventas@mochicas.com, URL: www.mochicas.com.

Hostel Colonial (Rooms: $19 - 29)
Small, but attractive rooms and an inviting courtyard decorated with Huanchaco's reed boats set Hostel Colonial apart from other hotels in Trujillo. An intimate reading area downstairs is the perfect place to thumb through guidebooks or plan an itinerary, and the hotel's restaurant/café will ensure that you don't go to bed on an empty stomach. Room service is also available. If you prefer a little more peace and quiet, be sure to ask for a room away from the street. Independencia 618, Tel: 52-44-258-261.

HIGH-END
Real Hotel Pizarro (Rooms: $27 and up)
The Real Hotel Pizarro is close to Trujillo's main square and historic buildings, and offers its guests Internet access, breakfast, room service and airport pick-up. Yet, with all that, the single rooms offered here at $27 a night are singularly unattractive: small, cramped and narrow. The double-sized rooms and matrimonial suites fare better. It also has laundry service and accepts all credit cards, which is not often the case with many other hotels in Trujillo. Still, there are better places in the area—with cheaper rates. Jr. Pizarro 651, Tel: 51-44-257-416.

La Alameda del Peregrino (Rooms: $30 - 40)
Of the hotels in Trujillo, La Alameda de Peregrino is one of the few that offers a tranquil atmosphere away from the noise of honking *taxistas* and city traffic. All rooms are clean and attractive, equipped with phone, cable TV, and refrigerators, and some enjoy excellent views of the city. The hotel also has internet and laundry service, a tour agency, safe, money exchange, café, bar and a restaurant offering a variety of Peruvian dishes ($2-6). The English-speaking owner is also very helpful. Pizzaro 879, Tel: 51-44-470-512, E-mail: alamedaperegrino@via-bcp.com, URL: www.perunorte.com/alamedaperegrino.

Peregrino Hotel (Rooms: $30 - 40)
Travelers in Trujillo looking for a more upscale accommodation and willing to spend more for it should consider the Peregrino Hotel. Besides such usual amenities as cable TV (with DVD players) and breakfast, the rooms come with a fridge-bar. The hotel has its own restaurant and bar, offers a "business center" and a conference room, Internet access, airport pickup and drop-off, medical service, laundry service, tourist information, as well as tours. They take all credit cards, and you will feel like you got your money's worth. Jiron Independencia 978, Tel: 51-44-203-989, E-mail: hotelperegrino@mixmail.com, URL: www.peregrinohotel.com.

Korianka Hotel (Rooms: $30 - 65)
The Korianka is not only a luxury hotel—and priced accordingly—but one that actively seeks to outdo the competition in Trujillo. For example: not only does it have internet access, but WiFi. With rooms priced rather high, you can expect everything else, including air conditioning (useful in this hot and humid city), rather than just an electric fan. The matrimonial suites have their very own Jacuzzis. There is also room service, bar and restaurant, and swimming pool. Independencia 808, Tel: 51-44-295-931, E-mail: informes@korianka.com, URL: www.korianka.com.

Hotel Libertador (Rooms: $80 - 121)
Hotel Libertador is a small chain of luxury hotels in Peru. The Hotel Libertador Trujillo is right on the Plaza de Armas, convenient to the airport, downtown and the ruins at Chan Chan. The hotel offers everything you would expect from a luxury hotel: good service, decadent surroundings, sauna, jewelry store and more. Even if you're not staying here, you may want to consider eating at the Las Bovedas restaurant, which offers good local cuisine and seafood. The Malabrigo bar affords a great view of the square. Prices do not include taxes and service

NORTHERN COAST

fees. Breakfast is included. Jr. Independencia 485, Tel: 51-44-232-741, Fax: 51-44-235-641, E-mail: trujillo@libertador.com.pe, URL: www.libertador.com.pe/ingles/libereng.htm.

TRUJILLO RESTAURANTS

Trujillo offers a variety of culinary options to visitors, and is a great place to sample a bit of everything. To test your palate with some of the local food, head towards the restaurants around Plazuela El Recreo, where you'll find less expensive traditional dishes like *cabrito de leche* (goat cooked in milk), *arroz con pato* (rice with duck), or *shambar* (wheat soup with beans and pork). If you've got money to burn and are looking for something with a bit more class, then take your pick of international cafés lining the seventh block of Pizarro. Although the nearby town of Huanchaco is better known for its seafood, Trujillo also has a few cheap seafood restaurants, located near Plazuela El Recreo.

The *menú*, or daily special, is served mostly at lunch. The price ranges from $1.35 to $5, with cheaper eateries being found on Orbegoso and along Ayacucho, as well as near the bus terminals. The mercado is at Ayacucho and Gamarra.

Café y Museo del Juguete ($.50 - 7)

At Café y Museo del Juguete you can sip on a cup of coffee while you stroll through the Peruvian past. Perhaps the classiest café in Trujillo, this place has an old-world-Paris feel accented by walls covered with photographs of Mario Vargas Llosa and numerous Peruvian intellectuals who have frequented the joint. In addition to the ambience, you will surely enjoy their house drink, *mistella*, or any one of their sandwiches, tamales or soups. A portion of the proceeds go upstairs to the Museo del Juguete. Open Monday through Saturday from 10 a.m. to midnight. Closed Sunday. Jr. Independencia 701, Tel: 51-44-297-200.

Restaurant Romano (Entrees: $1 - 9)

Of the restaurants in Trujillo, Restaurant Romano offers visitors a mixed-bag of options. Choose to relax in its smaller café where you can sample some of Trujillo's best coffee and desserts, or head over to the larger dining room where you can eat to the beat of trendy dance music. The restaurant offers a variety of menu options, available in both sections, from meat dishes to vegetarian sandwiches. Open daily from 7:30 a.m. to midnight. Pizzaro 747, Tel: 51-44-252-251.

El Sol (Entrees: $1.50 - 5)

If you prefer carrots to *carne* (meat) then head over to El Sol, one of the best vegetarian restaurants in Trujillo. Offering cheap set vegetarian meals in addition to other dishes, this restaurant is the perfect compromise for meat lovers and vegetarians alike. Pizarro 671.

El Tambo (Entrees: $2 - 5)

Grabbing a table outside El Tambo, however, is like having ringside seats to nightlife in the city center. As one of the main footpaths between the city center and nearby bus stations, the *plazuela* is a constant parade of bus bound commuters, corn and *parrilla* street vendors, and giggling teenagers. Although occupying an outdoor table is an open invitation for frequent sales pitches from candy-peddling kids, most of them are more interested in practicing their English than actually selling anything. If you're uninterested in conversation with local children, take a seat indoors, where the proprietors like to rock out to Bowie and Madonna circa 1985. With a traditional Peruvian menu to help you wash down some ice cold Pilsen Trujillo, the highlight of the menu is the platter of *pescado y chicharrones*, which at only $3 easily feeds three people. The woman who owns the place is a gracious host who doesn't forget a face. Food is served from 10 a.m. to 3 p.m., and drinks are available until 10 p.m. Francisco Pizarro 922.

Canana (Entrees: $3 - 6)

A popular dish served up by many restaurants in Trujillo is *criollo*, and at Canana you can enjoy this traditional entree with a side of traditional Peruvian dance. If you're brave enough to test your foot-stomping skills, you can bust a move with some of Trujillo's best *bailadores*

NORTHERN COAST

in the enormous stage-and-dance area. To limber up you may want to order *una jarra de cerveza* (a pitcher of beer) or try one of the enticing mixed drinks. After 11 p.m. on Friday and Saturday, traditional Peruvian music is played. San Martín 791, Tel: 51-44-295-422.

Restaurante Romano Rincón Criollo (Entrees: $4 - 10)

Restaurante Romano Rincón Criollo is a great place to taste the local cuisine. This is where Trujillians go to enjoy the most important meal of the day, lunch. Specializing in northern Peruvian cuisine, this restaurant offers several traditional favorites for you to sample, among which the *tacu tacu,* served with a rich shrimp sauce comes highly recommended. Los Estados Unidos 162, Tel: 51-44-244-207.

V!VA Member Review- Restaurante Romano Rincón Criollo

I love the restaurant location, prices, great menu, and service. I spend a month in Peru and I went back to Romano's at least 10 times during our stay. I recommend the *ceviches and tacu tacu,* but my favorite was "The Causa Trujillana." Tasty, colorful, simple, perfection!

USA, Jun 25, 2007

Mochica (Entrees: $4 - 10)

Occasional live music and heaping plates of traditional criolla cooking make Mochica a popular choice among restaurants in Trujillo. Characterized by white plastic chairs, a large TV in the front room and waiters decked out in black ties, this place is praised for providing well-prepared food at a reasonable price. A few of the favorite dishes include roasted guinea pig and *parilladas* (mixed grilled meats), and for the sea-struck customer fresh fish like *corvina* (sea bass). If you're feeling like a big meal in the middle of the day, you can also try one of their inexpensive fixed lunch menus. Open daily from 8 a.m. to 10:30 p.m. Bolívar 462, Tel: 51-44-224-247.

THINGS TO SEE AND DO NEAR TRUJILLO

The Pyramids of the Sun and Moon

For those interested in archaeological activities, the massive Moche pyramids of Huaca del Sol and Huaca de la Luna located 5 kilometers (13 mi) south of Trujillo are a must see. At 45 meters (148 ft) high, Huaca del Sol was the largest man-made structure in the western hemisphere before it was partly destroyed by Spaniards during a massive treasure hunt.

Sitting at the base of Cerro Blanco, these mud-brick remains of the ceremonial capital of the Moche State afford visitors a rare glimpse into ancient Moche civilization. These two massive structures were once divided by the homes of nearly 15,000 of the city's nobles, while suburbs housing over 20,000 commoners stretched outward from the central city.

While meandering through these ancient structures be sure to keep an eye out for repeated images of the anthropomorphic god Aie-Paec, endearingly nicknamed the Decapitator, which often adorn the pottery and frescoes of surrounding sites.

Archaeologists are peeling away layers to discover more about these ancient ruins and are constantly discovering and displaying new friezes of stylized figures. Reproductions of some murals are on display at Trujillo's Museo de Arqueología (Archaeology Museum).

From the *paradero* (bus stop) at Jirón Suárez, one block from Avenida Los Incas, or from Terminal Terrestre Interurbano, take a van to Campo de Moche. Note: The neighborhoods around the bus terminal and bus stop are not safe; take a taxi. Walking between the sites, there is a risk of assault and robbery as well. To avoid all this hassle, most people take a tour ($10).

Chan Chan

Chan Chan, five kilometers (3 mi) west of Trujillo, the largest pre-Columbian city in South America, was the capital of the Chimú kingdom. It dates from around 1300 AD. Some archaeologists believe Chan Chan was the largest adobe city ever. There were also nine sub-cities each ruled by a different sovereign. Around 100,000 residents inhabited 10,000 buildings in the main city. The city was used to store large quantities of gold, silver and ceramics, that were completely looted within two decades of the Spanish arrival. Sadly, not much remains of the original city due to heavy downpours and tomb robbers, or *huaqueros*. The best-preserved section of the city today is the Tschudi Complex. The complex still features friezes and courtyards as well as some original walls; the other walls have been restored.

Tours go to all four sites on the ticket, though some outfits omit Huaca Esmeraldas, for the danger ($7 average). To go on your own, hop on a Huanchaco combi and alight at the site or the museum ($0.35). Taxi to Chan Chan, Huaca Esmeraldas and Huaca Arco Iris costs between $1.70-7 per person (depending on size of group and ability to negotiate), with wait. It is best to take another combi between the museum and site, or go in a large group, due to robberies and assaults.

El Brujo

Once an important site used by the witches of Chicama, El Brujo (The Sorcerer) is a network of ruins and mounds dating back over 5,000 years. Situated in the Chicama Valley 60 kilometers (37 mi) from Trujillo, this archaeological gem remains remarkably unscathed by the grave robbers and tourists who destroyed many of the ruins closer to Trujillo.

The complex, which is considered to be one of the most important archaeological sites on the northern coast, served as a ceremonial center and meeting place for nearly ten cultures, among them the Moche. Stretching across 2 kilometers (1.2 mi), El Brujo consists of a long wall decorated with high-relief, stylized figures, and three pyramidal temples, Huaca Prieta, Huaca Corta and Huaca Cao Viejo.

Cao Viejo is one of the most popular attractions, where inside you'll encounter polychromatic reliefs that

Chan Chan—The Rise and Fall of a Kingdom

Comprised of high walled citadels decorated with religious motifs, and featuring a tangle of passages leading to ceremonial rooms, reservoirs, burial chambers, and temples, this archaeological ghost town is now a haunting token of what once was the mighty Chimú kingdom. In addition, Chan Chan is not only larger than Machu Picchu, but is the largest pre-Columbian city in South America.

The Chimú was the last Peruvian civilization before the rise of the Incan empire, and Chan Chan was its heart, whose inhabitants – the Chimor – numbered up to 30,000. Spread across the northern coast of Peru, Chan Chan extends 5 km (3 mi) west of Trujillo and roughly about 20 km (16 mi) wide.

As a society, the Chimor lasted for over six hundred years. Legend has it that their first ruler, Taycanamo, arrived on a log raft, wearing a cotton breechcloth and bringing magic yellow powers, proclaiming "a great lord sent him to govern this land from across the sea." Chan Chan began with Taycanamo's construction of a shrine upon which he used his yellow powders to perform rituals.

Through a combination of military force and irrigation mastery, the city and kingdom founded Aycanamo, which expanded and prospered through a succession of nine emperors. Much of what had once been arid land was converted into fertile fields through creative irrigation. In the course of events manifesting a renaissance in artwork and pottery amongst the Chimor.

The Chimú kingdom prevailed until falling to Incan conquerors in the 15th century, and shortly thereafter the Spanish. However, in Chan Chan the legacy of their culture has survived. In 1986, UNESCO officially declared Chan Chan a World Heritage Center.

display scenes from Mochica life. Among these archaeological attractions, you'll find depictions of prisoners, warriors, dancers and human sacrifices, in addition to well-preserved remains that highlight the burial practices implemented by Mochican royalty.

NOTE: To see the site, you must begin your journey to the site no later than 1 p.m.

HUANCHACO

Just 14 kilometers (8.7 mi) north of the popular tourist city of Trujillo is Huanchaco, a laid-back beach town that is definitely worth the trip for anyone seeking a respite from the rigors of travel. According to Chimú mythology, this peaceful fishing village was the landing-spot of Takaynamo, the founder of the ancient empire who supposedly ordered the construction of the famous adobe city of Chan Chan around 1200 AD.

Today, Huanchaco is a beloved *playa* hang-out for Peruvians and foreigners alike. Due to its popularity among beach bums, this modest town offers a variety of hotels and restaurants to suit any traveler's budget. In addition to accommodation, there exist a variety of attractions
in town, including an artisan market, mouth-watering seafood (check out Lucho del Mar), relaxed nightlife and surfing lessons, to name a few.

Early risers can observe the town's fishermen mounting their *caballitos de totora*, beautifully crafted, narrow, pointed fishing rafts that appear on both Mochica and Chimú pottery. Or, if you're up for a climb, head up to Santuario de la Virgen del Socorro, reportedly the second-oldest church in Peru. Regardless of where you stay or what you do, the general attitude in Huanchaco is that you can have a lot of fun doing very little.

Help other travelers. Publish your favorite places at www.vivatravelguides.com

Getting To and Away from Huanchaco

Three combi routes run between Trujillo and Huanchaco: A, B and H-Corazón (daily 6:30 a.m.-8 p.m. $0.40-0.50). From this coastal village into the city, Ruta B passes by Avenida El Ejército, where the Cruz del Sur, Civa and other bus offices are (see Getting To and Away From Trujillo). Ruta H-Corazón swings by Línea and Móvil on Avenida América. All pass within a few blocks of those terminals on Avenida Mansiche near Óvalo Cassinelli. You can catch any of them along the seafront. A taxi costs $3.35 one way.

Safety in Huanchaco

Please remember that regardless of where you choose to pull up a piece of sand for a little beachside relaxation, be sure your belongings are always attached to your person and never leave anything unattended while you swim. A number of clever robberies have recently occurred on Huanchaco's beaches, and in most cases, it was the theft of a bag sitting right beside its owner. Don't forget the sunscreen. Even on cloudy days the sun at Huanchaco is deceptively strong.

While wild camping on the beach is not recommended, due to safety concerns, it is okay to do so during the Christmas-New Years holidays, at either end of the beach, when safety comes in numbers. However, still use common sense to protect your gear.

The village has evacuation plans in the case of tsunamis. Green signs along Avenida la Ribera point out the routes. Follow instructions and head for higher ground, like the Santuario de la Virgen del Socorro up on the hill.

Getting Around

Taxis and mototaxis cruise Huanchaco's few streets, charging $1 and $0.50 respectively. In 2003, the city renumbered street addresses, making it a bit confusing to find establishments, especially as most still use the old number.

HUANCHACO SERVICES

Only during the summer months (December-March) does the tourism information kiosk next to the pier operate.

Two ATMs serve Huanchaco: to the left of the Municipalidad (La Ribera 725) is a Global Net one, accepting Visa, Plus, Cirrus, MasterCard, American Express and Diners Club cards. To the right of city hall is a BBVA *cajero*, taking only Visa and Plus. Several businesses along Avenida La Ribera change US dollars and Euros, including Huanchaco Multiservice (Av. La Ribera 284, Tel.: 51-62-462-407).

Only a few internet cafés are to be had in the village. Internet Primavera (Las Gardenias 242) and Internet Speedy (Los Pinos 185) are closed Sundays. Kmek on the main drag has Skype and exchanges money (daily 8 a.m.-10 p.m. Av. La Ribera 733). *Locutorios* are common. Serpost is here to drop a quick line to family and friends (Monday-Friday 2-6:30 p.m., Saturday 1-6 p.m. Manco Cápac 306).

Centro de Salud, Huanchaco's basic health post, provides round-the-clock service (Jirón Atahualpa 128, Tel.: 51-62-461-547). Four boticas, or pharmacies, exist. Two are on Los Pinos, between Los Helechos and Los Sauces, a third on the corner of the Plaza de Armas, and the fourth near the corner of Unión and Huáscar.

Chill Out has next-day laundry service at $1.70 per kilogram (Los Pinos 437, Tel.: 46-2320).

Gran Feria Artesenal

For a town that hosts thousands of national and international tourists year round, there's not much shopping to be done in Huanchaco. The largest collection of souvenirs in one spot is at the Gran Feria Artesenal on La Ribera, open daily from 8 a.m. to 7 p.m. Compared to the artisanal markets in larger Peruvian cities, this one may be a bit disappointing in terms of size. In fact, if you're not looking for it, it's certainly possible to miss it altogether as the entrance from the street is a small understated door in a larger complex that includes Western Union and several restaurants.

Typical wares include t-shirts, leather sandals, jewelry, key chains, purses and knick-knacks. The nearly two dozen booths all sell seemingly identical merchandise, but the market does have two advantages over other shopping areas off the beach. First is its proximity to one of the few ATMs in town, which happens to be just out front, and second is its beachside restaurant, which is one of two restaurants in Huanchaco located directly on the beach rather than across the street from it. The menu is typical Peruvian seafood, but the majority of the clientele is more interested in sipping ice cold Inca Kola and Pilsen Trujillo while watching the beach scene than having a bite to eat.

Artesanía Shopping
A few different outlets provide decent shopping along the *malecón*. In Huanchaco, the souvenir of all souvenirs is something to remind you of the distinctive reed boats used for fishing. Try Galería Artesanal Takaynamo, a market of about 20 shops that's just north of the pier, Av. Victor Larco 620.

THINGS TO SEE AND DO IN HUANCHACO
Huanchaco is the ultimate in relaxed atmosphere, good surfing and great seafood. The weekends and high seasons get lively with Trujillanos and other Peruvians looking for their yearly dose of rest and relaxation. The rest of the year is made for the foreigners, though. The kilometers of beaches, like Playa Varadero, make for great beachcombing strolls, and at the north end of the beach you can see how tortora reeds, used in the *caballitos* grow. Sit on the seawall with your honey and watch the sunset, then have a romantic dinner and some drinks. Life's uncomplicated here.

Playa El Varadero
It doesn't take long to figure out that the Playa El Varadero is where most of the action happens in Huanchaco. Tourists and locals alike converge on the sidewalk bordering the beach, beating a path from one end to the other and back. Weekends are especially chaotic when busloads of tourists empty onto the beach, which is little more than a sliver between high tide and the tall sea wall.

It's here where wannabe surfers make their first forays into the breaking waves, but you'll have to be brave to endure the chilly water without a wet suit. If sunbathing is more your speed, you may want to head about 100 meters (328 ft) south, just beyond the pier where it's a bit less crowded.

Playa El Varadero is also the place to catch a ride on Huanchaco's infamous caballitos, or reed boats. The boats line the sea wall and their owners are always willing to paddle tourists around for a small fee. Surprisingly, one of the most popular things to do at Varadero is simply take a seat on the sea wall and hang out. From there, you can watch the action on the beach, sort through the goods of passing street vendors, enjoy an ice cream, and if you're lucky, eavesdrop on an impromptu concert from local beach bums just enjoying the sun. And on the subject of sun, don't forget the sunscreen while soaking in the powerful Peruvian *sol*.

Surfing Lessons ($10.50 - 15 / 2 hours of instruction)
The surf is up in Huanchaco if you can handle it. Peruvian long board champions of long ago now give lessons to those eager enough to learn. Beware, the water is freezing and requires a wetsuit, and what's more, the beach is rough on the feet. Nonetheless, the prices and the instructional knowledge are worth it. Walk along the malecón (beach boardwalk) to compare prices offered at the different surf shops. Guide, surfboard and

NORTHERN COAST

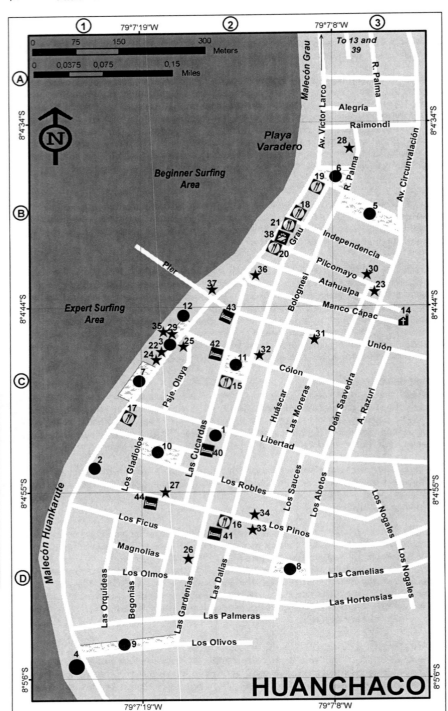

HUANCHACO

Activities ●
1 Área Cultural C2
2 Galería de Arte Club Colonial C3
3 Gran Feria Artesanal C2
4 Parador Turístico Quibisich D1
5 Parque Centenario B3
6 Parque El Pescador B3
7 Parque Huankarute C1
8 Parque Las Camelias D2
9 Parque Los Olivos D1
10 Parque Los Robles C2
11 Plaza de Armas C2
12 Plaza San Martín C2
13 Totorales A3

Churches ⛪
14 Nuestra Señora del Socorro C3

Eating 🍴
15 Casa Tere C2
16 Chill Out D2
17 El Kero C1
18 El Mochica B2
19 La Mamacha B2
20 Lucho del Mar B2
21 The Wave B2

Services ★
22 BBVA ATM C2
23 Centro Médico B3
24 GlobalNet ATM C2
25 Huanchaco Multiservices C2
26 Internet Primavera D2
27 Internet Speedy D2
28 Jean Louis Studio B3
29 Kmek C2
30 Mercado Zonal B3
31 Pharmacy C2
32 Pharmacy C2
33 Pharmacy D2
34 Pharmacy D2
35 Policía C2
36 Serpost B2
37 Tourism Kiosk B2

Shopping 🛍
38 Galería Artesanal Takaynamo B2

Sleeping 🛏
39 Hostal Camping Naylamp A3
40 Hostal Los Tres Delfines C2
41 Hostal Solange D2
42 Huanchaco Hostal C2
43 La Esquina C2
44 My Friend Hospedaje D2

wetsuit are usually part of the deal. To start, try The Wave, which is just north of the pier. Av. Larco 640, Tel: 51-62-587-005.

Cultural Activities
It isn't just all surf and sun in Huanchaco. There is a rising tide of fine art and other cultural spaces in this fishing village. Galería de Arte Club Colonial has regular exhibits featuring national artists. The opening night receptions are bound to be tasteful affairs, as Club Colonial is also one of Huanchaco's oldest up-scale restaurants (Open daily 1-11 p.m. Av. La Ribera 514, Tel: 51-44-461-015, 41-44-471-639).

Drop by Chiclayano Joan Louis' studio to view his works and chat about his contemporary paintings, based on classical Peruvian symbology (Irregular hours. Ricardo Palma 240, Tel: 949-33-5076, E-mail: arte@joanlouis.com, URL: www.joanlouis.com).

Huanchaco's Area Cultural has a permanent exhibit of photographs and artesanía, hosts cultural events and presentations, and shows a free video every Friday at 6:30 p.m. (Monday-Friday 8 a.m.-4 p.m. Libertad 204). The public library is next door.

STUDYING SPANISH
Spanish lessons ($3 - 6 / hour)
One can't surf all day. Why not use your time wisely and give Spanish lessons a good old college try? A number of places offer quality classes at a fraction of the price you would find back home. Where Spanish lessons and surfing go hand-in-hand, try negotiating a good price at The Wave. Larco 525, 51-44-587-005. Additionally, the recently opened Idiomatrix Language Academy in Huanchaco charges about $3 an hour for group lessons. They are open every day until 9:00 pm, so you can earn your certificate in the evenings while surfing during the day. Larco 502, Tel: 51-44-232-664, E-mail:spanish@idiomatrix.net, URL: www.idiomatrix.net.

NORTHERN COAST

Help other travelers. Publish your favorite places at www.vivatravelguides.com

VOLUNTEERING IN HUANCHACO

Volunteer at Serendipity Kids

A great way to really help the poorest local kids, while learning Spanish. To get there, go north along the beach front street until you get to Otra Cosa and ask for Juany Murphy. Las Camelias 431 (Headquartered in Trujillo, Av. Larco 385), Tel: 51-44-232-664, E-mail: info@serendipitykids.org, URL: www.serendipitykids.org.

HUANCHACO LODGING

This blossoming tourist spot is not without a large selection of accommodations to cater to every traveler that comes through. You will find some very budget places in the northern end of town and a few guesthouses at the southern end of town, near the beach. Most hotels increase prices in the high season. Try to negotiate in the low season for a better rate.

My Friend Hospedaje (Rooms: $3 - $7.50)

This new hospedaje-restaurant is in good with the foreigners, probably because it's run by a sweet, motherly lady. It also doesn't hurt that the prices are the best in town for backpackers and breakfast is only a walk downstairs. The owners can help set you up with a tour of the local beaches as well. To get there, walk up Los Pinos, the street with the gazebo on the beach. Los Pinos 533, Tel: 51-44-461-080, E-mail: magowave@hotmail.com.

La Esquina (Rooms: $3 - 11)

This corner joint with restaurant below has austere rooms but with ocean views. All rooms have their own bathroom with hot water. Head downstairs for the catch of the day. Unión 299, Tel: 51-44-461-081.

Hostal Camping Naylamp (Rooms: $3 - 17)

Hostal Camping Naylamp is another near-budget lodging option in Huanchaco, and one of the few that offers campsites. (If you don't have a tent, you can rent one.) The hostel is in two parts: the older one, with dorms and private rooms, on Avenida Víctor Larco. The second part, with private rooms, campgrounds and common kitchen, is just a back door away, across Jirón Pescador. Rooms are pleasant and clean. Throughout are hammocks to laze away hot afternoons. When coming from Trujillo, stay on the combi as it swings through the upper part of town. When it returns to the seafront, hop off. Naylamp is right there on the corner. Av. Víctor Larco 1420. Tel: 51-44-461-022, E-mail: maylamp@terra.com.pe, URL: www.hostalnaylamp.com.

Hostal Solange(Rooms: $4 - 8)

Hostal Solange is an old-time favorite of budget travelers. Señora Solange is a bit deaf, but eager to sit in the courtyard garden and talk with her guests about their lives, dreams and adventures. She has clean rooms on two floors around the patio, for one to four persons. All have private hot-water baths. You can ask politely to use the kitchen, or enjoy breakfast from the cafeteria. Los Ficus 258. Tel: 51-44-461-410, E-mail: hsolange@yahoo.es, URL: www.geocities.com/hostalsolange/solange.

Hostal Los Tres Delfines (Rooms: $6 - 21)

As far as hostels go, this four-story place a couple blocks from the beach is one of the nicer ones. Clean but dry in character, the beds are comfy and the hot water is always a crowd pleaser. Only doubles and quads have private bathrooms. All rooms come with cable TV. Las Cucardas 129-133, Tel: 51-4-446-1599.

Huanchaco Hostal (Rooms: $24 - 40)

Located on the main square, Huanchaco Hostal is a clean, respectable place. Each room has cable TV and is decorated with Peruvian art to boot. If you walk to the back patio, you will find a nice but rather small pool. To get there, walk two blocks up Los Pinos from the beach, take a left, continue 1.5 blocks. Víctor Larco 287, Tel: 51-44-46-1272, Fax: 51-44-461-688, E-mail: huanchaco_hostal@ yahoo.es.

Huanchaco Restaurants

If you are a seafood lover, you have come to the right place! This little surf town serves up cheap dishes that are super tasty and many come with a relaxing beach view. Restaurants dot the shore and are mostly open for lunch and dinner (a few for breakfast). Be sure to try the Peruvian treats, after you've tired of the seafood!

Although meals are quite pricey in Huanchaco, the lunch special can help a long way in staying on budget ($1.35-4). The further from the beach you go, the cheaper the restaurants, especially along Dean Saavedra, as well as near and in the market on Pilcomayo. Several hostels have common kitchens where you can whip up fare.

My Friend (Entrees: $2 - 4)
The restaurant side of the business does all the basics: sandwiches, soups, chicken, spaghetti, fish, lasagna and -even- fondue. Lots of the surfers come for breakfast at My Friend, since it's one of the only places open at 8 a.m. and it includes a medium-sized pitcher of juice. The strawberry-banana smoothies are a hit. Open daily until 11 p.m. Los Pinos 533, Tel: 51-44-461-080.

La Mamacha (Entrees: $2 - 4)
La Mamacha is the get-away for vegetarians seeking refuge from Huanchaco's sea food menus. This small bistro serves vegetarian sandwiches and blue plate specials, as well as hamburgers and a menú criollo (so your meat-eating friends don't feel left out). La Mamacha also hosts a Happy Hour. Natural yogurt can be picked up here, too. Open 5-10 p.m. (or later, if the energy is high). Calle Túpac Amaru 117, Tel: 51-44-462-347.

Chill Out (Entrees: $2 - 8)
Chill Out may be the most appropriately named destination on the northern coast. Situated around an empty above-ground swimming pool are two low tables surrounded by heavily cushioned wicker chairs and couches, a few racks filled with English magazines, and plenty of candles, plants and funky lights to gawk at. Inside, a giant TV is the big draw, in addition to the huge selection of DVDs that includes movies as well as televisions series. Kick off your shoes and cozy up on the mattresses and pillows at one of the three tables and order from a menu that offers various burger-fry-soda combinations for $2-3.50, as well as a variety of mains and munchies. Don't let the uber-relaxed atmosphere fool you when it comes to the food and service, however. Run by a young friendly couple, the service is quick, the water free, the food fresh and fast and the napkins linen. Slightly classy and super comfortable, Chill Out is a good stop for a nightcap during an old episode of "Friends," or a good hearty meal on a quiet patio. Open Monday-Saturday, 9 a.m.-noon, 7-11 p.m. Los Pinos 437, Tel: 51-44-462-320.

Casa Tere (Entree: $3 - 6)
Now here's a classy place. Gladly stuck in coastal elegance, this long-running restaurant serves delicious pizzas, pastas and parrillas but with a dose of history. Black and white photos depict the history of Huanchaco, giving you a quasi-museum tour while eating. The photos are so popular that the owners also have to post that the photos are, in fact, not for sale. This cozy joint on the southwest corner of the main plaza is perfect for a romantic dinner for two. Share a pizza or try the spinach ravioli. Open daily from 4-10 p.m. Víctor Larco 280, Tel: 51-44-461-197.

Wave (Entrees: $3 - 6)
Part surfer hangout, part surf school and part Mexican restaurant, Wave is the cool kids' hangout from sun up to sun down. The restaurant is located upstairs with a few tables and a small bar inside, and three tables wedged on a balcony so small you have to be really unsociable not to get to know the table next you as you bump elbows. Travelers craving a little Mexican food may have a hard time choosing what to order, as all the usual suspects, from quesadillas to tacos and enchiladas to burritos, make an appearance on the menu. Do order just one plate, however, as the portions are enormous. The waitstaff is comprised of surf instructors pulling double duty, and again, you have to be really unsociable not to strike up a conversation with these friendly guys. The wait for food seems interminable for those who

NORTHERN COAST

walk in ready to eat, but between the chilled tunes of Jack Johnson, a small dartboard and the view of the sunset, there's plenty of distraction to increase your patience level. Open Monday-Saturday from 9 a.m.-5 p.m., and Sunday from noon-5 p.m. Av. Victor Larco 640.

V!VA Member Review- Wave

The food is probably among the best food I've had in South America. Daytime chillout and night-time party spot.

Aug 12, 2007

El Mochica (Entrees: $5 - 10)
Mochica stays true to its cultural roots and name, serving seafood and typical criollo dishes from the northern coast. If you've found a dish you love, delight in the fact that this chain has more locations in the area. Open daily noon-6 p.m. Corner of Larco and Independencia, Tel: 51-44-224-401.

Lucho del Mar (Entrees: $6 - 10)
As soon as it's caught, your fish is sent to the kitchen. This is another on-the-beach seafood restaurant, minus much of a decor. Luckily, you'll be looking seaside anyway. Lucho is a good place to try Peruvian *ceviche*, a typical dish in which the shrimp, crab or fish is served in lemon juice. You have to roll up your sleeves also because it's served on a platter ready to be mixed. Open Tuesday-Sunday from 11 a.m.-6 p.m. Larco 600, Tel: 51-44-461-460.

El Kero (Entrees: $5 - 25)
Trendier than most along the beach, El Kero dishes up *desayuno* (breakfast) and coffee by day... and at night you'll need the extra caffeine, as the second floor is devoted to a *discoteca*. Wine, cocktails and beer are on tap as well as a sit-down meal of pizza, seafood or steak. Open daily from 9 a.m.-midnight. La Ribera 115, Tel: 51-44-461-184, E-mail: ksalinas@elkero.com, URL: www.el-kero.com.

CHICLAYO
Chiclayo, located in the northern part of Peru, has a mix of everything—sun, oasis and a cool breeze. Its prime location attracts business from around the area, and its optimal weather attracts vacationers. However, its latest claim to fame is its recent archaeology findings.

Just 35 km (22 km) from Chiclayo is Huaca Rajada, a complex where archaeologists discovered the tomb of the Moche Lord, otherwise known as the Lord of Sipán, a high-ranking leader whose body was accompanied by gold relics and jewelry. Now you can check out the treasures found at the tomb at the Royal Tombs of Sipan by taking a short drive to the small city of Lambayeque. Other archaeological finds of the Chiclayo area are displayed in the Brüning Archaeological Museum, and the Sicán National Museum.

Make time to visit Túcume, also known as the Valley of the Pyramids, where you can see 26 pyramids. Explore the archaeological sites and the natural landscape, as well as experience folk healing and a culture interchange in general. The active participation of the community in the preservation has made it possible for travelers to learn about their natural and cultural heritage.

Another site not to miss is Pimentel, a modern beach resort which provides opportunities for water sports such as surfing. You can also see local fishermen, who make use of thousand year old fishing practices. Naturally enough, Chiclayo is also famous for its fine cooking. One of the most popular dishes is *arroz con pato* (duck served with rice) and ceviche (raw fish marinated in lemon juice).

Getting To and Away from Chiclayo

Chiclayo's airport is Aeropuerto Capitán FAP José Abelardo Quiñones Gonzales (Avenida Bolognesi s/n, Tel.: 51-74-233-192). LanPeru (Monday-Friday 9 a.m.-7 p.m., Saturday 7 a.m.-2 p.m. MM Izaga 770, Tel.: 51-74-223-124) has thrice-daily service to Lima ($128, 1 hour 10-25 minutes) and once daily to Tumbes ($56, 1 hour).

There are buses departing Chiclayo at least once per day from the major bus terminals near the corner of Balta and Bolegnesi. Lima (12 hours) costs about $15 and leaves hourly from Transportes Línea. They also offer hourly service to Trujillo (3 hours) for $5. Chachapoyas (12 hours) costs $8. It's worth it to try and arrange a day bus for this trip, as the scenery is beautiful. Tombes (9 hours) costs $7 and there are two buses daily through Tepsa. Cajamarca (6 hours) is $5 with multiple departures daily with a variety of carriers. Jaén (6 hours) costs about $5, with two companies offering twice daily departures.

Most bus companies have offices on Avenida Bolognesi. Between 7 de Enero and A. La Point are Cruz del Sur, Cial, Civa and Línea. Near Colón is a terminal housing Kuélap, Sol, Zelada, El Cumbe and other companies with service to Chachapoyas, Jaén, Tarapoto, Cajamarca and other Eastern destinations. Between Avenida Luis González and Avenida Grau are Móvil, Flores and Ittsa. Another cluster of depots is on Avenida Leonardo Ortiz and Avenida Cuneo, including Transporte Chiclayo, Oltursa and combis for Pimentel, Santa Rosa and Lambayeque. Terminal Terrestre Epsel (Avenida Sáenz Peña and Avenida Pedro Ruiz) is the interdepartmental bus terminal.

To Lambayeque: $0.50, 15-20 minutes.
To Túcume: Go to Lambayeque first, then take a minivan from the market there, $0.50, 20 minutes.
To Ferreñafe: Bus from Epsel Interurbano terminal, $0.70, 1 hour.
To Monsefú: Combis from bus stop on Avenida Bolognesi, in front of Real Plaza Mall, $0.50, 15-20 minutes.
To Santa Rosa/Pimentel: leaves when full, 0.50 / $0.30.
To Máncora/Tumbes: $8/$9, 6/9 hours—Transporte Chiclayo (9:30 p.m., 10 p.m.), El Dorado (11:30 a.m., 9:30 p.m.)
To Piura: $4, 3 hours—Línea (hourly 5 a.m.-8:15 p.m.), Transporte Chiclayo (every 15-30 minutes 5 a.m.-9 p.m.). Also El Dorado
To Trujillo: $4, 3 hours—Línea (hourly 6 a.m.-7 p.m.). Also Transporte Chiclayo, El Dorado.
To Lima: Most buses leave 6:30-9 p.m.,12 hours—Móvil ($30), Cruz del Sur (also 8a.m., $14-38), Civa ($14-17), Cial ($14-27), Línea ($17-30), Flores ($14-24), Ittsa ($24-30)
To Cajamarca: 7.5-9 hours, $7-10—Línea (10:45 a.m., 10 p.m., 10:45 p.m.), El Cumbe (6:45a.m., 7 a.m., 2 p.m., 9:30 p.m.)
To Jaén: $6-9, 5-6.5 hours—Civa (10 a.m.-continues to San Ignacio, 9:30 p.m.), Línea (1:15 p.m., 11 p.m.), Móvil (2 p.m., 11 p.m.)
To Chachapoyas: All buses depart 6-7 p.m., $10-15, 9 hours—Móvil, Civa, Kuélap
To Moyobamba / Tarapoto: Most buses leave 6-7 p.m.,13-14 hours—Cial ($14), Civa ($16-20), Sol (also at noon, 2:30 p.m., $14-17), Móvil ($22)
To Yurimaguas, go to Tarapoto first and catch transport from there.

Getting Around

Public transportation costs $.35 and taxi cabs run between $.80-1. Mototaxis are allowed in the outlying areas of the town, but not in downtown ($0.50). A cab to the airport charges $1.

CHICLAYO SERVICES

Chiclayo's iPeru tourism office is the place to go for information on all that the city and its neighboring villages have to offer. Open Monday-Saturday 9 a.m.-7 p.m., Sunday 9 a.m.-1 p.m. Avenida Sáenz Peña 838, Tel.: 51-74-205-703, E-mail: iperuchiclayoromperu.gob.pe, URL: www.peru.info/eng/lambayeque). The tourism police station is located right next door (Avenida Sáenz Peña 830, Tel.: 51-74-235-181). Motorists might drop by Touring y Automóvil Club del Perú for maps and assistance (Manuel Arteaga 357, Urbanización Los Parques, Tel.: 51-74-603-131, Fax:

51-74-237-848, E-mail: chiclyoouringperu.com. Other useful websites are www.canaturper.org and www.regionlambayeque.gob.pe.

Chicalyo's money district is on Avenida Balta Sur, south of the Plaza de Armas. Here you'll find a few casas de cambio strewn among the banks. Street money changers also hang out here, though beware of fake bills. The following banks change American Express travelers' checks and have ATMs that accept MasterCard, Visa, Plus and Cirrus cards:
• BCP (Monday-Thursday 9 a.m.-6:30 p.m., Friday 9 a.m.-7:30 p.m., Saturday 9 a.m.-1 p.m. Avenida Balta, between Aguirre and Izaga).
• Scotiabank (Monday-Friday 9:15 a.m.-6 p.m., Saturday 9:15 a.m.-12:30 p.m. Avenida Balta, between Aguirre and Izaga)—Also Western Union agent.
• Interbank (Monday-Friday 9 a.m.-6:15 p.m., Saturday 9:15 a.m.-12:30 p.m. Corner of Aguirre and Colón, ATMs on Colón)—Its Global Net ATM also takes American Express cards.
• Banco de la Nación is a MoneyGram outlet (Monday-Friday 8 a.m.-5 :30 p.m., Saturday 9 a.m.-.1 p.m. Corner of Aguirre and Ortiz).

Phone shops are common. Most charge $0.10 for national calls and start from $0.20 for international calls. Internet cafés are concentrated along Jirón Aguirre and Jirón San José, east of the Plaza de Armas. Many have Skype. Their average cost is $0.35 per hour. Serpost is ready to stamp and send your postcards seven days a week (Monday-Saturday 8 a.m.-8:30 p.m., Sunday 8 a.m.- 1 p.m. Jirón Aguirre 140).

Two medical facilities provide round-the-clock attention: Hospital Nacional Almanzor Aguinaga Asenjo (Calle Hipólito Unanue 180, Tel.: 51-74-237-776) and Hospital Regional Docente Las Mercedes (Avenida Luis González 635, Tel.: 51-74-238-232 / 51-74-237-411). Pharmacies are all over, especially on Avenida José Balta, north of the main plaza. Deliveries are made by Botica Arcangel (Tel.: 51-74-205-999) and InkaFarm (51-74-208-648). Use Lavandería Burbujas for quick, reliable laundry service (daily 8:30 a.m.-7:30 p.m. 7 de Enero 639, Tel.: 51-74-273-944. $1 per kilo).

Feria Artesanal Permanente Mi Perú is a mini mall of ten shops selling a good selection of woolens, postcards and miscellaneous knick knacks (daily 8 a.m.-9 p.m. Bolognesi 590).

REGIONAL FINDS

The desert around Chiclayo continues to prove itself as one of Peru's most archaeologically rich regions. Year after year, with the patient brushing away of sand, more ruins come to the light of modern day. How do archaeologists make these discoveries? Sometimes it's just like out of a novel of spies, crimes and intrigues. Someone may notice pottery, jewelry and other artifacts starting to hit the black market, the fruits of huaqueros. Sleuthing around, the archaeologist may—with luck—find the source of those riches. This is the history of Walter Alva and the Lord of Sipán.

One recent discovery on the horizon for ruins rats is Huaca Ventarrón. In August 2007, Walter Alva and his team of young scientists began working to uncover this 4,000-year-old temple. A broad, 11-level staircase leads to the top platform. Decorations of the adobe holy place include red zig-zag bands and murals of deer captured in nets. Another is a tomb whose discovery was announced in July 2008 by Bruno Alva Meneses and Canadian Steve Bourget. The 1,700-year-old Mochica tomb is in the Úcupe archeological complex, some 40 kilometers (24 miles) from Chiclayo. So far, a body, gold jewelry and ceramics have been unearthed.

The Úcupe site cannot presently be visited. Visits to Huaca Ventarrón are semi-restricted. Write to Dr. Walter Alva, director of the Museo de Tumbas Reales de Sipán in Lambayeque, expressing the reason for wanting to see the ruins and a date / time for the visit.

Things to See and Do in Chiclayo

In recent years Chiclayo has begun to be recognized as an important area of archaeological sites. There are three major sites in the vicinity, each with its own museum: The Royal Tombs of Sipán Museum, located about ten minutes from Chiclayo, exhibits an impressive collection of artifacts from the Mohica Culture. The Brüning Archaeological Museum, named after the German architect that begun excavating the museums contents, has over 1500 artifacts on display. The Sicán National Museum, which is around 40 kilometers (25 miles) from Chiclayo, has various displays that showcase the Sicán culture and way of life.

Within the town of Chiclayo there is less to do, but it is worth spending a day or so wandering around here. There is an interesting flea market in town, and other various shops that might have something to pique your interest.

Pasaje Woyke

In this passage that runs alongside the bank to the main plaza you will find peddlers selling their handicrafts, such as earrings, necklaces and other jewelry. They also might bring their hairless Peruvian dogs—not for sale. Pasaje Woyke Route.

Paseo de las Musas

In a park along a brook, as close to the Springs of Helicon as this desert city could provide, reside the nine Muses of Greek mythology. Their pavilions of Classical Greek architecture are surrounded by well-manicured gardens. Clio, the muse who inspired the documentation of history's stories, just could be the great inspiration local or visiting writers are in search of.

Mercado Modelo

Looking for a tiara? Party decorations? Underwear? This wacky flea market gives you endless aisles to meander through. You probably won't find that one, special sought-after Peruvian souvenir, but it's an entertaining place. One can easily get lost here for a few hours. Lots of amateur alchemists are at work here if you're into alternative medicine. Go in the morning, to avoid afternoon pickpockets. Balta and Arica.

Chiclayo Cultural Centers

Culture in Chiclayo exists beyond the time and space of the numerous ancient ruins. For a taste of modern creativity, check out the cultural centers. Most events are free, and $2 is the usual cost for concerts.

• Instituto Nacional de Cultura (INC): This cultural institute has art exhibits, movies and concerts. Avenida Luis González 345, Tel: 51-74-237-261 / 51-74-225-848, E-mail: eventosinclambayeque@gmail.com, URL: inc-lambayeque.org.
• Alianza Francesa: The French Alliance has free movies Fridays at 7 p.m., in addition to lectures and cultural events. Cuglievan 644, Tel: 51-74-237-571, E-mail : afchiclayo@netcourier.com.
• Instituto Cultural Peruano Norteamericano: The North American Peruvian Culture Institute has art exhibits, movies, concerts and literary readings, which occur most evenings, and during the day there are also children's programs. MM Izaga 807, Tel: 51-74-231-241, Fax : 51-74-227-166, URL : www.icpnachi.edu.pe.

Coastal Tour

If you feel like you have visited enough ruins after the many archaeological sites around Chiclayo, then take an afternoon to explore the living culture of some of the nearby villages, like Monsefú, Santa Rosa or Pimentel. Begin the journey with a stop in Monsefú, an artisan village 14 kilometers (7.5 miles) south of Chiclayo. On the main plaza is a high relief mural sculpture by William Buendía, which honors the craftspeople of this pueblo. Around the Plaza de Armas is the brown and pale ochre church (1896), a small museum next door (open only before and after masses) and the central food market. While wandering down the streets, peer into the workshops of the artists and stop in to talk about their work. Four blocks from the plaza,

Activities ●

1 Instituto Cultural Peruano C4
   Norteamericano
2 Palacio Municipal C4
3 Paseo de las Musas E3
4 Paseo de los Kingkones D3
5 Plaza de Armas C4
6 Plazuela Elías Aguirre C2

Sleeping 🛏

26 Garza Hotel D4
27 Hospedaje San Lucas C3
28 Hostal Real C3
29 Hostal Sol Radiante C3
30 Hostal Victoria C5
31 Hotel Central C5
32 Hotel Paraíso C4
33 Hotel Sicán C3
34 Hotel Tumi de Oro B5

NORTHERN COAST

Churches 🏠

7   Basílica San Antonio C2
8   Iglesia La Verónica C3

Eating 🍴

9   Cafetería Trébol C4
10   Govinda B5
11   Las Américas C4
12   Restaurant Romana C4
13   Restaurante El Hebrón C4

Services ★

14   Banco de Crédito C4
15   Banco de la Nación C2
16   Correo C2
17   Interbank C3
18   Lavandería Burbujas C4
19   ScotiaBank C4
20   Tourism Office B5
21   Tourism Police C5

Shopping 🔀

22   Feria Artesanal Permanente D3
23   Mall Real Plaza
24   Mercado Central
25   Mercado Modelo A3

Transportation 🚌

35   Cial D4
36   Civa D4
37   Combis for Monsefú
38   Cruz del Sur D4
39   El Dorado C1
40   Emtrafesa D4
41   Epsel Terminal
42   Flores D3
43   Ittsa D3
44   Línea D3
45   Móvil Tours D3
46   Oltursa B1
47   Terminal for Costern Routes D3
48   Transportes Chiclayo B1

at Calle Izaga and Avenida Venezuela, is the large artisans market. For several blocks, stalls display the straw, cotton and wool weavings noted in Monsefú.

After picking up on a few gifts, wait by the side of Avenida Venezuela for a combi to take you down the road. As you near the coast, the landscape changes drastically. Now ribbons of greenery drape the desert. Fourteen kilometers (7.5 miles) of prime beach hug the coast here, from Puerto Etén to Pimentel. Midway is Santa Rosa, a hamlet devoted to fishing. The beach is lined with wooden boats being refurbished by its residents and caballitos de totora. The church (1918) has been eaten by the salt and wind. Stroll through the narrow streets and chat with the men crafting new caballitos and mending nets. South of the beach is El Farol, a popular surfing place. There are a few basic accommodations. To continue your coastal expedition, head to the roundabout a block past the seafront market and wait for the combi to Pimentel.

Pimentel, only two kilometers (1.2 mi) from Santa Rosa and 11 kilometers (6.5 miles) from Chiclayo, was once known as Caleta de la Concepción de Chiclayo. This is the most popular beach destination for the city slickers. Along the broad, pale gray beach is Malecón Seoane, the seafront promenade with gardens and modern low-rise condos. Throughout the town are the remnants of when this was Chiclayo's port, controlled by the powerful Compañía de Ferrocarril y Muelle. Good examples of the late 19th-early 20th century mansions are the train station and a long pier (Entrance into the fishing area is prohibited during work hours; other times, $0.30 entry fee). The big draw is the surfing. On the boardwalk in the center of town several shops offer board rentals and lessons.

The south end of the beach is home to colorfully painted wooden boats and the totora reed rafts. Near the village are the Pampas de Pimentel, the location of several archaeological sites. To the north of the beach, is Huaca Agujereada and to the south is Huaca Blanca. To end your afternoon outing, pull up a table on restaurant row and enjoy a fresh seafood dinner while watching the sun set over the Pacific. It is worth spending a few days to relax in Pimentel. Of the four hotels, the most reasonably priced are Hospedaje Pizzería All Incontro (Quiñones 51-

NORTHERN COAST

74-241-243, Tel.: 51-74-45-3410; $3.35 per person) and Hostal Garuda (Quiñones 109, Tel.: 51-74-45-2964; shared bath $5-6.70 per person, two persons with private bath $15-27.70).

Each of the villages has fiestas. Try to make it for one to experience the region's living culture more in depth.

• **Last week of February**—Pimentel—Caballo de Mar, races and other exhibitions of the *caballito del mar*, folk dances, beach sports, artisan, gastronomic and sand castle competitions as well as a beauty pageant.
• **March 24**—Monsefú—Señor Cautivo de Monsefú, a mid-year salute to the village's saint
• **June 24**—Santa Rosa and Pimentel—San Pablo y San Pedro, the festivities devoted to the patron saints of fishermen, with processions, seaside masses, regattas and other events.
• **Last week of July**—Monsefú—Fexticum, a salute to the artistic and artisan production of the village, with food, marinera dancing and the election of Señorita Fexticum
• **September 14**—Monsefú—Señor Cautivo de Monsefú, Monsefuanos procession the statue of the captive Christ is through the streets of their village. Artisan and gastronomic fairs help round out the festivities.

Needless to say, the beach towns are very popular with Peruvians during the summer holidays (mid-December through March) and Fiestas Patrias (end of July) vacations. Prices on lodging rise during this time.

CHICLAYO TOURS
Chiclayo itself does not have that many tour operators as most operate (and start) out of Trujillo. However, you can visit both cities on a single tour. Some Trujillo tours end in Chiclayo, giving you an opportunity to stay and explore the city and its surrounding attractions; others start in Chiclayo and end in Trujillo.

Go2Peru.com Tours
The tour company Go2Peru.com offers a combined tour of Chiclayo and Trujillo. It's a good option, because Go2Peru arranges for you to see the highlights of both cities and for your transportation between Chiclayo and Trujillo. This tour company really sets you up—arranging all meals, accommodation, and entrance fees into the various historical and archaeological sites the tour visits. If you're short on time and want to cruise through several of Northern Peru's archaeological highlights efficiently, Go2Peru.com is your best bet. Av. Casimiro Ulloa 333, San Antonio, Miraflores, Lima, Tel: 51-1-446-6981, E-mail: Monica@Go2Peru.com, URL: www.Go2Peru.com.

InkaNatura Tours
The InkaNatura tour company offers multi-day excursions in northwestern Peru. It emphasizes "conservation through tourism," thus appealing to those keen on seeing the sights but wanting to do so in a way that promotes conservation. The tours range from two to six nights. All accommodation is arranged, as are most lunches and dinners. Excursions visit the Sipán archaeological site, Túcume and other pre-Inca sites in the Northern Coast region. In Chiclayo, InkaNatura's office is located in the lobby of the Gran Hotel Chiclayo. Av. Federico Villarreal 115, Tel: 51-74-209-948, Fax: 51-74-270-797, E-mail: opcix@Inkanatura.com.pe, URL: www.InkaNatura.com.

Peruvian Secrets
Peruvian Secrets is a British company operating a different style of tour in the Chiclayo area. Guests sleep and eat in a homestead near the village of Salas north of Chiclayo. From there, tours are taken to see the various museums, ruins and archaeological treasures of the Chiclayo area. It promises to be a unique experience because instead of bunking in Chiclayo each night, guests see Peru in a more authentic context. Not only that, if you are experiencing an ailment you can't seem to fix, Salas is known as the shaman center of Peru. E-mail: mailquery@peruviansecrets.co.uk, URL: www.peruviansecrets.co.uk.

CHICLAYO LODGING

Some of the hotels in Chiclayo might not be the fanciest in the world, but they are very reasonably priced. Amenities, such as hot water and a television, tend to come standard, but if these are important to you, you might want to clarify before booking. If you prefer a bit of luxury, there are a couple of more expensive hotels in Chiclayo. Even those, however, are not expensive in comparison to hotels of similar grade in the U.S. or Europe.

BUDGET

Hospedaje San Lucas (Rooms: $4 - 10)

Run by a kind-hearted woman, the former Hostal Lido is its old self. Backpackers can shoestring their trip one more night in a room here. If you've found yourself in a room on the roof, enjoy the view, though it's likely to be overcast. Both common and private baths have hot water. Other amenities include free internet, book exchange, and common kitchen. Three blocks west of the plaza, E. Aguirre 412, Tel: 51-74-206-888, E-mail: pamelacalambrogio@hotmail.com.

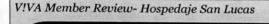

V!VA Member Review- Hospedaje San Lucas

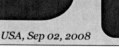

San Lucas has to be the best place to stay in Chiclayo for backpackers. It has all we need: free internet, book exchange & kitchen use. And, to top it off, the owners are really knowledgeable about the sites.

USA, Sep 02, 2008

Hotel Tumi de Oro (Rooms: $8 - 18)

Hotel Tumi de Oro is a bit far from the center of town and the bus terminals, but the price is right. It is one of the cheaper hotels for someone traveling alone in Chiclayo. The large, modern building has rooms that are a bit small and impersonal, but clean. The tiled, private baths have something you don't find in most city hotels: solar-heated water. Leonicio Prado 1145. Tel: 51-74-227-108 / 51-74-237-767.

Hostal Joel (Rooms: $9 - 15)

Spanning the second and third floors above outlet shopping stores, this hostel is very clean and comfortable. The floors are carpeted, and all rooms come with television, private bathroom with hot water and fan. Balta 1355, Tel: 51-74-225-953, Fax: 51-74-222-047, E-mail: hostaljoel@hotmail.com.

Hostal Victoria (Rooms: $10 - 15)

Hostal Victoria is a great deal for people traveling in pairs. Its large rooms are generously furnished with a desk, fan, reading lamp, cable TV and a very comfortable overstuffed chair. There is hot water and clean floors. Another plus of Hostal Victoria is the location, four blocks from the bus companies on Avenida Bolognesi.MM Izaga 933. Tel: 51-74-225-642.

Hostal Sol Radiante (Rooms: $15 - 20)

It seems all hotels in Chicalyo come wrapped up in a glass-paneled modern architecture. Hostal Sol Radiante is no exception. The rooms are good-sized and amply furnished. Besides central-heated hot water, some of the private bathrooms have tubs—a great way to soak away the dirt of the archaeological sites. Hostal Sol Radiante has 24-hour service, which is nice since it is close to the bus station if you arrive to Chiclayo in the middle of the night. MM Izaga 392. Tel: 51-74-237-858.

Hostal Sicán (Rooms: $15 - 20)

Hostal Sicán offers single and double rooms with private bathroom (very good hot showers) and cable TV. The hostel can be noisy - ask for rooms on upper floors. A simple breakfast (and all tax) is included in the price. The management have a safety deposit box for valuables and a few leaflets with information and maps on the city. Four blocks north of bus terminals on Avenida Bolognesi. M M Izaga 356. Tel: 51-74-237-618.

MID-RANGE
Hotel Paraíso (Rooms: $15 - 30)
Professionally-run Paraíso attracts a business clientele. They charge mid-range prices and deliver on cleanliness and comfort. Rooms come with television and hot water. A couple blocks west of Balta on Ruíz, 1064. Tel: 51-74-228-161, Fax: 51-74-222-070, E-mail: reservascix@hotelesparaiso.com, URL: www.hotelesparaiso.com.

Hotel Central (Rooms: $22 - 35)
Two blocks off the main plaza, Hotel Central runs a tight ship. Rooms have comfortable beds, private bathrooms with hot water and television. Some sport a mini-fridge, Jacuzzi and air conditioning. Two blocks east of the plaza, San José 976, Tel: 51-74-231-511, E-mail: hotelcentralchiclayo@yahoo.com.

HIGH-END
Garza Hotel (Rooms: $71 - 90)
Garza Hotel in Chiclayo is a modern hotel conveniently located five blocks from the main square, near the city's commercial center. The hotel offers a restaurant, bar/casino, pool, business center and conference facilities, making it a good option for both business and leisure travelers. In the area are lots of attractions, including a witch market, disco and mall. Av. Bolognesi 756, Tel: 51-74-228-172, Fax: 51-74-228-171, E-mail: reservas@garzahotel.com, URL: www.garzahotel.com.

CHICLAYO RESTAURANTS
The people of Chiclayo regard a few of their Peruvian dishes to be superior to similar plates in other regions. When visiting a restaurant in Chiclayo, be sure to try at least one of these dishes. Some of the most popular are arroz con pato, or rice with duck, *seco de cabrito*, a goat meat stew, and *espesado*, a dish made with meats and served with rice. If you aren't in the mood for traditional food, there are a couple of places in the area you can get international foods, such as sandwiches and pastas.

REGIONAL FOOD

All over the Chiclayo region the King Kong is a popular treat. This gigantic *alfajor* is made of thick wafers layered with fillings of *manjar blanco* (soft caramel) as well as pineapple and *cachaca* (peanut-molasses) jams. How did the King Kong earn its name? Was it because the great ape wanted to win the love of Fay Wray with one of these gigantic cookies? Not quite. Official history says it all began back in the 1920s. In her home, Victoria Mejía de García of Lambayeque made all sorts of traditional sweets which she sold to raise money to feed the poor. From the money she made, twice a year she provided breakfast and groceries to the destitute: on June 13, the feast day of San Antonio de Pádua, patron saint of the poor, and on Christmas day. Her giant-sized alfajor was a hit—just like the recently-released movie King Kong... thus the treat's name! Another version of history says that because the war, women would make their alfajors large, to save on ingredients.

In Chiclayo, the stretch of Avenida Bolognesi sandwiched between Avenida Balta Sur and Colón is dubbed Paseo de los Kingkones or Passageway of the King Kongs. Here are shop after shop selling the pastry prepared by a horde of local bakeries. Be sure to grab one before you hop your bus to sweeten that long journey to Lima or Amazonas.

The daily lunch special runs $1.35-3.70. Inexpensive dining choices are a bit scarce in the downtown area. If in a pinch, try one of the two markets: Mercado Central (Vicente de la Vega, between A La Point and Avenida Balta Norte) and the famed Mercado Modelo (Jirón Arica and Avenida Balta Norte). Amongst their stalls are produce stands and cheap eateries serving until about 3 p.m. Many small shops offer cheap, quick ceviche and *papa rellena* plates for $0.50-0.70 from early morning to mid-afternoon. A handy supermarket is Hipermercado Metro at San José 320.

Las Américas

This stalwart among Chiclayano restaurants serves all the local dishes, including the lusted-after duck with rice. Slip into one of their round booths and watch the comings and goings of passersby in the main plaza, as Américas is on the southeast corner. É. Aguirre 824.

Govinda (Entrees: $1 - 3)

This vegetarian score will impress you with its savory meals at bargain prices. The menu of the day is always tasty, or try their Hindu dishes a la carte. Open Monday through Saturday from 8 a.m. to 10 p.m., and Sunday from 8:30 a.m. to 4 p.m. Various locations throughout Peru. In Chiclayano, Vicente de la Vega 982-988.

El Trebol Cafe (Entrees: $1 - 9)

Fill your sweet tooth and coffee addiction here, while enjoying a pretty view of main plaza. They offer simple breakfasts and snack food, too. It's next door to Las Américas in the southeast corner of the plaza. Open daily from 7 a.m. to 11 p.m. E. Aguirre 816, Tel: 51-74-206-490.

Romana (Entrees: $3 - 8)

Romana is another longtime favorite for taste buds favoring the local delights. Like many other haunts in town, you get the feeling of Chiclayo circa 1965. Open Monday through Saturday from 7 a.m. to 1 a.m., and Sunday from 7 a.m. to 8 p.m. Balta 512.

Las Américas (Entrees: $3 - 8)

This stalwart among Chiclayano restaurants serves all the local dishes, including the lusted-after duck with rice. Nestle into one of their round booths and watch the comings and goings of passersby in the main plaza, as Américas is on the southeast corner. Open daily from 7 a.m. to 11 p.m. É. Aguirre 824.

Hebron (Entrees: $3 - 11)

A flurry of yuppified restaurants and cafes have entered Chiclayo. This one claims to have the flavor of Chiclayo, as it reads from the menu. Indeed, Hebron serves typical parrilladas akin to the area. Pull up to your grilled dish in a comfy sofa. (By yuppified, it's to say free WiFi is included with your meal.) Open daily from 7:30 a.m. to midnight Balta 605. Tel: 51-74-222-709.

THINGS TO SEE AND DO NEAR CHICLAYO

Brüning Archaeological Museum

Named after the German engineer who was head of the archaeology project that bore the majority of the contents of the museum, The Brüning Museum opened in 1966. More than 1500 pieces are on display, which originate from various cultures found in the surrounding area. Its collection of gold items is especially impressive and consists of an expansive display of golden funeral masks, vases and jewelry. The museum is located 17 kilometers (10.5 mi) north of Chiclayo in Lambayeque. Avenida Huamachuco, cuadra 8 s/n. Tel: 51-74-282-110 / 51-74-283-440.

Sipán

Approximately 28 kilometers (17 mi) east of Chiclayo, the formidable complex of Sipán is a great place for archaeology aficionados and history buffs. Since 1987, excavations of the site have uncovered more than 12 royal tombs brimming with sacrificial offerings, pottery, textiles, precious metals and an extensive collection of funerary objects. Some of these objects are considered to be some of the best examples of pre-Columbian art. The pyramids and adjacent mounds mark an important Moche burial site, which was only discovered after priceless artifacts from the area began to appear on the black market. Fortunately, the most extravagant tombs seem to have escaped the attention of local huaqueros (grave robbers).

Among the richest and most interesting tombs located at Sipán is the one belonging to El Señor de Sipán. Archaeologists believe El Señor was an important civil and religious figure in ancient Moche society around 300 A.D. A mere 5 meters (16.4 mi) long, this tomb was full of archaeological objects, including food offerings, gold and turquoise jewelry, and the bodies of those lucky enough to accompany El Señor in his life after death. Excavations of other tombs uncovered an equally interesting cache of objects, including metal and ceramic artifacts, copper decorations, and sacrificed animals. In its entirety, the site provides important clues about Moche society.

The site also has a small museum, and three tombs containing replicas of the objects originally discovered inside, are on display. A brief jaunt up the large ceremonial pyramid across from Sipán offers excellent views of the site. The site is open daily 8 a.m. - 4 p.m. and the museum is open 9 a.m. - 5 p.m. Entrance: $2.70 for adults, and $.35 for national students. Guides can be hired for a few dollars, though they might not speak English. Plan to spend between 3-4 hours exploring the site.

To get there, take a combis from the Epsel terminal (Terminal Terrestre Interdistrital) in Chiclayo for $0.70, which will take approximately one hour.

Royal Tombs of Sipán Museum

A stunning, informative and atmospheric exhibition on the discovery and subsequent excavation of the tomb of the "Lord of Sipán". Along with a replica of the tomb itself, the museum displays the remarkable collection of artifacts found buried with the Lord. The highlights of the exhibition are undoubtedly the painstakingly restored gold and silver jewelry, and towards the end of the exhibition there are interesting displays on the restoration work itself as well as on efforts made to recover Moche artifacts previously lost to international smuggling. Tuesday-Sunday, 9 a.m-5 p.m. Lambayeque can be reached from Chiclayo by shared taxi for 1.50 soles ($0.48) per person, which is much quicker than a *combi* (minibus). Guides are available for another 20 soles ($6.40), but if you can read Spanish there is no need, as the displays are very well described. Av. Juan Pablo Vizcardo and Guzmán, Tel: 51-7-428-3978, URL: http://sipan.perucultural.org.pe.

Sicán National Museum

Located in Ferreñafe about 25 minutes from the city of Chiclayo, this museum showcases artifacts from the Sicán culture. A replica of a Sicán tomb displays some of its contents, including the many gold pieces there were found at the site. The other exhibits are of more commonplace items for the Sicán culture, including pottery, textiles and metal crafts. There is even an instructional video about how the metal crafts were produced. Tuesday-Sunday, 9 a.m-5 p.m. Take a one-hour bus ride from the Epsel Interurbano terminal in Túcume for $0.70. Av. Batán Grande s/n, Carretera a Pitipo. Tel: 51-74-286-469, E-mail: celera27@yahoo.es.

Túcume

Stretching across the countryside 35 kilometers (22 mi) north of Chiclayo, along the old Panamericana, are the extensive ruins of Túcume. Dating back nearly 1,000 years the ruins at Túcume consist of a vast network of 26 pyramids, residential complexes and sacred cemeteries organized around a ceremonial center. Considering the number of pyramids spread across the area, Túcume is often referred to as Valle de las Pirámides (Valley of the Pyramids). Archaeologists believe that the site was constructed between 1000 and 1375 AD by the Lambayeque people who occupied the area until they were conquered by the Chimú.

The site is also home to the longest adobe structure in the world. Measuring an astonishing 700 meters (2296 ft) long, 280 meters (919 ft) wide and over 30 meters (98 ft) high, Huaca Larga is truly an impressive site. This pyramid and others in the area tell an interesting story of occupation and change in the area. Like the structures of Huacas de la Luna y Sol near Trujillo, these pyramids were constructed in stages, added to with each new wave of conquerors. The Chimú left their mark in 1375, followed by the Incas in 1470. At Huaca Larga, for example, archaeologists discovered the Chimú Temple of the Mythical Bird, beneath an Inca tomb housing the body of a warrior buried with two other men and 19 women.

Excavations led by the late Norwegian explorer-archaeologist Thor Heyerdahl uncovered a number of new and contradictory facets of Peruvian culture, and some experts believe that future excavations will reveal that Túcume was an even grander center of civilization than Chan Chan. For more information regarding the area and its history, visit the site museum near the entrance (8 a.m.-4:30 p.m., Tel: 51-74-800-052, E-mail: museotucume@hotmail. com, $2.70 for adults, $1.00 for students with ISIC card. Closed Christmas). While not spectacular, the museum does contain some interesting photographs and drawings of the area.

Besides the pyramids themselves, the most inspiring aspect of Túcume is the surrounding landscape. If you're up for a bit of a climb, head up to the lookout on Cerro La Raya (also known as El Purgatorio), a massive mountain poking out of the otherwise-flat desert. The views from here are stunning: a complete panorama of all 26 pyramids and accompanying structures.

To get to Túcume you must first head to Lambayeque, and then take a minivan for about $.50 from the market there, which should take about 20 minutes. If you're around in February, definitely check out the town's Fiesta de la Purísma Concepción, which takes place eight days before Carnival. If you'd like to stay a bit longer near the site, Los Horcones is a great option.

PIURA

Spanish conqueror Francisco Pizarro founded Piura as the first Spanish city in Peru in 1532. In a country where Inca ruins and trekking rule the scene, this first city is now a mere stop before heading north to Ecuador or south to Huaraz. If ruins and hiking have left you dazed, Piura isn't the resting place you're looking for. It's a hot commercial city located inland but welcoming enough with options for budget travelers as well as for high rollers.

Piura is well known for the tondero, a lively folk dance in which barefoot performers in multicolored outfits dance to strong, rhythmic music. This part of the culture isn't, however, all that obvious. From day to day, the downtown area is packed with people, cars, taxis and motorcycles scurrying left and right. The Plaza de Armas is a good place to sit back and decide what will be your next destination. At night, the city roars and yet has a generally safe feel. Families pour into the florescent-lit department stores and couples walk the sidewalks.

A common day trip from Piura is to the town of Catacaos 12 km (7.5 mi) south. There you will find crafts made of hay and cotton and also gold and silver filigree. About 5 km (3 mi) south of Catacaos, you can find the archeological remains of Narihualá. What's left of the Tallan culture there has, like other ruins, fallen prey to culprits such as huaqueros, time and weather damage.

Altitude: 29 meters (95 ft), Population: 248,000

Piura History

Piura was inhabited by two indigenous nations called the Tallán, of Caribbean origin, and the Yunga. These peoples lived without organization or a leader until the Mochica conquered them. These groups evolved into the Vicús Culture, and they controlled the area for centuries. The Vicús culture is revered by archaeologists and collectors for the intricate and beautiful pottery they created. At least 40 years before the Spanish conquest, Piura was taken over by Inca Yupanqui, the tenth ruler of the Inca Empire. When the Spanish arrived in 1532, they

NORTHERN COAST

founded Piura, which is the oldest Spanish city in South America. Piura also served as the first main port at which the Spaniards shipped out the Inca gold they had rifled.

After the Spanish Conquest the area developed a strong *mestizo* or mixed culture, which included influences from Spaniards, African slaves from Madagascar, Chinese rice field workers and Roman Gypsies who had come to the area as pirates.

When to Go
Piura is nicknamed "La Ciudad de Eterno Calor" (the city of eternal heat). All year this desert-oasis city is hot during the day and cool at night. January through March is summertime, with temperatures reaching 29-33°C (84-92°F) with rain. The rest of the year is a bit cooler with *garúa* (fine mist). The city observes its founding October 1-9, with Peruvian paso horse shows, music serenades and a folk dance festival. Tourism week is celebrated the last week of August with special tours and cultural exhibits. Piura honors the Virgen de Perpetuo Socorro (June 27-July 5) and the Virgen de las Mercedes (September 22-30).

Getting To and Away from Piura
Piura is the crossroads of northern Peru. Many travelers pass through on their way north to Ecuador or south to the heartlands of the country.

Piura is home to Guillermo Concha Iberico International Airport, the second busiest airport in Peru. The airport is located about 2 km (1.2 mi) from the main square in from the city's Plaza de Armas (Av Córpas s/n, Tel.: 51-73-344-503 /51-73-344-505). LAN has three flights per day to Lima ($144-190 one way, 1 hr, 15 min). The airline accepts Visa, MasterCard, Diners Club and American Express (Monday-Friday 9 a.m.-6:50 p.m., Saturday 9 a.m.-2 p.m., Tel.: 51-73-305-727 / 51-73-302-145, URL: www.lan.com).

The city has no central bus terminal. In general, interprovincial buses—to Sullana, Tumbes, Chiclayo, Trujillo and small neighboring towns—leave from Sánchez Cerro, cuadras 11 to 14. A few companies on Sánchez Cerro (Transporte Chiclayo, Ittsa and Línea) also offer direct Lima service.

To Máncora: Eppo—hourly 4 a.m.-9 p.m., $4, 3.5 hours; El Dorado—every 2 hours 6:30 a.m.-8 p.m., $5
To Chiclayo: El Dorado, Línea, Transporte Chiclayo—hourly 5 a.m.-8 p.m., $4, 3 hours
To Trujillo: El Dorado, Línea, ITTSA and others—afternoon and evening departures, $8-14, 6 hours
Combis for Catacaos, Paita, Sullana and smaller villages leave from Terminal Terrestre El Bosque. Collective taxis for Catacaos depart when full from the corner of Calle Lima and Jirón Huancavelica, and from Avenida Loreto and Jirón Tumbes (daily 8 a.m.-9 p.m., $0.50).
Flores, Cial, Civa and other companies providing direct service to Lima leave from the neighborhood around Óvalo Bolognesi ($14-37, 14 hours). Cruz del Sur is a few blocks away at Avenida Circunvalción 161. Most leave 5-8 p.m.
For Huancabamba and Chulucanas, go to Terminal Terrestre de Castilla on the other side of the river.
To Huancabamba: Civa—daily 8:30 a.m. Etipthsa—daily 7:45 a.m., 5:45 p.m. Turismo Express—7:30 a.m., 6:30 p.m. All buses take 6-10 hours depending on weather and road conditions and cost $8.35.

Getting Around
There are a variety of ways of getting around Piura. Combis run on major streets ($0.35). Taxis cost $1-1.65, depending on distance. Motorcycle rickshaw taxis are a cheaper ($0.50), but are prohibited from running on Avenida Grau and in the downtown area. The main stop for motos is at Parque Colón, also known as Parque Infantil, a block from Óvalo Grau. To the Terminal Terrestre de Castilla, mototaxis should charge $0.65 and taxis $1. Combis and collective taxis for Castilla leave from the corner of Sánchez Cerro and Loreto ($0.35).

PIURA SERVICES

The iPeru tourist information office is extremely helpful and has information on lodging, bus schedules and attractions in Piura and the region (Monday-Saturday 8:30 a.m.-7 p.m., Sunday 8:30 a.m.-2 p.m. Jr Ayacucho 377, Tel.: 51-73-320-249, URL: www.peru.info/piura). Additionally, iPeru staffs a booth at the airport when flights arrive. The Comisaría de Piura, or police department, is at Av Sánchez Cerro, cuadra (block) 12 (Tel.: 51-73-307-641).The following countries have representatives in Piura:

•Consulado de Alemania (Los Ampolas K6, Urb. Miraflores, Tel.: 51-73-343-149)
•Consulado del Ecuador (Av Chirichigno 505, Urb. El Chipe, Tel.: 51-73-308-027 / 51-73-309-959)
•Viceconsulado de España (Grau 370, Tel.: 51-73-327-741).
Most banks in Piura are located near the Plaza de Armas or on Av Grau. The following cash American Express travelers checks and have ATMs that handle Cirrus, Plus, Visa, Master-Card and American Express cards:
•BCP (Banco de Crédito)—has special window for travelers check transactions (Monday-Thursday 9 a.m.-6:30 p.m., Saturday 9 a.m.-1 p.m. Av Grau and Jr Tacna)
•Interbank—also exchanges cash US dollars and Euros (Monday-Friday 9 a.m.-6:15 p.m., Saturday 9:15 a.m.-12:30 p.m. Av Grau 160)
•ScotiaBank (Monday-Friday 9 a.m.-6:15 p.m., Saturday 9:15 a.m.-12:30 p.m. Jr Libertad 825).

All have branch offices and ATMs throughout the city, including near the bus depots on Av Sánchez Cerro. Western Union money wires can be picked up at ScotiaBank. Banco de la Nación handles MoneyGram (Monday-Friday 8 a.m.-5:30 p.m., Saturday 9 a.m.-1 p.m. Calle Libertad 959). *Casas de cambio* are concentrated on Jr Arequipa and Jr Ica, and are generally open Monday-Friday 8 a.m.-2 p.m., 4-8 p.m. Changing money on the street is not advisable.

Locutorios, or phone offices (calls $0.03 per minute for local to $0.30 per minute international) and internet cafés ($0.35-0.70 per hour) are common. Internet Acasa has Skype (Monday-Friday 8 a.m.-11 p.m. Tacna 646, next to Museo Grau). Serpost is the place to drop a post card, pick up general delivery or send a package (Monday-Saturday 8 a.m.-8 p-.m. Calle Ayacucho and Calle Libertad). Piura's phone code is 73.

Piura has several medical facilities. The main public hospital is Hospital I Santa Rosa (Prolongación Av. Grau and Chulucanas s/n, San Martín, Tel.: 51-73-361-075). *Boticas* (pharmacies) are found along Av Grau, between Óvalo Grau and the cathedral, and on Av Sánchez Cerro, between Av Loreto and Sullana. Normal hours are 7 a.m.-10 p.m. The chain drugstore Boticas Felicidad delivers (Tel.: 51-73-308-300 / 51-73-304-750).

Many towns near Piura are known for crafts. A good one-stop gallery to appreciate these artisan works is Centro Artesanal Norte, with 16 shops dedicated to a separate village and its products (daily 10 a.m.-1 p.m., 4-8 p.m. Calle Libertad 501, Tel.: 51-73-300-175).

THINGS TO SEE AND DO IN PIURA

Piura may not offer quite as many options of things to do as other cities in Peru, and what it does offer may not be thrilling, but it will prove to be entertaining. There is a small selection of museums in town which can waste an afternoon or two. A walk in the Plaza de Armas also proves entertaining. It is a wonderful place to find a bench and watch the locals continue on their daily business. There are also day trips options available. One of the most popular is to the Catacaos, where you can see and buy crafts made out of hay, cotton, gold and silver. Another popular destination is the archaeological remains of Narihualá, which is what is left of the Tallan culture. Chulucanas is also renowned for its ceramics.

Museo Municipal de Oro (Entrance: $0.90)

This is the city's cultural gem. A wide variety of archaeological finds are displayed here, accompanied by explanations of the development of the Tallán, Yunga and Vicús cultures.

Help other travelers. Publish your favorite places at www.vivatravelguides.com

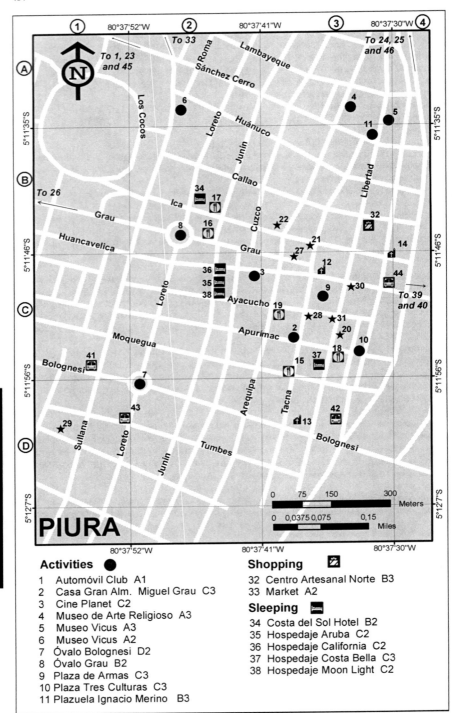

PIURA

Activities ●

1 Automóvil Club A1
2 Casa Gran Alm. Miguel Grau C3
3 Cine Planet C2
4 Museo de Arte Religioso A3
5 Museo Vicus A3
6 Museo Vicus A2
7 Óvalo Bolognesi D2
8 Óvalo Grau B2
9 Plaza de Armas C3
10 Plaza Tres Culturas C3
11 Plazuela Ignacio Merino B3

Shopping 📰

32 Centro Artesanal Norte B3
33 Market A2

Sleeping 🛏

34 Costa del Sol Hotel B2
35 Hospedaje Aruba C2
36 Hospedaje California C2
37 Hospedaje Costa Bella C3
38 Hospedaje Moon Light C2

NORTHERN COAST

Churches ⛪	Transportation 🚌
12 Catedral C3	39 Airport C4
13 Perpetuo Socorro D3	40 Civa C4
14 San Francisco C3	41 Civa C1
Eating 🍴	42 Cruz del Sur D3
	43 Paradero a Catacaos D1
15 Capuccino C3	44 Paradero a Patacaos C3
16 Heladería El Chalán B2	45 Terminal El Bosque A1
17 La Esquina del Sabor B2	46 Terminal Terrestre de Castilla A4
18 Picantería Los Santitos C3	
19 Restaurante Vida y Salud C3	

Services ★

20 Banco Nacional C3
21 BCP B3
22 Casa de Cambios B3
23 Comisaría A1
24 Consulado de Alemania A4
25 Consulado Ecuatoriano A4
26 Hospital Santa Rosa B1
27 InterBank C3
28 i-PERU C3
29 Migraciones D1
30 ScotiaBank C3
31 Serpost C3

Though a small museum, it has a quite impressive collection of gold artifacts, housed in the basement. Tuesday-Sunday, 9 a.m.-5 p.m. Huánuco 896 and Sullana, Tel: 51-73-309-267.

Casa Museo Gran Almirante Grau (Free, but donations accepted)

This house-turned-museum exhibits naval paraphernalia and other belongings of Miguel Grau Seminario, a war hero applauded for his accomplishments during the Marina de Guerra. Distinguished portraits, historical documents and antique furniture are on display. Daily, Monday-Friday 8 a.m.-1 p.m., 3-6 p.m., Saturday, Sunday 8 a.m.-noon. Just one block from the Plaza de Armas, Tacna 622.

Museo Municipal Vicús

This is the city's cultural gem that houses a wide variety of archaeological finds made of gold. Open Tuesday-Saturday 9 a.m.-5 p.m., Sunday 9 a.m.-1 p.m. Two blocks east from Urb Club Grau Huánuco 896 y Sullana. Tel: 51-73-309-267.

Museo de Arte Religioso

The Iglesia del Carmen is still used for masses, but its role has grown with the years. Now this venerable 18th century church is also a religious art museum, showcasing its Baroque altar screen and pieces from the Quiteña and Cusqueña schools of art. Adjoining the nave are two more galleries exhibiting fine silver and gold filigree models of churches, inlaid wooden crosses and other crafts by regional artisans, as well as religious items from Piura's other churches. Pope Juan Pablo II's chair from his visit is also displayed. Included in the admission is a visit to the Sala Bolívar Periodista, a journalism museum showing the history and technology behind Peru's oldest newspaper, El Peruano. Jirón La Libertad 366, Plazuela Merino.

PIURA LODGING

Piura has lodging options for any budget. From cheap no-nonsense hostels to the elegant but costly there is a place to suit any taste and pocketbook. Some hotels are located in the busier parts of town, near the Plaza de Armas, others on more residential quiet streets. Cheaper *hospedajes* often do not have hot water, but considering Piura's hot climate, you might not find

NORTHERN COAST

this an issue. In choosing a place to stay think not only about what area suits your needs, but also the concept of value. Some hotels may be cheaper, but rather run down and not conducive to a good night's rest. It might be worth spending a few more bucks for comfort's sake.

Hospedaje California (Rooms: $5 - 12)

For backpackers, Hospedaje California continues to be the best value. The rooms are cheery, the beds are comfortable and the staff is helpful. Seems like everything is great in sunny California, with the top floor terrace and balcony providing the ultimate chill-out area. There are however, no private bathrooms nor hot water. A fan can be provided. Three block west of Plaza de Armas, Junín 835 and Huancavelica, Tel: 51-7-332-8789, E-mail: ohema2003@hotmail.com.

Hospedaje Costabella (Rooms: $17 - 20)

With well-kept rooms and close proximity to popular eateries, Costabella is a good find for those willing to pay mid-range prices. Gringos and Peruvians alike stay here. All rooms have a private bathroom, hot water, cable television, wireless internet, telephone and fan. Hospedaje Costabella also offers laundry service and a restaurant. A security guard is always at the door. 2 blocks south of the Plaza de Armas, Libertad 1082 and Moquegua, E-mail: hostal_costabella@hotmail.com.

Costa del Sol Hotel (Rooms: $75 - 135)

Costal del Sol is owned by a chain of five luxury hotels of the same name in Northern Peru. There may be no notable, cultural character to the place, but it does have Jacuzzis. Come here to unwind and live the good life. Between the Plaza de Armas and the Gold Museum. Loreto 649 and Ica, Tel: 51-7-330-2864, Fax: 51-73-302-546, E-mail: ventaspiura@costadelsolperu.com, URL: www.costadelsolperu.com.

PIURA RESTAURANTS

While in Piura expect to partake in the sampling of a lot of traditional Peruvian foods, such as ceviche, (raw fish soaked in lemon juice), chicken or beef—and lots of rice. You will find restaurants serving this sort of food on every street corner. Some are better than others; use your best judgment and choose one that looks clean and reliable. Don't be too picky though, sometimes those hole-in-the-wall places have the best food. If you are craving food from home, there are a few options in the area that dish up international fare, such as pizza, sandwiches and salads.

Art Rock Café

Queen, Prince and Shakira posters grace the walls of this new breakfast and live-music eatery. Strangely, this place holds the reins in Piura as far as simple American breakfasts go, as well as happy hour. Small but tasty dishes are served from 8 a.m. to noon every day but Sunday. At night, patrons are served a healthy dose of rock, latin, jazz, pop, blues and funk—not to mention 2-for-1 cocktails from 8 to 10 p.m., Thursday to Sunday, and a mix of Peruvian and Swiss dishes. Live music plays from time to time, while pool and darts keep you occupied for the rest. The café is located inside the Plaza Rejas. Apurímac 341, Tel: 51-73-345-567.

El Rincón del Sabor (Entrees: $1 - 4)

Many of the diners of El Rincón del Sabor are regulars—not only for the inexpensive price ($1.35 for the special), but also because of the variety. The meal starts with your choice of appetizer or soup, and then moves into the main course accompanied by a *cebada* (barley) drink. Special menus are available at dinner, also. À la carte specialties include ceviche in three serving sizes ($1-3.35). Open for breakfast 7-10 a.m., lunch noon-3 p.m. and dinner 7-10 p.m. Calle Junín 692.

Restaurant Vegetariano Vida y Salud (Entrees: $1 - 5)

In the crowded market of vegetarian restaurants in Piura, Vida y Salud stands out for its economical meals and closeness to the lodging district. You can always count on the food here being creative, excellent and nutritious. Breakfasts include juice, a sandwich of choice, fruit salad and coffee or tea ($1.35). The set lunch offers several choices for appetizer and main course, and comes with dessert and drink ($1.70). At dinner, only à la carte entrees are served ($2.20-3). Open daily 7 a.m.-10 p.m. (although sometimes it does close earlier). Arequipa 509.

Heladería El Chalán (Entrees: $2 - 5)

This chain burger joint has a few locations in the downtown area. The ice cream is the main draw. Open daily 7:30 a.m.-11 p.m. Tacna 520, Grau 173.

Capuccino (Entrees: $3 - 9)

If stuck in the meat and rice rut, Capuccino is just the place to break up the routine: a gourmet cafe with a trendy European flare. Though primarily a pastry and coffee shop, the menu features a wide selection of salads, sandwiches and other specialty dishes, though it's all a bit pricey. Open Monday-Saturday 10 a.m.-2 p.m., 5-11 p.m. Tacna 786, Plaza Rejas. Tel: 54-73-301-111.

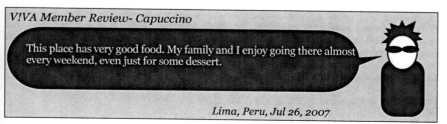

V!VA Member Review- Capuccino

This place has very good food. My family and I enjoy going there almost every weekend, even just for some dessert.

Lima, Peru, Jul 26, 2007

Picantería Los Santitos (Entrees: $4 - 11)

For more than 20 years, Santitos has been building its clientele, serving the typical fare of the northern coast of Peru, including ceviche, seafood, chicken and steak dishes. Enjoy the tasty cuisine, coastal music and traditionally-dressed friendly servers. Open daily 10 a.m.-11 p.m. Libertad 1040, Plaza Rejas, Tel: 51-733-09-475.

La Cabaña (Entrees: $4 - 12)

It may not be little Italy, but La Cabaña should fulfill your need for pizza and other traditional Italian dishes. This somewhat stylish corner restaurant is located close to many cheap hostels. Many locals come to eat and drink at later hours. Open daily 7 p.m.- Midnight Ayacucho 598, Tel: 51-73-306-610.

CATACAOS

Traveling southwest out of Piura the desert oasis fans into fields of cotton and forests of carob lining either side of the highway. Some 12 kilometers (7.2 miles) away is Catacaos, called the *Tierra de Encanto, Sol y Algarroba* (Land of Enchantment, Sun and Carob). This area had long been inhabited by the Tallán nation, who in turn had been conquered by the Chimú, Inca and Spaniards. In 1615 the priest Juan de Mori y Alvarado bought from the crown great extensions of land in the region which he then gave to the indigenous people.

Today the flower-filled central park of this small village is a pleasant place to sit beneath the trees and take a breather after wandering through the crafts markets. On one side is a white-trimmed green Iglesia de San Juan Bautista, said to be a replica of Rome's Sistine Chapel. Along the roofline are statues of Jesus and his twelve apostles, including Judas Iscariot clutching a bag of shekels, an ancient unit of currency. Inside, the nave is broad with no columns to separate it from the aisles. Painted on the barrel vaulting are scenes from Christ's life.

Surrounding the plaza and down Jirón Comercio are dozens of shops and stalls offering the artisan work for which Catacaos is renowned. You can spend hours wandering along the

NORTHERN COAST

streets and into the labyrinthine mini-malls. The ceramics are produced with pre-Hispanic techniques. Straw items, like hats and fans, are another famous product produced by the village's craftswomen, some of whom are willing to give lessons in weaving to visitors. Spectacular jewelry and statuary created with silver and gold filigree are surprisingly affordable. Other artisans now also do woodcarving and leatherwork. On Jirón Comercio is the Casa de la Cultura, which has a small museum displaying local *artesanía*, paintings and archaeological finds (Monday-Friday 8 a.m.-1 p.m., 2-8 p.m., Saturday 8 a.m.-1 p.m. Jirón Comercio 748. Entry: Free).

Catacaos showcases its traditions during its founding day celebrations on March 24. Additionally, it has one of the more rollicking pre-Lent carnivals in the region. As well, its Semana Santa is noteworthy, with masses, processions and a gastronomic fair featuring the *algarroba*, or carob products it is also well-known for. Another major religious festivity is the Bajada de Reyes, or the arrival of the Three Kings on January 6, in the near-by settlement of Narihualá.

A mere five kilometers (3 miles) away from Catacaos is the ancient village of Narihualá, dating to 1000 BC. The partially excavated adobe ruins include a ceremonial plaza and several buildings. Atop a hillock the Spaniards had built a church, which is now abandoned. The entire site is now scarred by erosion. The small museum displays ceramics and other articles found at the site, and an explanation of Tallán culture. Open daily 8 a.m.-5 p.m. Site entry: adults $0.70, high school and university students $0.35, primary school students $0.20. Local children will guide for a tip.

Population: 54.171, Altitude: 25 meters (81 feet), Phone Code: 073

Getting To and Away From Catacaos
From Piura, collective taxis leave from Calle Lima and Jirón Huancavelica, and from Avenida Loreto and Jirón Tumbes ($0.50). Combis depart from Terminal Terrestre El Bosque on Cerro Sánchez (6 a.m.-9 p.m., $0.35). From Catacaos, combis and collective taxis for Piura depart from opposite the plaza.

Even though Narihualá is within walking distance of the Catacaos, locals warn it is not safe for strangers to walk to the ruins. Motocycle rickshaw taxis leave from the corner of Jirón Comercio and Avenida Heredia ($1 one way, beware of overcharging). If returning to Piura from the archaeological site, it is said to be safe to walk the 700 meters (half mile) to the highway and flag down a passing bus.

CABO BLANCO
From late morning on, the winds kick up in Cabo Blanco, blowing sand into small dunes. The fishermen come ashore, their boats anchored in the steely-blue waters. Against the backdrop of the clear sky soar the bright chutes of paragliders surf the waves.

Few come to this small fishing village, located 29 kilometers (17.5 miles) south of Máncora. For many decades, however, this was the stomping ground of the richest US families, the Rockefellers, DuPonts and Firestones. The famous also came, sports great Ted Williams and Hollywood elites like Carole Lombard, Gregory Peck, Spencer Tracy and Jimmy Stewart. The most famous guest of the exclusive Fishing Club Hotel of Cabo Blanco hide-away was Ernest Hemingway, who had stayed here a month during the filming of his novella, *The Old Man and the Sea*, in 1956. (The movie was shot at a number of locations. Only about 10 minutes of footage from Cabo Blanco made it in the final cut.) Because of the meeting of the warm El Niño and cold Humboldt currents, the sea here is rich in plankton, thus drawing the much-prized sports fish, the black marlin. Many weighing over 1,000 pounds (455 kilograms) were caught. The largest was by Alfred C. Glassell, Jr., weighing in at 1,560 pounds (708 kilograms). Yellow fin tuna is another big catch here for sport fishers.

The Fishing Club has been closed since 1992. Plans are to open the renovated hotel over Easter Week 2009. Room 5—Mr. Hemingway's quarters—will be a museum showcasing the typewriter and other items he left behind. At present, the hamlet has only one lodge, Hotel El Merlín (URL: http://hotelmerlin.blogspot.com).

During the summer vacations (mid-December through March), Cabo Blanco picks up in visitors. At the end of the year, Billabong hosts a major surfing competition here. Mid-March is neighboring El Alto's Tourism Week and Founding Celebrations, with regattas and other events taking place in Cabo Blanco. The Southern summer is also the best season to try your hand at landing one of those prized black marlins. Yate Cristina, out of Los Órganos, offers these deep sea expeditions (51-73-257-600, E-mail: hangaroaperu@yahoo.com, URL: www.vivamancora.com/cristina). In the low season, though, few arrive. The fishermen continue to haul in their catches, now mostly albacore. North of the fishing pier is a cove where boats are dry-docked for repair. Windsurfers come to practice their sport.

While in Cabo Blanco, stop by Restaurant Cabo Blanco, owned by Hemingway's bartender Pablo Córdova. While serving you an absolutely exquisite *chicharrón de mariscos* (or any other seafood delight), he will tell you all about Papa's stay at the Fishing Club (Open daily 10 a.m.-6 p.m., Tel.: 51-73-256-121).

Population: 212, Altitude: 29 meters (94 feet), Phone Code: 073

Getting To and Away from Cabo Blanco

From Máncora, take an Eppo bus to El Alto (half-hourly 4 a.m.-7:15 p.m., $0.85, 40 minutes). Upon arriving in El Alto, catch a pick-up truck for Cabo Blanco from the park next to the city hall across the street (2 a.m.-6 p.m., $0.50, 20 minutes).

To get to the Fishing Club, follow the dirt road from the modern glass building at the entrance to the fishing hamlet. This track will go up over the hill, past the oil reserve. It is the white and blue building about a half-mile on. At low tide, you can walk there along the beach. On the heights of the cliffs, you will see nesting blue-footed boobies.

PAITA AND AROUND

Since at least 1700 BC, the coasts to the west of Piura have been premier fishing grounds. The Tallán lived here, and later the Chimú. On March 30, 1532, Spanish Conquistador Francisco Pizarro established San Francisco de Payta de Buena Esperanza in the main bay of the region. Payta, or Paita (as it is spelled today) is derived from Quechua and means "a just desolate desert." It was an important Spanish port, although with time, it lost its place to the city of Callao, further south. Once more, though, Paita is booming. It is the major port for the Interoceanic Highway, a continental project that creates a river and road shipping route from the Pacific to Atlantic.

After the Wars of Independence and the death of Simón Bolívar, Generala Manuela Sáenz (the Liberator's confidante) settled here in exile. She eked out a living by embroidering and making sweets. Her house still stands, and there are hopes are to make it into a museum (Jirón Nuevo del Pozo 390). Another famous face, Pacific War hero Miguel Grau, was a Paiteño by birth.

There are still a handful of colonial buildings that bedeck the labyrinth of streets, like the Iglesia de la Merced, the old customs building and the Club Liberal. Museo Elba Aranda de Sarango has archaeological, paleontological and historical exhibits. The palm tree-lined Malecón Almirante Miguel Grau and Playa El Toril along Mar de Grau are favorite strolling places for families and lovers. Stop at the tourism office at the new pier for more information (Monday-Friday 8 a.m.-3 p.m. Tel: 51-73-211-043, Anexo 205, E-mail: ofiturpaita@hotmail.com, URL: www.munipaita.gob.pe / www.paitavirtual.com). Have lunch next door to the office at Restaurante El Grifo (Jirón Los Cáramo s/n, Tel: 51-73-211-404, E-mail: vseseija@hotmail.com. Lunch special Monday-Friday, $ 2.35; daily à la carte $4.70-15). Tourism Week is the last part of March. Lodging in Paita is expensive, yet poor in quality. The best lodging choice seems to be Hostal Miramar, an old red mansion on the seafront (Single $13.35, Double $17. Avenida Jorge Chávez, Tel: 51-73-611-083).

Fishing continues to play a major role in the economy of Paita and its neighboring coastal villages. But beyond this veneer are kilometers-long grey sand beaches with great bird watching (including the Humboldt penguin) and sea lion colonies. Paita is the hub from which to visit these other hamlets.

Colán, 15 kilometers (9 miles) to the north, has long been one of northern Peru's great *balnearios*, or beach resorts. For decades the country's richest families have had vacation homes here. Colán has been around for much longer. It was a principle Tallán village. Spanish conquerors built San Lucas church—said to be the oldest on the Pacific coast of South America—atop a Chimú temple one kilometer inland. In 1983, flooding of the Chira River destroyed much of the resort. In recent years it has been rebuilt, with several expensive hotels. Budget travelers are not left out, though. In the low season, basic hostels like Restaurante-Hospedaje Los Cocos de Colán let rooms for as little as $6.70 per night (Avenida Costera s/n, Tel.: 51-73-778-519 / 96-926-1590, E-mail: loscocosdecolan@hotmail.com), and houses can be rented for $100 per month. Ask Secundino Ruiz of Restaurant-Hospedaje San Felipe, Paita's tourism office representative, about where is safe to camp. Colán's Playa Esmeraldas stretches five kilometers (3 miles). Beware of *rayas* (rays) if swimming. At the southern end, fossil-rich bluffs meet the sea. Oystercatchers, several species of gull, whimbrels, pelicans, frigate birds and blue-footed boobies are frequent visitors. The patron saint, Santiago Apóstol, is honored July 17-27 with traditional dances and other activities.

To the south of Paita are more pristine beaches. Yacila is a fishing village on a small, rocky cove 17 kilometers (10 miles) away from Paita. When the boats come in with their harvest of fish and *pota* (giant squid), the pelicans, man-of-war birds and sea lions come in for the castoffs. As well as modern wooden boats, men here use *balsillos*, traditional rafts made of five logs. Some travelers boogie board the waters, and everyone stops to watch the spectacular sunsets. Although accommodation is limited, there are two inns nearby for roughly $7-10.

When the tide is out (and if the sea isn't too rough) you can walk along the coast to the next beach, Los Cangrejos. With a bit of luck, you'll spot Humboldt penguins that live in caves worn into the rock cliffs. Otherwise, take the inland road to get to this beach for 2 kilometers (1.2 miles). Los Cangrejos is busy in the summer, but the rest of the year the only hotel is boarded up and sand dunes form around the vacation cottages. If you come in the off-season, ask around about renting a room from one of the dozen resident families or about camping. The many kilometers of sand afford great beachcombing and observation of birds and tidal pools.

Off-shore is Isla Foca, easiest reached from La Islilla hamlet, 22 kilometers (13 miles) south of Paita. A ride around the island to see its sea lion, guanero bird and penguin colonies costs about $10 per boat. Other southern beaches are La Laguna, Hermosa, Gramitas, Té para Dos and Las Gaviotas. These are very isolated during the low season; ask locally about safety. Playa Tortuga has a tourism officer who can orientate you to lodging and camping sites.

In many villages, Fiesta de San Pedro y San Pablo is a very large affair. From June 28-30, these patron saints of fishermen are feted with dances, maritime processions with San Pedro, regattas and masses. The summer months (mid-December through March) draw many vacationers, with prices rising sharply.

Paita—Population: 87,500, Altitude: 3 meters (10 ft), Phone Code: 073. Colán— Population: 13,000, Altitude, village: 45 meters (146 ft), Phone Code: 073. Yacila— Population: 800, Altitude: approx. 5 meters (16 ft), Phone Code: 073

Getting To and Away From Paita

In Paita, the Dora bus terminal is on the corner of Jirón Zanjón and Loreto. Buses run every half hour from 6 a.m. to 6 p.m., 40 minutes ($1). Other transport for Piura and other nearby beach towns leave from the brick-wall lot on the opposite corner.

Paita-Colán: Combis and collective taxis every half hour from 6 a.m.-9 a.m., then every one to two hours until 6 p.m. ($0.70, 20 minutes)

Paita-Yacila: Collective taxis and combis leave when full 5 a.m.-8 p.m. ($0.70, 20 minutes)

Paita-Islilla: Collective taxis leave when full 6 a.m.-5 p.m. ($1, 30 minutes)

Paita-Tortuga: Collective taxis leave when full 6 a.m.-5 p.m. ($1, 30 minutes)

HUANCABAMBA

Heading east from the Panamericana, the land stretches flat for hours. Ahead, between the folds of the mountains is Huancabamba. This road is mostly unpaved and it is necessary to ford a river. (In the wet season, small boats take passengers across to a waiting bus.) Soon, the road will be paved all the way to Huancabamba and beyond, to the new copper mines at Río Blanco.

Huancabamba is called the "City that Walks"—or, in local tongue *Ciudad Resbalabamba* (Slipping City). The town is built on a stratum of rock that is slowly sliding towards the river. Since at least the mid-19th century, there has been talk of relocating the village to more stable ground. People are now building higher up the hillside. Like any colonial-era town, the major buildings are around the Plaza de Armas. Along one side is the village church, Iglesia San Pedro, which is pretty colorful against the mountain backdrop. The Plaza and church gardens are full of topiary, shrubs sculpted into animals (including a band of critters playing in front of the church). In the center of the Plaza is a statue of La Samaritana, who represents the hospitality shown by the Huancabambinos. The region abounds with ruins of the former inhabitants. The most noteworthy is the Templo de los Jaguares. Many of the stone roads were used by the Spaniards to connect Huancabamba with Cabeza, Socha and other settlements. The most important spot is the Lagunas de las Huaringas, a traditional center for shamanism.

According to Dr. Felipe Paz Soldán, the name comes from Aymara. *Huancas* means large stones and *pampa* signifies plains. According to Incan chronicles written by Garcilaso de la Vega, the Huancabamba region was inhabited by an "empire of peoples of many languages and nations" who supposedly practiced cannibalism. Even though these peoples lived separately, they successfully captured an army sent by Inca Túpac Yupanqui. The Inca ruler decided to come with a force of more than 40,000 soldiers. Finally the nations here were conquered and many forced into relocation villages (*miqmaqs*). The Inca incorporated it into the Chinchay Suyo quadrant of the empire.

Spanish Captain Hernando de Soto and his soldiers followed the stone roads to Huancabamba and settled in the region. During the colonial period this was an important stop on trade routes. It earned a reputation as a hospitable town. When the cry for independence rose, Huancabambinos fervently joined the fight. The municipality was formally decreed by Libertador José de San Martín in 1821.

The village still opens its doors to visitors who come to have a healing ceremony done by the region's renowned healers. Lodging and dining options are basic, but sincere. Spend a while to explore the many natural and cultural wonders tucked into the valleys of this stretch of the Andes.

Altitude: 1957 meters (6360 ft), Population: 14,000, Phone Code: 073

NORTHERN COAST

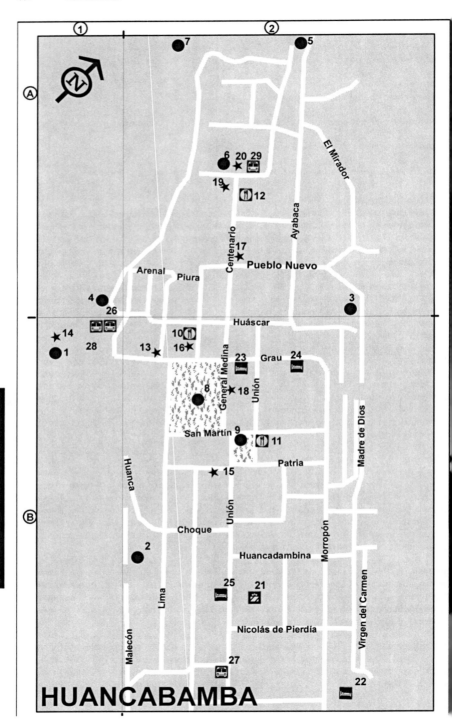

HUANCABAMBA

Activities ●

1 Jardín Botánico B1
2 Malecón B2
3 Mirador A2
4 Mirador A1
5 Mirador A2
6 Museo Mario Polia Meconi A2
7 Playa La Perla A2
8 Plaza de Armas B2
9 Plazuela Los Héroes B2

Eating 🍴

10 Café New York B2
11 Casa Blanca B2
12 El Tiburón A2

Services ★

13 Banco de la Nación B2
14 Hospital A2
15 Internet B2
16 Internet B2
17 Internet A2
18 Police B2
19 Serpost A2
20 Tourism Office A2

Shopping 🗺

21 Market B2

Sleeping 🛏

22 Albergue Turístico Municipal B2
23 Hospedaje El Dorado B2
24 Hospedaje Virgen del Carmen B2
25 La Cabaña B2

Transportation 🚌

26 Carros para Mitupamba B1
27 Combis to Sander B2
28 Combis to Sander B1
29 Terminal Terrestre A2

When to Go

The weather in Huancabamba is temperate and humid. In the higher altitude zones, it is cold and very humid. From January to April the region typically experiences rains, sometime perhaps even into May. Generally it is dry from May to December. The hottest month is December and the coldest is March. July is very busy with visitors who come for the local festivities in Huancabamba and Sapalache.

Festivals in Huancabamba are:
• **Second week of January**—Aniversario de Huancabamba—Arts fairs and cultural events
• **February 5-15**—Virgen de Lourdes
• **March / April**—Semana Santa (Easter Week)
• **July 13-20**—Fiesta Patronal de la Virgen del Carmen—Agricultural, cattle and artisan fairs, Danza de los Diabólicos and International Shaman Conference to honor the village's patron saint
• **August 15**—Virgen de la Asunción
• **September 14-30**—Fiesta de la Virgen de las Mercedes

Getting To and Away from Huancabamba

To Piura: Buses depart from the Terminal Terrestre. All companies charge $8.35 and take six to nine hours, depending on road conditions: Civa (8:30 a.m.), Etipthsa (7:30 a.m., 5 p.m.), Turismo Express (7:30 a.m., 5 p.m.).
To Chiclayo: Etipthsa has a bi-weekly service that is suspended during the rainy season.
Trucks for Piura and Chiclayo leave from the new bridge early in the morning. Carros (collective taxis) for neighboring villages also leave from there.
To Sondorillo: every half hour from 6 a.m.-3 p.m., $1.70, 1 hour.
To Sondor: Combis (mini-vans) depart from the corner of Calle Unión and Puente Porvenir, just past the market ($1, 45 minutes).
To Lagunas de las Huaringas (Salalá and San Antonio villages): Legitimate transport leaves from inside the bus terminal (4 a.m., 5 p.m., $3.35).
To Jaén: Transporte Cruz Chiquita (Calle 2 de mayo s/n)—8 a.m. and a later one 10 a.m.-

NORTHERN COAST

noon, leaving when full, $12, 9-10 hours. If you miss one of these, go to Tamborapa (3-4 daily, $5, 5 hours) and transfer from there.

Getting Around
A motorcycle rickshaw taxi costs $0.35 within the city and $0.50-0.70 to outlying areas. Always ask the price before boarding and insist on paying the real price. There is a shop that rents dirt bikes, if you want to explore the villages on your own (Grau 100, Tel: 51-73-207-919).

Safety in Huancabamba
Many conmen hang outside the bus terminal arranging trips to the Lagunas. The tourism office says to avoid them for your own safety. Ask the tourism office for assistance in taking legitimate transportation and a list of registered healers.

The tourism office also suggests you go on hikes with a local so you don't get lost. Trails to many attractions are not well marked.

Although the view of the sunset over the mountains is fantastic from the lookout, be careful here from dusk to dawn.

THINGS TO SEE AND DO IN HUANCABAMBA
Huancabamba's most famous attraction is the Lagunas de las Huaringas, nationally and internationally renowned for its *curanderos*, or shamans. The entire region, however, abounds with things to do and see—much of it yet undeveloped. Pre-Columbian ruins and waterfalls paint the countryside around quaint villages like Sondorillo and Sondor. For those with their own gear and experience, paragliding and rock climbing are sports that'll get the adrenaline pumping. (Unfortunately, no tour operators as yet offer these adventures). You can also trek to the Lagunas, Cascadas de Sipán, Infiernillo and Pariacaca. In town, don't miss the tourism office's Museo Mario Polío Meconi, or the Jardín Botánico de Plantas Medicinales (Monday-Friday 9 a.m.-noon. Granja CIPA, near Pronamach and the hospital. Entry: Free). You can hang out with the locals watching *telenovelas* on the public TV posted in Plazuela de los Héroes (Daily 7 p.m.-Midnight, extended viewing when there is a soccer game on the tube).

Templo de los Jaguares
The path off the road leads along a blue agave cactus hedge. From afar, this site, dating from about 1200 AD, doesn't look like much, just an old stone wall. But once reaching the Templo de los Jaguares, a wooden catwalk takes you around this ceremonial center sunken into the earth. The ancient cultures had performed rituals and left offerings upon the altars for the two reposing stars of this site—a female jaguar and a male carved in the sand-colored rock.

From the new bridge in Huancabamba, take a collective taxi to Sondorillo (half-hourly 6 a.m.-3 p.m., $1.70, 1 hour). Tell the driver to let you off at Mitupampa. From the blue sign, follow the road to the left. At the first turn-off, go left. At the next crossroads, turn left; the next two crossroads go straight. At the fifth, go right. The path will go down hill to the site, which is under a large zinc roof. The walk to the site takes about 30 minutes. There are few people to ask directions, and you can easily be lead to wrong paths or long ways around. The above instructions detail the most direct route. The site is at an altitude of 2800 meters (9100 feet).

Lagunas de las Huaringas
The Lagunas de las Huaringas are 14 lagoons that are said to have magical waters charged with positive energy and minerals. There are fields of green grasses and medicinal herbs. One of the principal lakes is Shimbe, also known as Lago de Turquesa (Turquoise Lake), where the Huancabamba River begins. Another well-known lagoon is Laguna la Negra, or Laguna del Inca. The whole area is at an altitude of 3,500-3,900 meters (11,375-12,675 feet) and has been declared an ecological, cultural and tourism reserve.

An almost undeveloped aspect of tourism to the Lagunas is trekking. The tourism office has a hand-drawn map of the region, including the distances and villages. Legitimate transport for Salalá and San Antonio leave from inside the bus terminal (4 a.m., 5 p.m., $3.35). From there you can trek to the lakes, or choose to do so from Huancabamba. Many hucksters hang outside the bus terminal arranging trips to the Lagunas. The tourism office cautions, for your own safety, to avoid them. Such offers could possibly lead to robberies. Ask the tourism office for assistance in taking legitimate transportation and a list of registered healers (if you also plan to have a ceremony done).

Remember you will be at high altitude, with a cold and humid climate. Be properly prepared against hypothermia and take precautions against sunburn. Because you will be trekking across unsigned territory with poor maps, you may want to hire a local guide; ask Huancabamba's tourism office for suggestions.

Note: Tourism is mostly a do-it-yourself affair in Huancabamba. It is best to consult with the tourism office to arrange your journey to Lagunas de las Huaringas or elsewhere. The only operation in town offering tours to the Lagunas is the all-inclusive *curandero* package (transportation with Civa, lodging, food and ceremony) that Restaurant Casa Blanca offers (Calle Unión 302, Tel: 51-73-473-157).

Do not defile the waters of the Lagunas, as these are sacred places.

Huancabamba Lodging

Most Peruvians coming to Huancabamba immediately go on to Lagunas Huaringas to have a healing ceremony done. Few spend a night in this village. It is surprising, therefore, that there are so many hostels here. Most are in the budget to low-mid-range price categories and are simple, family-run inns. The majority have hot water of the showerhead-heater variety. (Take care not to touch the wires or showerhead, lest you have a bit of a shock.)

Albergue Turística de la Municipalidad (Rooms: $3 - 5)
For travelers looking for a bucolic retreat, the village has a guesthouse on the outskirts of town. The hill-top lodge, set within a garden, has tremendous views over the valley below and the mountains beyond. The wood-paneled reception area has a TV. There are two wings of 12 large, sunny rooms furnished with beds and table. Hire a mototaxi to take you ($0.50-0.70). To walk there, follow Calle 2 de Mayo past the market to the end, then turn left, cross the bridge and about 150 meters (500 feet) on, before the Transporte Cruz Chiquita bus office is a green gate. Follow the road up, past the school IST Nestor Marlos Garrido. The Albergue Turística is across from the cemetery. 1 kilometer from town, off 2 de Mayo.

Hospedaje El Dorado (Rooms: $5 - 8)
Hospedaje El Dorado is an an old building teeming with character. All the guestrooms share common baths that are a bit worn but have hot water. Those rooms for solo travelers are on the first floor and a bit musty and claustrophobic. For pairs and groups, rooms on the second floor have views over the Plaza or balconies above the side street. All rooms also come with chamber pots, in case nature calls in the middle of the night. The owner and staff are very knowledgeable about the region. General Medina 116, Plaza de Armas, Tel: 51-73-473-016.

Hospedaje Virgen del Carmen (Rooms: $7 - 15)
Hospedaje Virgen del Carmen is considered the best of Huancabamba. The front of the hostel is classic colonial architecture. A back addition has two levels of new, nicely tiled rooms. Some of these accommodations are on the small side, so ask to see a few rooms before settling. Both private and shared baths have hot water. The common ones are the cleanest you'll find in town. You can ask the señora to use the kitchen to heat water. 1.5 blocks from the Plaza de Armas, across from Colegio María Inmaculada Calle Grau s/n, Tel: 51-73-473-017.

Help other travelers. Publish your favorite places at www.vivatravelguides.com

HUANCABAMBA RESTAURANTS

Eating is pretty basic in Huancabamba. A few restaurants do turn up the grill for special treats aimed to the tourist crowds that flock to the region for festivals and healing sessions. For the most part, though, diners offer the daily special, which averages $1.35. To warm up in the brisk evenings, have a local nightcap of *rompope* (an eggnog-like drink with a Grade-A aguardiente kick), or an *algarrobina* (carob) or *miel de México* (made of blue agave cactus juice) cocktail.

Café New York (Drinks: $.70 - 2)

Once upon a time, Felix went to New York City and fell in love with the "Center of the World." When he came back, he and his wife, Tula, opened up the intimate bistro Café New York. This quaint café has bright-orange and yellow decorated booths. Sit down on the cushioned benches at a table and ring the bell for service. You can draw the curtain and dim the light for a more romantic ambience. The music is kept low (requests accepted) so you and your companions can enjoy a laid-back conversation over empanadas and sandwiches, washed down by one of the local cocktails. Entrées / drinks $0.70-2. Open daily 4-10 p.m. Calle 2 de Mayo 206, Tel: 51-73-473-786.

La Cabaña (Entrees: $1 - 3)

Etched-glass doors mark the entrance to La Cabaña, one of Huancabamba's many inexpensive restaurants. Original paintings and shelves of Chulucanas and Catacaos ceramics deck the walls. Many locals and visitors choose this eatery above the others, whether for breakfast ($1-1.35), lunch special $1-35-1.70) or dinner (special $1.35, broasted chicken $2.50). Open for breakfast 7-10 a.m., lunch noon-3 p.m., dinner 7-10 p.m. Calle La Unión 516, Tel: 51-73-473-461.

El Tiburón (Entrees: $2 - 8)

El Tiburón has all bases covered. It's a restaurant that specializes in typical Peruvian food, like all manners of fish, seafood and the omnipresent broaster chicken. Plus, there is the disco. Its space is large—almost cavernous—and filled with the energy of families. This is definitely not a place to enjoy a romantic meal, but rather to soak in the energy of vacationing Peruvians having a good time. Open daily 8 a.m.-8 p.m. Avenida Centenario 211, Tel: 51-73-473-203.

ZORRITOS

Traveling southward from Tumbes, the Pan-American Highway threads together one fishing village after another, accentuated with the occasional resort town. Warm waters wash onto the pale grey beaches. Surfing is a prized sport on these shores, as is fishing and bird watching. A mere 27 kilometers (16 miles) south of Tumbes is Zorritos, one of Peru's best kept secrets. Here three hamlets string together for about five kilometers (three miles) along the Pan-American Highway. They provide a much more pleasant introduction to Peru than Tumbes.

Balneario Zorritos at Kilometer 1241.5 is the first sector of town. A monument to the first oil rig drilled in South America greets the visitor. Going southward are the village's only bank and a small plaza surrounded by municipal buildings and a church. The Balneario is where most hotels and restaurants can be found. The Pan-Am here is called Av. Faustino Piaggio. Contralmirante Villar (Kilometer 1238), simply known as Villar, is the next link in the Zorritos necklace. Along Av. República del Perú (so the highway is now called) are bus company offices, the fishing port and the market. This stretch also has less expensive hotels and restaurants. Parque Grau, with a chapel, is the center of this hamlet and the stop for combis and collective taxis to Tumbes. Kilometer 1237 marks the beginning of Los Pinos, the last of Zorritos' principal beaches. Here the Pan-Americana is known as Avenida Los Pinos.

Zorritos used to be a bustling petroleum town. It was here that in 1863, the first oil rig in South America was sunk. Faustino Piaggio is credited with establishing Peru's national petroleum industry. Up into the 1940s the headquarters were here. About 22 oil platforms are still offshore, though few are in actual operation. Nowadays Zorritos' economy is based on fishing and tourism. In the austral summer, vacationing Peruvians and Ecuadorians arrive to ride the surf and partake of the warm waters of this coast. During the rest of the year, a few foreign tourists come to learn surfing, laze on the beach or soak in the nearby hot springs.

When to Go

Zorritos is a popular Peruvian vacation destination from mid-December through March and for the Fiestas Patrias at the end of July. Prices double during these times. The rest of the year the beaches are quiet and the town is laid-back.

The village as a whole, as well as its various beaches, has many religious special masses and processions.

May 13 (Los Pinos)—Nuestra Señora de Fátima
June 29 (Villar)—San Pedro
August 11-12 (All Zorritos, especially in the countryside)—Santa Clara
September 24 (Villar)—Nuestra Señora de las Mercedes
Mid-October (All Zorritos)—El Señor de los Milagros

Getting To and Away from Zorritos

Bus companies are located north of the park, along the Panamericana. South of Puente Los Pozos are El Dorado and Flores; north, Cial and Civa. You can flag down a bus or combi (van) heading your direction anywhere along the highway.

To Tumbes: Combis and shared taxis — 20 minutes ($.70)
To Máncora: Minivans or buses — mostly 7-9 a.m. and in mid-afternoon, 1.5 hours ($1.70)
To Piura: Frequent buses (especially El Dorado), 3.75-4 hours ($5-6)
Fares for destinations farther away are about the same as from Tumbes.

Getting Around

Most people zip around Zorritos in three-wheel motorcycle rickshaw taxi ($0.50-0.70).

ZORRITOS SERVICES

Zorritos' tourism office in the Municipalidad operates only in the summer high season.

The only bank in Zorritos is Banco de la Nación, changing US cash dollars and providing MoneyGram services (Monday-Friday 8 a.m.-5:30 p.m., Saturday 9 a.m.-1 p.m. Avenida Faustino Piaggio 194, Balneario Zorritos). There are no casas de cambios. Some businesses, like Restaurante Turístico El Brujo, exchanges cash US dollars. The nearest ATM and traveler check facilities are in Tumbes.

A few locutorios and even fewer internet cafés operate in Zorritos. Kumb@l.net handily provides both services, including international calls. Internet costs $0.35 per hour (Daily 8:30 a.m.-11 p.m. Corner of Plaza Grau, Villar). Serpost, the post office, is near the market (Monday, Wednesday, Friday 9-10:30 a.m. Avenida Grau 519)

Centro de Salud Zorritos provides medical assistance to the village (daily 8 a.m.-8 p.m. Avenida República del Perú, across from the gas station, Villar, Tel.: 51-72-544-158). Zorritos has few pharmacies, most located in the Villar sector.

Lavandería Ferny can do up your dirty duds for $1.70 per kilo (daily 8 a.m.-10 p.m. Avenida República del Perú 088, Tel.: 51-72-9-712-978).

At Hands and Amp; Surf Escuela, established by the international organization Surfing Solidaridad, Coco teaches newbies how to ride the waves (Restaurant Sun Beach, Avenida República del Perú 088, Tel.: 51-72-9-712-978, E-mail: cocobighead@msn.com).

Help other travelers. Publish your favorite places at www.vivatravelguides.com

ZORRITOS LODGING

Zorritos has a full range of lodging options for its visitors, from camping on up to luxury resorts. All are located along the Pan-American Highway. Further south are fewer inns, but a guaranteed tranquil, uncrowded stay. In additional to more traditional hotels, a less-formal arrangement is a room let by local families. Just look for the "Se alquila habitaciones" signs. Room prices can be negotiated in the low season.

Hostal Grillo Tres Puntas (Rooms: $4 - 19)

Hostal Grillo Tres Puntas is the younger sister of Casa Grillo, both owned by the same family. A mosaicked front archway greets visitors to this sprawling complex of bungalows mad of adobe-plastered bamboo (the traditional materials of this region). Baths, both common and private, are tiled in stone and shell. Each room has a balcony with hammock. A central building has the restaurant, common room and bar all surrounded by a broad verandah. Pass the day in a hammock or in one of the *enramadas* (palm-thatched shelters) on the beach. Be sure to ask León about his bevy of Viringos (Peruvian hairless dogs). To get there, ask the bus driver to let you off at Km 1235 of the Highway. You will see the gateway and sign. Panamericana Norte Km 1235, Tel: 51-72-97-642-836, E-mail: reserves@casagrillo.net, URL: www.casagrillo.net.

Casa Grillo (Rooms: $5 - 7)

Casa Grillo isn't as fancy as it once was, but it is still a backpacker's haven. The four rooms of this ecological hotel are constructed of bamboo with bamboo furnishings. Most have poster beds for easy hanging of your mosquito net. (If you don't have your own, the staff can provide you with one.) Windows are screened. Spend the afternoon swaying in the front patio's hammocks and come evening whip up your dinner over the kitchen's wood fire. It's a simple life at Casa Grillo, popular not only with budget travelers, but also local lovers looking for seclusion. Guests here can join tours from Hotel Grillo Tres Puntas. Avenida los Pinos 563, Panamericana Norte Kilometer 12356.5, Tel: 51-72-794-828 /51-72- 544-222, E-mail: casagrillo@yahoo.es, URL: www.casagrillo.net.

Arrecife Hotel (Rooms: $16 - 24)

This upscale hotel is located right on the beach and affords pleasant views of the Pacific. Amenities offered include: internet access, cable TV, and direct dial telephone service. The tropical garden bar and restaurant serves as a great meeting point. Breakfast is included and all credit cards are accepted. Faustino Piaggio 158, Zorrito District, Tel: 51-72-544-46, E-mail: www.arrecifehotel.com.

M-Zen Beach Cottage (Rooms: $60 for 2 people)

Ideally located 30 minutes from Máncora on a private kms-long immaculate beach, offers simplicity, rest, amazing views and food. Paradise found! Drive north of Máncora for approximately 30 km, the hotel is on your left-hand side, just passing the bridge, Puente Huacura. M-Zen has a bamboo fence and visible sign. Puente Huacura, Panamericana Norte km 203, Tel: 01-99-980-944, E-mail: mzenonline@gmail.com, URL: www.mzen-online.com.

V!VA Member Review- M-Zen Beach Cottage

Silence relax sun, warmest waters ever, amazing food. Play beach volley, swim, read a book, stargaze. We had the best time here, a place to find your real self. Exceptional--truly.

Italy, Jan 07, 2008

ZORRITOS RESTAURANTS

As can be expected in a village whose principal products come from the ocean, the main feature on Zorritos menus is naturally seafood. Restaurants are all along the Panamericana, with cheaper ones in Villar hamlet. These provide set meals at \$1.20-1.70. There are scant diners in Los Pinos. Zorrito's central market is at Avenida Grau and Paseo Orlando Herrera A., one block east of the highway, in the Villar district. It has the usual produce stands and cheap eateries. The better stocked general stores are nearby. Fresh fish can be bought at the Terminal Pesquero.

Restaurant Arriba Perú (Entrees: \$1 - 9)

Restaurant Arriba Perú is just off the Panamericana. This orange-trimmed, blue and white diner sports a wraparound porch that's great for dining on home-cooked Peruvian food. The menu offers typical fishing village fare: fish, conch and other seafood ceviches. All are prepared in a variety of manners, including simple *á la plancha* (grilled) to *macho* (seafood sauce with a spicy kick). A few token chicken and meat dishes also appear. Open daily 9 a.m.-9 p.m. South edge of Villar sector.

Restaurant Sun Beach (Entrees: \$3 - 5)

After a day of surfing lessons with Coco, refuel through the food, view and refreshing breeze at this family-run rustic restaurant. The family serves generous portions of local fish and seafood. The ceviche is superb. Open daily 8 a.m.-10 p.m. Restaurant Sun also offers laundry sevices, so don't forget to pick up your clean clothes on your way out. Av. República del Perú 088, Tel: 51-72-505-265.

Restaurante Turístico El Brujo (Entrees: \$5 - 15)

Restaurante Turístico El Brujo is a tourist getaway from the crazy border and the town of Tumbes. The apple-green and white round restaurant on the beach is open-sided and provides unhindered views of the sea. The second floor balcony is an intimate space or tuck in at one of the tables surrounding the swimming pool. El Brujo's menu specializes in all types of fish and seafood, but doesn't forget chicken and beef dishes. Open Tuesday to Sunday and holidays, 10 a.m.-5 p.m., 7:15 p.m.-11 p.m. Av. Faustino Piaggio s/n (north of Puente Panteo), Tel: 51-72-544-140 / 51-9-72-638-428, E-mail: anilu299@hotmail.com.

THINGS TO SEE AND DO IN ZORRITOS

Travelers find themselves spending more time in Zorritos than they originally planned, not only chilling on the beach and surfing, but also taking in the many alluring attractions nearby. Bocapán, just five kilometers (three miles) south, has good fishing and lagoons perfect for bird watching. Mangroves both north and south are other good places for observing feathered creatures. In the eastern hills are two hot springs: the mud pools of Los Hervideros and the crystalline ones of El Tubo. Zorritos is an access point for Cerros de Amotape National Park.

Cerros de Amotape National Park

With its four different ecosystems, the Cerros de Amotape National Park, south of Tumbes, stands out as one of the finest models of an equatorial dry forest on the Pacific coast. Here you can enjoy a 100 different types of birds, amphibians, butterflies, and mammals (including the giant sloth bear, boa constrictors, and the American Crocodile, the latter an endangered species), along with 44 varieties of trees, 47 different types of bushes, and 61 species of plants, (including four varieties of orchids).

Amotape is at its most humid from December to April, and generally drier throughout the rest of the year. This park is 30 to 40 minutes from Tumbes, but can only be accessed through a tour agency. Permission to enter this park must be obtained from the Instituto Nacional de Recursos Naturales (INRENA) in Tumbes (Av. Tarapacá 427, Tel.: 52-6489). It is easier to go on tour to this reserve, as the agency takes care of the permit.

Los Hervideros

Surrounded by the ragged desert hills southeast of Zorritos, in this broad valley along the Quebrada El Grillo, the five natural pools of Los Hervideros provide an additional heat to the

South American sun. Los Hervideros are not your typical hot springs, though. The springs are full of fine clay muds that are rich in chlorides, iodine, iron and other salts. Each small pond has a different temperature and type of soil. One has green waters and black mud and another has reddish-brown clay. Locals swear to the springs' medicinal properties.

Near Bocapán south of Zorritos is the signed turn-off for Los Hervideros. From there it is five kilometers (three miles). Follow the road from the turn-off two kilometers (1.2 miles) to Cañaveral. Then head north three kilometers (1.8 miles) north to Quebrada El Grillo. Tour companies in Tumbes and Zorritos offer excursions. Daylight hours are best, though some tour operators do have night excursions. Be ready to get down and dirty. Some pools are clearer, allowing one to wash off (a bit).

El Tubo

If your idea of soaking in hot springs is a pure-water affair, then head for El Tubo. Here, when you exit the pools you'll drip water, not mud. Although a different experience than the other nearby hot springs, these are another wondrous place to just soak away. The thermal waters of El Tubo are full of natural salts, which give them medicinal properties. From Zorritos market, Paseo Orlando Herrera A. lends its way to El Tubo. You can hire a mototaxi to take you there ($6.70 roundtrip, with wait; 10 minute ride) or walk it in about 1.5 hours (one way). Daylight hours are best for coming to El Tubo, though some tour operators go in the evening.

ZORRITOS TOURS

You don't have to go all the way into Tumbes to arrange excursions to Cerros de Amotape and the other national parks in the area, or to local attractions like Los Hervideros and El Tubo. In Zorritos a few tour companies operate. Biosfera offers eco-tours to these sights (Avenida Faustino Piaggio 094, Tel.: 51-72-544-390 / 51-97 -917-149, E-mail: reserves@biosferatours. com, URL: www.biosferatours.com). León of Hotel Grillo Tres Puntas also takes people on a full range of expeditions (Panamericana Norte Km. 1235, Tel.: 97-642-836, E-mail: reserves@casagrillo.net, URL: www.casagrillo.net).

MÁNCORA

The surf is sweet in Máncora, and its growing reputation as a surfer's paradise has transformed this once small fishing village into a hopping resort town. During the summer, from late December to March, the city's characteristic sandy beaches swell with surfers and sandbunnies alike. Due to its popularity (or more precisely, the popularity of its beaches), the town boasts a number of budget hotels and cheap restaurants. A variety of surf schools and bars ensure that any visitor will have plenty to do, both day and night. Máncora is also one of the few Peruvian towns to have surfable waves almost all year-round; even in the off season the city's streets and beaches are bustling with travelers from around the world.

For a slightly quieter scene head south of town to Las Pocitas, a long strip of sand traced by lush green vegetation. Harboring less people and a distinctly more laid-back atmosphere than the main beach in Máncora, Las Pocitas has become a popular spot for families and anyone who enjoys long walks and lounging on the beach in relative peace.

Further down on the dirt road leading from Las Pocitas is Vichayito. In contrast to Máncora and Las Pocitas, the accommodation here is more spread out and consists mainly of quiet bungalows close to the beach. Large groups and families may want to look into renting out one of the houses in the area.

When to Go

Locals report that it never rains and the sun shines every day of the year in Máncora. With this in mind, note that the heat swells from January to March, just like the crowd of vacationing Peruvians. This is also a prime destination during most national holidays, especially the

Fiestas Patrias (mid-July to the first weekend of August). In the high seasons, prices double or triple and lodging is difficult to find, so make reservations in advance during the busier times. The town celebrates its founding day with celebrations November 4 to 14, which include artisan exhibits, gastronomic fairs and regattas.

Getting To and Away from Máncora

All bus companies are located on Av. Grau, as the Pan-American Highway is known north of the church.

To Piura: Eppo (stopping in Los Órganos, El Alto, Talara and Sullana, half-hourly 4 a.m.-7:15 p.m., $4). Also El Dorado and Transporte Chiclayo, 3 hours.

To Chiclayo: Transporte Chiclayo (seven buses daily, $10), El Dorado (9 a.m., three buses 9:30 p.m.-midnight, $7-9), Flores (12:30 p.m., 2:30 p.m., $10), Emtrafesa (9:30 p.m., $8), 5-6 hours.

To Trujillo: El Dorado (9:30 p.m., 11 p.m., $15), Emtrafesa (9:30 p.m., $10), Transporte Chiclayo (5:30 p.m., 10 p.m., $13), Flores (12:30 p.m., 2:30 p.m., $14), 8-9 hours.

To Lima: Roggero (6 p.m., $20), Cruz del Sur (5:30 p.m., $47-57), Flores (five buses 12:30-8:30 p.m., $24-40), 16-18 hours.

In Máncora you can catch the CIFA bus direct to Machala or Guayaquil, Ecuador, getting you safely through the problematic Aguas Verdes / Huaquillas border (daily 2 p.m. and 9 p.m., $13.35-16.70, 4-6 hours).

Getting Around Máncora

The Panamerican Highway is the main street in Máncora. North of city hall and the church, it is referred to as Avenida Grau. Then, south of the town center, it is known as Avenida Piura. Motorcycle rickshaw taxis whip passengers around the village for $0.35 per trip.

Safety in Máncora

Because Máncora attracts local and international tourists, it also attracts the thieves. Several armed robberies have been reported on the trail that leads to the northern sector of the beach. While at the beach, take special care with any belongings and camping on the beach is not recommended.

If roughing it, and sleeping outside, be aware of the *araña casera* (a poisonous spider with legs about an inch long). It hides in vegetation and clothes, so be sure to shake out clothing and footwear before putting them on. If you have been bitten, seek medical attention.

MÁNCORA SERVICES

In the Máncora city hall is an iPeru information booth that is sometimes staffed. You can also visit www.vivamancora.com for more information about Máncora hotels, restaurants and nearby attractions.

The only bank in town is Banco de la Nación. It changes US cash dollars and is the MoneyGram agent; its ATM accepts only Visa and Plus (Monday-Friday 8a.m.- 5:30 p.m., Saturday 9 a.m.-1 p.m. Av. Piura 641). Two GlobalNet ATMs, which take Visa, Plus, MasterCard, Cirrus and American Express cards, are found next to Hotel Sol y Mar and at Commercial Marlon (both on Av. Piura). A BCP ATM that excepts all the same plastic is across the street from Restaurant Espada. Many bus offices and tour agencies exchange US cash dollars.

Internet and *locutorios* (phone offices) are common. The internet costs $0.50-0.70 per hour. Phone calls, per minute, are $0.07-0.10 for local / national land lines, $0.20 and up for international landlines, and $0.30-0.50 for cell phone calls. Ushpa internet café has all services, including Skype (daily 9 a.m.-11 p.m. Av. Piura 372). There is no post office.

Máncora's public hospital is Centro de Salud Máncora (Tel.: 25-8130). On the road to the beach is an emergency health post. Many pharmacies are on Av. Piura and Av. Grau.

Help other travelers. Publish your favorite places at www.vivatravelguides.com

Laundry services abound here, allowing visitors more time to enjoy the surf and sand. The English-speaking staff of Lavandería El Espumón provides two-hour service for $1.70 per kilo (Monday-Saturday 8:30 a.m.-1 p.m., 3-6 p.m. Av. Piura 216, Tel.: 9954-812).

On the West side of the Pan-American is Máncora's *malecón*. Here all types of artisans set up shop, selling everything from crocheted bikinis to palm-fiber hats to jewelry. Some, however, have sea horses and other protected species for sale; it is advised not purchase these.

THINGS TO SEE AND DO IN MÁNCORA

Surfing
In Máncora, there is surfing and then there are all other activities. Surfing is practiced by men and women, young and old, a religion of sorts. There are reliable swells at most all times of the year and the *playas* are blessed with the same warm waters as Ecuador's Galápagos Islands. The several different breaks satisfy surfers of all abilities. Surf camp and lessons for beginners are available on many of Máncora's beaches.

Kite Surfing and Kite Boarding
In addition to surfing, there is a growing kite-surfing scene in Máncora. The wind is consistent, the waves always present and the water is usually warm – making Máncora a hot new spot for kitesurfers. During some months of the year, surfers may need to wear wet suits as the water can be colder than in more northern places like Zorritos. Be warned that sharing the water and the waves with local surfers is not always the most pleasant of experiences, but if you know what you're doing, and are respectful of others, you shouldn't have problems.

La Escuela de Wawa (Classes: $15)
La Escuela de Wawa is sponsored by Peruvian surfing champion Fernando Paraud, also known as Wawa. Pro instructor, Alan Roberto Valdiez, will guide you through all phases of aquatic aptitude, from "sand zaboob" to "trimming it on the stick," until you can "snap up and ice a wave". Alan guarantees no accidents and you proceed at your own pace. Classes are 70 minutes long, at a very reasonable $15 each, with all profits going to help local children. Hotel del Wawa, Av. Piura, Tel: 51-7-385-8258, E-mail: alansurf85@hotmail.com.

MÁNCORA TOURS

One Earth ($20 - 100)
Nature calls in Máncora—literally, from the songs of migrating whales in the Pacific to the low call of the egret in the nearby biosphere reserve. There are quieter attractions as well, such as a natural tar pit, with genuine hot tar. Working with local scientists, One Earth sponsors progressive, educational outdoor exploration. Eduardo Chamochumbi can accommodate every skill level, from beginning to advanced, on excursions ranging from boat tours and snorkeling, to one-day treks to multi-day camping trips. Its office is open seven days a week. Av. Piura, Tel: 51-1-231-5390, E-mail: lalo@oneearthperu.com, URL: www.oneearthperu.com.

Iguana's Trips
The Cerros de Amotape National Park in northern Peru features 404 species of bushes, reeds, herbs and epiphytic plants, as well as 44 species of trees, 63 species of mammals, 28 species of amphibians and 44 species of reptiles. Ursula Behr of Iguana's Trips is happy to teach you about every single one. There is more as well: Ursula has nearly two decades experience as a whitewater rafting guide. Iguana's Trips offers expertise in all areas of natural adventure, from mountain biking to snorkeling, or just visiting natural hot springs for a day of relaxation and serenity. Av. Piura 245, Tel: 51-9-853-5099 URL: www.vivamancora.com/igunastrips.

MÁNCORA LODGING
A surfer's paradise, Máncora has no lack of resort-style accommodation. Máncora's growing recognition as a surfer's paradise has transformed this once-small fishing village into a hopping resort town. During the summer, from late December to March, the city fills to the

max with people who want to enjoy the town's sun and sand. Due to its popularity, the town has a good amount of budget hotel options. Pricing tends to be reasonable, but you should shop around to find the best deal. If you are visiting during high season, be sure to make a reservation as far in advance as possible, just to ensure you will have a decent place to end up at after a long day of surfing and soaking up the rays.

BUDGET

Casa-Hospedaje Crillón (Rooms: $4 - 10)

Near the bus stations and one block from the highway, Casa-Hospedaje Crillón is a gem of a place to spend your nights while in Máncora. It is on a pedestrian street, which guarantees a more tranquil rest than at most hostels in this village. The clean, good-size rooms have comfortable beds and screened windows. Some accommodations have private bath. It is, admittedly, a bit far from the beach access road. Although, for those who are here for a spell of simple relaxation, Crillón is the best of Máncora's budget lodging. Paita 172, Tel: 51-73-258-017.

Hostel Casa Samara (Rooms: $4 - 20)

Right across the highway from the beach access road down is Walter Palomino's Hostel Casa Samara, owned by surfing great Walter Palomino. The few simple rooms are enough for a night's rest. All is kept clean and ready for guests to rest between waves. Surfing equipment is for sale or rent and lessons, tours and board repairs are available. Plunk down at one of the tables on the front porch to enjoy a quick breakfast or snack at the hotel's restaurant, El Burrito. Av. Piura 336, Tel: 51-73-258-145, E-mail:palominow@yahoo.com / palominowalter@hotmail.com.

Hostal Sol y Mar (Rooms: $7 - 12)

For all you surfers out there, the good news is that Sol y Mar is just a few meters from the beach! And if you don't surf, walk a few minutes in the other direction and you'll wind up in downtown Máncora. The swimming pool, bar/restaurant (with specialty seafood dishes), private parking, racquet court, ping pong and kids' game area will fill those off-beach hours. The single, double, triple, quads and sextuple rooms all have private bath, electric light and hot water. Know that this hostel and its guests LOVE to party and do so most nights, especially on the weekends. Av. Piura s/n, Tel: 51-73-258-106, E-mail: hsolymar@hotmail.com, URL: www.vivamancora.com/solymar.

MID-RANGE

Hotel del Wawa (Rooms: $20 - 30)

Fernando Paraud picked up the moniker "Wawa," a Quechua word for "little child," by always being the smallest in his class; the name stuck even as he became a tall, hunky, world-renowned surfer, competing from Sydney to Santa Cruz. His reputation in his native Peru is such that when he purchased the Casa del Mar people kept referring to it as "Wawa's hotel," so he finally just gave in and called it Hotel del Wawa (though he still refuses to have the name on a sign). No matter: everyone will tell you where it is... and if not, you can find it just before Puente Cabo Blanco on the south edge of Máncora. Follow the concrete road on the right heading towards the beach. At the end of the road, turn right. It is the low, salmon-colored building, third on the left. This first-rate beachfront hotel, complete with air conditioning, houses a restaurant as well as a surfing school whose profits go to help local children. Av. Piura, Tel: 51-73-258-427, E-mail: delwawa@hotmail.com, URL: www.delwawa.com.

Hotel Puerto Palos (Rooms: $35 - 75)

Hotel Puerto Palos is a Máncora beauty. The new, modern and clean inn is right on the beach, with permanent sun umbrellas for guests to use. If you get tired of the white sand and ocean, and need to refresh yourself in fresh water, Puerto Palos also has a pool surrounded by tables and umbrellas. Additionally, the hotel's ubiquitous hammocks provide plenty of places to kick back, suntan or do whatever you came to Máncora to do. Price includes breakfast. Km. 1216, Antigua Panamericana North, Tel: 51-7-325-8199, Fax: 51-73-258-198, E-mail: puertopalos@terra.com.pe, URL: www.puertopalos.com.

HIGH-END
Hotel Sunset (Rooms: $54 - 130)
The best part about Hotel Sunset is it's right on the beach, the reason for visiting Máncora. It's a cute little place that only has six rooms, pretty much guaranteeing you a quiet time. The rooms can sleep up to five people and each one has a little porch looking out onto the ocean — pretty ideal. The on-site restaurant also serves typical Peruvian and seafood cuisine, along with several Italian dishes. The folks at the hotel can arrange various excursions. Av. Antigua Panamericana Norte 196, Tel: 51-73-258-111, E-mail: sunset@amauta.rcp.net.pe, URL: www. hotelsunset.com.pe.

Las Arenas de Máncora (Rooms: $100 - 110)
Las Arenas de Máncora is a luxurious, beachside hotel that prides itself on its ability to serve couples for weddings, anniversaries or romantic retreats (and tempting them with couples discounts). That said, it's no inverted Club Med and there is plenty of space for all types. All rooms have at least a partial sea-view from their private terraces. No matter who is staying in the room, the employees will gladly stock it with candles, flowers or anything else you might fancy to spice up your dwellings. Tax not included. Antigua Panamericana Norte Km 1213, Tel:51-73-258-240 / 51-73-258-029, E-mail: reservas@lasarenasdemancora.com, URL: www.lasarenasdemancora.com.

MÁNCORA RESTAURANTS
As to be expected in a fishing-village-meets-beach-resort kind of town, fish and seafood are the main items on menus in Máncora. Prices are higher than in other areas of the country. The daily lunch special costs $1.35-4.70. Ceviche is a commonly offered appetizer to these meals. On the road to the beach are several simple eateries with good lunch-dinner menu for $1.70. The market is at Micaela Bastidas and Calle Los Incas, one block east of Avenida Grau. It has the usual produce and juice stands, and basic eateries operating from 6 a.m.-6 p.m.

Bar Rojo
Bar Rojo is a good place for cheap eats. Again, spaghetti and pizzas are the most common options, but they're good and economical. What's more, Bar Rojo's happy hour offers two drinks for $3.35-5. However, the real reason to visit is to show your moves once the sun dips below the horizon. Bar Rojo comes to life with a lively dance floor and an all-around happening scene. They stay open until the wee hours of the morning so if you've got energy to burn, this is the place to do it. Open from 7 p.m. to 2 a.m. Av. Piura 232, E-mail: fabiola-mancora17@hotmail.com.

Cafetería de Angela/Angela's Place (Entrees: $1 - 5)
Originally from Austria, Angela Schmitzberger considers it was her destiny to relocate to Peru and manage the only vegetarian restaurant in the northern coast region. Going both by the name of Angela's Place and Cafetería de Angela, this small but hip and bohemian bistro makes its own whole-grain bread, including rye, Turkish, banana and gluten-free rice and corn. Her menu is comprised of a creative variety of healthy vegetarian plates, such as quinoa, lentils, and curried vegetables. There is soy milk here too, and a concession to beef goulash due to Angela's native expertise with the dish. Inside a large, multi-language book exchange fills no less than three long shelves. Open daily from 8 a.m. to 6 p.m. Av. Piura 396, Tel: 51-73-278-603, E-mail: cafeteriadeangela@yahoo.com, URL: www.vivamancora.com/deangela.

Banana's Café (Entrees: $1.25 and up)
This little charmer, featuring a straw roof and bamboo siding offers inexpensive but very tasty sandwiches, courtesy of its owner, Elsa Ramos Salazar, as friendly and welcoming a local you'll meet in Máncora. Here, a cup of coffee costs no more than 60 cents. Especially recommended are the chicken, beef and ham sandwiches, served on toasted, but still very fresh buns. Elsa also makes fresh juices, from papaya to pineapple. This is not exactly haute cuisine, but very likeable with a distinct personal touch, and perfect for a tourist conserving time and money. It is open for breakfast, lunch and dinner. Open daily from 8 a.m. to 1 p.m. Graus 104.

Café Mengú (Entrees $3 - 6)

This bright, friendly restaurant in the heart of the Piuras Avenida strip along the beach in Máncora offers hamburgers and seafood platters for very affordable prices. A beer typically starts at $1.50. Juan Vega Ramirez and his brother are the owners and they take pride in offering a clean, convivial atmosphere, with a seating capacity of up to 24. They also point to their large selection of fruit shakes, appropriate for the humid and tropical climate of Máncora. Café Mengú is open for breakfast, lunch and dinner, daily from 8 a.m. to 11 p.m. Av. Piuras 6-17. Tel: 51-73-258-270.

Pizzería Volentieri (Entrees: $5 - 10)

Máncora seems to have a strangely high number of Italian restaurants and Pizzería Volentieri is one of the best. The pizzas are great of course, served to you fresh out of the wood-fired over. However, Chef Volentieri (while using mostly national ingredients, imports some of the finer items from Italy) can whip up several other great dishes such as gnocchi, lasagna or ravioli. If you've had enough of the traditional Peruvian fare and are looking to spice it up a bit, this is a great option. Open daily from 7:30 to 10 p.m. Talara 331, Tel: 73-962-1575, (01) 9822-9019.

Turismo Restaurant Espada (Entrees: $5 - 12)

Turismo Restaurant Espada is recognized as one of the best restaurants in Peru and has received a slew of awards to prove it. The specialty is anything that has been pulled out of the sea. There are other options on the menu, but you're missing out if you skip the seafood. Try the *enrollado de mero con pulpa de cangrejo* (grouper fish stuffed with crab meat). As would be expected, the food here is a little pricey, but it's certifiably some of the best seafood available in the country and worth the financial ding. Open daily from 8 a.m. to 10 p.m. Piura 501, Tel: 51-73-258-304 / 51-73-258-338.

La Sirena (Entrees: $7 - 10)

Would you care for goat sautéed in black beer or raw tuna marinated in teriyaki sauce? Or, how does potato pasta sound? Your expert chef at the La Sirena restaurant, Juan Seminario, has incorporated exotic combinations of native Peruvian dishes with Japanese and European cuisine to offer something special for the adventurous palette. The menu also comes with an epicurean selection of wines and spirits. Juan's creative flair also extends to desserts such as "Bananita's Flambé." La Sirena combines a restaurant with an elegant gift shop, gallery and clothing store, the latter features homemade fabrics and designs. This is an oasis of originality on the beach strip of Piura Avenida. Open Tuesday through Sunday from 7 to 11 p.m. Closed Monday. Av. Piura 326, E-mail: juanchichef@hotmail.com.

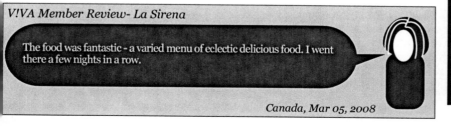

V!VA Member Review- La Sirena

The food was fantastic - a varied menu of eclectic delicious food. I went there a few nights in a row.

Canada, Mar 05, 2008

TUMBES

This coastal military garrison (taking pictures strictly circumscribed) is the northernmost town in Peru, a common transition point for travelers coming to—or heading from—Ecuador. Here is where tourists can get on busses such as CIFA and Ormeño and head further south to Trujillo, Huaraz, and Lima. It is not uninteresting as a destination point itself, a place from which three different ecosystems can be accessed: the Natural Sanctuary Los Manglares de Tumbes, the National Park Cerro de Amotape, and the tropical wood National Forest of Tumbes.

The very pleasant beaches, particularly Caleta la Cruz (16 kilometers south), and Zorritos (27 kilometers south), are not only great swims, but are also home to 200 species of exotic birds, including species listed as endangered. Local fisherman will also rent out their boats. In the city itself, near its Plaza de Armas, a library hosts some ancient pottery discovered on the site. In the same area are some historical 19th century homes.

TUMBES SERVICES

Centro Información Turística, Tumbes' tourism office, is on the second floor of Malecón Milenium (Monday-Friday 8 a.m.-4:30 p.m. Tel: 52-1757,URL: www.tumbesinfo.com).

Another place to obtain information is DICETUR (Monday-Friday 7 :30a.m.-1 p.m., 2-4:30 p.m. Calle Bolognesi 194, Centro Cívico, 2nd floor, Tel: 52-4940 / 52-3699, URL: www.dicetur-tumbes.org). Other useful websites are www.canaturperu.org and wwwregiontumbes.gob.pe.

When to Go

The City of Eternal Summer lives up to its name. The mean annual temperature is 26°C (79°F) during the day, dipping to 19°C (66°F) at night. The hottest months are January through March. When El Niño comes calling, rains can be torrential with temperatures that rise above 40°C (104°F).

Weekends are busy in Tumbes, shoppers cross to either side of the border in search of deals. Vacation months (mid-December-March, mid-July-early August) see many visitors looking to enjoy the warm waters off this coast. Tumbes celebrates its tourism week in October (dates vary) through cultural and tourist activities.

Getting To and Away from Tumbes

Long distance buses to Lima and points between (including Máncora, Piura, Chiclayo and Trujillo) depart from Avenida Tumbes, *cuadras* (blocks) 1 to 11.

To Piura: Cruz del Sur, El Dorado and other companies, $6-10, 4-5 hours.

To Chiclayo: Cruz del Sur, El Dorado, Emtrafesa, Transporte Chiclayo, $8-12, 9 hours.

Safety in Tumbes

The city of Tumbes is fairly safe, well safer than the route north to the border. Of course, take care around the bus terminals on Avenida Tumbes and even more so in the market district on Mariscal Castilla, where transportation departs for the border and coastal villages south of Tumbes.

Please see the Border Crossings to Ecuador-Aguas Verdes / Huaquillas for safety issues along that frontier.

MANGLARES DE TUMBES NATIONAL SANCTUARY

The Manglares de Tumbes National Sanctuary, one half hour north of Tumbes, gives travelers access to 200 species of birds, rare mammals (such as the crab-eating raccoon and the neo-tropical otter), and over 40 varieties of plants. As of yet, this constitutes one of the less-discovered treasures of northern Peru, popular with tourists, but not so that it is overcrowded or spoiled.

The most verdant time to go is from April to November; from December to March much of the Manglares wetlands dries up, and becomes a rich opportunity for harvesting shellfish. Permission to enter this park must be obtained from the Instituto Nacional de Recursos Naturales (INRENA) in Tumbes (Avenida Tarapacá 427, Tel.: 52-6489). It is easier to go on tour to this reserve, as the agency takes care of the permit. Getting there by either bus or taxi is very inexpensive.

TUMBES TOURS

The Tumbes area harbors many attractions for visitors. Besides the kilometers-long beaches with year-long warm seas, there are several natural parks and pre-Columbian ruins. Tour operators in the city specialize in excursions to these sights.

Mayte Tours promotes trips to the three national parks, the beaches and a city tour, as well as rafting on Río Tumbes. Avenida Piura 752, Hotel Smay Wasi, Tel.: 51-72-525-355 / 51-9-72-619-478, E-mail: reservas_maytetours@yahoo.es.

Cocodrilos Tours specializes in sustainable tourism and provides ticket sales and other services. San Martín 131, Tel.: 961-9204 / 960-8387, E-mail: ams_toto@yahoo.es / ams_toto@hotmail.com, URL: www.cocodrilotours.com.

TUMBES LODGING

Hotels in Tumbes are as varied as anywhere else in Peru. You are best advised, as always, to ask the manager to give you a tour of the facility before deciding.

Hospedaje Los Viñedos (Rooms: $4 - 14)

Two blocks from Tumbes' Plaza de Armas, Hospedaje Los Viñedos is a resting stop that promises the four most important things for the weary budget traveler: inexpensive prices, cleanliness, comfort and safety. The 1960s-style hotel has basic rooms with private or common bathrooms, as well as dorms. Hospedaje Los Viñedos also has a tour agency, in case you want to spend a while longer exploring the national parks and beaches. Calle Bolognesi 420, Tel: 51-72-522-868, E-mail: cfvvservice@yahoo.es, E-mail: www.losvinedosperu.com.

Hostal Samay Wasi (Rooms: $7 - 19)

The centrally located Hostal Samay Wasi is one of Tumbes' budget lodging options. The large rooms are well-furnished with comfortable beds. The bathrooms may be a bit worn, but they are very clean. Travelers on a tight budget overnighting in this city should ask about the special economical rooms that share a bathroom. All accommodations have cable TV, fan, and hot and cold water showers. Av. Piura. Tel: 52-5355.

Hostal Florian (Rooms: $10 - 20)

This hostel, two blocks from the Plaza de Armas in Tumbes, offers private rooms, hot and cold water, and television at reasonable rates. Prices are consistent all year-round. The hostel is near plenty of restaurants and diners. Piura 414, Tel: 51-72-522-464.

Arrecife Hotel (Rooms: $15 - 33)

This upscale hotel in the Zorrito district of Tumbes is located right at the beach with pleasant views of the Pacific, and is surrounded by tropical garden landscapes. Among its amenities are internet access, cable TV, direct dial phone service, bar and restaurant. Breakfast is included. All credit cards are accepted. Prices are slightly more during the high season. Faustino Piaggio 158, Zorrito, Tel: 51-72-544-462, URL: www.arrecifehotel.com.

Hotel Costa del Sol (Rooms: $75 - 90)

A luxury hotel at Plaza Bolognesi in the heart of Tumbes, the Costa del Sol has the reputation of having the best accommodations in town, complete with 56 rooms with cable TV, minibars, a Jacuzzi and safety deposit boxes. It also features a casino and pool, along with a restaurant. The staff will organize trips to Manglares. Jr. San Martín 275, Tel: 51-74-523-991.

TUMBES RESTAURANTS

Tumbes features some great places to eat, and is especially noteworthy for its *concha negra*, a particular black clam indigenous to the coast of northern Peru. Tumbes culinary specialties are based on fish and seafood. Yes, land-lubbing animals make it on the menus here, but don't miss out on dishes like black conch ceviche, *ají de langos-*

Photo by Freyja Ellis

tinos (spicy prawns), *chupe de cangrejo* (crab chowder) and *caldo de bolas* (a soup of green plantain dumplings with olives and raisins). The daily special, most often served at lunch, costs $1.35-3. Tumbes' market is on the third block of Avenida Mariscal Castillo.

Budabar Restaurant-Lounge (Entrees: $2 - 12)

Budabar is the place to go anytime of the day, for anything from breakfast to a nightcap. This corner restaurant on the Plaza de Armas has both inside and front patio seating. Lunch specials are a $1.70 and feature a *menú marino* (seafood menu) on Saturdays and holidays. À la carte dishes run $3.35-11.70. Buddha, however, would have a trying time dining here; there are very few vegetarian choices on the menu. Open Monday-Saturday 8:30 a.m.-1:30 a.m.; closed Sundays.

Cevichería El Sol Ñato (Entrees: $4 - 10)

This lunch-time only restaurant offers a large selection of marine platters. Their black clam ceviche is especially recommended, as is their *sudado de pescado*, despite its unsavory name which literally means "fish sweat." Open from 11 a.m. to 3 p.m.

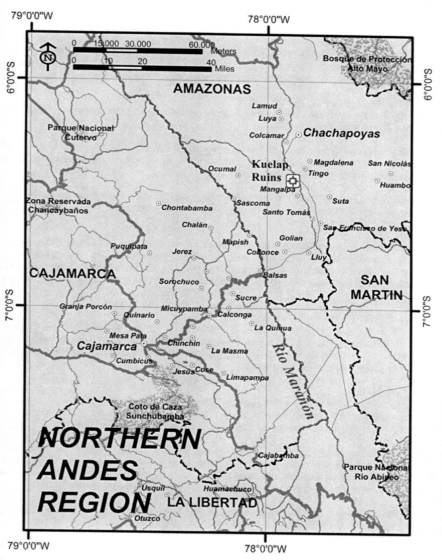

NORTHERN PERUVIAN ANDES

The Northern Peruvian Highlands are one of Peru's least traveled areas, but not for lack of attractions. Two popular destinations are the Chachapoyas (p.465) and Cajamarca (p.460) regions of Peru. Chachapoyas is surrounded by recently discovered Inca ruins while Cajamarca is dotted with classic colonial architecture. The beauty of the two areas is that they are much less visited than other colonial and ruin destinations due to the windy, bumpy and generally shoddy roads that lead into the region.

Hidden within the lush, virgin jungle surrounding Chachapoyas are a plethora of Inca and pre-Inca treasures—many of which have been recently found, though certainly there are many yet to be discovered. For ruin lovers there are several remote Inca sites that carry with them a more adventurous feeling than busier areas like Machu Picchu. The most popular site is Kuélap (p.472), perched atop a limestone peak. Getting to many of the sites is not easy, but it certainly is fun: some require a combination of 4x4 vehicle and horseback.

The colonial history of Cajamarca can't be missed during a stroll through the town's central area. With cobblestone streets and numerous colonial-era buildings, the city's beauty is easy to appreciate. Outside the city, crumbling ruins belie earlier Inca influence.

Northern Peruvian Andes–Highlights
• Kuélap–a massive ruin built with much more material than Machu Picchu but visited by a fraction of the crowds.

• Celedín–just one of the villages in the area worth the extra-bumpy trip outside the main cities. This little town is truly off the beaten track. Here you are sure to see a side of Peru that is not possible in the more popular destinations.

• Los Baños del Inca–hot springs never go out of style, and these even have some history. The Inca kings of 500 years ago soaked themselves in these same springs.

When to Go
The best time to visit the Northern Peruvian Andes is between May and October. The rest of the months are considered the rainy season (especially in Chachapoyas), when traveling to the Northern Peruvian Andes can be difficult because of the road conditions. Given the shaky status of many of the roads heading up to Chachapoyas and Cajamarca, a lot of rain can significantly slow travel.

Safety In The Northern Peruvian Andes
There are no major safety concerns in the Northern Peruvian Andes. So few visitors visit the region that locals tend to be a bit more curious and friendly. Though in general there is less petty crime, you should still take care of your valuables and don't leave yourself open to pickpockets on buses and in crowded areas.

CAJAMARCA
Cajamarca is located in the beautiful Andean countryside in a valley with the same name. This was an important area for the Inca Empire. The first encounter between Inca Atahualpa and the Spanish conqueror Francisco Pizarro took place in Cajamarca.

In the center of the city you will find several colonial houses, beautiful churches with attractive fronts, modest museums like the Museo Arqueológico y Etnográfico (Archaeological and Ethnographic Museum) and the famous Cuarto de Rescate (Ransom Room) which Atahualpa filled with silver and gold in exchange for his liberation from Pizarro.

The city has a special charm and you can join the local community by participating in their Carnival.

There are different places around the city that you should visit : The thermal Baños del Inca (hot springs), the amazing Cumbe Mayo with its impressive Inca Aqueduct, the Ventanillas de Otuzco (necropolis with a window-like appearance) and several picturesque towns like Llacanora and Porcón.

V!VA Member Review- Cajamarca

For a side of Peru that you will no longer find in really touristy places like Cusco, head to Cajamarca. This town is as beautiful as Cusco and there is lots to see and do, but with 1 percent of the tourists that you will find in Cusco. Cajamarca can be used as a base for exploring the northern part of the Peruvian Andes, including Kuélap.

London, England, Jan 23, 2008

NORTHERN ANDES

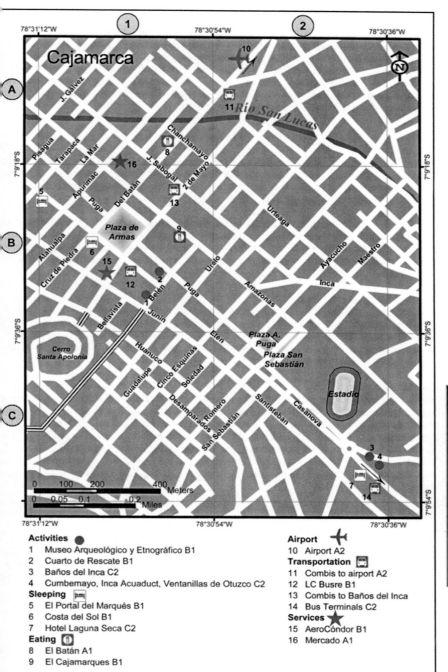

Activities ●
1 Museo Arqueológico y Etnográfico B1
2 Cuarto de Rescate B1
3 Baños del Inca C2
4 Cumbemayo, Inca Acuaduct, Ventanillas de Otuzco C2

Sleeping 🛏
5 El Portal del Marqués B1
6 Costa del Sol B1
7 Hotel Laguna Seca C2

Eating 🍴
8 El Batán A1
9 El Cajamarques B1

Airport ✈
10 Airport A2

Transportation 🚌
11 Combis to airport A2
12 LC Busre B1
13 Combis to Baños del Inca
14 Bus Terminals C2

Services ★
15 AeroCóndor B1
16 Mercado A1

NORTHERN ANDES

Getting To and Away From Cajamarca

The best way to get to Cajamarca is by plane. Daily flights run to Cajamarca from Lima on Aero Condor Perú (076-855-674, $60-$100 average one way) and LC Busre, Monday to Saturday, with limited service on Sunday. Another option is renting a car, but this is not for the faint of heart, as roads in the Northern Highlands are difficult and often unreliable. Rental agencies and buses leading to Cajamarca can be found in Huaraz, on Highway 109 (accessed via the Pan-American Highway). From there Highway 8 will lead you to Cajamarca. Once in Cajamarca, you can hire a tour guide or a driver to lead you to the ruins.

THINGS TO SEE AND DO IN CAJAMARCA

Los Inca Baths

Legend has it that when the Spanish conquistadors arrived in Cajamarca, Inca Atahualpa was relaxing in his favorite place: the Inca Baths. You too can experience these baths, which are located about six kilometers east of the city. Although the old pools remain intact and can be seen, only the new pools are allowed to be used by visitors.

Locals claim that the waters, which are full of minerals and can reach temperatures of 70 degrees Celsius, have medicinal and healing powers. They are said to have a positive effect on fatigue, rheumatism, respiratory and nervous system problems. It may not be proven that the waters offer miraculous cures, but guests are sure to feel relaxed and refreshed after a dip in the pools.

Las Ventanillas de Otuzco

Located 8 km (5 miles) north of Cajamarca, the small town of Otuzco is known for *las ventanillas* (little windows) carved into the mountainside. These beautiful stone windows were actually used by the Incas as tombs. The rock hillside looks like an ancient ghost town, abandoned since it was used as a burial ground between 300 and 800 A.D. Visiting hours are Monday through Sunday, 9 a.m. to 5 p.m.

Cumbe Mayo

In the indigenous language, Quechua, *Cumbe Mayo* means fine river, which is a quite fitting name for this ancient aqueduct. It is located about 12 miles southwest of Cajamarca, and stretches on for nearly five miles. It is believed that it was built around 1500 B.C. Its function seems to be for aesthetic and religious reasons, rather than to provide irrigation. It is said that it is meant to make people recognize the natural rock formations in the area, which mimic a stone forest, by allowing them to meditate on the movement of the water. Trips to this site can be organized in Cajamarca. You can either take a bus to the site or take part in an organized tour.

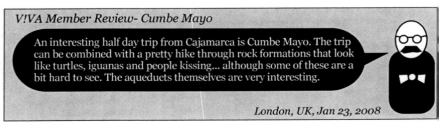

V!VA Member Review- Cumbe Mayo

An interesting half day trip from Cajamarca is Cumbe Mayo. The trip can be combined with a pretty hike through rock formations that look like turtles, iguanas and people kissing... although some of these are a bit hard to see. The aqueducts themselves are very interesting.

London, UK, Jan 23, 2008

CAJAMARCA TOURS

A handful of tour operators line Cajamarca's Plaza de Armas, each offering generally the same half-day tours to Cumbe Mayo, Los Baños del Inca, and Las Ventanillas de Otuzco at similar prices. It seems that regardless of which one you pick, you will end up getting more or less the same experience, especially because the tour companies work together to fill up seats in their vans.

InkaNatura Travel

InkaNatura Travel, is owned by the nonprofit group Peru Verde, and operates on the slogan of "conservation through tourism," with all net proceeds benefiting conservation efforts of national parks, reserves, and archaeological sites in Peru. InkaNatura organizes unique tours focused on nature, culture, or archaeology to Tambopata National Reserve, Manu, Manu National Park, the Inca Trail to Machu Picchu, Choquequirao, Chiclayo, The Lord of Sipán and The Royal Tombs of Sipan Museum, Tucume, Trujillo, Chan Chan, Chachapoyas, Lake of the Condors, the impressive Kuélap fortress, Máncora and Punta Sal. Stay in one of their world famous jungle lodges or sign up for one of their special interest archaeology or biology study tours and workshops. Offices in Lima, Chiclayo, Puerto Maldonado and Cusco. Manuel Bañon 461, San Isidro, Lima, Tel: 51-1 4-402-022 / 228-114, Fax: 51-14-229-225, E-mail: postmaster@inkanatura.com.pe, URL: www.inkanatura.com.

Cumbe Mayo Tours

One of several tour companies with their offices on the main plaza, Cumbe Mayo Tours offers inexpensive half-day tours to all of the fascinating sites around Cajamarca, including Cumbe Mayo, Otuzco, and Los Baños del Inca. Cumbe Mayo tour guides are passionate and knowledgeable, and the "Cumbe Mayo tour" in particular, which involves half a day of hiking, is a great choice. Cumbe Mayo Tours can also arrange multi-day trips to the fortress of Kuélap, which is difficult to get to on your own. Amalia Puga 635, Plaza de Armas, Tel: (76) 36-2938 / 968-4989, E-mail: Cumbemayo7@Hotmail.

Panorama Viajes

Panorama Viajes offers a few different tour options to Cajamarca and the surrounding areas. The agency was founded in 1968 and is a Peruvian Tour operator, IATA agent, member of the Peruvian Association of Incoming Tour Operators and of the American Society of Travel Agents. They have agents that speak Spanish, English and French. They offer both half day and package tours. Prices depend upon the type and length of tour. If none of the packages offered are quite what you are looking for, the tour agency is also willing to assist with custom tours. Please note that the office of this tour operator is located in Miraflores, Lima. Bellavista 210, Miraflores, Tel: 51-1-444-4485, Fax: 51-1-445-0910, E-mail: info@panorama-peru.com, URL: http://www.panorama-peru.com.

CAJAMARCA LODGING

As Cajamarca is relatively unnoticed on the tourist circuit, it's not bursting with dirt-cheap youth hostels like its southern sister, Cusco. Instead, Cajamarca features several large, old, mid-range hotels, the kind that may have once been beautiful, but today are due for a facelift. Nonetheless, they retain a certain charm.

El Portal Del Marques (Rooms: $34 - 44)

El Portal Del Marques is conveniently located in Cajamarca, only blocks away from the Plaza de Armas. If you want to be amidst the action, this is a great place for you. The hotel has many onsite amenities, such as the restaurant El Meson Gourmet, a bar, a convention room, casino and computers with internet. The rooms all have private bathrooms, cable TV, a fridge and a Jacuzzi. Even with all of these amenities, the hotel is one of the more reasonably priced in the area. Price includes 10% of service fees. Jr. Del Comercio 644, Tel: In Cajamarca: (076) 368464 / (076) 343339. In Lima: 9-9880-5440, RPM #530581 Fax: 51-76-368-464 / 51-76-343-339, E-mail: reservas@portaldelmarques.com / portaldelmarques@terra.com, URL: http://www.portaldelmarques.com/.

Hotel Casa Blanca (Rooms: $40)

Located right on the Plaza de Armas, the Casa Blanca is a good option for those who'd like to stay in Cajamarca's charming center. Featuring wooden banisters and floors, stained glass windows and a funky lobby, the hotel gives you a taste of what it once was. Unfortunately, actual hotel rooms are rather plain and old-fashioned, with surprisingly thin walls. Still, if you find yourself arriving to Cajamarca late at night and are looking for a decent lodging option, Hotel Casa Blanca will do the trick. Jr. Dos de Mayo 446, Plaza de Armas, Tel: 076-362-141, E-mail: hotelcasablanca446@hotmail.com,

Posada del Puruay (Rooms: $75 - 138)

Set in the countryside, this Spanish Colonial house in undoubtedly quaint. Originally built in 1822, its current owners seriously renovated it in the late 90s, keeping true to its colonial heritage. The 14 rooms in the Posada are all uniquely sized and shaped due to the original layout of the house. There are five categories of rooms: single, double, executive (2 beds), suite duplex, and suite senior. Extra beds are available for the suites. There is a restaurant on site named Restaurant El Mason, which serves a mix on traditional and international dishes, priding itself in its use of locally grown natural ingredients. Some activities such as horseback riding, trout fishing and gardening are available on site. The hotel also offers daily trips to the Inca Baths. The Posada del Puruay offers one of the most relaxing and charming getaways in the Andes. Carretera Porcón-Hualgayoc Km 4.5, Tel: Lima: (51-1) 3367869 / In Cajamarca: (51-76) 367028, E-mail: informes@posadapuruay.com.pe, URL: http://www.posadapuruay.com.pe/indexen.htm.

Hotel Laguna Seca (Rooms: $96 - 166)

Hotel Laguna Seca's main selling point is its location. It is located so near to the Inca Baths that there are thermal pools on their property and the thermal waters are pumped into the rooms allowing you to enjoy a relaxing bath in the privacy of your own room. Another perk of its placement is the fact that it is surrounded by lush green countryside. The atmosphere makes it a great place to go to relax and get away from all your worries. There is even a spa on site to further lend to a relaxing holiday. The hotel has two places to eat: El Fogón, an exclusive restaurant serving local and international fare and El Toril Café, a great place to get breakfast or an afternoon snack. The hotel offers horseback and bicycle excursions on their property. They also can assist you in arranging a tour of nearby sites. All taxes, airport transfer, breakfast in the cafeteria "El Toril," use of thermal and Turkish baths are included in price. Av. Manco Cápac 1098, Baños del Inca, Tel: 51-76-584-300, Fax: 51-76-584-311, E-mail: hotel@lagunaseca.com.pe, URL: http://www.lagunaseca.com.pe/.

CAJAMARCA RESTAURANTS

El Cajamarques (Entrees: $2 and up)

With a definite old-Spanish feel, this is one of the more elegant restaurants in Cajamarca. The prices, however, do not reflect its elegance. Instead, they tend to be reasonable, in particular during lunch time; the daily fixed menu for lunch costs about $2.00. The rest of the menu reflects a nice mix of both Peruvian and international dishes, so no matter what you are in the mood for you are sure to find something that suits you. Amazonas 770, Tel: 51-76-822-128 / (076) 36-2128.

Gran Bufet del Arte "El Batán" (Entrees: $3.50 and up)

El Batán, which is located in an 18th century colonial house, is considered to be the nicest restaurant in town, serving regional and international dishes. The prices tend to reflect this; the items on the menu are rather expensive for the area. However, they have a daily *menú ejecutivo* (fixed menu) which will only run you $3.50 or so. Vegetarians be aware that the menu is catered toward meat lovers, with the only non-meat offerings being appetizers or salads. They also have an art gallery and live music on Fridays and Saturdays. Jr. del Batán 369, Tel: 076 - 366025, E-mail: anabufet@hotmail.com.

Pizzeria Vaca Loca

As a major regional producer of dairy, it's no surprise that Cajamarca is home to an excellent pizza joint by the name of Vaca Loca. Get past the place's dubious name, Mad Cow, and you'll be treated to a warm and inviting place where the booths are covered in cow print and cow cartoons punctuate the walls. A wide variety of pizzas and other Italian dishes are offered. San Martín 320, Tel: (44) 82-8230.

Spaghetti Om-Gri

Half a block from Cajamarca's Plaza de Armas, with small glass door barely noticeable if you aren't looking for it, Spaghetti Om-Gri is a warm, tiny, family-run Italian restaurant worth a try. With maximum seating for 10, a menu that is one page long, and an open kitchen space behind the bar just big enough for one person to cook in, Om-Gri has a comfortable, uncomplicated atmosphere--the kind of place you can become a local in. Friendly owner/chef Tito (affectionately known by gringo customers as "the spaghetti man") can cook up a variety of pastas with traditional sauces like Alfredo and Bolognese, and makes a mean garlic bread. Don't be surprised, however, if half the items on the menu aren't available -- with such tiny facilities, Tito can only cook a couple of things each night. Jr. San Martin 360, half a block from the Plaza de Armas, Tel: 367-619 / 827-619.

Querubino

A fairly recent addition to the dining scene in Cajamarca, the Querubino is not lacking in hipness; it is decorated with bright colors and modern art and a live band often plays during dinner. The menu is attractively varied, but tends to be meat-oriented, which depending on your tastes will either make or break the place. The prices are a bit high by Peruvian standards, but reasonable from a Western perspective. Jr. Amalia Puga 589, Tel: (76) 34-0900 / (76) 976-333824.

CHACHAPOYAS

Chachapoyas is a small town containing several little-known archaeological sites as well as the fifth largest waterfall in the world: Yumbilla Catarata. The most accessible and spectacular site is the fortress at Kuélap. Also worth a visit are the burial buildings at Revash, and the Leymebamba Mummy Museum. Nearby towns are far from the tourist traffic, a rarity in the Peruvian Andes. As there is no air service, the best way to get the area is from Chiclayo. There are different tour agencies in Peru that can help you organize your trip.

Getting To and Away from Chachapoyas

Bus

To Celendín: Virgen del Carmen (Salamanca 650)—Tuesday, Friday, Saturday 5 a.m.; 30 soles/$10; 14 hours. Transportes Chuquibamba (Salamanca and Merced)—Monday, Friday.

To Chiclayo, Trujillo or Lima: Kuélap (Ortiz Arrieta 412)—Chiclayo (daily 7 p.m.; 33 soles/$11; 9 hours; snack). Civa (Salamanca 956)—Chiclayo (daily 6 p.m.; 25 soles/$8.30; 11 hours); Lima (Monday, Wednesday, Friday, noon; 70 soles/$23.30; 24 hours; meals). Movil Tours (Libertad 464)—Chiclayo and Trujillo (daily 8 p.m.; 45 soles/$15, 9 hours, and 60 soles/$20, 12 hours, respectively; snack); Lima (daily noon; 105 soles/$35; 22 hours; meals). Zelada (Ortiz Arrieta 310)—Chiclayo (daily 8 p.m.; 25 soles/$8.30; 9 hours); to Lima (daily 11:30 a.m.; 75 soles/$25 US; 22 hours; dinner).

To Rodríguez de Mendoza: Transportes Guayabamba (400-block, Ortiz Arrieta) daily 5 a.m.-midnight; 22 soles/$7.30 US; 3 hours. Fátima (Salamanca 914) daily 7:30 a.m., 2:00 p.m.; 15 soles/$5 US; 4 hours. Zelada—daily 4 p.m.; 12 soles/$4; 4 hours. There are terminals on Ortiz Arrieta (400-block); Hermosura (300-block) and Grau (200-300-block). Every type of transportation leaves to all points (including Kuélap and Rioja) from Libertad (700-900 blocks) at 4 a.m. - 7 a.m. and 3 p.m. - 5 p.m.

For Moyobamba and Tarapoto, go to Pedro Ruiz and transfer from there.

Air

Chachapoyas has an airport, located two kilometers north of the city, but there are no regular flights. The next closest airports are in Tarapoto, Chiclayo and Cajamarca.

THE PEOPLE OF THE CLOUDS

For centuries, clouds have blanketed the Chachapoya people. Inca and Spanish conquerors described them as fierce warriors, tremendous shamans, skilled builders and beautiful women. But Chachapoya origins, beliefs and fate remain obscure. All that is left behind from this ancient civilization are burial sites with mummies, ruins of homes and temples, and petrographs.

The Chachapoya realm extended west to Río Marañón, east to Huallaga, north to the Utucubamba flood plain and south to Pías. Human occupation began ±8000 BC. The classic Chachapoya period was from ±800 AD until the Spanish conquest.

The most-accepted Chachapoya origin theory states they were several jungle nations, perhaps of different language groups, that migrated towards the sierra and together developed similar traditions. We must understand Chachapoya was a blanket term for those who lived in this region. When asked by the arriving Spaniards what the peoples of these northern Andes were called, the Inca responded, Chachapoya (*sacha* + *puyu*). But this word's roots are vague. "Sacha" is translated as tree, mountain or cloud, depending on the language; "puyu" as cloud. Linguists have studied what remains of the Chachapoya language: place and family names. They note similarities with Jíbaro and Amazon River basin languages.

It is unknown how much of the celebrated traditions are from the original Chachapoya culture, as other indigenous and Spanish groups had significant impact on the area. However, Chachapoya worship probably centered on lagoons and mountains, as many burial sites are located at such places. The snake was probably significant; it appears in many carvings and other representations.

Chachapoya architecture was engineered for its cloud-forest climate: "terraces" and cornices to channel water away from building foundations, with steep thatch roofs to allow rain to run off. East of the Utucubamba River and south of Gran Vilaya, the stone buildings have intricate friezes in zigzag and rhomboid designs. Yálape, Kuélap and La Congona are examples of this.

The Chachapoya mummified their dearly departed; some skeletons reveal the practice of trepanation, surgery in which a hole is drilled into the skull. Sarcophagi burials are evidenced in Luya province from Kuélap northward, e.g. Karajía and Pueblo de los Muertos. Southward, *chullpas*, or mausoleums, are more common, though also found in Luya. Frequently petrographs decorate such sites. Burial finds show the Chachapoya as skilled weavers and potters, though no gold or silver artifacts produced by them have been encountered.

By studying mummies, scientists have discovered the genetic markers that make the Chachapoya, described by the Spaniards as being distinctly white-skinned. Findings show the modern rural population is about 65 percent Chachapoya. Thirty descendent communities have been identified in Peru and Bolivia, thus proving the Inca massively relocated this "rebellious" nation. The greatest depletion of their populations, however, came with the Spaniards' diseases: within 200 years, over 90 percent of Chachapoya were decimated.

Little by little the veils are lifting, revealing who the Chachapoya were. Yet many of their traditions, like the mountains and lagoons they worshiped, will only be glimpsed through the clouds.

La Balsa Border Crossing

Due north of Chachapoyas is a crossing into Ecuador, convenient for getting to Vilca-bamba, Ecuador. Passing through a landscape of cloud-bathed jungle mountains strewn with orchids, this journey is as beautiful as it is adventuresome. Expect delays due to landslides (especially December through April) and roadwork. You will need two days travel time; hotels exist in every transfer point. In Chachapoyas, catch a *colectivo* taxi to Bagua Grande from the 500-block of Jr. Grau (3:30 a.m. - 6 p.m. daily; $7.10, 3 hours). A cheaper alternative is a *combi* to Pedro Ruiz, leaving from the 400-block of Ortiz Arrieta (8 a.m. - 5 p.m., every two hours; $2.10, 1.5 hours) and then a combi to Bagua Grande ($2, 1.5 hours). The one-hour combi ride from Bagua Grande to Jaén costs $1.60; a moto taxi between the terminals is $0.30. Another combi takes you to San Ignacio ($4, 3 hours); then a colectivo to La Balsa, the Peruvian border post ($4, 1.5 hours). On the other side of the bridge is La Balsa, Ecuador. Immigration is open on both sides from 6 a.m. - 6 p.m., where moneychangers can be found. From La Balsa, several *chivas* a day go to Zumba ($1.75; 2 hours), and three buses from Zumba to Vilcabamba ($6.50; 5 hours).

Chachapoyas Services

As befitting the capital of a Peruvian department, Chachapoyas offers a full-range of services. As money facilities do not exist in other settlements in the region, it is important to stock up on soles here. The Banco del Crédito (BCP) on the Plaza de Armas changes US dollars and travelers' checks (Monday - Friday, 9:30 a.m. - 1 p.m., 4 p.m. - 6:30 p.m., Saturday 9:30 a.m. - 1:00 p.m.), and has a Master Card / Visa ATM. Several stores around the plaza change cash US dollars and Euros.

The post office, Serpost, (Jr. Ortiz Arrieta 638) is open Monday - Saturday 8 a.m. - 8 p.m. Chacha has a plethora of internet cafés and *locutorios* (telephone offices), with at least one on every block.

The helpful tourism office is at Jr. Ortiz Arrieta 588, on the Plaza; (Monday - Friday, 8 a.m. - 7 p.m., Saturday, 8 a.m. - 1 p.m.). There are at least a half-dozen tour agencies vying for your business. Shop around, as prices can vary and last-minute discounts may be had.

The city claims two hospitals. *Boticas* (pharmacies) are plentiful.

Two laundromats also operate, charging 3 soles /$1 per kilo; the better is Speed Clean (Jr. Ayacucho 964).

The large daily market is open dawn to 4 p.m. At Rusti-K (Jr. Ortiz Arrieta 676), you can buy products and crafts from the area villages' collectives.

Things To See and Do in Chachapoyas

Pinturas Rupestres of Amazonas

Circles within circles. Men with alpacas. Are they suns? Are they hunting? To this day it's unknown what the ancient peoples of the Amazonas region were saying with the thousands of *pinturas rupestres*, or petroglyphs, that adorn their burial sites. Some guides claim the petroglyphs are 20,000-40,000 years old, though radiocarbon dating of remains associated with the sites reveals that none are older than 4,000 years; most archaeologists believe they are from the Chachapoya period (1000-1500 AD).

According to archaeologist Klaus Koschmieder, 60 to 70 percent of the burial sites are adorned with paintings. *Huaqueros* (looters), often identify grave locations by them. Only three sites—Sonche, Yamón and Tambolik—are not associated with *chullpas* (mausoleums) or sarcophagi. When you go to Chanqui, Yamón or any of the dozens of other pinturas rupes-tres-decorated sites, you can ponder pictures of red-plumaged birds singing a song frozen in time. Were these artists telling the life history of their dearly departed? Were they relating the latest events? Or were they contemporary Chachapoya artists at their best?

Enter photo competitions at www.vivatravelguides.com

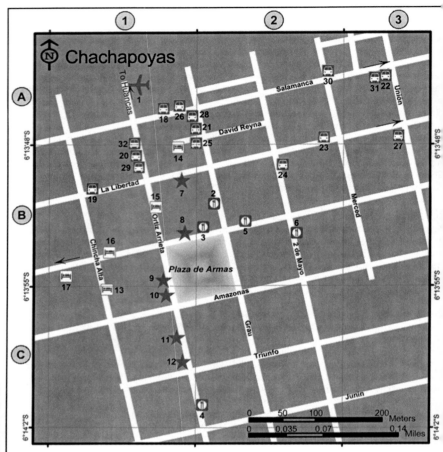

NORTHERN ANDES

Airport ✈
1 Airport A1
Eating 🍴
2 Nature Center New Eden B2
3 Las Rocas B2
4 La Tushpa C2
5 Mari Pizza B2
6 Bar B2
Services ★
7 Market B1
8 Speed Clean B1
9 Banco de Crédito (BCP) B1
10 i Peru C1
11 Serpost C1
12 Rusti-K C1
Sleeping 🛏
13 Casa Vieja Peru C1
14 Hospedaje Jenny B1
15 Hostal Continental B1
16 Hostal El Dorado B1
17 Orquídeas Hospedaje Turístico B1

Transportation 🚌
18 Chiva A1
19 Colectivo taxis to Luya and Lámud B1
20 Combis and colectivos to Huancas & Bagua Grande B1
21 Combis and colectivos to Pedro Ruiz A1
22 Combis to Jalca Grande, Cheto & Malinopampa A3
23 Combi to Kuélap A2
24 Combis to Leymebamba B2
25 Combis to Montevideo, Yerbabuena & Leymebamba A1
26 Fátima A1
27 Movil Tours A3
28 Roller A1
29 Transportes Guayabamba B1
30 Transportes Chuquibamba A2
31 Virgen del Carmen A3
32 Zelada A1

CHACHAPOYAS TOURS

Chachapoyas Tours SAC

Chachapoyas Tours offers the full gamut of tours available in northern Peru. Archaeological tours, orchid tours, trips to waterfalls, sacred tours, horseback and trekking expeditions, jungle tours, and birdwatching are available. Most of their trips are multi-day, as the region is remote and the destinations are spread out. Visitors can also take an interesting (if somewhat morbid) 7-day Tajopampa Tombs tour that involves going deep into largely untouched Andes to see cliff-side mausoleums complete with bones and burial wrappings. Chachapoyas tours is highly recommended and can provide you with nearly any type of tour in the area (pre-planned or custom) that you could dream of. The tours range in price, but in general the multi-day trips cost about $150 per day, including most meals, all transportation, entrance fees and a bilingual guide. Jr. Santo Domingo 432, Tel: (051-41) 478078 / (cell) 051-41-941963327 / (toll-free) 1-866-396-9582 / (international) 001-407-583-6786, E-mail: kuelap@msn.com / chachapoyastoursreceptivo@ hotmail.com, URL: www.kuelapperu.com/index.html.

Inka Tours

Explore the Inca ruins at Kuélap, along with the monumental cloud fortress of the Chachapoyas. This area is part of the Inca's last conquest. Fixed departures to / from Chiclayo take about 12 hours ($10 on public buses) on a partially paved road. To travel from Lima the trip takes around 30 hours and costs about $25 using public bus services. Av. Primavera 264, Of. 108 B, Zip: C.C. Chacarilla - Surco, Tel: 255 4193 / 255 4488, E-mail: reservas@inkatoursperu.com, URL: http://www.inkatoursperu.com/.

CHACHAPOYAS LODGING

Hospedaje Jenny (Rooms: $2 - 2.60)

Hospedaje Jenny is a no-frills, friendly inn that offers *habitaciones* (rooms) for one or two people. All rooms are good-sized and have large windows. The ones that look onto the hallway of the main building, unfortunately, are dark; however, the rest are light and airy. Five rooms off the courtyard are of earthy-smelling adobe. All rooms share common baths (one with a tepid shower). If you ask nicely, you may be able to wash a few pieces of laundry. While it could be kept a bit cleaner, Hospedaje Jenny is worth the price. Pasaje David Reina 285.

Hostal El Dorado (Rooms: $5 - 13)

El Dorado is an intimate and comfortable hostel close to the Plaza de Armas. Rooms, available with common or private bathroom, are a bit worn but clean. Some have balconies. Behind the hostel is a beautiful courtyard garden you can enjoy while washing your clothes. Hostal El Dorado is a good deal for the price. Jr. Ayacucho 1060, Tel: 51-4-147-7047.

Hostal Continental (Rooms: $5 - 22.60)

Labyrinthine hallways lead to the rooms of the Hostal Continental. The four stories echo with the comings and goings, the conversations and music of its guests. The rooms are a bit cramped, but have cable and some come with private bathrooms. The common baths are a bit austere but clean, and luckily there is hot water. The staff is friendly and helpful. A bit overpriced. Price includes taxes. Jr. Ortiz Arrieta 431, Tel: 51-41-478-352.

Las Orquídeas Hospedaje Turístico (Rooms: $6.80 - 18.30)

Tucked a few blocks away from the Plaza de Armas is Las Orquídeas Hospedaje Turístico. The staff is bilingual and generally pleasant; rooms are clean and spacious with carpeting and cable TV. Unfortunately, use of the common kitchen costs an additional $3.30 per day. Camping is also offered in the backyard (with access to communal bathroom). Jr. Ayacucho 1231, Tel: 51-41-478-271, Cellular: 041-941-708158, E-mail: hostallasorquideas@ hotmail.com, URL: www.hostallasorquideas.com.

Spatuletail Lodge (Rooms: $30 - 60)

The Spatuletail Lodge is located just outside the village of Choctámal and the Kuélap ruins. It is managed by the village and the income is split between the employees. The real attraction of the lodge is its proximity to the Kuélap ruins. The ruins can even been seen from one of the lodges large balconies. However, there is also a hot tub and a telescope for visitors to use. Also, if you like hummingbirds, the management has placed several hummingbird feeders around the hotel attracting several of the fluttering little birds. Take day trips from the lodge to Shubet Mountain, Cuchacuella Lake, or the Gran Vilaya valley. Located on the way to Kuélap (35 minutes). Prices do not include tax. Tel: (USA) 1-866-396-9582, (INT'L) 001-407-583-6786, (Chachapoyas) 001-41-478838, (Cell) 041-996-3327, E-mail: lostambos@hotmail.com, kuelap@msn.com, URL: www.marvelousspatuletail.com.

La Casona Monsante (Rooms: $59 - 180)

La Casona Monsante is a quaint little hotel just one block from Chachapoyas' Plaza de Armas. It is charmingly situated in a 19th century building, and received a national award for their restoration of the building. The hotel also boasts a massive garden featuring some 1500 of the exotic plants and flowers of the region. The wooden floors, balconies and staircases give the hotel a warmer feel than the usual concrete construction of the rest of the region. This hotel is a great option for reasonable prices, convenient location and Peruvian charm. Jr. Amazonas 746, Tel: 51-41-777-702, E-mail: info@lacasonamonsante.com.

Casa Vieja Peru

Casa Vieja Peru, while not quite from the Colonial era, is a beautifully converted house that has served as both a monastery as well as a dwelling for generations of families. As with many transformed hotels, each room has a different layout, giving the house a unique appeal. If you arrive and it's not busy, you might be able to tour the different rooms and pick the one that charms you most. You can also rent a 4x4 truck from Casa Vieja Peru to explore the Chachapoyas region. Jr. Chincha Alta 569, Tel: 51-41-477-353, E-mail: reservas@casaviejaperu.com, URL: www.casaviejaperu.com.

CHACHAPOYAS RESTAURANTS

La Roca (Entrees: $1.80 - 3)

Head to La Roca for regular, traditional Peruvian fare. There's nothing too special about this place, but the prices are good and the portions are huge, with soups, chicken, *flautas*, and tortillas as staples on the daily menu. Open for breakfast, lunch and dinner from 7 a.m. to 9 p.m. Ayacucho 932, Tel: 51-4-147-8158.

Mari Pizza (Entrees: $1.30 - 8)

This two-room pizza parlor is a beloved Chachapoyas meeting place. If one of the 14 varieties of pizza Mari offers doesn't strike your fancy, you can special order one. The pastas are all homemade and include lasagna, ravioli and fettuccini. A few vegetarian options are available. A glass case displays the wines and locally distilled fruit liqueurs Mari Pizza offers. There are also fresh fruit juices. To top off your meal, try one of Mari's luscious desserts. Service is excellent. Open daily, from the early evenings until 2 a.m. Phone delivery is available. Prices include tax. Jr. Ayacucho 912-916, Tel: 51-4-147-8876.

La Tushpa (Entrees: $2 - 4.50)

This is the hot-spot if you're craving a steak. The chefs at La Tushpa are experts on the grill and can make a wide variety of grilled items cooked to order. Get there early or be prepared to wait, as locals storm the doors for the delicious carnivore fare. Ortiz Arrieta 753, Tel: 51-4-180-3634.

505 Pizza Bar

Cheap, good pizza is what this place does. And they do it well. That's not all that it has going for it though, because when the sun goes down the energy goes up. When they crank the music, this tiny little place fills with people who want to shake their legs and cut a rug. 2 de Mayo 505, Tel: 51-4-147-7328.

Nature's Center New Eden

The only "meat" served at New Eden is soya, prepared with traditional Peruvian recipes. The lunch and dinner menus are vegan. Both vegetarian and vegan dishes are served à la carte. However, New Eden is much more than a mere vegetarian restaurant. Health supplements, herbal teas, wholemeal cookies and Christian literature are also sold here. To relax after trekking to Gran Vilaya or Laguna de los Cóndores, you can enjoy the rustic sauna fired with eucalyptus (Sunday and Thursday evenings; $2.60, unlimited time). Despite its English name, the wait staff is not bilingual. Jr. Grau 448.

Restaurant-Pollería El Sabor Chiclayano

Lunch and suppertimes are busy in this large, well-lit restaurant, and the waitresses are quick and attentive. Lunch is always a set *menú*: soup and a choice of four main dishes (usually chicken or beef), accompanied by the requisite rice, a dollop of vegetables and a drink. Only one dish is offered at dinner: rotisserie chicken (*pollo broaster*) with a heap of hot French fries and fresh salad. You can wash this repast down with a free glass of Peru's famous Inca Kola. Jr. Ortiz Arrieta 404, on the corner with Jr. Libertad.

AROUND CHACHAPOYAS

Huancas

Huancas, 5 kilometers north of Chachapoyas, derives its name from the Huancas nation. Originally from the Mantaro valley east of Lima, they were sent by Inca ruler Huayna Cápac as *mitmaq*, or colonists, to the Chachapoya realm. Huancas has become renowned for its pottery, made exclusively by women, giving them an economic power uncommon in Andean societies. You can visit the workshops of Asociación Comunal de Artesanos La Cusana. Just ten minutes walking from the plaza is a *mirador* with a breathtaking view of the Sonche River canyon and a four-step waterfall tumbling through the cloud forest. Follow Jr. Ortiz Arrieta north, past the airport: 1 hour walking; 20 minutes by collective taxi (leaving from the 300-block of Jr. Ortiz Arrieta).

Levanto and Yálape (Entrance: free)

Yálape, built 1100-1350 AD, was a major Chachapoya city. During Inca rule it served as the region's administrative center. With the Spanish conquest, Levanto was founded close-by as the capital of Amazonas; about nine years later, it was moved to its present site, Chachapoyas.

Today Levanto is a quiet town with a rose garden plaza and an ancient church. Recent excavations have revealed the stunning friezes of Yálape ruins from beneath heavy vegetation. The four-hectare site is a half-hour walk uphill from Levanto (ask for directions). Along the pre-Inca road that leads back to Chachapoyas is Colla Cruz, a restored *tambo*, or dwelling.

To Levanto: Collective taxis leave mornings from the Chachapoyas market and from the 100-block of Jr. Sosiego. The entire outing will take about 8 hours if traveling by *colectivo* to Levanto, so be sure to give yourself enough time for the return. The 16-kilometer pre-Inca road enters the Chachapoyas highway at La Molina, five kilometers south of the city. The *colectivo* costs $2. A guide can be hired in Chachapoyas for $6.60 - 8.30. Open from dawn to dusk.

Catarata de Gocta (Entrance: $1)

Quick—where's the third-highest waterfall in the world? According to the National Geographic Society, it is northwest of Chachapoyas, near the villages of Cocachimba and San Pablo. Gocta's two-step cascade plunges 771 meters through the jungle to a pool guarded by a blond mermaid. Legends say she is the mother of the river's fish and she will bewitch all those who dare to bathe in her waters, to protect the treasure that lies in their depths. The name Gocta is thought to come from the cry of the endemic yellow-tailed woolly monkey. While it's possible to go on your own, same-day transport back to Chachapoyas is difficult. Going with a tour is probably best. A local guide costs about $6.60; a tour from Chachapoyas is $16.60 - 23.30.

KUÉLAP

Clouds wrap around the mountains and enshroud the stones of the *fortaleza*. A silence pervades the air. What did these massive walls of Kuélap protect?

Photos cannot accurately portray this ancient citadel. The perimeter wall, containing a number of human and animal burials, measures 20 meters high and more than a half-kilometer long. You enter the site through one of three entries cut through the stone. Soon the passage narrows, allowing only one person to enter at a time, with carvings of faces staring as you pass.

Within, the jungle-covered four-hectare city, divided into Pueblo Bajo and Pueblo Alto, is comprised of more than 400 one-time circular homes, some with the intricate Chachapoya stone friezes. To the South is El Tintero, a towering construction with a hollow core shaped like an inverted inkwell. In Pueblo Alto are two buildings of note. The Castillo, a rectangular building, may have been a mausoleum. In the extreme northern end is a defensive tower, El Torreón, where many weapons were unearthed. The only fully restored building is in Pueblo Bajo. In the entire site, only four quadrangular, probably Inca, edifices exist.

Recent excavations have dramatically changed our understanding of what Kuélap was and who its inhabitants were. No longer are they viewed as a warrior tribe who practiced no farming. Instead they are seen as a people whose agricultural production was so great as to allow trade from coast to jungle. Further, El Tintero is now known to have been a ceremonial site, not a torture chamber. It is much older than the 900 years previously thought; occupation began around 400 BC. Archaeologist Alfredo Narváez believes it was a holy site to which Chachapoya peoples from all over the realm came to bury their dearly departed.

Little by little the silence is broken. The stones of Kuélap speak, revealing their history to us.

Getting To and Away from Kuélap

Tours to Kuélap from Chachapoyas cost up to 75 soles/$25. Alternatively, take the daily Transporte Roller (Jr. Grau and Salamanca) service to Kuélap (4 a.m.; 15 soles/$5; 3 hour trip), and buy tickets the night before. Another combi leaves at 3 p.m. from the gas station on Libertad.

From Leymebamba, go to Tingo, then by colectivo to Nuevo Tingo (1 sol/$0.30); await the combi from Chachapoyas (5 a.m., 4 p.m.; 8 soles/$2.60). Or from Tingo, climb the steep trail (3-4 hour up, 1½-2 hours down; horses, 20-25 soles/$6.60-8.30).

María to Kuélap is 1½-2 hours walking, or 1 sol/$0.30 in a cab.

KUÉLAP SERVICES

Tingo is 36 km south of Chachapoyas on the main highway and serves as a starting point for the trek to Kuélap. A mule trail goes up the mountain to the legendary site. A separate road zigzags up the Petaca range, through the villages of Nuevo Tingo, Choctámal, Lónguita, María and Quisango, before reaching Kuélap.

There are no banks, internet cafes, post offices or pharmacies in any of these hamlets. Each has a health post with basic services; there is a doctor in María. Nuevo Tingo, Choctámal and María have telephone service.

Only in Tingo, Choctámal, María, Quisango and Kuélap is lodging available. Power and water outages are common; Kuélap has no electricity. Locally produced woven and knitted goods may be purchased from the Asociación Comunal de Tejadoras, with workshops in Choctámal, Lónguita and María.

No tourism offices or agencies exist in this area. Local guides may be contracted in Choc-ámal for a trek into the Gran Vilaya, or in Kuélap for a tour of the ruins.

Things To See and Do In Kuélap

Macro

An enigma among the hundreds of Chachapoya ruins in the region, Macro is one of only two known sites built on the side of a hill, rather than atop. The walls, extending at least one kilometer, are made of finely finished yellow stone. Some are of circular buildings, others appear to hug the contours of the land, thus lending its name to the site: Macro means undulating. According to ethnohistorian Peter Lerche, this site probably had ceremonial purposes. From Tingo, a 10-minute walk along the road towards Chachapoyas takes you to the *oroya*, or cable car, across the river. Ask directions to Macro, it's quite easy to find. A pre-Inca road connects Macro with Yálape, near Levanto (a 3-hour walk).

Gran Vilaya

In 1985 a great discovery hit the headlines: Gran Vilaya. Reported to the authorities by Silverio Visalot Chávez and investigated by US explorer Gene Savoy, these ruin complexes extend west from the Río Utcubamba to the Río Marañón. The actual number of sites may be around 150, with 30 being important. They include Paxamarca, Pueblo Nuevo, Pueblo Alto, Pirquilla, Yumal and Machu Llacta. Connected by ancient stone roads and trails winding through pristine forests at the edge of the Andes, little excavation has been done.

Treks of four to five days of the Gran Vilaya can be arranged in Chachapoyas, Lámud or Cohechán. All expenses—horses, guide, lodging and food—are included in the price (up to $40 per day, per person). The journeys usually include visits to Karajía and Huaya Belén, Gran Vilaya itself, Congón and Kuélap. You can opt for an extension to include Revash and Centro Mallqui in Leymebamba. Treks can also be planned in Choctámal, near Kuélap. If your Spanish is good and you have the gear, you could do it on your own. However, trails are often unmarked and the ruins are difficult to find in the lush vegetation.

Kuélap Lodging

El Mirador de Kuélap (Rooms: $1.60 - 5 per person)

This hostel offers four warm rooms, two with private bathrooms and two with common bathrooms, for a bargain introductory price. Each room has a large picture window. The small baths all have hot showers. El Mirador de Kuélap earns its name with views of the fortress on the other side of the Utcubamba River valley. The wrap-around balcony is also a great place from which to watch the sunset. Jr. San Felipe and N. de Arriola, on corner of the Plaza Low.

Casa Hospedaje León (Rooms: $3.30 per person)

Sitting on the balcony overlooking the river, you can watch the waters flow. Though beautiful, this inn suffers from the periodic flooding of that *río*. The adobe walls are cracked, the ceiling is falling. Within, the Leon's sloping, terraced hallways make it feel like an amusement park funhouse. The floors are dirty throughout, as if the river's spirit wanders through each room. Rooms are common bath only. Beware of extra charges (e.g. hot shower). Located around the corner from Bar-Restaurant Kuélap, Tingo.

Casa Hospedaje Cucha Cuella (Rooms: $3.30 per person)

The courtyard is a working area for the family, with wash areas and, in one corner, a beehive adobe stove where the *doña* bakes traditional bread. But step into one of the half-dozen rooms up on the second floor, and you enter a sanctuary. The large rooms, for one or two persons, have wood floors and private bath with hot water (when there is electricity, when there is water). You will sleep well with the many blankets on the bed and the comfortable price. Near end of main road, on the right, in María.

Casa Huéspedes El Lirio (Rooms: $3.30 per person)
This hostel is much like the other ten that follow it along the main road through María—but with one distinction: from the common balcony you can watch the nightly soccer game in the village field across the road. The rooms are modest. The private, hot-water baths are clean. El Lirio's owner is friendly and knowledgeable about the different archaeological sites and natural features (e.g., Laguna Cucha Cuella, 10 kilometers away) that you can get to know in this region. On the right as you enter the village, next to the Centro de Salud, in María.

Hostal "El Bebedero" (Rooms: $6.60 per person)
This ecological-cultural inn, owned by the family of archaeologist Arturo Ruiz Estrada, offers six basic rooms, each with two beds. It is a typical country-style house with unpainted adobe, a red-tiled roof, dirt floor and central courtyard garden. There is no electricity; candles are provided. There is also the option to camp. Currently there is only an outhouse and throw-water "shower," but there are plans to install bathrooms in the main building. Upon arriving at Kuélap, ask for José Alba, who runs the hostel. 200 m downhill from the ruins, Tel: 51-4-181-3172 (Kuélap) / 51-1-471-1039 (Lima), E-mail: infokuelap@yahoo.es.

KUÉLAP RESTAURANTS
El Mirador (Entrees: $0.50 - 1.30)
El Mirador lives up to its name, with large windows bestowing incredible views of the Petaca mountain range. To watch the sunset is the perfect "dessert" to top off your evening meal. Doña Olga serves a delicious menu for lunch and dinner. She also offers breakfasts that come with locally baked unleavened corn-wheat bread and her homemade jams ($0.50 - 1). Every meal includes your choice of herbal tea or coffee. There is a popular *hospedaje* downstairs. Last building on the left, direction Kuélap, in María.

Bar-Restaurant Kuélap (Entrees: $1 and up)
This family-style restaurant is popular with transport and tour groups making rest stops at Tingo. Service is on-the-mark and friendly. Sit right down, and the señor will be at your table, giving it a quick wiping, and taking your order. Before you know it, a generous plateful of home cooked food will be steaming before you, and all for only 3 soles. The owner is helpful also, dishing up information on Kuélap and lesser-known local sites. Located on the main highway, diagonal from the National Police (PNP) in Tingo.

Restaurant y Hospedaje Kuélap (Entrees: $1.30)
This restaurant is just your typical Peruvian diner, right down to the low lighting and the plastic-covered tables with a cupful of silverware and brown-paper napkins. It serves the typical Peruvian fare, hot off the wood fire, with a mountain of rice and even a touch of salad, which is plenty to fill your hungry belly after the long journey to Kuélap, or after a day spent at those magnificent ruins. The price is relatively easy on your pocket: 4 soles. And to rest those weary bones, there is an inn upstairs. Near the end of the main road, direction Kuélap, on the right, in María.

JALCA GRANDE
Jalca Grande is the most traditional village in the region. Women still wear their centuries-old clothing. Most still spin wool and weave. Their goods are sold at the Club de Madres La Navidad (Jr. San Pedro, facing the plaza; no sign) and at Pacha Maituna (Jr. Arriola, one block from the plaza).

Friday is the traditional bartering market. The San Juan Bautista feast days, June 24-26, include the Danza del Oso, or Spectacled Bear Dance. The Museo de Jalca Grande has good information about the culture and history of this town, and an excellent scale model of Óllape ruins ($0.60). Irregular hours; contact Tourism Secretary Gladys Basán at Jr. Alvarado 550.

La Jalca's stone church with Chachapoya friezes, built in 1538, is the oldest in the Amazonas Department (open weekend nights). The famed Choza Redonda is now a ruin. Nearby attractions include Laguna de Mamacocha, and the archaeological sites Óllape and Putqueroloma.

Jalca Grande has limited services. There is no bank, post office or pharmacy. There is a dirt-floor internet "café" (Jr. San Felipe 589; $0.60 per hour) that also has phone service. The health post is on Jr. Arriola, a half block from the church. This town is also known as La Jalca.

Getting To and Away from Jalca Grande
From Chachapoyas, a combi leaves Monday-Saturday at 2 p.m. from Jr. Hermosura, near Jr. Salamanca (10 soles/$3.30US; 4 hours), passing through Tingo at 3 p.m. - 3:30 p.m. and the Ubilón crossroad at 4 p.m. - 4:30 p.m. To Chachapoyas, the combi leaves La Jalca at 4:30 a.m. From Leymebamba, catch the Celendín - La Jalca truck as it passes through on Friday, or a truck from the Sunday market in Yerbabuena (until 1 p.m.). Otherwise, go to Ubilón and await the combi or walk (3 hours uphill). Saturday between 11 a.m. - 12 p.m. a truck leaves Jalca Grande for Rioja and Moyobamba. Sunday at 8 a.m. another leaves for Yerbabuena, Leymebamba and Celendín.

THINGS TO SEE AND DO IN JALCA GRANDE
Óllape
Up on Cerro Ushparán, near Jalca Grande, lie more Chachapoya ruins. The walls of Óllape's one-time circular homes peek from beneath blackberry bushes, exhibiting these ancient peoples' classic stonework designs. Atop the knoll is a D-shaped structure with a wooden cross, the base of which is original and typical of religious Chachapoya structures. This site, dating from the Late Intermediate Period (800 - 1470 AD) had covered at least three hectares. Jalca Grande may have been a *llacta* (town) associated with Óllape. Open sunrise to sunset; admission is free. Follow the road out of town, towards Ubilón; the trailhead is marked. Keep to your right at each fork. Wear long pants, as there are a number of brambles.

Laguna Mamacocha
Laguna Mamacocha is just one of many natural wonders that speckle the Amazonas region. A sparkling gem hidden deep in the cloud-swathed mountains, it has three islets. It is a four to five-hour walk from Jalca Grande. Due to the terrain, littered with sinkholes, and the heavy vegetation, a guide is necessary. Fernando Guiop in the La Jalca may be contracted. The laguna may also be reached on horseback (3 hours) from the village of San Pedro, near Montevideo to the south. The cost of a guide would be about $10. Open sunrise to sunset. Bring water and food, as there is no place to acquire any along the way. Also wear a hat and sunblock.

JALCA GRANDE LODGING
El Mirador de Kuélap (Rooms: $1.60 - 5)
This hostel, still under construction, is already offering four warm rooms, two with private bathrooms and two with common bathrooms, for a bargain introductory price. Each room has a large picture window. The small baths all have hot showers. When completed there will also be a garage. El Mirador de Kuélap earns its name with views of the Fortress on the other side of the Utcubamba River valley. The wrap-around balcony is also a great place from which to watch the sunset. Jr. San Felipe and N. de Arriola, on the corner of the Plaza.

Rumi Huasi (Rooms: $3.30 per bed, hot showers $0.30 extra)
The stone façade of this home-away-from-home is amusing. An occasional face smiles down at you, inviting you to come in and relax. But it is only that: a façade. Behind that wall, Rumi Huasi's (Stone House) 13 rooms are small and shabby. Many of them are gloomy. All come with common, cold-water bath; one is nicely tiled, but the others are dark and dank. The price for a night of dreaming here, though, won't cause you a nightmare. Jr. San Pedro 352, 1.5 blocks from the church.

JALCA GRANDE RESTAURANTS
Restaurant Sarita (Entrees: $0.80)
A popular eatery, Restaurant Sarita serves up a pleasant ambience that is clean and orderly. Lace cloths decorate the half-dozen tables in this bright room. Service can be a bit slow. But give a call

out back to the kitchen and Doña Sara will present you today's blue plate special (menú) of large portions. All meals—breakfast, lunch, or dinner—won't put a hole in your pocket, either. They are reasonably priced at $0.80. Prices include tax. The Doña also prepares an amazing *escabeche de pollo* (stewed chicken). Jr. Alonso de Alvarado, 1 block from the Plaza, direction Ubilón.

Restaurant Rocío (Entrees: $1 - 1.15)

Restaurant Rocío is a small operation in the front room of a sky-blue house that also functions as a small store. But don't let the primitive feel of this popular *comedor* or its plastic-tarp ceiling put you off. The drinks are made with boiled water, and the regional foods are tasty. (Try the chicken with *olluco*—a type of potato—and peas.) Yes, it will come with the obligatory mountain of rice. The menú is $1. Trout and *cuy* are also prepared à la carte ($1.15). Prices include tax. Jr. San Roque 708, on the corner of Jr. San Pedro.

YERBABUENA

A 45-minute bus ride north of Leymebamba is the village of Yerbabuena. A dusty backwater during the week, come Sunday it bustles to life with the region's largest market. All services in this hamlet are located along the "main street": the only *hospedaje*, several restaurants, the public health center, drugstores and telephone offices. There is no bank or internet. Near the

---

YAVARÍ: SONG AND SOUL OF A PEOPLE

"There are pains that little by little
Pass without being felt . . ."

"We really need a guitar," Meider Díaz says as we sit in the smoke-darkened interior patio of his home. Horse tackle lies against one wall. Ducks preen in their cage. *Don* Meider wraps his red wool poncho closer around himself. With a chill-cracked voice, he begins to sing a *yaraví*. Its sorrowful melody warms this space.

"Love, love that takes away life
Thief, thief that stole my soul . . ."

In the old days, men conquered women's hearts with a serenade. Yes, that is how he won his wife's. If a lass broke his heart, the rejected beau would sing to her. Or he would croon one last good-bye, before seeking his destiny.

"Now I leave for far-off lands
To a country where no-one knows me . . ."

His teenage daughter and niece sit on low stools with us, giggling behind their hands. I ask them, "If a young man came to serenade you, what would you think?" "Oh, that he's *cursi*—old-fashioned," they reply.

With their young generation, the yaraví is dying. It is quaint, "not like the rock and reggaeton that is invading with globalization," Meider explains. Few still sing the old songs. Some, like Meider, write new ones. He penned *Campesino* while recovering from a horse accident. His sister Nimia is the first woman composer. Every July there is a song festival.

As Meider sings one song after another, the girls shyly join in. Perhaps, deep down, these songs aren't so *cursi*. Perhaps they will be the next generation to sing the yaraví—and conquer their lovers' hearts.

---

orth end of town is the turn-off that leads past the municipal buildings, the basic church, nd on to Revash.

Getting To and Away from Yerbabuena

Signs along the highway designate the *paraderos* (stops) for transport to other villages: Chachapoyas (p.465), Leymebamba, Santo Tomás and Jalca Grande (p.474), among others. On Sundays combis and trucks are frequent until the end of the market. On other days, here is only transport for other villages directly along the Leymebamba-Chachapoyas road. Any transportation plying this route passes through Yerbabuena from Leymebamba early in the morning (daily 3:45 a.m. - 5:45 a.m.; $1.30) and from Chachapoyas in the afternoon (daily 2:30 p.m. and 6:30 p.m., approximately; $2.60).

THINGS TO SEE AND DO IN YERBABUENA

Revash

High up on an escarpment you can see Revash, a group of white and red buildings. Some have likened them to dwellings of Southwest US *pueblos*, but these were no apartment houses for the living. These are *chullpas*, (mausoleums), built by the Chachapoya people during the Late Intermediate Period (probably in the 12th and 13th centuries). Constructed of stone, adobe mud and straw with a smooth plaster finish, some of the structures stand two-stories tall. Above, on the rock wall, are petroglyphs.

The original number of burials is unknown. By the time Henri and Paule Reichlen excavated here in 1948, the tombs had already been looted, save one lower chamber. The Reichlens recovered the skeletons of one infant and 11 adults along with a quantity of bone tools, pottery, musical instruments, combs and feather ornaments. A kilometer away they found a cave containing the remains of about 200 individuals. Due to an earthquake in the 1970s, that grotto was sealed. As you climb you can see at least seven other chullpa groups on the surrounding cliffs. Soon you arrive at Revash, its buildings marred by graffiti and scattered with bones. It is now forbidden to enter the site itself.

Getting there: To find Revash, travel along the road from Chachapoyas to Santo Tomás. Tours cost $25 and include entrance to Centro Mallqui (the mummy museum), transportation, a guide and lunch. Open dawn to dusk. A great Sunday trip from Leymebamba is to go to the Yerbabuena Sunday Market, then to Revash. Take plenty of water, sunblock and hat, as there is no shade along the road or trail.

Yerbabuena Sunday Market

In the dawn twilight, dozens of trucks from every village between Leymebamba and Chachapoyas disgorge passengers bowed beneath heavy bundles. Tarps are strung over rickety stands and goods are quickly displayed. This is Yerbabuena's Sunday *trueque* (bartering) market, the region's largest. Soon all's a-bustle—a Jalca Grande woman trades half a saddlebag of corn for plantains here; a family is landing a deal on their calf over there. No, you don't have to bring your pottery or *chacra*'s produce. Money is also used here. So step up and join the action. You might go home with fresh chicken for your dinner. Open from dawn until between noon and 1:30 p.m. A good outing is to combine this with a trip to Revash.

YERBABUENA LODGING

Hospedaje del Rocío (Rooms: $2.60 per bed)

The sign states, "Spacious rooms—Reservations for national and international tourists." The five rooms *are* spacious, but the ceilings are draped with blue tarp and sparse furnishings. Though visitors may be a bit dismayed after seeing the bathrooms and sagging beds, you can't beat the price. And, as the only lodging option in town, it's best to make a reservation if you need somewhere to crash, as it fills up Saturday nights before the market and clears out by Sunday afternoon. On the main highway, a half block north of the market.

YERBABUENA RESTAURANTS
Restaurant de Señora Wilma (Entrees: $1.15)
In this large, dimly lit restaurant with greasy, plastic-covered tables, Señora Wilma serves an uninspiring *menú* for lunch, though there aren't many better options in Yerbabuena. The plate has a healthy helping of rice, slightly undercooked *menestra* (lentils) and just enough meat to remind you the meal comes with it. A drink is included with this repast that costs $1.15. Evening meals are à la carte for the same price. You may choose either local trout or *cecina* (dried beef or pork, a regional specialty); drinks are separate. Across from the market, with the ENSA water and light sign.

LEYMEBAMBA
Called "The Land of the Millenium Gods," Leymebamba is a friendly, relaxed town on the banks of the Río Utcubamba. It is a convenient stopping point between Chachapoyas and Celendín, providing many opportunities to explore the ruins and southern villages of the Amazonas Department. Mornings here dawn over misty mountains ringing with the cries of green parrots. Atop those ridges lie numerous archaeological sites, including La Congona, La Joya and Torre Puco. Centro Mallqui, the "mummy museum," houses finds from the *chullpas* (burial tombs) of Laguna de los Cóndores.

The Plaza de Armas is stone-paved with Chachapoya designs. In one corner is a fountain replica of the Laguna de los Cóndores. The rough-stone church with twin stout towers is reputed to be the second oldest in the region (open nightly). Leymebamba is known as a center for *yaraví* music. Musicians play near the Plaza in the evenings. The patron saint is the Virgen del Carmen; her feast days are July 11-16, and feature traditional dances and the Festival de la Canción. Market day is Saturday.

Getting To and Away From Leymebamba
Leymebamba is accessible by unpaved road from Celendín and Chachapoyas (p.465). Virgen del Carmen has buses to Celendín (Sunday noon, Tuesday, 8 a.m. and 7 p.m., Friday 8 a.m.; $6.60; 10-12 hours), Chachapoyas (Sunday, Thursday, Friday 7 p.m.;$3; 3.5 hours), and Rioja (Sunday 7 p.m.; $8.30; 12 hours). Tours Marañón has combis to Celendín (Tuesday, Friday 7:30 a.m.; $6.60; 8 hours).

Several other companies run daily combis to Chachapoyas and villages between for the same price as the bus. *Carros* (collective taxis) charge $4.60 per person to Chachapoyas. Several times a week, trucks pass through to Rioja and Cajamarca (p.460).

LEYMEBAMBA SERVICES
There are no banks in Leymebamba; be sure to have plenty of soles before leaving Chachapoyas or Cajamarca. Three internet cafés offer services ($0.60 per hour): an unnamed one, (Jr. La Verdad 521, across from Cely Pizza; daily 9 a.m. - 10 p.m.); another unnamed one (Ayacucho 525); and the Casa de la Cultura (Jr. Sucre, a half block from the Plaza). The Telefónica on the Plaza is open 7 a.m. - 10 p.m. everyday. There is no post office. On or near the Plaza de Armas are several boticas (drugstores). The hospital is at La Verdada and Ayacucho, two blocks from the church.

Tourism information may be obtained from the Instituto Nacional de Cultura on the Plaza (irregular hours). There are no tour companies; tours may be booked through hotels. Recommended guides are Javier Farje and Daniel Aguilar.

The weekly market is Saturday, at the corner of Jr. Sucre and Próspero. Local weavings and other crafts may be bought at the Asociación de Mujeres Artesanas de Leymebamba (AMAL) store, near the church.

THINGS TO SEE AND DO IN LEYMEBAMBA
Centro Mallqui (Admission: $1.60)
Upon discovery of the chullpas (mausoleums) at Laguna de los Cóndores in 1996, a massive operation was launched to save the mummies from tomb robbers. With the assistance of

Austrian archaeologists, Centro Mallqui was founded to house and study the remains. The museum has four exhibition halls with well-laid-out displays. Explanations are in Spanish; also, much is in English and there is some in German. Sala 1 has information about Chachapoya culture, society and architecture, including the different burial structures (mausoleums and sarcophagi) encountered in the Amazonas region. Sala 2 is on the Chachapoya-Inca period, with some of the largest *quipus* ever found. Sala 3 consists of the bio-archaeological room. Behind a glass wall you can watch scientists studying and conserving the 219 mummy bundles contained therein. Sala 4 discusses the ethnography of the Chachapoya peoples and their cultural expressions in the modern era. The complex also has a botanical and orchid garden and a gift shop for souvenirs. What makes Centro Mallqui so amazing, however, is that the staff and guides are locals; in this way the importance and value of sites like Laguna de los Cóndores are taught to the *pueblo,* preventing future sacking of archaeological ruins. The admission price includes the services of a guide (Spanish only). Open daily, 9:30 a.m. - 4:30 p.m. Closed Mondays; Christmas, New Years Day. Located 4.5 kilometers from Leymebamba plaza. To get there, walk (uphill) or take a taxi ($1.60 for up to 3 persons). Av. Austria s/n, San Miguel, Leymebamba Tel: (041) 816803, (041) 816806, URL: http://centromallqui.org.pe/.

La Congona (Entrance: free)

Spread out upon a ridge near Leymebamba, La Congona is an as-yet unexcavated town. About 30 houses with zigzag, rhomboid and step-fret friezes rise out of the heavy bramble vegetation. They are of typical Chachapoya design of the Late Intermediate Period (800-1470 AD). You can still see the stone cornices that served to channel water away from the terrace foundations. At the edge of the ridge is a three-story structure, assumed by some to have been a watchtower. Climb the steps for a wide-angle view of the Utcubamba River valley below. If you have the eyes of a condor, you can see Kuélap and Yálape in the distance. La Congona lies far from the transited road. To walk there, take the path that zigzags like a vertical Chachapoya design up the hill at the end of Jr. 16 de Julio (3 hours there, 2 hours return). Ask for directions frequently. Alternately, take a Celendín-bound bus or the daily milk truck (*el lechero*) to Las Palmas ($1) and walk 1.5 - 2 hours downhill to La Congona; continue that path back to Leymebamba (2 hours). Ask for directions frequently. You could hire a guide to take you; however, it will cost about $8.30 for a five hour trip on foot, and you will spend only a little time at the site. Take water and a bit of food, as there are no stores along the entire route. Also, if it is a sunny day, take sunblock and a hat; if it is a day threatening rain, you can expect the path to be muddy. Open sunrise to sunset.

Laguna de los Cóndores

In late 1996, a group of farmers clearing land discovered 219 tombs. Soon after that, a combined Peruvian-Austrian scientific team began a rescue operation to save this national patrimony. Unfortunately, *huaqueros* (tomb robbers) cleaned out 18 other near-by sites before archaeologists could arrive.

Made of stone, adobe and straw and covered with a layer of mud plaster, some of the chullpas are painted white with red and yellow ochre designs. Most of these structures date from the Chachapoya Late Intermediate Period (800-1470 AD); two were built during the Inca occupation. The site was used until after the Spanish conquest. Ruins of Llaqtacocha, a residential *llacta*, or town, associated with these tombs, were excavated in 1998.

The artifacts found at Laguna de los Cóndores are on display at Centro Mallqui, the museum in Leymebamba. These tombs have been the topic of a Discovery Channel documentary and *Archaeology* magazine articles. It is a 10-12 hour journey on horseback and foot to Laguna de los Cóndores. The entire adventure lasts three to five days, according to your desires. A guide is essential and may be contracted in Leymebamba or Chachapoyas. Prices for the trek begin at about $67 per person, including horses, guide, lodging and food.

Lámud, you can walk by way of Shipata or Trita in 2-2.5 hours; ask directions. Transport from Chachapoyas to Luya is $2.30; Luya to Cruz Pata, $1.60. Open sunrise to sunset. You can go on a day tour from Chachapoyas, also visiting Pueblo de los Muertos or Huaya Belén, for $25.

Pueblo de los Muertos (Entrance: $1)

Pueblo de los Muertos (Village of the Dead) lies 30 kilometers north of Chachapoyas, near Lámud. The stout *purunmachus,* or sarcophagi, have suffered extensively at the hands of looters. Be advised not all these structures are original. The *chullpas* (mausoleums), also victims of plundering, long ago lost their roofs. The exposed adobe walls now melt in the elements. Some of the niche designs are said to be the exact same as Egyptian hieroglyphics. But whatever you may believe of possible cultural interchanges, these funerary monuments were crafted by the Chachapoya (Luya-Chilloa) between 1100 and 1350 AD. It is an 18 km walk (2 hours) from Lámud. Ask for directions. Open sunrise to sunset. You can go on day tour from Chachapoyas, also visiting Karajía, for $25.

LÁMUD LODGING

Hostal Forteleza de Kuélap (Rooms: $3.30 - 8.30)

The accommodations of this hostel are situated on the second floor of a classic colonial building. Rooms with common bath (cold water shower) are large and sparsely furnished. The common bathrooms could be cleaner. Also available are rooms with balconies and private bath. However, these add a new dimension to the term "private bath." Instead of being attached to the room itself, the bath is located in a cabinet on the other side of the hall, designated by room number. Av. G. de la Vega 452, on the Plaza, Tel: 51-4-183-0111 / 51-4-183-0112.

Hospedaje L and L (Rooms: $3.30 - 13.30)

Hospedaje L and L is a new inn sporting white-washed walls and fine-wood trim. The rooms are large and simply furnished. The bathrooms are of sparkling tile with hot water showers. There are rooms for one to three persons, with single and matrimonial beds and shared bath. Also there are four suites with private bath and television; towels and toiletries are provided. Other amenities include hot water for tea or coffee upon request, and a locked garage. Prices include tax. Jr. San Martín 477, Cellular: (01) 9536-2815, (01) 9056-1806.

LÁMUD RESTAURANTS

Restaurant Turístico El Paraíso (Entrees: $1.15 - 2.30)

If it doesn't appear open, just knock on the door. Soon you'll be attended to by Trinidad and Carola. No, it isn't a speakeasy, just a popular restaurant that serves set meals ($0.80-1.15) and regional specialties like *cecina, cuy* and *chicharrón* ($1.30-2.30). The front room is intimate, and the service is quick. There is optional seating in the hillside gardens. *Doña* Carola crafts her creations in the kitchen that includes a grotto and small waterfall. Prices include tax. Jr. Grau 539, Tel: 51-41-997-8085.

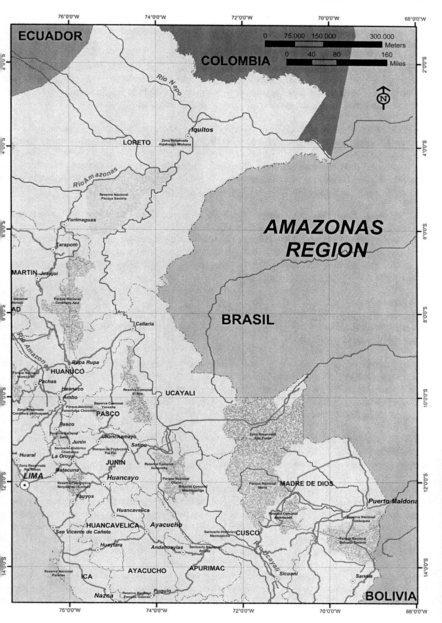

THE PERUVIAN AMAZON BASIN

Machu Picchu and the Incan ruins may claim most of Peru's popularity, but the Amazon Basin boasts most of Peru's land space. Much of the Peruvian Amazon Basin is untouched, but tourism is beginning to carve out a spot for itself here. In this vast and wild area, it is now possible to take a dugout canoe with an outboard motor through the winding tributaries to the Napo and Amazon Rivers, view toucans and squirrel monkeys directly overhead and, if you're lucky, pink river dolphins, caiman, giant otters and much more.

There are several different tour options. The main choice is between river tours on which you travel for several days in a row and stop to camp out or sleep with indigenous communities, and multi-day stays in jungle lodges, which range in quality from rustic to hotel standard. Most Amazon tour companies are located in Iquitos.

Iquitos, on the banks of a mile-wide river in the Amazon, features a floating market, various floating restaurants, some interesting architecture and several crafts markets. It is close to some highlights in the Peruvian Amazon Basin like Lake Quistococha and a few protected nature reserves, including one of the largest protected areas in Peru, the Reserva Nacional Pacaya-Samiria. Freshwater dolphins, turtles and monkeys are just a few of the many animals that live within this reserve.

The Peruvian Amazon is also where you will find the Manu Biosphere Reserve, one of the largest and most important nature reserves in the world. Approximately the size of New Hampshire, the biosphere is home to thousands of species of plants and animals, the most spectacular of which are monkeys, jaguars, caimans, macaws and giant otters, to name a few. It is also a birdwatcher's paradise: some estimate that there may be more than 1,000 species of bird in the region.

Environmental Issues

There are two principle environmental issues facing the Peruvian jungle: oil exploration and deforestation. Though they are not mutually exclusive, they impact the jungle separately to a large degree.

In the past few years there have been some scary developments for the future of Peru's jungle and its inhabitants. As late as 2005 only 20 percent of Peru's Amazon had been handed over to oil and natural gas companies for exploration. However, the current percentage is hovering around 70 percent. This figure represents about 97 million acres, an area larger than Italy or Japan.

What caused the change? One not-so-coincidental development has been an investment made by the U.S. Trade and Development Agency in Perupetro, the state-owned oil company, to push the development and marketing of Peru's oil concessions.

The Peruvian Amazon has been under siege by both foreign and national oil companies for decades. However, it appears production (and subsequent environmental devastation) will be ramped up in the coming years. Despite agreements between the Peruvian government and indigenous groups protecting areas inhabited by Peru's indigenous population, some of which live in complete isolation from other groups, PeruPetro is offering up oil and natural gas concessions to bidding by foreign companies.

The other major environmental threat to the Peruvian jungle is deforestation. One of the principle casualties of the oil exploration in the Peruvian rainforest is the trees. However, agriculture, cattle farming, mining and other resource-extraction activities contribute to the decimation of the rainforest as well.

Illegal logging presents many of the same issues as oil extraction. Many indigenous communities are being displaced from their traditional hunting and fishing grounds being ruined through uncontrolled, reckless logging. Although logging does not pollute with the same intensity as oil extraction, the activity itself is illegal and therefore there isn't any consideration for environmental issues or regulations.

Although inhabitants of the effected areas are employed by the companies carrying out the extraction, little money (if any) remains in the communities after the resources have been carted away to their foreign destination.

There has been significant protest by the indigenous inhabitants of the areas at risk (especially those being auctioned for oil exploration). In February 2007, when Perupetro attended an industry trade-show in Houston, Texas, it was met by multiple indigenous groups who had also made the trip. These groups have joined with the international community seeking to protect not only Peru's rainforest but endangered forests around the world. Also, there is talk that due to previous protests and occupations of oil concessions, First World companies are hesitant to make large investments in the jungle of South America.

Peruvian Amazon Basin Highlights

• Manu Biosphere Reserve—One of the world's largest areas of protected rainforest, the Manu Biosphere Reserve is one of the last pieces of truly virgin rainforest left in the world. As such, visitors explore deep into the untouched jungle in hoping to see jaguars and other exotic animals.

• Tambopata Candamo Reserve—If you're short on time or money, the Tambopata Candamo Reserve is an excellent alternative to Manu. Tambopata boasts a protected area of nearly 1.5 million hectares (about 1/3 the size of Costa Rica). In addition to endangered jaguars, giant otters and giant armadillos, the Reserve contains more species of birds and butterflies than any other area of similar size on the planet.

• Pacaya-Samiria National Reserve—The Pacaya-Samiria National Reserve is the largest protected area in Peru. Given its inaccessibility, those willing to make the journey into Pacaya-Samiria will not be disappointed. Taking advantage of the community immersion opportunities offered by some of the community-based tourism agencies will make for an unforgettable experience.

When to Go

May through November is the dry season for Peru's Amazon, and is the best time to visit. Outside of these times travel to the two most popular reserves, the Manu Biosphere Reserve and Tambopata Candamo Reserve, is restricted due to high water levels (not to mention the increased swarms of mosquitoes). It is also easier to see animals during the dry season as the rivers are lower and wildlife tends to hang out closer to the banks. If you can't make it during the dry season, there are still plenty of opportunities during the rest of the year. The rain usually lasts for only a few hours in the afternoon. Those willing to tolerate sporadic downpours may be more restricted, and rubber boots will be more of a necessity, but they will have the added benefit of fewer tourists, allowing for a more isolated experience.

Safety in The Peruvian Amazon Basin

While in the jungle heed the warnings and advice of your guides. Don't go swimming in jungle rivers without first asking if it is safe. Rivers that look placid on the surface can sometimes have strong currents or animals hiding below the surface. Ask your guide or tour operator before jumping in.

Travelers to the Peruvian Amazon should not have any concerns about run-ins with drug traffickers. The Amazon Basin is hundreds of kilometers from the nearest foothills (where coca plants are grown) and any traffickers that might be operating in the Amazon will have no interest in drawing any attention to themselves. With more than 400,000 inhabitants, Iquitos is the largest city in the world without road access. However, it feels like a small town, and when crime occurs it is big news.

Despite this, visitors should still exercise common-sense precautions. Avoid wearing expensive jewelry or flashing around large amounts of money. Don't let yourself be caught off guard

AMAZON

by opportunistic criminals. Carry your money and documents in your front pocket or money belt and don't leave valuables unattended. Probably the most serious safety consideration in the Amazon Basin of Peru is having all the necessary shots and vaccinations. See the immunization section for more information.

THINGS TO SEE AND DO IN THE PERUVIAN AMAZON

Although not the most popular destination in Peru, the Amazon Basin occupies most of Peru. The fact that tourism is less popular here means most of the activities in the area have a less touristy, more back-to-nature feel. Most things to do involve the area's amazing flora and fauna. During your trip to the Amazon you will surely see plants and animals unlike any you have ever seen before. At Lake Quistococha, near Iquitos, there are large nature reserves including one of the largest protected areas in Peru, the Reserva Nacional Pacaya-Samiria, which is not easy to get to, but those who are determined enough to visit it are sure to have an unforgettable experience. In the Peruvian Amazon you will also find the Manu Biosphere Reserve, which is considered to be one of the most important nature reserves in the world. It is home to thousands of species of plants and animals. It is most famous for its bird watching: there are said to be more than 1,000 species of birds in the area. Other activities in the area involve shopping for crafts in the floating market of Iquitos on the banks of a mile-wide river.

PERUVIAN AMAZON TOURS

The Amazon Jungle sprawls across most of Peru and is a hot spot for birdwatchers, nature lovers and anyone looking to explore the verdant forest and come eye to eye with exotic wildlife.

Photo by Kris Dressen

Tours usually consist of traveling by boat down the Amazon to see local jungle communities or of setting up camp for a few days at one of the many jungle lodges and taking short excursions from there.

Itineraries are endless and choices abundant, more than enough to cover all tastes and travel types—from natural adventures to cultural encounters. One of the most popular spots to arrange a tour is Iquitos, located in the northern jungle on the Amazon River. Amazon jungle sites not to miss include the Pacaya-Samiria Reserve, Lake Quistococha, Bellavista, Nahua-Kugapakori Reserved Zone and Manu Biosphere Reserve.

PERUVIAN AMAZON LODGING

When planning a trip to the Peruvian Amazon you will find that most of the hotels and lodges are in the cities of Iquitos, Manu and Tambopata.

AMAZON

The variety of hotels in Iquitos means that everyone from backpackers to first-class travelers will find a place that appeals to them. However, be aware that for every decent, clean hotel there is a run-down, noisy hole in the wall, so choose wisely. Budget travelers, in particular, need to take care to find the few exceptional hostels among the less-than-desirable ones. By doing some research before arrival, they can be assured they are picking a place that offers both a fair price and a nice room.

Once you've made up your mind, make reservations, as the best places tend to fill up. Also, if you make arrangements ahead of time your hotel may pick you up at the airport, saving you the hassle of dealing with cabbies. If you're staying for several days, you may want to reserve your first night in a more reputable hotel and then explore the area to find a nice budget hotel.

If you are looking for more immersion into the Amazon, a jungle lodge is just the thing for you. The lodges, which are generally close to Manu and Tambopata, are situated away from the city, offering a less tainted view of the Amazon. Many of the resorts are all-inclusive, meaning all meals are included in the lodging price, often due to the fact that there are few or no places to eat in the area. The lodges all also offer guided excursions and other activities in the surrounding area.

PUERTO MALDONADO
A dusty little town located just a half-hour plane ride from Cusco, Puerto Maldonado is the last stop for travelers heading into the infinitely more interesting Amazon jungle. Like many jungle towns, Puerto Maldonado has survived a series of boom and bust cycles, the first being a prosperous rubber industry in 1902. Gold mining and lumber soon followed suit and continue today, though to a large extent tourism and Brazil nut production are on the rise.

Characterized by wide avenues that narrow into mud lanes lined with unremarkable wooden buildings, the town offers little more to see than three-wheeled *motocarros* (motorcycle rickshaws) and scooters. For the most part, travelers use Puerto Maldonado as a jumping-off point to nearby attractions like Lago Sandoval, the Tambopata National Reserve and Bahuaja-Sonene National Park. Vastly more relaxed than its larger jungle-town relative Iquitos, Puerto Maldonado is a popular stop for Tambopata package tours.

Those keen to learn *más español* should definitely check out Tambopata Education Centre, one of the best language schools in the Peruvian Amazon. If you'd rather roll up your sleeves and delve into some much-needed volunteer work, there are a range of opportunities in the area, including being a field assistant at a biological research station, working on a local farm or helping to reforest the rainforest. Though most people blow through town without giving it much notice, it does have an alluring frontier atmosphere that some intrepid individuals may find interesting—at least for a night or two before heading into the heart of the Amazon.

NOTE: Because Puerto Maldonado is listed as part of the yellow fever endemic zone, travelers will need to be vaccinated. If you have already been vaccinated, don't forget to carry your card. Additionally, tourists will only be admitted to the National Reserve and Lake Sandoval with a certified guide.

Getting To and Away from Puerto Maldonado
There are two main forms of transport to Puerto Maldonado: truck or plane. Given the poor condition of the road connecting Cusco and Puerto Maldonado, most travelers choose to hop on a plane rather than endure the bumpy two-day journey via truck. Aeropuerto Internacional Padre Aldamiz Puerto Maldonado is located just eight kilometers outside the city.

Flights can be booked through Lan (www.lan.com). The best way to get to town from the airport is to hire a *motocarro*. Those armed with unflagging patience and plenty of pluck (or anyone who is just plain crazy) can catch a truck from Cusco to Puerto Maldonado. This route covers more than 500 kilometers of rugged Andean landscape—passing through Ocongate

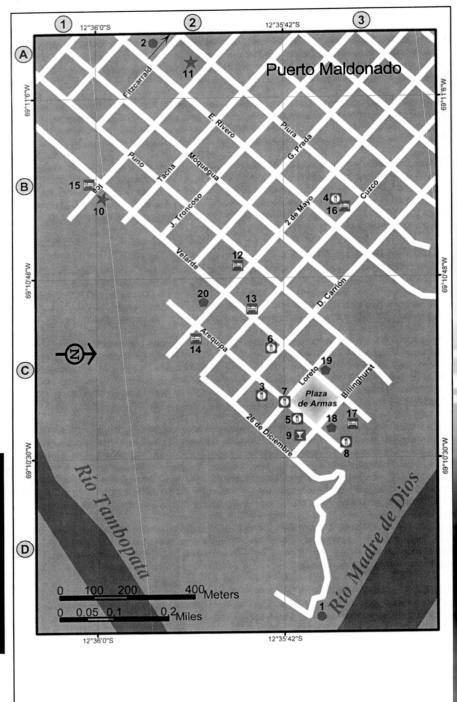

Puerto Maldonado

Activities ●	Services ★
1 Docks D3	10 Correo B2
2 Obelisk A2	11 Mercado Modelo A2
Eating 🍴	**Sleeping** 🛏
3 Carne y Brava C2	12 Hospedaje La Bahía B2
4 Hotel Cabaña Quinta Restaurant B3	13 Hospedaje Luciana C2
5 Karambola Restaurant C3	14 Hospedaje Tres Fronteras C2
6 Leña y Carbon C2	15 Hotel Don Carlos B1
7 Vaka Loka C3	16 The Cabaña Quinta Hotel B3
8 Wasai Lodge Restaurant C3	17 The Wasai Lodge C3
Nightlife 🍸	**Tour Operator** ⬟
9 Karambola Disco Pub C3	18 The Wasai Lodge Tours C3
	19 Ceiba Tours C3
	20 Tropical Nature Tours C2

village and over the peak of Ausangate before dropping over the east side of the Andes—and is by far one of the worst roads in Peru.

During the dry season the journey takes two to three days, and it can take up to ten days in the wet season. With less than zero comfort to speak of, this mode of transportation is in a class all its own. Trucks cost around $15 and leave from Plaza Túpac Amaru in Cusco. Should you survive this jaw-knocking journey, you'll be dropped off at the Mercado Modelo on Calle Ernesto Rivero. Besides a sore backside, the journey will leave you with a lifetime of stories and plenty of bragging rights.

THINGS TO SEE AND DO IN PUERTO MALDONADO

ProNaturaleza Butterfly Conservation Center Japipi

The Butterfly Conservation Center was established in 1996 by two Peruvian scientists who wanted to create Peru's first commercial butterfly farm. ProNaturaleza took over in 2002 and reopened the doors in 2004 as a well-run non-profit butterfly conservation center. Profits go towards the program and its environmental education activities. A few minutes walk from the airport in Puerto Maldonado. Tel: 51-14-479-032, Fax: 51-14-468-593, E-mail: pronaturaleza@pronaturaleza.org, URL: http://www.pronaturaleza.org.

Madre de Dios Ferry

Set out on the Madre de Dios ferry to get a good look at the Peruvian jungle river that is approximately 500 meters wide at the crossing. Drivers who need to ferry their vehicles across to Brazil can also do this here. The river traffic is not bad for people- and vehicle-watching as boats travel between the shores of the Madre de Dios river. The ferry is open from dawn to dusk. Located in Puerto Capitanía (near the Plaza de Armas).

Puerto Maldonado Obelisk (Entrance: $0.70)

Someone, somewhere came up with the idea of building a five-story-high obelisk in downtown Puerto Maldonado, giving both locals and visitors an opportunity to take in the vast and verdant Peruvian jungle from a unique perspective. The tower itself is an eyesore, but the view from the top is breathtaking. Entrance is an inexpensive 2 soles, or $0.70. Sometimes the elevator works, and sometimes it doesn't; you are better off walking up the steps in any case. Avenida Madre de Dios and Fitzcarraldo.

PUERTO MALDONADO TOURS

Motorcycle Tour of Puerto Maldonado ($2.70)

This is not an official activity, but it is a lot of fun, and in a jungle town where you can ride around on the back of a motorcycle, why not? Simply ask any *mototaxista* for a general tour of what there is to see in Puerto Maldonado, and he'll do so for about 8 soles, or $2.70. The tour will generally last an hour, and will include visits to the ports on the rivers Tambopata and Madre de Dios, the town Obelisk, and the area's parks. Just hold on tight.

Tropical Nature Tours & Travel SAC

Tropical Nature Tours and Travel SAC proudly boast that they are capable of all tours. That means taking advantage of all that Puerto Maldonado has to offer, from excursions along the various tributaries and rivers that cross through it to camping on Lake Sandoval. It works with a variety of lodges, and rent tents and other camping gear. It offers both from one-day to multi-day-and-night trips to areas (Paria Manu, Río Piedras) that have not been over-discovered by tourists. It also dispenses free tourist information, can book flights and offers discounts to members of the South American Explorers Club. Av. 2 de Mayo 287 / Av. Leon Velarde 537, Tel: 51-82-571-5821 / 51-82-574-439, E-mail: tropicalnaturemj@yahoo.es, www.tropicalnatureperu.com.

The Wasai Lodge Tours

The Wasai Lodge offers as comprehensive a tour and expedition program as you will find in Puerto Maldonado, focused on birdwatching, ayahuasca sessions, fishing trips and eco-tours. One-trip ventures to its hostel in the Tampopata, giving you an opportunity to experience waterfalls, howler monkeys, caimans, tapirs, deer, jaguars and exotic birds such as parrot, parakeet and macaw. Prices run an average of a $100 per person per day. The Wasai Lodge also offers "adventure from heaven to paradise in bicycle," a combination mountain biking and white water rafting escapade that takes you from Cusco to Puerto Maldonado. Plaza Grau 1, Tel: 51-14-368-792, E-mail: info@wasai.com, URL: www.wasai.com.

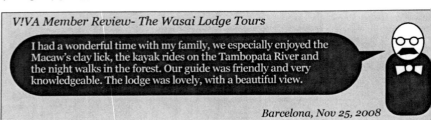

V!VA Member Review- The Wasai Lodge Tours

I had a wonderful time with my family, we especially enjoyed the Macaw's clay lick, the kayak rides on the Tambopata River and the night walks in the forest. Our guide was friendly and very knowledgeable. The lodge was lovely, with a beautiful view.

Barcelona, Nov 25, 2008

Ceiba Tours

Ceiba Tours is the authorized owner of the Mejía Lodge in Lake Sandoval that attracts tourists from all over the world. It will take you by boat, and its excursions include hikes along natural groves of medicinal plants and opportunities to do some crocodile watching. Eco- and mystic tours can also be arranged. Ceiba Tours serves as a travel agency as well, capable of booking flights on such local airlines as Lan Perú and Aero Cóndor. Tour prices start at $40 per day. Ceiba does not, at this point, accept credit cards. Av. León Velarde 420, Puerto Maldonado, Tel: 51-82-573-567, E-mail: davysandoval@yahoo.es.

Sergeturs Colpa Travel

Sergeturs Colpa Travel offers combined tours. On one-day excursions to a turtle reserve, you can observe turtles, under the protection of staff, hatch their offspring. Other tours include visits to monkey islands; parakeet sanctuaries in the lakes and tributaries around Puerto Maldonado; and the Marquisapa, a virgin jungle with a hauntingly beautiful lake, only four hours away by boat. Prices range from $70 to $80 for individual day trips, and $130 for a two-day trip that includes lodging. Sergeturs also offers trips to neighboring Brazil and can book flights. Av. León Velarde 411, Tel: 51-82-573-698, E-mail: colpatravel1@yahoo.com.

PUERTO MALDONADO LODGING

From no-frills hostels to jungle lodges, there is a variety of hotels in Puerto Maldonado. They tend to be a bit on the pricey side, with incredibly simple hostels starting at about nine dollars per night. Nicer hotels are anywhere from $15 to $60 per night. If amenities are important to you, check and make sure that your choice has what you need.

Most have rooms with the standard air conditioning, television, phone and hot water. But not all their rooms may have these things, so be sure to specify what the room you are reserving does and does not have.

Puerto Maldonado is on the edge of the Amazon Jungle, and is often a last stop for travelers heading into *la selva*. It also has a couple of lodges, for those who want to see some of the jungle but do not have either the time or the desire to dive too deeply into the area.

Anaconda Lodge (Rooms: $6.50 - 92)

If you're looking for a unique place to stay, Anaconda Lodge is a great place to start. A cozy lodge that offers bungalow-style accommodations and camping spots, the lodge is rustic luxury at its best. With both a Thai Restaurant and swimming pool on-site, there are enough creature comforts to feel at home. But make no mistake, the lodge's ready access to rain forest hikes are the main draw. Prices range from $6.50 (camping) to $92 for a four-bed bungalow with private bath. Airport Road. Tel: 51-82-792-726, E-mail: info@anacondajunglelodge.com, URL: www.anacondajunglelodge.com.

Hospedaje Luciana (Rooms: $8 - 14)

Hospedaje Luciana was constructed in 2007, and its main advantage for those seeking a bargain while visiting Puerto Maldonado is its fresh, clean rooms, all of which have bathrooms, new beds and new bedspreads. They start at eight dollars, with a matrimonial room going for $14. There are no televisions, but the owners promise that such amenities as laundry service and a cafeteria will be added soon. Jirón Cusco 263, Tel: 51-82-574-481, E-mail: mtorresbolivar@yahoo.es.

Hospedaje La Bahía (Rooms: $9 and up)

This mid-range, by Puerto Maldonado standards, hostel in the Abraham Aguirre Apazabusiness district offers better-than-average rooms, complete with television, table, dresser and even a telephone for as low as nine dollars per single unit. Breakfast is also included. There is a mini convenience shop where you can pick up such tourist staples as sunblock, toothpaste and rolls of film. The owners promise a new facility out in the jungle by 2008, so if you stay here you might consider asking about it. Av. Dos de Mayo 710, Tel: 51-82-572-127.

Hospedaje Tres Fronteras (Rooms: $15 - 18)

There are many inexpensive hostels in Puerto Maldonado. Hospedaje Tres Fronteras is recommended for its newness—it was constructed in 2004—and the high quality of the rooms for $15 a night. A larger, matrimonial room is only $18. Prices remain constant throughout the year. Laundry service, breakfast and cable television all come with the package, and there is an electric fan in every unit. All of the rooms are internal, in a somewhat prison-like manner, which shelters you from the ongoing roar of motorcycles outside. But to allow air to circulate, the windows facing the halls have screens instead of glass, and you can hear your fellow travelers clearly, as they can hear you, not to mention the loud hostel door buzzer at any hour of the night. Jirón Arequipa 357, Tel: 51-82-300-011 / 82-970-3377, E-mail: hospe-tresfronteras@hotmail.com.

Hotel Cabaña Quinta (Rooms: $20 - 67)

Hotel Cabaña Quinta is probably the most popular and recognized accommodation in all of Puerto Maldonado. Its selling points: air conditioning, stocked fridges in every room, free Internet access (including wireless), a bar, restaurant and cafeteria, a sauna, a mini-gymnasium, a Jacuzzi, two swimming pools (one for little kids) a buffet breakfast, a conference room, its own travel agency, not to mention the usual, such as calling and faxing services, laundry, safety box, and they take credit cards, though not MasterCard, which is not accepted anywhere in Puerto Maldonado. The price for a room, minus air conditioning (though with a fan), starts at $15, with AC at $30. Jirón Cuzco 535, Tel: 51-82-571-045, Fax: 51-8-257-3336, E-mail: cabanaquinta_reservas@hotmail.com.

Hotel Don Carlos (Rooms: $35 and up)

Don Carlos claims that it is "a hotel for people who like nature and adventure," and to that end its setting atop a small hill providing a great view of the Tambopata Nature Reserve is to its credit. It is one of the few high-priced (by Puerto Maldonado standards), as well as one of the oldest, hotels in town. Besides the air-conditioned rooms and stocked fridges, it also offers an airport shuttle, a swimming pool, room service (which includes delivering pizzas and grilled chickens), card tables, organized soccer games and even babysitting. Av. León Velarde 1271, Tel: 51-82-571-029, E-mail: reservations@hotelesdoncarlos.com, URL: www.hotelesdoncarlos.com.

The Maldonado Wasai Eco-Lodge (Rooms: $36 and up)

Taking advantage of Puerto Maldonado's reputation as one of THE places to go for jungle expeditions in Peru, the Wasai Eco-Lodge welcomes its guests with a thatched hut entrance worthy of a Tarzan movie. As for the rooms, well, their overall high quality and the view they offer of the Madre de Dios River justifies their high price: $36 for a single room, with a bathroom, air-conditioning and access to their swimming pool. A continental breakfast is included, of course, and the dining area also offer lunch and dinner (at an additional cost). Ask the desk about their tours. Jirón Guillermo Billinghurst, Tel: 51-14-368-792 / 82-571-355, E-mail: wasai@wasai.com, URL: www.wasai.com.

PUERTO MALDONADO RESTAURANTS

In this little jungle town don't expect to find high class restaurants or gourmet dishes. Do expect to find cheap Peruvian eats, chicken shops and delicious-smelling pizzerias at great prices. There are plenty of regional specialties around served with fresh juices, coffee and cakes, and though far from the ocean, the ceviche shouldn't be missed.

Vaka Loka (Entrees: $5)

The name means "mad cow," but don't be put: the food is not only safe, but exceptionally tasty. Steak marinated in Peruvian pisco, garlic-honey chicken wings and tacacho (green plantain, rolled, fried and served with Creole sauce) are among the many delicious items served up in a funky boho ambience, complete with local art work displayed and on sale, and one of the more original and interesting gift shops. Vaka Loka is open every day from noon to 11:30 p.m., and will take Visa cards. The average price for a dish is five dollars—quite a bargain considering the very high value of the food. Jirón Loreto 224.

Karambola Restaurant (Entrees: $6)

Karambola is part of the large, air-conditioned, fun and stylish Karambola Disco Pub near the Plaza de Armas in the center of Puerto Maldonado. It offers a varied selection of international cuisine, such as sweet and sour pork, or a very tasty chicken marinated in white cream and mushrooms and cooked in aluminum foil. Desserts includes its own specialty, Karambola Mousse, made from locally grown karambola (starfruit). Meals average at a very reasonable price of six dollars. Jirón Arequipa 162.

Carne y Brava (Entrees: $6 - 18)

Grilled platters such as beef and chicken are a given in most Peruvian restaurants, but this new eatery in Puerto Maldonado's main square, the Plaza de Armas, offers a more haute-cuisine version of the same, along with an upscale, mod, stained-wood appearance. Curiously, there are no fish items. Prices average about six dollars, except for, that is, their Super Carne Brava, a monster carnivore platter piled with grilled beef, pork, chicken, sausage and a side order of potatoes—all for $18. Bon appétit! Jirón Arequipa 297.

AMAZON

Wasai Lodge Restaurant (Entrees: $7 - 9)

The Wasai Lodge Restaurant is small—only five tables—but it is worth coming both for the well-prepared continental and Andean cuisine, as well as the great setting: a patio overlooking the Madre de Dios River. Dishes include fillet mignon and pickled beef, not to mention chicken or fish pizzaiola, which are served with cheese, oregano, yucca and salad. The small number of tables makes for a higher likelihood of speedier service, and the prices are very reasonable, running about seven or eight dollars a plate. Jirón Guillermo Billinghurst, Tel: 51-82-572-290.

Hotel Cabaña Quinta Restaurant

Located in one of the best hotels in Puerto Maldonado, this restaurant offers a great breakfast buffet with a wide variety of pastries, exotic tropical fruit, sausages and cheeses, among other items. Its lunch and dinner offerings are more standard but well-prepared Peruvian and international fare, such as grilled steak, steamed trout and curried chicken. It also offers some vegetarian dishes. The price for most items averages at a very reasonable five dollars. Don't be put off by the hotel's exterior or the dirt road leading up to the entrance; once you get in it is really an upscale environment. Jirón de Cuzco 535, Tel: 51-82-571-045, E-mail: cabana@ hotelcabanaquinta.com.

PUERTO MALDONADO NIGHTLIFE

Karambola Disco Pub

The Karambola is the newest and best dance club in Puerto Maldonado, which also happens to be an excellent restaurant and tavern. This modern, air-conditioned club claims to have "the best DJ in town," and offers prizes for the "most animated" couple and discounts for university students. Other contests include a battle of the sexes strip contest, in which a pair of male and female strippers compete for a prize doled out by the voting club members. The music starts pumping at 10:00 p.m., and the party lasts until the last dancer drops. Jirón Arequipa 162.

TAMBOPATA

Situated upstream from Puerto Maldonado in the department of Madre de Dios, the Tambopata-Candamo Nature Reserve is a bastion of natural beauty and biodiversity. Spanning 6,000 square kilometers, this UNESCO reserve includes the Bahuaja-Sonene National park and Las Pampas de Heath National Sanctuary. Covering an area about one-third the size of Costa Rica, Tambopata is home to approximately 595 species of birds, more than 1,200 species of butterflies and at least 13 different endangered species, including the jaguar, giant otter, ocelot, harpy eagle and giant armadillo.

The reserve also boasts spectacular oxbow lakes and over a dozen different forest types. In short, it is a great place to get out and explore the jungle.

A highlight of any visit to Tambopata is the macaw clay lick, one of the largest clay licks in the country. Also known as Collpa de Guacamayos, this famous clay lick attracts numerous birds that come to feed off the different mineral salts; scientists, birdwatchers and nature-lovers also seem to flock to this natural hot spot.

Besides the birds, beauty and biodiversity, Tambopata boasts a number of jungle lodges, which tend to be slightly more accessible than those in Manu in terms of cost and travel time. Tambopata tours and jungle lodge stays can be arranged with agencies in Cusco or Puerto Maldonado.

If you're pressed for time, 2-day/1-night packages are available, but longer stays are highly recommended if you want to see a wider range of plants and animals. Among the jungle lodges available, some of the more established ones include Sandoval Lake Lodge, Explorer's Inn, Posada Amazonas and the Tambopata Jungle Lodge. Backpackers and budgeters should

AMAZON

check out Inotawa. Rainforest Expeditions operates the Tambopata Research Center, which offers five to seven day tours of the reserve.

Regardless of where or how long you stay, Tambopata-Candamo Nature Reserve is sure to surprise and delight.

Sandoval Lake Lodge (Room & Board: $145 - 165)

Located deep in Peru's Tambopata National Reserve, Sandoval Lake Lodge sits on the shores of sparkling, palm-rimmed Sandoval Lake. The ox-bow lake's immediate area is rich with bird and wildlife, including macaws, monkeys, caimans and giant otters. You have access to the lake at dawn and dusk, prime hours for wildlife viewing and photography. Sandoval Lake Lodge is operated by the non-profit conservation organization InkaNatura Travel and five local indigenous families. It offers two to four-day packets, including lake, forest and night excursions, as well as evening slide shows, for small groups and families. The lodge boasts 25 double rooms with private bath, hot-water showers, screens, fans and electricity. Prices include roundtrip transportation from Puerto Maldonado airport, meals, purified beverages, bilingual naturalist guide, all excursions and the Tambopata National Reserve entrance fee. You can fly from Cusco or Lima on daily planes operated by Lan Perú. Once there you will be met and transferred by car to the port and then by boat to the lodge. Lima 27, Tel: 51-14-402-022, Fax: 51-14-229-225, E-mail: postmaster@inkanatura.com.pe, www.inkanatura.com/sandovallakelodge.asp.

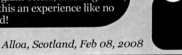

V!VA Member Review- Sandoval Lake Lodge

This was an amazing place: very humid and sticky but crawling with wild life and unexpected surprises. It was a very surreal place to be. The food was excellent, the guide was great. The giant otters, amazing birds, turtles, monkeys, caimens and more, made this an experience like no other! I wouldn't have missed it for the world!

Alloa, Scotland, Feb 08, 2008

MANU

This immense 1.5-million-hectare park has successive canopies of vegetation rising from 150 to 4,200 meters above sea level. The tropical forest in the lower tiers contains an unrivaled variety of animal and plant species. Some 850 species of birds have been identified and rare species such as the giant otter and the giant armadillo have found refuge there. Jaguars are often sighted in the park.

Recognized as a natural heritage of mankind and a biosphere reserve by UNESCO, Manu is an example of intact jungle—the virgin Amazon far from civilization.

Getting To and Away from Manu

Most people traveling to Manu do so with a tour which assists them in getting from Cusco to Manu. It is possible to get to the area without an organized tour, but it is much more difficult and not usually worth it. Most of the lodging in the area includes the trip to Manu in the price. Generally the transport is done in a car or bus, depending on the group size. The drive takes from six to eight hours from Cusco. There is some fabulous scenery along the way, making the ride rather enjoyable. A few boats and planes make the trip to Manu as well, but these tend to operate less often and be more costly.

THINGS TO SEE AND DO IN MANU

Manu Biosphere Reserve

As one of the largest conservation units on earth, this immense 1.5-million-hectare park contains an unrivaled variety of animal and plant species, including some 850 species of birds and numerous animal species. Roughly the size of New Hampshire, this World Heritage Site stretches from 200 to 4,100 meters above sea level, and is easily reached from Cusco. From high-altitude grasslands the landscape spirals downwards through dense cloud forest towards a dizzying stretch of rainforest below. The tropical forest in the lower tiers is home to jaguars, giant otters, ocelots and 13 species of primates—the largest number in the country.

On entering the labyrinth of rivers and *cochas* (lakes) that carve serpentine routes through the landscape, the traveler enters a universe of repeated surprises and delights. As opposed to other places in the jungle where man has hunted, Manu's wildlife shows little fear in the presence of humans. From May to June, during the colder, drier season, jaguars drape themselves over river logs, while from August to November, towards the end of the dry season, macaws, parrots and parakeets flock to the riverside clay licks. The rainy season is November to March. Boasting a whopping 15 percent of the world's bird population, it's no wonder Manu is also one of the world's top birding destinations. Besides feather-clad and four-legged friends, the park also has 15,000 plants, 1,300 butterflies, and more than a million undocumented insects.

Today the biosphere is divided into several regions. Manu National Park is only open for government-sponsored biologists and anthropologists with permits from the Ministry of Agriculture in Lima. The Reserved Zone, which is located within the Manu National Park, is allocated for scientific research and ecotourism. The Multiple Use Zone is home to a number of eco-lodges and acculturated native groups that continue to practice their traditional ways of life. Ethnic groups inhabiting this zone include the Harakmbut, Machiguenga and Yine. Each of these groups has established its own ecotourism activities, which cater to visitors and promote sustainable development within the community infrastructure. The Nahua-Kugapakori Reserved zone was established for the Nahua and Kugapakori nomadic native groups, and includes the area north of the Alto Madre de Dios between the headwaters of the Río Manu and Río Urubamba.

Manu National Park contains some of the most pristine tracts of rainforest in the biosphere, and for this reason is extremely well-protected. To enter the park, visitors must be part of one of the eight licensed tour operators in Manu. These companies own comfortable safari camps and offer five- to ten-day trips ranging from $500 to $2,000. Of course, the more you pay the more comfortable you're apt to be on your trip. Outdoor enthusiasts and adrenaline junkies should scout out the companies that now offer adventure activities, which range from mountain biking and llama-cart touring to rafting and kayaking.

A handful of tour operators offer reliable (and sustainable) service in this amazing area. Manu Nature Tours, Manu Expeditions, InkaNatura, and Pantiacolla Tours are among the best. Three budget tour operators are also licensed to operate in Manu: Manu Ecological Adventures, SAS Travel, and Expediciones Vilca. Tours through these companies can be booked at short notice, and often can be combined with Inca Trail trips at little additional cost.

Word to the wise budgeteer: anyone short on time or money may want to head to Puerto Maldonado, which offers cheaper lodging without skimping on the wildlife. This section of Peruvian jungle is more accessible than Manu, and can be reached in just a few hours via plane from Cusco.

Mountain Biking ($40 - 50)

Mountain biking is a relatively new activity in Peru. The trips range from onesthose within the Manu area, to those that go from Cusco to Manu. A popular route is from Tres Cruces to La Unión. In general only experienced bikers should consider this trip, since the terrain can be very rough. Most of the lodges in the areas offer bicycle equipment rentals for short treks around the area. Pricing on rentals is usually $40-$50.

AMAZON

Llama Carting

Llama taxis are offered at the most southern point of Manu National Park in the grasslands. They are let by local peasants and are a great opportunity to get off a bus and ride from the Andean grasslands to the elfin forests. Bird watching conditions are ideal on a llama, which moves at about 5 kilometers per hour. At certain times of the year llama taxis are not available due to occasions such as community festivities and national holidays.

Rafting and Kayaking

If you are looking to experience the thrill of navigating down treacherous waters while vacationing at Manu, you are in luck. Many lodges offer rafting and kayaking as an optional activity for their visitors. Most of the rafting in the area is considered to be class-three rapids, which generally require an intermediate paddling skill level. The pricing on this activity varies from lodge to lodge, but expect to pay around $100-$150. For the more adventurous there are companies that offer multi-day rafting tours. These tours generally run from five to seven days and cost around $700-$800.

MANU TOURS

Manu Nature Tours

Manu Nature Tours are nature tourism pioneers that have been operating in Manu since 1985 and own the only lodge inside Manu National Park. Both the Manu Lodge and Manu Cloud Forest Lodge are equipped with excellent facilities and come with spectacular views of the surrounding area. Unfortunately, due to restrictions set forth by the Peruvian Park Service, the company has recently suspended its more adventurous tented camp service.

Owner Boris Gómez Luna has actively participated in the conservation movement in southern Peru, particularly in the Madre de Dios region where he has worked since 1984. He was part of the local conservation group involved in drawing up the original proposal for the creation of the Tambopata-Candamo Reserve in 1986. The company is firmly committed to promoting sustainable, responsible ecotourism in the Manu area and to providing local communities with economically viable working models for ecotourism projects.

Recently, Manu Nature Tours implemented the Llama Taxi project with the Jajahuana community located in the high grasslands near Manu. A portion of the company's gross income is allocated to projects in and conservation of the Manu Reserve; its facilities are often used as bases for scientific research. With one of the largest and best-kept trail systems in Manu National Park, the company promises guests unparalleled views of rainforest habitats, birds, and mammals. Guides are dedicated conservationists and knowledgeable biologists with university degrees in both biology and tourism.

Manu Nature Tours also offers a wide variety of side-trip options, including mountain biking, river rafting, canopy climbing and trekking. The company has recently starting using speedboats to travel around the Reserve, which has the added benefit of cutting both travel time and fuel emissions in half. All packages are designed for people of any age, and combine visits to the protected Manu National Park and other natural and cultural attractions outside the Reserve. The five-day / four-night Manu Lodge and Manu Cloud Forest Lodge packages costs $1,403 per person, while the three-day / two-night Manu Cloud Forest Lodge short itinerary costs $466 per person. For more specifics on tour packages and costs, check out their website. Av. Pardo 1046, Tel: 51-84-252-721, E-mail: info@manunaturetours.com, URL: www.manuperu.com.

Manu Expeditions

A highly reputable company run by the husband and wife team Barry Walker and Rosario Velarde, Manu Expeditions operates a variety of excursions throughout the Manu Reserve. Birding enthusiasts will be happy to hear that Barry is a knowledgeable ornithologist who personally leads private birding tours to Manu and throughout Peru and Bolivia.

In conjunction with Peru Verde, a non-profit Peruvian conservation group, Manu Expeditions owns the Manu Wildlife Center, which facilitates rainforest research and conservation programs. The center boasts 35 kilometers of trails, oxbow lakes with giant otters and floating observation platforms, and two, 35-meter-tall canopy platforms. A natural salt lick near the lodge provides visitors a great opportunity to spy the 250-kilogram tapir, a cousin of the hippopotamus.

An active contributor to Manu preservation, Manu Expeditions continues to invest time, money and resources in environmental programs. Recently, the company has teamed up with the Association for Andean Ecosystems to execute the Polylepsis Project, which aims to preserve this endangered Andean woodland species. They also run a tented camp at Cocha Salvador, located in the depths of the Manu Biosphere Reserve. Most trips involve a stay at the Cock of the Rock Lodge, from where guests head into the rainforest for a couple nights at Madre de Dios Lodge near Boca Manu and the company's safari camp near Cocha Salvador in Manu National Park.

In addition to jungle tours, Manu Expeditions offers a variety of other activities and side-trips including butterfly watching, bird watching and horse trekking. Watch Macaws cling to clay at the Manu Wildlife Center, explore Machu Picchu, or ride the Inca Trail with the Pony Express. One of its trips even involves exploring off-the-beaten-trail routes in search of lost cities! If you can't find what you want in a tour package, Manu Expeditions will gladly make travel arrangements for you. Guides are experts in their fields and include experienced naturalists, biologists and ornithologists. Besides providing great service and an unforgettable Amazon experience, Manu Expeditions is dedicated to educating visitors about Peru, its people and history, and the unique wilderness that surrounds it. Avenida Pardo 895, Tel: 51-84-226-671 / 239-974, E-mail: manuexpeditions@terra.com.pe, URL: www.manuexpeditions.com.

InkaNatura

Inka Natura is one of Peru's leading eco-tour operators and offers itineraries to a wide range of places, including Tambopata National Reserve, Manu, the Inca Trail, Machu Picchu, and a number of others. You can choose to combine an archeological tour or Inca Trail trek with a visit to the Peruvian Amazon rainforest, where you can relax in one of their famous jungle lodges: Sandoval Lake Lodge, Manu Wildlife Center, Heath River Wildlife Center or Cock of the Rock Lodge.

Inka Natura also offers a four-day excursion to a tented camp near Cocha Salvador, which includes a round-trip flight between Cusco and Boca Manu. Perched on a hillside overlooking Urubamba River, the Machiguenga Center is a community-based lodge owned by the local Machiguenga Indians. The lodge is located in the mist-covered cloud forest of the Pongo de Mainique river canyon and is near three of the best Macaw clay licks in the region. Staying at this lodge is a great way to get a feel for traditional life in the Amazon.

In the United States InkaNatura is affiliated with Tropical Nature Travel (877-827-8350, www.tropicalnaturetravel.com), which can organize tours and places to stay before you leave. Travelers with specials interests in archaeology, thermal springs, anthropology, botany, photography or adventure can also organize tailor-made tours through InkaNatura. It can also customize itineraries for areas like Chiclayo, Trujillo, Piura, Tumbes, Chachapoyas, Cajamarca, Cusco, Tambopata and Manu. Manuel Bañón 461, Tel: 51-14-402-022 / 228-114, E-mail: www.postmaster@inkanatura.com.pe, URL: www.inkanatura.com.pe.

MANU LODGING
Pantiacolla Lodge ($55)

Pantiacolla Lodge is located in the rain forest overlooking the Alto Madre de Dios river. It sits at the base of the Pantiacolla mountains, which rise up more than 1,200 meters behind the lodge. The lodge contains bungalows with a total of 14 double-occupancy rooms, making a maximum occupancy of only 28 people. A path from the bungalow leads to showers and flush

AMAZON

toilets, as well as the dining area and bar. Pantiacolla Lodge offers something for all types of rain forest adventurers. There is an especially high amount of bird species for bird watchers, and for first time visitors to the jungle, there are many trails with opportunities for spotting wildlife. Pantiacolla Lodge is for those who wish to have a relaxing and comfortable experience in the rain forest. Accommodation costs $55 per person per day and includes three meals a day. Transport and guide service can be arranged separately by Pantiacolla Tours. Local transportation is also an option. Tel: 51-84-238-323, Fax: 51-84-252-696, E-mail: pantiaco@pantiacolla.com / pantiac@terra.com.pe, URL: www.pantiacolla.com.

Manu Paradise Lodge ($55 - 80)

Manu Paradise's eco-lodge is set in within the beautiful cloud forest between the Kosñipata and San Pedro Rivers, which lends to spectacular views. There are two houses on site: one with double rooms with the capacity for a roll-away and another with more double rooms, kitchen and dining rooms. Every room has a private bath with hot water. Food is included according to the package you choose. The lodge accommodates specialty dietary needs, such as vegetarian and macrobiotic. The bar serves spirits, beer, wine, juices and other cold drinks. Jirón Ricardo Palma N-9, Urbanización Santa Mónica, Tel: 51-84-224-156, E-mail: reservas@manuparadiselodge.com, URL: www.manuparadiselodge.com.

Amazonia Lodge ($60 and up)

Amazonia Lodge is located in the tropical rainforest lowlands of the Manu Biosphere Reserve. Before, in the 1980s, the lodge was the home of a tea plantation. The lodge contains 15 rooms, each with two beds. There are eight bathrooms with toilets and hot-water showers. The lodge also holds a dining area. Amazonia Lodge is said to be excellent for bird watching. Its website contains an extensive list of more than 600 birds seen in the area, in addition to eight species of monkeys. The price of a room includes all meals. Private transportation can be arranged to the lodge. Tel: 51-84-816-131, Fax: 51-84-231-370, E-mail: amazonialodge1@yahoo.com, URL: www.amazonialodge.com/lodge.html.

Cock of the Rock Lodge ($399 - 475)

The Cock of the Rock Lodge, located in the Kosñipata Valley of southeastern Peru, is named for its large displays of Peru's national bird: the Cock of the Rock. It is located with the Manu cloud forest, which is relatively cool and mosquito-free. The lodge has ten double-occupancy rooms with private bathrooms, screened windows and mosquito nets, and a private balcony to take in the amazing views. Meals at the lodge are served in a screened dining room. Vegetarian and other special-diet foods can be provided upon request. The Cock of the Rock Lodge is a 110-mile car ride from Cusco which takes 6 to 8 hours. The views along the road are amazing, so many prefer that the car ride last longer in order to fully enjoy the sights.

Manu Lodge and Manu Cloud Forest Lodge ($498 - 1680)

The Manu Lodge and Manu Cloud Forest Lodge are owned and operated by Manu Nature Tours. Both offer all-inclusive services within Manu. The Manu lodge boasts that it is the only lodging within the Manu National Park that is not just a tented campsite. The Manu Lodge is divided into two parts, block A and block B. Block A's three levels contain a bar, meeting area, dining room, two double rooms and an observation room. Block B holds 10 double rooms. The kitchen, showers and bathrooms are located away from the main area. The Manu Cloud Forest Lodge sits between mountains covered with cloud forests and a 400-foot-high waterfall. The lodge is small, with only 16-20 beds. Some of the amenities at Manu Cloud Forest Lodge include private bathrooms with hot water, private verandas and a sauna. The lodges offer various activities such as mountain biking, night walks and rafting for extra fees. The short Manu Lodge tour departs on Fridays. The long tours to the Manu Lodge depart on Thursdays. Tours to the Cloud Forest Lodge depart daily. All tours depart from Cusco. Tel: 51-84-252-721, Fax: 51-84-234-793, E-mail: info@manunaturetours.com, www.manuperu.com.

Manu Wildlife Center ($990+ / Person)

Manu Wildlife Center is close to the world's most approachable, photographable clay licks of macaws and tapirs. Here you will also find giant otters, several species of birds, ten species of monkeys and more. Trip options include 4- or 5-day fly in and out packages (from Cusco), or a six-day package that spends two days traveling overland from Cusco through the spectacular Manu cloud forest before arriving at the Center for three nights. Prices range from $990 to $1,290 per person. Tel: 51-1-440-2022, Fax: 51-1-422-9225, E-mail: postmaster@manu-wildlife-center.com, URL: www.manu-wildlife-center.com.

Manu Wildlife Tented Camps ($1,255 per person and up)

For birders and wilderness enthusiasts, Manu Wildlife Tented Camp is located on Manu river near Cocha (Lake) Salvador—the largest and most beautiful of the 13 oxbow lakes of the Manu National Park. InkaNatura Travel owns and manages this tented camp. It offers different five to seven day tourism packages. The cost is between $1255-1455 per person, including airfare from Boca Manu to Cusco, bus and boat transportation, all meals and snacks, entrance fee to Manu National Park, a bilingual naturalist guide to accompany you and more. Tel: 51-14-402-022, Fax: 51-1-422-9225, E-mail: postmaster@inkanatura.com.pe, URL: www.inka-natura.com/manu_wildlife_tented_camp.asp.

MANU RESTAURANTS

There are really no restaurants within the Manu area. Instead, the resorts in the area all have their own dining areas. Many of the resorts are all-inclusive, meaning that meals are included as part of the total cost of the stay. A couple of the resorts charge for meals separately, allowing travelers to choose which meals they would like to eat. Most also have a bar area, but drinks such as beer, wine and soda generally cost extra. If you have special dietary restrictions, let the lodge at which you are staying know in advance and it should be able to accommodate your needs.

TARAPOTO

San Martín Province is a zone full of fertile valleys and rough terrain that is spread out between the Andean mesa and a small area of lower jungle. There are 980 species of flora, in particular bromeliads, orchids and ferns, more than 220 species of birds, and nearly fifty species of mammals, like the yellow-tailed woolly monkey, Andean deer, spectacled bear and jaguar—species nearing extinction. Tarapoto, located just upstream from Yurimaguas, is a convenient stopping point for the journey from Iquitos to Chachapoyas.

THINGS TO SEE AND DO AROUND TARAPOTO

Abiseo River National Park

Abiseo River National Park (274,520ha) is part of the select UNESCO World Cultural and Natural Heritage List, and it contains eight live zones and 36 registered archaeological sites. The park also has fascinating archaeological remnants of the Chachapoya, like the Gran Pajatén, Los Pinchudos and La Playa archaeological site with the characteristically circularly -shaped stone buildings decorated with geometric designs and diverse figures in relief.

Blue Lagoon

Fifty kilometers (31mi) from Tarapoto (2 hours and 30 minutes), in the city of Sauce. Blue Lagoon covers an area of 350 hectares, and the deepest part is 35 meters (115ft). The water temperature varies from 25ºC (77ºF) to 28ºC (82ºF), and the color runs from green to blue. The lagoon is home to herons, common kingfishers, muscovy ducks, eagles, different amphibians, reptiles and fish. The place is surrounded by orchards, corn, beans, bananas, yucca, rice fields and pasture land for cattle.

Polish Petroglyphs

These are figures of animals, plants and some linguistic symbols in low relief. It is still not possible to date them accurately, even though some believe they correspond to the early period of the Chachapoya. You find more petroglyphs at Cabo Leveau, 30 kilometers (19mi) from Tarapoto (1 hour).

AMAZON

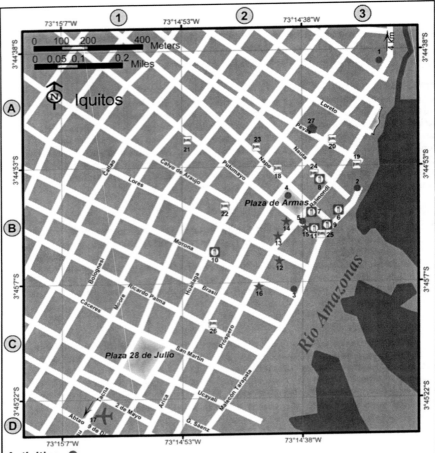

Activities ●

1 Amazon Animal Orphanage
  and Pipintuwasi Butterfly Farm A1
2 Malecón Maldonado B3
3 Museo Etnográfico C2
4 Plaza de Armas B2
5 The Iron House / Casa de Fierro B3

Eating 🍴

6 Arandú Bar B3
7 Ari's Burger B3
8 Chez Maggy B3
9 Fitzcarraldo Restaurant and Bar B3
10 Shambo B2
11 The Yellow Rose of Texas B3

Airport ✈

17 Iquitos Airport D1

Tour Operator ⬟

27 Paseos Amazónicos A3

Services ★

12 Banco Continental B2
13 Banco Weise B2
14 BCP B2
15 Mad Mick's Trading Post B3
16 Supermercado Los Portales C2

Sleeping 🛏

18 El Dorado Plaza Hotel B2
19 Hospedaje La Pascana A3
20 Hostal Ambassador A3
21 Hostal Jhuliana A2
22 Hotel Acosta B2
23 Hotel El Dorado A2
24 Hotel Marañón B3
25 Hotel Real Iquitos B3
26 Victoria Regia C2

AMAZON

huashiyaku Waterfalls

his 40-meter (131ft) waterfall is located on the hill *La Escalera* (the Stairs) at 465 meters
1,526ft) above sea level. The water flows over rocks densely surrounded by ferns, orchids
nd diverse species of trees. In the surroundings, there are plenty of butterflies, birds and
1sects to watch.

own of Lamas

ounded in 1656, it is one of the oldest towns in the Peruvian jungle, located at 1,000 mters
3,281ft) above sea level, at the top of a hill. This town's mos interesting characteristic is the
osition of its terraces. They say that the first floor belonged to the Chancas who came from
1e south, the second story to the *mestizos*, and the third level was used as a lookout. To-
ay, they maintain this division between the Indians, the Lamistas, and population of mixed
aces, who celebrate their patron saints separately. In spite of its jungle location, the town has
1e structure of a highland village, probably due to the origin of its inhabitants. The Wayku
eighborhood is populated by descendents of the fierce Chanca Indians, who maintain their
:aditional ancestral customs.

amas Ethnic Museum

'he Lamas Ethnic Museum shows part of the history and folklore of the Quechua-Lamista
ulture. You can witness different cultural expressions and customs like the *lanta-tipina*, the
rst hair cut, the making of clothes from native cotton and other vegetable fibers, dyeing, and
he dances of the Lamas people. Twenty-two km from Tarapoto.

QUITOS

'he jungle city of Iquitos is one of Peru's most fascinating burgs. Although commonly viewed
y visitors as a mere stopover on the way to Amazonian lodges and reserves, the city itself is
vorth a visit.

'he history of Iquitos is a fascinating portrait of boom / bust cycles. In the late nineteenth
entury, the region produced much of the world's rubber, which resulted in a huge economic
oom that lasted from about 1880 to 1910, when rubber plantations in Asia undercut Peru in
he international rubber market. During this period, incredibly wealthy Peruvians built pal-
ces and grand hotels in Iquitos, some of which survive to this day. The most notable of these
s the Casa de Fierro, or Iron House, designed by Gustave Eiffel and first built in Paris. It was
urchased by rubber baron Anselmo del Águila, dismantled, and shipped piece by piece to
quitos, where it was painstakingly reconstructed. Today it contains a café and English pub.
ie sure to stop for a look.

Getting To and Away from Iquitos

'he best and only really viable option for getting to and from Iquitos is by air. Lan offer four
lights per day from Iquitos to Lima and back. Its flights from Cusco to Iquitos all connect
hrough Lima. Aero Cóndor also offers a daily flight from Lima. The airport is 8 kilometers
ut of town.

t is not possible to travel to Iquitos by bus. It is possible to travel by boat to a number of
owns in the Peruvian Amazon, Brazil and Colombia from port Puerto Masusa, a little way
1orth of Iquitos. For long journeys, take a hammock and ropes to secure it. Alternatively, you
:an sleep in a cabin for a little bit extra. Tickets can be bought at the dock. Head down there
:arly in the day to ensure that there is still space for your hammock. Bring food and water for
ong trips, as there is not much for sale on the boat.

THINGS TO SEE AND DO IN IQUITOS

\lthough most who visit Iquitos do so for what lies outside of the town, there is a whole host
)f activities in Iquitos to keep tourists occupied during their time in this jungle city. There are
\andful of museums, such as the Museo Etnográfico, which features more than 70 statues

AMAZON

of indigenous women, children and men. The Iron House, a house made out of, well, iron, is another interesting site. It was designed by Gustave Eiffel, the man who created the Eiffel Tower. It was originally built in Paris and then shipped to Peru in the late 1800s.

If shopping is a must for you during a vacation, there are a few options of places to go in Iquitos. The Belén Street Market is located in a poor neighborhood, but don't let that stop you from visiting. It is crowded, busy and a wonderful example of daily life for many Peruvians. Other places to shop in Iquitos tend to cater more toward tourists, offering souvenirs such as jewelry and paintings.

Outside of the actual town of Iquitos is where the activities that cater toward nature lovers lie. The Amazon Animal Orphanage and Pilpintuwasi Butterfly Farm give tourists an opportunity to see wildlife that would otherwise be very difficult, if not impossible, to see. The Reserva National Pacaya-Samiria is the largest national reserve in Peru. Here one can see a fascinating mix of flora and fauna, with about 100 species of mammals, 500 species of birds and 250 of fish. Anyone who is interesting in wildlife would be crazy to miss this wonderfully preserved reserve.

Azulejos
When Europeans discovered the rubber tree in the late 1800s, entrepreneurs and money poured into the Amazon for a time. Wealthy rubber barons built grand mansions in Iquitos and indulged in such extravagances as ordering exquisitely painted ceramic tiles from Portugal called *azulejos*. They used them to adorn walls, inside and out. The rubber boom soon went bust, but azulejos can still be seen on many buildings in Iquitos, many along Raimondi, Malecón Maldonado and Malecón Tarapacá. Tile designs are intricate, colorful and weave in many delicate lines on a single tile in reds, blues, golds, greens and other colors. One of the best examples of azulejos is a three-story mansion across from the dolphin statue on Tarapacá. The former mansion is now home to the military. Tiles of blue, turquoise and tan dominate the entire façade, which is highlighted with classic architecture and more than a dozen arched doorways and dozens of tall windows. Azulejos also brighten a courtyard centerpiece in the Museo Etnográfico, at the intersection of Tarapacá and Morona.

Shopping in Iquitos
Visitors looking for indigenous crafts, expedition gear, books or a bargain can find it in Iquitos. The Anaconda craft market makes souvenir shopping a breeze, with some 30 vendors selling their wares under one roof. The market is on the Malecón Maldonado riverside, between Nauta and Napo. There's a large sign on the walkway; the market is down a flight of stairs and in a wooden pavilion. Everything from blow guns to hand-dyed shirts and handmade masks are sold here.

Shoppers can watch artists carving, painting or making jewelry, and go home with an original piece signed by its creator. Seeds are common canvases in the Amazon. Crafters use them as the base for smaller items like key chains and necklaces or to adorn carvings, belts and heftier pieces. A necklace on a simple black string with a blue bead and clay design costs less than 75 cents (2 soles), or a half-dollar-sized key chain with a small clay snake or monkey on top is the same price. Visits to isolated communities can be difficult to arrange, but crafts made by indigenous peoples are readily available in the market. A corn-husk doll made by members of the Muñeco community on the Río Momón costs $1.50 (5 soles). A painted mask made from natural materials is $3 (10 soles). One or two sellers may have blow guns and darts. The gun is about $30 (93 soles). The darts are stored in a wood cylinder, attached to a hollowed-out gourd and slung over the shoulder with a fabric strap. Hunters dip darts into poison, stored in the gourd. Since taking deadly weaponry through customs isn't a good idea, travelers can buy the entire outfit, minus the poison, for about $14 (about 44 soles).

Most items are handmade crafts, but there are also some animal products for sale, such as butterflies, spiders, piranhas and other jungle critters that were killed and sealed under glass.

It's easy to find jewelry, Iquitos T-shirts and preserved wildlife on the main streets, such as Malecón Maldonado and around the Plaza de Armas. Prices and quality vary. It's illegal to hunt jaguars and many other jungle animals, but it's not uncommon to be offered a necklace made from a jaguar claw.

Mad Mick's Trading Post, (upstairs, Putamayo 184, 8 a.m. to 8 p.m.), is a good place to find mosquito nets, expedition hats, long-sleeved shirts or flashlights for jungle expeditions, used and new. The stock is a bit sparse and varies, but what there is can be a lifesaver if you've forgotten something. Mad Mick will even buy back your gear when you're finished if it's in good condition. A new, packable canvas hat with a wide brim to block out the intense sun and a chin strap costs about $9 (about 30 nuevo soles).

The La Castellana librería (Arica 6), or bookstore, sells notebooks, pens and other writing supplies as well as some books.

Buy bread, yogurt and other staples at Supermercado Los Portales (at the corner of Próspero and Morona). There are several banks around Plaza de Armas: Banco Continental (on Lores, between Próspero and Malecón Maldonado), BCP (in Plaza de Armas at the corner of Próspero and Putamayo) and Banco Wiese (on Próspero, by Lores). Some have cash machines; lines for tellers can be long.

Amazon Animal Orphanage and Pilpintuwasi Butterfly Farm

Few travelers get to see stealthy jaguars, solitary anteaters and rare red uakari monkeys in the jungle, but at the Amazon Animal Orphanage and Pilpintuwasi Butterfly Farm, you can visit with wildlife and see the fragile insects in all stages of life. Chances are, a gregarious monkey will take a ride on your head on the grand tour, too.

The animal orphanage and butterfly farm are separate projects that share the same home on a forest farm on the Nanay River, outside Iquitos. Owners Austrian Gudrun Sperrer and Peruvian Roblar Moreno are passionate about their work and educating others about Amazonian flora and fauna. Butterflies fly in a large enclosure and some animals, like the monkeys and anteaters, are free to roam in their natural element. Here, you get an up-close look and an opportunity to help endangered, uncommon and fragile animals.

The orphan Pedro Bello, or "beautiful Pedro," was delivered to the Amazon Animal Orphanage by a man who had been trying to sell him, with no luck. The jaguar was emaciated, injured and near death. Sperrer and Moreno nursed him back to health. Now he's one of the orphanage's most popular residents.

The farm is home to some 20 animals, including tapirs, anteaters, turtles, parrots and six species of monkeys, including two red uakaris. All of the animals were abandoned, rescued after their mothers were killed or dropped off at the orphanage as a last resort. You can see the animals easily, at an arm's distance, or in spacious pens. Tony the capuchin monkey is the exception. He was raised by children in Iquitos so he's used to people and mighty curious. He's got a penchant for climbing up your legs or plunking down out of a tree to perch on your shoulders. Lucky visitors may see Rose the six-foot-anteater saunter by on her way to look for ants. Full-grown, she prefers to be alone.

More than 40 species of butterflies are raised at Pilpintuwasi, all in full view. Bright brick-red and yellow caterpillars nibble on leaves as they make their way to adulthood in a small building, along with other juveniles as they go from egg to caterpillar to chrysalis. Once they emerge, the butterflies flutter about in a large enclosure.

Fist-sized, electric-blue morphos twitter beside your head. Green and red swallowtails drink nectar from fruit. Someone with a keen eye can spot eggs the size of pin pricks on the underside of leaves. The enclosure is fenced in with a screen top to protect the butterflies

AMAZON

from predators and the monkeys, who like attention and cling to the sides wondering what the guests are doing.

The farm and orphanage share the same location at a private sanctuary in Padre Cocha, on the Nanay River. The easiest way to reach the site is to rent a private motor boat from the Bella Vista port in Iquitos for about $10. It's a 20-minute boat ride. Tel: 51-63-232-665, E-mail: pilpintuwasi@hotmail.com, URL: www.amazonanimalorphanage.org, www.amazonanimalorphanage.org/pilpintuwasi.htm.

Belén Street Market

The Belén neighborhood in Iquitos is one of the poorest in this Amazon city but also the most colorful. During flood season, water reaches the doorsteps of simple homes and shacks that are built on stilts or float on rafts in the path of the Amazon River. Families get around in canoes or walk on elevated wooden walkways.

The Belén market is on dry land and is the destination for rice and other staples, household goods, and everything from dried frogs to whole *largatos*—caimans, which are a type of alligator—cut up into steaks. You can find anything and everything in the chaotic street market, which goes nonstop from early morning until afternoon, when vendors and shoppers pack up shop and take a siesta. Late afternoon brings another round of haggling and sensory overload.

Shops line the booth-filled streets and add to the jumble. In just one block, travelers can watch women roll tightly-packed cigarettes lickety-split behind a basketball-sized pile of tobacco and a stack of paper. Dried fish bake in the tropical sun, a hardware store sells sheets of plastic, and rolls of toilet tissue are stacked a dozen high. Black caimans are hacked into hunks, clawed-hands, tail and all. There may be freshly hunted turtles, large rodents and other animals for sale, and not all of them are legal.

It's okay to take pictures, but as a courtesy, ask permission at a vendor's stall or get a friendly nod. It's safe to meander around in daytime, but keep your money in a neck pouch or other secure place and leave your valuables at the hotel. Hire a local guide to paddle around the floating area for a few soles at the end of Ugarte at Puerto Itaya for a look at Belén life. The market is also a good place to find souvenirs or experience the culture of the street markets found all over South America. You can also try salted giant grubs as a snack.

The market is south of the Plaza de Armas, along the river. Walk south on Próspero to 9 de Diciembre or Ugarte. A more scenic route is to head south on Malecón Tarapacá alongside the river. You can't miss the market.

Belén Canoe Tour ($1.50 - 10 / hour)

During the rainy season in Belén, houses built on stilts or rafts rise and fall with the Amazon river. Water creeps up to doorways and families get around in wooden canoes. Closer to shore, residents carry their satchels, book bags, groceries and sacks of rice along a series of rickety wooden walkways to steer clear of the river. Belén is home to upwards of 5,000 of Iquitos' poorest residents, who live in simple homes and shacks off the mainland. Water is their front and back yard, bathtub, swimming hole, wash basin, latrine and transportation.

When the water level drops during summer, the river takes away some of the refuse. What's left behind is stuck in the muck. Belén is sometimes called the "Venice of Peru" for its size and countless passageways accessible only by boat. It's easy to hire a local canoe guide's services for tour in the Belén market at the shore. Dozens of paddlers are waiting for passengers at Puerto Itaya, at the end of Ugarte.

Allow at least an hour to paddle through the flooded streets and past the rows of houses, bakeries, churches and bars—many are run out of private homes, or even windows. Bananas, bread and other wares are also sold right from boats and canoes. Students attend elementary and secondary schools—which are built on concrete pillars—in shifts. Wave hello as they pass by on their way to class. Kids often jump off higher floors of homes or decks into the river for a thrill, or swim past the canoe. Belén is crowded, but the jungle is just beyond. Outer edges of the village are surrounded by lily pads, birds and big patches of bright-green reeds. In open water, dozens of canoes, small fishing boats and *colectivos*, or collective boats that function like water buses, weave around each other aimed for different destinations. The collective boats often carry a roof full of plantains or other cargo.

Because life in Belén is so open and homes often don't have curtains or screens (or sometimes four walls), taking a canoe tour is an intimate experience and look into Belén life.

Malecón Maldonado

Malecón Maldonado is a pedestrian-only zone and a magnet for crowds that gather to watch the sun set below the horizon in shades of bright and burnt orange, then celebrate the night. The main drag in Iquitos is part romantic river walk, part carnival. Young couples hold hands on the concrete railings and street performers toss blazing batons into the air to catch the flaming rods behind their backs for applause and donations.

Some nights, a woman and a few small girls decorate their skin with traditional indigenous white paint and dance with 10-foot-long anacondas. They wow the crowd, then slide the serpents into sacks for safe keeping. Travelers off their budget are also known to market their talents, selling homemade rope and bead jewelry or juggling. Slap-stick comedians dress in drag and put on goofy skits to pass the hat.

Sightseers, beggars, performers, families, adventurers—they are all here. The promenade is always a great place to people-watch and meet other travelers and locals. Arandú Bar (Malecón Maldonado 113) and Fitzcarraldo Restaurant and Bar next door (Napo 100) have patio tables that are great locations from which to watch the fiesta. Beside the Amazon River, on the city's east side, south of Pevas.

Plaza de Armas

It seems everyone passes through Plaza de Armas in this Amazon outpost, whether they are on their way to work, taking a stroll, on their way to dinner or zipping by in mototaxis. The plaza spans four square blocks and is the heart of Iquitos. A park is the centerpiece. A fountain sprays geysers of water in the center, and serves as a popular meeting spot. Travelers come here to sightsee, but Plaza de Armas is an important part of life for residents, too.

Crowds gather in the evenings in restaurants that ring the plaza or in the park. Photographers are always on hand with an instamatic camera to snap keepsakes for a couple of soles, and visitors can often buy inexpensive popcorn and other snacks from street carts. The butter-colored Iglesia de Matriz dominates the southwest corner of Plaza de Armas, with its tall steeples and ornate architecture accented in brick red. Peek in for a look or contemplate in a pew.

Tellers at BCP bank will gladly exchange money (at the corner of Próspero and Putamayo). Perhaps the fanciest hotel in Iquitos, the El Dorado Plaza, faces the northern side. Anyone can stop in the bar for a drink. A tourist office (Napo 232) isn't well marked but is open for information and can provide maps. Have your pick of meals at Ari's Burger, a chicken joint or Peruvian restaurant on the eastern side of the plaza. The ice-cream parlor with the *Helado* sign specializes in flavors made with *guanábana*, passion fruit and other regional fruits.

Don't miss the Iron House (at the corner of Putamayo and Prospero). Called the *Casa de Fierro*, it really is made of iron. The constant parade of mototaxis—motorcycles with carts attached to the back for passengers—assures a steady serenade of engine roar. Because it's a busy place, people often come to sell what they think tourists want: butterflies, tarantulas and other insects and wildlife sealed under glass. Street vendors are on corners selling homemade popsicles and drinks made from the *aguaje* palm fruit, and police are usually around and

helpful to ask for directions. Between Napo and Putamayo to the north and south an
Arica and Próspero to the west and east.

Pasaje Paquito

The Shipibo, Asháninka and other indigenous tribes in Peru have relied on a prickly vin
to remedy ills for some 2,000 years. Named for its hook-like thorns that resemble felin
claws, uña de gato—or cat's claw—is drunk in tea or taken in capsule form to stimulat
the immune system, cleanse the bowels, lower cholesterol and even kill cancer cells. On
of the most common medicinal plants, uña de gato is found with other natural remedie
on grocery store shelves, in several forms.

Travelers in Iquitos can buy it direct from makers and vendors in the Belén street mar
ket's Pasaje Paquito. Pasaje Paquito is a small alleyway in the middle of the chaoti
market dedicated to all things medicinal. Snake heads pickled in cane liquor, big tubs o
dried bark, homemade tinctures and fresh-cut herbs piled several feet high fill the nar
row passage, lined on either side with booths. Natural medicine is an integral part of lif
in isolated communities and many traditional medicines have a laundry list of uses, from
pain reliever to aphrodisiac.

Vendors in Pasaje Paquito are happy to share information about what the bottles, powders
plants and other items are designed for. Plants, herbs and barks are labeled with large pa
per signs. The *chuchuhuasi* tree grows tall in the rainforest canopy. Its reddish-brown bark
is sold in finger-length slices and is believed to reduce arthritis pain and treat a number of
conditions such as bronchitis, rheumatism and stomach aches. Bark from the *huacapura-
na* tree is boiled in water to make a drink to alleviate arthritis and rheumatism symptoms,
relieve diarrhea and other conditions. Women buy abuta bark for menstrual pain, but it
also has several other uses, including reducing high blood pressure. In the middle of the
Belén market. Walk south along Malecón Maldonado, which turns into Malecón Tarapacá.
It leads you to Belén, around 9 de Diciembre or Urgate.

Museo Etnográfico ($1)

The more than 70 statues of indigenous women, children, men and high chiefs of western Amazonia are the highlight of the Museo Etnográfico in Iquitos. Their creator preserved tribe members for all time in traditional dress and poses, as the region developed
and these peoples lost their foothold. The statues ring the museum courtyard, gleaming
gold in the tropical sun. Members of the Shipibo, Iquitos, Yagua, Bora and several other
tribes are represented. They are fiberglass but look bronzed. One is frozen in time as
he looks down and another is ready to let loose an arrow. A bare-chested chief in a 65-
feather head dress holds his arms outstretched, his neck and wrists heavy with jewelry.
He's captured with his eyes closed and his head tilted to the sky.

The museum is a restored 19th century government building, designed with the flair of
early Iquitos architecture. Visitors can tour the elegant dining room and side rooms that
feature art, historic weaponry and a series of historic photographs of Iquitos. Take a seat
in the rows of wooden chairs in the historic meeting hall, and soak up ordered colonial
ambiance. Hand-painted ceramic tiles imported from Portugal, called *azulejos*, brighten
the centerpiece of the museum's central courtyard, glazed in blue, gold, green and red.
Malecón Tarapacá 386, at the corner of Tarapacá and Morona.

The Iron House / Casa de Fierro

The Casa de Fierro in Iquitos is just that—a house made of iron. Gustave Eiffel, the same
architect who created the Eiffel Tower, built the Iron House for the Paris Exhibition in
1889. Tycoon Anselmo del Águila bought it and shipped it in pieces from Europe during
the rubber-boom period. Natural rubber made from trees tapped in the jungle was big
business for Iquitos during the late 19th century and early 20th century.

Wealthy rubber barons built elegant mansions and could afford indulgences, such as transporting an entire house overseas. The Iron House was reconstructed in the Plaza de Armas in the southeast corner. Its steely, rugged exterior is a standout, but its history is more regal than its appearance today. The building looks like it's covered in sheets of tin patched together. The sun shines off the iron in late afternoon, lighting it up with a warm glow

Downstairs there is a small pharmacy/drugstore, a restaurant and an ice cream vendor. Walk upstairs for a drink or meal at the Regal Bar and Restaurant, which is run by the British consulate. The bar doubles as the consulate's office. Plaza de Armas offers a good view of the entire house. At the corner of Próspero and Putamayo, at the southeast corner of the Plaza de Armas.

Reserva Nacional Pacaya-Samiria

Sitting a hefty journey south of Iquitos in a flooded rainforest between the Ucayali and Marañón Rivers, Reserva Nacional Pacaya-Samiria is the largest and one of the best conserved protected areas in Peru. Conservation in the area began in the 1940s and the reserve was extended to its present size in 1982. This pristine patch of rainforest and wetlands is nearly twice the size of Yellowstone National Park in the United States and comprises nearly 1.5 percent of Peru's total surface area.

Characterized by the convergence of rivers and waterways, this intriguing landscape is home to a host of flora and fauna, including black caimans, pink dolphins, giant river turtles, Amazon manatee, tapir, twelve species of monkeys, the endangered paiche fish and nearly 500 species of birds. To break it down, this nearly 2 million hectare section of rainforests boasts approximately 100 species of mammals, 500 species of birds, 250 kinds of fish and 22 species of orchids. Did we mention the giant water lilies large enough to hold a small child?

In fact, Reserva Nacional Pacaya-Samiria has more wildlife than Parque Nacional Manu, and is thus a great place for plant and animal fanatics alike. One of the best times to visit is between July and December when various creatures can be spotted catching some rays on the riverbanks. A number of colonists and indigenous tribes also live in the reserve, including the Cocamas, Huitotos, Boras and Yaguas Indians.

Getting to Reserva Nacional Pacaya-Samiria is a challenge, and certainly requires more than the simple hop-skip-and-a-jump. Its relative remoteness, however, is what helps keep this place unspoiled—something to keep in mind when you're up to your neck in travel-weary woes. Visitors must come with a guided tour, so your best bet is to book a tour with one of the agencies in Iquitos. Although no official lodging or campgrounds exist in the reserve, most guides can help you find a dry spot to pitch a tent.

Camping and canoeing through the reserve is a spectacular experience, especially if you're keen to immerse yourself in the sights and sounds of jungle life. You may also want to look into arranging a stay at one of the community-based lodges located within the reserve. In short, if you don't mind getting a little dirty and are ready to delve deep into the Peruvian jungle, the Reserva Nacional Pacaya-Samiria is sure not to disappoint.

A number of tour companies have packages to the area. The following are some of the most reliable: Paseo Amazónicos, ProNaturaleza and Pascana Amazon Tours. You can also arrange to stay at the inviting Pacaya Samiria Amazon Lodge.

IQUITOS LODGING

When staying in Iquitos you will find the hotels are very varied. There may be a large number of backpacker dives, but there is also a selection of high-end, luxury hotels.

If you are traveling on a budget it is best to do an ample amount of research before your stay to make sure that you don't wind up in a total dive. Reviews from other travelers on sites like

AMAZON

ours will prove very helpful for you. It is best to make a reservation before you come, in particular during the summer months which tend to be very busy for this area.

If Iquitos is a jumping off point for other travel, ask your hotel for some recommended tour agencies and lodges. Hotels deal with many tourists every year, and are sure to have heard the latest good and bad things that they can relay to you.

BUDGET
Mad Mick's Bunk Hostel (Rooms: $4)
Mad Mick's is simple, but clean and cheap. It is 10 pesos a night, has 8 beds and it is reasonably quiet, despite its central location. The showers are cold and there is no kitchen. Your backpack can be securely stowed away in the large lockers under your bed. Mad Mick, an English Ex Pat, is a likable guy. He rents jungle safari equipment at reasonable prices and can organize jungle tours. Located in the Plaza de Armas, the hostel is directly opposite The Yellow Rose of Texas restaurant. You can't miss it.

MID-RANGE
La Casa Fitzcarraldo (Rooms: $20 - 40)
La Casa Fitzcarraldo, birthplace of the Werner Herzog films Fitzcarraldo and Aguirre, offers a premier, unique and unrivaled housing and jungle oasis leisure refuge for tourists and locals alike within chaotic Iquitos. Whether you are coming to Iquitos for volunteer work, a jungle adventure, a medicinal Ayahuasca quest or just to get away from it all, this hotel offers comfortable accommodations within the city, including a naturally cooled and very clean swimming pool. They offer great food, drinks, free WiFi and an impressive tri-level treehouse to lounge about with panoramic views. Price includes breakfast and tax. Av. La Marina 2153, Zip: 065, Tel: 51-65-601-138/9, E-mail: lacasafitzcarraldo@gmail.com, URL: www.lacasafitzcarraldo.com.

Hotel Real Iquitos (Rooms: $20 - 80)
The Hotel Real Iquitos is a venerable Iquitos institution. Built more than 50 years ago, what was once an elegant, upscale hotel right on the river is now somewhat run-down and quirky. The rooms vary greatly in size and price—be sure to look at several before you choose. The best ones are enormous and have a balcony and a good view of the river and even a balcony. The interior rooms are more gloomy but less expensive. Perfect for those who prefer history and uniqueness to comfort and luxury. It ain't the Ritz—at least not anymore—but for some, that's the whole point, right? Malecón Tarapacá, Tel: 51-65-231-011, Fax: 51-65-231-011.

Hotel Marañón (Rooms: $25 - 40)
Though small, the Hotel Marañón offers a comfortable place for visitors to stay. The hotel is simple, with tile floors and undecorated walls. However, it offers extras such as a small pool and terrace in the back of the hotel. If you're staying here, try to snag a room in the back, not only to be closer to the pool, but also to avoid the nighttime noises coming from the street. Prices include breakfast and airport transfers. Nauta 289, Tel: 51-65-242-673, E-mail: hmaranon@ec-red.com.

Hostal Ambasador (Rooms: $30 - 40)
Hotel Ambasador is an especially good value if you are a member of Hostelling International, as you will get special discounts. Hostal Ambasador is also a member of the Peruvian Youth Hostel Association. It has a great location, and includes amenities such as free breakfast, transport to and from the airport and a cafeteria. For the price you pay, it is definitely a cut above some of the other hostels found in Peru. Pevas 260, Tel: 51-65-233-110, Fax: 51-65-231-618, E-mail: info@paseosamazonicos.com, http://www.peru-hotels.com/iquiamba.htm.

Hospedaje La Pascana (Rooms: $35 - 50)
Hospedaje La Pascana is located near the Iquitos *malecón* (river walk) and is one of the better bargains in town. The rooms are simple and neat. The pleasant, plant-filled courtyard is

opular with visitors. Make reservations, as the place tends to fill up. Price includes
reakfast. Calle Pevas 133, Tel: 51-65-235-581 / 231-418, Fax: 51-65-233-466, E-mail:
ascana@tsi.com.pe, URL: http://www.pascana.com/hospedaje.htm.

Hotel Acosta (Rooms: $42 - 64)

Hotel Acosta is a comfortable choice for young tourists who plan on staying for an ex-
ended period. The rooms are clean and comfortable, and they have all the requisite
menities: cable TV, fridge and in-room safes. The on-site Las Orquídeas Restaurant is
quite appetizing, serving Peruvian specialties and fresh juices. Breakfast is included in
he room prices, as well as airport transportation. This hotel is smaller than its sister
Regia Victoria, but what it lacks in size, it compensates with in charm. Huallaga 254,
Tel: 51-65-231-761, E-mail: info@hotelacosta.com, URL: www.hotelacosta.com.

HIGH-END

Victoria Regia (Rooms: $63 - 122)

The Victoria Regia is a comfortable, modern hotel about ten minutes from the center
of town. Popular with tourists as well as business travelers, it's the place to stay if you
want to be sure the air conditioning works. There is also a restaurant and a pool and
courtyard on the premises. The rooms are large and pleasant. According to the website,
it makes the best cappuchinos in Iquitos, a serious consideration for caffeine addicts.
Avenida Ricardo Palma 252, Tel: 51-01-421-9195 / 14-424-515, Fax: 51-65-231-983, E-
mail: reservas@victoriaregiahotel.com, URL: www.victoriaregiahotel.com.

Hotel El Dorado (Rooms: $66 - 150)

Hotel El Dorado encapsulates charm in the heart of Iquitos. If you're looking to get away
from the mainstream hotels, this option is a few blocks away from the plaza. Like its sister
hotel, the El Dorado Plaza Hotel, it offers cable TV, airport shuttle and a good restaurant,
Las Rocas. The pool is also open to restaurant diners. The difference between the two ho-
els is the upkeep. While the Plaza Hotel remains modern, this hotel has been around for
a while longer, which shows in its rooms. Calle Napo 362, Tel: 51-65-232-574, E-mail: do-
rado@hoteldoradoiquitos.com, URL: www.hoteldoradoiquitos.com.

Hostal Jhuliana (Rooms: $90)

Though the rooms at Hostal Jhuliana are nice, you can get a room at a more upscale ho-
el for the price. However, many travelers find this location to be a comfortable choice,
slightly away from the hustle of the plaza area. Rates include 24-hour hot water, refrigerator and cable TV. The hotel also offers a pool, bar and café. Putumayo 521, Tel:
51-65-233-154.

Amazon Muyuna Lodge (Rooms: $120)

Muyuna Lodge is located 140 kilometers from Iquitos up the Amazon River. It's a small
rainforest lodge, secluded and intimate, that guarantees sightings of birds, sloths, pink
dolphins and monkeys in the wild. 163 Putumayo St., Zip: 065, Tel: 51-65-242-858, E-
mail: reservas@muyuna.com, URL: www.muyuna.com.

Hotel Safari (Rooms: $120)

The hotel is unique in that most rooms only have interior windows that open into an
open-air courtyard, which is about 5' x 5'. It is a little noisy at night—you can hear everyone coming down the hallways—but it's not unbearable. It does not have cable TV, but it
includes a free breakfast consisting of toast and jelly, available in the small dining area.
The third floor has great views of the river, from the hallway. The Safari is in a great
central location just one block from the Plaza Del Armas. The staff is friendly and the
hotel is small, but clean. There is also a small casino connected to the hotel. Napo #118-
128, Tel: 51-65-223-000, Fax: 51- 65-232-149, E-mail: irasacsafari@hotmail.com.

AMAZON

El Dorado Plaza Hotel (Rooms: $220 - 600)

Location, location, location. Set in the middle of Plaza Mayor, the El Dorado Plaza Hotel is one of the nicest hotels in Iquitos, with rooms featuring great views of the square. It is within walking distance of the downtown area. Not to be confused with the smaller El Dorado, which has the same owners, this hotel boasts top-of-the-line accommodations and impeccable service. In addition to clean, spacious rooms, there is an outdoor pool with a swim-up bar. The hotel also arranges package deals with lodges in the Amazon. For a place like this in cities such as New York or London, you would pay twice as much. Calle Napo 252, Plaza de Armas, Tel: 51-65-222-555, anexo 13, E-mail: administrador@eldoradoplazahotel.com, URL: www.eldoradoplazahotel.com.

IQUITOS RESTAURANTS

Ice Cream in Iquitos

Amazonian fruits make cool sweets in Iquitos as unique ice-cream flavors. Travelers can take a taste at several businesses around the city's central park, Plaza de Armas. Giornatta is the most popular parlor and announces its stock simply, with a big *helado* sign above its entrance on Próspero 127, on the plaza's east side. *Helado* is ice cream in Spanish, and here there are more than 25 flavors to sample.

Giornatta features ice cream made in the only ice-cream factory in Iquitos. Scoops cost less than $1 (about 3 nuevo soles). There's usually a line, especially when school lets out and on weekends. There's a dozen or so tables if you want to eat in. Satisfy your sweet tooth with cones or dishes of aguaje, guanábana and camu camu—all fruits found locally.

The camu camu ice cream is made from the reddish-purple, vitamin-C-packed berries of a low-growing shrub found in the jungle. The flavor is part citrus, part sour. Aguaje ice cream is made from the tangerine-sized fruit of female aguaje palm trees. The fruits fetch a high price at market, and debate about the effect its harvesting has on the forest and animals is heating up. People don't pick the fruits; they collect them by cutting down the trees, which can reach 40 meters in heigt. Lowland tapirs, grey brocket deer and other wildlife rely on the fruit for subsistance. The guanábana fruit is dark green. Split it open and it has a creamy flesh with a horseshoe pattern of black seeds. The ice cream is more mild than the fruit, and is sweet and a tad sour. Maracuyá, or passionfruit, is extra sweet in this parlor while managing to still taste natural, and coconut is close to pure coconut juice. Because fruits are native and always fresh, the flavors are punchy and authentic. Street vendors are usually at Plaza de Armas or on main streets selling homemade aguaje popsicles on carts, though if they used water, there's no way to be sure it's safe to consume.

Ari's Burger (Próspero 127, at the corner of Próspero and Napo, 7 a.m. to 3 a.m.) serves traditional chocolate, vanilla and local flavors, as does the chicken joint on the same side of the street.

Many restaurants such as Fitzcarraldo Restaurant and Bar (Napo 100) on the riverside promenade and Chez Maggy (Raymundi 218, Tel: 51-065-231637) offer ice cream on their dessert menu. Of course, there's less variety than dedicated ice cream parlors.

Another eatery, Shambo, three blocks off Plaza de Armas (Morona 394, at Huallaga) has a variety of homemade popsicles made from local and common fruits.

Arandú Bar (Beer: $1.25 - 3)

On Malecón Maldonado, the riverside walkway in Iquitos, crowds of people gather each night to watch the sun set and to hang out with street performers who often dance with snakes. At Arandú Bar, you're so close it's like being part of the action. The bar is beside the walkway and a few steps from one of its well-known landmarks—what looks like a giant picture frame decorated with colorful tiles and set in a fountain (it frames the Amazon beyond). You don't even have to get up from your table to take a picture of it. The artwork is modern and the rock

AMAZON

music can get loud. At the indoor seats, you may have to holler to be heard. Share tales of recent travels with other adventurers who make Arandú a popular stop. Malecón Maldonado 113, Tel: 065-243-434.

Artica Restaurant (Entrees: $3 - 9)

Several large wood ovens dominate the entire back wall of Artica, a restaurant in central Iquitos that specializes in wood-fired pizzas, pasta dishes and steaks. There are two dining rooms—one upstairs, one downstairs. Diners gather around large, round, wooden tables. Everything in here is wooden and rustic-looking. Large wooden beams dominate the ceiling that towers two stories overhead.

Pizzas are hand tossed and thin crust. The menu features several cuts of steaks. A good portion of sirloin is grilled and served with french fries and a salad. Pasta is also on the menu as well as salads and gnocchi dishes with meat. Fresh juices, bottled juices, mixed drinks and beer, such as the Crystal and Pilsen name brands, are served. As with other restaurants in Iquitos, don't be surprised if kids walk in and take leftovers off tables after diners have paid their bills and left. Diners who ask for a doggie bag can take them back to the hotel for a late-night snack or easily give them away to kids who are waiting outside in hopes you'll bring some out. Located on Calle Napo, right off the Plaza de Armas, toward the promenade.

Chez Maggy (Entrees: $3.75 - 6)

Pizzas baked in wood ovens are Chez Maggy's specialty. The ovens are, in fact, the first thing diners see coming through the door. Everything is wood in Chez Maggy, including the 20 or so tables that fill the first-floor dining room. A wooden stairway leads to the second floor, where more rustic-looking wooden tables are lit for ambiance with candles. Tables by open windows facing the street have a cool breeze. The second floor also has a bar; servers get the drinks. Maggy's is known for its pizza, but also offers pasta dishes. There are two sizes of pizza—small and large. The small stretches across a dinner plate and is hearty enough to fill a traveler after a day spent trekking in the jungle. Large pizzas are good to split with a friend. The dough is fresh and hand-tossed, the pizza thin-crust. Toppings range from mushrooms and ham to pineapple, pepperoni and many other ingredients.

Pizza needs soda and Peru's national soft drink, Inca Kola, is definitely on the menu. For the uninitiated, Inka Cola is bright-yellow, tastes a bit like bubble gum—or cough syrup, depending on who you ask—and packs enough sugar in one glass to have you bouncing off the walls. Fresh passion fruit, pineapple and other local fruit juices are served, as well as beer and mixed drinks. Pilsen and Crystal are popular brands of beer. Take-out is available, with the added bonus that customers pick up their pies at a counter beside the chefs who are creating them. Hours: 6 p.m. to 11:30 p.m. (Raymundi 218, between Nauta and Napo, Tel: 51-065-231-637).

The Yellow Rose of Texas (Entrees: $5 and up)

Got the munchies at 3 p.m. or 3 a.m.? The Yellow Rose of Texas has got you covered. Ex-Texan Gerald Mayeaux owns the restaurant, lounge and bar that's going 24 hours a day. He is the ex-director of tourism for Iquitos and is full of useful tidbits, like how to rent a canoe guide in Belén and where to get your laundry done. He touts his diverse home-cooked meals; and, The Yellow Rose has a huge menu. Helpings are generous, fairly priced and good, if not gourmet.

Diners find everything here from English fish and chips to Mayeaux's own Texas-style barbecue, Tex-Mex, or thick-cut French toast, made from a family recipe. The Yellow Rose's decór is even more diverse, there's enough memorabilia and mementos to fill a barn. Check out the massive amounts of native drums, leg-long bee hives, 15-foot anaconda skins, stuffed piranhas, taxidermy lizards and indigenous masks. Staff and patron photos tacked to the wall tell The Yellow Rose's story. Appropriately for a Texan, Mayeaux has a longhorn skull mounted prominently on the wall. The life-size dummy dressed as a Mexican mariachi beside the bar is a nice, and nicely weird, touch.

Share your travel experiences online at www.vivatravelguides.com

The Yellow Rose boasts more than 100 different drinks and features horse saddle seats instead of standard stools. Beers are served ice-cold. Waitresses take orders in University of Texas cheerleading uniforms—white shirts and fringed skirts. Diners are surrounded by the garden's native plants and vines. At night, it's lit by kerosene lamps for a more tranquil atmosphere. It's definitely more rowdy in the bar, among the animal skins and "the largest armadillo shell ever." The Yellow Rose is also a good place to meet travelers, especially from the United States. There's cable TV, a game room with Monopoly, checkers, comfy Adirondack-style chairs and a well-stocked book exchange. Located a few stores off Plaza de Armas at Putamayo 180, Tel: 51-65-231353.

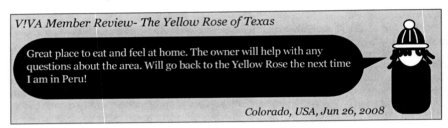

V!VA Member Review- The Yellow Rose of Texas

Great place to eat and feel at home. The owner will help with any questions about the area. Will go back to the Yellow Rose the next time I am in Peru!

Colorado, USA, Jun 26, 2008

Restaurant Fitzcarraldo (Entrees: $5 - 9)

One of the most popular restaurants on the main Iquitos promenade is Fitzcarraldo Restaurant and Bar, which pays homage to one of the region's most famous entrepreneurs. During the rubber boom in the late 19th and early 20th centuries, Irishman Brian Sweeney Fitzgerald was a rubber baron who had a wild dream—to open an opera house in the Amazon, in Manaus, Brazil. Called Fitzcarraldo because the locals couldn't pronounce his name, he became famous for how he tried to make his fortune: he dismantled and moved a 32-ton boat from one river to another, through the jungle, to reach rubber trees. His story was inspiration for German director Werner Herzog's 1982 film, "Fitzcarraldo," starring Klaus Kinksi.

Herzog got famous for having his own crazy ideas, like pulling a heavy steel boat across a small mountain during filming. Kinski's shock-blonde hair leaps out at diners in photo stills from the film that hang on the walls in Fitzcarraldo. Fitzcarraldo has a reputation as one of the best quality restaurants in town and offers a varied menu. Lunch includes hot and cold options, such as a grilled steak sandwich served on a submarine-like roll. Dinner features grilled meats, traditional dishes and some meals from the jungle for the more adventurous, such as grilled caiman (alligator). The chef also serves up ceviche, which is fresh raw fish or shrimp, marinated in lemon juice and chili peppers and served chilled. A restaurant like Fitzcarraldo is a good place to try ceviche because of the stock turnover and its reputation for high-quality food. Other regional dishes are made with dorado, a regional fish, and the giant paiche, the largest freshwater fish in the world. Grilled steaks are available as is lomo salteado—strips of stir-fry beef. Pork and chicken are also staples, served grilled or with sauces. Meals are often accompanied by french fries and ensalada palmito, which is a light, cold salad of hearts of palm. Drinks include pisco sour cocktails (the main ingredients are brandy, lemon and egg whites), beer, coffee and juice. Daily cohices of fresh-squeezed juices vary from pineapple to passion fruit.

The main room is cozy, with about 20 tables, and a small bar at one end. There is a patio dining area and two open-air entrances at Fitzcarraldo, which give diners a good view of the action on the promenade, where street performers are drawing crowds a few feet away. This openness, however, is also a magnet for people to congregate in the doorway asking for money or selling everything from gum to hand-dyed tablecloths, although restaurant staff usually ask them to leave. Fitzcarraldo is a mid-range to high-end restaurant in Iquitos, but laid-back enough that visitors can feel comfortable ordering a drink and relaxing. Napo 100, at the corner of Napo and Malecón, Tel: 51-65-243-434.

AROUND IQUITOS

If you don't want to do a river cruise, the best way to see the Peruvian Amazon near Iquitos is to visit one of the many jungle lodges in the area. Some of them are only a few kilometers from Iquitos and can be visited overnight, but most are more remote and require visits of several days. The lodges offer similar activities: guided walks, shamanic tours (including use of the hallucinogenic *ayahuasca*), canoe rides, swimming, fishing, bird watching, visits to local communities and more. You can establish your activities with the lodge guides upon arrival. Although activities vary little, the lodges differ from one another in several respects, including quality of naturalist guides and shamans, cost, comfort and location. If comfort is important to you—if you want to see the Amazon without really roughing it—you may want to check out one of the more luxurious lodges closer to Iquitos. But if what you really want is to see animals like monkeys, toucans and maybe even jaguars, you'll want to select a very remote jungle lodge.

Iquitos is a city of a half-million inhabitants, and there are not many wild animals within about 80 kilometers or so. Costs generally reflect levels of comfort, and you can expect to pay significantly more for a luxury lodge. A little bit of bargain shopping can go a long way: there is a lot of competition among the lodges, and you can often find discounts and special rates, especially if you're in a group or can make last-minute plans. Be sure to do your last-minute lodge shopping in the reputable agencies in Iquitos; guides who approach you on the street or in the airport are most likely con artists and should be avoided at all costs. Paseo Amazónicos has more than 25 years experience in taking tours in and around Iquitos and the Amazon rain forest. It is the proprietor of three Amazon lodges: Amazonas Sinchicuy Lodge, Tambo Yanayacu Lodge and Tambo Amazónico Lodge. It also owns the Hotel Ambasador in Iquitos. All three lodges are within 200 kilometers of Iquitos and feature similar activities: guided jungle walks, birdwatching, river trips, visits to local communities, etc. The activities are generally included in the price of a multi-day trip to the lodge, although tips are extra. Paseo Amazónicos also organizes different expeditions and day trips from Iquitos. There are multi-day visits that go to one or more of its lodges, as well as city tours of Iquitos and day trips to areas of interest in the region.

Tambo Amazónico Lodge

The most remote jungle lodge (121km / 75mi from Iquitos), operated by the reputable Paseo Amazónicos, Tambo Amazónico is also the one where you're most likely to see some of the more spectacular Amazonian birds and mammals. It is located on the Yarapa River, not far from the Pacaya-Samiria National Reserve. The lodge is for the most adventurous types: there are only two dormitory-style rooms, each of which holds ten beds, each equipped with mosquito netting. The communal dining room offers a superb view of the river and there are plenty of hammocks for lounging. Lights are kerosene lanterns. A favorite of birdwatchers--a one-week trip can result in sighting up to 300 species--the Tambo Amazónico is also good for those who like their jungle trips down and dirty. Guides often take guests to visit some of the nearby lakes and lagoons, hidden in the dense jungle. If the water isn't high enough, you may find yourself dragging the canoe along a muddy trail to get to where you want to go! The Tambo Amazónico Lodge has one extra feature: interaction with locals. Guides from the lodge are often locals and can take you to visit nearby villages. Tel: 51-12-417-576 / 417-614, Fax: 51-14-467-946, E-mail: info@paseosamazonicos.com, URL: www.paseosamazonicos.com.

Tambo Yanayacu

On the banks of the Yanayacu River, 38 miles (61 kilometers) from Iquitos, the Tambo Yanayacu lodge is another good option for those wishing to spend some quality time in the jungle. Smaller than Amazonas Sinchicuy, Tambo Yanayacu has only ten rooms (each with private bathroom) and space for 30 guests. The Tambo Yanayacu is known for being near a population of huatzines, a bizarre, turkey-like bird that has a hook-like talon on its wings that allows it to climb trees. Iquitos Office: Calle Pevas 246, Tel: 51-94-231-618 /51-65-231-618, Fax: 51-1-446-7946 / 51-65-233-110, E-mail: info@paseosamazonicos.com, URL: www.paseosamazonicos.com.

AMAZON

Amazonas Sinchicuy Lodge

Amazonas Sinchicuy is located only 32 kilometers (20mi) from Iquitos. Because it is so close to town, Amazonas Sinchicuy is a good option for those who only want to spend one or two nights in the jungle. It features 32 rooms, each of which can accommodate one to four guests. It features the usual jungle lodge activities, such as guided hikes, canoe trips, etc. Amazonas Sinchicuy is operated by Paseo Amazónicos. This lodge has facilities for handicapped guests. Calle Pevas 246. Tel: 51-94-231-618 / 233-110, Fax: 51-14-467-946, E-mail: p-amazon@ amauta.rcp.net.pe, URL: www.paseosamazonicos.com/index.html.

Tahuayo Lodge

Although it is still less than ten years old, Tahuayo Lodge (135 km / 90 miles from Iquitos) is one of the region's most acclaimed sites. It is located in the spectacular Tamshiyaco-Tahuayo Reserve, considered to be home to the greatest mammal diversity in all of South America. The region is believed to be a Pleistocene refuge, which means that during the last Ice Age it remained forested, instead of turning into grassy savannah like much of the rest of South America. It thus became a haven of sorts where wildlife could survive. The Tamshiyaco-Tahuayo Reserve was created in 1991 to protect the habitat of the extremely rare red uakari monkey, although countless other species also make their home there. Tahuayo Lodge's owner, Amazonia Expeditions, is the only tour operator licensed to take visitors into the reserve.

Tahuayo Lodge is attractive and comfortable, yet rustic. There is no electricity except for a small generator, the primary function of which is to recharge camera batteries. The lodge boasts 15 comfortable cabins, all of which are screened-in to keep unwelcome nocturnal visitors out, and well-maintained communal areas. Kerosene lamps provide light at night. Reviews of Tahuayo Lodge tend to be glowing: Outside Magazine rated it one of its top ten travel finds.

Tahuayo offers the usual range of jungle lodge activities, such as guided walks, swimming, visits to local communities, etc. It also offers specialty trips, such as honeymoon packages, but its best known trip is without doubt the wilderness survival program, in which rain forest novices are taken in to the heart of the jungle with nothing but a machete and are taught to survive: some skills include how to use poison sap to stun fish, identify and prepare edible nuts and roots, and build shelter. Tel: 1-800-262-9669 (US), Fax: 1-813-907-8475 (US), E-mail: Amazonia.Expeditions@verizon.net, URL: www.perujungle.com.

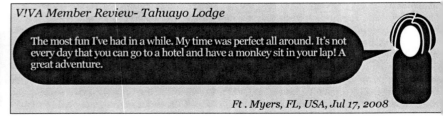

V!VA Member Review- Tahuayo Lodge

The most fun I've had in a while. My time was perfect all around. It's not every day that you can go to a hotel and have a monkey sit in your lap! A great adventure.

Ft . Myers, FL, USA, Jul 17, 2008

SANTA ROSA

On a island directly across from Leticia is the smallest of the triple-border towns, Santa Rosa. In reality, it is so small, it doesn't seem to be worth the census taker's time to make a call and count. The town isn't much, but it is the jumping off point for travelers looking for a boat up the Amazon River to Iquitos. A paved way parallels the riverbank. The walk frays into dirt paths disappearing into the dense vegetation. This main "street," though is as far as you ever need to go in Santa Rosa. Your launch from Leticia or Tabatinga will pull up amongst the many other canoes shoved against the shore. To the left is where the next boat for Iquitos may be loading up. Also along this stretch are the Peruvian migración post, about a half-dozen basic hotels, a handful of restaurants and other businesses. From the street vendors you can pick up a comic book or other last-minute item for your sojourn.
Alt: 50 meters (164ft), Pop: several hundred, City Code: 065

Getting To and Away from Santa Rosa

The only way to get to or from Santa Rosa is by launch, leaving from the main street.

To Leticia: daily 6 a.m.-8 p.m., $1.10.

To Santa Rosa: daily 6 a.m.-8 p.m., $2.80.

Santa Rosa is a more convenient departure point for cargo ships than Islandia, and as such most leave from here. Several agencies on the main drag sell tickets for the *rápido* boat and the weekly flight to Iquitos. See Colombia-Brazil-Peru Border Crossings for more information.

SANTA ROSA SERVICES

The most important office in Santa Rosa is immigration, about 50 meters (180ft) to the right of the boat docks, past Hotel Diana (Monday-Saturday 8 a.m.-noon, 2-6 p.m.). There are no banks in Santa Rosa. Hospedaje El Mirador, about 120 meters (400ft) from the boat dock changes money. To stay in touch with the outside world, the main phone office is 30 meters (100ft) to the right of immigration, in the Snack Bar Sabor Peruano "mall." There is no internet in Santa Rosa.

Index

A

Abimael Guzmán, 23-24, 242
Abiseo River National Park, 499
Abra Málaga, 56
Abraham Aguirre Apazabusiness, 491
Academia Castellana, 85
Academia Latinoamericana de Español, 266
Acclahuasi, 258
Acclimatization, 52, 300
Achoma, 197, 212
Acllahuasi, 263
Acobamba, 303
Acoma, 212
Action Valley, 275
Acuchimay, 242, 246
Acupari Language School, 267
Adventure Travel, 48
Aero Club del Peru, 102
Aero Condor, 221, 347, 462
Aeropuerto Carlos Ciriani Santa Rosa, 175
Aeropuerto Carlos Martínez de Pinillos, 402
Aeropuerto Internacional Jorge Chávez, 80, 243
Aeropuerto Internacional Padre Aldamiz, 487
Aeropuerto Internacional Velasco Astete, 253
Aeropuerto Rodríguez Ballón, 206
Aeroxtreme, 143-144
Aeródromo de Ica, 160
Agencia de Viajes Caminos, 174
Aguas Calientes, 323-331, 333, 339
Aguada Blanca, 212, 214
Aguas Verdes, 451
Ahuashiyaku Waterfalls, 501
Aie-Paec, 411
Aiko Restaurant, 330
Alan García, 23, 35-36
Albergue Las Cabañas, 364
Albergue Miraflores House, 121
Albergue Suasi, 367
Albergue Turística, 445
Alberto Fujimori, 23-25, 35, 73
Alcanfores, 124
Aldea Yanapay, 270-271, 293
Alegría Tours, 180
Alianza, 174, 221, 227-228,

423
All Saints Day, 34, 212
All Ways Tours, 367
All Ways Travel Agency, 355
Alma Mestiza, 276
Almacén Metro, 97
Almudena Cemetary, 325
Alpamayo, 49, 52, 383-386, 395
Altitude Sickness, 49, 67
Amantaní, 366
Amaru Hostal, 289
Amauta Spanish School, 269
Amazon, 483-489
Amazon Animal Orphanage, 502-503
Amazon Muyuna Lodge, 509
Amazon Tours, 47, 486, 507
Amazonas Explorer, 275
Amazonas Sinchicuy Lodge, 513-514
Amazonia Lodge, 498
Amigos Spanish School, 266
Ampato, 211
Anaconda Lodge, 491
Anapia, 367
Andahuaylillas, 298-299
Andean Life Adventure, 276-277
Andes Nature Tours, 277
Andes Top, 391-392
Andes Tours, 47, 377
Andex Adventure, 48, 88
Andino Club Hotel, 389
Año Nuevo, 34
Año Viejo, 34
Antica Pizzería, 110
Antigua Taberna Queirolo, 138
Aobamba Valley, 334
APU Expediciones, 273
Apu Auzangate, 276
Apu Salkantay, 330, 362
Apumayo, 275
Arandú Bar, 505, 510
Arco Deustua, 355
Architecture, 28-29
Arena Milano, 97
Arequipa, 186-213
Ari's Burger, 505, 510
Arizaga, 225
Arqueólogo Exclusive Selection Hotel, 286
Arrecife Hotel, 448, 457
Arrieros, 288, 376, 382
Art, 28-29, 42
Art Rock Café, 436

Artesanía Shopping, 415
Artesanías Pachacútec, 264
Artica Restaurant, 511
Ary Quepay, 207
Arúgula, 126
Asociación Comunal de Artesanos La Cusana, 471
Asociación Comunal de Lácteos, 480
Asociación de Operadores, 197
Asociación San Marcelo de Chiquián, 391
Asociacíon Pukllasunchis, 268
Atahualpa, 22, 28
Atocsaycuchi, 289
Ausunción, 363-364
Auto de Fé, 80
Aventuras de Oro, 48
Awana Kancha, 306
Ayabaca, 162, 167
Ayacucho, 243-248
Ayahuasca, 22, 28, 513
Aycanamo, 413
Aymara, 25
Azulejos, 502, 506

B

Babieca Tratoria, 295
Backpackers Inn, 133
Bagua, 467
Bahuaja-Sonene National Park, 493
Bahía de Paracas, 153
Bait Sababa Lodge, 138
Ballestas Islands, 56, 156-157
Baltazar La Torre, 39
Balthazar, 125
Banco Central, 85
Banco Continental, 82, 194, 503
Bar Mochileros, 135
Bar Restaurant Indigo, 292
Bar Restaurant Trujillo, 349
Bar Rojo, 454
Bar-Restaurant Kuélap, 473-474
Barranco, 78, 90, 112, 129-130, 132-136, 139-140
Basadre Suites Hotel, 108
Basilica of Our Lady of Copacabana, 369
Baños Intihuatana, 245
Belén, 504-506
Biking, 54-55
Bioferia, 118
Birdwatching, 55-56

Bistro de Los Andes, 390
Blue House, 288
Blue Lagoon, 499
Blueberry Lounge, 293
Blues Bar Cafe, 322
Bocapán, 449-450
Boccatto, 230
Bodega Bar Juanito, 136
Bodega El Catador, 165-166
Bodega Santiago Queirolo, 137
Bodegas Tacama, 63
Body Shop Spa Cusco, 264
Bohème Bar, 295
Boleto Turístico General, 258
Boli-Bar, 138
Bolivian Islands, 369
Bolivian Side of Lake Titicaca, 368
Border Crossing, 38, 42, 44
Borrachito, 159
Bothy Hostel, 201
Botica Arcangel, 422
Botica Divino Niño Jesús, 154
Boticas Arángel, 224
Boticas Felicidad, 433
Brava, 492
Bridge of Sighs, 129-130
Brujas, 127
Budabar Restaurant-Lounge, 458
Buena Vista Hostal, 202
Bunk Hostel, 508
Business Visas, 41
Butterfly Conservation Center, 489

C

Cabalgatas Horseback Riding, 144
Caballo de Mar, 426
Caballo Peruano de Paso, 144
Cabanaconde, 219-220
Cachora, 250, 304
Cactus Bar, 321
Cafe Genova, 231
Cafetería de Angela, 454
Caframi Tours, 198
Café Andino, 382-383, 390
Café Café, 126
Café Casa Verde, 206
Café Cecovasa, 355
Café Creperie, 389
Café Genova, 231
Café Haití, 124
Café Mengú, 455
Café New York, 446

Café Plaza, 313
Café Restaurant Pizzería Pacha, 372
Café Thespis, 225
Café Trotamundos, 296
Cahuachi, 182
Cajabamba, 46
Cajamarca, 460-465
Calana, 227
Caleta, 228, 425, 456
California Café, 390
Calixto, 240
Callao, 142
Callejón de Conchucos, 385
Callejón de Huaylas, 378, 385
Calling Abroad, 71
Camacho, 83, 141
Camaná, 95-96, 99, 101
Camelids, 306
Camera Repair, 76
Caminante School, 86
Camping, 60-61
Campo de Alianza, 228
Campo de Moche, 411
Campo Santo, 394
Canana, 410
Canchayoc, 56
Canchipata, 276
Candelabro de Los Andes, 145, 157
Cannie Pacheco, 330
Cantalloc, 179
Cantayo Aqueduct, 184
Canticle, 246
Cantuarias, 127, 273
Cantuta, 277
Cao Viejo, 412
Capac Cocha, 194
Capichica, 358
Cappuccino Café, 296
Car Rental, 45
Carabaya, 97, 99-101
Caraz Dulzura Hostal, 396
Caraz, 395-397
Cardenale, 230
Caretas, 73
Carhuaz, 392-393
Carmen Alto, 210, 266, 287, 289
Carmen de Nasca, 174
Carros, 443, 478, 481
Casa Andina Miraflores,123
Casa Andina Nasca, 181
Casa Andina Puno Plaza, 360
Casa Andina-Colca, 217
Casa Arequipa, 193

Casa Barranco, 132
Casa Bella, 108
Casa Blanca, 445, 463-464
Casa Bolívar, 161
Casa Bracamonte, 406
Casa Checa Eguren, 130
Casa Ciclista, 46
Casa de Aliaga, 95
Casa de Arena, 171
Casa de Avila Spanish School, 195
Casa de Clara, 408
Casa de Cultura, 226
Casa de Fierro, 501, 505-506
Casa de Guías, 381-383, 390
Casa De La Abuela, 241
Casa de Melgar, 204
Casa de Mi Abuela, 204
Casa de Mujer Artesana Nasca, 176
Casa de Sillar, 203
Casa de Zela, 225
Casa de Ávila, 202
Casa Del Zela, 225
Casa Ecológica, 318
Casa Fitzcarraldo, 508
Casa Ganoza Chopitea, 406
Casa Garcilaso, 258, 260
Casa Goyeneche, 95
Casa Grande, 282
Casa Grillo, 448
Casa Horno, 318
Casa Hospedaje Cucha Cuella, 473
Casa Hospedaje León, 473
Casa Huéspedes El Lirio, 474
Casa Kolping, 229
Casa Marfil, 138
Casa Museo Basadre, 226
Casa Museo Gran Almirante Grau, 435
Casa Nash, 130
Casa Parodi, 363
Casa Rada, 95
Casa Real, 241
Casa Riva-Agüero, 95
Casa San Blas Boutique Hotel, 289
Casa Tere, 419
Casa Torre Tagle, 95
Casa Tristán, 194
Casa Verde, 111, 206
Casa Vieja Peru, 470
Casa-Hospedaje Crillón, 453
Casa-Museo Maria Reiche, 179-180

Casablanca Hostal, 203
Cascadas de Sipán, 444
Cascapara, 324
Cashapampa, 384-385
Casma, 379
Casona de Jerusalén Hospedaje, 202
Casona de Leymebamba, 480
Casona Monsante, 470
Casona Real, 284-285
Catarata Chacchar, 481
Catarata de Gocta, 471
Cathedral, see Churches, Chapels, and Cathedrals
Cava de San Blas, 289
Cava de San Rafael, 290
Cayma, 197, 206, 209
CECOVASA Café, 361
Ceiba Tours, 490
CEICA Centro Estudios, 195
Cell Phones, 71, 75, 107
Cely Pizza, 478, 480
Cementerio Streets, 259
Cemetery of Chauchilla, 179
Center New Eden, 471
Central Lima, 90
Centro Andino de Tecnología Tradicional, 318
Centro Artesanal Norte, 433
Centro Cívico, 241, 456
Centro Comercial, 139, 141, 206, 275
Centro Comercial Cayma, 206
Centro Comercial El Polo, 141
Centro Comercial Plaza Lima Sur, 139
Centro Cultural Chávez, 194
Centro Cultural de La Católica, 31
Centro Cultural Teatro Orfeón, 225
Centro de Idiomas, 59, 86
Centro de Interpretación, 158
Centro de Medicina Integral, 299
Centro de Salud, 154, 158
Centro de Salud Máncora, 451
Centro de Salud Zorritos, 447
Centro Empresarial Real, 109
Centro Histórico, 280
Centro Información Turística, 456
Centro Mallqui, 473, 477-479
Cerpa, 26
Cerrito, 238, 240
Cerrito de Huajsapata, 355

Cerro Acuchimay, 242
Cerro Azul, 51, 143
Cerro Blanco, 173, 176, 411
Cerro Colorado, 195
Cerro de Pasco, 46
Cerro de San Cristóbal, 94
Cerro La Raya, 431
Cerro Supramarca, 220
Cerro Sánchez, 438
Cerro Ushparán, 475
Cerros de Amotape, 449-450, 452
Cervantes Spanish School, 265
Ceviche de Lenguado, 126
Cevichería A Todo Vapor, 230
Cevichería Edith, 158
Cevichería El Sol Ñato, 458
Chacaltana, 120
Chacas, 214
Chacchar, 481
Chacha, 467
Chachani, 53, 210-211
Chachapoyas, 465-472
Chachas, 219
Chachini, 187, 198
Chaco, 153
Chacón Tours, 407
Chahual, 46
Chaksi Inn Hostal, 282
Chala, 21, 135
Chalco, 307
Chalet Suisse, 389
Chanapata, 299
Chancas, 501
Chan Chan, 412
Chanqui, 467, 481
Chapel, see Churches, Chapels, and Cathedrals
Chaquihuayjo, 272
Charqui, 64
Chastity Bono, 26
Chauchilla, 173, 176, 179
Chavín de Huantar, 49
Che Guevara, 119
Chez Maggy, 295, 329, 510-511
Chicalyo, 422, 427
Chicama, 50, 401, 412
Chicha, 62, 321
Chiclayo, 420-431
Chicón, 272
Chifa Fuc Seng, 101
Chifa Nam Kug, 183
Chilca Railroad Station, 239
Children, 77
Chili Rivers, 198

Chilina Valley, 210
Chilli Heaven, 386, 390
Chilligua, 358
Chimbote, 72
Chimor, 413
Chimú Temple, 431, 440
Chinacocha, 376
Chinchero, 298
Chiquián, 391-392
Chira River, 440
Chivay, 215-218
Chiwata, 195
Chopicalqui, 53, 376
Choquequirao, 250, 299, 301, 303-304
Choquetico Stone, 218
Chorillos, 89, 139
Choza Redonda, 474
Chuakay, 183
Chucuito, 363-364
Chugay, 46
Chula Vista, 87
Chuquipalta, 304
Churajon, 189
Churches, Chapels, and Cathedrals
Catedral de Lima, 94
Catedral de Tacna, 225
Chapel of El Señor, 258, 481
Chapel of San Antonio Abad, 258
Chapel of San Ignacio de Loyola, 193
Church of Latter-Day Saints, 27
Church of San Francisco, 88, 188
Church of Santa Domingo, 88
Compañía Catholic Church, 281
Cusco Cathedral, 258
Iglesia de Cristo Rey, 234
Iglesia de Jesús, 96
Iglesia de La Merced, 96, 234, 439
Iglesia de Matriz, 505
Iglesia de Merced, 94
Iglesia de San Cristóbal, 234
Iglesia de San Francisco, 78-79
Iglesia de San Juan Bautista, 437
Iglesia de San Pedro, 96
Iglesia de Santa Teresa, 258
Iglesia Espíritu Santo, 227
Iglesia La Merced, 347
Iglesia San Blas, 252, 258-259
Iglesia San Cristóbal, 234

Iglesia San Francisco, 234
Iglesia San Juan Bautista, 210
Iglesia San Pedro, 250, 441
Iglesia San Pedro Apóstol, 250
Iglesia Santa Catalina, 347
Iglesia Santiago Apóstol, 350
Iglesia Soledad, 378
Iglesias de Quinua, 247
San Francisco Church, 82, 88, 97, 194
San Juan Bautista Church, 355
Santo Domingo Church, 35, 253
Cielo Hotel, 216-217
Cieneguilla, 81
CIFA, 42, 451, 455
CIMA Hyperbaric Center, 257
Circuito de Playas, 128, 135
CISPES, 26
City of Eternal Summer, 456
City of Kings, 79, 90
Ciudad Resbalabamba, 441
Ciudadela Warpa Picchu, 247
Climate, 21
Climbing, 52-53
Clinton Place New Rochelle, 88
Clorinda, 278, 311
Clorinda Matto de Turner, 278
Club Colonial, 417
Club de Madres La Navidad, 474
Club Liberal, 439
Club Med, 454
Clínica San Borja, 83
Coca Kintu, 363
Cocachimba, 471
Cocamas, 507
Cocha Salvador, 497
Cochas Chico, 235-236
Cochas Grande, 235-236
Coco de Mer, 125
Cocodrilos Tours, 457
Cocolat Café, 100
Cohechán, 473
Colán, 440
Colca Canyon, 186-188, 211-215
Colca Inn Hotel, 216
Colca Lodge Hotsprings, 216
Colegio María Inmaculada
Calle Grau, 445
Colla Cruz, 471
Colla Raymi, 327
Collacocha, 108
Collagua, 211-215
Collao Plateau, 348

Collpa de Guacamayos, 493
Colonia Hotel, 388
Colonial House II, 203
Colonial House Inn, 201
Colonial Inn, 122
Colón Inn, 360-361
Colquecruz, 304
Columbus, 210
Comandante Espinar, 121-122
Comedy, 32-33
Comedor Manuelita, 138
Comisaría de Piura, 433
Comisión Jurídica, 226
Communication, 69
Communist Party of Peru, 24
Compañía de Ferrocarril, 425
Compañía de Jesús, 258
Complejo Arqueológico Wari, 245
Complejo Cultural Simón Bolívar, 246
Comunidad Campesina de Ticapata, 276
Comunidades de Ollantay-tambo, 318
Concepción de Chiclayo, 425
Conchamarca, 334
Conde de Lemos, 344, 351
Conde de Superunda, 96
Conde Monclova, 148
Condor Tours, 273
Condor Travel, 273
Condor Wasi, 216
Conexus Language Institute, 86
Confitería Meli Melo, 349
Confraternidad Este, 378
Congón, 473
Coniraya, 343
Consulates, 39, 402
Convent of Mercy, 259
Convent of Santa Catalina, 258
Convent of Santo Domingo, 263
Convento de San Francisco, 258
Copa Sudamericana, 50
Copacabana, 368-372
Coporaque, 218
Cordillera Apolobamba, 342
Cordillera Blanca, 375-378
Cordillera Huayhuash, 376
Cordillera Huaytapallana, 236
Cordillera Negra, 375-376, 378
Cordillera Real, 342, 371
Cordillera Urubamba, 303
Cordillera Vilcabamba, 303-304
Cordillera Vilcanota, 250, 304

Córdova, 137, 439
Coricalle, 279-280
Corire, 210
Coroico, 342, 371
Coropuna, 214, 220
Corpus Christi, 34, 253
Correo Central de Lima, 69, 90
Corricalle, 279
Corrigedor, 282
Corvina, 135, 411
Cosentino Gourmet, 100
Costa Verde, 115, 135, 143
Costabella, 436
Costarica, 39
Cotahuasi, 220
Couch Bar, 297
Country Club Lima Hotel, 109
Crillón, 453
Cristina Hostal, 284
Cross Cultural Solutions, 88
Cross Keys Pub, 297
Crucero, 147
Cruces de Camino, 130
Cruz Blanca, 220
Cruz de Socos, 174
Cruz Pata, 481-482
Cruz Verde, 200, 265
Crystals Restaurant, 109
Cuarto de Rescate, 460
Cuchacuella Lake, 470
Cúcuta, 402
Cúpula, 371
Cuenca, 42, 47
Cuernavaca, 87
Cuero Sánchez, 96
Cuesta de San Blas, 294
Cuesta Santa Ana, 280
Cuglievan, 423
Cuichipunco, 274
Culinary Vocabulary, 64
Culture, 28
Cultural Institute of Peru, 351
Cumbe Mayo, 462
Cusco, 249-298
Cusco Café, 313
Cusco Mania Spanish School, 268
Cusi Coyllor, 315
Cusi Q, 325
Cusipata Viajes, 198
Cusqueña School, 193, 260, 263, 299, 364

D

Da Silva House, 172
Daily Newspapers, 73
Dance, 30-31
Day of San Pedro, 34
De César Restaurant, 101
Declaration of Nasca, 174
Deja Vu, 206
DELE Certificate, 87
Dengue Fever, 68
Departure Tax, 44, 221
Deústua Memorial, 355
Diablo Club Huaraz, 391
Diarrhea, 67-68
Dircetur, 224
Disabled Travelers, 77
DJ Tattoo Machines, 91
Domeyer Hostel, 133
Don Julio Youth Hostel, 359
Dragón Internet, 114
Dress, 74
Drink, 61
Dutch Hope Foundation, 289

E
Earthwatch Institute, 88
Eco Inn, 360-361
Eco Tours, 197
Eco Trek Peru, 276
Eco-lodges, 59, 61, 495
Eco-Tourism, 61, 75
Economy, 24-25
EDEAQ Escuela de Español Ari
Quipay Arequipa, 195
Edgar Adventures, 356
Edo Sushi Bar, 141
EEC Spanish School, 85
El Ekeko Café Bar, 136
El Abuelo Hostal, 393
El Abuelo Restaurant, 393
El Albergue, 320
El Alto, 439, 451
El Balcón Dorado, 99
El Balcón Hostal, 284
El Batán, 464
El Bebedero, 474
El Bocón, 73
El Bolivariano, 138
El Brujo, 412-413
El Buen Sabor, 111
El Cajamarques, 464
El Cartujo, 112
El Catador, 165-166
El Cerrojo, 206
El Chipe, 433
El Chorito, 159
El Comercio, 59, 73

El Condado Hotel and Suites, 123
El Correo Central de Lima, 69
El Cumbe, 421
El Delfín, 135
El Dorado Plaza Hotel, 509-510
El Dragón, 136
El Ekeko Café Bar, 136
El Escudero Lodge, 408
El Estadio Fútbol Club, 101
El Faro de la Marina, 115
El Farol, 425
El Grand Hotel Huánuco, 234
El Hornero, 140
El Huarango, 183
El Kapallaq, 127
El Kero, 420
El Latino, 129
El Lava, 98
El Malecón, 139
El Manu, 329
El Manzano, 358
El Marqués Hotel, 108
El Mirador de Kuélap, 473, 475
El Mochica, 420
El Mortal, 134
El Niño, 438, 456
El Olivar, 105, 109
El Parquetito Café, 125
El Patio de Monterrey, 389
El Peruano, 73, 435
El Planetario, 139
El Popular, 73
El Portal Del Marques, 463
El Rincón, 436
El Sol Spanish School, 86
El Suizo, 135
El Tambo, 410
El Templo de Santiago Apóstol de Coporaque, 218
El Tiburón, 446
El Trebol Cafe, 429
El Tren Macho, 239
El Truco Restaurant, 294
El Tubo, 449-450
El Tunqui, 330
El Turko I, 208
El Turko II, 208
El Viñedo, 209
El Virrey, 97, 107
Embassies, 39, 105, 108
Emergency Medical Care, 82
Environmental Awareness, 75
Environmental Issues, 33-38, 332, 484

Epsel Interurbano, 421, 430
Eric Adventures, 277
Ermita, 129-130, 135
Escribano, 214
Esmeralda, 96
España Restaurant, 101
Espíritu Pampa, 301, 304
Estacion de Bus Hacia Chucuito, 364
Estación Central, 240
Etapa, 276, 278
Ethmopesa, 401-402
Etiquette, 74-75
Euskara, 172
Excel Spanish Language Center, 265
Expedición Libertadora, 148
Explorandes, 386

F
Fair Trade Association, 318
Fair Trade Folk Art, 355
FairPlay Spanish School, 267
Fallen Angel, 259, 290
Faro Inn Hostel, 121
Fauna, 21-22
Fay Wray, 428
Fe Café, 290
Félix Arenas Mariscal, 162
Feria Artesanal Permanente Mi Perú, 422
Feria Manos Artesanas, 97
Fermín Tangüis, 149
Fertur Peru Travel, 89
Festival, 35
Fiestas, 34
Filtélico, 226
Fishing, 56
Flor de Canela, 402
Flora & Fauna, 21
Flying Dog Backpackers, 120
Fondo Tres Esquinas, 165
Food, 61-64
Food Manners, 74
Fort of San Felipe, 142
Fountain of Health, 390
Franciscan Recoleta Monastery, 193
Freyja Ellis, 80, 92, 345, 412, 458
Friend Hospedaje, 418
Friend's House, 181
Fu-Lin Restaurant Vegetariano, 230
Fulica Americana, 226
Fundación Selva Inka, 271

G

Galaxia Expeditions, 386
Galeria La Merced, 293
Galerias Gamesa, 217
Galería de Arte Carmen Porras, 154
Galería de Arte Club Colonial, 417
Galería de Arte Señor Mérida, 292
Galería Lucía de la Puente, 130
Garden House, 286
Garza Hotel in Chiclayo, 428
Gay and Lesbian travelers, 76-77, 193, 259
Geography, 21-22
Giornatta, 510
Global Crossroad, 269
Global Net, 414, 422
Global Systems for Mobiles, 71
Global Volunteers, 87
Globos de los Andes, 275
Gloria Pareja Guest House, 281
Glorieta Hotel, 363
Go2Peru.com Tours, 426
Gocta, 471
Gold's Gym Peru, 83
Gran Feria Artesenal, 414
Gran Hostal Miraflores, 234
Gran Hotel Huayhuash, 391
Granja Heidi Restaurant, 293
Gringo Alley, 262
Gringo Bill's, 327
GSA Arequipa, 197
Guillermo Charum, 402
Guillermo Concha Iberico International Airport, 432
Guía Tours, 407

H

Hacienda San José, 167
Haku Trek, 272
HAPE, 257
Hathun Rumiyoq, 258
Hatuchay Tower Bar, 327
Hatun Rumiyoc, 259-260, 262
Hatunrumiyoc, 259
Hatún Luya, 481
Health, 67-68
Hearts Café, 322
Heat Exhaustion, 67
Heath River Wildlife Center, 497
Heladería El Chalán, 437
Helados Huascarán, 393
Helena Inn Hostal, 358

Hepatitis, 68
Hiking, 48
Hilton Hotel, 157-158
Hipermercado Metro, 429
Hippodrome, 141
Hiram Bingham, 36, 250, 304, 324, 328, 330-331, 337
Hispana Spanish Language School, 86
History, 22-23
Hitchhiking, 45
Holidays, 34
Home Sweet Home Hostel, 197
Home Sweet Home Ollantaytambo, 320
Horseback Riding, 51-52
Hospedaje Bon Amigo, 229
Hospedaje California, 436
Hospedaje Costabella, 436
Hospedaje El Artesano, 287, 307
Hospedaje El Conde de Arce, 407
Hospedaje El Dorado, 445
Hospedaje El Mirador, 515
Hospedaje Emanuel, 280
Hospedaje Félix, 279
Hospedaje Granada, 287
Hospedaje Huascar, 408
Hospedaje Inka, 288
Hospedaje Jenny, 469
Hospedaje Kinsa Cocha, 307
Hospedaje Kuélap, 474
Hospedaje L, 482
Hospedaje La Bahía, 491
Hospedaje La Pascana, 508
Hospedaje Laguna, 480
Hospedaje Latino, 180
Hospedaje Linda Flor, 309
Hospedaje Loreto, 166
Hospedaje Los Andenes, 318, 320
Hospedaje Los Viñedos, 457
Hospedaje Luciana, 491
Hospedaje Mach, 312
Hospedaje Nasca Sur, 181
Hospedaje Pizzería All Incontro, 425
Hospedaje Posada, 280
Hospedaje Pumamarka, 319
Hospedaje Q, 280
Hospedaje Residencial Santa Fé, 138
Hospedaje Sambleño, 287
Hospedaje San Lucas, 427
Hospedaje Shalom, 157

Hospedaje Tres Fronteras, 491
Hospedaje Tumi, 279
Hospedaje Turístico San Blas, 289
Hospedaje Virgen del Carmen, 445
Hospital de Apoyo de Nasca, 176
Hospital Félix Torrealva Gutiérrez, 161
Hospital I Santa Rosa, 433
Hospital Nacional Almanzor Aguinaga Asenjo, 422
Hospital Regional Docente Las Mercedes, 422
Hospital Regional Hipólite Unanue, 224
Hospital San Juan de Dios, 149
Hostal Alegría, 181
Hostal Alfredo, 388
Hostal Ambasador, 508
Hostal Andino, 370
Hostal Baldeón, 240
Hostal Belén, 98
Hostal Buena Vista, 122
Hostal Camping Naylamp, 418
Hostal Casa Grande, 282
Hostal Casona Solar, 202
Hostal Colca Wasi Kopling, 216
Hostal Collacocha, 108
Hostal Continental, 469
Hostal Corihuasi, 283
Hostal Desert Nights, 171
Hostal Eiffel, 121
Hostal El Bosque, 319
Hostal El Dorado, 469
Hostal El Marquez de Valdelirios, 247
Hostal El Patio, 121
Hostal Florian, 457
Hostal Forteleza de Kuélap, 482
Hostal Gabriel, 370
Hostal Garuda, 426
Hostal Gemina, 133
Hostal Grau, 247
Hostal Grillo Tres Puntas, 448
Hostal Hatun Wasi, 288
Hostal Ima Sumac, 326
Hostal Inclán, 228
Hostal Jhuliana, 509
Hostal Joel, 427
Hostal La Compañia, 201
Hostal La Cúpula, 371
Hostal La Florida, 247
Hostal La Ñusta, 319
Hostal Las Orquídeas, 320

Hostal Leyenda, 370
Hostal Lido, 427
Hostal Los Frayles, 157
Hostal Los Tres Delfines, 418
Hostal Los Uros, 358
Hostal Luquini, 349
Hostal Machu Picchu, 326
Hostal Mami Panchita, 98
Hostal Mandor, 325
Hostal Marani, 289
Hostal Miramar, 440
Hostal Ollanta, 319
Hostal Perla, 396
Hostal Posada, 151, 282
Hostal Posada Hispana, 151
Hostal Procurador, 279
Hostal Puno Plaza, 360
Hostal Rocha, 171
Hostal Rojas, 282
Hostal Roma, 98
Hostal Salvatierra, 171
Hostal Samana Wasi, 309
Hostal Samay Wasi, 457
Hostal San Isidro, 151
Hostal Santa María, 159, 281
Hostal Sauce, 321
Hostal Sicán, 427
Hostal Sol de Nasca, 181
Hostal Sol Radiante, 427
Hostal Solange, 418
Hostal Solar, 203
Hostal Suecia I, 279
Hostal Taquile, 359
Hostal Torreblanca, 122
Hostal Valle, 219
Hostal Varayoc, 340
Hostal Varayoq, 309
Hostal Vía Morburg, 181
Hostal Victoria, 427
Hostal Villa Manuelita, 152
Hostal Yungay, 394
Hostel Casa Samara, 453
Hostel Colonial, 409
Hostel Jerusalen, 203
Hostelling International, 282,
359, 364, 508
Hostería Suiza, 171
Hotel Acosta, 509
Hotel Ambasador, 508, 513
Hotel Antigua Miraflores, 123
Hotel Apu Majestic, 327
Hotel Arqueólogo, 286
Hotel Ballestas Island, 157
Hotel Basadre Suites, 108
Hotel Britania, 141
Hotel Cabaña Quinta, 491

Hotel Cáceres, 280
Hotel Cantayo, 182
Hotel Carlos V, 284
Hotel Casa Blanca, 463-464
Hotel Casa Kolping, 229
Hotel Central, 428
Hotel Collahua, 217
Hotel Colomba, 388
Hotel Colonial Inn, 122
Hotel Copacabana, 229
Hotel Costa, 457
Hotel Diana, 515
Hotel Don Carlos, 492
Hotel El Dorado, 509
Hotel El Merlín, 439
Hotel Escobedo, 480
Hotel España, 97, 101
Hotel Ferrocarril, 359
Hotel Gloria, 371
Hotel Gran Tacna, 227
Hotel Grillo Tres Puntas, 448,
450
Hotel Hacienda Ocucaje, 167
Hotel Huaraz, 387
Hotel Huascarán, 377
Hotel Incatambo Hacienda, 52
Hotel Inka Path, 98
Hotel Italia, 359
Hotel Kamana, 99
Hotel La Posada, 205
Hotel Laguna Seca, 464
Hotel Lari House, 200
Hotel Las Dunas, 52, 167
Hotel Libertador Arequipa, 205
Hotel Libertador Palacio, 286
Hotel Libertador Puno, 361
Hotel Libertador San Isidro
Golf, 108
Hotel Libertador Trujillo, 409
Hotel Los Delfines, 109
Hotel Lima Sheraton, 99
Hotel Mamatila, 138
Hotel Marañón, 508
Hotel Marqueses, 285
Hotel Maury, 99
Hotel Meson, 229
Hotel Monasterio, 286
Hotel Mossone, 171
Hotel Munay Tika, 320
Hotel Nasca Lines, 182
Hotel Oblitas, 283
Hotel Ocucaje Sun, 52
Hotel Olaya, 140
Hotel Pakaritampu, 321
Hotel Paracas, 158
Hotel Paraíso, 428

Hotel Pirámide, 388
Hotel Pisaq, 309
Hotel Posada, 166
Hotel Primavera, 408
Hotel Puerto Palos, 453
Hotel Qelqatani, 360
Hotel Qenwa, 247
Hotel Real Iquitos, 508
Hotel Restaurant La Cabaña,
327
Hotel Rosario, 371
Hotel Royal Inka I, 285
Hotel Royal Inka II, 285
Hotel Royal Inka Pisac, 52, 310
Hotel Rumi Punku, 285
Hotel Safari, 509
Hotel Sakura, 349
Hotel Smay Wasi, 457
Hotel Sol, 451
Hotel Sunset, 454
Hotel Tumi de Oro, 427
Hotel Turismo Huancayo, 241
Hotel Urubamba, 312
Hotel Zarcillo Paradise, 153
House Hostel, 138, 181
Huaca Agujereada, 425
Huaca Arco Iris, 402, 412
Huaca Blanca, 425
Huaca Cao Viejo, 412
Huaca Corta, 412
Huaca del Sol y Huaca del
Luna, 400, 411
Huaca El Brujo, 402
Huaca Esmeraldas, 402, 412
Huaca Huallamarca, 88, 105
Huaca Larga, 431
Huaca Prieta, 412
Huaca Pucllana, 112, 114
Huaca Rajada, 420
Huaca San Borja, 140
Huacachina Lake, 164
Huacachina Oasis, 168-173
Huacas Luna, 402
Hualanca, 384
Hualca Hualca, 211
Hualgayoc, 85, 94
Hualhuas, 235-236
Huánaco, 46
Huambo, 220
Huancabamba, 441-446
Huancacalle, 304
Huancahuasi, 242
Huancas, 441, 471
Huancayo, 236-242
Huanchaco, 413
Huandoy, 376, 388

Huanoca Pampa, 391
Huanta, 243
Huánuco, 233-235
Huaraz, 378-391
Huari, 261, 374
Huaringas, 441, 443-445
Huarmihuañusca, 334
Huarochirí, 27
Huasacache, 210
Huascarán, 374, 385
Huatanay River, 353
Huaya Belén River, 480
Huayhuash Mountains, 391-392
Huayllabamba, 334
Huayllapa, 384
Huayna Cápac, 217, 471
Huayna Picchu, 331, 336-338
Huayno, 30-31
Huayoccari, 301, 304, 313
Hugo Chávez, 24
Huitotos, 507
Humala, 24, 36
Humboldt Penguin, 56, 156, 440
Humedales de Ite, 225-226
Huttese, 27

I

Ibero Librerías, 83
Ica, 159-168
Ichma, 140
Ichocán, 32
Ichu, 211, 239
Ichupampa, 212
ICPNA Spanish School, 87
Ideal Travels SAC, 199
Idiomatrix Language Academy, 417
Il Capuccino, 323
Ilaria, 107
Imma Sumack, 32
Immaculate Conception, 258
Imperial Palace, 281
INABIF Children, 196
Incas
Inca Atahualpa, 460, 462
Inca Baths, 243, 261, 462, 464
Inca Bridge, 331
Inca Chieftan, 263
Inca Civilization, 252, 344, 369
Inca Culture, 28, 159, 251, 263, 266, 299, 337, 339
Incan Empire, 250, 253, 315-316, 355, 413
Inca Fortress of Ollantaytambo,
312
Inca Fountain, 370
Inca General, 315
Inca Jungle Trail, 274, 325
Inca Mythology, 342-344
Inca Pachacútec, 285, 356
Inca Princess, 32
Inca Ruins of Paredones, 184
Inca Sundial, 252-253
Inca Town, 315
Inca Túpac Yupanqui, 304, 441
Inca Uyo, 363
Inca Yupanqui, 282, 431
Inca Kola, 63
Inca Land Adventures, 277
Inca Manco Cápac International Airport, 347
Inca Mayta Cápac, 188, 211
Inca Trail, 250, 330-336
Inca Trail Tours, 47, 273
Incabar, 362
Incachillasca Pass, 303
Incahaus, 120
Inka Adventure, 274
Inka Express, 273, 353
Inka Fe, 290
Inka Fest, 199
Inka Frog Hostel, 121
Inka Grill, 292
Inka Jungle Trail, 325
Inka Legacy Tours, 274
Inka Lodge Hostel, 121
Inka Natura, 497
Inka Tours, 469
Inka Trail, 325, 335
Inka Traveler, 323
InkaFarm, 422
InkaNatura, 426
Inrena, 154, 449, 456
Instituto Cultural Peruano Norteamericano, 423
Institute for Field Research Expeditions, 270
Instituto Nacional de Cultura, 224, 301, 336, 478
Instituto Nacional de Recursos Naturales, 449, 456
Inter-American Court of Human Rights, 26
Inter-American Development Bank, 342
International Schools, 59
International Student Identification Card, 302
Internet Acasa, 433
Internet Primavera, 414
Internet Speedy, 414
Inti Raymi Classic, 275
Inticahuarina Spanish School, 268
Intihuatana, 243-245, 336-337
Intipata, 335
Intipunku, 335-336, 338
Intiq Samana, 281
Iquitos, 501-512
Iron House, 501-502, 505-507
Isla Amantaní, 351, 366
Isla Anapia, 364, 367
Isla Del Sol, 342, 367-369, 371
Isla Foca, 440
Islas Ballestas, 56, 156-157
Isla Suasi, 367
Isla Taquile, 366-367
Isla Uros, 364-365
Isla Yuspique, 364, 367
Islas Guaneras, 145, 156
Ishinca, 53, 383
Izcuchaca, 243

J

Jahuacoa Lagoon, 391
Jajahuana, 496
Jalca Grande, 474-475, 477
Jampa, 304
Jardín Botánico de Plantas Medicinales, 444
Jauja, 239
Jedi Travel Service, 114
Jerónimo de Aliaga, 95
Jíbaro, 466
Jorge Chávez International Airport, 121, 138
Judas Iscariot, 437
Juli, 364
Juliaca, 347-350
Juliaca International Airport, 348
Junín, 235
Junín National Reserve, 235
JW Marriot, 124

K

Kachivache, 296
Kallpa Wasi Spa, 60
Kamisaraki Inn, 365
Kanlu Wantan, 183
Karajía, 481-482
Karambola, 492-493
Karambola Disco Pub, 492-493
Karambola Restaurant, 492
Kayaking, 53

KB Tours, 318-319
Kero Café, 286
Khipus Restaurant, 291
King Kongs, 428
King Tut, 399
Kinski, 512
Kintaro Japanese Restaurant, 292
Kiribati, 38
Kiskapata, 288
Kite Boarding, 452
Kite Surfing, 452
Kiteni, 304
Kmek, 414
Koala Bar, 99
Kolibri Expeditions, 89
Kollasuyo, 174
Korianka, 409
Kotosh Temples, 233
Krishna, 292
KTM Peru Adventure Tours, 119
KTM Peru Motorcycles, 119
Kuélap, 472-474
Kugapakori, 495
Kumb, 447
Kuntur Wassi, 355
Kurkurpata, 288
Kusicoyllor Café-Bar, 323

L

La Alameda de Peregrino, 409
La Aurora, 89
La Balsa Border Crossing, 47, 467
La Bóveda Social Club, 208
La Calera, 216
La Capilla de San Sebastián, 218
La Carreta, 110
La Casona de Leymebamba, 480
La Castellana, 503
La Catedral Restaurant, 104
La Central Ongoro, 211
La Cholita, 265
La Ciudad de Eterno Calor, 432
La Congona, 466, 478-479
La Crillonesa, 247
La Cruz, 214, 456
La Dalmacia, 126
La Escuela de Wawa, 452
La Esquina, 418
La Fiesta de San Juan, 212
La Florida Inn, 167
La Fonda de Santiago, 363

La Glorieta, 363-364
La Gruta Hotel, 204
La Hosteria del Monasterio, 151
La Ibérica Chocolates, 205-206
La Islilla, 440
La Italiana, 207
La Luna Café, 390
La Mamacha, 419
La Mansión, 210
La Noche, 136
La Oroya, 46, 240
La Pampilla, 118
La Pergola, 138
La Plaza de Armas, 193
La Plazuela, 204
La Posada del Cacique, 200
La Punta Grande, 397
La Quinta de Allison, 133
La Quinua, 243
La Rana Verde, 100
La Raya, 346, 348, 431
La Roca, 470
La Rosa, 194
La Rosa Náutica, 127
La Salchichería Alemana, 206-207
La Samaritana, 441
La Sirena, 170-171, 173, 455
La Taberna, 184
La Tina, 42
La Tushpa, 470, 480
La Universidad San Cristobal de Huamanga, 242
La Virgen de Candelaria, 212
La Virgen Imaculada, 212
La Yarada, 228
Lakes
Lago de Turquesa, 444
Lago Junín, 235
Lago Junín National Reserve, 235
Lago Mamacocha, 214
Lago Mitacocha, 385
Lago Sandoval, 487
Lago Titicaca, 341-347, 351, 371
Laguna Churup, 383
Laguna Cucha Cuella, 474
Laguna de Mamacocha, 474
Laguna Dorada, 103
Laguna Mamacocha, 475
Laguna Parón, 395
Laguna Salinas, 214
Laguna Umayu, 346
Laguna Viconga, 391
Lagunas de Llanganuco, 376

Lagunas Huaringas, 444
Lagunillas, 146, 158
Lake Huacachina, 171
Lake Quistococha, 484, 486
Lake Sandoval, 487, 490
Lake Titicaca, 341-347
Lakshmivan, 206
Lalo's, 111
Lamas, 501
Lamistas, 501
Lampa, 350
Lámud, 473, 480-482
Land Adventures, 197, 201, 274, 277
Land of Enchantment, 437
Language, 25
LanPeru, 402, 421
Lara, 392, 396
Larapa Grande, 286
Laras, 392
Larcomar Mall, 119
Lares, 49, 274, 276, 302-303
Lari House, 200
Las Arenas de Máncora, 454
Las Begonias, 76, 83
Las Bovedas, 409
Las Brujas de Cachiche, 127
Las Casitas, 217
Las Cañas, 183
Las Gardenias, 414
Las Gaviotas, 440
Las Hamacas, 134
Las Palmeras, 39, 402
Las Pampas de Heath National Sanctuary, 493
Las Pocitas, 450
Las Portadas, 319
Las Quenas, 208
Las Rocas, 509
Las Ventanillas de Otuzco, 462
Latin American Culture, 269
Laykakota Mines, 344
Lazy Dog Inn, 388
LC Busre, 44, 243, 462
Le Nomade, 295
Lemycha, 480
Leonicio Prado, 427
León of Hotel Grillo Tres Puntas, 450
Leptasthenura, 56
Lesbian Travelers, 76-77, 259
Leticia, 43, 514-515
Leucophaeus, 226
Levanto, 471, 473
Leymebamba, 478-480
Librería El Virrey, 97

Licores Leymebamba, 480
Lima, 78-142
Lima Airport, 81
Lima Cathedral, 94
Lima Centro, 89
Lima Golf Club, 105
Lima SAE Clubhouse, 66
Lima Sur, 139
Lima Visión, 88
Lima-Huancayo Train, 240
Limatambo Valley, 303
Lindley Corporation, 63
Lingua Cusco Spanish School, 268
Lista de Correos, 70
Little Italy, 128-129, 437
Llacanora, 460
Llachón, 350-351
Llactapata, 334
Llacuabamba, 46
Llama Carting, 496
Llama Education, 195
Llamac, 384
Llanganuco, 384, 376
Llankay Peru Travel, 277
Llostay, 228
Llulluchapampa, 334
Llullucharoc, 334
Lodge Los Uros, 365
Loja, 42, 47
Loja Internacional, 42
Loki Hostel Cusco, 280
Loki Hostel Lima, 120
Lonchera, 33
Lónguita, 472
Lord of Luren Sanctuary, 163
Lord of Qoyllur Rit, 253
Lord of Sipán, 420, 422, 429
Lorena, 259
Lores, 503
Lori Berenson, 26
Lorán, 481
Los Alisos, 46
Los Ampolas, 433
Los Andes, 145, 157, 192, 200, 214, 275, 390, 396
Los Apus, 289
Los Balcones de Moral, 203
Los Cangrejos, 440
Los Chankas, 243
Los Ficus, 418
Los Fieles Difuntos, 212
Los Helechos, 414
Los Hervideros, 449
Los Horcones, 431
Los Inca Baths, 462

Los Nogales Hotel, 392
Los Palos, 228
Los Perros Wine and Couch Bar, 297
Los Pinos Lodge, 396
Los Sauces, 414
Los Tombos, 188
Los Uros, 358, 365-366
Los Vitrales de Gemma, 104
Los Yuncas, 370
Los Órganos, 439, 451
Lovera, 168
Lucar, 387, 389-390
Lucho Ramírez, 46
Lurén, 162
Lurín, 30, 143
Luya, 466, 481-482
Luz, 309, 311
Luzuriaga, 378, 381, 387, 397
Luís Rojas Lara, 396

M

Maca, 102, 212-213, 218
Macará, 42
Machu Picchu, 336-340
Machu Picchu Sanctuary Lodge, 339
Machu Picchu Spanish School, 267-268
Macondo, 259, 294
MacPlanet Internet Café, 114
Mad Cow, 464, 492
Mad Mick, 503, 508
Madre de Dios, 489
Maikhana Namaskar Indian Restaurant, 292-293
Majes River Lodge, 211
Makaha, 118
Malaria, 43
Maldonado Wasai Eco-Lodge, 492
Mall Saga Falabella, 206
Mama Africa, 298
Mami Panchita, 98
Manay Raqay, 317-318
Manco Capac, 252, 328-329, 344, 355
Máncora, 450-455
Mandala Vegetarian Restaurant, 207
Mandor Gardens, 328
Manglares de Tumbes National Sanctuary, 456
Manos Cruzadas, 234
Mantaro Valley, 235-236
Manu Cloud Forest Lodge,

496, 498
Manu Ecological Adventures, 495
Manu Nature Reserve, 357
Manu Nature Tours, 273, 495-496, 498
Manu Wildlife Center, 497-498
Manu Wildlife Tented Camp, 499
Manuel Ascensio Segura, 32
ManuExpeditions, 276, 497
Maoist Shining Path, 22, 24
Mar de Grau, 439
Maras, 277, 314
Marañón River, 46
Marcos Zapata, 260
Mari Pizza, 470
Maria Reiche, 173-174, 176, 178-180
Mario Vargas Llosa, 28, 32, 410
Márquez de Mancera, 151
Marquis of Torre Hermosa House, 161
Mercado El Molino, 264
Mercado La Palma, 167
Mercado Modelo, 423, 429, 489
Mercado Mollina, 264
María Reiche Planetarium, 179
Matacancha, 384
Matarani, 148
Matia Angola, 259
Matseui, 112
Mayte Tours, 457
Mayuc Tours, 54
Mayupata, 322
Médecins Sans Frontières, 58
Meider Díaz, 476
Mejía Lodge, 490
Meléndez, 183
Melgar, 195, 204, 347
Meli Melo, 349
Mendivil, 258, 288
Mesquita Bab-Ul-Islam, 227
Mía Pizza, 248
Miculla, 227-228
Milagros Fair, 94
Millma, 191
MINCETUR, 224, 336
Minestroni Argentino, 209
Minimercado Santa Rosa, 146

Minor Health Problems, 67
Mirador de Carmen Alto, 210
Mirador de Kuntur Wasi, 355
Mirador de Los Andes, 192, 214

Mirador de Yanahuara, 202
Mirador Del Monasterio, 204
Mirador Hanan Qosco, 280
Miraflores, 112-129
Miraflores House, 121
Miraflores Park Hotel, 124
Miski Mijuna Wasi, 310
Miski Wasi, 103
Misky Uno, 322
Misterios Peru Travel, 277
Misti Volcano, 55, 198, 205
Mitupampa, 444
Moche, 400-401, 411-412
Mojsa Restaurant, 362
Molina, 79, 84, 239, 471
Molino de Sabandia, 210
Mollepata, 303
Moloko, 291
Momia Juanita, 187
Monasterio de Santa Catalina, 188, 193, 252, 258, 263
Monasterio El Carmen, 400
Money & Costs, 74
Monica, 426
Monsefú, 421, 423-426
Monte Blanco, 211
Monterrey, 397
Monterrico, 141-142
Monttrek, 387
Monumento Nacional Wilcahuaín, 377
Moon Islands, 369-370
Morales Guest House, 388
Moray, 277, 311, 314, 316, 321
Moray Ruins, 316
Moriya Daisuke, 292
Morro Solar, 139
Morsesky, 176, 180-181, 357
Motocycle, 438
Motorbike Tours, 386
Motorcycle Tour of Puerto Maldonado, 489
Motorists, 421
Mountain Biking, 54-55
Mountain Cacique, 56
Mountain Climbing, 48, 52-53
Móvil Tours, 379, 401, 465
Mr. Koala Restaurant, 99
Mt. Ampato, 187
Mt. Pinculluna, 304
Mullu, 310
Munay Wasi, 279
Munaypata, 305
Mundo Verde Spanish School, 265
Muralla, 79, 95, 103

Musas, 423
Muse, 145, 313, 423
Museums, 29-30
Andean Sanctuary Museum, 192
Adolfo Bermúdez Jenkins Regional Museum, 163
Brüning Archaeological Museum, 429
Bullfighting Museum, 85
CATCCO Museum, 317
Julio C. Tello Museum, 156
Lamas Ethnic Museum, 501
Larco Herrera Museum, 88
Manuel Chávez Ballón Site Museum, 328
Maritime Museum, 142
Municipal History Museum, 192
Museo Arqueológico, 84, 137, 242, 381, 400, 460
Museo Arqueológico de Ancash, 381
Museo Arqueológico Hipólito Unánue, 245Museo Arqueológico Rafael Larco Herrera, 84, 137
Museo Casa, 226
Museo Cassinelli, 406-407
Museo Catedrálico, 407
Museo de Arqueología, 406, 411
Museo de Arte Contemporáneo, 188, 194
Museo de Arte de Lima, 78, 85
Museo de Arte Italiano, 94
Museo de Arte Moderno, 406-407
Museo de Arte Popular Joaquín López Antay, 245
Museo de Arte Religioso, 258-259, 435
Museo de Cerámica, 258
Museo de Ciencias, 234
Museo de Historia Natural, 105, 406
Museo de Historia Natural UNMSM, 105
Museo de Jalca Grande, 474
Museo de La Nación, 29, 78-79, 84, 140
Museo de Oro, 78, 84
Museo de Piedras Grabadas de Ica, 161
Museo de Sitio Las Peañas, 227
Museo de Sitio Qoricancha, 260

Museo de Tumbas Reales de Sipán, 422
Museo de Zoología Juan Ormea Rodríguez, 406
Museo del Banco Central, 85
Museo Didactico Antonini, 178
Museo Dreyer Municipal, 351
Museo Elba Aranda de Sarango, 439
Museo Etnográfico, 501-502, 506
Museo Ferroviario, 226
Museo Galería Arte Popular de Ayacucho, 130
Museo Grau, 433
Museo Histórico Municipal, 188, 194
Museo Histórico Regional, 252, 258, 260
Museo Inka, 37, 258, 261, 263
Museo Larco, 84
Museo Mario Polío Meconi, 444
Museo Municipal de Oro, 433
Museo Municipal Vicús, 435
Museo Nacional de Antropología, 137
Museo Palacio Municipal, 258
Museo Peruano de Ciencias, 140
Museo Postal, 226
Museo Regional de Ancash, 378
Museo Regional de Ica, 161-162
Museo Regional Histórico, 226
Museo Santuarios Andinos, 187-188, 194
Museo Sicán, 399
Museo Sitio Campo, 227
Museo Taller Hilario Mendivil, 258
Museo Taurino, 85, 94
Museum of National History, 137
Museum of Natural History, 29, 105
Museum of Natural History Javier Prado, 29
National Anthropology Museum, 137
National Archaeology Museum, 37, 84
National Museum, 37, 78, 84, 420, 423, 430
Peabody Museum, 37
Puma Museum, 370

Rafael Larco Herrera Archaeological Museum, 137
Royal Tombs of Sipán Museum, 423, 430
Sicán National Museum, 420, 423, 430
Music, 30
Muyuna Lodge, 509
Mystery Peru, 180
Mystical Tour, 216
Mythology, 298, 300, 342-344, 368, 413, 423

N

Nahua-Kugapakori Reserved Zone, 486, 495
Nanay River, 503-504
Napa Valley, 63
Napo River, 43
Narguila, 295
Narihualá, 433, 438
Nasca, 173-185
Nasca Lines, 176-178
Nasca Trails, 180
National Forest of Tumbes, 455
National Historical Treasures, 142
National Library, 141
National Park Cerro de Amotape, 455
National Paso Horse, 144
National Pisco Sour Day, 147
Natural Sanctuary Los Manglares de Tumbes, 455
Natural Spa Aqlla, 340
Naturaleza Activa, 199
Nauta, 502, 508, 511
Nazcatel, 175
Nevado Ampato, 199
Nevado Ausangate, 301, 304
Nevado Chachani, 199
Nevado Champará, 385
Nevado Salkantay, 303
News Café, 110
Nicolás de Ribera El Viejo, 100, 102, 105
Nimbo Café Restaurant, 372
Niños Hotel, 283-284
Nobu Restaurants, 112
Nobuyuki Matsuhisa, 112
North American Peruvian Culture Institute, 423
Northern Andes, 466
Northern Atacama Desert, 225
Northern Coast, 68, 145, 399-400, 412-413, 419-420, 426,
437, 454
Northern Highlands, 376, 462
Northern Pacific Coast, 398-400
Northern Peruvian Andes, 459-460
Nowadays Zorritos, 446
Nuestra Señora Asunción, 215
Nuestra Señora de Fátima, 447
Nueva Acrópolis, 356
Nueva Alta, 265
Nueva Era, 248
Nuevo Horizonte, 241
Nuevo Pacto Universal, 27
Nuevo Rocafuerte, 43
Nuevo Tingo, 472

O

Oasis Net, 171
Occucaje Desert, 162
Oceanus Lounge, 111
Ocucaje, 52, 63, 161, 167
OFEC Avenida El Sol, 258
Oktoberfest, 102
Old Mountain, 331
Old Pub, 128
Ollantay Bar, 323
Ollantaytambo, 314-323
Ollantaytambo Adventure Center, 318
Ollantaytambo Temple Ruinsand Pisac Fortress, 250
Olleros, 49, 377, 384
Om-Gri, 465
Omagua, 21-22
Orange Tree Cloister, 194
Orbegoso, 401, 407, 410
Orient Express, 60, 124, 286-287, 324, 339
Oriente, 253
Orinoco, 38
Ortiz Arrieta, 465, 467, 469-471
Oscar Ramirez Durand, 24
Ostrich House Restaurant, 108
Otuzco, 460, 462-463

P

Pablo Tour, 199
Pacamayo Valley, 334
Pacaya Samiria Amazon Lodge, 507
Pacha, 35, 343, 372, 474
Pacha Mamá, 343
Pacha-Papa, 290-291
Pachacutec, 291, 315, 326
Pachacámac, 143
Pachacútec Restaurant, 291
Pacific Coast North of Lima, 398-400
Pacific Coast South of Lima, 145-147
Pacífico Centro de Idiomas, 86
Paita, 439
Palace of Inca Yupanqui, 282
Palace of Suitcases, 97
Palacio Arzobispal, 259
Palacio de Gobierno, 94, 100, 240
Palacio de Mamacuña, 144
Palacio de Sancochado, 104
Pallardelli, 183, 224, 227
Palpa Lines, 179
Pampa Galenas Nature Reserve, 183
Pampas de Pimentel, 425
Panadería El Buen Pastor, 297
Panamanian, 26
Panchamanca, 239
Pancho Fierro, 109-110, 112
Panorama Viajes, 463
Pantanos de Villa, 139
Pantiacolla, 495, 497-498
Paquita Siu Gourmet, 209
Para Chico, 229
Paracas Bay, 157
Paracas, 152-159
Paracas National Reserve, 156
Paracas Reserve, 149
Parades, 34, 63, 159, 221, 246, 362, 378, 381
Paragliding, 48, 88, 143, 197-198, 277, 312, 378, 444
Parcuapata, 210
Paredones, 173, 176, 180, 184
Pariacaca, 444
Parque Artesanal Turístico de Vista Alegre, 176
Parque Ayacucho, 138
Parque Colón, 432
Parque Combate de Altao, 107
Parque Curina, 217
Parque El Olivar, 109
Parque Ginebra, 383, 386, 388, 390
Parque Grau, 446
Parque Gálvez, 100
Parque Huajsapata, 351
Parque Infantil, 432
Parque Libertad de Expresión, 203

Parque Miraflores, 127-128
Parque Municipal, 133
Parque Nacional Huascarán, 378, 383, 385
Parque Nacional Manu, 507
Parque Nacional Río Abiseo, 46
Parque Pino, 351, 354
Parque Principal, 132
Parque Reducto, 118
Parque San Juan, 355
Parque San Martín, 396
Parón Lake, 395
Pasaje Woyke, 423
Pascana Amazon Tours, 507
Paseo Bolognesi, 225, 227
Paseo Colón, 85, 98
Paseo Sáenz Peña, 130, 132
Paso Santiago, 325
Passports, 38, 41, 221, 375
Pastoruri Glacier, 378, 383, 385
Pastoruri Hotel, 389
Patacancha, 300, 305, 315, 318, 323
Patagonia Art-Bar, 126
Patio Del Ekeko, 192
Patrimonio Cultural, 174
Pedemonte, 148-149
Pepe Zeta Bistro Lounge, 295
Perol Chico, 276
Peru Adventure Tours, 180
Peru Andes Travel, 387
Peru Bergsport, 386
Peru Bus, 147, 159-160
Peru Incas Explorer, 197
Peru Inkas Adventures, 274
Peru Instituto de Idiomas, 87
Peru Quick Facts, 41
Peru Travel Sustainable Tourism, 277
Peru Treks, 271, 303, 335
Peru Verde, 463, 497
PeruRail, 187, 191, 316, 324, 353
Peruvian Amazon Basin, 483-485
Peruvian Andes Adventures, 387
Peruvian Army, 96, 236
Peruvian Association of Adventure, 199
Peruvian Association of Incoming Tour Operators, 463
Peruvian Beer Festival, 102
Peruvian Handicraft, 137
Peruvian Islands of Lake Titicaca, 364
Peruvian Nuevo Sol, 41

Peruvian Tour, 271, 339, 463
Peruvian Yacht Club, 142
Peruvian Youth Hostel Association, 508
Perúrail, 191
Pescados Capitales, 127
Petit Thouars, 111, 119, 123, 127
Photography, 75
Picantería Los Santitos, 437
Piccolo Restaurant, 389
Picturesque Redondo, 118
Piedra de Huamanga, 364
Pikillacta, 261
Pilcocaina Temple, 370
Pilpintuwasi Butterfly Farm, 502-503
Pinculluna, 49, 304
Pino Park, 354
Pinturas Rupestres Chanqui, 481
Pinturas Rupestres of Amazonas, 467
Pirámide de Garcilaso, 395
Pirámide Tours, 357
Pirámides Sol, 407
Pisac, 305-311
Pisac Bridge, 310
Pisac Market, 250, 298, 300, 305-306
Pisac Ruins, 306-307, 309
Piscac, 316
Pisco, 148-152
Pisco Earthquake, 146, 148, 150, 167
Pisco Sour, 152
Pitipo, 430
Piura, 431-437
Piura-Emtrafesa, 402
Piuras Avenida, 455
Pizzaría Villanova, 152
Pizzeria Vaca Loca, 464
Pizzería El Buho, 362
Pizzería Volentieri, 455
Plateros Hostal, 282
Playa Chaco, 146, 153-154, 157-158
Playa El Toril, 439
Playa El Varadero, 415
Playa Esmeraldas, 440
Playa La Herradura, 135
Playa Norte, 143
Playa Pisco, 153
Playa Punta Rocas, 134
Playa Tortuga, 440
Playa Varadero, 415

Playa Yumaque, 158
Plaza Araccama, 323
Plaza Bolognesi, 98, 154, 158, 175-176, 347-349, 457
Plaza Bolívar, 84-85, 137, 205
Plaza Constitución, 309, 311
Plaza de Acho, 94
Plaza de Arma, 354
Plaza de Armas of Puno, 354
Plaza de Armasis, 291
Plaza de Gobierno, 98, 104
Plaza de San Francisco, 258
Plaza de San Martín, 96, 99
Plaza de San Pedro, 31
Plaza Del Armas, 509
Plaza Grau, 447, 490
Plaza Guru, 350
Plaza Huamanmarca, 241
Plaza Limacpampa, 266
Plaza Low, 473
Plaza Manco II, 313
Plaza Melgar, 347
Plaza Nazarenas, 258
Plaza Pizarro, 94
Plaza Regocijo, 258, 260, 275, 283, 285, 294
Plaza Regocio, 294
Plaza Rejas, 436-437
Plaza San Blas, 259, 291
Plaza San Francisco, 79, 94, 194
Plaza San Martin, 98
Plaza San Martín, 89, 96, 98, 101
Plaza Sucre, 369
Plaza Túpac Amaru, 489
Plaza Vea, 139
Plazas de Armas, 366
Plazoleta de San Blas, 288
Plazoleta Nazarenas, 286, 290
Plazoleta San Blas, 268, 287, 296
Plazoleta Santo Domingo, 263, 286
Plazuela de Santa Ana, 246-247
Plazuela El Recreo, 410
Plazuela Merino, 435
Plazuela Quiñónez, 153-154, 157
Plazuela San Cristóbal, 234
Plegadis, 226
Plus Café, 282
Pocollay, 227
Point Arequipa, 201
Point Backpacker, 133
Point Hostel, 196
Police, 71

Police Station, 149, 171, 192, 224, 330, 421
Policía de Turismo, 379
Polish Petroglyphs, 499
Politics, 23
Polylepsis Project, 497
Pomata, 346, 367
Pongo De Mainique, 276, 497
Pongo Mainique, 275
Pontífica Universidad Católica, 87
Pony Express, 497
Pope Juan Pablo II, 435
Portachuelo Llanganuco, 384
Porteadores Inka Nan, 333
Posada Amazonas, 493
Posada Hispana, 151
Posada Hospedaje Gino, 150
Posada Spa Wary Nayra, 359
Poste Restante, 70
Potosí, 364
President Alberto Fujimori, 24-25
President García, 36
President Juan Velasco, 60
Presidente Hotel, 326
Presidential Palace, 78-79, 90, 94
Prince Hotel Suites Spa, 141
Prince Suite, 141
Procadores, 296
Pronamach, 444
ProNaturaleza Butterfly Conservation Center Japipi, 489
Prospero, 505
Provincia de Leoncio Prado, 235
Proyecto Peru Language Centre, 268
Présbitero Andía, 224
Pub Cubano, 128
Puca Pucara, 261
Pueblo Alto, 472-473
Pueblo Bajo, 472
Pueblo Libre, 84, 90, 137-138
Pueblo Nuevo, 149, 473
Pueblo Viejo, 179
Puente Bolognesi, 203
Puente Cabo Blanco, 453
Puente Cervantes, 197
Puente de Los Suspiros, 129-130, 134-135
Puente Grau, 200-201, 205
Puente Huacura, 448
Puente Panteo, 449
Puente Porvenir, 443

Puerto Maldonado, 487-495
Pukaventana, 378
Pumacurco, 250, 286
Pumamarca, 49, 301, 305
Pumamarca Ruins, 301, 305
Puman Shimin, 387
Puna, 21, 46, 56, 226, 240, 304, 375
Puna Tapaculo, 56
Puno, 342-344, 351-363
Puno Plaza Restaurant, 360
Puno Week, 351
Punta Hermosa, 142-143, 367
Punta Negra, 143
Punta Rocas, 134, 142-143
Punta Sal, 112, 463
Punta Unión, 384
Punta Yanashallash, 384
Puntarenas Restaurant, 140
Punto Blanco, 135
Punto Italiano, 112
Puruay, 464
Purísma Concepción, 431
Putamayo, 503, 505-507, 512
Putqueroloma, 474
Putucusi, 328
Putumayo, 509
Puyupatamarca, 338
Pyramid Adventures, 387

Q

Qaluyu, 342
Qoricancha Temple, 355
Qoricancha Templo, 252, 258, 263
Quad Bike Tours, 272
Quechua, 57
Quechua Blues Bar Cafe, 322
Querubino, 465
Queñua, 220
Quinua, 247
Quiocta Caverns, 480
Qunuq Restaurant, 339

R

Rabies, 68
Raft Peru, 187
Rafting, 53-54
Raimondi, 84, 350, 502
Rainforest Expeditions, 494
Rancho San Antonio Restaurant, 230
Raqchi, 342, 353, 356
Ras El Hanout, 209
Raulito, 103, 183

Raymundi, 510-511
Real Hotel Pizarro, 409
Real Plaza Mall, 421
Recoleta, 193, 277
Recuay, 378, 381
Redondo, 118
Regal Bar, 507
Regia Victoria, 509
Religion, 27-29
Reserva Nacional de Aquada Blanca, 197
Reserva Nacional de Paracas, 152-154, 157-158
Reserva Nacional Junín, 235
Reserva Nacional Pacaya-Samiria, 507
Reserva Nacional Salinas, 212, 214
Reserva National Pacaya-Samiria, 502
Reserve Manu, 272, 463, 497
Reserve Tambopata, 272
Responsible Tourism, 75, 197-198, 271, 278, 289
Restaurant Aldea Yanapay, 293
Restaurant Aries, 124
Restaurant Arriba Perú, 449
Restaurant Cabo Blanco, 439
Restaurant Casa Blanca, 445
Restaurant Comida Pakistaní, 231
Restaurant Cámara Comercio, 248
Restaurant de Señora Wilma, 478
Restaurant Doña Clorinda, 311
Restaurant El Manu, 329
Restaurant El Mason, 464
Restaurant El Portón Colonial, 362
Restaurant Espada, 451, 455
Restaurant España, 101
Restaurant Fitzcarraldo, 512
Restaurant Huaca Pucllana, 184
Restaurant La Kañada, 184
Restaurant La Sirena, 172
Restaurant La Tushpa, 480
Restaurant Mayupata, 322
Restaurant Miranda, 323
Restaurant Moroni, 172
Restaurant Narguila, 295
Restaurant Nuevo Horizonte, 241
Restaurant Olímpico, 241
Restaurant Puerta, 372
Restaurant Riollo, 168

Restaurant Rocío, 476
Restaurant Romano, 410
Restaurant Rosa Náutica, 82
Restaurant Row, 158
Restaurant Samana Wasi, 310
Restaurant Sarita, 475
Restaurant Sun Beach, 447, 449
Restaurant Turístico El Paraíso, 482
Restaurant Valle Sagrado, 311
Restaurant Vegetariano El Paraíso, 168
Restaurant Vegetariano Vida, 436
Restaurant Venezia, 168
Restaurant Vía La Encantada, 184
Restaurant-Bar Desert Nights, 172
Restaurant-Pollería El Sabor Chiclayano, 471
Restaurant-Pub-Bar, 372
Restaurante El Grifo, 439
Restaurante La Rana Verde, 100
Restaurante Museo La Casona, 362
Restaurante Romano Rincón Criollo, 411
Restaurante Turístico El Brujo, 447, 449
Restaurante Vida, 134
Restaurante-Hospedaje Los Cocos de Colán, 440
Rey Antares Mystic Hotel, 283
ReyBus, 243
Ribera, 100, 414, 417
Rincón Cervecero, 102
Rincón Chileno, 101
Río Andagua, 214
Río Apurímac, 54, 304
Riobamba, 47
Río Blanco, 441
Río Caplina, 228
Río Colca, 215, 218
Río Colga, 187
Río Cotahuasi, 54
Río Cusichaca, 334
Río Grande, 46
Río Ica, 161
Río Majes, 187
Río Mantaro, 239
Río Manu, 495
Río Marañón, 466, 473
Río Moche, 401
Río Momón, 502
Río Nasca, 182

Río Patacancha, 300, 305
Río Piedras, 490
Río Quilcay, 377-378
Río Rímac, 79, 85, 95, 240
Río Sama, 228
Río Santa, 376, 378, 395
Río Santa Valley, 376, 378
Río Tambopata, 54
Río Tumbes, 457
Río Urubamba, 53, 250, 320, 330, 334, 337-338, 495
Río Utcubamba, 473, 478
Riva-Agüero, 95
Rivera Navarrete, 110
ROCIO Spanish Language Program, 195
Rock Lodge, 497-498
Rosa Náutica Restaurant, 118
Royal Inka I, 285
Royal Inn, 349-350
Royal Inn Restaurant, 350
Royal Tomb, 336-338
Ruinas Vilcashuamán, 245
Ruins of Llaqtacocha, 479
Rumbos de Sol, 73
Rumi Bar, 286
Rumi Huasi, 475
Rumicolca, 251, 261
Runcuracay, 334
Rupa Wasi Eco-Lodge, 327
Rusti Bar, 102
Rusti-K, 467

S
S. I. I. E School, 87
Sabancaya, 211, 214, 218
Sabandía Mill, 210
Sábado de Gloria, 246
Sacred Land Adventures Tour Operators, 274
Sacred Valley, 249, 299-305
Sacred Virgin, 393
Sacsayhuamán Ruins, 250, 261
SAE, 66-67, 71, 181-182, 269
Safety, 67
Salalá, 443, 445
Salamanca, 465, 472, 475
Salinas, 197, 212, 214, 311, 314
Salkantay, 303
Salomon Islands, 38
Samana Wasi, 309-310
Samatours, 228
San Andrés, 153, 402
San Augustín, 267
San Blas, 287

San Blas Spanish School, 268
San Borja, 140-141
San Clemente, 148-149, 154, 160, 243
Sánchez Cerro, 432-433
San Cristóbal, 94, 234, 242, 481
San Fernando, 126
San Francisco De Miculla Petroglyphs, 227
San Francisco de Payta de Buena Esperanza, 439
San Isidro, 104-112
San Jerónimo de Tunán, 235-236
San Jorge Residencial, 151
San Juan de Marcona Marine Reserve, 184
San Juan River, 304
San Judas Chico, 278
San Lorenzo, 139, 142
San Lucas, 427, 440
San Marino, 38
San Martín de Porres, 96
San Martín Province, 499
San Miguel, 83, 98-99, 479
San Miguel de Miraflores, 112
San Pablo, 34, 426, 440, 471
San Paolo, 102
San Pedro, 298-299
San Pedro Alcán, 219
San Pedro Market, 257
San Pedro Mártir, 364
San Ramon, 128, 349
San Remo, 100
San Sebastian, 271
San Vincente de Paul, 196
Sanctuary Lodge, 286-287, 290, 339
Sandboarding, 49-50, 162-164
Sandoval Lake, 493-494, 497
Sangalle Oasis, 219
Sanseviero, 107
Santa Ana, 218, 242, 246-247, 280
Santa Beatriz, 40
Santa Catalina Ancha, 280-282, 290
Santa Catalina Angosta, 263, 281
Santa Catalina Convent, 197
Santa Catalina Monastery, 204
Santa Clara, 324, 447
Santa Cruz, 48-49, 82, 364, 384-387, 396, 453
Santa Luisa, 110, 112

Santa Rosa, 514-515
Santiago Apóstol, 212, 218, 313, 317, 350, 440
Santiago Queirolo Winery, 137-138
Santo Tomás, 477
Santuario de Kiocta, 481
Santuranticuy, 257
Sapalache, 443
SAS Travel, 272, 326, 495
Sebastián Salazar Bondy, 31
Semana Santa, 34, 159, 198, 246, 438, 443
Semana Turística de Ica, 159
Seminario Ceramics, 264-265
Senderistas, 24
Sendero Luminoso, 24, 114, 130, 232
Senior Travelers, 77
Señor de Luren, 159
Señorita Fexticum, 426
Señoritas Beach, 142
SERENAZGO, 175
Sergeturs Colpa Travel, 490
Shehadi NYC, 125
Sheraton Lima, 99
Shopping, 64
Shubet Mountain, 470
Siduith Ferrer, 89
Sierra Verde Spanish, 390
Siete Cuartones, 280, 287
Siete Diablitos, 268
Silverio Lujano Jilapa, 365
Silverio Visalot Chávez, 473
Silvio Rodríguez, 134
Sipia Falls, 54
Sipán, 429-430
Sirena de Huacachina, 170
Sky Bar, 122
Sky Restaurant, 291
Snack Bar Sabor Peruano, 515
Social Issues, 33
Socorro, 413-414, 432
Sol Hotel, 436
Sol Plaza Inn, 283
Solmartour, 357
Sonccollay Restaurante Café Bar Pizzeria, 321
Sonche, 467, 471
Sonche River, 471
Sonesta Lima Hotel El Olivar, 109
Sonesta Posada, 60, 205, 285, 361
Sonia Mercado, 282
Sor Ana, 194

Soroche, 213, 240, 299-300, 333
Soul Mate Inn Hotel, 122
South American Explorers, 66-67, 269
South American Spanish School, 266
South of Puente Los Pozos, 447
Southern Coast, 145, 147, 367
Southern Cross, 337
Southern Pacific Coast, 146
Southern Peruvian Andes, 232-233
Spaghetti Om-Gri, 465
Spanish Café Arequipa, 195
Spanish Captain Hernando de Soto, 441
Spanish Conquistador Francisco Pizarro, 28, 94, 439
Spanish El Valle Sagrado, 299
Spanish Language Café, 195
Spatuletail Lodge, 470
Sport Fishing, 56
Sports & Recreation, 48
Spring Festival, 212
Springs of Helicon, 423
St. Martin of Porras, 27
St. Turibius of Mongrovejo, 27
Standard Spanish Course, 265
StarPeru, 44, 347
Stilos Spa, 60
Stone Puma, 262
Stop and Drop Lima Backpacker Hotel and Guest House, 120
Student Visas, 38, 41-42, 58
Studio Bacán, 74
Studying Quechua, 57
Studying Spanish, 56, 85, 195, 265, 417
Suecia I, 279
Suite Antique, 108
Sumac Wasi, 282
Sumaq Machu Picchu Hotel, 339
Sun God Expeditions Tours, 274
Super Rueda, 124
Supermarket Raulito, 183
Supermercado Los Portales, 503
Suquy Café-Bar, 339
Surcillo, 114
Surf Escuela, 447
Surfing, 50-51
Surfing Sufari, 51
Sushi Ito, 142

Swiss Los Apus Hotel, 289
Swissôtel, 109

T
Tacama, 63, 165-166
Tacna, 221-231
Tacna Gran Hotel, 230
Tahuayo, 514
Tahuayo Lodge, 514
Tai Lounge, 111
Tajopampa Tombs, 469
Takana Inn Hotel, 229
Takaynamo, 413, 415
Tallan, 431, 433
Taller de Cerámica Emilia, 176
Taller de Fotografia Profesional, 76
Talleres Los Andenes, 318
Tambo Amazónico Lodge, 513
Tambo Bar, 390
Tambo Colorado Ruins, 166
Tambo de Montero, 284
Tambo Machay, 261
Tambo Yanayacu, 513
Tambo Yanayacu Lodge, 513
Tambolik, 467
Tambopata, 493-494
Tambopata Candamo Reserve, 54, 485
Tambopata Education Centre, 487
Tambopata Jungle Lodge, 493
ambopata River, 275, 490
Tambopata-Candamo Nature Reserve, 493-494, 496
Tampu, 290, 315
Tampu Restaurant Bar, 290
Tamshiyaco-Tahuayo Reserve, 514
Tankanamarka, 307
Tapay, 213-214, 219
Tarapoto, 499-501
Tarata, 114
Tatoo Outdoors, 119
Tattoo Parlour, 91
Taypa, 183
Tayta Pizzeria-Trattoria, 322
Teaching English, 58, 196, 270-271
Teatro Británico, 31
Teatro Colón, 96
Teatro de Exposición, 103
Teatro Municipal, 31
Teatro Orfeón, 225
Teatro Street, 284
TEFL, 59

INDEX

Teleperu, 90
Telephone Services, 81
Temblores, 257-258
Temple of Kotosh, 234
Temple of Santiago Apóstol, 317
Templo de Coporaque, 218
Templo de los Jaguares, 444
Tenochtitlán, 251
Teodoro Valcárcel, 358
Teqsiqocha Hostal, 281
Teriyaki Alpaca, 293
Terminal Bolognesi, 221, 226, 228
Terminal de Ica, 159
Terminal Pesquero, 174, 221, 449
Terminal Terrestre de Castilla, 432
Terminal Terrestre El Bosque, 432, 438
Terminal Terrestre Epsel, 421
Terminal Terrestre Francisco Bolognesi, 174
Terminal Terrestre Interdistrital, 430
Terminal Terrestre Interurbano, 402, 411
Terminal Terrestre Manuel A. Odría, 174, 221
Terminal Terretsre El Kollasuyo, 174
The Discovery Internet Café and Snack Bar, 328
Theater, 31
Thermal Baths of Aguas Calientes, 328
Thomas Cook, 224
Tierra de Encanto, 437
Tierras Inkas, 277-278
Tika Bistro Gourmet, 292
Tika Wasi, 367
Tinajani Canyon, 350
Tingüina, 166
Tinkuy Buffet Restaurant, 290
Tipón, 251, 258, 262, 277
Tiquina Strait, 369
Titicaca, 341-347
Titikayak, 358
Tiwanaku, 346, 367
Tombs of Sipán, 399-400, 423, 430
Toribio Pacheco, 122
Toro Muerto, 196, 199, 210, 214
Toro Muerto Petroglyphs, 210

Torre de Parón, 395
Torre Parque Mar, 40
Torres Belón, 350
Totora Reed, 345
Tourist Information Office Cusco, 257
Tourist Police, 45, 71, 257
Tourist Visas, 41, 58
Tours Marañón, 478
Tours of Vilcashuamán, 242
Transporte Chiclayo, 421, 432, 451, 456
Transporte Cifa, 42
Transporte Cruz Chiquita, 443, 445
Transporte Roller, 472
Transportes Chuquibamba, 465
Transportes Guayabamba, 465
Transportes Línea, 421
Trattoria San Ceferino, 112
Travel SAC, 490
Trekperu, 272
Tropical Nature Tours, 490
Truco Restaurant, 294
Trujillo, 400-413
Try Galería Artesanal Takaynamo, 415
Tschudi Complex, 412
Tumbes, 455-458
Tumshukaiko, 395
Túpac Amaru, 33, 36, 401, 419, 489
Tupac Amaru Revolutionary Movement, 24, 26
Tupana Wasi, 294
Tupana Wasi Grill Bar, 294
Túpac Yupanqui, 304, 402, 441
Tuqsana Pass, 304
Turisbus, 371
Turismo Express, 443
Turismo Inkaiko, 271
Turismo Restaurant Espada, 455
Typhoid, 68

U
Unidad de Salvamento de Alta Montaña, 383
Universidad Autónoma de Madrid, 162
Universidad Nacional, 227
Universidad Ricardo Palma, 29
Universidad San Antonio de Abad, 263
Urmiri Hot Springs, 371
Uros Islands, 344-345, 356

Urpicha, 248
Ursula Behr of Iguana, 452
Urubamba, 311-313
Utcubamba River, 49, 466, 473, 475, 479
Uyuni Salt Flats, 370

V
Vaca Loca Pizzeria, 464
Vaka Loka, 492
Vallecito, 195, 199, 201-202, 204
Velasco Astete International Airport, 253, 289
Ventanillas de Otuzco, 460, 462
Victoria Mejía de García of Lambayeque, 428
Vicuña National Park of Pampas Galeras, 185
Vicuña Reserve of Pampas Galeras, 184
Vilcabamba, 304
Vilcanota, 250, 304, 331
Vilcashuamán, 242, 245
Villa Jennifer Eco-Lodge, 235
Villa Mayor, 283
Villa Natura, 102
Villa Swamps, 139
Villa Trujillo, 401
Visas, 38, 41-42, 57-58
Vista Alegre, 165-166, 176
Volcano Ubinas, 199
Volcanoes, 188-189, 194, 197, 199, 201-202, 204-205, 210-211, 214-215, 220
Volunteering, 58, 87-88, 196, 269-271, 356, 418
VolunTourism, 87

W
Wari Empire, 377
Wari Kayan, 153
Warm Valley, 21
Wars of Independence, 153, 439
Wasai Lodge, 490, 493
Waterfalls, 261, 328, 342, 358, 391, 444, 469, 480-481, 490, 501
Waykuna Andean, 123
Ways Travel, 347, 355-357, 364, 367
White City, 188, 198
White Mountain, 50, 373
Whitewater Rafting, 53-54

Wine, 63
Winery, 137-138, 165-167
Wiracocha Hotel, 98
Wiracocha Inn, 326
Wiracocha Spanish School, 269
Witches Garden, 293
Women Travelers, 76, 172
Woodside House, 87
Working in Peru, 58
World Challenge Expeditions, 357
World Challenge Organization, 356
World Heritage Center, 413
World Heritage Site, 80, 178, 189, 338, 374, 495
World Heritage Trust, 377, 385

X

Xauxa, 236

Y

Yakumama II Restaurant, 329
Yanacocha Lake, 304
Yanahuara, 210
Yanashallash Pass, 377
Yanayacu River, 513
Yanque, 218
Yarapa River, 513
Yate Cristina, 439
Yellow Fever, 68
Yellow Rose of Texas, 508, 511-512
Yerbabuena, 475-478
You Tours, 370
Youth Hostel Malka, 107
Yucay, 313
Yumbilla Catarata, 465
Yungay, 393-394
Yuspique, 367
Yálape, 471

Z

Zarumilla Bloque, 268
Zoila Augusta Emperatriz Chávarri, 32
Zárate Expeditions, 199, 358

PACKING LISTS
(* indicates something that might not be available in Peru)

GENERAL PACKING LIST
There are a number of items that every traveler should consider bringing to Peru as follows:

- ☐ **Medicines and prescriptions** (Very important. Bringing all relevant medical info and medicines may well save you a lot of grief in Peru)
- ☐ **Photocopies of passport** and other relevant ID documents
- ☐ Paperback novels (sometimes you'll be sitting on buses, in airports, or some where else for a long time. Bring some books with you so you're not bored. It is possible to find and / or exchange books in several places in Peru, but don't count on much selection)
- ☐ Plug converter
- ☐ A good camera (see photography section)
- ☐ Water bottle (bottled water is readily available in Peru, but you may want your own bottle)
- ☐ Sunglasses
- ☐ Motion sickness medicine
- ☐ Lip balm
- ☐ *Tampons (difficult to find outside the major cities)
- ☐ Sun hat
- ☐ Condoms and other contraceptives
- ☐ *Foot powder
- ☐ Antacid tablets, such as Rolaids
- ☐ Mild painkillers such as aspirin or ibuprofen
- ☐ *GPS device (especially for hikers)
- ☐ Watch with alarm clock
- ☐ Diarrhea medicine (i.e. Imodium)
- ☐ Warm clothes (the highlands are cooler than you think)

BACKPACKER PACKING LIST:
- ☐ All of the above, plus,
- ☐ Rain poncho
- ☐ Plastic bags
- ☐ *Swiss army knife / leatherman
- ☐ Toilet paper
- ☐ *Antibacterial hand gel
- ☐ Small padlock

RAIN FOREST PACKING LIST
- ☐ Rubber boots (most jungle lodges have them, call ahead)
- ☐ *Bug spray (with Deet)
- ☐ Flashlight
- ☐ Waterproof bags
- ☐ Rain poncho
- ☐ First aid kit
- ☐ *Compass
- ☐ Whistle
- ☐ Long-sleeved shirt and pants
- ☐ Malaria / yellow fever medicine
- ☐ Original passport
- ☐ Mosquito net (if your destination does not have one; call ahead)
- ☐ Biodegradable soap

INDEX

ADDITIONAL ITEMS

- ☐ _____
- ☐ _____
- ☐ _____
- ☐ _____
- ☐ _____
- ☐ _____
- ☐ _____
- ☐ _____

ANTI-PACKING LIST: THINGS NOT TO BRING TO PERU

- x   Expensive jewelry. Just leave it home.
- x   Nice watch or sunglasses. Bring a cheap one you can afford to lose.
- x   Go through your wallet: what won't you need? Leave your drivers' license (unless you're planning on driving), business cards, video-club membership cards, 7-11 coffee club card, social security card and anything else you won't need at home. The only thing in your wallet you'll want is a student ID, and if you lose it you'll be grateful you left the rest at home.
- x   Illegal drugs. You didn't need us to tell you that, did you?
- x   Stickers and little toys for kids. Some tourists like to hand them out, which means the children pester every foreigner they see.
- x   Really nice clothes or shoes, unless you're planning on going to a special event or dining out a lot.

INDEX

USEFUL SPANISH PHRASES

CONVERSATIONAL

Hello	Hola
Good morning	Buenos días
Good afternoon	Buenas tardes
Good evening	Buenas noches
Yes	Sí
No	No
Please	Por favor
Thank you	Gracias
It was nothing	De nada
Excuse me	Permiso
See you later	Hasta luego
Bye	Chao
How are you (formal)	¿Cómo está?
" " " (informal)	¿Qué tal?
I don't understand	No entiendo
Do you speak English?	¿Habla inglés?
I don't speak Spanish.	No hablo español.
I'm from England	Soy de Inglaterra
" " " the USA	Soy de los Estados Unidos

FOOD AND DRINK

Breakfast	Desayuno
Lunch	Almuerzo
Dinner	Cena
Check please	La cuenta, por favor
Main Course	Plato Fuerte
Menu	La Carta
Spoon	Cuchara
Fork	Tenedor
Knife	Cuchillo
Bread	Pan
Fruit	Fruta
Vegetables	Verduras
Potatoes	Papas
Meat	Carne
Chicken	Pollo
Beer	Cerveza
Wine	Vino
Juice	Jugo
Coffee	Café
Tea	Té

HEALTH/EMERGENCY

Call a....	¡Llame a...!
Ambulance	una ambulancia
A doctor	un médico
The police	la policía
It's an emergency	Es una emergencia
I'm sick	Estoy enfermo/a
I need a doctor	Necesito un médico
Where's the hospital?	¿Dónde está el hospital?
I'm allergic to...	Soy alérgico/a a
Antibiotics	los antibióticos
Nuts	nuez
Penicillin	la penicilina

GETTING AROUND

Where is...?	¿Dónde está...?
The bus station?	la estación de bus?
The train station?	la estación de tren?
A bank?	¿Un banco?
The bathroom?	¿El baño?
Left, right, straight	Izquierda, derecha, recto
Ticket	Boleto
Where does the bus leave from?	¿De dónde sale el bus?

ACCOMMODATION

Where is a hotel?	¿Donde hay un hotel?
I want a room	Quiero una habitación
Single / Double / Marriage	Simple / Doble / Matrimonial
How much does it cost per night?	¿Cuanto cuesta por noche?
Does that include breakfast?	¿Incluye el desayuno?
Does that include taxes?	¿Incluye los impuestos?

!VA TRAVEL GUIDES BRINGS YOU A TEAR-OUT LIST OF USEFUL CONTACTS IN PERU

free to photocopy this sheet for your use, to give to your dog, or to wallpaper your room.

:RGENCY NUMBERS

eral Emergencies	116	Police	105
	116	Medical Emergencies	117

SPITALS / DOCTORS

na: Clínica El Golf
Aurelio Miro Quesada 1030
Isidro
: 264 3300, 319 1500

Cusco: Essalud Clinic
Av. Anselmo Alvarez s/n, Cusco
Tel: 51-84-234724
24 hr emergency room

GLISH-SPEAKING LAWYERS

rcia de Piccetti, Consuelo
Carabaya 1011 of 208
na
: 428-1647, Cell: 9-630-2029
mail: cpiccetti@yahoo.com

Benites, Forno y Ugaz
Jr. Jiron Guillermo Marconi 165
San Isidro, Lima
Tel: 444-4966, 615-9090
E-mail: bmu@bmu.com.pe

AVELER GUIDANCE:

VA Travel Guides: www.vivatravelguides.com

uth American Explorers' Club:

ma contact details: Calle Piura 135, Miraflores, Lima, Peru, Tel/Fax: (51-14) 453-306,
mail: limaclub@saexplorers.org.

usco contact details: Choquechaca 188, No. 4, San Blas, Mailing Address: Apartado 500,
Isco, Peru, Tel: (51-84)245-484, E-mail: cuscoclub@saexplorers.org

ost Offices:

ima´s Main Post Office: Plaza de Armas at Camaná 195, Tel: 427-0370
ima DHL/Western Union: Nicolás de Piérola 808, Tel: 424-5820

usco´s Main Post Office: Av. El Sol 802, Tel: 224-212
usco DHL/Western Union: Av. El Sol 627-A, Tel: 244-167

axis

ima:
axi Plus: 578-4555, 24-hrs

Cusco
Cusco Taxis: 422-2222

harmacy: Pharmax, Av. La Encalada 1541, Monterrico, Lima (across street from Em-
assy), Delivery: 434-1460

Dentist: Ramón Castillo (and son), Av. La Fontana 291, La Molina, Lima Tel: 437-8084

EMBASSIES & CONSULATES

Canada
Bolognesi 228, Miraflores Lima
Tel: 51-1-319-3200
E-mail: lima@international.gc.ca
http://geo.international.gc.ca/latin-america/peru/

France
Av. Arequipa 3415, San Isidro, Lima
Tel: 51-1-215-8400, Fax: 51-1-215-8441
E-mail: france.embajada@ambafrance-pe.org
URL: www.ambafrance-pe.org/

Germany
Av. Arequipa 4210, Miraflores, Lima
Tel: 51-1-212-5016, Fax: 51-1-422-6475 / 51-1-440-4048
E-mail: kanzlei@embajada-alemana.org.pe
URL: www.embajada-alemana.org.pe

Italy
Venida Gregorio Escobedo 298, Jesus Maria, Lima
Tel: 51-1-463-2727, Fax: 51-1-463-5317
E-mail: italemb@chavin.rcp.net.pe

Japan
Av. San Felipe 356, Jesús María, Lima 11
Tel: 51-1-219-9550 / 219-9551
Fax: 51-1-219-9544
URL: http://www.pe.emb-japan.go.jp/
Email: consjapon@embajadajapon.org.pe

Netherlands
Torre Parque Mar, Av. José Larco 1301, 13th floor, Miraflores, Lima
Tel: 51-1-213-9800 / 51-1-213-9800
Fax: 51-1-213-9805
E-mail: nlgovlim@terra.com.pe
URL: http://www.nlgovlim.com/

Switzerland
Av. Salaverry 3240, San Isidro, Lima
Tel: 51-1-264-0305
Fax: 51-1-264-1319
URL: www.eda.admin.ch/lima

Spain
Calle Los Pinos, 490, San Isidro, Lima
Tel: 51-1-513-7930, Fax: 51-1-422-0347
E-mail: cog.lima@mae.es
URL: www.consuladolima.com.pe/

United Kingdom
Torre Parque Mar, 22nd floor, Av. Jose Larco 1301, Miraflores, Lima
Tel: 51-1-617-3000, Fax: 51-1-617-3100
Consular: consular.lima@fco.gov.uk
URL: http://ukinperu.fco.gov.uk/es

United States of America
Av. La Encalada, block 17, Surco, Lima
Tel: 51-1-434-3000, Fax: 51-1-618-2397
URL: http://lima.usembassy.gov/

Complete the sections below for your convenience:

My Tour Operator:

My Hotel Address:

Taxi Directions to
the hotel:

www.vivatravelguides.com

Printed in the United States
137738LV00004B/14/P